HISTORY OF PSYCHOTHERAPY

HISTORY OF PSYCHOTHERAPY

CONTINUITY AND CHANGE

SECOND EDITION

EDITED BY

JOHN C. NORCROSS, GARY R. VANDENBOS, and DONALD K. FREEDHEIM

American Psychological Association • Washington, DC

Published by
American Psychological Association
750 First Street, NE
Washington, DC 20002
www.apa.org

To order
APA Order Department
P.O. Box 92984
Washington, DC 20090-2984
Tel: (800) 374-2721; Direct: (202) 336-5510
Fax: (202) 336-5502; TDD/TTY: (202) 336-6123
Online: www.apa.org/books/
E-mail: order@apa.org

In the U.K., Europe, Africa, and the Middle East, copies may be ordered from
American Psychological Association
3 Henrietta Street
Covent Garden, London
WC2E 8LU England

Typeset in Goudy by Circle Graphics, Columbia, MD

Printer: United Book Press, Inc., Baltimore, MD
Cover Designer: Naylor Design, Washington, DC

The opinions and statements published are the responsibility of the authors, and such opinions and statements do not necessarily represent the policies of the American Psychological Association.

Library of Congress Cataloging-in-Publication Data

History of psychotherapy : continuity and change / edited by John C. Norcross, Gary R. VandenBos, and Donald K. Freedheim. — 2nd ed.
    p. ; cm.
 Includes bibliographical references and index.
 ISBN-13: 978-1-4338-0762-6
 ISBN-10: 1-4338-0762-9
 1. Psychotherapy—United States—History. 2. Psychotherapy—History. I. Norcross, John C., 1957- II. VandenBos, Gary R. III. Freedheim, Donald K. IV. American Psychological Association.
 [DNLM: 1. Psychotherapy—history. 2. History, 19th Century. 3. History, 20th Century. WM 11.1 H6776 2011]

 RC443.H57 2011
 616.89'14—dc22

                          2009046231

British Library Cataloguing-in-Publication Data

A CIP record is available from the British Library.

Printed in the United States of America
First Printing

To all the courageous participants in psychotherapy—
patients, practitioners, researchers, and educators.

CONTENTS

CONTRIBUTORS

Norman Abeles, PhD, ABPP, is a professor emeritus of psychology at Michigan State University. He has published in the area of ethics and has given numerous workshops on that topic. He and his students were involved in research on mood and memory concerns of older adults. He was president of the American Psychological Association in 1997.

Diane B. Arnkoff, PhD, is a professor of psychology at The Catholic University of America. She is a member of the Steering Committee of the Society for the Exploration of Psychotherapy Integration and has published in the areas of psychotherapy integration, clients' perceptions of their psychotherapy, and cognitive processes in social–evaluative anxiety.

Rodney R. Baker, PhD, retired as chief of psychology after 40 years in the Veterans Administration (VA). He has coauthored a history of VA psychology and edited a book of stories by past VA psychology leaders. He received the American Psychological Association Award for Distinguished Contributions to Practice in the Public Sector in 2004.

Scott Baldwin, PhD, is an assistant professor of psychology at Brigham Young University. His research focuses on methodological and statistical issues involved in evaluating psychotherapy. He and two colleagues received the 2008 American Psychological Association Division 29 (Psychotherapy)

Research Paper of the Year Award for their research on the therapeutic alliance.

Jacques P. Barber, PhD, ABPP, is a professor at the Center for Psychotherapy Research, University of Pennsylvania School of Medicine, and past president of the Society of Psychotherapy Research. His publications include five books, more than 100 journal articles, and 50 chapters. He has received National Institute of Mental Health and National Institute on Drug Abuse grants to conduct psychotherapy research.

Michael Barkham, PhD, is a professor of clinical psychology and director of the Centre for Psychological Services Research at the University of Sheffield. He has an abiding commitment to developing and delivering practice-based evidence for the psychological therapies. He was editor of the *British Journal of Clinical Psychology* from 2005 to 2009.

Anthony W. Bateman, FRCPsych, is a consultant psychiatrist in psychotherapy, Halliwick Unit, Barnet, Enfield, and Haringey Mental Health Trust, as well as a visiting professor at University College London. His recent books include *Psychotherapy for Borderline Personality Disorder* and *Mentalization-Based Treatment for Borderline Personality Disorder*.

Larry E. Beutler, PhD, is a distinguished professor at Pacific Graduate School of Psychology. He is a consulting professor of psychiatry at Stanford University School of Medicine and past president of the American Psychological Association Division of Clinical Psychology, Division of Psychotherapy, and Society for Psychotherapy Research. He is the author, editor, or coauthor of approximately 400 publications and 21 books.

Laura S. Brown, PhD, founded and directs the Fremont Community Therapy Project and maintains a private practice in Seattle. Her most recent work includes *Cultural Competence in Trauma Therapy* and *Feminist Therapy*, as well as a DVD, *Feminist Therapy Over Time*. She is the 2009 recipient of the Society for Clinical Psychology's Lifetime Contributions to Diversity in Practice Award.

Gary M. Burlingame, PhD, is a professor of psychology at Brigham Young University and the president of the group psychotherapy/psychology division of the American Psychological Association (APA). His contributions to group psychotherapy have been acknowledged by career awards from the American Group Psychotherapy Association and APA.

Franz Caspar, PhD, is a professor of clinical psychology and psychotherapy at the University of Bern, Switzerland. He is a past president of the Society for Psychotherapy Research and president-elect of the International Federation for Psychotherapy.

Robin L. Cautin, PhD, is an associate professor of psychology at Manhattanville College. She authored a chapter on David Shakow in *Portraits of Pioneers in Psychology, Volume VI*, and several articles on the history of clinical psychology. She received the 2008 Early Career Award from

American Psychological Association Division 26 (Society for the History of Psychology).

David R. Chabot, PhD, is an associate professor of psychology at Fordham University and past director of clinical training in the clinical psychology program at Fordham. He authored the Chabot Emotional Pursuer-Distance Movement Scale as well as the Chabot Emotional Differentiation Scale.

Lillian Comas-Díaz, PhD, is a psychologist in private practice and a clinical professor at the George Washington University Department of Psychiatry and Behavioral Sciences. Former director of the American Psychological Association's Office of Ethnic Minority Affairs, she was a faculty member at the Yale University Department of Psychiatry, where she also directed its Hispanic Clinic. The author of over 100 publications, her writings focus on gender issues, culture, spirituality, ethnicity, social class, and creativity. She serves on several editorial boards and is an associate editor of *American Psychologist*.

Paul Crits-Christoph, PhD, is a professor of psychology in psychiatry and director of the Center for Psychotherapy Research at the University of Pennsylvania. He has published over 200 journal articles and chapters and has served as president of the Society for Psychotherapy Research.

Eugene J. D'Angelo, PhD, ABPP, is chief of the Division of Psychology and director of the Outpatient Psychiatry Service at Children's Hospital Boston. He is also an assistant professor of psychiatry at Harvard Medical School. He is interested in enhancing treatment outcomes for youth and families in community settings.

Patrick H. DeLeon, PhD, MPH, JD, is Chief of Staff for U.S. Senator Daniel Inouye (D-HI) and was president of the American Psychological Association in 2000. He is a clinical psychologist and lawyer specializing in public policy.

Stephen T. DeMers, EdD, is professor emeritus in the Educational, Counseling, and School Psychology Department at the University of Kentucky and currently serves as the executive officer of the Association of State and Provincial Psychology Boards. He previously served on the American Psychological Association (APA) Council of Representatives and on APA's Committee for the Advancement of Professional Practice and Board of Professional Affairs.

Carlo C. DiClemente, PhD, is a professor of psychology and director of the MDQUIT tobacco resource center and the Center for Community Collaboration at the University of Maryland, Baltimore County. He is a codeveloper of the transtheoretical model and author of *Addiction and Change: How Addictions Develop and Addicted People Recover*.

Raymond DiGiuseppe, PhD, received his doctorate from Hofstra University. He is a professor and chairperson of the Psychology Department at

St. John's University and director of education at the Albert Ellis Institute. He was elected a fellow of American Psychological Association Divisions 12, 16, 29, and 43. His most recent book is *Understanding Anger Disorders*.

Sheila Eyberg, PhD, is a distinguished professor of clinical and health psychology at the University of Florida and creator of parent–child interaction therapy. She received the Distinguished Contributions to Education and Training Award from the American Psychological Association and the Distinguished Career Award from the Society of Clinical Child and Adolescent Psychology.

Daniel B. Fishman, PhD, is a professor of clinical psychology at the Graduate School of Applied and Professional Psychology, Rutgers University. He is editor of the peer-reviewed, open-access e-journal *Pragmatic Case Studies in Psychotherapy*. Among his five books are *Paradigms in Behavior Therapy* and *The Case for Pragmatic Psychology*.

Edna B. Foa, PhD, is a professor of psychiatry at the University of Pennsylvania School of Medicine. She has been recognized with lifetime achievement awards from the International Society for Traumatic Stress Studies and the Association for Behavioral and Cognitive Therapies. She chaired the *DSM–IV* Subcommittee for Obsessive–Compulsive Disorder and Posttraumatic Stress Disorder.

Beverly W. Funderburk, PhD, is an associate professor of research at the Center on Child Abuse and Neglect in the University of the Oklahoma Health Sciences Center's Department of Pediatrics. She conducts treatment and training in parent–child interaction therapy (PCIT). Her research interests include issues of training and dissemination in PCIT.

Linda Garcia-Shelton, PhD, MHSA, ABPP, is the executive director of the California Psychology Internship Council and visiting professor at the California School of Professional Psychology at Alliant University. She has worked in integrated co-located family medicine practice for 30 years and trained psychologists in those settings.

Mary Beth Connolly Gibbons, PhD, is an assistant professor of psychology in psychiatry, University of Pennsylvania, and recipient of the Society for Psychotherapy Research Outstanding Early Career Achievement Award in 2002. Her program currently focuses on interventions for major depressive disorder in the community mental health system.

Carol R. Glass, PhD, is a professor of psychology at The Catholic University of America. She serves on the editorial board of the *Journal of Psychotherapy Integration*, is a member of the Steering Committee of the Society for the Exploration of Psychotherapy Integration, and is a founding fellow of the Academy of Cognitive Therapy.

Marvin R. Goldfried, PhD, distinguished professor of psychology at Stony Brook University, is the author of numerous articles and books, a cofounder of the Society for the Exploration of Psychotherapy Integration, and founder of AFFIRM: Psychologists Affirming Their Lesbian, Gay, Bisexual, and Transgender Family.

Rhonda N. Goldman, PhD, is an associate professor of clinical psychology at Argosy University Schaumburg Campus and is affiliated with the Family Institute at Northwestern University in Evanston, Illinois. She has coauthored and edited four texts on emotion-focused therapy and conducts therapy with individuals and couples.

Carol D. Goodheart, EdD, is a health psychologist in independent practice in Princeton, New Jersey, and a clinical supervisor for the Graduate School of Applied and Professional Psychology, Rutgers University. She is the 2010 president of the American Psychological Association.

Leslie S. Greenberg, PhD, is a professor of psychology at York University in Toronto and director of York University Psychotherapy Research Clinic. He has authored many texts on emotion-focused therapy and received the Society of Psychotherapy Research Distinguished Research Career award. He conducts a private practice and offers training in emotion-focused approaches.

Alan S. Gurman, PhD, is a professor emeritus of psychiatry and director of family therapy training, University of Wisconsin, School of Medicine. He is a former editor of the *Journal of Marital and Family Therapy* and the author or editor of *Clinical Handbook of Couple Therapy*, *Essential Psychotherapies*, and *Theory and Practice of Brief Therapy*.

Gillian E. Hardy, PhD, is a professor of clinical psychology at the University of Sheffield. She has published extensively on process and outcome psychotherapy research and worked with clinicians and researchers in a research clinic for the treatment of depression. She is also coeditor of the *British Journal of Clinical Psychology*.

Allen K. Hess, PhD, ABPP, is a professor of psychology at the University of Alabama, where he was department head for 15 years. He is editor of *Psychotherapy Supervision*, now in its second edition, and coeditor of three editions of the *Handbook of Forensic Psychology*. He has presented workshops on psychotherapy supervision for three decades.

Clara E. Hill, PhD, a professor of psychology at the University of Maryland, has been president of the Society for Psychotherapy Research (SPR) and editor of the *Journal of Counseling Psychology* and *Psychotherapy Research*. She has received awards from the Society of Counseling Psychology, American Psychological Association Division of Psychotherapy, and SPR.

Steven D. Hollon, PhD, is a professor of psychology at Vanderbilt University. His research focuses on the nature and treatment of depression. He is a past president of the Association for Behavior Therapy and the recipient of a Distinguished Scientist Award from the Society for a Science of Clinical Psychology.

Judith V. Jordan, PhD, is director of the Jean Baker Miller Training Institute and founding scholar of the Stone Center at Wellesley College. She is an assistant professor of psychology at Harvard Medical School and was founding director of the Women's Treatment Program. Dr. Jordan authored *Relational–Cultural Therapy* and coauthored *Women's Growth in Connection*.

Florence W. Kaslow, PhD, ABPP, is president of Kaslow Associates in Palm Beach Gardens, Florida. She is editor or author of 30 books, 60 chapters, and 190 articles as well as a past president of the International Family Therapy Association, American Psychological Association Divisions of Family Psychology and Media Psychology, and the American Board of Family Psychology of the American Board of Professional Psychology.

Nadine J. Kaslow, PhD, ABPP, is a professor, chief psychologist, and director of postdoctoral training in Emory University's Department of Psychiatry and Behavioral Sciences. She is a past chair of the Association of Psychology Postdoctoral and Internship Centers and president of the American Psychological Association's Division of Psychotherapy and the American Board of Clinical Psychology.

Alan E. Kazdin, PhD, ABPP, is the John M. Musser professor of psychology and child psychiatry at Yale University and director of the Yale Parenting Center and Child Conduct Clinic, an outpatient treatment service for children and families. He was the 2008 president of the American Psychological Association.

Mary Beth Kenkel, PhD, is the dean of the College of Psychology and Liberal Arts at the Florida Institute of Technology. For the past 30 years she has been involved with the education and training of professional psychologists and with the broader societal and human resource issues affecting psychology practice. Her research, writing, and editorial work (as editor of *Professional Psychology: Research and Practice*) have focused on finding effective ways to bring behavioral health services to underserved populations and new settings.

Elizabeth A. Klonoff, PhD, ABPP, is a professor of psychology (San Diego State University [SDSU]) and psychiatry (University of California, San Diego [UCSD]) and codirector of clinical training at the SDSU–UCSD joint doctoral program in clinical psychology. Her research is in the area of ethnicity and disease, with an emphasis on the role of discrimination in health and illness.

Bob G. Knight, PhD, is Merle H. Bensinger professor of gerontology and professor of psychology at the University of Southern California. His book *Psychotherapy With Older Adults* has been translated into four languages. He was the 2009 recipient of the American Psychological Association Committee on Aging Award for the advancement of psychology and aging.

Gerald P. Koocher, PhD, ABPP, is a professor of psychology and dean of the School of Health Sciences at Simmons College. Prior to 2001 he was chief of psychology at Boston's Children's Hospital and Judge Baker Children's Center, and executive director of the Linda Pollin Institute at Harvard Medical School. He served as president of the American Psychological Association in 2006.

Michael J. Lambert, PhD, is a professor of psychology and the Susa Young Gates University Professor at Brigham Young University. He has been in private practice as a psychotherapist throughout his career. He is editor of *Bergin and Garfield's Handbook of Psychotherapy and Behavior Change.*

Marsha M. Linehan, PhD, is a professor of psychology and an adjunct professor of psychiatry and behavioral sciences at the University of Washington and director of the Behavioral Research and Therapy Clinics. Her primary research is in the application of behavioral models to suicidal behaviors, drug abuse, and borderline personality disorder.

T. J. McCallum, PhD, is an associate professor of psychology at Case Western Reserve University. He teaches courses in clinical interviewing, aging, and psychopathology. His research examines cognitive enhancement in older adult populations and stress proliferation among older adults and families dealing with dementia.

Kim T. Mueser, PhD, is a professor of psychiatry and of community and family medicine at Dartmouth Medical School. He has published numerous peer reviewed articles and conducted many workshops on the psychiatric rehabilitation of severe mental illness. In 2007 he won the Ken Book Award for *The Complete Family Guide to Schizophrenia: Helping Your Loved One Get the Most Out of Life* (with Susan Gingerich) from the National Alliance on Mental Illness of New York City Metro.

Katherine L. Muller, PsyD, is an assistant professor in the Department of Psychiatry and Behavioral Sciences at Albert Einstein College of Medicine and the director of psychology training at Montefiore Medical Center in Bronx, New York. She is also the director of Montefiore's Cognitive–Behavioral Therapy Program.

Peter E. Nathan, PhD, is University of Iowa Foundation professor emeritus of psychology and public health at the University of Iowa. He has devoted the bulk of his career to studying and writing about the etiology, diagnosis, treatment, and prevention of alcohol abuse and dependence.

Greg J. Neimeyer, PhD, is a professor of psychology at the University of Florida. A fellow of the American Psychological Association, he has served as director of training and graduate coordinator in the Department of Psychology and was inducted as a lifetime member of the Academy of Distinguished Teaching Scholars.

David E. Orlinsky, PhD, teaches at the University of Chicago. His coauthored books include *How Psychotherapists Develop, Varieties of Psychotherapeutic Experience,* and *The Psychotherapist's Own Psychotherapy.* He and Kenneth Howard developed the generic model of psychotherapy and cofounded the Society for Psychotherapy Research.

Wade E. Pickren, PhD, is associate chair of psychology at Ryerson University and American Psychological Association historian. His historical work includes two volumes documenting the importance of the National Institute of Mental Health and the Veterans Administration for psychology since World War II. He serves as president of the Society for the History of Psychology and editor of *History of Psychology.*

Mark B. Powers, PhD, received his doctorate at the University of Texas in Austin. He was an assistant professor at the University of Amsterdam in the Netherlands from 2006 to 2008. He recently joined the Center for the Treatment and Study of Anxiety at the University of Pennsylvania as an assistant professor.

Simon A. Rego, PsyD, is an assistant professor in the Department of Psychiatry and Behavioral Sciences at Albert Einstein College of Medicine, associate director of the Psychology Training Internship Program, and director of quality management and development at University Behavioral Associates.

Lynn P. Rehm, PhD, is a professor emeritus at the University of Houston. He received his doctorate from the University of Wisconsin–Madison. The papers from the festschrift honoring his retirement will appear in a special issue of the *Journal of Clinical Psychology* on the topic of depression in women and girls.

Emil Rodolfa, PhD, is director of the University of California–Davis Psychological Services, a California Board of Psychology member, president of the Association of State and Provincial Psychology Boards, and editor of *Training and Education in Professional Psychology.* His interests lie in legal and ethical issues and professional training.

Michael Helge Rønnestad, PhD, is a professor of clinical psychology at the University of Oslo in Norway. He received his doctorate from the University of Missouri–Columbia. Many of his publications are within the areas of the professional development of psychotherapists and counselors, clinical supervision, and process–outcome research.

Ronald H. Rozensky, PhD, ABPP, is a professor and associate dean for international programs in the College of Public Health and Health Professions and the Department of Clinical and Health Psychology at the University of Florida. He is the founding editor of the *Journal of Clinical Psychology in Medical Settings*.

Morgan T. Sammons, PhD, ABPP, is dean of the California School of Professional Psychology at Alliant International University. He is a retired U.S. Navy captain, a prescribing psychologist, a fellow of the American Psychological Association (APA), and president of APA Division 55 (American Society for the Advancement of Pharmacotherapy). He lectures extensively on issues pertaining to prescriptive authority and the professional practice of psychology.

Jack B. Schaffer, PhD, recently retired after a career in full-time practice and teaching in two medical schools and a professional school. He has diplomates in clinical psychology and clinical health psychology from the American Board of Professional Psychology. He is the 2010 president of the Association of State and Provincial Psychology Boards.

David A. Shapiro, PhD, was a research clinical psychologist for 35 years. He led psychotherapy research groups in Sheffield and Leeds from 1977 to 1999, published about 150 articles, and served as editor of the *British Journal of Clinical Psychology* and managing editor of *Psychotherapy Research*. He now works as a photographer.

Anne Helene Skinstad, PhD, is an associate professor of community and behavioral health at the University of Iowa. Her principal research interests include studying and writing about the diagnosis, treatment, and prevention of alcohol abuse and dependence.

Douglas K. Snyder, PhD, is a professor and director of clinical psychology training at Texas A&M University. He received the American Psychological Association Distinguished Contributions to Family Psychology Award. He has published several books, including *Getting Past the Affair*, *Treating Difficult Couples*, and *Emotion Regulation in Couples and Families*.

George Stricker, PhD, is a professor of psychology at Argosy University, Washington, DC. His most recent book is *A Casebook of Psychotherapy Integration*, with Jerry Gold. He has also completed a DVD, *Psychotherapy Integration Over Time*, which will be accompanied by a monograph.

Stanley Sue, PhD, is a distinguished professor of psychology at the University of California, Davis, and 2010 president of the Western Psychological Association. His publications include the coauthored review, "The Case for Cultural Competency in Psychotherapeutic Interventions," in the 2009 *Annual Review of Psychology*.

Jennifer M. Taylor, MS, is a doctoral student in the counseling psychology program at the University of Florida in Gainesville.

Jennifer Titus, MPH, is a senior research analyst in the Public Health Department of the National Opinion Research Center at the University of Chicago. Prior to that, she was a project director at the Institute for Juvenile Research at the University of Illinois at Chicago.

Patrick Tolan, PhD, is director of the Institute for Juvenile Research, University of Illinois at Chicago, and professor of psychiatry and public health. He has published over 120 articles and book chapters and edited four books. Dr. Tolan chaired the American Psychological Association Work Group on Advancing Psychology's Agenda for Children's Mental Health.

Bruce E. Wampold, PhD, ABPP, is a professor and chair of the Department of Counseling Psychology and clinical professor of psychiatry at the University of Wisconsin–Madison. His work involves understanding psychotherapy from empirical, historical, and anthropological perspectives. He is a recipient of the American Psychological Association Distinguished Professional Contributions to Applied Research Award.

Jeanne C. Watson, PhD, is a professor of counseling psychology at the University of Toronto. She has coauthored and edited six books on humanistic and experiential psychotherapy. She received the Outstanding Early Achievement Award from the Society for Psychotherapy Research. She conducts training in experiential psychotherapy and maintains a part-time private practice.

Carol Webb, PhD, ABPP, is the director of internship training at Emory University School of Medicine, Department of Psychiatry and Behavioral Sciences at Grady Health Systems. She serves on the board of directors of the Association of State and Provincial Psychology Boards and on the Georgia State Board of Examiners of Psychologists.

Danny Wedding, PhD, is a professor of psychiatry for the University of Missouri–Columbia School of Medicine and director of the Missouri Institute of Mental Health, a research, policy, and training center. He wrote his chapter while serving as a 2008–2009 Fulbright distinguished scholar teaching at Yonsei University in Seoul, Korea.

Ulrike Willutzki, PhD, is a professor of clinical psychology and psychotherapy at the Ruhr-University in Bochum, Germany. Her research foci are on the professional development of psychotherapists, psychotherapy training, and supervision as well as social anxiety disorder and resources in psychotherapy. She regularly gives workshops on these topics.

Barry E. Wolfe, PhD, is president of the Center for Training in Psychotherapy Integration, a psychologist in limited private practice, and adjunct professor of clinical psychology at the Uniformed Services University of the Health Sciences. His most recent book is *Understanding and Treating Anxiety Disorders: An Integrated Approach.*

David L. Wolitzky, PhD, is a faculty member and former director of the PhD program in clinical psychology and the psychology clinic at New York University. He is also clinical supervisor and former codirector there of the postdoctoral program in psychotherapy and psychoanalysis. He is editor of *Psychological Issues*.

Everett L. Worthington, Jr., PhD, professor of psychology, has published on forgiveness, marital enrichment, and religion and spirituality. He authored *Forgiveness and Reconciliation* and edited *Handbook of Forgiveness* and *Spiritually Oriented Interventions for Counseling and Psychotherapy*.

Nolan Zane, PhD, is a professor of psychology at the University of California, Davis, and director of the Asian American Center on Disparities Research. His research focuses on the design of culturally based socio-behavioral interventions, ethnocultural moderators of change in psychotherapy, and the determinants of addictive behaviors among Asian Americans.

Hansjörg Znoj, PhD, is a professor of clinical psychology at the University of Bern in Switzerland. His research interests include the psychotherapy process, coping and regulation of emotion following traumatizing life events, health psychology, and bereavement.

ABBREVIATED FOREWORD
TO THE FIRST EDITION

From the time of the cavemen, we have needed people who played the role of the psychotherapist. We can find in the history of different centuries this cry for help, this begging for an understanding of the inner person. We seek an understanding of the consciousness and the unconsciousness where we think our most serious thoughts and where we experience our deepest joy.

When we endeavor to clarify our methods of "ministering to a mind diseased" as Shakespeare puts it, there comes to mind the heroic days in the infancy of our own profession. My memory goes back to the years of 1955 and 1956, when there were only a handful of us in the whole state of New York practicing psychotherapy.

We thought of those as the "dangerous years." We few psychologists were continually under the threat of being declared outlaws in our conflict with the narrow wing of the American Medical Association (AMA). I recall those days when the legislature for New York State was in session. We knew the legislators had before them a bill introduced by the conservative wing of the AMA that would make all psychotherapy a branch of medicine. If this passed, we would be explicitly outlawed and possibly arrested for practicing medicine.

My own office was on the 25th floor of the Master Hotel overlooking the Hudson River and the skyline of New York. Whenever a depressed client would tell me that he or she was contemplating suicide, I secretly glanced to see that my windows were tightly locked, for I had fantasies of the patient jumping out and being squashed on the sidewalk far below.

For six or eight years, intense anxiety visited me and my colleagues almost continually when the legislature was in session. We employed a part-time psychologist, Arthur Combs, as our representative on the floor of the state legislature. I recall a special day, when we were to have a crucial meeting that evening in the ballroom of the Hotel New Yorker, on which I did not dare answer the phone for fear it would be Art Combs in Albany to announce that the "outlawing" legislation had gone through and we psychologists were all about to be arrested. When I did finally answer the phone, it was Art simply wanting to tell us that he had gained promises from the leaders of the legislature that the medical bill would not be passed, at least in that session.

Several months later, I concluded, along with a psychiatrist who sympathized with our cause, that the best step for us as psychologists would be to clarify all the different branches of psychotherapy. The plan we then developed was to bring together selected members of the five professions that practice psychotherapy: psychiatrists, psychologists, social workers, ministers, and educators. The five professions would appoint commissions and prepare for an inclusive conference on psychotherapy in one year's time. Preparatory to this major conference, the five groups would study what kind of training was necessary for its members, and the aims each group sought. Each commission met bimonthly. The members of each group undertook to find out what persons in the other fields did in the form of training and practice, what safeguards they honored, and so on.

The psychology group consisted of Nevitt Sanford, Harry Bone, Peter Blos, George Klein, and myself. The psychiatry group consisted of Frederich Allen, William Cooper, Louis Fraud, Florence Powdermaker, Robert Sooley, and Exie Welsch.

The results were available in the regular *Annals of the New York Academy of Sciences*. I do not know how many states made concrete use of the published results of the conference; I can only say that from that moment on, the fact that psychotherapy was conducted by psychologists and by each of the above groups was eventually accepted in the various legislatures around the country.

In my task as head of the Joint Council, I telephoned Carl Rogers to get his ideas on licensing. I had never met Carl, who was then in Chicago. Expecting his enthusiastic help, I was taken aback by his stating that he was not sure whether it would be good or not to have psychologists licensed. Although I could not understand then why he had this hesitation, I think I do understand it now.

During the following years, I kept thinking of Carl Rogers' doubts about our campaign for licensing. I think he foresaw that we psychologists could be as rigid as any other group, and this certainly has been demonstrated. We have discovered that we also tend to lose our sensitivity and that we also face dangers similar to those faced by the AMA before us.

There is a serious dilemma occurring in our vocation and in our practice of helping people with their personal problems. The question is, Are we training technicians or professionals?

The leaders and seminal thinkers in psychoanalysis and psychotherapy—Freud, Jung, Adler, Rank, and others—treated psychological problems as opportunities for the therapist and patient to discover the deeper levels of human experience. These leaders used crises as ways to find the unexpressed possibilities in the client's behavior. It means uncovering the buried talents in the mysterious depths of the human mind and personality. In his famous statement, Freud called dreams the "royal road to the unconscious." He and those who followed found free associations and myths not only in dreams or as goals in themselves but also as ways of revealing the mental and emotional difficulties of their clients.

In our day, however, the goals of therapy have often been radically changed. I have taught a student seminar for seniors who are about to graduate from the California School of Professional Psychology. This school graduates each year a substantial number of therapists who will work with individuals and groups in this country. These students are excellent in intelligence and experience. In the seminar, each student presents one case for discussion. Last year, not one student mentioned a dream or a free association of the client, and this year there was only one. Never was a free association brought up; indeed, I often had to explain what is meant by the term *free association*. These students are learning to be very good technicians; my fear is that they will join the great flood of professionals whose task is to help clients who are to be adjusted only, and they will never get to the deeper level our original explorers described.

Although I would be the last person in the world to recommend withholding information from anyone who would be helped by it, the problem here is different. It is, rather, that we in America have become a society devoted to the individual self. The danger is that psychotherapy becomes a self-concern, fitting what has recently been called the narcissistic personality. Robert Bellah has rightly stated in his book *Habits of the Heart* (University of California Press, 1985) that we have made of psychotherapy a new cult, a method in which we hire someone to act as a guide to our success and happiness. Rarely does one speak of duty to one's society—almost everyone undergoing therapy is concerned with individual gain, and the psychotherapist is hired to assist in this endeavor.

Some therapists recognize this problem chiefly through the fact that therapy gets boring. There are only so many practical problems in our day—

sex, family, financial support; soon therapists begin to feel that they are hearing the same story again and again. One of the graduates with whom I dealt spoke dolefully of his work as "the McDonald's of therapy." No wonder one of them writes, "Some of the fire that used to make therapy creative and fun seems to have diminished."

I well remember five decades ago, when I was getting my training in psychoanalysis, that we were chiefly open to *surprise*. We were never certain what interesting data were going to come out in work with this or that client. We were so filled with *wonder* that we could scarcely wait to get to our home-formed little discussion group of therapists one night a week to share what we had discovered that day.

The blocking of one's capacity for wonder and the loss of the capacity to appreciate mystery can have serious effects on our psychological health, not to mention the health of our whole planet. Psychologically, this "psychic numbing," to borrow Robert Lifton's phrase, the dulling or absence of sensitivity, leads to a loss of a sense of the grandeur of life and death. The personality type called compulsive-obsessional in some quarters and narcissistic personality in others comes to mind when we consider psychological numbing. Frighteningly, this type is increasing in our time. Caused generally by an inability to reach out and relate more than superficially to other people, it is the type of the mechanical man or woman, the "man in the gray suit," atrophied of emotions, inwardly lonely and outwardly detached. All of this appears externally as the boredom in the loss of the capacity to wonder.

Psychotherapy and the problems that lead people to come for psychological help emerge when the values held by the culture break down and disintegrate. And as these values are mediated by myths, it is in the breakdown of the myths that we can most clearly discern the conflicts that lead people to come to psychotherapists. A dream is a private myth; a myth is a public dream.

These thoughts are offered with the hope of restoring, so far as we can, the richness, the mystery, the fascination that the original leaders of the movement gave us. Although everyone must endure some boredom, which indeed is part of experience, I am proposing that we examine the deeper levels of the human adventure where this sense of awe and wonder is present.

Rollo May (1992)
Saybrook Institute

FOREWORD TO
THE SECOND EDITION

There are many important and exemplary books that make major contributions to the field of psychology. Great books, however, are difficult to find. The first edition of *History of Psychotherapy: A Century of Change* (1992) was a great book, widely acclaimed as necessary reading for researchers, practitioners, and students. Any revision of a great book would be subject to high expectations but fraught with perils: Can a second edition meet the standards of the first edition?

Before commenting on the revised edition of the book, I want to provide a context for the book's contribution. There is increasing realization that mental disorders and psychological discomfort affect an alarmingly large number of individuals. In the United States, the 1-year prevalence of mental disorders hovers between 20% and 30%, and a significant number of that percentage suffer from multiple conditions. Worldwide, mental disorders are a leading cause of health disabilities.

Given that psychotherapy and medication are the main resources to treat mental disorders, understanding psychotherapy is critical. Over half a century ago, Hans Eysenck asserted that psychotherapy had not proven its effectiveness. Not surprisingly, his view fueled widespread discussion and criticism, which provoked the debate over whether psychotherapy was effective.

Then in 1967, the debate was reformulated by Gordon Paul, who penned the classic question, "What treatment, by whom, is most effective for this individual, with that specific problem, and under what specific set of circumstances?" Paul's reformulation placed in bold relief the complexities of the practice of psychotherapy and the challenges for researchers.

As a researcher interested particularly in the effectiveness of psychotherapy for members of ethnic and racial minorities, I have been confronted with these challenges for decades. Is psychotherapy effective with ethnic minorities? Under what conditions are treatment outcomes favorable? Let me try to answer these questions by giving a brief history of psychotherapy involving ethnic minorities.

Concerns regarding the effectiveness of psychotherapy for ethnic minority clients have existed for at least half a century. Some studies demonstrated high treatment dropout rates. Early pioneers such as Robert Williams, Robert Guthrie, and George Sanchez noted that assessment of ethnic minority persons was often biased and ethnocentric. In the 1960s and 1970s, a number of psychologists and psychiatrists argued that racism and cultural bias often made it difficult for members of ethnic minority groups to receive effective mental health care. My own research showed that African Americans, Asian Americans, Latinos, and Native Americans tended to drop out of treatment quickly and to have poorer treatment outcomes. Not all ethnic clients fared poorly, of course. These findings underscored the significant role played by client, therapist, treatment, and situational factors in psychotherapy success.

At that time, many psychotherapeutic strategies were suggested to improve treatment outcomes for ethnic minority clients. These included "cultural responsiveness," "cultural sensitivity," and using bilingual and bicultural therapists. However, in the 1960s and 1970s, no large-scale treatment outcome studies or even rigorously designed experimental studies examined the effects of culturally responsive interventions. The paucity of research was understandable, given the imprecise specification of cultural responsiveness, inherent difficulties in studying relatively small ethnic populations, questions over the cultural equivalence of assessment and outcome measures, lack of funding for ethnic minority research, and a whole host of other factors.

Progress was also limited by the dearth of ethnic minority psychologists who could bring cultural experiences to bear in psychotherapy. For example, it was not until 1920 that an African American first earned a doctorate in psychology. It still surprises me it was not until 1943 that an Asian American, Robert Chin, received a PhD in psychology; in 1951, Efrain Sanchez-Hidalgo was the first Puerto Rican to earn a psychology doctorate; Martha Bernal was the first Chicana to receive a psychology doctorate in 1962; and in 1975, Gail Wyatt became the first African American woman licensed to practice psychology in California.

The 1980s ushered in major inroads in defining cultural responsiveness and in promoting policy changes in psychotherapy. The terms *multiculturalism* and *cultural competency* were increasingly used in place of *cultural responsiveness*. Derald Sue and colleagues conceptualized cultural competency into three therapist components: cultural awareness, cultural knowledge, and cultural skills. This conceptualization formed the basis for many of the multicultural guidelines later adopted by the American Psychological Association (APA) as well as the multicultural counseling competencies established by APA Division 17 (Society of Counseling Psychology). The guidelines were hortatory or aspirational in nature, indicating how therapists should act or what they ought to do in treating ethnic clients. Little was said about how to implement cultural competency.

During the 1990s, research findings increasingly demonstrated disparities in the quality of services received by ethnic minority clients. Early in 2000, the U.S. Surgeon General issued the supplement *Mental Health: Culture, Race, and Ethnicity*, which became the most authoritative analysis of the mental health status and treatment outcomes for ethnic minorities. The significant works of the present decade have asked variants of Gordon Paul's seminal question: How do cultural competent therapists behave? What is cultural competency? Does it reside in the person or is it a skill that can be manualized? Can it be added to current treatments or is it a separate form of treatment? Is there evidence that culturally competent therapies result in better client outcomes? If so, how do they work? These are the challenges being studied today—a full circle to the complexities embodied in Paul's reformulation of the effectiveness of psychotherapy.

My analysis is intended to lay the groundwork for how I view psychotherapy and how to evaluate contributions to the field. Any discussion of historical developments in psychotherapy must address specific questions raised by Paul's reformulation, on which I have elaborated:

- What is psychotherapy?
- How does one conduct effective psychotherapy?
- What are its methods and theories?
- Does it work?
- How does it work?
- Who were some of the main contributors to psychotherapy research and practice?
- How can psychotherapists and students improve their psychotherapy skills?
- How has the field changed over time?

How well does the second edition of *History of Psychotherapy* accomplish this? As in the case of the first edition, it is encyclopedic in scope to address these fundamental questions. Chapters are organized according to similar categories used to great advantage in the first edition. Some of the authors contributed to both editions. Thus, there is continuity with the first edition. One cannot help but be impressed with the overall quality of the contributions.

Much has occurred since the first edition was published in 1992. The field now uses, and depends heavily on, clinical trials; adopts a wide range of qualitative and quantitative methods; attempts to balance efficacy and effectiveness research; and employs advanced analytic strategies such as meta-analysis, effect sizes, and structural equation modeling. Psychotherapists increasingly endorse integrative or systematic eclectic treatments. Evidence-based practices are routinely emphasized in training programs, and multiculturalism is widely embraced throughout the profession, at least in attitude if not always in skill. These are but a few of the important changes that have occurred over the past 20 years, changes that are presented in an impressive manner by the contributors in this second edition.

It is difficult to appreciate that the first edition was published about 20 years ago, because it is still widely regarded as the most authoritative source on the history of psychotherapy, and the issues raised then are still being examined today. In all likelihood, this second edition, this monumental contribution, will be viewed in a similar manner 20 years from now.

Stanley Sue
University of California, Davis

PREFACE

A warm welcome to the second edition of *History of Psychotherapy*. The first edition was published in 1992 to commemorate the centennial of the American Psychological Association (APA). This second edition appears almost 20 years later and reflects both continuity and change in psychotherapy. Two decades are a mere blink in terms of history, but in the science and profession of psychotherapy, are nearly a lifetime.

William Shakespeare, a great psychologist, once wrote, "What's past is prologue" (*The Tempest*, Act II, Scene 1). In the hope of not repeating our prologue and of moving us forward, this volume endeavors to canvass the history of modern psychotherapy. Although the use of psychological methods to ease human suffering is as old as humanity itself, modern psychotherapy established its roots in the latter part of the 19th century.

The book begins with two chapters devoted to the broad historical outlines of the field from 1860 to the present. Thereafter, the *History* is divided into four major areas: theory, research, practice, and training. Each chapter therein highlights historical roots, current manifestations, and future directions. To end the volume, we briefly speculate on the future of psychotherapy.

So much has transpired in the field since the first edition that we had to carefully pick and choose what to include and what to leave for another project. The result is both a continuation of topics included in the first edition and the addition of areas barely suggested in the earlier book. We commissioned entirely new chapters on multicultural theories (Chapter 8), psychotherapy with adolescents (Chapter 13b), psychotherapy with health conditions (13d), couples therapy (Chapter 14a), integration of spirituality and religion into psychotherapy (14e), and pharmacotherapy (14d). Twenty years ago few would have predicted the routine use of medications with psychotherapy (combined treatment) or the idea that psychologists would prescribe psychoactive medications to their clients. We also added an entirely new section on psychotherapy for specific disorders: depression, anxiety, substance abuse, borderline personality disorders, and psychosis. The section on psychotherapy education and training has been overhauled to address licensing and credentialing (Chapter 16d), continuing education (16e), psychotherapy supervision (Chapter 17), and psychotherapy ethics (Chapter 18).

In the first edition, we featured 12 centers where major research programs contributed to an understanding of psychotherapy process and outcome from 1975 to 1992. In this second edition, we again feature 12 psychotherapy research centers that are advancing knowledge in the 2000s. Only two of the research centers—Chicago and Penn—appear again. Reports on the original research centers, along with all chapters in the previous edition, are available online via the PsycBOOKS full-text database.

The first edition of *History of Psychotherapy* was widely adopted as a textbook for undergraduate and particularly graduate courses. With this audience in mind, we worked to reduce redundancy among chapters, use straightforward chapter titles, cross-reference the chapters, and invite only seasoned authors with a documented record of clear writing. We also heard the pleas of instructors lamenting the large number of psychotherapist names mentioned in select chapters. Thus, in this edition we worked with our authors to place the names of most authors in parentheses and to invoke only the most-known names in the text.

In addition to students, the second edition will prove of interest to psychotherapy practitioners, educators, and researchers who seek to understand the historical roots and current state of the art and science of psychotherapy. We hope this volume will advance the field's understanding of how it arrived at where it is today. In the words of William Faulkner, another great psychologist, "The past is not dead. In fact, it is not even past."

A large edited book of this ambitious scope requires the cooperation of many individuals and the support of several organizations. First, we appreciate the enthusiastic support of the American Psychological Association's Division of Psychotherapy, which initially sponsored the book and which now receives its royalties. Second, we gratefully acknowledge the contributors to this edition and its predecessor. Of the 63 authors in the first edition, 17 have passed away as of this writing. Third, the first edition prospered because of the diligence of its associate editors—Herbert Freudenberger, Jane Kessler, Stanley Messer, Donald Peterson, Hans Strupp, and Paul Wachtel—and this second edition has indirectly profited from their contributions as well. Fourth, we extend our thanks to Lizette Ann Royer from the Archives of the History of American Psychology for her help with the photo images. Fifth, we have had the good fortune of working with accomplished professionals at APA Books, including Susan Reynolds and Dan Brachtesende. Sixth, but never final, we thank our spouses, who saw us through yet another book project with grace and encouragement.

We extend our gratitude to all of them for the second edition of the *History of Psychotherapy*, which is intended to clarify the field's past, understand its present, and propel it, more informed and prepared, into the future.

John C. Norcross
Gary R. VandenBos
Donald K. Freedheim
April 2010

I

PROLOGUE: PSYCHOTHERAPY FROM 1860 TO TODAY

1

A CENTURY OF PSYCHOTHERAPY, 1860–1960

ROBIN L. CAUTIN

Broadly defined, *psychotherapy* refers to the treatment of emotional or physical ills by psychological means, implying a belief in the influence of the mind on the mind and of the mind on the body. Although often associated with the work of Freud, the origins of psychotherapy in America significantly predate psychoanalysis proper. Psychotherapy—or *mental therapeutics, psychotherapeutics,* or *mental healing,* as it was variously called—traces its roots to the second half of the 19th century and what came to be known as *moral treatment.* By the time of Freud's famous 1909 visit to the United States, an American psychotherapy movement had already gained considerable momentum (Burnham, 1967). It comprised various methods, which were for the most part ungrounded in a unifying theory or in empirical research, including suggestion, persuasion, reeducation, and hypnosis, all of which terms were often used interchangeably or "simply descriptively without any technical connotation" (Burnham, 1967, p. 76). Freudian psychoanalysis was simply considered another variant within the movement.

The scientific community generally eschewed psychological treatments, owing to the prevailing somatic model of illness. Moreover, certain aspects of psychotherapy were rooted in mind-cure and American spiritualism, both of which were incompatible with the scientific paradigms of the medical field.

Academic psychology, for its part, had only recently emerged from its philosophical and physiological parentage as a laboratory-based science, and most psychologists were thus not interested in the treatment of mental disorders or maladaptive behavior.

Various contextual factors, however, prompted the medical community to embrace psychotherapy, and from 1910 through 1940, psychoanalysis and psychiatrists would dominate the American psychotherapy scene (Cushman, 1992). Following World War II, the psychotherapy marketplace would change dramatically, as professional psychology would flourish and psychiatry would lose its dominion over psychotherapy practice. As consumer demand for psychotherapy steadily increased, the practice of psychology would begin to gain professional status and legal recognition, and psychotherapy would become an integral part of American psychology and American culture (Cushman, 1992; VandenBos, Cummings, & DeLeon, 1992).

MORAL TREATMENT, 1860–1890

Developed around the turn of the 19th century, what became known as moral treatment signified an important shift in the care and treatment of people with mental illness. Such individuals had previously been disregarded or punished for "deviant behavior" that was believed to be the result of demonic possession or sinful transgression. However, the intellectual changes that marked the Enlightenment era—an emphasis on naturalistic observation and a widespread sense of optimism—engendered growing compassion for human problems, including mental illness, and effectively set the stage for treatment reform (Grob, 1966).

Although many individuals contributed to the reform effort, moral treatment can rightly be traced to the therapeutic work of Philippe Pinel (1745–1826), an empirically minded French psychiatrist who directed the Bicêtre and Salpêtrière asylums in Paris beginning in the 1790s. Pinel eschewed standard medical treatments such as bloodletting and corporal punishment because they had proved ineffective (Grob, 1966). Instead, he initiated a nonviolent and nonmedical treatment regimen for patients that emphasized compassionate individualized care and the ameliorative effects of new surroundings, both of which are embodied in various aspects of modern-day psychotherapy. Not grounded in any comprehensive or unified theory, moral treatment, at its core, aimed to establish "a warm and trusting familial environment in which [patients] could feel that their mental condition did not in any way preclude participation in normal human activities" (Grob, 1966, p. 11). Patients were involved in occupational therapy, religious exercises, and entertainment and leisure activities, and had meaningful conversations with hospital staff. It was believed that the special milieu of the hospital setting "could reverse traits acquired because of improper living in an abnormal environment" (Grob, 1966, p. 66). Moreover, patients' treatment plans were devised in accordance with their own particular needs and interests. The ideas underlying this approach anticipated modern psychotherapeutic efforts, such as skills training and milieu therapy.

Moral treatment found a warm reception in the United States during the 1830s, as the American asylum movement began to emerge (Benjamin & Baker, 2004). Its use greatly characterized institutional psychiatric practice during the movement's early decades. By 1860, although the use of moral treatment still existed, particularly at private institutions, its use had already begun to wane (Grob, 1966). Admission rates continued to swell and cure rates dwindled; mental hospitals increasingly became symbols of hopelessness and despair, as chronic cases overpopulated their wards. The character of these institutions changed from therapeutic to custodial in nature, and by 1890, moral treatment had become virtually unworkable (Benjamin & Baker, 2004). Hospital superintendents, never having been able to justify the use of moral therapy on theoretical grounds, increasingly grew pessimistic about the curability of mental illness; institutional psychiatry, for the most part, embraced a staunch somaticism (Grob, 1966). It was against this backdrop that the American psychotherapy movement would emerge.

THE AMERICAN PSYCHOTHERAPY MOVEMENT, 1880–1920

In postbellum America, science underwent a paradigmatic shift as positivistic materialism gained supremacy. Medicine reflected this change as all illness, mental and physical, sought to rid itself of its metaphysical origins (Coon, 1992). This materialistic approach was lent significant momentum by the discovery of the anthrax microbe and the later acceptance of germ theory (Caplan, 1998). As with germ theory, according to which diseases were associated with specific microbes, vigorous efforts were made to associate different mental diseases with specific forms of neuropathology. Even with respect to the functional nervous disorders—seemingly organic disorders for which no neuropathology could be found—most physicians adhered to somatic explanations. One revered neurologist commented that if physicians were to take mental therapeutics seriously, they might as well "go back to the monkery—give up [their] instruments, give up [their] medicines and enter a convent" (Hale, 1995, p. 66). Physicians acknowledged psychological and behavioral symptoms, but mental therapeutics as a means of alleviating these symptoms were relatively unpopular. Indeed, prior to the 1st decade of the 20th century, most treatments for mental and physical illnesses, including diet cures, rest cures, electricity, and hydrotherapy, reflected the medical community's staunch allegiance to the somatic paradigm. Mental therapeutics were eschewed by physicians in order to protect the scientific legitimacy of their profession. Yet in spite of this resistance on the part of the medical community as a whole, mental therapeutics had strong appeal to a few professionals within scientific circles and to large segments of the general population.

The mind-cure movement that emerged in America represented a backlash against the hegemony of materialism in American medicine. The movement aroused widespread popular enthusiasm as increasing numbers of people sought lay practitioners for relief from various emotional, behavioral, and physical symptoms. Although many in medical circles would dismiss the various manifestations of the movement as unscientific, even fraudulent, some were inclined to consider psychological factors in healing. William James, for example, declared, "What the real interest of medicine requires, is that mental therapeutics should not be stamped out, but studied, and its laws ascertained" (James, 1894, as cited in Caplan, 1998, p. 63). As part of the vanguard of the medical community that would come to embrace mental healing, an influential minority of neurologists, psychiatrists, and psychologists in the late 19th century would study the agents of mental therapeutics and their implications for understanding psychopathology. In fact, one contingent of the psychotherapy movement (the Emmanuel movement) would ultimately help to inspire the medical community at large to embrace the possibility of mental therapeutics (Caplan, 1998). In addition, at the end of the 19th century, Lightner Witmer, a charter member of the American Psychological Association (APA), established the first psychological clinic. Here psychological principles were applied to assist children with educational impairments. Thus, in turn-of-the-century America, a psychotherapy movement was growing within the scientific community, stimulated by popular fascination and enthusiasm for mental therapeutics. By the end of the 1st decade of the 20th century, psychotherapy had obtained a prominent place in mainstream American culture, and American medicine had embraced it as within its professional domain (Burnham, 1967; Caplan, 1998). Despite its increasing prominence, psychotherapy at this time consisted only of a collection of techniques that practitioners implemented in accordance with their own relatively disjointed theories; this provides an important context within which to understand the subsequent development of the practice.

Franz Anton Mesmer and Mesmerism in America

Many of the early efforts at mental healing can be traced to the "medical" practices of Franz Anton Mesmer (1734–1815), an Austrian physician who developed the theory and practice of animal magnetism, later known as mesmerism and later still as hypnotism. Mesmer believed that the bodily fluids were magnetized and their imbalance resulted in disease. Consequently, he believed that placing magnets on a patient's body could restore a normal balance of fluid and therewith the health of the patient. Mesmer described patients' early reactions to the magnets as unpleasant, even painful, but ultimately beneficial: An initial "crisis" involving convulsions would give way to a trance-like (or somnambulistic) state. He later dispensed with the use of magnets, insisting that the simple laying of his hands on the patient, by virtue of the magnetism of his own body, was sufficient to effect positive therapeutic change. On the basis of his clinical experiments, Mesmer claimed that the effects of animal magnetism did not depend on contact with the magnetizing agent and that proper balance could be hastened with a variety of devices, including water, mirrors, and music. He reported that with his method he had successfully treated a range of medical conditions, including what would later be referred to as functional nervous disorders (Crabtree, 1993).

Though animal magnetism was a popular success in France, opposition to it was growing from within the medical community (Bruce, 1911). In 1784, King Louis XVI of France appointed a committee, chaired by Benjamin Franklin, to study the empirical validity of animal magnetism. The commission condemned the concept of animal magnetism, concluding that the observed effects were attributable to imitation and suggestion. Mesmer's injured self-esteem notwithstanding, the repercussions were minimal (Benjamin & Baker, 2004). Although criticism persisted, particularly in scientific circles, animal magnetism continued to be practiced by a growing number of nonprofessionals (Fancher, 1996).

The greatest champion of animal magnetism in the United States was Charles Poyen, a Frenchman who immigrated to the United States in the 1830s. During this time he galvanized the masses with public demonstrations of animal magnetism, emphasizing magnetic clairvoyance and healing; in the following decade animal magnetism became a popular movement in the United States. Despite Mesmer's vigorous efforts to explain the phenomenon of animal magnetism in purely naturalistic terms, mesmerism became associated with the occult and spiritual traditions (Bruce, 1911; Crabtree, 1993). This was in part because an influential minority of practitioners emphasized paranormal experiences that accompanied the somnambulistic state.

Mental Healing and Lay Practitioners

Mesmerism is considered the precursor to modern hypnosis, but it also precipitated the emergence of American spiritualism, the mind-cure movement, and the Emmanuel movement, all of which contributed to early popular psychotherapies in the United States practiced largely by nonphysicians.

American Spiritualism

American spiritualism as a therapeutic movement originated with the "Hydesville Rappings" of March 31, 1848 (Taylor, 1999, p. 139), when the young Fox sisters claimed that noises in their bedroom were caused by the spirit of a man who was purportedly buried in the basement. Their assertions drew hordes of people to their home to listen to the sounds and speculate as to their source. Although they eventually confessed to chicanery, their story captured wide media attention (Taylor, 1999). Moreover, the Fox sisters held many public engagements in which they acted as mediums for spiritual communication, increasing public interest in the paranormal. The supply of mediums increased as did the number of means of communicating with the dead: automatic writing, moving tables, and the use of the medium's own voice (Crabtree, 1993). By the 1890s, the movement could claim as many as 11 million followers (Taylor, 1999). Although the mediums' main source of income was spiritual communication, they also provided counseling to their clients regarding various emotional ills or work- and family-related problems (Benjamin & Baker, 2004).

The Mind-Cure Movement

The mind-cure movement may be traced to the efforts of Phineas Parkhurst Quimby (1802–1866), a clockmaker who was inspired to master the technique of mesmerism after hearing a lecture demonstration by Poyen in Portland, Maine. Beginning in 1843, Quimby embarked on a 4-year tour of New England with Lucius Burkmar, a readily mesmerized volunteer, with whom he gave public demonstrations of the diagnostic and healing powers of mesmerism. Quimby in fact claimed to have cured himself of semi-invalidism (Meyer, 1980). Reflecting on his clinical experience with patients, Quimby came to believe that the agent of successful treatment was not the mesmeric technique per se but instead involved the patient's convictions. In his practice he thus abandoned the use of mesmerism in favor of mental suggestion. He eventually claimed to have treated more than 12,000 patients in this fashion (Caplan, 1998).

One of Quimby's patients was Mary Baker Eddy (1821–1910), who had sought Quimby's services in 1862 for her own infirmity. Her successful treatment at the hands of Quimby was a watershed experience in her life, after which she would devote herself to the practice of mental healing. That all diseases and their cures are mental became her mantra. In 1875, she published *Science and Health*, in which she expounded the "absolute healing power of God alone" and the evils of materialism, and suggested that her technique and philosophy were superior to all other contemporaneous healing approaches (Taylor, 1999, p. 152). In 1879, she founded the Church of Christ

Scientist, known today as Christian Science. Shortly thereafter she founded the Metaphysical College, an instructional school for her healing philosophy and methods. Though the mind-cure movement enjoyed great popular support (Hale, 1995), it was largely dismissed or criticized within the scientific community. By contrast, the success of a subsequent movement, the Emmanuel movement, would not only capture the attention of the medical community but also compel physicians to wrest control of psychotherapy from lay practitioners (Caplan, 1998).

Elwood Worcester and the Emmanuel Movement

In 1904, Elwood Worcester (1862–1940), who 15 years earlier had earned his doctorate under Wilhelm Wundt at Leipzig, became the head minister of the Emmanuel Church in Boston. There he developed a program that "fused religious faith and scientific knowledge" in the treatment of functional nervous disorders (Caplan, 1998, p. 118). His program, initiated in 1906, comprised free weekly medical examinations; lectures on health-related topics given by distinguished physicians, clergymen, and psychologists; and private psychotherapy sessions conducted by the minister. It would develop into a spirited nationwide movement. Two years later, Worcester, Samuel McComb, Worcester's assistant, and Isador Coriat, a prominent neurologist who would become one of the leading first-generation American psychoanalysts, published *Religion and Medicine*, offering an elaborate treatment of the movement (Sicherman, 1978). The book was reviewed in "virtually every major newspaper and medical and religious periodical and soon became the single most important text of so-called scientific psychotherapy in the United States" (Caplan, 1998, p. 130). Although religion remained a fundamental element of the movement, Worcester insisted that it was grounded in modern science:

> While psychotherapy is by no means a new method of treatment . . . its scientific and rational application has been the work of only recent years. . . . With the advent of physiological psychology, of sound experiment instead of hazy generalizations, with the modern advances in the study of hysteria and the various aspects of the dissociations of consciousness, it was soon perceived that a rational psychic treatment was indicated in purely psychic disorders. (Worcester, McComb, & Coriat, 1908, p. 260)

In large part because of the Emmanuel movement's success, the medical community became acutely aware of its competition. As one prominent New York neurologist warned his colleagues:

> We as neurologists are confronted with the fact that an enormous number of mentally sick people are running around and getting their psychotherapeutics from the wrong well. . . . We must find out the good behind these false methods and organize it into some wise scientific measure which we

can prescribe. Until we do this there will be a continual succession of new cults, Christian Science, Osteopathy, etc., to the discredit of medicine and more especially psychiatrists and neurology. (Caplan, 1998, p. 134)

Many academic psychologists also took umbrage at the Emmanuel movement. Lightner Witmer, for example, argued, "Whatever Dr. Worcester's practice may be in his own church clinic, the principles of psychotherapy to which he and his associates adhere, are based upon neither sound medicine, sound psychology, nor to our mind, upon sound religion" (as cited in Benjamin & Baker, 2004, p. 51).

Largely as a result of the mounting intense opposition from within the medical and psychology communities, by 1910 the Emmanuel movement had essentially dissolved. Yet, its short-lived success had a significant impact on American medicine, as the psychiatry profession wrested control of psychotherapy from lay practitioners. "By offering the imprimatur of respectable science to psychotherapy American physicians contributed to a radical transformation in the role that mental therapeutics would play in mainstream American culture" (Caplan, 1998, p. 149). Before psychiatrists took possession of psychotherapy, however, an influential minority of academic psychologists and physicians from the Boston area were developing ideas about and undertaking studies of mental therapeutics and their implications for psychopathology; this group has been referred to as the Boston school of psychotherapy (Burnham, 1967; Gifford, 1978).

The Boston School of Psychotherapy (Psychopathology)

The Boston school of psychotherapy, an informal network of prominent academic psychologists and physicians, has been identified as the epicenter of the development of American scientific psychotherapy (Gifford, 1978; Taylor, 2000). The Boston school investigated functional nervous disorders, relevant explanatory concepts such as dissociation and the subconscious, and psychotherapeutic techniques such as hypnosis and suggestion. These studies were inspired by the French psychopathologists, in particular, Charcot and Janet, as well as by the claims of the mental healers and spiritualists (Taylor, 2000). Partly inspired by his controversial interest in psychic phenomena, William James (1842–1910) spearheaded such investigations in 1884 as the cofounder of the American Society for Psychical Research (Coon, 1992). James discussed different levels of consciousness and how the subconscious mind could be harnessed for therapeutic good (Crabtree, 1993), and his influential writings on habit inspired the psychotherapeutic method of reeducation.

At the same time, investigations of functional nervous disorders and psychotherapeutic treatments were being undertaken at various Harvard laboratories of experimental psychology, physiology, and neuropathology. These efforts culminated in the development of the new specialty of experimental psychopathology in the mid-1890s; these investigations also justified the use of such methods at local hospitals and outpatient clinics (Taylor, 2000).

Many prominent individuals were associated with the Boston school of psychotherapy, including Boris Sidis (1867–1923), Adolf Meyer (1881–1929), and Morton Prince (1854–1929). Sidis, who earned his PhD at Harvard in experimental psychopathology, published *The Psychology of Suggestion* in 1898. He was among the first American scientists to study unconsciously motivated behavior and to employ hypnosis and suggestion in the treatment of functional nervous disorders (Benjamin & Baker, 2004; Caplan, 1998). Meyer, possibly the most important psychiatric figure in the development of psychotherapy (Caplan, 1998), was a leader in the development of dynamic psychiatry, or what he termed *psychobiology*. He was an evangelist for psychogenetic explanations of mental illness and warned against strict reliance on purely materialistic conceptions. Morton Prince, a neurologist who specialized in multiple personality, founded the *Journal of Abnormal Psychology* in 1906 and later the Harvard Psychological Clinic. Prince was very influential in promoting psychogenesis, and his journal provided an important venue in which psychologists published their ideas on dynamic psychopathology and mental therapeutics (Marx, 1978).

Lightner Witmer and Clinical Psychology

Lightner Witmer, who in 1896 established the first psychological clinic in the United States at the University of Pennsylvania, is recognized as the founder of clinical psychology. He was the first to use the term *clinical psychology* to denote a distinct profession (McReynolds, 1997), and in 1907 he inaugurated the first scholarly journal in the field, *The Psychological Clinic*. Witmer's clinical psychology would apply scientific principles to the prevention, diagnosis, and treatment of mental and behavioral impairments. The work of his clinic focused primarily on children with educational impairments and on their families. The clinical psychology as envisaged by Witmer was thus quite different from the profession that actually emerged post-World War II (Routh, 1996). Nevertheless, Witmer's conception of the field was far broader than his initial clinical work—primarily with mentally retarded children—might have suggested:

> I would not have it thought that the method of clinical psychology is limited to mentally and morally retarded children. . . . The methods of clinical psychology are necessarily invoked wherever the status of an individual mind is determined by observation and experiment, and pedagogical treatment applied to effect a change, i.e., the development of such individual mind. Whether the subject be a child or an adult, the examination and treatment may be conducted and their results in the terms of the clinical method. (Witmer, as cited in McReynolds, 1997, p. 131)

Witmer's professional vision aside, it is important to note that pre-World War II, *clinical psychology* was a term that was used broadly, variously encompassing what today are referred to as the subfields of school psychology, counseling psychology, clinical child psychology, pediatric psychology, and clinical health psychology.

As Caplan (1998) wrote, "When Freud first set foot on American soil, psychotherapy was already integrally woven into the fabric of American culture and American medicine" (p. 151). This situation was indeed conducive to the assimilation of Freud's psychoanalysis (Burnham, 1967). Psychoanalysis would, in turn, have a profound effect in America on psychotherapy, psychology (see Hornstein, 1992; Shakow & Rapaport, 1964), psychiatry, and the general public.

AMERICAN PSYCHOANALYSIS

Although Freud's psychoanalytic writings date back to the 1890s, his work did not receive considerable attention within American scientific circles until the middle of the 1st decade of the 20th century. The term *psychoanalysis* first appeared in print in the United States in 1906 (Burnham, 1967), and articles specifically devoted to Freud's work began to appear in Prince's *Journal of Abnormal Psychology* during that same year. In fact, Prince's journal "became in effect almost a psychoanalytic journal" (Burnham, 1967, p. 28). American physicians, particularly in psychiatry and neurology, would become increasingly familiar with Freud's work as the medical literature contained more and more expositions on Freudian concepts and psychoanalytic techniques. In 1909, the first English translation of Freud's writings, by A. A. Brill, appeared in print, and the importance of these texts' availability in English cannot be overstated (Burnham, 1967). However, perhaps it was Freud's first and only visit to the United States in the fall of 1909 that ultimately catapulted Freudian theory into the limelight, within both the medical community and the public at large. To the dismay of many academic psychologists who considered psychoanalysis unscientific (Hornstein, 1992), a psychoanalytic movement established itself in the United States and, moreover, was understood by the public to be the "one legitimate science of psychology" (Benjamin & Baker, 2004, pp. 46–47).

Sigmund Freud and the Clark Conference, 1909

In December 1908, Sigmund Freud (1856–1939) was invited by G. Stanley Hall, the founder of the APA and then president of Clark University, to receive an honorary degree and deliver a series of lectures at a conference to be held in celebration of the university's 20th anniversary. Freud ultimately accepted the invitation, despite the apprehension he expressed to a colleague that "once [the Americans] discover the sexual core of our psychological theories they will drop us" (Hale, 1971, p. 234). Carl Gustav Jung (1875–1961), who was a coleader of the Freudian movement until he and Freud split in 1912, traveled with Freud to America and also lectured at the conference. On Tuesday, September 7, 1909, Freud gave the first of his five Clark lectures on psychoanalysis, which were all delivered in German and later published in the *American Journal of Psychology* (Freud, 1910). In his lecture series, Freud described Breuer's famous case of Anna O. and the success of the "talking cure." He subsequently outlined his theory of hysteria, discussing his topographical theory of mind and the key role of repression in the development of nervous symptoms. He described his views on childhood sexuality and transference as well as his therapeutic methods, including free association and dream analysis. Freud concluded with a cautionary tale of the dangers of excessive sexual repression and affirmed the individual's ultimate capacity to exert conscious control over impulse (Hale, 1971).

Freud was pleased with the reception he and his ideas received, particularly in contrast to his European audience: "In Europe I felt like someone excommunicated; [in America] I saw myself received by the best as an equal. . . . [P]sychoanalysis was not a delusion any longer; it had become a valuable part of reality" (Gay, 2006, p. 206). Indeed, in America Freud found his most receptive audience, detractors notwithstanding. In the year following his Clark lectures, second editions of three of his books were published (Makari, 2008). He and his colleagues enjoyed a spate of new trainees, supporters, and case referrals. Although initially considered just another variant method within the existing psychotherapy movement (Burnham, 1967), psychoanalysis would quickly come to dominate the psychotherapy landscape. In the words of Morton Prince in 1929, psychoanalysis "flooded the field like a full rising tide, and the rest of us were left submerged like clams in the sands at low water" (as cited in Hale, 1971, p. 434). In addition, psychoanalysis would profoundly affect the theory and practice of American psychiatry, providing an alternative etiological model and treatment method (see Hale, 1971). This influence was realized in no small part through the psychoanalytic movement that established itself in this country.

The American Psychoanalytic Movement

By virtue of key, indefatigable advocates and informal professional networks, a psychoanalytic movement established itself in the United States (Burnham, 1967). This movement, which included professional societies and psychoanalytic journals, distinguished psychoanalysis from competing schools of psychotherapy. A. A. Brill and Ernest Jones, both of whom had studied with Freud in Vienna, were its chief promoters.

Modeled after the International Psychoanalytic Association, which was founded in 1910, American psychoanalytic organizations were established to address the need for training and to prevent the misuse of psychoanalysis. Ernest Jones, at Freud's urging, established the American Psychoanalytic Association in Baltimore on May 9, 1911. Brill established the New York Psychoanalytic Society on February 12, 1911. According to Hale (1971), it "became the most cohesive, active, and orthodox center of psychoanalysis" (p. 323). In addition to their other functions, the professional societies served to provide a safe environment in which basic postulates would not be continually questioned. The psychoanalysts needed to discuss their work, in the words of Meyer, "*en famille*" (as cited in Hale, 1971, p. 317). A Psychoanalytic Society was founded in Boston in 1914. Indeed, many of the hubs of psychoanalytic activity were along the East Coast, particularly in the Northeast, but interest spread as far as California by 1915 (Burnham, 1967).

In addition to a proliferation of important American books, translations of foreign language works, and journal articles, specialty journals were initiated to facilitate the communication and dissemination of psychoanalytic theories and techniques. In 1913, William A. White and Smith Ely Jelliffe, both American neurologists, founded the *Psychoanalytic Review*. The New York Psychoanalytic Society adopted the *Review* as its official publication. The journal was intended to be eclectic and inclusive; a striking case in point was that in its inaugural edition, the journal featured an article by Jung, who by that time had separated from Freud (Burnham, 1967). In contrast, the *Psychoanalytic Quarterly*, founded in 1933, was started "with the express purpose of promoting doctrinal orthodoxy" (Hale, 1971, p. 330).

During the first 2 decades of the 20th century, psychoanalytic training was personal and informal. However, owing to factors both internal and external to the movement, the nature of psychoanalytic training would change. What constituted psychoanalysis proper was a debatable issue, as Freud's dissident followers, such as Adler and Jung, proposed alternative theories and therapies. In addition, World War I further increased the prominence of psychoanalysis as Freudian concepts were employed in the understanding and treatment of "shell shock," a war neurosis that was newly understood to be psychological in nature. Physicians thus became increasingly interested in learning about Freudian psychology. Moreover, the general popularity of psychoanalysis threatened the integrity of the nascent movement as the number of lay practitioners—pastors, journalists, and mental healers—increased. The eclectic nature of the psychoanalytic movement, growing interest in psychoanalysis on the part of American physicians, and increasing lay competition brought into focus the need for systematic training (Hale, 1995).

Psychoanalytic training institutes began to form in America in the 1930s. Institutes were established in Chicago, Baltimore–Washington, Boston, New York, and San Francisco during the 1930s and early 1940s (VandenBos et al., 1992). These institutions fostered a crystallization of Freudian orthodoxy, which in turn provoked the creation of official neo-Freudian schools (Hale, 1995). Concurrent with the inauguration of training institutes was the establishment of psychoanalytic clinics, some of which earned worldwide notability, including the Austen Riggs Center in Stockbridge, Massachusetts (Howard, 1978; Riggs, 1978), Chestnut Lodge near Washington, D.C., and the Menninger Clinic in Topeka, Kansas. The staffs of these clinics were prolific advocates of the psychoanalytic approach. These facilities trained psychoanalytic psychiatrists (and later psychologists) in the treatment of those with severe mental illness; they also served to popularize psychotherapy in this country (VandenBos et al., 1992).

Psychiatry and psychoanalytic treatments dominated the psychotherapy landscape in America throughout the first half of the 20th century (Garfield & Bergin, 1994). Psychoanalysis had no important rival in this regard (Garfield, 1981). To be sure, both behaviorism and Carl Rogers's client-centered therapy were emerging in the 1920s and 1930s, respectively. Neither one, however, would exercise substantial influence within the psychotherapy community until after World War II.

AMERICAN BEHAVIORISM

In 1913, J. B. Watson (1878–1958) redefined psychology by repudiating the study of consciousness and the use of introspection, both of which he deemed unscientific. He claimed that psychology "is a purely objective experimental branch of natural science. Its theoretical goal is the prediction and control of behavior" (Watson, 1913, p. 158). Behaviorism would prevail in academic psychology beginning in the 1920s (Samelson, 1981), but it would be decades still before behavior therapy gained ascendancy.

Nevertheless, its roots can be traced to the 1920s. During that time, Watson and Rayner (1920), applying Pavlovian principles, conditioned the fear of a white rat in an 11-month-old boy, "Little Albert." They also demonstrated that Albert's learned fear of a white rat generalized to similar objects, including a white rabbit and a Santa Claus mask. The case is often cited as initial evidence of the clinical utility of classical conditioning principles, its methodological shortcomings notwithstanding (Harris, 1979). Mary Cover Jones (1897–1987), a graduate student of Watson, is considered "the mother of behavior therapy" (Rutherford, 2006, p. 189). Jones successfully employed social imitation and pairing the presence of the feared stimulus with that of a pleasant one, a method she termed *direct conditioning*, in order to decondition the fear of a rabbit in her young subject, Peter (Jones, 1924a, p. 312). Jones also tested several other fear-removal methods, concluding that only social imitation and direct conditioning were unequivocally effective (Jones, 1924b). Although Jones would come to be regarded as a pioneer for her deconditioning work, this work did not generate much interest at the time (Rutherford, 2006). Indeed, behavior therapy was incongruent with the therapeutic zeitgeist, which emphasized the value of an intensive and long-term therapeutic process dedicated to the uncovering of unconscious material (Garfield, 1981). Behavior therapy, which was largely based on the laboratory work of academic psychologists, was perhaps less influential with psychiatrists, who dominated the psychotherapy arena before World War II. Moreover, academic psychologists typically were not interested in clinical applications, as psychological practice was thought to undermine the status of psychology as a scientific discipline. Behavior therapy, though it had limited influence in the early years of the 20th century, would ultimately be instrumental in ending the predominance of the psychoanalytic approach. By the 1960s it would assume a more central place in the psychotherapy arena.

CARL R. ROGERS AND CLIENT-CENTERED THERAPY

Carl Rogers's client-centered therapy was the major alternative to psychoanalytic psychotherapy during the first 2 decades following World War II. Although it had a relatively limited impact on psychiatry as compared with the influence of psychoanalysis (Garfield, 1981), client-centered therapy had considerable influence in other domains, such as university counseling centers (VandenBos et al., 1992), and had far-reaching application beyond the psychotherapy context (see Lakin, 1998; Zimring & Raskin, 1992).

Client-centered therapy can be traced to the work of Carl R. Rogers (1902–1987), who in the late 1930s directed the Rochester Child Guidance Center and published *The Clinical Treatment of the Problem Child* (1939), based on his decade of clinical experience with troubled youth. In 1940, Rogers began his professorial appointment in clinical psychology at Ohio State University. There he wrote *Counseling and Psychotherapy* (1942), in which he articulated the key components of his nondirective therapeutic approach: the therapist's acceptance of the client's feelings and the therapist's responding to feelings as opposed to content. In the 1950s, Rogers (1951, 1957) emphasized therapeutic process over technique, maintaining that a therapist's attitude, characterized by unconditional positive regard, genuineness, and empathic understanding, was necessary and sufficient to mobilize the individual's self-actualizing tendency, or "a fundamental, basic motivating force for [positive] change" (Zimring & Raskin, 1992, p. 636).

Rogers was one of the first to investigate systematically the therapeutic process and outcome (Lakin, 1998), and for this groundbreaking work he earned the APA's Distinguished Scientific Contribution Award in 1956. It is ironic that critics have described Rogers's conceptions of personality and psychotherapy as simplistic and vague, charges that argue against the theory's suitability as an object of scientific scrutiny. Rogers's theory inspired the development of the Q-sort technique, for example, which was designed to measure the way individuals perceive themselves. Researchers used the Q-sort to compare subjects' self-perceptions with how they would ideally see themselves. The discrepancy between these two measurements was presumably an indication of self-esteem. Rogers viewed the Q-sort, particularly the self-ideal discrepancy, as an indication of personality change as a function of psychotherapy. Critics aside, the extent of his influence on the field of psychotherapy is arguably second only to that of Freud (Carducci, 2009).

PSYCHOPATHOLOGY AND PSYCHOTHERAPY: BETWEEN THE WARS

Although psychiatry represented the chief source of psychotherapy— and psychiatrists were dominant in the diagnosis and treatment of psychopathology—a growing number of psychologists would assume responsibilities in a variety of clinical settings during the early decades of the 20th century. During this time, applied psychology would expand dramatically. Indeed, by the mid-1930s, one in every three APA members was employed in an applied setting (Capshew, 1999). Prior to World War I, clinical psychologists were mostly employed in mental hospitals and schools for the feebleminded (this term is historical, and not intended to offend readers; see Zenderland, 1998), where they were primarily engaged in research and assessment. However, though mental testing remained the primary function of the clinical psychologist during the 1920s and 1930s, some psychologists began to push the boundaries of the field (Reisman, 1976), fueling interdisciplinary tensions between psychology and psychiatry.

Clinical Psychology and Mental Testing

Although today clinical psychology is associated with a wide range of activities, the field was initially rooted in mental testing (see Benjamin & Baker, 2004). James McKeen Cattell (1860–1944), inspired by the work of Francis Galton (1822–1911), developed measures of various sensory and motor abilities that he believed would have clinical utility in educational institutions. Although one of Cattell's students ultimately demonstrated that Cattell's tests evidenced no predictive validity (Zenderland, 1998), Cattell's efforts prompted others to devise measures of intellectual functioning. In this regard, the work of Alfred Binet (1857–1911), who measured intelligence by assessing abilities associated with academic success, was extremely influential in America. Binet's test was translated into English by Henry Herbert Goddard (1866–1957), who also restandardized it for American use. Goddard published his version in 1908 as the Binet–Simon Measuring Scale for Intelligence. In 1916, Lewis Terman (1877–1956), a Stanford University psychologist, revised the Binet–Simon, renaming it the Stanford–Binet. Goddard and Terman, among others, developed intelligence measures that would be used in the assessment of military personnel and recruits during World War I.

Psychologists' service in World War I affirmed the usefulness of psychological testing and as a consequence testing became popular (Camfield, 1992). Psychologists' assessment interests would expand into the areas of aptitude and career preferences, and later into the personality domain, first with projective tests such as the Rorschach and the Thematic Apperception Test, and later with objective personality measures, most notably the Minnesota Multiphasic Personality Inventory. Proficiency in personality assessments, particularly those requiring statistical knowledge and skilled interpretation, conferred on psychologists a potentially new role—that of diagnostician (Benjamin & Baker, 2004; Reisman, 1976). As Ernest Hilgard described, "if the psychologist was an expert on the Rorschach, which required subtle interpretation, the psychologist had secrets to share and was listened to with some deference because the psychologist now made clinical diagnoses that had been previously disallowed" (as cited in Benjamin & Baker, 2004, p. 62).

As psychologists' expertise in clinical assessment came to encompass that of personality functioning, tensions between psychology and psychiatry began to intensify, for psychologists were pushing the boundaries of their field beyond those of research and assessment into the physicians' domains of diagnosis and treatment. This trend would persist as the field of clinical psychology continued to flourish throughout the 1930s, owing in part to the emergence of the child guidance movement, which afforded clinical psychologists exposure to a broad range of problems and patient populations and to opportunities to experiment with therapeutic techniques (Reisman, 1976; VandenBos et al., 1992).

The Child Guidance Movement

The child guidance movement, characteristic of progressive reform in America, developed within the context of the mental hygiene movement (Horn, 1989). The mental hygiene movement began with Clifford W. Beers

(1876–1943), a former mental patient whose famous book, *A Mind That Found Itself* (1908), chronicled his negative experiences at the Hartford Retreat and the Connecticut Hospital for the Insane. The movement called for improving the treatment of those with mental illness and for preventing mental illness through early intervention (Horn, 1989). With the support of psychologist–philosopher William James and psychiatrist Adolf Meyer, Beers's story popularized the call for asylum reform; the National Committee for Mental Hygiene (NCMH) was formally inaugurated in 1909 (Grob, 1994). As part of its efforts, the NCMH conducted nationwide surveys of mental health facilities (Napoli, 1981).

On the advice of Meyer, the focus of the organization's agenda shifted from that of institutional reform to the promotion of mental hygiene and the prevention of psychopathology. This change in emphasis "opened entirely new vistas [for psychiatrists] and suggested roles outside of isolated mental institutions with chronic populations" (Grob, 1994, p. 154). Such an agenda represented a broadening of psychiatrists' sphere of influence, which would not only improve psychiatry's professional status but would have profound implications for other developing mental health professions, particularly social work and clinical psychology. For although the mental hygiene movement is judged by historians to have had little positive influence on the outcomes of people with chronic mental illness (Grob, 1983), it precipitated the child guidance movement and the establishment of child guidance clinics, which served as fertile ground for the development of allied mental health fields and modern psychotherapy (VandenBos et al., 1992).

The child guidance movement formally began in 1922, as part of the Commonwealth Fund's Program for the Prevention of Delinquency (Horn, 1989). The private Commonwealth Fund, in conjunction with the NCMH, established a series of demonstration child guidance clinics to tackle the problem of juvenile delinquency through prevention. The movement embraced the belief that criminality and mental illness were not inevitable; it held that early intervention could mitigate or even prevent serious problems in the long term. Although the term *child guidance clinic* was not coined until 1922, these demonstration clinics were inspired by the earlier work of psychiatrist William Healy and psychologist Augusta Bronner, who in Chicago in 1909 established what might be considered the first child guidance clinic, the Juvenile Psychopathic Institute (Ridenour, 1961). Though this clinic was expressly devoted to the problem of juvenile delinquency, the child guidance clinics of the 1920s served a much broader range of children and families because children presented with a wide range of educational, behavioral, and emotional difficulties (Horn, 1989; Napoli, 1981; VandenBos et al., 1992). From the late 1920s through the following decade, the number of child guidance clinics increased dramatically. By 1933, 27 U.S. cities had established full-time clinics and several hundred were created to provide part-time service (Ridenour, 1961).

The child guidance clinics employed innovative interdisciplinary treatment of at-risk children. Earlier efforts to address child health and welfare were seen as inadequate, in part because they were unsynchronized and too compartmentalized. Ralph P. Truitt (1926), who served as director of the NCMH's Division on Prevention of Delinquency, explained that

> these activities to date were uncoordinated, that each group was taking only a fractional interest in the child and treating him either as a mind to be educated, a physical organism to be safeguarded or an offender to be disciplined. It was felt that a coordinated attack from the physical, mental, educational, and social angles was essential if the child as a whole was to be understood and his adjustment worked out in accordance with the best standards developed in each of the separated fields. (p. 23)

These clinics thus used a team approach in which psychiatrists, psychiatric social workers, and clinical psychologists worked together, each group performing the duties consistent with its specific training at that time. The psychiatric social worker was responsible for obtaining case histories and for working with parents and social agencies; the psychologist was in charge of test administration and interpretation; and the psychiatrist, who usually directed the clinic, conducted the full physical and psychiatric assessments, made the diagnoses, and provided psychotherapy (Ridenour, 1961).

The child guidance clinics commonly embraced the psychodynamic perspective, specifically the theories of Sigmund Freud and Adolf Meyer (Horn, 1989). Although in the early 1920s many clinics emphasized behavior theories and techniques, by 1930 these were quickly supplanted by a focus on intrapsychic factors within the child and parent. It is interesting that this shift in theoretical emphasis cannot be attributed to any evidenced superiority of effectiveness of psychodynamic therapy, as practitioners' own evaluations did not bear this out. Rather, it is likely that a causal factor in psychiatrists' embracing of the psychodynamic perspective was the increasing popularity of Freud's ideas. Embracing the dynamic approach, moreover, conferred on psychiatrists professional benefits, for "psychiatrists sought exclusive claim to the newer, esoteric form of treatment" (Horn, 1989, p. 147).

Although mental testing was the primary function of the clinical psychologist, the clinics also provided psychologists with opportunities to broaden their spheres of activity and expertise. The Commonwealth Fund endowed a training program for child guidance professionals, including clinical psychologists. One prominent psychologist trained under the auspices of this program was Carl R. Rogers (1902–1987), who began his professional work in 1930 at the Rochester Child Guidance Center. As previously mentioned, he would later conduct the first controlled research on psychotherapy and develop client-centered psychotherapy (Rogers, 1942, 1951, 1957). These clinics offered psychologists opportunities to provide individual psychotherapy, most typically for problems of an educational rather than an emotional nature (Horn, 1989). In any case, psychiatrists always supervised the psychologists' psychotherapeutic work. Though "participation in treatment enhanced the status of psychologists," it did so "only within clear limits that preserved the dominance of psychiatrists in child guidance practice," thus planting the seeds for interdisciplinary tensions (Horn, 1989, p. 105).

Turf Battles Between Psychiatry and Clinical Psychology

The child guidance movement illustrates a larger trend within American psychiatry: As the psychoanalytic approach in psychiatry gained ascendancy, psychiatrists in increasing numbers left the asylums for employment in community-based clinics and private practice. Here patients tended to be higher functioning, presenting with varying forms of neurosis, in contrast to the severe and persistent mental illnesses endemic to the asylums (Grob, 1994). Psychiatrists' exodus from the mental hospitals into the community would prove a mixed blessing for clinical psychologists, whose field was rooted in remedial work with children in educational institutions. On the one hand, clinical psychologists enjoyed growing opportunities to expand their professional roles, such as in the child guidance clinics. Furthermore, beginning in the early 1920s, some clinical psychologists ventured into private practice as trained psychoanalysts (VandenBos et al., 1992). On the other hand, professional boundaries became more and more obscured, fueling interdisciplinary tensions, as it became increasingly difficult to discriminate between educational and psychiatric problems (Napoli, 1981; Reisman, 1976). Psychiatrists, in response, sometimes went to great lengths to control the scope of psychologists' jurisdiction because they strongly believed that they should hold dominion over the treatment of mental illness and problems of adjustment. Though many psychologists felt particularly qualified to treat adjustment difficulties, "clinical psychologists often found themselves operating in the reflected light of psychiatry rather than shining on their own" (Napoli, 1981, p. 62).

The practice of psychoanalysis offers a relevant case in point. Many analysts, though not Freud, believed that psychoanalysis was a medical practice, and a fierce controversy over "lay analysis" ensued within the psychoanalytic movement. A. A. Brill, for example, was strongly opposed to nonphysicians practicing psychoanalysis, publishing an article to this effect in a New York newspaper in 1925 (Reisman, 1976). In contrast, Freud insisted, "Psychoanalysis is not a particular branch of medicine. I do not see how anyone can refuse to recognize this. Psychoanalysis is a part of psychology" (as cited in Reisman, 1976, p. 185).

In 1926, Theodor Reik, a young European lay analyst who had received his PhD in psychology from the University of Vienna in 1912 and had trained for several years with Freud, was sued in Vienna by one of his patients on charges of harmful treatment and quackery. Freud defended Reik, whose ordeal prompted Freud to publish *The Question of Lay Analysis* (1926/1978). Reik was subsequently acquitted, and no trained psychologist was ever prosecuted on the same grounds (Buchanan, 2003).

In any event, the controversy over lay analysis continued within the psychoanalytic community. In the 1920s, there were attempts by the New York state legislature and the American Medical Association to ban lay analysis, although "no law explicitly outlawing lay analysis ever existed in the United States" (Buchanan, 2003, p. 228; Reisman, 1976). Many psychoanalytic training institutes, however, became increasingly exclusive, denying entry to nonphysicians, brief exceptions notwithstanding (Hale, 1995).

Despite growing frictions between the two groups, psychiatrists and psychologists continued to cooperate within interdisciplinary clinical settings. However, psychiatrists had to be, in the words of William Menninger, "the quarterback of a team that works together" (as cited in Grob, 1994, p. 238). Be that as it may, the landscape would change significantly in the years following World War II. Psychiatry would lose its prior dominion over the provision of psychotherapy as clinical psychology established itself as a bona fide profession.

WORLD WAR II, CLINICAL PSYCHOLOGY, AND PSYCHOTHERAPY

During the early decades of the 20th century, clinical psychology was a young field, ambiguously defined and wanting professional status and legal recognition (Cautin, 2006). The term *clinical psychology* held a number of meanings, most of which were broadly conceived as dealing with practical problems in a variety of settings. Although psychological testing was the primary function of the clinical psychologist, conceptions of the nature and scope of the work of the clinical psychologist varied. Training in clinical psychology was largely piecemeal and informal, reflecting the inchoate nature of the field. Indeed, standards guiding training and accreditation did not exist, nor were there means to enforce such standards (Routh, 2000).

Improving clinical psychology's professional standing would not be easy, given resistance from sources both external and internal to the field. As observed earlier, psychiatrists made concerted efforts to restrict the province of the clinical psychologist (Reisman, 1976). At the same time, the APA, psychology's umbrella organization, did not consider professional issues to be particularly relevant to its mission. APA's bylaws, after all, prescribed the promotion of psychology as a science, not practice, and the dominant core of the APA, which was committed to advancing an academic scientific psychology, experienced the burgeoning success of applied psychologists as a threat to the scientific foundation of the association (Cautin, 2009). Applied psychologists often felt marginalized as they failed to secure APA resources to address the professional needs of defining the boundaries of their field and its training standards. As a consequence, various splinter groups, such as the American Association of Applied Psychologists (AAAP), formed throughout the 1930s to try to meet the needs of a growing number of clinical psychologists (Cautin, 2009; Dewsbury & Bolles, 1995). However, partly because most psychologists were employed in academic settings (Tryon, 1963), the progress of clinical psychologists to secure a professional identity and improve their professional status was arduous and slow. These efforts, however, would gather significant momentum from the challenges of World War II (Cautin, 2009).

World War II was a watershed event in the history of psychology, and of clinical psychology in particular, as a confluence of institutional, environmental, and economic influences transformed the field. The intradisciplinary tensions between academics and practitioners that gave rise to splinter groups throughout the 1930s were tempered as academic purists and applied psychologists joined forces to serve their country during wartime. Psychologists both within and outside the umbrella organization, motivated by their wartime collaboration, merged into a newly reformulated APA. Originally established in 1892 as an elite academic society, the APA now had as a mission "the advancement of psychology as a science, as a practice, and as a means of promoting human welfare" (Wolfle, 1946, p. 3). Within this new APA, applied psychologists achieved equal rank with their academic counterparts. This structural reorganization would significantly reduce the internal impediments to the pursuit of the professional psychologist's agenda.

World War II brought with it an unprecedented number of neuropsychiatric casualties—the U.S. Army in fact reported that almost half of its first 1.5 million medical discharges were due to neuropsychiatric disabilities—and changed the way psychiatrists understood psychological dysfunction (Farrell & Appel, 1944). The ensuing need for psychological services, bolstered by the advocacy of key individuals, led clinical psychologists to play an integral part on the neuropsychiatric treatment teams during the war. Psychiatrist William C. Menninger, who by 1943 was the chief of the Neuropsychiatry Branch of the Surgeon General's Office in the U.S. Army, was a particularly ardent champion of psychologists' involvement. Lt. Col. Robert J. Carpenter, executive officer of the Medical Corps in the Surgeon General's Office, observed that psychologists were "invaluable assistants to the hard pressed neuropsychiatrists. . . . The services of these clinical psychologists are needed more than ever before because of the increasing scarcity of neuro-psychiatrists" (as cited in Moore, 1992, p. 782). Indeed, following World War II there were five times as many veterans in the United States as before the war (Miller, 1947).

The psychiatrist was the authority in this setting, but acute demand for psychological treatment required that other mental health professionals be trained to assume duties beyond their usual responsibilities (VandenBos et al., 1992). More than 400 clinical psychologists served in the military's neuropsychiatric services (Menninger, 1947). Although only a small minority of clinical psychologists had provided psychotherapy prior to World War II, "the door was largely opened by the military, which allowed psychologists to be put to the test as psychotherapists" (Benjamin & Baker, 2004, p. 68). In this way psychologists came to regard their role of psychotherapists as both reasonable and significant (VandenBos et al., 1992). Although the psychiatric community would continue to resist psychologists' growing claim on psychotherapy (Buchanan, 2003), psychologists, through their wartime service, earned respect and approval from allied professions and the public at large.

Growing national awareness of psychological disorders and the daunting expectation of an unprecedented need for mental health services for the 16 million discharged veterans of World War II prompted the Veterans Administration (VA) and the National Institute of Mental Health (NIMH) to fund programs that produced training and employment opportunities for clinical psychologists and others, expressly including opportunities to conduct psychotherapy. These circumstances had profound implications for psychology, and for clinical psychology in particular, as "the orientation of American psychology changed from an academic, laboratory-based science to a science-based profession" (Pickren, 2003, p. 760).

Veterans Administration and Clinical Psychology Training

The unprecedented need for mental health care among newly discharged veterans underscored the demand for more mental health professionals. Indeed, in spring 1946, almost 60% of patients in the VA hospitals were neuropsychiatric. The VA, which was established in 1930 as the sole organization in charge of veterans' issues, was justifiably concerned that traditional American medical care would prove inadequate to care for the psychiatric needs of its veterans (Moore, 1992). The VA thus assumed this social responsibility by committing itself to "the most advanced and efficient medical care in all fields, including psychiatry" (Miller, 1946, p. 182). This included an integral role for clinical psychologists, who had demonstrated their usefulness during the war. By virtue of their diagnostic skills . . . and their superior understanding of the principles of normal behavior and how these can be applied to problems of personal adjustment . . . [clinical] psychologists in the Army, Navy, and other military organizations were given tasks of great responsibility and professional importance. (Miller, 1946, p. 181)

However, the resolution to recruit qualified clinical psychologists into the VA was complicated by the fact that there was "no corps of solidly trained clinical psychologists available" (Moore, 1992, p. 788). Training in clinical psychology varied tremendously in terms of form and rigor (Sears, 1947), reflecting the myriad definitions of the clinical psychologist and the fledging status of the field (Cautin, 2008b; Sears, 1946). To be sure, applied psychologists had long been concerned with training standards, particularly throughout the 1930s (Cautin, 2008b; Farreras, 2005). However, efforts to address training issues did not gain much traction, as the APA often dismissed such concerns as irrelevant to the organization's mission.

The VA's strong appeal (and financial support) for more adequately trained clinical psychologists, however, impelled organized psychology to articulate training standards (Shakow et al., 1945) and to evaluate existing graduate training programs and facilities (Sears, 1946, 1947). In fall 1946, the VA, under the directorship of James Grier Miller (1916–2002), initiated a training program in clinical psychology. At Harvard, Miller had earned his medical degree in psychiatry in 1942 and his doctoral degree in psychology the following year. As a member of the psychological evaluation staff of the Office of Strategic Services, the predecessor of the Central Intelligence Agency, Miller became a consultant to General Bradley in anticipation of the great demand for mental health services for discharged veterans. In 1946, Miller was put in charge of the clinical psychology section of the VA, where he initiated the VA training program in conjunction with the 22 educational institutions recognized by the APA as providing adequate training (Miller, 1946; Pickren, 2003).

In all VA treatment settings, clinical psychologists would perform diagnostic, therapeutic, and research functions. Miller (1946) maintained that diagnosis would be the primary task of the psychologist, but that the psychologist would also have therapeutic responsibilities:

If the case involves such fields as readjustment of habits; personality problems within the normal range; educational disabilities such as reading defects, speech impairments, or similar difficulties requiring re-education; or relatively minor psychoneurotic conditions without important somatic components, the patient may be referred to a clinical psychologist for individual or group treatment. (p. 184)

Miller was particularly enthusiastic about the clinical psychologist's research function. Owing to their specialized training in test construction, experimental design, and scientific method, clinical psychologists could make their most important contribution developing clinical materials and evaluating patient outcomes. With such research endeavors, "tremendous opportunities for advancing mental sciences [were] available" (Miller, 1946, p. 184).

Miller established the doctoral degree in psychology as the minimum requirement for clinical psychologists' entry into the field. Staff psychologists who previously had been hired at the predoctoral level could not be promoted without earning their doctoral degrees, and by 1951 all of these employees had received their doctorates, entered the training program, or left the VA (Moore, 1992). As part of the VA training program in clinical psychology, students were expected to work part-time in the VA; they were paid at hourly rates commensurate with their number of years in training. Students received their academic preparation from the universities, which determined the training curriculum and the required number of training hours. Miller added that faculty at affiliated psychology departments would be hired as part-time consultants. In this role, they would supervise students in their clinical work and "supervise students and other staff in the conducting of psychological research, as well as conduct research themselves" (Baker & Pickren, 2007, p. 24).

During its 1st year, the training program funded 215 students from affiliated universities. In the ensuing years, the VA training program grew rapidly in terms of staff, supervision, and trainees; by 1950 there were 650 trainees. Moreover, a formal evaluation of the program conducted in 1956 observed that most of the graduates of the program tended to take staff positions in the VA, even though this was not a stipulation of their training (Wolford, 1956).

Students, veterans, universities, and the profession of clinical psychology all profited from the VA training program, which called for a strong collaboration between the VA and the university. It was a mutually advantageous situation: Veterans received services that were hitherto lacking, and universities enjoyed governmental funding and increased opportunities for its psychology professors to expand their knowledge base and clinical expertise. The VA training program also helped to define training standards in clinical psychology, as necessity pushed training issues to the fore.

National Institute of Mental Health and Clinical Psychology

The VA was not the only federal institution to help transform clinical psychology into a bona fide profession. The passage of the National Mental Health Act (NMHA) of 1946 signaled the federal government's commitment to prioritizing mental health. The NMHA authorized funding for basic and applied research and for the training of mental health professionals. The Division of Mental Hygiene of the U.S. Public Health Service (USPHS) was initially responsible for the implementation of the NMHA initiatives, but was eliminated when the NIMH was officially inaugurated in 1949 (Pickren, 2005).

In January 1947, the USPHS established the Training and Standards Section, or what was known as the Committee on Training, to be responsible for developing an adequate supply of mental health service professionals (Baker & Benjamin, 2005). The committee was charged with distributing training grants and stipends. Among other things, the training grants enabled institutions to hire clinical faculty who could offer advanced degrees in clinical psychology. Also, individual graduate students in approved university-based training programs could earn training stipends to help subsidize their education (Baker & Benjamin, 2005).

The Committee on Training was divided into four subgroups: psychiatry, psychiatric social work, psychiatric nursing, and clinical psychology. The ratio of psychiatrists to psychologists on the committee was 4:1, as was the ratio of psychiatrists to psychiatric social workers; there was only one psychiatric nurse. The National Advisory Mental Health Council was the final arbiter of funding allocations and, reflecting psychiatry's dominance, ultimately apportioned 40% of the approximate $1 million in available funds to psychiatry, equally dividing the remaining resources among the three other subgroups (Baker & Benjamin, 2005; Pickren, 2005).

However, clinical psychology earned a prominent place on the committee, psychiatry's supremacy notwithstanding. Its inclusion was owed to the discipline's demonstrated usefulness in the treatment of mental disorders in America and to the work of key individuals who helped to bolster the field's legitimacy by establishing training standards (Baker & Benjamin, 2005). David Shakow (1901–1981), who was appointed to the USPHS's Committee on Training and was elected chair of its clinical psychology subgroup (Baker & Benjamin, 2005), contributed a great deal in this regard. As an active participant in the myriad committees and conferences devoted to training standards in clinical psychology throughout the 1940s, Shakow was in the vanguard of clinical psychology's path to professionalization (Cautin, 2006, 2008a). He began to formulate his own ideas on clinical psychology training during his tenure at Worcester State Hospital (WSH) as chief psychologist and director of psychological research from 1928 to 1946 (Cautin, 2008b; Shakow, 1938, 1942, 1969). Drawing on his experiences at WSH, Shakow exerted substantial influence on the national debate regarding clinical psychology training. In 1941, as a member of the Committee on the Training of Clinical Psychologists convened by the AAAP, Shakow drafted a 4-year training program that integrated academic training in scientific methodology and clinical training in diagnosis and psychotherapy (Shakow, 1942). Following the integration of the AAAP and the APA, Shakow chaired the Subcommittee on Graduate Internship Training, which met at the Vineland

Training School in 1944 (Baker & Benjamin, 2000). The report that resulted from this meeting—what came to be known as the Shakow Report—reflected what Shakow considered to be the primary functions of the clinical psychologist: diagnosis, research, and psychotherapy. Two years later, as chair of the newly established APA Committee on Training in Clinical Psychology (CTCP), Shakow solicited feedback from all committee members on the Shakow Report, receiving nearly unanimous approval. In 1947, the APA officially endorsed the report (APA, 1947), which likely constituted the most thorough description of a recommended program of training for clinical psychology ever written (Baker & Benjamin, 2000).

Prompted by the VA and the USPHS, the CTCP was also charged with visiting and evaluating institutions providing training in the field, an undertaking that was funded by the Mental Hygiene Division of the USPHS. The committee initiated its evaluative task in 1948, publishing two reports on doctoral training programs and facilities (APA, 1948, 1949; Baker & Benjamin, 2000). The CTCP commended the psychologists, with whom they visited, expressing confidence in the preparedness of the students they were graduating. In addition, in characterizing the current state of graduate education in clinical psychology, the CTCP delineated several problems that confronted the field. Most relevant to the current discussion, the committee stressed the need for psychotherapy training throughout the doctoral program, not just during the internship or postdoctoral years. Also, although the committee "t[ook] no stand on the question," it mentioned many departments' growing concern of the "extent to which their students will go into the private practice of clinical psychology" (APA, 1949, p. 340). The committee also bemoaned the overly narrow conception of the field, which focused almost exclusively on psychiatric hospitals and people with severe disturbances (APA, 1947). Indeed, Shakow's ideas on clinical psychology training were largely inspired by the medical–psychiatric settings in which he worked, reflecting his close alliance with psychiatry (Cautin, 2006).

Boulder Conference, 1949

Despite the accomplishments of the CTCP, there remained a need for greater consensus with regard to "the principles and procedures for the training of the clinical psychologist" (Baker & Benjamin, 2005, p. 244). Thus, in a collaborative effort, the NIMH and the APA prepared for the Boulder Conference on Graduate Education in Psychology (Raimy, 1950), which was held at the University of Colorado in August and September 1949. Its 73 participants represented "each of 42 institutions granting the Ph.D. . . . in Clinical Psychology, interested government agencies [including James G. Miller from the VA], field training institutions, related professions and relevant APA Committees [including all members of the CTCP]" ("Boulder Conference," 1949).

University departments were concerned about giving external funders authority over their programs, particularly the curricula. Furthermore, many academic psychologists did not support the strengthening of applied psychology programs, lest scientific training and research, the presumed cornerstone of a doctoral degree in psychology, be compromised (Baker & Benjamin, 2005). The major result of the Boulder Conference was an affirmation of the scientist–practitioner model of training (also referred to as the Boulder model), according to which clinical psychologists were to be trained as researchers and as service providers, thus acquiring a unique set of skills among mental health professionals (Cautin, 2006; Farreras, 2005). Some conference participants opposed this training paradigm, particularly its psychiatric emphasis, but for a variety of reasons the Boulder model prevailed (Farreras, 2005). Detractors and alternative training models notwithstanding, it arguably remains the predominant training model in clinical psychology today (Baker & Benjamin, 2000).

Psychotherapy Research

In addition to funding the training of clinical psychologists, the NIMH championed and funded research in mental health. Psychotherapy research, in particular, was an emerging specialty area, prompted in part by Hans Eysenck's (1952) provocative article in which he bemoaned the lack of experimental rigor in studies on psychotherapy's effects. Although the practice of psychology had existed as long as had human suffering (Benjamin & Baker, 2004), the scientific understanding of psychotherapy was in its infancy. Research on psychotherapy, financially supported by the government, was motivated as much by the desire to understand its process and outcome as by the desire to legitimize its practice as science-based.

The NIMH committed significant resources to fund psychotherapy research, spending over $55 million on approximately 530 psychotherapy research grants between 1959 and 1977 (Rosner, 2005). In its early years, the NIMH invested considerable resources in David Shakow's psychoanalytic film study. In 1954, Shakow had become the first director of the Intramural Psychology Laboratory at the NIMH. His film study was an ambitious project in which he attempted to film an entire course of psychoanalysis in order to examine its process objectively. However, mired in a deluge of unforeseen obstacles, the film project ultimately was considered, by Shakow himself, "a failure, a very expensive failure" (as cited in Rosner, 2005, p. 128). Its very existence, however, "reflected the unparalleled generosity of Congress in supporting creative basic research and the unparalleled optimism of some psychoanalysts that subjectivity, objectivity, and democracy could work hand in hand in the creation of a new, 'objective,' psychotherapeutic science" (as cited in Rosner, 2005, p. 128).

During this period of flexibility and financial support, epistemological debates regarding the proper method by which to investigate psychotherapy scientifically began to emerge (Rosner, 2005), with some researchers valuing naturalistic methods over experimental, and vice versa; such debates continue to this day (see Chapters 10 and 11, this volume). The NIMH, at least at this time, remained impartial in the face of these controversies (Rosner, 2005), as the government was more interested in finding answers than in taking sides.

The NIMH financed three invitation-only conferences on research in psychotherapy. The first, in 1958, was initiated and organized by an ad hoc subcommittee of the APA's Division 12 (Clinical Psychology), chaired by Eli A. Rubinstein, who was at the time a member of the NIMH's Committee on Training. A "select group of research workers who [had] been most active in actual research activities . . . were brought together to present and mutually discuss the status of their various research projects" (Ad Hoc Subcommittee, 1957). In so doing, various critical issues related to the effects of psychotherapy were highlighted and discussed, including the goals of therapy, the problem of controls, and measures of change and outcome ("Summary Statement," 1957). The conference helped to create a "new spirit of collaboration between groups of different persuasions" (Rosner, 2005, p. 131). In many respects, the conference was considered a success by most of the attendees.

The NIMH funded two similar conferences, in 1961 and 1966. It is, however, noteworthy that the socioeconomic milieu changed considerably in the years following the 1958 conference, as Congress (and insurance companies) became increasingly interested in quantitative approaches and demonstrable results with respect to the efficacy of psychotherapy. Meanwhile, the field witnessed a proliferation of psychotherapeutic theories and techniques, thus further incentivizing psychologists to demonstrate the relative superiority of their particular method. Nevertheless, throughout the 1950s the NIMH offered significant financial support for psychotherapy, in terms of both training and research (VandenBos et al., 1992).

Professionalization of Clinical Psychology

With the Boulder model, the burgeoning field of clinical psychology had endorsed a training paradigm and had articulated training standards, and it had initiated an accreditation program, prompted by the needs and interests of the VA and the NIMH. Contrary to the original intentions of the CTCP (APA, 1947) and the framers of the Boulder model (Raimy, 1950), psychotherapy increasingly became the predominant activity of clinical psychologists, as the availability, use, and acceptance of psychotherapeutic services steadily increased after World War II (Garfield, 1981).

In the face of escalating conflicts with psychiatry over medical claims to the exclusive practice of psychotherapy (Buchanan, 2003; Napoli, 1981), clinical psychologists endeavored to amass additional indicators of genuine professional status and legal recognition, markers that psychiatry had previously achieved. In 1945, Connecticut became the first state to certify psychologists, and in the following year, Virginia passed the first licensing law for psychologists (Dörken, 1979; see chap. 16d, this volume). Licensure defines the practice of psychology and restricts that practice to competent, qualified individuals. Certification, in contrast, specifies the criteria used to determine who is entitled to use the title *psychologist*; it may or may not define the practice of psychology (VandenBos et al., 1992). In addition to protecting the public from uncredentialed practitioners, these regulations conferred legal recognition on psychologists as mental health providers, a necessary step in their battle for parity with their medical counterparts.

Organized psychiatry had long resisted the expansion of the psychologist's practitioner role. The tensions, however, became ever more inflamed throughout the 1950s, as psychologists' initial legislative successes elicited retaliation by the psychiatric community in the form of legislative actions and threats of litigation across several states (Buchanan, 2003; Grob, 1991, Chapter 5). Within the psychiatric community, to be sure, there were differing opinions with regard to the psychologist's claim over psychotherapy. Biologically oriented psychiatrists saw little value in psychotherapy, considering it a threat to psychiatry's image: They considered the issue irrelevant to their discipline's agenda. Psychoanalytically oriented psychiatrists, in contrast, were more amenable to cooperating with psychologists, although there were disagreements among them with respect to the degree of inclusiveness that psychologists should be afforded. However, even the most inclusive among them fought to maintain their superior place in the professional hierarchy (Buchanan, 2003).

The interdisciplinary battles of the 1950s ended in a standoff, as neither side could provide an adequate definition of psychotherapy—either legally or intellectually. Neither side was willing to "force a court test of their exclusive right to practice psychotherapy because the burden of definition would fall on the side initiating legal action" (Buchanan, 2003, p. 242). Defining the enterprise too broadly undermined any one discipline's exclusive claim on the practice, as there were other nonmedical professions, such as social work and psychiatric nursing, engaged in similar activities. Exceedingly narrow and specific definitions, on the other hand, "had little currency beyond the fragile consensus found within each intellectual tribe" (Buchanan, 2003, p. 234). Moreover, the virtual absence of comparative studies offered no empirical basis from which either profession could argue for its own superiority (Grob, 1991). The impasse inevitably favored clinical psychology. Despite aggressive maneuvers on the part of organized psychiatry, which continued to insist that lay psychotherapy be conducted only under medical supervision, psychologists continued to gain legislative ground. By 1960, 15 states had enacted licensing or certification laws, and this figure would nearly triple in the following decade (VandenBos et al., 1992). Indeed, psychiatry was losing its proprietary claim on the provision of psychotherapy—a trend that continues today (Mojtabai & Olfson, 2008). At the same time, growing numbers of psychologists were entering private practice. This tendency would only accelerate in the decades to come.

CONCLUSION

Although commonly associated with Freudian psychoanalysis, the roots of American psychotherapy actually have their origins in moral treatment and the mental therapeutics of the late 19th century. The medical community, previously dismissive of psychotherapeutic methods, began to take interest only once the Emmanuel movement had garnered significant national public enthusiasm (Caplan, 1998). Although a vibrant psychotherapy movement existed in the United States well before Freud's 1909 visit (Burnham, 1967), Freud did introduce psychoanalysis, which ultimately came to dominate the American psychotherapy scene in the first half of the 20th century. Psychiatry, holding that psychoanalysis was a medical specialty, laid exclusive claim to its practice. In the 1920s, applied psychologists, whose professional contributions were typically limited to psychological testing, slowly began to expand their professional role into the domains of diagnosis and treatment, psychiatrists' proprietary claims notwithstanding. The challenges of World War II irrevocably changed the American psychotherapy landscape, as the work of key individuals and an unprecedented demand for psychotherapy hastened the development and professionalization of clinical psychology and weakened psychiatry's dominion over the provision of psychotherapy.

There have always been psychological explanations of maladaptive behavior and illness, and such explanations imply psychological treatments. Between 1860 and 1960, the scientific community and the public were variably receptive to these treatments, as scientific, economic, and cultural factors collaboratively influenced both public attitudes and the development of psychotherapy as a professional enterprise. By 1910, the medical community had claimed the practice of psychotherapy as the province of the medical profession (Caplan, 1998). Around 1920, a small number of applied psychologists began to provide psychotherapy, and following World War II, the development of clinical psychology as a profession accelerated, partly as a result of an unparalleled need for psychotherapeutic services. The contemporaneous development of the Boulder model, which identified psychotherapy as one of the defining functions of the clinical psychologist, cemented the relationship between the development of clinical psychology and the growth of psychotherapy. By 1960, psychotherapy had been embraced by American culture, and an ever-increasing number of licensed psychologists were providing these services.

The psychotherapy scene in the United States would continue to change in the ensuing decades as the number of alternative psychotherapies, most notably cognitive, behavioral, and integrative approaches, would increase dramatically. The decline of psychoanalysis within psychology and psychiatry can be attributed to several factors (Hale, 1995). Mounting competition among extant psychotherapies played a critical role. In addition, the advent of psychotropic medications ushered in a resurgence of the somatic paradigm in psychiatry, challenging the tenets of psychoanalysis. Moreover, the basis for psychotherapy evaluation changed: The scientific community's staunch commitment to objective studies using quantifiable data, as opposed to the case study method, challenged the psychoanalytic movement's claims of validity and effectiveness. Furthermore, growing criticism of psychoanalysis from both within and without the psychoanalytic movement would be instrumental in tempering its dominance in psychology and psychiatry (Hale, 1995).

In addition to the developments in psychotherapy itself, the succeeding decades would witness social, economic, and political changes that would contribute to the increasing provision of psychotherapy by medical and nonmedical mental health professionals alike. Governmental initiatives, such as the Community Mental Health Program and Medicare and Medicaid programs, and further legislative successes, such as third-party reimbursement for psychologists conducting psychotherapy, would be instrumental in the expansion of psychotherapy practice in the United States (VandenBos et al., 1992). Environmental factors thus would play a critical role in the further development of psychotherapy and its continued relationship with psychology.

REFERENCES

Ad Hoc Subcommittee, Division 12. (1957, March 1). *Letter to D. Shakow*. (Shakow Papers, M1370). Archives of the History of American Psychology, University of Akron, Akron, OH.

American Psychological Association, Committee on Training of Clinical Psychologists. (1947). Recommended graduate training program in clinical psychology. *American Psychologist, 2,* 539–558. doi:10.1037/h0058236

American Psychological Association, Committee on Training of Clinical Psychologists. (1948). Training facilities: 1948. *American Psychologist, 3,* 317–318. doi:10.1037/h0056261

American Psychological Association, Committee on Training of Clinical Psychologists. (1949). Doctoral training programs in clinical psychology: 1949. *American Psychologist, 4,* 331–341. doi:10.1037/h0057831

Baker, D. B., & Benjamin, L. T., Jr. (2000). The affirmation of the scientist-practitioner: A look back at Boulder. *American Psychologist, 55*, 241–247. doi:10.1037/0003-066X.55.2.241

Baker, D. B., & Benjamin, L. T., Jr. (2005). Creating a profession: The National Institute of Mental Health and the training of psychologists, 1946–1954. In W. E. Pickren & S. F. Schneider (Eds.), *Psychology and the National Institute of Mental Health: A historical analysis of science, practice, and policy* (pp. 181–207). Washington, DC: American Psychological Association.

Baker, R. R., & Pickren, W. E. (2007). *Psychology and the Department of Veterans Affairs: A historical analysis of training, research, practice, and advocacy.* Washington, DC: American Psychological Association.

Beers, C. W. (1908). *A mind that found itself.* Pittsburgh, PA: University of Pittsburgh Press.

Benjamin, L. T., Jr., & Baker, D. B. (2004). *From séance to science: A history of the profession of psychology in America.* Belmont, CA: Wadsworth/Thomson Learning.

Boulder Conference: Major Topics and Samples of Specific Questions. (1949). (Shakow Papers, M1383). Archives of the History of American Psychology, University of Akron, Akron, OH.

Bruce, H. A. (1911). *Scientific mental healing.* Boston, MA: Little, Brown, and Company.

Buchanan, R. D. (2003). Legislative warriors: American psychiatrists, psychologists, and competing claims over psychotherapy in the 1950s. *Journal of the History of the Behavioral Sciences, 39*, 225–249. doi:10.1002/jhbs.10113

Burnham, J. C. (1967). Psychoanalysis and American medicine, 1894–1918: Medicine, science, and culture. *Psychological Issues, 4* (Monograph No. 20).

Camfield, T. M. (1992). The American Psychological Association and World War I: 1914 to 1919. In R. B. Evans, V. S. Sexton, & T. C. Cadwallader (Eds.), *100 years: The American Psychological Association. A historical perspective* (pp. 91–118). Washington, DC: American Psychological Association.

Caplan, E. (1998). *Mind games: American culture and the birth of psychotherapy.* Berkeley, CA: University of California Press.

Capshew, J. H. (1999). *Psychologists on the march: Science, practice, and professional identity in America, 1929–1969.* New York, NY: Cambridge University Press.

Carducci, B. J. (2009). *The psychology of personality* (2nd ed.). Malden, MA: Wiley.

Cautin, R. L. (2006). David Shakow: Architect of modern clinical psychology. In D. Dewsbury, L. T. Benjamin, Jr., & M. Wertheimer (Eds.), *Portraits of pioneers in psychology* (Vol. VI, pp. 207–224). Washington, DC: American Psychological Association.

Cautin, R. L. (2008a). David Shakow and schizophrenia research at Worcester State Hospital: The roots of the scientist-practitioner model. *Journal of the History of the Behavioral Sciences, 44*, 219–237. doi:10.1002/jhbs.20312

Cautin, R. L. (2008b, August). *Clinical training comes of age: David Shakow and the Worcester State Hospital internship program.* Paper presented at the American Psychological Association, Boston, MA.

Cautin, R. L. (2009). The founding of the APS: Part 1. Dialectical tensions within organized psychology. *Perspectives on Psychological Science, 4*, 211–223. doi:10.1111/j.1745-6924.2009.01120.x

Coon, D. J. (1992). Testing the limits of sense and science: American experimental psychologists combat spiritualism, 1880–1920. *American Psychologist, 47*, 143–151. doi:10.1037/0003-066X.47.2.143

Crabtree, A. (1993). *From Mesmer to Freud: Magnetic sleep and the roots of psychological healing.* New Haven, CT: Yale University Press.

Cushman, P. (1992). Psychotherapy to 1992: A historical situated interpretation. In D. K. Freedheim (Ed.), *History of psychotherapy: A century of change* (pp. 21–64). Washington, DC: American Psychological Association.

Dewsbury, D. A., & Bolles, R. C. (1995). The founding of the Psychonomic Society. *Psychonomic Bulletin & Review, 2*, 216–233.

Dörken, H. (1979). Current legal and legislative status of professional psychology. In C. A. Kiesler, N. A. Cummings, & G. R. VandenBos (Eds.), *Psychology and national health insurance: A sourcebook* (pp. 175–189). Washington, DC: American Psychological Association.

Eysenck, H. J. (1952). The effects of psychotherapy: An evaluation. *Journal of Consulting Psychology, 16*, 319–324. doi:10.1037/h0063633

Fancher, R. E. (1996). *Pioneers of psychology* (3rd ed.). New York, NY: Norton.

Farrell, M. J., & Appel, J. W. (1944). Current trends in military neuropsychiatry. *The American Journal of Psychiatry, 101*, 12–19.

Farreras, I. G. (2005). The historical context for National Institute of Mental Health support of American Psychological Association training and accreditation efforts. In W. E. Pickren & S. F. Schneider (Eds.), *Psychology and the National Institute of Mental Health: A historical analysis of science, practice, and policy* (pp. 153–179). Washington, DC: American Psychological Association.

Freud, S. (1910). The origins and development of psychoanalysis. *The American Journal of Psychology, 21*, 181–218. doi:10.2307/1413001

Freud, S. (1978). *The question of lay analysis.* New York, NY: Norton. (Original work published 1926)

Garfield, S. L. (1981). Psychotherapy: A 40-year appraisal. *American Psychologist, 36*, 174 183.

Garfield, S. L., & Bergin, A. E. (1994). Introduction and historical overview. In A. E. Bergin & S. L. Garfield (Eds.), *Handbook of psychotherapy and behavior change* (pp. 3–18). New York, NY: Wiley.

Gay, P. (2006). *Freud: A life for our time.* New York, NY: Norton.

Gifford, G. E., Jr., (Ed.). (1978). *Psychoanalysis, psychotherapy, and the New England medical scene, 1894–1944.* New York, NY: Science History Publications.

Grob, G. N. (1966). *The state and the mentally ill: A history of Worcester State Hospital in Massachusetts, 1830–1920.* Durham: University of North Carolina Press.

Grob, G. N. (1983). *Mental illness and American society, 1875–1940.* Princeton, NJ: Princeton University Press.

Grob, G. N. (1991). *From asylum to community: Mental health policy in modern America.* Princeton, NJ: Princeton University Press.

Grob, G. N. (1994). *The mad among us: A history of the care of America's mentally ill.* Cambridge, MA: Harvard University Press.

Hale, N. G., Jr. (1971). *Freud and the Americans: The beginnings of psychoanalysis in the United States, 1876–1917.* New York, NY: Oxford University Press.

Hale, N. G., Jr. (1995). *The rise and crisis of psychoanalysis in the United States: Freud and the Americans, 1917–1985.* New York, NY: Oxford University Press.

Harris, B. (1979). Whatever happened to Little Albert? *American Psychologist, 34*, 151–160. doi:10.1037/0003-066X.34.2.151

Horn, M. (1989). *Before it's too late: The Child Guidance Movement in the United States, 1922–1945.* Philadelphia, PA: Temple University Press.

Hornstein, G. A. (1992). The return of the repressed: Psychology's problematic relations with psychoanalysis, 1909–1960. *American Psychologist, 47*, 254–263. doi:10.1037/0003-066X.47.2.254

Howard, E. M. (1978). Early vicissitudes of psychoanalysis at the Austen Riggs Center. In G. E. Gifford, Jr., (Ed.), *Psychoanalysis, psychotherapy, and the New England medical scene, 1894–1944* (pp. 273–281). New York, NY: Science History Publications.

Jones, M. C. (1924a). A laboratory study of fear: The case of Peter. *Pedagogical Seminary, 31,* 308–315.

Jones, M. C. (1924b). The elimination of children's fears. *Journal of Experimental Psychology, 7,* 382–390. doi:10.1037/h0072283

Lakin, M. (1998). Carl Rogers and the culture of psychotherapy. In G. A. Kimble & M. Wertheimer (Eds.), *Portraits of pioneers in psychology* (Vol. III, pp. 245–258). Washington, DC: American Psychological Association and Lawrence Erlbaum.

Makari, G. (2008). *Revolution in mind: The creation of psychoanalysis.* New York, NY: Harper-Collins.

Marx, O. M. (1978). Morton Prince and psychopathology. In G. E. Gifford, Jr. (Ed.), *Psychoanalysis, psychotherapy, and the New England medical scene, 1894–1944* (pp. 155–162). New York, NY: Science History Publications.

McReynolds, P. (1997). *Lightner Witmer: His life and times.* Washington, DC: American Psychological Association.

Menninger, W. C. (1947). Psychiatric experience in the war, 1941–1946. *American Journal of Psychiatry, 103,* 577–586.

Meyer, D. (1980). *The positive thinkers: Religion and pop psychology from Mary Baker Eddy to Oral Roberts.* New York, NY: Pantheon Books.

Miller, J. G. (1946). Clinical psychology in the Veterans Administration. *American Psychologist, 1,* 181–189. doi:10.1037/h0055143

Miller, J. G. (1947). The Veterans Administration and clinical psychology. *Journal of Clinical Psychology, 3,* 1–3. doi:10.1002/1097-4679(194701)3:1<1::AID-JCLP 2270030102>3.0.CO;2-M

Mojtabai, R., & Olfson, M. (2008). National trends in psychotherapy in office-based psychiatrists. *Archives of General Psychiatry, 65,* 962–970. doi:10.1001/archpsyc.65.8.962

Moore, D. L. (1992). The Veterans Administration and the training program in psychology. In D. K. Freedheim (Ed.), *History of psychotherapy* (pp. 776–800). Washington, DC: American Psychological Association.

Napoli, D. S. (1981). *Architects of adjustment: The history of the psychological profession in the United States.* New York, NY: Kennikat Press.

Pickren, W. E. (2003). James Grier Miller (1916–2002). *American Psychologist, 58,* 760. doi:10.1037/0003-066X.58.9.760

Pickren, W. E. (2005). Science, practice, and policy: An introduction to the history of psychology and the National Institute of Mental Health. In W. E. Pickren & S. F. Schneider (Eds.), *Psychology and the National Institute of Mental Health: A Historical analysis of science, practice, and policy* (pp. 3–15). Washington, DC: American Psychological Association.

Raimy, V. C. (1950). *Training in clinical psychology.* New York, NY: Prentice Hall.

Reisman, J. M. (1976). *A history of clinical psychology.* New York, NY: Irvington.

Ridenour, N. (1961). *Mental health in the United States: A fifty-year history.* Cambridge, MA: Harvard University Press for the Commonwealth Fund.

Riggs, B. C. (1978). Austen Fox Riggs: Pioneer in the psychotherapy of the neuroses. In G. E. Gifford, Jr. (Ed.), *Psychoanalysis, psychotherapy, and the New England medical scene, 1894–1944* (pp. 282–292). New York, NY: Science History Publications.

Rogers, C. R. (1939). *The clinical treatment of the problem child.* Boston, MA: Houghton Mifflin.

Rogers, C. R. (1942). *Counseling and psychotherapy.* New York, NY: Houghton Mifflin.

Rogers, C. R. (1951). *Client-centered therapy: Its current practice, implications, and theory.* Boston, MA: Houghton Mifflin.

Rogers, C. R. (1957). The necessary and sufficient conditions of therapeutic personality change. *Journal of Consulting Psychology, 21,* 95–103. doi:10.1037/h0045357

Rosner, R. I. (2005). Psychotherapy research and the National Institute of Mental Health, 1948–1980. In W. E. Pickren & S. F. Schneider (Eds.), *Psychology and the National Institute of Mental Health: A historical analysis of science, practice, and policy* (pp. 113–150). Washington, DC: American Psychological Association.

Routh, D. K. (1996). Lightner Witmer and the first 100 years of clinical psychology. *American Psychologist, 51*, 244–247. doi:10.1037/0003-066X.51.3.244

Routh, D. K. (2000). Clinical psychology training. *American Psychologist, 55*, 236–241. doi:10.1037/0003-066X.55.2.236

Rutherford, A. (2006). Mother of behavior therapy and beyond: Mary Cover Jones and the study of the "whole child." In D. A. Dewsbury, L. T. Benjamin, Jr., & M. Wertheimer (Eds.), *Portraits of pioneers in psychology* (Vol. VI, pp. 189–204). Washington, DC, and Mahwah, NJ: American Psychological Association and Lawrence Erlbaum.

Samelson, F. (1981). Struggle for scientific authority: The reception of Watson's behaviorism. *Journal of the History of the Behavioral Sciences, 17*, 399–425. doi:10.1002/1520-6696(198107)17:3<399::AID-JHBS2300170310>3.0.CO;2-2

Sears, R. R. (1946). Graduate training facilities. I. General information II. Clinical psychology. *American Psychologist, 1*, 135–150. doi:10.1037/h0058566

Sears, R. R. (1947). Clinical training facilities: 1947. *American Psychologist, 2*, 199–205. doi:10.1037/h0061605

Shakow, D. (1938). An internship year for psychologists. *Journal of Consulting Psychology, 2*, 73–76. doi:10.1037/h0055488

Shakow, D. (1942). The training of the clinical psychologist. *Journal of Consulting Psychology, 6*, 277–288. doi:10.1037/h0059917

Shakow, D. (1969). The Worcester Internship Program. In D. Shakow (Ed.), *Clinical psychology as science and profession: A forty-year odyssey* (pp. 87–98). Chicago, IL: Aldine.

Shakow, D., Brotemarkle, R. A., Doll, E. A., Kinder, E. F., Moore, B. V., & Smith, S. (1945). Graduate internship in psychology: Report by the Subcommittee on Graduate Internship Training to the Committee on Graduate and Professional Training of the American Psychological Association and the American Association for Applied Psychology. *Journal of Consulting Psychology, 9*, 243–266. doi:10.1037/h0058618

Shakow, D., & Rapaport, D. (1964). *The influence of Freud on American psychology. Psychological Issues, 4* (Monograph No. 13).

Sicherman, B. (1978). Isador H. Coriat: The making of an American psychoanalyst. In G. E. Gifford, Jr. (Ed.), *Psychoanalysis, psychotherapy, and the New England medical scene, 1894–1944* (pp. 163–180). New York, NY: Science History Publications.

Summary Statement on the Conference of Psychotherapy Research. (1957). (Shakow Papers, M1370). Archives of the History of American Psychology, University of Akron, Akron, OH.

Taylor, E. (1999). *Shadow culture: Psychology and spirituality in America.* Washington, DC: Counterpoint.

Taylor, E. (2000). Psychotherapeutics and the problematic origins of clinical psychology in America. *American Psychologist, 55*, 1029–1033. doi:10.1037/0003-066X.55.9.1029

Truitt, R. P. (1926). The role of the child guidance clinic in the mental hygiene movement. *American Journal of Public Health, 16*, 22–24. doi:10.2105/AJPH.16.1.22

Tryon, R. C. (1963). Psychology in flux: The academic-professional bipolarity. *American Psychologist, 18*, 134–143. doi:10.1037/h0046989

VandenBos, G. R., Cummings, N. A., & DeLeon, P. H. (1992). A century of psychotherapy: Economic and environmental influences. In D. K. Freedheim (Ed.), *History of psychotherapy: A century of change* (pp. 65–102). Washington, DC: American Psychological Association.

Watson, J. B. (1913). Psychology as the behaviorist views it. *Psychological Review, 20,* 158–177. doi:10.1037/h0074428

Watson, J. B., & Rayner, R. (1920). Conditioned emotional reactions. *Journal of Experimental Psychology, 3,* 1–14. doi:10.1037/h0069608

Wolfle, D. (1946). The reorganized American Psychological Association. *American Psychologist, 1,* 3–6. doi:10.1037/h0061125

Wolford, R. A. (1956). A review of psychology in VA hospitals. *Journal of Counseling Psychology, 3,* 243–248. doi:10.1037/h0049356

Worcester, E., McComb, S., & Coriat, I. H. (1908). *Religion and medicine: The moral control of nervous disorders.* New York, NY: Maffat, Yard, and Company.

Zenderland, L. (1998). *Measuring minds: Henry Herbert Goddard and the origins of American intelligence testing.* New York, NY: Cambridge University Press.

Zimring, F. M., & Raskin, M. J. (1992). Carl Rogers and client/person-centered therapy. In D. K. Freedheim (Ed.), *History of psychotherapy: A century of change* (pp. 629–656). Washington, DC: American Psychological Association.

2

PSYCHOTHERAPY, 1960 TO THE PRESENT

PATRICK H. DeLEON, MARY BETH KENKEL,
LINDA GARCIA-SHELTON, AND GARY R. VANDENBOS

Today, in 2010, psychotherapy increasingly is being viewed as an integral component of our overall health care delivery system. This is a substantial change from how most mental health practitioners have historically viewed themselves. To a significant extent, this is the result of modifications over time in the reimbursement status of psychotherapy and other mental health services, as well as evolving standards of what is deemed by society to be "quality health care." With this new status comes increasing governmental oversight and societal responsibility.

No longer can any one or two professional disciplines (e.g., psychology or psychiatry) claim exclusive expertise for serving the mental, emotional, behavioral, psychological, and psychiatric needs of Americans. Today's mental health landscape includes psychiatric nurses, clinical social workers, marriage and family therapists, clinical pharmacists, and a range of provider extenders, in addition to psychologists and psychiatrists. Each of these disciplines has become increasingly involved in the public policy and legislative process as it has sought to expand its traditional scope of practice, be reimbursed under various private and governmental payment systems, and gain access to vital professional training support.

At the same time, legislative and judicial bodies have increasingly held that individuals receiving mental health care possess the same constitutional and civil rights as those diagnosed with other "medical disorders," thereby possessing the unalterable right of patients (now frequently referred to as "educated consumers") to determine their own course of care. As a nation, however, we have not yet adopted the fundamental policy that all citizens are entitled to the quality health care that they require (i.e., national health insurance).

This chapter traces the history of the growth in recognition and utilization of psychotherapy from the 1960s to the present day. These years marked the tremendous growth and diversification of psychotherapy. More people sought psychotherapy for an increasingly broad array of mental health problems. The demographics and backgrounds of both therapists and clients became more diverse. The settings for psychotherapy practice multiplied, as did the forms and theories of psychotherapy. Psychotherapy research blossomed, and the research results on the effectiveness of psychotherapy played a key role in advancing the recognition of psychotherapy as a standard health care service. These years also marked the greater recognition of psychotherapy by private insurance companies and state and federal governments, providing access to psychotherapy for a greater number of people and more ways to finance therapy services. The practice of psychotherapy became more complex, regulated, and affected by changes occurring not only in mental health services but also in the broader health care industry—a trend that continues today and will be greatly heightened in the future, as behavioral health care becomes an integral part of health care.

THE 1960s

There were perhaps 20,000 trained and practicing psychotherapists in the United States in 1960. World War II demonstrated the need for additional mental health providers, particularly clinical psychologists and psychiatrists. Federal mental health policy during the 15 years after the conclusion of World War II was to increase the supply of trained mental health professionals. By 1960, the number of trained and practicing clinical psychologists had grown to 7,104, with about half employed in universities, 2,800 working in organized care settings such as hospitals and clinics, and 600 to 900 working in private practice mostly in and around a few large cities (Albee, 1963). The membership of the American Psychiatric Association was 11,037, with perhaps 8,300 clinically active and primarily engaged in the delivery of services (VandenBos, Cummings, & DeLeon, 1992). The number of trained psychotherapists among social workers and psychiatric nurses was relatively small at that time, perhaps as low as 2,000 total individuals.

By 1960, psychotherapy as a clinical activity was beginning to be recognized by consumers as a meaningful mental health service. Because there was no legal definition of psychotherapy or specification of the type of training needed to provide it, the title of *psychotherapist* was open to whoever might wish to use it. Psychotherapists were being trained in the 1960s within three broad clinical approaches: psychodynamic (which was the most common), client centered (which was rapidly expanding), and behavioral (which was just beginning to emerge). However, the recognition of psychotherapy as a clinical service that should be reimbursed by insurance companies or provided by the government through organized care settings was not universally accepted.

Several federal policy initiatives in the 1960s led to the dramatic shift in the locus and clients of mental health services. The Joint Commission on Mental Illness and Health was established in 1955, and in 1961, published its influential *Action for Mental Health: Final Report of the Joint Commission on Mental Illness and Health* (Joint Commission on Mental Illness and Health, 1961). This report reviewed the status of mental health services and research and made recommendations to improve both. The passage of the Community Mental Health Centers Act of 1963 established the goal of transferring the care of the mentally ill from the state psychiatric hospitals to community-based centers, authorized the development of such centers throughout the United States, and provided local grants to develop such centers. This report and this legislation, jointly, provided a consensus regarding the desirability of diminishing the central role of state mental hospitals in mental health care and strengthening outpatient and community facilities in order to better integrate the mentally ill into society (Grob, 1991). The passage of Medicaid and Medicare in the mid-1960s further hastened the exodus of aged patients from hospitals to chronic nursing homes. Additionally, the rapid expansion of third-party insurance reimbursement plans stimulated the use of outpatient psychotherapy as well as inpatient psychiatric services in general hospitals (Grob, 2001).

As a result, the location of patient-care episodes shifted dramatically in the 1960s. In 1955, there were 1,675,352 patient-care episodes in the United States, with 22.6% occurring in outpatient facilities, 48.9% occurring in state mental hospitals, and the remainder in other institutions. By 1968, there was over a 100% increase in patient episodes to 3,380,818, with 52.7% occurring in outpatient facilities (of which 8% were in community mental health centers [CMHCs]), 23.4% in state hospitals, and 23.9% in other institutions (Grob, 2001). Outpatient facilities grew rapidly because they were used by new groups of patients who in the past had no access to mental health service and who were, for the most part, not persons with long-term severe psychiatric problems.

Although CMHCs originally were instituted to enable the deinstitutionalization of mental health patients from state hospitals to community care, they ended up serving a very different population. Most centers made little effort to provide coordinated aftercare services to persons with long-term mental illnesses. This omission was partially due to federal budgetary pressures caused by the Vietnam War. Instead, CMHCs emphasized psychotherapy, an intervention especially adapted to individuals with emotional and personal problems as well as one that appealed to a professional constituency. As a result, an expanding number of people were able to access psychotherapy for the first time, and the stigma associated with seeking psychotherapeutic services began to lessen.

The efforts during the 1960s to make psychotherapy more accessible were not just within the federal government. Many major labor unions lobbied to include mental health care in the health plans for their members. Professional psychology began working enthusiastically on a range of health insurance reimbursement issues, particularly on implementing freedom-of-choice legislation at the state level (Dörken et al., 1986). Freedom-of-choice legislation required insurance companies to allow the insured consumer to choose among all licensed psychotherapy providers rather than being restricted to only one discipline (e.g., psychiatrists). As more resources were becoming available to psychotherapists, the American Psychological Association's (APA's) Division 29 began publishing the journal *Psychotherapy* in 1963, and APA launched the journal *Professional Psychology*, which covered a variety of practice and professional issues, in 1969 with Donald K. Freedheim as first editor.

THE 1970s

By 1970, the number of trained and practicing psychotherapists in the United States had grown to at least 30,000. Federal policy during the preceding decade had been to continue to expand the number of psychologists and psychiatrists trained as researchers, practitioners, or both. The number of doctoral psychologists had grown to over 24,000, with 88% belonging to APA, with another 10,667 master's level individuals available who had been trained in the previous 20 years (Boneau & Cuca, 1974). More than half of these psychologists were trained in "applied areas," and slightly over half were employed in college and universities. Over 11,723 were employed in an array of practice settings, including about 1,800 in private practice. The membership of the American Psychiatric Association was 18,407 in 1970, with perhaps 13,805 clinically active and primarily engaged in the delivery of services (VandenBos, Cummings, & DeLeon, 1992). The number of trained psychotherapists among social workers and psychiatric nurses was still relatively small but also increasing, perhaps totaling around 4,000 individuals. Early in the 1970s, some national leaders began to question whether federal policy should continue to focus merely on expanding that number of trained mental health professionals.

Although little action was taken on mental health issues by the federal government in the first part of the 1970s, renewed attention surfaced in the later half. During the early 1970s, the focus of federal mental health policy shifted dramatically because of a growing perception that substance abuse represented major threats to public health. Beginning in 1968, Congress enacted legislation that sharply altered the role of CMHCs by adding new services for substance abusers, children, and elderly persons. Between 1970 and 1972, the Nixon Administration worked to scale back National Institute of Mental Health (NIMH) programs, many of which survived only because of a sympathetic Congress. By 1973, however, the Watergate scandal was preoccupying the attention of the White House and resulted in Nixon's resignation in summer 1974. In the months preceding and following Nixon's resignation, Congress undertook a reassessment of the CMHC program and renewed mental health legislation in mid-1975, over President Gerald Ford's veto.

The practice of psychotherapy flourished in the 1970s. The *Report of the Research Task Force of the National Institute of Mental Health* (NIMH, 1975) referred to the growth in the number of psychotherapies that occurred during the 1960s and early 1970s. The growth seemed to be due to the more benign attitude toward mental illness in the United States (Garfield, 1980) and the funds provided during the previous 30 years by the federal government for training and research in mental health. Psychotherapists were addressing an expanded range of human problems, and psychotherapy was being provided for disorders beyond the psychoses and neurotic disorders, including alcoholism, delinquency, psychosomatic illnesses, and so forth (Garfield, 1980). Also, in keeping with an optimistic view of human potential in the 1970s, there was an emphasis on solving "problems in living." Within mental health care, there was a general shift in emphasis from psychological illness to psychological health. Psychotherapy was regarded as a means not only to ameliorate distress but also to enhance functioning.

CMHCs continued to expand in all areas of the country, increasing the public's access to psychotherapy. Moreover, a larger number of people, especially the better educated who were more knowledgeable about mental health, began to seek psychotherapy services. Growing referral sources included social service and welfare agencies seeking to help their clients deal with psychological issues. HMOs were recognized in federal legislation in the 1970s as a new type of health facility that incorporated mental health services as an integral part of their health services. With the exponential growth in psychotherapy, NIMH began to raise questions about the essential change processes in psychotherapy and whether one approach was more beneficial than another. Psychotherapy research was still in its early development, but NIMH funding for psychotherapy research was increasing, with a greater percentage going to research on behavior therapies (NIMH, 1975).

Jimmy Carter's presidency renewed attention to mental health issues and hope of substantial change. In one of his first acts, on February 17, 1977, President Carter signed Executive Order No. 11973, which formally established the President's Commission on Mental Health. Representatives from each of the four traditional mental health disciplines and the general public actively participated in developing the commission's report (President's Commission on Mental Health, 1978).

DeLeon and VandenBos (1980), in reviewing this major initiative, felt that not since the enactment of the original community mental health center legislation (PL 88-164) in 1963 had the subject of mental health, and psychotherapy in particular, received such public and professional attention at the local and national level, especially within the popular media. The commission's overall findings were startling. Nearly 15% of the nation was in need of some form of mental health services, but only 21% of these individuals were receiving specialty mental health care. Instead, 54% of those with identifiable mental health problems were being seen in primary health care settings by general practitioners. Twenty percent of those with identifiable symptoms were not in contact with any health or mental health provider. The commission further pointed out that general practitioners, who are the mainstay of the general health care system, received fewer than 20 hr of introductory training in mental health during their medical school education and approximately 17 hr of training over the 4-year period in clinical psychopharmacology. Moreover, within any particular subset of patients (e.g., children, older adults, women, rural America, people of color), their unique needs were especially and dramatically unattended to.

DeLeon and VandenBos (1980) concluded the following:

> In essence, regardless of from what vantage point one looks, there can be no question that the delivery of high-quality mental health services *should* be a priority for our nation. Further, if one takes into account the already available cost-effectiveness data (such as that 60% or more of the physician visits are currently made by patients who demonstrate an emotional rather than an organic etiology for their physical symptoms), it becomes quite evident that it is extremely costly not to accord mental health services broader recognition. (p. 250)

Prophetically, the authors also noted the following:

> In our judgment, the specter of ever-rising health care costs will be the most significant factor influencing the delivery of health care and the

development of national health insurance. It would appear that national health insurance will be enacted in the United States for pragmatic financial reasons and not necessarily because of any particular philosophical commitment to the right to adequate health care. (p. 252)

A second late 1970s initiative came from the Senate Finance Committee. It had historically taken the position that Medicare should not directly reimburse nonmedical providers as the program was expressly to have a medical, in contrast to a social service, orientation. Such a position was endorsed in 1968 by then-Secretary of Health, Education, and Welfare Wilbur Cohen. In August 1978, the Senate Finance Committee held hearings for the first time in 7 years on the specific topic of "Proposals to Expand Coverage of Mental Health Under Medicare-Medicaid." Representatives from the various mental health professions were invited to testify, with Joan Willens and Nick Cummings representing APA.

At the request of the Finance Committee, the then-Health Care Financing Administration had funded a special demonstration project in Colorado reimbursing psychologists, and those data were made available. Following up on the hearing, the Finance Committee staff drafted a targeted mental health amendment that would have incorporated provisions from the ongoing Food and Drug Administration (FDA) and other legislation. This proposal would have required demonstrated safety and efficacy, as well as appropriateness—in order to ensure that the most cost-effective treatment would be utilized. It was proposed that a 13-member, truly interdisciplinary commission, balanced for both practitioner and scientific/research expertise, would be established. The commission would be charged with the responsibility of making concrete recommendations for what types of mental health services, including under what conditions, met the stringent FDA-type tests. In the short term, the commission would be expected to rely primarily on its members' clinical and scientific judgment, as well as the technical expertise of the department.

Under the proposed legislation, the then-restrictive Medicare copayment for mental health would be modified from its 50:50 rate to the 20:80 rate of physical health services; the $250 ceiling on mental health services would be raised to $1,000, and, immediately upon enactment, Medicare would for the first time allow for the direct reimbursement of clinical psychologists, clinical social workers, and psychiatric nurse practitioners. The commission's recommendations for reimbursement were to be gradually phased in, with practitioner clinical judgment being the initial sole determinant of what was to be reimbursed. Although this far-reaching proposal was endorsed by the three nonmedical mental health professions and the National Association of State Mental Health Program Directors, the House of Representatives was unwilling to accept it in a subsequent conference.

Although this proposal for expanding the coverage of psychotherapy did not become law, during the 1970s, psychology consolidated many of its early legislative initiatives related to the reimbursement of psychotherapy, focusing on universal state-level licensure and certification, large-scale adoption of freedom-of-choice legislation, and the steady increase of federal recognition of psychotherapeutic services (DeLeon, VandenBos, & Kraut, 1984). For example, in 1973, the Internal Revenue Service clarified the federal income tax instructions to expressly indicate that the psychotherapy services of psychologists qualified under the medical expenses deduction provision of the code. A federal freedom-of-choice statute was enacted for federal employees, annuitants, and their dependents under the Federal Employee Health Benefit Program in 1974. Psychology's first statutory recognition under Medicare occurred in 1972, when the Health Secretary was authorized to determine "whether the services of clinical psychologists may be made more generally available . . . in a manner consistent with quality of care and equitable and efficient administration." (42 U.S.C. § 1395b-1[c][1][I]; DeLeon, VandenBos, & Kraut, 1984, p. 940).

THE 1980s

By 1980, the number of trained and practicing psychotherapists in the United States had exploded to at least 65,000. Federal mental health policy had shifted from merely producing more mental health providers to addressing problems in the maldistribution of mental health providers, as psychotherapists were more likely to be concentrated around bigger cities as well as towns with colleges and universities as compared with the general public. Federal training support was now limited to training individuals to serve specific patient populations or geographic areas. The number of doctoral psychologists who provided mental health services had now reached at least 30,000 by 1980 (Stapp, Tucker, & VandenBos, 1985). The membership of the American Psychiatric Association was 25,345 in 1980, with perhaps 19,008 clinically active and primarily engaged in the delivery of services (VandenBos, Cummings, & DeLeon, 1992). The number of trained psychotherapists among social workers and psychiatric nurses was rapidly expanding, perhaps totaling around 15,000. Marriage and family therapists, professional counselors, addiction specialists, and psychosocial rehabilitation specialists were beginning to grow in numbers.

The mood of the United States changed dramatically in the 1980s. The freewheeling 1970s, with the emphasis on experimentation, turned more conservative in the 1980s. The report of the President's Commission on Mental Health resulted in the passage by Congress of the Mental Health Systems Act a month before the 1980 presidential election. Its provisions were complex but advocated for a national system that would ensure the availability of mental health care and psychotherapy in community settings (Grob, 1994). But the act hardly had become law when its provisions became moot.

With the election of Ronald Reagan to the presidency, the federal government's involvement with mental health services changed dramatically. Preoccupied with campaign promises to reduce both taxes and federal expenditures, the new administration proposed a 25% cut in federal funding. More important, it called for a conversion of federal mental health programs into a single block grant to the states carrying few restrictions and without policy guidelines.

When the Omnibus Budget Reconciliation Act was signed into law in summer 1981, most of the provisions of the Mental Health Systems Act were repealed. Federal funding for mental health and substance abuse services was provided through block grants to states. The new legislation also reduced federal funding for mental health, fulfilling campaign promises to reduce the "activist" government and to do away with the "failed" social engineering of the 1960s' Great Society. This reversed 3 decades of federal leadership in mental health care. With the focus of mental health policy and funding shifting back to the states in the 1980s, the tradition that had prevailed until World War II was restored in part. However, the reduction in federal funding and the transfer of authority occurred at precisely the same time that states were confronted with massive social and economic problems that increased their fiscal burdens, leading them to seek ways to reduce expenditures on mental health services (Grob, 1994, 2001).

However, mental health professionals continued the push for psychotherapy to be covered under health insurance plans. Many more professionals were going into private practice on a full-time or part-time basis. Psychologists also had successes in their bids to have their psychotherapy skills recognized. Under President Reagan's Comprehensive Crime Control Acts of 1982 and 1984, psychologists (and ultimately other nonphysician mental health providers by regulation) were recognized as fully qualified to provide diagnostic and treatment functions for federal courts. In addition, in signing Executive Order No. 12586, President Reagan similarly modified the Department of Defense *Manual for Courts-Martial* to ensure that psychological expertise would be appropriately utilized, which over time resulted in all other relevant military regulations being modified, whenever an individual's mental capacity was in question.

The domains within which psychological and behavioral interventions were being applied also expanded during the 1980s. In 1982, the APA Division of Health Psychology established a new journal, *Health Psychology*, to better showcase the clinical efforts and empirical research related to the application of psychological methods to physical health problems. The division itself had only been formed in 1976, although at least one "medical psychology" program had existed in a university since the late 1950s. In May 1983, the National Working Conference on Education and Training in Health Psychology was held, and the conference report was published in *Health Psychology* before the end of the year ("Special Issue: Proceedings of the National Working Conference," 1983). This marked the early modern recognition within psychology of the interplay between psychological and physical health and health processes.

Toward the end of the 1980s, business and government concerns about health care costs increased. In an effort to contain costs, a variety of managed care arrangements began to appear. Mental health services in managed care organizations (MCOs) were increasingly provided through carve outs, in which the MCO would contract with a specialized behavioral health managed care organization to provide psychological services. Patients of the MCOs had to go to a mental health professional in the MCOs' provider panel or else pay much higher out-of-network rates for psychotherapy. Mental health professionals who wanted to be on MCO provider panels had to accept specified, typically discounted, rates for their services; limits on the number of sessions provided; and utilization review procedures. Many mental health providers began to worry about the impact of managed care on their ability to provide high quality and appropriate psychotherapy services for their clients.

THE 1990s

By 1990, the number of trained and practicing psychotherapists in the United States had grown to somewhere between 125,000 and 175,000 individuals. Federal support for training additional mental health providers was now quite limited, often focusing on training individuals from specific ethnic and cultural backgrounds. The number of health services providing doctoral-level psychologists had grown to at least 58,000 (NIMH, 1990). The membership of the American Psychiatric Association was 37,777 in 1990, with perhaps 25,000 clinically active and primarily engaged in the delivery of services (VandenBos, Cummings, & DeLeon, 1992). And, the U.S. government was now acknowledging at least 81,500 clinical social workers and 10,000 psychiatric nurses as mental health providers (NIMH, 1990). Marriage and family therapists, professional counselors, addiction specialists, psychoeducational specialists, and psychosocial rehabilitation specialists were exploding in numbers and were becoming legally recognized.

A major Medicare legislative victory was achieved at the beginning of the 1990s, ending a 25-year political struggle to eliminate the cap on mental health benefits for older adults and disabled people. Psychologists and clinical social workers were also recognized as providers of psychotherapy for older adults and disabled people, who could be directly reimbursed under Medicare.

However, mental health care was still only reimbursed on a 50/50 percentage basis, rather than the 20/80 basis used with physical health care (Buie, 1990).

The 1990s brought rapid expansion of managed care in health and mental health. Concerns about the deleterious impact of managed care on the provision of psychotherapy were raised by all of the mental health disciplines (Fox, 1995; Karon, 1995). A survey of psychology practitioners (Phelps, Eisman, & Kohout, 1998) indicated that four out of five professionals reported that managed care was having a negative impact on their psychotherapy practices. A survey in one state found that higher involvement in managed care by independent practitioners resulted in greater changes in morale, professional identity, and approach to therapy compared with practitioners with lower involvement levels (P. Rothbaum, Bernstein, Haller, Phelps, & Kohout, 1998).

There were many concerns about people's ability to access psychotherapy because of managed care policies. It was unclear whether psychiatrists would still be able to provide psychotherapy to their clients or be relegated to providing only psychopharmacological treatment. Data from 587 psychiatrists who participated in the American Psychiatric Institute for Research and Education's Practice Research Network 1999 Study of Psychiatric Patients and Treatments indicated that only 56% of patients of psychiatrists received some form of psychotherapy from the psychiatrist. More than half of those individuals with schizophrenia did not receive psychotherapy (Wilk, West, Rae, & Regier, 2006). The percentage of psychiatrists who provided psychotherapy to all of their patients would decline to 10.8% by 2005. There were fewer psychiatrists specializing in psychotherapy, and a corresponding increase in those specializing in pharmacotherapy, because of the financial incentives and growth in psychopharmacological treatments during the 1990s.

Managed health care had other impacts on psychotherapy. It drove the movement toward shorter and more evidence-based therapies and demanded more accountability of the profession, forcing therapists to justify the effectiveness of their treatment approach. This emphasis on accountability was forecasted in the NIMH 1975 report (Segal, 1975). In response to the push for evidence-based practice, a task force of APA's Division 12 (Clinical Psychology) developed a manual listing all the forms of psychotherapy that had strong evidence for their effectiveness (Chambless et al., 1996).

U.S. Senator Daniel K. Inouye urged psychologists at the November 1984 annual meeting of the Hawaii Psychological Association to seek prescriptive authority in order to improve the availability of comprehensive, quality mental health care. During the congressional deliberations on the Fiscal Year 1989 Appropriations Bill for the Department of Defense [Pub. L. 100-463], the conferees directed the department to establish a "demonstration pilot training project under which military psychologists may be trained and authorized to issue appropriate psychotropic medications under certain circumstances." In 1989, the APA Board of Professional Affairs endorsed immediate research regarding the feasibility and the appropriate curricula in psychopharmacology so that psychologists might provide broader service to the public and more effectively meet the psychological and mental health needs of society. An ad hoc Task Force on Psychopharmacology was established in 1990. Their 1992 report concluded that practitioners, with combined training in psychopharmacology and psychosocial treatments, could be viewed as a new form of health care professional, expected to bring to health care delivery the best of both psychological and pharmacological knowledge. At its August 1995 meeting in New York, the APA Council of Representatives formally endorsed prescriptive privileges for appropriately trained psychologists and called for the development of model legislation. By the beginning of 1998, prescription privileges legislation was either pending or about to be introduced in seven states: California, Florida, Georgia, Hawaii, Louisiana, Missouri, and Tennessee.

On December 30, 1998, the Guam legislature made B.695 public law, allowing a clinical psychologist to administer, prescribe, and dispense any licensed drug with the delegated authority of a Collaborative Practice Agreement. In March 2002, New Mexico Governor Gary Johnson signed HB 170 into public law, setting the stage of psychologists' prescriptive authority in that state. Louisiana Governor Kathleen Blanco signed HB 1426 into public law on May 6, 2004, providing psychologists with prescriptive authority in that state. Such legislation allows psychotherapists with a broader array of tools to assist and support their patients.

In 1997, U.S. Surgeon General David Satcher authorized the preparation of the *U.S. Surgeon General's Report on Mental Health* (U.S. Department of Health and Human Services, 1999). This was the first surgeon general's report ever issued on the topic of mental health and mental illness, and its bold opening message was that mental health is fundamental to health. The report noted that just as Americans assign high priority to preventing illness and promoting physical health, so should they be promoting better mental health and preventing mental disorders. No longer should mental health be viewed as separate and unequal to general health. The report called for a public health model to promote mental health by instituting a number of effective prevention programs for people of all ages. After an extensive review of the literature, the report emphatically stated that the efficacy of psychotherapy and other mental health treatments was well documented and a range of treatments exists for most mental disorders. On the strength of these findings, the single, explicit recommendation of the report was to encourage people to seek help if they have a mental health problem.

There was also a growing awareness in the 1990s of the lack of culturally competent treatment for ethnic minorities. The *U.S. Surgeon General's Report on Mental Health* (U.S. Department of Health and Human Services,

1999) highlighted how individuals' mental health is influenced by their age, gender, race, culture, socioeconomic status, sexual orientation, physical disability status, as well as other forms of diversity. Therefore, to be effective, treatments had to be tailored to these characteristics. The report called for culturally competent mental health services that would incorporate understanding the histories, traditions, beliefs, and value systems of different ethnic and racial groups and would be structured to overcome the groups' reluctance to access psychotherapy because of stigma, mistrust, inappropriate methods, and costs. Reinforcing the necessity of providing culturally competent therapy, in 1990, APA approved the *Guidelines for Providers of Psychological Services to Ethnic, Linguistic, and Culturally Diverse Populations* (APA, 1990). These guidelines were followed by others addressing treatment with other diverse groups, including the treatment of lesbian, gay, and bisexual clients (APA, 2000); older adults (APA, 2004); and girls and women in the next decade (APA, 2007). An updated and more comprehensive guidelines covering multicultural education, training, research, practice, and organizational change was released at the end of the decade (APA, 2003).

Psychotherapists began to develop and implement culturally competent therapies (cf. Comas-Díaz, 2000; Fuertes & Gretchen, 2001; Helms & Cook, 1999; McGoldrick, Giordano, & Pearce, 1996; Sue, Ivey, & Pedersen, 1996; Sue & Sue, 1999), and such models were incorporated into the education and training programs for mental health professionals (Lee et al., 1999; Ponterotto, 1997; Quintana & Bernal, 1995; Rogers, Hoffman, & Wade, 1998) and accreditation guidelines (APA, 2002).

THE 2000s

By 2000, it was harder than ever to determine the exact number of trained psychotherapists in the United States or the total size of the overall workforce identified with the mental health field. There were perhaps between 200,000 and 250,000 trained and practicing psychotherapists in the United States in 2000 (and a mental health industry workforce of 535,000; Bureau of Labor Statistics, 2010). The number of doctoral psychologists was estimated to be between 78,000 and 85,000. The number of psychiatrists was estimated to be around 41,000, but the number of psychiatrists who were trained and practicing as psychotherapists was declining rapidly, as most provided psychopharmacological agents with some counseling and supportive contact. Mental health social workers were estimated to number between 100,000 and 200,000. Advanced practice psychiatric nurses numbered at least 15,000, and the overall total of nurses providing some types and levels of mental health care was even larger. Professional counselors were estimated at 100,000, and marriage and family therapists were estimated at around 50,000 (Bureau of Labor Statistics, 2010; Center for Mental Health Services, 2006).

In February 2001, President George W. Bush announced his New Freedom Initiative, and in May 2003, the final report of the President's New Freedom Commission on Mental Health was released. The commission concluded that mental illnesses rank first among illnesses that cause disability in the United States but found that the American mental health delivery system was fragmented and in disarray—leading to unnecessary and costly disability, homelessness, school failure, and incarceration. The commission also concluded that it was necessary to fundamentally transform how mental health care was delivered in the United States, such that care would focus on increasing consumers' ability to successfully cope with life's challenges, facilitating recovery, and building resilience, not just on managing symptoms. Understanding that mental health is essential to overall health was viewed as fundamental for establishing a health system that treats mental illness with the same urgency as it treats physical illness. Among the commission's highest recommendations were promoting the mental health of young children and the screening for mental disorders in primary health care across the entire life span (New Freedom Commission on Mental Health, 2003).

In 2002, the Center for Medicare and Medicaid Services expanded the set of Current Procedural Terminology (CPT) codes that gave greater recognition to psychological and behavioral services provided to physically ill patients. CPT codes refer to a system of codes developed by the American Medical Association that are used for describing and billing for health and medical services. They are used by almost all third-party payers to reimburse for health care services, including Medicare and Medicaid. This new set of CPT codes was collectively referred to as *health and behavior* (H&B) codes, and they could be used to capture behavioral, psychophysiological, and social procedures for the management, treatment, and prevention of physical health problems and overall adjustment to physical illness, adherence to medical treatment, and prevention efforts (Dittmann, 2004). This recognition allowed psychologists and other health providers to bill for assessment and interventions related to physical health problems, rather than trying to fit such services under mental health treatment codes. These H&B codes allowed for a brief visit of 15 min, as well as longer visits that are simply coded by noting the number of 15-min units of assessment and or intervention during the visit. The H&B CPT codes were especially valuable for psychotherapists working in integrated colocated health care settings. The psychologist could be available in the clinic to see a patient with a health problem immediately at the request of the physician, providing focused behavioral assessment or intervention. In 2006, additional CPT codes were created for psychological and neuropsychological testing, including the reimbursement for the professional time spent interpreting the test data.

During the 2000s, one of the critical policy themes the Institute of Medicine (IOM; and the Congress, and both the Bush and Obama administrations) has highlighted is the unprecedented growth in digital and electronic communications, which had had a direct impact on almost all phases of life. Yet, the health care industry was slow to systematically incorporate such technology in the health care environment. In 2001, the IOM noted the following:

> Health care delivery has been relatively untouched by the revolution in information technology that has been transforming nearly every other aspect of society. The majority of patient and clinician encounters take place for purposes of exchanging clinical information: patients share information with clinicians about their general health, symptoms, and concerns, and clinicians use their knowledge and skills to respond with pertinent medical information, and in many cases reassurance. Yet it is estimated that only a small fraction of physicians offer e-mail interaction, a simple and convenient tool for efficient communication, to their patients. (IOM, 2001, p. 15)

Even as late as 2009, the Congressional Budget Office estimated that only 12% of physicians were using electronic tools. *The New England Journal of Medicine* reported that only 1.5% of U.S. hospitals have a comprehensive electronic records system available in all clinical units, and just another 7.6% have a basic system available in at least one clinical unit. But, 17.0% of hospitals did let doctors prescribe medications electronically (Jha et al., 2009).

Within behavioral health care, some technologies, such as the telephone, have been widely adopted as a vehicle for the occasional provision of psychotherapy, whereas other technologies still are scarcely used. The term *telehealth* is used to describe the use of electronic and communications technology to accomplish health care over a distance (Jerome et al., 2000). A survey of 596 health-service provider members of APA (VandenBos & Williams, 2000) showed that a substantial percentage of psychologists occasionally used the telephone to provide individual psychotherapy (69%) or group/family therapy (22%), whereas a smaller percentage used e-mail or fax to provide individual therapy (8%) or family/group therapy (15%). Only about 2% used Internet technology, such as video/audio connections, to provide therapy.

Psychotherapy via interactive televideo (IATV) began being used successfully in the 2000s to reduce many of the traditional barriers to mental health services, including geographical barriers, stigma, lack of transportation, availability of providers, waiting times, and costs. Such IATV psychotherapy was first applied in rural settings to augment mental health human resources, reduce travel, and provide access to specialty care providers (Stamm, 1998). Psychotherapy via IATV also began being used to reach underserved populations, such as in correctional facilities, to lessen the costs of transporting inmates (Magaletta, Fagan, & Ax, 1998), to connect military personnel on aircraft carriers to therapists on base, and to connect patients at remote locations with specialized behavioral health providers (Glueckauf & Ketterson, 2004).

Telehealth initiatives began to explore web-based psychotherapeutic interventions, that is, treatments that were developed and operationalized specifically for Internet delivery (Ritterband et al., 2003). Many of them used highly structured, cognitive–behavioral approaches to behavioral medicine issues, such as smoking cessation, weight loss, diabetes management, pediatric encopresis, insomnia, and physical activity. Initial studies on these interventions showed them to be feasible and effective (Ritterband et al., 2003). Handheld computers were also used as adjuncts to treat panic disorders (M. G. Newman, Kenardy, Herman, & Taylor, 1997) and social phobia (Gruber, Moran, Roth, & Taylor, 2001). Such research demonstrated that a handheld computer can promote self-monitoring and use of standard cognitive–behavioral therapy methods for anxiety disorders, thus partially reducing the need for therapist time (Wright, 2008). The most dramatic form of computer-assisted therapy is virtual reality exposure therapy in which patients are immersed in a virtual environment to help extinguish fears of flying, heights, social situations, or other anxiety-provoking situations (B. O. Rothbaum, Hodges, Ready, Graap, & Alarcon, 2001; B. O. Rothbaum, Hodges, Smith, Lee, & Price, 2000). Such technology was also used to assist individuals with posttraumatic stress disorder following the 9/11 attacks (Difede et al., 2007), with good success.

There are questions, however, as to whether these electronic interventions are as effective as working directly with a therapist and whether clients are less likely to complete the web-based programs when there is no therapist guidance. A recent meta-analysis (Spek et al., 2007) found that computer-assisted therapies with no therapist contact produced fewer robust changes in symptoms than those that integrated the work of the clinician and the computer.

More controversial aspects of telehealth include the provision of psychotherapy via the Internet. Some individual psychotherapists, as well as Internet companies, began to provide online counseling for a fee in the early 2000s. Such practices raised a number of clinical, ethical, and legal issues, including concerns about patient safety and confidentiality, federal and state regulations regarding telehealth, and demonstrations of clinical effectiveness (Koocher & Morray, 2000; Maheu & Gordon, 2000). Nonetheless, an increasing number of resources became available to psychotherapists as they ventured into the area of telehealth, including interdisciplinary guidelines for the use of telehealth (Reed, McLaughlin, & Milholland, 2000), a framework for assessing knowledge and skills for using telehealth services (Glueckauf, Pickett, Ketterson, Loomis, & Rozensky, 2003), and guides for instituting the best technology practices (Maheu, Pulier, Wilhelm, McMenamin, & Brown-Connolly, 2005; Maheu, Whitten, & Allen, 2001). At the federal level, the Joint Working Group on Telehealth was an interagency group comprising 11 agencies that coordinated members' telehealth activities, including grant funding and developing specific actions to reduce barriers to the effective use of telehealth technologies. In the decades ahead, technology will continue to be used to expand the reach, effectiveness, and efficiency of psychotherapy.

The Health Insurance Portability and Accountability Act (HIPAA), a federal law enacted in 1996 but implemented in the 2000s, provides rights and protections for health care recipients and protects the privacy of health data. The intent of this act was to help people keep their health information private by regulating the use and disclosure of "protected health information," including information about health status, provision of health care, or payment for health care. The standards also were meant to improve the efficiency and effectiveness of the nation's health care system by encouraging the widespread use of electronic data exchange and electronic health records. Although the intent of HIPAA was to guard the privacy of health records, in practice, providers and health insurance plans quickly came to require the waiver of HIPAA rights as a condition of service. Therefore, psychotherapists were very concerned about confidentiality of therapy treatment. In response to this concern, psychotherapy notes were granted a special protection under HIPAA because of the likelihood that they contain particularly sensitive information. *Psychotherapy notes* were defined as records by a mental health professional documenting or analyzing an individual or group counseling session (typically called *process notes*) and that can be maintained separately from the medical record. HIPAA granted special protection for psychotherapy notes requiring specific authorization to release them in addition to any consent an individual may have given for the disclosure of other protected health information.

In 2006, the IOM released its Quality Chasm Series report on mental and substance abuse. The report noted that each year, more than 33 million Americans received health care for mental or substance use conditions, or both. The IOM report observed that although effective treatments exist, services are frequently fragmented, and there are barriers that prevent many from receiving these services. The evidence of a link between mental health/substance use illnesses and general health (and health care) was seen as very strong, especially with respect to chronic illnesses and injury. The IOM report concluded that improving the nation's general health and resolving the quality problems of the overall health care system would require attending equally to the quality problems of mental health/substance use health care (IOM, 2006, p. 10).

Among the mental health disciplines, psychology fully embraced the transition to an integrated health care model. In his 2005 APA presidential address, Ronald Levant (2006) took a futuristic stance with his "Health Care for the Whole Person" initiative. He argued that it was critical to the future of psychotherapy and other behavioral interventions to promote the integration of physical and psychological health care in a reformed health care system, one in which health care professionals team up to treat the whole person. To achieve this, he argued, required abandoning the idea of the separation of mind from body, the notion pervasive in many concepts of health and illness.

The inevitability of viewing the provision of psychotherapy as moving from a historically isolated, solo practice model to an integrated and systems approach has also been reflected in the views of the APA senior Practice Directorate professional staff. Then-Executive of the APA Practice Directorate Russ Newman, in keynoting the 2007 State Leadership Conference, stated the following:

> Consumer-driven healthcare can come together with government engagement for universal coverage; one thing continues to be clear—the health care system's fixation with treating disease must give way to a greater priority to prevent disease and promote good health. What policy makers and the public are now beginning to appreciate, psychology has know for years, if not decades—the research, the knowledge base, and technologies to change behavior in ways that promote good health do exist. And, much of the research, the knowledge base and technologies are psychology's work. (R. Newman, 2007, p. 26)

And, at the APA 2009 State Leadership Conference, the new executive director of the APA Practice Directorate, Katherine Nordal (2009), stated in the keynote address:

> It is *foolhardy* for us to focus narrowly on mental health issues when the real opportunities to make a significant difference in the quality of life for most of our citizens are in the broader domain of general health care and in delivery systems that will have stringent demands for accountability with a focus on quality and outcomes. *It is time for us to view our discipline more broadly as a health care profession*, with mental health as a subset of our expertise, and to communicate the breadth of our expertise to the public and policy makers.

Similarly, in 2009, APA President James Bray testified before the IOM as it formulated its recommendations to the Agency for Healthcare Research and Quality as to how to prioritize the $1.1 billion for comparative effectiveness research provided under the Obama Administration Economic Stimulus legislation (The American Recovery and Reinvestment Act of 2009):

> Comparative effectiveness research is a critically important tool for advancing an evidence-based approach to health care decision-making.

However, the full public health benefits of such research will only be realized if behavioral, psychosocial, and medical interventions for the prevention and treatment of mental and physical health conditions are evaluated individually and in combination. Even when strictly medical treatments are compared, it is important to expand the range of outcome measures to include behavioral and psychological outcomes, such as quality of life and adherence to treatment protocols. It is also essential to evaluate promising new models of care, such as the use of integrated, interdisciplinary behavioral and medical teams in primary care settings. And finally, the effectiveness of health interventions across the life span and for different minority and gender groups must be considered. (Bray, 2009)

Integrated health care is not a new idea for psychology. Work in this area began several decades ago in the field of clinical health psychology. In 1965, there were few psychological interventions offered in general medical settings (Wagner, 1968). Since then, psychotherapeutic interventions with nonmental health clients have increased dramatically.

In July 2008, the mental health field achieved another major Medicare legislative victory—parity in reimbursement between mental health care and physical health care. Medicare Improvement for Patients and Providers Act of 2008 lowered the 50/50 reimbursement rate to 20/80 of physical health care (Novotney, 2008).

2010 AND BEYOND

Over the past 50 years, there has been a substantial growth in all the mental health professions, with federal reports estimating the overall human resources in the mental health field at over 702,000 in 2008 (Bureau of Labor Statistics, 2010) and expected to exceed 750,000 by 2010. The greatest growth over the past 10 years has been in mental health counselors, clinical social workers, marriage and family therapists, and other subdoctoral providers. Currently women comprise a larger percentage of each profession, except psychiatry, but that profession too is shifting to become more female dominated. The professions continue to be largely White, with some gains in increasing ethnic and racial representation. The provision of psychotherapy and/or counseling continues to be a central role for each of the mental health professionals, though it has become only a small percentage of the job activities for psychiatrists.

Such growth in the number of psychological service providers could not occur without a public demand for such services. Gurin, Veroff, and Feld (1960) found that in the late 1950s only 14% of Americans had ever received psychological treatment at any point in their lifetime. Twenty years later, this figure had grown to 26% (Kulka, Veroff, & Douvan, 1979). Now, in 2010, our best integration of survey data suggests that 50% of Americans have received psychological services at some point in their life. Psychotherapy is now a popular, understood, and highly desired health care service, with relatively little stigma attached to it.

Psychological treatment is increasingly being referred to as *behavioral health care*, rather than as psychotherapy per se. Psychotherapy still exists and represents a major clinical service for specific types of presenting problems. But more and more psychoeducational and behavioral interventions are being developed and empirically tested for application with specific symptoms, including ones previously considered in a global manner as psychological or mental. Increasingly, specific symptoms of a mental disorder, such as schizophrenia, are being treated (e.g., delusions) separate from the overall larger disorder. The interventions themselves are being viewed more and more as techniques or procedures being done to treat a problem, rather than as occurring in a broader therapeutic relationship. The nature of the contact, and contract, between therapist and patient is changing. And with it, there will be changes in the training of psychological behavioral health specialists and the accreditation of their programs.

With the increasing use of various text, voice, and video communications by all members of society, it seems likely that a great deal of psychotherapy, behavioral counseling, and other psychological interventions, as well as assessment, will be mediated by digital technology. How to do this effectively, and maintain the confidence of the public with respect to confidentiality within a system vulnerable to hacking by determined third parties, will likely challenge the field. It may require time for the profession to shift into the hands of psychologists who began using this media in nursery school for us to feel capable of making full use of the technology—a true paradigm shift for the descendents of James and Freud.

The rapid expansion of neuroscience knowledge, both basic and applied, is providing hints and answers to questions heretofore only responded to with statements of belief. Interventions will be developed on the basis of this growing body of information, and continuing education will be increasingly essential, and specific, in order to stay current in the field. Such advances in neuroscience, combined with the increasing emphasis on the integration of physical health care and mental health care, point to changes in the conceptualization of psychotherapy and how, where, and when it will be delivered. Within such a context, prescriptive authority for psychologists, and the related knowledge of the effects of psychoactive medications on the brain and behavior, will take on increasing significance for all psychotherapists.

REFERENCES

Albee, G. W. (1963). American psychology in the sixties. *American Psychologist, 18*, 90–95. doi:10.1037/h0041088

American Psychological Association. (1990). *Guidelines for providers of psychological services to ethnic, linguistic, and culturally diverse populations.* Washington, DC: Author.

American Psychological Association. (2000). Guidelines for psychotherapy with lesbian, gay, and bisexual clients. *American Psychologist, 55*, 1440–1451. doi:10.1037/0003-066X.55.12.1440

American Psychological Association. (2002). *Guidelines and principles for accreditation.* Washington, DC: Author.

American Psychological Association. (2003). Guidelines on multicultural education, training, research, practice, and organizational change for psychologists. *American Psychologist, 58*, 377–402. doi:10.1037/0003-066X.58.5.377

American Psychological Association. (2004). Guidelines for psychological practice with older adults. *American Psychologist, 59*, 236–260. doi:10.1037/0003-066X.59.4.236

American Psychological Association. (2007). Guidelines for psychological practice with girls and women. *American Psychologist, 62*, 949–979. doi:10.1037/0003-066X.62.9.949

Boneau, A. C., & Cuca, J. M. (1974). An overview of psychology's human resources: Characteristics and salaries from the 1972 APA survey. *American Psychologist, 29*, 821–840. doi:10.1037/h0037460

Bray, J. H. (2009, March 20). Testimony presented at the Institute of Medicine's Committee on Comparative Effectiveness Research Priorities Public Meeting, Washington, DC.

Buie, J. (1990, January). President signs Medicare bill. *Monitor on Psychology, 21*(1), 17–18.

Bureau of Labor Statistics. (2010). *Occupational employment statistics.* Retrieved from http://www.bls.gov/oes/oes_dl.htm

Center for Mental Health Services. (2006). *Mental Health, United States, 2004* (R. W. Manderscheid & J. T. Berry [Eds.]; DHHS Pub No. [SMA]-06-4195). Rockville, MD: Substance Abuse and Mental Health Services Administration.

Chambless, D. L., Sanderson, W. C., Shoham, V., Bennett Johnson, S., Pope, K. S., . . . McCurry, S. (1996). An update on empirically validated therapies. *Clinical Psychologist, 49*, 5–18.

Comas-Díaz, L. (2000). An ethnopolitical approach to working with people of color. *American Psychologist, 55*, 1319–1325. doi:10.1037/0003-066X.55.11.1319

DeLeon, P. H., & VandenBos, G. R. (1980). Psychotherapy reimbursement in federal programs: Political factors. In G. R. VandenBos (Ed.), *Psychotherapy: Practice, research, policy* (pp. 247–285). Beverly Hills: Sage.

DeLeon, P. H., VandenBos, G. R., & Kraut, A. G. (1984). Federal legislation recognizing psychology. *American Psychologist, 39*, 933–946. doi:10.1037/0003-066X.39.9.933

Difede, J., Cukor, J., Jayasinghe, N., Patt, I., Jedel, S., Spielman, L., . . . Hoffman, H. G. (2007). Virtual reality exposure therapy for the treatment of posttraumatic stress disorder following September 11, 2001. *The Journal of Clinical Psychiatry, 68*, 1639–1647. doi:10.4088/JCP.v68n1102

Dittman, M. (2004, October). CPT codes: Use them or lose them. *Monitor on Psychology, 35*(9), 58.

Dörken, H., Bennett, B. E., Carpenter, L. G., Jr., Cummings, N. A., DeLeon, P. H., Fox, R. E., et al. (Eds.). (1986). *Professional psychology in transition: Meeting today's challenges.* San Francisco, CA: Jossey-Bass.

Fox, R. (1995). The rape of psychotherapy. *Professional Psychology, Research and Practice, 26*, 147–155. doi:10.1037/0735-7028.26.2.147

Fuertes, J. N., & Gretchen, D. (2001). Emerging theories of multicultural counseling. In J. G. Ponterotto, J. M. Casas, L. A. Suzuki, & C. M. Alexander (Eds.), *Handbook of multicultural counseling* (2nd ed., pp. 509–541). Thousand Oaks, CA: Sage.

Garfield, S. L. (1980). *Psychotherapy: An eclectic approach.* New York, NY: Wiley.

Glueckauf, R. L., & Ketterson, T. U. (2004). Telehealth interventions for individuals with chronic illness: Research review and implications for practice. *Professional Psychology, Research and Practice, 35,* 615–627. doi:10.1037/0735-7028.35.6.615

Glueckauf, R. L., Pickett, T. C., Ketterson, T. U., Loomis, J. S., & Rozensky, R. H. (2003). Preparation for the delivery of telehealth services: A self-study framework for expansion of practice. *Professional Psychology, Research and Practice, 34,* 159–163. doi:10.1037/0735-7028.34.2.159

Grob, G. N. (1991). *From asylum to community. Mental health policy in modern America.* Princeton, NJ: Princeton University Press.

Grob, G. N. (1994). *The mad among us: A history of the care of America's mentally ill.* New York, NY: Free Press.

Grob, G. N. (2001). Mental health policy in 20th century America. In R. W. Manderscheid & M. J. Henderson (Eds.), *Mental Health, United States, 2000* (DHHS Pub No. [SMA] 01-3537). Washington, DC: Superintendent of Documents, U.S. Government Printing Office.

Gruber, K., Moran, P. J., Roth, W. T., & Taylor, C. B. (2001). Computer-assisted cognitive behavioral group therapy for social phobia. *Behavior Therapy, 32,* 155–165. doi:10.1016/S0005-7894(01)80050-2

Gurin, G., Veroff, J., & Feld, S. (1960). Americans view their mental health: A nationwide interview survey. *Joint Commission on Mental Illness and Health. Monograph Series No. 4.* New York, NY: Basic Books.

Helms, J. E., & Cook, D. A. (1999). *Using race and culture in counseling and psychotherapy: Theory and process.* Boston, MA: Allyn & Bacon.

Institute of Medicine (IOM). (2001). *Crossing the quality chasm: A new health system for the 21st century.* Washington, DC: National Academies Press.

Institute of Medicine (IOM). (2006). *Improving the quality of health care for mental and substance use conditions: Quality chasm series.* Washington, DC: National Academies Press.

Jha, A. K., DesRoches, C. M., Campbell, E. G., Donelan, K., Rao, S. R., Ferris, T. G., . . . Blumenthal, D. (2009). Use of electronic health records in U.S. hospitals. *The New England Journal of Medicine, 360,* 1628–1638. doi:10.1056/NEJ Msa0900592

Jerome, L. W., DeLeon, P. H., James, L. C., Folen, R., Earles, J., & Gedney, J. J. (2000). The coming age of telecommunications in psychological research and practice. *American Psychologist, 55,* 407–421. doi:10.1037/0003-066X.55.4.407

Joint Commission on Mental Illness and Health. (1961). *Action for mental health: Final report, 1961.* New York, NY: Basic Books.

Karon, B. (1995). Provision of psychotherapy under managed health care: A growing crisis and national nightmare. *Professional Psychology, Research and Practice, 26,* 5–9. doi:10.1037/0735-7028.26.1.5

Koocher, G., & Morray, E. (2000). Regulation of telepsychology: A survey of state attorneys general. *Professional Psychology, Research and Practice, 31,* 503–508. doi:10.1037/0735-7028.31.5.503

Kulka, R. A., Veroff, J., & Douvan, E. (1979). Social class and the use of professional help for personal problems: 1957 and 1976. *Journal of Health and Social Behavior, 20,* 2–17.

Lee, R. M., Chalk, L., Conner, S. E., Kawasaki, N., Janetti, A., LaRue, T., & Rodolfa, E. (1999). The status of multicultural training at counseling center internship sites. *Journal of Multicultural Counseling and Development, 27,* 58–74.

Levant, R. F. (2006). Making psychology a household word. *American Psychologist, 61,* 383–395. doi:10.1037/0003-066X.61.5.383

Magaletta, P. R., Fagan, T. J., & Ax, R. K. (1998). Advancing psychology services through telehealth in the Federal Bureau of Prisons. *Professional Psychology, Research and Practice, 29,* 543–548. doi:10.1037/0735-7028.29.6.543

Maheu, M., & Gordon, B. (2000). Counseling and therapy on the Internet. *Professional Psychology, Research and Practice, 31,* 484–489. doi:10.1037/0735-7028.31.5.484

Maheu, M. M., Pulier, M. L., Wilhelm, F. H., McMenamin, J., & Brown-Connolly, N. (2005). *The mental health professional and the new technologies: A handbook for practice today.* Mahwah, NJ: Erlbaum.

Maheu, M. M., Whitten, P., & Allen, A. (2001). *E-health, telehealth, and telemedicine: A guide to start-up and success.* San Francisco, CA: Jossey-Bass.

McGoldrick, M., Giordano, J., & Pearce, J. K. (Eds.). (1996). *Ethnicity and family therapy* (2nd ed.). New York, NY: Guilford Press.

National Institute of Mental Health. (1975). *Report of the Research Task Force of the National Institute of Mental Health: Research in the service of mental health* (DHEW Publication No. [ADM] 75-236). Rockville, MD: Author.

National Institute of Mental Health. (1990). *Mental Health, United States, 1990* (R. W. Manderscheid & M.A. Sonnenschein [Eds.]; DHHS Pub. No. [ADM] 90-1708). Washington, DC: Superintendent of Documents, U.S. Government Printing Office.

New Freedom Commission on Mental Health. (2003). *Achieving the promise: Transforming mental health care in America. Final report* (DHHS Pub. No. SMA-03-3832). Rockville, MD: U.S. Department of Health and Human Services.

Newman, M. G., Kenardy, J., Herman, S., & Taylor, C. B. (1997). Comparison of palmtop-computer-assisted brief cognitive- behavioral treatment to cognitive-behavioral treatment for panic disorder. *Journal of Consulting and Clinical Psychology, 65,* 178–183. doi:10.1037/0022-006X.65.1.178

Newman, R. (2007, May). Moving beyond reform. *Monitor on Psychology, 38*(5), 46.

Nordal, K. C. (2009, March). Keynote address at the 2009 State Leadership Conference, Washington, DC. Retrieved from https://securenet.apa.org/news/2009/,DanaInfo=www.apapracticecentral.org+slc-keynote.aspx

Novotney, A. (2008, September). Parity nears reality. *Monitor on Psychology, 39*(8), 14.

Phelps, R., Eisman, E., & Kohout, J. (1998). Psychological practice and managed care: Results of the CAPP practitioner survey. *Professional Psychology, Research and Practice, 29,* 31–36. doi:10.1037/0735-7028.29.1.31

Ponterotto, J. G. (1997). Multicultural counseling training: A competency model and national survey. In D. B. Pope-Davis & H. L. K. Coleman (Eds.), *Multicultural counseling competencies: Assessment, education and training, and supervision* (pp. 111–130). Thousand Oaks, CA: Sage.

President's Commission on Mental Health. (1978). *Report to the President from the President's Commission on Mental Health* (Vol. 1). Washington, DC: U.S. Government Printing Office.

Quintana, S. M., & Bernal, M. E. (1995). Ethnic minority training in counseling psychology: Comparisons with clinical psychology and proposed standards. *The Counseling Psychologist, 23,* 102–121. doi:10.1177/0011000095231010

Reed, G., McLaughlin, C., & Milholland, K. (2000). Ten interdisciplinary principles for professional practice in telehealth: Implications for psychology. *Professional Psychology, Research and Practice, 31,* 170–178. doi:10.1037/0735-7028.31.2.170

Ritterband, L. M., Gonder-Frederick, L. A., Cox, D. J., Clifton, A. D., West, R. W., & Borowitz, S. M. (2003). Internet interventions: In review, in use, and into the future. *Professional Psychology, Research and Practice, 34,* 527–534. doi:10.1037/0735-7028.34.5.527

Rogers, M. R., Hoffman, M. A., & Wade, J. (1998). Notable multicultural training in APA-approved counseling psychology and school psychology programs. *Cultural Diversity & Ethnic Minority Psychology, 4,* 212–226.

Rothbaum, B. O., Hodges, L. F., Ready, D., Graap, K., & Alarcon, R. D. (2001). Virtual reality exposure therapy for Vietnam veterans with posttraumatic stress disorder. *The Journal of Clinical Psychiatry, 62,* 617–622.

Rothbaum, B. O., Hodges, L., Smith, S., Lee, J. H., & Price, L. (2000). A controlled study of virtual reality exposure therapy for the fear of flying. *Journal of Consulting and Clinical Psychology, 68,* 1020–1026. doi:10.1037/0022-006X.68.6.1020

Rothbaum, P., Bernstein, D., Haller, O., Phelps, R., & Kohout, J. (1998). New Jersey psychologist's report on managed mental health care. *Professional Psychology, Research and Practice, 29,* 37–42. doi:10.1037/0735-7028.29.1.37

Segal, J. (Ed.). (1975). *Research in the service of mental health: Report of the research task force of the National Institute of Mental Health* (DHEW Publication No. ADM 75-236). Washington, DC: Government Printing Office.

Special Issue: Proceedings of the National Working Conference on Education and Training in Health Psychology. (1983). *Health Psychology 2*(Suppl. 5).

Spek, V., Cuijpers, P., Nyklícek, I., Riper, H., Keyzer, J., & Pop, V. (2007). Internet-based cognitive-behaviour therapy for symptoms of depression and anxiety: A meta-analysis. *Psychological Medicine, 37,* 319–328. doi:10.1017/S0033291706008944

Stamm, B. H. (1998). Clinical applications of telehealth in mental health care. *Professional Psychology, Research and Practice, 29,* 536–542. doi:10.1037/0735-7028.29.6.536

Stapp, J., Tucker, A. M., & VandenBos, G. R. (1985). Census of psychological personnel: 1983. *American Psychologist, 40,* 1317–1351. doi:10.1037/0003-066X.40.12.1317

Sue, D. W., Ivey, A. E., & Pedersen, P. B. (1996). *A theory of multicultural counseling and therapy.* Pacific Grove, CA: Brooks/Cole.

Sue, D. W., & Sue, D. (1999). *Counseling the culturally different: Theory and practice* (3rd ed.). New York, NY: Wiley.

U.S. Department of Health and Human Services. (1999). *Mental health: A report of the Surgeon General—Executive summary.* Rockville, MD: U.S. Department of Health and Human Services, Substance Abuse and Mental Health Services Administration, Center for Mental Health Services, National Institutes of Health, National Institute of Mental Health.

VandenBos, G. R., Cummings, N. A., & DeLeon, P. H. (1992). A century of psychotherapy: Economic and environmental influences. In D. K. Freedheim, H. Freudenberger, D. R. Peterson, J. W. Kessler, H. S. Strupp, S. B. Messer, & P. L. Wachtel (Eds.), *History of psychotherapy: A century of change* (pp. 65–102). Washington, DC: American Psychological Association. doi:10.1037/10110-002

VandenBos, G. R., & Williams, S. (2000). The Internet versus the telephone: What is telehealth, anyway? *Professional Psychology, Research and Practice, 31,* 490–492. doi:10.1037/0735-7028.31.5.490

Wagner, N. N. (1968). Psychologists in medical education: A 9-year comparison. *Social Science & Medicine, 2,* 81–86. doi:10.1016/0037-7856(68)90103-0

Wilk, J. E., West, J. C., Rae, D. S., & Regier, D. A. (2006). Patterns of adult psychotherapy in psychiatric practice. *Psychiatric Services, 57,* 472–476. doi:10.1176/appi.ps.57.4.472

Wright, J. H. (2008). Computer-assisted psychotherapy: Human therapists still needed. *Psychiatric Times, 25*(14), 14–15.

II

PSYCHOTHERAPY THEORY

3

PSYCHOANALYTIC THEORIES OF PSYCHOTHERAPY

DAVID L. WOLITZKY

In the chapter on this topic in the previous edition of this volume (Eagle & Wolitzky, 1992), psychoanalytic therapies were presented primarily from the perspective of several major theorists, starting with Freud. In the current chapter, I refer to most of those theorists but organize the discussion more around key issues and trends in contemporary psychoanalytic treatments, particularly as they bear on therapeutic action.

For nearly 4 decades, it has been an era of theoretical pluralism in psychoanalytic theory. Some observers celebrate and sharpen the differences among these diverse perspectives (Greenberg & Mitchell, 1983), whereas others urge an appreciation of the common ground (e.g., a focus on transference) that unites different psychoanalytic theories (Wallerstein, 1988, 1990b). Whatever one's position, it is clear that one can no longer speak of *the* psychoanalytic theory of treatment.

Actually, there have been theoretical schisms, often bitter, virtually since the inception of psychoanalysis and certainly commencing with major theorists (e.g., Jung, Adler, Ferenczi, Rank, Horney) who deviated from Freud's views. Only in recent years has the denigration of rival theoretical points of view diminished substantially in a context in which claims about treatment outcomes have become more modest; for example, today one hears of more adaptive means of dealing with conflict rather than of complete conflict resolution or "cure." At the same time, it is uncertain whether the current theoretical pluralism in psychoanalysis actually aids therapeutic efforts.

To a significant extent, the history of theoretical developments in psychoanalysis can be understood as a series of successive reactions to Freudian drive theory, with its emphasis on libidinal and aggressive wishes as the primary motives for behavior. The main foci of theorizing in psychoanalysis subsequent to Freud's final theory of libidinal and aggressive drives were theories emphasizing ego structures and functions (ego psychology), object relations, and the self (Pine, 1990). Each of these theoretical developments entailed modification of or abandonment of Freud's drive theory.

The following offers a condensed presentation of the basic theoretical concepts of the major psychoanalytic treatments. I focus on the three most often considered to be in the psychoanalytic mainstream: contemporary Freudian theory and practice (current versions of traditional Freudian psychoanalysis), relational approaches to psychoanalysis (primarily American and British relational theories), and self psychology. Of course, a concentration on these three approaches omits other psychoanalytic therapies, such as interpersonal psychoanalysis (Sullivan, 1953), the French psychoanalysts (e.g., Green, 2000), and the work of Lacan and Bion and the contemporary Kleinians of London (Schafer, 1994).

A WORD ABOUT TERMINOLOGY

For many years, psychoanalysts spilled a lot of ink on the distinction between *psychoanalysis* and *psychoanalytic psychotherapy* (Wallerstein, 1986, 1990a). Psychoanalysis was considered the most ambitious of the analytic therapies, the gold standard, because it aimed at an intensive, in-depth investigation, analysis, and alteration of the patient's overall personality functioning. Traditional Freudian analysts focused on the patient's unresolved, unconscious, mainly oedipal conflicts as these became manifest in the so-called transference neurosis (Freud, 1912/1958) along with the associated defenses and resistances. The term *transference neurosis*, seldom used today, referred to the presumed replacement (or at least recapitulation) of the patient's neurosis by its activation and reenactment in relation to the analyst. Frequent sessions, the supine position on the couch, and the relative anonymity of the analyst were designed to facilitate the flowering of the patient's transference neurosis and the uncovering of and resolution of the patient's unconscious conflicts.

Today, most analytic therapists practice psychoanalytic psychotherapy on a once- or twice-a-week basis, with the patient sitting facing the therapist, and do not exclusively or systematically focus on the transference. All else being equal, more frequent sessions and the use of the couch are considered to facilitate, but not define, the analytic process.

In addition to insight-oriented therapy, some therapists practice deliberately *supportive psychotherapy* based on general psychoanalytic principles. In this approach, frankly supportive methods (e.g., reassurance, praise, advice) are primary and analysis of defenses and of transference is minimal. This form of treatment tends to be used primarily with patients who do not have the ego resources and capacities (e.g., psychological mindedness) to engage in a more exploratory therapy (Luborsky, 1984). In some instances insight-oriented, exploratory therapy focused on the transference has been used successfully with more disturbed patients (Kernberg, Yeomans, Clarkin, & Levy, 2008).

As a result of these shifts in practice over the past 3 decades, fewer analysts attempt to maintain as sharp a distinction between psychoanalysis and psychoanalytic psychotherapy (or between transference neurosis and transference reactions). Accordingly, in this chapter, I refer to *psychoanalysis* and *psychoanalytic psychotherapy* interchangeably and refer to *transference* in the sense of transference reactions (Wallerstein, 1990a).

As is evident from these distinctions, psychoanalytic treatments can be arranged on a continuum of expressive–supportive treatment. At the one end is psychoanalysis proper, with its emphasis on the interpretation of transference, defense, and unconscious conflicts. At the other end of the continuum is supportive psychotherapy informed by psychoanalytic concepts. Supportive therapy aims to strengthen the patient's defenses and to help the patient cope with current realities and stresses, but includes minimal attempts to analyze defenses and to promote insight. This is not to say that psychoanalysis proper offers no elements of support. However, the support is more implicit (e.g., listening to the patient in a nonjudgmental manner) than explicit. In practice, most treatments are an admixture of exploratory and supportive interventions.

Where possible, most analysts prefer an emphasis on insight-oriented rather than supportive approaches on the grounds that insight will have a more lasting impact than will results that rely on the suggestive influence of the therapist. Long ago, Freud resigned himself to the inevitability that the "pure gold of analysis" would be mixed "freely with the "copper of suggestion" (Freud, 1919/1955, p. 167). However, his primary concern in wanting to avoid cure by suggestion was that his theoretical claims would be vulnerable to the charge that his results were simply due to suggestion. Freud also wanted to minimize the influence of suggestion in order to facilitate the patient's liberation from reliance on authority.

A WORD ON PSYCHOANALYTIC RESEARCH

Although there is a small cadre of psychoanalytic researchers who investigate the process and outcome of psychoanalytic therapy, most psychoanalytic clinicians tend to ignore, or be disdainful of, empirical research. The rationale for such a dismissive attitude is that in meeting the requirements for systematic, controlled observations, empirical studies sacrifice the complexity and subtlety of what transpires in the psychoanalytic situation. Furthermore, whatever generalizations might emerge from psychotherapy research are regarded as offering little guidance to the clinician dealing with the exigencies of a particular case. Thus, most analysts are not consumers of research, let alone contributors to it, because such research also is generally felt to be an unacceptable intrusion into the sanctity of the analytic relationship.

Ever since Freud's masterful handful of case studies, analysts relied on the case study method as the basis for their clinical and theoretical views. Some clinicians might occasionally grudgingly acknowledge the limitations of this methodology for drawing conclusions about cause and effect but nonetheless find case reports stimulating and illuminating. They do not seem concerned that such reports could entail inaccurate reporting by the author. Thus, the clinical vignette or anecdote continues to be the main source of information in the clinical literature. Such a state of affairs led Fonagy (2003a) to write that "there is some truth to the quip that analytic clinicians understand the word data to be a plural of the word anecdote" (p. 15).

Although psychoanalytic practitioners by and large ignore empirical research, psychoanalytic researchers have assembled evidence for the viability of several Freudian concepts (e.g., Westen, 1998). In more recent years, there also have been efforts to draw links between psychoanalysis and neuroscience (Westen & Gabbard, 2002a, 2002b). Another influential trend is the effort to integrate psychoanalytic and cognitive–behavioral therapies (e.g., Wachtel, 1997).

There is a strong evidence base for the effectiveness of brief psychodynamic psychotherapies; there are stable, meaningful effect sizes for target symptoms, social functioning, and general psychiatric symptoms. With respect to long-term psychodynamic therapies, significant effect sizes have been found with individuals who have complex disorders that are not responsive to short-term therapy (e.g., Leichsenring & Rabung, 2008; Sandell et al., 2000; Yager, 2008). At the same time, it should be noted that there are no controlled trials of psychoanalysis, nor have the effects on psychodynamic therapies been found more substantial than the effects of other treatments. In general, research findings support the argument for common factors in diverse therapies as the ingredients most relevant to favorable outcomes (see also Chapter 10, this volume).

As of now, there is still no solid, unified theory about how treatment works. Rosenbaum (2009) echoed the view of most psychoanalysts when he wrote that "despite many attempts to discover an answer, the question of what 'really' constitutes the curative factor of psychotherapy remains at the center of incessant discussion and controversy and, to a large extent, continues to be the enigma of psychoanalysis" (p. 188).

With these considerations in mind, I turn to a presentation of the three major psychoanalytic therapies. Because all psychoanalytic approaches take Freud's theories as their point of departure, I begin with a brief synopsis of his basic concepts.

TRADITIONAL FREUDIAN PSYCHOANALYSIS

Sigmund Freud (1856–1939) founded psychoanalysis as a theory, as a method of investigating the human mind, and as a method of treatment. As a theory, psychoanalysis was, and remains, the most ambitious, comprehensive, and complex attempt to understand human behavior, both normal and pathological. It aims not only to explain psychopathology but also to explicate key cognitive, emotional, and motivational aspects of personality development and the possible biological bases of these processes. It also ventures into virtually every aspect of human experience, such as interpersonal functioning; creativity in art, music, and literature; history; politics; and religion. The essential defining characteristic of psychoanalysis is a view of mental life as influenced by inner conflict, particularly unconscious conflicts related to unacceptable and threatening wishes.

Freud changed aspects of his theory many times in his long, productive career, as one can see from a study of the 23 volumes of his collected works, published as the definitive *Standard Edition*. Freud's impact on 20th-century thought is unrivaled by any other conception of personality. His influence has penetrated Western cultural experience to the point that many of his ideas no longer seem radical but have become an assimilated, common part of Westerners' implicit conceptions of personality. At the same time, certain of his views, such as the centrality of the Oedipus complex, remain controversial and objectionable.

Freud started with the theory that the symptoms of neurosis were the result of repressed memories of childhood sexual seduction and (later) of repressed sexual wishes and fantasies. In *Studies on Hysteria*, Freud stated, "I have shown how, in the course of our therapeutic work, we have been led to the view that hysteria originates through the repression of an incompatible idea from a motive of defense" (Breuer & Freud, 1893–1895/1955, p. 285).

Over the next several decades, he expanded his theory to encompass all aspects of personality functioning. With regard to neurotic symptoms, Freud posited that the affects associated with the repressed memories were "strangulated," that is, cut off from associative connection with other mental contents. Both the strangulated status of the affect and the associative isolation of the mental content result in hysterical symptoms. In other words, central to Freud's early thinking was that mental contents that are isolated and remain unintegrated into one's personality constitute pathogens that can result in various kinds of symptoms. "It turns out to be a *sine qua non* for the acquisition of hysteria that an incompatibility should develop between the ego and some idea presented to it" (Freud, 1916–1917/1963, p. 122).

The pathogenic memories needed to be unearthed and the associated affects needed to be abreacted—that is, consciously experienced. As Freud (1916–1917/1963, p. 17) put it, psychotherapy allows "strangulated affect [of the idea] to find a way out through speech" and also subjects the idea to "associative correction by introducing it into normal consciousness." Hypnosis was initially the preferred means of retrieving repressed, split-off memories. Later, Freud turned to the quasihypnotic "pressure" technique of placing his hand on the patient's forehead and insisting that the patient would recall the forgotten memory. These procedures evolved into psychoanalysis when, instead of hypnosis and the pressure technique, Freud instructed patients to free associate, that is, to refrain from deliberately censoring their thoughts and to say whatever spontaneously came to mind. The method of free association became the fundamental rule in psychoanalytic treatment.

It was quickly apparent to Freud that the flow of thoughts and the accompanying expression of feelings were far from a random sequence of utterances. Furthermore, there were sequences of verbalization in which the patient's associations stopped at various points or went off in directions in which they had no obvious manifest connection with one another. The initial aim of this method was to recover the concealed memories that Freud previously attempted to retrieve via hypnosis and the pressure technique. However, in tracing the course of the patient's free associations, Freud saw that they did not immediately lead directly back to the repressed memories; instead, he assumed that the patient's "free" associations were influenced by such memories. On this basis, Freud posited two central assumptions of his theory: psychic determinism and unconscious motivation.

Psychic determinism refers to the idea that there are lawful regularities in mental life. *Unconscious motivation* postulates that what is in awareness is only one portion of the psyche and that conscious thoughts and behavior are influenced by motives of which the patient is unaware and that he or she cannot bring to awareness by a simple act of will. In other words, there are thoughts and feelings about which people are conflicted and regarding which people are motivated to prevent their entry into awareness. This is what Freud meant by the *dynamic unconscious*.

Psychoanalytic theory views behavior as representing intrapsychic conflict between opposing aims and aspects of the personality. According to Freud, the instinctual drives of sex and aggression are represented in the mind as wishes seeking immediate gratification, an aspect of personality Freud (1923/1961) later termed the *id*. *Ego* refers to part of the personality that tests reality, learns how to delay gratification, and as the executive portion, decides which wishes can be safely expressed and which need to be the target of defense, lest they arouse too much anxiety, guilt, or other negative affects. Thus, the ego operates according to the *reality principle*, in which delay of gratification is essential, whereas the id operates according to the *pleasure principle*, seeking immediate discharge of tension. Part of the ego's judgment is its assessment of the dictates of the superego. The *superego* is the moral aspect of the personality and includes the conscience (internalized standards of right and wrong) and the ego ideal (internalized aspirations that regulate one's level of self-esteem).

Conflicts between these personality aspects can lead to pathological solutions. Most accounts of this tripartite, structural theory make it sound like the id, ego, and superego are concrete entities doing battle with one another. However, the proper way of thinking about them is simply as different aspects of the personality that, in the absence of conflict, function in a relatively harmonious, seamless manner.

This model of behavior is one of *wish* (the mental representation of an instinctual drive that aims to restore a previous memory of gratification) versus *defense* (which seeks to disavow or disguise or block the wish from awareness). This basic model has been used to explain symptom formation, dreams, character traits, and other aspects of behavior. With the advent of ego psychology (Hartmann, 1958), analysts began paying attention to conflict-free spheres of ego functioning.

TRADITIONAL, CLASSICAL PSYCHOANALYTIC THERAPY

At the height of the dominance of the orthodox Freudian approach to psychoanalysis in the 1950s, Gill's (1954) definition was often quoted: "Psychoanalysis is that technique which employed by a *neutral* analyst, results in the development of a *regressive transference neurosis* and the ultimate resolution of this neurosis by techniques of *interpretation alone*" [emphasis added;

original entirely in italics] (p. 775). In the gradual shift from this conception of classical psychoanalysis to contemporary Freudian analysis, the italicized elements in the definition above came to be regarded, in many respects, as no longer essential, or at least as an overly restrictive conception of the psychoanalytic process.

The term *regressive transference neurosis* refers to the reenactment and centering of the patient's childhood conflicts on the person of the analyst. The term *transference* refers to the

> experiencing of impulses, feelings, fantasies, attitudes, and defenses with respect to a person in the present which do not appropriately fit that person but are a repetition of responses originating in regard to significant persons of early childhood, unconsciously displaced onto persons in the present. (Greenson & Wexler, 1969, p. 28)

Transference reactions to emotionally significant persons in the present are fairly ubiquitous and are not restricted to experiences in analysis. In fact, in everyday life they often are a common source of considerable difficulty in interpersonal relationships. What is distinctive about psychoanalytic treatment is that they are analyzed.

The idea that transference "ignores or distorts reality" and is "inappropriate" (Greenson & Wexler, 1969, p. 28) came to be vigorously opposed by relational analysts because the emphasis on "distortion" places the analyst in the position of the final arbiter of reality. Many post-Freudians prefer a relativistic position in which transference seems to be regarded as synonymous with the patient's experience of the relationship (Gill, 1982). In this view, patients' reactions are plausible constructions of aspects of the analyst's real behavior. Thus, normative analyst behaviors (e.g., silence) are not to be regarded simply as neutral technical devices but are actual ways of relating that patients can react to in ways that are not necessarily distorted or inappropriate.

Neutrality refers to the analyst taking a position equidistant from the different sides of the patient's conflicts and doing so in a nonjudgmental manner. The term *neutrality* was perhaps an unfortunate choice of words in that it can be misunderstood to mean indifference and a lack of caring. In fact, even though it is missing from the definition, caring (nonjudgmental, respectful affirmation of the patient's worth in a way that promotes the patient's autonomy and individuality) is considered an effective, implicit element in the therapeutic process.

At the same time, the notion of neutrality also is linked to Freud's (1912/1957) recommendation that the analysis be conducted in an atmosphere of abstinence, that is, in a manner that does not include transference gratification beyond that which is inherent in the analyst's caring attitude. To avoid transference gratification that would allegedly offer temporary solutions and to facilitate the full flowering of the transference, the traditional analyst also maintained a relative anonymity (e.g., did not offer deliberate, personal self-disclosures). Freud used the metaphors of the "blank screen," the "mirror," and the "surgeon" to describe the analytic stance of being more of an observer than a participant. This position led classical analysts to a "one-person" psychology in which they believed erroneously that they could somehow stand outside the field of observation. During this period of psychoanalysis (until about 1970) it was assumed that analysts were interchangeable, that is, the patient's transference would unfold in essentially the same manner with any well-trained, competent analyst (Stone, 1961).

In processing the patient's communications, the analyst tries to listen with an attitude of "evenly hovering attention" while engaged in a partial, transient identification with the patient. This empathic attunement to the patient, which includes listening "between the lines" or "with a third ear," facilitates the analyst's apprehension and appreciation of the patient's intrapsychic reality. This "analytic attitude" (Schafer, 1983) involves an oscillation between empathic immersion in the patient's inner experience and a stepping back to process and make sense of the patient's communications. This vacillation between an experiential mode and an observational mode (Sterba, 1934) includes monitoring one's own subjective experience and potential biases (i.e., countertransference reactions).

This mode of reacting to the patient's free associations prepares the way for what has been assumed to be the decisive, curative element in psychoanalysis, namely, interpretation leading to insight. The other common verbal interventions in the course of treatment (e.g., clarifications, questions, confrontations) are preparatory to interpretation. The most (and some would argue only) mutative interpretations are considered to be transference interpretations with regard to unconscious fantasies from the past linked to "here and now" interpretations, which bring to light how the past is being reenacted in relation to the analyst. In emphasizing the emotional immediacy of transference interpretations, Freud (1912/1958) noted that one cannot slay anyone "in absentia or in effigie" (p. 108).

Freud maintained that the patient was motivated to expel from consciousness mental contents that arouse anxiety. This formulation of a dynamic unconscious is closely linked to *resistance*. Although the term has a pejorative connotation, it is an inevitable aspect of the treatment. As Freud (1912/1958) put it, "The resistance accompanies the treatment step by step. Every single association, every act of the person under treatment must reckon with the resistance and represents a compromise between the forces that are striving towards recovery and the opposing ones" (p. 103). It can be regarded as defense expressed in the transference, as resistance both to the awareness of transference reactions and to the resolution of the transference (Gill, 1982). Defense analysis focuses on what the patient is resisting, how he is resisting, and why he is resisting. According to Freud (1937/1964), the sources of resistance include the "adhesiveness of the libido," the repetition compulsion, and the so-called negative therapeutic reaction and its connection to unconscious guilt.

In the evolution from traditional psychoanalysis to the contemporary Freudian view, there has been an increasing focus on (a) the working or therapeutic alliance, (b) countertransference, (c) the role of extratransference interpretation, and (d) the noninterpretive elements in psychoanalytic treatment.

The Working or Therapeutic Alliance

In a paper on technique, Freud (1912/1957) wrote of the necessity of rapport and of the desired attitude of the patient toward the analyst:

> It remains the first aim of the treatment to attach him [the patient] to it and to the person of the doctor. To ensure this, nothing need be done but to give him time. If one exhibits a serious interest in him, carefully clears away the resistances that crop up at the beginning and avoids making certain mistakes, he will of himself form such an attachment and link the doctor up with one of the imagoes of the people by whom he was accustomed to be treated with affection. (pp. 139–140)

This is essentially what is now called the *therapeutic* (Zetzel, 1966) or *working alliance* (Greenson, 1965).

According to Greenson (1967), the working alliance is the "relatively non-neurotic, rational relationship between patient and analyst which makes it possible for the patient to work purposefully in the analytic situation" (p. 45). The alliance between the analyst's analytic attitude and the patient's reasonable ego is not a once-and-for-all achievement but one that is prone to disruption by the patient's transference reactions and narcissistic vulnerabilities as well as by the analyst's lapses in empathy. Ruptures in the alliance can lead to a temporary deterioration of mutual agreements concerning the tasks and goals of treatment as well as to heightened resistance and an increase in negative transference. Ruptures can take the form of subtle avoidance and withdrawal or explicit hostility and confrontation (e.g., questioning the analyst's competence). Though the ruptures might shake the patient's trust in the analyst, successful repairs can teach the patient that a relationship can survive some psychic pain and misunderstanding when the analyst is a person of fairness and decency.

Countertransference

Countertransference was originally considered a serious obstacle to effective treatment; that is, insofar as the analyst's unconscious conflicts led to unchecked and therefore unmanaged distortions of the patient's reactions, the analyst's interpretations would not be accurate and not lead to genuine insights. Over the years, the definition of countertransference has been broadened to refer to all of the analyst's reactions (conscious and unconscious) not only to the patient's transference but also to all aspects of the patient's personality and behavior. With this shift in how countertransference was conceptualized it was no longer seen as a hindrance to the analytic work. In fact, it has come to be regarded as an essential means by which the analyst gains understanding of the patient.

At issue among psychoanalysts is the extent to which the analyst's reactions to the patient should be used as a source of information or also be shared with the patient. Some analysts apparently disclose their reactions fairly routinely, whereas others are more apt to do so only when there is a rupture in the therapeutic alliance or an impasse in the treatment.

Extratransference Interpretation

Most classical analysts argued that only transference interpretations were mutative. The classic interpretation would link the patient's conflictual patterns in three relationships: past relationships, the relationship with the therapist, and current relationships with significant others. In more recent years, many Freudian analysts have come to acknowledge that interpretations focusing only on conflicts and fantasies relevant to current relationships with significant others can have therapeutic impact.

Noninterpretive Elements in Psychoanalytic Therapy

Though the traditional Freudian explanation of change in psychoanalysis strongly emphasized the vital importance of emotional insight, it was recognized early on that other aspects of the therapeutic relationship had curative properties, perhaps more important than insight, at least for some patients. Ferenczi (1926) was one of the first and most influential analysts to depart from a strictly interpretive stance. He experimented with "active techniques" that included restricting and indulging patients in various ways, both to break through repression and to provide some of the love they missed in childhood (e.g., platonically kissing the patient). He also experimented with mutual analysis in which he and the patient took turns free associating and analyzing one another. He believed that the patient's experience of the relationship was crucial.

Without deliberately departing from an interpretive stance, analysts came more and more to recognize the implicit, inherent features of the therapeutic relationship that could have healing properties. These factors included (a) the reduction in the harshness of the patient's superego as a result of being accepted by a calm, nonjudgmental parent-like authority figure; (b) the safe, supportive base that provides a "holding environment" for the patient (Modell, 1976) that fosters exploration; and (c) the opportunity to form an identification with the analyst as well as the analyst's analytic attitude, and to embrace the analyst's conception of the patient's potential for growth. In addition to these kinds of largely silent factors, some analysts (e.g., Schachter & Kachele, 2007) have advocated for "psychoanalysis-plus," the judicious use of explicitly supportive methods of the kind one would typically employ in a supportive therapy (e.g., reassurance, praise). In short, many contemporary Freudians have joined relational analysts in making a theoretical place for relationship factors in treatment (Wolitzky, 2003).

CONTEMPORARY FREUDIAN THEORY AND PRACTICE

Contemporary Freudians subscribe to many of the foregoing concepts of traditional Freudian theory but with modifications and extensions. Contemporary Freudians still accept the formulation of the tripartite, structural theory of id, ego, and superego as the three main psychological structures of the mind and the central importance of defenses against sexual and aggressive conflicted wishes. They also focus on the role of anxiety in triggering the ego's defensive operations (as well as the ego's autonomous, conflict-free coping efforts). Signals of anxiety trigger the activation of defense, currently understood to include not only the classic mechanisms of defense (e.g., projection, denial, repression, and reaction formation) but also any aspect of ego functioning that can be used for defensive purposes (Brenner, 1982). Following Freud, the primary anxieties or "danger situations" of childhood are loss of the object, loss of the object's love, castration anxiety, and superego anxiety (guilt). The failure of signal anxiety to activate adequate defenses leads to traumatic anxiety and an extreme state of unpleasure in which the ego is totally overwhelmed and rendered helpless. It is this traumatic situation of overstimulation that some (e.g., A. Freud, 1936) regard as the basic, bedrock anxiety.

Since Anna Freud's (1936) *The Ego and the Mechanisms of Defense*, the treatment focus has been increasingly on the analysis of defense against disturbing affects, impulses, and conflicts. Perhaps the strongest contemporary example of this approach is Gray's (1973) emphasis on helping the patient become an observer of his or her defensive maneuvers and the affect signals that trigger them.

Within the framework of the tripartite, structural theory, Mahler (1968), Erikson (1950), and Jacobson (1964), with their respective concepts of separation–individuation, ego identity, and the self and the object world, began to make room for issues of self-hood and object relations within a

Freudian framework. These theorists paid more attention to early mother–infant interactions as a vital crucible for personality development. In contrast to a strong emphasis on oedipal conflicts in adult pathology, early childhood trauma and deprivation became seen as determinants of more severe adult pathology, a view that resulted in a widening scope of psychoanalysis (Stone, 1954, 1961) in which such patients were treated with modified forms of psychoanalysis. Interpretation alone started to give way to a broader conception of the ingredients of therapeutic change.

The theoretical contributions of psychoanalysts in the second half of the 20th century increasingly focused on aspects of self-hood and object relations, even among theorists who grew up in the Freudian tradition. Kernberg (1975, 1976, 1980) developed a theory of borderline personality organization in which he integrated drive theories, ego psychology, and object relations. His developmental theory emphasized self and object representations and their affective links. He emphasized the transference patterns of borderline patients in which splitting of self and object representations is prominent. Such patients cannot integrate "good" and "bad" and therefore alternate between attitudes of idealization and devaluation of self and others. Excessive oral aggression caused by marked early deprivation or strong constitutional factors, or both, is characteristic of borderline patients. Kernberg's transference-focused psychotherapy aims at dealing, via interpretation, with the split-off components of the patient's self and object representations.

A recent phase of theorizing among those who previously characterized themselves traditional Freudians might be called *modern structural theory* or *contemporary conflict theory* (Richards & Lynch, 1998). Based primarily on the writings of Brenner (1982, 1994), this approach views all of mental and emotional life as the expression of conflicting intrapsychic forces, originating in childhood, that result in compromise formations. Adaptive compromise formations are characterized by relatively less depression, anxiety, and self-punishment, and greater pleasure, compared with maladaptive ones. All behavior can be seen as reflecting the combined, interactive influences of instinctual wishes, defenses, superego factors, reality considerations, coping and defensive devices, tolerance for anxiety, and so on. The concept of intrapsychic conflict is still regarded as the main vantage point for understanding the patient. However, this focus is now supplemented with attention to how the patient experiences his or her sense of self in the context of interpersonal relationships. Although the traditional Freudian approach still is regarded by most contemporary Freudians as a one-person psychology, there are definite trends toward viewing the analyst as a participant–observer and broadening the definition of countertransference to refer to all of the analyst's feelings toward the patient. Contemporary Freudian analysts also considered the potential therapeutic value of self-disclosure (Jacobs, 1986).

These developments led increasingly to an interest in the here-and-now relationship between patient and analyst and to the importance of the analyst's attunement to mutual transference–countertransference enactments. The past is still of interest to contemporary analysts but only insofar as it is being maladaptively repeated in the present.

Conception of Therapeutic Action

The main implications of contemporary Freudian theory for treatment can be stated in abbreviated form as follows:

- Significant aspects of mental life are unconscious for defensive reasons. This can result in pathological compromise formations that have a repetitive quality. Therefore, analytic attention is directed to unconscious conflicts, wishes, and fantasies.
- The interaction of childhood experiences and genetic predispositions shapes the nature of internal, mental representations of interpersonal relationships, which, in turn, shape the adult personality. The child's mental representations of its interpersonal relationships are an admixture of veridical and distorted perceptions of significant others.
- The distinctions between psychoanalysis and psychoanalytic therapy are less sharply drawn than previously. Extrinsic criteria (e.g., use of the couch, frequency of sessions) should not be used to make the distinction. Rather, the distinction should be based on the degree to which the transference is the major focus of the treatment (Gill, 1994).
- The structuring of psychoanalytic therapy is such that it facilitates a regressive pull and the emergence of transference reactions. The encouragement to free associate, the supine position on the couch out of view of the analyst, the relative restraint shown by the analyst, and the optimal frustration (or abstinence) in relation to the patient's desires for gratification from the analyst keep old and conflicted desires alive, emotionally vivid, ready for transference, and potentially analyzable.
- Interpreting the transference is the key way of elucidating the patient's intrapsychic life. When possible, such interpretations can occur in the context of a triangle of insight (Malan, 1976) in which the patient comes to appreciate how he or she is repeating the same dynamic patterns in his or her relationship with the therapist, with significant figures from the past, and in current relationships with significant others.

- Insight is still regarded as the main curative factor. Insight is not a once-and-for-all achievement but needs to be repeated in the context of repeated "working through" of core issues.
- The analytic process is facilitated by appropriate tact, timing, and dosage of interpretations of the patient's core conflicts in the context of an effective therapeutic alliance. Ideally, analysts appreciate the irreducibly subjective nature of their experience, monitor their countertransference, and do not set themselves up as the arbiter of their patients' psychic reality or seek to impose their preferred theory or values on their patients.
- The value of therapists' countertransference reactions as a source of information about their patients' dynamics is emphasized. The challenge for therapists is to monitor their own reactions to avoid automatically assuming that what they are feeling is necessarily what their patients intended to induce them to feel (Jacobs, 1986).
- Transference–countertransference enactments are an inherent, inevitable, ongoing aspect of the analytic relationship and can be a fruitful source of information about the interpersonal and intrapsychic dynamics of both members of the analytic dyad.
- A major focus of the treatment continues to be the patient's resistance, both to the awareness of transference and to its resolution (Gill, 1994). Resistance is best thought of as defense expressed in the transference rather than simply as opposition to the procedures of the treatment.
- There is less interpretive emphasis on derivatives of unconscious drives and more stress on the complexity and conflicted nature of interpersonal relationships. Nonetheless, contemporary Freudians claim that these two facets of personality are intimately related and that they always have been interested in patients' relationship struggles.
- The development and maintenance of a therapeutic or working alliance is necessary for the patient to be receptive to the analyst's interventions. Ruptures in the alliance are inevitable, and the successful repair of such ruptures often offers significant opportunities for therapeutic progress (Messer & Wolitzky, in press; Safran & Muran, 2000).
- Many psychoanalysts believe that more disturbed patients require more supportive and fewer exploratory methods. Others believe that patients with severe disorders can benefit from transference-focused interpretations (e.g., Kernberg, Yeomans, Clarkin, & Levy, 2008). Many analysts now recommend the

judicious use of explicitly supportive measures even with the average patient.

- Whereas in the past Freudian analysts gave primacy to the Oedipus complex, contemporary Freudians have become more interested in the significance of early parent–child interactions in the development of psychopathology. In turn, they are somewhat more willing to depart from a classical analytic stance. Previously, deviations from the analytic frame were regarded as "parameters" (Eissler, 1953) that had to be clearly justified, temporary, and eventually interpreted, lest they provide unanalyzed transference gratification. These days, so-called parameters seem to be used more freely and probably often go unanalyzed.
- The influence of object relations theories and self psychology is certainly evident, and many analysts believe concepts from these theories enrich their contemporary Freudian perspective.
- Contemporary Freudians, as well as analysts of all persuasions, agree that the patient needs to experience the analyst as an old object for transference to develop and as a new object for it to be worked through and resolved. It also is accepted that the experience of the analyst as a new object can be therapeutic in its own right; for example, being nonjudgmental offers the patient a new experience. It was recognized early on that the analyst's nonjudgmental attitude facilitated a diminution in the patient's harsh superego (Loewald, 1960; Strachey, 1934).
- Freudian analysts increasingly acknowledge that environmental deficits, such as child abuse and neglect, can lead to associated ego defects, which have to be addressed in treatment along with unresolved conflicts.
- Many analysts are enthusiastically exploring the implications of Bowlby's (1969) attachment theory for their clinical work (e.g., Eagle & Wolitzky, 2008; Fonagy, 2001).

The stereotyped image of traditional or classical psychoanalysts persists today in relation to contemporary Freudians. As late as the 2000s (e.g., Fiscalini, 2004), commentators depicted Freudian analysts as "authoritarian," "rigid," "controlling," "hierarchical," and "generally silent" (p. 45). Others saw Freudians as trying to impose an absolute, singular, allegedly correct view of reality in an "accusatory" manner (e.g., Wile, 1984).

However, most Freudian analysts today no longer position themselves as nonparticipating, detached observers oblivious to the constantly interactive nature of the analytic relationship which, of course, includes their contribution to the way the patient experiences the situation and the analyst. For example, in offering an interpretation, the analyst considers the possible multiple meanings to the patient of the fact that an interpretation was presented at a particular moment. Is it being experienced as a gift, an intrusion, a penetration, or a moralistic criticism? Such considerations often are more important than the content of the interpretation. In general, contemporary Freudian analysts respond to their patients with less formality and personal restraint than was the case for prior generations.

Unfortunately, there is not yet a solid body of research that could shed definitive light on the relative benefits of a more pure interpretative psychoanalysis versus a treatment that blends exploratory and supportive features. For example, the ambitious, long-term Menninger study compared patients who received standard psychoanalysis with those who received modified analysis. The latter treatments, which included more frankly supportive measures and less attention to the interpretation of transference, were equally effective in promoting long-term benefits (Wallerstein, 1986). Supportive strategies resulted in structural changes just as durable as those brought about by interpretive approaches. In other words, there are alternative paths to structural change.

In conclusion, one can say that, relatively speaking, Freudian approaches locate therapeutic action primarily in the patient's insights into transference reactions, whereas relational psychoanalysis, my next topic, focuses relatively more on the healing properties of a good therapeutic relationship.

RELATIONAL PSYCHOANALYSIS

Object relations theories were first formulated in Great Britain, mainly by Klein (1948), Fairbairn (1952), and Winnicott (1965). Fairbairn and Winnicott were considered part of the British independent school. American relational theory (Greenberg & Mitchell, 1983) is an amalgam of British object relations theories and Sullivan's (1953) interpersonal theory. Sullivan argued that it is misleading to think about personality traits or states as though they were self-contained intrapsychic entities. With respect to treatment, this view implies that the therapist is always as much a participant in the interaction as is the patient. In Mitchell's (1988) view, the relational model is "an alternative perspective which considers relations with others, not drives, as the basic stuff of mental life" (p. 2), always expressed in an (interpersonal and intrapsychic) interactional field or intersubjective context (Stolorow, Brandchaft, & Atwood, 1987).

The varieties of object relations theories are held together by common threads:

- the limitations of Freud's theories, in particular his theory of instinctual drives;

- the idea that the primary aim of the infant is to seek and maintain relatedness to others. As Fairbairn (1952) famously put it, "libido is primarily object seeking (rather than pleasure-seeking, as in the classic theory)" (p. 82);
- the importance of the early mother–infant relationship in facilitating or arresting personality development;
- the view that psychopathology results from environmental failure leading to the faulty internalization of early interpersonal relationships; and
- the centrality given to the development of the self. The evolution of self-hood and the internalization of the object world is based on the infant's formation of mental representations of self and others, and the affective tone of their interaction (Kernberg, 1975). These units are the building blocks of psychic structure, which consists largely of relational configurations. Sexuality, aggression, and conflict are still considered important, but are conceptualized in relational terms.

According to Fairbairn (1952), although it is natural for the infant to internalize objects, it is mainly under the impact of negative, depriving, and frustrating experiences that objects are internalized. The infant does this to take in the badness of the environment in order to experience the caretakers as more benevolent and controllable. However, such internalized objects often are not fully integrated into one's self-organization; they are experienced as "presences" or introjects (e.g., "my conscience tells me . . . ") rather than as natural, seamless parts of the self, as is the case in identification (e.g., *I* believe . . . "). Thus, a major aim of object relations therapy is the exorcism of the internalized bad objects.

Winnicott (1965) stressed the importance of "good enough" mothering in an adequate "holding environment" as facilitating the "capacity to be alone," leading to eventual independence. Emphasizing early object relationships as crucial to personality development is now accepted by all psychoanalytic approaches, not only object relations theories. Although some research evidence supports this view, it is a position that does not give sufficient consideration to other factors (e.g., genetic variables) that influence the development of adult pathology (Fonagy & Target, 2003).

In the United States, the principal theorists who have incorporated object relations concepts into their theories are Mahler (1968), Jacobson (1964), and Kernberg (1975). Starting in the 1980s, in the United States, what came to be called American relational theories began to be developed. Created primarily by Mitchell (1988), this approach is a blend of British object relations theory and Sullivan's (1953) interpersonal theory. For purposes of this chapter, in what follows the terms *object relations* and *relational* are used interchangeably.

As Wachtel (2008) observed, "A new wind is blowing in psychoanalysis" (p. vii). The wind, sparked by Greenberg and Mitchell's (1983) comparative studies of psychoanalytic theories, is the promulgation of a relational point of view that draws on British object relations theories, Sullivan's interpersonal theory, and American relational theory. It has reached gale force status in the past 2 decades and has become the dominant psychoanalytic theory (Fonagy & Target, 2003). What most clearly distinguishes relational theories from traditional and contemporary Freudian theories is aptly captured by Fairbairn's dictum, cited above, that libido is object seeking, not pleasure seeking. This assertion rejects Freud's idea that a person's initial turning toward objects is based primarily on the object's role in serving instinctual discharge.

As stated by Greenberg and Mitchell (1983),

> The most significant tension in the history of psychoanalytic ideas has been the dialectic between the original Freudian mode, which takes as its starting point the instinctual drive, and an alternative comprehensive model initiated in the work of Fairbairn and Sullivan, which evolves structure solely from the individual's relations with other people. (p. 20)

From a relational perspective, the building blocks of mental life and psychological structure are to be found in the constant relational matrix in which the self evolves. Object relations units (e.g., victim–abuser) become internally represented and become models for interpersonal relationships.

This view is linked to perhaps the single, overarching trend in psychoanalytic treatment over the past 2 decades: the significant demise of the conviction that interpretation leads to insight as the main curative factor in treatment and the concomitant emphasis on the therapy relationship as a central ingredient in therapeutic change. As Strupp and Binder (1984) reminded us, Frieda Fromm-Reichmann said that patients seek and need an experience, not an explanation. One need not, however, think of experience and explanation as dichotomous. For example, feeling empathically understood following an interpretation by the therapist is, after all, an experience (Eagle & Wolitzky, 1982). Thus, explanation and experience can be intimately linked. This view is echoed by Kohut (1984), who believed that the therapeutic impact of an interpretation derives not so much from the content of the interpretation but from the fact that it can lead to a feeling of being understood and thereby strengthen the patient–therapist bond.

The Relational, Hermeneutic, Postmodern Turn in Psychoanalysis

Relational writings indicate a deliberate attempt to democratize the therapeutic relationship, to emphasize its mutuality, to not see it as a relationship between a sick person and a healthy one (Racker, 1968). While recognizing the irreducibly asymmetrical nature of the analytic relationship, one can conduct it in a nonadversarial manner (Aron, 1996).

One reason for the popularity and dominance of relational treatments is their attempt to liberate analysts from adherence to the Freudian default position that includes a near-exclusive emphasis on interpretation, including its focus on transference "distortions." This position is seen as that of a nonegalitarian analyst who sets him- or herself up as arbiter of the patient's reality in the near-delusional belief that he or she has infallible access to "truths" about the patient that will be delivered in a single set of canonical interpretations.

The writings of many relational therapists tend to portray Freudian analysts as oblivious to the fact that the analyst and patient are engaged in a relationship and are in an ongoing interaction with one another. From a relational perspective, traditional analysts are regarded as being stuck in an antiquated adherence to a "one-person psychology" in contrast to what is deemed to be the necessary "two-person psychology" that reflects an appreciation of the inevitable, constantly interactive nature of the patient–analyst dyad, of two subjectivities interacting in an intersubjective field. Although defined somewhat differently by different theorists, the principal meaning of the term *intersubjectivity* is the often unconscious, mutual regulation of the psychological experiences of each member of the analytic dyad (Aron, 1996). In this vein, relationalists offer a reminder that an interpretation is a form of interpersonal interaction; so is silence, as well as any other activity on the part of the analytic dyad.

The relational turn and its focus on the two-person nature of the analytic situation brought an emphasis on the coconstruction of new meanings that emerge in the intersubjective field and that lead to coherent, narrative truths. This hermeneutic, postmodern view is contrasted with what is considered an outmoded, positivist view that assumes a singular, correct reality to which the analyst has privileged access. Instead, there are retellings of lives (Schafer, 1992), persuasive narratives to be constructed or coconstructed, new perspectives to be taken (Renik, 2006), and new meanings to be created (Mitchell, 1998).

Consistent with the deemphasis on interpretation and an increased focus on the intersubjective field (Stolorow, Brandchaft, & Atwood, 1987) are a number of concepts that have been developed by relational analysts. These include the therapeutic value of *implicit relational knowing*, the *analytic third*, the virtues of *self-disclosure*, and *dissociation and multiple self-states*. Each is considered briefly in the sections that follow.

Implicit Relational Knowing

The Boston Change Process Study Group (1988, 2002, 2005) has advanced the idea that therapeutic change requires "something more" than interpretation. The something more is a change in implicit relational knowing.

To understand this concept, one needs to note the distinction between explicit and implicit forms of knowledge, the latter usually eluding conscious awareness. Implicit relational knowing is acquired quite early in life. For example, before they have language skills to use in navigating and negotiating social interactions, children know implicitly what they have to do and what they cannot do if they want to elicit a positive response from mother. In this view, verbally articulated insights in the context of recovered memories are not the sole road to personality change, perhaps not even the most important road. As Fonagy (2003b) noted, "The therapeutic action of psychoanalysis is unrelated to the 'recovery' of memories of childhood" (p. 219). It works by modifying procedures rather than by creating new ideas. In other words, procedural knowledge is not easily translatable into reflective (symbolized) knowledge and therefore not always susceptible to change via interpretation and insight. Although some analysts would agree with Fonagy's (2003b) point regarding childhood memories, most analysts would still emphasize the importance of uncovering unconscious fantasies and wishes, including those originating in childhood.

One interesting treatment question arising from the concept of implicit relational knowing is whether it might be preferable for the therapist not to interpret and bring into the patient's awareness aspects of implicit relational knowing. For example, Weiss and Sampson (1986) and Silberschatz (2005) emphasized the importance of the therapist "passing" the patient's "tests" as a precondition for the patient gaining access to previously warded-off mental contents. Should the therapist allow passed tests to occur without interpreting to the patient the connection between the passed test and the patient's subsequent behavior, or is it better for the therapist to comment on the connection between the passed test and the nature of the patient's subsequent associations? Under what circumstances are positive patient–therapist interactions better left at the implicit level?

The Analytic Third

In recent years, Ogden (1994) and others have focused on the idea of the analytic third. This concept refers to the analyst's attempt simultaneously to track both his or her own subjectivity and that of the patient while also being attuned to the intersubjectivity of the analytic dyad that is the unconscious experience of the analytic pair. It is this intersection of the unconscious psychic activity of the analytic pair that is called the analytic third. As Ogden (1994) put it, "I believe that, in an analytic context, there is no such thing as an analysand apart from the relationship with the analyst, and no such thing as an analyst apart from the relationship with the analysand" (p. 3). This view is heavily influenced by Winnicott's (1960) idea that "there is no such thing as an infant [apart from the maternal provision]" (p. 39, fn). Patient and analyst are encouraged to consider that the thoughts and feelings that occur to them in the course of their interaction are not random but reflect, indirectly, unverbalized and unconscious reactions they are having to one another. For example, if the analyst finds him- or herself gazing at an envelope on the desk and has thoughts regarding the intimate versus impersonal nature of the letter he or she received from a colleague, this experience likely reflects feelings about his or her interaction with the patient. It is not clear to what extent this represents an advance over what analysts have been presumably doing for years, that is, monitoring their own reactions for clues not only about the patient's intrapsychic life but also about how patient and analyst are experiencing their interaction on various levels.

Dissociation and Multiple Self-States

In the past 2 decades, influenced largely by the relational movement in American psychoanalysis, there has been an upsurge of interest in dissociation and in multiple self-states as important phenomena. Although the concept of dissociation was prominent in the early history in psychoanalysis, it was relatively neglected for many years because of the overriding emphasis on the repression of mental contents. The revived interest in dissociation is closely linked to the renewed emphasis on the role of external trauma in pathology. Experiences that might be excluded from awareness in some contexts but emerge in others can be thought of as dissociated rather than permanently repressed.

The person more or less automatically monitors his or her degree of safety versus danger of traumatic anxiety and via dissociation selects the most adaptive self-state in a given moment. The desire to avoid anxiety-arousing conflict and preserve a sense of self-continuity and self-cohesiveness can lead to the dissociative segregation of incompatible self-states. Relational analysts also question the notion of a unitary self. Alterations in so-called self-states seem to be viewed as indicating that the person becomes a new and different self (Bromberg, 1997).

The Potential Value of Self-Disclosure

Ever since the articulation of the blank screen model with its emphasis on analytic anonymity and reserve, therapists have grappled with the questions of whether and when to disclose, how much to disclose of a personal nature to which patients at which point in treatment, and for what purpose.

We are referring here to intentional self-disclosures (e.g., spontaneously or in response to direct questions). Recall that in the blank screen model the main rationale for nondisclosure was that it provided a screen for the projection of the patient's infantile wishes. In addition, providing gratification allegedly reduced the incentive for further exploration of the meanings involved in what the patient wants to know. Also, there were concerns that therapists not use intentional self-disclosure (a) as a means of gratifying their narcissistic needs (e.g., stories of war exploits) or (b) in a way that unnecessarily burdened the patient (e.g., a recital of personal problems). These factors were part of the objection to Ferenczi's experiments with mutual analysis (apart from the issue of who gets to bill whom!).

The essence of the relational view on self-disclosure is not that one is *required* to self-disclose but that one is *permitted* to (Wachtel, 2008). In other words, if analysts do not have to worry about maintaining abstinence or contaminating the transference or interfering with exploration, then they can feel freer to express their feelings and reactions. Of course, this does not mean that anything goes.

From the literature, one gets the impression that relational therapists are more willing to depart from the default position and to loosen the restrictions or inhibitions on self-disclosure that were more common among traditional analysts. The relational analyst is probably more inclined to adopt a flexible attitude and make the clinical judgment in each instance concerning what degree and type of self-disclosure is likely to advance the therapy.

Conception of Therapeutic Action

In the past 2 decades, relational models have become increasingly influential in psychoanalytic psychotherapy. As indicated earlier, these models put relationships with others, both in actuality and as internalized representations, front and center in conceptions of human development, core motivations, psychopathology, and treatment. Relational psychoanalysts share the central idea that humans are inherently relational, that is, that people's primary motivational aim is to seek and maintain fulfilling, meaningful relatedness to others.

Relational theories have several important implications for how one approaches psychoanalytic treatment and for what is considered curative.

- One sees a number of attitudinal shifts under the rubric of a more egalitarian spirit in conducting treatment, compared with (stereotyped) views of traditional analysis. This attitude of "irreducible subjectivity" (Renik, 2006) of both patient and analyst calls for an attitude of cooperative mutuality. Because analysts in the relational model cannot expect to be neutral and objective even if they want to be, they are freer to speak their mind. They also are freer to be more self-disclosing when deliberate personal revelations are thought to be helpful.

- Interpretation leading to insight is deemphasized in favor of a corrective emotional experience (Alexander & French, 1946), in which the therapist is a benign, reparative parent. Corrective emotional experience is not meant to refer to deliberately playing a parental role more benign than that of the patient's parent, as was the case for Alexander and French (1946). The relational therapist naturally acts like a new, benign object rather than the transference-eliciting old object. With this approach, the patient has new experiences in implicit relational knowing (Lyons-Ruth, 1998)—how to be with another in a good way.

- With the deemphasis on interpretation leading to insight comes greater freedom to depart from the default position of traditional analysis to include a variety of noninterpretive interventions, such as explicit praise, support, and suggestions—psychoanalysis-plus (Schachter & Kachele, 2007).

- Seeing every aspect of the therapeutic relationship as the interaction of two subjectivities makes it harder to maintain that the analyst can be an objective observer who knows "the truth" and therefore knows when the patient is engaged in a distortion. Thus, relational theorists prefer to speak of the patient and therapist coconstructing a negotiated reality (Pizer, 1992). Transference is not seen as a distortion but as a plausible perspective taken by the patient based on perceptions of the analyst's personality and behavior. Differences in inferences between patient and analyst are negotiated in an effort to reach some consensus.

- Relational analysts do not make a big point of the therapeutic alliance. Unlike many traditional analysts who saw it as a necessary addition to the basic phenomena of therapy, relational analysts try to always be attuned to the nature and quality of the therapeutic relationship. This stance includes being alert to actual and potential ruptures in the alliance and the realization that repairing the inevitable ruptures that occur is an essential aspect of the curative power of analysis. What is being modeled here is that disagreements that ordinarily lead to angry withdrawal or confrontation (Safran & Muran, 2000) can become occasions for the clarification of misunderstandings, for apologies when indicated, and for improved communication.

- From a relational (as well as from a Kohutian) perspective, the importance of feeling understood takes precedence over the explanation.
- The idea of multiple self-states can be seen as a corollary of the variety of interacting subjectivities, not only with different people in different settings but with the same person over time in the same setting, that is, with the analyst. When the intersubjective context shifts in the course of an analytic session, different aspects of the self may recede while others become activated. The emphasis on what emerges in the dyadic interaction versus the personality that the patient brings into the consulting room accords well with the stress on multiple self-states.
- From a relational perspective, there are several presumed active ingredients in analytic therapy: (a) increasingly coherent, plausible narratives are coconstructed from the intersubjective experiences of both patient and therapist; (b) the "holding environment" provided by the therapist can constitute a corrective emotional experience that can liberate the patient to risk new ways of relating to others; (c) the patient can experience different aspects of self and learn how his or her various self-states are influenced by the interpersonal contexts in which the patient finds him- or herself; and (d) the patient can learn to modify tendencies to split images of self and other into good and bad; as a result, the patient emerges with a more balanced, integrated view of self and other. In the process of making these changes, the patient struggles to loosen his or her devotion and loyalty to internalized "bad" objects. As Fairbairn (1952) put it, the difficult task in treatment is "the overcoming of the patient's devotion to his repressed [internalized] object" (p. 73), particularly one that is exciting but ultimately rejecting. A common clinical manifestation of this problem is seen in the tendency of patients to seek out love partners who are alluring and intriguing but inaccessible and emotionally unavailable.

SELF PSYCHOLOGY

Considerations concerning the self and self-development were of interest to psychoanalysis almost from the beginning. For example, in his paper "On Narcissism," Freud (1914/1958) addressed the increasing differentiation between self and object. However, in most of his writings, Freud paid little attention to the concept of self. Although Erikson's (1950) concept of ego identity and Jacobson (1964) and Mahler (1968) focused on selfhood, it was Kohut (1971, 1977, 1984) who founded a highly influential theory of the self. He made the self the centerpiece of his self psychology by postulating a narcissistic line of development as the central dimension of personality formation and the development of a cohesive, vital sense of self. Kohut (1971) originally presented his self psychology as a supplement to traditional Freudian theory, applicable only to narcissistic personality disorders in which so-called self-defects were prominent. Over time, Kohut (1977, 1984) proposed that the development of a cohesive, integrated self is the major motivational aim of all patients. In this view, narcissism is healthy to the extent that there is a joyful, productive, zestful expression of one's talents, skills, ambitions, ideals, and values. Kohut presented the concept of the *bipolar self* to describe the individual's ambitions (one pole) and goals (the other pole) and suggested that these two poles are linked by the person's skills and talents. He later proposed the concept of the *tripolar self* in which skills and talents were considered a third pole.

Kohut's formulation of a healthy self as one that is robust, joyful, and vital sounds a lot like the striving for self-actualization (e.g., Maslow, 1954; Rogers 1951). Kohut considered archaic grandiosity and exhibitionism to be pathological expressions of ambitions and goals and, along with proneness to disintegration anxiety, to impair the individual's capacity to carry out his or her "nuclear program." In this view, self-cohesiveness and positive self-esteem are superordinate motives that are more important than instinctual gratification or object relations.

According to Kohut (1977), the development of a cohesive self requires adequate empathic attunement on the part of the parents. The major experiences the parents need to provide are to serve as mirroring self-objects and idealizing self-objects. *Self-object experiences* refer to the infant's sense of partial merging with the parents; that is, the self-object is not fully one's self or the other. In self-object experiences, as the blended terms suggest, the individual experiences the other person as an extension of the self, although the experience need not be a conscious one. It is an experience of the other as providing functions that contribute to one's sense of self-cohesiveness. The experience of mirroring and idealized self-objects enables the child to feel normal grandiosity and exhibitionism by feeling admired (through being mirrored) and feeling powerful and vital (by having idealized self-objects). Kohut (1984) believed that self-object experiences are crucial not only to early personality development but also throughout life. However, an important aspect of psychological growth and maturity is to cope with the inevitable lapses in the provision of self-object functions by others. Through a process of *transmuting internalization* the individual grows psychologically by being able to maintain self-cohesion in the face of optimal failures in empathy by others. In other words, aspects of positive self-object experiences are internalized, thereby strengthening the self. This capacity for transmuting internalization marks a shift from excessive reliance on archaic self-objects to a normal reliance on mature self-objects and a corresponding decrease in narcissistic vulnerability. When self-object failures exacerbate conflicts and fears, these reactions are regarded as breakdown products. For example, if a person reacts with rage rather than anger, one assumes there has been a significant narcissistic injury that the person might feel can be remedied only by exacting revenge.

From a Kohutian perspective, most psychological difficulties in life ultimately are traceable to early failures in parental empathy. For example, the oedipal period or phase can pass relatively uneventfully and not result in an oedipal "complex" if the parents are and have been empathically attuned to the child's needs.

In summary, to the extent that there is deficiency in parental empathy the child will have difficulty developing the intrapsychic structures that serve to regulate self-esteem and anxiety. The individual is then overly dependent on the provision of self-object functions. Such a deficient, narcissistically vulnerable self will be prone to fragmentation. Such individuals are inclined to develop particular styles of coping. For example, there are "mirror hungry" personalities who have a desperate need for admiration and approval and whose self-esteem rises or falls as a function of whether those needs are met, "contact-shunning" personalities who fear that close involvement with others threatens a loss of the sense of self, as well as individuals who search for idealized parental imagos to feel safe, calm, and strong.

Conception of Therapeutic Action

- From a self-psychology perspective, the goals of treatment include the provision of a therapeutic environment in which the arrested development of the self can belatedly resume a normal course and an understanding of how the early failures of significant others to provide those experiences damaged the self.
- The primary focus of self psychological treatment is not on the interpretation of unconscious conflicts but on helping the patient restore or develop a sense of self-cohesion and to be less vulnerable to narcissistic injury, especially when there is a disruption in self-object ties. From this perspective, symptomatic behaviors

(e.g., compulsions) are seen as efforts to ward off a depressed or fragmenting self. For example, shoplifting is seen not as an attempt at gratifying some instinctual impulse but as an effort to forestall a depleted self or impotent rage by an act that momentarily creates a sense of self-empowerment.

- Transferences play a central role in self psychological treatment. Some of the main types of transferences are mirroring, idealizing, and twinship patterns. The analyst develops an appreciation of the extent to which patients need the analyst's approval and admiration as a basis for regulating their self-esteem and self-worth (the mirroring transference), need to admire and idealize the analyst as a way of enhancing the value of the self (idealizing transference), or need to feel a kinship with the analyst (twinship transference).

- Transference patterns are eventually interpreted, usually in contexts where the patient feels lapses in the analyst's empathic attunement to one of his or her self-object needs. When the analyst engages in empathic lapses, he or she acknowledges his or her role in the patient's reaction and hopes the rupture of the therapeutic alliance is not serious and is readily repairable. These inevitable experiences are not unfortunate disruptions. In fact, although not intended, they are necessary so that the patient has opportunities for transmuting internalization. This is especially important for narcissistic patients.

- The essential factor in treatment is the patient's poignant effort to resume developmental growth, not the relinquishment of infantile wishes. For this resumption to occur patients have to feel they are in a safe atmosphere, one that does not threaten retraumatization at the hands of the therapist. Experiencing the therapist as an accepting, empathic, nonjudgmental presence allows patients to reduce their resistance to the formation and expression of mirroring and idealizing transferences. As Kohut (1984) put it, after each empathic failure "new self structure will be acquired and existing ones will be firmed" (p. 69). The essential therapeutic ingredient is feeling understood and that experience solidifies the empathic bond between patient and therapist and thereby meets a traumatically unfulfilled developmental need, which, in turn, facilitates the resumption of developmental growth and the realization of one's nuclear program. Thus, for Kohut, empathic understanding and the repeated working through of failures in empathy constitute the basic therapeutic unit of treatment.

CONCLUDING COMMENTS

Trends in psychoanalytic psychotherapy over the past 2 decades are characterized by three distinctive movements. First is the increasing and dominant popularity of relational treatments. American relational analysts (principally Mitchell, 1988) have emphasized what they regard as a major paradigm shift from the "drive/structure" to the "relational/structure" model of the mind and have formed separate institutes, associations, and journals to promulgate their approach.

Second, closely linked to this trend is the emphasis on a two-person (vs. a one-person) psychology with its associated features of a hermeneutic, postmodern, constructivist, narrative approach to psychoanalytic understanding. In this view, it is a myth to assume that there is a knowable, objective reality that the analyst is in a privileged position to ascertain. The relational approach gives primary emphasis to the interaction of two subjectivities (patient and analyst) in the intersubjective field of the therapeutic relationship. Relational and intersubjective analysts object to what they regard as the outmoded view of the isolated, bounded mind.

Third, the psychoanalytic scene, although still characterized by different schools and psychoanalytic institutes, allows for greater mutual tolerance and dialogue between different approaches than was the case in the past. The nature of therapeutic change is seen by most contemporary clinicians as complex and multidetermined. No one factor or set of factors is considered curative for all patients. Still unattained is a definitive, research-based integration of the different psychoanalytic conceptions of therapeutic effectiveness.

In Table 3.1, I summarize multiple trends in psychoanalytic theory and practice over the past several decades. The items listed in the left-hand column are characteristic of more traditional Freudian analysts, whereas those characteristics listed in the right-hand column are more often found among relational, intersubjective, interpersonal, and self psychologists as well as many contemporary Freudians.

Finally, I highlight some probable trends over the next decade in psychoanalytic therapies:

- Further research on the process and outcome of psychoanalytic treatment. This trend will include (a) additional attempts to specify key patient and therapist variables and their interaction, (b) improved measures of therapist interventions (e.g., interpretations, contributions to the quality of therapeutic alliance), (c) specification of the kinds of interpretations that are more and less helpful, (d) studies of diverse patient populations, (e) research relating changes in treatment to alterations in brain functioning,

TABLE 3.1
Changes in Emphasis in Psychoanalytic Theory and Practice

Traditional Freudian view	Contemporary view
Traditional Freudian theory	Relational theory and self psychology
Traditional Freudian theory	Modern conflict theory
Oedipal	Pre-oedipal
Conflict	Deficit (and conflict)
Psychoanalysis	Psychoanalytic psychotherapy
Neurosis	Borderline and narcissistic disorders
Insight	Relationship factors and corrective emotional experience
Transference neurosis	Transference reactions
Interpretation	Coconstructed narratives
Singular theories	Theoretical pluralism
Transference as "distortion"	Transference as "plausible" view
One-person psychology	Two-person psychology
Intrapsychic focus	Intrapsychic and interpersonal focus
Genetic transference interpretation	"Here and now" transference interpretation
Transference interpretation key	Transference and extratransference interpretation
Focus on intrapsychic conflict that is expressed to a "blank screen" analyst	Focus on mutual transference-counter transference enactments
Search for early pathogenic memories	Implicit relational knowing
Analytic anonymity	Analyst self-disclosure
Neutrality	Less neutrality
Adherence to "default position" to maintain analytic frame	Less analytic restraint and less worry about transference gratification
Countertransference as hindrance and as flaw in the analyst	Countertransference as source of vital information
Therapeutic alliance important as precursor to effective interpretation	Analyst attunement to "rupture and repair" of the alliance as therapeutic
Correspondence theory of truth— "historical truth"	Coherence theory of truth— "narrative truth"
Unitary self	Multiple selves and self-states
Repression	Dissociation
Empathy as source of information	Empathy as curative (Kohut)
Essentialism	Social constructivism
Analyst as "blank screen" observer	Intersubjectivity of the analytic pair

and (f) studies matching patient and therapist on personality variables and matching patients to different forms of treatment. An important question to be answered is whether insight versus supportive methods (e.g., those that lead to identification with the analyst and feeling empathically validated) yield differential long-term benefits.

- Attempts to synthesize Freudian, relational, and self psychological perspectives in ways that reflect a decreasing polarization. In line with this anticipated trend, the personal qualities of the therapist are likely to become even more emphasized than particular theories or techniques. Correlated with this trend one can expect to see a continuation of more modest claims of therapeutic efficacy and few claims of superior outcomes by any one school.

A continued trend toward a relative deemphasis on interpretation and insight and an increased stress on the healing aspects of the therapeutic relationship. It seems that the disillusionment with the therapeutic value of insight, particularly among relational analysts, led to philosophical positions that maintain that there are no truths about the patient's mind to be discovered, but only persuasive narratives to be coconstructed by the unique analytic dyad. However, over time, the pendulum might swing back, at least partially, to the recognition that some patients benefit from accurate insight about conflicts that existed before the start of treatment.

- Attachment theory continuing to inform clinical practice.
- Further efforts to study psychoanalytic concepts in relation to neurobiology.
- More work to integrate psychoanalytic techniques with cognitive–behavioral therapies.
- More clinical and research work on (a) brief analytically oriented treatments; (b) psychoanalytic child, family, and couple therapy; and (c) specific approaches to individual treatment (e.g., control mastery theory and mentalization-based therapy).
- Progress in formulating a comprehensive theory of therapeutic action. Such a theory would address the changes analytic therapists hope to facilitate and the strategies considered likely to promote those changes. Such a theory of therapeutic action would need to (a) offer a fine-grained analysis of why and how insight and relationship factors are effective, (b) address the varieties of insight (e.g., intellectual versus emotional, insights into the present versus the past), (c) study the process of clinical inference so more can be learned about how analysts arrive at their interpretations, (d) assess the impact of different types of countertransference reactions, (e) evaluate the relative efficacy of transference versus extratransference interpretations, (f) consider the pros and cons of different types of therapist self-disclosure, and (g) assess how the above factors interact with a variety of patient variables (e.g., degree and type of psychopathology, quality of object relations).

Psychoanalytic researchers have begun to respond to the demands for accountability and the competition from rival treatment methods. Many of the kinds of empirical studies suggested earlier have been done and yield promising results, particularly for short-term treatment. However, more studies are needed on longer term treatments.

In envisioning the future, I realize that I have presented an ambitious agenda rather than a set of confident predictions. However, it is my view that significant progress on this agenda is necessary for psychoanalytic treatments to earn a secure place among the viable methods of mental health intervention in the 21st century.

REFERENCES

Alexander, F., & French, T. M. (1946). *Psychoanalytic therapy: Principles and application*. New York, NY: Ronald Press.

Aron, L. (1996). *A meeting of minds: Mutuality in psychoanalysis*. Hillsdale, NJ: Analytic Press.

Boston Change Process Study Group. (1988). Non-interpretive mechanisms in psychoanalytic therapy: The "something more" than interpretation. *The International Journal of Psycho-Analysis, 79*, 903–921.

Boston Change Process Study Group. (2002). Explicating the implicit: The local level and the microprocess of change in the analytic situation. *The International Journal of Psycho-Analysis, 83*, 1051–1062. doi:10.1516/B105-35WV-MM0Y-NTAD

Boston Change Process Study Group. (2005). The "something more" than interpretation revisited. *Journal of the American Psychoanalytic Association, 53*, 693–729.

Bowlby, J. (1969). *Attachment and loss: Vol. 1. Attachment*. New York, NY: Basic Books.

Brenner, C. (1982). *The mind in conflict*. Madison, CT: International Universities Press.

Brenner, C. (1994). Mind as conflict and compromise formation. *Journal of Clinical Psychoanalysis, 3*, 473–488.

Breuer, J., & Freud, S. (1955). *Studies on hysteria: Vol. 2. The standard edition of the complete psychological works of Sigmund Freud* (J. Strachey, Ed). London: Hogarth Press. (Original work published 1893–1895)

Bromberg, P. M. (1996). Standing in the spaces: The multiplicity of self and the psychoanalytic relationship. *Contemporary Psychoanalysis, 32*, 509–535.

Bromberg, P. (1997). *Standing in the spaces*. Hillsdale, NJ: Analytic Press.

Eagle, M., & Wolitzky, D. L. (1982). Therapeutic influences in dynamic psychotherapy: A review and synthesis. In S. Slipp (Ed.), *Curative factors in dynamic psychotherapy* (pp. 321–348). New York, NY: McGraw-Hill.

Eagle, M., & Wolitzky, D. L. (1992). Psychoanalytic theories of psychotherapy. In D. Freedheim (Ed.), *History of psychotherapy* (pp. 109–158). Washington, DC: American Psychological Association.

Eagle, M., & Wolitzky, D. L. (2008). Adult psychotherapy from the perspectives of attachment theory and psychoanalysis. In J. H. Obegi & E. Berant (Eds.), *Attachment theory and research in clinical work with adults* (pp. 351–378). New York, NY: Guilford Press.

Eissler, K. R. (1953). The effect of the structure of the ego on psychoanalytic technique. *Journal of the American Psychoanalytic Association, 1*, 104–143. doi:10.1177/000306515300100107

Erikson, E. H. (1950). *Childhood and society*. New York, NY: Norton.

Fairbairn, W. R. D. (1952). *Psychoanalytic studies of the personality*. London: Tavistock Publications and Kegan Paul, Trench, & Trubner.

Ferenczi, S. (1926). *Further contributions to the theory and technique of psychoanalysis*. London: Hogarth Press and the Institute of Psycho-Analysis.

Fiscalini, J. (2004). *Coparticipant psychoanalysis*. New York, NY: Columbia University Press.

Fonagy, P. (2001). *Attachment theory and psychoanalysis*. New York, NY: Other Press.

Fonagy, P. (2003a). Some complexities in the relationship of psychoanalytic theory to technique. *The Psychoanalytic Quarterly, 72*, 13–47.

Fonagy, P. (2003b). Memory and therapeutic action. *The International Journal of Psycho-Analysis, 80*, 215–223. doi:10.1516/0020757991598620

Fonagy, P., & Target, M. (2003). *Psychoanalytic theories: Perspectives from developmental psychopathology*. New York, NY: Brunner-Routledge.

Freud, A. (1936). *The ego and the mechanisms of defense*. Madison, CT: International Universities Press.

Freud, S. (1955). Lines of advance in psycho-analytic therapy. In J. Strachey (Ed. and Trans.), *The standard edition of the complete psychological works of Sigmund Freud* (Vol. 17, pp. 157–168). London: Hogarth Press. (Original work published 1919)

Freud, S. (1957). On beginning the treatment (Further recommendations on the technique of psycho-analysis). In J. Strachey (Ed. and Trans.), *The standard edition of the complete psychological works of Sigmund Freud* (Vol. 14, pp. 73–102). London: Hogarth Press. (Original work published 1912)

Freud, S. (1958). The dynamics of transference. In J. Strachey (Ed. and Trans.), *The standard edition of the complete psychological works of Sigmund Freud* (Vol. 12, pp. 97–108). London: Hogarth Press. (Original work published 1912)

Freud, S. (1958). On narcissism: An introduction. In J. Strachey (Ed. and Trans.), *The standard edition of the complete psychological works of Sigmund Freud* (Vol. 14, pp. 121–144). London: Hogarth Press. (Original work published 1914)

Freud, S. (1961). The ego and the id. In J. Strachey (Ed. and Trans.), *The standard edition of the complete psychological works of Sigmund Freud* (Vol. 19, pp. 3–68). London: Hogarth Press. (Original work published 1923).

Freud, S. (1963). *Introductory lectures on psycho-analysis: Vols. 15 and 16. The standard edition of the complete psychological works of Sigmund Freud* (J. Strachey, Ed). London: Hogarth Press. (Original work published 1916–1917)

Freud, S. (1964). Analysis terminable and interminable. In J. Strachey (Ed. and Trans.), *The standard edition of the complete psychological works of Sigmund Freud* (Vol. 23, pp. 255–269). London: Hogarth Press. (Original work published 1937)

Gill, M. M. (1954). Psychoanalysis and exploratory psychotherapy. *Journal of the American Psychoanalytic Association, 2*, 771–797. doi:10.1177/000306515400200413

Gill, M. M. (1982). Analysis of transference, Volume 1: Theory and technique. *Psychological Issues* [Monograph 53]. Madison, CT: International Universities Press.

Gill, M. M. (1994). *Psychoanalysis in transition*. Hillsdale, NJ: Analytic Press.

Gray, P. (1973). Technique and the ego's capacity for viewing intrapsychic activity. *Journal of the American Psychoanalytic Association, 21*, 474–494. doi:10.1177/000306517302100302

Green, A. (2000). The intrapsychic and intersubjective in psychoanalysis. *The Psychoanalytic Quarterly, 69*, 1–39.

Greenberg, J. R., & Mitchell, S. A. (1983). *Object relations in psychoanalytic theory*. Cambridge, MA: Harvard University Press.

Greenson, R. R. (1965). The working alliance and the transference neurosis. *The Psychoanalytic Quarterly, 34*, 155–181.

Greenson, R. R. (1967). *The technique and practice of psychoanalysis* (Vol. 1). Madison, CT: International Universities Press.

Greenson, R. R., & Wexler, M. (1969). The non-transference relationship in the psychoanalytic situation. *The International Journal of Psycho-Analysis, 50,* 27–39.

Hartmann, H. (1958). *Ego psychology and the problem of adaptation.* Madison, CT: International Universities Press. (Original work published 1939)

Jacobs, T. J. (1986). On countertransference enactments. *Journal of the American Psychoanalytic Association, 34,* 289–307. doi:10.1177/000306518603400203

Jacobson, E. (1964). *The self and the object world.* Madison, CT: International Universities Press.

Kernberg, O. F. (1975). *Borderline conditions and pathological narcissism.* New York, NY: Jason Aronson.

Kernberg, O. F. (1976). *Object relations theory and clinical psychoanalysis.* New York, NY: Jason Aronson.

Kernberg, O. F. (1980). *Internal world and external reality.* New York, NY: Jason Aronson.

Kernberg, O. F., Yeomans, F. E., Clarkin, J. F., & Levy, K. N. (2008). Transference focused psychotherapy: Overview and update. *The International Journal of Psycho-Analysis, 89,* 601–620. doi:10.1111/j.1745-8315.2008.00046.x

Klein, M. (1948). *Contributions to psychoanalysis (1921–1945).* London: Hogarth Press.

Kohut, H. (1971). *The analysis of the self.* Madison, CT: International Universities Press.

Kohut, H. (1977). *The restoration of the self.* Madison, CT: International Universities Press.

Kohut, H. (1984). *How does analysis cure?* Chicago: University of Chicago Press.

Leichsenring, F., & Rabung, S. (2008). Effectiveness of long-term psychodynamic psychotherapy: A meta-analysis. *JAMA, 300,* 1551–1565. doi:10.1001/jama.300.13.1551

Loewald, H. (1960). On the therapeutic action of psychoanalysis. *The International Journal of Psycho-Analysis, 2,* 17–33.

Luborsky, L. (1984). *Principles of psychoanalytic psychotherapy: A manual for supportive-expressive treatment.* New York, NY: Basic Books.

Lyons-Ruth, K. (1998). Implicit relational knowing. *Infant Mental Health Journal, 19,* 282–289.

Mahler, M. (1968). *On human symbiosis and the vicissitudes of individuation: Vol. I. Infantile psychosis.* Madison, CT: International Universities Press.

Malan, D. H. (1976). *The frontier of brief psychotherapy.* New York, NY: Plenum Press.

Maslow, A. H. (1954). *Motivation and personality.* New York, NY: Harper & Row.

Messer, S., & Wolitzky, D. L. (in press). The therapeutic alliance: A psychodynamic perspective. In J. C. Muran & J. P. Barber (Eds.), *The therapeutic alliance: An evidence-based approach to practice & training.* New York, NY: Guilford Press.

Mitchell, S. A. (1988). *Relational concepts in psychoanalysis: An integration.* Cambridge, MA: Harvard University Press.

Mitchell, S. A. (1998). The analyst's knowledge and authority. *The Psychoanalytic Quarterly, 67,* 1–31.

Modell, A. H. (1976). "The holding environment" and the therapeutic action of psychoanalysis. *Journal of the American Psychoanalytic Association, 24,* 285–307. doi:10.1177/000306517602400202

Ogden, T. H. (1994). The analytic third: Working with intersubjective clinical facts. *The International Journal of Psycho-Analysis, 75,* 3–19.

Pine, F. (1990). *Drive, ego, object, and self: A synthesis for clinical work.* New York, NY: Basic Books.

Pizer, S. A. (1992). The negotiation of paradox in the analytic process. *Psychoanalytic Dialogues, 2,* 215–240.

Racker, H. (1968). *Transference and countertransference*. Madison, CT: International Universities Press.

Renik, O. (2006). *Practical psychoanalysis for therapists and patients*. New York, NY: Other Press.

Richards, A. D., & Lynch, A. A. (1998). From ego psychology to contemporary conflict theory: An overview. In C. S. Ellman, S. Grand, M. Silvan, & S. J. Ellman (Eds.), *The modern Freudians: Contemporary psychoanalytic technique* (pp. 3–23). Northvale, NJ, and London: Jason Aronson.

Rogers, C. R. (1951). *Client-centered therapy*. Boston: Houghton Mifflin.

Rosenbaum, M. S. (2009). *Dare to be human*. New York, NY: Routledge.

Safran, J., & Muran, J. C. (2000). *Negotiating the therapeutic alliance: A relational treatment guide*. New York, NY: Guilford Press.

Sandell, R., Blomberg, J., Lazar, A., Carlsson, J., Broberg, J., & Schubert, J. (2000). Varieties of long-term outcome in patients in psychoanalysis and long-term psychotherapy: A review of findings in the Stockholm outcome of psychoanalysis and psychotherapy project (STOPP). *The International Journal of Psycho-Analysis, 81*, 921–942. doi:10.1516/0020757001600291

Schachter, J., & Kachele, H. (2007). The analyst's role in healing. *Psychoanalytic Psychology, 24*, 429–444. doi:10.1037/0736-9735.24.3.429

Schafer, R. (1983). *The analytic attitude*. New York, NY: Basic Books.

Schafer, R. (1992). *Retelling a life: Narration and dialogue in psychoanalysis*. New York, NY: Basic Books.

Schafer, R. (1994). The contemporary Kleinians of London. *The Psychoanalytic Quarterly, 63*, 409–432.

Silberschatz, G. (Ed.). (2005). *Transformative relationships: The control-mastery theory of psychotherapy*. New York, NY: Routledge.

Sterba, R. (1934). The fate of the ego in analytic therapy. *The International Journal of Psycho-Analysis, 15*, 117–126.

Stolorow, R. D., Brandchaft, B., & Atwood, G. E. (1987). *Psychoanalytic treatment: An intersubjective approach*. Hillsdale, NJ: Analytic Press.

Stone, L. (1954). The widening scope of indications for psychoanalysis. *Journal of the American Psychoanalytic Association, 2*, 567–594. doi:10.1177/000306515400200402

Stone, L. (1961). *The psychoanalytic situation: An examination of its development and essential nature*. Madison, CT: International Universities Press.

Strachey, J. (1934). The nature of the therapeutic action of psycho-analysis. *The International Journal of Psycho-Analysis, IV*, 127–159.

Strupp, H. H., & Binder, J. L. (1984). *Psychotherapy in a new key*. New York, NY: Basic Books.

Sullivan, H. S. (1953). *The interpersonal theory of psychiatry*. New York, NY: Norton.

Wachtel, P. L. (1997). *Psychoanalysis, behavior therapy, and the relational world*. Washington, DC: American Psychological Association.

Wachtel, P. L. (2008). *Relational theory and the practice of psychotherapy*. New York, NY: Guilford Press.

Wallerstein, R. S. (1986). *Forty-two lives in treatment. A study of psychoanalysis and psychotherapy*. New York, NY/London: Guilford Press.

Wallerstein, R. S. (1988). One psychoanalysis or many? *The International Journal of Psycho-Analysis, 69*, 5–21.

Wallerstein, R. S. (1990a). Psychoanalysis and psychotherapy: An historical perspective. *The International Journal of Psycho-Analysis, 70*, 563–592.

Wallerstein, R. S. (1990b). Psychoanalysis: The common ground. *The International Journal of Psycho-Analysis, 71*, 3–20.

Weiss, J., & Sampson, H. (1986). *The psychoanalytic process: Theory, clinical observations, and empirical research.* New York, NY: Guilford Press.

Westen, D. (1998). The scientific legacy of Sigmund Freud: Toward a psychodynamically informed psychological science. *Psychological Bulletin, 124,* 333–371. doi:10.1037/0033-2909.124.3.333

Westen, D., & Gabbard, G. O. (2002a). Developments in cognitive neuroscience: I. Conflict, compromise, and connectionism. *Journal of the American Psychoanalytic Association, 50,* 53–98. doi:10.1177/00030651020500011501

Westen, D., & Gabbard, G. O. (2002b). Developments in cognitive neuroscience: II. Implications for theories of transference. *Journal of the American Psychoanalytic Association, 50,* 99–134. doi:10.1177/00030651020500011601

Wile, D. B. (1984). Kohut, Kernberg, and accusatory interpretations. *Psychotherapy (Chicago, Ill.), 21,* 353–364. doi:10.1037/h0086097

Winnicott, D. W. (1960). The theory of the parent-infant relationship. *The International Journal of Psycho-Analysis, 41,* 585–595.

Winnicott, D. W. (1965). *The maturational processes and the facilitating environment.* London: Hogarth Press.

Wolitzky, D. L. (2003). The theory and practice of traditional psychoanalytic treatment. In A. S. Gurman & S. B. Messer (Eds.), *Essential psychotherapies: theory and practice* (pp. 24–67). New York, NY: Guilford Press.

Yager, J. (2008). The emerging evidence base for psychodynamic psychotherapies, *JW Psychiatry, 15*(1), 4.

Zetzel, E. R. (1956). Current concepts of transference. *International Journal of Psycho-analysis, 37,* 369–375.

Zetzel, E. R. (1966). The analytic situation. In R. E. Litman (Ed.), *Psychoanalysis in the Americas* (pp. 86–106). New York, NY: International Universities Press.

4

BEHAVIORAL THEORIES
OF PSYCHOTHERAPY

DANIEL B. FISHMAN, SIMON A. REGO,
AND KATHERINE L. MULLER

All major systems of psychotherapy—behavior therapy, psychoanalysis, family systems, humanistic therapy, and so forth—are embedded in a broad paradigm that involves a number of dimensions. These dimensions include (a) adherence to certain epistemological, philosophy-of-science assumptions; (b) a particular set of theoretical positions; (c) a body of scientific and other data; (d) particular collections of techniques and technologies; (e) specific values and ethical positions; and (f) a particular sociological, political, and historical context (Fishman, Rotgers, & Franks, 1988; Kuhn, 1962). In this chapter, the focus is on the evolution of behavior therapy in terms of epistemology and theory. However, because a full understanding of behavior therapy demands a consideration of the interrelationships among the various components of the entire paradigm, as just defined, we also devote some space to these relationships.

We view behavior therapy as closely linked to the patterns of thought and values first developed during the Age of Enlightenment of the 17th and 18th centuries and later expanded in 20th-century terms. These include a focus on rationally and scientifically derived, "value-neutral" technology used in the service of promoting individual growth and freedom from irrational authority and arbitrary privilege (see Fishman et al., 1988; Woolfolk & Richardson, 1984).

In theoretical terms, we view behavior therapy as an approach to understanding behavior and behavior change that relies in large part on the traditional methodology of behavioral science, with significant links to learning theory, cognitive psychology, and experimental psychology. Behavior is defined broadly to include both overt actions and observable manifestations of covert affective and cognitively mediated processes. These aspects of behavior may occur at several levels and contexts: psychophysiological, individual, small group, organizational, and community.

In practical terms, we regard behavior therapy as a data-based application of theory to generate a technology, the primary goal of which is cost-effective, constructive behavior change. By constructive, we mean behavior change that is endorsed by all concerned and considered ethical. From the points of view of theory and practice, we view behavior therapy as a major conceptual advance rather than as simply another therapeutic innovation.

It is important to point out that in this book on the history of psychotherapy, there is this chapter on behavior therapy and another chapter on cognitive therapy. In practice, the procedures of these two systems are frequently merged into *cognitive behavior therapy (CBT)*. Their conceptual separation is based in part on theoretical differences between these two. Behavior therapy began by focusing on directly observable, overt behaviors and their interactions with the directly observable, immediate physical and social environment. This focus derived from the behavioral change principles of operant conditioning (Thorndike and Skinner) and respondent conditioning (Pavlov) that came out of learning experiments with animals, such as dogs, cats, pigeons, and rats, in which cognition was generally not considered (Davison & Neale, 1990). In contrast, cognitive therapy in the work of theorists such as Beck (1963), Ellis (1962), and Mahoney (1974) is based on the assumption that "the human organism responds primarily to cognitive representations of its environments rather than to these environments per se" (Kendall & Bemis, 1983). This way of thinking is rooted in experiments in cognitive psychology with human beings who—unlike experimental animals—have highly developed languages for capturing complex and nuanced meanings and representations of the world. Thus, the focus in cognitive therapy is on the personal meaning of the environment to an individual rather than to the objective characteristics of those environments per se.

Hayes (e.g., Hayes, Masuda, Bissett, Luoma, & Guerrero, 2004) proposed that the original focus on observable behavior and the objective environment be considered a "first wave" in behavior therapy and that the subsequent focus on cognitive representations of the environment be considered a "second wave." Hayes has also been a leader in a new approach, which he calls a "third wave" of behavior therapy, that focuses on internal cognitive processes, like the second wave, but views the focus of understanding on how these processes are functionally related to the objective environment, like the first wave. In addition, third-wave behavior therapy emphasizes the distinctive theme of a client learning to accept certain aspects of his or her behavior, cognitions, feelings, or a combination of these. Adopting Hayes's terminology, this chapter primarily concentrates on first-wave and third-wave movements in behavior therapy, whereas another chapter focuses on second-wave cognitive therapy. Specifically, in the first part of the chapter, we focus mainly on first-wave developments; in the second part, we address contemporary trends, focusing primarily on third-wave developments together with a consideration of the interrelationships among the three waves.

With regard to terminology, we use the term *behavior therapy* to refer to all three waves of the field or just to first-wave behavior therapy, depending on the context; the term *cognitive therapy*, or *cognitive behavior therapy*, to refer to second-wave behavior therapy; and the term *third-wave behavior therapy* to refer to that particular movement.

LEARNING THEORY BEGINNINGS

Behavior therapy as it is known today began to emerge in the 1950s. However, its origins can be traced to the Enlightenment, the period of European history emphasizing reason and scientific study of the natural world. For example, the British empiricists, who spanned the period from 1600 to 1900, emphasized four main principles: (a) that knowledge comes from experience with the world rather than introspective rumination or divine inspiration; (b) that scientific procedures have to be based on systematic observation rather than opinion, intuition, or authority; (c) that the mind of the child is a blank slate (tabula rasa) on which experience writes, so that adult mental life is primarily a recording and unfolding of the previous environmental and experiential history of the person; and (d) that consciousness is best viewed in terms of "mental chemistry" in which thoughts can be broken down into basic elements connected through various laws—such as continuity, similarity, and contrast—into more complex ideas (Kimble, 1985).

These principles of the British empiricists were linked to the thinking of the early psychologist J. B. Watson, who is frequently viewed as launching the system of *behaviorism*. The birth of this movement was marked by Watson's 1913 manifesto in the *Psychological Review*, titled "Psychology as the Behaviorist Views It":

> Psychology as the behaviorist views it is a purely objective branch of natural science. Its theoretical goal is the prediction and control of behavior. Introspection forms no essential part of its methods, nor is the scientific value of its data dependent on the readiness with which they lend themselves to interpretation in terms of consciousness. The behaviorist, in his

efforts to get a unitary scheme of animal response, recognizes no dividing line between man and brute. The behavior of man, with all of its refinement and complexity, forms only a part of the behaviorist's total scheme of investigation. (p. 158)

Thus, according to Watson, if psychology were to become a science, it must become materialistic (as opposed to mentalistic), mechanistic (as opposed to anthropomorphic), deterministic (as opposed to accepting of free will), and objective (as opposed to subjective). For example, Watson viewed thinking as "laryngeal habits," that is, tiny movements of the vocal chords.

During this period Pavlov demonstrated that dogs could learn to salivate at the ringing of a bell through a process of contiguous associations between the bell and direct access to food. Thus, a previously neutral stimulus (the bell) could become a conditioned stimulus because of its association with an inherently positive, "unconditioned" stimulus (the meat powder). Likewise, this process could include a previously neutral stimulus (e.g., the sight of a stove) becoming a negative stimulus if associated with an inherently negative stimulus (e.g., the burning of one's finger on the stove).

Another closely related development was the establishment in 1913 of Thorndike's general principles of human and animal learning. Cats learned to escape from a puzzle box to obtain release or bits of food as rewards. Studies such as these led to the formulation of Thorndike's (1911) law of effect:

Of several responses made to the same situation, those which are accompanied or closely followed by satisfaction of the animal will, other things being equal, be more firmly connected with the situation, so that, when it recurs, they will be more likely to recur; those which are accompanied or closely followed by discomfort to the animal will, other things being equal, have their connections with that situation weakened, so that, when it recurs, they will be less likely to occur. . . . By a satisfying state of affairs is meant one which the animal does nothing to avoid, often doing such things as to attain and preserve it. (pp. 244–245)

Pavlovian classical conditioning and Thorndike's (and, later, Skinner's) operant conditioning, in which the subject is rewarded for making the desired response and punished whenever an undesired response is elicited, became the foundation of behavioral learning theory for the next 50 years.

FORMATION OF BEHAVIOR THERAPY AS A DISTINCT MOVEMENT

In the first article devoted exclusively to behavior therapy in the *Annual Review of Psychology*, Krasner (1971) suggested that 15 streams of development came together during the 1950s and 1960s to form this new approach to behavior change. These streams may be summarized as follows:

1. the concept of behaviorism in experimental psychology;
2. the operant conditioning work of Thorndike and Skinner;
3. the development of Wolpe's (1958) systematic desensitization;
4. the emergence of behavior therapy as an experimental science at the University of London Institute of Psychiatry, Maudsley Hospital, under the direction of Eysenck;
5. the application of conditioning and learning concepts to human behavior problems in the United States from the 1920s to the 1950s;
6. the interpretation of psychoanalysis in terms of learning theory (e.g., Dollard & Miller, 1950);
7. the application of Pavlovian principles in explaining and changing both normal and deviant behavior;
8. theoretical concepts and research studies of social role learning and interactionism in social psychology and sociology;
9. research in developmental and child psychology emphasizing vicarious learning and modeling;
10. social influence studies of demand characteristics, experimenter bias, hypnosis, and placebo;
11. an environmentally based, social-learning model as an alternative to the disease model of human behavior (Bandura, 1969; Ullmann & Krasner, 1965);
12. dissatisfaction with the prevailing psychoanalytic model, particularly as articulated in Eysenck's (1952) critical empirical study of therapy outcome;
13. the development of the idea of the clinical psychologist as a scientist–practitioner;
14. a movement within psychiatry away from the orthodox focus on internal dynamics and pathology toward human interaction and environmental influence; and
15. a Utopian emphasis on the planning of social environments to elicit and maintain the best of human behavior (e.g., Skinner's [1948] *Walden Two*).

As Krasner (1982) pointed out, these streams of development were neither independent nor static, and, as we shall show, new streams of influence are continually emerging.

From an earlier perspective, in the United States the possibility of explaining behavioral abnormalities in conditioning terms was first outlined in the 1910s and 1920s (e.g., Dunlap, 1932/1972; Watson, 1924), with the 1930s through the 1950s exhibiting many attempts to explore the nature of neurosis by inducing so-called neurotic behavior in various animals such as the pig (Liddell, 1958) and the cat (Masserman, 1943; Wolpe, 1952). Of note at this time from a practical point of view was the application of conditioning concepts to the development of a method to prevent a child's bed-wetting by O. H. Mowrer and W. M. Mowrer (1938). In the procedure, a special pad with an alarm bell was placed under the child during sleep. The moment any moisture reached the pad, the alarm bell was triggered. The feeling of a full bladder (a conditioned stimulus) was then automatically paired with an alarm (an unconditioned stimulus) that woke the child. Over time, the feeling of a full bladder became associated with waking up.

Within universities, the integration of experimental research with clinical procedures, coupled with a general dissatisfaction with prevailing psychodynamic formulations, led to the development of behavior therapy as a viable psychological intervention. As recounted from the personal experience of Cyril Franks, a coauthor of the first edition of this chapter (Fishman & Franks, 1992), one notable origin of these developments was in the United Kingdom at the Maudsley Hospital, the physical home of the University of London Institute of Psychiatry, in the clinical psychology unit headed by Hans Eysenck. At that time, the only available and generally acceptable form of psychotherapy was based on psychoanalytic models carried out under the supervision of a physician; the conceptual context of treatment was the medical model, which views mental and emotional problems as diseases for which an "etiology" had to be found, leading to some form of "treatment" and the possibility of a "cure." The clinical psychologist, as a nonmedical professional, was seen, at best, as a useful ancillary worker.

In this context, clinical psychologists began to question the utility of spending years studying a body of knowledge that stressed the methodology of the behavioral scientist only to find that their professional work rested on the goodwill and psychodynamic tutelage of physicians. Moreover, on the basis of their rigorous training as behavioral scientists, the Maudsley psychologists developed critiques of the reliability, validity, and general utility of traditional psychiatric diagnoses; of the psychometric viability of the psychodynamically based tests they were required to use in their assessment role; and of the efficacy of psychodynamic therapy. These psychologists concluded that a promising alternative that avoided all these problems was stimulus–response (S-R) learning theory—in particular, the work of Pavlov, which was rooted in scientific experimentation and rigorous data collection and analysis. The goal was learning theory–based assessment and intervention grounded in the idea that psychopathological behavior was learned like any other behavior and that it could be unlearned (i.e., changed or eliminated) by using the proper learning principles. So it was that the concept of behavior therapy was born (Franks, 1987).

Over the years, Eysenck's many students established Maudsley enclaves and offshoots throughout the world, with accomplishments such as publication of the first behaviorally based textbook of abnormal psychology (Eysenck, 1960) and one of the first collections of case studies in behavior therapy (Eysenck, 1964). This group was also responsible for the creation of the first journal devoted exclusively to behavior therapy, *Behaviour Research and Therapy*, and the invention of a name for this treatment, *behavior therapy*. (See Eysenck's 1990 autobiography for a more detailed account of these events.)

During the late 1950s and early 1960s, a parallel development was proceeding in South Africa led by a Johannesburg physician dissatisfied with both the theory and clinical usefulness of psychodynamic concepts. First in South Africa, and later in the United States, Joseph Wolpe (1958) used Pavlovian principles to develop his widely disseminated psychotherapy by reciprocal inhibition and the technique of systematic desensitization for the treatment of fears. Wolpe's ideas were pragmatically expanded by his South African colleague Arnold Lazarus to new populations, such as school phobia (Lazarus, 1959), and in new formats, such as group therapy (Lazarus, 1961).

In Wolpe's systematic desensitization technique, the patient first learns how to achieve a state of deep muscle relaxation (Jacobson, 1938). Then a hierarchy of specific situations and scenes related to the patient's fear is created in terms of intensity of anxiety elicited by the situation. For example, a patient with agoraphobia might assess being near the door of his or her house as mildly anxiety arousing, walking in the neighborhood as moderately anxiety arousing, and driving 10 miles from home as extremely anxiety arousing—with a variety of associated situations filling in points along the hierarchy. The therapist then begins the formal desensitization process. In it, the client first engages in progressive muscle relaxation and then imagines the mildest scene on the hierarchy that elicits anxiety. After 5 seconds or so, this experience is followed by a period of terminating the scene image and returning to a state of relaxation, such that the patient starts to learn to associate relaxation rather than anxiety to the previously feared situation. Each scene in the hierarchy is repeated until the patient reports experiencing virtually no anxiety while visualizing it. In this way, the patient works his or her way stepwise through the complete hierarchy.

Systematic desensitization was the first viable "talk therapy" alternative to traditional psychodynamic forms of psychotherapy. Before the advent of systematic desensitization, conditioning was applied exclusively to animals, small children, seriously impaired individuals, or perhaps those suffering from a highly focalized disorder. Now, an alternative to psychodynamic therapy became available, an alternative that could be meaningfully and efficiently applied to the sophisticated patients who came to a mental health professional's private office for treatment of complex problems. In the years since, Wolpe's laborious procedures have been modified many times as a result of subsequent study. However, their practical significance remains undiminished.

The 1950s and 1960s was a pioneering era characterized by ideology and polemics in which behavior therapists strove to present a united front against the common psychodynamic "foe." As behavior therapy established itself in the 1970s as a respected treatment, behavior therapists gradually abandoned their missionary zeal and searched for new frontiers within which to extend their approach. These included outpatient psychotherapy practice, biofeedback, health psychology, community psychology, and the worlds of business, administration, and government. For example, jobs were subjected to careful, systematic analysis, comparing those behaviors that were actually rewarded by salary and promotions against those that were most desirable for achieving the goals of the overall organization. By changing incentive systems, work behaviors could then be brought into closer correspondence with organizational objectives (Gilbert, 1978). It was an era of intellectual expansion into concepts, methods, and ways of viewing data beyond those of traditional learning theory. As mentioned earlier, it was also the era that ushered in the second wave of behavior therapy—the rise of CBT—in part a reflection of the cognitive revolution in psychology as a whole (Baars, 1986).

EMERGENCE OF SUBMOVEMENTS

In the 1970s, behavior therapy began to cohere into more or less distinct streams, all sharing a common methodological and learning theory core. At least five were noteworthy (see Wilson & Franks, 1982). The first three were applied behavioral analysis, a neobehavioristic S-R model, and psychological behaviorism. All three led to interventions that would fall into the category of first-wave behavioral theories. The second two—social learning theory and cognitive theory—fall into the more cognitively focused second wave. All five continue to exist in some form today.

Applied behavior analysis (e.g., Austin & Carr, 2000) describes the application of principles derived from Skinner's operant conditioning to a wide range of clinical and social problems, particularly mental retardation, autistic spectrum disorders, and brain injury. For the most part, applied behavior analysts are radical behaviorists, that is, their basic assumption is that behavior is a function of its consequences and not of the individual's particular interpretation of the environment. There are few intervening variables, mentalistic inferences are disavowed, and treatment methods are evaluated primarily in terms of quantitative, single-case experimental designs in which the participant serves as his or her own control. The emphasis is on the manipulation of environmental variables to bring about behavioral change and on the use of laboratory-based principles, such as reinforcement, punishment, extinction, and stimulus control.

The neobehavioristic–mediational S-R model (Wilson & Franks, 1982) is particularly connected with the works of Pavlov, Mowrer, and Wolpe. Intervening variables and hypothetical constructs are acceptable, and publicly unobservable processes, such as the imaginal representation of anxiety-eliciting stimuli in systematic desensitization, are accepted and even encouraged.

Psychological behaviorism, which was originally called *social behaviorism* and then *paradigmatic behaviorism* by its developer Staats (1975, 1988), emphasizes the integration of conditioning theory with traditional concepts in personality, clinical, and social psychology (Staats, 2005). Staats viewed the principles of reinforcement and contiguity as always present and interacting in the development of personality, with operant conditioning affecting overt behavior patterns and classical conditioning affecting emotional and cognitive response patterns. Staats's concept of cumulative–hierarchical learning and development explains how complex combinations of simple behaviors learned by basic conditioning can evolve, over time, into three complex personality repertoires of responses: sensory–motor, emotional–motivational, and language–cognitive. Staats applied the principles of conditioning to all areas of traditional psychology, including such clinically relevant domains as personality assessment, psychopathology, and psychotherapy.

Social learning theory, developed by Albert Bandura and his colleagues (e.g., Bandura, 1969), constitutes, along with the cognitive theory (e.g., Beck, 1963), the mainstream of second-wave, contemporary, CBT. In its more advanced form (e.g., Bandura, 1982), social learning theory is interactional, interdisciplinary, and multimodal. Behavior is influenced by stimulus events (primarily through classical conditioning), by external reinforcement (through operant conditioning), and by cognitive mediational processes. Behavior change is brought about largely through observational learning, a process in which people are influenced by observing someone else's behavior. The term *model* is reserved for the exemplar, the person who demonstrates the behavior that the observer views. Live modeling occurs when the exemplar is directly seen, whereas symbolic modeling takes place when the model is observed indirectly, as in movies, on television, by reading, through an oral description of someone else's behavior, or even by imagining a model's behaviors. Social learning emphasizes reciprocal interactions between the individual's behavior and the environment. The individual is considered capable of self-directed behavior change. Bandura's theory of perceived *self-efficacy* was one of the first major attempts to provide a unified theoretical explanation of how behavior therapy and other psychotherapies work. Self-efficacy is the individual's belief or expectation that he or she can master a particular situation and bring about desired outcomes. It is viewed as a common cognitive mechanism that mediates the effects of all psychological change procedures; that is, these procedures are postulated to be effective because they create and strengthen a client's expectations of personal efficacy.

Cognitive theories, especially those developed by Beck (e.g., 1963), Ellis (e.g., 1962), and Mahoney (e.g., 1974), emphasize the central role of cognitive processes and private events as mediators of behavior change, as nicely summarized into six basic assumptions (Kendall & Bemis, 1983, pp. 565–566):

1. the human organism responds primarily to cognitive representations of its environments rather than to these environments per se;
2. most human learning is cognitively mediated;
3. thoughts, feelings, and behaviors are causally interrelated;
4. attitudes, expectances, attributions, and other cognitive activities are central to producing, predicting, and understanding psychopathological behavior and the effects of therapeutic interventions;
5. cognitive processes can be cast into testable formulations that are easily integrated with behavioral paradigms, and it is possible and desirable to combine cognitive treatment strategies with enactive techniques [such as behavioral rehearsal] and behavioral contingency management; and
6. the task of the cognitive–behavioral therapist is to act as diagnostician, educator, and technical consultant, assessing maladaptive cognitive processes and working with the client to design learning experiences that may ameliorate these dysfunctional cognitions and the behavioral and affective patterns with which they correlate.

As we discuss subsequently, today these five submovements have coalesced into two broader movements characterized by the different waves in the field just discussed. Specifically, applied behavior analysis and the neobehavioristic S-R model have coalesced into the first wave and psychological behaviorism, social learning theory, and cognitive theory into the second wave. As mentioned earlier, a third wave has also emerged, led by Marsha Linehan's dialectical behavior therapy (DBT) and Steven Hayes's acceptance and commitment therapy (ACT). The third wave represents a creative integration of Skinner's radical behaviorism and other behavioral principles with concepts from cognitive, experiential, and Eastern approaches, emphasizing acceptance, mindfulness, cognitive defusion, dialectics, spirituality, and relationship. In addition, their therapeutic methods often use more experiential techniques and place a greater emphasis on contextual factors.

WORLDWIDE ORGANIZATION OF BEHAVIOR
AND COGNITIVE THERAPY

Behavior therapy, together with cognitive therapy, CBT, and the more recent third-wave therapies, has grown into a large, worldwide movement. The largest behavior therapy association in the United States, the Association for Behavioral and Cognitive Therapies (ABCT; http://www.abct.org) is more than 40 years old, and in 2009 had more than 5,000 members (approximately 60% professionals and 40% students). It embraces practitioners, researchers, trainers, and students of both traditional behavior therapy and CBT, as well as the newer third-wave approaches. The largest association of applied behavior analysts in the United States is the Association for Behavior Analysis International (ABAI; http://www.abainternational.org), which has a membership of approximately 4,500 in the United States and 7,000 in its 29 non-U.S. affiliated chapters.

The European Association for Behavioural and Cognitive Therapy (EABCT; http://www.eabct.com) was formally established in 1976 and brings together 41 individual associations from 29 countries. EACBT includes 25,000 individual clinician and researcher members.

There have been 12 World Congresses devoted to behavior therapy (the first held in 1980), cognitive therapy (the first in 1983), or—since 1992—a combination of cognitive and behavior therapies. Run by a World Congress Committee (WCC; http://www.wcbct.org/index.htm), the last World Congress of Behavioural and Cognitive Therapies as of this writing was held in Barcelona in 2007, with an attendance of more than 1,000; the next is planned for Boston in 2010. The WCC was established by mutual agreement of seven organizations, each of which is represented on the WCC, including ABCT, EABCT, the Australian Association for Cognitive and Behaviour Therapy, La Asociación Latinoamericana de Análisis y Modificación del Comportamiento, the International Association of Cognitive Psychotherapy, the Japanese Association of Behavior Therapy, and the South African Behaviour Therapy Association.

Finally, a large number of journals, many in English, are devoted primarily or exclusively to behavior therapy in all its various waves. For example, in Thomson Reuters's ISI Web of Knowledge (2009) listing of important, English-language journals in clinical psychology, there are 14 such journals (16%) among the 87 listed. Those among the 14 with the top three highest 5-year citation impact factors in English are *Behaviour Research and Therapy*,

Journal of Behavior Therapy and Experimental Psychiatry, and *Cognitive Therapy and Research*.

DEFINITIONS OF BEHAVIOR THERAPY

Interestingly, the term *behavior therapy* was introduced more or less independently by three widely separated groups of researchers: (a) by Skinner, Solomon, and Lindsley in the United States in a 1953 status report to refer to their application of operant conditioning to increase simple social behaviors in chronically hospitalized psychotic patients; (b) by Lazarus (1958) in South Africa to refer to Wolpe's application of his reciprocal inhibition technique to neurotic patients; and (c) by Eysenck's (1959) Maudsley group in the United Kingdom to describe their "new look at clinical intervention" in which "behavior therapy" was defined as the application of modern learning theory to the understanding and treatment of behavioral disorders.

Many authors (e.g., Erwin, 1978; Franks, 1990; O'Leary & Wilson, 1987; Spiegler & Guevremont, 2003) have pointed out that it is difficult to articulate a succinct definition of contemporary behavior therapy that does justice to the field. The definitional dilemma results from the fact that behavior therapy, like many areas in the behavioral sciences, consists of a series of overlapping domains, as represented in the five circles of Figure 4.1 (Fishman, 1988). The first four circles include the following:

1. therapeutic principles derived from operant and respondent learning theory principles;
2. therapeutic principles derived from experimental psychology, including cognitive psychology;
3. therapeutic techniques originated by behaviorally oriented clinicians, such as contingency contracting and systematic desensitization; and
4. ideas and strategies adapted from the general psychotherapy literature, such as the relationship-enhancement methods of Rogerian therapy that have been further developed by experiential therapists (e.g., Elliott, Watson, Goldman, & Greenberg, 2003) and therapy process models taken from systems theory (e.g., Kanfer & Schefft, 1988).

In Figure 4.1, the partial overlap among the circles is noteworthy. For example, Circle 3 only partially overlaps Circles 1 and 2. This reflects the fact that some of the techniques in Circle 3, such as contingency contracting, are clearly deducible from the contemporary experimental principles associated with Circles 1 and 2, whereas other accepted techniques in Circle 3, such as

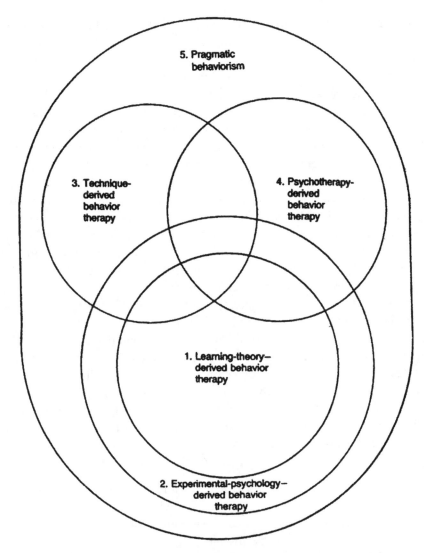

Figure 4.1. The overlapping domains of the behavioral movement. From *Paradigms in Behavior Therapy: Present and Promise* (p. 268), edited by D. B. Fishman, F. Rotgers, and C. M. Franks, 1988, New York, NY: Springer. Copyright 1988 by Springer Publishing Company. Reprinted with permission.

systematic desensitization, are not (Wilson & O'Leary, 1980). As another example, Circle 4 overlaps only parts of Circles 1, 2, and 3. This reflects the fact that, although some of the approaches from general psychotherapy, such as goal setting, are clearly deducible from traditional behavioral techniques and contemporary experimental principles, others, such as client-centered relationship facilitation, are not.

Circle 5 embraces the other four and involves the methodological principles of behavioral science, such as empiricism, operational definition, quantification, and experimental research design. As we describe in the next section, these principles can be framed in epistemological terms either within the positivist paradigm (traditional experimental science) or within the alternative epistemology of pragmatism and social constructionism (Fishman, 1988).

As an example of Circle 5, consider how behavior therapy experienced the addition of cognitive approaches into its purview. Cognitive therapy deals with internal experiences that are more inferential and can be only indirectly observed, and thus requires a stretch of behavioral emphases on overtly observable actions. However, cognitive behavioral therapists are more committed than other therapists to linking these internal cognitive phenomena—even at a deep, "underlying" level (Persons, 2008)—to overt behavioral and environmental referents. Also, in concert with behavior therapy and unlike insight-oriented therapies, cognitive therapy focuses primarily on present interactions and relationships rather than developmentally historical ones, for the latter are particularly difficult to link directly to observable behavioral and environmental data. Finally, cognitive therapy is similar to behavior therapy in preferring relatively "value neutral" data and phenomena that involve less emotionally and socially loaded concepts and that are "nearer" to the empirical data. Thus, cognitive therapy favors more observationally based and less inferential data that is more likely to be agreed on by different observers.

Recognizing the difficulty of succinctly defining behavior therapy, O'Leary and Wilson (1987) provided a useful list of nine common "core" assumptions that behavior therapists hold. In our view, these beliefs are held by the majority of contemporary behavior therapists:

1. Most abnormal behavior is acquired and maintained according to the same principles as normal behavior.
2. Most abnormal behavior can be modified through the application of social learning principles.
3. Assessment is continuous and focuses on the current determinants of behavior.
4. People are best described by what they think, feel, and do in specific life situations.
5. Treatment methods are precisely specified, replicable, and objectively evaluated.
6. Treatment outcome is evaluated in terms of the initial induction of behavior change, its generalization to the real life setting, and its maintenance over time.
7. Treatment strategies are individually tailored to different problems in different individuals.

8. Behavior therapy is broadly applicable to a full range of clinical disorders and educational problems.
9. Behavior therapy is a humanistic approach in which treatment goals and methods are mutually contracted [between client and therapist]. (O'Leary and Wilson, 1987, p. 12)

Another way of broadly summarizing the distinctive themes of behavior therapy is represented by Kanfer and Schefft's (1988) six "think rules" that help to capture important attitudes and skills that behavior therapists model and teach their clients. These include the following:

- *Think Behavior*—Assist the client to redefine problems [and goals] in terms of [concrete] behaviors [rather than in abstract concepts like traits, e.g., "My goal is to overcome my social anxiety by meeting with non-family members at least once a week in nonwork situations" rather than "My goal is to overcome my social anxiety by trying to understand why I've always been such a shy, withdrawn person."].
- *Think Solution*—Get the client to ask continuously, "What is the least I can do to improve the situation?"
- *Think Positive*—Have the client identify personal strengths and the positive aspects of any event or change effort.
- *Think Small Steps*—Set limited goals to enhance the probability of success and permit continuing reappraisal.
- *Think Flexible*—Help the client to develop alternatives and back-up plans and to be prepared for the unexpected.
- *Think Future*—Focus on the future and encourage rehearsal and planning. (Kanfer & Schefft, 1988, p. 122)

A METATHEORY OF CONTEMPORARY BEHAVIOR THERAPY

A theory in psychology is a conceptual framework that identifies important dimensions of human experience and behavior and that describes relationships among these dimensions. A metatheory is a fundamental viewpoint that stands "behind," or logically prior to, the theory. Thus, a metatheory consists of those assumptions that are made before the creation, validation, and refinement of a specific theory.

Table 4.1 presents an overview of the metatheoretical location of earlier and later versions of behavior therapy, relative to other systems of psychotherapy and applied psychology theory. The table thus highlights the different underlying assumptions among therapy systems. It is organized as a grid formed by two cross-cutting typologies of metatheoretical assumptions: epistemological

TABLE 4.1

Metatheoretical Location of Behavior Therapy Within Applied Psychology[a]

Dominant theoretical worldview	Epistemological paradigm		
	Logical positivism	Social constructionism	
	Positivist paradigm	Pragmatic paradigm	Hermeneutic paradigm
Trait	McCrae & Costa's (2003) five-factor theory of personality	Psychometric polling models for predicting voter preferences in presidential elections (e.g., Zogby International, 2008).	Freud's theory of oral, anal, and phallic character types (e.g., Freud, 1924)
Interactional	Earlier and later behavior therapy theory	Later behavior therapy theory only	
Organismic	General systems theory as applied to living systems (e.g., Miller, 1978)	Program evaluation theory (e.g., Patton, 2008)	Structural family therapy theory (e.g., Minuchin, 1974)
Transactional		Qualitative research (Patton, 2002)	Constructivist psychotherapy theory (Neimeyer & Mahoney, 1995)

[a]Empty cells involve logically incompatible perspectives and thus cannot support viable theories.

paradigms (divided into the positivist, pragmatic, and hermeneutic; Fishman, 1999) and worldviews (divided into trait, interactional, organismic, and transactional; Altman & Rogoff 1987). (Note that the discussion that follows focuses on the position of behavior therapy in Table 4.1. For more details about how the nonbehavioral examples of applied psychology fit into Table 4.1 and for more details about the table generally, see Fishman & Franks, 1992.)

Epistemological Paradigms

Epistemology is the branch of philosophy that investigates the origins, nature, methods, and limits of human knowledge. An epistemological paradigm sets forth the criteria according to which the relevance and validity of a particular body of knowledge are judged. In other words, philosophically speaking, no knowledge is given in any absolute sense. Rather, a variety of possible, coherent epistemological systems are set forth, and the evaluation of a statement's truth or falsity will depend, in part, on the epistemological criteria chosen for the evaluation and not just on the content of the statement per se (Fishman, 1999; Gergen, 1985).

Until recently, American psychology was dominated by the epistemology of conventional natural science, that of logical positivism. In broad terms, logical positivism contends that there is an external world independent of human experience and that objective, "scientific" knowledge about this world can be obtained through direct sense experience, as interpreted within the framework of theory-embedded, hypothesis-testing laboratory experiments. The data on which this knowledge is founded consist of discrete, molecular, sensorily based "facts," all of which can eventually be quantified. Knowledge is in the form of a cumulative body of context-free, universal laws about the phenomenon studied. Psychologists who have adopted a positivist perspective generally assume that the universal laws that emerge from scientific study will have a form such that they can eventually be applied to help solve significant psychological and social problems in a unique, rationally based manner.

In contrast to logical positivism, social constructionism posits that the reality of an individual or group experience is, to a substantial degree, conceptually constructed rather than sensorily discovered by that group. Objective knowledge about the world is significantly limited because "facts" and "raw data" can be known only within a particular, pre-empirically established cultural, social, and linguistic context. As reflected in Table 4.1, social constructionism has encouraged the growth of two types of nonpositivist epistemological paradigms. The more radical is a hermeneutic paradigm that emphasizes qualitative interpretation, experiential and symbolic meaning, a place for subjectivity and intuition, and a historically situated psychology. This model views the goals and proper methods of psychology as similar to those of history, literary criticism, and investigative reporting (Messer, Sass, & Woolfolk, 1988).

The alternative approach spawned by social constructionism is that of the pragmatic paradigm (Fishman, 1999, 2005; Polkinghorne, 1992), a hybrid between the experimental and hermeneutic approaches. Like the hermeneutic paradigm, the pragmatic paradigm is based on social constructionism and rejects the theory-based laboratory experiment and the search for general psychological laws, advocating instead for contextually embedded, case-based knowledge. However, like the experimental paradigm, the pragmatic paradigm values a quantitative, atomistic, observational approach and adapts some of the research methods of the laboratory into quasi-experimental and single-subject research designs.

The origins of the behavior therapy movement are clearly embedded in logical positivism. Watson's original model for behavioristic theory was that of experimental animal psychology, and this model was continued by Hull, Skinner, Tolman, Guthrie, and other learning theory researchers in the so-called Age of Grand Theory (Kimble, 1985). Applying the model of physics and chemistry, these researchers assumed that there are a few basic, universal laws of learning that apply to both animals and humans. In line with this view, these researchers pursued scientific psychology by focusing on publicly observable, circumscribed behaviors such as the food-seeking activities of white mice or pigeons under controlled laboratory conditions. As also shown in Table 4.1, whereas some groups in later behavior therapy theory have remained within the experimental paradigm (Baars, 1986; Wilson & Franks, 1982), others have moved away from the experimental epistemological paradigm into the pragmatic paradigm (Fishman, Rotgers, & Franks, 1988).

There are at least three reasons that many behavior theorists have moved from the experimental to the pragmatic paradigm. First, as behavior therapy began in the 1960s, the experimental paradigm was coming to an unsuccessful end. Its demise was derived in large part from the failure of animal-based learning theorists to agree on a single theory and the failure to apply and validate models of learning theory to complex human behavior in rigorous ways (Baars, 1986; Erwin, 1978; Kimble, 1985). A second reason came from the experiences of most behavior therapy practitioners. They discovered that they could practice effectively without having to show a tight link between their practices and the experimental literature (e.g., Hayes, Barlow, & Nelson-Gray, 1999). A third reason for behavior therapy's movement away from the experimental paradigm, beginning in the 1960s, was the loss of support for logical positivism in the philosophical community (Erwin, 1978; Fishman, 1999).

One of the clearest and most explicit, early statements of the move by behavior therapists toward the pragmatic paradigm was made by Azrin (1977). This applied researcher began his career solidly aligned with the positivist paradigm but was led to an identification with the pragmatic paradigm after focusing on the development of effective change programs for significant human problems in areas such as controlling aggression, toilet training, marital adjustment, alcoholism, tics, and job finding. In line with the pragmatic paradigm, Azrin took his measurement methods from the experimental tradition, but the substance of what he did was pragmatically focused, with an emphasis on emergent clinical techniques and practical success with specific problems in specific situations, not on the derivation of theory-based, general laws.

In a similar vein, an early, important textbook on behavior therapy by Spiegler (1983) also reflects pragmatic thinking. He described his approach as "operational," viewing behavior therapy "in terms of how it functions and what it accomplishes (rather than in terms of theoretical explanations of why it works)" (Spiegler, 1983, p. xvii).

Also around this time, Edwin Erwin (1978), a philosopher of behavior therapy, argued on epistemological grounds against the positivist view of behaviorism, which asserts that in principle, only publicly observable behavior is worthy of scientific study. Rather, Erwin introduced the concept of "pragmatic behaviorism," which he defined as

> the philosophical assumption that clinical problems should generally be analyzed in behavioral terms. . . . In treating a client, behavioral counterparts should generally be sought that correlate with (but are not equivalent to) any relevant problematic mental state. Treatment should focus primarily on behavior, not because the mind is behavior, but for practical reasons. . . . It may be of some use to learn, for example, that an obese patient has a craving for food, but it is even more useful to learn how many eating responses are engaged in each day and under exactly what conditions. (1978, p. 80)

Building on this view and that of Mahoney (1974), Fishman (1988) defined pragmatic behaviorism in terms of a commitment to a variety of methodological principles for the conduct of behavior therapy, as embodied in Circle 5 in Figure 4.1. These principles include an emphasis on (a) empiricism; (b) variables that are objective, specific, and concrete; (c) the analysis of problems into smaller parts to be dealt with one at a time; (d) quantification; (e) a view of behavior as a sample (rather than a sign) of personality; (f) functional analysis of the relationship between behavior and the environment; and (g) linkage of all cognitive and affective variables used to behavioral and environmental referents.

Worldviews

On the basis of the work of philosophers John Dewey and Steven Pepper, Altman and Rogoff (1987) posited four distinct worldviews for categorizing the core content of various types of psychological theories, as shown in Table 4.1.

The trait view—for example, as associated with the well-known five-factor theory of personality—sees behavior as emerging from the individual. In other words, individuals act as they do primarily because of their inherent natures, without much attention to the temporal aspects of behavior or to the contexts within which the behaviors are embedded.

The interactional view—associated particularly with behavior therapy—treats the person and the environment as separate underlying entities that interact in a linear, causal, predictable manner, like the parts of a watch or dynamo. Psychological phenomena are analyzed in terms of the antecedent conditions that lead to certain behaviors, which in turn lead to various consequences, which in turn become antecedents for certain subsequent events.

The organismic view—associated particularly with systems theory—conceives of both the person and the social environment as a system with complex, reciprocal, and dynamic relationships and influences among its various parts and subsystems. Change usually occurs in accord with underlying regulatory mechanisms such as homeostasis and long-range directional teleological mechanisms (e.g., psychological development from birth to adulthood).

Finally, the transactional view emphasizes the role of varying perspectives on a particular purposive action or pattern of such actions in a person's life, such as deciding to apply to graduate school or to go out on a date. The act is viewed as intrinsically embedded in the individual's surrounding life context and unfolding in time. Thus, the event is viewed as a complex and holistic phenomenon.

Although behavior therapy began as narrowly focused within a positivist interactional worldview, over time the field has branched out to add interactional view components from the other worldviews to its root. Brief illustrations of the root and its branches follow.

Interactional Theories

Perhaps the clearest examples of pure, interactional theory are Watson's behaviorism and the animal-based conditioning research in the Age of Grand Theory. The metatheory behind both of these projects involves a mechanistic, billiard-ball, linear causal model that focuses on functional links between present environmental stimuli and an organism's responses. This view was carried over into the early development of behavior therapy procedures by Skinner, Solomon, and Lindsley (1953), who applied animal-based operant learning theory to the alleviation of socially unresponsive schizophrenic behavior.

Although cognitive components were present early in behavior therapy's development in the form of covert conditioning (e.g., Cautela, 1970), Mahoney (1974) described how this model conformed to the interactional worldview:

> Thoughts, images, memories, and sensations are described as covert stimuli, covert responses, or covert consequences. The skull becomes a rather crowded Skinner box in which such conventional principles as reinforcement, punishment, and extinction are said to describe the function and patterning of [these covert events]. (p. 61)

Interactional Theories With Trait Components

Persons (1989, 2008) developed a highly recognized theory that emphasizes underlying, traitlike mechanisms—such as core beliefs and basic skill deficits—behind overt dysfunction and distress. Young has developed a typology of these underlying beliefs and created schema-focused therapy. He posited five major themes or domains in dysfunctional schemas: Disconnection and Rejection; Impaired Autonomy and Performance; Impaired Limits; Other-Directedness; and Overvigilance and Inhibition. More about schema therapy can be found in the chapter on cognitive therapy and also on the schema therapy website, http://www.schematherapy.com/id73.htm.

Another example of behavior therapy's incorporation of trait-based approaches is its general acceptance of the psychopathology categories embodied in the *Diagnostic and Statistical Manual of Mental Disorders* (DSM) published by the American Psychiatric Association.

Interactional Theories With Organismic Components

Because of the importance of the environment in the interactional approach, and because of the social context of much behavior, behavior therapists became interested early on in social interaction, social relationships, and the social environment generally. In his 1968 book, Peterson demonstrated how functional analysis could be applied using a similar perspective for solving dysfunction in an individual, a family, and a social system (such as a state psychiatric hospital). To show the link between individual and group behavior, Peterson (1968) pointed out that social interaction (as distinct from the "interactional" worldview)

> refers to a class of social phenomena involving mutuality of stimulation and effect. . . . Explicit behavior by person 1 serves as a stimulus for person 2, who reacts in some way. This either terminates the interchange or leads to a further reaction on the part of person 1, perhaps to an action-reaction chain of indefinite length. . . . [Thus] in his motives and cognitive beliefs, each person takes the other, who has his own motives and beliefs, into account. When relatively stable patterns of [social] interaction develop between two individuals, a relationship has been formed. . . . Groups of people [socially] interacting can be studied as emergent units. A different class of phenomena can be examined, and with this a new order of comprehension may result. (pp. 82–84)

Many later behavior theorists built on this type of reasoning to integrate concepts from family systems therapy into cognitive behavior therapy with couples (e.g., Baucom, Epstein, LaTaillade, & Kirby, 2008) and families. An excellent example of the latter is behavioral-family systems therapy for negotiating parent-adult conflict (Robin & Foster, 2002). In this therapy, a detailed analysis of contingency arrangements from the interactional, behavioral tradition provided an excellent starting point for a functional analysis of family members' behavior with each other. This then is combined with organismic elements to address "the circular nature of [social] interaction patterns and the hierarchical structure of families, which overlay contingency arrangements" (Robin & Foster, 2002, p. 7).

In addition, behavior therapists have embedded their principles within the concepts of community psychology, designing interventions to have an impact on communities as systems. For example, Henggeler, Schoenwald, Borduin, Rowland, and Cunningham's (1998) multisystemic therapy with antisocial children and adolescents involves managing and reengineering the antecedent stimuli and consequences of a youth's total environment that are associated with acting-out behavior by coordinating with all relevant caregivers (e.g., parents and guardians, school personnel, child welfare workers, police officers, recreational workers, probation officers, and psychotherapists). In the process, new and more positive social support systems are created for the youth.

Interactional Themes With Transactional Elements

As mentioned earlier, many behavior therapists have conceptualized behavior therapy within a social constructionist, pragmatic metatheory (e.g., Azrin, 1977; Fishman, 1999; Kanfer & Schefft, 1988; Nelson, 1983; Persons, 2008). A major aspect of this perspective is the emphasis on the contextual specificity of behavior. The focus is on solving particular problems in particular situations, not on the derivation of empirically confirmed general laws. This perspective leads to a focus on the individual case study (Fishman, 1999), which in turn highlights the fact that each treatment program with a client—be it an individual, group, or organization—consists of a social interactional process over time between a particular client and a particular behavior change agent.

This process involves a series of sequential, interdependent steps or phases. How such phases link with transactional thinking is outlined in Kanfer and Schefft's (1988) process model of therapeutic change. It consists of seven phases: (1) role structuring and creating a therapeutic alliance; (2) developing a commitment for change; (3) behavioral analysis; (4) negotiating treatment objectives and methods; (5) implementing treatment and maintaining motivation; (6) monitoring and evaluating progress; and (7) maintenance, generalization, and termination of treatment.

These phases generally take place in an interdependent, sequential manner, although progress through the phases is not consistently linear. The evolution of these phases reflects a transactional worldview because, given the great variety of patterns created by different choice point decisions, each case brings its own idiosyncratic particularities.

BEHAVIOR THERAPY TODAY

As mentioned in the introductory portion of this chapter, we have organized the history of behavior therapy into three distinct waves: a first wave that focuses on functional relationships between observable behavior and the objective environment; a second wave that focuses on cognitive representations of the environment rather than on characteristics of the objective environment per se; and a third wave that encompasses the cognitive processes and inner experience of the second wave, while focusing on how these internal processes are functionally related to the objective environment (sometimes called *functional contextualism*), like the first wave.

Given the separate chapter in this book on second-wave cognitive therapy, we consider four main topics in the remainder of this chapter: the status of first-wave behavior therapy, the status of third-wave behavior therapy, contrasts and complementarities between second-wave and third-wave therapies, and the rediscovery by behavior therapy of the research potential of the case study.

Today's First-Wave Behavior Therapy

Today's first-wave behavior therapy can be organized around individualized assessment and treatment planning for particular, contextualized behavior problems. The focus (Spiegler & Guevremont, 2003) is on (a) operationalizing problems and goals in behavioral terms, (b) assessing the maintaining conditions of the problem behaviors through direct observation and the functional analysis of their relevant environmental antecedents and consequences, (c) using the assessment to develop a treatment plan, and then (d) conducting and monitoring the results of implementing the treatment plan, with revisions of earlier steps made if necessary on the basis of monitoring data. First-wave behavior therapy entails a large menu of techniques and strategies from which to choose for treatment planning, all directly traceable to aspects of operant and respondent conditioning principles. These include procedures such as (a) stimulus control (reducing the antecedent cues that trigger problematic behavior); (b) differentially reinforcing behaviors for which increase is desirable through the use of strategies such as contingency contracting and token economies; (c) reducing undesirable behaviors through aversive punishment and/or nonaversive techniques such as response cost, overcorrection, and time out; (d) decreasing anxiety through in vivo and imaginal desensitization; and (e) teaching social and problem-solving skills through modeling.

A noteworthy example of first-wave behavior therapy is the work of Gordon Paul and associates (e.g., Paul & Lenz, 1977; Rhoades, 1981). Although the work was completed between 35 and 40 years ago, it represents a gold standard for what can be accomplished with a particularly difficult population such as the severely and chronically mentally ill—namely, increasing patient functioning along with impressive cost savings. That it has rarely been replicated is, unfortunately, a testament to the power of politics over rational program design (Rhoades, 1981; for one of the replications, see Silverstein et al., 2006). Using social learning principles, Paul and colleagues redesigned and restructured a traditional state hospital ward that housed patients with chronic schizophrenia who had been hospitalized for an average of 17 years and who were functioning at such a low level of self-care or who had manifested such excesses in bizarre behavior that they had been rejected for extended-care community placement. Paul et al. randomly assigned patients to their social learning program and to a treatment-as-usual (TAU) condition. After 2 years, 25% of the social-learning patients were indistinguishable from the normal population on reliable, observation-based measures of self-care and social functioning (Rhoades, 1981, p. 15). At the end of the program, of the 40 social-learning patients who were treated, 36 (90%) were released to board-and-room homes, and three others (7.5%) achieved self-supporting, independent living. In contrast, of the 29 patients receiving the TAU, only 13 (45%) were released to board-and-room homes and none (0%) to independent living (Rhoades, 1981, p. 3). Because of the lower cost of non-hospital alternatives, the social-learning program was found to be 4 times as cost-effective as TAU (Rhoades, 1981).

Paul's success was based on extending operant principles in an explicit, systematic, sophisticated manner. For example:

- Paul correctly hypothesized that the residents' dysfunctional behavior was maintained by the interactions with high-school-equivalent, aide-level staff (whom he called "change agents" to properly highlight their role), who before Paul's intervention responded with negative attention to residents' disturbing behaviors and by ignoring residents' less frequent incidents of nondisturbing behavior. Thus, Paul's main intervention was to train the staff in responding to specific resident behaviors in the opposite way—by reinforcing residents' approximations of functional behaviors and by either ignoring dysfunctional behaviors or using time-out when residents' engaged in aggressive, harming behaviors.

- The program was designed to maximize ongoing contact between staff and residents, including meals and morning and evening routines, which provided a time for explicit training in self-care skills and structured skill-training groups during the day in areas such as prosocial behavior and communication, functional arithmetic, reading, writing, speaking, homemaking, and grooming. This resulted in 85% of each resident's waking hours devoted to structured time with staff in acquiring skills to overcome specific deficits in behavior, compared with only 36.2% of such structured time in the TAU.

- Staff fidelity to the treatment was assessed by the detailed, structured observation of representative samples of staff–resident interaction. The direct observation of client behaviors is a preferred mode of measurement in first-wave behavior therapy, because self-report instruments—typical of second-wave and third-wave approaches—are mediated by complex cognitive and linguistic processes of memory and generalization that are required of the client. These processes are viewed by advocates of first-wave approaches as typically distorting and simplifying the gold standard results achieved by direct, third-party observation of behavior.

Another distinctive and successful first-wave behavior therapy is parent–child interaction therapy (PCIT; Brinkmeyer & Eyberg, 2003). PCIT is a parenting skills training program for young children with disruptive behavior disorders that targets change in parent–child interaction patterns. In a first, child-directed interaction phase of treatment—that integrates elements from play therapy and attachment theory—parents learn positive attention skills in a play situation with their child. These skills include (a) describing rather than criticizing the child's behavior, (b) praising the child's behavior when warranted, and (c) ignoring when possible the child's negative behavior. The emphasis is on increasing positive parenting and warmth in the parent–child interaction as the foundation for discipline skills that are introduced in the second, parent-directed phase of treatment. In this second phase, and within the child-directed context, parents learn and practice giving clear instructions to their child when needed and following through with praise or time-out during in vivo discipline situations. Parents are taught to apply the skills calmly and consistently in the clinic until they achieve competency and are ready to generalize the skills to their home environment. Parent-directed homework assignments proceed gradually from brief practice sessions during play to application at just those times when it is necessary for the child to obey.

Today's Third-Wave Behavior Therapy

Steven Hayes (2004) has been a leading advocate of third-wave therapies, which focus on internal cognitive processes, like the second wave, but view the focus of understanding on how these processes are functionally related to the objective environment, like the first wave.

The following are generally considered third-wave therapies: acceptance and commitment therapy (ACT; Hayes, 2004); dialectical behavior therapy (DBT; Linehan, 1993); behavioral activation (BA; Martell, Addis, & Jacobson, 2001); functional analytic psychotherapy (Kohlenberg & Tsai, 1991);

cognitive behavioral analysis system of psychotherapy (McCullough, 2000); and mindfulness-based cognitive therapy (Segal, Williams, & Teasdale, 2002). As examples, we briefly consider the first three of these.

Acceptance and Commitment Therapy

The difference between second-wave and third-wave therapies can be illustrated by a client, Ms. X, who has the thought, "People in my team's group meeting at work will look down on me when they see that I am blushing because of my social anxiety." Second-wave cognitive therapy contends that such thoughts contain thinking errors that should be challenged and eventually replaced by alternative, more functional thoughts, such as, "My team members might notice that I am blushing but will also pay attention to the substance of what I have to say as it relates to why our team is meeting." Third-wave therapies, such as ACT, take a different approach and contend that the problem is not in the content of Ms. X's thought but rather in the context of the thought—that is, how Ms. X views the thought. Specifically, if Ms. X. can distance herself from the thought—realizing that the thought is just a thought and does not necessarily correspond to objective reality—then the power of the thought to amplify Ms. X's anxiety and thus perhaps to prevent her from attending the meeting will be importantly lowered. In Hayes's (2005) terms, the original upsetting thought will be defused from reality and thus defanged of some of its potency:

> When you learn to view your thoughts as thoughts, occurring in the here and now, you still "know what they mean" (the verbal relations are still there; that is, you still know to what you thoughts refer). But the illusion dissolves that the thing being thought about is present merely when you think about it. This greatly reduces the impact of the symbols . . . [Thus,] the thought, "I am having the feeling that I am anxious," is quite different from the thought, "God, I am so anxious!" The first statement is more defused than the second. For that reason, it is less anxiety-provoking. When you learn to defuse language, it becomes easier to be willing to be present, to be conscious, and to live the life you value, even with the normal [cognitive] chatter going on in your head. (p. 70)

ACT offers a variety of techniques through which a client such as Ms. X can distance herself from her negative thoughts, for example, by looking at her thoughts as though they were floating leaves on a moving stream or by "watching the mind-train"—that is, looking down from a bridge at a slow freight train with each car labeled on top with a negative thought (Hayes, 2005, pp. 66–67). This defusion process, along with acceptance (nonjudgmental awareness), being in contact with the present moment ("showing up"), and viewing one's self as context ("contacting the transcendental sense of self in which all experience is safe") constitute crucial acceptance and mindfulness processes in ACT therapy.

The commitment and behavior change dimensions of ACT for a client like Ms. X would include her selecting and engaging in behaviors that are consistent with her personal values—that is, doing what she wants to do. Thus, if Ms. X. wants to do well at work and to advance, she will be encouraged to pursue these activities behaviorally while also accepting and being mindful (through distancing and defusing) of such anxious thoughts as, "I am anxious" and "I am blushing, and this makes me even more anxious." As can be seen by the demands of ACT on the individual client, at the core of the various ACT processes is the need for psychological flexibility.

Dialectical Behavior Therapy

In working with parasuicidal borderline clients in the late 1970s, Marsha Linehan found that these clients experienced the first-wave and second-wave therapy emphasis on change as invalidating. In studying session tapes of such therapy with borderline clients, Linehan's team noticed that therapists would abandon change-oriented interventions when a patient demonstrated a negative response (e.g., anger, withdrawal, shame, threatened self-harm) and that clients would "reward" a therapist with social connection or warmth when they were allowed to move to another subject the clients preferred.

Linehan responded to these observations by making modifications to second-wave CBT and creating DBT. On the basis of dialectical philosophy, in which polar opposites are considered an intrinsic part of reality, Linehan added acceptance-oriented validation strategies to balance dialectically the change-oriented strategies that were already part of the therapy. To help borderline patients, who have particular problems with emotional regulation, DBT teaches patients to recognize and accept the existence of simultaneous, opposing forces, such as the experience of not wanting to engage in a certain behavior and yet knowing that one has to engage in it to reach a certain desired goal. To help patients on the acceptance side of the equation, DBT—like ACT—uses mindfulness procedures. Another distinctive third-wave theme in Linehan's multifaceted, DBT approach includes seeing therapy as a multistage process that links directly to a patient's environment, including systematic, behavior-based efforts to (a) enhance and maintain a client's motivation to change, (b) enhance a client's capabilities, (c) augment individual therapy with behavioral skills groups and phone coaching, and (d) structure the environment so that treatment can effectively take place—for example, by working with local hospital emergency rooms so that patients are not highly reinforced for making parasuicidal gestures (Linehan, 1993).

Behavioral Activation for Depression

BA in the third wave (Martell, Addis, & Jacobson, 2001) expands on earlier behavioral interventions recommended in both the first and second waves of behavior therapy. BA emphasizes the relationship between activity and mood and the role of contextual changes associated with decreased access to reinforcers, which are hypothesized to be a major cause of depression. BA highlights the centrality of behavioral patterns of avoidance and withdrawal by patients with depression from situations such as interpersonal relationships, occupational and other daily-life demands, or distressing thoughts and feelings. Because approaching potential antidepressant reinforcers—such as seeking out new and unfamiliar social contacts—is often initially punishing, avoidance of contact minimizes distress in the short term but is associated with increasing long-term difficulty (e.g., isolation from others). Thus, increased activation is a tactic used to break this cycle.

Like ACT, BA seeks to identify and promote engagement with activities and contexts that are reinforcing and consistent with an individual's long-term goals. Activation strategies include self-monitoring, structuring and scheduling daily activities, rating the degree of pleasure and accomplishment experienced during engagement in specific daily activities, assessing the function of avoidance behaviors, exploring alternative behaviors related to achieving participant goals, and using role-playing to address specific behavioral deficits. In addition, BA can include behavioral strategies for targeting rumination, including an emphasis on the function of ruminative thinking and on moving attention away from the content of ruminative thoughts toward direct, immediate experience.

Contrasts and Complementarities Between Second-Wave and Third-Wave Therapies

The differences between adherents of the two waves have at times become politicized, with a battle for dominance in the field (Cloud, 2006; Hayes, 2008; Hoffman, 2008). Here we attempt to offer balanced arguments documenting contrasts and complementarities between second-wave therapy (hereafter "CBT") and third wave therapy (hereafter "ACT," a leading representative; for more details on the arguments, see Arch & Craske, 2008; Heimberg & Ritter, 2008).

From the perspective of ACT, CBT's cognitive restructuring excessively focuses on the content per se of cognition, further embedding clients into anxiety-arousing thoughts and pushing clients toward trying to avoid and suppress their upsetting thoughts—a process Hayes (2005) called *experiential avoidance*. In contrast, from the perspective of CBT, "the acceptance of thoughts in ACT, which includes 'letting go' of thoughts as they arise . . .

could be misunderstood and misused as encouragement of thought suppression" (Arch & Craske, 2008, p. 267). Each side cites studies to support its position. In fact, both ACT and CBT use methods of coping with anxious cognition that require additional thinking not to get too tied up in the anxious cognition. The additional thinking takes the form of self-talk or coaching at a bare minimum. Even on a silent meditation, self-talk in the form of verbal coaching is readily present.

Both ACT and CBT use procedures for encouraging patients to stay in contact with their upsetting thoughts: in ACT, the goal is to immerse one-self in such thoughts using a distancing perspective, and in CBT, it is first to focus on and articulate them (e.g., by monitoring automatic thoughts) and then challenge and change them. A possible common pathway here is that both ACT and CBT involve the exposure of patients to previously avoided negative thoughts, which blocks experiential avoidance. Thus, a common mechanism of change could be through the behavioral principle of extinction, such that exposure to upsetting thoughts without the occurrence of a negative outcome will lead to the extinction of those thoughts.

The debate between ACT and CBT adherents sometimes includes the contrasting goals of valued living versus symptom reduction, respectively, as the desired outcomes of therapy. ACT's stated goal is to have the patient accept anxious and other emotionally disturbing thoughts by distancing and defusing from them, freeing the patient to then concentrate on pursuing his or her behavioral goals. CBT's stated goal is to identify dysfunctional thoughts and then to challenge and change their content so that the content no longer generates upset. However, it seems unlikely that CBT therapists aim to reduce anxiety so that their clients can do nothing all day. Nor is there any hard evidence that promoting anxiety symptom reduction in CBT versus valued living in ACT results in different therapy outcomes (Arch & Craske, 2008). Moreover, it would seem that successfully reducing symptoms through CBT would free clients to pursue their goals successfully and, in a parallel way, that successfully pursuing goals via ACT would help clients to think differently about themselves and the world and thus to reduce their symptoms.

Back to Metatheory

The battles between third-wave adherents (e.g., Hayes, 2008) and second-wave adherents (e.g., Hoffman, 2008) are occasionally framed as a debate about the nature of the laws that govern objective reality. In this context, each side claims that scientific data show that their movement corresponds more closely to this objective reality. For example, Hayes (2005) claimed that ACT is logically derived from a distinctive epistemology (functional contextualism) and a distinctive theory of language (relational frame theory, or RFT) and that based on conducting experiments empirically testing aspects of this theory, "we think we've found what is at the core of the human mind itself" (p. 17). In addition, Hayes (2008) argued that because CBT goes against the laws of RFT, CBT is just wrong. In fact, he claimed that CBT is not based on scientific theory but on "tribal tradition" (p. 286). On the other side, the CBT adherent Hoffman (2008) argued not only that CBT is based on a coherent scientific theory but that there is clear empirical evidence supporting the efficacy of cognitive restructuring and the fundamental notion that change in cognitions mediates (i.e., causes) changes in emotions and overt behaviors. Moreover, Hoffman argued, "although . . . acceptance strategies are not routinely used in CBT, they are certainly compatible with the CBT model" (p. 283). In fact, Hoffman claimed, third-wave therapies are not really new, and we should therefore "abandon the terms 'new wave' and 'third wave'" (p. 284).

In terms of the earlier discussion about metatheory, as summarized in Table 4.1, the Hayes–Hoffman dialogue is located in the positivist-paradigm column, which is quite different from the social constructionist, pragmatic-paradigm column. (Note that at some points Hayes [e.g., 2008] has stated that ACT is based on a constructionistic and pragmatic epistemology, but for the present discussion, we are focusing on the positivist aspects of his statements about ACT.) Epistemological pragmatists view theories as conceptual tools, whose value and validity are based not on their correspondence to objective reality but on their capacity to solve real-world problems (Fishman, 1999, 2005). In line with this perspective, for many years within CBT, clinicians have combined strategies associated with first- and second-wave practice—for example, cognitive restructuring and behavioral activation approaches in working with depressed and anxious clients—and the practical effectiveness of this combination has led to its rapid acceptance and proliferation. Also in line with this perspective, more recently, behavioral clinicians have begun to integrate second- and third-wave treatments in their case conceptualizations and practice. (For a thorough example of such integration, see Persons, 2008.)

It should also be noted that the main claims for the efficacy and effectiveness of all three waves of behavior therapy are based on their pragmatic capacity to result in better outcomes in randomized clinical trials compared with control treatments—not on their theoretical validity or persuasiveness per se. Lists of therapies determined to be empirically supported treatments (Society of Clinical Psychology, 2009; http://www.div12.org) on the basis of their successful performance in randomized clinical trials reveal that not only are all of the first-wave and third-wave approaches described in this chapter on the lists, but many second-wave approaches are as well (see the chapter on cognitive therapy in this volume for a discussion of these). In fact, for the some disorders—such as depression, borderline personality, and bulimia—not only behavior and cognitive therapies but also psychodynamic therapies are on the lists. From the pragmatist's point of view, this simply means that different conceptual tools can lead to similar results, just as different carpenter tools can get similar jobs done.

Back to Definition

In reviewing the differences and similarities between second-wave and third-wave therapies, we have seen clear theoretical and political differences between them, for example, in some of the contrasts between their positions on cognitive restructuring versus cognitive defusion. This is reflected in separate professional and scientific associations of CBT, such as the International Association of Cognitive Psychotherapy (http://www.the-iacp.com), and of third-wave therapy, such as the Association for Contextual Behavioral Science (http://www.contextualpsychology.org). However, both waves have a commitment to the methods of psychological science, for example, using concepts that can be operationally defined in the descriptions of their therapy, including the creation of therapy manuals; quantitatively measuring relevant variables to monitor the therapy process and to assess its outcome; and conducting randomized clinical trials to assess the efficacy of the treatment. Thus, it is particularly within pragmatic behaviorism—that is, Circle 5 of Figure 4.1—that the continuity among the various waves of behavior therapy can be found.

REDISCOVERING THE CASE STUDY

The origins of behavior therapy are replete with the importance of case studies. For example, in the 1920s, J. B. Watson and Rayner (1920) demonstrated the principle of learned fear by showing how the nine-month-old Little Albert became afraid of white rats when their presence was associated with loud noises and how this fear generalized to the sight of other animals, such as rabbits and dogs. A few years later, Mary Cover Jones (1924) clinically demonstrated counterconditioning by helping young Peter, who began with a fear of rabbits, to lose this fear through the experience of being fed in the presence of a rabbit—first placed a few feet away from Peter, then gradually moved closer on subsequent occasions.

From the 1930s to the 1960s, behavior therapy continued to focus on the individual case. Examples are Skinner's (1938) research on the functional analysis of the individual organism in context as the basic unit of research, the case study approach to behavior therapy at the Maudsley Hospital in London (Jones, 1956), and Ullmann and Krasner's (1965) *Case Studies in Behavior Modification*, which persuasively demonstrated the effectiveness of behavior change through particular cases.

In the 1970s, Goldfried and Davison's (1976) groundbreaking book *Clinical Behavior Therapy* connected behavior therapy to the whole psychotherapy tradition. The authors did so by providing detailed case examples throughout and by presenting the extended case illustration of "Ann," a 35-year-old woman with multiple diagnoses.

In the 1980s, we find this illustrative statement by the editor (Nelson, 1983) of the journal, *Behavioral Assessment*, who reminded us of the case-based, idiographic tradition in the behavioral movement:

> [Nomothetic] psychometric criteria . . . are antithetical to behavior theory. . . . Given the assumption that behavior is situation-specific, concurrent validity across different assessment situations should not be predicted. Given the assumption that behavior frequently varies across response systems, concurrent validity across different assessment methods should be not expected. . . . For each client, an assessment process must be delineated that takes into account his or her unique problematic situations and response systems. (pp. 199, 201)

However, in the 1990s, behavior therapy moved away from individual case study toward the group-based, nomothetic direction. Although the applied behavior analysis branch of behavior therapy—following from Skinner's work—continued to have a commitment to experimental work at the individual case level through single-subject research designs (Hayes, Barlow, & Nelson-Gray, 1999), this era saw the rest of behavior therapy move strongly toward large group designs. Federal grants were plentiful for conducting randomized clinical trials of manualized treatment procedures designed to address patients whose problems ideally were delimited to a particular psychopathological category of the *DSM*. In 1995, the Society of Clinical Psychology (Division 12 of the American Psychological Association) used the results of these randomized clinical trials to create its first public list of empirically supported treatments, and in 1998, the theoretical and empirical background of this list was described and discussed in detail in Nathan and Gorman's (2007) book, *A Guide to Treatments That Work*. The Division 12 list thrives today on its website (Society for Clinical Psychology, 2009; http://www.div12.org), and the third edition of the Nathan and Gorman book was published in 2007.

Nevertheless, as clinical experience with manualized therapy has accumulated, in recent years the superiority of exclusively following the nomothetic model has been increasingly questioned, and alternatives have been developed. Consider the following examples.

- Experts have learned in using treatment manuals that they must augment and revise the manuals on the basis of individual patient needs, values, and preferences and that they must address obstacles, such as patients who will not do the homework (Huppert &

Abramowitz, 2003; Rego et al., 2009). For example, the use of metaphors and the nuances of language are reviewed as arenas that go beyond manuals but are crucial in engaging and communicating with patients.

- Some researchers have developed "manualized principles" (Rego et al., 2009) that provide a conceptual guide to therapy but do not dictate a linear sequence of specific "manualized protocols" to be followed, as in earlier work. Two examples are Henggeler et al.'s (1998) manual for working with oppositional youth and Linehan's manual (1993) for working with patients with borderline disorder.

- Seasoned clinicians have discovered the inherent set of trade-offs between highly prescriptive manuals and clinician flexibility in adapting therapy to the individual case. Five examples of these trade-offs (Addis et al., 1999), respectively, include (a) a focus on a general diagnostic category versus on the individual client, (b) a focus on therapeutic techniques versus on the therapeutic relationship, (c) a focus on adherence to a manual versus on integration of the manual with the client's individual situation, (d) a focus on adherence to the manual versus being genuine with the client, and (e) a focus on the therapist believing in what the manual says about positive outcome versus on recognizing that an individual client may not improve as much as the manual says.

- A recent movement toward unified, transdiagnostic treatment manuals—for example, for emotional disorders (Barlow, Allen, & Choate, 2004) and eating disorders (Fairburn, Cooper, & Shafran, 2003). Barlow and colleagues (2004) explained that they developed their unified manual that cuts across emotional disorders in part because of the reality that diagnostically specific, manualized protocols have become overly numerous and complex, logistically restricting effective training and dissemination. They also pointed out that a deepening understanding of the nature of emotional disorders reveals commonalities in etiology and latent structure among them that supersedes their differences. The transdiagnostic treatments are designed to be adaptable to the idiographic complexities of each individual case and thus fall into the category of manualized principles rather than manualized protocols.

A final example of the trend away from a primary focus on manualized treatments for specific diagnoses has been the growing interest in the field in individualized case formulation and treatment planning. In 1989, Jacqueline Persons published a book laying out a case formulation approach in CBT, drawing on both first- and second-wave theory. For the next 19 years, this book was a highly popular seller and was recently published in a new, revised version (2008), integrating third-wave therapies. Moreover, Persons is now the editor of a book series on individualized evidence-based treatments, with eight titles as of November 2008, including first-, second-, and third-wave therapies.

In Person's (1989) book, she discusses the dialectic of nomothetic, manualized treatment versus idiographic, individualized formulation and treatment planning as follows:

> I struggle in this book to rely on the empirically supported therapies (ESTs). . . . The EST protocol assumes that the mechanisms causing and maintaining the symptoms of the patient who is being treated at that moment match the mechanisms that underpin the design of protocol. The protocol also assumes that the patient's goal is to treat the DSM disorder targeted by the protocol. These assumptions often appear to be incorrect.
>
> My solution to these problems, described in detail in this book, is to recommend that clinicians examine the EST protocols to understand the formulations that underpin them and how the interventions in the protocol flow out of the formulations. Then they can use that information (not the step-by-step procedures of the protocol itself) to guide their work. To facilitate those tasks, this book includes three chapters that lay out in detail the principles of the three major groups of models that underpin most ESTs: [second-wave] cognitive models (especially Beck's theory), [first wave] learning theories, and [third wave] basic models of emotion. The approach to cognitive-behavior therapy described here is [designed to be] . . . responsive to the situation at hand, guided by clear thinking, and evidence based. (p. vii)

As behavior therapists refocus on the importance of integrating nomothetic treatment manuals with individualized treatments, the field has rediscovered its earlier interest in nonexperimental case studies. This is reflected in the recent establishment of two peer-reviewed journals publishing cases studies of this type, the print journal *Clinical Case Studies* (CSS; Hersen, 2002) and the online, open-access journal *Pragmatic Case Studies in Psychotherapy* (PCSP; Fishman, 2005; http://pcsp.libraries.rutgers.edu). Although both journals are multitheoretical, it is important to note that both were started by editors associated with behavior therapy, both have prominent behavior therapy researchers and practitioners on their editorial boards, and both have published a substantial number of behavior therapy case studies from all three waves.

CONCLUSION

Behavior therapy started in the dog laboratory of Pavlov, the cat laboratory of Thorndike, and later the pigeon laboratory of Skinner. The discipline then developed by applying the respondent and operant learning principles that emerged from these laboratories to complex human behaviors. During this application process, researchers and practitioners retained from the experience of the animal laboratory a commitment to the experimental method, including the operational definition of key variables, quantification, and reliable observation of animal and then human behavior. These aspects of what we have called pragmatic behaviorism have continued.

At the same time, behavior therapy has incorporated into its first wave of learning theory the cognitive theory that emerged from the cognitive revolution, forming the field's second wave. In addition, a third wave has recently developed, focusing on accepting emotional experience through mindfulness, which emerged by linking cognition and emotional processes back to a first-wave concern with how internal experience functionally relates to the objective environment. Along the way, behavior therapy has extended itself from individual, to group, to community, to business settings; it has diversified its epistemology from a positivist base to include a pragmatic perspective; and it has developed both nomothetic, manualized and idiographic, case-based intervention models.

We will not be surprised to see additional theoretical waves and new methodological developments in the future. However, we believe the core of behavior therapy will endure in a commitment to theory that is scholarly, logically clear, directly linked to data, and primarily rooted in the interactional worldview (see Figure 4.1); to therapy principles and procedures that are evidence-based; to measurement methods designed to ensure accountability; and to a focus on outcomes that result in concrete improvement in patients' lives.

REFERENCES

Addis, M. E., Hatgis, C., Soysa, C. K., Zaslavsky, I., & Bourne, L. S. (1999). The dialectics of manual-based treatment. *The Behavior Therapist, 22,* 130–132.

Altman, I., & Rogoff, B. (1987). World views in psychology: Trait, interactional, organismic, and transactional perspectives. In D. Stokols & I. Altman (Eds.), *Handbook of environmental psychology* (pp. 7–40). New York, NY: Wiley.

American Psychological Association, Society of Clinical Psychology, Division 12 (2008). Website on research-supported psychological treatments. Retrieved from http://www.psychology.sunysb.edu/eklonsky-/division12/index.html

Arch, J. J., & Craske, M. G. (2008). Acceptance and commitment therapy and cognitive behavioral therapy for anxiety disorders: Different treatments, similar mechanisms? *Clinical Psychology: Science and Practice, 15*, 263–279.

Austin, J., & Carr, J. E. (Eds.). (2000). *Handbook of applied behavior analysis*. Reno, NV: Context Press.

Azrin, N. H. (1977). A strategy for applied research: Learning based but outcome oriented. *American Psychologist, 30*, 469–485.

Baars, B. J. (1986). *The cognitive revolution in psychology*. New York, NY: Guilford Press.

Bandura, A. (1969). *Principles of behavior modification*. New York, NY: Holt, Rinehart & Winston.

Bandura, A. (1982). Self-efficacy mechanisms in human agency. *American Psychologist, 37*, 122–147. doi:10.1037/0003-066X.37.2.122

Barlow, D. H., Allen, L. B., & Choate, M. L. (2004). Towards a unified treatment for emotional disorders. *Behavior Therapy, 35*, 205–230. doi:10.1016/S0005-7894(04)80036-4

Baucom, D. H., Epstein, N. B., LaTaillade, J. J, & Kirby, J. S. (2008). Cognitive–behavioral couple therapy. In A. S. Gurman (Ed)., *Clinical handbook of couple therapy* (4th ed., pp. 31–72. New York, NY: Guilford Press.

Beck, A. T. (1963). Thinking and depression. *Archives of General Psychiatry, 9*, 324–333.

Beck, A. T., Rush, A. J., Shaw, B. F., & Emery, G. (1979). *Cognitive therapy of depression*. New York, NY: Guilford Press.

Brinkmeyer, M. Y., & Eyberg, S. M. (2003). Parent–child interaction therapy for oppositional children. In A. E. Kazdin & J. R. Weisz (Eds.), *Evidence-based psychotherapies for children and adolescents* (pp. 204–223). New York, NY: Guilford Press.

Cautela, J. R. (1970). Covert reinforcement. *Behavior Therapy, 1*, 33–50. doi:10.1016/S0005-7894(70)80055-7

Cloud, J. (2006). Happiness isn't normal—What's the best form of psychotherapy? How can you overcome sadness? Controversial psychologist Steven Hayes has an answer: embrace the pain. *Time Magazine*. Retrieved fromhttp://www.time.com/time/magazine/article/0,9171,1156613,00.html

Davison, G. C., & Neale, J. M. (1990). *Abnormal psychology* (5th ed.). New York, NY: Wiley.

Dollard, J., & Miller, N. E. (1950). *Personality and psychotherapy*. New York, NY: McGraw-Hill.

Dunlap, K. (1972). *Habits: Their making and unmaking*. New York, NY: Liveright. Original work published 1932.

Ellis, A. (1962). *Reason and emotion in psychotherapy*. New York, NY: Lyle Stuart.

Erwin, E. (1978). *Behavior therapy: Scientific, philosophical, and moral foundations*. New York, NY: Cambridge University Press.

Eysenck, H. J. (1952). The effects of psychotherapy: An evaluation. *Journal of Consulting Psychology, 16*, 319–324. doi:10.1037/h0063633

Eysenck, H. J. (1959). Learning theory and behaviour therapy. *The Journal of Mental Science, 195*, 61–75.

Eysenck, H. J. (Ed.). (1960). *Handbook of abnormal psychology: An experimental approach*. London, England: Pitman.

Eysenck, H. J. (Ed.). (1964). *Experiments in behavior therapy: Readings in modern methods of treating mental disorders derived from learning theory*. Elmsford, NY: Pergamon Press.

Eysenck, H. J. (1990). *Rebel with a cause*. London, England: W. H. Allen.

Fairburn, C. G., Cooper, Z., & Shafran, R. (2003). Cognitive behaviour therapy for eating disorders: A "transdiagnostic" theory and treatment. *Behaviour Research and Therapy, 41*, 509–528. doi:10.1016/S0005-7967(02)00088-8

Fishman, D. B. (1988). Pragmatic behaviorism: Saving and nurturing the baby. In D. B. Fishman, F. Rotgers, & C. M. Franks (Eds.), *Paradigms in behavior therapy: Present and promise* (pp. 254–293). New York, NY: Springer.

Fishman, D. B. (1999). *The case for pragmatic psychology.* New York, NY: NYU Press.

Fishman, D. B. (2005). Editor's introduction to PCSP—from single case to database: A new method for enhancing psychotherapy practice. *Pragmatic case studies in psychotherapy, 1*, 1–50. Retrieved from http://hdl.rutgers.edu/1782.1/pcsp_journal

Fishman, D. B., & Franks, C. M. (1992). Evolution and differentiation within behavior therapy: A theoretical and epistemological review. In D. K. Freedheim (Ed.), *History of psychotherapy: A century of change* (pp. 159–196). Washington, DC: American Psychological Association.

Fishman, D. B., Rotgers, F., & Franks, C. M. (Eds.). (1988). *Paradigms in behavior therapy: Present and promise.* New York, NY: Springer.

Franks, C. M. (1987). Behavior therapy and AABT: Personal recollections, conceptions, and misconceptions. *The Behavior Therapist, 10*, 171–174.

Franks, C. M. (1990). Behavior therapy: An overview. In C. M. Franks, G. T. Wilson, P. C. Kendall, & J. P. Foreyt (Eds.), *Review of behavior therapy: Theory and practice* (Vol. 12, pp. 1–43). New York, NY: Guilford Press.

Freud, S. (1924). Character and anal eroticism. In *Collected papers: II.* London, England: Institute of Psychoanalysis and Hogarth Press.

Gergen, K. J. (1985). The social constructionist movement in modern psychology. *American Psychologist, 40*, 266–275. doi:10.1037/0003-066X.40.3.266

Gilbert, T. F. (1978). *Human competence: Engineering worthy performance.* New York, NY: McGraw-Hill.

Goldfried, M. R., & Davison, G. C. (1976). *Clinical behavior therapy.* New York, NY: Holt, Rinehart & Winston.

New York, NY:Hayes, S. C. (2004). Acceptance and commitment therapy, relational frame theory, and the third wave of behavioral and cognitive therapies. *Behavior Therapy, 35*, 639–665. doi:10.1016/S0005–7894(04)80013–3

Hayes, S. C. (2005). *Get out of your mind & into your life.* Oakland, CA: New Harbinger.

Hayes, S. C. (2008). Climbing our hills: A beginning conversation of the comparison of acceptance and commitment therapy and traditional cognitive behavioral therapy. *Clinical Psychology: Science and Practice, 15*, 286–295.

Hayes, S. C., Barlow, D. H., & Nelson-Gray, R. O. (1999). *The scientist practitioner: Research and accountability in the age of managed care.* Boston, MA: Allyn and Bacon.

Hayes, S. C., Luoma, J. B., Bond, F. W., Masuda, A., & Lillis, J. (2006). Acceptance and commitment therapy: Model, processes and outcomes. *Behaviour Research and Therapy, 44*, 1–25. Medline doi:10.1016/j.brat.2005.06.006

Hayes, S. C., Masuda, A., Bissett, R., Luoma, J., & Guerrero, L. F. (2004). DBT, FAP, and ACT: How empirically oriented are the new behavior therapy technologies? *Behavior Therapy, 35*, 35–54. doi:10.1016/S0005–7894(04)80003-0

Heimberg, R. G., & Ritter, M. R. (2008). Cognitive behavioral therapy and acceptance and commitment therapy for the anxiety disorders: Two approaches with much to offer. *Clinical Psychology: Science and Practice, 15*, 296–298.

Henggeler, S. W., Schoenwald, S. K., Borduin, C. M., Rowland, M. D., & Cunningham, P. B. (1998). *Multisystemic treatment of antisocial behavior in children and adolescents.* New York, NY: Guilford Press.

Hersen, M. (2002). Rationale for *Clinical Case Studies*: An editorial. *Clinical Case Studies, 1*, 3–5. doi:10.1177/1534650102001001001

Hoffman, S. G. (2008). Acceptance and commitment therapy: New wave or Morita therapy? *Clinical Psychology: Science and Practice, 15*, 280–285.

Huppert, J. D., & Abramowitz, J. S. (2003). Special series—Going beyond the manual: Insights from experienced clinicians. *Cognitive and Behavioral Practice, 10*, 1–2. doi:10.1016/S1077-7229(03)80002-0

ISI Web of Knowledge. (2009). Retrieved from http://www.isiwebofknowledge.com

Jacobson, E. (1938). *Progressive relaxation* (2nd ed.). Chicago, IL: University of Chicago Press.

Jones, H. S. (1956). The application of conditioning and learning techniques to the treatment of a psychiatric patient. *Journal of Abnormal and Social Psychology, 52*, 414–419.

Jones, M. C. (1924). A laboratory study of fear: The case of Peter. *Psychological Seminar, 31*, 308–315.

Kanfer, F. H., & Schefft, B. K. (1988). *Guiding the process of therapeutic change.* Champaign, IL: Research Press.

Kendall, P. C., & Bemis, K. M. (1983). Thought and action in psychotherapy: The cognitive behavioral approaches. In M. Hersen, A. E. Kazdin, & A. S. Bellak (Eds.), *The clinical psychology handbook* (pp. 565–592). Elmsford, NY: Pergamon Press.

Kimble, G. A. (1985). Conditioning and learning. In S. Koch & D. E. Leary (Eds.), *A century of psychological science* (pp. 284–321). New York, NY: McGraw-Hill.

Kohlenberg, R. J., & Tsai, M. (1991). *Functional analytic psychotherapy: Creating intense and curative therapeutic relationships.* New York, NY: Plenum.

Krasner, L. (1971). Behavior therapy. In P. H. Mussen (Ed.), *Annual Review of Psychology* (Vol. 22, pp. 483–532). Palo Alto, CA: Annual Reviews.

Krasner, L. (1982). Behavior therapy: On roots, contexts, and growth. In G. T. Wilson & C. M. Franks (Eds.), *Contemporary behavior therapy: Conceptual and empirical foundations* (pp. 11–62). New York, NY: Guilford Press.

Kuhn, T. S. (1962). *The structure of scientific revolutions.* Chicago, IL: University of Chicago Press.

Lazarus, A. A. (1958). New methods in psychotherapy: A case study. *South African Medical Journal, 32*, 600–664.

Lazarus, A. A. (1959). The elimination of children's phobias by deconditioning. *Medical Proceedings. Mediese Bydraes, 5*, 261–265.

Lazarus, A. A. (1961). Group therapy of phobic disorders by systematic desensitization. *Journal of Abnormal and Social Psychology, 63*, 504–510. doi:10.1037/h0043315

Liddell, H. S. (1958). A biological basis for psychopathology. In P. H. Hoch & J. Zubin (Eds.), *Problems of addiction and habituation* (pp. 183–196). New York, NY: Grune & Stratton.

Linehan, M. M. (1993). *Cognitive-behavioral treatment of borderline personality disorder: The dialectics of effective treatment.* New York, NY: Guilford Press.

Mahoney, M. J. (1974). *Cognition and behavior modification.* Cambridge, MA: Ballinger.

Martell, C. R., Addis, M. E., & Jacobson, N. S. (2001). *Depression in context: Strategies for guided action.* New York, NY: Norton.

Masserman, J. M. (1943). *Behavior and neurosis.* Chicago, IL: University of Chicago Press.

McCrae, R. R., & Costa, P. T., Jr. (2003). *Personality in adulthood: A five-factor theory perspective* (2nd ed.). New York, NY: Guilford Press.

McCullough, J. P., Jr. (2000). *Treatment for chronic depression: Cognitive behavioral analysis system of psychotherapy (CBASP).* New York, NY: Guilford Press.

Messer, S. B., Sass, L. A., & Woolfolk, R. L. (Eds.). (1988). *Hermeneutics and psychological theory.* New Brunswick, NJ: Rutgers University Press.

Miller, J. G. (1978). *Living systems.* New York, NY: McGraw-Hill.

Minuchin, S. (1974). *Families and family therapy*. Cambridge, MA: Harvard University Press.

Mowrer, O. H., & Mowrer, W. M. (1938). Enuresis: A method for its study and treatment. *American Journal of Orthopsychiatry, 8,* 436–459.

Nathan, P. E., & Gorman, J. M. (Eds.). (2007). *A guide to treatments that work* (3rd ed.). New York, NY: Oxford University Press.

Nelson, R. O. (1983). Behavioral assessment: Past, present, and future. *Behavioral Assessment, 5,* 195–206.

O'Leary, K. D., & Wilson, G. T. (1987). *Behavior therapy: Application and outcome*. Englewood Cliffs, NJ: Prentice Hall.

Patton, M. Q. (2002). *Qualitative research & evaluation methods* (3rd ed.). Thousand Oaks, CA: Sage.

Patton, M. Q. (2008). *Utilization-focused evaluation* (4th ed.). Thousand Oaks, CA: Sage.

Paul, G. L., & Lenz, R. J. (1977). *Psychosocial treatment of chronic mental patients: Milieu versus social-learning programs*. Cambridge, MA: Harvard University Press.

Persons, J. B. (1989). *Cognitive therapy in practice: A case formulation approach*. New York, NY: Norton.

Persons, J. B. (2008). *The case formulation approach to cognitive-behavior therapy*. New York, NY: Guilford Press.

Peterson, D. R. (1968). *The clinical study of social behavior*. New York, NY: Appleton-Century-Crofts.

Polkinghorne, D. E. (1992). Postmodern epistemology of practice. In S. Kvale (Ed.), *Psychology and postmodernism* (pp. 146–165). Thousand Oaks, CA: Sage.

Rego, S. A., Barlow, D. H., McCrady, B. S., Persons, J. B., Hildebrandt, T. B., & McHugh, R. K. (2009). Implementing empirically supported treatments in real-world clinical settings: Your questions answered! *The Behavior Therapist, 32,* 52–58.

Rhoades, L. J. (1981). *Treating and assessing the chronically mentally ill: The pioneering research of Gordon L. Paul*. Rockville, MD: U.S. Department of Health and Human Services, Division of Scientific and Public Information.

Robin, A. L., & Foster, S. L. (2002). *Negotiating parent–adolescent conflict: A behavioral-family systems approach*. New York, NY: Guilford Press.

New York, NY:Segal, Z. V., Williams, J. M. G., & Teasdale, J. D. (2002). *Mindfulness-based cognitive therapy for depression: A new approach to preventing relapse*. New York, NY: Guilford Press.

Silverstein, S. M., Hatashita-Wong, M., Wilkniss, S., Bloch, A., Smith, T., Savitz, A., et al. (2006). Behavioral rehabilitation of the "treatment-refractory" schizophrenia patient: Conceptual foundations, interventions, and outcome data. *Psychological Services, 3,* 145–169. doi:10.1037/1541–1559.3.3.145

Skinner, B. F. (1938). *The behavior of organisms: An experimental analysis*. Englewood Cliffs, NJ: Prentice-Hall.

Skinner, B. F. (1948). *Walden two*. New York, NY: Macmillan.

Spiegler, M. D. (1983). *Contemporary behavior therapy*. Palo Alto, CA: Mayfield.

Spiegler, M. D., & Guevremont, D. C. (2003). *Contemporary behavior therapy* (4th ed.). Belmont, CA: Thomson-Wadsworth

Staats, A. W. (1975). *Social behaviorism*. Homewood, IL: Dorsey Press.

Staats, A. W. (1988). Paradigmatic behaviorism, unified positivism, and paradigmatic behavior therapy. In D. B. Fishman, F. Rotgers, & C. M. Franks (Eds.), *Paradigms in behavior therapy: Present and promise* (pp. 211–253). New York, NY: Springer.

Staats, A. W. (2005). A road to, and philosophy of, unification. In R. J. Sternberg (Ed.), *Unity in psychology: Possibility or pipedream?* (pp. 159–177). Washington, DC: American Psychological Association.

Thorndike, E. L. (1911). *Animal intelligence*. New York, NY: Macmillan.

Ullmann, L. P., & Krasner, L. (Eds.). (1965). *Case studies in behavior modification*. New York, NY: Holt, Rinehart & Winston.

Watson, J. B. (1913). Psychology as the behaviorist views it. *Psychological Review, 20*, 158–177. doi:10.1037/h0074428

Watson, J. B. (1924). *Behaviorism*. Chicago, IL: The People's Institute.

Wilson, G. T., & Franks, C. M. (Eds.). (1982). *Contemporary behavior therapy: Conceptual and empirical foundations*. New York, NY: Guilford Press.

Wilson, G. T., & O'Leary, K. D. (1980). *Principles of behavior therapy*. Englewood Cliffs, NJ: Prentice Hall.

Wolpe, J. (1952). Experimental neuroses as learned behavior. *The British Journal of Psychology, 43*, 243–268.

Wolpe, J. (1958). *Psychotherapy by reciprocal inhibition*. Stanford, CA: Stanford University Press.

Woolfolk, R. L., & Richardson, F. C. (1984). Behavior therapy and the ideology of modernity. *American Psychologist, 39*, 777–786. doi:10.1037/0003-066X.39.7.777

Zogby International. (2008). http://www.zogby.com

5

HUMANISTIC AND EXPERIENTIAL THEORIES OF PSYCHOTHERAPY

JEANNE C. WATSON, RHONDA N. GOLDMAN,
AND LESLIE S. GREENBERG

Humanistic and experiential psychotherapies coalesced around the humanistic movement that emerged in the United States and Europe in the 1950s and 1960s. A number of psychologists, including Maslow, Rogers, Moustakas, and May, dissatisfied with the dominant paradigm, began to critique the values, assumptions, and methods of psychological practices and thought (Misiak & Sexton, 1973). These writers were at odds with the nomothetic and reductionistic stance of the natural sciences being applied to the study of human experience. They called for a more human science that would incorporate naturalistic methods and description. There was also a growing concern that psychology was focusing on behavior and the observable dimensions of human experience as opposed to the inner, subjective processes that humanistic psychologists saw as core to human functioning.

The theories of psychotherapy that coalesced around this movement include client-centered, experiential, existential, and gestalt. These psychotherapies are based on shared values and principles that differentiate them from other major approaches, including psychodynamic, cognitive–behavioral, and family systems.

Although there is much variability within and across humanistic approaches, they share a number of fundamental assumptions about human functioning: first, a phenomenological perspective with an emphasis on subjective experiencing; second, a belief in the actualizing or growth tendency; third, a view of the person as an agent capable of self-awareness, self-determination and choice; and fourth, a style of interpersonal relating that respects and values the other while struggling to fully understand the other's experience.

One of the most important tenets of humanistic–experiential psychotherapies is the emphasis placed on humans' phenomenological experience. *Phenomenology* is the study of consciousness from a first-person perspective and the ability to think about prereflective experience and bring it into conscious awareness. It is the attempt to understand people's subjective worldviews, including their feelings, perceptions, values, and construals.

A second major assumption underlying humanistic approaches is a belief in a growth tendency. Human beings are capable of evolving and striving toward growth and development. They are not concerned with the maintenance of stability only but dream and aspire to different ways of being. According to this view, human beings are forward-looking, influenced by their goals for the future as well as the present moment and their past experiences. Carl Rogers saw the actualizing tendency as a biological imperative, with all systems moving toward greater and greater complexity. Others saw it as more than a biological tendency operating within the individual's consciousness and awareness; they saw it as a directional tendency that places the self at the center in a more or less intentional search for meaning (Tageson, 1982).

The third assumption sees human beings as self-reflective agents with the capacity to symbolize and use language so that they can reflect on experience and choose between different courses of action. The capacity to be self-reflective distinguishes humans from other sentient beings and provides them with the capacity to grow and change. People are beings who symbolize experiences and for whom things matter and have significance (Taylor, 1990). People become alerted to the significance and importance of things by their feelings and desires. Through their feelings, people come to understand the impact of their experiences, gain an understanding of how they need to respond, and communicate with others (Greenberg, Rice, & Elliott, 1993; Rogers, 1959; Taylor, 1990; Watson & Greenberg, 1996). According to this view, people are agents who have the capacity to choose among competing wishes, desires, needs, and values. Taylor (1990) referred to this capacity to choose as *second-order valuing*: a type of reflection that is more than just understanding and is based on making choices that are consistent with a person's deepest values and desires. The capacity for self-reflection is fostered in humanistic psychotherapy as clients come to know their feelings, desires, values, and assumptions and develop their capacity to choose among these competing experiences to live in ways that are more personally meaningful and fulfilling (Watson & Greenberg, 1996).

The term *agent* refers to the human capacity for choice and self-determination as well as the ability to represent experience symbolically and to reflect on that experience in terms of higher order values and goals (Fagan, 1974; May & Yalom, 1989; Perls, 1973; Taylor, 1990; Tiryakian, 1962). There is a dynamic interaction between language and other forms of symbolic expression and feelings such that as each is formed it influences the other in an ongoing dialectic (Gendlin, 1962; 1984; Taylor, 1990; Watson & Greenberg, 1996). Moreover, there are two ways of evaluating experience: the first is in accord with one's immediate needs and desires, and the second is in accord with another value framework that has the capacity to override the more immediate concerns and evaluate them in terms of higher order values (Taylor, 1990). This dual framework for evaluating experiences provides humans with the capacity to choose between alternative courses of action (Watson & Greenberg, 1996).

The fourth assumption concerns the centrality of relationship. Humanistic psychotherapists believe in the uniqueness and value of every human being and emphasize respect and caring for each person's subjective experience. Sharing in the private world of another is regarded as a privilege that can potentially turn every encounter into an "I–Thou" exchange as opposed to one between a subject and object (Buber, 1957; Rogers 1959). Humanistic therapists struggle to understand the subjective worldview of the other without judgment and to treat each person with deep respect and caring. Given their commitment to respecting the other, humanistic therapists are committed to developing authentic, egalitarian relationships.

In this chapter, we trace the history of four psychotherapies that fall under the humanistic umbrella: client-centered or person-centered, experiential, gestalt, and existential. All four share the basic assumptions outlined previously. We provide an overview of the major proponents of each approach, followed by a brief explication of the humanistic and experiential perspective of the therapeutic process, including the client–clinician relationship. We conclude with several recent developments that have contributed to the continuation of humanistic and experiential therapies.

CLIENT-CENTERED THERAPY

Carl Rogers was the developer and leading proponent of the person-centered approach in the United States. He was born on January 8, 1902, in Oak Park, a suburb of Chicago. His father was a civil engineer and his mother a homemaker. Carl was the fourth of six children and received a strict religious education. Initially he thought he would study agriculture, but then he changed to religion and spent 2 years at Union Theological Seminary in New

York City. However, after a trip to China when he was 20, he began to question his faith and decided to transfer to Columbia Teachers College and pursue a degree in clinical psychology under the supervision of Goodwin Watson, an expert in group leadership training. Rogers received training in psychological assessment and psychoanalytic psychotherapy during his internship at the Institute for Child Guidance. His thinking was influenced by the ideas of John Dewey, and his training had left him with a strong commitment to the principles and methods of scientific research (Kirschenbaum, 2007; Rice & Greenberg, 1992).

When he finished graduate school, Rogers began working at the Society for the Prevention of Cruelty to Children, in Rochester, New York, where he was appointed director in 1930. While at the agency he became acquainted with the ideas of psychoanalyst Otto Rank. Rank's emphasis on the here and now and the healing power of the therapeutic relationship, as well as the constructive forces within the individual, was consonant with Rogers's own direction and thinking about psychotherapy. In 1939, Rogers published his first book, *The Clinical Treatment of the Problem Child.* The following year he was offered a faculty position at Ohio State University, where he taught until 1944. It was during his period at Ohio State that Rogers and his colleagues began to study psychotherapy audiotapes and transcripts intensively to understand the process of psychotherapy more fully. Rogers was a pioneer with respect to audiotaping psychotherapy sessions (Kirschenbaum, 2007; Rogers, 1961). The product of these intensive and inductive attempts to understand psychotherapy and to document the process of change was presented in Rogers's 1942 book *Counselling and Psychotherapy,* which contained a complete transcript of an individual's psychotherapy.

Rogers continued his intensive analysis of psychotherapy when he moved to the University of Chicago in 1945. The primary objective during those years was to reflect on and listen to tapes in order to identify and describe the essential change processes in psychotherapy and to understand how these were facilitated by therapists. Rogers was not so much interested in the content of the sessions or the client's specific insights as he was in the process of change in clients with successful outcome. From this work Rogers developed a number of hypotheses about therapy that he subjected to empirical verification and testing. Much of this work was conducted at the Counseling Center at the University of Chicago.

The work of Rogers and his colleagues had quite an impact on the field, with an entire issue of the *Journal of Consulting Psychology* devoted to the research conducted by Rogers's graduate students in 1949. The work at the University of Chicago resulted in the publication of a third book in 1951, titled *Client-Centered Therapy,* in which he presented his theory of psychotherapy and personality development. This was a major development in his theory and practice that built on his earlier work and laid the foundation for his later work. In recognition of his scholarly work, Rogers was awarded the Distinguished Scientific Contributions to Psychology Award by the American Psychological Association (APA) in 1956.

Kurt Goldstein and Martin Buber were two important influences on Rogers's work (Rice & Greenberg, 1992). Kurt Goldstein, an eminent neuropsychologist at the Institute for Brain Damaged Soldiers in Germany, had been impressed by the capacity of brain-injured soldiers to reorganize their own modes of functioning. Goldstein's observations that people reorganized in constructive ways confirmed Rogers's view of the basic human motivation toward wholeness and his belief in an actualizing tendency, which became a motivational concept in his theoretical system. These ideas of reorganization and growth were revolutionary in the middle of the 20th century; it would be several decades later before the idea of neural plasticity would be fully recognized along with the extraordinary powers of the brain to reorganize and adapt to environmental demands (Doidge, 2007).

The writings of Martin Buber (1957) were brought to Rogers's attention by graduate students in theology at the University of Chicago. Rogers recognized that the I–thou relationship discussed in Buber's writings was exactly the type of relationship and experience that emerged in good psychotherapy. In 1957, Rogers moved to the University of Wisconsin and began an extensive research project on the processes and effectiveness of client-centered therapy with hospitalized patients diagnosed with schizophrenia (Rogers, Gendlin, Kiesler & Truax, 1967).

A number of problems developed during the course of the research, including tension among the collaborators; research data being stolen; and research participants who, after benefiting from therapy, refused to complete the final set of outcome measures because they were a painful reminder of their experience in hospital (Kirschenbaum, 2007). As a result of these difficulties it took 10 years for the book about the study to be published. The findings were mixed, though there was support for the relationship between good outcome and therapist congruence and empathy. Moreover, there was evidence to suggest that the absence of the two conditions was related to relapse.

In 1964, Rogers moved to California, first to the Western Behavioral Sciences Institute and then to the Center for the Studies of the Person. During these years he moved away from focusing on individual therapy and became interested in working with groups and with a wide range of social and political challenges, including teaching, international relations, conflict resolution, and the prevention of nuclear war. It was during this period that he decided client-centered therapy should be renamed *person-centered approach*. Rogers's influence on the field was well recognized by his fellow psychologists, and in 1972 he received the APA Award for Distinguished Contributions to Professional Practice.

EXPERIENTIAL PSYCHOTHERAPIES

Experiential psychotherapy emphasizes the role of experiencing or emotional processing in the change process. There are a number of different variants of experiential therapy, including focusing oriented psychotherapy developed by Eugene Gendlin; process experiential psychotherapy, an emotion-focused approach for individuals developed by Greenberg, Rice, and Elliott; the symbolic–experiential therapy of Carl Whitaker; and the experiential psychotherapy of Alvin Mahrer.

Rogers placed much value on what he had learned from graduate students and colleagues. One very important influence at the University of Chicago was Eugene Gendlin, a graduate student and later a colleague, who formulated the concept of *experiencing* (Gendlin, 1962). In contrast to those who emphasized nondirectiveness with clients, experiential clinicians try to guide clients' process while retaining the basic tenets of the person-centered tradition. Eugene Gendlin was born in Vienna, Austria, on December 25, 1926. He and his family fled Austria in the 1930s after Hitler's rise to power. His family moved to Holland and later to the United States, where Gendlin attended school. The young Gendlin learned to appreciate and value the wisdom of the body by watching his father weigh different escape routes and devise plans to keep his young family safe during their flight from Austria. His desire to explicate and share this way of knowing with others would later become Gendlin's lifework. Gendlin pursued a career in philosophy and received his doctorate in philosophy at the University of Chicago in 1958. Five years later, in 1963, he returned to teach at the University of Chicago in the Department of Philosophy, where he remained until he retired in 1995. Subsequently, he set up the Focusing Institute (www.focusing.org/gendlin/) with his wife, Marion Hendricks. The mandate of the Institute is to share focusing with the population at large.

Another important figure to emerge from Rogers's influence at the University of Chicago was Laura Rice, who continued to develop the idea of promoting clients' experiencing in the session and broaden Rogers's therapeutic approach. In this respect, Rice represented both a post-Rogers person-centered therapist and an early experiential therapist. Laura Rice was born in 1920 in New England to parents of Puritan descent. Both parents were intellectuals; her father was a lawyer, and her mother home-schooled their children to ensure that they received a quality education. Rice was in her early teens before she went to a public school with other children her own age. She regretted that she had been schooled at home, as it left her with a sense of being out of step with her peers (Watson & Wiseman, in press). At university Rice initially studied botany but switched to psychology. Prior to her doctoral studies, Rice worked in Human Resources for an airline company, conducting aptitude and cognitive assessments for pilots and other employees. In 1951, she returned to the University of Chicago to pursue her doctoral studies because of the presence of Carl Rogers and its strong research focus (Rice, 1992). After graduating, Rice worked at the Counseling Center at the University of Chicago before moving to a faculty position in the newly formed Department of Psychology at York University in Toronto, Canada. There she held a dual appointment with the Department of Psychology and the University Counselling and Development Centre, combining teaching, research, and clinical work. She died in 2004 at the age of 84. Her contribution to psychotherapy research was recognized by her colleagues when she was awarded the Senior Research Career Award by the International Society for Psychotherapy Research (Watson & Wiseman, in press).

Rice, with her graduate student and later colleague Leslie Greenberg, developed a research paradigm called *task analysis* to help describe and better understand clients' processes in therapy. While Rice was a firm adherent of Rogers's client-centered therapy, Greenberg was integrating her influence with that of gestalt therapists. Together, in their book *Patterns of Change*, they articulated a method of examining micro-change events in psychotherapy in order to explicitly state the steps that clients need to engage in to resolve problematic issues. They each developed models of specific in-session change processes, including systematic evocative unfolding for problematic reactions, two-chair dialogues, and empty-chair dialogues that they subjected to empirical testing and verification (Greenberg, 1979; 1980; 1983; Greenberg & Webster, 1982; Rice & Greenberg, 1984). Subsequently, they incorporated their ideas and techniques to form process experiential psychotherapy, an emotion-focused approach to psychotherapy (Greenberg et al., 1993).

Carl Whitaker was one of the first to use the term *experiential therapy* (Whitaker & Malone, 1953; 1969). He emphasized the nonrational aspects of human experience and saw change in psychotherapy as emanating from patients' feelings as opposed to their intellects. Whitaker was born on February 20, 1912, in Raymondville, New York. He received an MD and an MA from Syracuse University in 1936 and 1941, respectively. After completing his residency at Syracuse, he worked with the Veterans Administration Hospital in Georgia from 1945 to 1955. While there, he joined the faculty at Emory University, becoming a full professor in 1947; subsequently, he was appointed head of psychiatry at the University of Wisconsin. Like other experiential psychotherapists, Whitaker emphasized the importance of the therapeutic relationship in facilitating change through the resolution of transference and countertransference reactions, with change occurring as a result of new experiences either with the therapist or in the outside world. He saw healthy functioning as an increasing capacity to choose, reflecting sincerity and congruence (Whitaker & Malone, 1969).

Another important figure in the experiential movement was Alvin Mahrer, a professor emeritus at Ottawa University in Canada. Mahrer graduated from Ohio State University in 1954 and later held positions at Miami University, the University of Waterloo, and the University of Ottawa, Canada. In the 1970s he began to develop his variant of experiential psychotherapy. Mahrer (1983, 1986, 1998) conceives of the person in terms of potentials for experiencing, which are the building blocks of personality. The primary goal in psychotherapy is to assist the person to become aware of hidden potentials and encourage his or her expression so that new ways of experiencing can occur (Mahrer, 1998). Mahrer characterizes experiential psychotherapy as comprising a series of five steps: first, a focus on bodily experience; second, a carrying forward of the experience by means of symbolization and expression; third, developing an awareness of deeper levels of experience through the therapeutic relationship; fourth, becoming immersed in the deeper experience; and fifth, incorporating the new experience into current behavior in the world outside of therapy (Mahrer, 1983). He sees experiential psychotherapists as focusing on and facilitating the role of experiencing in the change process.

The concept of experiencing and the role of affect are central to the change process in experiential psychotherapy. Although all proponents emphasize the importance of the therapeutic relationship, their interventions are also directed toward evoking and facilitating clients' access to their inner experience within the session, to evoke alternative experiential states. An important influence on the development of experiential psychotherapy was Fritz Perls, the father of gestalt therapy.

GESTALT THERAPY

The early development of gestalt therapy emphasized personal experience and the experiential episodes understood as the "safe emergencies" of experiments; indeed, half of the content of Perls, Hefferline, and Goodman's 1951 classic *Gestalt Therapy* consists of such stylized experiments. A second theoretical emphasis emerged that emphasized contact between self and other, and ultimately the dialogical relationship between therapist and client (Polster & Polster, 1973). This was followed by an emphasis on field theory (Wheeler, 1991). Gestalt therapy focuses on the individual's experience in the present moment, the therapist–client relationship, and the environmental and social contexts in which these things take place, as well as the self-regulating adjustments people make as a result of the overall situation. Currently, gestalt therapy is based on three fundamental principles: field theory, denoting that everything is relational and in flux; phenomenology, which emphasizes subjective experience and the creation of meaning; and dialogue, involving open engagement between the client and therapist for therapeutic purposes (Resnick, 1995).

Gestalt therapy was cofounded by Fritz and Laura Perls in the 1940s and 1950s. Frederick Perls was born in Germany in 1893. After acquiring medical training, he worked as an assistant to Kurt Goldstein and was strongly influenced by Goldstein's ideas about the organism and the self-actualizing tendency. It was in Germany where he met Laura Perls, who became his wife and collaborator and who introduced him to the work of the Gestalt psychologists, Kaffka, Kohler, and Wertheimer. She herself had also been influenced by the existential writings of Buber and Tillich.

Fritz Perls became a psychoanalyst and was especially influenced by his own analyst, Wilhelm Reich. He was also informed by the works of psychoanalysts Karen Horney and Otto Rank. Like her husband, Laura Perls had trained in psychoanalysis and was interested in the body and movement. Dissatisfied with psychoanalytic dogmatism, and working within a European zeitgeist of phenomenology and existentialism, the Perlses made revisions to psychoanalytic theory (Perls, 1947). In 1951, Perls, Hefferline, and Goodman proposed a new integration of gestalt theory, existential, and analytic approaches in the form of a gestalt therapy, originally called *concentration therapy*.

Two additional influences on the Perlses' thinking were that of the philosopher Friedlander and the South African statesman and prime minister, Jan Smuts. Impressed by Friedlander's (1918) work on holism and Kurt Lewin's (1951) field theory, they came to view the person as part of an organism–environment field with the mind and body as holistic. Zen also has had an influence on the development of gestalt therapy, especially in its later years.

When Fritz Perls arrived in the United States after his stay in South Africa, where he and Laura had fled as war approached in Europe, he actively promoted gestalt therapy. The New York Institute for Gestalt Therapy was formed in the 1950s, and workshops and study groups were established throughout the country. Later Fritz Perls moved to the West Coast in the 1960s and settled for awhile at the Esalen Institute in California, where he established training workshops. Subsequently, he moved to Canada to establish a new institute.

EXISTENTIAL PSYCHOTHERAPY

The other important wing of humanistic psychotherapy is existential psychotherapy, which was introduced to the United States in the late 1940s (Misiak & Sexton, 1973; Rice & Greenberg, 1992). It was after the translation of existential works into English that existential psychotherapies began to emerge in North America.

One of the first people to introduce the ideas was Paul Tillich, who published an article on existential philosophy in 1944. Tillich was a German-born professor of philosophy who taught first at Union Theological Seminary in New York, then at Harvard before moving to the Divinity School at Chicago. It was only later in the 1950s that existential ideas began to take root in psychiatry and psychology under the stewardship of Rollo May and Adrian van Kaam (Misiak & Sexton, 1973). In 1958, May published an edited text, *Existence: A New Dimension in Psychiatry and Psychology*, which presented the ideas of Binswanger and other existential writers (Cooper, 2008).

Existential psychology was rooted in the ideas of European existential philosophy as led by the works of Kierkegaard (1954), Husserl (1977), Sartre (1956), Marcel (1951), Jaspers (1963), and Heidegger (1962). Many early existential psychotherapists were psychoanalytically trained psychiatrists critical of how human nature was portrayed in psychoanalytic theory and seeking an alternative view. Two of the most influential existential approaches were those of Binswanger (1963) and Boss (1963), who rejected Freud's mechanistic and biological view of human functioning. Instead, they adopted Heidegger's concept of *Dasein* (existence) and developed an approach called *Daseinanalyse* or *phenomenological anthropology*, in which they attempted to understand the human sufferer's way of being-in-the-world and emphasized people's capacity for loving relationships as the highest and most original form of human existence. Subsequently, Heidegger denounced Binswanger as having misinterpreted his work and encouraged Medard Boss to spell out the implications of his work and promote Daseinanalyse. Boss dismissed the intellectual contortions required by psychoanalytic thought and replaced it with an analytical practice that was grounded in the phenomenological reality of human existence (Cooper, 2008).

Rollo May, born in 1909 in Ada, Ohio, was primarily responsible for introducing existential therapy to the United States (May, Angel, & Ellenberger, 1958). He had a difficult childhood, during which his parents divorced. May graduated with a degree in English from Michigan State College and taught in Greece for some years. When he returned to the United States, he completed a bachelor's degree in divinity at Union Theological Seminary in 1938 and then went to Teacher's College at Columbia University, graduating with a PhD in clinical psychology in 1949. He was a close friend of Paul Tillich.

May trained as a psychoanalyst at the William Alanson White Institute in New York, where he was influenced by the work of Sullivan, Fromm, and Horney. After practicing as a psychoanalyst he became dissatisfied with some of the methods and underlying assumptions of psychoanalysis. May (1960) focused on what he thought was missing, drawing on the work of existential philosophers, specifically the person's relationship with him or herself. May observed that while the neo-Freudians had incorporated an interpersonal view of the self, they had not developed an account of one's relationship with oneself (Rice & Greenberg, 1992).

May wrote 12 books in which he explored his ideas. His first book, *The Meaning of Anxiety*, published in 1950, was based on his doctoral dissertation and incorporated the ideas of Soren Kierkegaard. In this book, May defined *anxiety* as a threat to some value that the individual holds essential to his or her existence as a person. Three of May's students—James Bugental, Irvin Yalom, and Kirk Schneider—continued his work, each becoming a leading proponent of existential psychotherapy in North America.

James Bugental (1969; 1987) was born on December 25, 1915, the older of two brothers. A formative influence when he was a child was his family's experience of economic hardship which necessitated that they split up. May, his mother, and brother went to live with his grandmother in Michigan while his father went west to California to find work. In 1931, the family was reunited. His education was interrupted by the war, but he eventually graduated with his PhD from Ohio State University where he worked with George Kelly. He had chosen to study at Ohio State because Carl Rogers was there, but on the eve of his entering the program Rogers moved to Chicago. After he graduated, Bugental joined the faculty of the University of California, Los Angeles. He wrote five books and many articles on existential psychotherapy. Bugental's contribution to the development of humanistic existential thought was recognized by the field when he became the first recipient of the APA's Division of Humanistic Psychology's Rollo May Award.

Another existential analyst was Victor Frankl, who developed logotherapy (1963, 1967, 1969), based on some of his experiences as a prisoner in a Nazi death camp at Auschwitz. Frankl's work seems to have developed independently of other existential writers of his day (Cooper, 2008). Two aspects of Frankl's work are particularly important: first, the idea that people can discover the true meaning of a situation through intuitively experiencing the qualities of things; second, that human reality can be divided into body, mind, and spirit. The primary objective in logotherapy was to have clients find the meaning or purpose of their existence in order to overcome feelings of emptiness and despair.

Irvin Yalom is another existential psychotherapist of note. Yalom was born on June 13, 1931, to Russian immigrant parents in Washington, DC. He recalls a secluded childhood; the neighborhood in which he grew up was inhospitable and unsafe for children, so he spent much of his time reading. He decided early on that he would like to be a writer. Subsequently, he trained as a medical doctor with the intent of becoming a psychiatrist. He graduated from the Boston University School of Medicine in 1956 and, after completing his residency requirement, joined the faculty at Stanford University in 1962, where he remained and is currently professor emeritus (Yalom, 2007). Yalom is the author of 11 books, including *The Theory and Practice of Group Psychotherapy* (1995). Disillusioned by the direction of psychiatry with its focus on treating symptoms and developing brief psychotherapy interventions, he turned his attention to writing teaching novels, which have been very well received and widely translated. His second such book, *When Nietzsche Wept*, won the Commonwealth Gold Medal for best fiction in 1993 (Yalom, 2007).

THE THERAPEUTIC PROCESS

Humanistic psychotherapists share a number of therapeutic goals. The most important of them is to facilitate clients' awareness and promote self-reflective agents who exercise choice. They emphasize a phenomenological, discovery-oriented approach in which clients are the experts on their inner experience. To this end, humanistic therapists are encouraged to bracket their assumptions and restrain the tendency to impose solutions and meaning on their clients' experiences. Instead, the core task is to be fully present with their clients so as to understand their experiences from the inside out and to provide clients with a responsive, safe, and empathic therapeutic relationship to facilitate self-exploration, growth, and healing.

Client-Centered

Rogers (1959) viewed pathology as arising from a conflict between the person's organismic experience and internalized conditions of worth. Thus, inner experiencing inconsistent with internalized conditions of worth leads to anxiety and denial of conflicting feelings. Rogers suggested that in an environment of acceptance and empathy clients would let go their conditions of worth and develop more authentic and satisfying ways of being in the world (Rogers, 1959). Rogers saw clients as having the gift of self-awareness as well as a capacity to self-actualize. In a safe, prizing, and empathic atmosphere, clients could know their organismic experience, symbolize it in awareness, and thereby become more congruent both with themselves and others. If therapists could stand back and help clients to explore their experience and symbolize it in awareness, then clients would become aware of their inner and outer reality and how they perceive the world. With this increased clarity and knowledge, clients would then be in a position to make more informed decisions about their lives, to live with greater satisfaction and authenticity.

Three distinct strands in Rogers's thought continue to inform the work of client-centered psychotherapists. The first is the emphasis on nondirectivity and the therapeutic relationship, together with a fundamental trust in the client's capacity to reorganize and develop without any need for direct guidance and input from the therapist; second is the recognition of and emphasis on the concept of clients' experiencing and how therapists can facilitate that process; and third is the focus on groups and the wider social context. These three foci spawned different camps within the person-centered tradition, with each one weighting the importance of these ideas in slightly different configurations. We will discuss the first two as they relate to psychotherapy.

Nondirectivity and the Relationship

Rogers (1957) emphasized the role of the therapeutic relationship in facilitating clients' changes in psychotherapy. He posited six necessary and sufficient conditions for personality change to occur. These conditions required the therapist and client to be in contact and the therapist to create a warm, safe, nnonjudgmental environment and to respond showing a deep understanding of the client's emotional experience. Therapists were free to set limits on behavior, but not on attitudes and feelings, and should restrain themselves from blaming, interpreting, reassuring, or persuading clients (Wyatt, 2001). Researchers and clinicians from diverse orientations have come to accept that the relationship conditions are essential for effective psychotherapy; however, only a few have argued that the Rogerian facilitative conditions are both necessary and sufficient for change (Bozarth, 1990; Brodley, 1990; Lambert & Barley, 2002; Norcross, 2002; Wyatt, 2001).

Initially, Rogers (1951, 1975) promoted the use of reflections to mirror clients' experience and make their outer and inner worlds more visible and hold their views up for self-reflection. He suggested that by providing the optimal conditions to enable clients to engage in deep reflection they would be able to challenge conditions of worth and resolve incongruities between their own organismic valuing process and introjected views of how they should feel and behave (Rogers, 1951). This was seen as an important change mechanism because it provided the antidote to clients' internalized conditions of worth and mistrust of their own inner experience.

Rogers saw people as symbolizing their experience and reflecting on it to construct meaning, plan, learn, and choose. When functioning well, people can revise their perceptions by remaining open to new information. They differentiate their experiences and accurately locate them in time and space. At this level people are acting as self-reflective agents who are aware of different levels of abstraction and are able to test their inferences and perceptions against reality. Client-centered therapists characterize people as well-functioning when they perceive in a comprehensive and thorough manner, are nondefensive, accept responsibility for their own behavior, differentiate from others, make evaluations in accord with their own senses and organismic valuing, accept others as unique, and prize themselves and others (Meador & Rogers, 1979).

Early in his career Rogers was convinced that therapists should stay as close to their clients as possible and reflect what they were expressing in the moment. However, later he became less restrictive and suggested that therapists could be more open and freer in what they expressed in order to be more genuine and congruent within the relationship.

He saw the realness of the therapist in the relationship as the most important element. He suggested that therapists are most effective when they are natural and spontaneous (Rogers, 1961).

Among contemporary scholars there is disagreement about the relative importance of Rogers's six necessary and sufficient conditions. Some scholars have viewed the relationship as central to the change process and emphasize the role of acceptance in particular (Bozarth, 2001; Brodley, 1990; Freire, 2001), whereas others have adopted a more interpersonal focus in their interactions with clients and view congruence as the most important facilitative condition or at least an overarching one that presupposes empathy and unconditional positive regard (Lietaer, 2001; Mearns & Thorne, 2000; Schmid, 2003).

Those client-centered therapists who view acceptance, as opposed to empathy or genuineness, as the essential ingredient of change have argued that it provides the optimal conditions to activate clients' capacity for growth (Barrett-Lennard, 2002; Bohart & Tallman, 1999; Bozarth, 2001; Freire, 2001). The goal of therapy in this respect is to respond to the whole person as clients tell their story. In this manner, the nondirective client-centered therapist provides a unique environment in which individuals are maximally free to reflect on themselves and pursue their own trajectory of growth and self-healing. These therapists deemphasize technique in favor of the quality of relationship between clients and therapists and a belief in the clients' actualizing tendency (Bohart & Tallman, 1999; Bozarth 2001; Schmid, 2003).

Contemporary client-centered therapists who emphasize genuineness note that being genuine does not mean that therapists disclose all their feelings to their clients but, rather, that they do not deny those feelings to themselves (Mearns & Cooper, 2005). Lietaer (1993, 2001) distinguished between *inner genuineness* and *outer genuineness*. Inner genuineness refers to the degree to which therapists have conscious access to, or are receptive to all aspects of their own flow of experiencing. This is referred to as *congruence*. The outer aspect refers to explicit communication by therapists of conscious perceptions, attitudes, and feelings, and it is referred to as *transparency*. Client-centered therapists are willing to be transparent about any persistent feelings that exist in their relationships with their clients and share these with their clients.

These scholars emphasize the importance of clients' contexts and relationships outside of therapy. They have moved away from Rogers's unidimensional view of the self toward a conception that recognizes a plurality of voices made up of dissonant self-experiences that need to be worked with in therapy (Mearns, 2002). According to this view, the person's actualizing tendency is seen as constantly in the process of configuring and reconfiguring a state of equilibrium between social restraint and social mediation (Mearns, 2002).

Experiential Psychotherapy

The second strand in Rogers's (1958) thought, the emphasis on client experiencing, has developed into experiential psychotherapy. Experiential therapists see people as actively organizing their view of reality on the basis of experiential referents (Gendlin, 1996; Greenberg et al., 1993; Greenberg & Watson, 2006; Elliott, Watson, Goldman, & Greenberg, 2003; Lietaer, 1990; Mahrer, 2001). The capacity for self-awareness is seen as a uniquely human attribute that allows people to experience themselves as both the subject and object of their experience (James, 1981; Rennie, 1992; Taylor, 1990; Watson & Greenberg, 1996). People can thus be immersed in the process of acting and being and simultaneously stand back and view themselves as objects. In this way, people make their emotion schemes available to awareness so that they can be examined and revised as new information becomes available.

Experiential therapists are concerned with clients' becoming more aware of their own organismic experience to make meaning and understand themselves and their worlds and to develop more satisfying ways of being with themselves and others. However, experiential practitioners are more process-guiding in their approach with clients than are their client-centered counterparts (Elliott et al., 2003; Greenberg and Watson, 2006; Leijssen, 1998; Mahrer, 2001).

Gendlin, along with Rogers and their colleagues at the University of Chicago, developed the technique of *focusing*. Gendlin (1962, 1996) posited that there was an ongoing flow of experiencing within human beings to which they can turn to discover the "felt meanings" of experiences. They observed that clients who did well in therapy could turn their attention inward to the body and label the impact of experience, by representing their feelings, beliefs, and inner worldviews. In so doing, they posed questions about their experience and their ways of functioning to understand why they acted and felt the way they did. In this way they were able to come up with solutions. Some clients engaged in this experiential search of their own accord; however, others who did not fare as well did not. To assist those clients who did not, Gendlin and colleagues began to teach them how to turn attention inward and focus on their inner-bodily-felt referent in order to understand the impact of events and access their feelings. Seven levels of awareness of inner experience, ranging from a focus on incidental and external experience to focusing on inner experience and posing questions about it and exploring it to achieve felt shifts in behavior, feelings, and perceptions, were identified (Gendlin, 1962; Klein, Mathieu-Coughlan, & Kiesler, 1986). Today the approach is known as *focusing oriented psychotherapy* and has an extensive Web-based organization devoted to the training and development of the approach (Friedman, 2003; Leijssen 1990; 1998; Weiser-Cornell, 1996).

Another colleague of Rogers from the University of Chicago, Laura Rice, examined other variables that reflected clients' productive engagement in psychotherapy in an attempt to facilitate clients' experiencing process. She identified clients' vocal quality and the quality of their descriptions as important indicators of when they were aware of and engaged in symbolizing and exploring their experience freshly to create new meaning (Rice, 1974, 1992). To help clients access the poignant aspects of their experience, Rice (1974) developed the technique of evocative reflections, thereby helping clients access the live, vulnerable aspects of their experiences that have been denied to awareness.

Rice also developed the technique of *systematic evocative unfolding* (SEU) to help clients resolve problematic reactions. She observed that clients would identify certain reactions as problematic if they were puzzled by a reaction of theirs or viewed it as too intense. She saw these *problematic reactions* as indications that clients were becoming more reflective about their own behavior and potentially ready to turn inward to explore their experience more systematically (Rice & Saperia, 1984). SEU enabled clients to create vivid, graphic, and idiosyncratic descriptions of situations in which their problematic reactions occurred and identify the triggers for the reactions so as to better understand their behavior and devise new ways of acting (Rice, 1974; Rice & Saperia, 1984).

Rice's work, together with that of her student and colleague Leslie Greenberg, formed the foundation of process experiential psychotherapy, an emotion-focused approach (Greenberg et al., 1993). Process experiential psychotherapy was based on the intensive study of productive change episodes. Models of micro-change events were developed, to show the steps involved in helping clients to resolve specific problems and facilitate productive processing. The first interventions that were developed included the resolution of problematic reactions, conflict in the two-chair task, and unfinished business in the empty-chair task (Greenberg, 1983; Greenberg et al., 1993) and empathy at markers of vulnerability (Greenberg et al., 1993). Subsequently other tasks have been modeled and added to the approach, including the creation of meaning (Clarke, 1993); clearing a space (Elliott et al., 2003); and processing vulnerability (Elliott et al., 2003). Numerous empathic responses have been differentiated and markers identified for their specific use within the session (Watson, 2002).

Process experiential psychotherapy sees difficulties arising from problematic emotion schemes. The latter are made up of specific autobiographical memories, perceptions, feelings, needs, and actions that are used to interpret different situations. When experience is not processed, it can be the source of intense reactions that may be incommensurate with current situations. The primary objective for experiential therapists is to assist clients to access their organismic experience and become aware of how they are blocking or distorting it from awareness, so that they can become aware of all aspects of their experience and discover ways of expressing and balancing their needs and feelings with a system of values that they own fully (Elliott et al., 2003; Greenberg & Watson, 2006). Once they are aware of their emotional responses, clients can discriminate between responses that are healthy and useful to guide them and those which are maladaptive and need to be changed (Elliott et al., 2003; Greenberg et al., 2003; Greenberg & Paivio, 1997).

In process experiential psychotherapy, change is seen to occur as a result of a dialectical synthesis occurring from the coconstruction of new meaning in a dialogue between client and therapist in which the therapist plays an active role in confirming clients' emotional experiences while assisting them to synthesize a new experience of self based on their strengths and possibilities (Greenberg & Pascual-Leone, 1997). The client is seen as an active agent constantly organizing or configuring experience and reality into meaningful wholes, with the active ingredients of change being the client's emerging internal experience and the interpersonal support provided by the therapist. Like their more nondirective counterparts, experiential therapists adhere to the notion of an inherent growth tendency, and they view the person's awareness of their organismic experience as the ultimate guide.

Experiential theorists see the relationship as important in bringing about change, but they tend to be more didactic and process-directive. Like their client-centered counterparts, experiential psychotherapists provide an interpersonal relationship characterized by empathy, warmth, and prizing. However, these therapists emphasize empathic attunement to capture the poignant, vulnerable aspects of clients' experiences (Elliott et al., 2003; Watson, 2002). In addition, experiential therapists observe how clients treat themselves and share aspects of the process that they have observed (Elliott et al., 2003; Watson, Goldman, & Greenberg, 2007). Specific tasks have been designed that can be offered to clients to assist them to become aware of their experience or process it in different ways.

Gestalt Therapy

Perls considered self-regulation essential to healthy functioning (Perls et al., 1951; Yontef & Simkin, 1989). As they become moral agents, humans learn to establish a balance among their organismic needs and desires, their values, and environmental demands. Perls insisted that individuals should come to own and incorporate their experience and introject values into their self-concept. To do so, they need to evaluate their experiences before they can be assimilated and owned as part of their self-systems. Experience that is not assimilated gives rise to conflict. Healthy individuals trust their own nature and capacities and are able to meet their needs. They are not bound by unnecessary rules and constraints but function in a fluid and permeable way that allows them to adjust and adapt (Yontef & Simkin, 1989).

Gestalt therapists view life as a process of needs arising and being satisfied in a continual cycle. A dominant need emerges as figural from a background, claims attention, is satisfied, and fades into the background again. The cycle continues as new needs emerge into the foreground. Pathology or dysfunction occurs when this need-satisfaction cycle is interrupted. The cycle is viewed as consisting of four major stages: awareness, excitement, action, and contact. Much of the focus in gestalt therapy is on becoming aware of different points at which the cycle is interrupted. Thus, the emergence of a clear need can be blocked at the initial stage by dulled sensation and poor awareness of inner or outer stimuli. Therapeutic work involves helping people become more aware of sensation or experience. Blocking that occurs at the arousal or excitement stage results from a dampening or disavowal of emotional experience. The focus of therapeutic work at this stage is on increasing awareness of muscular constriction and other ways that clients suppress their emotional experience. At the action stage, need satisfaction is seen as being interrupted by introjected values. Finally, interruption can occur at the contact stage by the person not experiencing the satisfaction of the need and completion of the cycle (Greenberg, Elliott, & Lietaer, 2003).

Initially the gestalt approach tended to be confrontational, using somewhat abrasive techniques, including deliberately frustrating clients. Perls operated from a view, drawn from his psychodynamic roots, that people manipulated the environment for support, rather than developing self-support. Thus, he intentionally frustrated behaviors that he saw as clients' manipulations. The graded experiment was another intervention used by gestalt therapists. These experiments, like two-chair work and dream work, were initiated to facilitate discovery. Other creative experiments included asking the client to express resentment to an imagined other, to assert or disclose something intimate to the therapist, to curl up into a ball, or express a desire in order to make it more vivid. The clients' experience and expression were then analyzed for what prevented completion of these experiments.

After Perls's death in 1970, the Gestalt movement shifted toward a softer form of therapy, with less emphasis on frustrating clients and more emphasis on the I–Thou dialogue. Contemporary forms of gestalt therapy place more emphasis on respecting the client, providing support, validating clients as authentic sources of experience, and relating to clients less authoritatively. One source of influence in this development has been gestalt therapy with people with more fragile processes and self-disorders. With these people it became apparent that the relationship with the therapist and an empathic bond were crucial to therapeutic success.

Contemporary gestalt therapists use the phenomenological method of working with awareness in the here and now (Yontef, 1993). Gestalt therapists pay particular attention to what is occurring at the contact boundaries between self and others, and they work to enhance clients' awareness of their own processes, needs, and wants. Increasing awareness by focusing on feelings, sensations, and motoric processes is core. Awareness is seen as a continual process that changes moment by moment, as a need is recognized, acted on, and satisfied and as a goal is met or an interest followed. To facilitate this process, gestalt therapists often focus on people's nonverbal behavior and their use of language. They may, for example, direct clients' attention to a sigh or a sneer of the lip, or ask clients to experiment with the effect on their experience of changing the word *it* to *I*.

Gestalt therapists also use key questions designed to reveal particular aspects of clients' functioning and promote creative adjustment. Some questions are oriented toward clients' experiences in the moment: for example, "What are you aware of?" Or "What do you need?" Other questions are related to identity: for example, "Who are you"? Or "What do you want to be"? With more fragile clients who have not developed a strong sense of self or boundary between self and other, the development of awareness is a long-term objective. Focusing on immediate experience and asking these clients questions such as "What do you feel?" or "Can you stay with this feeling?" is not helpful because they have yet to develop an awareness of their internal world. With these clients a more relational form of work may be necessary with contact with the therapist as the primary focus.

Awareness is seen as leading to choice, thus allowing the person to choose how to behave. Initially the emphasis in gestalt therapy on self-determination and independence led to an overemphasis on self-sufficiency and to an underemphasis on interdependence. More recently, gestalt therapists have proposed *self-support* as more desirable than *self-sufficiency*. If people are self-supportive, then they can ask for what they need and thereby maintain a sense of both autonomy and connectedness.

While contemporary practitioners still adopt active, didactic, and confrontational stances at times, today they view clients as the experts on their own experience (Greenberg et al., 2003). They value self-discovery and believe that clients must discover for themselves the ways in which they block or interrupt their experience. They recognize that there might be conflict between aspects of clients' experiences and their introjected values that can interfere with functioning. Consequently, they view confrontation between different aspects of the personality as essential to growth and development. The dual function of gestalt therapists is to connect individuals to each other and to preserve individuals' autonomy and separation (Yontef, 1969, 1993).

Gestalt therapists believe in an actualizing tendency, drawing on Goldstein's (1939) view that the individual's search for ways to maintain and enhance the self was never ending. To the gestalt therapist, self-actualization becomes possible when people fully identify with themselves as growing, changing organisms, and clearly discern their needs. The theory particularly emphasizes self-regulation, which is seen as a natural or organismic tendency. Effective self-regulation depends on discriminating feelings and needs by means of sensory awareness. This leads to awareness of intuitive appraisals of what is good for the person and should be assimilated, or of what is bad and should be rejected. This organismic wisdom works by a spontaneous emergence of needs to guide action.

Perls did not emphasize the curative nature of the therapy relationship as much as Rogers did, but he did subscribe to Buber's view of an I–Thou relationship. In practice, Perls was more interested in helping clients see what they were doing and how they were treating themselves and less attentive to helping clients explore their experience in nonthreatening ways. In its early formulation, gestalt therapy posited that problems in the relationships between clients and therapists reflected projection and transferential processes. Thus, they were worked on, not as interpersonal problems with the therapist but as projections that needed to be re-owned. Gestalt therapists did not view the relationship as the only vehicle for stimulating change; rather, they experimented by inviting clients to put their therapists in an empty chair and dialogue with their imagined therapists. Instead of the therapeutic relationship, Perls emphasized awareness, experiencing, and the gestalt experiment in facilitating change.

A more interpersonal form of dialogical gestalt therapy has now replaced the classical approach in which the active experiment was the cornerstone of treatment. Problems in the relationship between client and therapist are now responded to supportively; dealing with them in the here and now is seen as a source of new learning for both client and therapist. Clients' growth is thought to be facilitated by the therapist's working with the client to heal the ruptures that occur in the relationship. Therapists are highly aware of their own impact on clients' momentary experience, focusing on disruptions in relational contact as both a source of discovery and an opportunity for new experience. Client awareness of patterns in their experiences and awareness of how they interrupt themselves, as well as the corrective experience of a helping dialogue, are all seen as curative.

Existential Psychotherapy

Like other humanistic therapists, existential therapists see the goal of therapy as helping their clients live more authentic and fulfilling lives (Bugental & Stirling, 1995; Cooper, 2008; Yalom, 1980; 1995). Nonetheless, existential therapists disagree among themselves on what is authentic. Some existentialists see the acceptance of struggle and the loss of self-delusion as authentic, while others see it as developing purpose and finding meaning in existence, and yet others define it as becoming more open and relating to others in authentic ways. Notwithstanding these differences, they do not have preconceived notions of how clients should arrive at living more authentically but believe clients need to work this out for themselves.

Bugental and his followers believed that the fact of being is the central issue of life. It is only through the recovery of one's lost sense of being that one can alleviate the psychological distress that brings an individual to psychotherapy. As in all humanistic approaches, existential psychotherapy contends that significant life change resides in the subjectivity of the client. Bugental held that the main vehicle to help clients become genuinely aware of their own inner processes, including their attitudes, emotions, thoughts, and intentions, was the actual interpersonal encounter between the client and therapist. He saw this as the only way in which true life-changing therapy could occur (Bugental & McBeath, 1973).

It is through awareness that individuals implicitly experience the basic conditions of living, each of which confronts individuals with a particular challenge or dilemma that invariably gives rise to existential anxiety. Bugental saw pathology as developing from constricted patterns of living employed to reduce or avoid the inevitable anxieties of existence. If individuals find life's issues too devastating, a constrictive and dysfunctional pattern of living may evolve as a means of attempting to avoid existential anxiety. Change occurs through confrontation and acceptance of life's fundamental conditions of change, death, individual responsibility, loss, and separateness. If integrated into peoples' lives, anxiety can become a strong and healthy motivation to live fully and in accord with their needs and values (Bugental, 1999).

Yalom (1980, 2007) joined a wave of European psychiatrists and psychoanalysts who objected fundamentally to Freud's model of psychic functioning and his attempts to understand the human being through a lens borrowed from the physical sciences. Yalom placed primacy on the importance of understanding the patient's phenomenological experience—and his or her own unique subjectivity. He, along with other existential psychotherapists, differed from traditional psychoanalysts in the kinds of basic conflicts he emphasized. Yalom was not so much concerned with conflict between suppressed instinctual strivings and society or with internalized significant adults as he was with conflicts flowing from the individual's confrontation with the givens of existence. The individual's confrontation with each of these facts of life constitutes the content of the existential dynamic conflict. Yalom (1980, 2007) believed that individuals need to discover the nature of these givens and that productive psychotherapy is focused on clients coming to terms with the four ultimate concerns of existence: death, freedom, isolation, and meaninglessness.

Existential therapists draw on Husserl's phenomenological method to help their clients address their problems in living (Bugental, 1987; Cooper, 2008; Yalom, 1980). The phenomenological method requires that therapists bracket their assumptions and attend intently to their clients' experiences. Like client-centered therapists, they are concerned with unpacking clients' experiences, understanding their different nuances, and facilitating an inner search (Bugental, 1987). Bugental (1987) observed that as the focus of psychotherapy is continual attention to the patient's inner experience, the primary instrument needed for that attention is the therapist's own subjectivity. Early on, the phenomenological method was a more intellectual exercise. However, recently, existential psychotherapists have emphasized that it requires a holistic type of listening, demanding that its practitioners focus on the emotional, cognitive, and embodied aspects of clients' experience to develop an accurate understanding of their inner world (Mearns & Cooper, 2005). The second step in the phenomenological method is to help clients describe in detail aspects of their experiences. Working in this way, existential therapists are less likely to inquire about early experiences but rather to have the client explore their current experience.

While it is recognized that clients are capable of becoming aware, some existential therapists believe that some clients need to be confronted to face existential realities. With confrontation, existentialist therapists heighten clients' awareness of how they block their experience and limit themselves, by identifying inconsistencies in clients' behavior either in the session or in the conduct of their lives (Cooper, 2008; Schneider, 1998). Existential therapists see people as engaged in a process of discovery and invention (Bugenthal & Stirling, 1995). The self is an evolving process, and people are capable of learning and growing throughout their lives. As people interact with the world, they make sense of their experiences and form identities in order to differentiate between self and other. Existential therapists see healthy functioning as represented by sensitivity, flexibility, and choice. Dysfunction occurs when people chronically employ one mode or the other (Bugental & Stirling, 1995).

Existential theorists see meaning creation as a central goal of therapy. The existential concerns of death, isolation, freedom, and meaninglessness are central (Yalom, 2007). Thus, existential therapists focus on helping clients find meaning in their existences and confronting the ways in which the human condition limits them from pursuing possibilities that would lead to more satisfying ways of being. Existentialists see individuals as responsible agents capable of choosing and directing the course of their lives. It is through exercising choice that people become authentic (Schneider & May, 1995). To act responsibly, human beings create meaning and construct value systems to guide their actions. The desire for meaning and order is seen as innate; however, the desire is challenged as people confront the givens of existence, including isolation and the inevitability of death. Human beings are born with a capacity to be aware, to relate to others, to be autonomous and agentic, and to remain separate (Bugenthal & Stirling, 1995; Cooper, 2008); however, separateness and autonomy are counterbalanced by a need for relatedness.

To facilitate the development of a real encounter, some existential therapists, like R. D. Laing (1962), dispensed with outside restrictions, rules, and boundaries in order to be more spontaneous and with their clients (Cooper, 2008). For example, Laing did not restrict sessions to 1 hour and would meet clients outside the consulting room. Rollo May and Irvin Yalom construe the relationship as direct and nonformal—it is a relationship of equals in which first names are used and therapists are free to self-disclose. They view this type of relationship as healing in itself and as an example of the kind of intimacy that can teach clients how fulfilling it is to be cared for in this way (Yalom, 1980). Unlike client-centered therapists, existential therapists focus on helping clients become aware of blocks and the ways in which they are avoiding taking responsibility for their well-being. Thus, they sometimes challenge clients' expressed goals and ways of viewing themselves and their experience from the position of the expert.

Contemporary existential theorists have seen a real, genuine relationship as a crucial ingredient of psychotherapy. They strive to be responsive to their clients' concerns, as opposed to imposing a prescribed agenda or set of norms (Bugental, 1987; Cooper, 2008). This allows therapists to be more creative, spontaneous, and flexible with their clients. The objective is to pare away clients' props, lies, self-deception, defenses, and anxieties in order to encounter themselves and their therapists in a real and authentic fashion. Bugental (1987) described the relationship as one of copresence, drawing on Buber's notion of an I–Thou dialogue.

RECENT AND FUTURE DEVELOPMENTS

A number of recent developments deserve mention in addressing current and future developments in humanistic psychotherapy. These include, first, recent developments in neuroscience that support a number of the assumptions underlying humanistic psychotherapy; second, the growing use of qualitative research methodologies that fit with the epistemological assumptions of the approach; and third, the development of humanistic treatments with specific populations.

Neuroscience

Recent developments in cognitive neuroscience have provided insights into the nature of empathy and the actualizing tendency. Brain mapping has spurred the discovery of mirror neurons in which similar brain regions are activated in an observer as those activated in a person who is experiencing a particular sensation or performing a certain action (Decety & Jackson, 2004; Gazzola, Aziz-Zadeh, & Keysers, 2006; Rizzolatti, 2005). This occurs with emotion as well, as regions in the brain associated with feeling a specific emotion are activated by seeing that emotion in another or witnessing the other in a situation that might elicit the emotion. However, these reproductions are not one-to-one simulations. Certain areas of the brain that would alert us to our own personal experience are not activated in observers, thus preserving the *as if* condition that Rogers (1967) and other psychotherapists have emphasized in their writings on empathy. These findings provide support for the ways in which empathy has been conceptualized by humanistic and experiential psychotherapists and suggest ways of enhancing empathic resonance (Bohart et al., 2002; Watson & Greenberg, 2009).

With respect to the actualizing tendency, recently neuroscientists have accorded greater credence to brain plasticity. Norman Doidge (2007), for example, brought together numerous lines of research in *The Brain That Changes Itself*. The evidence suggests that the brain changes and reformulates its processing capacity depending on the senses it has available, often colonizing areas of the brain for alternative functions if the requisite organ has been incapacitated. The growing understanding of the brain's plasticity echoes Kurt Goldstein's observations of healing in injured soldiers and provides some support for the notion of a biological actualizing tendency or the capacity of the brain to maximize its potential.

Other important developments have to do with the burgeoning research on emotion and particularly on affect regulation (Bradley, 2000; Kennedy-Moore & Watson, 1998). Although numerous approaches to psychotherapy facilitate affect regulation, client-centered and experiential approaches are particularly focused on helping clients articulate their implicit organismic experience. This facilitates awareness of emotion as well as its labeling, two important skills in the development of affect regulation (Elliott et al., 2003; Kennedy-Moore & Watson, 1998).

Contemporary humanistic researchers are intensively studying emotion in the change process (Pos, Greenberg, Goldman, & Korman, 2003; Watson & Bedard, 2006) as well as differences in psychotherapeutic process among client-centered therapy, process experiential psychotherapy, and cognitive behavior psychotherapy (Greenberg et al., 2003; Watson et al., 2003). By extending the tradition begun by Rogers and his colleagues, the ongoing process analysis of change points may provide a key to improving our understanding of how change occurs in psychotherapy.

Qualitative Research

There has been a proliferation of qualitative research methodologies consonant with the tenets of humanistic and experiential therapy, particularly with an emphasis on phenomenology and the need for more intensive description of human experience (see Polkinghorne, 2001; Schneider, 2001; Toukmanian & Rennie, 1992). These phenomenological approaches to inquiry have increased our understanding of clients' experience during psychotherapy, including the role of clients' deference (Rennie, 1994), congruence (Grafanaki, 2002), and pain (Bolger, 1999), and the resolution of problematic reactions (Watson & Rennie, 1994).

Humanistic Treatments for Specific Populations

Over the past decade, humanistic practitioners have elaborated theory and practice and developed specific ways of working with different populations. Rogers's concept of psychological contact has been extended in work with persons with schizophrenia and those who are mentally challenged or have dementias (Prouty, 1998, 2001). These populations are seen as contact-impaired, and pretherapy interventions have been developed to help them develop contact functioning (Prouty, 2002). Other differential treatment applications include dissociative and fragile processes (Warner, 1998, 2002); trauma (Elliott, Davis & Slatik, 1998; Greenberg & Paivio, 1997); anxiety (Wolfe & Sigl, 1998); depression (Greenberg & Watson, 2006); borderline process (Eckert & Biermann-Ratjen, 1998); psychosomatic disorders (Sachse, 1998); those with special needs (Portner, 2002); cross-cultural counseling (Vontress & Epp, 2001); families (Gaylin, 2002); children (Behr, 2003, 2009); and couples (Greenberg & Johnson, 1988; Greenberg & Goldman, 2008). The focus on specific populations has served to bring the approach more into the mainstream and relevant to practitioners from other orientations while still remaining true to the basic tenets of humanistic theory and practice.

CONCLUSION

Humanistic and experiential psychotherapies continue to grow and develop as evidence accrues with respect to their effectiveness in treating clients dealing with a variety of conditions, including depression, posttraumatic stress, and marital difficulties. The fundamental insights and relational methods of humanistic therapies are too important to lose. In the expanding perspectives emerging in neuroscience and qualitative research, we are confident that humanistic psychotherapy will continue to enrich our understanding of people and how they change.

REFERENCES

Barrett-Lennard, G. T. (1997). The recovery of empathy: Toward others and self. In A. C. Bohart & L. S. Greenberg (Eds.), *Empathy reconsidered: New directions in psychotherapy* (pp. 103–121). Washington, DC: APA Press.

Barrett-Lennard, G. T. (2002). The helping conditions in their context: Expanding change theory and practice. *Person-Centered & Experiential Psychotherapies, 1* (1&2), 144–155.

Behr, M. (2003). Interactive resonance in work with children and adolescents: A theory based concept of interpersonal relationship through play and the use of toys. *Person-Centered & Experiential Psychotherapies, 2*(2), 89–103.

Behr, M. (2009). Constructing emotions and accommodating schemas: A model of self-exploration, symbolization, and development. *Person-Centered & Experiential Psychotherapies, 8*(1), 44–62.

Binswanger, L. (1963). *Being in the world.* New York, NY: Basic Books (J. Needleman, Trans.). (Originally published 1951)

Bohart, A., Elliott, R., Greenberg, L. S., & Watson, J. C. (2002). Empathy redux. In J. Norcross & M. Lambert (Eds.), *Psychotherapy relationships that work* (pp. 89–108). Oxford: Oxford University Press.

Bohart, A., & Tallman, K. (1999). *How clients make therapy work: The process of active self-healing.* Washington, DC: American Psychological Association.

Bolger, L. (1999). A grounded theory analysis of eotional pain. *Psychotherapy Research, 9,* 342–362. doi:10.1093/ptr/9.3.342

Boss, M. (1963). *Psychoanalysis and daseinanalysis* (L. B. Lefebre, Trans.). New York, NY: Basic Books. (Originally published 1957)

Bozarth, J. (2001). Client-centered unconditional positive regard: A historical perspective. In J. Bozarth & P Wilkens (Eds.), *Unconditional positive regard* (pp. 5–18). London: PCCS Books.Bozarth, J. D. (1990).

The essence of client-centered therapy. In G. Lietaer, J. Rombauts, & R. Van Balen (Eds.), *Client-centered and experiential psychotherapy in the nineties* (pp. 59–64). Leuven, Belgium: Leuven University.

Bradley, S. (2000). *Affect regulation and the development of psychopathology.* New York, NY: Guilford Press.

Brodley, B. T. (1990). Client-centered therapy and experiential: Two different therapies. In G. Lietaer, J. Rombauts, & R. Van Balen (Eds.), *Client-centered and experiential psychotherapy in the nineties* (pp. 87–108). Leuven, Belgium: Leuven University.

Buber, M. (1957). *I and thou.* New York, NY: Scribner.

Bugental, J. F. T. (Ed.). (1969). *Challenge of humanistic psychology*. New York, NY: McGraw-Hill.

Bugental, J. F. T. (1987). *The art of the psychotherapist*. New York, NY: Norton.

Bugental, J. F. T. (1999). *Psychotherapy isn't what you think*. Pheonix, AZ: Zeig, Tucker.

Bugental, J., & McBeath, B. (1973). Depth existential therapy: Evolution since World War II. In B. Bongar & L. Beutler (Eds.), *Comprehensive textbook of psychotherapy* (pp. 11–122). New York, NY: Oxford University Press.

Bugental, J. F. T., & Stirling, M. (1995). Existential psychotherapy. In A. S. Gurman & S. B. Messer (Eds.), *Essential psychotherapies* (pp. 226–260). New York, NY: Guilford.

Clarke, K. M. (1993). Creation of meaning in incest survivors. *Journal of Cognitive Psychotherapy, 7*, 195–203.

Cooper, M. (2008). Existential psychotherapy. In J. Lebow (Ed.), *Twenty first century psychotherapies: Contemporary approaches to theory and practice* (pp, 237–276). New York, NY: Wiley.

Decety, J., & Jackson, P. L. (2004). The functional architecture of human empathy. *Behavioral and Cognitive Neuroscience Reviews, 3*, 71–100.doi:10.1177/1534582304267187

Doidge, N. (2007). *The brain that changes itself*. New York, NY: Penguin.

Eckert, J., & Biermann-Ratjen, E. (1998). The treatment of borderline personality disorder. In L. S. Greenberg, J. C. Watson, & G. Lietaer (Eds.), *Handbook of experiential psychotherapy* (pp. 349–367). New York, NY: Guilford.

Elliott, R., Davis, K., & Slatik, E. (1998). Process-experiential therapy for posttraumatice stress difficulties. In L. Greenberg, G. Lietaer, & J. Watson (Eds.), *Handbook of experiential psychotherapy* (pp. 249–271). New York, NY: Guilford.

Elliott, R., Watson, J. C., Goldman, R. N., & Greenberg, L. S. (2003). *Learning emotion-focused therapy: The process-experiential approach to change*. Washington, DC: American Psychological Association.

Fagan, J. (1974). Personality theory and psychotherapy. *The Counseling Psychologist, 4*(4), 4–7. doi:10.1177/001100007400400404

Frankl, V. (1963). *Man's search for meaning: An introduction to logotherapy*. New York, NY: Pocket Books.

Frankl, V. (1967). *Psychotherapy and existentialism: Selected papers on logotherapy*. New York, NY: Washington Square Press.

Frankl, V. (1969). *The will to meaning: Foundations and applications of logotherapy*. Ohio: World Publishing.

Freire, E. (2001). Unconditional positive regard: The distinctive feature of client-centered therapy. In J. Bozarth & P. Wilkens (Eds.), *Unconditional positive regard* (pp.145–155). London: PCCS Books.

Friedlander, S. (1918). *Schopferische indifferenz* [Creative indifference]. Munich, Germany: Georg Muller.

Friedman, N. (2003). Eugene Gendlin's theory and practice of psychotherapy, a personal account. *Person-centered and experiential psychotherapies, 2*(1), 31–42.

Gaylin, N. (2002). The relationship: The heart of the matter. In J. C. Watson, R. N. Goldman, & M. Warner (Eds.), *Person-centered and experiential psychotherapy in the 21st century* (pp. 339–347). Ross-on-Wye, England: PCCS Books.

Gazzola, V., Aziz-Zadeh, L., & Keysers, C. (2006). Empathy and the somatotopic auditory mirror system in humans. *Current Biology, 16*, 1824–1829.doi:10.1016/j.cub.2006.07.072

Gendlin, E. (1962). *Experiencing and the creation of meaning*. New York, NY: Free Press.

Gendlin, E. (1984). *Focusing* (Rev. ed.). New York, NY: Bantam Books.

Gendlin, E. T. (1996). *Focusing-oriented psychotherapy: A manual of the experiential method*. New York, NY: Guilford Press.

Goldstein, K. (1939). *The organism: A holistic approach derived from pathological data in man.* New York, NY: American Books.

Grafanaki, S. (2002). On becoming congruent: How congruence works in person-centered counselling and practical applications for training and practice. In J. C. Watson, R. N. Goldman, & M. Warner (Eds.). *Person-centered and experiential psychotherapy in the 21st century* (pp. 278–290). Ross-on-Wye, England: PCCS Books.

Greenberg, L. S. (1979). Resolving splits: Use of the two-chair technique. *Psychotherapy: Theory, Research and Practice, 16,* 316–324.

Greenberg, L. S. (1980). An intensive analysis of recurring events from the practice of gestalt therapy. *Psychotherapy: Theory, Research and Practice, 17,* 143–152.

Greenberg, L. S. (1983). Toward a task analysis of conflict resolution. *Psychotherapy: Theory, Research and Practice, 20,* 190–201.

Greenberg, L. S., Elliott, R., & Lietaer, G. (2003). The humanistic-experiential approach. In G. Stricker & T. Widiger (Eds.), *Handbook of psychology: Vol. 8. Clinical psychology* (pp. 301–326). Hoboken, NJ: Wiley.

Greenberg, L. S., & Goldman, R. N. (2008). *Emotion-focused couples therapy: The dynamics of emotion, love and power.* Washington, DC: American Psychological Association.

Greenberg, L. S., & Johnson, S. (1988). *Emotionally focused therapy for couples.* New York, NY: Guilford.

Greenberg, L., & Paivio, S. (1997). *Working with emotion in psychotherapy.* New York, NY: Guilford.

Greenberg, L., & Pascual-Leone, J. (1997). Emotion in the creation of personal meaning. In M. Power & C. Brewin (Eds.), *Transformation of meaning* (pp. 157–174). London: Wiley.

Greenberg, L. S., Rice, L. N., & Elliott, R. (1993). *Facilitating emotional change.* New York, NY: Guilford.

Greenberg, L. S., & Watson, J. C. (2006). *Emotion-focused therapy for depression.* Washington, DC: American Psychological Association.

Greenberg, L. S., & Webster, M. (1982). Resolving decisional conflict by means of two-chair dialogue and empathic reflection at a split in counseling. *Journal of Counseling Psychology, 29,* 468–477. doi:10.1037/0022-0167.29.5.468

Heidegger, M. (1962). *Being and time* (J. Macquarrie & E. S. Robinson, Trans.). New York, NY: Harper and Row. (Original work published 1949)

Husserl, E. (1977). *Phenomenological psychology* (J. Scanlon, Trans.). The Hague: Nijhoff. (Original work published 1925)

Jaspers, K. (1963). *General psychopathology.* Chicago: University of Chicago Press.

James, W. (1981). *The principles of psychology.* Cambridge: Harvard University Press. (Original work published 1890)

Kennedy-Moore, E., & Watson, J. C. (1999). *Expressing emotional myths, realities, and therapeutic strategies.* New York, NY: Guilford.

Kierkegaard, S. (1954). *Fear and trembling and the sickness unto death* (W. Lowrie, Trans.). Garden City, NY: Doubleday Anchor. (Original work published 1843)

Kirschenbaum, H. (2007). *The life and work of Carl Rogers.* Ross-on-Wye, England: PCCS Books.

Klein, M., Mathieu-Coughlan, P., & Kiesler, D. (1986). The experiencing scales. In L. Greenberg & W. Pinsof (Eds.), *The psychotherapeutic process: A research handbook* (pp. 21–71). New York, NY: Guilford.

Laing, R. D. (1962). *The divided self: An existential study in sanity and madness.* New York, NY: Pantheon Books.

Lambert, M., & Barley, D. (2002). Research summary on the therapeutic relationship and psychotherapy outcome. In J. Norcross (Ed.), *Psychotherapy relationships that work: Ther-*

apist contributions and responsiveness to patients (pp. 17–36). New York, NY: Oxford University Press.

Leijssen, M. (1990). On focusing and the necessary conditions of therapeutic personality change. In G. Lietaer, J. Rombauts, & R. Van Balen (Eds.), *Person-centered and experiential psychotherapy in the nineties* (pp. 225–250). Leuwen, Belgium: Leuwen University Press.

Leijssen, M. (1998). Focusing microprocesses. In L. S. Greenberg, J. C. Watson, & G. Lietaer (Eds.), *Handbook of experiential psychotherapy* (pp. 121–154). New York, NY: Guilford.

Lewin, K. (1951). *Field theory in social science: Selected theoretical papers.* New York, NY: Harper & Row.

Lietaer, G. (1990). The client-centered approach after the Wisconsin project: A personal view on its evolution. In G. Lietaer, J. Rombauts, & R. Van Balen (Eds.), *Client-centered and experiential therapy in the nineties* (pp. 19–46). Leuven, Belgium: Leuven University Press.

Lietaer, G. (1993). Authenticity, congruence, and transparency. In D. Brazier (Ed.), *Beyond Carl Rogers: Towards a psychotherapy for the twenty-first century* (pp. 17–47). London: Constable.

Lietaer, G. (2001). Being genuine as a therapist: Congruence and transparency. In G. Wyatt (Ed.). *Rogers' therapeutic conditions: Evolution, theory and practice* (pp. 36–54). Ross-on-Wye, England: PCCS Books.

Mahrer, A. (1983). *Experiential psychotherapy: Basic practices.* New York, NY: Brunner/Mazel.

Mahrer, A. (1986). *Therapeutic experiencing: The process of change.* New York, NY: Norton.

Mahrer, A. (1998). How can impressive in-session changes become impressive post-session changes. In L. S. Greenberg, J. C. Watson, & G. Lietaer (Eds.), *Handbook of experiential psychotherapy* (pp. 201–226). New York, NY: Guilford Press.

Mahrer, A. (2001). If you are ready to undergo these awful moments, then have an experiential session. In K. J. Schneider, J. E. T. Bugental, & J. Fraser Pierson (Eds.), *The handbook of humanistic psychology: Leading edges in theory, research, and practice* (pp. 411–420). Thousand Oaks, CA: Sage.

Marcel, S. (1951). *Homo Viator: Introduction to a metaphysic of hope.* Chicago: Regnery.May, R. (1950/1977). *The meaning of anxiety* (Rev. ed.). New York, NY: Norton.

May, R. (Ed.). (1960). *Existential psychology.* New York, NY: Random House.

May, R., Angel, E., & Ellenberger, H. (Eds.). (1958). *Existence: A new dimension in psychiatry and psychology.* New York, NY: Basic Books.

May, R., & Yalom, J. (1989). Existential therapy. In R. J. Corsini & D. Wedding (Eds.), *Current psychotherapies* (4th ed., pp. 363–402). Itasca, IL: Peacock.

Meador, B., & Rogers, C. (1979). Person-centred therapy. In R. Corsini (Ed.), *Current psychotherapies* (pp. 131–184). Itasca, IL: Peacock.

Mearns, D. (2002). Theoretical propositions in regard to self theory within the person-centered approach. *Person Centered and Experiential Psychotherapies, 1* (1 & 2), 14–27.

Mearns, D., & Cooper, M. (2005). *Working at relational depth in counselling and psychotherapy.* London: Sage.

Mearns, D., & Thorne, B. (2000). *Person-centered counselling in action.* Newbury Park, CA: Sage.

Misiak, H., & Sexton, V. (1973). *Phenomenological, existential and humanistic psychologies.* New York, NY: Grune & Stratton.

Norcross, J. C. (Ed.). (2002). *Psychotherapy relationships that work: Therapist contributions and responsiveness to patients.* New York, NY: Oxford University Press.

Perls, F. S. (1947). *Ego, hunger, and aggression.* London: Allen & Unwin.

Perls, F. S. (1973). *The Gestalt approach and eyewitness to therapy.* New York, NY: Science and Behavior Books.

Perls, F. S., Hefferline, R. F., & Goodman, P. (1951). *Gestalt therapy*. New York, NY: Julian Press.

Polkinghorne, D. (2001). The self and humanistic psychology. In K. J. Schneider, J. E. T. Bugental, & J. Fraser Pierson (Eds.), *The handbook of humanistic psychology: Leading edges in theory, research, and practice* (pp. 81–100). Thousand Oaks, CA: Sage.

Polster, E., & Polster, M. (1973). *Gestalt therapy integrated*. New York, NY: Bruner/Mazel.

Portner, M. (2002). Psychotherapy for people with special needs: A challenge for client-centered therapists. In J. C. Watson, R. N. Goldman, & M. Warner (Eds.). *Person-centered and experiential psychotherapy in the 21st century* (pp. 278–290). Ross-on-Wye, England: PCCS Books.

Pos, A. E., Greenberg, L. S., Goldman, R., & Korman, L. (2003). Emotional processing during experiential treatment of depression. *Journal of Consulting and Clinical Psychology, 71,* 1007–1016. doi:10.1037/0022-006X.71.6.1007

Prouty, G. (1998). Pre therapy and pre-symbolic experiencing: Evolutions in person-centered/experiential approaches. In L. S. Greenberg, J. C. Watson, & G. Lietaer (Eds.), *Handbook of experiential psychotherapy* (pp. 388–409). New York, NY: Guilford.

Prouty, G. (2001). The practice of pre-therapy. *Journal of Contemporary Psychotherapy, 31*(1), 31–40. doi:10.1023/A:1010226814792

Prouty, G. (2002). Humanistic psychotherapy for people with schizophrenia. In D. Cain & J. Seeman (Eds.), *Handbook of research and practice in humanistic psychotherapies* (pp. 579–601). Washington, DC: American Psychological Association.

Rennie, D. (1994). Clients' deference in psychotherapy. *Journal of Counseling Psychology, 41,* 427–437. doi:10.1037/0022-0167.41.4.427

Rennie, D. L. (1992). Qualitative analysis of the client's experience of psychotherapy: The unfolding of reflexivity. In S. Toukmanian & D. Rennie (Eds.), *Psychotherapy process research: Paradigmatic and narrative approaches* (pp. 211–233). Newbury Park, CA: Sage.

Resnick, R. (1995). Interviewed by Malcolm Parlett. Gestalt therapy: Principles, prisms and perspectives. *British Gestalt Journal, 4,* 3–13.

Rice, L. N. (1974). The evocative function of the therapist. In D. A. Wexler & L. N. Rice (Eds.), *Innovations in client-centered therapy* (pp. 282–302). New York, NY: Wiley.

Rice, L. N. (1992). From naturalistic observation of psychotherapy process to micro theories of change. In S. Toukmanian & D. Rennie (Eds.), *Psychotherapy process research: Paradigmatic and narrative approaches* (pp. 1–21). Newbury Park, CA: Sage Publications.

Rice, L. N., & Greenberg, L. S. (1992). Humanistic approaches to psychotherapy. In D. K. Freedheim (Ed.), *History of psychotherapy: A century of change* (pp. 197–224). Washington, DC: American Psychological Association.

Rice, L. N., & Greenberg, L. S. (Eds.). (1984). *Patterns of change: Intensive analysis of psychotherapy process*. New York, NY: Guilford.

Rice, L. N., & Saperia, E. (1984). Task analysis of the resolution of problematic reactions. In L. N. Rice & L. S. Greenberg (Eds.), *Patterns of change: Intensive analysis of psychotherapy process* (pp. 29–66). New York, NY: Guilford.

Rizzolatti, G. (2005). The mirror neuron system and imitation. In S. Hurley & N. Chater (Eds.), *Perspective on imitation: From neuroscience to social science: Vol. 1. Mechanisms of imitation and imitation in animals* (pp. 55–76). Cambridge, MA: MIT Press.

Rogers, C. R. (1951). *Client-centered therapy*. Boston: Houghton Mifflin.

Rogers, C. R. (1957). The necessary and sufficient conditions for therapeutic personality change. *Journal of Consulting Psychology, 21,* 95–103. doi:10.1037/h0045357

Rogers, C. R. (1958). A process conception of psychotherapy. *American Psychologist, 13,* 142–149. doi:10.1037/h0042129

Rogers, C. R. (1959). A theory of therapy, personality, and interpersonal relationships, as developed in the client-centered framework. In S. Koch (Ed.), *Psychology: A study of science; formulations of the person and the social context* (pp. 184–256). New York, NY: McGraw-Hill.

Rogers, C. R. (1961). *On becoming a person.* Boston: Houghton Mifflin.

Rogers, C. R. (1967). The necessary and sufficient conditions of therapeutic personality change. *Journal of Consulting Psychology, 21,* 97–103.

Rogers, C. (1975). Empathic: An unappreciated way of being. *The Counseling Psychologist, 5,* 2–10. doi:10.1177/001100007500500202

Rogers, C. R., Gendlin, G. T., Kiesler, D. V., & Truax, C. (Eds.). (1967). *The Therapeutic relationship and its impact: A study of schizophrenics.* Madison: University of Wisconsin Press.

Sachse, R. (1998). Goal-oriented client-centered therapy of psychosomatic disorders. In L. S. Greenberg, J. C. Watson, & G. Lietaer (Eds.), *Handbook of experiential psychotherapy* (pp. 295–327). New York, NY: Guilford Press.

Sartre, J. P. (1943/1956). *Being and nothingness* (H. Barnes, Trans.). New York, NY: Philosophical Library. Schmid, P. F. (2003). The characteristics of a person centered approach to therapy and counseling: Criteria for identity and coherence. *Person-Centered and Experiential Psychotherapies, 2,* 104–120.

Schneider, K. (1998). Existential processes. In L. S. Greenberg, J. C. Watson, & G. Lietaer (Eds.), *Handbook of experiential psychotherapy* (pp. 103–120). New York, NY: Guilford.

Schneider, K. (2001). Multiple-case depth research: Bringing experience near closer. In K. J. Schneider, J. E. T. Bugental, & J. Fraser Pierson (Eds.), *The handbook of humanistic psychology: Leading edges in theory, research, and practice* (pp. 305–314). Thousand Oaks, CA: Sage.

Schneider, K. J., & May, R. (1995). *The psychology of existence: An integrative clinical perspective.* New York, NY: McGraw-Hill, Inc.

Tageson, W. C. (1982). *Humanistic psychology: A synthesis.* Homewood, IL: Dorsey.

Taylor, C. (1990). *Human agency and language.* Port Hope, ON: Cambridge University Press.

Tiryakian, E. (1962). *Sociologism and existentialism.* Englewood Cliffs, , NJ: Prentice-Hall.

Toukmanian, S., & Rennie, D., Eds. (1992). *Psychotherapy process research: Paradigmatic and narrative approaches.* Newbury Park, CA: Sage.

Vontress, C. E., & Epp, L. R. (2001). Existential cross-cultural counselling: When hearts and cultures share. In K. J. Schneider, J. E. T. Bugental, & J. Fraser Pierson (Eds.), *The handbook of humanistic psychology* (pp. 371–387). Thousand Oaks: Sage.

Warner, M. (1998). A client-centered approach to therapeutic work with dissociated and fragile process. In L. S. Greenberg, J. C. Watson, & G. Lietaer (eds.), *Handbook of experiential psychotherapy* (pp. 368–387). New York, NY: Guilford.

Watson, J. C. (2002). Revisioning empathy: Theory, research and practice. In D. Cain & J. Seeman (Eds.), *Handbook of research and practice in humanistic psychotherapies* (pp. 445–473). Washington, DC: American Psychological Association.

Watson, J. C., & Bedard, D. (2006). Clients' emotional processing in psychotherapy: A comparison between cognitive-behavioral and process-experiential psychotherapy. *Journal of Consulting and Clinical Psychology, 74,* 152–159. doi:10.1037/0022-006X.74.1.152

Watson, J. C., Goldman, R. N., & Greenberg, L. S. (2007). *Casebook in the treatment of emotion focused therapy: Comparing good and poor outcome.* Washington, DC: American Psychological Association.

Watson, J. C., Gordon, L. B., Stermac, L., Steckley, P., & Kalogerakos, F. (2003). Comparing the effectiveness of process-experiential with cognitive-behavioral psychotherapy in the treatment of depression. *Journal of Consulting and Clinical Psychology, 71,* 773–781. doi:10.1037/0022-006X.71.4.773

Watson, J. C., & Greenberg, L. S. (1996). Emotion and cognition in experiential therapy: A dialectical-constructivist position. In H. Rosen & K. Kuelwein (Eds.), *Constructing realities: Meaning-making perspectives for psychotherapists* (pp. 253–276). San Francisco: Jossey-Bass.

Watson, J. C., & Greenberg, L. S. (2009). Empathic resonance. In J. Decety & W. Ickes, (Eds.). *The social neuroscience of empathy* (pp. 125–138). Cambridge: MIT Press.

Watson, J. C., & Rennie, D. L. (1994). A qualitative analysis of clients' reports of their subjective experience while exploring problematic reactions. *Journal of Counseling Psychology, 41,* 500–509. doi:10.1037/0022-0167.41.4.500

Watson, J. C., & Wiseman, H. (in press). Laura Rice: Naturalistic observer of psychotherapy process. In L. Castonguay, C. Muran, L. Angus, J. Hayes, N. Ladany, & T. Anderson (Eds.), *Bringing psychotherapy research to life: Understanding change through the work of leading clinical researchers.* Washington, DC: American Psychological Association.

Weiser-Cornell, A. (1996). The power of focusing: A practical guide to emotional self healing. Oakland, CA: New Harbinger.

Wheeler, G. (1991). *Gestalt reconsidered.* New York, NY: Gardner.

Whitaker, C. & Malone, T. (1953). *The roots of psychotherapy.* New York, NY: Blakiston.

Whitaker, C. & Malone, T. (1969). Experiential or nonrational psychotherapy. In W. Sahakian (Ed.), *Psychotherapy and counseling: Studies in techniques* (pp. 416–431). Chicago: Rand McNally.

Wolfe, B., & Sigl, P. (1998). Experiential psychotherapy of the anxiety disorders. In L. S. Greenberg, J. C. Watson, & G. Lietaer (Eds.), *Handbook of experiential psychotherapy* (pp. 272–294). New York, NY: Guilford Press.

Wyatt, G. (2001). Introduction to the series. In G. Wyatt (Ed.), *Rogers' therapeutic conditions: Evolution, theory and practice: Vol. 1. Congruence* (pp. i–vi). Ross-on-Wye, England: PCCS Books.

Yalom, I. (1980). *Existential psychotherapy.* New York, NY: Basic Books.

Yalom, I. (1995). *The theory and practice of group psychotherapy* (4th ed.). New York, NY: Basic Books.

Yalom, I. (2007). http://www.yalom.com

Yontef, G. (1969). *A Review of the practice of gestalt therapy.* Los Angeles, CA: Trident Books.

Yontef, G. M. (1993). *Awareness, dialogue and process: Essays on gestalt therapy.* Highland, NY: Gestalt Journal Press.

Yontef, G. M., & Simkin, J. S. (1989). Gestalt therapy. In R. J. Corsini & D. Wedding (Eds.), *Current psychotherapies* (4th ed., pp. 323–361). Itasca, IL: Peacock.

6

FAMILY SYSTEMS THEORIES
OF PSYCHOTHERAPY

DAVID R. CHABOT

This review of the developments in systems psychotherapy is organized into two sections. The first section covers the *initial period* up to the classical period (1980s), when there was a shift from an individual perspective to a systems perspective. This shift represented a theoretical revolution with a corresponding radically different way of approaching the therapeutic process. This revolution was begun in the 1950s by small groups of mental health professionals working separately and in disparate places who made the *family unit* a primary focus of research and clinical intervention. Much of the early work was characterized by efforts to avoid thinking in traditional *individual* terms, which would have been reflective of existing theories. Rather, these pioneers explained behavior by using new, ecologically valid interpersonal concepts. For this initial period, I present those theoretical concepts that have received consensual validation and that form the foundation of the family systems psychotherapy.

The second section covers *conceptual changes* that built on the original concepts but expanded them in response to two main forces. Some of these conceptual changes and additions were directly related to changing social and cultural conditions. Other conceptual changes resulted from integrating the core concepts of the original theories with one another as well as combining them with established social and psychological theories.

THE INITIAL PERIOD

The early clinical researchers in family systems were well versed in the prevailing individual theories of their day. Foremost among these theories were psychoanalytic (Freud) and humanistic (Rogers) theories, within one of which most of the early pioneers had been professionally trained. To be sure, these individual theories recognized the role that negative family relationships played in the development of individual pathology. However, the treatment of these problems tended to avoid direct involvement with family members; rather, treatment focused on the dysfunctional or distressed individual, emphasizing a "corrective emotional experience" with the therapist.

The early family pioneers asked these questions: "What would happen if we were to focus on the family relationships in a direct manner to conceptualize and treat problems that presented in an individual?" "What concepts would we need to both understand how problems develop and to intervene successfully?" "To what extent would we have to reject and/or accept prevailing theoretical concepts and techniques from individual theories to succeed?" Their answers to this last question in particular provided a basis for a classification framework that organizes the diverse early contributions to family therapy theory.

An early classification of family systems theories (Guerin, 1979) proposed a metaphor of two branches of a tree: those practitioners who based their clinical methods on traditional psychoanalytic (individual) theory and those practitioners who attempted to formulate a *systems* conceptual framework using new, nonpsychoanalytic concepts. This latter approach was first represented in the early 1950s by the Bateson Project with its emphasis on the communication process between family members. It continued with the work of Jackson and Weakland (1961) and Haley (1976) and extended to the Brief Therapy Project of Watzlawick, Weakland, and Fisch (1974). Later, Ackerman's brief therapy and the work of the Milan Associates (Selvini-Palazzoli, Boscolo, Cecchin, & Prata, 1978) also branched from this, as did Minuchin's (1974) structural therapy.

The psychoanalytic branch of the early family theory tree involved a wide range of relatively independent groups, all of whom retained some psychoanalytic elements in their concepts. This branch included theorists who maintained a direct connection to psychoanalytic theory (Ackerman, 1958; Boszormenyi-Nagy & Framo, 1965), theorists who approached family systems from a group process framework (Bell, 1961; Wynne, 1988), and a group that embraced multigenerational systems (Bowen, 1966, 1976, and his descendents, Guerin, Fogarty, and Kerr). It also included a more experiential group of pioneers who shared a common humanistic framework overlaying primarily psychoanalytic beginnings. This group was typically more interested in technique rather than theory (Satir, 1967; Whitaker, 1976).

Communication Theorists

The communication theorists began their work with the Bateson project at Palo Alto, California. In addition to the original members of this project, there were other significant early theorists who remained true to communication concepts but who went on to produce additional seminal concepts within communication theory.

Bateson Project and Mental Research Institute

In 1954, Gregory Bateson, a cultural anthropologist, studied patterns of communication in schizophrenics. He was joined in the research by Jay Haley (communication), John Weakland (chemical engineering), and Don Jackson (psychiatry). In the early phases of their work, they interviewed individual hospitalized patients at the Palo Alto Veterans Hospital. A few years later (1959) Jackson founded the Mental Research Institute (MRI) and invited Virginia Satir (social work) to join him. After Jackson's death in 1968, Watzlawick (psychology) and Weakland were joined by Richard Fisch (psychiatry) to form the Brief Therapy Project at the MRI.

From these interdisciplinary researches emerged several seminal concepts of family systems. One of the most basic concepts was *family homeostasis*, a concept borrowed from biology. The concept of family homeostasis described how families resist change, and how, when challenged, these relationship systems strive to maintain the status quo even at considerable emotional cost to one of their members. Jackson was among the first to observe the camouflaging function that a child's symptoms provide for covert parental conflict. Thus, the child becomes the *identified patient* instead of the dysfunctional family process.

Another core idea that emerged from these projects was the concept of the *double bind*. It was based on the family homeostasis and multiple, often contradictory, levels of communication in relationships. In certain relationship situations, an overt and explicit meaning of a communication is contradicted by the implied or *metamessage*. The six basic characteristics of the double bind may be summarized as follows (Nichols, 2008):

1. Two or more persons are involved in an important relationship.
2. The relationship is a repeated experience.
3. A primary negative injunction is given, such as "do not do X, or I will punish you."
4. A second injunction is given that conflicts with the first but at a more abstract level. This injunction is also enforced by a perceived threat. This second injunction is often nonverbal and frequently involves one parent's negating the injunction of the other.

5. A third-level negative injunction exists that prohibits escape from the field while also demanding a response.
6. Once the victim is conditioned to perceive the world in terms of a double bind, the necessity for every condition to be present disappears, and almost any part is enough to precipitate panic or rage.

In 1967, Watzlawick, Beavin, and Jackson published *Pragmatics of Human Communication*. In this text they explained a "calculus" of human communications, that is, a series of principles about communication and metacommunication. They defined disturbed behavior as a communicative reaction to a particular family relationship rather than evidence of a disease of the individual mind. Further, they emphasized both the pathological and potentially therapeutic aspect of paradox in human communications and the value of the therapeutic double bind, an intervention wherein the therapist attempts to use the natural oppositional forces within the family system to resist continuing dysfunctional behavior. They demonstrated no interest in triangles, the transmission of anxiety, or the role of situational stress.

In 1974, Watzlawick, Weakland, and Fisch reported on their work at the MRI's Brief Therapy Center. Core concepts were problem formation, problem resolution, first-order change, second-order change, and reframing. A summary of the principles of first-order and second-order change reveals the importance of this contribution:

1. First-order change occurs within a given system, which itself remains unchanged. It is a logical, commonsense solution to a problem. If Johnny is failing in school, mother must supervise his schoolwork more closely.
2. Second-order change is applied when the first-order change (the logical, commonsense solution) is clearly demonstrated to be at the center of an escalating problem. In other words, use second-order change when first-order change is making the problem worse. The mother's hovering in the previous example is the escalating problem.
3. Second-order change based on reframing and paradox flies in the face of logic and common sense and usually is perceived as weird and unexpected. The second-order change in the preceding example is defining the mother's escalating behavior as desirable and as required in greater amounts to produce the desired result.
4. The use of second-order changes lifts the situation out of the trap created by the commonsense solution and places it in a different frame. The entrapping, repetitive cycle of mother's pres-

sure and son's responsive passivity is replaced by a new sequence
of behaviors, which eliminates the symptoms.

The work of the interdisciplinary Bateson Project and the MRI produced groundbreaking contributions to family systems thinking. The concepts of homeostasis, double bind, reframing, paradoxical injunctions, first- and second-order change, metacommunication, and prescribing the symptom owe their origins to these overlapping groups. Of the persons contributing to these research programs, those most directly influential on the clinical behavior of succeeding generations of family therapists have been Haley and Satir. Satir's contribution is presented in the section on experiential systems theorists.

Jay Haley

Jay Haley emerged from his work on the Bateson Project with a two-fold conviction that clinical symptoms were a by-product of context and that a power struggle for control was behind relationship patterns. A logical consequence of his thinking was the view that a person's symptom is a strategy for obtaining control within a relationship. The covert nature of the process, its being out of awareness, and the function it serves for the symptomatic individual and the family homeostasis render direct confrontation of the symptom and attempts to make the process explicit fruitless. Therefore, counterstrategies that bypass or confuse the homeostatic mechanism, creating chaos and allowing for spontaneous reorganization, represent the optimal clinical methodology. From the beginning of his work, Haley paid close attention to hierarchal structure as it relates to power distribution and advocated therapeutic strategies to defeat entrenched patterns of dysfunctional behavior.

Haley's work with Minuchin and Montalvo at the Philadelphia Child Guidance Clinic helped fashion structural family therapy, a method described later in this chapter. In the 1970s, Haley left Philadelphia and with Cloe Madanes established the Family Institute in Washington, DC. From then on his focus shifted away from structural family therapy to the pursuit of a more refined understanding of hierarchy, power, and strategic intervention. By the 1980s, Haley's (1984) and Madanes's (1981) contributions to strategic family therapy made it the most popular approach to family therapy.

Two predominant characteristics of Haley's methods are his firm belief in the uselessness of direct educational techniques and his corollary commitment never to explain himself but rather to operate covertly on the process of power by giving directives to the family that are specific to the presenting problem. Together, Haley (1984) and Madanes developed a clinical method for working strategically with severe marital dysfunction called ordeal therapy. In this method, a strategic ordeal is fashioned that provides, on the one hand, a ritual of penance and absolution, and on the other, a bond formed between the two people who experience an ordeal together. A recent shift in the Haley and Madanes form of therapy involves *strategic humanism*. Here, directives are still given by the therapist, but these directives are designed to help family members be more loving to each other rather than to gain greater control over others.

Milan Associates

The Milan Associates (Selvini-Palazzoli et al., 1978) consisted in its early years of four principals: Selvini-Palazzoli, Boscolo, Cecchin, and Prata. The Milan model is an interesting method, with fibers from the work of the Bateson Project, the strategic therapists, and Minuchin all woven together into a creative fabric. The early work of this group involved seeing families typically once a month to avoid dependency on the therapist and used techniques that were direct derivatives of the earlier communication theorists. Family problems were framed with a *positive connotation*—a positive reframing of the symptomatic behavior without the earlier connotation that someone else in particular was benefiting from the symptom. This was done by the therapist to lower family resistance to the reframing. *Circular questioning* was used by the therapist to address differences in perceptions about events and relationships. This technique was designed to help the family member see their behavior as interpersonal. The Milan group stressed the importance of defining the *family rules*, an approach similar to that of Jackson in his early work. *Rituals* (initially involving paradox) were directed to the family to more clearly manifest these family rules and counter their negative consequences.

Later the group stopped using paradoxical prescriptions and replaced this technique with *invariant prescriptions*. This technique assumed that a child's symptomatic behavior was the result of his or her being caught in the power struggle between the parents with the child trying to side with one parent over the other. The invariant prescription involved having the parents tell the child that they had a secret (not available to the child). In addition, the parents were to spend more alone time with one another to foster the parental dyad and detriangulate the child. In this country, the Milan Associates' methods were built on and modified at the Ackerman Institute, which led to an American version of the Milan method.

Salvatore Minuchin

Minuchin began to develop his family theory in 1962 at the Wiltwyck School for Boys in New York. The staff of the Wiltwyck Project included E. H. (Dick) Averswald, Richard Rabkin, Bernice Russman, and Braulio Montalvo. Averswald was strongly influenced by Bateson's ideas, and Rabkin brought a certain irreverence for traditional psychotherapy theories and methods best documented in his text *Inner and Outer Space* (Rabkin, 1970) and in an essay titled "Is the Unconscious Necessary?" (Rabkin, 1968).

Minuchin formed his model of the family as a relationship system. His model rests heavily on the notion that most symptoms, whether they present as a dysfunction in an individual (such as anorexia) or as a conflict in a relationship, are a byproduct of structural failings within the family organization. The family is normally determined by structure, power, function, boundaries between subsystems, and degrees of functional attachment among individuals. The family, as defined by Minuchin, is the nuclear family or household. Minuchin would include the grandparental generation in his observational lens only when the grandparent was a part of the household.

His description of the family system as a whole relates to the degree to which a family structure demonstrates appropriate boundaries. Those families with dysfunctional structures are grouped into two categories. *Enmeshed* is the term used for those families characterized by overly permeable or absent boundaries, and the term *disengaged* is used for families with rigid boundaries between individuals that do not allow enough flexibility or attachment. The *structure* of structural family therapy can be best understood by examining boundaries and triangles or *conflict detouring triads*, as triangles have been termed within this model. After *joining* with the family and having them *enact* their typical process, the therapist maps out the structure of the family highlighting specific interactions and then attempts to unbalance the interactions to create healthier boundaries.

Minuchin's (1974) model was a major breakthrough in the history of family therapy. His video training tapes demonstrated the systemic aspects of clinical problems formerly conceptualized as residing within the individual. The impact was to turn the attention of the mental health movement toward the developing field of family therapy. One of the most admirable aspects of Minuchin's work has been the ability to make his conceptual formulations and clinical methodology effective with underprivileged populations.

The early work described previously initially resulted in a *communication* school of family systems therapy. The concepts were so important, so fundamental that they were readily incorporated into other major schools of family therapy. As a result, the communication school lost its separate identity. By the 1980s, the two major schools of family therapy that contained these original ideas were the strategic and the structural schools, which were the most popular theories at that time. A central characteristic of all this work was its emphasis on overt behaviors between family members rather than internal processes (thinking and feeling) within individual family members. The family systems theorists described in the section that follows emphasized *emotional* processes consistent with their psychoanalytic foundations but extended them to more fully account for the family from a systems point of view.

Psychoanalytic Theorists

The next group of early theorists to be considered is implicitly defined by their relative weddedness to psychoanalytic formulations. This is not surprising for two major reasons: First, most of these theorists were trained in psychoanalytic theory, which was the dominant clinical theory in the 1950s when their family theory efforts were initiated. Second, much of psychoanalytic knowledge about how and why people behave had already been incorporated into the mental health field. Thus, one did not have to be a psychoanalyst to be using psychoanalytic thinking. Although this group started by drawing from psychoanalytic theory, its core contributions viewed the family from a systems perspective. The psychoanalytic group can be divided into three subcategories: those with a group therapy focus (Bell and Wynne), an object relations group (Ackerman, Framo, and Boszormenyi-Nagy), and the Bowen group (Bowen, Guerin, Fogarty, and Kerr).

Group Focus

It was only natural for some early theorists to draw on group therapy and add it to their psychoanalytic base in their efforts to formulate family systems theory. Serious work dating back to the 1920s had already been completed regarding the process of organized groups. Gestalt psychology had demonstrated how the group was more than the sum of its parts, thus necessitating that individual concepts alone would not suffice in understanding family functioning. Role theory was already well established. More important, the process–content distinction had gained wide acceptance, indicating that it may be more important to focus on how something is said rather than what is said. The contributions of John Bell and Lyman Wynne are particularly important here.

Bell was a psychologist at Clark University who began his clinical work with families in the early 1950s. He is important because many consider him to be one of the founders of family therapy along with Ackerman, Bowen, and Jackson. Bell's (1961) work focused on pragmatic ways to deal with the power differential between parents and children when seeing them all in family sessions. He orchestrated a three-phase therapeutic process in which he first focused on the children to prepare them for conjoint family meetings, then focused on the parents, and finally, the entire family. His stages to therapy demonstrate his investment in traditional analytic theory: defining a therapeutic contract, testing limits, shifting of power within the group, achieving success on a common task, and termination issues. Reflecting his psychoanalytic base, Bell strongly believed in the importance of maintaining effective boundaries between the therapist and the family group.

Lyman Wynne received his doctor of medicine in psychiatry and his doctorate in social relations at Harvard. He worked with Bowen at the National Institute of Mental Health, where both shared a commitment to studying schizophrenia from a family process perspective. The development of his major concepts *pseudomutuality* and *pseudohostility* (Wynne, Ryckoff, Day, & Hirsch, 1958) described distorted emotional processes within the family. Pseudomutuality describes a surface appearance of agreement and attachment among family members, while in reality the family members are tightly locked into dysfunctional roles that did not permit individuation from the family or truly close relationships within it. Behind the pseudomutality is a strong fear of separateness. Although pseudomutuality reflects a deficit in expressing positive affect in the family, pseudohostility reflects a disturbance of negative affect. Pseuodohostility is behavior that also speaks to problems in intimacy, affection, and fear of separateness but masks this deficit by hostility and bickering rather than by false connectedness.

Wynne's third major concept, the "rubber fence," describes how dysfunctional families are socially isolated and only open a tight boundary around themselves to permit minimal extrafamilial involvement with others. Thus, an "outside" person, such as a psychotherapist seeking to engage family members, might feel a certain ease of entry into the family, only to be bounced out later as if by a rubber fence if certain unwritten rules were violated. Developed in a research program, these important concepts have yet to be interpreted into a more elaborate clinical model of family therapy

Although important contributions were made to family therapy by early pioneers espousing group therapy model, there are inherent limitations in how much one could transfer group concepts to family systems. These limitations are largely due to the fact that group therapy involves an ad hoc group, whereas family therapy involves a natural group. "Continuity, commitment and shared distortions all make family therapy different from group therapy" (Nichols, 2008, p. 16).

Object Relations

As mentioned earlier, Freudian theory has long been influential in understanding the impact of family relationships on the psychological functioning of its individual members. In the early days of family therapy, attempts to formulate a separate theory for family were resisted by the psychoanalytic community. Family therapy was viewed as a method or technique, similar to group therapy, which had successfully adapted traditional Freudian theory.

Clinical work with families, from the perspective of the analytic community, was indicated in two situations. One situation was when family members needed education about the ways in which they were potentially defeating the transferential therapy of an individual. The other situation was one in which there was a need to open communications around tension-filled conflicts within the family. Initially there was considerable skepticism about seeing families because of the possible effects on the transference, but eventually a group committed to psychoanalytic theory began to experiment with such methods. The child psychoanalyst Nathan Ackerman, who many consider to be one of the founders of family therapy, began to see families as early as the mid 1940s. He used the traditional psychoanalytic model of drives and defenses as a framework for his clinical efforts with the family. Later, those in the analytic community who maintained both an allegiance to analytic theory and an interest in family therapy moved toward object relations as their primary conceptual base.

The theoretical underpinnings of the object relations approach to family therapy rest on the work of Klein (1946) and Fairbairn (1952). The Kleinian concept of *good breast/bad breast* refers to infantile ambivalence about the mother derived from the developmental experiences of nurturance and deprivation. Fairbairn developed the idea of internalized relationship structures. Contained within these proposed structures were partial objects, that is, a portion of the ego and the affect associated with the relationship. The external object was perceived as either all good, all bad, or both, in alternating cycles, which Fairbairn referred to as *splitting*. Fairbairn believed that when the splitting process was not resolved, the individual's ability to objectify relationships was impaired. This concept of splitting has been developed further in the notion of *projective identification*.

Projective identification is defined as a process whereby an individual first projects onto another person certain denied behaviors or characteristics of his or her own personality. Then, in the interaction, the person behaves in ways that either provoke such behaviors from the other or reacts as if the other possesses these characteristics, which thereby reinforces the projective perception. A simple example from a marital relationship is when a wife with an internalized judgmental and negative image of herself projects the perception of a harsh, critical, unloving person onto her husband and then behaves in ways that predictably bring forth critical and withholding behaviors on his part.

Family therapists working with these concepts can track this interactional process within the session and interpret the object relation forces that are driving the conflict. These methods closely resemble those used early on in psychoanalytically based family therapy wherein the existence of naturally occurring *transferences* in the family was hypothesized and interpreted clinically to explain relationship conflict and dysfunction.

The most prominent individual in the early years to blend psychoanalytic theory with family therapy theory was Nathan Ackerman. A man of broad interests, Ackerman was a prolific writer on a variety of topics. Early in his medical career he published on the psychological aspects of hypertension and on the impact of the economic depression of the 1930s on coal miners' families. A psychoanalyst, he maintained his commitment to psychoanalytic thought and practice. Ackerman's belief in the primacy of analytic theory resulted in his not developing a conceptual model for his clinical work with families. A study of his filmed clinical interviews suggests three themes in his work consistent with his use of analytic theory: nurturance and dependency, control and anger, and sexuality and aggression. These themes can be viewed as corresponding to the different stages of psychosexual development of the individual: oral, anal, and phallic. Operationalizing the oral theme, Ackerman would challenge family members on their excessive need to be fed, on their "sucking" behavior, and on their desire to be a baby. He would provoke them into expressing their anger and would openly discuss their unconscious oedipal strivings. Ackerman quickly took charge and made contact with each family member after playfully teasing the children, flirting with the women, and challenging the men in a fairly aggressive style. He was an activist stirring up emotion by a process he called "tickling the defenses." He believed it was healthy to let emotion out, especially to express anger openly.

Today, Ackerman's contribution to family systems is experienced by many as remote, in much the same way most people experience the process in their own extended families—interesting but irrelevant to the present. Nonetheless, Ackerman's contribution remains relevant to the major issues in family therapy. For one example, he was sensitive to the impact of the social context on families far earlier than most. His study of the families of coal miners enduring the lingering depression of the late 1930s remains a model for studying the impact of social context on the internal dynamics of the family. It raises questions still pertinent today, such as what constitutes a functional adaptation versus a maladaptation? What are the premorbid or preevent characteristics of those families that adapt well as opposed to those families that are thrown into chaos and fragmentation? For another example, Ackerman contributed a typology of families. In his 1958 book *The Psychodynamics of Family Life*, Ackerman presented a preliminary typology: disturbance of marital pairs, disturbance of parental pairs, disturbance of childhood, disturbance of adolescence, and psychosomatic families. A clinical typology, even one that is symptom focused as is this one, is essential to the development of corresponding clinical methodologies.

Ivan Boszormenyi-Nagy, a psychiatrist, and James Framo, a psychologist, edited a volume titled *Intensive Family Therapy: Theoretical and Practical Aspects* (Boszormenyi-Nagy & Framo, 1965) that brought together papers from most of the leading family researchers at that time. Framo adopted Fairbairn's object relations theory as the basis for his work. In his practice, this position led to his inviting significant extended family members into the sessions, especially when dealing with marital conflict. Framo also expended considerable effort in integrating his work with that of others whose theoretical stance derived primarily from psychoanalytic theory.

Boszormenyi-Nagy also maintained his psychoanalytic orientation when he changed from the study of schizophrenia to the study of loyalty in families, particularly as it influences coalitions and alliances over multiple generations. This work is described in his book *Invisible Loyalties: Reciprocity in Intergenerational Family Therapy*, written with his colleague Geraldine Spark (Boszormenyi-Nagy & Spark, 1973). Boszormenyi-Nagy offered the concept of the family ledger, an invisible ledger of mutigenerational accounts of obligations, debts, and events perceived as relationship atrocities. These firmly entrenched emotional wounds require retribution of some kind over the generations. If a problem's genesis is reframed in terms of old wounds and loyalties, family members have a face-saving mechanism that allows them to give up their present-day conflict (Hoffman, 1981).

In 1987 Boszormenyi-Nagy made additional contributions with his *contextual therapy*, which places ethical behavior between family members center stage for adaptive family functioning. His reminder that relationships have to be fair to be functional is most important. Around the same time, the Washington School of Psychiatry was refining the psychoanalytic method of treating families. David Scharff and his wife, Jill Scharff (1987), published their work in a book titled *Object Relations Family Therapy*.

The Bowen Group

Bowenian family systems therapy evolved directly from psychoanalytic principles and practices. It is the most comprehensive model of family systems insofar as it consists of a defined number of concepts with a corresponding clinical methodology. Murray Bowen, its originator and major contributor, began with an interest in studying the problem of schizophrenia and brought to his study of the family extensive training in psychoanalysis, including 13 years of personal training analysis.

In the early years of the family therapy movement, many of the pioneers trod lightly in the area of theory. Bowen was the exception to this rule, both in his emphasis on the importance of theory and in his belief that his ideas could form a new theory of human emotional functioning. He hoped his theory would be viewed as evolving from Freudian theory but be seen as distinctly different from it in its systems orientation. Bowen kept an essential element of psychoanalytic theory, emotional process, but moved it beyond an intrapersonal domain to a transgenerational domain. In this sense his theory does evolve from Freudian theory but becomes something distinctively different. Because of the emphasis on the emotional process in the system rather than in the individual, the techniques of Bowenian therapy are substantially different from psychoanalytic therapy techniques in spite of their similar beginnings. Bowen (1978) believed that the task of the theorist was to find the smallest number of congruent concepts that could fit together as a working blueprint for understanding the human experience. He designated eight concepts as central to his theory: differentiation of self, triangles, nuclear family emotional system, family projection process, emotional cutoff, multigeneration transmission process, sibling position, and societal regression. He repeatedly warned of the pitfalls of lowest common denominator eclecticism.

Bowen dated the beginning of his theory to his clinical work with schizophrenia at the Menninger Clinic from 1946 to 1954. During that time he studied mothers and their schizophrenic offspring who lived together in small cottages on the Menninger campus. From this clinical research he was hoping to gain a better understanding of mother–child symbiosis. Observations from these studies led to the formation of his concept of differentiation (Bowen, 1972). Bowen's concept of differentiation consists of two interrelated parts, an interpersonal differentiation and an intrapsychic differentiation. To be differentiated on the interpersonal level one has to achieve a balance between a well-defined sense of self while simultaneously being able to be in an intimate relationship with another. To the extent that one fails to do this, one is either fused to the other at the expense of having a well-defined sense of self or one is without a functional close relationship because one is attempting to acquire or preserve a well-defined sense of self. When one has a poor level of differentiation interpersonally it is accompanied by a poor level of differentiation intrapsychically. A poor level of differentiation on the intrapsychic level involves a lack of integration between one's feelings and one's thinking. An individual who is poorly differentiated intrapsychically does not behave in a functional manner because of excessive emotionality or the lack thereof. Bowen's concept of differentiation has been well received by family therapists and researchers. There are a number of scales that measure interpersonal differentiation. Chabot has developed an intrapsychic scale of Bowen's concept (Licht & Chabot, 2006).

From the Menninger Clinic, Bowen moved to the National Institute of Mental Health, where he formed a project to hospitalize and study whole families with a schizophrenic member. It was this project that expanded the concept of mother–child symbiosis to involve fathers that inevitably led to the Bowen concept of *triangulation*. Triangulation is another central concept in Bowen theory and has become an essential concept in any systems theory of psychotherapy. Triangles get created when there is a lack of differentiation interpersonally and intrapsychically. As one is unable to achieve a balance between a well-defined sense of self and a simultaneous functional close relationship anxiety is experienced. One seeks to stabilize the anxious situation by moving off the relationship and involving a third person or thing. A triangle is an abstract way of thinking about a structure in human relationships, and triangulation is the reactive emotional process that goes on within that triangle.

For example, when a couple presents for treatment, the triangle with their son may have become relatively fixed so that the mother and the son are overly close and the father is in the distant, outside position. This alignment may occasionally shift so that there are times when either the mother or the son is in the outside position and the father has some closeness with his son or his wife, but then it shifts back to its usual dysfunctional structure. Triangulation is the emotional process that occurs among the three people who make up the triangle. For example, in the triangle just described the father might desire a connection with his son and resent his wife's monopoly of the boy's affection; the mother may be angry at the father's distance from her and compensate by substituting closeness with her son. The child, in turn, may resent his father's inattention and criticism and may move toward his mother but, at the same time, be anxious about his overly close relationship with her. As the emotional process of triangulation moves around the triangle it can produce changes in its structure.

In 1959, Bowen left the National Institute of Mental Health and went to Georgetown Medical School, where he was a professor of psychiatry until his death in the fall of 1990. In his 31 years at Georgetown, Bowen refined his theory by applying it to less dysfunctional populations and developing a clinical methodology that he could pass on to the psychiatric residents at Georgetown. Bowen saw the need for a corresponding method that would assist the psychotherapist in the development of his or her own personal autonomy. For this purpose, Bowen began to research and experiment with the emotional process within his own personal family system. A documentation of his research on his own family of origin was first presented at a national family therapy conference in 1967 and published in 1972; in the published study Bowen spelled out his method and its four steps in detail. First, know the facts about your family relationship system. Bowen encouraged his trainees to construct comprehensive family diagrams to document the structural relationships among members of the family and to gather facts about the timing of important events such as deaths and births. Second, he coached his trainees to become better observers of their families and to learn to control their emotional reactivity to these people. Third, he taught them how to detriangulate themselves from emotional situations. This part of the method entails developing an ability to stay nonreactive during periods of intense anxiety within one's own family. Last, he advocated the development of person-to-person relationships with as many family members as possible.

Over the years Bowen trained many psychiatrists. Among the most influential are Phil Guerin, Tom Fogarty, and Mike Kerr. Kerr remained at Georgetown as Bowen's closest associate, and his theoretical contributions are reflective of that association. One of his major contributions has been the further development of the role of anxiety in the family system. Fogarty (1976a, 1976b, 1984) has become most widely known for his contributions detailing the repetitive patterns of pursuit and distance (with the corresponding concepts of the emotional pursuer and the emotional distancer). These patterns reflect the preferred styles that individuals manifest in a relationship as they struggle to achieve a balance between autonomy and closeness. Chabot (1996) has operationalized these concepts into a brief test useful for both clinical work and research. Guerin, Fay, Burden, and Kautto's (1987) most important contributions to family therapy are the clarifications and elaborations of Bowen's concepts as well as the application of the theory to the treatment of marital conflict and child and adolescent centered families. In his work Guerin has focused on the development of the individual's "adaptive level of functioning" to operationalize the more fixed and innate aspects of differentiation as described by Bowen.

Experientialist Theorists

Experiential family therapy is characterized by its emphasis on intuition, feelings, unconscious processes, and an atheoretical stance. The foundations of this approach stem from the existential–humanistic tradition, which emphasizes personal freedom, honest expression of emotion, and the underlying natural goodness of individuals. The two major figures in this branch of the family therapy movement are Carl Whitaker (Whitaker & Keith, 1981) and Virginia Satir (1967). Both of them drew on quite different epistemologies for their therapies, but they shared a common set of experiential assumptions and techniques in their clinical work that parallels the work of Carl Rogers in individual therapy in its underlying assumptions.

Carl Whitaker's approach to family therapy was predicated on the belief that family problems are due to emotional suppression of individuals. Thus, his goal was to help individuals better express themselves emotionally as a way of improving family functioning. His approach was pragmatic and atheoretical (to the point of being antitheoretical). Whitaker (1976) considered theory to be useful only for the beginning therapist. He believed that the real role of theory for the novice therapist is to control his or her anxiety about managing the clinical situation. Whitaker preferred to use the support of a cotherapist and a supervisor to deal with these stresses rather than relying on theory. When a family functions well it is cohesive which, in turn, fosters individual growth. Honest affective expression is critical both for individual growth and for family cohesion.

The basic goal of therapy for Whitaker is to facilitate individual autonomy and a sense of belonging within the family. The emphasis is on the emotional experience, not conceptual understanding. Above all, the process of therapy is a very personal experience for the therapist. The more expressive and genuine the connection between the therapist and the family members in the session, the more successful the therapy is considered to be.

Existential encounter is believed to be the most important therapeutic process for both the therapist and the family. Early in his career Whitaker tended to present himself in a provocative manner as he attempted to break through the clients' defenses and relate to them in an emotionally honest manner. In his own interviews, Whitaker's highest stated priority was to "get something out of it for myself." What he did clinically, on a fairly consistent basis, was to seize on a perception of the family's "craziness" and attempt to escalate this state of affairs to the level of the absurd. One can see an example of Whitaker's method in his statement to a young man who had recently made a suicide gesture. Whitaker turned to the young man and said to him that he should consider taking his therapist with him the next time he felt suicidal. Whitaker explained this maneuver as an attempt at augmenting the pathology of the family until the symptoms disappeared (Hoffman, 1981). Although Whitaker's contributions to the family therapy movement have been considerable (Whitaker, 1976; Whitaker, Felder, & Warkentin, 1965), his contribution to a formalized system of family psychotherapy has been minimal. He was, however, a master at being able to get the family to improve by engaging each family member in the session and helping family members to express themselves emotionally more fully. In this way he worked at changing the family by changing individual members.

Virginia Satir, like Whitaker, represents a clinical method that is highly personalized, experiential, and immensely popular. Satir began her work with families in Chicago and in 1959 came to California to join Don Jackson at the MRI. There she organized what may have been the first formal training program in family therapy. Although she left the MRI to work at the Esalen Institute, where she further developed her humanistic–experiential therapy, much of her conceptual framework is based on the Bateson Project, especially in the formulations of Jackson concerning the rules that govern relationships and the forces of family homeostasis. Satir speaks of the family as a *balanced* system and, in her assessment, seeks to determine the price individual family members pay to maintain this balance. She views symptoms as blockages to growth, which help to maintain the family status quo. She is more important as a skilled clinician and teacher than as an original theorist. However, her impact on the practices of family therapists was far from minor. Indeed, she may be the most influential of all the family pioneers mentioned in this chapter.

Despite the fact that Satir did not primarily concern herself with theory, there are several theoretical premises in her work. First, there is a strong emphasis on individual growth stemming from positive self-esteem. Second, Satir emphasizes communication patterns among family members. Third, she addresses the rules by which the family members interact with one another, and fourth, she emphasizes the family linkage to society.

These four aspects of family life are viewed as universal needs and forces operating in all families. In Satir's definition of healthy families, the individual member has positive self-esteem and communication is clear, emotionally honest, and direct. The family rules by which the system maintains itself are conducive to individual growth. Thus, family rules are human, flexible, and appropriate to the situation at hand.

A fifth premise is that the family does not function as a closed emotional system but is open to larger systems in society and hopeful in its outlook. As a counterpoint, Satir believes that troubled families do not foster positive self-worth; communication patterns are indirect and vague; rules are not flexible but absolute; and the family functions as a closed emotional system in a defensive and negative manner.

Satir (1972) stated her goals in family therapy,

> We attempt to make three changes in the family system. First, each member of the family should be able to report congruently, completely, and obviously on what he sees and hears, feels and thinks, about himself and others, in the presence of others. Second, each person should be addressed and related to in terms of his uniqueness, so that decisions are made in terms of exploration and negotiation rather than in terms of power. Third, differentness must be openly acknowledged and used for growth. (p. 120)

Although Satir conceptualized the family in these ways, her therapy technique involved heavy use of herself in a direct, pragmatic, and supportive way. She described herself both as a "mirror," allowing the family to see how it was functioning, and as a "teacher" suggesting ways to grow by offering specifics on how to improve self-esteem and communication patterns.

There is some suggestion that Satir may have overworked self-esteem and communication in her attempts to account for both normal and pathological family functioning. Again, like Whitaker, her highly individual and powerful persona makes reproducibility a problem for descendant generations. On the other hand, her optimistic view of the potential for growth in families and her dynamic teaching of many other family therapists make her a major personality in family therapy.

Conclusions From the Initial Period

Even though the work of the early systems theorists started from different vantage points, the end result was agreement on a number of core assumptions about how to understand family functioning. Perhaps the most fundamental assumption is that the whole is greater than the sum of its parts. Related to this is the assumption that pathology is not only within the individual, but is in the system (often across multiple generations). Functional behavior is characterized by development of healthy individual differentiation as well as appropriate dyadic relationships. The dysfunctional aspects of a family can be understood by considering the structure and process of triangles, boundaries, communications, power, and rules. Causality is not linear but circular among family members. The tendency to maintain homeostasis involves feedback loops. Effective improvement of functioning often necessitates second-order change.

Although a single comprehensive theory did not emanate from this early work, three major models emerged with a strong systemic perspective: the strategic (Haley and colleagues), the structural (Minuchin), and the multigenerational (Bowen). Each of these models had its strengths as well as its weaknesses. The strategic model, although clearly demonstrating the power of context and the magic of paradox and reframing, failed to consider the internal developmental struggles of the individual. Therefore, it overvalued context in much the same way that a theory of the individual undervalues it.

The structural model of Minuchin (1974) was the clearest and most easily understood of the three. However, it was much more a model of doing therapy than a comprehensive theory of family psychotherapy. In addition, although it was eminently teachable and reproducible, it was almost entirely a method for working with child-focused families. It offered little assistance for working with the problems of a relationship conflict between adults and/or working with an individual.

The multigenerational model of Bowen and his descendents represented the most consistent effort at developing a broad-based theory of family psychotherapy, including attention to the development of individual autonomy. However, Bowen's models became somewhat murky in attempts to define and describe differentiation and triangulation. In addition, their clinical technique can become overly ritualized and constricted.

CONCEPTUAL CHANGES IN SYSTEMS THEORY

Since the initial period (and the emergence of these three dominant theories), family therapy has profited from a number of important contributions. In the next section of this chapter, I summarize these contributions as stemming from two major sources: (a) changing social conditions and (b) the integration of theories.

Changing Social Conditions

The concepts of clinical theory that are used to provide direction for the treatment of families did not get developed in a vacuum but were constantly being influenced by changing social and economic conditions. Concepts relevant to the psychoeducation, solution-focused, feminist, and multicultural approaches to family therapy have been particularly influenced by changing social and economic conditions.

Psychoeducation

Perhaps the major social force in the 1960s that had an impact on the mental health field was the movement toward deinstitutionalization and community care. Related to these movements was an enlarged focus on well-being, rather than on pathology, and on prevention, rather than on tertiary treatment. These changes in social philosophy resulted in the development of the psychoeducational approach to the treatment of emotional dysfunction.

The history of psychoeducation in family therapy goes back at least to the early 1970s. At that time, the Center for Family Learning, directed by Phil Guerin, received a federal grant from the National Institute of Alcohol and Alcohol Abuse to conduct multiple family groups for family members at risk for alcohol abuse. This program, called Family Systems Training, taught families the principles of family systems theory and how families function emotionally. The program targeted families with a history of alcohol abuse. In the same period, at Albert Einstein College of Medicine, family therapists at the Family Studies Section under the direction of Israel Zwerling were formulating a psychoeducation multifamily group approach for schizophrenics and their families.

The difference between these efforts was that the Center for Family Learning program was primary prevention that attempted to teach family systems principles to those at risk for alcohol abuse as determined by cultural background and family history. The Einstein program, on the other hand, was tertiary prevention created to teach families with a schizophrenic member about the phenomenon of schizophrenia. It aimed to help them cope with the emotional fallout of the disease and to relieve them of misplaced guilt that they had caused the condition in their family member. In addition, it attempted to educate family members in specific ways to relate to the schizophrenic member to promote better functioning in that person and prevent the exacerbation of symptoms that would require rehospitalization.

This latter model is consistent with methods that took hold in the early 1980s and has continued to develop in various centers through the country. Of special note is the work of Carol Anderson (Anderson, Reiss, & Hogarty, 1986) and Michael Goldstein (Goldstein, Rodnick, Evans, May, & Steinberg, 1978). Research showed that multiple family psychoeducation groups for schizophrenics and their families are more effective than medication alone at preventing rehospitalization and more effective than a combination treatment of medication and family sessions with their individual families (McFarlane, Dixon, Lukens, & Luckstead, 2003).

This early work with schizophrenia was extended to families with chronic medical problems. Medical family therapists such as McDaniel, Hepworth, and Doherty (1992) and Doherty (1996) have mapped out the relationship between the clinical aspects of a specific medical condition and specific family dynamics. These programs drew heavily from concepts contained in Bowenian and structural family theory and combined them with social support theory and expressed emotion. The work with expressed emotion has highlighted the particularly destructive nature of criticism, hostility, and emotional over-involvement. These elements have been consistently correlated with the relapse of schizophrenia (Milkowitz, 1995).

Solution-Focused Therapy

In the mid-1980s, simultaneous with the managed care focus in the health industry, the solution-focused approach to family therapy made a significant impact on the field (Berg, 1994; de Shazer, 1985; O'Hanlon & Weiner-Davis, 1989).

Managed care was an attempt to equate psychological and counseling treatments to medical treatments. By designating specific treatments for specific disorders, insurance companies sought to save money by limiting services as much as possible. Practitioners accepting managed care patients were increasingly told who they could see, what services they could provide, and how many sessions would be reimbursed. Treatments that were quick (particularly if they could be demonstrated to be effective) were preferred.

Solution-focused therapy was based on a reemergence of constructivism, a philosophical position dating back to Immanual Kant. An essential feature of constructivism is that individuals "construct" their own reality. They use their individual lens to perceive a problem in a specific way. The solution to a problem is not to analyze how a problem began or how individuals are trapped in recurring behavioral processes but to acquire new ways of solving the problem by challenging assumptions and activating solutions. This *reframing* is essentially a cognitive activity and has much in common with the earlier work of the communication theorists at the MRI. Unlike the earlier communication theorists, solution-focused therapists do not accept the notion of resistance or ulterior motives for symptomatic behavior but believe that family members *want* to change.

Here are seven assumptions that solution-focus therapists make as a basis for their interventions (from Selekman, 1993):

1. Resistance is not a useful concept. Clients want change, and the therapist should join with the family in its efforts at change.
2. Change is inevitable. The problem is to be viewed optimistically, and the therapy emphasizes possible solutions to the problems.

3. Only a small change is necessary. Therapy should proceed in a fashion that links one small change to another.
4. Clients have the strength and resources to change. Therapy emphasizes a health perspective.
5. Problems are unsuccessful attempts to resolve difficulties. Families need new consultation to get unstuck from old attempts at problem solving.
6. Therapists do not need to know a great deal about the problem in order to solve it. Understanding why the problem initially began is not necessary to finding a solution to the current problem.
7. There are multiple perspectives. There is no one way to view the problem. There is no one solution to the problem.

In addition to focusing on how the clients are framing the problem and assuming that they have the strength to change, solution-focused family therapists ask specific questions in concrete behavioral terms to get individuals to take responsibility for new actions in their relationships.

Feminism and Multiculturalism

Changing social and cultural conditions impacted the ways that family psychotherapy was conceptualized and practiced in a number of significant ways beyond the psychoeducational approach and solution-focused therapy. Feminism was a major force in getting theorists to reconceptualize family life. Rachel Hare-Mustin and Jeanne Marecek (1988) challenged whether systems theory was intrinsically predicated on concepts that were in opposition to feminist principles. Although some maintained that being a feminist therapist involved more than being sensitive to gender issues and necessitated taking an active political position, there is no question that therapists of all orientations benefited from the insights provided by feminist writings.

Multiculturalism alerted family therapists to the power of culture, race, and ethnicity in influencing family behavior. Therapists could no longer be mere technicians implementing specific techniques but had to be concerned with broader contextual issues. Therapists needed to distinguish between cultural, racial, and ethnic differences and pathology. The work of McGoldrick, Giordano, and Pearce (1996) on ethnic patterns and Boyd-Franklin (1993) on racial issues was particularly effective in raising consciousness. Cultural changes that resulted in greater awareness of the plight of marginalized groups in our society (gay and lesbian families, economically disadvantaged families, immigrant families, single-parent families) have influenced therapist thinking and practice significantly.

Integration of Theories

Once the family therapy field moved beyond its initial period there was a natural integration of these family theories with relevant preexisting psychological theories as well as with other family theories both old and new. As therapists using the new family theories became more secure about their contributions to the mental health field they were less resistant to additions, modifications, and integration of concepts and techniques drawn from multiple sources. A major force driving these changes was the desire to make theory more comprehensive to achieve greater clinical effectiveness. Indeed, integration or eclecticism is the modal position of therapists in the United States.

In this section I comment on the integration of early family therapy theories: behavioral family theory, internal family systems therapy, narrative therapy, and developmental theory. Last, I comment on family therapy theories that are a combination of elements from various family therapy theories.

Behavioral Family Therapy

Behavior therapists have a long history of applying their principles to a variety of problems that occur within the family. However, early attempt by behavior therapists to address symptoms in the family tended to occur using well-established behavior techniques that kept these efforts contained within behavior theory. Family systems therapists, for the most part, left the established theoretical groups with which they were originally associated to form their own informal, and later formal, organizations. These organizations were committed to the development of new theoretical formulations of family functioning. Thus, initially, behavior therapists and systems therapists belonged to two different professional groups and tended to use their respective techniques to address family problems. However, with time there has been a beneficial blending of the techniques of behavior therapy and systems therapy. Early on, as behaviorists attempted to move from an individual perspective to a systemic perspective, they used social exchange theory (e.g., Homans, 1961; Thibaut & Kelly, 1959). Some of the underlying assumptions of this theory include the facts that people are motivated by self-interest, that they will try to maximize their rewards at minimal cost, and that each member of a group has to expect some reward for maintaining the relationship with the group.

Jacobson and Margolin (1979), building on the earlier work of Stuart (1969), used these principles in constructing a view of reinforcement that is both circular and reciprocal. An example is the following: A wife asks her husband for more time together; the husband is not so inclined and does not respond. The wife begins to become angry and demanding, and the husband says, "There is no way I'm going to spend time with you when you act like such a shrew." This only serves to increase the wife's anger and behavioral tirade. Finally, in exhaustion, the husband gives in, saying, "Okay, if you just stop, we will go out somewhere to eat."

In this sequence, the wife has been reinforced for delivering the tirade, and the husband has been reinforced for giving in to the wife's negative behavior by stopping her tirade after he agrees to go out. In behavior exchange, each partner's behavior is both being affected by and influencing the other. Thus, the model maintains the centrality of behavior modification by intervening to alter the reinforcement contingencies while at the same time attempting to deal with a relationship focus by looking at how both spouses participate in the process of reinforcement.

Further contributions to behavioral family therapy were made when cognitive techniques were added to the original behavioral paradigm to form cognitive–behavioral therapy. The work of Beck (1988) and Dattilio (1998) has been widely received. The basic premise of these theories is that cognitions are essential along with behaviors and emotions in understanding and modifying the interactions between individuals. Cognitions, emotions, and behaviors all interact in a mutually influential manner. Beliefs can be perpetuated across generations and can result in personal schemas about self, others, and the world at large. If these schemas are predicated on false assumptions, the result is dysfunctional behavior.

Gordon and Davidson (1981) were among the first to acknowledge the limitations of behavior therapy and stressed the importance of broad-based assessment and treatments that went beyond traditional behavioral techniques. They called for an integrative model that would extend the focus of treatment to other areas of the family system beyond the presenting complaint. Today, there is general agreement that behavioral family therapy not only addresses specific symptoms but also broader systemic concerns of the family to effectively improve family functioning. As behavior therapists began to acknowledge these broad problems in the family, they began to incorporate more traditional family systems concepts and techniques into their efforts (Birchler & Spinks, 1980; Jacobson & Christensen, 1996). Thus, as behavior therapists deal with the complex problems of families, they are not only modifying their procedures but are also incorporating systemic principles, which has made their efforts more successful.

Internal Family Systems Therapy

When the family therapy movement began in the 1950s, there was a strong effort by the early theorists to avoid established individual theory. Indeed, many of the dominant leaders of the family therapy movement were allergic, if not hostile, toward existing individual theory. Those family theorists who used a psychoanalytic underpinning to their family psychotherapy were the major exception. The relentless focus on an interpersonal perspective, however, resulted in inadequate consideration of internal processes of the individual to the family process. By the mid-1980s, enough time had passed that family theorists could reconsider individual processes without fear that they were losing their systems identity. The self had rejoined the system. A strong example of this is Schwartz's (1995) internal family systems theory.

Schwartz's understanding of individuals and their relationship began when he observed that clients talked about *parts* of themselves. He conceptualized that each of these parts had a full range of feelings and beliefs and functioned as autonomous personalities, almost independent of the person in whom they existed. The goal of therapy was to help the individual to establish trust and harmony among these parts so that an integrated self could relate in a functional manner to others. These inner parts function as a system, thereby allowing the therapist to use the same principles used to treat family members to treat the subparts of an individual. Therapist tracking of the internal processes across parts is done simultaneously with the tracking of the interpersonal process between people.

Schwartz conceptualized parts of an individual into three categories, each with its own function or role. There are the *manager* parts, whose role is to be responsible and protective. There are the *exile* parts, whose role is to be containers of hurt, pain, and wounds. And there are the *fire fighter* parts, whose role is to put out the fire of the pain and hurt when it surfaces from the exiles. Overuse of fire fighter behavior does not solve the problem, and in fact it creates other problems, such as alcoholism. In addition to the parts of an individual, there is the *self*. When the self is in charge it can balance and heal the parts of the individual and thereby not be at the mercy of extreme behavior from any one part.

Narrative Therapy

Narrative therapy has its base in symbolic interactionism theory, which began in the early 1900s (Thomas & Znaniecki, 1920) and is one of the most influential theories for studying and understanding the family. These philosophical principles were used by Michael White (1991), considered to be the founder of the narrative movement in family therapy. In narrative therapy, primary import is given to the stories that families tell themselves to make sense of their experiences. These stories are core for families and are a primary source of both functional and dysfunctional behavior.

White appeared uninterested in what causes peoples' problems. Rather, he focused on how the therapist can empower them to overcome "the oppression" of their "negative lives." In doing this work, White used two main techniques. The first is the construction of a new narrative story in which the therapist helps the family members fashion a more functional and more hopeful storyline for their lives. The second technique centers on the externalization of the problem outside of the individual and the family in a way that makes the problem the external common enemy. In this way, the family as a group can join forces and become empowered to change.

The manner in which narrative therapists work with families takes its cues from the earlier work of Anderson and Goolishiam (1988) known as the collaborative-conversational model. This method is reminiscent of the 1970s when Carl Whitaker challenged therapists to abandon "dummy–expert" theories and use more collaborative methods in which family and therapist come together in a joint effort at healing. This idea of working collaboratively and supportively has been extended by many narrative family therapists (e.g., Epston, 1994; Madigan & Epston, 1995), who emphasize the need for the family to acquire supportive communities after therapy to help them sustain their new narratives.

Developmental Theory

Soon after the basic concepts of family psychotherapy became established, theorists began to study the family from a clinical perspective over time. They drew on developmental theory based on psychological and sociological theories of the family, which came into their own in the 1950s. One of the first contributions to developmental theory was made by Duvall and Hill (1948), who took the systems position that families developed as a dynamic unit not merely as a collection of individuals. In this early work, the distinction was made between the functioning of the family at a particular stage of development and the functioning of the family as they experienced the transition period between stages. Duvall's eight stages of the family life cycle, beginning with a married couple has been the most widely accepted format for family development. Each of his stages involves roles and developmental tasks for the various family members. Others have expanded the life cycle to a *life course* (e.g., Bengtson & Allen, 1993), which adds the social context in which change occurs as well as the individual meaning family members gave to the changes occurring in their life course. These contributions take into account that all families do not follow the same path on the same time table.

Contributions by family therapists to family theory have been substantial since the early 1970s. Wynne (1988) proposed an epigenetic model of family process that involved four processes: attachment, communication, joint problem solving, and mutuality. He pointed out that relational processes usually proceed at a pace that is different from individual life cycle changes. Breunlin (1988) helped to explain why families experience stress during transition periods during their life cycle. His oscillation theory proposes that transitions are not made clearly from one stage to the next but involve a period of time in which there is oscillation between levels of functioning. This back-and-forth involvement between levels of functioning is frustrating for family members. Olson has shown how his core dimensions of cohesion and adaptability need to change in a family depending on external stress and developmental stage. A family starting out with infant children may need to have a higher level of cohesion to be functional than a family that is at the stage of launching its children. Carter and McGoldrick (1980), working from their multigenerational Bowenian beginnings, have contributed substantially in demonstrating how anxiety develops in families over time particularly in response to major life transitions.

Integrative Family Psychotherapy

The preceding integrative developments draw heavily from theories outside the mainstream of family psychotherapy, such as individual psychology and developmental theory. But many developments have resulted directly from integrating different theories and techniques of family psychotherapy. Some of these integrative therapies have been in existence for a considerable period of time, and others have recently been proposed. Over the past 30 years, integrative approaches to family therapy have combined elements from the early models (structural, strategic, Bowenian, experiential) with each other as well as with elements from relatively newer models (behavioral, narrative, solution focused). It is to be expected that no one model could do full justice to the complexity of the human condition or the difficulties inherent in clinical problems. As such, approaches that integrate elements from various theories are indicated provided that they reflect conceptual integrity and clinical relevance.

An exemplar of well-developed integration is the problem-centered therapy of Pinsof (1995) and his colleagues. Working from a strategic family theory base, Pinsof added emotional expressive procedures from the experientialists, family-of-origin procedures from Bowen, or intrapsychic procedures from psychoanalytic family therapy as the course of treatment warrants. He often employed a team of therapists, each of whom had his or her own competencies to provide the needed services to a given family.

Eron and Lund (1996) proposed a well-developed therapy protocol that has been developed over the past 20 years. Their approach combines strategic elements from the earlier MRI model with narrative techniques. The use of this combination of techniques can be more easily mastered by a single therapist than can the wide range of techniques used in the Pinsof model. In combining the behavioral focus of the strategic model with the cognitive approach (organizing story line or *preferred view* of oneself) of the narrative approach, Eron and Lund broadened their focus of the therapy to more fully account for the multiple dimensions of the family problem.

Other problem-centered integrative approaches have been developed from major research program designed to address specific clinical problems. Henggeler and Borduin (1990) developed a multisystemic model that is designed to treat juvenile offenders and their families. In addition to using established procedures aimed at improving family relationships they extended their efforts to school and peer systems, two critical systems beyond the family. They also paid close attention to relevant developmental issues that may be critical to the presenting problem. The movement toward integrative therapies is a dominant characteristic of current family psychotherapy. Often these integrated models are the results of pragmatic concerns about which combination will work for a specific presenting problem. Recent experimentation with combinations is highlighting the strengths of the respective theories. This can eventually result in the identification of overarching principles of treatment interventions. Knowledge about these principles and which techniques from specific therapies can best address them should result in more effective treatments.

CONCLUSION

Family systems therapy has grown over the past 60 years in theory, research, and application. Overall, this growth has been quite positive. There has been a general acceptance of family therapy by both the public and professionals in the mental health field and beyond. The broader context of family functioning (e.g., ethnicity, gender, race) continues to be addressed and incorporated into clinical practice. The range of clinical issues that are addressed by family therapy continues to be expanded. Research continues to refine procedures so that treatments can be more effective.

Although there are many positives about this growth, there is no consensus on a comprehensive theory of family. If family systems theory is to continue as a comprehensive model for understanding the individual's emotional, cognitive, and behavioral functioning in relationship context, several eventualities must occur. There must be a continued sophistication and refinement of the characteristics of functional compared with dysfunctional systems, a systemic model of the individual including a continuum linking his or her "inner and outer space," and a model for tracking dyadic interaction and triangle formation. Guerin, Fogarty, Fay, and Kautto (1996) in their book *Working With Relationship Triangles* proposed one such model. The goal of these refined family concepts is to reach the point where the pioneers of family therapy began: to develop an integrated system of interventions that would enhance better functioning for individuals as well as the family system as a whole.

REFERENCES

Ackerman, N. (1958). *The psychodynamics of family life*. New York, NY: Basic Books.

Anderson, C. M., Reiss, D., & Hogarty, G. E. (1986). *Schizophrenia and the family: A practitioner's guide to psychoeducation and management*. New York, NY: Guilford Press.

Anderson, H., & Goolishian, H. (1988). Human systems as linguistic systems: preliminary and evolving ideas about the implications for clinical theory. *Family Process, 27,* 371–393. doi:10.1111/j.1545-5300.1988.00371.x

Beck, A. T. (1988). *Cognitive therapy and the emotional disorders*. New York, NY: International Universities Press.

Bell, J. E. (1961). Family group therapy. *Public Health Monograph No. 64*. Washington, DC: U.S. Government Printing Office.

Bengtson, V. I., & Allen, K. R. (1993). The life course perspective applied to families over time. In P. G. Boss, W. J. Doherty, R. LaRossa, W. J. Schumm, & S. K. Steinmetz (Eds.), *Sourcebook of family theories and methods: A contextual approach* (pp. 469–499). New York, NY: Plenum Press.

Berg, I. K. (1994). *Family-based services: A solution focused approach*. New York, NY: Norton.

Birchler, G. R., & Spinks, S. H. (1980). Behavioral-systems marital therapy: Integration and clinical application. *The American Journal of Family Therapy, 8,* 6–28. doi:10.1080/01926188008250354

Boszormenyi-Nagy, I. (1987). *Foundations of contextual therapy*. New York, NY: Brunner/Mazel.

Boszormenyi-Nagy, I., & Framo, J. (Eds.). (1965). *Intensive family therapy: Theoretical and practical aspects*. New York, NY: Harper & Row.

Boszormanyi-Nagy, I., & Spark, G. (1973). *Invisible loyalties: Reciprocity in intergenerational family therapy*. New York, NY: Harper & Row.

Bowen, M. (1966). The use of family theory in clinical practice. *Comprehensive Psychiatry, 7,* 345–374. doi:10.1016/S0010-440X(66)80065-2

Bowen, M. (1972). On the differentiation of self. In J. Framo (Ed.), *Family interaction: A dialogue between family researchers and family therapists* (pp. 111–173). New York, NY: Springer.

Bowen, M. (1976). Theory in the practice of psychotherapy. In P. Guerin (Ed.), *Family therapy: Theory and practice* (pp. 42–90). New York, NY: Gardner Press.

Bowen, M. (1978). *Family therapy in clinical practice*. New York, NY: Jason Aronson.

Boyd-Franklin, N. (1993). Race, class, and poverty. In F. Walsh (Ed.), *Normal family processes* (pp. 260–279). New York, NY: Guilford Press.

Breunlin, D. C. (1988). Oscillation theory and family development. In C. Falicov (Ed.), *Family transitions: Continuity and change over the life cycle* (pp. 133–155). New York, NY: Guilford Press.

Carter, E. A., & McGoldrick, M. (1980). *The family life cycle: A framework for family therapy*. New York, NY: Gardner Press.

Chabot, D. R. (1996). Chabot pursuer—Distancer movement scale. Unpublished manuscript, Fordham University, New York, New York.

Dattilio, F. M. (1998). *Case studies in couple and family therapy: Systemic and cognitive perspectives*. New York, NY: Guilford Press.

de Shazer, S. (1985). *Keys to solutions in brief therapy*. New York, NY: Norton.

Doherty, W. (1996). *The intentional family*. Reading, MA: Addison-Wesley.

Duvall, E. M., & Hill, R. L. (1948). *Reports of the committee on the dynamics of family interaction*. Washington, DC: National Conference on Family Life.

Epston, D. (1994). Extending the conversation. *Family Therapy Networker, 18,* 30–37.

Eron, J., & Lund, T. (1996). *Narrative solutions in brief therapy*. New York, NY: Guilford Press.

Fairbairn, W. D. (1952). *An object-relations theory of the personality*. New York, NY: Basic Books.

Fogarty, T. F. (1976a). Marital crisis. In P. J. Guerin (Ed.), *Family therapy: Theory and practice* (pp. 325–334). New York, NY: Gardner Press.

Fogarty, T. F. (1976b). Systems concepts and the dimensions of self. In P. J. Guerin (Ed.), *Family therapy: Theory and practice* (pp. 144–153). New York, NY: Gardner Press.

Fogarty, T. F. (1984). The individual and the family. In E. Pendagast (Ed.), *Compendium II: The best of the family, 1978–1983* (pp. 71–77). New Rochelle, NY: Center for Family Learning.

Goldstein, M. J., Rodnick, E. H., Evans, J. R., May, P. R., & Steinberg, M. (1978). Drug and family therapy in the aftercare treatment of acute schizophrenia. *Archives of General Psychiatry, 35,* 1169–1177.

Gordon, S. B., & Davidson, N. (1981). Behavioral parent training. In A. S. Gurman & D. P. Kniskern (Eds.), *Handbook of family therapy* (pp. 517–555). New York, NY: Brunner/Mazel.

Guerin, P. (1979). System, system, who's got the system? In E. Pendagast (Ed.), *Compendium I: The best of the family, 1973–1978* (pp. 9–16). New Rochelle, NY: Center for Family Learning.

Guerin, P., Fay, L., Burden, S., & Kautto, J. (1987). *The evaluation and treatment of marital conflict: A four-stage approach.* New York, NY: Basic Books.

Guerin, P. Fogarty, T. F., Fay L. & Kautto, J. (1996). *Working with relationship triangles: The one-two-three of psychotherapy.* New York, NY: Guilford Press.

Haley, J. (1976). *Problem solving therapy.* San Francisco, CA: Jossey-Bass.

Haley, J. (1984). *Ordeal therapy.* San Francisco, CA: Jossey-Bass.

Hare-Mustin, R. T. (1978). A Feminist approach to family therapy. *Family Process, 17,* 181–194.

Hare-Mustin, R. T., & Mareck, J. (1988). The meaning of difference: Gender theory, postmodernism, and psychology. *American Psychologist, 43,* 455–464.

Henggeler, S., & Borduin, C. (1990). *Family therapy and beyond: A multisystemic approach to treating the behavior problems of children and adolescents.* Pacific Grove, CA: Brooks/Cole.

Hoffman, L. (1981). *Foundations of family therapy.* New York, NY: Basic Books.

Homans, G. (1961). *Social behavior: Its elementary forms.* New York, NY: Harcourt, Brace & Jovanovich.

Jackson, D. D., & Weakland, J. H. (1961). Conjoint family therapy: Some considerations on theory, technique and results. *Psychiatry, 24,* 30–45.

Jacobson, N., & Christensen, A. (1996). *Integrative couple therapy.* New York, NY: Norton.

Jacobson, N., & Margolin, G. (1979). *Marital therapy: Strategies based on social learning and behavioral exchange principles.* New York, NY: Brunner/Mazel.

Klein, M. (1946). Notes on some schizoid mechanisms. *The International Journal of Psycho-Analysis, 27,* 99–110.

Licht, C., & Chabot, D. (2006). The Chabot emotional differentiation scale: A theoretically and psychometrically sound instrument for measuring Bowen's intrapsychic aspect of differentiation. *Journal of Marital and Family Therapy, 32,* 167–180. doi:10.1111/j.1752-0606.2006.tb01598.x

Madanes, C. (1981). *Strategic family therapy.* San Francisco, CA: Jossey-Bass.

Madigan, S., & Epston, D. (1995). From "spychiatric gaze" to communities of concern: From professional monologue to dialogue. In S. Friedman (Ed.), *The reflecting team in action: Collaborative family practice* (pp. 257–276). New York, NY: Guilford Press.

McDaniel, S. Hepworth, J., & Doherty, W. (1992). *Medical family therapy.* New York, NY: Basic Books.

McFarlane, W. R., Dixon, L., Lukens, E., & Luckstead, A. (2003). Family psychoeducation and schizophrenia: A review of the literature. *Journal of Marital and Family Therapy, 29,* 223–245.

McGoldrick, M. Giordano, J., & Pearce, J. (1996). *Ethnicity and family therapy* (2nd ed.). New York, NY: Guilford Press.

Milkowitz, D. J. (1995). The evolution of family-based psychopathology. In R. H. Mikesell, D. D. Lusterman, & S. H. McDaniels (Eds.), *Integrating family therapy: Handbook of family psychology and systems theory* (pp. 183–197). Washington, DC: American Psychological Association.

Minuchin, S. (1974). *Families and family therapy*. Cambridge, MA: Harvard University Press.

Nichols, M. (2008). *Family therapy: Concepts and methods*. Boston, MA: Allyn & Bacon.

O'Hanlon, W., & Weiner-Davis, M. (1989). *In search of solutions: A new direction in psychotherapy*. New York, NY: Norton.

Pinsof, W. (1995). *Integrative problem-centered therapy*. New York, NY: Basic Books.

Rabkin, R. (1968). Is the unconscious necessary? *American Journal of Psychiatry, 125,* 313{3n}319. doi:10.1176/appi.ajp.125.3.313

Rabkin, R. (1970). *Inner and outer space*. New York, NY: Norton.

Satir, V. (1967). *Conjoint family therapy*. Palo Alto, CA: Science & Behavior Books.

Satir, V. (1972). *Peoplemaking*. Palo Alto, CA: Science & Behavior Books.

Scharff, D., & Scharff, J. (1987). *Object relations family therapy*. New York, NY: Jason Aronson.

Schwartz, R. C. (1995). *Internal family systems therapy*. New York, NY: Guilford Press.

Selekman, M. D. (1993). Solution-oriented brief therapy with difficult adolescents. In S. Friedman (Ed.), *The new language of change: Constructive collaboration in psychotherapy* (pp. 138–157). New York, NY: Guilford Press.

Selvini Palazzoli, M., Boscolo, L., Cecchin, G., & Prata, G. (1978). *Paradox and counterparadox*. New York, NY: Jason Aronson.

Stuart, R. B. (1969). An operant-interpersonal treatment for marital discord. *Journal of Consulting and Clinical Psychology, 33,* 675–682. doi:10.1037/h0028475

Thibaut, J., & Kelly, H. H. (1959). *The social psychology of groups*. New York, NY: Wiley.

Thomas, W. I., & Znaniecki, F. (1920). *The polish peasant in Europe and America* (Vol. 5). Boston, MA: Badger.

Watzlawick, P., Beavin, J., & Jackson, D. (1967). *Pragmatics of human communication*. New York, NY: Norton.

Watzlawick, P., Weakland, J., & Fisch, R. (1974). *Change: Principles of problem formation and problem resolution*. New York, NY: Norton.

Whitaker, C. (1976). The hindrance of theory in clinical work. In P. J. Guerin (Ed.), *Family therapy: Theory and practice*. New York, NY: Gardner Press.

Whitaker, C., Felder, R., & Warkentin, J. (1965). Counter-transference in the family treatment of schizophrenia. In I. Boszormenyi-Nagy & J. Framo (Eds.), *Intensive family therapy* (pp. 323–342). New York, NY: Harper & Row.

Whitaker, C., & Keith, D. (1981). Symbolic experiential family therapy. In A. Gurman & D. Kniskern (Eds.), *Handbook of family therapy* (pp. 187–225). New York, NY: Brunner/Mazel.

White, M. (1991). Deconstruction of family therapy. *Dulwich Center Newsletter, 3,* 21–40.

Wynne, L. (1988). An epigenetic model of family process. In C. Falicov (Ed.), *Family transitions: Continuity and change over the life cycle* (pp. 81–106). New York, NY: Guilford Press.

Wynne, L., Ryckoff, I., Day, J., & Hirsch, S. (1958). Pseudomutuality in the family relations of schizophrenics. *Psychiatry, 21,* 205–220.

7

COGNITIVE THEORIES OF PSYCHOTHERAPY

STEVEN D. HOLLON AND RAYMOND DiGIUSEPPE

The cognitive psychotherapies emerged from a theory positing that what people believe influences how they feel and act. Cognitive theories of disorder emphasize the role of maladaptive beliefs and information processing. It logically follows that cognitive theories of change involve the notion that correcting these erroneous beliefs and information processing errors can ameliorate negative affect and facilitate adaptive behavior. In this chapter, we trace the history of cognitive therapies, but note that more extensive material on newer, "third wave" therapies is provided in Chapter 4 of this volume.

THE PIONEERS

Cognitive behavior therapies (CBTs) can be viewed as a subfield of the wider field of behavior therapy. Behavior therapy developed from the application of learning principles to clinical problems. The inclusion of cognitive interventions within behavior therapy occurred in the first volume of *Behavior Therapy*, the official journal of the new Association for the Advancement of Behavior Therapy (AABT). The first issue included an article by Cautela

(1970) on the use of covert reinforcement, or the use of covert or imaginal reinforcement to strengthen behaviors. The second issue of *Behavior Therapy* included an article by Aaron Beck (1970) on cognitive therapy and its relation to behavior therapy. Ullmann (1970) responded to Beck's article by noting that behavior therapists should treat cognitions as any other form of human behavior and were therefore targets for change by this new form of therapy. Ullmann pointed out that cognitive approaches such as Beck's were scientific and fell within the field of behavior therapy because Beck had provided a clear definition of the cognitions he targeted and the techniques he used in psychotherapy.

The introduction of the cognitive method was largely embraced (and often debated) by behavior therapy. Today, CBT forms the most popular theoretical orientation among psychologists (after eclecticism/integration). However, CBT is a hyphenated moniker. Virtually all advocates of cognitive interventions integrate them with the behavioral interventions identified elsewhere in this book (Chapter 4).

Although CBT remains a part of behavior therapy, it has emerged from several disparate traditions within psychotherapy. The first tradition started from within behavior therapy when practitioners became disappointed with their strictly behavioral methods and theories. An influential event in moving the field of behavior therapy toward a cognitive perspective was Albert Bandura's *Principles of Behavior Modification* in 1969. The final chapter of Bandura's classic text reviewed his and others' work on the pervasiveness of learning through modeling. The research evidence questioned the reliance on conditioning to explain human learning and as the primary method to explain behavior change. Michael Mahoney (1974) followed Bandura's book with several influential publications, including *Cognition and Behavior Modification*, reviewing the place of language, modeling, and cognitive factors in learning and psychotherapy. These works in behavior therapy both reflected and reinforced the growth of cognitive models in psychology as a whole.

In 1976, Albert Ellis organized and underwrote the expenses for the first conference on cognitive behavior therapies, which met in New York City at his institute. Seminal CBT figures, such as Aaron Beck, Marvin Goldfried, Michael Mahoney, Don Meichenbaum, and George Spivack, attended this conference. Both authors of this chapter attended as postdoctoral fellows of their respective mentors. This conference and a similar one the following year helped several theoretical positions unite under the term *CBT*. After the conference, the journal *Cognitive Therapy and Research* began publication, with Mahoney as its inaugural editor.

Some researchers within behavior therapy vehemently challenged the emergence of cognitive interventions and claimed that cognitions were epiphenomena that played no role in the mediation of disturbance. In fact, several behavior therapists argued that cognitive methods added nothing to the effectiveness of behavior therapy (e.g., Ledwidge, 1978; Wolpe, 1978). Mahoney (1977a, 1977b; Mahoney & Kazdin, 1979) served as the academic champion of CBT, answering these challenges by providing theoretical and empirical arguments for cognitive constructs and interventions.

Some behavior therapists noticed that their interventions, such as token economies, produced poor generalization across time and place and attempted to remedy the limited generalization of the treatment results (e.g., O'Leary & Drabman, 1971). Even assertiveness training, which involved rehearsing a client's new adaptive skills, provided limited generalization. The exigencies of life presented clients with so many variations of problematic situations that it was impossible to rehearse an adaptive response for all the events that could cue maladaptive behavior. If behavior therapists thought of cognitions as covert operants that could be manipulated and influenced as other forms of behavior, they needed to use language to instruct their clients when to practice these covert acts, or when to use covert reinforcers, as Cautela (1970) and Ullmann (1970) had recommended. In addition, behaviorists could not always be present to provide the reinforcement for adaptive behavior. Behavior therapists wanted to teach a skill that included cuing the desired behaviors and self-reinforcing for their occurrence. This would require language-based rules to generate effective coping across a wide variety of situations and provide the self-reinforcement necessary to internalize the response. An early CBT method involved teaching people self-instructional and self-control skills for responding outside of therapy sessions (Kanfer & Goldstein, 1975; Meichenbaum, 1977).

This behavioral tradition can be characterized as a cognitive deficit model (Braswell & Kendall, 2001). These models of therapy asserted that normal development involves the acquisition of certain cognitive processes to guide adaptive behavior. Well-adjusted people develop cognitive processes and structures that guide adaptive behavior when they encounter stressful situations, whereas disturbed individuals fail to develop these cognitive processes. Cognitive deficit model methods originally focused on children with externalizing disorders and seriously disturbed patients. These psychotherapies include cognitive–behavior modification, self-instructional training, and stress inoculation (Meichenbaum, 1977, 1993), as well as social problem-solving (Spivack, Platt, & Shure, 1976).

Donald Meichenbaum worked with hospitalized psychiatric patients during his internship and noticed the limitations of token economies in producing generalization of improvements. He used the patients' self-speech to guide adaptive behavior. Meichenbaum based his treatment on the then recently translated work of the Soviet psychologist Vygotsky (1962). Vygotsky explored the interface of thought and language. He discovered that the dominant cortex influenced people's language and sequential processing. Because most complex adaptive behavior requires the performance of a series of behaviors, Vygotsky believed that adaptive behavior required the encoding of a sequence of behaviors, the rehearsal of the sequence, and decoding of the language-based instructions when presented with the appropriate cue. The behavior guiding subroutines would eventually become overlearned, occur quickly, and not reach consciousness when performed.

Vygotsky noticed that children learned to use language to guide behavior by following a sequence. First, children encoded the complex, sequential task in language. Then, they spoke the words aloud as they performed the behavior. Then, they lowered their voice and spoke in a whisper to guide the behavior. Finally, children reported using subvocal speech to guide their behavior. Meichenbaum discovered that some people failed to follow this process at all and others had encoded behavior patterns in some ways but not others (Meichenbaum, 1977; Meichenbaum & Cameron, 1973, 1974). By training in this skill, people could learn to talk to themselves to guide more adaptive behavior. This flexible method has been used across all ages and has been applied to a wide variety of problems, from impulsive classroom behavior and aggression to anxiety, depression, and pain management.

Another method stemming from the cognitive deficit model is the social problem-solving model (SPS). SPS emerged from two different groups. Spivack, Platt, and Shure (1974) developed a curriculum to prevent adjustment problems in poor, inner-city children at what was then Hahenmann Medical School in Philadelphia. They demonstrated that focusing on kindergarten and first-grade children could prevent the development of problems and reduce referrals to mental health professions. The success of this program expanded the use of these methods as psychotherapy applied to other problems and patient groups. Working independently, D'Zurilla and Goldfried (1971), at the State University of New York at Stonybrook, developed similar principles of problem solving within behavior therapy. SPS involves a process that defines and formulates the problem, generates a variety of response alternatives, considers the possible consequences for the alternatives, and chooses the most likely successful plan of action. Training in problem solving was considered a self-control skill for the individual to learn how to solve problems and discover the most effective way of responding.

SPS methods represent one of the most researched areas in CBT and are a good first-line intervention for most problems. An extensive research literature supports the efficacy and effectiveness of SPS in all age groups with many different problems and disorders (D'Zurilla & Nezu, 2006).

A second stream of ideas that merged into CBT focused on changing dysfunctional thoughts. We could characterize these approaches as the cognitive dysfunction model. Albert Ellis (1962) and Aaron Beck (1970, 1976) led this tradition. Both of them received their initial training in psycho-analytic therapy and became dissatisfied with the outcome and length of such treatment. The clinical and then scientific failure to confirm unconscious processes led these therapists to focus on clients' present and conscious thoughts. Both Ellis and Beck based their psychotherapy on the idea that emotional disturbance emerged from thoughts that were illogical, anti-empirical, irrational, or incorrect. More scientific, accurate methods of thinking would free people from their disturbed emotions. Both cognitive therapies focused on what people think in the present, incorporated directive techniques into practice, and initiated a number of the specific methods used today. A more detailed discussion of these two cognitive therapies appears below.

A third stream forming CBT was George Kelly's personal construct therapy (PCT) (1955). Kelly recognized that humans evolved and survived because of their ability to impose order on a chaotic world. Understanding the world provides the first steps in developing coping and survival strategies. Kelly based PCT on understanding the constructs individuals design about their personal world; PCT helped clients become flexible in relinquishing constructs that fail to explain the world and lead to maladaptive behavior. PCT involves assessing and understanding clients' systems of constructs and helping them evaluate whether those constructs help them maneuver in the world effectively.

Kelly's theory led to the development of treatment methods based on scientific reasoning and correcting maladjustment (Mahoney, 1979). It also laid the foundation for constructivist methods that conceptualize therapy as a task of understanding a person's epistemology or philosophy of understand-ing the world (e.g., Mahoney, 1991; Mahoney & Lyddon, 1988; Neimeyer, 1993). A meta-analysis reviewed the outcomes of studies on PCT (Metcalfe et al., 2007). The results concluded that PCT was modestly effective compared with no-treatment controls and other alternative methods. Clients receiving PCT improved more than clients receiving no active treatment but were not different from clients who received other treatment methods.

Kelly's PTC served as a basis for cognitive therapies. Ellis and Beck stated that irrational beliefs, automatic thoughts, and dysfunctional attitudes emerge from the schemas people develop to understand major life events (A. T. Beck, 2005; Ellis, 1962). Changing explanatory schema has become the primary focus of a form of CBT (Young, Klosko, & Weishaar, 2004).

Another influence on CBT from the perspective of human attempts to understand the world is attribution theories. Seligman's (Seligman & Maier, 1967) experiments with dogs and his resulting theory of learned helplessness (Seligman, 1975) represented a more nomothetic approach to understand-ing humans' explanatory thinking. Seligman found that dogs who received inescapable electric shock learned to be helpless and exhibited symptoms similar to clinical depression. Later research discovered that the original theory of learned helplessness failed to account for people's varying reactions to situations that cause learned helplessness. Learned helplessness can remain specific to one situation, or these attributions can generalize across situations. A person's attributional or explanatory style presents the means to understand why people respond differently to adverse events. Although people may experience similar negative events, each person's interpretations of the event affect the likelihood of acquiring learned helplessness and depression (Abramson, Seligman, & Teasdale, 1978). People with pessimistic explanatory style who perceive negative events as permanent ("It will never change"), personal ("It's my fault"), and pervasive ("I can't do anything correctly") are more likely to suffer from learned helplessness and depression.

Weiner, a cognitive psychologist, developed a similar attribution theory (1979, 1985) based on research from children's academic achievement motivation. Weiner proposed that people attribute a cause or explanation to an unpleasant event. Attribution theory includes the dimensions of globality versus specificity, stability versus instability, and internality versus externality (Weiner, 1985). A global attribution occurs when the individual believes that the cause of negative events is consistent across different contexts. A specific attribution occurs when the individual believes that the cause of a negative event is unique to a particular situation. A stable attribution occurs when the individual believes the cause to be consistent across time. An unstable attribution occurs when the individual thinks that the cause is specific to one point in time. An external attribution assigns causality to situational or external factors, whereas an internal attribution assigns causality to factors within the person (Abramson et al., 1978).

Despite the vast number of research publications on the attributional model and early reviews touting the effectiveness of attribution-based interventions (Försterling, 1985), they have failed to become a major brand of CBT (Harvey, & Galvin, 1984). A review of the attribution model questions its clinical effectiveness (Henkel, Bussfeld, Möller, & Hegerl, 2002); the majority of studies in this area have been conducted in subjects who were healthy or only mildly depressed and not with psychotherapy clients. Research with actual psychotherapy clients would help test the usefulness of attribution interventions. CBT has always prospered from its commitment to science and the empirical testing of its theories and techniques.

The therapy wars between behavior therapy and the more established psychodynamic and humanistic psychotherapies resulted in behavior therapy and CBT not finding a congenial home in any of the divisions of the American Psychological Association. Instead, they created their own home with AABT. Commitment to the scientist–practitioner model and the development of evidence-based treatments has been a primary mission of AABT. Wilson (1997) characterized behavior therapy and the association's mission as "a commitment to apply the principles and procedures of experimental psychology to clinical problems, to rigorously evaluate the effects of therapy, and to ensure that clinical practice was guided by such objective evaluation." The list of early behavior therapists who served as president of AABT and who made significant research contributions to the validation of CBT is impressive indeed. These include David Barlow, Edward Craighead, Gerald Davison, Marvin Goldfried, Alan Kazdin, Rosemery Nelson, Daniel O'Leary, and Terrence Wilson.

As the popularity of cognitive therapy grew, a debate ensued within AABT concerning the movement away from basic experimental science and the inclusion and integration of cognition into behavior therapy. In the 1990s, some members of AABT desired to change the name of the organization to acknowledge the cognitive additions. A special issue of *Behavior Therapy* summarized opposition to such a name change (Forsyth & Hawkins, 1997). The argument proceeded that

> (a) cognition is not behavior, (b) behavior principles and theory cannot account for events occurring within the skin, and most important, (c) we therefore need a unique conceptual system to account for how thinking, feeling, and other private events relate to overt human action. (Forsyth, 1997, p. 621)

This debate continued until 2004, when the association members added the word *cognitive* to the name (Antony, 2003): Association for Behavioral and Cognitive Therapies (G. Beck, 2005).

Two figures stand out among the cognitive theorists of the last 50 years: Albert Ellis (1913–2007) and Aaron Beck (1921–). We have chosen to highlight the work of these figures because their variants of CBT represent comprehensive psychotherapy systems with a broad literature applying their methods to many populations and disorders. Ellis was a psychologist and Beck a psychiatrist. Both received their training initially in psychoanalytic therapy. Each broke with that theoretical orientation and founded schools of psychotherapy that emphasized the role of cognition in the etiology of distress and the process of change.

Ellis was a charismatic clinician and the consummate New Yorker. He lived for decades on the top floor of a brownstone on the upper east side of New York, over an institute that trained hundreds of psychotherapists and treated tens of thousands of patients. Ellis published numerous books and articles regarding psychotherapy and was, in his time, one of the most famous and recognizable psychologists in the world. He also was outspoken, irreverent, and inclined to say things that shocked the more genteel and somewhat stodgy psychotherapy community of the 1950s. His insights grew from his interests in philosophy and his clinical practice, and he grew restless with the orthodoxy of the day. Never one to blindly do as he was told, Ellis rebelled at the slow pace of therapy and struck off in new directions because it seemed the right thing to do for his patients. Ellis advocated for but did not do research. He did not work at a university and chose to focus on clinical work, teaching, and writing. He authored many theoretical works, clinical materials, and self-help books. Ellis's choice has had negative implications for his approach, which he termed *rational emotive behavior therapy* (REBT), as we have entered an era of evidence-based practice that relies on randomized clinical trials. However, Ellis's REBT became one of the most widely practiced therapies in the second half of the 20th century.

Beck was a clinical scientist who spent his entire career on the faculty at the University of Pennsylvania. He maintained a clinical practice throughout his career and, like Ellis, was struck by the incongruity between the orthodoxy he was taught and what he observed with his patients. He set about trying to confirm one of the basic principles of dynamic theory: Depression represents anger turned inward on the self. However, all he could find in his patients' dreams and free associations were the same themes of loss and self-blame that he heard in their conscious verbalizations. When he found in his experiments that sadness and behavioral passivity were ameliorated by success and exacerbated by failure (the exact opposite of what would be expected if depression were motivated by an unconscious masochism), Beck turned this theory upside down and posited that his patients became depressed because they believed they were inadequate and unlovable. He began to experiment with clinical strategies that targeted those erroneous beliefs and arrived at a model of change that was much the same as that espoused by Ellis. Beck called his treatment *cognitive therapy* and rapidly expanded its tenets to a wide range of disorders.

Despite the similarity in their perspectives, the two pioneers approached the change process in somewhat different ways. Ellis focused on the irrationality of his patients' beliefs and used logic and persuasion to help them see the error of their thinking and to adopt more rational philosophies. Beck saw his patients' beliefs as being more inaccurate than illogical and used empirical disconfirmation. Both attended to patient behaviors out of sessions but in somewhat different ways: Ellis reinforced the process of change by getting his patients to act on their new beliefs, and Beck had his patients run behavioral experiments to test the accuracy of their beliefs. In essence, Ellis acted as a philosopher in disputing his patients' beliefs, whereas Beck acted as a scientist by getting his patients to test their beliefs. However, their respective therapies were more similar than different. Together, REBT and cognitive therapy formed one of the dominant therapy systems in recent decades.

ALBERT ELLIS AND RATIONAL EMOTIVE BEHAVIOR THERAPY

Albert Ellis is considered the grandfather of CBT because of his development of REBT, probably the first formal system in the genre. Ellis was instrumental in transforming psychotherapy to the point where CBT represented a major paradigm for behavioral change. A 1982 survey of U.S. and Canadian psychologists ranked Ellis as the second most influential psychotherapist in history (Carl Rogers ranked first in the survey; Sigmund Freud ranked third; Smith, 1982). In addition, in that year, an analysis of psychology journals published in the United States found that Ellis was the most cited author after Rogers. More recently, in a survey of more than 2,500 psychotherapists (Cook, Biyanova, & Coyne, 2009), Ellis ranked as the sixth most influential psychotherapist. Psychotherapists rated CBT as the most popular theoretical orientation. Carl Rogers remained the most influential psychotherapist; Aaron Beck came in second. At his death at age 93 (July 2, 2007), Ellis had authored and coauthored more than 80 books and more than 800 articles in peer-reviewed journals (for a complete bibliography, see http://www.albertellis institute.org/ellisbibliography).

Ellis was born in Pittsburgh, Pennsylvania, in 1913, the eldest of three children. Shortly thereafter, his family moved to the Bronx in New York City. In his youth, Albert Ellis suffered numerous health problems. At age 5, he was hospitalized for an extended period for a kidney ailment. He required eight hospitalizations between the ages of 5 and 7, one of which lasted almost a year. Ellis's literary interests nurtured his psychotherapy writings. Many of his psychotherapy principles first appeared in an unpublished autobiographical novel (Ellis, 1933) that recounted his attempts to overcome his shyness, anxiety, and shame concerning his family's poverty. During his youth, Ellis became interested in romantic and sexual relationships and read voraciously on the topic. In 1941, he found the nonprofit LAMP (Love and Marriage Problems) Institute to dispense advice on such topics, mostly to friends and relatives. On the advice of his lawyer, he sought a professional degree to provide him with professional recognition of his expertise. He enrolled in the doctoral program in clinical psychology at Columbia University's Teachers College at the age of 40.

After completing graduate school, Ellis started psychoanalytic training and simultaneously started to practice. He quickly evolved two separate practices. One group of clients received traditional psychoanalysis on the couch, whereas a second group of clients with marital and sex problems received a more active set of interventions sitting face to face with Ellis. Ellis became discouraged with the effectiveness of psychoanalysis in the early 1950s. He discovered that he helped clients in his sex and marital therapy practice more quickly than those he treated with psychoanalysis. Initially, Ellis thought that he needed to dig deeper into his patients' pasts before they would relinquish their neuroses. Yet after they gained insight, they still failed to improve. Ellis concluded that insight into childhood experiences failed to help patients and reasoned that insight alone led to change in only a small percentage of individuals.

Ellis recognized that he behaved differently with clients in his marital and sex therapy practice. He actively taught these clients to change their attitudes. Ellis's earlier interest in philosophy had led him to read the works of the great Asian and Greek thinkers, including Confucius, Lao Tze, Marcus Aurelius, and Epictetus. When freed from the constraining psychoanalytic role, he provided advice to his clients based on these philosophical works. Ellis contemplated the stoic philosophers' notion that people could choose whether to become disturbed, or in the words of Epictetus (90 BC/1996), "Men are not disturbed by things, but by the view which they take of them" (from the Enchiridion). Ellis utilized philosophy as the foundation for his new therapy and always credited classical and modern philosophers as the source of his ideas. In 1955, he formulated his theory in a paper delivered at the annual convention of the American Psychological Association.

Despite Ellis's critical attitude toward psychoanalysis, clearly his REBT built on some psychoanalytic skills and principles. Astutely, Ellis focused on his clients' emotions during the therapy sessions. As a trainee, an author of this chapter (R. D.) was amazed to watch the small shifts in clients' vocal intonation and gestures that Ellis perceived and then used to redirect therapy. Although Ellis rejected the passive stance of the psychoanalyst, he was aware of the relationship between him and his clients. He was dedicated to clients and displayed tremendous powers of concentration during the sessions. It is often surprising to those who saw him only on the lecture and workshop circuit, where he was brash and flamboyant, to imagine that Ellis could build a therapeutic alliance. Having co-led a therapy group with Ellis for 2 years, R.D. observed his clients' attitude toward him. He behaved in the clinical context in a manner inconsistent with his stage personality, and his clients perceived him as attentive, empathic, and dedicated to helping them.

Ellis's psychoanalytic training may have influenced his theory, especially the centrality of demandingness. REBT postulates that people become disturbed when they make a want or desire into an absolute demand on the universe. When people are disturbed, they think that what they want must be, and they fail to distinguish between what they desire and what is. Emotional adjustment involves recognizing the distinction between what one wants and the fact that the universe has no obligation to provide it. Ellis once noted that demanding reflects the psychoanalytic construct of primary process. Adjustment involves the distinction between desires and reality, which Freud called *secondary process thinking*. REBT, Ellis maintained, differs from psychoanalysis in that REBT focuses like a laser on the primary process thinking, and actively tries to change it, whereas psychoanalysis relies on more subtle change processes.

Ellis was among the first psychotherapists to advocate actively changing clients' beliefs to induce emotional or behavioral change. He was also among the first psychotherapists to use between-sessions homework assignments, including in vivo behavioral exposure. Ellis provided workshops, lectures, books, and written assignments to identify, challenge, and replace irrational ideas (primary process) and to reinforce the rational ideas (secondary process) that he covered in therapy. Ellis was among the first psychotherapy integrationists. Although REBT obviously had a strong cognitive component, from the onset of his practice and writings, Ellis (1955) advocated many types of therapy methods to help people change. He encouraged the use of imagery, hypnosis, group sessions, family sessions, humor, psychoeducational readings, interpersonal support, writing assignments, singing, behavioral rehearsal, exposure assignments, action assignments, metaphors, parables, and cathartic experiences. According to Ellis (1957b), psychotherapy should include any activity that could convince the client to change.

When Ellis entered the profession in the late 1940s and began to publish on psychotherapy in the 1950s, two major theoretical orientations dominated psychotherapy: psychoanalysis and client-centered therapy. Psychotherapy research was in a rudimentary stage. Both of the major theoretical orientations prescribed a passive, nondirective role for the therapist. Ellis was instrumental in changing much of that. Ellis's (1957a) first study of the effectiveness of what he then called *rational therapy* came between Eysenck's (1952) classic evaluation of the outcomes of psychoanalytic treatments and Wolpe's (1961) pioneering report on the outcomes of behavior therapy.

It was not until 1961 that Ellis wrote his most influential self-help book (with Robert Harper), *A Guide for Rational Living*. It is now in its third edition and has sold more than 2 million copies. The following year, Ellis (1962) published his first professional book, *Reason and Emotion in Psychotherapy*. Ellis published dozens of self-help and professional books advancing REBT until his death in 2007 (Kaufman, 2007).

In 1965, Ellis founded the Institute for Advanced Study in Rational Psychotherapy for professional training. It survives today as the Albert Ellis Institute. Affiliated training centers that train mental health professionals exist in Argentina, Australia, Bosnia, Canada, Colombia, England, France, Germany, Greece, Japan, Israel, Italy, Mexico, the Netherlands, Peru, Romania, Serbia, and Taiwan.

Ellis originally named his treatment rational therapy because of his focus on cognitions. He later realized that he had underemphasized the role of emotions in the label and renamed it *rational emotive therapy*. He finally changed the name to rational emotive behavior therapy (Ellis, 1994) at the urging of his longtime friend Ray Corsini. Corsini (1994) was revising his classic psychotherapy textbook when he recognized that Ellis usually used behavioral methods in therapy. He suggested that Ellis (1999) rename his approach to reflect what he practiced.

During the early days, the profession considered CBT to be on the lunatic fringe of psychotherapy. Psychoanalysts ridiculed cognitive theories as superficial and shallow, and they portrayed the active directiveness of the therapy as caustic, brutish, and harmful. Behavior therapists mocked the focus on cognition as foolish. They relegated thoughts to unimportant epiphenomena. As a young psychologist, R. D. recalls accompanying Ellis to conferences where he debated B. F. Skinner and Joseph Wolpe, paragons of anti–cognitive behavior therapy, on the impact of cognition in emotional disturbance. Despite the anticipated excitement and friction in these debates, it was clear that the adversaries did not differ as much as they thought they did.

In 1974, Wolpe and Ellis debated the role of cognition in psychopathology and psychotherapy at Hofstra University. Wolpe spoke first. He drew a human head on the blackboard and identified visual and auditory stimulus channels. He said that there were two pathways to anxiety problems. The first pathway ran from the senses to the lower levels of the brain and the hypothalamus. This pathway, he said, occurred through conditioning. Exposure and systematic desensitization effectively treated disturbed anxiety mediated by this pathway. The second pathway involved information from the senses going through the cortex and back down the thalamus and onto the hypothalamus. The reaction time for this pathway was slower and required learning through faulty assumptions. Treatment of disturbed emotions that formed through this pathway involved the testing and replacement of disturbed ideas. Wolpe stated that the first conditioning-formed pathway accounted for about 90% of all anxiety disorders.

Ellis then walked to the podium. The audience expected him to challenge Wolpe, as Ellis's reputation for debate had preceded him. Ellis agreed with everything Wolpe had said, except for one thing. Yes, there were two pathways mediating emotional disturbance. One was lower, quicker, and resulted from conditioning. The other pathway was cognitive, slower, and based in the cortex. However, Ellis said the cognitive pathway mediated 90% of emotional disturbance and the conditioning pathway mediated 10%. The remainder of the debate consisted of what proportions involved the two pathways. This debate clarified that CBT and REBT clearly existed within the larger context of behavior therapy. REBT still holds that the mechanisms of psychopathology and the mechanisms of change are multiple; different strategies are often required for effective therapy. This dual-pathway theory identified by Wolpe and Ellis remains an active area of inquiry within CBT (Power & Dalgleish, 2008).

The Theorist's Role in the Theory

A journal reviewer once remarked that REBT was whatever Albert Ellis said it was. His personality became synonymous with the theory. No history of cognitive psychotherapies would be complete without mentioning the personality of Albert Ellis. Ellis was a tireless promoter of his theory and therapy. His life consisted almost exclusively of doing therapy, writing about therapy, or teaching about therapy. He started seeing patients each day at 9:30 a.m. and continued until 10:00 p.m., with a half hour off each for lunch and dinner. He traveled extensively to give workshops and presentations. He once said, "I wouldn't go to the Taj Mahal unless I could give a workshop."

Each presentation included a live demonstration of therapy. Ellis sought volunteers from the audience to come on stage and present a personal problem, with which he would demonstrate the application of REBT. These demonstrations also occurred each week at his famous Friday night workshops. At a time when the activities of psychotherapists remained shrouded in secrecy, Ellis fostered transparency. He was willing to demonstrate what he did for anyone who was interested. These demonstrations attracted large crowds for more than 40 years and exposed many to the advantages of CBT. The demonstrations persist to this day at the Albert Ellis Institute.

Ellis was renowned for his colorful, foul language and his directness. He championed sexual libertarian ideas when people considered such views scandalous. He was a devout atheist. He could be described at best as irreverent. He enjoyed jousting with conventional wisdom. Many people would laugh at his off-color remarks, while others would walk out of his presentation when he spoke in such a fashion. Whether Ellis's personal style helped or hurt the dissemination of REBT is uncertain. He clearly was a person of renown, and his appearance at national conferences drew standing room only crowds.

Ellis's private personality, however, contrasted markedly with his public personality. He was a generous and accepting mentor. He encouraged dissent and debate among his staff, and he was accepting of them professionally and personally. Ellis always listened carefully and remained nonjudgmental (W. B. Johnson, DiGiuseppe, & Ulven, 1999).

Philosophical Assumptions

REBT differs from other forms of CBT in several distinctive ways. Ellis (2001, 2005a, 2005b) often used the term *classic REBT* to refer to the distinct features of REBT, while using the term *general REBT* to refer to these distinct aspects plus the inclusion of other forms of CBT. Most REBT practitioners incorporate the distinctive features of REBT while using the techniques of the wider field of CBT. However, they usually try the distinctive features first.

REBT rests on several philosophical assumptions. The first of these is commitment to the scientific method. Ellis believed that applying the scientific method to one's personal life results in less emotional disturbance and ineffectual behavior. People would be better adjusted if they recognized that all of their beliefs, schemata, perceptions, and cherished truths could be wrong. Testing one's assumptions, examining the validity and functionality of one's beliefs, and posing a willingness to entertain alternative ideas promotes mental health. Rigid adherence to a belief or schema of the world prevents one from revising one's thinking and dooms one to behave as if the world is as one hopes it will be, rather than the way it is. For Ellis, people are better off if they hold all beliefs *lightly*.

REBT theory posits (DiGiuseppe, 1986; Ellis, 1994) that humans function best when they use the philosophy of science to guide their thinking, specifically the positions of Popper (1962) and Bartley (1987). Popper noted that humans cannot help but develop hypotheses. Holding preconceived hypotheses distorts the data people collect and results in confirmatory biases. People cannot stop themselves from forming hypotheses, nor from remembering data that fit their conclusions. This brings into question the objectivity of inductive reasoning. REBT, Ellis, and Popper relied little on the inductive method of logic. Popper's solution is to acknowledge our hypotheses and attempt to falsify them as soon as possible. Popper maintained that knowledge accumulates most quickly when people deduce predictions from their hypotheses and attempt to disprove them. REBT recommends that we adopt Popper's model of falsifiability personally for our emotional health and professionally as psychotherapists. Thus, REBT relies more on hypothetico-deductive proofs and theory testing and less on inductive reasoning. Ellis believes that it is best to apply all means to challenge one's thinking as a theorist, as a therapist, and as an individual.

Over time, Ellis incorporated elements of constructivism into his theory. He repeatedly credited George Kelly's (1955) *The Psychology of Personal Constructs* as a foundation for REBT. In the 1980s, Ellis moved away from the traditional social learning, which espoused that people learn their disturbed behavior and their disturbed thinking from their parents and society. Ellis thought that humans could create their irrational beliefs even if they had sane, loving parents. This may explain why he abandoned searching for insights from the memories of clients' experiences. The clients may have invented the thoughts.

Although Ellis thought of humans as capable of constructing ideas as an explanation for human disturbance, he failed to adopt much of the epistemology of the postmodernist philosophers and the constructivist cognitive therapists such as Mahoney (1991) and Neimeyer (1993). Constructivist therapists believed that the almost exclusive criterion to evaluate beliefs was their utility or viability. Empirical reality or veracity remained unimportant to them because they believed reality was ultimately unknowable. REBT posited that empirical reality was one of several criteria used to assess one's beliefs along with their utility/viability and logical consistency. In addition, constructivist therapists maintained that therapists should allow and encourage clients to develop alternative thoughts on their own and should not provide alternative beliefs for clients. As a philosophy of life, REBT posited that some rational beliefs are likely to promote emotional adjustment. Although REBT valued learning though self-discovery, if clients failed to generate alternative rational beliefs, the therapists offered alternatives for them and taught the clients to assess the veracity and viability of these alternatives.

Distinctive Features of REBT

REBT's trademark emphasizes teaching people to learn their ABCs of emotional disturbance: identifying the *activating* events, their *beliefs* about those events, and the resulting emotional *consequences*. REBT teaches that disturbed emotional and behavioral consequences result from irrational beliefs individuals hold rather than from activating events.

The distinctive features of REBT (Dryden, 2008) are as follows. First, the A-B-C model focuses on underlying irrational beliefs, not automatic thoughts. REBT would argue that automatic thoughts concern the probabilistic occurrence of negative reality. They are about the world and are part of the activating event, whether they are exaggerated or not. Second, rigidity is at the core of psychological disturbance; flexibility is at the core of psychological health. Third, extreme beliefs are derived from rigid beliefs; nonextreme beliefs emerge from flexible beliefs. Fourth, the distinction between unhealthy negative emotions and healthy negative beliefs is qualitative, not quantitative. Fifth, self-esteem is a dangerous, elusive concept. Sixth, there is a distinction between ego disturbance and discomfort disturbance. Seventh, people get upset about their emotional experience. That is, emotional consequences can become activating events. Eighth, humans are both biologically rational and irrational.

Ellis maintained that negative automatic thoughts emerged from a person's more tacitly held irrational beliefs. Intervening at the level of the automatic thoughts would work to reduce a person's emotional disturbance. However, such an intervention failed to provide a coping mechanism when the automatic thought was true. Ellis maintained that clients would have a more elegant, comprehensive, and generalizable coping strategy and would stop generating the automatic thoughts if they challenged the tacit, nonconscious beliefs. This required the psychotherapist to identify the beliefs that generated the automatic thoughts. REBT recommends that therapists not challenge the truth of negative automatic thoughts. Rather, REBT proposes that the hypothetical assumptions might be true, and if they were true, what thoughts would the client have? In this way, REBT tried to get at more tacit, evaluative beliefs.

Ellis (1962) originally identified 11 irrational beliefs that he commonly found in his clients. Research in REBT at that time attempted to demonstrate that measures of the 11 irrational beliefs predicted emotional disturbances such as anxiety and depression. Over time, the 11 irrational beliefs were distilled to four. These were demands (i.e., shoulds, oughts, and musts), awfulizing and catastrophizing statements, low frustration-tolerance beliefs (e.g., I can't stand it; It's too hard), and global evaluations of human worth (Walen, DiGiuseppe, & Wessler, 1980). Eventually, Ellis (Ellis & Dryden, 1997) changed his theory again to posit that the demands were the primary core of emotional disturbance. The other three types of irrational beliefs were psychological derivatives of the demands. Thus, clients enter therapy with a demand and one of the other irrational beliefs. As of yet, this theoretical model has not been challenged and has dominated the REBT literature.

REBT theory and practice have changed in other important ways. Early in his career, Ellis was an avid atheist. He distinguished between religion and religiosity (see Ellis, 1986). Religious beliefs could be benign. However, he believed religiosity—the rigid, absolutistic adherence to dogma—to be a source of psychopathology. Over the years, Ellis (2000) mellowed toward religion. Although he never surrendered his atheism, when asked about his religious belief while he was in the rehab facility before he died, he said, "Still an atheist" (J. C. Norcross, personal communication, 2009). He did recognize that his fierce attacks on faith alienated many. When some people of faith would require psychotherapy, he was unlikely to help them if he took such a strident antireligious position. Ellis cultivated several trainees with widely varying religious backgrounds; these collaborations resulted in a major book on practicing REBT with religious clients (Nielsen, Johnson, & Ellis, 2001), a therapist manual for treating religious clients, using scripture quotes to support rational beliefs, and research studies on the effectiveness of REBT with religious patients (B. W. Johnson, DeVries, Ridley, Pettorini, & Peterson, 1994).

Influence of REBT on Modern Psychotherapy

Perhaps REBT's most influential idea to infiltrate psychotherapy and CBT has been the concept of demandingness and its antidote, acceptance. Ellis proposed that demanding that the world be different than it is results in a failure to cope with or change the adverse situation. People do not attempt to solve a problem they think should not exist. REBT encourages clients to accept the existence of adversity, cope with it, and possibly try to change it.

Ellis noted that he borrowed this idea from the Stoic philosophers, particularly Epictetus (90 BC/1996).

REBT's focus on acceptance has had a lasting influence on couples and relationship therapy. Ellis believed that attempts to change one's partner resulted in more coercion and disagreement. He recommended that therapists teach clients to accept their partners as fallible human beings (Ellis & Harper, 1961). When clients would recite their partner's faults, Ellis would respond, "That's what you get for being attracted to a mere mortal." This work preceded by several decades the acceptance methods that emerged in behavioral marital therapy (Baucom & Hoffman, 1986), integrative marital therapy (Christensen, Wheeler, & Jacobson, 2008), and the "third wave" of behavior therapy (Hayes, 2004; Chapter 4, this volume).

Ellis also proposed that people make demands concerning their thoughts and feelings and thus create a spiral of more negative emotions and irrational thoughts. A person might condemn himself or herself for having the thoughts or emotions and then cause more disturbed emotions. A client who does not accept his or her emotions spirals into even more emotional disturbance. In this way, the emotional consequences become a new activating event. This pattern results in people becoming depressed about their depression, or anxious about their anxiety. REBT referred to these iterative thoughts and emotions as secondary problems.

Raimy (1975) reviewed the early evidence for this spiraling or augmenting process. The concept has become a crucial aspect of REBT (Walen, DiGiuseppe, & Dryden, 1992; Walen, DiGiuseppe, & Wessler, 1980) under the name *experiential avoidance* and represents a major component in the third-wave therapies (Hayes, 2004). The REBT strategy is for practitioners to focus on the secondary problems first. Clients learn to accept disturbed emotions and learn that they could stand them until either the emotion passes or they learn better ways to divert them. Ellis's therapy preceded many of the interventions included in the standard CBT treatments of anxiety disorders (Warren, 2007). Like modern treatments of anxiety disorders, REBT treats the worry about the anxiety, challenges the catastrophic thoughts, and encourages clients to face the feared stimuli with exposure. Velten (2007) edited an entire volume on the contributions of Ellis and REBT to contemporary therapies.

As psychotherapy has entered the era of evidence-based practice, REBT has ceded popularity to therapies for which a large number of randomized clinical trials have been published. Ellis was not a researcher, and relatively few of his protégés pursued careers in academia or research. Ellis focused on practice and the training of practitioners. Despite this, a large number of outcome studies do support REBT. In fact, 502 outcome studies, of which more than 300 include random assignment to REBT versus a no-treatment, waiting-list, placebo, or alternative treatment control condition, have appeared corroborating the efficacy and effectiveness of REBT with many clinical problems.

Although this research literature is extensive, it has major flaws. Most contributing authors produced just one study. Few studies are part of programmatic research that explored a problem in depth with follow-up studies. Many of the studies do not include a control group, and more compare REBT to a wait list or placebo control. Few studies have tested REBT against an alternative treatment. In addition, the definitions of clinical populations and controls lack the rigor that the criteria for empirically based treatments require. (For a searchable database of REBT studies, see http://www.rebtinstitute.org/professionals/).

AARON BECK AND COGNITIVE THERAPY

Like Ellis, Aaron Beck came of age at a time when psychoanalytic theory was monolithic and psychoanalysis the dominant treatment. He began his career by trying to confirm the primacy of unconscious motivations and ended up formulating a theory of inaccurate beliefs and thinking errors that were largely accessible to conscious introspection. This cognitive theory led him to formulate principles of change that he codified into a cognitive therapy that has become one of the most widely practiced and most widely tested interventions in the world (DeRubeis & Crits-Christoph, 1998). The capstone of his career to date came when he became the recipient of the Lasker Award, probably the nation's most prestigious medical prize. In announcing the award, Joseph L. Goldstein, chairperson of the Lasker jury, called cognitive therapy "one of the most important advances—if not the most important advance—in the treatment of mental diseases in the last 50 years" (Altman, 2006).

Early History and Theory Development

Aaron Beck was the youngest of five children of parents who both emigrated from Russia (for an expanded discussion, see Weishaar, 1993). His father was a printer by trade and an intellectual by nature who was a strong supporter of socialistic principles. His mother was a strong-willed woman from a prominent Rhode Island family who gave up her dream of going to medical school to care for her younger siblings after the untimely death of her own mother.

Beck himself nearly died at age 7 after a broken bone became infected and he developed an infection of the blood that was nearly always fatal at that time. The surgery itself was traumatic; he was separated from his mother without warning and put under the knife before the anesthetic had taken effect. This experience led to fears of abandonment and health-related phobias that he mastered only by testing the accuracy of his beliefs by exposing himself to the situations that he feared. He missed so much time from school that he was held back a grade and came to think of himself as "dumb and stupid." He nonetheless excelled in school by dint of effort and came to believe that he could overcome any misfortune through hard work and turn "adversity to advantage." In many respects, the seeds of his later theoretical innovations were sown by his own early life experiences.

Like most psychiatrists in the middle part of the past century, Beck was trained in the psychoanalytic model (A. T. Beck, 2006). Early in his career, he embarked on a program of research designed to test Freud's notion that depression was a consequence of unconscious anger directed against the self. In a series of experimental and clinical studies, he found little evidence of the retroflected anger posited by dynamic theory in the performance of his depressed patients or in their dreams and free associations. What he found instead were consistent themes of loss and personal failing that were wholly consistent with the waking verbalizations and conscious ruminations of his patients. Struck by the consistency of this content, he proposed a major reformulation that held that depression was not at its core a product of unconscious drives and defenses, but rather the consequence of unduly negative beliefs and biased information processing. In so doing, Beck emphasized the causal role of one class of symptoms of depression, a causal role that had been largely overlooked by the major theoretical perspectives of the day.

It is easy to forget just how revolutionary this perspective was at the time or how controversial it proved to be. Psychoanalytic theory dating to Freud held that unconscious motivations lay at the root of all psychopathology and that these aberrant wishes and goals could not be directly addressed without triggering defenses that led the patient to resist all efforts at change. Behavior therapy, the major alternative at the time, held that psychopathology was a consequence of aberrant cues and consequences and could best be resolved by reordering the external environment. Both treatments largely dismissed the notion that what a patient believed could affect how he or she felt or behaved. Putting cognition at the core of psychopathology was truly revolutionary, and cognitive theory paved the way for some of the most efficacious treatments of the modern era. As might be expected, it was actively resisted at the time, and the larger psychoanalytic community regarded Beck's views (like those of Ellis) as heretical at best.

In 1967, Beck published a monograph on depression that became a classic in the field (A. T. Beck, 1967). In it, he summarized his work over the preceding decade that suggested that depression was a consequence of a systematic tendency to perceive things in a negative and biased fashion. He introduced the concept of the negative cognitive triad: negative views about the self, the world, and the future. He also explicated the role of schema, organized knowledge systems that bias the way information is processed in the direction of maintaining existing beliefs. He laid out the rudiments of a treatment in which patients were taught how to examine the accuracy of their own beliefs and how to protect themselves from the biasing effects of schema-driven processing. In the process, he drew heavily on cognitive psychology to explicate how existing beliefs could bias information processing and developed a sophisticated set of clinical procedures to offset those proclivities.

By the early 1970s, Beck had developed a treatment based on a coherent set of principles that he called *cognitive therapy*. He summarized these principles and strategies in a talk at the AABT in Denver and began a long and productive interaction with many theorists and therapists with a more behavioral perspective (A. T. Beck, 1970).

There was no evidence at that time that any psychosocial intervention was as efficacious as medications in the treatment of depression or even superior to pill-placebo controls. Back at the University of Pennsylvania, he was challenged by a young resident named John Rush to compare cognitive therapy with antidepressant medications, then the standard of treatment for depression. By the end of the decade, Beck and his colleagues had published the first controlled trial in which any psychotherapy was found to be at least the equal of medications (Rush, Beck, Kovacs, & Hollon, 1977). Patients in that trial were not only as likely to respond to cognitive therapy as to medications, but they also were considerably more likely to remain well after treatment termination (Kovacs, Rush, Beck, & Hollon, 1981). This was not only the first time that any psychosocial treatment had held its own with medication in the treatment of depression, it also was the first clear evidence of an enduring effect for psychotherapy, something that had long been claimed but never before demonstrated.

Forty years of subsequent research has substantiated most of those early claims (A. T. Beck, 2005). Cognitive therapy is now widely recognized as an empirically supported psychotherapy for depression. Its enduring effects, not found for medications, are well supported in the literature (Hollon, Stewart, & Strunk, 2006).

Moreover, its efficacy is not limited to depression. In a major monograph published in 1976, Beck laid the framework for extending cognitive theory and therapy to the understanding and treatment of a variety of other disorders (A. T. Beck, 1976). There now is evidence for its efficacy and enduring effects in many of the nonpsychotic disorders, as well as emerging work in the personality disorders and the psychoses (Butler, Chapman, Forman, & Beck, 2006). In randomized clinical trials, cognitive therapy has proven the most broadly efficacious of the existing psychotherapies, and it has largely eclipsed psychodynamic psychotherapy and even the more purely behavioral methods in terms of the support for its efficacy and the number of its adherents.

Beck has a long-standing commitment to empirical evaluation that has generated the evidence that fueled the widespread acceptance of his psychotherapy. He views his theories as hypotheses to be tested and seeks to subject them to empirical disconfirmation in as timely and as powerful a manner as possible. His clinical trials have consistently pitted cognitive therapy against the best existing treatments in the field, and he has done whatever possible to ensure that each treatment tested has a fair chance at success. The quality and impartiality of his studies have contributed greatly to their impact on the field. The ease with which they have been replicated speaks to the generalizability of cognitive therapy. Cognitive therapy has been revised on the basis of experimental findings and clinical insights, allowing it to be generalized to numerous other disorders. There is even emerging evidence that cognitive therapy can be taught to persons at risk to prevent the emergence of subsequent distress (see, e.g., Garber et al., 2009).

Beck and colleagues also played a major role in developing treatment manuals for use in research and practice. As he and his colleagues identified the cognitive underpinnings of a given disorder and formulated specific strategies that could be used in its treatment, they would collate these materials into treatment manuals that could be used in subsequent controlled trials and disseminated to therapists elsewhere. This approach was first developed in his work on depression and led to the publication of what is probably the prototypical and most widely cited treatment manual, *Cognitive Therapy of Depression* (A. T. Beck, Rush, Shaw, & Emery, 1979). This same approach was subsequently applied to the study and treatment of panic and the anxiety disorders (Beck, Emery, & Greenberg, 1985), personality disorders (A. T. Beck, Freeman, & Associates, 1990), and substance abuse (A. T. Beck, Wright, Newman, & Liese, 1993).

Beck evidences a long-standing interest in suicide and its prevention. He found that persons with elevated levels of hopelessness were at significant risk of ultimate suicide and that predictors of subsequent risk among suicide attempters included expressions of regret over the failure of their attempt(s) and increasing intensity of ideation across attempts (R. W. Beck, Morris, & Beck, 1974). This work culminated in the development of a brief cognitive therapy for suicide that has been shown to cut the frequency of subsequent attempts in half among high-risk patients with a recent history of attempts (Brown et al., 2005).

In the late 1970s, Beck joined with other cognitive behavioral theorists, including Albert Ellis, to found the journal *Cognitive Therapy and Research*. The seminal depression treatment study by Rush et al. (1977) was published in the inaugural issue of the journal, and it has been one of the most widely cited articles in the history of psychology. The journal played a major role in bringing CBT to the attention of the field in its early years, and it survives today as a major outlet for high-quality research.

During the 1970s and 1980s, Beck made extended visits to Oxford University, where the chairperson of psychiatry, Michael Gelder, was supportive of cognitive therapy. There he met John Teasdale, who conducted a number of early trials with cognitive therapy (Paykel et al., 1999; Teasdale, Fennell, Hibbert, & Amies, 1984) and later joined with Mark Williams and Zindel Segal in Toronto to develop a mindfulness-based approach to cognitive therapy (Kuyken et al., 2008; Ma & Teasdale, 2004; Teasdale et al., 2000). Beck also had a strong influence on David M. Clark and Paul Salkovskis (later joined by Anke Ehlers from Germany), who adapted cognitive therapy to the treatment of a variety of anxiety disorders, including panic, social phobia, hypochondriasis, posttraumatic stress disorder, and obsessive–compulsive disorder. This trio of clinical researchers subsequently moved to the Institute of Psychiatry in London (the Maudsley) and is doing some of the most elegant treatment development in the field today. Clark is overseeing a particularly ambitious effort by the National Health Service to train therapists across the whole of Great Britain in CBT. Dominic Lam, another former trainee, adapted cognitive therapy to the prevention of recurrence in bipolar disorder, and Christopher Fairburn at Oxford and Kelly Bemis Vitousek in Hawaii have each been strongly influenced by cognitive therapy in their respective work with eating disorders.

David Kingdon and Douglas Turkington (1994) in England adapted cognitive therapy to the treatment of residual symptoms in schizophrenia, and other groups in the United Kingdom similarly have found promising results in the treatment of both acute and chronic patients. This work has been slow to penetrate the United States (where clinical lore has long presumed that you cannot reason with a delusion) but is beginning to make its way to the new world (A. T. Beck & Rector, 2005). Much of the work in the United States (including that by Robert J. DeRubeis and Steven D. Hollon) has focused on depression; Martin Seligman at the University of Pennsylvania and Judy Garber at Vanderbilt have each investigated the role of cognitive interventions in the prevention of depression in at-risk children and adolescents.

Specific Disorders

Depression is seen by cognitive theory as a consequence of unduly negative beliefs about the self, world, and future (the negative cognitive triad) and maladaptive information processing. Cognitive therapy for depression typically starts by using behavioral strategies to get the patient moving (with behavior change often framed in the context of hypothesis testing regarding current beliefs) and then teaches the strategies for examining the accuracy of specific automatic thoughts and underlying assumptions and core beliefs. The emphasis is kept on current life situations for patients with uncomplicated depressions, whereas attention also is paid to childhood antecedents and the therapeutic relationship for patients with depressions superimposed on underlying personality disorders (the "three-legged stool"). Early studies suggested that cognitive therapy might be more efficacious than medication in the treatment of major depression but did not implement pharmacotherapy in an adequate fashion (Blackburn et al., 1981; Rush et al., 1977). Subsequent studies that did a better job of implementing medication typically found that cognitive therapy was as efficacious as medication (Hollon et al., 1992; Murphy et al., 1984). The National Institute of Mental Health's Treatment of Depression Collaborative Research Program found antidepressant medication (and interpersonal psychotherapy) to be superior to cognitive therapy in the treatment of patients with more severe depression (Elkin et al., 1995) but may not have implemented cognitive therapy in an adequate fashion at all of its sites (Jacobson & Hollon, 1996). The same can be said for a recent comparison with behavioral activation that also found that cognitive therapy was less efficacious than medication in the treatment of patients with more severe depression (Dimidjian et al., 2006). A placebo-controlled trial among more severely depressed patients found cognitive therapy as efficacious as medication treatment when implemented by experienced cognitive therapists (DeRubeis et al., 2005). Across virtually all of these trials, prior exposure to cognitive therapy reduced risk of relapse by about half relative to medication withdrawal following treatment termination (Blackburn et al., 1986; Dobson et al., 2008; Evans et al., 1992; Hollon, DeRubeis, et al., 2005; Simons et al., 1986; for the sole exception, see Shea et al., 1992). (See Chapter 14d for a fuller discussion of pharmacotherapy.)

Panic disorder has been transformed in the past 2 decades in terms of our understanding of its etiology and our ability to treat the disorder, with David M. Clark joining Beck in the lead. Whereas behavior theory views panic disorder as a conditioned response to external cues, and biological theory views it as a spontaneous discharge of neural centers involved in stress response, a cognitive model of panic suggests that patients panic when they misinterpret benign bodily sensations as signs of impending physical or mental catastrophes (A. T. Beck, Emery, & Greenberg, 1985; Clark, 1986). Cognitive therapy of panic disorders encourages patients to drop the safety behaviors they use to forestall the feared outcome (usually a heart attack or going crazy) and to do whatever they can to bring about the catastrophic event. In essence, patients are encouraged to disconfirm their catastrophic beliefs by doing everything they can to bring them about. An early trial found that cognitive therapy focused on the disconfirmation of catastrophic cognitions was superior to either imipramine or applied relaxation, which were in turn superior to a waiting-list control in the treatment of panic disorder (Clark et al., 1994). A subsequent study found that a brief five-session version of cognitive therapy (supplemented by self-study modules) was as efficacious as the full 12- to 15-session intervention (Clark et al., 1999). Barlow and colleagues found that 3 months of CBT (that emphasized repeated exposure to interoceptive cues) was as efficacious as and more enduring than imipramine (Barlow, Gorman, Shear, & Woods, 2000). Findings from these and other related studies have led the National Institute for Health and Clinical Excellence (NICE), an independent advisory body to the National Health Service in Great Britain, to certify cognitive therapy as the primary psychosocial treatment for panic disorder.

Social phobia also has undergone a renascence in the past decade, with David M. Clark and colleagues again in the lead. Social phobia involves not only the operation of inferential biases in social situations but also an undue focus on internal processes and a tendency to overweight those cues in monitoring interpersonal interactions (Clark & McManus, 2002). In brief, persons with social phobia attend too much to themselves in social situations (especially their own visual representations of how they think they are coming across) and rely too much on safety behaviors that produce the very social oddities that they are trying to avoid. In addition to standard cognitive and behavioral strategies for dealing with inaccurate beliefs and unskilled social behaviors, patients watch videotapes of themselves engaging in social interactions with and without their safety behaviors and rate the way they come across. Invariably, patients find themselves more pleased with how they appear when they drop their safety behaviors than when they try to protect themselves from social embarrassment. Cognitive therapy was superior to either fluoxetine or placebo plus self-exposure after 3 months of active treatment and more enduring than fluoxetine over a 12-month follow-up (Clark et al., 2003). A subsequent study by that same group found cognitive therapy superior to applied relaxation, with both superior to a waiting-list control (Clark et al., 2006). Group CBT was as efficacious as and more enduring than phenelzine in the treatment of social phobia (Heimberg et al., 1998; Liebowitz et al., 1999). As was the case for panic disorder, the NICE guidelines certify only CBT as a treatment for social phobia among the psychosocial interventions.

Hypochondriasis is common in medical settings and is generally considered difficult to treat. Its central feature is a tendency to misinterpret innocuous physical signs and symptoms as evidence of serious disorder (Warwick & Salkovskis, 1990). Whereas panic disorder involves the anticipation of an imminent catastrophe that might be medical or psychiatric (e.g., heart attack, psychosis), hypochondriasis involves the anticipation of a catastrophic medical illness with a longer temporal delay (e.g., cancer). This propensity not only leads to considerable anxiety, it also tends to focus one's attention on health issues and leads to excessive efforts to seek reassurance from the medical community. As with panic disorder, the therapy focus is to get patients to drop their safety behaviors and to examine the basis for their beliefs. Behavioral experiments are used to induce "symptoms" by deliberate body focus and to prevent body-checking and reassurance-seeking behaviors. Cognitive therapy has been found superior to a waiting-list control, with gains maintained at a 3-month follow-up (Warwick, Clark, Cobb, & Salkovskis, 1996), and superior to both behavioral stress management and a waiting-list control (Clark et al., 1998). These are the first controlled trials suggesting the efficacy of any intervention in the treatment of hypochondriasis.

Generalized anxiety disorder has long presented a problem for behavior theory since there is no clear external referent for the pervasive worry that is the hallmark of the disorder. CBT of the disorder historically has combined relaxation training or meditation with cognitive restructuring to bring the process of worry under control. None of these methods have fared that well, and the specificity of CBT is less compelling for generalized anxiety disorder than it is for either panic or social phobia (Siev & Chambless, 2007). Some cognitive therapists dropped relaxation training entirely to focus more intensely on purely cognitive targets, such as intolerance of uncertainty and avoidance, and found cognitive therapy superior to a delayed treatment control (Ladouceur et al., 2000). Whether this more purely cognitive approach will improve on the rather modest and nonspecific gains typically found for this disorder remains to be determined.

Specific phobias respond particularly well to both behavioral and cognitive–behavioral therapies, with exposure the key apparent mechanism. Recent studies suggest that tailoring the exposure to the specific and often idiosyncratic beliefs that underlie the fears of a given individual can accelerate the pace of treatment and often result in a one-session cure (Öst, Alm, Brandberg, & Breitholtz, 2001; Öst, Svensson, Hellström, & Lindwall, 2001). Just as in panic and social phobia, cognitive strategies can be used to make exposure-based interventions even more powerful and long lasting.

Obsessive–compulsive disorder (OCD) is a particularly refractory disorder that appears to be less susceptible to nonspecific effects than the other anxiety disorders (Huppert et al., 2004). NICE certifies both behavioral exposure and CBT with behavioral exposure (along with select antidepressants) for the treatment of OCD (see, e.g., Foa et al., 2005). CBT appears to have an enduring effect in OCD following treatment termination not found for medications (Simpson et al., 2004). Nonetheless, it is clear that none of the current interventions are as efficacious in absolute terms for OCD as they are for disorders like panic or social phobia. An exaggerated sense of personal responsibility can lead to the generation of anxiety and motivate a desire to engage in neutralizing strategies that serve as safety behaviors in OCD (Salkovskis, 1999). It remains to be seen whether this reworking at a theoretical level will lead to the generation of therapeutic interventions with greater specificity for this disorder.

Posttraumatic stress disorder involves increased arousal and persistent avoidance combined with other symptoms like flashbacks or intrusive recollections following exposure to traumatic events outside the range of normal human experience. NICE certifies three types of treatments for posttraumatic stress disorder: prolonged exposure, CBT, and eye-movement desensitization and reprocessing (Bisson et al., 2007). All involve exposure to avoided memories of the traumatic event, and that appears to be the key element in successful treatment. Recent theoretical formulations have emphasized the role of exaggerated concerns of danger and unwarranted beliefs about diminished personal worth and focused more on cognitive strategies that target those beliefs (Ehlers & Clark, 2000). It remains to be seen whether this greater attention to the meaning system that develops in conjunction with the traumatic event will enhance the effects of treatment.

Eating disorders are an area in which CBT represents the current standard of treatment, in particular for bulimia and binge eating disorder; less is known about the treatment of anorexia nervosa, although a specific form of family therapy shows some promise (Wilson, Grilo, & Vitousek, 2007). NICE certifies only CBT and certain antidepressants in the treatment of bulimia. Fairburn and colleagues have done some of the best work in the area. An early study found that CBT focusing on aberrant beliefs about weight and shape as well as eating behaviors was superior to interpersonal psychotherapy (IPT) and more enduring than behavior therapy in the treatment of bulimia (Fairburn et al., 1995). A subsequent study found CBT both superior to and more enduring than IPT in that same population (Agras, Walsh, Fairburn, Wilson, & Kraemer, 2000). CBT was also found superior to fluoxetine in the treatment of binge eating disorder (Grilo, Masheb, & Wilson, 2005). CBT was found to be superior to nutritional counseling in the treatment of patients with anorexia nervosa during the first year post-hospitalization (Pike et al., 2003). Fairburn recently proposed a transdiagnostic treatment within the eating disorders that emphasizes the elements they share rather than the ways in which they differ (Fairburn, Cooper, & Shafran, 2003).

Borderline personality disorder is a particularly problematic disorder that is exasperating to both patients and clinicians alike. NICE certifies only dialectical behavior therapy in the treatment of borderline personality disorder (see Linehan et al., 2006; Chapter 12L), although a recent study out of the Netherlands suggests a good effect for schema-focused cognitive therapy, if it replicates at other sites (Giesen-Bloo et al., 2006). Schema-focused cognitive therapy adopts a "three-legged stool" in which early childhood antecedents and the therapeutic relationship are incorporated with a more conventional focus on current life situations. Treatment tends to be longer than for less complicated patients with depression or anxiety disorders (up to 3 years in the Dutch study), but given the lack of success with most treatments, this may be necessary in the treatment of borderline personality disorder.

Bipolar disorder and the schizophrenias remain the province of medication treatment, with psychotherapy playing an adjunctive role at best. Patients with a history of mania are generally well advised to stay on mood stabilizers, although family-focused therapy, CBT, and social rhythm IPT all look promising as adjuncts (Miklowitz, 2008). For example, adding cognitive therapy can reduce the frequency of depressive relapse in medicated bipolar patients (Lam et al., 2005). Patients with schizophrenia are typically maintained on antipsychotic medications, although CBT does appear to have an adjunctive role to play in dealing with delusions and hallucinations (A. T. Beck & Rector, 2005). This conclusion is based on nearly a dozen randomized controlled trials with schizophrenic populations (all done in England) and represents one of the most exciting developments in cognitive therapy in the past decade.

Childhood disorders largely show the same patterns of response as do the adult disorders. Behavior therapy and CBT generally produce impressive results in the nonpsychotic disorders and play a more adjunctive role in the psychotic disorders (Weisz, Jensen-Doss, & Hawley, 2006). Cognitive therapy has been found superior to either behavioral family therapy or nondirective supportive therapy in the treatment of depressed suicidal adolescents (Brent et al., 1997), and CBT was nearly as efficacious as (and safer than) fluoxetine in the treatment of depressed adolescents (March et al., 2004). Kendall and colleagues have found CBT at least as efficacious as psychosocial or pharmacological interventions in the treatment of a variety of different childhood anxiety disorders (Kendall, Hudson, Gosch, Flannery-Schroeder, & Suveg, 2008; Walkup et al., 2008).

Influence of Cognitive Therapy on Modern Psychotherapy

Cognitive therapy is probably the best researched and most frequently taught approach to psychotherapy in the field today. Cognitive restructuring is represented in most of the cognitive behavioral interventions, but the combination of Socratic dialogue and empirical hypothesis testing pioneered by Beck is widely imitated and considered by many to be the sine qua non of the approach. Cognitive therapy is widely practiced in every corner of the globe, and training institutes and opportunities can be found in virtually every industrialized country. The Beck Institute in suburban Philadelphia remains the center of this worldwide network, and its extramural program has trained many clinical researchers in the field today. The Academy of Cognitive Therapy offers performance-based certification in cognitive therapy and maintains a website that lists the names and contact information of cognitive therapists around the country and the world. Beck's daughter Judy Beck has emerged as a major figure in her own right as a training director and author of several popular books, including a recent treatise applying cognitive therapy to weight management (J. S. Beck, 2007).

There is little doubt that Beck's insistence on empirical testing has promoted the visibility of cognitive therapy and helped ensure that it is more than just a passing fad. Beck and his disciples have consistently tested their approach against the most powerful clinical alternatives, and in the process they have provided strong data that often serve to convince the skeptics. Not everything works, and the approach is in a constant state of evolution, but the commitment to subjecting the approach to potential disconfirmation ensures that weaknesses are uncovered and open to correction. This is perhaps best exemplified by the evolution of schema-based approaches designed to provide a means of working with patients with the kinds of chronic personality disorders that make them particularly unlikely to respond to standard approaches to specific disorders (A. T. Beck, Freeman, & Associates, 1990).

Many of the people who trained with Beck have gone on to hold the kinds of positions in academic and clinical research settings that ensure that they will train the next generation of clinicians and researchers. This provides a multiplicative effect that ensures that the principles developed by Beck and his associates will be broadly represented in the larger clinical community. Cognitive therapy is broadly applicable clinically and well validated empirically. This combination makes it likely that the approach will be more than just a passing fad.

INTO THE FUTURE

In the 40-plus years since its first formal conference, CBT has become a major force and a pluralistic orientation in psychotherapy. Several different theoretical constructs and methods fall within the CBT rubric. The constructs include negative automatic thoughts, dysfunctional attitudes, irrational beliefs, underlying schema, attributional styles, problem-solving skills, and behavior guiding self-statements. The brand-name interventions include REBT, cognitive–behavioral modification, CBT, cognitive therapy, and multiple variations thereof. A substantial amount of controlled research supports the efficacy of CBT for multiple disorders and patient presentations. Along with behavior therapy, CBT has garnered the largest amount of supportive research.

The psychotherapies of Beck and Ellis represent the most systematic applications of CBT. Cognitive therapy and REBT practitioners rely on the entire armamentarium of CBT techniques, plus behavioral methods and a healthy dose of empathy, but they do follow a defined plan of action and use techniques in planned order. However, CBT as practiced and researched often includes a hodgepodge of different techniques. Each practitioner and researcher constructs a unique combination of CBT methods that includes different components with a different dose.

The emerging questions for both practice and research concern the optimal number of ingredients and the sufficient dose for CBT's effectiveness. Some CBT leaders advocate a specificity hypothesis. That is, they believe that psychotherapists should target one set of beliefs relatively specific to a disorder and focus their clinical attention on it. However, many practitioners feel no such allegiance to a particular variant of CBT and want to individualize the treatment for the individual client.

This diversity of constructs and techniques and the lack of comparative research raise critical questions. Do all of the cognitive constructs exert independent influences on emotional disturbance? Or perhaps all the constructs are highly correlated—similar phenomena labeled with different names? Should a psychotherapist provide a single CBT method or include multiple CBT techniques, targeting automatic thoughts, irrational beliefs, problem-solving deficits, and underlying schema? Integrating too many CBT constructs and methods may overwhelm the psychotherapist and the client alike and may decrease their effectiveness (Hollon, Garber, & Shelton, 2005). Providing too many methods in a single psychotherapy may dilute the impact of any one and may lead to clients learning too many methods poorly rather than learning one or two strategies well.

Another critical question concerns the specificity of cognitive therapy. If you aim your interventions at a specific cognition, say, negative automatic thoughts, does the intervention change only that construct, or will other cognitive constructs show change as well? A recent comparative study of cognitive therapy, REBT, and medication for the treatment of depression demonstrated that cognitive therapy and REBT produced changes in both negative automatic thoughts and irrational beliefs (Szentagotai, David, Lupu, & Cosman, 2008). If this finding is replicated and expanded to comparisons of other forms of CBT, perhaps all forms of CBT influence all of the cognitions hypothesized to influence emotional disturbance.

An additional problem encountered by the CBT practitioner is the growing number of treatment manuals for particular disorders and the inability of people to commit them all to memory. Practitioners face the choice of specializing in a few disorders or applying broad principles of CBT across clients with diverse problems.

To address these problems, CBT may become less dependent on treatment manuals for specific problems and more prescriptive in the future. Theoreticians and researchers likely will develop principle-based, transdiagnostic methods (Allen, McHugh, & Barlow, 2008). Case conceptualization as developed by Persons (2006) likely will become a cornerstone of CBT. Practitioners will develop assessment strategies to uncover which cognitive constructs contribute to the problems of particular clients. They will use this information to develop case conceptualizations of the client and then select the appropriate methods that target the individual client's needs. Thus, CBT will become more prescriptive, advocating that practitioners apply empirically based principles to the assessment and treatment of the individual.

Will CBT continue to be dominated by the great, charismatic psychotherapists? We think not. We have probably witnessed the last of the great theoreticians with Beck and Ellis. While visionaries will integrate what has come before and develop new treatments, we think it likely that controlled research, rather than charismatic theorists, will lead the way in the future.

CONCLUSIONS

Several factors account for the rise of CBT into its position of prominence in psychotherapy today. First, cognitive therapies have always represented a compromise between psychoanalytic psychotherapy's focus on clients' internal experiences and behavior therapy's focus on observable behavior and empiricism. From the outset, CBT represented an integration of techniques that allowed for the theorists and practitioners to best focus on clients' subjective experiences and their external, observable reality.

Second, CBT has advocated and promoted research. CBT continued the research tradition established by one of its parents, behavior therapy. The constructs identified by CBT allowed for the easy development of self-report measures. Automatic thoughts, dysfunctional attitudes, irrational beliefs, and problem-solving skills were all operationalized into measures that can assess change over the course of psychotherapy. These factors culminated in an avalanche of research on CBT and may have fulfilled the dream set forth in the Boulder model for a scientist–practitioner (see Chapter 16a). This empirical tradition of CBT attracted academics who train new generations of psychotherapists. The research commitment of cognitive therapies will remain one of its legacies to psychotherapy.

Third, both cognitive therapy and REBT are relatively brief and structured treatments that fit well in an era of cost effectiveness and evidence-based practice. Fourth, the determined personalities of Ellis and Beck shaped CBT in particular and psychotherapy in general. Both were strong visionaries.

Beck set an example for high scientific standards in testing the efficacy of therapies. Ellis modeled the quintessential skeptic, advocating the challenging of every idea.

CBT has moved into a state of slow growth, similar to what Thomas Kuhn (1996) called *normal science*. This is the period in the history of any science when a paradigm is accepted and people work out the details of the paradigm. Researchers and practitioners are making small, fine-tuned changes to theory and technique. Comparative research will most likely help us learn which aspects of CBT are most helpful for different disorders and types of patients. CBT will probably dominate the field for a while.

CBT does not help all clients. Practitioners' insights and researchers' findings will gradually expand our knowledge, but just so far. Smart people will focus on the limits of CBT, and a new paradigm will probably emerge. We hope that CBT advocates and all those committed to science will accept change when it comes.

REFERENCES

Abramson, L. Y., Seligman, M. E., & Teasdale, J. D. (1978). Learned helplessness in humans: Critique and reformulation. *Journal of Abnormal Psychology, 87,* 49–74. doi:10.1037/0021-843X.87.1.49

Agras, W. S., Walsh, T., Fairburn, C. G., Wilson, G. T., & Kraemer, H. C. (2000). A multicenter comparison of cognitive-behavioral therapy and interpersonal psychotherapy for bulimia nervosa. *Archives of General Psychiatry, 57,* 459–466. doi:10.1001/arcpsyc.57.5.459

Allen, L. B., McHugh, R. K., & Barlow, D. H. (2008). Emotional disorders: A unified protocol. In D. H. Barlow (Ed.), *Clinical handbook of psychological disorders: A step-by-step treatment manual* (4th ed., pp. 216–249). New York, NY: Guilford Press.

Altman, L. K. (2006, September 17). Psychiatrist is among five chosen for medical award. *The New York Times.* Retrieved from http://www.nytimes.com

Antony, M. (2003). Is it time for AABT to change its name? *Behavior Therapist, 26,* 361–371.

Barlow, D. H., Gorman, J. M., Shear, M. K., & Woods, S. W. (2000). Cognitive-behavioral therapy, imipramine, or their combination for panic disorder: A randomized controlled trial. *JAMA, 283,* 2529–2536. doi:10.1001/jama.283.19.2529

Bartley, W. W. (1987). In defense of self applied critical rationalism. In G. Radnitzky & W. W. Bartley (Eds.), *Evolutionary epistemology, theory of rationality and sociology of knowledge* (pp. 279–312). LaSalle, IL: Open Court.

Baucom, D. H., & Hoffman, J. A. (1986). The effectiveness of marital therapy: Current status and applications to the clinical settings. In N. S. Jacobson & A. S. Gurman (Eds.), *Clinical handbook of marital therapy* (pp. 597–620). New York, NY: Guilford Press.

Beck, A. T. (1967). *Depression: Clinical, experimental, and theoretical aspects.* New York, NY: Hoeber.

Beck, A. T. (1970). Cognitive therapy: Nature and relation to behavior therapy. *Behavior Therapy, 1,* 184–200. doi:10.1016/S0005-7894(70)80030-2

Beck, A. T. (1976). *Cognitive therapy and the emotional disorders.* New York, NY: Meridian.

Beck, A. T. (2005). The current state of cognitive therapy: A 40-year retrospective. *Archives of General Psychiatry, 62*, 953–959. doi:10.1001/archpsyc.62.9.953

Beck, A. T. (2006). How an anomalous finding led to a new system of psychotherapy. *Nature Medicine, 12*, 1139–1141. doi:10.1038/nm1006-1139

Beck, A. T., Emery, G., & Greenberg, R. (1985). *Anxiety disorders and phobias: A cognitive perspective.* New York, NY: Basic Books.

Beck, A. T., Freeman, A., & Associates. (1990). *Cognitive therapy of personality disorders.* New York, NY: Guilford Press.

Beck, A. T., & Rector, N. (2005). Cognitive approaches to schizophrenia: Theory and therapy. *Annual Review of Clinical Psychology, 1*, 577–606. doi:10.1146/annurev.clinpsy.1.102803.144205

Beck, A. T., Rush, A. J., Shaw, B. F., & Emery, G. (1979). *The cognitive therapy of depression.* New York, NY: Guilford Press.

Beck, A. T., Wright, F. D., Newman, C. F., & Liese, B. S. (1993). *Cognitive therapy of substance abuse.* New York, NY: Guilford Press.

Beck, G. (2005). What's in a name? *Behavior Therapist, 28*, 16.

Beck, J. S. (2007). *Beck diet weight loss workbook.* New York, NY: Oxmoor House.

Beck, R. W., Morris, J. B., & Beck, A. T. (1974). Cross-validation of the Suicidal Intent Scale. *Psychological Reports, 34*, 445–446. Bisson, J. I., Ehlers, A., Matthews, R., Pilling, S., Richards, D., & Turner, S. (2007). Psychological treatments for chronic post-traumatic stress disorder: Systematic review and meta-analysis. *British Journal of Psychiatry, 190*, 97–104. doi:10.1192/bjp.bp.106.021402

Blackburn, I. M., Bishop, S., Glen, A. I. M., Whalley, L. J., & Christie, J. E. (1981). The efficacy of cognitive therapy in depression: A treatment trial using cognitive therapy and pharmacotherapy, each alone and in combination. *British Journal of Psychiatry, 139*, 181–189. doi:10.1192/bjp.139.3.181

Blackburn, I. M., Eunson, K. M., & Bishop, S. (1986). A two-year naturalistic follow-up of depressed patients treated with cognitive therapy, pharmacotherapy and a combination of both. *Journal of Affective Disorders, 10*, 67–75. doi:10.1016/0165-0327(86)90050-9

Braswell, L., & Kendall, P. (2001). Cognitive-behavior therapy with children and adolescents. In K. Dobson (Ed.), *Handbook of cognitive-behavior therapies* (2nd ed., pp. 246–294). New York, NY: Guilford Press.

Brent, D. A., Holder, D., Kolko, K. J., Birmaher, B., Baugher, M., Roth, C., et al. (1997). A clinical psychotherapy trial for adolescent depression comparing cognitive, family, and supportive treatments. *Archives of General Psychiatry, 54*, 877–885.

Brown, G. K., Have, T. T., Henriques, G. R., Xie, S. X., Hollander, J. E., & Beck, A. T. (2005). Cognitive therapy for the prevention of suicide attempts: A randomized controlled trial. *JAMA, 294*, 563–570. doi:10.1001/jama.294.5.563

Butler, A. C., Chapman, J. E., Forman, E. M., & Beck, A. T. (2006). The empirical status of cognitive-behavioral therapy: A review of meta-analyses. *Clinical Psychology Review, 26*, 17–31. doi:10.1016/j.cpr.2005.07.003

Cautela, J. R. (1970). Covert reinforcement. *Behavior Therapy, 1*, 33–50. doi:10.1016/S0005-7894(70)80055-7

Christensen, A., Wheeler, J. G., & Jacobson, N. S. (2008). Couple distress. In D. H. Barlow (Ed.), *Clinical handbook of psychological disorders: A step-by-step treatment manual* (4th ed., pp. 662–689). New York, NY: Guilford Press.

Clark, D. M. (1986). A cognitive approach to panic. *Behaviour Research and Therapy, 24*, 461–470. doi: 10.1016/0005-7967(86)90011-2

Clark, D. M., Ehlers, A., Hackmann, A., McManus, F., Fennell, M., Grey, N., et al. (2006). Cognitive therapy versus exposure and applied relaxation in social phobia: A randomized controlled trial. *Journal of Consulting and Clinical Psychology, 74,* 568–578. doi:10.1037/0022-006X.74.3.568

Clark, D. M., Ehlers, A., McManus, F., Hackmann, A., Fennell, M., Campbell, H., et al. (2003). Cognitive therapy versus fluoxetine in generalized social phobia: A randomized placebo-controlled trial. *Journal of Consulting and Clinical Psychology, 71,* 1058–1067. doi:10.1037/0022-006X.71.6.1058

Clark, D. M., & McManus, F. (2002). Information processing in social phobia. *Biological Psychiatry, 51,* 92–100. doi:10.1016/S0006-3223(01)01296-3

Clark, D. M., Salkovskis, P. M., Hackmann, A., Middleton, H., Anastasiades, P., & Gelder, M. (1994). A comparison of cognitive therapy, applied relaxation and imipramine in the treatment of panic disorder. *Journal of Consulting and Clinical Psychology, 164,* 759–769.

Clark, D. M., Salkovskis, P. M., Hackmann, A., Wells, A., Fennell, M., Ludgate, J., et al. (1998). Two psychological treatments for hypochondriasis: A randomized controlled trial. *British Journal of Psychiatry, 173,* 218–225. doi:10.1192/bjp.173.3.218

Clark, D. M., Salkovskis, P. M., Hackmann, A., Wells, A., Ludgate, J., & Gelder, M. (1999). Brief cognitive therapy for panic disorder: A randomized controlled trial. *Journal of Consulting and Clinical Psychology, 67,* 583–589. doi:10.1037/0022-006X.67.4.583

Cook, J. M., Biyanova, T., & Coyne, J. C. (2009). Influential psychotherapy figures, authors, and books: An Internet survey of over 2,000 psychotherapists. *Psychotherapy: Theory, Research, Practice, Training, 46,* 42–51.

Corsini, R. J. (Ed.). (1994). *Encyclopedia of psychology* (2nd ed.). New York, NY: Wiley.

DeRubeis, R. J., & Crits-Christoph, P. (1998). Empirically supported individual and group psychological treatments for adult mental disorders. *Journal of Consulting and Clinical Psychology, 66,* 37–52. doi:10.1037/0022-006X.66.1.37

DeRubeis, R. J., Hollon, S. D., Amsterdam, J. D., Shelton, R. C., Young, P. R., Salomon, R. M., et al. (2005). Cognitive therapy vs. medications in the treatment of moderate to severe depression. *Archives of General Psychiatry, 62,* 409–416. doi:10.1001/archpsyc.62.4.409

DiGiuseppe, R. (1986). The implications of the philosophy of science for rational emotive theory and therapy. *Psychotherapy, 23,* 634–639. doi:10.1037/h0085668

Dimidjian, S., Hollon, S. D., Dobson, K. S., Schmaling, K. B., Kohlenberg, R. J., Addis, M. E., et al. (2006). Behavioral activation, cognitive therapy, and antidepressant medication in the acute treatment of major depression. *Journal of Consulting and Clinical Psychology, 74,* 658–670. doi:10.1037/0022-006X.74.4.658

Dobson, K. S., Hollon, S. D., Dimidjian, S., Schmaling, K. B., Kohlenberg, R. J., Gallop, R. J., . . . Jacobson, N. S. (2008). Randomized trial of behavioral activation, cognitive therapy, and antidepressant medication in the prevention of relapse and recurrence in major depression. *Journal of Consulting and Clinical Psychology, 76,* 468–477. doi:10.1037/0022-006X.76.3.468

Dryden, W. (2008). *Rational emotive behaviour therapy: Distinctive features.* Hove, England: Routledge.

D'Zurilla, T. J., & Goldfried, M. R. (1971). Problem solving and behavior modification. *Journal of Abnormal Psychology, 78,* 107–126. doi:10.1037/h0031360

D'Zurilla, T., & Nezu, A. M. (2006). *Problem-solving therapy: A positive approach to clinical intervention* (3rd ed.). New York, NY: Springer.

Ehlers, A., & Clark, D. M. (2000). A cognitive model of posttraumatic stress disorder. *Behaviour Research and Therapy, 38,* 319–345. doi:10.1016/S0005-7967(99)00123-0

Elkin, I., Gibbons, R. D., Shea, T., Sotsky, S. M., Watkins, J. T., Pilkonis, P. A., & Hedeker, D. (1995). Initial severity and differential treatment outcome in the National Institute of Mental Health Treatment of Depression Collaborative Research Program. *Journal of Consulting and Clinical Psychology, 63,* 841–847. doi:10.1037/0022-006X.63.5.841

Ellis, A. (1933). *Youth against the world: A novel.* Unpublished manuscript.

Ellis, A. (1955). New approaches to psychotherapy techniques. *Journal of Clinical Psychology, 11,* 207–260. doi:10.1002/1097-4679(195507)11:3{207::AID-JCLP2270110302}3.0.CO;2-1

Ellis, A. (1957a). Outcome of employing three techniques of psychotherapy. *Journal of Clinical Psychology, 13,* 344–350.

Ellis, A. (1957b). Rational psychotherapy and individual psychology. *Journal of Individual Psychology, 13,* 38–44.

Ellis, A. (1962). *Reason and emotion in psychotherapy.* New York, NY: Lyle Stuart.

Ellis, A. (1986). Do some religious beliefs help create emotional disturbance? *Psychotherapy in Private Practice, 4,* 101–106.

Ellis, A. (1994). *Reason and emotion in psychotherapy: A comprehensive method of treating human disturbance: Revised and updated.* New York, NY: Birch Lane Press.

Ellis, A. (1999). Why rational emotive therapy to rational emotive behavior therapy? *Psychotherapy: Theory, Research, Practice, Training, 36,* 154–159.

Ellis, A. (2000). Can rational emotive behavior therapy (REBT) be effectively used with people who have devout beliefs in God and religion? *Professional Psychology, Research, and Practice, 31,* 29–33. doi:10.1037/0735-7028.31.1.29

Ellis, A. (2001). The rise of cognitive behavior therapy. In W. T. O'Donohue, D. A. Henderson, S. C. Hayes, J. E. Fisher, & L. J. Hayes (Eds.), *A history of the behavioral therapies: Founders' personal histories* (pp. 183–194). Reno, NV: Context Press.

Ellis, A. (2005a). Discussion of Christine A. Padesky and Aaron T. Beck, "Science and philosophy: Comparison of cognitive therapy and rational emotive behavior therapy." *Journal of Cognitive Psychotherapy: An International Quarterly, 19,* 181–185.

Ellis, A, (2005b). Why I (really) became a therapist. *Journal of Clinical Psychology, 61,* 945–948.

Ellis, A., & Dryden, W. (1997). *The practice of rational emotive behavior therapy.* New York, NY: Springer.

Ellis, A., & Harper, R. (1961). *A new guide to rational living.* Englewood Cliffs, NJ: Prentice-Hall.

Epictetus. (1996). *The Enchiridion.* Raleigh, NC: Alex Catalogue [also available as an e-book: Boulder, CO: NetLibrary]. (Original work dated 90 BC)

Evans, M. D., Hollon, S. D., DeRubeis, R. J., Piasecki, J. M., Grove, W. M., Garvey, M. J., & Tuason, V. B. (1992). Differential relapse following cognitive therapy and pharmacotherapy for depression. *Archives of General Psychiatry, 49,* 802–808.

Eysenck, H. J. (1952). The effects of psychotherapy: An evaluation. *Journal of Consulting Psychology, 16,* 319–324. doi:10.1037/h0063633

Fairburn, C. G., Cooper, Z., & Shafran, R. (2003). Cognitive behaviour therapy for eating disorders: A "transdiagnostic" theory and treatment. *Behaviour Research and Therapy, 41,* 509–528. doi:10.1016/S0005-7967(02)00088-8

Fairburn, C. G., Norman, P. A., Welch, S. L., O'Connor, M. E., Doll, H. A., & Peveler, R. C. (1995). A prospective study of outcome in bulimia nervosa and the long-term effects of three psychological treatments. *Archives of General Psychiatry, 52,* 304–312.

Foa, E. B., Liebowitz, M. R., Kozak, M. J., Davies, S., Campeas, R., Franklin, M. E., et al. (2005). Treatment of obsessive compulsive disorder by exposure and ritual prevention, clomipramine, and their combination: A randomized, placebo-controlled trial. *American Journal of Psychiatry, 162,* 151–161. doi:10.1176/appi.ajp.162.1.151

Försterling, F. (1985). Attributional retraining: A review. *Psychological Bulletin, 98,* 495–512. doi:10.1037/0033-2909.98.3.495

Forsyth, J. (1997). In the name of the "advancement" of behavior therapy: Is it all in a name? *Behavior Therapy, 28,* 615–627. doi:10.1016/S0005-7894(97)80021-4

Forsyth, J., & Hawkins, R. (Eds.). (1997). Thirty years of behavior therapy: Promises kept, promises unfulfilled [Special issue]. *Behavior Therapy, 28(3–4).*

Garber, J., Clarke, G. N., Weersing, V. R., Beardslee, W. R., Brent, D. A., Gladstone, T. R. G., . . . Iyengar, S. (2009). Prevention of depression in at-risk adolescents: A randomized controlled trial. *JAMA, 301*, 2215–2224. doi:10.1001/jama.2009.788

Giesen-Bloo, J., van Dyck, R., Spinhoven, P., van Tilburg, W., Dirksen, C., van Asselt, T., . . . Arntz, A. (2006). Outpatient psychotherapy for borderline personality disorder: Randomized trial of schema-focused therapy vs transference-focused psychotherapy. *Archives of General Psychiatry, 63*, 649–658. doi:10.1001/archpsyc.63.6.649

Grilo, C. M., Masheb, R. M., & Wilson, G. T. (2005). Efficacy of cognitive behavioral therapy and fluoxetine for the treatment of binge eating disorder: A randomized double-blind placebo-controlled comparison. *Biological Psychiatry, 57*, 301–309. doi:10.1016/j.biopsych.2004.11.002

Harvey, J. H., & Galvin, K. S. (1984). Clinical implications of attribution theory and research. *Clinical Psychology Review, 4*, 15–33. doi:10.1016/0272-7358(84)90035-7

Hayes, S. C. (2004). Acceptance and commitment therapy, relational frame theory, and the third wave of behavioral and cognitive therapies. *Behavior Therapy, 35*, 639–665. doi:10.1016/S0005-7894(04)80013-3

Heimberg, R. G., Liebowitz, M. R., Hope, D. A., Schneier, F. R., Holt, C. S., Welkowitz, L. A., . . . Klein, D. F. (1998). Cognitive behavioral group therapy vs phenelzine for social phobia: 12-week outcome. *Archives of General Psychiatry, 55*, 1133–1141. doi:10.1001/archpsyc.55.12.1133

Henkel, V., Bussfeld, P., Möller, H. J., & Hegerl, U. (2002). Cognitive-behavioural theories of helplessness/hopelessness: Valid models of depression? *European Archives of Psychiatry and Clinical Neuroscience, 252*, 240–249. doi:10.1007/s00406-002-0389-y

Hollon, S. D., DeRubeis, R. J., Evans, M. D., Wiemer, M. J., Garvey, M. J., Grove, W. M., & Tuason, V. B. (1992). Cognitive therapy and pharmacotherapy for depression: Singly and in combination. *Archives of General Psychiatry, 49*, 774–781.

Hollon, S. D., DeRubeis, R. J., Shelton, R. C., Amsterdam, J. D., Salomon, R. M., O'Reardon, J. P., . . . Gallop, R. (2005). Prevention of relapse following cognitive therapy versus medications in moderate to severe depression. *Archives of General Psychiatry, 62*, 417–422. doi:10.1001/archpsyc.62.4.417

Hollon, S. D., Garber, J., & Shelton, R. C. (2005). Treatment of depression in adolescents with cognitive behavior therapy and medications: A commentary on the TADS project. *Cognitive and Behavioral Practice, 12*, 149–155. doi:10.1016/S1077-7229(05)80019-7

Hollon, S. D., Stewart, M. O., & Strunk, D. (2006). Cognitive behavior therapy has enduring effects in the treatment of depression and anxiety. *Annual Review of Psychology, 57*, 285–315. doi:10.1146/annurev.psych.57.102904.190044

Huppert, J. D., Schultz, L. T., Foa, E. B., Barlow, D. H., Davidson, J. R., Gorman, J. M., . . . Woods, S. W. (2004). Differential response to placebo among patients with social phobia, panic disorder, and obsessive-compulsive disorder. *American Journal of Psychiatry, 161*, 1485–1487. doi:10.1176/appi.ajp.161.8.1485

Jacobson, N. S., & Hollon, S. D. (1996). Cognitive behavior therapy vs. pharmacotherapy: Now that the jury's returned its verdict, it's time to present the rest of the evidence. *Journal of Consulting and Clinical Psychology, 64*, 74–80. doi:10.1037/0022-006X.64.1.74

Johnson, B. W., DeVries, R., Ridley, C. R., Pettorini, D., & Peterson, D. R. (1994). The comparative efficacy of Christian and secular rational-emotive therapy with Christian clients. *Journal of Psychology and Theology, 22*, 130–140.

Johnson, W. B., DiGiuseppe, R., & Ulven, J. (1999). Albert Ellis as mentor: National survey results. *Psychotherapy: Theory, Research, Practice, Training, 36*, 305–312.

Kanfer, F. H., & Goldstein, A. P. (1975). *Helping people change: A textbook of methods.* Oxford, England: Pergamon Press.

Kaufman, M. T. (2007, July 25). Albert Ellis, influential psychotherapist, dies at 93. *The New York Times*. Retrieved from http://www.nytimes.com

Kelly, G. (1955). *The psychology of personal constructs* (Vol. 1). New York, NY: Norton.

Kendall, P. C., Hudson, J. L., Gosch, E., Flannery-Schroeder, E., & Suveg, C. (2008). Cognitive-behavioral therapy for anxiety disordered youth: A randomized clinical trial evaluating child and family modalities. *Journal of Consulting and Clinical Psychology, 76*, 282–297. doi:10.1037/0022-006X.76.2.282

Kingdon, D. G., & Turkington, D. (1994). *Cognitive-behavioral therapy of schizophrenia*. New York, NY: Guilford Press.

Kovacs, M., Rush, A. J., Beck, A. T., & Hollon, S. D. (1981). Depressed outpatients treated with cognitive therapy or pharmacotherapy: A one-year follow-up. *Archives of General Psychiatry, 38*, 33–39.

Kuhn, T. S. (1996). *The structure of scientific revolutions*. Chicago, IL: University of Chicago Press.

Kuyken, W., Byford, S., Taylor, R. S., Watkins, E., Holden, E., White, K., et al. (2008). Mindfulness-based cognitive therapy to prevent relapse in recurrent depression. *Journal of Consulting and Clinical Psychology, 76*, 966–978. doi:10.1037/a0013786

Ladouceur, R., Dugas, M. J., Freeston, M. H., Léger, E., Gagnon, F., & Thibodeau, N. (2000). Efficacy of a cognitive–behavioral treatment for generalized anxiety disorder: Evaluation in a controlled clinical trial. *Journal of Consulting and Clinical Psychology, 68*, 957–964.

Lam, D. H., Hayward, P., Watkins, E. R., Wright, K., & Sham, P. (2005). Relapse prevention in patients with bipolar disorder: Cognitive therapy outcome after 2 years. *American Journal of Psychiatry, 162*, 324–329. doi:10.1176/appi.ajp.162.2.324

Ledwidge, B. (1978). Cognitive behavior modification: A step in the wrong direction? *Psychological Bulletin, 85*, 353–375. doi:10.1037/0033-2909.85.2.353

Liebowitz, M. R., Heimberg, R. G., Schneier, F. R., Hope, D. A., Davies, R., Holt, C. S., . . . Klein, D. F. (1999). Cognitive-behavioral group therapy versus phenelzine in social phobia: Long-term outcome. *Depression and Anxiety, 10*, 89–98.

Linehan, M. M., Comtois, K. A., Murray, A. M., Brown, M. Z., Gallop, R. J., Heard, H. L., . . . Lindemboim, N. (2006). Two-year randomized controlled trial and follow-up of dialectical behavior therapy vs therapy by experts for suicidal behaviors and borderline personality disorder. *Archives of General Psychiatry, 63*, 757–766. doi:10.1001/archpsyc.63.7.757

Ma, S. H., & Teasdale, J. D. (2004). Mindfulness-based cognitive therapy for depression: Replication and exploration of differential relapse prevention effects. *Journal of Consulting and Clinical Psychology, 72*, 31–40. doi:10.1037/0022-006X.72.1.31

Mahoney, M. (1991). *Human change processes: The scientific foundations of psychotherapy*. New York, NY: Basic Books.

Mahoney, M. J. (1974). *Cognition and behavior modification*. Cambridge, MA: Ballinger.

Mahoney, M. J. (1977a). On the continuing resistance to thoughtful therapy. *Behavior Therapy, 8*, 673–677. doi:10.1016/S0005-7894(77)80198-6

Mahoney, M. J. (1977b). Reflections on the cognitive-learning trend in psychotherapy. *American Psychologist, 32*, 5–13. doi:10.1037/0003-066X.32.1.5

Mahoney, M. J. (1979). *Self-change: Strategies for solving personal problems*. Oxford, England: Norton.

Mahoney, M. J., & Kazdin, A. E. (1979). Cognitive behavior modification: Misconceptions and premature evacuation. *Psychological Bulletin, 86*, 1044–1049. doi:10.1037/0033-2909.86.5.1044

Mahoney, M. J., & Lyddon, W. J. (1988). Recent developments in cognitive approaches to counseling and psychotherapy. *Counseling Psychologist, 16,* 190–234. doi:10.1177/0011 000088162001

March, J., Silva, S., Petrycki, S., Curry, J., Wells, K., Fairbank, J., et al. (2004). Fluoxetine, cognitive-behavioral therapy, and their combination for adolescents with depression: Treatment for Adolescents with Depression Study (TADS) randomized controlled trial. *JAMA, 292,* 807–820. doi:10.1001/jama.292.7.807

Meichenbaum, D. (1977). *Cognitive behavior modification: An integrative approach.* New York, NY: Plenum.

Meichenbaum, D. (1993). Changing conceptions of cognitive behavior modification: Retrospect and prospect. *Journal of Consulting and Clinical Psychology, 61,* 202–204. doi:10. 1037/0022-006X.61.2.202

Meichenbaum, D., & Cameron, R. (1973). Training schizophrenics to talk to themselves: A means of developing attentional controls. *Behavior Therapy, 4,* 515–534. doi:10.1016/ S0005-7894(73)80003-6

Meichenbaum, D., & Cameron, R. (1974). The clinical potential of modifying what clients say to themselves. *Psychotherapy: Theory, Research and Practice, 11,* 103–117.

Metcalfe, C., Winter, D., & Viney, L. (2007). The effectiveness of personal construct psychotherapy in clinical practice: A systematic review and meta-analysis. *Psychotherapy Research, 17,* 431–442. doi:10.1080/10503300600755115

Miklowitz, D. J. (2008). Adjunctive psychotherapy for bipolar disorders: State of the evidence. *American Journal of Psychiatry, 165,* 1408–1419. doi:10.1176/appi.ajp.2008.08040488

Murphy, G. E., Simons, A. D., Wetzel, R. D., & Lustman, P. J. (1984). Cognitive therapy and pharmacotherapy, singly and together, in the treatment of depression. *Archives of General Psychiatry, 41,* 33–41.

Neimeyer, R. A. (1993). Constructivist psychotherapy. In K. T. Kuehlwein & H. Rosen (Eds.), *Cognitive therapies in action: Evolving innovative practice* (pp. 268–300). San Francisco, CA: Jossey-Bass.

Nielsen, S. L., Johnson, W. B., & Ellis, A. (2001). *Counseling and psychotherapy with religious persons: A rational emotive behavior therapy approach.* Mahwah, NJ: Erlbaum.

O'Leary, K. D., & Drabman, R. (1971). Token reinforcement programs in the classroom: A review. *Psychological Bulletin, 75,* 379–398. doi:10.1037/h0031311

Öst, L. G., Alm, T., Brandberg, M., & Breitholtz, E. (2001). One vs five sessions of exposure and five sessions of cognitive therapy in the treatment of claustrophobia. *Behaviour Research and Therapy, 39,* 167–183. doi:10.1016/S0005-7967(99)00176-X

Öst, L. G., Svensson, L., Hellström, K., & Lindwall, R. (2001). One-session treatment of specific phobias in youths: A randomized clinical trial. *Journal of Consulting and Clinical Psychology, 69,* 814–824. doi:10.1037/0022-006X.69.5.814

Paykel, E. S., Scott, J., Teasdale, J. D., Johnson, A. L., Garland, A., Moore, R., . . . Pope, M. (1999). Prevention of relapse in residual depression by cognitive therapy: A controlled trial. *Archives of General Psychiatry, 56,* 829–835. doi:10.1001/archpsyc.56.9.829

Persons, J. B. (2006). Case formulation-driven psychotherapy. *Clinical Psychology: Science and Practice, 13,* 167–170. doi:10.1111/j.1468-2850.2006.00019.x

Pike, K. M., Walsh, B. T., Vitousek, K., Wilson, G. T., & Bauer, J. (2003). Cognitive behavior therapy in the posthospitalization treatment of anorexia nervosa. *American Journal of Psychiatry, 160,* 2046–2049. doi:10.1176/appi.ajp.160.11.2046

Popper, K. (1962). *Conjecture and refutation.* New York, NY: Harper.

Power, M. J., & Dalgleish, T. (2008). *Cognition and emotion: From order to disorder* (2nd ed.). New York, NY: Psychology Press.

Raimy, V. (1975). *Misunderstandings of the self: cognitive psychotherapy and the misconception hypothesis.* San Francisco, CA: Jossey-Bass.

Rush, A. J., Beck, A. T., Kovacs, M., & Hollon, S. (1977). Comparative efficacy of cognitive therapy and pharmacotherapy in the treatment of depressed outpatients. *Cognitive Therapy and Research, 1,* 17–37. doi:10.1007/BF01173502

Salkovskis, P. M. (1999). Understanding and treating obsessive-compulsive disorder. *Behaviour Research and Therapy, 37*(Suppl. 1), S29–S52.

Seligman, M. E. P. (1975). *Helplessness: On depression, development, and death.* San Francisco, CA: W.H. Freeman.

Seligman, M. E. P., & Maier, S. F. (1967). Failure to escape traumatic shock. *Journal of Experimental Psychology, 74,* 1–9. doi:10.1037/h0024514

Shea, M. T., Elkin, I., Imber, S. D., Sotsky, S. M., Watkins, J. T., Collins, J. F., et al. (1992). Course of depressive symptoms over follow-up: Findings from the National Institute of Mental Health Treatment of Depression Collaborative Research Program. *Archives of General Psychiatry, 49,* 782–787.

Siev, J., & Chambless, D. L. (2007). Specificity of treatment effects: Cognitive therapy and relaxation for generalized anxiety and panic disorders. *Journal of Consulting and Clinical Psychology, 75,* 513–522. doi:10.1037/0022-006X.75.4.513

Simons, A. D., Murphy, G. E., Levine, J. E., & Wetzel, R. D. (1986). Cognitive therapy and pharmacotherapy for depression: Sustained improvement over one year. *Archives of General Psychiatry, 43,* 43–48.

Simpson, H. B., Liebowitz, M. R., Foa, E. B., Kozak, M. J., Schmidt, A. B., Rowan, V., . . . Campeas, R. (2004). Post-treatment effects of exposure therapy and clomipramine in obsessive-compulsive disorder. *Depression and Anxiety, 19,* 225–233. doi:10.1002/da.20003

Smith, D. (1982). Trends in counseling and psychotherapy. *American Psychologist, 37,* 802–809. doi:10.1037/0003-066X.37.7.802

Spivack, G., Platt, J., & Shure, M. (1974). *The social adjustment of young children: A cognitive approach to solving real life problems.* San Francisco, CA: Jossey-Bass.

Spivack, G., Platt, J., & Shure, M. (1976). *The social problem solving approach to adjustment.* San Francisco, CA: Jossey-Bass.

Szentagotai, A., David, D., Lupu, V., & Cosman, D. (2008). Rational emotive behavior therapy versus cognitive therapy versus pharmacotherapy in the treatment of major depressive disorder: Mechanisms of change analysis. *Psychotherapy: Theory, Research, Practice, Training, 45,* 523–538.

Teasdale, J. D., Fennell, M. J., Hibbert, G. A., & Amies, P. L. (1984). Cognitive therapy for major depressive disorder in primary care. *British Journal of Psychiatry, 144,* 400–406. doi:10.1192/bjp.144.4.400

Teasdale, J. D., Segal, Z. V., Williams, J. M., Ridgeway, V. A., Soulsby, J. M., & Lau, M. A. (2000). Prevention of relapse/recurrence in major depression by mindfulness-based cognitive therapy. *Journal of Consulting and Clinical Psychology, 68,* 615–623. doi:10.1037/0022-006X.68.4.615

Ullmann, L. P. (1970). On cognitions and behavior therapy. *Behavior Therapy, 1,* 201–204. doi:10.1016/S0005-7894(70)80031-4

Velten, E. (Ed.). (2007). *Under the influence: Reflections of Albert Ellis in the work of others.* Tucson, AZ: See Sharp Press.

Vygotsky, L. S. (1962). *Thought and language.* Oxford, England: Wiley.

Walen, S., DiGiuseppe, R., & Dryden, W. (1992). *A practitioner's guide to rational emotive therapy* (2nd ed.). New York, NY: Oxford University Press.

Walen, S., DiGiuseppe, R., & Wessler, R. (1980). *A practitioner's guide to rational emotive therapy.* New York, NY: Oxford University Press.

Walkup, J. T., Albano, A. M., Piacentini, J., Birmaher, B., Compton, S. N., Sherrill, J. T., . . . Kendall, P. C. (2008). Cognitive behavioral therapy, sertraline, or a combination in childhood anxiety. *New England Journal of Medicine, 359,* 2753–2766.

Warren, R. (2007). Modern cognitive-behavior treatments of anxiety disorders began in 1933. In E. Velten (Ed.), *Under the influence: Reflections of Albert Ellis in the work of others* (pp. 47–62). Tucson, AZ: See Sharp Press.

Warwick, H. M. C., Clark, D. M., Cobb, A. M., & Salkovskis, P. M. (1996). A controlled trial of cognitive-behavioural treatment of hypochondriasis. *British Journal of Psychiatry, 169,* 189–195. doi:10.1192/bjp.169.2.189

Warwick, H. M. C., & Salkovskis, P. M. (1990). Hypochondriasis. *Behaviour Research and Therapy, 28,* 105–117. doi:10.1016/0005-7967(90)90023-C

Weiner, B. (1979). A theory of motivation for some classroom experiences. *Journal of Educational Psychology, 71,* 3–25. doi:10.1037/0022-0663.71.1.3

Weiner, B. (1985). "Spontaneous" causal thinking. *Psychological Bulletin, 97,* 74–84. doi:10.1037/0033-2909.97.1.74

Weishaar, M. E. (1993). *Aaron T. Beck.* Thousand Oaks, CA: Sage.

Weisz, J. R., Jensen-Doss, A., & Hawley, K. M. (2006). Evidence-based youth psychotherapies versus usual clinical care: A meta-analysis of direct comparisons. *American Psychologist, 61,* 671–689. doi:10.1037/0003-066X.61.7.671

Wilson, G. T. (1997). Behavior therapy at century close. *Behavior Therapy, 28,* 449–457.

Wilson, G. T., Grilo, C. M., & Vitousek, K. M. (2007). Psychological treatment of eating disorders. *American Psychologist, 62,* 199–216. doi:10.1037/0003-066X.62.3.199

Wolpe, J. (1961). The prognosis in unpsychoanalysed recovery from neurosis. *American Journal of Psychiatry, 118,* 35–39.

Wolpe, J. (1978). Cognition and causation in human behavior and its therapy. *American Psychologist, 33,* 437–446. doi:10.1037/0003-066X.33.5.437

Young, J. E., Klosko, J. S., & Weishaar, M. E. (2004). *Schema therapy: A practitioner's guide.* New York, NY: Guilford Press.

8
MULTICULTURAL APPROACHES TO PSYCHOTHERAPY

LILLIAN COMAS-DÍAZ

"From many, one." This principle infuses the United States with a diversity of cultures, races, ethnicities, classes, and religions. Like Pandora's box, our diversity releases doubts, fears, and a hopeful sense of unity. A contemporary expression of diversity, multiculturalism promotes unity through diversity. Critics may argue that multiculturalism threatens the preservation of a uniform national identity (Clausen, 2000), but multiculturalism is a dynamic process that encourages inclusion and enhances our ability to recognize ourselves in others. In fact, multiculturalism has been identified as the "fourth force" in psychology (Pedersen, 1991).

Cultural influences permeate our concepts of health, illness, and healing. However, culture remains the proverbial elephant in the middle of the therapeutic room. As a product of Western civilization, psychotherapy frequently reflects the values of its cultural context. Practitioners listening with a Western therapeutic ear frequently hear their clients' narratives without listening to them. The increasing number of culturally diverse individuals, such as people of color, immigrants, internationals, and others, benefit from multicultural treatments. These types of clients are growing. For instance, I see a number of White European American clients who experience changes in their cultural identity after a sojourn abroad and, consequently, seek multicultural psychotherapy.

Regrettably, dominant psychotherapy lacks diverse cultural and ecological validity (Bernal & Scharrón-del-Río, 2001) and therefore does not fully address the needs of diverse populations. Although multiculturalism has reached mainstream institutions, psychotherapy has been slow to respond to this cultural phenomenon. For example, therapeutic themes such as family relations, interpersonal boundaries, emotional space, intimacy, relationships, and identity are culturally embedded. Lamentably, mainstream psychotherapy seldom reflects cultural variability or analyzes power and privilege. Moreover, psychotherapy can be ethnocentric, decontextualized, ahistorical, and apolitical (Brown, 1997). Indeed, when practitioners pathologize multicultural worldviews, dismiss ethnic values, neglect indigenous spirituality, and ignore cultural strengths, they engage in cultural imperialism. As a result, multiculturalists question the applicability of dominant psychotherapy to diverse populations.

In this chapter, I discuss the early emergence and historical development of multicultural approaches to psychotherapy. To achieve these goals, I review both historical and contemporary influences on multicultural psychotherapies. Then, I discuss cultural competence as an impetus for the establishment of multicultural psychotherapies. Afterward, I examine the cultural adaptation of dominant psychotherapy. Finally, I present examples of ethnic psychotherapies, followed by a discussion of the current status of multicultural psychotherapies.

EARLY THEORETICAL CONTRIBUTIONS

The relationship between self and others has been a source of inquiry among philosophers, historians, politicians, theologians, and other scholars. The fascination with the stranger reached the mental health fields during the 1950s and 1960s. The relationship between culture and psyche resulted in the collaboration of anthropology and psychoanalysis. Consequently, the interdisciplinary origins of multicultural psychotherapies included psychological anthropology, ethnopsychology, cultural anthropology, psychoanalytic anthropology, and folk healing.

Psychoanalytic Anthropology

Proponents of the anthropology–psychoanalysis movements applied psychoanalytic understandings to social and cultural phenomena. Moreover, they interpreted cultural symbols, such as dreams, rituals, and myths, through a psychoanalytic lens. Practitioners adhering to a psychoanalytic anthropological framework used qualitative analyses, such as clinical studies and ethnographic methods. Some of the notable names associated with this movement include

Georges Devereux (1979), who studied cross-cultural mental health–illness, and Abram Kardiner (Kardiner, Linton, Du Bois, & West, 1945), who examined the effects of oppression on ethnic minorities' mental health. Additionally, proponents of this movement questioned the universal application of psychoanalytic concepts. For example, cultural anthropologists (e.g., Spiro, 1984) challenged the cross-cultural application of the Oedipus complex and called attention to the adaptive mechanisms of culture.

Several psychoanalysts departed from Freudian precepts during the middle of the 20th century to form the cultural school of psychoanalysis. Proponents of this school believed that human development is rooted in environmental factors that vary across cultural contexts and historical periods (Seeley, 2000). Exponents of this approach, such as Eric Fromm, Karen Horney, and Harry Stack Sullivan, argued that culture shapes behavior because individuals are contextualized and embedded in social interactions.

Psychiatric and psychological anthropologists studied the interaction between culture and mental health. For instance, the study of culturalism, or the emphasis on culture-specific themes and techniques to treat culture-bound syndromes, gave birth to transcultural mental health (Kiev, 1972). Transcultural psychiatry and psychology proposed mental health practitioners' collaboration with community resources, such as paraprofessionals, clergy, teachers, folk healers, and the network of individuals residing in and/or delivering services to ethnic minority communities. Decades later, the American Psychiatric Association (1994, 2000) provided a glossary of culture-bound syndromes, such as *susto* (i.e., fright causing the soul to leave the body), as part of its cultural formulation. Indeed, anthropology offered psychiatry a cultural lens to understand mental health issues. As an illustration, Arthur Kleinman (1980), both a psychiatrist and an anthropologist, developed the explanatory model of distress based on ethnographic research. An ethnographic tool, the explanatory model of distress yields clients' perspectives on their problem, treatment, expectations of the therapist, and perceptions regarding the course of treatment.

Psychoanalytic anthropology, psychiatric anthropology, and the cultural school of psychoanalysis developed theories and methods for the study of culture and mental health. Although these orientations enriched the culture and behavior discourse, they largely failed to develop specific methods that could be applied to clinical practice (Seeley, 2000). Cultural psychology, a contemporary brainchild of the cultural mental health movements, continues the legacy of promoting pluralism in psychological theory and research (Shweder, 1993). Like its predecessors, however, cultural psychology's impact on psychotherapy is limited because of its current lack of clinical applications.

Into this collection of early theoretical influences came the 1960s and several movements that informed multicultural psychotherapies. Two discrete sociopolitical influences can be identified: minority empowerment movements and the psychology of colonization.

Minority Empowerment Movements

The minority empowerment movements, starting in the 1960s, nurtured the development of multicultural psychotherapies. These movements examined the power–powerlessness and oppression–privilege dynamics between dominant group members and minorities. Also known as *identity politics,* the minority empowerment movements, such as women's rights, Black power, Chicano–Brown power, and the gay, lesbian, and bisexual movement, highlighted the civil rights and needs of marginalized groups. These groups raised their consciousness and attempted to redress the social and political inequities afflicting marginalized minority groups.

The empowerment identity movements transcended politics. These perspectives provided alternative models for understanding oppression, resistance, and liberation. Adherents of these movements examined minorities' collective self-esteem, individual development, and relationships between dominant and nondominant groups, as well as definitions of normality and pathology. For instance, the minority identity developmental models describe the minority group members' relationship with the majority group members. In brief, racial and cultural identity theories propose that members of minority groups initially value the dominant group and devalue their own group, then proceed to value their own group while devaluing the dominant group, and, in a final stage, evolve to integrate and value both groups (Atkinson, Morten, & Sue, 1998; W. E. Cross, 1991). The cultural identity development of mixed-race individuals focuses on the individual's journey into an integration of his or her diverse ethnocultures, ranging from (a) personal identity, (b) choice of group categorization, (c) enmeshment–denial, (d) appreciation, and (e) integration (Poston, 1990).

Cultural identity development theories abound for diverse cultural groups. For example, women's identity development theory articulates that females continuously struggle and work through their reactions to their experiences with sexism, prejudice, and discrimination. Such processes culminate in the development of a positive feminist identity. Therefore, feminist identity develops through the following stages: (a) passive acceptance, (b) revelation, (c) embeddedness–emanation, (d) synthesis, and (e) active commitment (Downing & Roush, 1985). Likewise, gay and lesbian identity developmental stages frequently entail (a) confusion, where questions around sexual orientation arise; (b) comparison, where individuals accept the possibility that they may be members of a sexual minority; (c) tolerance, characterized by the person's acceptance that he or she is gay or lesbian; (d) acceptance, where there are increased contacts with other gays and lesbians; (e) pride, where the person prefers to be gay or lesbian; and (f) synthesis, where the person contacts allies and supportive heterosexuals and is reconciled with his or her own sexual orientation (Cass, 2002).

Janet Helms (1990) proposed an influential European American identity developmental theory in which members are familiar with their whiteness and journey through stages. The developmental trajectory includes (a) contact, in which they are aware of minorities but do not perceive themselves as racial beings; (b) disintegration, in which they acknowledge that prejudice and discrimination exist; (c) reintegration, in which they blame the victim and believe in reverse discrimination; (d) pseudoindependence, in which they accept minority group members at a conceptual level and become interested in understanding differences; and (e) autonomy, in which they become knowledgeable about cultural similarities and differences and accept, respect, and appreciate both minority and majority group members. This journey culminates with individuals' understanding the role of White privilege in a European American–dominated society.

A decontextualized, apolitical, and ahistorical psychotherapy may lead members of minority groups to internalize oppression and compromise their agency (Freire, 1973). Clinicians embracing empowerment examine the relationship between sociopolitical factors and mental health to address racism, sexism, classism, homophobia, heterosexism, ethnocentrism, ableism, ageism, and other forms of oppression. Feminist therapists, for instance, promote transformation and social change through the dictum, "the personal is the political." Similarly, clinicians endorsing a gay and lesbian affirmative therapy address heterosexism and homophobia, foster empowerment, and help clients to differentiate between functional and dysfunctional coping styles. As a result, psychotherapists working within a multicultural perspective address the sociopolitical context and oppression. They examine clients' internalized oppression and racially generated horizontal hostility (toward minority group members) to promote awareness and empowerment.

Psychology of Colonization

In the search for understanding the effect of oppression on mental health, some scholars examined the psychology of colonization. Articulated by the Caribbean Frantz Fanon (1967), the psychology of colonization uses the constructs of imperialism, dominance, and exploitation to examine the relationship between the colonizer and the colonized. Whereas Fanon argued that the colonial relationship entails the psychological nonrecognition of the subjectivity of the colonized, Albert Memmi identified the colonial relationship as the chaining of the colonized to the colonizer through an economic and emotional dependence (Comas-Díaz, 2007).

The psychology of colonization is intimately related to multiculturalism because a significant number of culturally diverse individuals have been exposed to historical colonization, political oppression, and neocolonialism. Moreover, many people of color in the United States are exposed to colonization through cultural imperialism. Kenneth B. Clark, the first president of color of the American Psychological Association (APA), called attention to the similarity of colonization and the condition of people of color in the United States (Comas-Díaz, 2007). The United States' history of medical mistreatment toward people of color, also known as a "medical apartheid" (Washington, 2007), adds to Clark's assertion. The Tuskegee project chronicled how African American men suffering from syphilis were treated with a placebo, whereas European American men received the curative medication (penicillin), despite the fact that a cure for syphilis was found during the course of the research (Washington, 2007). Medical apartheid extended to other Americans of color. Because of their historical trauma, ungrieved losses, internalized oppression, suffering, and learned helplessness, many Native Americans suffer from a "soul wound" (Duran & Ivey, 2006). African Americans' soul wound is related to their history of slavery, which has created a rupture of continuity and an annihilation of their past (Grier & Cobbs, 1969).

Current mental health practices often reinforce people of color's distrust of dominant healing institutions. For instance, clinicians' ignorance of ethnoracial differences in metabolizing drugs may lead to psychopharmacological mistreatment (Melfi, Croghan, Hanna, & Robinson, 2000; Rey, 2006). Furthermore, many people of color suspect that dominant psychotherapy is an instrument of acculturation and cultural imperialism.

The psychology of colonization dovetailed with the Latin American movement of education for the oppressed. Paulo Freire, a Brazilian scholar, coined the term *conscientization,* or critical consciousness, as part of his paradigm for educating the oppressed. According to Freire (1973), traditional models of education are instruments of oppression that reinforce and maintain the status quo and social inequities. As a process of personal and social transformation, conscientization teaches oppressed individuals to become aware of their circumstances and change them through a dialectical conversation with their world. Within this process, people learn to assume control of their lives, overcome their negative internalized conscience, and achieve a critical knowledge of themselves.

EARLY CLINICAL CONTRIBUTIONS

In the same time period that the psychology of colonization and minority empowerment movements were emerging as vital theoretical influences, three healing perspectives were also setting the stage for a practical system of multicultural psychotherapy. They were reevaluation counseling, feminist therapy, and ethnic family therapy, all coming into their own during the 1960s and 1970s.

Reevaluation Counseling

Originally a labor organizer, Harvey Jackins founded reevaluation counseling to empower people within a social justice context. This therapy involves co-counseling, when two or more individuals take turns listening to each other without interruption to recover from the effects of racism, classism, sexism, and other types of oppressions (Roby, 1998). Reevaluation counseling theory assumes that everyone is born with tremendous intellectual and loving potential but that these qualities have become blocked as a result of accumulated distress. The recovery entails a catharsis—a natural discharge process where the "counselor" encourages the "client" to discharge his or her emotions. The counselor's position is one of appreciative attention with nonjudgmental active listening. The client talks, discharges, and reevaluates. Afterward, the process is reversed, and the client becomes the counselor, whereby he or she listens to the client. When the person emotionally discharges, he or she is liberated from the rigid pattern of dysfunctional behavior. A major component of reevaluation counseling is examining the role of racism at the individual, collective, and societal levels (see http://www.rc.org).

Feminist Therapy

Feminist therapy and multicultural theories influence each other because they both embrace diversity as a foundation for practice. Feminist consciousness attempts to empower all people, women as well as men, and promotes equality at individual, interpersonal, institutional, national, and international levels. Feminists asserted that dominant psychotherapists act as agents of the status quo, encourage women to adapt to traditional gender roles, pathologize women's ways of being, and neglect female mental health needs. As a reaction to these concerns, feminist therapy emerged to promote women's empowerment, collaboration, self-reflection, transformation, and social change (Worrell & Johnson, 1997). In addition to dominant psychotherapy's tools, feminist therapists use consciousness raising, self-help groups, self-analysis, and power analyses (Worrell & Remer, 2003).

The development of a multicultural feminist therapy was a challenge because feminism tended to reflect middle class, European American women's experiences. Many culturally diverse women—particularly, women of color—did not see their experiences addressed by feminism (Silverstein, 2006). Indeed, many women of color feared that feminists asked them to choose which identity (i.e., gender or race–ethnicity) needed liberation at the expense of the other. Accordingly, different branches of feminist therapy developed. Two of these branches, cultural feminist therapy and women of color feminist therapy, relate to multicultural feminist therapy. Cultural feminist therapists use the empathic relationship to increase women's ability to be self-empathic and to connect to others in a mutually empathic manner. They reaffirm women's orientations, such as connection, subjectivity, interdependence, generativity, and other feminine values. Women of color's feminist therapists focus on the interactions among racism, sexism, classism, heterosexism, ethnocentrism, ableism, and other forms of oppressions. They address values endorsed by many women of color, such as collectivism, holism, and spirituality. Women of color's feminist therapy incorporates the womanism–African American women feminism and *mujerismo*–Latina feminism (Comas-Díaz, 2008) movements. Womanism and *mujerismo* are dynamic paradigms that view the interaction of race, ethnicity, gender class, sexual orientation, nationality, and other diversity variables at the center of healing and liberation.

Ethnic Family Therapy

Family therapy has a legacy of incorporating contextual factors, such as ethnicity and culture, into its theory and practice (McGoldrick, Giordano, & Garcia-Preto, 2005). Emerging from this tradition, ethnic family therapy addresses the cultural context of family and uses ethnic values in treatment. A classic example of this perspective is Boyd-Franklin's (2003) multisystemic approach in *Black Families in Therapy: Understanding the African American Experience*.

Family therapy places individuals in contexts through the use of genograms (McGoldrick, Gerson, & Shellenberger, 1999); ethnic family therapists use cultural genograms (Hardy & Laszloffy, 1995). In addition to family dynamics, cultural genograms examine culture-specific information, such as cultural translocation, adaptation, acculturation, ethnic–racial identity development, historical and current trauma, racial socialization, oppressive experiences, in-group–out-group member dynamics, relations with dominant society, geopolitics, ecological influences, and many other contextual factors. Likewise, the culturagram is an ethnic family therapy tool used with immigrant families to explore their reason for relocation; legal status; time in community; languages spoken at home and in the community; health beliefs, trauma, and crises; contact with cultural and religious institutions; exposure to oppression, discrimination, racism, and xenophobia; values about education and work; and values about family (Congress, 1994).

As a multicultural approach, ethnic family therapy asks therapists to develop cultural competence. Therapists can do so by knowing their own culture, avoiding ethnocentric attitudes and behaviors, achieving an insider status, using intermediaries, and having selective disclosure (Ariel, 1999).

CULTURAL COMPETENCE AND MULTICULTURAL GUIDELINES

The voices of the identity, feminist, and civil rights movements helped to create legislation to address the needs of minority group members. In 1969, the United States Congress mandated the National Institute of Mental Health to establish the Minority Fellowship Program to support the education of professionals of color in psychiatry, psychology, social work, sociology, and psychiatric nursing. The program allowed many culturally diverse individuals to enter mental health fields and provided them with financial support and mentorship.

This era witnessed a sociopolitical tipping point that promoted cultural competence in clinical practice. Cultural competence enables practitioners to work effectively in most psychotherapeutic situations. Cultural competence refers to a set of congruent behaviors, attitudes, and policies that reflect an understanding of how cultural and sociopolitical influences shape individuals' worldviews and related health behaviors and how such factors interact at multiple levels of therapeutic practice (Betancourt, Green, Carrillo, & Ananch-Firempong, 2003). Therefore, culturally competent therapists develop the capacities to value diversity and manage the dynamics of difference. They also acquire and incorporate cultural knowledge into their interventions, plus adapt to diversity and to the cultural contexts of their clients.

The American Psychiatric Association and the American Psychological Association responded to the need to increase cultural competence in psychotherapy. The American Psychiatric Association (1994, 2000) published the cultural formulation, a model for incorporating culture into diagnosis and treatment. A process-oriented tool, the cultural formulation examines (a) cultural identity, (b) cultural explanations for individual illnesses, (c) cultural factors related to the psychosocial environment and levels of functioning, (d) cultural elements of the therapist–patient relationship, and (e) overall cultural assessment for diagnosis and treatment (American Psychiatric Association, 1994). Although grounded in a medical model that emphasizes pathology, the cultural formulation fosters clinicians' cultural competence (Comas-Díaz, 2001). The cultural formulation recognizes the contextual expression of distress through a glossary of culture-bound syndromes (American Psychiatric Association, 1994).

In their discussion of the application of the cultural formulations, Lo and Fung (2003) identified the domains of self, relations, and treatment. In brief, the self domain refers to the cultural influences on the self, such as affect, cognition, behavior, body, self-concept, and individual goals and motivations.

The relations domain explores the cultural influence on clients' relationships with family, groups, others, society, possessions, environment, spirituality, and time. Finally, the treatment domain highlights therapy elements influenced by culture, such as communication (both verbal and nonverbal), problem solving, and the clinician–client relationship.

Before the 1960s, the American Psychological Association did not pay systematic attention to ethnic minority psychology and failed to address the needs of people of color both as psychologists and as consumers of psychology. However, in the 1980s, the American Psychological Association created the Ad Hoc Committee on Equality of Opportunity in Psychology, sponsored the Dulles Conference: Expanding the Roles of Culturally Diverse People in the Profession of Psychology, and established the Society for the Psychological Study of Ethnic Minority Issues (Division 45), among others (Comas-Díaz, 1990).

In 1990, the American Psychological Association formulated its *Guidelines for Providers of Psychological Services to Ethnic, Linguistic, and Culturally Diverse Clients*. These guidelines pointed out the importance of the role of culture, sociopolitical contexts, racial identity, communication, spirituality, and cultural competence in treatment models, among several other topics. More specifically, these guidelines asked practitioners to (a) recognize cultural diversity; (b) understand the central role culture, ethnicity, and race play in culturally diverse individuals; (c) appreciate the significant impact of socioeconomic and political factors on mental health; and (d) help clients understand their cultural identification (American Psychological Association, 1990; see http://www.apa.org/pi/oema/guide.html).

Over a decade later, the American Psychological Association (2003) approved its *Guidelines on Multicultural Education, Training, Research, Practice, and Organizational Change*. Multicultural Guideline 5—"Psychologists are encouraged to apply culturally appropriate skills in clinical and other applied psychological practices"—is highly relevant to the practice of multicultural psychotherapies (American Psychological Association, 2003, p. 390). This guideline highlights the importance of placing clients in a context, calls for the use of culturally appropriate assessment tools and psychological testing, encourages the inclusion of a broad range of psychological interventions, and advocates for the use of therapeutic pluralism through the incorporation of culture-specific healing interventions. Therapists who work in organizational settings need to pay special attention to Multicultural Guideline 6: "Psychologists are encouraged to use organizational change processes to support culturally informed organizational (policy) development and practices" (American Psychological Association, 2003, p. 392).

Along these lines, cultural competence in psychotherapy ranges along a continuum. At one end are cultural destructiveness—attitudes, practices, and policies destructive to cultures—and cultural incapacity—dominant group members' paternalistic mode toward culturally diverse groups. In the middle of the continuum sits cultural blindness—the belief that culture makes no difference. Approaching the other end is cultural precompetence—an awareness of cultural sensitivity but ignorance as to how to proceed—followed by cultural competence (T. Cross, Bazron, Dennis, & Issacs, 1998).

Both sets of American Psychological Association guidelines highlight psychology's commitment to cultural competence. Research has shown that clients who perceive their therapists as being culturally competent tend to adhere to and complete treatment and to be satisfied with it (Knipscheer & Kleber, 2004). Culturally competent psychotherapists obtain training on specific behaviors, attitudes, and policies that respect and value the cultural uniqueness of individuals and groups (Hansen, Pepitone-Arreola-Rockwell, & Greene, 2000). Multiculturalists urged practitioners to promote cultural competence within health and mental health organizations by asking these groups to

- evaluate the institution's mission statement and policies to determine whether they include diversity issues,
- assess policies with regard to diversity,
- evaluate how people of color may perceive specific policies,
- acknowledge within-group diversity,
- be aware that diversity requires examination from both the individual and the institutional levels, and
- recognize that multicultural sensitivity may mean advocating for culturally diverse people (Howard-Hamilton, Phelps, & Torres, 1998).

The commitment to cultural competence fostered a coalition among ethnic minority psychological associations to advocate for the delivery of effective psychological services to people of color. In 2000, the American Psychological Association's Society for the Psychological Study of Ethnic Minority Issues joined the Asian American Psychological Association, the Association of Black Psychologists, the National Hispanic Psychological Association, and the Society of Indian Psychologists to establish the Council of National Psychological Associations for the Advancement of Ethnic Minority Interests.

CULTURAL ADAPTATION IN PSYCHOTHERAPY

The history of multiculturalism in psychotherapy has alternated between adapting extant psychotherapy systems to marginalized populations (culturally adapted psychotherapy) and developing new systems of psychotherapy that specifically fit those marginalized client populations (ethnic and indigenous psychotherapies). The earliest cultural adaptations probably occurred in psychoanalysis. Some psychoanalysts incorporated sociocentric values and communal and spiritual elements into their practices. Neil Altman (1995), a pioneer in this approach, measured clients' progress by their use of relationships to grow rather than by the insights gained. Others used education, empathy, interest, and warmth in their psychoanalytic practice with East Indian clients. Some humanistic psychotherapists modified their practices to contextualize the sociohistorical experiences of culturally diverse clients. Similarly, existential psychotherapy's liberation approach seemed congruent with many African Americans' life experiences, as well as with Latinos' legacy of Latin American humanism and Native American spiritual worldviews (Schneider, 2008).

With the ascendancy of cognitive–behavioral therapy (CBT), many practitioners began adding multicultural awareness and culture-specific strategies to it (Bernal & Scharrón-del-Río, 2001). To illustrate, Ricardo Muñoz incorporated Latino values into CBT (Muñoz & Mendelson, 2005). His cultural adaptation involved culturally diverse people in the development of interventions. The ensuing treatment included collectivistic values and attended to religion–spirituality. During treatment, the therapists acknowledged the relevance of acculturation, as well as the effects of oppression on mental health (Muñoz & Mendelson, 2005). Although specific to Latinos, this cultural adaptation is applicable to other people of color. Moreover, some principles in CBT seem congruent with collectivistic worldviews. These principles include the use of education in treatment, the mind and body connection, emphasis on self-healing, and the relevance of thoughts in developing illness and maintaining health.

Research has reported therapeutic gains in the application of CBT to culturally diverse populations (Voss Horrell, 2008). A meta-analysis of 76 studies and 25,225 patients found a moderately strong benefit ($d = .45$) of culturally adapted interventions (Griner & Smith, 2006). Culturally adapted therapy resulted in significant client improvement across a variety of conditions and outcome measures.

At the same time, there is a dearth of empirical research on the cultural applicability of empirically supported treatments validated almost exclusively on European American populations (Hall, 2001; Roselló & Bernal, 1999; S. Sue et al, 2006). What research does exist suggests that many clients of color tend to drop out of CBT as compared with European American clients (Miranda et al., 2005). Even those clients of color who endorsed positive mental-health-seeking expectations found psychotherapy less positive than their European American counterparts after receiving such services (Diala et al., 2000).

How can these findings be explained? Culture may affect the psychotherapeutic process more than the therapeutic outcome (Whaley & Davis, 2007), a position that affirms the need to recognize context. Several multicultural scholars lamented mainstream psychotherapy's lack of a contextual–ecological perspective to address social and environmental problems, such as poverty, poor health, violence, and racism (Johnson, Bastien, & Hirschel, 2008; Rogers, 2004).

An American Psychological Association Presidential Task Force attempted to address some of these issues by defining evidence-based practice as the "integration of the best available research with clinical expertise in the context of patient characteristics, culture and preferences" (American Psychological Association Presidential Task Force on Evidence-Based Practice, 2006, p. 273). Nonetheless, psychotherapists still tend to ignore ethnopolitical realities (Comas-Díaz, 2007). Thus, multicultural practitioners have stressed the need to address oppression in psychotherapy, in addition to the need to reconnect with ethnic and indigenous roots. To achieve these goals, some practitioners have resorted to ethnic and indigenous psychotherapies.

ETHNIC AND INDIGENOUS PSYCHOTHERAPIES

The American Psychological Association's Multicultural Guideline 5 urges psychologists to expand the range of their interventions by acknowledging ethnic and indigenous psychologies. When appropriate, multicultural psychotherapists endorse pluralism, use holistic models of health in psychotherapy, acknowledge spirituality as a dimension in healing, and use narrative approaches that predicate on multicultural people's oral legacies. Ethnic and indigenous psychotherapies operate within a cultural context that facilitates therapist's responsiveness to clients' life experiences. Ethnic psychologies are holistic, empowering, and transformative.

Ethnic psychotherapies appeal to many culturally diverse individuals. For example, the family structure among many people of color honors ancestors by including the deceased because relationships do not necessarily end with death. Dominant psychotherapy seldom addresses the domain of relationships with the deceased in assessment and/or treatment. In contrast, ethnic psychotherapies promote ancestral and sacred affiliations in healing. Because many ethnic psychotherapists interpret distress as a result of a disconnection from cultures of origin, treatment usually involves helping clients to reconnect with their ethnicity and culture.

The following are six prominent examples of ethnic psychotherapies: folk healing, network therapy, Morita therapy, Naikan therapy, ethnic narratives, and liberation psychology–psychotherapy. Each is discussed in turn.

Folk Healing

Many ethnic individuals rely on indigenous practices during times of crisis, particularly when dominant treatment fails. Folk healers incorporate clients' cultural and personal strengths into a holistic treatment focusing on context, interpersonal relationships, cultural and spiritual health, and collective well-being. Moreover, healers supplement their contextual approaches with a shared language and worldview. The U.S. Office of the Surgeon General (2000) concluded that Western psychological interventions could benefit from incorporating aspects of indigenous healing. In fact, the American Psychological Association's (2003) multicultural guidelines recommended the use of indigenous healing when working with people of color.

Folk healing is both a historical antecedent of multicultural psychotherapies and a form of ethnic psychotherapy. Folk healing addresses discontinuity by grounding individuals to the past, present, and future. Therefore, this approach promotes sufferers' reestablishment of their sense of cultural belonging and continuity. As such, folk healing is congruent with sociocentric societies because it fosters self-healing and encourages a balance between the sufferer, family, community, and cosmos (Comas-Díaz, 2006). A meaning-making process, folk healing supports liberation and promotes spiritual development.

The main difference between psychotherapy and folk healing is the latter's philosophical–religious belief system and its commitment to spiritual evolution. For example, folk healers tend to perceive life as sacred, do not attempt to dominate nature, recognize a creative energy, believe in the circular nature of time, and accept life's mysteries (Cowan, 1996). Folk healers obtain knowledge through honoring, listening, respecting, being humble, accepting, revering, and collaborating (Comas-Díaz, in press).

Most ancient cultures have an indigenous legacy of shamanism. Tedlock (2005) identified five fundamental elements in all shamanic worldviews. First, shamans believe that all animate and nonanimate entities contain a life force, energy, soul spirit, and/or consciousness that transcends their physicality. Second, a "web of life" connects all things, making them interdependent and creating a cause and effect relationship between different dimensions and entities. Third, a central axis connects the multilayered web of life. Shamans "journey" though the central axis (sometimes symbolized by a tree or mountain) to heal, foretell, and engage in other shamanic practices. Fourth, communities recognize and designate certain individuals as shamans. Finally, shamans identify and interact with forces, whose behavior in an alternative reality affects individuals and events in our ordinary world. These indigenous beliefs permeate many of the ethnic and multicultural psychotherapies.

Network Therapy

Many Native American communities have preserved their healing approaches despite being subjected to cultural imperialism. Network therapy is one of these healing approaches. Based on Native American indigenous practices, psychologist Carolyn Attneave (Speck & Attneave, 1973) developed network therapy. Attneave designed this ethnic healing as an extended family and group psychotherapy. Infused with sociocentric values, network therapy involves the client's social context by recreating the entire network to activate and mobilize a person's family, kin, clan, and relationships in the healing process.

Morita Therapy

Another ethnic psychotherapy is Morita therapy, developed by Shoma Morita (Reynolds, 1980). A Japanese psychiatrist, Morita also called his treatment *experiential therapy* because he prescribed rest, life renormalization, rehabilitation, and related experiences to his patients. During the first treatment stage (1 to 2 weeks) of Morita therapy, patients are deprived of sensory and social activity and are confined to bed to rest. During the second stage, patients engage in housework tasks to experience appreciation of life instead of obsessing about their symptoms. During this stage, patients are encouraged to write a daily diary. Therapists comment on the journal to help patients accept reality. To change their life attitudes, patients learn to accept things as they are, become action oriented, and accept Zen teachings, such as "perceive every day as a good day" (Reynolds, 1980). Many Chinese clinicians use Morita therapy, partly because of Morita therapy's Zen philosophy.

Naikan Therapy

Ishin Yoshimoto, a Japanese Buddhist monk, developed Naikan therapy (Reynolds, 1980). Self-inspection is the central principle of this ethnic approach, in which clients examine their lives with a focus on significant relationships, particularly parental figures (Tseng, 2001). This self-evaluation helps clients to change their views of life through the development of insight, appreciation, and joy and the expression of gratitude toward others. Naikan therapists use cultural values such as parent–child relationships to restore relations through the reappraisals of primary relationships and a discouragement of narcissistic views. The root of Naikan therapy may be the Japanese spiritual Shinto concept of *sunao* or a harmonious state of mind associated with honesty, humility, and simplicity (Tseng, 2001).

Ethnic Narratives

Many ethnic psychotherapists use narrative approaches congruent with multicultural people's oral and storytelling legacies. Storytelling has been found to be effective in cross-cultural psychotherapy (Semmler & Williams, 2000). For example, many medical providers use *telenovelas* (soap operas) for health promotion and education among low-income Latinos. There are several ethnic narrative tools. However, I limit my discussion to *dichos, cuento*, and *testimonio*.

Dichos psychotherapy involves Spanish proverbs or idiomatic expressions that capture folk wisdom. Also known as *refranes, dichos* have cultural resonance, credibility, and validity. *Dichos* are a type of flash therapy that offers the therapist a window into Latinos' worldviews (Comas-Díaz, 2006). For example, the *dicho* "*No por mucho madrugar se amanance mas temprano*" (loosely translated as, "You cannot hurry dawn by getting up before sunrise"), refers to the importance of timing and the need to coordinate actions with reality. Several multicultural clinicians have used *dichos* in adapting dominant psychotherapy to foster culturally relevant cognitive restructuring and address cultural obstacles in managing interpersonal conflicts (Comas-Díaz, 2006).

Cuento therapy promotes culturally relevant models of adaptive interpersonal behavior (Costantino, Malgady, & Rogler, 1986). *Cuentos* are Latino folk tales that foment youngsters' identification with a culturally relevant hero or heroine, for instance, El Zorro. *Cuentos* also have antiheroes, such as Juan Bobo, a fool (*bobo*) who teaches valuable lessons. The goal of *cuento* therapy is to promote a bicultural adaptation and synthesis to youngsters who live in two cultures. Research has demonstrated the efficacy of *cuento* therapy with Puerto Rican children (Costantino et al., 1986). This healing narrative has evolved to include mothers and their offspring in group therapy.

Another ethnic narrative, *testimonio*, or testimony, means bearing witness to traumatic experiences. *Testimonio* emerged in Latin America, during the dictatorship of August Pinochet, to focus on how the traumatic experiences have affected the individual, family, and community (Cienfuegos & Monelli, 1983). An ethnic healing approach, *testimonio* addresses the sociopolitical context of oppression through a verbal healing journey.

Liberation Psychology–Psychotherapy

Liberation psychology emerged from Latin American liberation theology. Indeed, the architect of psychology of liberation, Ignacio Martin-Baro, was both a psychologist and a priest. Liberation psychology resonates with Black liberation theology and with Afrocentric American psychology. As an ethnic approach grounded in spiritual–social action, liberation psychology collaborates with the oppressed in developing critical analysis and engaging in a transforming practice (Comas-Díaz, Lykes, & Alarcon, 1998). Consequently, liberation psychologists work with people in context through strategies that enhance awareness of oppression and the ideologies and structural inequalities that have kept them subjugated and oppressed. Liberation practitioners focus on oppression because domination robs victims of their critical thinking. Consequently, liberation psychologists use conscientization, or critical consciousness, to help individuals recognize the relationship between intra–interpersonal dynamics and the sociopolitical context (Blanco, 1998). Conscientization involves asking critical questions, such as, What? Why? How? For whom? Against whom? By whom? In favor of whom? In favor of what? and To what end? (Freire & Macedo, 2000). As a result, liberation practitioners become change agents instead of status quo representatives. Liberation psychology combines critical dialogue and reflection with social action. To illustrate, a transforming action can culminate in an African American man's commitment to community organization, to running for an elected office, and, finally, to becoming the first president of color of the United States.

CURRENT STATUS OF MULTICULTURAL PSYCHOTHERAPIES

Multicultural psychotherapists have transcended the question of whether therapy works for culturally diverse individuals. Instead, they ask, which type of therapy for which kind of clients under which conditions (Fisher, Jome, & Atkinson, 1998)? The current status of multicultural psychotherapies involves an integration of ethnic psychotherapies, non-Western practices, cultural studies, empowerment approaches, and dominant psychotherapy. Indeed, several practitioners have recommended a multicultural integration when working with culturally diverse clients (Comas-Díaz, 2006).

Adherents to the integrative perspective recognize the impact of culture, oppression, cultural identity, history, and other contextual factors on mental health. They view treatment through multicultural lenses because these reflect the interacting influences of psychological, spiritual, and contextual factors on the psychotherapeutic process. For example, Bernal, Bonilla, and Bellido (1995) recommended the integration of a multicultural lens through eight dimensions—language, persons, metaphors, content, concepts, goals, method, and context—into psychotherapy. Therapists need to use language and relationships culturally appropriate to the client's worldview and life experiences. The metaphors dimension refers to concepts shared by members of a cultural group. The therapist's cultural knowledge (e.g., Does the client feel understood by the therapist?) entails the dimension of content. Goals examine whether therapeutic objectives are congruent with clients' adaptive cultural values. Methods refer to the cultural adaptation and validation of methods and instruments. Finally, context comprises clients' environment, including history and sociopolitical circumstances.

Consequently, multicultural psychotherapists integrate cultural domains into psychotherapy. For example, Pamela Hays (2001) suggested addressing cultural complexities by highlighting identity with overlapping cultural influences. Her ADDRESSING framework helps psychotherapists to better recognize the complex cultural influences of Age, Developmental and acquired Disabilities, Religion, Ethnicity, Socioeconomic status, Sexual orientation, Indigenous heritage, National origin, and Gender. Another example of addressing cultural complexities in treatment, culturally sensitive psychotherapy, tailors psychotherapy to specific ethnocultural groups so that one group may benefit more from a specific intervention than from interventions designed for another ethnocultural group (Hall, 2001). This model requires the definition of race, ethnicity, and culture; the existence of a set of characteristics that are unique to certain groups relative to others; and the use of culturally sensitive interventions responsive to the specific characteristics of cultural diverse groups (Hall, 2001). Another multicultural healing, ethnocultural psychotherapy, integrates interactive cultural variables into diagnosis and treatment (Comas-Díaz & Jacobsen, 2004). Ethnocultural therapists pay special attention to the healing relationship to facilitate clients' truth, identity, and agency. As a result, psychotherapists examine clients' heritage, cultural transitions, explanatory models of distress, relationships, and context. They promote cultural consciousness, or individuals' awareness and reconnection to cultural resources, to empower, heal, and redeem (Comas-Díaz, 2007).

A major contribution of multicultural psychotherapies is empowerment among individuals and groups alike. A history of racial oppression frequently results in a struggle for survival. As part of this reality, people of color suffer from racial microaggressions—the assaults inflicted upon individuals on a regular and acute basis solely because of their race, color, and/or ethnicity (Pierce, 1995). Once in psychotherapy, clients of color can be exposed to racial microaggressions in the form of color blindness, denial of individual racism, myth of meritocracy, and pathologizing ethnic minority cultural values (D. W. Sue et al., 2007).

People of color's struggle against oppression offers an adaptive coping mechanism against terrorism. The struggle against racism and xenophobia often gave birth to cultural resilience—a group of culture-specific values and practices that promote coping mechanisms and adaptive reactions to sociopolitical trauma (Elsass, 1992). Multicultural psychotherapies affirm clients' cultural resilience and help them to restructure trauma, overcome adversity, enhance agency, and nurture hope. Moreover, cultural resilience activates self-expression because the oppressed need to find their own voices to name and describe their conditions. An example of self-expression as a form of cultural resilience is creativity. Throughout history, many people of color have used creativity to cope with trauma. Illustrations of such creative resilience include flamenco, hip hop, jazz, spoken word, urban art (murals, graffiti), literature–memoirs of color, folklore, and many other artistic manifestations.

As many culturally diverse individuals require a combined mind, body, and spirit approach, multiculturalists promote self-healing. To encourage self-healing, practitioners incorporate non-Western healing traditions into psychotherapy. For example, Cane (2000) reported a successful application in which she combined mind, body, and spirit self-healing practices with critical consciousness. Her research showed that self-healing practices such as Tai Chi, Pal Dan Gum, acupressure, visualization, breath work, ritual, polarity, massage, labyrinth, and body movement significantly reduced posttraumatic stress disorder symptoms among Central American clients.

In summary, multicultural theories of psychotherapy embrace multiple perspectives and promote an integrative holism. To implement these principles, multicultural therapists engage in self-reflection, conduct power differential analysis, challenge ethnocentrism, and question the applicability of Western psychological models to diverse worldviews. Additionally, they affirm clients' cultural strengths, foment cultural consciousness, use ethnic–indigenous practices, encourage critical analysis, and foster empowerment–liberation. Table 8.1 summarizes several multicultural psychotherapeutic processes and their corresponding interventions.

FUTURE DIRECTIONS

The future of multicultural psychotherapies will bring a full integration of holism into mental health treatment. Consequently, indigenous, ethnic, and folk healing approaches will become mainstream psychotherapy. More

TABLE 8.1
Processes and Interventions of Multicultural Psychotherapies

Process	Interventions
Assessment	Explanatory model of distress, cultural genogram, culturagram, cultural formulation–analysis
Treatment	Integration, multiple perspectives, holism: mind–body–spirit, liberation approaches, strength-based approaches—cultural consciousness
Therapeutic relationship	Cultural self-awareness, cultural empathy, power analysis, reflexibility–flexibility

than a third of adult and 12% of children in the United States use acupuncture, herbal remedies, breath work, meditation, yoga, and other alternative medicines (Stein, 2008). Dominant psychotherapy's integration of Eastern traditions, such as yoga, creative visualization, and meditation (Walsh & Shapiro, 2006), attests to the evolution of multicultural holistic approaches.

A holistic framework promotes spiritual development—a journey in which distress, illness, and adversity are viewed as opportunities for transformation. A classic example is the wounded healer, whose painful journey concludes with the attainment of healing abilities. When adversity strikes, individuals feel disoriented and lost. Multicultural psychotherapies offer a healing path—a cultural collectivistic therapy. In the future, culturally sensitive therapy will certainly become the standard of care for those suffering from natural disasters, ethnopolitical strife, and traumatic experiences of every genre.

Multicultural psychotherapies will move from culturally sensitive approaches to culturally derived healing. A current example is constellation family therapy, developed by Bert Hellinger, a former Catholic priest and missionary in South Africa, from the Zulu cultural and spiritual worldview. Constellation therapists address the family soul, a type of energy that includes clients' ancestors and future generations in case formulation and treatment. Healing involves becoming conscious of unconscious loyalties toward ancestors and generational burdens (Hellinger, Weber, & Beaumont, 1998). Constellation family therapy is popular in sociocentric societies such as Latin America as well as in some parts of Europe.

The global exchange will continue to enrich psychotherapy with cultural pluralism. In the near future, multicultural theories will facilitate the incorporation of holistic and integrative approaches into mainstream psychotherapy.

CONCLUSIONS

Multicultural psychotherapies foster a paradigm change in psychotherapy. They promote cultural competence in all practitioners. Psychotherapists demonstrate their cultural competence by becoming aware of their own and their clients' worldviews and by using appropriate interventions that reflect their cultural knowledge, skills, and beliefs. The integrative holistic nature of multicultural psychotherapies helps to accommodate cultural change and globalization. As the world changes, multiculturalism becomes a passport for effective cross-cultural encounters.

The emancipation of multicultural psychotherapies combats oppression and fosters liberation for individuals and groups. Practitioners acknowledge clients' contexts, help to reformulate identities, strengthen cultural resilience, and advance ecological adaptation. Moreover, liberation models keep everyone accountable and remind us of the limits of our contextualized reality. Within this framework, both client and therapist become critically conscious of their cultural embeddedness and of how to negotiate differences and similarities. Finally, multicultural theories can address the need to continuously rethink our theory, research, and practice. In sum, the multicultural principles of pluralism, inclusion, integration, holism, and liberation are consistent with the needs of an increasingly diverse world.

REFERENCES

Altman, N. (1995). *The analyst in the inner city: Race, class and culture through a psychoanalytic lens.* New York, NY: Analytic Press.

American Psychiatric Association. (1994). *Diagnostic and statistical manual of mental disorders* (4th ed.). Washington, DC: Author.

American Psychiatric Association. (2000). *Diagnostic and statistical manual of mental disorders* (4th ed., text rev.). Washington, DC: Author.

American Psychological Association. (1990). *Guidelines for providers of psychological services to ethnic, linguistic, and culturally diverse populations.* Washington, DC: American Psychological Association, Office of Ethnic Minority Affairs. Retrieved from http://www.apa.org/pi/oema/guide.html

American Psychological Association. (2003). Guidelines on multicultural education, training, research, practice, and organizational change for psychologists. *American Psychologist, 58,* 377–402. doi:10.1037/0003-066X.58.5.377

American Psychological Association Presidential Task Force on Evidence-Based Practice. (2006). Evidence-based practice in psychology. *American Psychologist, 6,* 271–285.

Ariel, S. (1999). *Culturally competent family therapy.* New York, NY: Greenwood.

Atkinson, D. R., Morten, G., & Sue, D. W. (Eds.). (1998). *Counseling American minorities* (5th ed.). Boston, MA: McGraw-Hill.

Bernal, G., Bonilla, J., & Bellido, C. (1995). Ecological validity and cultural sensitivity for outcome research: Issues for cultural adaptation and development of psychosocial treatments with Hispanics. *Journal of Abnormal Child Psychology, 23,* 67–82. doi:10.1007/BF01447045

Bernal, G., & Scharrón-del-Río, M. R. (2001). Are empirically-supported treatments valid for ethnic minorities? Toward and alternative approach for treatment research. *Cultural Diversity & Ethnic Minority Psychology, 7,* 328–342. doi:10.1037/1099-9809.7.4.328

Betancourt, J. R., Green, A. R., Carrillo, J. E., & Ananch-Firempong, O. (2003). Defining cultural competence: A practical framework for addressing racial/ethnic disparities in health and health care. *Public Health Reports, 118,* 293–302.

Blanco, A. (1998). *Psicología de la liberación de Ignacio Martín-Baró* (Liberation psychology of Ignacio Martin-Baro). Madrid, Spain: Editorial Trotta.

Boyd-Franklin, N. (2003). *Black families in therapy: Understanding the African American experience* (2nd ed.). New York, NY: Guilford Press.

Brown, L. S. (1997). The private practice of subversion: Psychology as Tikkun Olam. *American Psychologist, 52,* 449–462. doi:10.1037/0003-066X.52.4.449

Cane, P. (2000). *Trauma, healing and transformation: Awakening a new heart with body mind spirit practices.* Watsonville, CA: Capacitar Inc.

Cass, V. (2002). Gay and lesbian identity development model. In K. Y. Ritter & A. I. Terndrup (Eds.), *Handbook of affirmative psychotherapy with lesbians and gay men* (pp. 90–97). New York, NY: Guilford Press.

Cienfuegos, A. J., & Monelli, C. (1983). The testimony of political repression as a therapeutic instrument. *American Journal of Orthopsychiatry, 53*, 43–51.

Clausen, C. (2000). *Faded mosaic: The emergence of post cultural America.* Chicago, IL: Ivan R. Dee.

Comas-Díaz, L. (1990). Ethnic minority mental health: Contributions and future directions of the American Psychological Association. In F. C. Serafica, I. Schwebel, R. K. Russell, P. D. Issac, & L. B. Myers (Eds.), *Mental health of ethnic minorities* (pp. 275–301). New York, NY: Praeger.

Comas-Díaz, L. (2001). Building a multicultural private practice. *The Independent Practitioner, 21*, 220–223.

Comas-Díaz, L. (2006). Latino healing: The integration of ethnic psychology into psychotherapy. *Psychotherapy: Theory, Research, Practice, Training, 43*, 436–453. doi:10.1037/0033-3204.43.4.436

Comas-Díaz, L. (2007). Ethnopolitical psychology: Healing and transformation. In E. Aldarondo (Ed.), *Promoting social justice in mental health practice* (pp. 91–118). Mahwah, NJ: Erlbaum.

Comas-Díaz, L. (2008). *Spirita:* Reclaiming womanist sacredness in feminism. *Psychology of Women Quarterly, 32*, 13–21. doi:10.1111/j.1471-6402.2007.00403.x

Comas-Díaz, L. (in press). Interventions with culturally diverse populations. In D. Barlow (Ed.), *Oxford handbook of clinical psychology.* New York, NY: Oxford University Press.

Comas-Díaz, L., & Jacobsen, F. M. (2004). Ethnocultural psychotherapy. In E. Craighead & C. Nemeroff (Eds.), *The Corsini encyclopedia of psychology and behavioral science* (pp. 338339). New York, NY: Wiley.

Comas-Díaz, L., Lykes, B., & Alarcon, R. (1998). Ethnic conflict and psychology of liberation in Guatemala, Perú and Puerto Rico. *American Psychologist, 53*, 778–792. doi:10.1037/0003-066X.53.7.778

Congress, E. (1994). The use of culturagrams to assess and empower culturally diverse families. *Families in Society, 75*, 531–540.

Costantino, G., Malgady, R., & Rogler, L. (1986). *Cuento* therapy: A culturally sensitive modality for Puerto Rican children. *Journal of Consulting and Clinical Psychology, 54*, 639–645. doi:10.1037/0022-006X.54.5.639

Cowan, T. (1996). *Shamanism as a spiritual practice for daily life.* Freedom, CA: The Crossing Press.

Cross, T., Bazron, B., Dennis, K., & Issacs, M. (1989). *Towards a culturally competent system of care: A monograph on effective services for minority children who are severely emotionally disturbed.* Washington, DC: CASSP Technical Assistance Center, Georgetown University Child Development Center.

Cross, W. E. (1991). *Shades of Black: Diversity in African American identity.* Philadelphia, PA: Temple University Press.

Devereux, G. (1979). *Basic problems of ethnopsychiatry* (B. M. Gulati, Trans.). Chicago, IL: University of Chicago Press.

Diala, C., Muntaner, C., Walrath, C., Nickerson, K., LaVeist, T., & Leaf, P. (2000). Racial differences in attitudes toward professional mental health care in the use of services. *American Journal of Orthopsychiatry, 70*, 455–456.

Downing, N., & Roush, K. (1985). From passive acceptance to active commitment: A model of feminist identity development for women. *The Counseling Psychologist, 13*, 695–709. doi: 10.1177/0011000085134013

Duran, E., & Ivey, A. E. (2006). *Healing the soul wound: Counseling with American Indians and other native people.* New York, NY: Teachers College Press.

Elsass, P. (1992). *Strategies for survival: The psychology of cultural resilience in ethnic minorities.* New York: New York University Press.

Fanon, F. (1967). *Black skin, White masks*. New York, NY: Grove Press.

Fisher, A. R., Jome, L. M., & Atkinson, D. (1998). Back to the future of multicultural psychotherapy with a common factors approach. *The Counseling Psychologist, 26*, 602–606. DOI: 10.1177/0011000098264004

Freire, P. (1973). *Education for critical consciousness*. New York, NY: Seabury Press.

Freire, P., & Macedo, D. (2000). *The Paulo Freire reader*. New York, NY: Continuum.

Grier, W., & Cobbs, P. (1969). *Black rage*. New York, NY: Bantam Books.

Griner, D., & Smith, T. B. (2006). Culturally adapted mental health interventions: A meta-analytic review. *Psychotherapy: Theory, Research, Practice, Training, 43*, 531–548. doi:10.1037/0033-3204.43.4.531

Hall, G. C. N. (2001). Psychotherapy research with ethnic minorities: Empirical, ethical, and conceptual issues. *Journal of Consulting and Clinical Psychology, 69*, 502–510. doi:10.1037/0022-006X.69.3.502

Hansen, N. D., Pepitone-Arreola-Rockwell, F., & Greene, A. F. (2000). Multicultural competence: Criteria and case examples. *Professional Psychology: Research and Practice, 31*, 652–660. doi:10.1037/0735-7028.31.6.652

Hardy, K. V., & Laszloffy, T. (1995). The cultural genogram: Key to training culturally competent family therapists. *Journal of Marital and Family Therapy, 21*, 227–237.

Hays, P. (2001). *Addressing cultural complexities in practice: Assessment, diagnosis and therapy*. Washington, DC: American Psychological Association,

Hellinger, B., Weber, G., & Beaumont, H. (1998). *Love's hidden symmetry: What makes love in relationships*. Phoenix, AZ: Zeig, Tucker & Theisen.

Helms, J. E. (1990). *Black and White racial identity: Theory, research and practice*. Westport, CT: Greenwood.

Howard-Hamilton, M. F., Phelps, R. E., & Torres, V. (1998). *Meeting the needs of all students and staff members: The challenge of diversity—New directions for student services*. San Francisco, CA: Jossey-Bass.

Johnson, L. R., Bastien, G., & Hirschel, M. (2008). Psychotherapy in a culturally diverse world. In S. Eshun & R. Gurung (Eds.), *Culture and mental health: Sociocultural influences, theory, and practice* (pp. 115–148). New York, NY: Blackwell.

Kardiner, A., Linton, R. R., Du Bois, C., & West, J. (1945). *The psychological frontiers of society*. New York, NY: Columbia University Press.

Kiev, A. (1972). *Transcultural psychiatry*. New York, NY: The Free Press.

Kleinman, A. (1980). *Patients and healers in the context of culture: An exploration of the borderland between anthropology, medicine, and psychiatry*. Berkeley: University of California Press.

Knipscheer, J. W., & Kleber, R. J. (2004). A need for ethnic similarity in the therapist–patient interaction? Mediterranean migrants in Dutch mental health care. *Journal of Clinical Psychology, 60*, 543–554. doi:10.1002/jclp.20008

Lo, H.-T., & Fung, K. P. (2003). Culturally competent psychotherapy. *Canadian Journal of Psychiatry, 48*, 161–170.

McGoldrick, M., Gerson, R., & Shellenberger, S. (1999). *Genograms: Assessment and intervention*. New York, NY: Norton.

McGoldrick, M., Giordano, J., & Garcia-Preto, N. (Eds.). (2005). *Ethnicity and family therapy* (3rd ed.). New York, NY: Guilford Press.

Melfi, C. A., Croghan, T. W., Hanna, M. P., & Robinson, R. (2000). Racial variation in antidepressant treatment in a medication population. *The Journal of Clinical Psychiatry, 61*, 16–21.

Miranda, J., Bernal, G., Lau, A., Kohn, L., Hwang, W.-C., & La Framboise, T. (2005). State of the science on psychosocial interventions for ethnic minorities. *Annual Review of Clinical Psychology, 1*, 113–142.

Muñoz, R. F., & Mendelson, T. (2005). Toward evidence-based interventions for diverse populations: The San Francisco General Hospital prevention and treatment manuals. *Journal of Consulting and Clinical Psychology, 73,* 790–799. doi:10.1037/0022-006X.73.5.790

Pedersen, P. B. (1991). Multiculturalism as a generic framework. *Journal of Counseling and Development, 70,* 6–12.

Pierce, C. M. (1995). Stress analogs of racism and sexism: Terrorism, torture and disaster. In C. V. Willie, P. P. Reiker, & B. S. Brown (Eds.), *Mental health, racism and sexism* (pp. 277–293). Pittsburgh, PA: University of Pittsburgh Press.

Poston, W. C. (1990). The biracial identity development model: A needed addition. *Journal of Counseling and Development, 69,* 152–155.

Rey, J. (2006, December 1). The interface of multiculturalism and psychopharmacology. *Journal of Pharmacy Practice, 19,* 379–385. doi:10.1177/0897190007300734

Reynolds, D. K. (1980). *The quiet therapies: Japan pathways to personal growth.* Honolulu: The University Press of Hawaii.

Roby, P. (1998, January). Creating a just world: Leadership for the twenty-first century. *Social Problems, 45,* 1–20. doi:10.1525/sp.1998.45.1.03x0154x

Rogers, W. A. (2004). Evidence medicine and justice: A framework for looking at the impact of EBM upon vulnerable and disadvantage groups. *Journal of Medical Ethics, 30,* 141–145. doi:10.1136/jme.2003.007062

Roselló, J., & Bernal, G. (1999). The efficacy of cognitive–behavioral and interpersonal treatments for depression in Puerto Rican adolescents. *Journal of Consulting and Clinical Psychology, 67,* 734–745. doi:10.1037/0022-006X.67.5.734

Schneider, K. (Ed.). (2008). *Existential-integrative psychotherapy: Guideposts to the core of practice.* New York, NY: Routledge.

Seeley, K. M. (2000). *Cultural psychotherapy: Working with culture in the clinical encounter.* Northvale, NJ: Jason Aronson.

Semmler, P. L., & Williams, C. B. (2000). Narrative therapy: A storied context for multicultural counseling. *Journal of Multicultural Counseling and Development, 28,* 51–62.

Shweder, R. A. (1993). Cultural psychology: Who needs it? *Annual Review of Psychology, 44,* 497–523. doi:10.1146/annurev.ps.44.020193.002433

Silverstein, L. B. (2006). Integrating feminism and multiculturalism: Scientific fact or science fiction? *Professional Psychology: Research and Practice, 37,* 21–28. doi:10.1037/0735-7028.37.1.21

Speck, R. V., & Attneave, C. L. (1973). *Family networks.* New York, NY: Pantheon Books.

Spiro, M. E. (1984). Some reflections on cultural determinism and relativism with special reference to emotion and reason. In R. A. Schweder & R. A. Levine (Eds.), *Culture theory: Essays on mind, self and emotion* (pp. 323–346). Cambridge, England: Cambridge University Press.

Stein, R. (2008, December 11). 38% of adults use alternative medicine. *The Washington Post,* p. A02.

Sue, D. W., Copodilupo, C. M., Torino, G. C., Bucceri, J. M., Holder, A. M., Nadal, K. L., & Esquilin, M. (2007). Racial microaggressions in everyday life: Implications for clinical practice. *American Psychologist, 62,* 271–286. doi:10.1037/0003-066X.62.4.271

Sue, S., Zane, N., Levant, R. F., Silverstein, L. B., Brown, L. S., Olkin, R., & Taliaferro, G. (2006). How well do both evidence-based practices and treatment as usual satisfactorily address the various dimensions of diversity? In J. C. Norcross, L. E. Beutler, & R. F. Levant (Eds.), *Evidence-based practices in mental health: Debate and dialogue on the fundamental questions* (pp. 329–337). Washington, DC: American Psychological Association.

Tedlock, B. (2005). *The woman in the shaman's body: Reclaiming the feminine in religion and medicine.* New York, NY: Bantam Dell.

Tseng, W.-S. (2001). *Handbook of cultural psychiatry*. San Diego, CA: Academic Press.

U.S. Office of the Surgeon General. (2000). *Mental health, culture, race and ethnicity: A supplement to mental health—A report of the Surgeon General Disparities in mental health care for racial and ethnic minorities*. Rockville, MD: Author.

Voss Horrell, S. C. (2008). Effectiveness of cognitive–behavioral therapy with adult ethnic minority clients: A review. *Professional Psychology: Research and Practice, 39*, 160–168. doi:10.1037/0735-7028.39.2.160

Walsh, R., & Shapiro, S. (2006). The meeting of meditative disciplines and Western psychology: A mutually enriching dialogue. *American Psychologist, 61*, 227–239. doi:10.1037/0003-066X.61.3.227

Washington, H. A. (2007). *Medical apartheid: The dark history of medical experimentation on Black Americans from colonial times to the present*. New York, NY: Doubleday.

Whaley, A. L., & Davis, K. E. (2007). Cultural competence and evidence-based practice in mental health services: A complementary perspective. *American Psychologist, 62*, 563–574.

Worrell, J., & Johnson, N. G. (1997). *Shaping the future of feminist psychology: Education, research, and practice*. Washington, DC: American Psychological Association.

Worell, J., & Remer, P. (2003). *Feminist perspectives in therapy* (2nd ed.). New York, NY: Wiley.

9

INTEGRATIVE APPROACHES TO PSYCHOTHERAPY

MARVIN R. GOLDFRIED, CAROL R. GLASS,
AND DIANE B. ARNKOFF

Alas, our theory is too poor for experience.

—Albert Einstein

No, no! Experience is too rich for our theory.

—Niels Bohr

In contrast to the humility communicated by these two prominent scientists, the field of psychotherapy has tended to operate on the belief that we can develop a comprehensive theory of human functioning and therapy that can be applied to all situations. Some therapists have focused on the role of historically based conflicts, others on thinking processes, some on maladaptive behaviors, and still others on emotional responses. Yet, we contend that human behavior is far too complex to be explained by any one theory in that a host of variables typically come into play as causes of and as means to therapeutic change. The recognition that psychotherapy can be most effective when contributions from different approaches are integrated has steadily been growing. Indeed, "from its beginnings, psychotherapy integration has been characterized by a dissatisfaction with single-school approaches and the concomitant desire to look beyond school boundaries to see what can be learned—and how patients can benefit—from other forms of behavior change" (Norcross & Goldfried, 2005, p. v). The purpose of this chapter is to trace this trend over the years.

Portions of this chapter are based on "A History of Psychotherapy Integration," (Goldfried, Pachankis, & Bell, 2005).

269

The history of ideas often progresses gradually, and sometimes in fits and starts. Given the changing zeitgeist in psychology, "an idea too strange or preposterous to be thought in one period . . . may [later] be readily accepted as true" (Boring, 1950, p. 3). This has certainly been the case in the history of integrative psychotherapy.

Our historical review of psychotherapy integration extends over a period of approximately seven decades, covering trends up to the end of the 20th century. We provide not only an overview of what has appeared in the literature over the years but also of why the interest in psychotherapy integration may have occurred, offering private accounts from audiotaped interviews conducted by Carol R. Glass and Diane B. Arnkoff (in 1989) with many of the people who have been responsible for the integration movement. As we show, the establishment of a professional organization was responsible for raising the consciousness of the field about the importance of work in this area. We end with thoughts about the future that lies ahead.

INITIAL EFFORTS AT INTEGRATION

To our knowledge, one of the earliest attempts at psychotherapy integration took place at the 1932 meetings of the American Psychiatric Association, when Thomas French stood before his colleagues and drew links between the work of Freud and Pavlov. As an example, he described the parallel between Freud's concept of repression and Pavlov's notion of extinction. French's presentation was published a year later (French, 1933), along with commentaries from some of the audience members. It should come as little surprise that the reactions were very mixed, with one person being horrified at this integrative attempt, suggesting that "Pavlov would have exploded; and that Freud . . . would be scandalized by such a rapprochement made by one of his pupils" (French, 1933, p. 1201). Some of the reactions were more positive, such as the suggestion that one should "enjoy the convergences which show in such discussions as we have had this morning" (French, 1933, p. 1201). Gregory Zilboorg was even more enthusiastic about French's efforts at rapprochement, noting "that while dealing with extremely complex functional units both in the physiological laboratory and in the clinic, we can yet reduce them to comparably simple phenomena" (French, 1933, pp. 1198–1199).

In the very next year, Lawrence Kubie (1934) extended French's (1933) thinking by arguing that selected psychoanalytic methods could be understood in terms of the conditioned reflex. Specifically, Kubie suggested that certain unconscious associations were learned under a state of inhibition and that free association might function to remove that inhibition to let the associations emerge in consciousness.

In a very brief article that is as relevant today as when it was published, Rosenzweig (1936) argued that different approaches to intervention may be comparably effective because they contain common principles of change. Interestingly, he subtitled his paper with a line from *Alice in Wonderland*: "At last the Dodo said, 'Everybody has won and all must have prizes,'" a phrase that often appears in the contemporary therapy literature to highlight the probability that the failure to find efficacy differences across approaches may be a function of common principles of change. Also very timely was Rosenzweig's description of common principles of change: (a) The characteristics of the therapist are important to the change process because they inspire hope and motivation in the client; (b) the interpretations made during the course of therapy are important because they help the client gain a better understanding of his or her problems; and (c) although different therapy systems emphasize different aspects of the client's functioning (e.g., thinking, behavior, emotion), they may all be effective because a change in any given aspect of functioning can synergistically affect another.

Just a few years later, at the meeting of the American Orthopsychiatric Association, a group of therapists met to discuss those aspects of the change process on which they might agree—such as the importance of the therapeutic relationship (Watson, 1940). In commentary on the meeting, a conclusion emerged that many contemporary therapists would agree with, namely, "If we were to apply to our colleagues the distinction, so important with patients, between what they tell us and what they do, we might find that agreement is greater in practice than in theory" (Watson, 1940, p. 708). Another very contemporary-sounding view was put forth by Herzberg (1945), who suggested that giving the client "homework" might enhance psychodynamic therapy, as would the use of graded tasks for individuals whose avoidance behavior was motivated by anxiety. Also very much in the spirit of integration, Woodworth (1948) reviewed different schools of psychological thought (e.g., behaviorism, psychoanalysis) and concluded that "no one is good enough" in itself (p. 255) and wondered "whether synthesis of the different lines of advance [might] not sometime prove to be possible" (p. 10).

All of this early work may have set the stage for what appeared next—the landmark book by Dollard and Miller (1950), *Personality and Psychotherapy*. Dedicated to "Freud and Pavlov and their students," this classic makes use of learning theory to understand such psychoanalytic concepts as anxiety, repression, and displacement. Although some have claimed that Dollard and Miller only translated analytic language into learning terms, they nonetheless offered several useful insights on common factors, such as the importance of therapeutic empathy and the use of therapeutic support of clients' attempts at change. They also anticipated by several years what would come to be known as *behavior therapy*, suggesting such principles as setting up "a series of graded situations where the patient can learn" (p. 350) and the importance of therapists' "approval to reward good effort on the part of the patient" (p. 395).

In that same year, Thorne (1950) published his book *Principles of Personality Counseling*. Unlike Dollard and Miller's (1950) attempt at psychotherapy integration by linking two separate approaches, Thorne argued that integration might best be approached on the basis of what we know empirically about human functioning and how people change. A half-century before evidence-based practice, Thorne credits his experience as a medical student for the realization that the practice of medicine was not based on different schools of thought but rather on what was known empirically. In his book *Introduction to Clinical Psychology*, Garfield (1957) similarly underscored the importance of basing our intervention on research evidence and also outlined such common factors across orientations as the therapy relationship and the self-understanding provided to clients.

Although the contributions that were made in the 1950s to psychotherapy integration were clearly significant, they were not plentiful. This might be attributed to the more conservative social climate of the time, or perhaps simply to the fact that no dominant therapy had yet been developed as an alternative to psychoanalysis, or to the growing experiences of practicing therapists—especially the realization that there are limits to what can be achieved by following a single orientation. Indeed, a survey of members of Division 12 (then called the Division of Clinical and Abnormal Psychology) of the American Psychological Association found that of those engaged in psychotherapy, 35% endorsed "eclectic" as their school of therapy (Shaffer, 1953). However, it was not until the decade of the 1960s that alternative approaches were developed and therapists began questioning their theoretical paradigms.

THE 1960s

A landmark contribution to psychotherapy integration in the 1960s was Jerome Frank's (1961) classic book *Persuasion and Healing*. Frank wrote about the commonalities that existed among widely diverse approaches to change, including religious conversion, tribal healing, brainwashing, and the placebo effect. A key concept that tied all these approaches and phenomena together was their ability to facilitate an expectation for improvement, combat demoralization, and instill a sense of hope.

Another key contribution was made by Franz Alexander (1963). Alexander, a colleague of French's—whose groundbreaking article had appeared some 30 years earlier—came to the conclusion that psychoanalytic therapy may best be understood in terms of learning theory. As an outgrowth of his research with actual taped therapy sessions, Alexander concluded that "we are witnessing the beginnings of a most promising integration of psychoanalytic theory with learning theory, which may lead to unpredictable advances in the theory and practice of the psychotherapies" (p. 448).

In a little-known article, Carl Rogers (1963) wrote about the current status of therapy, observing that the field seemed to be moving beyond the limitations set by a given theoretical orientation—including client-centered therapy—and that it was important for the field to spend more energy in studying directly what went on in therapy sessions. Here again, we have some earlier stirrings about evidence-based practice.

Another important but overlooked contribution was London's (1964) *The Modes and Morals of Psychotherapy*, which reviewed the shortcomings of purely insight-oriented psychodynamic or action-oriented behavior therapy. As London observed,

> There is a quiet blending of techniques by artful therapists of either school: a blending that takes account of the fact that people are considerably simpler than the Insight schools give them credit for, but that they are also more complicated than the Action therapists would like to believe. (p. 39)

In 1967, Arnold Lazarus, one of the founders of behavior therapy, introduced the concept of *technical eclecticism*, which referred to clinicians using therapy methods advocated by different orientations without having to accept the theoretical underpinnings of those orientations. His thesis that the clinical utility of technical eclecticism was more important than theoretical explanation was later expanded on in his multimodal therapy (Lazarus, 1976), a broad-spectrum approach that takes into account the client's behaviors, affects, sensations, images, cognitions, interpersonal relationships, and drugs or physiological states.

In our interview, Lazarus described several of the reasons for his beginning to use techniques from nonbehavioral approaches:

> I kept feeling, and still feel, dissatisfied at not being able to help as many people as I think can be helped, and kept looking for ways and means of enhancing this thing. . . . So I began to borrow techniques like the empty chair. Now why would I use the empty chair instead of regular role-playing or behavior rehearsal? And so where I had somebody who appeared not to be owning up to, say, feelings of anger, and in the role playing these things were not coming out. But I began to do the empty chair and got the person to assume actively the identity of the other person. Out came the anger and things of this kind, I said, "Well this is a useful technique." (A. A. Lazarus, personal communication, November 3, 1989)

However, some in the behavior therapy community were displeased with Lazarus's advocating technical eclecticism and talking about broad-spectrum behavior therapy:

> This was the point of departure between Wolpe and I, where he saw this as some form of heresy, some sort of watering down of the purity of what he was doing. And Eysenck took up the cudgels on behalf of Wolpe and expelled me from the editorial board of *Behaviour Research and Therapy*. I was defrocked by virtue of asking for breadth, you see, and introducing cognitions in the 70s. (A. A. Lazarus, personal communication, November 3, 1989)

Appearing in the same year as Lazarus's (1967) landmark paper on technical eclecticism were several articles advocating the use of systematic desensitization in the context of psychoanalytic therapy (e.g., Weitzman, 1967). Also writing about systematic desensitization—a behavioral procedure that was rapidly gaining popularity at the time—Bergin (1969) suggested that the effectiveness of the procedure might be enhanced within the context of a good therapeutic relationship, especially where there was also a focus on relevant cognitive and emotional issues. The argument was that the combination of behavioral and dynamic interventions might be particularly well suited in complex clinical cases. Surveys of clinical psychologists in the 1960s showed that a substantial minority endorsed "eclectic" as their therapeutic orientation (Goldschmid, Stein, Weissman, & Sorrells, 1969; Kelly, 1961; Lubin, 1962). Percentages of "eclectics" in these surveys ranged from 24% to 48%; interestingly, the highest figure was among fellows of Division 12 of the American Psychological Association (Kelly, 1961).

THE 1970s

The popularity of behavior therapy came into its own in the United States in 1970 with the publication of the journal *Behavior Therapy*, 7 years after *Behaviour Research and Therapy* was founded. Even though *Behavior Therapy* was the inaugural issue of the journal published by the Association for Advancement of Behavior Therapy, it interestingly enough highlighted the need for psychotherapy integration. Several practitioners (e.g., Birk, 1970), for example, presented clinical cases that involved the integration of psychodynamic and behavior therapy. Acknowledging the importance of incorporating cognitive concepts into behavior therapy, Bergin (1970) accurately foresaw the important implications of this beginning trend:

> The sociological and historical importance of the movement should not be underestimated for it has three important consequences. It signifi-

cantly reduces barriers to progress due to narrow school allegiances, it brings the energies of a highly talented and experimentally sophisticated group to bear upon the intricate and often baffling problems of objectifying and managing the subjective, and it underscores the notion that a pure behavior therapy does not exist. (p. 207)

The accuracy of his prediction became apparent when many behavior therapists who were involved in incorporating cognition into behavior therapy in the 1970s (e.g., Davison, Goldfried, Lazarus, Mahoney, Meichenbaum) went on to contribute to the psychotherapy integration movement.

Marmor (1971), a steady contributor to the literature on integration, further strengthened his advocacy by indicating,

The research on the nature of the psychotherapeutic process in which I participated with Franz Alexander, beginning in 1958, has convinced me that all psychotherapy, regardless of the techniques used, is a learning process. . . . Dynamic psychotherapies and behavior therapies simply represent different teaching techniques, and their differences are based in part on differences in their goals and in part on their assumptions of the nature of psychopathology. (p. 26)

As behavior therapy has become more cognitive in nature, the nature of the learning process within these two approaches has become less distinct.

Following up on the growing interest within behavior therapy to look outside its orientation, London (1972) encouraged his behavioral colleagues—as did Lazarus before him—to take a pragmatic approach to integration. He argued that we should not get too caught up with theory but rather make use of treatments that work. Also appearing in that year were advocates of combining learning theory with client-centered therapy (Martin, 1972), as well as further illustrations of the integration of psychodynamic and behavior therapies (e.g., Feather & Rhoads, 1972). Hans Strupp (1973), in the first of his many contributions to psychotherapy integration—as we show later, his foresight would provide the impetus for forming a professional network dedicated to integration—wrote about change processes common to all therapy approaches. A psychodynamic therapist by training, Strupp's experience as both a practitioner and a researcher led him to conclude that a key aspect of therapeutic change involved corrective learning experiences that were inherent in the therapy relationship.

A number of important contributions to integration appeared in 1974, such as the suggestion that the way psychodynamic and behavioral approaches might be combined is by using the former approach to provide the insight that could set the stage for change, with the latter involving the implementation of a specific process to help change to occur (Birk & Brinkley-Birk, 1974). Kaplan (1974) offered her guidelines for similarly combining these two approaches in conducting sex therapy.

An account of the Menninger Foundation Psychotherapy Research Project concluded that psychodynamic therapists might need to consider treatment methods that do not fit into a dynamic model, an assertion that was quite radical at the time. This was expanded on by P. L. Wachtel (1975), in the first of his many writings, in which he advocated the incorporation of behavioral techniques into psychodynamic therapy. His integrative message also applied to behavior therapists, in that he suggested their approach could bring about more lasting change by viewing maladaptive behavioral patterns within more of a psychodynamic context. This idea was later expanded on in P. L. Wachtel's (1977) classic, *Psychoanalysis and Behavior Therapy*. Wachtel described the journey of discovery that led him to his integrative approach in our interview:

> The perennial question that patients would always ask, "Well, now that I understand this, what do I do about it?" was a more legitimate question than analysts are prone to acknowledge. And it seemed to me that behavior therapy offered possibilities for intervening more explicitly. I went to Philadelphia for a one-month, very intensive training program that Joseph Wolpe was running and had contact, not only with him, but with a number of other behavioral clinicians who were there . . . then I contacted Jerry Davison at Stony Brook and, once a week, went out to Stony Brook and met with him and Marv Goldfried who were running the postdoctoral program in behavior therapy. . . . In the beginning it was much easier, than it would be now, for me to identify very clearly, which portion of the session . . . was the psychodynamic part and which was the behavioral part. . . . Since I had just been learning behavioral techniques, and felt at that point relatively new to them, I wanted to be sure to be practicing them in the classical mode, so to speak . . . to be sure I was doing the right thing. I was exploring what were the possible ways of putting them together. . . . I was struggling, really, to find a personal style that felt comfortable to me, that felt kind of true to who I was and to the perspective that I was holding . . . what did happen is that both the psychodynamic and the behavioral aspects of the work, themselves, began to change . . . something that was more thoroughly synthesized began to appear. (P. L. Wachtel, personal communication, November 30, 1989)

Jerry Davison recalled the same period from his own perspective, noting that Wachtel's perspective influenced him as well:

> The Wachtel thing was mind blowing. . . . He said that he had been reading a lot about behavior therapy but wanted to *see* behavior therapy. Could I show him some behavior therapy? I told him I was seeing a case behind a one-way mirror for my four post-docs. . . . And then we'd have a rehash afterwards. And what began to happen early on was that Paul was seeing different things. . . . I was not surprised that he saw different

things, but how receptive I was to his analytic way of talking and thinking about things . . . in his '77 book. . . . he goes on quite accurately to
describe how I missed certain things with the case and how my not seeing it the way he was seeing it might have led to the problems in progress
with the patient. . . . He was seeing anger and hostility towards women
in a young boy that I was treating basically for heterosocial anxiety. That
had a big impact on me. (G. C. Davison, personal communication,
November 4, 1989)

Two important books appeared in 1975 that are rarely mentioned by
those who have contributed to psychotherapy integration. One was Raimy's
(1975) *Misunderstandings of the Self*, which described how most therapy systems involved changing clients' misconceptions of themselves and others.
Raimy indicated that all therapies are alike in that they call attention to
"evidence" that contradicts these misconceptions—even though the type of
evidence and how it is presented may differ across orientations. The other
book was a slim volume by Egan (1975), directed toward providing clinical
skills to helping professionals. Egan, whose original orientation was humanistic, described how client-centered contributions could readily be combined
with the action-oriented methods of behavior therapy.

Goldfried and Davison's (1976) *Clinical Behavior Therapy*, in addition
to describing how cognitive–behavior therapy can be implemented in clinical practice, also challenged behavior therapists to consider contributions
from other orientations. They suggested, "It is time for behavior therapists to
stop regarding themselves as an out-group and instead to enter into serious
and hopefully mutually fruitful dialogues with their nonbehavioral colleagues" (p. 15). In fact, this was already starting to happen because a plurality of clinical psychologists in the United States considered themselves to be
eclectic, combining learning and psychodynamic approaches (Garfield &
Kurtz, 1976).

In our interview, Goldfried recalled one of the times he first began to
realize the influence of other psychotherapies. At Stony Brook, American
Psychological Association site visitors suggested that students were not being
exposed to different points of view. So in a 1st-year course on psychotherapy,

> I went back to the texts that I used as a graduate student, dug those out,
> and assigned some of them, and reread some of that stuff. And as I reread
> it, I was struck by some of the similarities that I saw . . . started having
> discussions in class as to what kind of themes seem to be coming through
> that are similar to a behavioral approach when we started reading the
> psychodynamic stuff. Also what happened clinically is that as I started
> demonstrating some cases to graduate students behind a one-way screen,
> I realized that a lot of what I was doing was not straight behavior ther-
> apy. (M. R. Goldfried, personal communication, December 7, 1989)

With a most provocative title, "Has Behavior Therapy Outlived Its Usefulness?" Lazarus (1977) questioned whether behavior therapy as a separate treatment—or any other specific school of therapy—could continue to be justified for all clinical cases. After spending approximately 20 years in the clinical practice of behavior therapy, Lazarus maintained that the field needed to "transcend the constraints of factionalism, where cloistered adherents of rival schools, movements, and systems each cling to their separate illusions" (p. 11).

Prochaska's (1979) book describing different systems of psychotherapy was one of the first texts of this kind to end with a chapter that argued for the need to develop a transtheoretical approach that would incorporate effective features of the various orientations. The timeliness of this final chapter on integration can readily be seen from the results of a survey of leading cognitive and non–cognitive–behavior therapists (Mahoney, 1979). Among the questions asked was, "I feel satisfied with the adequacy of my current understanding of human behavior." On the basis of a 7-point scale, Mahoney (1979) found that the average rating of satisfaction was less than 2.

THE 1980s

The momentum of interest in psychotherapy integration increased even more in the 1980s, moving it from a fledgling interest to a clearly discernable movement. The number of publications and presentations increased severalfold, therefore requiring us to review only some of the highlights that occurred during this decade and thereinafter.

In an article appearing in the *American Psychologist* titled "Toward the Delineation of Therapeutic Change Principles," Goldfried (1980) argued that rapprochement could best be found at a level of abstraction somewhere between observable clinical procedures and the theoretical explanations for why these techniques might work. This middle level of abstraction, which may be thought of as a clinical strategy or principle of change, may exist across different schools of thought. An example of a change principle would be providing the client with corrective experiences, especially those that might be applied to fear-related behavior. To illustrate this, Goldfried cited a well-known psychoanalyst (Fenichel, 1941):

> When a person is afraid but experiences a situation in which what was feared occurs without any harm resulting, he will not immediately trust the outcome of his new experience; however, the second time he will have a little less fear, the third time still less. (p. 83)

The corrective experience as an important principle of change was acknowledged by a diverse group of well-known therapists of different orientations who presented their views in a special edition of the journal *Cognitive Therapy and Research* appearing in 1980 (Brady et al., 1980). Such therapists as Brady, Davison, Dewald, Egan, Frank, Gill, Kempler, Lazarus, Raimy, Rotter, and Strupp categorized the importance of new experiences from within their orientation as being "essential," "basic," "crucial," and "critical."

Noting that the integration of psychodynamic and behavioral approaches can be problematic, Messer and Winokur (1980) nonetheless acknowledged that the synergy between the two can facilitate therapeutically beneficial insights and actions. Confirming Bergin's (1970) earlier prediction that the introduction of cognition in behavior therapy could be a bridge to rapprochement, behavior therapists were beginning to acknowledge the existence of "implicit" cognitions, moving them closer to studying the psychodynamic concept of unconscious processes (Mahoney, 1980).

Also appearing in 1980 was an edited book by Marmor and Woods titled *The Interface Between Psychodynamic and Behavioral Therapies* and Garfield's (1980) *Psychotherapy: An Eclectic Approach*, which argued for an evidence-based, rather than a theory-based, approach to the practice of therapy. Agreeing with Bergin's (1970) earlier prediction, Garfield concluded that the introduction of cognition into behavior therapy would serve to facilitate a rapprochement. In our interview, Garfield noted the importance of "being flexible, paying attention to the research, trying to utilize what appears to be potentially feasible with a given patient, and also if something doesn't work, maybe you've made a mistake and you should reconsider and use something else" (S. L. Garfield, personal communication, December 4, 1989).

In 1981, several authors wrote about the complementary nature of different orientations. For example, the empty chair technique from gestalt therapy can profitably be used by cognitive–behavior therapists to identify and change affect-laden, maladaptive cognitions (Arnkoff, 1981). For another example, a multifaceted empirical approach could be used within the context of couple therapy (Gurman, 1981).

Although there had been periodic conference presentations that dealt with psychotherapy integration, most of what had been done involved published articles, chapters, and books. Seeing the need to extend a transtheoretical dialogue even further, a small group of psychotherapists of different orientations met in 1981 at an informal weekend retreat. The goal of this meeting was to facilitate direct communication, especially with regard to how different therapies would deal with the same clinical problem.

Goldfried's (1982) *Converging Themes in Psychotherapy* provided a collection of key papers on integration and included the suggestion that translating theoretical jargon into the vernacular could help advance the discovery of similarities across theoretical approaches. In P. L. Wachtel's (1982) edited book *Resistance: Psychodynamic and Behavioral Approaches*, well-known behavioral and psychodynamic therapists shared their views on how resistance was conceptualized and handled clinically from within these two orientations. Similarly, Arkowitz and Messer (1984) published a unique volume, *Psychoanalytic Therapy and Behavior Therapy: Is Integration Possible?* The 10 contributing authors had the opportunity to comment on each other's chapters, providing a lively exchange of ideas on various aspects of psychotherapy integration. Ryle's (1982) *Psychotherapy: A Cognitive Integration of Theory and Practice* described different orientations and procedures in terms of cognitive science. In his *Marital Therapy: A Combined Psychodynamic–Behavioral Approach*, Segraves (1982) similarly made use of a common language, cognitive psychology, to integrate different approaches to couples therapy. In the first of many contributions to integration, Beutler (1983) presented an empirical approach to eclecticism, emphasizing ways of matching clients to the technique and the therapist. Accounts of how psychotherapy integration was occurring in other countries also began to emerge (e.g., in Germany by Textor, 1983).

The 1980s was a time when numerous other books on integration appeared. For example, in *Cognitive Processes and Emotional Disorders: A Structural Approach to Psychotherapy*, Guidano and Liotti (1983) described a constructivist approach to cognitive therapy, in which the focus was on changing deep structures of the self and world. In Prochaska and DiClemente's (1984) *The Transtheoretical Approach: Crossing the Traditional Boundaries of Therapy*, the authors described the processes and stages of change that characterize the different approaches to therapy.

One of the most significant events of the 1980s was the formation of a professional organization dedicated to the advancement of psychotherapy integration. Formed in 1983, the Society for the Exploration of Psychotherapy Integration (SEPI) was established to create a professional community dedicated to the topic of integration. It was—and still is—an interdisciplinary and international organization that holds yearly conferences at which both researchers and clinicians can present their work and interact with each other. We have more to say about SEPI later in the chapter.

From the middle to the late 1980s, the integration movement developed considerable momentum, and an increasing number of professionals began contributing to the literature in this area. As might be expected, journals were created to deal directly with integration, such as the *International Journal of Eclectic Psychotherapy*, later renamed the *Journal of Integrative and Eclectic Psychotherapy*. In 1987, the *Journal of Cognitive Psychotherapy: An International Quarterly* was formed, inviting articles that would consider the integration of cognitive psychotherapy with other systems of treatment.

In an *American Psychologist* article appearing in 1986, Messer illustrated the similarities and differences that existed between psychoanalytic and behavior therapy by discussing how therapists from within each orientation responded to choice points in actual clinical work. Using a case illustration to make his point, Messer indicated, for example, how the former therapy spent more time on understanding and elaborating on a client's distorted thinking, whereas the latter moved more quickly in attempting to change the thinking. Which therapy is more effective remains open to empirical investigation. Such issues have been used by others to argue for future research, with the frequent finding that different approaches were comparably efficacious, suggesting that process research be undertaken to better understand the change process within different approaches (e.g., Goldfried & Safran, 1986).

With the increasing interest in integration, the topic of optimal training for integration began to receive consideration (Halgin, 1985) and was dealt with at length in Norcross's (1986a) edited volume on eclectic psychotherapy and in a 1986 special section of the *International Journal of Eclectic Psychotherapy* (Norcross, 1986b).

The year 1987 witnessed not only a marked increase in the number of books on integration but also a reminder of the international interest in this issue, with books from Italy (Guidano, 1987), Canada (LeComte & Castonguay, 1987), and the United States (e.g., Beitman 1987; Norcross, 1987). No longer was an integrative theory a novelty; instead, multiple integrative theories were being promulgated around the globe.

The proportion of practitioners endorsing an eclectic or integrative orientation remained substantial, from 26% to 56% (as reviewed by Arnkoff & Glass, 1992). An update of the earlier survey revealed that therapists were becoming increasingly more eclectic in their practice but that the therapy orientations being combined had changed (Norcross & Prochaska, 1988). Whereas the eclecticism of the 1970s was typically the combination of psychoanalytic and behavioral approaches, the typical therapy integration in the 1980s—therapists preferred the term *integration* to *eclecticism*—involved the combination of cognitive with behavioral and cognitive with humanistic approaches.

Bergin (1988), a long-term advocate of integration, provided an interesting rationale for combining the contributions of different orientations. He reminded us that no biologist would ever attempt to offer an understanding of how the body operated by using a single conceptual approach. Thus, to understand how the heart works, principles of fluid mechanics are required, and to understand neural transmission, one needs to use electrochemical principles. Indeed, this is the very observation by Neils Bohr that we quoted at the outset of this chapter: "Experience is too rich for our theory."

A number of authors wrote about the integration of individual and family–couples therapy (e.g., Feldman, 1989; Gurman, 1981; Lebow, 1984; E. F. Wachtel & Wachtel, 1986). The underlying rationale for combining these two formats was that there often exists a vicious cycle between an individual's expectations and perception of one's significant other, the person's actions that follow, and the impact on the other that could confirm the thoughts responsible for the negatively affecting behavior. Basically, the person initiating the vicious cycle needs to become aware of what the cartoon character Pogo once said: "We have met the enemy—and it is us!"

Much of what was written on psychotherapy integration was based on clinical experience and conceptual reasoning. As the decade of the 1980s was coming to a close, a number of professionals emphasized the importance of demonstrating the merits of integration empirically (e.g., Goldfried & Safran, 1986; Norcross & Grencavage, 1989; Safran, Greenberg, & Rice, 1988; Wolfe & Goldfried, 1988). Several researchers (e.g., Safran et al., 1988) argued that more could be learned by studying successful and unsuccessful cases than by investigating clients who had certain diagnostic labels. Several studies of clients' own explanations of the change process found evidence for both common and specific factors (e.g., Glass & Arnkoff, 1988).

The National Institute of Mental Health sponsored a conference that delineated directions for research on psychotherapy integration (Wolfe & Goldfried, 1988). Among the many recommendations that grew out of the conference, it was suggested that the availability of therapy tapes and transcripts would greatly facilitate research on the process of change and how it relates to different theoretical orientations. Moreover, it was concluded that psychopathology research was essential to the complete understanding of how change occurred.

Using transcripts and audiotapes of actual therapy sessions, a program of psychotherapy process research that compared what took place in psychodynamic and cognitive–behavioral interventions was carried out by Goldfried and his colleagues (e.g., Goldsamt, Goldfried, Hayes, & Kerr, 1989; Kerr, Goldfried, Hayes, & Goldsamt, 1989). Using a theoretically neutral coding system, points of similarity and difference between these two orientations emerged.

One of the common factors between psychodynamic and cognitive–behavioral approaches highlighted in the 1980s was the centrality of the therapy relationship. In her dialectical behavior therapy for the treatment of borderline personality disorder, Linehan (1987; see also Chapter 121, this volume) described the therapy relationship as being a key component of the treatment. An interesting article (Westen, 1988) conceptualized transference in terms of information-processing theory, a language that could readily be understood by cognitive–behavior therapists. Psychotherapists of diverse orientations were increasingly identifying—and researching—the therapeutic relationship as a pantheoretical, curative factor.

Mahrer (1989), in *The Integration of Psychotherapies*, described what was needed to teach, practice, and carry out research on an integrated approach.

An article appearing in the *American Journal of Psychiatry* by Beitman, Goldfried, and Norcross (1989) emphasized that "prescriptive treatment [could be] based primarily on patient need and empirical evidence rather than on theoretical predisposition" (p. 141). Research on this issue was carried out in Sheffield, England, where researchers found that sequencing clients from a psychodynamic to a cognitive–behavioral approach worked better than an approach that used the reverse order (Barkham, Shapiro, & Firth-Cozens, 1989).

Finally, Wolfe (1989) published one of his first articles on the integrative treatment of anxiety, which he would continue to develop over the next 15 years. During our interview, he recalled that he

> systematically tried on each of the three major schools of psychotherapy, in succession. It may surprise you to learn that during undergraduate school I was a rather dogmatic Skinnerian. That was after some flirtation with the psychoanalytic point of view. By the time I had my fill of the behavioral point of view at Illinois, I began to look at the Rogerian and other humanistically oriented points of view as an alternative to perceived limitations of both behaviorism and psychoanalysis. And after, again, an initial, almost convert-like reaction, I began to see real limitations to the humanistic approach, and at that point I had to ask myself, "Well, maybe there was something of value in each of the perspective that I tried to live out." . . . I began to wonder whether or not—if you could combine exposure therapy for the phobic symptoms themselves with some gestalt-dynamic-cognitive-oriented treatments to deal with the conflicts that seem connected—whether you wouldn't get a more durable and longer-lasting response in the treatment of phobias and panic. . . . I keep waiting to get hit by a two-by-four, and so far it has not happened. (B. E. Wolfe, personal communication, November 20, 1989)

THE 1990s

During the 1990s, the integration movement began to have a very definite impact on mainstream psychotherapy. Even those professionals not particularly interested in integration recognized that *integration* and *integrative* were good things with which to identify. A clear indicator of this was the increase in the number of books, chapters, and articles that used the term *integrative* in their titles—even if the material described was only remotely related to integration. A survey of four mental health professions found that a majority of respondents in each profession (ranging from 59% of psychiatrists to 72% of marital and family therapists) described themselves as eclectic, although the mix of orientations combined differed across the professions (Jensen, Bergin, & Greaves, 1990).

Although the integration of psychoanalytic and behavioral interventions had been occurring for decades, the shift in psychoanalytic circles toward a relational focus made it even easier to link interpersonal and cognitive–behavioral therapies. Safran and Segal (1990) clearly illustrated this in their book *Interpersonal Process in Cognitive Therapy*. Following up on his earlier work, Ryle (1990) published *Cognitive-Analytic Therapy: Active Participation in Change*, in which he offered a model of interventions that combines elements of psychodynamic, behavioral, and cognitive approaches. Guidelines for how to combine treatment approaches were outlined by Beutler and Clarkin (1990), taking into account such factors as client and therapy relationship variables. An interesting debate took place between Lazarus (1990) and Beitman (1990), presenting their respective views on eclectic and common-factor approaches to integration. And research continued on the common factors proposed by those advocating this approach to integration (Grencavage & Norcross, 1990).

In 1991, two particularly important books were published on integration. One was a revision of the classic work *Persuasion and Healing* (Frank & Frank, 1991), and the other was *Human Change Processes: The Scientific Foundations of Psychotherapy* (Mahoney, 1991), which provided a comprehensive analysis of how change occurred. Another significant event in 1991 was the founding of the *Journal of Psychotherapy Integration*, with Arkowitz as the first editor. The official publication of SEPI, the journal provided a dedicated forum for work on psychotherapy integration. The first edition of the present book (Freedheim, 1992) contained two chapters on the history of integration during the 20th century, one covering theory (Arkowitz, 1992) and the other covering practice (Arnkoff & Glass, 1992).

Several volumes appeared that were specifically devoted to a review of what had been happening in psychotherapy integration. The first edition of Norcross and Goldfried's (1992) edited *Handbook of Psychotherapy Integration* provided a comprehensive review of past and current work on integration. Dryden's (1992) edited *Integrative and Eclectic Therapy: A Handbook* included an overview of the work that had been done in the United Kingdom over the previous 25 years. In the following year, Stricker and Gold (1993) edited the volume *Comprehensive Handbook of Psychotherapy Integration*, to which a number of individuals actively working on integration contributed.

In the 1990s, more research on integration began to appear. For example, findings detailed both similarities and differences in psychodynamic and cognitive–behavioral therapies (Jones & Pulos, 1993). Comparative process analyses between these two orientations also looked specifically at the therapy alliance (Raue, Castonguay, & Goldfried, 1993) and clients' emotional experiencing (Wiser & Goldfried, 1993). Another example is Linehan's (1993) now classic book on dialectical behavior therapy—an integrative approach that has received considerable clinical and research attention.

Goldfried's (1995) book *From Cognitive-Behavior Therapy to Psychotherapy Integration* traced his involvement in the development of cognitive–behavioral approaches and its eventual implications for therapy integration. Davison (1995), an important figure in the history of cognitive–behavior therapy, similarly offered a personal and professional account of the past 20 years of his career. He elaborated on the therapeutic benefits of taking a broader therapeutic approach and discussed how his early cases may have had better outcomes if such a perspective had been taken.

In the manual for his Cognitive–Behavioral Analytic System of Psychotherapy, McCullough (1995) outlined an integrative treatment of chronic depression, which was later expanded into a book (McCullough, 2000) that detailed this clinically sophisticated integration of behavioral, cognitive, and interpersonal approaches, together with empirical findings that attested to its efficacy. Another important contribution to integration in 1995 was Pinsof's *Integrative Problem-Centered Therapy*, which involves a combination of clinical aspects of individual, family, and biological approaches to intervention.

During this decade, a number of publications attested to the international scope of integration. Approximately 87% of counselors in the United Kingdom could be characterized as integrative (Hollanders & McLeod, 1999). Reporting from the Netherlands (Trijsburg, Colijn, Collumbien, & Lietaer, 1998), South Africa (Eagle, 1998), Italy (Carere-Comes, 1999; Giusti, Montanari, & Montanarella, 1995), Germany (Christoph-Lemke, 1999), Spain (Caro, 1998), Argentina (Fernández-Alvarez, 1992), and Chile (Opazo, 1992, 1997), a number of professionals all described the involvement in integrative approaches in their countries.

Although the situation would begin to change just a few years later (see the next section), research on integration seriously lagged behind the work that had been done on theory and practice (Glass, Arnkoff, & Rodriquez, 1998). Acknowledging that some integrative therapies had been based on research findings, they argued that research was nonetheless needed to demonstrate their efficacy and effectiveness.

With the growing emphasis on evidence-based practice, some observers predicted that theoretical orientations might give way to interventions that have been shown to work and that these approaches are more likely to look integrative than like pure theory therapies (e.g., Smith, 1999). One such evidence-based model was described by Beitman and Yue (1999). Interestingly enough, this recognition that empirical findings about efficacy and effectiveness can form the basis of psychotherapy integration echoes the earlier writings (e.g., Beutler, 1983; Garfield, 1957; Thorne,

1950) and was later extended by Castonguay and Beutler (2006), who advocated viewing psychotherapy in terms of empirically based principles of change.

The end of the century found integrative therapies well established in the theoretical literature and in training programs, with the favored theories having evolved over time. The typical combinations in the late 1970s were psychoanalytic–behavioral and humanistic–behavioral; in the late 1980s, the most popular hybrids involved interpersonal and cognitive therapy; and in the early 2000s, cognitive therapy dominated the list of combinations (Norcross, Karpiak, & Lister, 2005). The relative popularity of constituent elements of integrative therapies closely parallels theoretical orientations in general.

OUTCOME RESEARCH ON PSYCHOTHERAPY INTEGRATION

Fortunately, more and more outcome studies are now available to guide clinicians interested in evidence-based practice of integrative–eclectic therapy, and integration is widely believed by experienced clinicians to improve the effectiveness of psychotherapy (Wolfe, 2001). One of the inherent difficulties in reviewing this outcome literature is the wide variety of ways in which therapists integrate, and we have chosen to organize approaches with empirical support by distinguishing among four types of psychotherapy integration (for a review, see Schottenbauer, Glass, & Arnkoff [2005]).

A variety of therapies have been developed within the framework of a particular system of psychotherapy, in which *assimilative integration* (Messer, 2001) consists of supplementing that primary therapy with specific techniques from other systems of psychotherapy. Those with the most empirical support are mindfulness-based cognitive therapy for depression (Segal, Williams, & Teasdale, 2002) and emotionally focused couples therapy (Greenberg & Johnson, 1988), but others of note include emotion-focused therapy (Greenberg, 2002), integrative cognitive therapy for depression (Castonguay et al., 2004), and functional analytic psychotherapy (Kohlenberg & Tsai, 1991).

We call *sequential and parallel-concurrent integration* those approaches in which separate forms of therapy (e.g., cognitive–behavioral and interpersonal) are given either in sequential order or during the same phase of treatment in separate sessions or separate sections of the same therapy session. The Sheffield Psychotherapy Project (Barkham et al., 1989) and cognitive–behavioral therapy and interpersonal–emotional processing therapy for generalized anxiety disorder (Newman, Castonguay, Borkovec, & Molnar, 2004) are examples of empirically investigated interventions.

Although *theoretical integration* has been defined in a variety of ways, our focus on theoretically driven integration consists of approaches in which a clear theory guides the choice of interventions, which may include techniques from one or more systems of psychotherapy. At least five examples of theoretically driven integration have received substantial empirical support: the transtheoretical model (Prochaska & DiClemente, 1984), acceptance and commitment therapy (Hayes, Strosahl, & Wilson, 1999), cognitive-analytic therapy (Ryle & Kerr, 2002), dialectical behavior therapy (Linehan, 1993), and multisystemic therapy (Henggeler, Schoenwald, Borduin, Rowland, & Cunningham, 1998). Other theoretically driven integrative therapies with empirical support include brief relational therapy (Safran, Muran, Samstag, & Stevens, 2002), Cognitive–Behavioral Analysis System of Psychotherapy (McCullough, 2000), and developmental counseling and therapy (Ivey, 2000).

Finally, a fourth type of psychotherapy integration is *technical eclecticism*, which has typically been defined as the use of psychotherapy techniques without regard to their theoretical origins (Lazarus, 1967) and which is often systematic in the choice of interventions. Several systems of client–treatment matching have been developed with the aim of improving therapy outcome, and Beutler and Harwood's (2000) systematic treatment selection has strong empirical support. Lazarus's (1997) multimodal therapy is probably one of the most widely known systems of eclectic psychotherapy, although less outcome research has evaluated its effectiveness.

We believe it vital to conduct research in the future on prominent integrative therapies that have not been subject to research (e.g., P. L. Wachtel, 1997), to investigate principles of change and common factors (Castonguay & Beutler, 2006; Norcross, 2002), and to examine the effectiveness of psychotherapy integration as it is carried out by clinicians in their usual practice to glean the principles of decision making.

WHY THE MOVEMENT TOWARD PSYCHOTHERAPY INTEGRATION?

Ideas and concepts in psychology develop slowly over the course of years, often depending on—and also changing—the zeitgeist. As can be seen from our review of the historical contributions to psychotherapy integration, involving writings on the topic that began in the early part of the 20th century, it took several decades before this literature made any impact. In addressing the question of why the latent theme of integration eventually developed into an ongoing movement, Norcross (2005) enumerated a number of factors that have probably contributed to this growing interest:

- the proliferation of different schools of therapy led to increasing confusion within the field, creating a need to reduce this fragmentation;
- practicing clinicians began to recognize—like Neils Bohr, whom we quoted at the outset of this chapter—that human behavior and the change process were far too complicated to be understood by any single theoretical approach;
- as managed care began to exert its influence on the practice of therapy, there was increasing pressure for the field to reach some consensus, preferably based on empirical finds of what worked for whom;
- with greater understanding of specific clinical problems came an emphasis on specialization, with professionals eager to draw on whatever could be used to address the clinical problem at hand;
- the available therapies became more clearly specified and readily observable to practitioners, in the form of workshops, videotapes, and therapy manuals;
- the discussions in the field about commonalities across the therapies were used to help understand those research findings that failed to find differences between different orientations; and
- the formation of a professional organization—SEPI—brought together those researchers and clinicians who had become interested in psychotherapy integration and constituted a network that would encourage others to recognize the advantage of not being limited by a single orientation.

SEPI started when Strupp (a psychodynamicist) and Goldfried (a cognitive–behaviorist) compiled a list of professionals whom they knew to be interested in rapprochement across the orientations. Goldfried began to meet with Wachtel (a psychodynamicist) to discuss the topic of integration and what could be done to further this latent issue. In 1982, the informal list of names had increased to 162 professionals, and Goldfried and Wachtel decided to poll them to ask what they thought a next step should be.

On the basis of the responses to the survey, it was clear that a newsletter was in order. Regarding the formation of an organization, some concerns were expressed, stating that it was important to encourage informal interaction and dialogue. In discussing this meeting of the Organizing Committee,

Goldfried and Wachtel (1983) reported, "It was concluded that we needed to achieve a delicate balance: a formal organization that would facilitate informal contacts among the members" (p. 3). SEPI has since grown into an interdisciplinary organization of international scope.

INTO THE FUTURE

As indicated at the outset of the chapter, we conclude this historical review with the end of the 20th century. Efforts to expand and deepen psychotherapy integration have continued to evolve since then. With the exception of those who continue to create schools of thought that they believe can encompass everything we are likely to see clinically, the field has become increasingly skeptical of finding any one psychotherapy that can deal with all psychological and relational problems. Indeed, the zeitgeist has changed since French stood before his colleagues in 1932 and hypothesized about the integration of Freud's and Pavlov's contributions. We have moved to a point where "an idea too strange or preposterous to be thought in one period [is now] accepted as true" (Boring, 1950, p. 3). We believe that clinical and research efforts in the 21st century will contribute to the further evolution of psychotherapy integration.

The vast majority of work that has been done on the topic of psychotherapy integration up until now has been theoretical and clinical in nature. Indeed, this originally characterized psychotherapy in general, with research efforts entering the field only during the second half of the 20th century. Within the past several decades, there has been a very clear emphasis on the need to demonstrate empirically that therapy works, and when it does, how it does. Although theoretical debates continue to exist, the shift has been in the direction of empirical evidence.

As we have indicated throughout this chapter, many of those interested in psychotherapy integration have argued for an empirical approach to integration, and indeed there has been an increase in research to demonstrate that integrated interventions have merit. With psychotherapy moving toward evidence-based practice, it is very likely that this will become more of the organizing force for integration. In essence, empirical pragmatism, not theory, will be the integrative theme of the 21st century.

The increasing emphasis on evidenced-based practice, which is informed by both research findings and clinical expertise, will probably extend the work on integration that has been done in the 20th century and move the field toward consensus. We anticipate that new generations of mental health professionals, whose initial psychotherapy training has occurred in a world in which integration is accepted and even encouraged on the basis of empirical evidence, will integrate effortlessly. In so doing, they will make increasingly important and exciting contributions to the field.

RECOMMENDED RESOURCES

Society for the Exploration of Psychotherapy Integration (SEPI): http://www.sepiweb.org

Beitman, B. D., & Yue, D. (1999). *Learning psychotherapy: A time-efficient, research-based and outcome-measured psychotherapy training program.* New York, NY: Norton.

Beutler, L. E., & Harwood, T. M. (2000). *Prescriptive psychotherapy: A practical guide to systematic treatment selection.* New York, NY: Oxford University Press.

Castonguay, L. G., & Beutler, L. E. (Eds.). (2006). *Principles of therapeutic change that work.* New York, NY: Oxford University Press.

Norcross, J. C., & Goldfried, M. R. (Eds.). (2005). *Handbook of psychotherapy integration* (2nd ed.). New York, NY: Oxford University Press.

Stricker, G., & Gold, J. R. (Eds.). (1993). *Comprehensive handbook of psychotherapy integration.* New York, NY: Plenum Press.

Wachtel, P. L. (1997). *Psychoanalysis, behavior therapy, and the relational world.* Washington, DC: American Psychological Association.

REFERENCES

Alexander, F. (1963). The dynamics of psychotherapy in light of learning theory. *American Journal of Psychiatry, 120,* 440–448.

Arkowitz, H. (1992). Integrative theories of therapy. In D. K. Freedheim (Ed.), *History of psychotherapy: A century of change* (pp. 261–303). Washington, DC: American Psychological Association.

Arkowitz, H., & Messer, S. B. (Eds.). (1984). *Psychoanalytic and behavior therapy: Is integration possible?* New York, NY: Plenum.

Arnkoff, D. B. (1981). Flexibility in practicing cognitive therapy. In G. Emery, S. D. Hollon, & R. C. Bedrosian (Eds.), *New directions in cognitive therapy* (pp. 203–223). New York, NY: Guilford Press.

Arnkoff, D. B., & Glass, C. R. (1992). Cognitive therapy and psychotherapy integration. In D. K. Freedheim (Ed.), *History of psychotherapy: A century of change* (1st ed., pp. 657–694). Washington, DC: American Psychological Association.

Barkham, M., Shapiro, D. A., & Firth-Cozens, J. (1989). Personal questionnaire changes in prescriptive vs. exploratory psychotherapy. *British Journal of Clinical Psychology, 28,* 97–107.

Beitman, B. D. (1987). *The structure of individual psychotherapy.* New York, NY: Guilford Press.

Beitman, B. D. (1990). Why I am an integrationist (not an eclectic). In W. Dryden & J. C. Norcross (Eds.), *Eclecticism and integration in counseling and psychotherapy* (pp. 51–70). Loughton, England: Gale Centre.

Beitman, B. D., Goldfried, M. R., & Norcross, J. C. (1989). The movement toward integrating the psychotherapies: An overview. *American Journal of Psychiatry, 146,* 138–147.

Beitman, B. D., & Yue, D. (1999). *Learning psychotherapy: A time-efficient, research-based and outcome-measured psychotherapy training program.* New York, NY: Norton.

Bergin, A. E. (1969). Technique for improving desensitization via warmth, empathy, and emotional re-experiencing of hierarchy events. In R. D. Rubin & C. M. Franks (Eds.), *Advances in behavior therapy, 1968* (pp. 117–130). New York, NY: Academic Press.

Bergin, A. E. (1970). Cognitive therapy and behavior therapy: Foci for a multidimensional approach to treatment. *Behavior Therapy, 1*, 205–212. doi:10.1016/S0005-7894(70)80032-6

Bergin, A. E. (1988). Three contributions of the spiritual perspective to counseling, psychotherapy and behavior change. *Counseling and Values, 32*, 21–31.

Beutler, L. E. (1983). *Eclectic psychotherapy: A systematic approach*. Elmsford, NY: Pergamon Press.

Beutler, L. E., & Clarkin, J. F. (1990). *Systematic treatment selection: Toward targeted therapeutic interventions*. Philadelphia: Brunner/Mazel.

Beutler, L. E., & Harwood, T. M. (2000). *Prescriptive psychotherapy: A practical guide to systematic treatment selection*. New York, NY: Oxford University Press.

Birk, L. (1970). Behavior therapy: Integration with dynamic psychiatry. *Behavior Therapy, 1*, 522–526. doi:10.1016/S0005-7894(70)80076-4

Birk, L., & Brinkley-Birk, A. (1974). Psychoanalysis and behavior therapy. *American Journal of Psychiatry, 131*, 499–510.

Boring, E. G. (1950). *A history of experimental psychology* (Rev. ed.). New York, NY: Appleton-Century-Crofts.

Brady, J. P., Davison, G. C., Dewald, P. A., Egan, G., Fadiman, J., Frank, J. D., . . . Strupp, H. H. (1980). Some views on effective principles of psychotherapy. *Cognitive Therapy and Research, 4*, 271–306.

Carere-Comes, T. (1999). Beyond psychotherapy: Dialectical therapy. *Journal of Psychotherapy Integration, 9*, 365–396. doi:10.1023/A:1023295311832

Caro, I. (1998). Integration of cognitive psychotherapies: Vive la difference! Right now. *Journal of Cognitive Psychotherapy, 12*, 67–76.

Castonguay, L. G., & Beutler, L. E. (Eds.). (2006). *Principles of therapeutic change that work*. New York, NY: Oxford University Press.

Castonguay, L. G., Schut, A. J., Aikins, D. E., Constantino, M. J., Laurenceau, J. P., Bologh, L., & Burns, D. D. (2004). Integrative cognitive therapy for depression: A preliminary investigation. *Journal of Psychotherapy Integration, 14*, 4–20. doi:10.1037/1053-0479.14.1.4

Christoph-Lemke, C. (1999). The contributions of transactional analysis to integrative psychotherapy. *Transactional Analysis Journal, 29*, 198–214.

Davison, G. C. (1995). A failure of early behavior therapy (circa 1966): or why I learned to stop worrying and to embrace psychotherapy integration. *Journal of Psychotherapy Integration, 5*, 107–112.

Dollard, J., & Miller, N. E. (1950). *Personality and psychotherapy*. New York, NY: McGraw-Hill.

New York, NY:Dryden, W. (Ed.). (1992). *Integrative and eclectic therapy: A handbook*. Buckingham, England: Open University Press.

Eagle, G. T. (1998). An integrative model for brief term intervention in the treatment of psychological trauma. *International Journal of Psychotherapy, 3*, 135–146.

Egan, G. (1975). *The skilled helper*. Monterey, CA: Brooks/Cole.

Feather, B. W., & Rhoads, J. M. (1972). Psychodynamic behavior therapy: II. Clinical aspects. *Archives of General Psychiatry, 26*, 503–511.

Feldman, L. B. (1989). Integrating individual and family therapy. *Journal of Integrative and Eclectic Psychotherapy, 8*, 41–52.

Fenichel, O. (1941). *Problems of psychoanalytic technique*. Albany, NY: Psychoanalytic Quarterly Press.

Fernández-Alvarez, H. (1992). *Fundamentos de un modelo integrativo en psicoterapia* [Fundamentals of an integrative model of psychotherapy]. Buenos Aires, Argentina: Paidós.

Frank, J. D. (1961). *Persuasion and healing*. Baltimore: Johns Hopkins University Press.

Frank, J. D., & Frank, J. B. (1991). *Persuasion and healing: A comparative study of psychotherapy*. Baltimore: Johns Hopkins University Press.

Freedheim, D. K. (Ed.). (1992). *History of psychotherapy: A century of change.* Washington, DC: American Psychological Association.

French, T. M. (1933). Interrelations between psychoanalysis and the experimental work of Pavlov. *American Journal of Psychiatry, 89,* 1165–1203.

Garfield, S. L. (1957). *Introductory clinical psychology.* New York, NY: MacMillan.

Garfield, S. L. (1980). *Psychotherapy: An eclectic approach.* New York, NY: Wiley.

Garfield, S. L., & Kurtz, R. (1976). Clinical psychologists in the 1970s. *American Psychologist, 31,* 1–9. doi:10.1037/0003-066X.31.1.1

Giusti, E., Montanari, C., & Montanarella, G. (1995). *Manuale di psicoterapia integrate* [Handbook of integrated psychotherapy]. Milano: FrancoAngeli.

Glass, C. R., & Arnkoff, D. B. (1988). Common and specific factors in client descriptions of and explanations for change. *Journal of Integrative and Eclectic Psychotherapy, 7,* 427–440.

Glass, C. R., Arnkoff, D. B., & Rodriquez, B. F. (1998). An overview of directions in psychotherapy integration research. *Journal of Psychotherapy Integration, 8,* 187–209.

Goldfried, M. R. (1980). Toward the delineation of therapeutic change principles. *American Psychologist, 35,* 991–999.

Goldfried, M. R. (Ed.). (1982). *Converging themes in psychotherapy: Trends in psychodynamic, humanistic, and behavioral practice.* New York, NY: Springer.

Goldfried, M. R. (1995). *From cognitive-behavior therapy to psychotherapy integration: An evolving view.* New York, NY: Springer.

Goldfried, M. R., & Davison, G. C. (1976). *Clinical behavior therapy.* New York, NY: Holt, Rinehart & Winston.

Goldfried, M. R., Pachankis, J. E., and Bell, A. C. (2005). A history of integration. In J. C. Norcross & M. R. Goldfried (Eds.), *Handbook of Psychotherapy Integration* (2nd ed., pp. 24–60) New York, NY: Oxford University Press.

Goldfried, M. R., & Safran, J. D. (1986). Future directions in psychotherapy integration. In J. C. Norcross (Ed.), *Handbook of eclectic psychotherapy* (pp. 463–483). New York, NY: Brunner/Mazel.

Goldfried, M. R., & Wachtel, P. L. (1983). *Newsletter of the Society for the Exploration of Psychotherapy Integration, 1,* 1–16.

Goldsamt, L., Goldfried, M. R., Hayes, A. M., & Kerr, S. (1989, April). *A comparison of three psychotherapies on the dimension of therapist feedback.* Paper presented at the annual meeting of the Society for the Exploration of Psychotherapy Integration, Berkeley, CA. (Subsequently published as Goldsamt, L. A., Goldfried, M. R., Hayes, A. M., & Kerr, S. [1992]. Beck, Meichenbaum, and Strupp: A comparison of three therapies on the dimension of therapist feedback. *Psychotherapy, 29,* 167–176.)

Goldschmid, M. L., Stein, D. D., Weissman, H. N., & Sorrells, J. (1969). A survey of the training and practices of clinical psychologists. *Clinical Psychologist, 22*(Winter), 89–94, 107.

Greenberg, L. S. (2002). *Emotion-focused therapy: Coaching clients to work through their feelings.* Washington, DC: American Psychological Association.

Greenberg, L. S., & Johnson, S. M. (1988). *Emotionally focused therapy for couples.* New York, NY: Guilford Press.

Grencavage, L. M., & Norcross, J. C. (1990). Where are the commonalities among the therapeutic common factors? *Professional Psychology: Research and Practice, 21,* 372–378.

Guidano, V. F. (1987). *Complexity of the self: A developmental approach to psychotherapy and theory.* New York, NY: Guilford Press.

Guidano, V. F., & Liotti, G. (1983). *Cognitive processes and emotional disorders: A structural approach to psychotherapy.* New York, NY: Guilford Press.

Gurman, A. S. (1981). Integrative marital therapy: Toward the development of an interpersonal approach. In S. H. Budman (Ed.), *Forms of brief therapy* (pp. 415–457). New York, NY: Guilford Press.

Halgin, R. P. (1985). Teaching integration of psychotherapy models to beginning therapists. *Psychotherapy, 22,* 555–563.

Hayes, S. C., Strosahl, K. D., & Wilson, K. G. (1999). *Acceptance and commitment therapy: An experiential approach to behavior change.* New York, NY: Guilford Press.

Henggeler, S. W., Schoenwald, S. K., Borduin, C. M., Rowland, M. D., & Cunningham, P. B. (1998). *Multisystemic treatment of antisocial behavior in children and adolescents.* New York, NY: Guilford Press.

Herzberg, A. (1945). *Active psychotherapy.* New York, NY: Grune & Stratton.

Hollanders, H., & McLeod, J. (1999). Theoretical orientation and reported practice: A survey of eclecticism among counsellors in Britain. *British Journal of Guidance & Counselling, 27,* 405–414.

Horwitz, L. (1976). New perspectives for psychoanalytic psychotherapy. *Bulletin of the Menninger Clinic, 40,* 263–271.

Ivey, A. (2000). *Developmental therapy.* Amherst, MA: Microtraining Associates.

Jensen, J. P., Bergin, A. E., & Greaves, D. W. (1990). The meaning of eclecticism: New survey and analysis of components. *Professional Psychology: Research and Practice, 21,* 124–130.

Jones, E. E., & Pulos, S. M. (1993). Comparing the process in psychodynamic and cognitive–behavioral therapies. *Journal of Consulting and Clinical Psychology, 61,* 306–316.

Kaplan, H. S. (1974). *The new sex therapy.* New York, NY: Brunner/Mazel.

Kelly, E. L. (1961). Clinical psychology—1960: Report of survey findings. *Newsletter: Division of Clinical Psychology of the American Psychological Association, 14,* 1–11.

Kerr, S., Goldfried, M. R., Hayes, A. M., & Goldsamt, L. (1989, June). *Differences in therapeutic focus in an interpersonal-psychodynamic and cognitive-behavioral therapy.* Paper presented at the Society for Psychotherapy Research, Toronto. [Subsequently published as: Kerr, S., Goldfried, M. R., Hayes, A. M., Castonguay, L. G., & Goldsamt, L. A. (1992). Interpersonal and intrapersonal focus in cognitive-behavioral and psychodynamic-interpersonal therapies: A preliminary analysis of the Sheffield Project. *Psychotherapy Research, 2,* 266–276.]

Kohlenberg, R. J., & Tsai, M. (1991). *Functional analytic psychotherapy: Creating intense and curative therapeutic relationships.* New York, NY: Plenum.

Kubie, L. S. (1934). Relation of the conditioned reflex to psychoanalytic technic. *Archives of Neurology and Psychiatry, 32,* 1137–1142.

Lazarus, A. A. (1967). In support of technical eclecticism. *Psychological Reports, 21,* 415–416.

Lazarus, A. A. (1976). *Multimodal behavior therapy.* New York, NY: Springer.

Lazarus, A. A. (1977). Has behavior therapy outlived its usefulness? *American Psychologist, 32,* 550–554.

Lazarus, A. A. (1990). Why I am an eclectic (not an integrationist). In W. Dryden & J. C. Norcross (Eds.), *Eclecticism and integration in counseling and psychotherapy* (pp. 34–50). Loughton, England: Gale Centre.

Lazarus, A. A. (1997). *Brief but comprehensive psychotherapy: The multimodal way.* New York, NY: Springer.

Lebow, J. L. (1984). On the value of integrating approaches to family therapy. *Journal of Marital and Family Therapy, 10,* 127–138.

Lecomte, C., & Castonguay, L. G. (Eds.). (1987). *Rapprochement et integration en psychotherapie* [Rapprochement and integration in psychotherapy: Psychoanalysis, behaviorism, and humanism]. Montreal: Gaetan Morin Editeur.

Linehan, M. M. (1987). Dialectical behavioral therapy: A cognitive-behavioral approach to parasuicide. *Journal of Personality Disorders, 1*, 328–333.

Linehan, M. M. (1993). *Cognitive-behavioral treatment of borderline personality disorder*. New York, NY: Guilford Press.

London, P. (1964). *The modes and morals of psychotherapy*. New York, NY: Holt, Rinehart & Winston.

London, P. (1972). The end of ideology in behavior modification. *American Psychologist, 27*, 913–920.

Lubin, B. (1962). Survey of psychotherapy training and activities of psychologists. *Journal of Clinical Psychology, 18*, 252–256.

Mahoney, M. J. (1979). Cognitive and non-cognitive views in behavior modification. In P.-O. Sjödén, S. Bates, & W. S. Dockens III (Eds.), *Trends in behavior therapy* (pp. 39–54). New York, NY: Academic Press.

Mahoney, M. J. (1980). Psychotherapy and the structure of personal revolutions. In M. J. Mahoney (Ed.), *Psychotherapy process* (pp. 157–180). New York, NY: Plenum.

Mahoney, M. J. (1991). *Human change processes: The scientific foundations of psychotherapy*. New York, NY: Basic Books.

Mahoney, M. J. (1993). Diversity and dynamics of development in psychotherapy integration. *Journal of Psychotherapy Integration, 3*, 1–13.

Mahrer, A. R. (1989). *The integration of psychotherapies*. New York, NY: Human Sciences Press.

Marmor, J. (1971). Dynamic psychotherapy and behavior therapy: Are they irreconcilable? *Archives of General Psychiatry, 24*, 22–28.

Marmor, J., & Woods, S. M. (Eds.). (1980). *The interface between psychodynamic and behavioral therapies*. New York, NY: Plenum.

Martin, C. G. (1972). *Learning-based client-centered therapy*. Monterey, CA: Brooks/Cole.

McCullough, J. P. (1995) *Manual for Cognitive Behavioral Analytic System of Psychotherapy (CBASP)*. Richmond: Virginia Commonwealth University.

McCullough, J. P. (2000). *Treatments for chronic depression: Cognitive Behavior Analysis System of Psychotherapy (CBASP)*. New York, NY: Guilford Press.

Messer, S. B. (1986). Behavioral and psychoanalytic perspectives at therapeutic choice points. *American Psychologist, 41*, 1261–1272.

Messer, S. B. (2001). Introduction to the special issue on assimilative integration. *Journal of Psychotherapy Integration, 11*, 1–19.

Messer, S. B. & Winokur, M. (1980). Some limits to the integration of psychoanalytic and behavior therapy. *American Psychologist, 35*, 818–827.

Newman, M. G., Castonguay, L. G., Borkovec, T. D., & Molnar, C. (2004). Integrative psychotherapy. In R. G. Heimberg, C. L. Turk, & D. S. Mennin (Eds.), *Generalized anxiety disorders: Advances in research and practice* (pp. 320–350). New York, NY: Guilford Press.

Norcross, J. C. (Ed.). (1986a). *Handbook of eclectic psychotherapy*. New York, NY: Brunner/Mazel.

Norcross, J. C. (Ed.). (1986b). Training integrative/eclectic psychotherapists [Special section]. *International Journal of Eclectic Psychotherapy, 5*, 71–94.

Norcross, J. C. (Ed.). (1987). *Casebook of eclectic psychotherapy*. New York, NY: Brunner/Mazel.

Norcross, J. C. (1997). Emerging breakthroughs in psychotherapy integration: Three predictions and one fantasy. *Psychotherapy: Theory, Research, Practice, Training, 34*, 86–90.

Norcross, J. C. (Ed.). (2002). *Psychotherapy relationships that work*. New York, NY: Oxford University Press.

Norcross, J. C. (2005). A primer on psychotherapy integration. In J. C. Norcross & M. R. Goldfried (Eds.), *Handbook of psychotherapy integration* (2nd ed., pp. 3–23). New York, NY: Oxford University Press.

Norcross, J. C., & Goldfried, M. R. (Eds.). (1992). *Handbook of psychotherapy integration*. New York, NY: Basic Books.

Norcross, J. C., & Goldfried, M. R. (Eds.). (2005). *Handbook of psychotherapy integration* (2nd ed.). New York, NY: Oxford University Press.

Norcross, J. C., & Grencavage, L. M. (1989). Eclecticism and integration in counselling and psychotherapy: Major themes and obstacles. *British Journal of Guidance and Counselling, 17*, 227–247.

Norcross, J. C., Karpiak, C. P., & Lister, K. M. (2005). What's an integrationist? A study of self-identified integrative and (occasionally) eclectic psychologists. *Journal of Clinical Psychology, 61*, 1587–1594.

Norcross, J. C., & Prochaska, J. O. (1988). A study of eclectic (and integrative) views revisited. *Professional Psychology: Research and Practice, 19*, 170–174.

Opazo, R. (Ed.). (1992). *Integración en psicoterapia* [Integration within psychotherapy]. Santiago, Chile: Ediciones CECIDEP.

Opazo, R. (1997). In the hurricane's eye: A supraparadigmatic integrative model. *Journal of Psychotherapy Integration, 7*, 17–54.

Pinsof, W. M. (1995). *Integrative problem-centered therapy: A synthesis of family, individual and biological therapies*. New York, NY: Basic Books.

Prochaska, J. O. (1979). *Systems of psychotherapy: A transtheoretical analysis*. Homewood, IL: Dorsey.

Prochaska, J. O., & DiClemente, C. C. (1984). *The transtheoretical approach: Crossing the traditional boundaries of therapy*. Homewood, IL: Dow Jones-Irwin.

Raimy, V. (1975). *Misunderstandings of the self*. San Francisco: Jossey-Bass.

Raue, P. J., Castonguay, L. G., & Goldfried, M. R. (1993). The working alliance: A comparison of two therapies. *Psychotherapy Research, 3*, 197–207.

Rogers, C. R. (1963). Psychotherapy today or where do we go from here? *American Journal of Psychotherapy, 17*, 5–15.

Rosenzweig, S. (1936). Some implicit common factors in diverse methods in psychotherapy. "At last the Dodo said, 'Everybody has won and all must have prizes.'" *American Journal of Orthopsychiatry, 6*, 412–415.

Ryle, A. (1982). *Psychotherapy: A cognitive integration of theory and practice*. London: Academic Press.

Ryle, A. (1990). *Cognitive-analytic therapy: Active participation in change*. Chichester, England: Wiley.

Ryle, A., & Kerr, I. B. (2002). *Introduction to cognitive-analytic therapy: Principles and practice*. New York, NY: Wiley.

Safran, J. D., Greenberg, L. S., & Rice, L. (1988). Integrating psychotherapy research and practice: Modeling the change process. *Psychotherapy, 25*, 1–17.

Safran, J. D., Muran, J. C., Samstag, L. W., & Stevens, C. (2002). Repairing alliance ruptures. In J. C. Norcross (Ed.), *Psychotherapy relationships that work* (pp. 235–254). New York, NY: Oxford University Press.

Safran, J. D., & Segal, Z. V. (1990). *Interpersonal process in cognitive therapy*. New York, NY: Basic Books.

Schottenbauer, M. A., Glass, C. R., & Arnkoff, D. B. (2005). Outcome research on psychotherapy integration. In J. C. Norcross & M. R. Goldfried (Eds.), *Handbook of psychotherapy integration* (2nd ed., pp. 459–493). New York, NY: Oxford University Press.

Segal, Z. V., Williams, J. M. G., & Teasdale, J. D. (2002). *Mindfulness-based cognitive therapy for depression: A new approach for preventing relapse*. New York, NY: Guilford Press.

Segraves, R. T. (1982). *Marital therapy: A combined psychodynamic–behavioral approach*. New York, NY: Plenum.

Shaffer, L. F. (1953). Of whose reality I cannot doubt. *American Psychologist, 8,* 608–623.

Smith, D. A. (1999). The end of theoretical orientations? *Applied and Preventive Psychology, 8,* 269–280.

Stricker, G., & Gold, J. R. (Eds.). (1993). *Comprehensive handbook of psychotherapy integration.* New York, NY: Plenum Press.

Strupp, H. H. (1973). On the basic ingredients of psychotherapy. *Journal of Consulting and Clinical Psychology, 41,* 1–8.

Textor, M. R. (Ed.). (1983). *Integrative psychotherapie.* Munich, Germany: Schobert.

Thorne, F. C. (1950). *Principles of personality counseling.* Brandon, VT: Journal of Clinical Psychology.

Trijsburg, R. W., Colijn, S., Collumbien, E. C. A, & Lietaer, G. (Eds.). (1998). *Dutch handbook of integrative psychotherapy.* Amsterdam: Elsevier.

Wachtel, E. F., & Wachtel, P. L. (1986). *Family dynamics in individual psychotherapy.* New York, NY: Guilford Press.

Wachtel, P. L. (1975). Behavior therapy and the facilitation of psychoanalytic exploration. *Psychotherapy: Theory, Research, and Practice, 12,* 68–72.

Wachtel, P. L. (1977). *Psychoanalysis and behavior therapy: Toward an integration.* New York, NY: Basic Books.

Wachtel, P. L. (Ed.). (1982). *Resistance: Psychodynamic and behavioral approaches.* New York, NY: Plenum.

Watson, G. (1940). Areas of agreement in psychotherapy. *American Journal of Orthopsychiatry, 10,* 698–709.

Weitzman, B. (1967). Behavior therapy and psychotherapy. *Psychological Review, 74,* 300–317.

Westen, D. (1988). Transference and information processing. *Clinical Psychology Review, 8,* 161–179.

Wiser, S. L., & Goldfried, M. R. (1993). A comparative study of emotional experiencing in psychodynamic–interpersonal and cognitive–behavioral therapies. *Journal of Consulting and Clinical Psychology, 61,* 892–895.

Wolfe, B. E. (1989). Phobias, panic, and psychotherapy integration. *Journal of Integrative and Eclectic Psychotherapy, 8,* 264–276.

Wolfe, B. E. (2001). A message to assimilative integrationists: It's time to become accommodative integrationists: A commentary. *Journal of Psychotherapy Integration, 11,* 123–131.

Wolfe, B. E., & Goldfried, M. R. (1988). Research on psychotherapy integration: Recommendations and conclusions from an NIMH workshop. *Journal of Consulting and Clinical Psychology, 56,* 448–451.

Woodworth, R. S. (1948). *Contemporary schools of psychology.* New York, NY: Ronald.

Woody, R. H. (1968). Toward a rationale for psychobehavioral therapy. *Archives of General Psychiatry, 19,* 197–204.

III

PSYCHOTHERAPY
RESEARCH

10

PSYCHOTHERAPY RESEARCH AND ITS ACHIEVEMENTS

MICHAEL J. LAMBERT

Psychotherapy research is an established branch of clinical research that is well documented in the highest quality psychological and medical journals. The earliest studies were published as far back as the 1920s, with an exponential rise in the number of studies since that time. By 1970, Meltzoff and Kornreich commented that it would take a person with the patience of Job and the mind of a bank auditor to summarize the accumulated research literature—and the decades since then have made mastering the material beyond even the keenest mind. Fortunately, the serious reader can access the five editions of the *Handbook of Psychotherapy and Behavior Change* (Bergin & Garfield, 1971, 1994 ; Garfield & Bergin, 1978, 1986; Lambert, 2004), serious compendia of psychotherapy research findings.

It is impossible in a mere chapter to discuss all of the achievements of the thousands of studies and decades of psychotherapy research that are now part of our history. As a consequence, I shall focus on those achievements that exerted the greatest relevance to practice and training. This focus is consistent with the major goals of psychotherapy research as an applied clinical science, namely, protecting and promoting the welfare of the client by identifying the principles and procedures that enhance positive outcomes. The research achievements are divided into two major categories: (a) those that have been attained directly in response to the goals of research and (b) those that are conceptual and methodological by-products of the research itself. Such a classification allows us to see how successful we have been in answering many of the questions we have asked and, at the same time, to examine the fortunate consequences of undertaking research.

ACHIEVEMENTS REFLECTED IN ANSWERS TO RESEARCH QUESTIONS

The discussion here is organized around questions of both historical and contemporary concern: Is psychotherapy effective? Is psychotherapy more effective than placebo controls? Are the effects of therapy enduring? Is one type of psychotherapy more effective than another type? What causes therapeutic effects? Are all patients helped by psychotherapy? Can psychotherapy research be used to improve client outcome? Do we know how to measure the effects of therapy?

The General Effects Question

The first question to be addressed in psychotherapy research is the general question of its effects: Is psychotherapy effective? Does psychotherapy help the client solve problems, reduce symptoms, and improve interpersonal functioning? Of course, these general questions were rarely the specific goal of any particular study. The specific questions addressed by researchers were connected to the specific therapy that they practiced. Is psychodynamic therapy effective? Is client-centered therapy effective? Literally thousands of studies have been directed at variations of the general effects question. Beginning in the 1930s and continuing through the 1960s, this was the question of importance. It was dealt with first in purely descriptive studies and later in quasi-experimental studies of patients who participated in any of a number of verbal psychotherapies.

Typical of this research was the Berlin Psychoanalytic Institute's report of their first 10 years of existence (Fenichel, 1930). The institute had 1,955 consultations (between 1920 and 1930), which led to the commencement of 721 analyses. At the time of the report, 363 patients had concluded treatment, while 241 terminated prematurely and 117 were still in analysis. Of those who had completed treatment, 47 were considered uncured, 116 were considered improved, 89 were considered very much improved, and 111 were considered cured. There are various ways of calculating the percentage of cases improved, depending on whether dropouts are included (they could be excluded, as one is interested in the effects of treatment, and dropouts were more or less untreated) and whether one considers those classified as "improved" as essentially equivalent to "much improved" and "cured." Reasonable estimates of outcome vary between 59% and 91% (see Bergin, 1971, for an extensive discussion). These rates of improvement are very similar to those obtained in contemporary treatments provided over much shorter durations.

A serious problem in this study (and similar single-group studies) is that although it allowed evaluation of the outcome of therapy as assessed by therapists and independent clinicians, it did not provide an estimate of change that might have occurred in patients with the passage of time. Many studies conducted in the ensuing years encountered the same problem, and those who were skeptical about the value of therapy were quick to point out that people who are disturbed and who do not undergo therapy also improve. In fact, Hans Eysenck (1952) published a challenging article in which he purported to show that the "spontaneous remission rate" in untreated patients was about two thirds, which was identical to the improvement rate for treated cases quoted by Fenichel and others who had published reports on psychotherapy outcome at the time. Eysenck's critical view did not go unchallenged and was ultimately refuted (e.g., Lambert, 1976). However, it was difficult to demonstrate the effects of therapy in those days because the usual research design did not include random assignment of patients to treatment and no-treatment comparison groups (a point to which I shall return). Following Eysenck's article, there was an increase in outcome studies that assigned patients to the treatment group, a wait-list group, or a no-treatment control group, thus allowing for a reasonable comparison of treated with untreated clients of comparable pathology over time.

This research is typified by a study of client-centered therapy reported by Rogers and Dymond (1954). Rogers and Dymond conducted one of the more important early studies of therapy that incorporated assessments of outcome for a group of untreated clients with which the treated group could be compared. Unfortunately, this study and many others of the same period had a critical flaw. They divided clients into two groups: One group received client-centered therapy, and the other group was assigned to a wait list. Clients in the treated groups were assessed on outcome measures at the beginning of therapy and after its completion. The wait-list group was assessed at the start of the waiting period (that lasted 60 days), after the wait period, and again when they finished their (delayed) therapy experience, but the wait period was not equivalent to the treatment time period. Clients were not assigned to groups randomly (or through some other method that assured their equivalence), but they were assigned to wait lists only if it were judged that they could wait for counseling without serious harm or discomfort. Wait-list clients were also allowed to enter treatment early if they felt a pressing need to do so. Also, a separate control group consisted of normal participants, and therefore the controls were not equivalent in pathology to the experimental group.

Researchers of the day were very concerned about the ethical problems associated with withholding psychotherapy from patients in need. The wait-list control group seemed to be a solution to this problem because, ordinarily, clients may well be delayed in entering treatment because of limited clinical resources. Early studies of therapy that used a comparison group to answer the general effects question often drew their comparison group from clients who needed therapy but refused it or who dropped out of therapy early in the process but who would agree to undergo posttesting. Unfortunately, these groups of clients were usually not equivalent to those who actually underwent treatment. Often, they were less motivated, less insightful, more disturbed, or sometimes less disturbed, than the treated clients. Often, the differences were not assessed or reported. Also, the time periods between pre- and posttesting were often not equal across treated and untreated groups.

How can we conclude that the after-treatment status of clients is due to therapy and not to an independent process within the client if the clients, as a group, are different from the start? The usual method for overcoming this problem is to randomly assign clients to therapy and control groups or to match clients on important dimensions (e.g., psychopathology) to ensure equivalence.

To a large extent, early psychotherapy research studies grappled with numerous methodological issues. The Rogers and Dymond (1954) study is but one example of the growing sophistication and effort of researchers to remediate the numerous obstacles in the empirical analysis of treatment outcomes. Progress was made in designing studies with adequate control groups that dealt with a variety of threats to internal validity such as maturation, instrumentation, statistical regression, selection bias, attrition, and/or combinations of these. Threats to external validity were also identified and overcome through the increased use of real patients and larger number of participants, unobtrusive measures, and assessment from a variety of sources, improved measurement instruments, and evaluation across varied time periods.

Psychotherapy research has been exemplary in facing nearly insurmountable methodological problems and finding ways of making the subjective more objective. In the use of literature-aggregation techniques, such as meta-analysis that integrate research evidence, psychotherapy research has been a highly productive leader in this scientific domain (e.g., Smith, Glass, & Miller, 1980). A vast number of studies—more than 5,000 published individual studies and more than 500 published meta-analyses—have been replicated and provide the general conclusion: Psychotherapy is effective at helping people to achieve their goals and overcome their psychopathology at a rate that is faster and more substantial than changes that result from the clients' natural healing processes and supportive elements in the environment.

This conclusion is limited because not all therapies have been empirically tested and new therapies are being developed with staggering rapidity. Clinicians develop, apply, and advocate therapies without any formal evaluation. In addition, not every psychotherapy has been studied with every patient disorder; therefore, one must be careful not to generalize too far about the empirical support for therapy's effects. However, to the extent that traditional therapies have been tested, there has been vast evidence accumulated to suggest that positive effects have been clearly demonstrated.

A simple expression of the impact of therapy in contrast to no-treatment controls is that produced by Smith, Glass, and Miller (1980), based on a meta-analysis of 475 controlled outcome studies, suggesting that at the end of treatment the average psychotherapy patient is better off than 80% of the untreated sample. Similarly, Lambert, Shapiro, and Bergin (1986) suggested a 70% to 75% improvement rate for treated patients and an improvement rate of about 35% to 40% in untreated patients, although these figures are abstractions in light of the variations due to diagnosis, severity, and so forth. In addition, the untreated group improvement rates are inflated for various reasons, including that the patients in these groups often seek help elsewhere (both formal and informal) while serving as controls in treatment studies!

The importance of demonstrating the general effects of therapy cannot be underestimated. It is not reasonable to move on to more specific questions of causality (e.g., by undertaking a microscopic examination of therapy process or therapist characteristics) without first showing that psychotherapy exerts a general effect. Specific causal relations are unimpressive unless the overall impact of therapy has been shown to be beneficial. The demonstration by researchers that many psychotherapies are effective opened the door to this next generation of questions—those concerned with the mechanisms of change. What is it in psychotherapy that facilitates patient improvement?

The Placebo Question

Some critics of psychotherapy (e.g., Prioleau, Murdock, & Brody, 1983; Rachman & Wilson, 1980) and many psychotherapy researchers themselves were interested in the possibility that psychotherapy embodied nothing more than a pseudotreatment that gave patients hope. Borrowing from medical research, largely in the area of psychopharmacology, outcome researchers started applying the concept of placebo controls. In medicine, the effects of an active chemical are contrasted with the effects of pharmacologically inert substances. This contrast allows researchers to rule out the effects of attention, belief by the patient that they are being treated or helped (because the patients do not know if they are actually receiving the active drug or the placebo drug), and belief in the treatment by the physician (who is also "blind" to which patients are actually getting the experimental drug; Shapiro, 1971). In psychotherapy, the placebo construct has been variously conceptualized and studied as the effects of attention, expectation for change, emotional support, and so on. This type of research calls for a placebo comparison group that controls for the "nonspecific aspects" of treatment that may be causing improvements, thereby helping to ascertain how much of the observed improvements can be attributed to such theory-based mechanisms as transference interpretations, exposure to fear- provoking stimuli, cognitive restructuring, biofeedback, and the like.

Historically, there has been considerable debate over the meaning and importance of the placebo concept in psychological treatment research (e.g., Critelli & Neumann, 1984; Kazdin, 1986). Much of the problem arises because of the difference between prescribing drugs and offering psychotherapy. Drugs presumably achieve their results directly through chemical activity as well as psychological mechanisms called *placebo effects*. The point of drug efficacy research is to separate chemical from psychological effects. By this criterion, it does not make much sense to use placebo controls in psychotherapy research because it amounts to trying to separate psychological effects from psychological effects.

Nevertheless, it is important to demonstrate that psychotherapy does more than raise hopes by virtue of being seen as a bona fide treatment (e.g., techniques accomplish more than can be achieved with nontechnical support, attention, belief in a procedure, or similar processes that are not unique to professional treatments). Psychotherapy research has produced a body of knowledge on this question. Clients in so-called placebo control groups typically show greater improvement than patients in wait-list or no-treatment control groups (Shapiro & Shapiro, 1982; Smith, Glass, & Miller, 1980; Wampold, 2008). However, patients in these groups show less improvement than those who are receiving specific psychological interventions (Blanchard, Andrasik, Ahler, Teders, & O'Keefe, 1980; Miller & Berman, 1983; Quality Assurance Project, 1983). In a review of 69 studies, comparing different forms of behavior therapy with placebo conditions to estimate the incremental contribution of specific interventions over the so-called nonspecific effects of placebo, Bowers and Clum (1988) concluded that the specific effects of psychotherapies are twice as great as the placebo effects.

The second important achievement of psychotherapy research, then, is the demonstration that many therapies contain components or active ingredients that are more powerful than a variety of placebo controls. This and the controversial nature of the placebo construct itself have allowed us to move beyond the placebo question to similar questions that deal with the comparative success of different psychotherapies. Which psychotherapy works best?

The Comparative Effects Question

Researchers have expended a great deal of energy and expense in testing hypotheses about the comparative effects of different therapies. Because different theories give diverse accounts of the way that psychopathology develops and the interventions to restore health, it is not surprising that the differential effect of therapies has been a focus of research for well over 4 decades. The polemics surrounding the questions asked, the conduct of research, and the interpretation of the results of comparative outcome studies are still matters of debate. As some people are still committed to a single theory-based treatment with underlying assumptions about the nature of humanity, the nature of change, and other philosophical–value positions, comparative outcome studies will continue to occupy psychotherapy outcome research in the near future (even though some researchers have deserted this approach in favor of examining mechanisms of change that may cut across therapies). This emphasis is likely not only because of emotional and intellectual commitments to school-based practice but also because the most suitable control group for many future studies will be the "best alternative treatment." Because of the ethical and methodological problems involved in no-treatment, wait-list, and placebo controls, contrasting a new therapy with an existing effective therapy has become more common. What has been achieved from conducting comparative studies?

A clear achievement of research is the demonstration (through a variety of psychotherapy research strategies) that some specific techniques have powerful and superior treatment effects on certain specific problems. The clearest superiority for a particular treatment is that which deals with phobic disorders. Research has suggested the necessary procedures to facilitate rapid reduction of anxiety to phobic situations. These procedures involve selecting patients with clearly identified fears that are evoked by specific stimuli. In addition to identifying the evoking stimuli, the patient must be motivated to seek and complete treatment. Early reports indicated that as many as 25% of patients may refuse or drop out of treatment (Marks, 1978), although this is not a high figure for a research protocol. In order for the treatment to work, clients must be willing to "make contact" (i.e., exposure) with the evoking stimuli until their discomfort subsides.

Numerous behavioral treatments were originally based on this exposure paradigm. Desensitization involves repeated brief exposure in fantasy or in vivo with a counteracting response, such as relaxation, during and between exposures. Prolonged exposure involves lengthy immersion (sometimes called *flooding*) in the avoided situation in fantasy or in vivo. Operant approaches have been used through systematic rewards for moving toward or staying in the feared situation. Modeling follows a similar paradigm in which the therapist models approach behaviors and then encourages the patient to do the same. Even in cognitive rehearsal and self-regulation, the patient is encouraged to face feared situations and attain mastery of those situations through the use of effective coping strategies. Therapies for some other anxiety-based disorders, such as sexual dysfunctions and compulsive rituals, are conducted through the use of similar exposure techniques. These include gradual practice in sexual situations and response prevention following exposure to the anxiety that precedes and accompanies rituals.

Although exposure does not necessarily explain the reasons for improvement, it does point to a successful therapeutic strategy: Identify the provoking stimuli, encourage exposure, help the patient remain exposed (response prevention) until his or her anxiety subsides, and assist in mastering thoughts and feelings linked with the disordered responses. Given enough contact with the feared situation, patients cease to respond with avoidance, anxiety, or rituals. Contrary to the expectations of some professionals and the patients themselves, increased sensitization to the anxiety-provoking situation is rare. Only 3% to 15% of patients experience such sensitization or symptom exacerbation among patients who completed a reasonable amount of treatment (e.g., Foa et al., 2002; Marks, 1978).

Numerous studies tried to sort out the specific procedures necessary for successful treatment. Is deep muscle relaxation necessary? Is response prevention required? Is high arousal necessary (as in prolonged exposure)? Should exposure be in vivo or through mental images? Does modeling enhance exposure? Will the addition of cognitive coping strategies enhance the effects of exposure treatments? The bulk of evidence on these and similar questions suggests that achieving lasting reductions in fears and rituals is a function of exposure. Time spent with deep muscle relaxation, the use of tranquilizers, and high levels of arousal add little to treatments that focus on any effective means of encouraging exposure until anxiety reduction occurs (Emmelkamp, 2004).

Although the earliest studies on anxiety reduction were undertaken with simple phobias and nonclinical populations, such as speech phobia, there is now an abundance of studies on clinical populations that substantiate the specific effects of exposure treatments when contrasted with other therapeutic methods that do not include an exposure component. Still, research has identified boundaries to these effects. Exposure treatments, although effective with agoraphobia, simple phobias, and compulsions, are not as effective or uniquely effective with social phobias, generalized anxiety disorders, or combinations of these. The exposure principle seems to have more limited applicability with sexual dysfunctions, where the short-term effects are not followed with the same long-term effects as exposure for agoraphobic persons (Emmelkamp, 2004). It is important to note that psychotherapy research is the only practical method for answering these questions and for discovering the boundaries or limits within which treatment effects operate. Certainly the research conducted by behavior therapists on anxiety disorders is a testimony to the powerful impact of research on theory, training, and practice.

Psychological Treatments for Depression

Another achievement of psychotherapy research is the demonstration of the efficacy of numerous treatments for unipolar depressed patients. It has now been demonstrated that many therapies, particularly cognitive–behavioral therapies and interpersonal psychotherapy (IPT), are at least equal to those of both the older and newer pharmacotherapy (perhaps the current standard of treatment). Furthermore, research clearly shows that relapse with cognitive therapy and IPT is less than with pharmacotherapy, making psychological interventions the treatment of choice for depression, either alone or in combination with pharmacotherapy (e.g., Frank, 1991; Hollon & Beck, 2004).

Still, these psychological treatments cannot be said to have proved their unique effects or to have clearly explained the mechanisms of their effects with depression. Cognitive–behavioral and IPT have rarely been compared with other therapies in the treatment of depression (other than pharmacotherapy), and the few comparisons that have been made have not shown a clear superiority for cognitive therapy or interpersonal therapy (Elliott, Greenberg, & Lietaer, 2004). The results of the National Institute of Mental Health collaborative study support this conclusion and suggest that the superiority of either cognitive therapy or IPT is questionable (Elkin et al., 1989).

Empirically Supported Psychotherapies

The most obvious achievement of psychotherapy research for contemporary practice is the degree to which research findings on comparative effects have come to dominate training and practice worldwide. The most aggressive of efforts in this area were those developed by the Division of Clinical Psychology (Division 12) of the American Psychological Association (Society of Clinical Psychology), which created criteria for what constitutes empirical support for psychological treatments. The agenda of the original Task Force on Promotion and Dissemination of Psychological Procedures (1995) was to consider methods for educating clinical psychologists, third-party funders, and the public about effective psychotherapies. This task force (now the Committee on Science and Practice) generated and disseminated criteria for levels of empirical support, identified relevant treatment outcome studies, and weighed evidence according to defined criteria. This resulted in highly controversial lists of treatments in the late 1990s that met criteria for different levels of empirical support (Chambless, 1996; Chambless & Hollon, 1998;

Chambless et al., 1996) and lists of resources for training and treatment manuals (Woody & Sanderson, 1998).

The controversies generated from the initial report came mainly from practitioners who saw the report as rigid and as having an agenda that was biased in favor of therapies that were promoted by task force members (e.g., criteria were set up that would give an advantage to structured short-term behavioral and cognitive-behavioral treatments advocated by many task force members). However, strong criticism came from psychotherapy researchers as well (e.g., Garfield, 1996; Westen, Novotny, & Thompson-Brenne, 2004). For example, Gavin Andrews (2000), a scholar and researcher with a behavioral orientation, stated the following view of empirically supported treatments:

> This is not to deny that identifying empirically supported treatments carried out by a profession does not have important political advantages for the profession. Funders, providers, and consumers all like to pretend that efficacy is the same as effectiveness, and lists of empirically supported treatments feed this delusion. (p. 267)

Nonetheless, the task force retained its criteria and mission with only a few revisions, such as changing from "empirically validated" to "empirically supported therapies" (Chambless, 1996). Their "methodolatry" did not seem like a hopeful way of bridging the gap between practice and research, creating greater distance rather than greater consensus. Despite the clash between "science" and "practice," the common goal of assuring positive patient outcomes and the dialogues between advocates of the two positions has proven to be a very important debate.

In the 2000s, the Division 12 Committee on Science and Practice has changed the name of its enterprise to "research supported therapies" and has pursued a three-part agenda (Weisz, Hawley, Pilkonis, Woody, & Follette, 2000): reliability of review procedures through standardization and rules of evidence, improved research quality, and increased relevance and dissemination to the professions and public (the most recent list can be found at http://www.PsychologicalTreatments.org). This work is an evolving movement that has toned down its rhetoric, but its productions are still seen in many quarters as too limited and doctrinaire.

The goal of the Division 12 lists of empirically or research-supported treatments converges with the international movement toward evidence-based practice and encourages rapprochement between research and practice communities. Psychotherapy research has taken center stage in identifying and perhaps limiting treatments to those that have empirical support; however, it is important to remember that treatments evolve, as do research strategies, and the search for final conclusions must always recognize the tentative nature of the results of research and practice. Given the large number of disorders, psychological treatments, and the varied means of measuring treatment effects, lists of empirically supported treatments are too static and may offer only a false guarantee of effectiveness. Although many practitioners and the public may be comforted by the notion that they are offering or receiving an empirically supported psychotherapy, the fact is that the success of treatment appears to be largely dependent on the client and the therapist, not on the use of proven evidence-based treatments. Proof of effective treatment needs to be based on the measurement of treatment response in real time rather than provision of the "right" treatment.

The Equal Outcomes Phenomenon

At first, the achievements of research on comparative psychotherapy may appear to be surprisingly meager. It can be simply stated: Differences in outcome among various psychotherapies are not as pronounced as many expected. Behavior therapy, cognitive therapy, and their hybrids occasionally show superior outcomes to traditional verbal therapies in studies of specific disorders, although this is by no means the general case. When such differences are reported in individual studies, those differences seem to be at least partially a function of the researchers' theoretical allegiance to their own, favored treatment (Luborsky et al., 1999; Wampold, 2008). Reviews of comparative outcome studies have been undertaken and reported by numerous authors with the same general conclusion—relative equivalence (e.g., Lambert, Shapiro, & Bergin, 1986; Luborsky, Singer, & Luborsky, 1975; Quality Assurance Project, 1983; Shapiro & Shapiro, 1982; Smith, Glass, & Miller, 1980; Wampold, 2008). The general failure to find differences between different theory-based individual psychotherapies is also reflected in failures to find such differences in different kinds of couple–family treatments (e.g., insight, vs. systemic, vs. behavioral interventions) and modality of treatment (e.g., individual therapy being equivalent to group psychotherapy and couple treatments; Burlingame, MacKenzie, & Strauss, 2004; Sexton, Alexander, & Mease, 2004). The finding of relative equivalence has had an impact on the practice of therapy and affected the future direction of theory, practice, and training. The following are several of the important consequences of these findings:

- the decline of single-theory practice, be it psychoanalytic, behavioral, experiential, or systemic;
- the growth of integrative therapies as a reflection of both the trend for equivalence and occasional superiority of certain techniques;
- the increase in short-term, time-limited, and group treatments that appear to be as effective as long-term approaches and individual approaches with a large portion of the client population;

- and a renewed focus on the mechanisms of change through process research.

The general findings of no difference in the treatment outcomes for clients who have participated in diverse psychotherapies have a number of alternative explanations: (a) Different therapies can achieve similar goals through different processes; (b) different outcomes do occur but are not detected by past research strategies; and (c) different therapies embody common factors that are curative although not emphasized by the theory of change of a particular school. At this time, any of the aforementioned interpretations can be advocated and defended because there is not enough evidence available to rule out alternative explanations. Different therapies require the client to undergo different experiences and engage in different behaviors. Diverse therapies could be effective for different reasons. However, we do not yet know enough about the boundaries of effectiveness for each therapy to discuss the first listed alternative explanation (i.e., [a]) and its merits.

The second alternative explanation (i.e., [b]), the inadequacy of past research, will not be fully discussed here because the emphasis is on achievements (for additional material on unresolved questions in psychotherapy research, see Chapter 11, this volume). Suffice it to say that there are many methodological reasons for failing to reject the null hypothesis (no differences). Kazdin and Bass (1989) questioned the value of the majority of past comparative studies on the basis of a "lack of statistical power." As they pointed out, these studies usually have patient samples that are too small to detect differences that may in fact exist. As researchers are well aware, one must be extremely careful in interpreting the failure to reject the null hypothesis because the lack of differences between experimental conditions could be due not only to actual equivalence but also to anyone of a host of methodological shortcomings (e.g., poor selection of outcome measures, failure to implement, differential attrition).

The third alternative explanation (i.e., [c]), emphasizing common factors in different therapies, is the possibility that has received the most research attention and the one that has the clearest implications for practice. It is not only an interpretation of the comparative outcome literature, but it is also based on other research aimed at discovering the active ingredients of psychotherapy.

The Common Factors Question

Interpersonal, social, and affective factors common across therapies loom large as stimulators of patient improvement. In fact, psychotherapy research suggests that these factors may be more important than "technique" factors in facilitating patient gains (Norcross, 2002; Wampold, 2008). This is true despite the fact that most research has been aimed at identifying the potency of particular techniques, most theories emphasize the place of interventions or techniques, and training programs devote the majority of their resources to the development of theoretical and technical skills rather than to common factors.

What common factors have been shown to be curative? A host of common factors have been identified under the microscope of good process studies: support, warmth, empathy, feedback, reassurance, suggestion, credibility, focus on avoided emotions, expectations for improvement, exposure to feared situations and objects, encouragement to face fears, and altering expectations for personal effectiveness or power. Several of these common factors have received considerable empirical support.

Of the common factors investigated in psychotherapy, none has received more attention and confirmation than a facilitative therapeutic relationship. Among the relationship variables that have received the most attention are the core conditions of empathy, warmth, and positive regard. Although they formed the core of client-centered therapy, they are also central to all therapies in which a similar therapeutic attitude is encouraged and described by terms such as acceptance, validation, therapeutic alliance, working alliance, therapist interpersonal skills, and support (Norcross, 2002). They are also alluded to in cognitive and behavior therapies (although often minimized) as an essential means for establishing the rapport necessary to motivate clients to complete treatment.

Research support for the relationship dimensions comes from a variety of research efforts. First, there is considerable consensus in studies that merely ask clients what was most helpful to them in their therapy. Clients tend to emphasize the importance of the therapist rather than specific technical interventions or interpretations (e.g., Strupp, Fox, & Lessler, 1969). For example, Sloane, Staples, Cristol, Yorkston, and Whipple (1975), in their study of behavior and insight therapies, administered a 32-item questionnaire 4 months following treatment. The items included statements descriptive of both behavior therapy techniques (e.g., training in muscle relaxation) and dynamic therapy techniques (e.g., explaining the relationship of one's problem to early life events) as well as others thought to be present in both therapies. The successful patients in both therapies placed primary importance on more or less the same items. Seventy percent or more of the successful clients listed the following items as *extremely important* or *very important* in causing their improvement:

1. The personality of the therapist.
2. The therapist's helping them to understand problems.
3. Encouragement to gradually practice facing the things that bothered them.
4. Being able to talk to an understanding person.
5. The therapist's helping them to greater self-understanding.

None of the items regarded as *very important* by the majority of either patient group described techniques specific to one therapy (although Item [3] is, in general, approached more systematically in behavior therapies). The foregoing suggests that, at least from the patient's point of view, effective treatment was due to factors associated with relationship variables, self-understanding, and active involvement. Although this type of data is limited by methodological problems (e.g., patients may not actually know how they are being helped), its repeated occurrence with different questionnaires not aimed at highlighting the importance of relationship factors suggests that they are prominent ingredients of change, at least from the client's point of view.

A second research strategy used to investigate relationship factors is the rating of therapist attitudes directly from clients or from transcripts of video or audiotape recordings of sessions, followed by assessments of outcome attained at the end of treatment. If a positive relationship is evident, then these results would be consistent with the hypothesis that the relationship plays a causal role in psychotherapy outcome. Studies showing both positive and equivocal support for the hypothesized relationship have been reviewed in depth elsewhere (e.g., Mitchell, Bozarth, & Krauft, 1977; Norcross, 2002; Patterson, 1984). Reviews are virtually unanimous in their opinion that the therapist–patient relationship is central to therapeutic change; however, studies using client-perceived ratings of the relationship factors, rather than those given by objective raters, obtain consistently more positive results, with recent studies demonstrating that the quality of the relationship can be attributed to therapists independent of the clients contribution (Baldwin, Wampold, & Imel, 2007).

It is becoming increasingly clear that the attributes of the patient, as well as the therapist, play an important part in creating the quality of the therapeutic relationship and in the outcome of psychotherapy. Strupp (1980a, 1980b, 1980c, 1980d) reported a series of four studies in which two patients were seen by one therapist in time-limited psychotherapy. In each instance, one of the therapist's patients was seen as having a successful outcome, whereas the other was considered to be a treatment failure. These individualized reports were part of a larger study that used extensive outcome measures and an analysis of patient–therapist interactions during the process of therapy. In each instance, the therapist was working with college males who were suffering from anxiety, depression, and social withdrawal. Although each therapist was seen as having good interpersonal skills, a different relationship developed with the two patients. In all reports (eight cases with four therapists), the patients who had successful outcomes appeared more willing and able to have a meaningful relationship with the therapist, whereas the patients who did not do well in therapy did not relate well to the therapist and had a tendency to keep the interaction on a more superficial level.

In Strupp's analysis, the contributions of the therapists remained relatively constant throughout therapy, and the difference in outcome was attributed to patient factors such as the nature of the patient's personality make-up, including ego organization, maturity, motivation, and ability to become productively involved in the verbal therapy being offered. On the other hand, the poorer outcomes with the less functional clients could be attributed just as well to the failure of the therapists to adapt their techniques to the more difficult problems presented by these cases.

Despite the many methodological limitations that can be raised, one finding remains clear: Relationship factors predict, if not cause, outcome. If we want an early estimate of the likelihood of the patient's ultimate success, it can be obtained by patient reports of the client-centered dimensions. Nevertheless, ratings of therapist attitudes such as *empathy, alliance, warmth,* and *genuineness* are far from perfectly correlated with outcome. Thus, research has identified a certain limit or boundary to the measured effects of therapist attitudes, casting doubt on the accuracy of Carl Rogers's (1957) bold attempt at specifying the "necessary" and "sufficient" conditions for positive personality change. Rogers's indifference to diagnosis precluded a clear demonstration of where these relationship factors did and did not make a major impact. Had research results actually supported his hypothesis, there would be many more client-centered practitioners, and the search for active ingredients would be all but over.

In summary, both the demonstration of the centrality of the relationship for therapy outcome and a gross specification of the limits that the relationship exerts are important achievements of psychotherapy research. Future research may eventually specify the extent to which positive relationship factors enhance the effects of specific techniques that are known to be effective. In studies that highlight the efficacy of specific techniques, therapeutic factors regularly correlate and predict treatment outcome (e.g., in vivo exposure; Emmelkamp & Van der Hout, 1983; Rabavilas, Boulougouris, & Perissaki, 1979). Research has also shown that the therapeutic alliance interacts with therapeutic techniques in such a way that if the alliance is high, adherence to treatment manuals is less important to outcome. However, if the therapeutic alliance is low, a moderate amount of adherence to the treatment manual appears to be needed to produce good outcomes (Barber et al., 2006). Much more needs to be done to unravel this interaction.

Research has identified other common factors that could account for the general equivalence of therapeutic outcomes. Zeiss, Lewinsohn, and Munoz (1979), for example, compared behavioral activation and interpersonal skills training (a reinforcement theory-based program to increase pleasant activities and the enjoyment of potentially pleasant activities) with cognitive therapy for depressive thoughts. Noting the improvements recorded by all the groups, they cited Frank's (1973) demoralization hypothesis as the most parsimonious explanation for the results. They suggested that the impact of treatment was due to the enhancement of self-efficacy through training in self-help skills, thus increasing expectations of mastery and perceptions of obtaining greater positive reinforcement as a function of the patient's greater skillfulness. Similar explanations for positive outcomes because of common factors were offered in a comparison of cognitive, behavioral, and brief dynamic therapies (Thompson, Gallagher, & Breckenridge, 1987). Additional elements common across treatments are probably *exposure* and *skill development*. Systematic exposure to fear-evoking stimuli probably has specific unique effects. It is also true, however, that virtually all therapies require patients to discuss and look at anxiety-provoking memories, situations, and relationships. Although this is done in a structured programmatic fashion in behavior therapy, it is also required in dynamic and humanistic therapies where emotional arousal and nonavoidance of facing painful affects are considered central aspects of effective treatment. All therapies attempt to help patients, or at least encourage patients, to develop new skills for coping with problematic reactions and interpersonal difficulties.

The common factors explanation for the general equivalence of diverse therapeutic interventions has resulted in the dominance of integrative practice in routine care by implying that the dogmatic advocacy of a particular theoretical school is not supported by research. Research also suggests that *common factors* can become the focal point for integration of seemingly diverse therapy techniques.

The Negative Effects Question

Although the general effects question of why improvement in psychotherapy occurs is widely discussed, the converse question of why deterioration of psychotherapy patients occurs is widely ignored. Simply put: Are all patients helped by psychotherapy? What can we do for those who are not?

As a consequence of carefully studying the progress and outcome of patients who are undergoing therapy, we know that the majority of patients improve, a minority remain unchanged, and still others actually deteriorate. It is a matter of some urgency to identify those patients who cannot benefit and those who may actually experience a negative outcome in therapy. Therapy research has used various quasi-experimental procedures to discover the correlates of treatment failure and deterioration. Negative effects are difficult to study in a scientifically controlled way, but research still indicates that some patients are worse after therapy than they were before treatment. This does not mean that all worsening is therapy produced. Some cases may be on a progressive decline that no therapeutic effort can stop. Other patients may undergo life traumas and untoward events extraneous to therapy that are not moderated by the therapeutic relationship or particular techniques. Research suggests that a variety of extra therapeutic events, patient characteristics, therapy interventions, and therapist attitudes are correlated with negative outcomes.

In early research reviews, Bergin and Lambert (1978) and Lambert, Bergin, and Collins (1977) cited evidence from more than 50 studies on the prevalence and magnitude of negative change. These reviews pieced together obscure sets of evidence, as there are few definitive studies on the topic and considerable hesitation even to address the issues directly. Many early outcome studies failed to include a "worse" category in ratings of change, and contemporary studies rarely analyze treatment failure data in their initial reports of outcome. It appears that rates for negative change (excluding no change), when they are reported, vary from 0% to 15%. They are widespread, occurring across a variety of treatment modalities, including group and family therapies, across theoretical orientations (e.g., behavioral, cognitive, dynamic, client centered), and across patient populations (e.g., phobic, encounter group participants, schizophrenics). Although the evidence is wide ranging, it is also sketchy and incomplete. Despite this incompleteness, nearly all practitioners and researchers believe that negative effects do occur (Strupp, Hadley, & Gomes-Schwartz, 1977). Information on the negative consequences of therapist maladjustment, exploitiveness, and immaturity can be gathered with ease from client reports. In a consumer report study (Striano, 1982), the personal experiences of 25 selected patients who had been to more than one therapist, one of whom was reported as being helpful and one of whom was said to be unhelpful or harmful. Through the reports of these clients Striano documented a variety of "horror stories" of the type that are often shared privately among clients and professionals but are rarely published. In a study of mental health professionals who described their own personal therapy experiences (Grunebaum, 1985), 10% reported being harmed by therapy. Such accounts lack documentation independent of client report; therefore, they could be laden with subjective biases to an unknown degree. However, such complaints are of social and clinical importance, and they provide reasons to continue inquiries into the therapist's contribution to negative change (e.g., Mohr, 1995).

Many other variables cause negative outcomes. Some of these are the subject of litigation, such as the sexual involvement of therapist with client, violations of the basic contract of therapy involving patients' rights to confidentiality, right to refuse treatment, and the like. Less obvious are issues related to treatment termination and abandonment of clients. The times at which patients are most vulnerable are referral and termination from treatment. Many issues couple the vulnerability and dependence of the patient with the naiveté, incompetence, negligence, or exploitativeness of the therapist. Past research (e.g., Bentley, DeJulio, Lambert, & Dinan, 1975; Lieberman, Yalom, & Miles, 1973) suggests that in group treatments therapists often underreport or are less sensitive to negative effects than both clients and other group members. More recent work indicates that it is commonplace for therapists to be unaware of negative changes even in individual therapy and that therapists build into their theory of effective treatment client worsening (Hannan, et al. 2005). Thus, the study of negative effects will be facilitated by a more open attitude on the part of clinicians as well as data collection from sources other than the therapist.

In the 2000s, psychotherapy research methods have been integrated into ongoing care to reduce deterioration rates and maximize outcome. Variously termed *patient-focused research, quality management,* and *outcome management,* these research strategies make use of statistical strategies for modeling expected patient treatment response in relation to actual treatment response and use definitions of clinically meaningful final outcome, such as those elaborated upon by Jacobson and colleagues (Jacobson, Follette, & Revenstorf, 1984; Jacobson & Truax, 1991). Outcome management strategies are aimed at helping clinicians formally monitor patient treatment response and then make adjustments to treatments in real time for those clients not on track for a positive outcome. Outcome management makes empiricism a viable part of routine practice, rather than a distant abstraction that practitioners find difficult to incorporate in practice. Simply put, therapists can use client progress data (mental health lab tests) to detect client deterioration.

These methods, which are being applied in numerous settings in the United States and around the world, promise to add to standard research paradigms. For example, if a therapist develops a treatment plan based on empirically supported treatment outcomes, monitoring a particular patient's response to this treatment, as offered, allows one to judge the degree of the patient's response and to shift treatments if the first, empirically supported treatment is not having its usual (expected) impact. Such modeling of expected recovery (and related techniques for providing real-time feedback to practitioners) has already been shown to enhance treatment outcome substantially (e.g., Harmon et al., 2007; Hawkins et al., 2004; Lambert et al., 2001, 2002; Slade et al., 2008; Whipple et al., 2003). On the basis of the initial applications of these research methods, it is clear that quality management research can be integrated into routine practice, thus narrowing the gap between practice and research while improving treatment outcomes.

The Dose–Effect Question

Of central concern is the proper number of treatment sessions for positive therapy outcome. Will psychological difficulties yield only to frequent sessions that occur over prolonged periods of time, or can they be brief? Who is an appropriate candidate for short-term therapy? How much therapy is, in fact, enough?

Research studies on short-term or time-limited therapy versus long-term or time-unlimited therapy have been conducted since the mid-1950s. Research then addressed the efficacy of brief dynamic therapy and patient selection. The consensus findings (e.g., Koss & Butcher, 1986; Luborsky, Chandler, Auerbach, Cohen, & Bachrach, 1971): Moderate doses of psychotherapy exert substantial impact on patient status.

The first meta-analytic review of 2,431 cases from published research covering a 30-year span showed a stable pattern across studies, reflecting the relationship of amount of therapy and improvement (Howard, Kopta, Krause, & Orlinsky, 1986). These data indicated that by the eighth session, approximately 50% of patients were measurably improved and that 75% of patients had shown measurable improvement by the end of 6 months of weekly psychotherapy. From the 26th session on, the percentage of patients who were improving approached an asymptote. This finding certainly raises questions about the general necessity of long-term treatments for the majority of patients. Long-term therapy cannot be easily justified on the basis of this research, but too brief courses of therapy may leave the majority of patients short of returning to normal functioning or even reliable improvement.

Following the original estimate of dose–response by Howard et al. (1986), several additional studies were published that reinforce their general findings and improve on their methodological shortcomings. Using data ($N > 6,000$ patients) from a variety of clinical samples across the United States that received routine clinical care, at least five additional studies have estimated the dose–effect relationship (Anderson & Lambert, 2001; Hansen, Lambert, & Forman 2002; Kadera, Lambert, & Andrews, 1996; Snell et al., 2001; Wolgast, Lambert, & Puschner, 2003). The findings suggest that limiting treatment to four sessions will result in insufficient treatment response for the vast majority of patients. Even policy decisions that permit more than twice this amount of treatment cannot be justified on the basis of research findings. Empirical findings suggest that limiting psychotherapy sessions to 10 is likely to be appropriate for less than half of the clients who seek treatment, even when the least rigorous criterion, reliable change, is used to define a positive treatment response. It is also clear that such a policy is particularly disadvantageous to the most disturbed clients whose time to recovery is slower and who are most at risk for personal failures, self-harm, and hospitalization. The composite results provide important guidance to policy decisions that limit the amount of psychotherapy a patient may receive and allow government agencies, insurance companies, employers, clinics, and consumers to understand the consequences of such policies. These data suggest the need for providers and policymakers to pay attention to empirical research, not just theoretical or economic rationales for decisions about dosage. The dose–response data suggest that the highest quality of care will be provided by monitoring each client's treatment response and making treatment length a function of treatment response and mental health status, rather than arbitrary or theory-driven limits. Defining treatment response and estimating dosage consequences is an important achievement of psychotherapy research. Limiting treatment or continuing treatment without formal assessment requires either frequent formal assessment of patient well-being as psychotherapy unfolds, or at the very least, reassessment at the time a decision is being contemplated.

The Permanence Question

Although research has focused primarily on the immediate posttreatment status of patients who are undergoing psychotherapy, there is considerable interest in the long-term effects of treatment. What kinds of change persist? For whom? For how long? What factors increase the likelihood of maintenance (and relapse)?

Research has demonstrated that most patients who undergo psychotherapy achieve healthy adjustments for long periods of time even when they have a long history of recurrent problems. This finding seems to hold even when treatments are quite brief. Haas, Hill, Lambert, and Morrell (2002) identified a subset of patients that responded rapidly and dramatically to treatment maintained their gains 6 months to 2 years following treatment. Typically when the outcome of treated groups is compared with control group outcome at termination and follow-up, differences between groups have washed out by the follow-up comparison, particularly if years have passed. The failure to find differences between groups at follow-up is usually because of improvement in control participants during the follow-up period rather than declines in the treated groups.

The most impressive review of this topic was published by Nicholson and Berman (1983), who summarized 67 follow-up studies of patients with a broad range of Axis I disorders. Their conclusion was that psychotherapy generally has lasting effects. Relapse rates vary by disorder, and therefore it is hard to provide exact estimates. For example, Ilardi, Craighead, and Evans (1997) reported that even within inpatient treatment for Axis I affective disorder relapse rates varied from 77% for patients with Axis II diagnoses to 14% in those without this complication.

Despite the overall tendency for gains to be maintained following treatment, a portion of patients who are improved relapse and continue to seek help or develop a different disorder that requires treatment. In fact, several problems such as addictions (e.g., alcohol abuse, smoking, obesity) are so likely to recur that they are not considered properly studied without data collection one year after treatment.

ACHIEVEMENTS REFLECTED IN THE PROCESS OF RESEARCH

A number of positive developments have resulted from decades of subjecting psychotherapies to empirical analysis. Because empirical studies require operational definitions of both independent and dependent variables, the process of carrying out research has demanded clear specification of theoretical constructs. Thus, the conduct of psychotherapy research has necessitated the specification of such theoretically diverse notions as transference interpretations, empathic understanding, reframing, positive personality change, and so forth. As a consequence of this specification, psychotherapy theory, practice, and training have all benefited. Several of the more important results of this specification or operationalization are now discussed.

Treatment Operationalization

The earliest studies of psychotherapy made little attempt to specify treatment beyond general titles such as *dynamically oriented*, *client centered*, or *gestalt*. Gradually, researchers became dissatisfied with this vagueness, especially because these general terms gave the artificial appearance of greater clarity and distinctness than the treatment actually offered. Furthermore, within each therapy orientation there was growing interest in exploring the specific effects of particular theoretically important aspects of the therapeutic endeavor. Efforts to operationalize and measure these aspects of treatment often resulted in the development of both *treatment manuals* and *rating scales* that could be applied not only in the research protocol but also later in training therapists. This development moved therapy from an art that was difficult to pass on to other artisans to a scientific technology that can be more easily and rapidly taught, learned, and replicated. Many examples of these developments could be presented; two examples are provided that illustrate the general achievement.

Therapy Manuals

Research on psychoanalytic psychotherapy has a long history. Many problems have been encountered in the empirical understanding of this treatment system, especially in defining what it entails and what its essential elements are thought to be. A number of different analytically trained therapists developed treatment manuals to train therapists more explicitly in the use of key analytic techniques for the purpose of conducting psychotherapy research. These manuals differ from traditional books on psychoanalytic technique by clearly operationalizing interventions and providing rating scales for measuring compliance and competence in treatment (cf. Strupp & Binder, 1984).

Lester Luborsky (1984), for example, developed a manual that rests on a long tradition of systematic research and practice. Luborsky's supportive-expressive psychotherapy manual is a prototype for the impact of research on practice and training. Foremost among the techniques made explicit in this manual is the identification of the patient's core conflictual relationship theme (viz., transference) and the therapist's curative focus, interpretation, and its role in helping the patient work through this problem. The manual provides a reliable method for problem conceptualization that can be formulated and judged by the therapist as well as independent raters. The procedure calls for the identification of instances within the therapy narrative in which the patient speaks of his or her relationships with various people. These "relationship episodes" are then separately rated with regard to the patient's wishes, the responses that the wishes elicit (or are imagined to elicit) in others, and the patient's characteristic response to what they get from the other. Once a conflict of central importance to the patient that appears across a number of relationships is identified, then the therapist and patient direct considerable energy toward its analysis. Transference interpretations are viewed in the context of this focal theme, which is expected to manifest itself within as well as outside the therapeutic relationship.

It is notable that such an explicit approach has been developed in psychoanalytic treatment. The manual enhances treatment efforts (that can now be offered in a brief rather than long-term format) and the training of therapists. The material assists not only in making the analysis of interpersonal problems more explicit but also in providing consensus among raters as well as feedback for the therapists' immediate consideration.

Treatment manuals have become commonplace, and although they vary in quality, most facilitate not only the testing of therapy but also the training of therapists. Behavioral manuals began appearing in the 1960s, but psychodynamic manuals did not appear until the 1980s and then only in response to the needs of research protocols, not to the needs of training programs. Just what is a part of psychotherapy and what is not can be made explicit and transferable because of the degree of specificity that is demanded by research.

Multiple studies have now been conducted to evaluate the potential benefits of using treatment manuals for both psychotherapy and training purposes. For example, the "transportability" of a manualized cognitive–behavioral treatment for panic disorder was examined (Wade, Treat, & Stuart, 1998). Using a 15-session CBT treatment protocol, 110 clients diagnosed with panic with or without agoraphobia were treated in group sessions at a community mental health center. Treatment outcomes were then compared with those of two clinical trials of CBT for panic disorder, using a "benchmarking" strategy. Comparison of the results revealed that clients who received the treatment within the community mental health center improved on every measure, and the magnitudes of improvement were comparable with those in the clinical trials. The investigators suggested that these findings support the idea that manualized treatments used in efficacy studies can be transported into clinical settings (Stuart, Treat, & Wade, 2000; Wade et al., 1998). A similar study was conducted, using a treatment manual for bulimia, again revealing outcomes that were comparable with controlled research (Tuschen-Caffier, Pook, & Frank, 2001) and reinforcing the notion that research-initiated treatment manuals have a place in training and clinical practice.

At the same time, controversy still swirls around whether the use of treatment manuals actually improves the success of psychotherapy (Norcross, Beutler, & Levant, 2006). Strong reliance on treatment manuals while conducting psychotherapy has been related to less successful therapy in several studies, probably owing to therapist rigidity. However, all partisans of the debate agree that treatment manuals prove invaluable for conducting research studies and for training therapists, as long as the manuals, like all tools, do not become the only source of guidance for the utterly human endeavor of psychotherapy.

Process Rating Scales

Another example of the valuable impact of researchers' attempts to operationalize treatment came from the research program of Rogers, Gendlin, Kiesler, and Traux (1967). Rogers, in the noble tradition of the scientist–practitioner model, made numerous attempts to phrase client-centered theory in terms that would lend itself to empirical investigation. He and his colleagues undertook serious and ambitious efforts to investigate empirically client-centered therapy. Early in their program of research, considerable energy was devoted to defining explicitly such elusive therapist attitudes as empathy, positive regard, and genuineness; the depth of client self-exploration was defined in terms of the Experiencing Scale; and positive personality change was measured with the Q-sort technique—aimed at illuminating discrepancies between real and ideal self.

Client-centered work on empathy is characteristic of the interaction between practice and research. The researchers developed a rating scale for quantifying the empathy observed in therapy sessions. The scale was explicit enough so that the ratings could be made by a layperson with no psychological training. Empathy was divided into a 9-point scale, with each point along the scale defined and exemplified. Raters were given transcripts or audiotape examples of the different levels of empathy to help them use the scales in a reliable manner. The researchers were successful in training raters to make reliable ratings. These rating scales proved to be of value in research studies examining the relationship between therapist behaviors and client improvement but had an even greater effect on training programs.

Many educators realized that these rating scales and teaching methods could be successfully used to train novice therapists. Many training programs quickly adopted them for training graduate students. Clinical and counseling trainees used the rating scales first to distinguish high and low levels of empathy and later to practice empathic responding and obtain feedback about their own empathic efforts. The scales, in various formats, came to be used as training outcome criteria and even as selection criteria (e.g., Ivey, 1988; Truax & Carkhuff, 1967). In less formal activities, the explicit definitions of empathy—developed originally for psychotherapy outcome studies—were used broadly in education, business, industry, and religion (Rogers, 1980). Even though the helping principles embodied in client-centered theory may have had this impact without a link to research, it is clear that the research made the theory more specific, concrete, and applicable.

Many similar examples of the impact of research on practice could be offered. Consider the research literature on the training of group leaders (through the identification of research-based curative factors or the application of group-process rating scales), training in cognitive therapy (through competence ratings), and marriage and family therapy training programs (use of family process scales), to name just a few. The bottom line is that research measures have improved clinical training and practice.

Outcome Operationalization

A final area of consideration is the development of scales for rating patient change and their use in both research and practice. In calling for reliable and accurate measures of treatment outcome, research was a primary stimulus behind the development of numerous assessment tools that have important clinical uses. As a consequence of psychotherapy outcome research, certain scales and practices that are still used in clinical settings (e.g., Rorschach, Thematic ApperceptionTest, Human Figure Drawings, Minnesota Multiphasic Personality Inventory) have been largely rejected as measures of change. These devices have not proven sensitive to change and to a large extent do not provide evidence for the effects of therapy. They are rarely used as outcome measures (Froyd, Lambert, & Froyd, 1996; Lambert, Christensen, & DeJulio, 1983). Instead, research has favored the use of behavioral measures, symptomatic scales, and other instruments specific to the disorder being modified or the therapy being tested. Thus, psychotherapy research resulted in redefining the assessment endeavor and the targets of treatment.

This focus has led to the development of hundreds of scales that have subsequently been applied more broadly in clinical practice. Most notable, perhaps, has been the use of diagnostic evaluations, often based on interviews. Research diagnostic criteria were originally developed for research protocols. Such criteria as those for depression, anorexia nervosa, and schizophrenia became the model for revisions and improvements in the *Diagnostic and Statistical Manual of Mental Disorders* (3rd ed., rev.; *DSM–III–R*; American Psychiatric Association, 1987). The manual in its revisions from *DSM* to *DSM–IV* has shown the increase in precision typical of that demanded in empirical research. These are rather remarkable indirect effects of research, as is the Structured Clinical Interview for *DSM* Disorders used in research to establish that patients are suffering from particular disorders.

Hundreds of new scales have been developed. The growing number of scales is most noticeable within both behavioral and cognitive orientations. The behavioral schools have contributed to general practice through such measures as the Fear Survey Schedule (Marks & Mathews, 1978), Behavioral Avoidance Test (McGlynn, 1988), Subjective Units of Discomfort (Kaplan, 2009), Pleasant Events Schedule (MacPhillamy & Lewinsohn, 1982), and a host of similar devices that often prove to be an integral part of treatment as well as a means of testing the effects of treatment.

The same can be said for new measures in the cognitive therapies. Here such devices as the Beck Depression Inventory (Beck, Ward, Mendelson, Mock, & Erbaugh, 1961), Irrational Beliefs Test (Nelson, 1977), the Autonomic Thoughts Questionnaire (Hollon & Kendall, 1980), and similar scales have gained widespread use in clinical practice. Similar developments are apparent in social leaning theory (e.g., Locus of Control Scale). More broadly, one can see that the advances in assessment measures necessitated by therapy research also affected clinical practice through the development of marital satisfaction inventories; measures of sexual satisfaction and performance; and measures of addictive behaviors, eating disorder symptoms, depression, and anxiety. Clearly significant contributions of outcome research have been the articulation of specific of treatment goals, more precise measurement of change, and well-defined links between these and the specific nature of interventions.

CONCLUSION

Much of psychotherapy research, like research in other sciences, has been devoted to making the subjective more objective. To a large extent, these efforts have proven successful. The long list of problems facing researchers who have applied experimental methods to the amorphous, organic, fluid process of psychotherapy has been gradually overcome. The most important methodological accomplishments of psychotherapy research include the following:

1. Experimental and control groups were equated and contrasted.
2. The problems of withholding treatment were overcome.
3. Treatment was defined, described, and offered in precise terms and actions.
4. Therapist cooperation for evaluation and recording of sessions was obtained, allowing for the systematic analysis of the therapy process.
5. Ethical problems in research were addressed, and guidelines for research were developed.
6. Suitable, reliable, and valid measures of change were developed and applied, resulting in higher standards for evaluating the effects of therapy.
7. The development of a variety of research designs (e.g., single participant designs, small sample designs, intensive designs) contributed to the sense that therapy process and outcome could be adequately studied.
8. The development of a variety of methods of estimating pre–post changes that are clear of bias from pretest scores, regression, and similar factors resulted in findings that were more acceptable to even the harshest critics.

As a partial consequence of the aforementioned achievements in methodology, psychotherapy research has gradually moved from the most general questions about the efficacy of therapy to specific questions that address more precisely the boundary conditions for therapeutic effects. Some of these findings have been embraced by the profession, whereas others remain an enigma that can only lead to further studies that attempt to clarify the picture we have of therapeutic effects. The current pressing matters in psychotherapy research hover around evidence-based practices in the broadest sense of this phrase. Certainly treatment guidelines will continue to be developed (NICE Guidelines: http://www.nice.org.uk; Cochrane Reviews: http://www.cochrane.org/reviews/), and these provide helpful suggestions for practice, but have many problems if applied without question (Stiles, Barkham, Twigg, Mellor-Clark, & Cooper, 2006; Wampold, 1997; Wampold & Brown, 2006).

The more important achievements of therapy research include

1. demonstrating that the general effects of psychotherapy exceeded spontaneous remission;

2. showing that therapy effects were generally positive;
3. providing evidence that therapy effects exceeded the effect of placebo controls;
4. helping to change the definition of placebo controls in psychological studies so that we have a precise and appropriate definition that includes the notion of common factors;
5. demonstrating the efficiency of psychotherapy and its long-lasting consequences;
6. revealing that outcomes varied even in homogeneous samples, because of relationship and therapist factors rather than technique factors;
7. demonstrating the relative equivalence in outcome for a large number of therapies, therapeutic modalities, and temporal arrangements;
8. suggesting the unique effectiveness of a few therapies with specific disorders;
9. demonstrating the possible interactive and synergistic role of medication and psychotherapy;
10. demonstrating the central importance of the therapist–patient relationship in predicting and possibly causing treatment success; and
11. uncovering negative effects in treatment and studying processes that lead to patient deterioration and ways of preventing such untoward outcomes.

Useful research has led to changes in theory and practice. For just one example, the failure of highly touted therapy methods to demonstrate dramatic results, when put to the test, has repeatedly resulted in questions about the actual mechanisms that cause change. The importance of transference interpretations, the need for an exposure hierarchy, and the centrality of self-talk have all been critically questioned by research. Other mechanisms that explain change have been offered as it becomes clear that a particular theory of change is not supported by empirical evidence. For another example, psychotherapy research often sets an empirical standard for innovations and provides a restraining effect (over time) on bizarre or unworthy therapy methods (e.g., Norcross, Koocher, & Garofalo, 2006). This same restraining force is exerted by research on the claims and beliefs of traditional practice as well. This has had an important impact on the credibility of therapy in the eyes of other scientists, insurance companies, government agencies, and possibly, even the public.

Further achievements of psychotherapy research are manifest in the identification of the salient role of patients and contextual factors in change and the resistance to change. Much of this research has examined gender issues, ethnic identity, and educational and economic status, along with a host of related variables. Surely we know now much about those patients who are most likely to drop out of therapy prematurely. We also understand methods of socializing these patients and their therapists so as to maximize the likelihood of success (Lambert & Ogles, 2004). Psychotherapy research has also made clear that few differences in outcome are evident as a function of field of professional training (whether psychiatry, social work, marital and family therapy, or psychology). In addition, research has suggested the similarity of behaviors across therapists with diverse orientations as well as the occasional marked behavioral differences between those who subscribe to the same theoretical orientations (Sundland, 1977).

We are gradually closing in on those variables that are most powerful in maximizing our treatment efforts. These variables are often not those that are touted as important prior to empirical scrutiny. Future research has a strong foundation provided by past achievements. Upon this foundation, scientifically based psychological interventions may continue to be built—to the mutual benefit of all.

REFERENCES

American Psychiatric Association. (1987). *Diagnostic and statistical manual of mental disorders* (3rd ed., rev.). Washington, DC: Author.

Anderson, E. M., & Lambert, M. J. (2001). A survival analysis of clinically significant change in outpatient psychotherapy. *Journal of Clinical Psychology, 57,* 875–888. doi:10.1002/jclp.1056

Andrews, G. (2000). A focus on empirically supported outcomes: A commentary on search for empirically supported treatments. *Clinical Psychology: Science and Practice, 7,* 264–268. doi:10.1093/clipsy/7.3.264

Baldwin, S. A., Wampold, B. E., & Imel, Z. E. (2007). Untangling the alliance-outcome correlation: Exploring the relative importance of therapist and patient variability. *Journal of Consulting and Clinical Psychology, 75,* 842–852. doi:10.1037/0022-006X.75.6.842

Barber, J. P., Gallop, R., Crits-Christoph, P., Frank, A., Thase, M. E., Weiss, R. D., et al. (2006). The role of therapist adherence, therapist competence, and the alliance in predicting outcome of individual drug counseling: Results from the NIDA Collaborative Cocaine Treatment Study. *Psychotherapy Research, 16,* 229–240. doi:10.1080/10503300500288951

Beck, A. T., Ward, C. H., Mendelson, M., Mock, J., & Erbaugh, J. (1961). An inventory for measuring depression. *Archives of General Psychiatry, 4,* 561–571.

Bentley, J. C., DeJulio, S. S., & Lambert, M., & Dinan, W. (1975). *The effects of traditional versus confrontative leadership styles in producing causalities in encounter group participants.* Unpublished manuscript, Brigham Young University, Provo, UT.

Bergin, A. E. (1971). The evaluation of therapeutic outcomes. In A. E. Bergin & S. L. Garfield (Eds.), *Handbook of psychotherapy and behavior change* (pp. 217–270). New York, NY: Wiley.

Bergin, A. E., & Garfield, S. L. (1971). *Handbook of psychotherapy and behavior change*. New York, NY: Wiley.

Bergin, A. E., & Garfield, S. L. (1994). *Handbook of psychotherapy and behavior change* (4th ed.). New York, NY: Wiley.

Bergin, A. E., & Lambert, M. J. (1978). The evaluation of therapeutic outcomes. In S. L. Garfield & A. E. Bergin (Eds.), *Handbook of psychotherapy and behavior change* (2nd ed., pp. 139–190). New York, NY: Wiley.

Blanchard, E. B., Andrasik, F., Ahler, T. A., Teders, S., & O'Keefe, D. O. (1980). Migraine and tension headache: A meta-analytic review. *Behavior Therapy, 11*, 613–631. doi:10.1016/S0005-7894(80)80001-3

Bowers, T. G., & Clum, G. A. (1988). Relative contribution of specific and nonspecific treatment effects: Meta-analysis of placebo-controlled behavior therapy research. *Psychological Bulletin, 103*, 315–323. doi:10.1037/0033-2909.103.3.315

Burlingame, G. M., MacKenzie, R., & Strauss, B. (2004). Small group treatment: Evidence for effectiveness and mechanisms of change. In M. J. Lambert (Ed.), *Bergin and Garfield's handbook of psychotherapy and behavior change* (5th ed., pp. 647–696). New York, NY: Wiley.

Chambless, D. L. (1996). In defense of dissemination of empirically supported psychological interventions. *Clinical Psychology: Science and Practice, 3*, 230–235.

Chambless, D. L., & Hollon, S. D. (1998). Defining empirically supported psychological interventions. *Journal of Consulting and Clinical Psychology, 66*, 7–18. doi:10.1037/0022-006X.66.1.7

Chambless, D. L., Sanderson, W. C., Shoham, V., Bennett Johnson, S., Pope, K. S., Crits-Christoph, P., et al. (1996). An update on empirically validated therapies. *Clinical Psychologist, 49*, 5–18.

Critelli, J. W., & Neumann, K. F. (1984). The placebo: Conceptual analysis of a construct in transition. *The American Psychologist, 39*, 32–39. doi:10.1037/0003-066X.39.1.32

Elkin, I., Shea, T., Watkins, J. T., Imber, S. D., Sotsky, S. M., Collins, F., et al. (1989). National Institute of Mental Health treatment of depression collaborative research program: General effectiveness of treatment. *Archives of General Psychiatry, 46*, 971–982.

Elliott, R., Greenberg, L. S., & Lietaer, G. (2004). Research on experiential psychotherapies. In M. J. Lambert (Ed.), *Bergin & Garfield's handbook of psychotherapy and behavior change* (5th ed., pp. 493–540). New York, NY: Wiley.

Emmelkamp, P. M. G. (2004). Behavior therapy with adults. In M. J. Lambert (Ed.), *Bergin & Garfield's handbook of psychotherapy and behavior change* (5th ed., pp. 393–446). New York, NY: Wiley.

Emmelkamp, P. M. G., & Van der Hout, A. (1983). Failure in treating agoraphobia. In E. B. Foa & P. M. G. Emmelkamp (Eds.), *Failures in behavior therapy* (pp. 58–81). New York, NY: Wiley.

Eysenck, H. J. (1952). The effects of psychotherapy: An evaluation. *Journal of Consulting Psychology, 16*, 319–324.

Fenichel, O. (1930). *Ten years of the Berlin Psychoanalytic Institute, 1920–1930*. Berlin, Germany: Berlin Psychoanalytic Institute.

Foa, E. B., Zoellner, L. A., Feeny, N. C., Hembree, E. A., & Alvarez-Conrad, J. (2002). Does imaginal exposure exacerbate PTSD symptoms? *Journal of Consulting and Clinical Psychology, 70*, 1022–1028. doi:10.1037/0022-006X.70.4.1022

Frank, J. D. (1973). *Persuasion and healing* (2nd ed.). Baltimore, MD: Johns Hopkins University Press.

Froyd, J. E., & Lambert, M. J., & Froyd. (1996). A review of practices of psychotherapy outcome measurement. *Journal of Mental Health, 5*, 11–15. doi:10.1080/09638239650037144

Garfield, S. L. (1996). Some problems associated with 'validated' forms of psychotherapy. *Clinical Psychology: Science and Practice, 3*, 218–229.

Garfield, S. L., & Bergin, A. E. (1978). *Handbook of psychotherapy and behavior change* (2nd ed.). New York, NY: Wiley.

Garfield, S. L., & Bergin, A. E. (1986). *Handbook of psychotherapy and behavior change* (3rd ed.). New York, NY: Wiley.

Grunebaum, H. (1985). Helpful and harmful psychotherapy. *The Harvard Medical School Mental Health Newsletter, 1*, 5–6.

Haas, E., Hill, R., Lambert, M. J., & Morrell, B. (2002). Do early responders to psychotherapy maintain treatment gains? *Journal of Clinical Psychology, 58*, 1157–1172. doi:10.1002/jclp.10044

Hannan, C., Lambert, M. J., Harmon, C., Nielsen, S. L., Smart, D. W., Shimokawa, K., et al. (2005). A lab test and algorithms for identifying clients at risk for treatment failure. *Journal of Clinical Psychology, 61*, 155–163.

Hansen, N. B., Lambert, M. J., & Forman, E. V. (2002). The psychotherapy dose-response effect and its implications for treatment delivery services. *Clinical Psychology: Science and Practice, 9*, 329–343. doi:10.1093/clipsy/9.3.329

Harmon, S. C., Lambert, M. J., Smart, D. M., Hawkins, E., Nielsen, S. L., Slade, K., et al. (2007). Enhancing outcome for potential treatment failures: Therapist-client feedback and clinical support tools. *Psychotherapy Research, 17*, 379–392. doi:10.1080/10503300600702331

Hawkins, E. J., Lambert, M. J., Vermeersch, D. A., Slade, K., & Tuttle, K. (2004). The effects of providing patient progress information to therapists and patients. *Psychotherapy Research, 14*, 308–327. doi:10.1093/ptr/kph027

Hollon, S. D., & Beck, A. T. (2004). Cognitive and cognitive-behavioral therapies. In M. J. Lambert (Ed.), *Bergin & Garfield's handbook of psychotherapy and behavior change* (5th ed., pp. 447–492). New York, NY: Wiley.

Hollon, S. D., & Kendall, P. C. (1980). Cognitive self-statements in depression: Development of the Automatic Thoughts Questionnaire. *Cognitive Therapy and Research, 4*, 383–395.

Howard, K. I., Kopta, S. M., Krause, M. S., & Orlinsky, D. E. (1986). The dose-effect relationship in psychotherapy. *The American Psychologist, 41*, 159–164. doi:10.1037/0003-066X.41.2.159

Ilardi, S. S., Craighead, W. E., & Evans, D. D. (1997). Modeling relapse in unipolar depression: The effects of dysfunctional cognitions and personality disorders. *Journal of Clinical and Consulting Psychology, 65*, 381–391. doi:10.1037/0022-006X.65.3.381

Ivey, A. (1988). *Intentional interviewing and counseling: Facilitating client development.* Pacific Grove, CA: Brooks/Cole.

Jacobson, N. S., Follette, W. C., & Revenstorf, D. (1984). Psychotherapy outcome research: Methods for reporting variability and evaluating clinical significance. *Behavior Therapy, 15*, 336–352. doi:10.1016/S0005-7894(84)80002-7

Jacobson, N. S., & Truax, P. (1991). Clinical significance: A statistical approach to defining meaningful change in psychotherapy research. *Journal of Consulting and Clinical Psychology, 59*, 12–19. doi:10.1037/0022-006X.59.1.12

Kadera, S. W., Lambert, M. J., & Andrews, A. A. (1996). How much therapy is really enough? A session-by-session analyses of the psychotherapy dose-effect relationship. *Journal of Psychotherapy Practice and Research, 5*, 132–151.

Kaplan, D. M. (2009). A validity study of the subjective unit of discomfort (SUD) score. *Journal of Counseling & Development, 87*, 241–256.

Kazdin, A. E. (1986). Research designs and methodology. In S. L. Garfield & A. E. Bergin (Eds.), *Handbook of psychotherapy and behavior change* (3rd ed., pp. 23–68). New York, NY: Wiley.

Kazdin, A. E., & Bass, D. (1989). Power to detect differences between alternative treatments in comparative psychotherapy outcome research. *Journal of Consulting and Clinical Psychology, 57,* 138–147. doi:10.1037/0022-006X.57.1.138

Koss, M. P., & Butcher, J. N. (1986). Research on brief psychotherapy. In S. L. Garfield & A. E. Bergin (Eds.), *Handbook of psychotherapy and behavior change* (3rd ed., pp. 627–670). New York, NY: Wiley.

Lambert, M. J. (1976). Spontaneous remission of adult neurotic disorders: A revision and summary. *Psychological Bulletin, 83,* 107–119. doi:10.1037/0033-2909.83.1.107

Lambert, M. J. (Ed.). (2004). *Bergin and Garfield's handbook of psychotherapy and behavior change* (5th ed.). Chicago, IL: Wiley.

Lambert, M. J., Bergin, A. E., & Collins, J. L. (1977). Therapist-induced deterioration in psychotherapy. In A. S. Gurman & A. M. Razin (Eds.), *Effective psychotherapy: A handbook of research* (pp. 452–481). New York, NY: Pergamon.

Lambert, M. J., Christensen, E. R., & DeJulio, S. S. (Eds.). (1983). *The assessment of psychotherapy outcome*. New York, NY: Wiley-Interscience.

Lambert, M. J., & Ogles, B. M. (2004). The efficacy and effectiveness of psychotherapy. In M. J. Lambert (Ed.), *Bergin and Garfield's handbook of psychotherapy and behavior change* (5th ed., pp. 139–193). New York, NY: Wiley.

Lambert, M. J., Shapiro, D. A., & Bergin, A. E. (1986). The effectiveness of psychotherapy. In S. L. Garfield & A. E. Bergin (Eds.), *Handbook of psychotherapy and behavior change* (3rd ed., pp. 157–212). New York, NY: Wiley.

Lambert, M. J., Whipple, J. L., Smart, D. W., Vermeersch, D. A., Nielsen, S. L., & Hawkins, E. J. (2001). The effects of providing therapists with feedback on patient progress during psychotherapy: Are outcomes enhanced? *Psychotherapy Research, 11,* 49–68. doi:10.1080/713663852

Lambert, M. J., Whipple, J. L., Vermeersch, D. A., Smart, D. W., Hawkins, E. J., Nielsen, S. L., & Goates, M. K. (2002). Enhancing psychotherapy outcomes via providing feedback on client progress: A replication. *Clinical Psychology & Psychotherapy, 9,* 91–103. doi:10.1002/cpp.324

Lieberman, M. A., Yalom, I. D., & Miles, M. B. (1973). *Encounter groups: First facts*. New York, NY: Basic Books.

Luborsky, L. (1984). *Principles of psychoanalytic psychotherapy: A manual for supportive-expressive treatment*. New York, NY: Basic Books.

Luborsky, L., Chandler, M., Auerbach, A. H., Cohen, J., & Backrach, H. M. (1971). Factors influencing the outcome of psychotherapy: A review of quantitative research. *Psychological Bulletin, 75,* 145–185. doi:10.1037/h0030480

Luborsky, L., Diguer, L., Seligman, D. A., Rosenthal, R., Krause, E. D., Johnson, S., et al. (1999). The researcher's own therapy allegiances: A "wild card" in comparisons of treatment efficacy. *Clinical Psychology: Science and Practice, 6,* 95–106. doi:10.1093/clipsy/6.1.95

Luborsky, L., Singer, B., & Luborsky, L. (1975). Comparative studies of psychotherapy. *Archives of General Psychiatry, 32,* 995–1008.

MacPhillamy, D. J. & Lewinsohn, P. M. (1982). The Pleasant Events Schedule: Studies on reliability, validity, and scale intercorrelation. *Journal of Consulting & Clinical Psychology, 50,* 363–375.

Marks, I. (1978). Behavioral psychotherapy of adult neurosis. In S. L. Garfield & A. E. Bergin (Eds.), *Handbook of psychotherapy and behavior change* (2nd ed., pp. 493–547). New York, NY: Wiley.

Marks, I. M., & Mathews, A. M. (1978). Brief standard self-rating for phobic patients. *Behavior Research and Therapy, 17,* 263–267.

McGlynn, F. D. (1988). Behavioral avoidance tests. In M. Hersen & A. Bellack (Eds.), *Dictionary of behavioral assessment techniques*. Oxford, England: Pergamon Press.

Meltzoff, J., & Kornreich, M. (1970). *Research in psychotherapy*. New York, NY: Atherton Press.

Miller, R. C., & Berman, J. S. (1983). The efficacy of cognitive behavior therapies: A quantitative review of the research evidence. *Psychological Bulletin, 94*, 39–53. doi:10.1037/0033-2909.94.1.39

Mitchell, K. M., Bozarth, J. D., & Krauft, C. C. (1977). A re-appraisal of the therapeutic effectiveness of accurate empathy, nonpossessive warmth, and genuineness. In A. S. Gurman & A. M. Razin (Eds.), *Effective psychotherapy: A handbook of research* (pp. 482–502). New York, NY: Pergamon.

Mohr, D. V. (1995). Negative outcome in psychotherapy: A critical review. *Clinical Psychology: Science and Practice, 2*, 1–27.

Nelson, R. E. (1977). Irrational beliefs in depression. *Journal of Clinical and Consulting Psychology, 45*, 1190–1191.

Nicholson, R. A., & Berman, J. S. (1983). Is follow-up necessary in evaluating psychotherapy? *Psychological Bulletin, 93*, 261–278. doi:10.1037/0033-2909.93.2.261

Norcross, J. C. (Ed.). (2002). *Psychotherapy relationships that work: Therapist contributions and responsiveness to patients*. New York, NY: Oxford University Press.

Norcross, J. C., Beutler, L. E., & Levant, R. F. (2006). *Evidence-based practices in mental health: Debate & dialogue on the fundamental questions*. Washington, DC: American Psychological Association.

Norcross, J. C., Koocher, G. P., & Garofalo, A. (2006). Discredited psychological treatments and tests: A Delphi poll. *Professional Psychology: Research and Practice, 37*, 515–522. doi:10.1037/0735-7028.37.5.515

Patterson, C. H. (1984). Empathy, warmth, and genuineness in psychotherapy: A review of reviews. *Psychotherapy, 21*, 431–438. doi:10.1037/h0085985

Prioleau, L., Murdock, M., & Brody, N. (1983). An analysis of psychotherapy versus placebo studies. *The Behavioral and Brain Sciences, 6*, 275–310.

Quality Assurance Project. (1983). A treatment outline for depressive disorders. *The Australian and New Zealand Journal of Psychiatry, 17*, 129–146. doi:10.3109/00048678309159997

Rabavilas, A. D., Boulougouris, J. C., & Perissaki, C. (1979). Therapist qualities related to outcome with exposure in vivo in neurotic patients. *Journal of Behavior Therapy and Experimental Psychiatry, 10*, 293–294. doi:10.1016/0005-7916(79)90005-3

Rachman, S. J., & Wilson, G. T. (1980). *The effects of psychological therapy: Second enlarged edition*. New York, NY: Pergamon Press.

Rogers, C. R. (1957). The necessary and sufficient conditions of therapeutic personality change. *Journal of Consulting Psychology, 21*, 95–103. doi:10.1037/h0045357

Rogers, C. R. (1980). *A way of being*. Boston, MA: Houghton Mifflin.

Rogers, C. R., & Dymond, R. (1954). *Psychotherapy and personality change*. Chicago, IL: University of Chicago Press.

Rogers, C. R., Gendlin, E. T., Kiesler, D. J., & Truax, C. B. (1967). *The therapeutic relationship and its impact*. Madison, WI: University of Wisconsin Press.

Sexton, T. L., Alexander, J., & Mease, A. L. (2004). Levels of evidence for the models and mechanisms of therapeutic change in family and couple therapy. In M. J. Lambert (Ed.), *Bergin and Garfield's handbook of psychotherapy and behavior change* (5th ed., pp. 590–646). New York, NY: Wiley.

Shapiro, A. K. (1971). Placebo effects in medicine, psychotherapy and psychoanalysis. In A. E. Bergin & S. L. Garfield (Eds.), *Handbook of psychotherapy and behavior change* (pp. 439–473). New York, NY: Wiley.

Shapiro, D. A., & Shapiro, K. (1982). Meta-analysis of comparative outcome studies: A replication and refinement. *Psychological Bulletin, 92*, 581–604. doi:10.1037/0033-2909.92.3.581

Slade, K., Lambert, M. J., Harmon, S. C., Smart, D. W., & Bailey, R. (2008). Improving psychotherapy outcome: The use of immediate electronic feedback and revised clinical support tools. *Clinical Psychology & Psychotherapy, 15*, 287–303. doi:10.1002/cpp.594

Sloane, R. B., Staples, F. R., Cristol, A. H., Yorkston, N. J., & Whipple, K. (1975). *Psychotherapy versus behavior therapy*. Cambridge, MA: Harvard University Press.

Smith, M. L., Glass, G. V., & Miller, T. I. (1980). *The benefits of psychotherapy*. Baltimore, MD: Johns Hopkins University Press.

Snell, M. N., Mallinckrodt, B., Hill, R. D., & Lambert, M. J. (2001). Predicting counseling center client's response to counseling: A 1-year follow-up. *Journal of Counseling Psychology, 48*, 463–473. doi:10.1037/0022-0167.48.4.463

Stiles, W. B., Barkham, M., Twigg, E., Mellor-Clark, J., & Cooper, M. (2006). Effectiveness of cognitive behavioural, person-centered, and psychodynamic therapies as practiced in UK National Health Service settings. *Psychological Medicine, 36*, 555–566. doi:10.1017/S0033291706007136

Striano, J. (1982). Client perception of "helpful" and "not helpful" psychotherapeutic experience. *Dissertation Abstracts International, 43*, 4303B. (University Microfilms No. 80-17, 382)

Stuart, G. L., Treat, T. A., & Wade, W. A. (2000). Effectiveness of an empirically based treatment for panic disorder delivered in a service clinic setting: 1-year follow-up. *Journal of Consulting and Clinical Psychology, 68*, 506–512. doi:10.1037/0022-006X.68.3.506

Strupp, H. H. (1980a). Success and failure in time-limited psychotherapy: A systematic comparison of two cases-comparison 1. *Archives of General Psychiatry, 37*, 595–603.

Strupp, H. H. (1980b). Success and failure in time-limited psychotherapy: A systematic comparison of two cases-comparison 2. *Archives of General Psychiatry, 37*, 708–716.

Strupp, H. H. (1980c). Success and failure in time-limited psychotherapy: With special reference to the performance of a lay counselor. *Archives of General Psychiatry, 37*, 831–841.

Strupp, H. H. (1980d). Success and failure in time-limited psychotherapy: A systematic comparison of two cases-comparison 4. *Archives of General Psychiatry, 37*, 947–954.

Strupp, H. H., & Binder, J. L. (1984). *Psychotherapy in a new key: A guide to time limited dynamic psychotherapy*. New York, NY: Basic Books.

Strupp, H. H., Fox, R. E., & Lessler, K. J. (1969). *Patients view their psychotherapy*. Baltimore, MD: Johns Hopkins University Press.

Strupp, H. H., Hadley, S. W., & Gomes-Schwartz, B. (1977). *Psychotherapy for better or worse*. New York, NY: Jason Aronson.

Sundland, D. M. (1977). Theoretical orientations of psychotherapists. In A. S. Gurman & A. M. Razin (Eds.), *Effective psychotherapy: A handbook of research* (pp. 189–219). New York, NY: Pergamon Press.

Task Force on Promotion and Dissemination of Psychological Procedures. (1995). Training in and dissemination of empirically validated psychologist treatments: Report and recommendations. *Clinical Psychologist, 48*, 3–23.

Thompson, L. W., Gallagher, D., & Breckenridge, J. S. (1987). Comparative effectiveness of psychotherapies for depressed elders. *Journal of Consulting and Clinical Psychology, 55*, 385–390. doi:10.1037/0022-006X.55.3.385

Truax, C. B., & Carkhuff, R. R. (1967). *Toward effective counseling and psychotherapy*. Chicago, IL: Aldine.

Tuschen-Caffier, B., Pook, M., & Frank, M. (2001). Evaluation of manual-based cognitive-behavioral therapy for bulimia nervosa in a service setting. *Behaviour Research and Therapy, 39*, 299–308. doi:10.1016/S0005-7967(00)00004-8

Wade, W. A., Treat, T. A., & Stuart, G. L. (1998). Transporting an empirically supported treatment for panic disorder to a service clinic setting: A benchmarking strategy. *Journal of Consulting and Clinical Psychology, 66*, 231–239. doi:10.1037/0022-006X.66.2.231

Wampold, B. E. (1997). A meta-analysis of outcome studies comparing bona fide psychotherapies. Empirically, 'All must have prizes'. *Psychological Bulletin, 122*, 203–215. doi:10.1037/0033-2909.122.3.203

Wampold, B. E. (2008). *The great psychotherapy debate: Models, methods, and findings.* Mahwah, NJ: Erlbaum.

Wampold, B. E., & Brown, G. S. (2006). Estimating variability in outcomes attributable to therapists. A naturalistic study of outcomes in managed care. *Journal of Consulting and Clinical Psychology, 73*, 914–923. doi:10.1037/0022-006X.73.5.914

Weisz, J. R., Hawley, K. M., Pilkonis, P. A., Woody, S. R., & Follette, W. C. (2000). Stressing the (other) three rs in the search for empirically supported treatments: Review procedures, research quality, relevance to practice and the public interest. *Clinical Psychology: Science and Practice, 7*, 243–258. doi:10.1093/clipsy/7.3.243

Westen, D., Novotny, C. M., & Thompson-Brenne, H. (2004). The empirical status of empirically supported psychotherapies: Assumptions, findings, and reporting in controlled clinical trials. *Psychological Bulletin, 130*, 631–663. doi:10.1037/0033-2909.130.4.631

Whipple, J. L., Lambert, M. J., Vermeersch, D. A., Smart, D. W., Nielsen, S. L., & Hawkins, E. J. (2003). Improving the effects of psychotherapy: The use of early identification of treatment failure and problem-solving strategies in routine practice. *Journal of Counseling Psychology, 50*, 59–68. doi:10.1037/0022-0167.50.1.59

Wilkins, W. (1984). Psychotherapy: The powerful placebo. *Journal of Consulting and Clinical Psychology, 52*, 570–573.

Wolgast, B. M., Lambert, M. J., & Puschner, B. (2003). The dose-response relationship in a college counseling center: Implications for setting session limits. *Journal of College Student Psychotherapy, 8*, 15–29.

Woody, S. R., & Sanderson, W. C. (1998). Manuals for empirically supported treatments: 1998 update. *Clinical Psychology Review, 51*, 17–21.

Zeiss, A. M., Lewinsohn, P. M., & Munoz, R. F. (1979). Nonspecific improvement effects in depression using interpersonal skills training, pleasant activity schedules, and cognitive training. *Journal of Consulting and Clinical Psychology, 47*, 427–439. doi:10.1037/0022-006X.47.3.427

11

UNRESOLVED QUESTIONS AND FUTURE DIRECTIONS IN PSYCHOTHERAPY RESEARCH

BRUCE E. WAMPOLD, STEVEN D. HOLLON, AND CLARA E. HILL

Psychotherapy is a remarkably complex practice. Much has been learned over the many decades of research, but it is clear that there are many unanswered questions. Some of the unresolved issues are critical to understanding how best to deliver psychotherapy and how best to train psychotherapists. The path to knowledge, however, is not entirely clear. To some, randomized clinical trials (RCTs) are the most useful design because they involve experimental manipulations, giving rise to causal statements. Others hew to the idea that looking at quantitative indices of outcome masks the rich material generated in the complex therapeutic interaction and focuses on the *process* of psychotherapy. Lately, there have been attempts to integrate process and outcome. As well, as neuroscience develops and researchers understand the neural substrate of much of human behavior, knowledge of psychotherapy will inevitably be informed by neuroscientific investigations. In this chapter, we review these four strands of research with an eye to what they can and cannot tell us about psychotherapy and what the future might hold for research in the field.

RANDOMIZED CLINICAL TRIALS

Clinical interventions are conducted in an effort to make things better, either to keep something bad from happening (prevention) or to remove the bad once it has occurred (treatment). RCTs are done in an effort to determine whether a particular intervention has made things better, that is, whether it has had the intended causal effect. The first question to ask about an intervention is, Does it have the intended effect? Can the state of affairs observed after providing an intervention be attributed to what was done? In short, the question is whether it caused things to be better than they otherwise would have been.

Clinical trials can take any of several forms, including within-subjects designs and between-groups comparisons, but they all involve some type of intentional manipulation(s) in a manner that allows a causal inference to be drawn. Someone or members of some group receive an intervention that they were not already receiving that may subsequently be taken away or staggered across problems (in the case of single-subject designs) or that is not provided to some other group (in the case of randomized controlled trials), and consequences are observed. Clinical trials are said to be *controlled* because of the quality of intentionality. Simply observing what happens to people going through psychotherapy in an uncontrolled fashion might provide useful information, but it does not allow for ruling out rival explanations as to what actually caused the outcomes observed. Anecdotal case reports can provide a wealth of useful information and often form the starting point for the process of discovery, but they cannot rule out the possibility that any changes observed would not have happened in the absence of the psychotherapy (Kazdin, 1981).

When the pivotal question is whether some intentional act can produce the consequences intended, that is, if the goal is to draw a causal inference regarding the effects of psychotherapy, then most powerful way to answer that question is to do an experiment (Cronbach, 1957). Not all experiments involve intentional manipulations. Causal inferences can be drawn about the effects of genes and other "experiments of nature" when it is reasonable to conclude that preexistent factors could not have accounted for the consequences observed; but when it comes to intentional acts, the controlled experiment is the most powerful design for ruling out rival plausible alternatives to the notion that the intervention had a causal effect.

Psychotherapy had been a going concern for over half a century when Eysenck claimed that there was no good evidence that it actually had a causal effect (Eysenck, 1952). In his critique, Eysenck (1952) cited evidence indicating that patients who pursued psychotherapy fared no better than people who did not. The problem with that critique is that people were not randomized to treatment or its absence; rather, people who chose to pursue treatment (often at considerable expense) were compared with people who did not make that choice. It was likely that those who pursued no therapy were not as troubled as those who did. The debate that was triggered by Eysenck led to a spate of RCTs, the vast majority of which suggested that any reasonable psychotherapy was better than its absence (Luborsky, Singer, & Luborsky, 1975). Eysenck was clearly wrong in his critique (because he allowed individual differences to determine whether someone received treatment, thereby confounding patients and procedures), but he did have the effect of spurring the field to actually test the efficacy of treatment in a systematic fashion.

Eysenck (1952) was somewhat disingenuous in his critique; it was not just that he thought that the psychotherapies of the time (largely psychodynamic or humanistic) were ineffective but rather that he preferred another treatment (behavior therapy) that he considered to be more scientific. Carl Rogers developed a theoretical orientation that is often labeled *humanistic*, and he believed that the role of the therapist was not to guide treatment in a deterministic fashion but rather to create the conditions in therapy that would facilitate psychological growth within each patient. At the same time, Rogers was firmly committed to the notion of testing his therapy in a scientific fashion; in fact, he and his colleagues produced some of the first RCTs that showed that psychotherapy had a causal effect (Rogers & Dymond, 1954).

The simplest RCT compares a treatment with its absence. Patients are selected on a systematic basis and randomly assigned to either treatment or control, usually some form of wait list or assessment-only condition. The results of literally hundreds of such experiments are clear; most reasonable approaches to treatment work better than their absence. Not all types of treatments have been tested as extensively as others, and there are major gaps in the literature with respect to more severe and complex populations (the behavioral and cognitive behavioral therapies tend to have been more extensively explored than the other major schools). Nonetheless, there is good consensus across the field that on average most treatments work better than their absence (see Chapter 10, this volume, for details).

Scientific Validity of Clinical Trials

Clinical trials resemble classical experiments in that the research manipulates an independent variable to determine effects on a dependent variable. This type of design rules out several threats to the validity of the conclusions and therefore has reasonable validity compared with alternative designs.

Internal validity refers to the extent to which one can be sure that the effects observed can be attributed to the intervention (Campbell & Stanley, 1963). A major source of variability in outcomes is the patients, given that they often change over time whether something is done to them or not (e.g., most people recover from the flu even without treatment). A control condition in the design enables spontaneous remission to be differentiated from the effect of treatment. Different patients are likely to change in different ways over time in response to the same psychotherapy. Allowing individual differences between patients to determine what type of intervention they receive can confound the process of interpretation; that is, any subsequent differences observed could be as much a consequence of differences between patients in maturational course as a consequence of treatment. Randomization provides a means of controlling for patient differences; ideally, in an RCT, different kinds of patients are distributed equally across the groups, and subsequent differences in outcome can be attributed to the effects of the intervention.

RCTs and their logical equivalents (single-subject designs that provide the necessary internal controls to rule out rival causal interpretations) are the most powerful tools researchers have for drawing causal inferences about the consequences of clinical interventions. Nonetheless, RCTs are far from perfect. Randomization does not always work, and groups can be unbalanced simply as a consequence of chance, especially when the number of patients sampled is small. That is why investigators test to determine whether the treatment groups differ on pretreatment characteristics (and control statistically for any such differences observed) and stratify prior to randomization on important variables likely to predict subsequent course. Similarly, attrition can undermine the balance produced by initial randomization. That is why the field has come to prefer analyses based on all patients initially randomized to treatment (intent to treat) rather than restricting analyses to only samples of those patients who started treatment (modified intent to treat) or finished treatment (completer). The basic principle recommended by statisticians is "once randomized always analyze"; investigators risk undermining the internal validity of the conclusions drawn when that principle is violated.

External validity refers to the extent to which the findings observed in a study generalize to the conditions of actual interest (Campbell & Stanley, 1963). College students with elevated symptom scores may be more accessible to researchers in academic settings, but questions can be raised as to whether the results from experiments conducted on such participants generalize to bona fide clinical populations. The therapists selected for a given trial may not be adequately trained to implement the intervention of interest, or restrictions may be imposed by the design or the setting that prevent the intervention from being implemented in a fully representative fashion. Generalization can vary across multiple dimensions (including patients, therapists, and settings), and much of the existing literature has been criticized for screening out the complicated patients often seen by experienced therapists in actual clinical settings (Westen, Novonty, & Thompson-Brenner, 2004).

A distinction has been drawn in recent years between *efficacy* studies, which are often done in controlled research settings that seek to maximize internal validity, versus *effectiveness* trials, which are often done in applied clinical settings in an effort to maximize external validity (Nathan, Stuart, & Dolan, 2000). All efficacy trials are by definition randomized experiments, but that is only true for some effectiveness designs (Seligman, 1995). Effectiveness designs that do not involve randomization can address important questions, but they cannot rule out rival plausible alternatives to the notion that treatment had a causal effect. Internal and external validity are not necessarily incompatible, and it is possible to do randomized trials in a clinically representative fashion. However, it proves difficult, and good examples of studies that are high on both dimensions are hard to find in the literature.

It is easier to detect an effect than it is to explain it. That is because any attempt to explain an effect necessarily requires identifying the causal mechanisms through which the intervention works and the links between those causal mechanisms; the outcomes observed are not themselves directly manipulated (Baron & Kenny, 1986). Nonetheless, explanation is an important part of science, and knowing how an intervention works can facilitate efforts to maximize its effects. *Construct validity* is defined as the extent to which researchers understand how an intervention exerts its causal effects (Cook & Campbell, 1979). For as long as people have believed that psychotherapy is efficacious, they have argued as to how it produces its effects. All psychotherapies are accompanied by a theory that attempts to explain how each works. Sometimes the theory precedes the development of the intervention, and sometimes the theory follows the serendipitous discovery that an intervention works, but in either event refinements in theory can be used to refine the intervention and vice versa in a synergistic fashion.

Issues Inherent in Clinical Trials of Psychotherapy

Although it is now well accepted that most psychotherapies work, it remains unclear precisely how they work. There are several major schools that each puts forth a different specific explanation for how treatment works, as described elsewhere in this book (see Chapters 3–8, this volume). All schools of therapy have given rise to numerous specific offshoots, and much literature has been devoted to distinguishing among them and singing the praises of each.

There is yet another perspective that says what makes psychotherapy work is not what separates the competing schools but the common elements they all share (Frank & Frank, 1991). This perspective emphasizes the role of nonspecific factors believed to be present in all therapies: the provision of a compelling rationale for treatment and the mobilization of hope that things can be made better. It is not the specific strategies and techniques that separate the schools but the nonspecific aspects that they all share that are the causal mechanisms that drive change. To the extent that this is true, the field would be better served by investigating elements that the different treatments share rather than the specific techniques that differentiate them.

Addressing the issue of specificity versus common factors is complex because it is not always possible to implement a nonspecific control with a compelling rationale in which therapists can believe. It is easier to implement a nonspecific control in the form of pill (e.g., placebos in pharmacotherapy trials) because patients and prescribers can be blinded as to whether the pills contain an active medication. Such dismantling studies are inherently difficult to conduct in psychotherapy because both patient and provider know what is being done, and it is harder to disguise the absence of the theoretically specified active ingredient(s). Nonetheless, many studies exist that do control for therapeutic contact and attempt to equate the conditions on such nonspecific factors as treatment credibility and expectations for change. Some would argue that such efforts are doomed to fail and that any control condition that is not itself a bona fide treatment implemented by therapists who believe in its effects cannot possibly serve as an adequate nonspecific control (Baskin, Tierney, Minami, & Wampold, 2003).

Comparisons between two or more bona fide treatments that do address this concern provide the additional benefit of addressing differential efficacy. If two or more treatments each implemented by competent adherents produce differential effects and one is ipso facto superior to the other, it is likely so for nonspecific reasons. Researchers qualify the latter because it is still possible that one treatment may just be better than another at mobilizing nonspecific factors and that may account for its advantage, not the different strategies and techniques specified by theory. As we indicated earlier, it is easier to detect an effect (even a differential effect) than it is to explain it. Evidence for differential efficacy is sufficient to prefer one treatment over another but not sufficient to prove that the superior treatment works for the reasons specified. That would require a more extensive program of research that ideally would involve systematic assessment and manipulation of both specific and nonspecific factors in an effort to test the underlying theory.

There is at this time no consensus in the field as to whether psychotherapy works for reasons specified by theory or even whether differential efficacy can be said to exist with respect to most disorders. There are more high-quality studies supporting the efficacy of the behavioral and cognitive behavioral therapies than the more traditional insight-oriented or humanistic therapies, but the absence of evidence is not necessarily evidence of absence of comparable or superior efficacy. Not that many studies have directly compared treatments across the different schools, and fewer still have implemented each of the interventions in a fully representative fashion. Box-score and meta-analytic summaries that include all available studies regardless of quality typically find little evidence for differential efficacy and conclude that "all have won and all must have prizes" (Luborsky et al., 1975; Smith & Glass, 1977; Wampold et al., 1997), whereas summaries that require support from a minimum number of clinically representative studies across different research groups have tended to certify a smaller number of treatments as empirically supported for any given disorder (Chambless & Ollendick, 2001; Task Force on Promotion and Dissemination of Psychological Procedures, 1995). Critics of the more inclusive quantitative approach complain that including weak studies in the larger pool dilutes the effects of strong treatments, whereas critics of the less inclusive exemplar approach complain that it ignores negative findings and the *file drawer* problem.

Independent governmental agencies like the National Institute for Health and Clinical Excellence in England try to integrate the two approaches by restricting quantitative reviews to those studies that meet minimum quality criteria and then asking representatives from different theoretical perspectives to arrive at a Delphic consensus based on reasoned judgments regarding the findings and the studies underlying them. The result of this process has been to yield an outcome somewhat closer to the exemplar approach with only certain types of therapies (mostly cognitive or behavioral) certified for specific disorders, although it has been done with the clear recognition that often excluded therapies have not so much been shown not to work as well as those that are certified as much as to say that they have not been adequately tested. For example, the National Institute for Health and Clinical Excellence certifies three types of treatments for the treatment of posttraumatic stress disorder: prolonged exposure, cognitive behavior therapy (CBT), and eye-movement desensitization and reprocessing (Bisson et al., 2007); whereas a recent meta-analysis suggested that any of several therapies (including more traditional dynamic and humanistic approaches) were all comparable in effect (Benish, Imel, & Wampold, 2008).

What Researchers Need to Know

In summary, there is a broad consensus that any reasonable psychotherapy works better than its absence. There is considerably less consensus as to whether psychotherapy works for specific as opposed to nonspecific reasons and whether there is any support for the notion of differential efficacy across the different therapies. Meta-analytic studies suggest that all are effective, whereas reviews that rely on a minimum number of exemplary studies or Delphic consensus methods typically certify a smaller number of therapies. Each approach has its adherents, and the issue is not one that will be resolved soon. What remains unclear from the use of clinical trials in psychotherapy is whether different kinds of patients respond best to different therapies and the processes through which each intervention works.

It has long been the goal of psychotherapy research to identify the best treatment for a given patient (Paul, 1967). Efforts to accomplish this goal rest on the detection of moderation (patient characteristics that predict differential response to different treatments), and the best way to detect moderation is to randomly assign patients who differ in their characteristics to different treatments (Fournier et al., 2009). Simply providing different patients with the same treatment and noting who does better provides prognostic information that can be useful, but it does not serve as a basis for treatment selection. In effect, such prognostic designs indicate what to expect as a consequence of treatment (and who to select to make a treatment look good), not which treatment to select to maximize response for a given patient.

Given the crises in the cost of health care, future research must focus on how to improve the quality of mental health care in routine practice. There are emerging potential topics in this area. First, research is increasingly being focused on transporting evidence-based treatments to routine care (e.g., Addis et al., 2004; Weisz, Jensen-Doss, & Hawley, 2006). Second, the effect of providing therapists feedback on their progress appears to improve outcomes (Lambert, Harmon, Slade, Whipple, & Hawkins, 2005; Miller, Duncan, & Hubble, 2005). Although increasing the benefits of psychotherapy in routine care is absolutely critical, determining the costs of such quality improvement programs is necessary. How can the benefits of psychotherapy be improved most efficiently?

PROCESS RESEARCH

Given that researchers have consistently demonstrated that psychotherapy is effective, the burning question for future research is, What makes it effective? From their review of the literature of the contributors of improvement in psychotherapy, Asay and Lambert (1999) suggested that the therapeutic relationship accounted for 30% of the variance; extratherapeutic factors (patient and environmental characteristics) accounted for 40% of the variance; therapist techniques accounted for 15% of the variance; and expectancy (patient's hope and therapist credibility) accounted for 15% of the treatment. Although the exact percentages can be questioned given researchers' lack of sophistication about how to measure these factors and their contribution to outcome, these figures provide some beginning indication about the important process contributors. In this section, then, we discuss the future directions and unresolved questions related to the contributions of patients, therapists, the therapeutic relationship, and the interaction among these factors to psychotherapy process.

Patient Characteristics

Several researchers have reviewed the multitude of variables (e.g., motivation, level of psychopathology, gender, and race) that have been assessed in the literature (e.g., Clarkin & Levy, 2004). Here, we focus on two variables that seem very promising: patient readiness for change and patient involvement.

Given that patients are the ones who come to psychotherapy seeking helping, who disclose their problems, who have to implement the changes suggested in psychotherapy, and who have to adjust to the changes in their lives, it is not surprising that patient motivation (or readiness for change) for participating in the therapy process has been found to relate to the outcome of psychotherapy. Patient readiness for change has been divided into several stages (Prochaska, Norcross, & DiClemente, 1994). In the *precontemplation stage*, patients have no desire to change and are unaware of their problems and impact on others. In the *contemplation stage*, patients are beginning to become aware of their problems, and they are thinking about changing. In the *preparation stage*, patients have decided they want to change and are taking small steps toward the change process. In the *action stage*, patients are in the process of actively modifying their behaviors or environments. In the *maintenance stage*, patients work to consolidate their changes and deal with lapses and problems as they arise. At the end of this process, patients are no longer troubled by the initial problem and have confidence that they can cope without relapse. Readiness to change has been assessed by a multitude of paper-and-pencil measures. Strong support has been shown for the importance of identifying which stage patients are in, and evidence indicates that therapists use different strategies when patients are in different stages (see Prochaska & Norcross, 2002).

A related variable that seems promising is patient involvement, which can be defined as openness, engagement, cooperation, and active participation in the psychotherapy process. Patient involvement probably reflects patient motivation for change, being in the action stage of readiness to change, and feeling good about working with the particular therapist (see more in the section that follows on the working alliance). Patient involvement can be assessed by having judges code the behavior of patients by listening to tapes of therapy sessions (e.g., Hill et al., 1992) or by having patients rate themselves or by therapists rating patients (e.g., Eugster & Wampold, 1996). Patient involvement has been related to the therapeutic alliance (e.g., Karver et al. 2008) and treatment outcome (e.g., Eugster & Wampold, 1996; O'Malley, Suh, & Strupp, 1983). The opposite of patient involvement is patient resistance (e.g., Mahalik, 1994), also an important construct in need of further study. Of particular interest is how to increase patient involvement and decrease patient resistance, that is, what can therapists do to help patients become more involved and less defended or resistant? Unfortunately, no consistent definition or measure of patient involvement or resistance has been used, so although intuitively appealing, these constructs deserve further exploration.

Therapist Characteristics

The person of the psychotherapist is a huge part of the process of therapy. Empirically, there is strong evidence of therapist effects (Beutler et al., 2004; Wampold, 2001), although there is less evidence for what aspects of therapists contribute to these results. In this section, we look at the therapist techniques and personal reactions as variables that merit attention.

We contend that what the therapist does within sessions has a huge impact on the immediate and long-term outcome of therapy, but investigating the connection between therapist actions and outcomes is extremely complex. First, therapist actions can be conceptualized in many ways—nonverbal behaviors, verbal response modes, overall treatment approach, flexibility in applying techniques to the individual patient, or ability to track the patient. Second, the context of the therapist action is critical because what works differs depending on the moment in therapy. These comments are not meant to imply that techniques are not important, only that researchers have not figured out well how to study them.

The most typical way that therapist techniques have been assessed is through coding verbal response modes (VRMs; e.g., reflection of feelings, interpretation) in transcripts or videotapes of therapy sessions. Much of the early research focused on correlating the frequency or proportion of VRMs with session or treatment outcome. Mixed and inconsistent results were found in these studies, probably because of the inappropriate use of a correlational strategy. In this regard, Stiles (1988) commented that it is not the number of VRMs (i.e., more is not necessarily better) but rather the therapist's responsiveness to giving the patient what he or she needs at the moment in therapy that should be related to outcome.

Given the concerns about correlational strategies, researchers moved to analyzing the immediate effects of therapist VRMs (e.g., how does the patient respond in the next speaking turn when the therapist uses an interpretation). For example, one study (Hill et al., 1988) examined all the immediate effects of therapist VRMs in 127 sessions of psychotherapy (eight therapist–patient dyads in brief therapy for 12 to 20 sessions). Therapist VRMs accounted for only 1% of the variance of immediate outcome (patient and therapist helpfulness ratings, patient experiencing in the subsequent speaking turn, and patient self-reported reactions). When added into the equation, therapist intentions and previous patient experiences accounted for more of the variance (but not a lot) than did therapist VRMs. One suggestion for the lack of effects for VRMs was that the complexity of therapy was not accounted for. In other words, it makes little sense that a reflection of feelings would have a uniform impact on therapy. Rather, the helpfulness of the reflection is probably dependent on how it is presented (quality, accompanying nonverbals), when it is presented (stage of therapy, the problem being discussed, and what interventions have preceded the reflection), and patient needs at the time. Thus, although this method of coding all the VRMs within several cases and examining the immediate impact is appealing, obvious problems arise is trying to interpret the data.

A more recent strategy for studying therapist techniques is to investigate specific techniques within a case study so that context can be taken into account. For example, Hill and colleagues recently conducted two case studies on therapist immediacy (Hill et al., 2008; Kasper, Hill, & Kivlighan, 2008), which they defined as working with the therapeutic relationship in the here and now. Immediacy involves such therapist actions as inquiring about reactions to the therapy relationship, drawing parallels between other relationships and the therapy relationship, processing ruptures or boundary crossings, and disclosing feelings of closeness to or lack of closeness to others. The positive effects across the two cases were very similar (facilitated negotiation of the therapeutic relationship, provided a corrective relational experience), although the therapist in the Kasper et al. study more often used challenging forms of immediacy that helped break down the patient's defenses and the therapist in the Hill et al. (2008) study more often used supportive forms of immediacy that helped build the patient's fragile ego. Thus, these two cases illustrate the benefits of using a qualitative case study methodology to study therapist techniques. Other therapist techniques that merit careful attention are interpretations, challenges, paradoxical interventions, self-disclosures, and reflections of feelings.

Personal reactions of therapists (e.g., countertransference) also seem to exert influence on the process and outcome of psychotherapy (Gelso & Hayes, 2007). It appears that it is important for therapists to be aware of these personal reactions and manage them in the therapy process to avoid harming patients (Williams, Hurley, O'Brien, & DeGregorio, 2003). Finding appropriate strategies for assessing personal reactions and management strategies is a challenge.

The Therapeutic Relationship

The therapeutic relationship has been characterized as one of the most robust predictors of outcome, although estimates are that the relationship accounts for only a modest amount of outcome variance (Horvath & Bedi, 2002). Thus, when patients perceive that they feel a bond with their therapists and agree with their therapists about the tasks and goals of therapy, the outcome is better than when patients do not feel such an alliance with their therapists.

Researchers know that the therapeutic relationship is related to outcome, although they do not know exactly what the mechanism is by which it leads to change. We propose that researchers need to know more about how the relationship is built and how it is fixed when broken. Given Bordin's (1979, 1994) ideas about tear and repair, repairing ruptures probably builds stronger therapeutic relationships (see also Hill & Knox, 2009). Safran, Muran, Samstag, and Stevens (2002) have done groundbreaking research on the repair of ruptures in therapy. Their research points to four stages in the resolution of ruptures. First, the therapist notices the rupture (e.g., patient withdrawal or hostility). Second, the therapist helps the patient explore feelings related to the rupture. Third, the therapist helps the patient examine avoidance related to discussing the rupture. Finally, the patient begins to be able to explore the precipitants of the rupture. Continued research is needed about which patients are most suited for this kind of work, as well as about when and how to do it.

Interaction Among Patient, Therapist, and Relationship Variables

Beyond determining the effectiveness of the individual components, it is important for researchers to investigate the intertwining of patient characteristics, therapy characteristics, and the relationship in terms of their impact on psychotherapy. Psychotherapists probably build the relationship through specific techniques with patients who are motivated, and then they use the relationship as a foundation for using other techniques to help patients change (Hill, 2005). But patients have to be involved and work outside of therapy, using the therapist as a consultant, and thus circumstances outside of therapy also facilitate or hinder the change process. Furthermore, therapy is probably a mediated process such that a certain amount of exploration is needed before the patient can gain insight, which is needed before the patient can take action; different therapist techniques undoubtedly facilitate these different steps. Although researching the interaction among the three components will be difficult, this is clearly a good direction for future exploration.

Furthermore, new methods are needed for linking process to outcome. As mentioned earlier, correlational strategies (i.e., correlating the frequency or proportion of process events to outcome) seem to be inappropriate. Sequential analyses (i.e., relating process events to immediate outcomes within sessions) are slightly better but ignore important contextual variables. Event analyses are useful for examining what takes place over different episodes (e.g., ruptures, talking about the relationship) within therapy, but it is difficult to summarize across events and make linkages with treatment outcome. Qualitative strategies (i.e., interviewing therapists and patients retrospectively) are useful from a descriptive perspective but cannot provide causal evidence. Clearly, new methods are needed.

What Researchers Need to Know

Clearly, researchers have learned much about the process of psychotherapy, yet there are a number of areas for which illuminating research is needed. As indicated, understanding is emerging with regard to patient readiness for change and involvement in the therapeutic process, but researchers need to know more about how patients can be motivated to seek psychotherapy, what perceived barriers exist, and how help seeking, motivation, and involvement can be increased. It may be that much of this process occurs prior to the commencement of therapy and sociocultural factors are involved.

At a microprocess level, personal reactions of patients to therapist techniques remains another area in which research can yield further knowledge. Determining how the therapeutic alliance is generated from complex interactions of therapist and patient is particularly important given the robust connection between alliance and outcome. Although it has been established that the alliance is critical to successful therapy, relatively little is known about optimal development of the alliance over time and role of the tear and repair of the alliance in psychotherapy.

Predominantly, psychotherapy research has relied on a linear causation assumption: patient and therapist characteristics→therapeutic process→outcome. However, most would agree that psychotherapy is a complex transaction between a therapist who has various characteristics and patients who have various characteristics, in a particular context and with various concomitant external events, that unfolds over time, creating reciprocal causal relations with chaotic and emergent properties. Process research has great potential for understanding this level of complexity.

Another important area for further process research involves examining the effects of various therapist interventions (e.g., interpretations, challenges) within a case study format. Once a number of case studies are done, meta-synthesis can be used to determine commonalities and differences across cases (Iwakabe & Gazzola, 2009).

Finally, the recent research on measuring outcome to provide feedback to therapists (Lambert et al., 2005) presents another opportunity for process researchers. If feedback is effective, as it appears to be, then it would be informative to know what therapists do when they receive feedback to improve their outcomes.

INTEGRATING PROCESS AND OUTCOME

To this point, we have presented two very different research strategies to understanding psychotherapy. On the one hand are RCTs focused on investigating whether a particular treatment affects outcomes vis-à-vis a control group. On the other hand are process studies that examine what happens within therapy. Although the paradigms might appear to be incommensurable, there have been increasing efforts to integrate the approaches to, in a sense, have the best of both worlds. Of course, the goals of the two paradigms are, in some ways, comparable. Clinical researchers are not solely on a mission to find the most efficacious treatment; they are keenly interested in how treatments work and ways to improve those treatments. A variant of the RCT involves the dismantling a design in which a full treatment is compared with the treatment without a purported critical ingredient (Borkovec, 1990) to test whether the ingredient is important for therapeutic benefits. Process researchers are not content to describe what happens in therapy but want to tie the various process variables to outcome. Clearly, the future ideal is an integration of process and outcome research.

One perspicuous difficulty in melding the two paradigms is that most process variables cannot be experimentally manipulated. The logic of RCTs depends on an experimental manipulation to establish causality; for the most part, process variables such as the alliance, patient readiness for change, and therapist responses to patients (except in a general theoretic manner as specified in manuals) cannot be manipulated. Nevertheless, these process variables may well be causal variables in the sense that they undoubtedly affect outcomes of psychotherapy. That is to say, the fact that practically or ethically a variable cannot be manipulated does not preclude causality, as in the example that there is a strong consensus that smoking causes certain human disease despite the fact that no one has experimentally manipulated nicotine inhalation in humans.

Transactional Nature of Process Variables

Most of the critical process variables are created in the transaction between the therapist and the patient. Consider the therapeutic alliance, which cannot exist independent of the transaction. The alliance, which is conceptualized as the bond as well agreement on the tasks and goals of therapy (Bordin, 1979, 1994), refers to a collaboration between patient and therapist (Hatcher & Barends, 2006). Surely, levels of the alliance cannot be experimentally manipulated; more cumbersome for understanding the alliance is the fact that it is not solely under the control of the therapist. Some patients come to therapy with reasonable set of social skills, have a decent attachment history, and are motivated to work in therapy; these patients will likely form a productive working alliance with most therapists. Other patients, however, will have a different profile—poor social skills, a disturbed attachment history, and a resistance to change—and they will have difficulty forming a bond with the therapist and may well resist setting goals and fail to comply with the tasks of therapy (Mallinckrodt, 1991). On the therapist side, some therapists will form alliances across a variety of patients: that is, a given patient will report a better alliance with some therapists than the patient would with other therapists. The therapist and the patient bring to therapy certain propensities, but nevertheless the alliance is built in the context of the therapy, changes over the course of therapy, and may well depend on the match of the therapist and patient (i.e., the "chemistry" of this particular patient–therapist pair). Moreover, the alliance may also be, to a large extent, *the result* of early benefit of therapy. So, the association of alliance and outcome could be due to (a) the patient's contribution to the alliance, (b) the therapist's contribution to the alliance, (c) the match of the therapist and the patient, or (d) early improvement in therapy (DeRubeis, Brotman, & Gibbons, 2005). Unfortunately, neither the typical RCT nor the typical process research can discriminate among the four explanations, limiting knowledge about psychotherapy process and outcome. However, as discussed in the following section, there are statistical methods coming on line that are suitable to investigating such questions, but first an ignored aspect of therapy should be included.

Therapist Effects

At the origins of the randomized design in agriculture, medicine, and education, the provider of the practice (viz., the farmer, the physician, and the teacher) was not considered an important factor to consider in the design and analysis of experiments that focused on outcomes (Danziger, 1990; Serlin, Wampold, & Levin, 2003; Wampold, 2001). This omission occurred despite the fact that the statistical machinery necessary for estimating the importance of the provider has been well-known since the origins of the analysis of variance (Serlin et al., 2003). Psychotherapy research has been no different (Wampold, 2001) despite evidence that psychotherapists, within treatments and in clinical trials and in practice, vary considerably in their outcomes (Huppert et al., 2001; Kim, Wampold, & Bolt, 2006; Wampold & Brown, 2005). Although the therapist is often a focus for process researchers, his or her presence in outcome research has largely been ignored.

Ignoring therapist effects in clinical trials has three pernicious effects. First, it is important to know whether some therapists consistently attain better outcomes than others. If this is the case, as it appears that it is, then future research should be addressed toward investigating the characteristics and actions of the more effective therapists. Second, ignoring therapist effects creates inferential problems for RCTs. Failing to consider that patients are nested within therapists (i.e., each therapist treats multiple patients) inflates treatment effects (Wampold & Serlin, 2000). As well, ignoring therapists limits the generalizability of evidence produced by RCTs because the results are specific to the therapists who conducted the treatment (Serlin et al., 2003); this is exacerbated by the fact that the number of therapists in RCTs is typically small, and the therapists are selected for their expertise and are provided training, supervision, and feedback. Third, ignoring therapists precludes investigating how process variables are related to outcome. That is, patient, therapist, and match contributions to a phenomenon cannot be disentangled if the therapist is not considered (Baldwin, Wampold, & Imel, 2007).

Multilevel Models

Multilevel statistical models can be applied in psychotherapy research to account for the fact that patients are nested within therapists (Hox, 2002; Snijders & Bosker, 1999). Multilevel models estimate the proportion of variability in outcomes due to variables at various levels (e.g., patient level, therapist level, and treatment level) so that the importance of the variables for outcome can be assessed. Thus, multilevel models address questions such as, How important are therapist variables vis-à-vis treatment variables? Multilevel models can then be used to disentangle therapist and patient contributions to various process variables. For example, Baldwin and colleagues (2007) used multilevel models and found that the therapist's contribution to the alliance was related to outcome, whereas the patient's contribution was not. That is, therapists who generally had higher alliances with their patients also generally had better outcomes, but patients who had better alliances with a given therapist did not have better outcomes than other patients seeing the same therapist.

The same method can also be used examine other process variables. Adherence to a treatment protocol is an important variable in psychotherapy research (Waltz, Addis, Koerner, & Jacobson, 1993). However, adherence to the protocol is not simply a therapist variable because cooperative and motivated patients permit their therapists to adhere to the typical sequence of a treatment, whereas and resistant and difficult patients can create havoc for adherence. Thus, multilevel models could illuminate the effects of adherence on outcome.

Multilevel models can also incorporate longitudinal data so that the process of psychotherapy can better be examined. These models are best applied when both process and outcome measures are measured regularly so that the cause and effect can be examined (Klein et al., 2003). Such examinations should always be nested within therapists so that both temporal and nested aspects of psychotherapy can be disentangled.

What Researchers Need to Know

Clinical trials have focused on particular treatments, whereas process research has mined the complexity of the interaction between therapist and patient. Future research needs to integrate the two strands to explore the complexities of psychotherapy. There is little doubt that the therapist delivering a particular treatment is critical to success; consequently, future investigations, including RCTs and process studies, will need to include therapists as a factor. This necessitates attention to power issues and an increase in the number of therapists in studies. A fundamental unanswered question in psychotherapy is, What are the characteristics and actions of effective therapists? Once that question is answered, attention can be focused on how to better train therapists to be effective.

To understand how the process of psychotherapy unfolds over time, various outcome and process variables will need to be collected over time. Recently there has been increased attention to studying the trajectories of change (e.g., Baldwin, Berkeljon, Atkins, Olsen, & Nielsen, 2009), and future research is needed in this area.

ATTENDING TO BIOLOGICAL PROCESSES IN PSYCHOTHERAPY

Biological variables can be just as relevant to understanding psychotherapy and selecting treatments as psychological ones. With the decoding of the human genome and the rapid advance in gene-processing technologies, it has become possible to relate genetic variation to treatment response. Many of the recent efforts to personalize medicine have been focused on identifying those genes that predict differential response to different medications. The same logic can be as readily applied to different psychotherapies and medications for mental disorders. Ideally, blood or tissue samples could be subjected to genetic analysis and related to variability in subsequent treatment response. We know of no study that has done so to date, but the technologies exist and the possible benefits are evident.

We know that genes are only part of the story (most nonpsychotic disorders are less than half heritable), but any strategy that helps account for even part of the variability in outcome will facilitate the detection of the remaining components. For example, detecting the presence of a gene–environment interaction facilitated specification of the causal role of negative life events in the etiology of depression (Caspi et al., 2003). The same kind of logic can be used to isolate the extent to which psychotherapy plays a causal role in the amelioration of psychological distress. Even in disorders as heritable as autism, insights gleaned from cognitive and developmental neuroscience have been used to develop psychosocial strategies that slow the expression of the disorder (Dawson, 2008).

Similarly, recent advances in neural imaging provide a means of refining what researchers know about how psychotherapy works and of developing novel psychosocial interventions. Any change in affect or behavior has underlying neural correlates, and any encoding of memories or learning of new information involves physical changes in the brain. Specifying the neural correlates of the changes induced by psychotherapy will contribute to a greater understanding of the mechanisms through which those treatments work and the patient process that contribute to the etiology and maintenance of the disorder. This will be true whether those neural mechanisms are specific to the particular intervention or not. For example, both CBT and medication for obsessive–compulsive disorder were found to be associated with decreased caudate activity in treatment responders and reduced linkage between the orbitofrontal cortex, the caudate, and the thalamus (Baxter et al., 1992). This suggests that these two very different treatments either mobilize similar neural mechanisms in the process of change or that changes in those specific neural regions are epiphenomenal consequences of successful treatment and do not play a causal role in the production of change.

Conversely, there are indications that CBT and medications may work through different neural mechanisms in the amelioration of depression (Goldapple et al., 2004). Depression is marked by hyperactive limbic and brainstem processes that contribute to emotional reactivity and hypoactive cortical processes that typically serve to regulate those lower processes. Antidepressant medications appear to work from the "bottom up" by turning down those hyperactive limbic and brainstem processes, whereas CBT appears to work from the "top down" by strengthening higher cortical regulatory processes (DeRubeis, Siegle, & Hollon, 2008). These differences in patterns of neural changes are particularly intriguing in that CBT appears to have an enduring effect not found for medications after treatment termination (Hollon, Stewart, & Strunk, 2006). Although it has yet to be tested explicitly, it would be interesting to relate neural changes specific to CBT to its enduring effects. Researchers do not yet know what neural processes mediate CBT's enduring effects, but they do know that something is different in the brains of patients who respond to CBT versus patients who respond to medications alone.

Neural imagining can not only help researchers refine their understanding of how different treatments work but also guide the development of novel treatments. For example, training patients to recognize bird calls serves to strengthen the anterior cingulate, a region of the brain that plays a role in regulating lower limbic processes, and leads to a reduction in affective distress (Siegle, Ghinassi, & Thase, 2007). The idea was suggested by an understanding of the ways that different neural systems interact and led to the adoption of a strategy that proved to be successful despite the complete lack of face validity. Adding to the intriguing possibilities is research on the neurochemical effects of placebos and expectations in real and sham treatments (Benedetti, 2009).

The growing understanding of the neural substrates of behavior may even deepen researchers' understanding of the mechanisms underlying effective prevention. Maier, Amat, Baratta, Paul, and Watkins (2006) showed that rats exposed to controllable stress are inoculated against the deleterious effects of subsequent exposure to uncontrollable stress. Moreover, they were able to identify the neural pathways that mediate this learned resilience. In brief, exposure to uncontrollable stress activates the raphe nucleus in the brainstem that in turns sends serotonergic projections to the amygdale and other limbic structures that activate the stress response. However, exposure to controllable stress activates the ventral medial prefrontal cortex (mPFCv), a higher cortical center that has direct inhibitory connections to the raphe nucleus. Pharmacological inhibition of mPFCv firing during exposure to controllable stress blocks the acquisition of this acquired resilience (the rats act as if they had been exposed to uncontrollable stress), whereas pharmacological facilitation of mPFCv firing during exposure to uncontrollable stress leads to resilience in the face of subsequent stress (the rats act as if they had been exposed to controllable stress). Researchers have long known that a sense of control provides a psychological buffer against stress, but they have not understood the neural mechanisms that underlie that effect. Researchers now have efficacious preventive interventions for disorders like depression (Garber et al., 2009). It would be of interest to see if those interventions mobilize the same neural processes that have been shown to facilitate resilience in animal experimentation.

There is no necessary incompatibility between biological and psychological explanations. Everything researchers do rests on a biological basis, and a better understanding of the neural substrates underlying human behavior will only facilitate the understanding of the processes that drive therapeutic change. That is not to say that all psychological processes must be explained in biological terms or that somatic or pharmacological interventions are necessarily superior to psychological ones, just that researchers enrich the understanding of what goes on in psychotherapy to the extent that they understand the neural processes that underlie those changes. With the advent of modern tools for exploring genetic variation and imaging neural processes, researchers move closer to realizing Freud's dream of understanding the neural processes underlying human behavior.

CONCLUSION

In this chapter, we have discussed two paradigms—clinical trials (outcome research) and process research—as well as means to integrate the two. As well, we have speculated about how neuroscience might inform the field about the process and outcome of psychotherapy. There are those who see another distinction, namely, the quantitative versus qualitative approaches. This distinction, alluded to in this chapter, is grounded in a philosophy of science argument, a full discussion of which is beyond the scope of this chapter (see Hunsberger, 2007; Schneider, 2008; Wendt & Slife, 2007). An argument can be made that quantifying discrete aspects of psychotherapy places the procedure in a positivist framework, although the phenomenon belongs in the humanistic and intersubjective realm, which only phenomenological-based investigation can capture. The exciting aspect of anticipating the future is the realization that research methods that cannot now be envisaged will be used in innovative and productive ways.

REFERENCES

Addis, M. E., Hatgis, C., Krasnow, A. D., Jacob, K., Bourne, L., & Mansfield, A. (2004). Effectiveness of cognitive–behavioral treatment for panic disorder versus treatment as usual in a managed care setting. *Journal of Consulting and Clinical Psychology, 72*, 625–635. doi:10.1037/0022-006X.72.4.625

Asay, T. P., & Lambert, M. J. (1999). The empirical case for the common factors in therapy: Quantitative findings. In M. A. Hubble, B. L. Duncan, & S. D. Miller (Eds.), *The heart and soul of change: What works in therapy* (pp. 23–55). Washington, DC: American Psychological Association.

Baldwin, S. A., Berkeljon, A., Atkins, D. C., Olsen, J. A., & Nielsen, S. L. (2009). Rates of change in naturalistic psychotherapy: Contrasting dose effect and good-enough level models of change. *Journal of Consulting and Clinical Psychology, 77*, 203–211. doi:10.1037/a0015235

Baldwin, S. A., Wampold, B. E., & Imel, Z. E. (2007). Untangling the alliance–outcome correlation: Exploring the relative importance of therapist and patient variability in the alliance. *Journal of Consulting and Clinical Psychology, 75*, 842–852. doi:10.1037/0022-006X.75.6.842

Baron, R. M., & Kenny, D. A. (1986). The moderator–mediator variable distinction in social psychological research: Conceptual, strategic, and statistical considerations. *Journal of Personality and Social Psychology, 51*, 1173–1182. doi:10.1037/0022-3514.51.6.1173

Baskin, T. W., Tierney, S. C., Minami, T., & Wampold, B. E. (2003). Establishing specificity in psychotherapy: A meta-analysis of structural equivalence of placebo controls. *Journal of Consulting and Clinical Psychology, 71*, 973–979. doi:10.1037/0022-006X.71.6.973

Baxter, L. R., Jr., Schwartz, J. M., Bergman, K. S., Szuba, M. P., Guze, B. H., Mazziotta, J. C., . . . Phelps, M. E. (1992). Caudate glucose metabolic rate changes with both drug and behavior therapy for obsessive-compulsive disorder. *Archives of General Psychiatry, 49*, 681–689.

Benedetti, F. (2009). *Placebo effects: Understanding the mechanisms in health and disease.* New York, NY: Oxford University Press.

Benish, S. G., Imel, Z. E., & Wampold, B. E. (2008). The relative efficacy of bona fide psychotherapies for treating post-traumatic stress disorder: A meta-analysis of direct comparisons. *Clinical Psychology Review, 28*, 746–758. doi:10.1016/j.cpr.2007.10.005

Beutler, L. E., Malik, M., Alimohamed, S., Harwood, T. M., Talebi, H., Noble, S., & Wong, E. (2004). Therapist variables. In M. J. Lambert (Ed.), *Handbook of psychotherapy and behavior change* (5th ed., pp. 194–226). New York, NY: Wiley.

Bisson, J. I., Ehlers, A., Matthews, R., Pilling, S., Richards, D., & Turner, S. (2007). Psychological treatments for chronic post-traumatic stress disorder: Systematic review and meta-analysis. *The British Journal of Psychiatry, 190,* 97–104. doi:10.1192/bjp.bp.106.021402

Bordin, E. S. (1979). The generalizability of the psychoanalytic concept of the working alliance. *Psychotherapy: Theory, Research and Practice, 16,* 252–260. doi:10.1037/h0085885

Bordin, E. S. (1994). Theory and research on the therapeutic working alliance: New directions. In A. O. Horvath & L. S. Greenberg (Eds.), *The working alliance: Theory, research, and practice* (pp. 13–37). New York, NY: Wiley.

Borkovec, T. D. (1990). Control groups and comparison groups in psychotherapy outcome research. *National Institute on Drug Abuse Research Monograph, 104,* 50–65.

Campbell, D. T., & Stanley, J. C. (1963). *Experimental and quasi-experimental designs for research and teaching.* Chicago, IL: Rand McNally.

Caspi, A., Sugden, K., Moffitt, T. E., Taylor, A., Craig, I. W., Harrington, H. L., . . . Poulton, R. (2003, July 18). Influence of life stress on depression: Moderation by a polymorphism in the 5-HTT gene. *Science, 301,* 386–389. doi:10.1126/science.1083968

Chambless, D. L., & Ollendick, T. H. (2001). Empirically supported psychological interventions: Controversies and evidence. *Annual Review of Psychology, 52,* 685–716. doi:10.1146/annurev.psych.52.1.685

Clarkin, J. F., & Levy, K. N. (2004). The influence of client variables on psychotherapy. In M. J. Lambert (Ed.), *Handbook of psychotherapy and behavior change* (5th ed., pp. 194–226). New York, NY: Wiley.

Cook, T. D., & Campbell, D. T. (1979). *Quasi-experimentation: Design and analysis issues for field settings.* Chicago, IL: Rand McNally.

Cronbach, L. J. (1957). Two disciplines of scientific psychology. *American Psychologist, 12,* 671–684. doi:10.1037/h0043943

Danziger, K. (1990). *Constructing the subject: Historical origins of psychological research.* Cambridge, England: Cambridge University Press.

Dawson, G. (2008). Early behavioral intervention, brain plasticity, and the prevention of autism spectrum disorder. *Development and Psychopathology, 20,* 775–803. doi:10.1017/S0954579408000370

DeRubeis, R. J., Brotman, M. A., & Gibbons, C. J. (2005). A conceptual and methodological analysis of the nonspecifics argument. *Clinical Psychology: Science and Practice, 12,* 174–183. doi:10.1093/clipsy/bpi022

DeRubeis, R. J., Siegle, G. J., & Hollon, S. D. (2008). Cognitive therapy versus medication for depression: Treatment outcomes and neural mechanisms. *Nature Reviews Neuroscience, 9,* 788–796. doi:10.1038/nrn2345

Eugster, S., & Wampold, B. (1996). Systematic effects of participant role on evaluation of the psychotherapy session. *Journal of Consulting and Clinical Psychology, 63,* 268–278.

Eysenck, H. J. (1952). The effects of psychotherapy: An evaluation. *Journal of Consulting Psychology, 16,* 319–324. doi:10.1037/h0063633

Frank, J. D., & Frank, J. B. (1991). *Persuasion and healing: A comparative study of psychotherapy* (3rd ed.). Baltimore, MD: Johns Hopkins University Press.

Fournier, J. C., DeRubeis, R. J., Shelton, R. C., Hollon, S. D., Amsterdam, J. D., & Gallop, R. (2009). Prediction of response to medication and cognitive therapy in the treatment of moderate to severe depression. *Journal of Consulting and Clinical Psychology, 77,* 775–787. doi:10.1037/a0015401

Garber, J., Clarke, G. N., Weersing, V. R., Beardslee, W. R., Brent, D. A., Gladstone, T. R. G., . . . Iyengar, S. (2009). Prevention of depression in at-risk adolescents: A randomized controlled trial. *JAMA*, *301*, 2215–2224. doi:10.1001/jama.2009.788

Gelso, C. J., & Hayes, J. A. (2007). *Countertransference and the therapist's inner experience: Perils and possibilities*. Mahwah, NJ: Erlbaum.

Goldapple, K., Segal, Z., Garson, C., Lau, M., Bieling, P., Kennedy, S., & Mayberg, H. (2004). Modulation of cortical-limbic pathways in major depression: Treatment-specific effects of cognitive behavior therapy. *Archives of General Psychiatry*, *61*, 34–41. doi:10.1001/archpsyc.61.1.34

Hatcher, R. L., & Barends, A. W. (2006). How a return to theory could help alliance research. *Psychotherapy*, *43*, 292–299. doi:10.1037/0033-3204.43.3.292

Hill, C. E. (2005). Therapist techniques, client involvement, and the therapeutic relationship: Inextricably intertwined in the therapy process. *Psychotherapy: Theory, Research, Practice, Training*, *42*, 431–442.

Hill, C. E., Corbett, M. M., Kanitz, B., Rios, P., Lightsey, R., & Gomez, M. (1992). Client behavior in counseling and therapy sessions: Development of a pantheoretical measure. *Journal of Counseling Psychology*, *39*, 539–549. doi:10.1037/0022-0167.39.4.539

Hill, C. E., Helms, J. E., Tichenor, V., Spiegel, S. B., O'Grady, K. E., & Perry, E. S. (1988). The effects of therapist response modes in brief psychotherapy. *Journal of Counseling Psychology*, *35*, 222–233. doi:10.1037/0022-0167.35.3.222

Hill, C. E., & Knox, S. (2009). Processing the therapeutic relationship. *Psychotherapy Research*, *19*, 13–29. doi:10.1080/10503300802621206

Hill, C. E., Sim, W., Spangler, P., Stahl, J., Sullivan, C., & Teyber, E. (2008). Therapist immediacy in brief psychotherapy therapy: Case Study II. *Psychotherapy: Theory, Research, Practice, Training*, *45*, 298–315.

Hollon, S. D., Stewart, M. O., & Strunk, D. (2006). Cognitive behavior therapy has enduring effects in the treatment of depression and anxiety. *Annual Review of Psychology*, *57*, 285–315. doi:10.1146/annurev.psych.57.102904.190044

Horvath, A. O., & Bedi, R. P. (2002). The alliance. In J. C. Norcross (Ed.), *Psychotherapy relationships that work: Therapist contributions and responsiveness to patients* (pp. 37–70). New York, NY: Oxford University Press.

Hox, J. (2002). *Multilevel analysis: Techniques and applications*. Mahwah, NJ: Erlbaum.

Hunsberger, P. H. (2007). Reestablishing clinical psychology's subjective core. *American Psychologist*, *62*, 614–615. doi:10.1037/0003-066X62.6.614

Huppert, J. D., Bufka, L. F., Barlow, D. H., Gorman, J. M., Shear, M. K., & Woods, S. W. (2001). Therapists, therapist variables, and cognitive–behavioral therapy outcomes in a multicenter trial for panic disorder. *Journal of Consulting and Clinical Psychology*, *69*, 747–755. doi:10.1037/0022-006X.69.5.747

Iwakabe, S., & Gazzola, N. (2009). From single case studies to practice-based knowledge: Aggregating and synthesizing case studies. *Psychotherapy Research*, *19*, 601–611. doi:10.1080/10503300802688494

Karver, M., Shirk, S., Handelsman, J., Fields, S., Crisp, H., Gudmundsen, G., & McMakin, D. (2008). Relationship processes in youth psychotherapy: Measuring alliance, alliance-building behaviors, and client involvement. *Journal of Emotional and Behavioral Disorders*, *16*, 15–28.

Kasper, L., Hill, C. E., & Kivlighan, D. M., Jr. (2008). Therapist immediacy in brief psychotherapy therapy: Case Study I. *Psychotherapy: Theory, Research, Practice, Training*, *45*, 281–297.

Kazdin, A. E. (1981). Drawing valid inferences from case studies. *Journal of Consulting and Clinical Psychology*, *49*, 183–192. doi:10.1037/0022-006X.49.2.183

Kim, D. M., Wampold, B. E., & Bolt, D. M. (2006). Therapist effects in psychotherapy: A random effects modeling of the NIMH TDCRP data. *Psychotherapy Research, 16*, 161–172. doi:10.1080/10503300500264911

Klein, D. N., Schwartz, J. E., Santiago, N. J., Vivian, D., Vocisano, C., Castonguay, L. G., . . . Keller, M. B. (2003). Therapeutic alliance in depression treatment: Controlling for prior change and patient characteristics. *Journal of Consulting and Clinical Psychology, 71*, 997–1006. doi:10.1037/0022-006X.71.6.997

Lambert, M. J., Harmon, C., Slade, K., Whipple, J. L., & Hawkins, E. J. (2005). Providing feedback to psychotherapists on their patients' progress: Clinical results and practice suggestions. *Journal of Clinical Psychology, 61*, 165–174. doi:10.1002/jclp.20113

Luborsky, L., Singer, B., & Luborsky, L. (1975). Comparative studies of psychotherapies: Is it true that "Everyone has won and all must have prizes"? *Archives of General Psychiatry, 32*, 995–1008.

Mahalik, J. R. (1994). Development of the Client Resistance Scale. *Journal of Counseling Psychology, 41*, 58–68. doi:10.1037/0022-0167.41.1.58

Maier, S. F., Amat, J., Baratta, M. V., Paul, E., & Watkins, L. R. (2006). Behavioral control, the medial prefrontal cortex, and resilience. *Dialogues in Clinical Neuroscience, 8*, 397–406.

Mallinckrodt, B. (1991). Clients' representations of childhood emotional bonds with parents, social support, and formation of the working alliance. *Journal of Counseling Psychology, 38*, 401–409. doi:10.1037/0022-0167.38.4.401

Miller, S. D., Duncan, B. L., & Hubble, M. A. (2005). Outcome-informed clinical work. In J. C. Norcross & M. R. Goldfried (Eds.), *Handbook of psychotherapy integration* (2nd ed., pp. 84–102). New York, NY: Oxford University Press.

Nathan, P. E., Stuart, S. P., & Dolan, S. L. (2000). Research on psychotherapy efficacy and effectiveness: Between Scylla and Charybdis? *Psychological Bulletin, 126*, 964–981. doi:10.1037/0033-2909.126.6.964

O'Malley, S. S., Suh, C., & Strupp, H. (1983). The Vanderbilt Psychotherapy Process Scale: A report on the scale development and a process–outcome study. *Journal of Consulting and Clinical Psychology, 51*, 581–586. doi:10.1037/0022-006X.51.4.581

Paul, G. L. (1967). Strategy of outcome research in psychotherapy. *Journal of Consulting Psychology, 31*, 109–118. doi:10.1037/h0024436

Prochaska, J. O., & Norcross, J. C. (2002). Stages of change. In J. C. Norcross (Ed.), *Psychotherapy relationships that work: Therapist contributions and responsiveness to patients* (pp. 37–70). New York, NY: Oxford University Press.

Prochaska, J. O., Norcross, J. C., & DiClemente, C. C. (1994). *Changing for good.* New York, NY: Guilford Press.

Rogers, C. R., & Dymond, R. F. (1954). *Psychotherapy and personality change.* Chicago, IL: University of Chicago Press.

Safran, J. D., Muran, J. C., Samstag, L. W., & Stevens, C. (2002). Repairing alliance ruptures. In J. C. Norcross (Ed.), *Psychotherapy relationships that work: Therapist contributions and responsiveness to patients* (pp. 235–254). New York, NY: Oxford University Press.

Schneider, K. (2008). *Existential-integrative psychotherapy: Guideposts to the core of practice.* New York, NY: Routledge.

Siegle, G. J., Ghinassi, F., & Thase, M. E. (2007). Neurobehavioral therapies in the 21st century: Summary of an emerging field and an extended example of cognitive control training for depression. *Cognitive Therapy and Research, 31*, 235–262. doi:10.1007/s10608-006-9118-6

Seligman, M. E. P. (1995). The effectiveness of psychotherapy: The *Consumer Reports* study. *American Psychologist, 50*, 965–974. doi:10.1037/0003-066X.50.12.965

Serlin, R. C., Wampold, B. E., & Levin, J. R. (2003). Should providers of treatment be regarded as a random factor? If it ain't broke, don't "fix" it: A comment on Siemer and Joorman (2003). *Psychological Methods, 8,* 524–534. doi:10.1037/1082-989X.8.4.524

Smith, M. L., & Glass, G. V. (1977). Meta-analysis of psychotherapy outcome studies. *American Psychologist, 32,* 752–760. doi:10.1037/0003-066X.32.9.752

Snijders, T., & Bosker, R. (1999). *Multilevel analysis: An introduction to basic and advanced multilevel modeling.* London, England: Sage.

Stiles, W. B. (1988). Psychotherapy process–outcome correlations may be misleading. *Psychotherapy), 25,* 27–35. doi:10.1037/h0085320

Task Force on Promotion and Dissemination of Psychological Procedures. (1995). Training in and dissemination of empirically-validated psychological treatments: Report and recommendations. *Clinical Psychologist, 48,* 3–23.

Waltz, J., Addis, M. E., Koerner, K., & Jacobson, N. S. (1993). Testing the integrity of a psychotherapy protocol: Assessment of adherence and competence. *Journal of Consulting and Clinical Psychology, 61,* 620–630. doi:10.1037/0022-006X.61.4.620

Wampold, B. E. (2001). *The great psychotherapy debate: Models, methods, and findings.* Mahwah, NJ: Erlbaum.

Wampold, B. E., & Brown, G. S. (2005). Estimating therapist variability: A naturalistic study of outcomes in managed care. *Journal of Consulting and Clinical Psychology, 73,* 914–923. doi:10.1037/0022-006X.73.5.914

Wampold, B. E., Mondin, G. W., Moody, M., Stich, F., Benson, K., & Ahn, H. (1997). A meta-analysis of outcome studies comparing bona fide psychotherapies: Empirically, "all must have prizes." *Psychological Bulletin, 122,* 203–215. doi:10.1037/0033-2909.122.3.203

Wampold, B. E., & Serlin, R. C. (2000). The consequences of ignoring a nested factor on measures of effect size in analysis of variance. *Psychological Methods, 5,* 425–433. doi:10.1037/1082-989X.5.4.425

Weisz, J. R., Jensen-Doss, A., & Hawley, K. M. (2006). Evidence-based youth psychotherapies versus clinical care: A meta-analysis of direct comparisons. *American Psychologist, 61,* 671–689. doi:10.1037/0003-066X.61.7.671

Wendt, D. C., Jr., & Slife, B. D. (2007). Is evidence-based practice diverse enough? Philosophy of science considerations. *American Psychologist, 62,* 613–614. doi:10.1037/0003-066X62.6.613

Westen, D., Novonty, C. M., & Thompson-Brenner, H. (2004). Empirical status of empirically supported psychotherapies: Assumptions, findings, and reporting in controlled clinical trials. *Psychological Bulletin, 130,* 631–663. doi:10.1037/0033-2909.130.4.631

Williams, E. N., Hurley, K., O'Brien, K., & DeGregorio, A. (2003). Development and validation of the Self-Awareness and Management Strategies (SAMS) Scale for therapists. *Psychotherapy, 40,* 278–288. doi:10.1037/0033-3204.40.4.278

12

PSYCHOTHERAPY RESEARCH
CENTERS AND GROUPS

The Stone Center and Relational–Cultural Theory

Judith V. Jordan

The Stone Center for Developmental Studies was established at Wellesley College in 1981 under the leadership of Jean Baker Miller. Miller had written her classic and influential book, *Toward a New Psychology of Women*, in
1976. In 1978, the original collaborative group began meeting twice monthly
to explore the interface of theory and practice in psychotherapy. Combining
two missions, the Stone Center group sought to better understand both women's
and men's development and also hoped to change some of the prevailing models
of psychotherapy and psychology. In the course of their investigations, members
of the Stone Center began to point to the need for a shift from the prevailing
paradigm of "the separate self" in Western psychology to a paradigm of "being-
in-relation." Over time, a distinctive theoretical and clinical approach emerged:
relational–cultural theory (RCT).

Although feminist in its origins and developed to better represent the
psychology of women, the Stone Center called for a new understanding of the
psychology of all people. This new depiction of development suggests that all

357

people grow through and toward connection throughout the life span. The model further asserts that isolation is a source of human suffering and that a primary goal of most therapies is to lessen that suffering. Miller and Stiver (1997) referred to this state of chronic disconnection as "condemned isolation," asserting that in this state, a person feels utterly alone, outside the human community, and immobilized, blaming him- or herself for this condition. It occurs when one has suffered chronic nonresponsiveness, ongoing empathic failures, humiliations, or more blatant violations from others. Together, these non-growth-fostering interactions produce a feeling of "not mattering," or of not being relationally competent or making a difference in the relationship.

The original group of scholars (Jean Baker Miller, Irene Stiver, Judith V. Jordan, and Janet Surrey) worked as a collaborative group, sharing cases and critiquing conventional wisdom about what created change in therapy. Over time, others were invited into the dialogue: Alexandra Kaplan, Maureen Walker, Amy Banks, Yvonne Jenkins, Elizabeth Sparks, and Wendy Rosen, among others. Some of the participants pointed to the White privilege of the original group, and since then, the work has explicitly attempted to honor the many different experiences and voices of women (and men). RCT has tried to represent the power of complex interlocking matrices of privilege, oppression, and stratification that differentially affect individuals (Collins, 1990).

From the outset, RCT sought to move beyond the individual construction of the consequences of disconnection to also study the societal ramifications of power imbalances and marginalization. In fact, Miller's (1976) book is largely aimed at depicting the impact of forces of domination and subordination on women and on all marginalized and disempowered groups.

Writing over 100 "Works in Progress"—so named to represent the emergent quality of this work—and eventually several well-regarded books (Jordan, 1997, in press; Jordan, Kaplan, Miller, Stiver, & Surrey, 1991; Jordan, Walker, & Hartling, 2004; Miller & Stiver, 1997; Walker & Rosen, 2004, to name a few), the collaborators disseminated their works in both mainstream and more alternative clinical circles. Many welcomed the model as "something I always knew in my heart but had not found validation for." For the last 10 years, the Relational–Cultural Research Forum has supported empirical as well as clinical research on the model and has increasingly provided validation for the original concepts.

The core therapeutic concepts of RCT suggest that people grow through and toward connection throughout the life span. No one ever achieves a state of complete independence or autonomy, which is often held out as the desired endpoint of traditional psychodynamic developmental theories. Internalization of structure and resources is not the goal RCT offers. Rather than building safety in gaining power over others, RCT suggests people achieve safety and a base for creativity by building growth-fostering relationships. These are relationships in which people experience a sense of zest, more clarity about themselves and others, the capacity to be creative, an increasing sense of worth, and a desire for more connection. The model strongly emphasizes the importance of the larger social context in shaping experience; thus, cultural forces of marginalization and disconnection are seen as having an enormous impact on people's well-being and functioning.

Mutual empathy provides one of the primary channels for healing in therapy as well as outside therapy. When a person represents his or her pain to another person and he or she can see, know, and feel that his or her pain affects the other person, that it matters to the other person (that he or she matters), there is a lessening of both the sense of isolation and helplessness. He or she feels that he or she matters and is in connection, making a difference, and having an impact. Parts that have been split off, inaccessible, or unavailable for interaction begin to come forward, back into connection.

In therapy, as in other relationships, there are multiple opportunities for empathic failures and misunderstandings. Although it is relatively easy for a therapist to be empathic with the injuries that are inflicted on clients by others (e.g., family member, coworkers, partners), one of the core tasks for the therapist is managing the empathic failures that take place in the therapy itself. Thus, when the therapist "fails" or misunderstands the client, the therapist must stay empathically present, open to acknowledging mistakes, and open to letting his or her pain about injuring the client be accessible. Thus, the client can be with a person who acknowledges causing the pain, is sorry for that, and will not jump into "blaming the victim" through the notion of projective identification or believing that "the client put his or her feelings into me." The therapist stays present with, witnesses, and is affected by the client's feelings. In these exchanges, the client experiences a significant sense of mattering and gains a feeling of relational competence.

RCT has been used primarily in individual psychotherapy, but group therapists have also found RCT helpful (Fedele, 1993). An eight-session group manual has been developed for using RCT in time-limited and semididactic settings (Jordan & Dooley, 2000). The eight-session psychoeducational approach has been used in a women's prison (with both inmates and staff), several inpatient treatment settings with trauma survivors, partial hospital programs, staff development groups, and facilities treating patients requiring chronic psychiatric care. Some family therapists (Mirkin, 1994; Mirkin & Geib, 1999) have worked with RCT. Therapists working with couples have found the language of "we" and the explicit focus on building the relationship helpful (Shem & Surrey, 1998). Although much RCT work is done in relatively long-term individual therapy, with increasing pressure for short-term work, therapists have found ways to apply RCT principles in time-limited therapy (Jordan,

Handel, Alvarez, & Cook, 2000). Consultants in organizational settings have also used RCT. New ways of understanding leadership and team building have been suggested as a result of RCT (Fletcher, 1999; Fletcher, Jordan, & Miller, 2000).

There has not yet been abundant empirical or outcome research on RCT therapy. A research team at the Brief Psychotherapy Centre for Women in Toronto conducted a 2-year outcome study that indicated that clients in short-term RCT-focused treatment improved significantly on all outcome measures and that those gains were maintained at 6 months after completion of RCT therapy (Oakley & Addison, 2005. RCT has also been applied to women coping with cancer; a relational coping pattern in couples dealing with cancer has been demarcated (Kayser, Watson, & Andrade, 2007; Kayser, Sormanti, & Strainchamps, 1999).

Several assessment instruments have also come out of the RCT framework. A Connection–Disconnection Scale assessed perceived mutuality in both community and clinical samples of eating disordered women (Sanftner & Tantillo, 2004), and a Mutual Psychological Development Questionnaire measured perceived mutuality with partners and friends in a college community sample of women (Genero, Miller Surrey, & Baldwin, 1992). In addition, the Relational Health Indices (RHI) assessed growth-fostering connections with peers, mentors, and communities and specifically named the factors of engagement, authenticity, and empowerment in creating relational health (Liang et al., 1998). In Liang et al.'s (1998) study, relational health, as measured by the RHI, was generally associated with mental health and adjustment, and mutuality was significantly related to women's higher level of quality of life and self-care. The RHI has also been found to strongly influence the success of mentoring in the lives of young women (Spencer, 2007; Spencer, Jordan, & Sazama, 2004).

Research carried out by neuroscientists (not directly affiliated with the Jean Baker Miller Training Institute) has provided some of the most cogent support for RCT (Banks, 2006; Cozolino, 2002; Doidge, 2007). It appears that people are hardwired to connect. Scientists have discovered the presence of mirror neurons in the brain, which most likely are at the core of empathic resonance (Begley, 2008; Goleman, 2006). Growth of the orbitofrontal cortex probably depends on relational experience (Schore, 1994; Siegel, 1999). When in empathic attunement, the brains of both mother and infant are changing. This fits well with the RCT notion of mutual growth.

Moreover, social pain from exclusion or even the anticipation of exclusion, registers in the same area of the brain as physical pain (the anterior cingulate). The conclusion is that people need relationships like they need air and water (Eisenberger & Lieberman, 2004). Further, these studies support a major contention of RCT: The personal and the political are linked. Social pain is real pain.

When the Stone Center's RCT was just emerging, it was greeted with much skepticism and concern. There were those who did not want to believe in the power of connection to form and transform people's lives. There were those who were committed to psychotherapy characterized by distance, objectivity, nongratification, and therapist neutrality or nonresponsiveness. Recent empirical work on the importance of therapist responsiveness has supported a shift from more analytically derived notions of nonengagement (Norcross, 2002). Two generations of Stone Center researchers and clinicians have shown that relationships are central to people's well-being and growth and that safety arises in building good connections. As neuroscience confirms, neuronal pathways are reworked in what RCT calls *growth-fostering relationships*. Change happens in relationship; in mutual empathic connection, people can move beyond restrictive and isolating images of their communities and themselves. In short, people can celebrate courage and nourish hope in relationships, which are mutually sustaining and liberating.

REFERENCES

Banks, A. (2006). *The neurobiology of connection. Presentation at Summer Training Institute.* Wellesley, MA: Jean Baker Miller Training Institute.

Begley, S. (2008). *Train your mind, change your brain.* New York, NY: Ballantine Books.

Collins, P. H. (1990). *Black feminist thought: Knowledge, consciousness and the politics of empowerment.* Boston, MA: Unwin Hyman.

Cozolino, L. (2002). *The neuroscience of psychotherapy: Building and rebuilding the human brain.* New York, NY: Norton.

Doidge, N. (2007). *The brain that changes itself.* New York, NY: Viking.

Eisenberger, N. I., & Lieberman, M. (2004). Why rejection hurts: A common neural alarm system for physical and social pain. *Trends in Cognitive Sciences, 8,* 294–300. doi:10.1016/j.tics.2004.05.010

Fedele, N. (1993). Relationships in groups: Connection, resonance and paradox. In J. Jordan, M. Walker, & L. Hartling (Eds.), *The complexity of connection: Writings from the Stone Center's Jean Baker Miller Training Institute* (pp. 194–219). New York, NY: Guilford Press.

Fletcher, J. (1999). *Disappearing acts: Gender, power and relational practice at work.* Cambridge, MA: MIT Press.

Fletcher, J., Jordan, J., & Miller, J. (2000). Women and the workplace: Applications of a psychodynamic theory. *American Journal of Psychoanalysis, 60,* 243–261. doi:10.1023/A:1001973704517

Genero, N., Miller, J., Surrey, J., & Baldwin, L. (1992). Measuring perceived mutuality in close relationships: Validation of the mutual psychological development questionnaire. *Journal of Family Psychology, 6,* 36–48. doi:10.1037/0893-3200.6.1.36

Goleman, D. (2006). *Social intelligence: The new science of human relationships.* New York, NY: Bantam Books.

Jordan, J. (Ed.). (1997). *Women's growth in diversity*. New York, NY: Guilford Press.

Jordan, J. (in press). *Relational–cultural therapy*. Washington, DC: American Psychological Association.

Jordan, J., & Dooley, C. (2000). *Relational practice in action: A group manual* (Project Report No. 6). Wellesley, MA: The Stone Center for Developmental Studies.

Jordan, J., Handel, M., Alvarez, M., & Cook, R. (2000). *Applications of the relational model of time-limited therapy* (Work in Progress No. 87). Wellesley, MA: The Stone Center for Developmental Studies.

Jordan, J., Kaplan, A., Miller, J., Stiver, I., & Surrey, J. (1991). *Women's growth in connection*. New York, NY: Guilford Press.

Jordan, J., Walker, M., & Hartling, L. (2004). *The complexity of connection*. New York, NY: Guilford Press.

Kayser, K., Sormanti, M., & Strainchamps, E. (1999). Women coping with cancer: The impact of close relationships on psychosocial adjustment. *Psychology of Women Quarterly, 23,* 725–739. doi:10.1111/j.1471-6402.1999.tb00394.x

Kayser, K., Watson, L., & Andrade, J. (2007). Cancer as a "we-disease": Examining the process of coping from a relational perspective. *Families, Systems, and Health, 25,* 404–418.

Liang, B., Taylor, C., Williams, L., Tracy, A., Jordan, J., & Miller, J. (1998). *The Relational Health Indices: An exploratory study* (Paper No. 293). Wellesley, MA: Wellesley Centers for Women.

Miller, J. (1976). *Toward a new psychology of women*. Boston, MA: Beacon Press.

Miller, J., & Stiver, I. (1997). *The healing connection: How women form relationships in therapy and in life*. Boston, MA: Beacon Press.

Mirkin, M. P. (1994). Female adolescence revisited: Understanding girls in the sociocultural contexts. *Journal of Feminist Family Therapy, 4,* 43–60. doi:10.1300/J086v04n02_03

Mirkin, M. P., & Geib, P. (1999). Consciousness of context in relational couples therapy. *Journal of Feminist Family Therapy, 11,* 31–51. doi:10.1300/J086v11n01_02

Norcross, J. (Ed.). (2002). *Psychotherapy relationships that work: Therapist contribution and responsiveness to patient*. New York, NY: Oxford University Press.

Oakley, A., & Addison, S. (2005, June). *Outcome evaluation of a community-based mental health service for women employing a brief feminist relational–cultural model*. Paper presented at the Jean Baker Miler Research Colloquium, Wellesley, MA.

Sanftner, J., & Tantillo, M. (2004, June). *Development and validation of the Connection–Disconnection Scale for measuring perceived mutuality in clinical and college samples of women*. Poster session presented at the Jean Baker Miller Training Institute Annual Research Forum, Wellesley, MA.

Schore, A. (1994). *Affect regulation and the origins of the self: The neurobiology of emotional development*. Hillsdale, NJ: Erlbaum.

Shem, S., & Surrey, J. (1998). *We have to talk: Healing dialogues between women and men*. New York, NY: Basic Books.

Siegel, D. (1999). *The developing mind: How relationships and the brain interact to shape who we are*. New York, NY: Guilford Press.

Spencer, R. (2007). I just feel safe with him: Emotional closeness in male youth mentoring relationships. *Psychology of Men & Masculinity, 8,* 185–198. doi:10.1037/1524-9220.8.3.185

Spencer, R., Jordan, J., & Sazama, J. (2004). Growth-promoting relationships between youth and adults: A focus group study. *Families in Society, 85,* 354–363.

Walker, M., & Rosen, W. (2004). *How connections heal: Stories from relational–cultural therapy*. New York, NY: Guilford Press.

Yale Parenting Center and Child Conduct Clinic

Alan E. Kazdin

I began conducting individual behavior therapy with adults and applying behavioral techniques in schools and institutions for children while in graduate school (Northwestern University, 1967–1970). When I moved to my first academic appointment (Pennsylvania State University), I continued my work by beginning research with shy and withdrawn adults and with children with social, emotional, and behavioral problems (1971–1979). During my tenure at Pennsylvania State University, two activities influenced the direction of my work. First, I completed a 4-year project for the National Academy of Sciences examining the historical and experimental underpinnings of behavior modification. Second, I was on leave for a year (1976–1977) at the Center for Advanced Study in the Behavioral Sciences (Stanford, CA) and joined others (Stewart Agras, Nathan Azrin, Walter Michel, Jack Rachman, and G. Terence Wilson) assembled to evaluate the status of therapy and broader issues related to treatment research. Both experiences conveyed the remarkable progress achieved in developing psychosocial interventions. They also helped move me in the direction of evaluating treatments with children and with seriously disturbed populations, areas that were not well developed at the time.

In 1980, I joined the faculty in the Department of Psychiatry (Western Psychiatric Institute and Clinic) at the University of Pittsburgh School of Medicine with the goal of shifting my work exclusively to children and families. Soon, and against my better judgment, I was placed in charge of an inpatient child service, Child Psychiatric Intensive Care. As the name suggests, severely impaired children (ages 5 to 12) were admitted. I began two programs of research, one on underpinnings of childhood depression and suicide and the other on the treatment of aggressive and antisocial behavior. I only focus on the latter in this chapter.

The most frequent referrals to the service were children with severe aggressive and antisocial behavior and a primary psychiatric diagnosis of conduct disorder (CD). Most of the children met criteria for multiple comorbid disorders and showed severe impairment at home, at school, and in the community. The situations from which they emerged were daunting (e.g., parent psychopathology, abusive relations).

Parent management training (PMT), with its heavy reliance on parent–child interactions, and applied behavior analysis, with its potent behavior-change techniques, seemed like a viable place to begin treatment. I had been using both of these since graduate school. However, PMT was not an option for many parents. They could not participate for a variety of reasons, including their own impairments (e.g., mental disorder, developmental disability), unavailability (e.g., because they were in prison), and/or activities (e.g., drug abuse, prostitution) that interfered with or precluded participation. For such cases, my group sought a treatment that could be provided to the child with little or no reliance on a parent figure. We elected to pursue problem-solving skills training (PSST) administered individually to children.

We began a series of studies including randomized controlled trials of PMT and PSST alone and in combination. Treatments began during hospitalization and were continued as children were released. After a few years, we developed an outpatient service, the Yale Child Conduct Clinic, specifically devoted to aggressive and antisocial behavior and continued our clinical work and treatment studies. In 1989, I joined faculty in the Department of Psychology at Yale University, where the clinical service and research have continued.

THE TREATMENTS

In PMT, the parents meet with a therapist who teaches them to use specific procedures to alter interactions with their child, to promote prosocial behavior, and to decrease deviant behavior. The intervention draws on the seminal work of Patterson and his colleagues that focused on sequences of coercive parent–child interactions in the home and how they can be altered (e.g., Patterson, 1982; Patterson, Reid, & Dishion, 1992) and advances in applied behavior analysis on how to foster and maintain behavior (e.g., establishing operations, functional analysis, reinforcement schedules to reduce and eliminate behavior). PMT extends beyond a set of techniques and integrates diverse facets related to parent, family, and peer functioning (e.g., parental stress, marital conflict) and their role in the development of disruptive behavior and the delivery of treatment. The intervention also draws from the basic and applied operant conditioning research.

PSST focuses on cognitive processes of the children—how they perceive, code, and experience the world. Children with conduct problems often show distortions and deficiencies in several cognitive processes (e.g., generating alternative solutions to interpersonal problems, means–ends thinking), and these relate to disruptive behavior, as reflected in teacher and peer evaluations as well as direct assessment of overt actions. We drew heavily on the pioneering work of Shure and Spivack (e.g., Shure, 1992; Spivack & Shure, 1982) to adapt the intervention to children with CD.

PSST is directed specifically at changing how the child responds in interpersonal situations at home, at school, and in the community and in interactions with teachers, parents, peers, siblings, and others. The children are taught to engage in a step-by-step approach to solve interpersonal problems. They make statements to themselves that direct attention to certain aspects of the problem and that lead to effective solutions. Prosocial behaviors are fostered through modeling and direct reinforcement as part of the problem-solving process. Structured tasks involving games, academic activities, and stories are used to teach the approach. Early in treatment, real-life situations are practiced within the sessions, and children apply the approach at home, at school, and in other settings. Therapists play an active role in treatment by modeling use of self-statements; applying the statements to interpersonal problems; and prompting, praising, shaping, and fading to develop use and application of the skills.

RESEARCH

The goals of both treatments are to reduce oppositional, aggressive, and antisocial behavior and to improve the children's functioning at home, at school, and in the community. We see children from 2 to 14 years of age. The families are European American, African American, and Hispanic American (approximately 60%, 30%, and 5%, respectively), with biracial families forming most of the remainder. Approximately 50% of our cases come from two-parent families. All socioeconomic–occupational levels are represented.

For purposes of summarizing our main findings, it is useful to consider five domains of our research. Each domain has multiple studies underlying the conclusions (see Kazdin, in press, for more details).

Outcome Effects

PMT and PSST alone and in combination produce reliable and significant reductions in aggressive behavior and increases in prosocial behavior among children. The combined treatment tends to be more effective than either treatment alone. Effects of treatment are evident in performance at home, at school, and in the community, both immediately after treatment and at 1- and 2-year follow-up assessments. Parent reports indicate that the changes are large for many (78%) of the cases. Commonly used measures of magnitude of effect on symptom scales (e.g., large mean effect sizes) and clinical significance (e.g., return of symptoms to within a normative range) are in keeping with such reports. Although not targeted directly, treatment also is associated with reductions in maternal depression and stress and improved relations among family members. Relationship-based therapy and treatment-contact control conditions in our studies have not led to reliable changes.

Experimental Interventions to Augment Therapeutic Change

The effects of PMT on changes in child functioning can be enhanced by providing supplementary sessions that focus on and alleviate parent sources of stress. Also, a motivational enhancement intervention can improve parent motivation for, adherence to, and attendance of treatment. The effects of PSST can be enhanced by including in vivo practice ("homework" assignments) as part of treatment.

Therapeutic Alliance

The child–therapist and parent–therapist alliances relate to several outcomes. The more positive the child–therapist and parent–therapist alliance during treatment, the greater the therapeutic change of the child and improvements of the parents in parenting practices in the home, the fewer barriers parents experience during the course of treatment, and the more acceptable parents view the treatment. None of this work has shown that alliance causes or is responsible for change; we are working on research to elaborate the precise role (e.g., moderator, mediator, mechanism; Kazdin, 2007).

Other Moderators of Treatment

We have completed studies on other moderators of therapeutic change, that is, those factors that influence the direction or magnitude of the relation between the treatment and therapeutic change. Several characteristics of parents and children influence therapeutic change, including severity of child dysfunction, child IQ, parent stress, and parent psychopathology. The relations are not always what might be expected. For example, severity of child dysfunction (comorbid diagnoses and total number of symptoms), severity of impairment of the parents, and family dysfunction are related to outcome. More severe cases show greater rather than less therapeutic change over the course of treatment; their endpoint is no different from that of less severe cases. An often-voiced but infrequently tested concern in clinical practice is that research findings from evidence-based treatments may not apply to complex or severe cases. This is not really tenable given the samples we study and is not supported in our direct empirical tests with children diagnosed with oppositional defiant disorder (ODD) or CD. The most robust moderator of our treatment has been parental experience of barriers to participation in treatment. Greater barriers experienced by the parents in coming to treatment are associated with less therapeutic change among the children. Even so, children of parents high in barriers change significantly over the course of treatment, and the magnitude of change is large (effect size > 1).

Family Participation in Treatment

Many factors relate to participation in treatment and to dropping out. For example, parental dysfunction, stress in the home, and the experience of barriers to participation in treatment are among the more robust predictors of dropping out early. It is interesting to note that dropping out early is not necessarily failing in treatment or premature termination. Approximately 33% of those who drop out of treatment early report large improvements in the behavior of their children. We have seen clinically that when parents see such stark gains that are sustained for a few weeks, they see no need to continue in treatment. We have no evidence to controvert the advisability of their actions.

Our psychotherapy research in each of the aforementioned areas has been supported by several sources. These include a Research Development Award, Research Scientist Award, MERIT Award, and other grants from the National Institute of Mental Health as well as grants from the Leon Lowenstein Foundation, the William T. Grant Foundation, and Yale University.

As we continue to develop, understand, and apply the treatments, our clinical service has changed, especially within the past 5 years. First, our clinic referrals have become younger. We began with an almost exclusive focus on CD among children (ages 5 to 12); however, younger children (< 5 years of age) are referred for treatment to us more frequently now and ODD, rather than CD, is their primary diagnosis. Second, community interest (and pressure) has led us to open the service to parents who wish help with the normal challenges of child rearing (e.g., toilet training, noncompliance, tantrums, homework completion, teenage "attitude" problems). In response, we changed the name of our service from the Yale Child Conduct Clinic to the Yale Parenting Center and Child Conduct Clinic. With that change, we now accommodate clinically referred cases (CD and ODD) and families whose children do not meet criteria for any diagnosis. Our treatment manual for professional therapists (Kazdin, 2005) has a version directed to parents for everyday parenting challenges (Kazdin & Rotella, 2008). Finally, our clinic currently dedicates a significant portion of time to therapist training. We provide ongoing therapist training and supervision locally and in other states in an effort to disseminate the treatments.

DIRECTIONS FOR FUTURE RESEARCH

There are several next steps for our research. First, evidence-based treatments like ours are not being adopted or trained very well and are not getting to the children and families in need. Our clinic devotes considerable time to training therapists and to the supervision of cases, but more and different dissemination efforts are needed. We are interested in developing more disseminable versions of our treatment. We do research at our clinic not only for the lofty goal of contributing to the body of knowledge but also to one we view as even loftier, namely, helping to reduce the burden of mental illness nationally. Outpatient one-to-one therapy, even if practitioners were trained in the evidence-based treatments, would not have much impact. One line of work is to pursue new avenues to get the treatments to the people in need.

Second, a high priority for our work is to understand the mechanisms of therapeutic change. By *mechanisms*, I refer to the processes that produce the change and how these processes unfold to improve child functioning. We still do not know how and why therapy works, and we have discussed and shown elsewhere that statistical analyses (e.g., mediation) and our usual designs cannot answer the mechanism question (Kazdin, 2007). We are trying to shed light on why and precisely how treatment works.

Third, we have not found ethnic differences in the effectiveness of our treatments among European American, African American, and Hispanic American families. However, we have found many other factors that moderate treatment. Some of these (parental stress, barriers to coming to treatment) we have altered with supplementary interventions to enhance treatment. A research priority is to understand how key moderators operate and, equally important, how they can be used for triage. Two ways to improve the effectiveness of treatment are to develop more potent interventions and to direct patients to the treatments from which they are most likely to benefit. Both of these occupy our research program (Kazdin, 2008).

Many of the directions and challenges of our program are broadly applicable across treatments for children and adolescents. Perhaps what is new now that influences our research and the parallel work of others is that palpable progress has been made in developing effective interventions for the full spectrum of oppositional children to seriously disturbed and adjudicated adolescents with CD and criminal behavior. Our own behavior will be criminal if we do not do more to get these interventions to the public.

REFERENCES

Kazdin, A. E. (2005). *Parent management training: Treatment for oppositional, aggressive, and antisocial behavior in children and adolescents.* New York, NY: Oxford University Press.

Kazdin, A. E. (2007). Mediators and mechanisms of change in psychotherapy research. *Annual Review of Clinical Psychology, 3,* 1–27.

Kazdin, A. E. (2008). Evidence-based treatments and delivery of psychological services: Shifting our emphases to increase impact. *Psychological Services, 5,* 201–215. doi:10.1037/a0012573

Kazdin, A. E. (in press). Problem-solving skills training and parent management training for oppositional defiant disorder and conduct disorder. In J. R. Weisz & A. E. Kazdin (Eds.), *Evidence-based psychotherapies for children and adolescents* (2nd ed.). New York, NY: Guilford Press.

Kazdin, A. E., & Rotella, C. (2008). *The Kazdin method for parenting the defiant child: With no pills, no therapy, no contest of wills*. Boston, MA: Houghton Mifflin.

Patterson, G. R. (1982). *Coercive family process*. Eugene, OR: Castalia.

Patterson, G. R., Reid, J. B., & Dishion, T. J. (1992). *Antisocial boys*. Eugene, OR: Castalia.

Shure, M. B. (1992). *I can problem solve (ICPS): An interpersonal cognitive problem solving program*. Champaign, IL: Research Press.

Spivack, G., & Shure, M. B. (1982). The cognition of social adjustment: Interpersonal cognitive problem solving thinking. In B. B. Lahey & A. E. Kazdin (Eds.), *Advances in clinical child psychology* (Vol. 5, pp. 323–372). New York, NY: Plenum.

University of Pennsylvania Center for Psychotherapy Research

Paul Crits-Christoph, Jacques P. Barber,
and Mary Beth Connolly Gibbons

The history of research on psychotherapy at the University of Pennsylvania (Penn) can be traced to the 1950s. Aaron Beck was already at Penn and was beginning to formulate his thoughts on the nature and treatment of depression when Lester Luborsky arrived in 1959 to launch a long and distinguished career as a psychotherapy researcher. Both Beck's and Luborsky's research programs on cognitive therapy and psychodynamic therapy, respectively, developed and flourished throughout the 1960s, 1970s, and 1980s as largely independent research programs. By the mid-1980s, Beck had created the first treatment manual for cognitive therapy for depression and completed an efficacy study of cognitive therapy in comparison with antidepressant medication in the treatment of major depressive disorder. Luborsky had conducted a naturalistic study of the factors influencing the outcome of psychotherapy, had written a treatment manual for supportive-expressive psychodynamic psychotherapy, and had engaged in several studies attempting to validate some of the key clinical concepts of psychodynamic psychotherapy. (Luborsky's early work on the specific Penn Research Project was summarized in the first edition of this book; Luborsky, 1992.)

Paul Crits-Christoph joined the faculty at Penn in 1984, working closely with Luborsky. Jacques P. Barber was added as a faculty member to the group in 1989. As a member of the newer generation of psychotherapy researchers, Crits-Christoph was interested in comparing the efficacy of different psychotherapies, understanding how such different psychotherapies work, and ultimately working to improve existing treatments through their integration. A large grant from the National Institute of Mental Health in 1990 established the Center for Psychotherapy Research. The grant provided funds for pilot studies and core resources (e.g., administrative, statistical, method development, assessment services) to a large team of investigators. Some of these researchers were located within the Center (Paul Crits-Christoph, Jacques P. Barber, Lester Luborsky, Mary Beth Connolly Gibbons, Robert Gallop, Madeline Gladis, Karla Moras, Leigh McCullough, Lynne Siqueland, Jennifer Jones), whereas others were part of collaborating units within the departments of Psychiatry, Psychology, and Epidemiology and Biostatistics at Penn (Aaron Beck, Greg Brown, Robert DeRubeis, Cory Newman, Xin Tu). As additional investigators (Marna Barrett, Shannon Wiltsey Stirman) were added over time, the Center's focus shifted in response to overarching trends that were occurring in the scientific literature, including a greater emphasis on studying not just the efficacy of psychotherapy but also the mechanisms of change and an initiative (described later) toward studying psychotherapy in real-world settings.

The existence of many psychotherapy studies and the collaborative synergy among investigators created a fertile ground for the productive development of many investigators. Of the 37 presidents of the international Society for Psychotherapy Research, seven were faculty in the Department of Psychiatry at Penn (Arthur Auerbach, Jacques P. Barber, Aaron Beck, Paul Crits-Christoph, Lester Luborsky, Jim Mintz, Karla Moras). In addition, four investigators affiliated with the Center (Jacques P. Barber, Mary Beth Connolly Gibbons, Paul Crits-Christoph, Karla Moras) received the Early Career Award from the Society for Psychotherapy Research.

CONTRIBUTIONS TO PSYCHOTHERAPY RESEARCH

Investigators at the Center for Psychotherapy Research have conducted a wide range of studies on the process and outcome of psychotherapy. One of the early studies was an investigation of the factors that predict the outcome of naturalistic (primarily psychodynamic) psychotherapy (Luborsky, Crits-Christoph, Mintz, & Auerbach, 1988). The main finding of this study was that psychotherapy outcomes were largely not predictable on pretreatment characteristics of the patient and therapist.

This finding led to numerous intensive investigations of the process of psychodynamic psychotherapy. As a first step, research needed to focus on the development of measures, including both observational coding systems and self-report scales, that captured key constructs of psychodynamic psychotherapy. We developed measures for assessing the therapeutic alliance, patients' core conflictual relationship themes, self-understanding of interpersonal patterns, and the accuracy of therapists' interventions. A variety of studies explored the role of these concepts in psychotherapy (e.g., Barber, Foltz, & Weinryb, 1998; Connolly et al., 1996, 1999; Crits-Christoph, Cooper, & Luborsky, 1988; Luborsky & Crits-Christoph, 1998). The role of the individual therapist was also investigated in terms of therapists' impact on treatment outcome and the methodological complications inherent in the study of a process like psychotherapy, which involves multiple levels of analysis (therapist, patients; Crits-Christoph & Mintz, 1991).

The next phase of research at the Center focused on developing and testing manual-driven interpersonal-psychodynamic psychotherapy (labeled *supportive-expressive psychotherapy*) for different patient populations. We conducted treatment development–pilot studies on the usefulness of supportive-expressive psychotherapy for generalized anxiety disorder, depression, certain personality disorders (obsessive–compulsive, avoidant), and panic disorder. As part of the manualization of psychotherapy, instruments were needed for measuring the extent to which therapists actually implemented the intended techniques of the psychotherapy. We therefore developed scales to assess both the frequency (adherence) and skillfulness (competence) of therapist techniques and studies examining whether increasing the frequency or skill-fulness of therapist interventions improved treatment outcome (e.g., Barber, Crits-Christoph, & Luborsky, 1996).

One major focus of the Center's activities during the 1990s was the completion of a large-scale, multicenter clinical trial evaluating the efficacy of supportive-expressive therapy, cognitive therapy, and drug counseling treatments for cocaine dependence (Crits-Christoph et al., 1999). In addition to the efficacy results, this study yielded a number of articles examining the role of theory-specific mediators of treatment outcome, patient pretreatment predictors of outcome, and key process dimensions (e.g., the alliance, adherence to treatment manual) as predictors of outcome.

A central aspect of supportive-expressive psychotherapy is the curative influence of the therapeutic alliance. Accordingly, we have teased out whether the alliance potentially has a causal role in relation to outcome or whether a positive alliance is simply a by-product of the patient's early improvement in psychotherapy (Barber, Connolly, Crits-Christoph, Gladis, & Siqueland, 2000). Additional studies found that (a) therapists could be trained to improve the quality of their alliances with patients (Crits-Christoph et al., 2006); (b) a positive alliance is associated with certain pretreatment characteristics of the patients, including positive expectations for therapy and lack of a hostile–dominant interpersonal style (Gibbons et al., 2003); and (c) that the alliance interacts with therapeutic techniques in such a way that if alliance is high, adherence to treatment manuals is less important to outcome, but if alliance is low, a moderate amount of adherence to the treatment manual appears to be needed to produce good outcomes (Barber et al., 2006).

Throughout the early 2000s, research at the Center continued in the areas described previously, but additional scientific questions emerged that reflected a wider perspective on psychotherapy. In particular, we conducted studies that explored cross-theoretical mechanisms of change in diverse psychotherapies (Gibbons et al., in press) and the impact of psychotherapy on patients' broader positive quality of life (Crits-Christoph et al., 2008).

CURRENT AND FUTURE STUDIES

We are currently conducting a full range of process and outcome studies on various psychotherapies. These include large-scale randomized clinical trials evaluating the efficacy of (a) psychodynamic therapy versus medication for major depressive disorder and (b) psychodynamic and cognitive–behavioral treatments for panic disorder. Research on substance abuse continues, with an ongoing evaluation of the efficacy of a system for providing feedback to therapists that is being conducted in 20 community-based substance abuse treatment clinics. Although individual psychotherapy has been the main focus of almost all of the studies conducted at the Center, the prevalence of group treatments for substance use disorders stimulated a large-scale study of the process of group drug counseling sessions in relation to treatment outcome.

A new initiative at the Center has been research on evidence-based psychotherapies for depression in a community setting through an academic–community partnership involving a large community mental health center in Philadelphia, Pennsylvania. This research program has two main goals. The first is to understand the nature of a persistent and costly problem for the agency as it attempts to deliver mental health services to a low-income population: Many patients fail to engage with the treatment delivery system (i.e., they contact the agency, or show up at an intake evaluation, but fail to follow through with treatment) or they drop out of psychotherapy quickly, before they have had an opportunity to receive a sufficient "dose" of psychotherapy. Although many studies have looked at the attrition problem in psychotherapy, we aim to take a new look at this issue, evaluating the role of patient, therapist, and agency factors as they impinge on engagement and retention in treatment. The second main goal of the academic–community partnership is to evaluate the effectiveness of evidence-based psychotherapies when implemented in a real-world community clinic, using the types of therapists and broad range of patients at such clinics. Once it has been determined from controlled clinical trials that a psychotherapy is effective, additional research questions about how best to disseminate such evidence-based treatments to actual clinical practice are relevant. New research at the Center is beginning to explore these questions as well.

In sum, the 50 years of research at the University of Pennsylvania Center for Psychotherapy Research has produced scientific advances in the study of the process and outcome of a variety of forms of psychotherapy. As we move into the next decade, our hope is to translate these findings into useful ways to improve the lives of patients seeking treatment in the community and to build on our knowledge about how psychotherapies achieve their effects.

REFERENCES

Barber, J. P., Connolly, M. B., Crits-Christoph, P., Gladis, M., & Siqueland, L. (2000). Alliance predicts patients' outcome beyond in-treatment change in symptoms. *Journal of Consulting and Clinical Psychology, 68,* 1027–1032. doi:10.1037/0022-006X.68.6.1027

Barber, J. P., Crits-Christoph, P., & Luborsky, L. (1996). Effects of therapist adherence and competence on patient outcome in brief dynamic therapy. *Journal of Consulting and Clinical Psychology, 64,* 619–622. doi:10.1037/0022-006X.64.3.619

Barber, J. P., Foltz, C., & Weinryb, R. M. (1998). The Central Relationship Questionnaire: Initial report. *Journal of Counseling Psychology, 45,* 131–142. doi:10.1037/0022-0167.45.2.131

Barber, J. P., Gallop, R., Crits-Christoph, P., Frank, A., Thase, M. E., Weiss, R. D., & Connolly Gibbons, M. B. (2006). The role of therapist adherence, therapist competence, and the alliance in predicting outcome of individual drug counseling: Results from the NIDA Collaborative Cocaine Treatment Study. *Psychotherapy Research, 16,* 229–240. doi:10.1080/10503300500288951

Connolly, M. B., Crits-Christoph, P., Demorest, A., Azarian, K., Muenz, L., & Chittams, J. (1996). The varieties of transference patterns in psychotherapy. *Journal of Consulting and Clinical Psychology, 64,* 1213–1221. doi:10.1037/0022-006X.64.6.1213

Connolly, M. B., Crits-Christoph, P., Shelton, R. C., Hollon, S., Kurtz, J., Barber, J. P., . . . Thase, M. E. (1999). The reliability and validity of a measure of self-understanding of interpersonal patterns. *Journal of Counseling Psychology, 46,* 472–482. doi:10.1037/0022-0167.46.4.472

Crits-Christoph, P., Connolly Gibbons, M. B., Crits-Christoph, K., Narducci, J., Schamberger, M., & Gallop, R. (2006). Can therapists be trained to improve their alliances? A pilot study of alliance-fostering therapy. *Psychotherapy Research, 13,* 268–281. doi:10.1080/10503300500268557

Crits-Christoph, P., Connolly Gibbons, M. B., Gallop, J., Stirman, S. W., Present, J., Temes, C., & Goldstein, L. A. (2008). Changes in positive quality of life over the course of psychotherapy. *Psychotherapy: Theory, Research, Practice, Training, 45,* 419–430.

Crits-Christoph, P., Cooper, A., & Luborsky, L. (1988). The accuracy of therapists' interpretations and the outcome of dynamic psychotherapy. *Journal of Consulting and Clinical Psychology, 56,* 490–495. doi:10.1037/0022-006X.56.4.490

Crits-Christoph, P., & Mintz, J. (1991). Implications of therapist effects for the design and analysis of comparative studies of psychotherapy. *Journal of Consulting and Clinical Psychology, 59,* 20–26. doi:10.1037/0022-006X.59.1.20

Crits-Christoph, P., Siqueland, L., Blaine, J., Frank, A., Luborsky, L., Onken, L. S., . . . Beck, A. T. (1999). Psychosocial treatments for cocaine dependence: National Institute on Drug Abuse Collaborative Cocaine Treatment Study. *Archives of General Psychiatry, 56,* 493–502. doi:10.1001/archpsyc.56.6.493

Gibbons, M. B., Crits-Christoph, P., de la Cruz, C., Barber, J. P., Siqueland, L., & Gladis, L. (2003). Pretreatment expectations, interpersonal functioning, and symptoms in the prediction of the therapeutic alliance across supportive-expressive psychotherapy and cognitive therapy. *Psychotherapy Research, 13,* 59–76. doi:10.1093/ptr/kpg007

Gibbons, M. B., Gallop, R., Barber, J. P., Temes, C., Goldstein, L., Stirman, S., & Crits-Christoph, P. (in press). Unique and common mechanisms of change across cognitive and dynamic psychotherapies. *Journal of Consulting and Clinical Psychology.*

Luborsky, L. (1992). The Penn Research Project. In D. K. Freedheim (Ed.), *History of psychotherapy: A century of change* (pp. 394–401). Washington, DC: American Psychological Association.

Luborsky, L., & Crits-Christoph, P. (Eds.). (1998). *Understanding transference: The core conflictual relationship theme method* (2nd ed.). Washington, DC: American Psychological Association.

Luborsky, L., Crits-Christoph, P., Mintz, J., & Auerbach, A. (1988). *Who will benefit from psychotherapy? Predicting therapeutic outcomes.* New York, NY: Basic Books.

Society for Psychotherapy Research Collaborative Research Program on the Development of Psychotherapists

David E. Orlinsky, Michael Helge Rønnestad, and Ulrike Willutzki

Psychotherapists are the trained professionals to whom large numbers of individuals in our society turn for help when they experience significant distress in their personal lives. We know a considerable amount about the effectiveness and process of psychotherapy after decades of research, but we still know relatively little about the trained professionals who practice their skills on behalf of those who seek their help. Who are the people who work as psychotherapists? What qualifications and qualities do they have as professionals? What kind of people are they as persons? How do they experience their work? Which of their professional and personal characteristics influence how they work with clients? What impact does the therapists' work have on them, professionally and personally? How do psychotherapists develop? What work-related or personal experiences influence their development, and what impact does their development have on their therapeutic work?

These questions have guided the Society for Psychotherapy Research Collaborative Research Network (SPR/CRN) since its inception in 1989, when members of the international Society for Psychotherapy Research began working together to study the development of psychotherapists. The SPR/CRN is a research co-op that consists of colleagues who collaborate voluntarily on projects of mutual interest. Aside from its substantive contributions to knowledge, the SPR/CRN is noteworthy for representing an innovative and perhaps unique model of research organization—one that is independent, self-supporting, and self-governing; that is, free to pursue its own intellectual interests because it does not depend on funds solicited from other sources.

Over the past 2 decades, some 70 to 80 doctoral-level colleagues and students in more than two dozen countries have participated in varying degrees as SPR/CRN members for varying lengths of time. They have mostly been clinical researchers with considerable experience as practicing psychotherapists and also trainers and supervisors of therapists. Together they designed a wide-ranging research instrument, made careful translations of it into multiple languages, and used it to collect data from an ever-growing group of professional psychotherapists and counselors (nearly 10,000 so far) in North and South America, Europe, Asia, the Middle East, Oceania, and Africa. Responsibility for coordination and continuity of SPR/CRN research is vested in a steering committee comprising approximately 10 or 12 of the most active and committed members.

The Development of Psychotherapists Common Core Questionnaire (DPCCQ) was created to survey the professional and personal experiences of clinical colleagues (Orlinsky et al., 1999). The original version of the DPCCQ included 392 items organized in various sections according to topic. These included questions about psychotherapists'

- professional characteristics (e.g., professional training and identity, theoretical orientation, amount and types of clinical experience);
- types of clients treated (e.g., ages, diagnoses, impairment levels);
- experiences of therapeutic work (e.g., typical treatment goals, skills, manner of relating, difficulties in practice, coping strategies);
- current and overall professional development and the influences on their development;
- use and evaluation of their own personal therapy; and
- personal characteristics (e.g., age, gender, marital status, levels of life satisfaction and stress, personal self-concept in the context of close relationships).

We tried to adapt the DPCCQ versions used in different countries to the social, cultural, and professional situations where therapists live and work. Most recently, the use of interactive, Internet-based versions of the DPCCQ is being explored and evaluated.

What kinds of people are asked to complete the DPCCQ? The problem of research design we encountered stems from the fact the universe of professional psychotherapists cannot be rationally defined, and, hence, a statistically representative sample cannot be collected. The world of professional psychotherapists includes clinical and counseling psychologists, psychiatrists and psychoanalysts, clinical social workers and counselors, and others in a mix of professions that varies from one country to another. The diversity is further compounded by the fact that therapists are divided into rival theoretical camps. Given this complex situation, we chose to invite a large number of people who self-identify as psychotherapists—of varied professions and theoretical orientations in various countries—to voluntarily give an hour or more of their time to reply to our questions.

Detailed reports of our findings and their interpretation are presented in *How Psychotherapists Develop: A Study of Therapeutic Work and Professional Growth* (Orlinsky & Rønnestad, 2005) and elsewhere (e.g., Ambühl, Orlinsky, & the SPR/CRN, 1997; Bae, Joo, & Orlinsky, 2003; Elliott, Orlinsky, Klein, Amer, & Partyka, 2003; Orlinsky et al., 1996, 1999; Orlinsky, Botermans, & Rønnestad, 2001; Orlinsky, Botermans, Wiseman, Rønnestad, & Willutzki, 2005; Rønnestad, Orlinsky, Parks, & Davis, 1997; Schroder & Davis, 2004; Smith & Orlinsky, 2004). Some of these are summarized in the sections that follow.

HOW DO THERAPISTS EXPERIENCE THERAPEUTIC WORK?

Analyses of multiple facets of therapeutic work demonstrate the presence of two broad dimensions named healing involvement and stressful involvement. The experience of healing involvement was marked by personal investment in affirming, receptive relationships with clients, high levels of clinical skill, and use of constructive coping strategies when confronting difficulties in practice. By contrast, the experience of stressful involvement was defined by frequent difficulties in practice, accompanied by defensive, therapeutically unconstructive coping strategies (e.g., withdrawal) and therapists' feelings of boredom and anxiety.

Both healing involvement and stressful involvement are experienced by all therapists, although to varying degrees. Nearly three fourths of approximately 5,000 therapists studied experienced relatively high levels of healing involvement in their therapeutic work. Combining varying levels of healing involvement and stressful involvement, therapists who were high in healing involvement and low in stressful involvement were said to have an effective practice—which included about 50% of all surveyed. Another 23% were high in healing involvement but also experienced comparatively high levels of stressful involvement, producing a pattern of challenging practice. Unfortunately, a small but significant minority (about 10%) of therapists showed a pattern of distressing practice, marked by much stressful involvement and not much healing involvement. These therapists did not appear to be helping many of their clients, were somewhat at risk themselves, and required special attention from supervisors and others responsible for quality of patient care. Another small but significant group (about 17%) appeared to have a personally neutral but unproductive pattern of disengaged practice, in which there was little stressful involvement but not much healing involvement.

The experience of healing involvement was most strongly predicted by theoretical breadth (use of multiple orientations), feelings of support and satisfaction in the primary work setting, and positive work morale, along with breadth and depth of case experience across individual, couples, family, and group therapy modalities. Thus, therapists who have broad-ranging experience, have a broad understanding of how therapy can be done, and feel a strong commitment to their work appear to be the most helpful to their clients.

Only a few therapist characteristics were associated with the experience of stressful involvement, suggesting that this may be more determined by client and caseload characteristics. However, it was clear that work stress was greater for therapists who felt little support or satisfaction in their main work setting, had no private practice, and were caught in a process of demoralization.

PROFESSIONAL DEVELOPMENT

The concept of psychotherapist development was the key idea and initial stimulus for the SPR/CRN study, but the meaning of *development* was far from clear at the outset. Analysis of the concept led to four observational frames of reference: (a) cumulative career development, as reflected directly and manifested indirectly in therapeutic work experience; (b) currently experienced development, felt by therapists as present change for better or worse in therapeutic activities; (c) comparative cohort development, based on differences detected between therapists at successive career levels; and (d) sequential individual development, based on repeated measures of therapeutic function over significant periods of time.

Therapists' cumulative career development was only modestly correlated with the length of time therapists had been in practice and was actually more closely related to the breadth and depth of the therapist's work experience—suggesting that development depends less on the passage of time in practice than on how much one has learned in that time. Two dimensions of present change were found. Currently experienced growth reflected a sense of enhanced skillfulness, deepening understanding of therapeutic process, an enthusiasm for practice, and an awareness of overcoming one's past limitations as a therapist. Therapists on average had high scores on this dimension at all career levels, contrary to expectations that the sense of current growth would level out after many years in practice. This fact led to interpreting the dimension largely as a reflection of the therapist's positive work morale, in addition to actual learning and improvement. By contrast, the second dimension of present change was one of currently experienced depletion. This reflected a sense of deteriorating skills, loss of empathic responsiveness to patients, routine performance in work, and a growing doubt about the effectiveness of therapy.

A MODEL OF THERAPIST DEVELOPMENT

The empirical relations we discovered between therapists' professional growth and their concurrent experiences in therapeutic work led us to formulate a theoretical model of psychotherapist development. We called this a *cyclical–sequential model* because it involves two simultaneous cycles, positive and negative, each varying in intensity, that jointly shape successive periods of growth (or decline) in therapeutic ability. The positive cycle reflects the reciprocal influence that was found between healing involvement and current growth. Therapists' experiences of healing involvement with patients gives rise to current growth, and that, in turn, imbues them with the assurance and endurance needed to engage effectively with patients. This cycle also acts over time to increase the therapist's overall career development, expanding the therapist's confidence, resourcefulness, and flexibility with patients.

Concurrently, a negative cycle reflects the potential for a self-reinforcing spiral of influence between stressful involvement in therapeutic work and therapists' currently experienced depletion. Therapists' experiences of stressful involvement with clients gives rise to currently experienced depletion, engendering a loss of interest and optimism in therapists that further undermines their work with clients. The therapist's demoralization thus reflects and reinforces the patient's own demoralization and, if it is not adequately compensated by other factors (e.g., supervisory support), may lead to a state of therapist burnout and diminish the therapist's overall career development.

The model does not envisage a fixed sequence of developmental stages through which all therapists pass. Instead, the pattern of development over time depends on the relative balance between positive and negative cycles, which are always present as potentials for development. The actual course of a therapist's development depends on contingencies that make one or the other cycle more intense. When the positive cycle is dominant, there is a period of positive growth in therapeutic ability; however, when the negative cycle prevails for a time, therapeutic ability may decline, leading the therapist to be awkward, insecure, and defensively rigid.

This empirically grounded model of therapist development has clear implications for psychotherapy training, supervision, and practice (discussed in detail in Rønnestad & Orlinsky, 2005a). The most important recommendations for training are to ensure that (a) therapists have an experience of healing involvement, especially in their initial work with patients, (b) stressful involvement is kept to a minimum and constructively compensated when unavoidable, and (c) adequate supervisory and peer support is available, especially for beginners. Provided there is appropriate training and supervision, an early introduction to clinical work is recommended (Orlinsky et al., 2001). Supervision is widely viewed by therapists as a very positive influence on their current growth and career development, but there is also a potential for negative influence from supervision when supervisors are seen as critical and unsupportive. This may combine with the supervisee's experience of stressful involvement with a client to create a situation of double traumatization for the trainee (Rønnestad & Orlinsky, 2005b).

For therapists at all career levels, the cyclical relationship between current development and therapeutic practice provides a strong argument for continually monitoring one's own development. Two brief self-rating forms for work involvement and professional development were constructed from the DPCCQ to aid therapists in this (see Orlinsky & Rønnestad, 2005, Appendixes E and F).

The SPR/CRN program of research on psychotherapists continues to add to its 20-year history with new studies. Additional data collections have recently been completed in Australia, Chile, Portugal, and India. Data analyses are currently underway to deepen our understanding of therapists' personal characteristics, identities, personal lives, and spirituality in relation to therapeutic work and professional development. Psychotherapists of different theoretical orientations and professions are being compared. The SPR/CRN remains an active and open voluntary association of clinicians–researchers, and it will continue to exist as long as old and new members combine their skills and resources in pursuing the shared goal of learning more about psychotherapists.

REFERENCES

Ambühl, H., Orlinsky, D. E., & the Society for Psychotherapy Research Collaborative Research Network. (1997). Zum einfluss der theoretischen orientierung auf der psychotherapeutische praxis [On the influence of theoretical orientation on psychotherapeutic practice]. *Psychotherapeut, 42*, 290–298. doi:10.1007/s002780050078

Bae, S., Joo, E., & Orlinsky, D. E. (2003). Psychotherapists in South Korea: Professional and practice characteristics. *Psychotherapy, 40*, 302–316. doi:10.1037/0033-3204.40.4.302

Elliott, R., Orlinsky, D., Klein, M., Amer, M., & Partyka, R. (2003). Professional characteristics of humanistic therapists: Analyses of the Collaborative Research Network sample. *Person-Centered and Experiential Psychotherapies, 2*, 188–203.

Orlinsky, D. E., Ambühl, H., Rønnestad, M. H., Davis, J. D., Gerin, P., Davis, M., . . . Eunsun, J. (1999). The development of psychotherapists: Concepts, questions, and methods of a collaborative international study. *Psychotherapy Research, 9*, 127–153. doi:10.1093/ptr/9.2.127

Orlinsky, D. E., Botermans, J.-F., & Rønnestad, M. H. (2001). Towards an empirically-grounded model of psychotherapy training: Five thousand therapists rate influences on their development. *Australian Psychologist, 36*, 139–148. doi:10.1080/00050060108259646

Orlinsky, D. E., Botermans, J.-F., Wiseman, H., Rønnestad, M. H., & Willutzki, U. (2005). Prevalence and parameters of personal therapy in Europe and elsewhere. In J. D. Geller, J. C. Norcross, & D. E. Orlinsky (Eds.), *The psychotherapist's own psychotherapy: Patient and clinician perspectives* (pp. 177–191). New York, NY: Oxford University Press.

Orlinsky, D. E., & Rønnestad, M. H. (2005). *How psychotherapists develop: A study of therapeutic work and professional growth.* Washington, DC: American Psychological Association.

Orlinsky, D. E., Willutzki, U., Meyerberg, J., Cierpka, M., Buchheim, P., & Ambühl, H. (1996). Die qualität der therapeutischen beziehung: Entsprechen gemeinsame faktoren in der psychotherapie gemeinsamen characteristika von psychotherapeutinnen? [Quality of the therapeutic relationship: Do common factors in psychotherapy correspond with common characteristics of psychotherapists?] *Psychotherapie, Psychosomatik, Medizinische Psychologie, 46*, 102–110.

Rønnestad, M. H., & Orlinsky, D. E. (2005a). Clinical implications: Training, supervision, and practice. In D. E. Orlinsky & M. H. Rønnestad (Eds.), *How psychotherapists develop: A study of therapeutic work and professional growth* (pp. 181–201). Washington, DC: American Psychological Association.

Rønnestad, M. H., & Orlinsky, D. E. (2005b). Therapeutic work and professional development: Main findings and practical implications. *Psychotherapy Bulletin, 40,* 27–32.

Rønnestad, M. H., Orlinsky, D. E., Parks, B. K., & Davis, J. D. (1997). Supervisors of psychotherapy: Mapping experience level and supervisory confidence. *European Psychologist, 2,* 191–201.

Schroder, T. A., & Davis, J. D. (2004). Therapists' experience of difficulty in practice. *Psychotherapy Research, 14,* 328–345. doi:10.1093/ptr/kph028

Smith, D. P., & Orlinsky, D. E. (2004). Religious and spiritual experience among psychotherapists. *Psychotherapy, 41,* 144–151. doi:10.1037/0033-3204.41.2.144

The Sheffield–Leeds Psychotherapy Research Program

Michael Barkham, Gillian E. Hardy, and David A. Shapiro

The Sheffield–Leeds Psychotherapy Research Program spans a 30-year period of work carried out at the University of Sheffield, Sheffield, England (Social and Applied Psychology Unit, 1977–1995); University of Leeds, Leeds, England (Psychological Therapies Research Centre, 1995–2007); and again at the University of Sheffield (Centre for Psychological Services Research, 2007 onward). In this chapter, we present the major research yield of this ongoing program under three headings: (a) comparative outcome trials, (b) process investigations, and (c) practice-based studies. The research program was founded by David A. Shapiro in 1977 and carried forward across much of this time frame with Michael Barkham and Gillian E. Hardy—as well as with other colleagues—together with the long-term international collaboration of William B. Stiles (Miami University), Robert Elliott (University of Toledo and University of Strathclyde, Glasgow, Scotland), and Marvin Goldfried (State University of New York).

A hallmark of the Sheffield–Leeds Psychotherapy Research Program has been our dual commitment to methodological pluralism and theoretical equipoise in relation to differing treatments. An overarching aim has been to increase the precision of outcome trials methodology as one possible resolution to the equivalence paradox. However, our commitment to examining explanatory models and psychotherapeutic processes, as well as investigating what happens in routine practice, reflects our core assumption that randomized clinical trials alone cannot build a robust science of psychotherapy. Here, we summarize the major research activity and findings from the Sheffield–Leeds program (for a full list of references, see http://www.shef.ac.uk/cpsr/).

COMPARATIVE OUTCOME TRIALS

A key impetus setting the research agenda for the Sheffield–Leeds program was a meta-analysis of 143 outcome studies published between 1975 and 1979, in which two or more psychological treatments were compared with a control group (Shapiro & Shapiro, 1982). Beyond the central finding that the mean effect size for treatment approached 1 standard deviation, the results suggested that the relatively modest differences between treatment methods were largely independent of other factors and that outcome research, at that time, was not representative of clinical practice. Further, it was concluded that the most promising application lay in same-experiment data, in which studies compared contrasting conditions within the same experiment.

The substantive and methodological yield of this meta-analysis provided the rationale for a quartet of successive trials, all of which were designed to compare two therapies—psychodynamic–interpersonal (PI) and cognitive–behavioral (CB)—as representative of the range of clinical therapies practiced in the United Kingdom. Although our studies held the comparison between PI and CB therapies constant, they variously used differing durations of treatment sessions considered as an independent variable: two, eight, and 16 sessions. The following sections provide a summary, in chronological order, of these trials.

(First) Sheffield Psychotherapy Project

The (first) Sheffield Psychotherapy Project compared prescriptive (CB) therapy with exploratory (PI) therapy within the same experiment and using a crossover design to control for patient, therapist, and common factors (Shapiro & Firth, 1987). The aim was to maximize the sensitivity of the design to any treatment differences that might exist and thereby address the equivalence paradox resolution asserting that differences are there but obscured by weak research design. Forty clients referred for depression were randomly assigned to receive eight sessions of either prescriptive or exploratory therapy followed by eight sessions of the alternative therapy. The results favored prescriptive therapy, although this difference was moderate, confirming views that equivalent outcomes may be due to poor control over extraneous therapist, technique, and patient variables that were well controlled in this study. However, further analysis showed that the differential effectiveness of the two treatments was confined to one of the two main therapists—a precursor of our current interest in therapist effects.

Second Sheffield Psychotherapy Project

The larger Second Sheffield Psychotherapy Project (SPP2) used a more complex design with five therapists and comparing CB and PI therapies by testing the impact of treatment length—eight or 16 sessions—and severity of depression—low, medium, high—on outcomes with a sample of 117 clients presenting with depression (Shapiro et al., 1994). More specifically, it focused on questions of therapy approach (e.g., Is CB more effective and rapid in its effects than PI when delivered by investigators having no prior allegiance to CB or PI?) and duration (e.g., Is 16 sessions more effective than eight sessions?). Crucially, the effect of initial severity was considered. A battery of standard outcome measures was used that included the Beck Depression Inventory (BDI), Symptom Checklist–90–R, and the Inventory of Interpersonal Problems. Overall, the study yielded slight but not robust advantages to CB therapy, with only the BDI yielding a medium-size treatment effect and no evidence that either therapy delivered a difference in rate of change. There was some evidence that 16 sessions were more effective than eight sessions, but process data also suggested that therapist–client dyads adjusted the pace of therapy according to the duration available. There was, however, a significant interaction between severity and duration that resulted in more severely depressed clients fairing worse when receiving eight rather than 16 sessions. It is important to note that this result held for both PI and CB treatments. At 1-year follow-up, eight sessions of PI performed significantly worse than eight sessions of CB and 16 sessions of PI or CB (Shapiro et al., 1995).

National Health Service Collaborative Project

In the context of results from the SPP2, there was interest in the extent to which findings would generalize to routine practice settings. To test this, Barkham, Rees, Shapiro, et al. (1996) carried out a smaller effectiveness trial in clinical settings across multiple sites to determine whether the outcome results could be generalized to National Health Service outpatients. A total of 36 clients and four National Health Service therapists took part. Although clients showed high levels of improvement, these were not as great as for the SPP2, nor were they maintained at 1-year follow-up. There was no advantage of CB over PI therapy in this study.

Two-Plus-One Project

The consistent finding of only small differences between differing therapies led us to design a trial that attempted to maximize the potential impact of technically specific treatment components. The resultant trial compared PI and CB therapies delivered in two sessions 1 week apart followed by a third session 3 months later (Barkham, Shapiro, Hardy, & Rees, 1999). The rationale was to package these treatments to a plausible minimum to maximize their impact as a cost-efficient intervention combining technical specificity and common factors. A total of 116 clients were randomly assigned to either PI or CB therapies and received treatment either immediately or after a short delay (enabling a controlled evaluation of the short-term impact of intervention). This very brief treatment, albeit for subsyndromal depression, was effective. Gains were greater in the CB treatment than in the PI treatment, but the advantage was modest.

Sigmund Freud's only visit to the United States, at Clark University's 20th anniversary conference, Worcester, MA, September 1909. *Courtesy of the Clark University Archives. Photo key courtesy of the Archives of History of American Psychology, University of Akron.*

1. Franz Boas	11. C. E. Seashore	22. B. T. Baldwin	32. S. P. Hayes
2. E. B. Titchener	12. Joseph Jastrow	23. F. L. Wells	33. E. B. Holt
3. William James	13. J. M. Cattell	24. G. M. Forbes	34. C. S. Berry
4. William Stern	14. E. F. Buchner	25. E. A. Kirkpatrick	35. G. M. Whipple
5. Leo Burgerstein	15. E. Katzenellenbogen	26. Sandor Ferenczi	36. Frank Drew
6. G. S. Hall	16. Ernest Jones	27. E. C. Sanford	37. J. W. A. Young
7. Sigmund Freud	17. A. A. Brill	28. J. P. Porter	38. L. N. Wilson
8. C. G. Jung	18. W. H. Burnham	29. Sakyo Kanda	39. K. J. Karlson
9. Adolf Meyer	19. A. F. Chamberlain	30. Kikoso Kakise	40. H. H. Goddard
10. H. S. Jennings	20. Albert Schinz	31. G. E. Dawson	41. H. I. Klopp
	21. J. A. Magni		42. S. C. Fuller

Wilhelm Wundt (1832–1920), founder of the discipline of psychology. *Courtesy of the Archives of the History of American Psychology, University of Akron.*

William James (1842–1910) founded the first psychological laboratory in America, at Harvard University in 1875. *Courtesy of the Archives of the History of American Psychology, University of Akron.*

Rollo May (1909–1994), renowned psychotherapist and popular writer. *Courtesy of the Archives of the History of American Psychology, University of Akron.*

Anna Freud (1895–1982). *Courtesy of the Archives of the History of American Psychology, University of Akron.*

Melanie Klein (1882–1960).
Courtesy of the Klein Trust/Wellcome Institute Library, London.

David Shakow (1901–1981), pioneer
clinical psychologist and researcher.
*Courtesy of the Archives of the History
of American Psychology, University of
Akron.*

Abraham Maslow (1908–1987) laid the
foundations for humanistic therapy.
*Courtesy of the Archives of the History
of American Psychology, University of
Akron.*

Lightner Witmer (1867–1956) founded The Psychological Clinic at the University of Pennsylvania in 1896. *Courtesy of the Archives of the History of American Psychology, University of Akron.*

John B. Watson (1878–1958) pioneered behaviorism. *Courtesy of the Archives of the History of American Psychology, University of Akron.*

Francis C. Sumner (1895–1954), the first African American to be awarded a PhD in psychology, from Clark University in 1920. *Courtesy of the Clark University Archives.*

1. Isabelle V. Kendig (St. Elizabeth's Hospital, Washington, DC)
2. R. A. Brotemarkle (University of Pennsylvania)
3. Robert G. Bernreuter (Pennsylvania State College)
4. Nicholas Hobbs (Columbia University)
5. Edward S. Bordin (University of Michigan)
6. C. Roger Myers (University of Toronto)
7. Joseph E. Brewer (Wichita Guidance Center, Kansas)
8. Arthur L. Benton (State University of Iowa)
9. Graham B. Dimmick (University of Kentucky)
10. E. J. Asher (Purdue University)
11. Delton C. Beier (Indiana University)
12. Robert E. Harris (University of California Medical School)
13. Earl E. Swartlander (Veterans Administration Hospital, Long Island, NY)
14. George F. J. Lehner (University of California)
15. H. M. Hildreth (Veterans Administration, Washington, DC)
16. J. Hildreth (APA staff, guest)
17. Robert R. Blake (University of Texas)
18. Cecil W. Mann (Tulane University)
19. Lyle H. Lanier (University of Illinois)
20. Albert I. Rabin (Michigan State College)
21. John Gray Peatman (APA Policy and Planning Board)
22. Ruth Tolman (Los Angeles VA Hospital)
23. Jerry W. Carter (National Institute of Mental Health)
24. Donald K. Adams (Duke University)
25. George E. Levinrew (American Association of Psychiatric Social Workers)
26. Robert C. Challman (Menninger Foundation)
27. Julian B. Rotter (Ohio State University)
28. Chester C. Bennett (Boston University)
29. John W. Stafford (The Catholic University of America)
30. Bertha M. Luckey (Cleveland Public Schools)
31. William R. Grove (Phoenix Elementary Schools)
32. Carrol A. Whitmer (University of Pittsburgh)
33. Howard F. Hunt (University of Chicago)
34. T. Ernest Newland (University of Tennessee)
35. M. E. Bunch (Washington University)
36. Starke R. Hathaway (University of Minnesota)
37. H. P. Longstaff (University of Minnesota)
38. Brian E. Tomlinson (New York University)
39. Paul Henry Mussen (University of Wisconsin)
40. Carlyle Jacobsen (State University of Iowa)
41. Marshall R. Jones (University of Nebraska)
42. C. L. Winder (Stanford University)
43. Helen M. Wolfle (Managing Editor, American Psychologist)
44. Rex M. Collier (University of Illinois)
45. Dael Wolfle (Executive Secretary, APA)
46. Randall (no further identification)
47. James W. Layman (University of North Carolina)
48. D. B. Klein (University of Southern California)
49. Lawrence F. Shaffer (Columbia University)
50. Paul E. Huston (State University of Iowa)
51. Mary Schmitt (National League of Nursing Education)
52. Virginia T. Graham (University of Cincinnati)
53. O. H. Mowrer (University of Illinois)
54. Eliot H. Rodnick (Worcester State Hospital)
55. Max L. Hutt (University of Michigan)
56. Martin Sheerer (University of Kansas)
57. David Shakow (University of Illinois)
58. Jean W. MacFarlane (University of California)
59. Bert Kaplan (Harvard University)
60. Thelma G. Alper (Clark University)
61. Lt. Col. Charles Gersoni (U.S. Army)
62. Joseph M. Bobbit (National Institute of Mental Health)
63. C. R. Strother (University of Washington)
64. James G. Miller (University of Chicago)
65. Wayne Dennis (University of Pittsburgh)
66. John C. Eberhart (National Institute of Mental Health)
67. E. Lowell Kelly (University of Michigan)
68. Karl F. Heiser (Associate Executive Secretary, APA)
69. William H. Hunt (Northwestern University)
70. V. C. Raimy (University of Colorado)
71. Dorothea McCarthy (Fordham University)
72. Seymour B. Sarason (Yale University)
73. Robert H. Felix (National Institute of Mental Health)
74. G. R. Wendt (University of Rochester)

Not pictured: Dwight Miles (Western Reserve University)

Second Psychotherapy Research Conference, Chapel Hill, NC, May 1961. *Courtesy of the Archives of the University of North Carolina, Chapel Hill.*

1. Maury Lorr	14. Dan Levinson	26. Martin Lakin
2. Hans Strupp	15. Stan Imber	27. Dave Hamburg
3. Dave Shakow	16. Donald Glad	28. Martin Wallach
4. Leon Bernstein	17. John Schlein	29. Jack Butler
5. Irwin Rosen	18. Henry Lennard	30. Lester Luborsky
6. Morris Parloff	19. Nevitt Sanford	31. J. McV. Hunt
7. Richard Siegal	20. Jerry Frank	32. Otto Will
8. George Mahl	21. Will Snyder	33. Ian Stevenson
9. Ed Bordin	22. Len Krasner	34. Ernest Haggard
10. George Saslow	23. Don Bloch	35. Jack Block
11. Barbara Betz	24. Ken Colby	
12. Mabel Cohen	25. Donald Gorham	
13. Hedda Bolgar		

Herbert Freudenberger (1927–1999), psychotherapy leader and writer. Coined the term "burnout." *Courtesy of the American Psychological Foundation.*

Hans H. Strupp (1921–2006), pioneer researcher in psychotherapy. *Courtesy of Karen Strupp.*

Donald R. Peterson (1925–2007), psychotherapy trainer and founder of PsyD programs in psychology. *Courtesy of Rutgers University.*

Colorado Conference on Graduate Education in Clinical Psychology, Boulder, CO, August 1949. The conference produced the well-known Boulder scientist–practitioner model of clinical education. *Courtesy of the Archives of the History of American Psychology, University of Akron. Photo key courtesy of Eliot H. Rodnick.*

The Evolution of Psychotherapy Conference (2000). Back row: Mary Goulding, Ernest Rossi, Alexander Lowen, Aaron Beck, James Hillman, Zerka Moreno, Jay Haley, William Glasser, Donald Meichenbaum, Irving Yalom, Paul Watzlawick, Jeffrey Zeig. Front row: Eugene Gendlin, Cloé Madanes, Michael White, James Bugental, Judd Marmor, Miriam Polster, Erving Polster, Sal Minuchin, James Masterson, Otto Kernberg, Thomas Szaz, Albert Ellis. *Courtesy of the Milton H. Erickson Foundation, Inc.*

The Evolution of Psychotherapy Faculty (2005). Back row: John and Julie Gottman, Michael White, Ernest Rossi, Arnold Lazarus, Jeffrey Zeig, Marsha Linehan, Donald Meichenbaum, Irvin Yalom, James Hillman, Thomas Szasz, James Masterson, Albert Bandura, Martin Seligman. Front row: Jean Houston, Erving Polster, Otto Kernberg, Mary Goulding, Albert Ellis, William Glasser, Salvador Minuchin, Cloé Madanes, Francine Shapiro, Aaron Beck. *Courtesy of the Milton H. Erickson Foundation, Inc.*

Dose–Effect Relations

Although this quartet of studies held the comparison between PI and CB therapies constant, they used differing durations of treatment sessions considered as an independent variable: two, eight, and 16 sessions. In terms of informing the dose–effect curve, aggregated results from two, eight, and 16 sessions suggested a greater degree of linearity than originally proposed by the work of Howard, Kopta, Krause, and Orlinsky (1986; see Shapiro et al., 2003). We used both nomothetic (i.e., BDI) and idiographic (i.e., personal questionnaire) data to investigate the rates of change and found evidence indicating classes of BDI items that changed more quickly than others. In addition, the personal questionnaire data, which was completed weekly throughout treatment, showed broadly linear improvements as well as faster improvements in symptoms, followed by relationships and then self-esteem (Barkham, Rees, Stiles, et al., 1996). Work on treatment comparisons and dose–effect relations continued within our practice-based studies drawing on large data sets from routine settings (see the Practice-Based Studies section).

PROCESS STUDIES

Underpinning the design of the comparative Sheffield trials was a focus on the underlying mechanisms of change. Intensive process work on the first Sheffield Psychotherapy Project showed that the immediate impacts of the two treatments were consistent with theoretical expectations, with exploratory sessions rated as deeper and more powerful and prescriptive sessions rated as smoother and easier. Differential impacts also showed that significant therapy events in prescriptive sessions were more likely to lead to problem solution and reassurance, whereas significant events in exploratory sessions led to awareness and a sense of personal contact with the therapist. Analyses using comprehensive process analysis on selected insight events in exploratory and prescriptive sessions led directly to informing the development of the assimilation model by William B. Stiles (Stiles et al., 1990).

Work arising from the SPP2 focused on investigations of common factors as a means of explaining the equivalence paradox as well as developing innovative research methods to study encompassing frameworks. An exemplar of this was devising an experimentally rigorous but clinically sensitive method for testing the assimilation model and showing how a problematic experience in PI therapy was successfully incorporated into a schema (for a fuller account, see Shapiro, 1995). It is interesting to note that much of the change occurred within a single session, a finding that predated subsequent work on sudden gains. A further example of encompassing frameworks was the exploration of responsiveness as an explanation for the limitations of process–outcome dose–effect relationships (Hardy, Stiles, Barkham, & Startup, 1998). A continued commitment to researching the therapeutic alliance led to the development of a new measure of the client–therapist relationship and its adoption in the trials (Stiles, Agnew-Davies, Hardy, Barkham, & Shapiro, 1998). We also developed innovative qualitative methods to develop alliance rupture markers and the cultural determinants of relationship development. Our subsequent research showed that both the alliance and therapist competence independently predicted outcome, with client interpersonal style influencing therapy processes—evidence that supported the importance of common mechanisms in psychotherapy change.

PRACTICE-BASED STUDIES

A research clinic was established in Leeds, modeled on the research clinic in Sheffield but staffed by National Health Service clinical psychologists working 1 day per week as part of a protocol-based trial—the Leeds Depression Project. The clinic originally offered both PI and CB therapy for depressed outpatients, but in pursuit of research funding and of efficient services, it became a CB therapy clinic for depression. That project yielded important further development of responsiveness and also showed that treatment outcome improved when therapists adjusted their interventions according to the interpersonal style of clients (Hardy et al., 2001). Work on sudden gains showed that 41% of clients experienced at least one sudden gain during treatment, and those who experienced a sudden gain showed greater overall improvement in outcome compared with those who did not experience a sudden gain (Hardy et al., 2005).

The development, implementation, and widespread adoption in the United Kingdom of a core outcome measure led to the collation of increasingly large data sets, which provided the basis for developing practice-based evidence (Barkham et al., 2001). These large data sets enabled further investigations of dose–effect relations as well as comparisons between differing treatments as delivered in routine practice settings. Contrary to the work of Howard et al. (1986), our dose–effect work suggested support for a good enough level model in which clients end therapy when a satisfactory level of gains has been achieved (Barkham et al., 2006).

In terms of differing treatments, comparisons were made between CB, person-centered, and psychodynamic therapies. Although CB therapy yielded better outcomes, the between-treatment differences were small (Stiles, Barkham, Mellor-Clark, & Connell, 2008). The high external validity obtained in these studies comes at a cost, as practice-based data is vulnerable to arguments relating to the quality of treatment and the impact of this noise in reducing sensitivity to treatment effects. In addition, securing high completion rates at the end of treatment is a major logistical challenge in capturing practice-based data. Our methodological pluralism incorporating data from both controlled trials and practice-based studies led us to compare their outcomes (Barkham et al., 2008). We compared data from controlled trials of depression with routine practice data, and our findings suggested that outcomes in trials were approximately 12% superior to those from routine practice—not an altogether surprising finding but important in establishing a better estimate of the difference, as this matter becomes crucial when adopting outcomes from trials as benchmarks for routine practice.

The 30 years of systematic research by members of the Sheffield–Leeds Psychotherapy Program has contributed to our understanding of psychotherapy outcome, process, relationship, responsiveness, and other crucial features of the healing enterprise. Overall, our findings suggest a modest and contingent edge for CB therapy but in the context of many exceptions at the case level. Evidence for treatment-specific change mechanisms has been achieved but amidst the pervasive impact of the therapeutic relationship, and the extent to which efficacy trials outperform "real-world" implementation is, at best, moderate.

REFERENCES

Barkham, M., Connell, J., Stiles, W. B., Miles, J. N. V., Margison, J., Evans, C., & Mellor-Clark, J. (2006). Dose–effect relations and responsive regulation of treatment duration: The good enough level. *Journal of Consulting and Clinical Psychology, 74*, 160–167. doi:10.1037/0022-006X.74.1.160

Barkham, M., Margison, F., Leach, C., Lucock, M., Mellor-Clark, J., Evans, C., . . . McGrath, G. (2001). Service profiling and outcomes benchmarking using the CORE-OM: Towards practice-based evidence in the psychological therapies. *Journal of Consulting and Clinical Psychology, 69*, 184–196. doi:10.1037/0022-006X.69.2.184

Barkham, M., Rees, A., Shapiro, D. A., Stiles, W. B., Agnew, R. M., Halstead, J., . . . Harrington, V. M. G. (1996). Outcomes of time-limited psychotherapy in applied settings: Replicating the Second Sheffield Psychotherapy Project. *Journal of Consulting and Clinical Psychology, 64*, 1079–1085. doi:10.1037/0022-006X.64.5.1079

Barkham, M., Rees, A., Stiles, W. B., Shapiro, D. A., Hardy, G. E., & Reynolds, S. (1996). Dose–effect relations in time-limited psychotherapy for depression. *Journal of Consulting and Clinical Psychology, 64*, 927–935. doi:10.1037/0022-006X.64.5.927

Barkham, M., Shapiro, D. A., Hardy, G. E., & Rees, A. (1999). Psychotherapy in two-plus-one sessions: Outcomes of a randomized controlled trial of cognitive–behavioral and psychodynamic–interpersonal therapy for subsyndromal depression. *Journal of Consulting and Clinical Psychology, 67*, 201–211. doi:10.1037/0022-006X.67.2.201

Barkham, M., Stiles, W. B., Connell, J., Twigg, E., Leach, C., Lucock, M., . . . Angus, L. (2008). Effects of psychological therapies in randomized trials and practice-based studies. *British Journal of Clinical Psychology, 47*, 397–415. doi:10.1348/014466508X311713

Hardy, G. E., Cahill, J., Shapiro, D. A., Barkham, M., Rees, A., & Macaskill, N. (2001). Client interpersonal and cognitive styles as predictors of response to time limited cognitive therapy for depression. *Journal of Consulting and Clinical Psychology, 69,* 841–845. doi:10.1037/0022-006X.69.5.841

Hardy, G. E., Cahill, J., Stiles, W. B., Ispam, C., Macaskill, N., & Barkham, M. (2005). Sudden gains in cognitive therapy for depression: A replication and extension. *Journal of Consulting and Clinical Psychology, 73,* 59–67. doi:10.1037/0022-006X.73.1.59

Hardy, G. E., Stiles, W. B., Barkham, M., & Startup, M. (1998). Therapist responsiveness to client attachment issues during time-limited treatments for depression. *Journal of Consulting and Clinical Psychology, 66,* 304–312. doi:10.1037/0022-006X.66.2.304

Howard, K. I., Kopta, S. M., Krause, M. S., & Orlinsky, D. E. (1986). The dose–effect relationship in psychotherapy. *American Psychologist, 41,* 159–164.

Shapiro, D. A. (1995). Finding out how psychotherapies help people change. *Psychotherapy Research, 5,* 1–21.

Shapiro, D. A., Barkham, M., Rees, A., Hardy, G. E., Reynolds, S., & Startup, M. (1994). Effects of treatment duration and severity of depression on the effectiveness of cognitive–behavioral and psychodynamic–interpersonal psychotherapy. *Journal of Consulting and Clinical Psychology, 62,* 522–534. doi:10.1037/0022-006X.62.3.522

Shapiro, D. A., Barkham, M., Stiles, W. B., Hardy, G. E., Rees, A., Startup, M., & Reynolds, S. (2003). Time is of the essence: The fall and rise of brief therapy research. *Psychology and Psychotherapy: Theory, Research and Practice, 76,* 211–236.

Shapiro, D. A., & Firth, J. (1987). Prescriptive vs. exploratory psychotherapy: Outcomes of the Sheffield Psychotherapy Project. *British Journal of Psychiatry, 151,* 790–799. doi:10.1192/bjp.151.6.790

Shapiro, D. A., Rees, A., Barkham, M., Hardy, G. E., Reynolds, S., & Startup, M. (1995). Effects of treatment duration and severity of depression on the maintenance of gains following cognitive–behavioral and psychodynamic–interpersonal psychotherapy. *Journal of Consulting and Clinical Psychology, 63,* 378–387. doi:10.1037/0022-006X.63.3.378

Shapiro, D. A., & Shapiro, D. (1982). Meta-analysis of comparative therapy outcome studies: A replication and refinement. *Psychological Bulletin, 92,* 581–604. doi:10.1037/0033-2909.92.3.581

Stiles, W. B., Agnew-Davies, R. M., Hardy, G. E., Barkham, M., & Shapiro, D. A. (1998). Relations of the alliance with psychotherapy outcome: Findings in the Second Sheffield Psychotherapy Project. *Journal of Consulting and Clinical Psychology, 66,* 791–802. doi:10.1037/0022-006X.66.5.791

Stiles, W. B., Barkham, M., Mellor-Clark, J., & Connell, J. (2008). Effectiveness of cognitive–behavioural, person-centred, and psychodynamic therapies in UK primary care routine practice: Replication with a larger sample. *Psychological Medicine, 38,* 677–688. doi:10.1017/S0033291707001511

Stiles, W. B., Elliott, R., Llewelyn, S. P., Firth-Cozens, J. A., Margison, F. R., Shapiro, D. A., & Hardy, G. (1990). Assimilation of problematic experiences by clients in psychotherapy. *Psychotherapy, 27,* 411–420.

The Bern Psychotherapy Research Group

Franz Caspar and Hansjörg Znoj

The Bern Psychotherapy Research Group was founded by Klaus Grawe in 1979 and is inseparably associated with his name. Grawe was born in 1943 and grew up in Hamburg, Germany, where he also completed most of his studies in psychology. He spent 10 years doing behavior therapy and psychotherapy research at the Hamburg University Psychiatric Hospital. These years gave him a solid practical background that contributed to his view that the noblest tasks of psychotherapy researchers are to answer the urgent questions of practitioners and to contribute directly to patient care.

Grawe had two major insights in these early times. First, dealing with interactionally difficult patients (many of whom would nowadays be diagnosed with a personality disorder), he experienced the limits of traditional behavior therapy and developed what he called *vertical behavior analysis*, an approach based on Miller, Galanter, and Pribram's (1960) plan concept. This concept emphasized the vertical structure of motives in addition to the horizontal relation of stimulus, reaction, and consequence on the time axis. Second, he concluded that it is much too general to examine average effects of treatments; instead, differential effects for different groups of patients would be more conclusive for research and more helpful for patients.

In 1979, Grawe moved to the newly created position of chair of clinical psychology at the University of Bern, Bern, Germany. His first assistants were Hans Peter Müller, now rector of the School of Education in Bern, and Franz Caspar, whom Grawe met in Hamburg and with whom a fruitful collaboration ensued. The first years in Bern were dedicated to setting up a teaching program and an outpatient clinic.

The Bern Psychotherapy Research Group continued under Grawe's direction for 25 years, until his sudden death in 2005. Hansjörg Znoj directed the department for the next 2 years. In 2007, Franz Caspar was elected to become Grawe's successor and now continues to pursue many of the research ideas that he developed and shared with Grawe for more than 2 decades.

MAJOR RESEARCH ACHIEVEMENTS

It is crucial to understand the Bernese research as an ongoing process, partially stimulated by concrete research projects, rather than as a product of individual, time-limited studies. It is a comprehensive endeavor, grounded in an infrastructure of collaborators, an outpatient clinic, a postgraduate training program, masters and doctoral theses, and extramurally funded grants.

The Bernese approach to psychotherapy is integrative. The commitment to clinical pragmatism and empirically sound procedures results in a preference for cognitive–behavioral therapy, but it is complemented by many theoretical orientations, including the interpersonal and systemic. Grawe always criticized narrow-mindedness and theoretical restrictions. In what he called *second generation approaches* or *general psychotherapy*, all research findings, theoretical concepts, and therapeutic procedures relevant for a particular patient should be considered. Nothing should be excluded just because it does not fit into the limited view of the original (*first generation*) approaches.

Integrative meant not only the integration of theoretical orientations but also concepts from social, cognitive, and emotion psychology and, above all, neuroscience. Examples are *attractors* in Grawe's (2004) thinking and *local minima* in terms of neural networks in Caspar's (Caspar & Berger, 2007; Caspar, Rothenfluh, & Segal, 1992) thinking. Grawe's interest in the neurobiological aspects of psychotherapy led to his 2007 book, *Neuropsychotherapy*. He postulated that every psychotherapist should be aware of and consider the neurobiological basis of disorders and of therapy. Our treatments are based on individual case conceptualizations that use the concepts of consistency theory (Grawe, 2004; discussed later) and plan analysis (Caspar, 2007). They are the basis for constructing individual therapy plans, in which manualized, disorder-specific treatments may be used as prototypes but do not ultimately determine the therapeutic procedure (Caspar, 2008).

Bern's large outpatient clinic maintains extensive records of thousands of current and completed psychotherapy cases. These therapies are available within a research strategy termed *selection within natural variation*. Our idea is that it is impossible to bring about specific data experimentally, especially if combinations of variables are of interest. For example, it is hard to imagine how the effect of a noncomplementary utterance of a therapist with patients in the eight extreme interpersonal positions according to the Inventory of Interpersonal Problems (Horowitz, Rosenberg, Baer, Ureno, & Villasenor, 1988) could be traced experimentally in comparing successful and failed therapies. If one has a large pool of therapy recordings, then there is a high chance of finding data corresponding to the demands, even when combining several criteria. Grawe argued that hypothesis testing within such a strategy comes close to experimental research and has a value that goes beyond mere explorative studies.

Our first randomized controlled trial, the Bernese Comparative Treatment Study (Grawe, Caspar, & Ambühl, 1990), was conducted in the 1980s. Patients presenting with mixed diagnoses were randomly assigned to three forms of explicit case conceptualization: traditional functional behavior analysis, plan analysis, and a treatment condition without explicit case conceptualization (represented by client-centered therapy). Large differences in process among the three therapies were found, but there were few differences in average patient outcomes. Above all, the results supported differential outcomes. Specifically, autonomy-seeking patients had better outcomes with client-centered therapy, whereas more support- and structure-seeking patients did better with traditional behavior therapy. The patient's interpersonal needs made no difference in the most individualized plan-based therapy condition. In general, correlations between patient variables and treatment outcome were the lowest in this last condition, suggesting that this is where psychotherapists were most responsive to patients' needs.

Evidence-based practice favors research-supported, disorder-oriented psychotherapies. Nevertheless, non-disorder-specific therapies, like process-experiential approaches (e.g., Greenberg, 2002; Sachse, 2003), focusing on conflicts and emotions have also proved to be effective. A Bernese fundamental principle of human information processing concerns striving for consistency between actual perceptions and expectations. Therefore, we postulated that inconsistency in psychological functioning contributes to the development and maintenance of psychological disorders. The specific focus on inconsistency was intended to improve the outcome for patients with internal conflicts (e.g., goals, losses) as compared with purely disorder-oriented therapies. We thus compared cognitive–behavioral therapy alone with cognitive–behavior therapy plus experiential therapy in the next randomized study (Grosse Holtforth, Grawe, Fries, & Znoj, 2008), which was completed and published after Grawe's death.

In this randomized controlled trial involving 67 outpatients with heterogeneous diagnoses, the hypothesis tested was whether the level of inconsistency would differentially predict outcome. The treatment phase included 20 sessions; after 20 sessions, the therapist was free to change his or her approach. Differential effects on inconsistency were examined using two different operationalizations: the degree of avoidance goals and the mean total of approach and avoidance goal discrepancy. Outcome was measured with a combination of direct measures (goal attainment, change of experience and behavior) and indirect measures (symptom distress, interpersonal problems, well-being). Results indicated that after 20 sessions, the two therapies demonstrated equal outcomes. The predicted differential effects were observed for only one measure of inconsistency, namely, the intensity of avoidance goals, and for two outcome measures, reduction of interpersonal goals and change of behavior. There were several limitations in this study, specifically the statistical power. However, there was preliminary evidence for the differential prediction of treatment outcome by patient severity of inconsistency.

Much of the reputation of the Bernese group is owed to its process and process–outcome research. We developed several rating systems over the years dedicated to what Grawe called *wirkfaktoren* (therapeutic factors). Among the most interesting results was that therapy sessions are most productive when problem and resource activation are balanced in every session. A practical consequence derived from this research is to never talk with a patient about his or her problems, or to activate these problems in other ways, without counterbalancing this with activating abilities and positive goals. Other process research done by Bern researchers relates to the quality of the therapeutic relationship, with a direct measure of therapist responsiveness related to outcome (Caspar, Grossmann, Unmüssig, & Schramm, 2005).

A vast meta-analysis conducted by Grawe and colleagues in the 1980s (Grawe, Donati, & Bernauer, 1994) was titled *Psychotherapy in Transition From Confession to Profession*. The book contributed much to his reputation but also to controversy. Grawe thought a sober evaluation of the effectiveness of various psychotherapy systems was needed. Grawe interpreted his meta-analytic results to mean that psychotherapies were not of equivalent effectiveness; rather, Grawe concluded with a more nuanced or differential view, namely, that the outcome depends on various variables (above all, patient variables) in interaction with treatment variables. Advocates of several psychotherapy systems felt that Grawe's meta-analysis did not present their approach in a favorable light. For many years, the old competitive race between psychotherapies seemed to have been replaced by battles about the proper way of conducting meta-analyses.

A variety of other topics have been studied over the course of 30 years by members of the Bernese group. Examples are a training program for emotional competencies entitled TEK (Berking et al., 2008), emotion regulation (Znoj, 2008), priming of therapist attention to patient resources (Flückiger & Grosse Holtforth, 2008), modules for feedback-intense training of psychotherapists (Caspar, Berger, & Hautle, 2004, and Internet-based therapy (Berger, Hohl, & Caspar, in press). Other groups using Bernese research data and concepts include one of the few worldwide experimental studies related to doctor–patient relationships (Schmitt, Kammerer & Holtmann, 2003), an evaluation of data from the Bernese pool (Beutler, Mohr, Grawe, Engle, & McDonald, 1991; see also Beutler, this chapter), and the use of plan analysis to develop treatment plans for complex patients (Kramer, Berger, & Caspar, 2009).

CONCLUSIONS

Since 1979, Grawe has been the inspirational source and research director of the prolific Bern Psychotherapy Research Group. Among the group's influential contributions are Grawe's meta-analysis, the first comparative treatment study demonstrating differences depending on case conceptualizations, work on the importance of consistency and the therapeutic relationship, and Grawe's and Caspar's outreach to neurobiology (Caspar, 2003; Grawe, 2007). Grawe's untimely death in 2005 changed but did not stymie the research contributions of the group.

Indeed, Grawe was restless in his questioning and revising of concepts while remaining faithful to the principles mentioned in this chapter. He would be deeply satisfied that the Bernese group has continued to work along these principles. However, he would also be pleased to learn that his colleagues and descendants have continued his heritage of moving into newer areas that simultaneously advance our research knowledge and patient care. His empirical commitment, integrative approach, and open example make it much easier to carry on his heritage.

REFERENCES

Berger, T., Hohl, E., & Caspar, F. (in press). Internet-based treatment for social phobia: A randomized controlled trial. *Journal of Clinical Psychology*.

Berking, M., Wupperman, P., Reichard, A., Pejic, T., Dippel, A., & Znoj, H. J. (2008). General emotion-regulation skills as a treatment target in psychological interventions for mental health problems: Preliminary results of a randomized controlled trial. *Behaviour Research and Therapy, 46*, 1230–1237.

Beutler, L. E., Mohr, D. C., Grawe, K., Engle, D., & McDonald, R. (1992). Looking for differential treatment effects: Cross-cultural predictors of differential psychotherapy efficacy. *Journal of Psychotherapy Integration, 1*, 121–142. doi:10.1037/0033-3204.38.4.431

Caspar, F. (2003). Psychotherapy research and neurobiology: Challenge, chance, or enrichment? *Psychotherapy Research, 13*, 1–23. doi:10.1093/ptr/kpg013

Caspar, F. (2007). Plan analysis. In T. Eells (Ed.), *Handbook of psychotherapeutic case formulations* (2nd ed., pp. 251–289). New York, NY: Guilford Press.

Caspar, F. (2008). Therapeutisches handeln als individueller konstruktionsprozess [Therapist action as an individual construction process]. In J. Margraf & S. Schneider (Eds.), *Lehrbuch der verhaltenstherapie* (Vol. 1, pp. 213–225). Berlin, Germany: Springer.

Caspar, F., & Berger, T. (2007). Insight and cognitive psychology. In L. Castonguay & C. Hill (Eds.), *Insight in psychotherapy* (pp. 375–399). Washington, DC: American Psychological Association.

Caspar, F., Berger, T., & Hautle, I. (2004). The right view of your patient: A computer assisted, individualized module for psychotherapy training. *Psychotherapy: Theory, Research, Practice, Training, 41*, 125–135.

Caspar, F., Grossmann, C., Unmüssig, C., & Schramm, E. (2005). Complementary therapeutic relationship: Therapist behavior, interpersonal patterns, and therapeutic effects. *Psychotherapy Research, 15*, 91–102. doi:10.1080/10503300512331327074

Caspar, F., Rothenfluh, T., & Segal, Z. V. (1992). The appeal of connectionism for clinical psychology. *Clinical Psychology Review, 12*, 719–762. doi:10.1016/0272-7358(92)90022-Z

Flückiger, C., & Grosse Holtforth, M. (2008). Focusing the therapist's attention on the patient's strengths—A preliminary study to foster a mechanism of change in outpatient psychotherapy. *Journal of Clinical Psychology, 64*, 876–890. doi:10.1002/jclp.20493

Grawe, K. (2004). *Psychological therapy*. Seattle, WA: Hogrefe.

Grawe, K. (2007). *Neuropsychotherapy*. Mahwah, NJ: Erlbaum.

Grawe, K., Caspar, F., & Ambühl, H. R. (1990). Die Berner therapievergleichsstudie: Zusammenfassung und schlussfolgerungen. In differentielle psychotherapieforschung: Vier therapieformen im vergleich [The Bernese therapy comparison study: Summary and consequences. In differential psychotherapy research: Four forms of psychotherapy compared]. *Themenheft der Zeitschrift für Klinische Psychologie, 4,* 362–376.

Grawe, K., Donati, R., & Bernauer, R. (1994). *Psychotherapie im wandel von der konfession zur profession* [Psychotherapy in transition from confession to profession]. Göttingen, Germany: Hogrefe.

Greenberg, L. (2002). *Emotion-focused therapy: Coaching clients to work through feelings*. Washington, DC: American Psychological Association.

Grosse Holtforth, M., Grawe, K., Fries, A., & Znoj, H. J. (2008). Inkonsistenz als differentielles indikationskriterium in der psychotherapie—Eine randomisierte kontrollierte studie [Inconsistency as a criterion for differential indication in psychotherapy—A randomized controlled trial]. *Zeitschrift für Klinische Psychologie und Psychotherapie, 37,* 103–111. doi:10.1026/1616-3443.37.2.103

Horowitz, L., Rosenberg, S., Baer, A., Ureno, G., & Villasenor, V. (1988). Inventory of Interpersonal Problems: Psychometric properties and clinical applications. *Journal of Consulting and Clinical Psychology, 57,* 599–606. doi:10.1037/0022-006X.57.5.599

Kramer, U., Berger, T., & Caspar, F. (2009). Psychotherapeutic case conceptualization using plan analysis for bipolar affective disorder. *Journal of Clinical Psychology, 65,* 352–367. doi:10.1002/jclp.20557

Miller, G. A., Galanter, E., & Pribram, K. H. (1960). *Plans and the structure of behavior*. New York, NY: Holt.

Sachse, R. (2003). *Klärungsorientierte psychotherapie* [Clarification oriented psychotherapy]. Göttingen, Germany: Hogrefe.

Schmitt, G. M., Kammerer, E., & Holtmann, M. (2003). Förderung interaktioneller kompetenzen von medizinstudierenden [Furthering interactional competencies of medical students]. *Psychotherapie, Psychosomatik, Medizinische Psychologie, 53,* 390–398. doi:10.1055/s-2003-42171

Znoj, H. J. (2008). *Regulation emotionaler prozesse in psychotherapie und verhaltensmedizin* [Regulation of emotional processes in psychotherapy and behavioral medicine]. Bern, Germany: Peter Lang.

Project MATCH

Carlo C. DiClemente

The history of alcoholism treatment research in the 20th century in many ways paralleled the history of psychotherapy. Formal treatments for alcoholism were based on extant theories of psychotherapy that shifted as the field moved from psychodynamic to humanistic and social-learning perspectives.

Several unique developments, however, diverged from the history of psychotherapy. One was the emergence of Alcoholics Anonymous (AA), which espoused personal recovery through Twelve Steps and a network of mutual support groups. By the 1980s, Twelve-Step support groups for individuals with alcoholism were ubiquitous throughout the United States and around the world. The other unique development was the discovery that brief interventions comprising advice and feedback could produce significant changes in drinking behavior without the intensive involvement of hospitals, physicians, and psychotherapists. Although self-help, brief interventions, and diverse inpatient and outpatient treatments were having some success, these interventions often failed to reach many individuals with problem drinking or to produce long-term success (see Chapter 15, this volume). The frequency of relapse made sustained abstinence and lasting change elusive.

Reviews on the effectiveness of alcoholism treatments indicated that no single intervention demonstrated consistently superior outcomes. Because many treatments experienced some success, a logical assumption was that specific treatments may be effective for some and not other types of individuals with problem drinking. Moreover, because of the vast heterogeneity of individuals engaging in excessive drinking, many attempts were undertaken to identify subtypes of drinkers and special phenotypes that could explain alcohol dependence and indicate those clients who might differentially benefit from one rather than another type of treatment. The idea of matching treatments to client characteristics emerged from the discontent with "one size fits all" approaches, the disillusionment with finding a single efficacious treatment, and the zeitgeist of treatment specificity and individualization.

The National Institute on Alcohol Abuse and Alcoholism (NIAAA) responded to the interest in treatment matching with a call to initiate a rigorous, large-scale, randomized trial. Investigators selected to participate had to abandon their single site proposals in favor of a large, multisite matching trial that would be conducted within the framework of a multiyear cooperative agreement. The Project MATCH Research Group, consisting of 23 investigators, NIAAA staff, and consultants, developed and implemented one of the largest randomized treatment trials in the history of alcoholism research. The project was funded for a total of 10 years at a cost of 28 million dollars and involved 1,726 clients in outpatient and residential treatment facilities at nine clinical research sites. Project MATCH generated well over 125 published articles, chapters, and monographs by the end of the funding period. The complete description of the trial and all its components is published in *Project MATCH: The Book*, written by members of the research team (Babor & Del Boca, 2003).

The design of the trial was unique in that it tested multiple matching hypotheses using three specific treatments adapted or created for the trial with a heterogeneous population of treatment-seeking clients. The research design consisted of two parallel matching studies conducted in outpatient and aftercare settings. The Clinical Research Units awarded the grants were nearly evenly split in their access to and collaboration with either outpatient or inpatient treatment facilities. These settings accessed client populations that differed along important matching dimensions and added to the breath of the matching characteristics that could be studied. The two arms also provided the ability to test replication of any findings across two distinct settings.

Because the study was focused on treatment matching and used three different treatments, the investigators decided that each treatment would serve as a control for the others when testing matching hypotheses. Therefore, the design did not include a wait-list, no-treatment, or other type of placebo control group.

The trial was executed by the MATCH Steering Committee. The Steering Committee, in collaboration with many co-investigators and consultants, delegated tasks and created teams of investigators to develop the design, treatments, inclusion criteria, assessments, schedule of assessments, implementation protocol of the trial, analytic strategies, and coordination of publications (see Connors et al., 1994; DiClemente, Carroll, Connors, & Kadden, 1994; Donovan et al., 1994; Donovan & Mattson, 1994; Longabaugh, Wirtz, DiClemente, & Litt, 1994). An external Data and Safety Monitoring Board monitored the trial for any danger to participant safety. The favorable follow-up rates at 1 year of over 90% and for blood samples of over 80% were due to the collaborative and multidisciplinary nature of the leadership and a true team approach to the project. The project has served as a model of organization and collaboration for multisite clinical trials.

Selection of therapies was challenging because the treatments had to possess documentation of clinical effectiveness and strong rationale for an interaction between the treatment and select client characteristics. In addition, the treatments had to be acceptable to practitioners, have active and measurable ingredients, be feasible to implement within the constraints of the trial, and address adequately the needs of heterogeneous patients with alcohol problems.

We offered three therapies that met these criteria. Cognitive–behavioral therapy (CBT) had demonstrated effectiveness and was becoming a standard treatment, focusing on coping skills and social-learning principles. Motivational enhancement therapy (MET) was based on the effectiveness of brief interventions and the favorable outcomes of the alcoholism checkup studies of William R. Miller (1985) and the newly developed motivational interviewing. Twelve-Step facilitation (TSF) was chosen because of its widespread use, its influence on rehabilitation programs such as the Minnesota Model, and the existence of the mutual support system of AA. Also, there were studies documenting the effectiveness of this approach for individuals with alcohol dependence who regularly attended and became involved in AA and its principles.

Manuals were developed for each of the treatments (available online at the NIAAA web site, http://www.niaaa.nih.gov). The manuals described the treatment protocol and adaptations for use in aftercare settings. Project MATCH included over 80 therapists who had some familiarity with each of the treatments and would be typical of those delivering the treatments selected. All three treatments were 12 weeks in duration but differed in intensity, with MET offering four sessions at Weeks 1, 2, 6, and 12, and the other two treatments offering 12 sessions in 12 weeks. All treatments allowed for several emergency sessions during the course of the treatment and were videotaped for coding by the coordinating center to evaluate the fidelity and validity of the treatments. Tape ratings indicated excellent internal validity of the treatments and good adherence to the treatment manuals. Tapes were also used to evaluate process variables and causal chains, described later.

Matching hypotheses were essentially Attribute × Treatment interactions (ATIs), based on hypothesized interactions between one of the treatments with measured characteristics of the clients (also see Beutler, this chapter). Table 12.1 presents the list of primary hypothesized interactions. For example, clients with higher levels of psychopathology were hypothesized to have better drinking outcomes when assigned to CBT because of its skills focus and problem-based approach in contrast to MET and TSF, which did not offer problem solving. Clients with more alcohol-involved social systems or who were searching for meaning should have better outcomes in TSF. Each hypothesis team had to hypothesize an ATI and also indicate which active ingredients of the treatment were responsible for the interaction. For example, CBT and MET focused on clients' abstinence self-efficacy in contrast to perspective of TSF that emphasized client powerlessness over alcohol, so that clients with low efficacy would do better in CBT and MET than in TSF. Outcomes as well as an analysis of the causal chains for these interactions were summarized in the MATCH monograph (Longabaugh & Wirtz, 2001).

TABLE 12.1
Primary Matching Hypotheses

Matching characteristic	Contrasts
Alcohol involvement	CBT, TSF > MET
Cognitive impairment	TSF > CBT, CBT > MET
Conceptual level	MET > TSF
Gender	Female CBT – TSF > Male CBT – TSF
Meaning seeking	TSF > CBT, MET
Motivation	CBT > MET
Psychiatric severity	CBT > MET
Sociopathy	CBT > MET, CBT > TSF, TSF > MET
Support for drinking	CBT > MET, TSF > CBT
Typology	Type B CBT, TSF mean > MET
	Type A CBT, TSF mean – MET mean

Note. CBT = cognitive–behavioral therapy; TSF = Twelve-Step facilitation; MET = motivational enhancement therapy.

In all, 23 matching hypotheses were tested with appropriate adjustment for multiple tests. Drinking outcomes were measured using two primary measures: percentage of days abstinent (PDA), measuring the frequency of drinking, and drinks per drinking day (DDD), measuring the intensity of drinking. Other outcomes were also examined using total abstinence and survival analyses and a categorical view of success that included both drinking frequency and drinking consequences measured over each 3-month follow-up period.

The matching hypotheses did not support to any significant degree the overall matching hypothesis. Basic matching results can be summarized as follows:

- TSF tended to be more effective than one or both the other treatments for outpatients without additional psychopathology and those with greater social support for continued drinking. TSF was also more effective for clients in the aftercare treatment arm who had higher alcohol dependence and, to a lesser extent, were higher in meaning seeking.
- MET was more effective than the other two treatments for outpatients with higher state–trait anger scores. This was the strongest matching effect statistically.
- CBT emerged as more effective than TSF with aftercare participants who were lower in alcohol dependence.

No matching effect or ATI emerged across both arms of the study. The largest of the matching effects produced what were considered clinically meaningful differences of 10% to 17% in days abstinent.

Treatment outcomes across all three treatments were statistically and clinically impressive. Drinking outcomes were significantly better and drinking reduced dramatically during the 1-year posttreatment period, in comparison with pretreatment drinking frequency and intensity. For outcomes that focused only on abstinence, the participants in TSF showed a slight superiority. In the period from baseline to the end of treatment (3 months later), outpatients in all three treatments increased abstinence (PDA) from 30% a month to 80% per month. Outpatients decreased DDD from baseline to end of treatment more than fourfold, from 13 drinks to about 3 drinks on days when they drank. For aftercare patients, the PDA went from 25% to 90% and DDD from 20 to about 2 from the baseline period to end of treatment.

During the 1-year follow-up, there was only a slight decrement in these outcomes for the three treatment groups. Thus, change was sustained over time for the majority of the participants. Continuous total abstinence from end of treatment to the end of the 1-year follow-up, however, was achieved by only a minority of the patients in the two arms of the trial: 16% of outpatients and 30% of aftercare patients.

MATCH investigators evaluated both therapeutic relationship dimensions as well as the therapists to see whether there were differences in outcomes on the basis of therapist dimensions. Client ratings of the therapeutic alliance in the outpatient treatment arm were related to better drinking outcomes but were also moderated by client motivation, with more motivated clients rating the alliance higher. Therapist effects were also discovered in each treatment in one or another arm of the trial. Differences were attributable in almost all cases to individual outlier therapists who had either better or worse outcomes than the average of the group. Thus, both the working alliance and individual therapists demonstrated an effect on treatment outcomes.

When evaluating Site × Drinking Outcome interactions, investigators found that each of the three treatments would have emerged as significantly better or worse in terms of drinking outcomes at a single site. The conclusions about superiority of a treatment would have favored one or another of these treatments based only on single site data. However, these differences evaporated when the outcomes were evaluated across sites.

Participation and involvement in AA predicted better drinking outcomes overall. Large numbers of the patients had some knowledge of AA, as 64% of outpatients and 92% of aftercare patients had been exposed to AA prior to the study. However, most of the positive changes in drinking outcomes for the CBT and MET clients were achieved with no involvement in AA.

Investigators also evaluated the prognostic value of various client characteristics (independent of treatment matching). No single variable captured a sizeable portion of unique outcome variance. The strongest predictor of drinking outcomes was client motivational readiness, which predicted a small but significant portion of the variance throughout the 1-year follow-up period and even at a 3-year follow-up. Only higher abstinence self-efficacy, a better ratio of temptation to drink minus abstinence efficacy, and less support for drinking in the environment were predictive of better drinking outcomes at 1 year in both arms of the study. In general, patient characteristics that were more problem oriented or stable did not predict drinking outcomes. The patient variables that demonstrated some predictive ability were those that involved the patient process of change.

In summary, Project MATCH represented a large-scale test of ATI matching with three treatments that differed significantly among heterogeneous individuals suffering from serious alcohol problems. Results were not strongly supportive of the matching hypothesis. However, treatments of differing intensities, conceptual frameworks, and clinical strategies produced similar significant changes in drinking behavior over time, with few differences among TSF, CBT, and MET. Results of the causal chain analyses for the matching hypotheses indicated that assumed mediators and moderators based on therapy type or client characteristics were elusive. The results argue for a better understanding of treatment mechanisms and the client process of change. Support was modest both for the popular idea of matching clients to optimal treatments (at least with these treatments and clients) and for the search for a single client characteristic, therapist dimension, or treatment interaction that would reliably account for drinking outcomes. More positively, Project MATCH is serving as a reminder of the effectiveness of several manualized treatments for alcohol dependence and as a model for multisite, collaborative trials.

REFERENCES

Babor, T., & Del Boca, F. (Eds.). (2003). *Project MATCH: The book*. London, England: Cambridge University Press.

Connors, G. J., Allen, J., Cooney, N. L., DiClemente, C. C., Tonigan, J. S., & Anton, R. (1994). Assessment issues and strategies in alcoholism treatment matching research. *Journal of Studies on Alcohol, 12*(Suppl.), 92–100.

DiClemente, C. C., Carroll, K. M., Connors, G. J., & Kadden, R. (1994). Process assessment in matching research. *Journal of Studies on Alcohol, 12*(Suppl.), 156–162.

Donovan, D. M., Kadden, R., DiClemente, C., Carroll, K., Longabaugh, R., Zweben, A., & Rychtarik, R. (1994). Issues in the selection and development of therapies in alcoholism treatment matching research. *Journal of Studies on Alcohol, 12*(Suppl.), 138–148.

Donovan, D. M., & Mattson, M. E. (Eds.). (1994). Alcoholism treatment matching research: Methodological and clinical approaches [Special issue]. *Journal of Studies on Alcohol, 12*(Suppl.).

Longabaugh, R., & Wirtz, P. W. (Eds.). (2001). *Project MATCH: A priori matching hypotheses, results, and mediating mechanisms. National Institute on Alcohol Abuse and Alcoholism Project MATCH Monograph Series* (Vol. 8; DHHS Publication No. 01-4238). Rockville, MD: National Institute on Alcohol Abuse and Alcoholism.

Longabaugh, R., Wirtz, P. W., DiClemente, C., & Litt, M. (1994). Issues in the development of patient–treatment matching hypotheses. *Journal of Studies on Alcohol, 12*(Suppl.), 46–59.

Miller, W. R. (1985) Motivation for treatment: A review with special emphasis on alcoholism. *Psychological Bulletin, 98,* 84–107.

Prescriptive Matching and Systematic Treatment Selection
Larry E. Beutler

Traditionally, being an eclectic psychotherapist has meant either one of two things: (a) that one uses two or more theories of psychotherapy to construct an integrated treatment (what is now called *integrative therapy*) or (b) that one develops a menu of techniques from multiple theories and from which to draw in designing a treatment for a particular patient (what has been called *technical eclecticism*). These early forms of eclecticism have given way, over the years, to more systematic forms of psychotherapy, based largely on principles of prescriptively fitting treatments to patient needs.

In contemporary practice, the focus is turning toward unifying and cross-cutting procedures in which research-informed principles are used to guide clinicians in tailoring treatments to each patient. This shift from eclecticism to prescriptive matching reflects an emerging awareness that the reliance on theoretical orientations, which continues to characterize much of psychotherapy practice, often results in ineffective treatment. With this awareness have come two defining concepts that characterize prescriptive eclecticism: (a) that research evidence rather than compliance with a particular theory best determines the effectiveness of therapeutic methods and (b) that establishing a fit among the participants, the treatment, the relationship, and the context requires a broader perspective than can be achieved by considering only patient diagnosis or a particular brand name of psychotherapy.

In this brief chapter, I review programmatic research on prescriptive matching and systematic treatment selection (STS). The development of an integrative model of practice has been the thread that has guided me during my career from the Medical School of Duke University to the Pacific Graduate School of Psychology–Stanford University, with many stops in between. This often twisted road has brought me into collaboration with dozens of research contributors, dozens of creative colleagues, and, literally, hundreds of interesting and informative patients. Collectively, these studies of prescriptive matching via research-informed principles of change have been supported by grants from the National Institute of Mental Health; the National Institute for Alcohol, Alcohol Abuse, and Alcoholism; the National Institute for Drug Abuse; and more than a dozen private foundations and benevolent groups that have supported validation and refinement studies on this system of selecting and applying psychotherapy. This research has made STS and prescriptive therapy among the most widely researched integrative treatments available today (Norcross & Beutler, 2008).

STS (Beutler & Clarkin, 1990; Beutler, Clarkin, & Bongar, 2000) is a prescriptive model of treatment explicitly based on research-informed principles that define, predict, and induce change across therapists' theoretical orientations, settings, and patient diagnoses. STS is marked by attending to and relying on a wide range of characteristics that uniquely identify the optimal fit between each patient and each prescribed treatment. These characteristics have been identified in studies of normal personality, situational determinants of behavior, psychopathology, and treatments of all types.

The birth of STS began with a simple assumption: Because virtually any psychotherapy that has been studied can be found to be effective for some people and ineffective for others, it should be possible to design and tailor a unique therapy that optimally fits each person who seeks treatment by drawing procedures and methods from multiple models. STS has emerged as a viable alternative to other eclectic models and has accumulated a sizeable number of supporting research studies and scientific findings.

STS shares with other integrative perspectives a reliance on empirical evidence as the means for assessing outcomes and comparing results with other approaches. This reliance on scientific methods firmly places STS within the domain of research-based practice, although STS looks to a broader range of work in defining useful research than do many other research-driven treatments. Indeed, STS challenges some cardinal assumptions often associated with conventional views of empirically supported treatments (ESTs; e.g., Chambless & Hollon, 1998) and research-informed practice (Norcross, Beutler, & Levant, 2006). For example, ESTs and evidence-based treatments are frequently characterized by a focus on discrete theoretical models of treatment, whereas STS is decidedly cross-cutting. The former methods rely on a structured, technique-oriented manual, whereas STS is driven by principles of change. In addition, the former are applied to patients who share a common diagnosis, whereas STS focuses on the power of a wide range of patient characteristics, including personality traits and situational states.

STS eschews theoretical models in favor of research-supported principles that enhance effectiveness and then applies these strategies to patients as wholistic beings. That is, treatment strategies are differentially based on both a patient's diagnostic and nondiagnostic characteristics. STS asserts that psychotherapy consists of more than what the therapist does and includes the therapist him- or herself, the patient, the relationship between them, and the environment of both the patient and the treatment. All of these characteristics, domains, and aspects of psychotherapy contribute meaningfully to improvement, but many of them are indelibly owned by the patient, the therapist, the setting, or the social environment and are not capable of being randomly assigned to patients, therapists, or environments. Patient or therapist gender, ethnicity, and social status, as well as patient coping styles, reactance level, readiness for change, and many other variables exemplify those that cannot be randomly assigned to participants or treatments. An optimal scientific test of psychotherapy, therefore, uses research designs that combine aspects of a randomized clinical trial design with quasiexperimental comparisons and correlational analyses.

Prescriptive therapies, like STS, advocate for aptitude treatment interaction research designs, which focus on patient aptitudes that moderate the effects of treatments. For example, patients can present with either high or low levels of resistance—a patient aptitude that varies from being benign to being reactant–oppositional. Patients can be randomly assigned to two or more treatments, and then researchers analyze the success of the treatments as a function of the patient's level of resistance–reactance.

Aptitude treatment interaction research considers psychotherapeutic treatment to be broader than merely that which is offered by therapists. Psychotherapy also includes aspects of the patient that mediate and moderate the interventions, the relationship that develops between patient and therapist, the stylistic qualities of the therapist who offers the treatment, and the context in which these things become blended.

STS was developed and validated in four steps. The first step was to initiate an extensive review of the research to identify patient, therapist, relationship, and treatment characteristics that consistently have predicted improvement across studies and settings (Beutler & Clarkin, 1990; Beutler et al., 2000). Variables that were so identified were then collapsed into small groups based on shared similarities and tested to ensure reliability. The results of studies using these cohesive groups of variables were then cross-tabulated with one another to highlight the presence of patterns of patient–therapy interaction that could index a good fit of treatments to patients. From this analysis of published research, 15 hypotheses to define principles that might predict good outcomes were extracted.

In the second step, researchers developed two measurement devices that could be applied to the anticipated predictive studies that were to follow. One instrument, the STS–Clinician Rating Form (Fisher, Beutler, & Williams, 1999; Corbella et al., 2003), was designed to measure the strength of the patient characteristics that had been identified in the earlier analysis of research literature. A second instrument, the Therapy Process Rating Scale (TPRS; Malik et al., 2003), was designed to provide an optimal profile of how treatment characteristics may complement the identified patient characteristics. Some aspects of treatment were easily defined, such as the type and dosage of medications, the format of treatment (group, individual, family), the frequency and duration of the intervention, the location, and the like. Other treatment aspects required a direct observation of the therapy session; examples were the level of therapist direction, the therapist's activity level, the use of insight-based interventions, and the use of behavior change interventions. Dimensions that described the therapist–patient relationship were also measured by the TPRS.

The third step in the development process used the STS–Clinician Rating Form and TPRS in a prospective test of the 15 hypotheses with 289 patients from different research programs. These patients represented a variety of diagnoses, types of therapy, formats of treatment, and outcomes (Beutler et al., 2000). Four of these programs had used a randomized clinical trial to test the efficacy of different types of psychotherapy and a pharmacological regimen. A fifth program was based on a naturalistic design, and patients were drawn from university-based clinic. The therapists represented a wide range of experience and training, and the therapies ranged from being highly manualized to being unstructured and theory driven. The patients had all undergone similar evaluation, and treatment had been videotaped. This allowed researchers to redo the design so that all patients were subject to the same predictive processes, procedures, and analyses.

To test the 15 hypotheses, researchers used structural equation and regression models. Therapist variables, patient variables, relationship variables, and the fit of the therapy to the patient (as hypothesized from the literature review) were all analyzed individually and within an interaction framework. Thirteen of the original 15 hypotheses were statistically supported. The relationships among all of these variables and positive outcome were restated in the form of 18 guiding principles that defined the basic and optimal conditions required to instigate change. These principles included aspects of treatment methods, setting, formats, and context that were most often present when improvement occurred and were framed as the conditions under which different strategies may be optimally effective.

The final step in developing STS has been a series of independent studies using a variety of methodologies. These studies have been designed to cross-validate the findings and extend them to an increasing number of populations and settings. Indeed, nearly 100 research and theoretical articles and several books have been published on the findings. Over 30 studies have been devoted to fitting patient resistance to therapist nondirective style alone (e.g., Beutler, Moleiro, & Talebi, 2002). The results strongly suggest that (a) an inverse level of patient resistance and therapist directiveness is predictive of treatment benefit and (b) these results appear to cut across cultures and settings. Indeed, a direct comparison of the size of these effects with standard assessments of ESTs consistently suggests that they are strong and replicable (Beutler, in press). Tested head to head, the average differential effect of models of psychotherapy is expressed by an effect size (d) of .11 (Beutler et al., 2003), as compared with an effect size (d) that varies from .60 to .80 for matching dimensions defined by STS. The effect associated with STS dimensions of fit between treatment and patient characteristics is at least as strong as the dominant brands of ESTs identified in the literature (Beutler, in press).

Nearly as many studies have focused on the advantages of fitting patient coping style to the selective use of insight versus skills training strategies (e.g., Beutler, Harwood, Alimohamed, & Malik, 2002). Patients who are characterized as having an internalizing style of coping tend to do markedly better with treatments that include both a skill-building and an insight focus, whereas those who adopt an externalize coping style are best treated with a symptom-focused, skill-building approach (Beutler, in press). Many other studies have looked at the validity of fitting multiple dimensions of patient and treatment at once (e.g., Beutler et al., 2000, 2003; Beutler, Blatt, Alimohamed, Levy, & Angtuaco, 2006). The results of the studies completed to date support the validity of the research-informed STS principles and the efficacy of strategic applications based on multiple principles. Additional principles, beyond the 18 that originally formed the STS treatment planning system, have also been identified over time as research has accumulated (e.g., Castonguay & Beutler, 2006; Norcross & Beutler, 2007), but these original 18 principles remain at the core of the system.

In 1998, the STS system was transferred to a web-based administration and for several years has been used by clinicians to help formulate a treatment plan for their patients and to track progress over time. In this approach, clinicians interviewed and assessed patients and then used a computer-based tool to construct a treatment plan and to project a course of treatment (Harwood & Williams, 2003). In 2008, the revised STS (now called *systematic treatment*) was placed in a self-report format and now can be accessed directly by patients using the Internet (see http://www.innerlife.com). Systematic treatment provides a report directly to patients to be used to help them find and use an effective treatment. The report identifies potentially important problem areas, offers recommendations to select an appropriate therapist and treatment, warns of potentially contraindicated or discredited therapies, suggests self-help materials based on the patient's preferences and problem areas, and presents additional web-based aids and references. The system also projects the course of change and tracks improvement over time. With the patient's permission, the report and associated materials are also accessible by therapists and by health-care administrators. These health care professionals may provide further assistance to the patient in developing meaningful treatments for those in need.

REFERENCES

Beutler, L. E. (in press). Making science matter in clinical practice: Redefining psychotherapy. *Clinical Psychology: Science and Practice*.

Beutler, L. E., Blatt, S. J., Alimohamed, S., Levy, K. N., & Angtuaco, L. (2006). Participant factors in treatment of conditions with dysphoria. In L. G. Castonguay & L. E. Beutler

(Eds.), *Principles of therapeutic change that work* (pp. 13–63). New York, NY: Oxford University Press.

Beutler, L. E., & Clarkin, J. F. (1990). *Systematic treatment selection*. New York, NY: Brunner/Mazel.

Beutler, L. E., Clarkin, J. F., & Bongar, B. (2000). *Guidelines for the systematic treatment of the depressed patient*. New York, NY: Oxford University Press.

Beutler, L. E., Harwood, T. M., Alimohamed, S., & Malik, M. (2002). Functional impairment and coping style. In J. Norcross (Ed.), *Psychotherapy relationships that work: Therapist contributions and responsiveness to patient needs* (pp. 145–170). New York, NY: Oxford University Press.

Beutler, L. E., Moleiro, C., Malik, M., Harwood, T. M., Romanelli, R., Gallagher-Thompson, D., & Thompson, L. (2003). A comparison of the Dodo, EST, and ATI indicators among co-morbid stimulant dependent, depressed patients. *Clinical Psychology & Psychotherapy, 10*, 69–85. doi:10.1002/cpp.354

Beutler, L. E., Moleiro, C., & Talebi, H. (2002). Resistance. In J. Norcross (Ed.), *Psychotherapy relationships that work: Therapist contributions and responsiveness to patient needs* (pp. 129–144). New York, NY: Oxford University Press.

Castonguay, L. G., & Beutler, L. E. (Eds.). (2006). *Principles of therapeutic change that work: Integrating relationship, treatment, client, and therapist factors*. New York, NY: Oxford University Press.

Chambless, D. L., & Hollon, S. D. (1998). Defining empirically supported therapies. *Journal of Consulting and Clinical Psychology, 66*, 7–18. doi:10.1037/0022-006X.66.1.7

Corbella, S., Beutler, L. E., Fernandez-Alvarez, H., Botella, L., Malik, M. L., Lane, G., & Wagstaff, N. (2003). Measuring coping style and resistance among Spanish and Argentine samples: Development of the systematic treatment selection self-report (STS-SR) in Spanish. *Journal of Clinical Psychology, 59*, 921–932. doi:10.1002/jclp.10188

Fisher, D., Beutler, L. E., & Williams, O. B. (1999). Making assessment relevant to treatment planning: The STS Clinician Rating Form. *Journal of Clinical Psychology, 55*, 825–842. doi:10.1002/(SICI)1097-4679(199907)55:7<825:AID-JCLP5>3.0.CO;2-3

Harwood, T. M., & Williams, O. B. (2003). Identifying treatment-relevant assessment: Systematic treatment selection. In L. E. Beutler & G. Groth-Marnat (Eds.), *Integrative assessment of adult personality* (2nd ed., pp. 65–81). New York, NY: Guilford Press.

Malik, M. L., Beutler, L. E., Gallagher-Thompson, D., Thompson, L., & Alimohamed, S. (2003). Are all cognitive therapies alike? A comparison of cognitive and non-cognitive therapy process and implications for the application of empirically supported treatments (ESTs). *Journal of Consulting and Clinical Psychology, 71*, 150–158.

Norcross, J. C., & Beutler, L. E. (2007). Integrative psychotherapies. In R. J. Corsini & D. Wedding (Eds.), *Current psychotherapies* (8th ed., pp. 481–511). Belmont, CA: Brooks/Cole.

Norcross, J. C., Beutler, L. E., & Levant, R. (Eds.). (2006). *Evidence-based practices in mental health: Debate and dialogue on the fundamental questions*. Washington, DC: American Psychological Association.

Center for the Treatment and Study of Anxiety

Edna B. Foa and Mark B. Powers

Edna B. Foa first made contact with behavior therapy at the University of Illinois, where she received her master of arts under the supervision of O. H. Mowrer. In the 1960s, the clinical program in the Department of Psychology at the University of Illinois, Urbana–Champaign, was one of the strongholds of behavior therapy and modification; their faculty included Leonard Ullman, Leonard Krazner, and Gordon Paul. There, Foa became acquainted with the work of Joseph Wolpe and with the integration of experimental psychology into psychopathology and treatment. Her graduate training at the University of Illinois, Urbana–Champaign, together with Uriel G. Foa's mentoring in research methodology and theory construction, marked the beginning of her professional career.

After completing her doctorate in 1970 at the University of Missouri at Columbia, Foa was awarded a National Institute of Mental Health postdoctoral fellowship to work with Joseph Wolpe at Temple University, the Mecca of behavior therapy at the time. While at Temple, she had the opportunity to meet leaders in the field, many of whom influenced her conceptual and empirical work. Of particular importance was the influence of Peter Lang and Stanley Rachman.

CENTER FOR THE TREATMENT AND STUDY OF ANXIETY

In 1979, Foa founded the Center for the Treatment and Study of Anxiety (CTSA) at Temple University, where she began her research program on anxiety disorders, with particular emphasis on obsessive–compulsive disorder (OCD) and later posttraumatic stress disorder (PTSD). It was at Temple University that she began developing emotional processing theory to provide a conceptual framework for the research. In 1986, she was invited to join the faculty of the Medical College of Pennsylvania, together with several faculty of the CTSA. There, she extended her research to social anxiety disorder. When she joined the Department of Psychiatry at the University of Pennsylvania (Penn) in 1998, she established the CTSA there, together with colleagues who moved with her to Penn. Thus, all her research and clinical activities have been conducted within the framework of the CTSA—first at Temple University, then at the Medical College of Pennsylvania, and now at Penn.

Foa began her research career by examining the efficacy of behavioral treatments for anxiety disorders and identifying the active processes involved in these treatments. She soon discovered the limitations of behavior therapy; not all patients were helped, and many remained quite symptomatic. Consequently, she embarked on an inquiry into treatment processes to distinguish patients who benefit from behavior therapy from those who do not (Foa & Emmelkamp, 1983).

As a natural sequel, she extended her interest from the study of treatment outcomes to the study of what treatment should correct. This inquiry was the impetus for developing emotional processing theory (Foa & Kozak, 1986). This theory has provided a framework to guide studies elucidating the mechanisms involved in pathological anxiety and their treatments. Foa's research has been characterized by the interplay among studies on therapy outcome, therapy processes, and the psychopathology of pathological anxiety. This work could not have been conducted without the collaboration of numerous colleagues. In particular, she recognizes Michael Kozak and Marty Franklin for their contribution to the work on the treatment of OCD and Barbara Rothbaum, Elizabeth Hembree, Shawn Cahill, Norah Feeney, and Lori Zoelner for their contribution to the work on the treatment of PTSD. Her work on the psychopathology of anxiety disorders was enriched by Richard McNally, Nader Amir, Jonathan Davidson, Eva Gilboa-Schechtman, Lori Zoelner, and Jonathan Huppert.

TREATMENT OUTCOME STUDIES

In the initial stage of her research career, Foa focused primarily on the treatment of OCD. In a series of studies supported by the National Institute of Mental Health, she developed and investigated the active ingredients of exposure and ritual prevention (EX/RP). At the same time, she was investigating the efficacy of various medications, both alone and together with cognitive–behavior therapy (CBT), in ameliorating OCD symptoms. These studies have advanced the knowledge of how best to conduct CBT for OCD and how to combine this therapy with medication. The treatment that emerged from this research has been disseminated to therapists and patients via articles, chapters, treatment manuals, and a self-help book titled *Stop Obsessing!* (Foa & Wilson, 2001). As chair of the *Diagnostic and Statistical Manual of Mental Disorders, Fourth Edition* Subcommittee for OCD, Foa also had the opportunity to help incorporate empirical research findings into the diagnostic criteria.

Despite the fact that by the 1970s the use of imaginal exposure in the treatment of anxiety disorders was practically abandoned, Foa's clinical experience persuaded her to pursue this method and to study its effects on reduction of OCD symptoms. In the first study, OCD patients with checking rituals were randomly assigned to treatment by exposure in vivo and response prevention or the same treatment that also included imaginal exposure. The results indicated that imaginal exposure to feared consequences promoted long-term maintenance of treatment gains. These results were replicated in a second study (Steketee, Foa, & Grayson, 1982). Accordingly, our EX/RP program today continues to include imaginal exposure, especially with patients whose obsessional fears are focused on disastrous consequences that will follow if they refrain from ritualizing.

During this stage of research, we also examined the relative contribution of in vivo EX/RP to OCD symptom reduction. Two studies converged to indicate that exposure reduced obsessional distress, ritual prevention reduced ritualistic behavior, and the combination of EX/RP yielded superior outcome relative to either treatment component alone.

Since 1990, we at the CTSA have begun a fruitful collaboration with the Anxiety Disorders Clinic at Columbia University, first with Michael Liebowitz and now with Blair Simpson. A series of large-scale multicenter studies have examined how best to treat adults with OCD. We compared the efficacy and durability of established treatments for OCD clomipramine (CMI) and EX/RP, comparing them with one another, with their combination, and with pill placebo. At Week 12, all active treatments were superior to placebo; EX/RP and EX/RP plus CMI did not differ from each other, and both were superior to CMI alone (Foa, Liebowitz, et al., 2005). Twelve weeks after treatment discontinuation, patients who received EX/RP (with or without CMI) maintained their gains better than did patients who received CMI alone.

We also investigated pharmacological and psychological augmentation strategies for OCD. The addition of EX/RP to pharmacotherapy was more effective than the addition of a psychological control therapy, stress management training (Simpson et al., 2008). We are now directly comparing the augmentation effects of the antipsychotic medication risperidone and EX/RP. Because after 6 to 8 weeks of antipsychotic or EX/RP augmentation most patients still have significant residual OCD symptoms, we are also examining whether patients who benefit from 8 weeks of augmentation maintain their gains or improve further with continued treatment. Parallel to the collaboration with Columbia University on the treatment of adult OCD, we have been collaborating with John March from Duke University Medical School on examining the efficacy of treatment for pediatric OCD.

Since 1983, Foa has been funded to study PTSD, pursuing both outcome and psychopathology investigations. As with her work in OCD, she began by developing a short-term CBT program for PTSD called prolonged exposure (PE) and conducted a series of controlled studies to evaluate its efficacy in ameliorating PTSD symptoms. PE consists of 9 to 12 sessions of breathing retraining, psychoeducation, imaginal exposure, and in vivo exposure (Foa, Hembree, & Rothbaum, 2007). In several studies, she discovered the following:

- PE outperformed both stress inoculation training and supportive counseling (Foa, Rothbaum, Riggs, & Murdock, 1991),
- PE showed superior outcome to stress inoculation training and combined PE and stress inoculation training (Foa et al., 1999), and
- PE and PE plus cognitive restructuring both produced an excellent but equivalent outcome and were superior to the wait-list control (Foa, Hembree, et al., 2005).

Other researchers found that the addition of cognitive therapy to PE did not augment the outcome of PE alone. As a result, we concluded that PE alone is an efficient and effective treatment for PTSD and that the addition of other cognitive components put unnecessary burden both on the patient and the therapist. Moreover, treatment that includes fewer components can be disseminated to therapists who are not CBT experts. Indeed, in 2002 and 2008, the treatment was recognized by the Substance Abuse and Mental Health Services Administration as a treatment to be targeted for dissemination. At present, PE is widely disseminated among metal health professionals in the Veterans Affairs and military systems in the United States. It has also been successfully disseminated internationally.

EMOTIONAL PROCESSING THEORY

The first exposition of emotional processing theory was articulated in two publications in 1985 and 1986 that Foa coauthored with Michael Kozak (Foa & Kozak, 1985, 1986). The theory presented a heuristic model for understanding pathological anxiety and the mechanisms involved in its treatment. Expanding on Lang's (1979) bio-informational model, the starting point of emotional processing theory is the supposition that fear is represented in memory as a cognitive structure that includes information about the fear stimuli, the fear responses, and their meaning. In contrast to Lang, who emphasized the role of response representations, emotional processing theory places particular emphasis on the meaning representations of the stimuli and responses.

According to emotional processing theory, two conditions are required for the modification of pathological fear structures (Foa & Kozak, 1986). First, the fear structure must be activated through exposure to information that is sufficiently similar to the information embedded in the fear structure. Second, information that is incompatible with the pathological elements of the fear structure must be available during exposure and incorporated into the fear structure. This modification, which is the essence of emotional processing, underlies the reduction in pathological fear across various disorders. The theory has been expanded to explain the psychopathology and treatment of PTSD in many articles and chapters (e.g., Foa, Steketee, & Rothbaum, 1989; Foa, Zinbarg, & Rothbaum, 1992).

TREATMENT PROCESS STUDIES

As a complement to developing effective treatments, Foa has been interested in the processes that make treatment work. One line of investigation followed from the three indicators of emotional processing: fear activation, habituation within sessions, and habituation across sessions. Our studies indicated that the level of fear activation during exposure sessions was consistently related to outcome in both OCD and PTSD—patients who showed greater fear activation benefited more from treatment. These results were consistent across different measures of fear: self-report, psychophysiological measures, and facial expression of fear.

This line of investigation has also shown that two partially independent processes occur during exposure treatment: habituation within sessions and habituation across sessions. Studies conducted at the CTSA demonstrated that, consistent with emotional processing theory, patients who show habituation across sessions benefit from treatment more than those who do not. However, inconsistent with the theory, habituation within sessions was not correlated with treatment outcome in either disorder.

In addition, we have endeavored to elucidate information-processing biases that characterize the anxiety disorders. We used cognitive experimental methods (e.g., dichotic listening, emotional Stroop test) to demonstrate cognitive bias in the processing of fear-relevant information in OCD, social anxiety disorders, and PTSD patients, a bias that does not appear in the processing of neutral or general anxiety-relevant information. These studies show biases favoring the processing of threatening information specific to the patient's fears. At the information-processing level, PTSD is similar to panic disorder and OCD. For example, rape victims with PTSD demonstrate disorder-specific interference on the Stroop test, reflecting the intrusiveness of trauma-related material. Rape victims without the disorder, however, do not exhibit such cognitive bias.

INTO THE FUTURE

Our future research will continue to focus on developing psychological treatments for OCD and PTSD and disseminating them into the community, as well as investigating therapy processes and psychopathology. In OCD, we are studying the augmentation effects of EX/RP in patients who are partial responders to medication. In PTSD, we are conducting studies that measure processes and outcome of exposure therapy. Some studies reflect Foa's interest in treating anxiety disorders that are comorbid with another disorder (e.g., PTSD with alcohol dependence), whereas other studies reflect our interest in understanding the relationship between psychological and biological factors underlying PTSD.

Encouraged by the efficacy of PE for adults suffering from PTSD, we have modified it to treating youth with PTSD (Foa, Chrestman, & Gilboa-Schechtman, 2009). Our results revealed that PE for adolescents was significantly more beneficial than psychodynamic psychotherapy in reducing PTSD severity. We are now conducting an effectiveness study in which community therapists are treating adolescent girls whose PTSD is related to sexual abuse using PE for adolescents and comparing the outcome with that of supportive counseling.

In the spirit of the scientist–practitioner model, the CTSA is committed to disseminating effective treatments for OCD and PTSD by means of lectures, workshops, and systematic study of their effectiveness by clinicians in community-based clinics. We have been systematically training psychotherapists in the Veterans Affairs and military systems to use PE.

REFERENCES

Foa, E. B., Chrestman, K. R., & Gilboa-Schechtman, E. (2009). *Prolonged exposure therapy for adolescents with PTSD: Emotional processing of traumatic experiences, therapist guide.* New York, NY: Oxford University Press.

Foa, E. B., Dancu, C. V., Hembree, E. A., Jaycox, L. H., Meadows, E. A., & Street, G. P. (1999). A comparison of exposure therapy, stress inoculation training, and their combination for reducing posttraumatic stress disorder in female assault victims. *Journal of Consulting and Clinical Psychology, 67*, 194–200. doi:10.1037/0022-006X.67.2.194

Foa, E. B., & Emmelkamp, P. M. G. (1983). *Failures in behavior therapy.* New York, NY: Wiley.

Foa, E. B., Hembree, E. A., Cahill, S. P., Rauch, S. A., Riggs, D. S., Feeny, N. C., et al. (2005). Randomized trial of prolonged exposure for posttraumatic stress disorder with and without cognitive restructuring: outcome at academic and community clinics. *Journal of Consulting and Clinical Psychology, 73*, 953–964. doi:10.1037/0022-006X.73.5.953

Foa, E. B., Hembree, E. A., & Rothbaum, B. O. (2007). *Prolonged exposure therapy for PTSD: Emotional processing of traumatic experiences.* New York, NY: Oxford University Press.

Foa, E. B., & Kozak, M. J. (1986). Emotional processing of fear: Exposure to corrective information. *Psychological Bulletin, 99,* 20–35. doi:10.1037/00332909.99.1.20

Foa, E. B., Liebowitz, M. R., Kozak, M. J., Davies, S., Campeas, R., Franklin, M. E., et al. (2005). Randomized, placebo-controlled trial of exposure and ritual prevention, clomipramine, and their combination in the treatment of obsessive–compulsive disorder. *American Journal of Psychiatry, 162,* 151–161. doi:10.1176/appi.ajp.162.1.151

Foa, E. B., Rothbaum, B. O., Riggs, D. S., & Murdock, T. B. (1991). Treatment of posttraumatic stress disorder in rape victims: A comparison between cognitive–behavioral procedures and counseling. *Journal of Consulting and Clinical Psychology, 59,* 715–723. doi:10.1037/0022-006X.59.5.715

Foa, E. B., Steketee, G., & Rothbaum, B. O. (1989). Behavioral/cognitive conceptualizations of post-traumatic stress disorder. *Behavior Therapy, 20,* 155–176. doi:10.1016/S0005-7894(89)80067-X

Foa, E. B., & Wilson, R. (2001). *Stop obsessing!* New York, NY: Bantam Books.

Foa, E. B., Zinbarg, R., & Rothbaum, B. O. (1992). Uncontrollability and unpredictability in post-traumatic stress disorder: An animal model. *Psychological Bulletin, 112,* 218–238. doi:10.1037/0033-2909.112.2.218

Lang, P. J. (1979). A bio-informational theory of emotional imagery. *Psychophysiology, 8,* 862–886.

Simpson, H. B., Foa, E. B., Liebowitz, M. R., Ledley, D. R., Huppert, J. D., Cahill, S., . . . Petkova, E. (2008). A randomized, controlled trial of cognitive–behavioral therapy for augmenting pharmacotherapy in obsessive–compulsive disorder. *American Journal of Psychiatry, 165,* 621–630. doi:10.1176/appi.ajp.2007.07091440

Steketee, G., Foa, E. B., & Grayson, J. B. (1982). Recent advances in the behavioral treatment of obsessive–compulsives. *Archives of General Psychiatry, 39,* 1365–1371.

Parent–Child Interaction Therapy

Beverly W. Funderburk and Sheila Eyberg

Parent–Child Interaction Therapy (PCIT) was originally developed in the 1970s by Sheila Eyberg for families of children ages 2 to 7 diagnosed with disruptive behavior disorders. Since that time, PCIT has evolved into a widely used, evidence-based treatment.

PCIT includes two sequential phases and requires an average of 15 weekly sessions. Goals of the first phase, the Child-Directed Interaction (CDI), are to improve the quality of the parent–child relationship and strengthen attention and reinforcement for positive child behavior. In the CDI, parents learn to follow their child's lead in dyadic play and provide positive attention combined with active ignoring of minor misbehavior. They are taught to use the PRIDE skills—Praise, Reflection, Imitation, Description, and Enthusiasm—to reinforce positive, appropriate behaviors. Parents also learn to avoid leading or intrusive behaviors—commands, questioning, criticism, sarcasm, and negative physical behaviors. This phase forms the foundation for effective discipline training in the second phase, the Parent-Directed Interaction (PDI). In the PDI, parents learn to lead their child's activity, first in dyadic play situations and later in real-life situations when it is important that their child obey. They learn to give effective instructions and to follow through with consistent consequences, including praise for compliance and a timeout procedure for noncompliance.

One distinguishing feature of PCIT is its intensive delivery—direct coaching of parent–child interactions. Live skills coaching of the parent during parent–child interactions is the hallmark of PCIT. For both the CDI and PDI phases, the principles and skills are introduced in one teaching session with the caregiver(s) alone. In subsequent coaching sessions, after a homework review, therapists coach each parent–child dyad in turn. In clinic-based PCIT, coaching is done via a wireless earphone through a one-way mirror. The parent and child interact in the therapy room while the therapist coaches from an adjacent room behind the one-way mirror.

EARLY DEVELOPMENT OF PCIT

PCIT was designed in the early 1970s at the Oregon Health Sciences University to integrate two prominent but theoretically distinct child treatments of the day into a sound intervention that retained important therapeutic elements of each. The first treatment was play therapy in which, as described by Virginia Axline (1947), the therapist followed and reflected the child's behavior and emotions during play to convey acceptance of the child. With the child able to express emotions safely through fantasy play, and with the child's emotions out in the open, the therapist helped the child in the immediacy of the child's play experience to try out alternative solutions to achieve inner resolution.

The second child treatment, then in its infancy but spreading rapidly, was child behavior therapy. This model focused on the child's parent as the direct change agent. The therapist and parent met weekly to design "programs"—that is, plans outlining concrete behavior change techniques based on learning theory that the parent would apply to specific behavior problems at home. The parent recorded the frequency of the problem behavior each day, and each week the frequency data were graphed for review. If the problem was decreasing, the plan would continue; if not, the plan was revised. The graphs were expected to show progress each week until each problem was resolved, defining treatment success.

Both play therapy and behavior therapy had unique strengths that PCIT sought to retain. One was the emotional calm produced by the play therapy experience. However, the calming effects of play therapy are a function of the bond that develops between therapist and child, which, for children with disruptive behavior, is often lacking in the parent–child relationship. Benefits for the child of a therapeutic interaction 1 hr a week with the therapist may be overshadowed by many contrasting hours of negative interaction experienced at home with their parents. By training the child's parents to deliver the treatment, as in behavior therapy, treatment benefits may be more lasting. Moreover, teaching parents to use play therapy skills could provide greater exposure to the calming play therapy and further enhance its benefits. Having parents conduct play therapy with their own child would not only strengthen the parent–child attachment but also reduce the underlying anger of children with disruptive behavior disorders; such changes were expected to attenuate behavior problems at home. Even if parents became highly skilled in play therapy interactions, though, these positive accepting behaviors would be difficult to sustain in the context of disciplinary interactions. Parents would still need the skills, provided by behavioral parent training, for setting limits and reversing coercive discipline.

This collection of play therapy and behavior therapy techniques was an intervention coalescing in the context of an outpatient clinic—an intervention in need of a unifying theory and structure. The theory appeared in the work of Diana Baumrind (1967), a developmental psychologist who studied parenting styles. Her research demonstrated that the authoritative parenting style, which combines nurturant and responsive interactions with clear communication and firm limit-setting, leads to the healthiest outcomes for children as they move into adolescence. This set of parenting behaviors bridged the gap between the prevailing child and behavior therapies of the time and added importantly to the foundation of PCIT.

The unifying structure of PCIT was found in the work of Constance Hanf (1969), a psychologist who developed a behavioral program for improving compliance in developmentally disabled children. She trained mothers in two stages: first to apply differential attention to the child's cooperative and uncooperative behavior, and then to use "controlling behavior"—to give the child direct commands and follow through with time out for noncompliance. She used bug-in-the-ear technology to cue and reinforce the mothers' use of the procedures while they played with their children in the clinic.

Hanf's program provided an overarching structure that was well suited to teaching the authoritative parenting style. Parents could be taught the play therapy skills directly with their child in treatment sessions and practice them at home to provide the child play therapy experience every day. Placing play therapy skills within a differential attention paradigm provided more guidance to parents for timing skill application as well as a more direct but still nonintrusive method of child behavior change. The same overarching structure provided a controlled means of ensuring the correct application of child management skills and the consistency in limit-setting that is essential to authoritative parenting.

This period of initial development of the treatment took place in the context of real-life clinical experiences with low-income families living in difficult, stressful circumstances and without exclusionary criteria. The treatment was named *PCIT* in 1974 in an application to the Alcohol, Drug Abuse, and Mental Health Administration to conduct a formal pilot study of its effectiveness. To that point, individual cases had been assessed only with behavior counts by parents at home and therapists in the clinic, and few standardized measures of treatment progress and outcome existed in the field.

The need to demonstrate change formally led to the development of three assessment tools: a behavioral coding system to assess changes in children's behavior and parents' skills in the clinic—the Dyadic Parent–Child Interaction Coding System (Eyberg & Robinson, 1983; Eyberg, Nelson, Duke, & Boggs, 2005), a parent rating scale to monitor and evaluate parents' report of behavior change at home—the Eyberg Child Behavior Inventory (Eyberg & Ross, 1978; Eyberg & Pincus, 1999), and a consumer satisfaction measure to assess the acceptability of treatment to families—the Therapy Attitude Inventory (Eyberg, 1974; 1993). The first decade of PCIT research involved standardizing these instruments and reporting early results on PCIT efficacy (Eyberg & Matarazzo, 1980; Eyberg & Robinson, 1982).

GROWTH OF PCIT

The second decade of PCIT was devoted to efficacy and generalization studies, many originating at the University of Florida Child Study Lab. Outcome studies demonstrated important changes in parents' interactions with their child at treatment completion, including increased reflective listening, physical proximity, and prosocial verbalization as well as decreased criticism and sarcasm, and children showed decreases in noncompliance and disruptive behaviors with parents and teachers (Eisenstadt, Eyberg, McNeil, Newcomb, & Funderburk, 1993). Rating scale measures also showed positive changes in parent psychopathology, personal distress, and parenting locus of control.

The success of these preliminary findings led, in the third decade of PCIT research, to funding by the National Institute of Mental Health (NIMH), enabling the first randomized controlled trial of treatment efficacy (Eyberg, Boggs, & Algina, 1995) and further examination of treatment generalization within the family (Brestan, Eyberg, Boggs, & Algina, 1997) and across time. A series of studies demonstrated maintenance of treatment gains up to 6 years (Hood & Eyberg, 2003). NIMH funding has supported continuing study at the University of Florida examining treatment maintenance strategies (Fernandez & Eyberg, 2009) and application of PCIT to children with disruptive behavior and comorbid mental retardation (Bagner & Eyberg, 2007).

In its third decade, PCIT extended significantly beyond the University of Florida laboratory and was adapted for application to diverse diagnostic and cultural groups. The PCIT website (http://www.pcit.org) currently lists more than 150 research studies related to PCIT. At the University of Oklahoma Child Study Center, researchers conducted the first randomized controlled trial of PCIT with physically abusive families. Results demonstrated significantly reduced recidivism during 2½ years after treatment compared with standard community parenting group intervention (Chaffin et al., 2004). PCIT has been designated an evidence-based practice in addressing child abuse (Chadwick Center, 2004) and was listed with the National Registry of Evidence-based Programs and Practices (NREPP) in 2009 (http://www.nrepp. samhsa.gov/listofprograms.asp; NREPP is a service of the Substance Abuse and Mental Health Services Administration).

DISSEMINATION OF PCIT

The mounting evidence base for PCIT has spurred national and international interest in its dissemination and application. The PCIT group at the University of California, Davis, Medical Center hosted the first PCIT conference in 2000, which has developed into a biennial national conference with several hundred participants, and the Second Norwegian Conference on Parent–Child Interaction Therapy was held in October 2007. The increasing demand on child mental health practitioners and agencies worldwide to provide evidence-based treatments for troubled children likely foretells increased use and research for PCIT in the decades to come.

REFERENCES

Axline, V. (1947). *Play therapy*. Boston: Houghton Mifflin.

Bagner, D. M., & Eyberg, S. M. (2007). Parent–child interaction therapy for disruptive behavior in children with mental retardation: A randomized controlled trial. *Journal of Clinical Child and Adolescent Psychology, 36*, 418–429.

Baumrind, D. (1967). Child care practices anteceding three patterns of preschool behavior. *Genetic Psychology Monographs, 75*, 43–88.

Brestan, E. V., Eyberg, S. M., Boggs, S. R., & Algina, J. (1997). Parent–Child Interaction Therapy: Parents' perceptions of untreated siblings. *Child & Family Behavior Therapy, 19*, 13–28. doi:10.1300/J019v19n03_02

Chadwick Center. (2004). *Closing the quality chasm in child abuse treatment: Identifying and disseminating best practices*. Retrieved from http://www.chadwickcenter.org

Chaffin, M., Silovsky, J. F., Funderburk, B., Valle, L., Brestan, E., Balachova, T., . . . Bonner, B. L. (2004). Parent–Child Interaction Therapy with physically abusive parents: Efficacy for reducing future abuse reports. *Journal of Consulting and Clinical Psychology, 72*, 500–510. doi:10.1037/0022–006X.72.3.500

Eisenstadt, T. H., Eyberg, S. M., McNeil, C. B., Newcomb, K., & Funderburk, B. (1993). Parent–Child Interaction Therapy with behavior problem children: Relative effectiveness of two stages and overall treatment outcome. *Journal of Clinical Child Psychology, 22*, 42–51. doi:10.1207/s15374424jccp2201_4

Eyberg, S. M. (1974). *Therapy Attitude Inventory*. Unpublished instrument. Oregon Health and Sciences University. Available online at http://www.pcit.org

Eyberg, S. M. (1993). Consumer satisfaction measures for assessing parent training programs. In L. VandeCreek, S. Knapp, & T. L. Jackson (Eds.), *Innovations in clinical practice: A source book* (Vol. 12, pp. 377–382). Sarasota, FL: Professional Resource Press.

Eyberg, S. M., Boggs, S. R., & Algina, J. (1995). Parent-child interaction therapy: A psychosocial model for the treatment of young children with conduct problem behavior and their families. *Psychopharmacology Bulletin, 31*, 83–91.

Eyberg, S. M., & Matarazzo, R. G. (1980). Training parents as therapists: A comparison between individual parent–child interaction training and parent group didactic training. *Journal of Clinical Psychology, 36*, 492–499.

Eyberg, S. M., Nelson, M. M., Duke, M., & Boggs, S. R. (2005). *Manual for the dyadic parent–child interaction coding system* (3rd ed.). Retrieved from http://www.PCIT.org

Eyberg, S. M., & Pincus, D. (1999). *Eyberg Child Behavior Inventory and Sutter-Eyberg Student Behavior Inventory: Professional manual*. Odessa, FL: Psychological Assessment Resources.

Eyberg, S. M., & Robinson, E. (1982). Parent–child interaction training: Effects on family functioning. *Journal of Clinical Child Psychology, 11*, 130–137.

Eyberg, S. M., & Robinson, E. (1983). Dyadic parent-child interaction coding system: A manual. *Psychological Documents, 13*, 2424, MS. No. 2582.

Eyberg, S. M., & Ross, A. W. (1978). Assessment of child behavior problems: The validation of a new inventory. *Journal of Clinical Child Psychology, 7*, 113–116. doi:10.1080/15374417809532835

Fernandez, M. A., & Eyberg, S. (2009). Predicting treatment and follow-up attrition in parent–child interaction therapy. *Journal of Abnormal Child Psychology, 37*, 431–441. doi:10.1007/s10802–008–9281–1

Hanf, C. (1969). *A two stage program for modifying maternal controlling during mother-child (M-C) interaction.* Paper presented at the meeting of the Western Psychological Association, Vancouver, B.C.

Hood, K. K., & Eyberg, S. M. (2003). Outcomes of Parent-Child Interaction Therapy: Mothers' reports of maintenance three to six years after. *Journal of Clinical Child and Adolescent Psychology, 32*, 419–429. doi:10.1207/S15374424JCCP3203_10

Asian American Center on Disparities Research

Stanley Sue and Nolan Zane

In 1988, we had the unprecedented opportunity to conduct research on the mental health of Asian Americans and other ethnic minority groups. We were awarded grants to establish the National Research Center on Asian American Mental Health, now called the Asian American Center on Disparities Research (AACDR). It is one of the longest surviving ethnic research centers funded by the National Institute of Mental Health (NIMH). During the center's 20-plus years, its researchers have made important contributions to understanding the mental health and treatment of ethnic minority populations in general and Asian Americans in particular. Dozens of professionals trained at the center have now assumed major roles in conducting ethnic research. In this chapter, we discuss the purpose, establishment, and research contributions of AACDR.

WHY WAS A CENTER NEEDED?

In the 1970s, there was increasing awareness of the mental health needs of Asian Americans, many of whom were immigrants and refugees. Yet, there was a lack of knowledge on the best treatment and prevention practices to use with this population.

Research suggested that mental health needs of Asian Americans had been underestimated and that services were relatively inaccessible and ineffective compared with those available to nonHispanic White Americans. Almost all studies demonstrated low rates of utilization of mental health services across Asian subgroups, whether students or nonstudents, inpatients or outpatients, adults or children, those living in one part of the country or another, and among different Asian ethnic groups. The underrepresentation did not occur because Asian Americans are somehow better adjusted than other populations. Every population underutilizes such resources because not all individuals with psychological disturbances seek or receive help from the mental health system. The question was whether Asian Americans with mental disorders had a greater propensity to avoid using services than other populations. The evidence suggested that this was the case.

In addition, the findings revealed that Asian Americans who used mental health services exhibited, on average, a higher level of severity of disturbance than did other ethnic groups within the client population. This suggested that moderately disturbed Asian Americans, unlike Caucasian Americans, were more likely to avoid using mental health care.

A number of factors affect utilization and effectiveness of mental health services. Some of the factors involve accessibility (e.g., ease of using services, financial cost of services, location of services), availability (e.g., existence of services), cultural and linguistic appropriateness of services, and knowledge of available services. Also important to consider are culturally based factors, such as shame and stigma, conceptions of mental health, willingness to use services, and access and desirability of alternative services. All have been implicated in low mental health service utilization among Asian Americans. Thus, both the mental health needs of Asian Americans and the adequacy of services available to them needed to be addressed.

The main impetuses for creating the center were thus to gain knowledge of the mental health problems and to find effective treatments for Asian Americans. While the separate research grants were critical to address specific research problems, we conceived the center as a viable mechanism for producing a broader and more lasting impact on the field in a number of ways. First, mental health research on Asian American communities often was constrained by the small number of researchers who were actually conducting research in these communities. Moreover, most of these researchers worked in isolation, severely limiting the growth and dissemination of knowledge. Second, because of this isolation, interaction among researchers was limited, funding opportunities were few, and the investigations produced few thematic research programs. Consequently, mental health research on Asian Americans tended to be "one-shot" opportunities that did not produce replicable service models or lead to the systematic development of scientific knowledge. Third, despite the general recognition of the diversity that exists within Asian American communities, mental health research failed to examine this heterogeneity in any substantial detail. Fourth, although the primary research focus involved Asian Americans, our interest in ethnicity and culture led us to study other ethnic minority groups such as African Americans, Americans Indians, and Hispanics (Sue et al., 2009).

We wanted to conduct programmatic research that could provide focus, form national collaborative research teams, and train new generations of researchers who could continue with these lines of research. We thus constructed a research center to address all of our concerns, resulting in numerous on- and off-site researchers, a national board of advisors, multiyear and multisite studies, multiple generations of researchers (e.g., graduate and undergraduate students, postdoctoral scholars, senior scholars), and sufficient resources in terms of funding, available expertise, and multiple, linked projects.

The aims of the center were to continue to conduct systematic and programmatic research on how specific cultural factors influence treatment outcomes and moderate the effects of evidence-based treatments; to make important theoretical and applied research contributions; to serve as a focal point for researchers and trainees; and to maintain a network of researchers, service providers, and policymakers. To achieve these aims, we organized the center so that its work could be examined within and between research programs in order to plan future research and to share resources and findings from our ongoing projects. The center encouraged widespread participation; for example, the center's research could be used for student dissertations and its database library could provide investigators with immediate access to current research on Asian American mental health. Finally, in AACDR's current funding cycle, the Internet-accessible Information Server (a computer network) has allowed easy communication among researchers, administrators, and practitioners interested in Asian American mental health issues.

The center was established by a NIMH center grant in 1988 at the University of California, Los Angeles. It was moved to the University of California, Davis, in 1996. AACDR was continuously funded by NIMH until 2002. From 2003 to 2007, the center received bridge funding from the University of California, Davis, until it was successful in regaining NIMH funding (2007–2012).

RESEARCH CONTRIBUTIONS

Since 1988, the center has made a number of contributions to the field. First, it linked and collaborated with different research programs and community organizations throughout the United States. Second, the research programs advanced knowledge about mental disorders, adjustment problems, acculturation, service utilization, and culturally competent interventions, as well as research methodology and assessment with Asian American and other ethnic minority populations (Sue, 1999). Hundreds of publications were generated at the center, and many of the findings have had a major applied and theoretical impact in the field. Third, the center secured $11 million in additional funding to support its research programs. Fourth, many researchers were trained at the center and are now independently conducting Asian American mental health research. Of these AACDR-trained researchers, most have pursued academic careers, and a large number have assumed positions in governmental agencies or research organizations. Many have subsequently distinguished themselves in research on Asian American, cultural diversity, and ethnic minority mental health.

Studies in Psychological Distress

AACDR is well known for its epidemiological studies on ethnic minority mental health. Under the leadership of David Takeuchi, we conducted several community and national psychiatric studies on Asian Americans using rigorous sampling designs and state-of-the-art epidemiologic methods. The Chinese American Psychiatric Epidemiological Study (CAPES) was the first-ever large-scale study of a major Asian American population. A household sampling of 1,700 respondents provided prevalence estimates of mental disorders for one of the largest Chinese American communities in the nation. This study assessed mental disorders using both *Diagnostic and Statistical Manual of Mental Disorders* (4th ed., *DSM–IV*; American Psychiatric Association, 1994) standards and criteria aligned with East Asian constructs of distress and disease (e.g., the culture-specific syndrome of neurasthenia). The center's second large-scale epidemiological study, the Filipino American Community Epidemiological Study (FACES), involved two population-based household surveys in Hawaii and the San Francisco Bay Area. Data were collected from 2,300 respondents. The National Latino and Asian American Study (NLAAS) was the largest population-based survey of Latinos and Asian Americans ever conducted in the United States. The objectives of NLAAS were to estimate prevalence of mental disorders and the rates of mental health services use for Latino and Asian American populations, assess risk factors involving social position, environmental context, and psychosocial variables, and compare the rates of disorders and utilization among Latinos and Asian Americans with national representative samples of non-Latino Whites (Takeuchi et al., 2007).

Much of the center's research indicated that, contrary to the "model minority" myth, Asian Americans indeed have serious needs for mental health care that have been inadequately addressed. Center researchers have consistently found that the rates of mental disorders and the extent of psychological distress were not lower for Asian Americans than Whites when cultural factors were taken into consideration.

The results of AACDR-related research in the area of psychological distress can be summarized as follows:

1. While rates of depression and other disorders may be somewhat lower for Asian Americans than other ethnic groups, including Whites, Asian Americans have comparable rates of dysthymia and higher rates of neurasthenia (a disorder not recognized in *DSM–IV*).

2. Among college students, foreign-born Asian Americans reported greater intrapersonal and interpersonal distress (indicating more psychological maladjustment) than U.S.-born Asian Americans and White Americans. Asian American college students also were significantly higher than White American college students on self-reports of depression and social anxiety.

3. Not only were rates of mental disorders much higher than previously believed, Asian Americans who entered into the mental health system tended to be more severely disturbed than other ethnic groups (Meyer et al., 2009).
4. Manifestations of psychological distress differed between Asian Americans and White Americans, particularly in the way they expressed social anxiety.
5. Ethnic differences in self-construal (independent vs. interdependent) accounted for coping style differences between Asian Americans and White Americans.

Utilization and Help-Seeking

A major trend documented by AACDR research was the lower utilization of mental health services among various Asian American populations. Some of our key findings are:

1. Studies consistently found that Asian Americans were underrepresented in the mainstream mental health system. Asian Americans may have delayed using mental health services until their emotional problems became very serious.
2. When clients utilized mainstream services, a higher percentage of Asian Americans (nearly half) dropped out after the first session of therapy, stayed for fewer sessions, and used fewer types of services than White clients.
3. For some Asian Americans, recovery from mental distress was not isolated to strictly therapeutic realms; recovery also necessitated the gradual replacement of damaged social networks, a critical issue given the clients' cultural context.

Cultural Competency

The notion that psychotherapists must be culturally competent has become a priority in mental health systems serving large numbers of ethnic minority clients. Unfortunately, there exists little consensus among practitioners and researchers on what constitutes cultural competence.

The center's principal efforts in research on cultural competence are reflected in the following findings:

1. Ethnic minority clients who were ethnically matched with their therapists tended to stay in therapy for more sessions than clients whose therapists were of a different ethnicity. Also, ethnic match appeared to be related to better treatment outcomes when the clients were not acculturated to American society.

2. Ethnic-specific services (ESS) or minority-oriented programs are those mental health programs specifically designed to accommodate Asian American clients' cultural and linguistic needs. Asian American clients treated in ESS programs showed better outcomes than those treated in mainstream programs. Moreover, we found a significant association between cost-utilization and outcome only at the ESS programs.
3. Although Asian Americans tended to underutilize the mainstream mental health system, their utilization rates for ESS were significantly higher. This suggests that ESS exerted a stronger therapeutic effect than mainstream services.
4. Clients in ESS programs rated sessions as more in-depth and reported stronger client-counselor alliance than those using non-ESS programs.
5. Therapists who exhibited *cultural cognitive match*—that is, similarity in problem perception, coping orientation, and treatment goals with their clients—had better treatment outcomes than those who tended to differ from their clients on these cognitive factors (Zane et al., 2005).

On the basis of these and other findings, most cultural competence models suggest that the therapist must in tangible and substantial ways address culture if the therapeutic experience is to be of major benefit to ethnic minority clients. Moreover, if the mechanisms by which ethnic matching and ESS improve client utilization and therapeutic alliance, these principles can be applied to mental health care to more effectively serve culturally diverse clientele (Zane et al., 2004).

AACDR is currently engaged in three major research programs. The first is designed to investigate the effectiveness of evidence-based treatments for depression for Asian American clients and identify the cultural variables that moderate the effects of these interventions (Gordon Hall, Nolan Zane, and Janie Hong, primary investigators). The second is aimed at determining if therapist characteristics associated with cultural competence and the use of evidence-based practices interact or independently affect treatment outcomes for mental health outpatient clients (Wei-Chin Hwang and Stanley Sue, primary investigators). The third will develop and test the effectiveness of a culturally targeted intervention designed to improve medication adherence among depressed Southeast Asian American clients (Tonya Fancher, Deborah Paterniti, Tony Jerant, and Ladson Hinton, primary investigators).

In sum, AACDR has been at the forefront of psychotherapy research for and with Asian Americans for more than 2 decades. It has been a deeply gratifying experience to establish the center and to work with its researchers in making significant empirical contributions to Asian American and ethnic minority mental health.

REFERENCES

American Psychiatric Association. (1994). *Diagnostic and statistical manual of mental disorders* (4th ed.). Washington, DC: Author.

Meyer, O., Dhindsa, M., Gabriel, C., & Sue, S. (2009). Psychopathology and clinical issues with Asian American populations. In N. Tewari & A. Alvarez (Eds.), *Asian American psychology: Current perspectives* (pp. 519–536). Mahwah, NJ: Erlbaum.

Sue, S. (1999). Science, ethnicity, and bias: Where have we gone wrong? *American Psychologist, 54*, 1070–1077.

Sue, S., Zane, N., Nagayama Hall, G. C., & Berger, L. K. (2009). The case for cultural competency in psychotherapeutic interventions. *Annual Review of Psychology, 60*, 525–548. doi:10.1146/annurev.psych.60.110707.163651

Takeuchi, D T., Zane, N., Hong, S., Chae, D. H., Gong, F., Gee, G. C., . . . Alegria, M. (2007). Immigration and mental disorders among Asian Americans. *American Journal of Public Health, 97*, 84–90. doi:10.2105/AJPH.2006.088401

Zane, N., Hall, G. N., Sue, S., Young, K., & Nunez, J. (2004). Research on psychotherapy with culturally diverse populations. In M. J. Lambert (Ed.), *Bergin and Garfield's handbook of psychotherapy and behavior change* (5th ed., pp. 767–804). New York, NY: Wiley.

Zane, N., Sue, S., Chang, J., Huang, L., Huang, J., Lowe, S., . . . Lee, E. (2005). Beyond ethnic match: Effects of client-therapist cognitive match in problem perception, coping orientation, and therapy goals on treatment outcomes. *Journal of Community Psychology, 33*, 569–585. doi:10.1002/jcop.20067

University of Washington Behavioral Research and Therapy Clinics

Marsha M. Linehan

The development of dialectical behavior therapy (DBT) began with an interest in understanding and treating suicidal behaviors. One of my advisors said that clinical psychologists did not receive adequate research training, so my graduate studies focused on social and experimental-personality psychology. The subsequent teaching and consistent review of social and personality research was one of the most important influences on my treatment development work and indirectly led to dialectical behavior therapy (DBT).

I had become interested in behavioral approaches in graduate school for two reasons. First, the behavioral assumptions of a continuity between normal and abnormal behavior and the parsimonious insistence on using psychological principles of normal behavior to explain problem (or abnormal) behaviors fostered both compassion and hope. Second, the emphasis on using psychological research to guide treatment and on using experimental analyses of behavior seemed most congenial to treatment effectiveness rather than the simple belief in effectiveness.

Following graduate school I went to the Buffalo Suicide Prevention and Crisis Center for a postdoctoral clinical internship. After that I was a post-doctoral fellow in behavior modification at the State University of New York (SUNY) at Stony Brook. Both of these experiences had important influences on the later development of DBT for suicidal individuals. First, basing my efforts on Bandura's (1969) book on behavior modification and Mischel's (1973) book on social learning theory, I tried to apply behavior therapy to all the suicidal and high-risk patients I was responsible for on internship. My efforts were ineffective, however. I could not seem to get behavior change and keep a good relationship going at the same time. (This central therapy dilemma is what first led me to developing a treatment that diverged from the "standard" behavior therapy of the time.) The emphasis on behavioral assessment in my postdoctoral training at SUNY led directly to an emphasis on chain analyses of behavior in my treatment. The emphasis on skills training in DBT derives from Marvin Goldfried's emphasis on desensitization and cognitive therapy as self-control treatments; the emphasis on cognitive restructuring in DBT is an outgrowth of the influence of nearby Albert Ellis on all of us at that time. The supervision from Jerry Davison on my fellowship, as well as his book with Marv Goldfried on clinical behavior therapy (1976), alerted me to the fact that much of the warmth, compassion, and empathy displayed by behavior therapists was not adequately described in behavior therapy treatment manuals and research publications. Because of this, I was determined to include all of the interpersonal communication strategies used in DBT in my own treatment manual.

FIRST RANDOMIZED CLINICAL TRIALS

My first job was on the faculty of the Catholic University. My view of suicidal behavior was that it often resulted from an inability of individuals to ask for and get help when needed. I received a small grant to compare rational restructuring to behavior rehearsal to a combination of both (with a patient-centered control condition) for treatment of nonassertiveness. The assertion study found, for the most part, that the two conditions with behavioral rehearsal had superior outcomes. This find presaged the development of opposite action in DBT as an integrative treatment across dysregulated emotions.

At the same time, I received a Catholic University grant to develop an intervention for suicidal patients. Roger Barton and I developed a behavioral assertiveness intervention for suicidal psychiatric inpatients and conducted a randomized clinical trial (RCT). We found that inpatients assigned to behavioral assertiveness training had significantly fewer suicide attempts and self-injury episodes than did those assigned to a client-centered condition. Without baseline measures of what to expect in an inpatient setting, I was not sure whether the patient-centered treatment had made people worse or the behavioral therapy had made them better. We did not publish the study. The 5 years at the Catholic University gave me a chance to start working with program staff at the National Institute of Mental Health (NIMH): Stephanie Stolz, Morris Parloff, Irene Elkin, and Barry Wolfe. These individuals mentored me in grant writing, which later had an enormous impact on my receiving sufficient funding to develop DBT.

DEVELOPMENT OF DIALECTICAL BEHAVIOR THERAPY

I went to the University of Washington in 1977. Like many other clinical psychology training sites, the psychology clinic would not accept suicidal or seriously disordered individuals as training clients for students. Such restrictions, combined with difficulties in being respected by physicians as an expert on suicide, led me to consider dropping suicide interventions as a research area. However, I simultaneously discovered that experts on suicide are extremely rare.

In 1980, I received funding from NIMH to develop a treatment for suicidal individuals. I began treating highly suicidal individuals myself, with graduate students and others on my research team observing the treatment on videotape or through a one-way mirror. I also started developing a behavioral skills training package by working with patient groups at a large community mental health clinic associated with a public teaching hospital. I was concerned that mildly suicidal or less disturbed people might respond to a placebo condition, so I selected only chronically suicidal individuals with histories of suicide attempts.

At the time, however, there were no assessment instruments that provided information on both the topography and severity of nonsuicidal self-injury and suicidal behaviors (e.g., ideation, suicide attempts, nonsuicidal self-inflicted injuries). Therefore, while developing the treatment I was also developing two assessment instruments: the Suicidal Behaviors Questionnaire (Linehan, 1981) and the Suicide Attempt Self Injury Interview (Linehan et al., 2006a). We called our small clinical research group at the University of Washington the Suicidal Behaviors Research Clinic, later renamed the Behavioral Research and Therapy Clinics (BRTC) when we began treating individuals with substance abuse and other disorders.

Although I had initially planned to cure all suicidal individuals with a 12-week behavior therapy/skills training program, the behavioral treatments I tried simply did not work and, at times, seemed to make things worse. As I kept trying to keep patients from either withdrawing from psychotherapy, becoming mute, or attacking me, the validation strategies now central to DBT developed. Still interested in how to teach patients what others did to survive in unbearably painful situations rather than killing themselves, I started looking around for who might know.

On the basis of a wide range of readings, I concluded that the secret to survival was in the ability of the individual in excruciating pain to somehow "radically" accept the fact or reality of the painful situation, concluding that others were not often able to save one from the pain. As a Roman Catholic trained in spiritual direction, I looked first to the Christian mystical tradition as a source of teaching on radical acceptance. Many of the people I treated, however, were not Christians or, if they were, they hated Christianity. Another drawback was that the language of Christianity was not acceptable to atheists and agnostics. I then looked to the client-centered theory of Carl Rogers. But Rogers had the concept of self-actualization, which implied that one was still in need of change. I was looking for radical acceptance.

Finally, a Zen monastery was suggested to me. Knowing nothing about Zen or Buddhism, I decided nonetheless to take a sabbatical and go to a Zen monastery for 6 months. I found that Zen practice included notions of absolute nonjudgmentalness and of being only "in-the-moment" and a focus on "skillful means." I knew almost immediately that I had found what I was looking for. My translation of Zen meditation and radical acceptance into behavioral skills and DBT strategies added a dimension to a treatment that was compatible with the focus on validation balanced by change strategies. The focus on distress tolerance, reality acceptance, mindfulness, and "wise mind" emerged from my subsequent visits back and forth with Willigis Jaeger, Koan Roshi, in Wurtzburg, Germany.

Once I had added in validation, mindfulness, and acceptance, I needed a name for the therapy that would reflect these additions. My secretary at the time (whose husband was a Marxist philosopher) suggested that the treatment seemed very dialectical. When I discovered that over the past 200 years social and physical sciences as a whole have become more dialectical, I decided that I was probably in good company. I made a tactical decision to use dialectics as a guiding philosophy for the treatment and for all further development decisions. In principle, I said if it is not dialectical, we will throw it out. This simple decision then transformed the treatment.

The first DBT manual never mentioned borderline personality disorder. (As a behaviorist to the core, I had not paid much attention to personality disorders since, at the time, diagnosis was quite unreliable.) Two events redirected my focus. First, my NIMH review committee said that my participants sounded just like patients meeting criteria for BPD. After looking at the literature I was struck by how similar my descriptions of my patients were to the descriptions of BPD patients by experts in that area. Second, John Gunderson published a structured interview for BPD that showed acceptable diagnostic reliability. I did not want to lose my focus on suicidal behavior and did not have funding for a large enough sample to stratify on presence or absence of BPD. So, when I started my first RCT evaluating DBT, I decided to require that participants both have a recent suicide attempt and meet criteria for BPD.

DBT CLINICAL TRIALS

To date there are nine published RCTs of DBT, seven with patients meeting criteria for BPD. Three clinical trials have specifically targeted highly suicidal patients. In our first study, results favoring DBT were found in each DBT target area. Compared with treatment-as-usual (TAU), DBT subjects were significantly less likely to attempt suicide or self-injure, reported fewer intentional self-injury episodes at each assessment point, had less medically severe intentional self-injury episodes over the year, had lower treatment dropout, tended to enter psychiatric units less often, and improved more on scores of global as well as social adjustment (Linehan et al., 1991; Linehan et al., 1993). In the most recent study (Linehan et al., 2006b), DBT reduced suicide attempts by half when compared with treatment by community experts and had less medically severe self-injurious episodes as well as fewer admissions to both emergency departments and inpatient units due to suicidality. In a third trial, Stanley and colleagues (Lynch et al., 2007) found that a 6-month version of the treatment was also effective. Among less severe patients (i.e., those with suicide risk but not necessarily a recent history of self-inflicted injury), DBT reduces suicide ideation, hopelessness, and depression (Koons et al., 2001; Lynch et al., 2003; Verheul et al., 2003). At present, it is the only evidence-based treatment that has been shown effective in reducing suicidal behaviors across multiple RCTs conducted at independent sites.

Since the original DBT studies, DBT has been adapted for other clinical problems such as depression (Lynch et al., 2003) and eating disorders (Safer et al., 2001). The outcomes of DBT skills training trials indicate they are effective across a wide range of functional areas (e.g., Feldman et al., 2009; Harley et al., 2008;). Because DBT is a multimodal treatment, components of DBT have been widely implemented either alone or as additions to other evidence-based treatments (e.g., Hesslinger et al., 2002; Koons et al., 2006; Miller et al., 2000; Telch et al., 2001).

The cost-effectiveness of DBT has been examined using data from both RCTs and naturalistic studies of community settings. Using data from the original Linehan RCT for suicidal BPD women, yearly health care costs for DBT were $9,291 versus $18,275 for TAU patients (Linehan & Heard, 1999). Similar results were reported in a naturalistic study of a DBT outpatient program for BPD patients, which found total annual treatment costs for patients receiving DBT were cut in half from $645,000 to $273,000 (American Psychiatric Association, 1998). In a naturalistic study of an Australian DBT intensive outpatient program for chronically suicidal and self-injuring adults with frequent hospital admissions (Arnott, 2005), costs associated with inpatient hospitalizations decreased by $314,500 for the 10 DBT patients.

BEHAVIORAL RESEARCH AND THERAPY CLINICS

The BRTC has been continuously funded to conduct treatment research on DBT since 1980. Our focus has been on determining critical factors responsible for the efficacy of DBT such that we can modify or simplify the treatment to make it more usable in community settings. We have also focused on evaluating DBT for nonsuicidal populations.

In 1994, a small group of graduate students and colleagues convened at the BRTC and formed the International Society for the Improvement and Teaching of DBT. In 2008, the group had its 13th annual meeting in association with the annual meeting of the Association of Behavioral and Cognitive Therapies. As interest in DBT grew among clinicians, requests for training quickly overwhelmed our resources, and in 1998 we formed the

Behavioral Technology Training Group, a company cofounded with and led by Kelly Koerner.

As interest in DBT also grew among researchers, we launched the DBT Strategic Planning Group in 2002. All DBT researchers worldwide and their graduate students and fellows are invited to come to the BRTC annually to share ideas about what research studies are most important to do next, evaluate what outcome measures should be used and/or developed, and agree on who should do what to advance treatment development and evaluations. In 2007, we launched a second strategic planning group, this time aimed at individuals interested in developing treatments for suicidal individuals. The aim here was to invite senior suicide intervention researchers to attend with the aim of assisting more junior researchers to develop successful suicide intervention research programs and grant proposals.

From the very beginning, a graduate student Treatment Development Clinic has been part of the BRTC. We recruit patients meeting criteria for BPD who are at very high risk of suicide, have chronic histories of suicidal behavior, or are otherwise out-of-control or treatment failures. The treatment team consists of graduate students, postdoctoral fellows at the BRTC, and any staff applying DBT to clients not in a specific research study. Students apply for our training program in their 1st or 2nd year and commit to at least 2 years of training.

INTO THE FUTURE

Our main aim continues to be the development and improvement of behavioral treatment for highly suicidal individuals and complex disorders. We continue to conduct clinical trials. We have recently organized an experimental training group in the BRTC to develop innovative methods of disseminating treatments into health care systems. We are examining the deficits of DBT and are attempting to develop ancillary protocols to improve outcomes. We are also working on developing standards for accreditation of DBT programs and certification of individual DBT therapists. Large and small versions of the BRTC are sprouting up at other academic institutions—led by DBT colleagues and former students. The generative effect of their work is substantial and, I believe, will continue to keep a research focus on developing psychological interventions for suicidal individuals.

REFERENCES

American Psychiatric Association. (1998). Gold Award: Integrating Dialectical Behavior Therapy into a community mental health program. *Psychiatric Services, 49,* 1338–1340.
Arnott, A. (2005). *Dialectical behavior therapy (DBT)*. Adult Mental Health Program—Dandenong [Australia]. Unpublished work.

Bandura, A. (1969). *Principles of behavior modification*. New York, NY: Holt, Rinehart & Winston.

Feldman, G., Harley, R., Kerrigan, M., Jacobo, M., & Fava, M. (2009). Change in emotional processing during dialectical behavior therapy-based skills group for major depressive disorder. *Behavior Research and Therapy, 47*, 316–321.

Goldfried, M. R., & Davison, G. C. (1976). *Clinical behavior therapy*. New York, NY: Holt, Rinehart & Winston.

Harley, R., Sprich, S., Safren, S., Jacobo, M., & Fava, M. (2008). Adaptation of dialectical behavior therapy skills training group for treatment-resistant depression. *Journal of Nervous and Mental Disease, 196*, 136–143. doi:10.1097/NMD.0b013e318162aa3f

Hesslinger, B., Tebartz van Elst, L., Nyberg, E., Dykierek, P., Richter, H., Berner, M., & Erbert, D. (2002). Psychotherapy of attention deficit hyperactivity disorder in adults: A pilot study using a structured skills training program. *European Archives of Psychiatry and Clinical Neuroscience, 252*, 177–184.

Koons, C. R., Chapman, A. L., Betts, B. B., O'Rourke, B., Morse, N., & Robins, C. J. (2006). Dialectical behavior therapy adapted for the vocational rehabilitation of significantly disabled mentally ill adults. *Cognitive and Behavioral Practice, 13*, 146–156. doi:10.1016/j.cbpra.2005.04.003

Koons, C. R., Robins, C. J., Tweed, J. L., Lynch, T. R., Gonzalez, A. M., Morse, J. Q., . . . Bastian, L. A. (2001). Efficacy of dialectical behavior therapy in women veterans with borderline personality disorder. *Behavior Therapy, 32*, 371–390. doi:10.1016/S0005-7894(01)80009-5

Linehan, M. M. (1981). Suicidal Behaviors Questionnaire (SBQ). Unpublished. University of Washington, Seattle, WA.

Linehan, M. M., Armstrong, H. E., Suarez, A., Allmon, D., & Heard, H. L. (1991). Cognitive-behavioral treatment of chronically parasuicidal borderline patients. *Archives of General Psychiatry, 48*, 1060–1064.

Linehan, M. M., Comtois, K. A., Brown, M. Z., Heard, H. L., & Wagner, A. (2006a). Suicide Attempt Self-Injury Interview (SASII): Development, reliability, and validity of a scale to assess suicide attempts and intentional self-injury. *Psychological Assessment, 18*, 303–312. doi:10.1037/1040-3590.18.3.303

Linehan, M. M., Comtois, K. A., Murray, A. M., Brown, M. Z., Gallop, R. J., Heard, H. L., . . . Lindenboim, N. (2006b). Two-year randomized controlled trial and follow-up of dialectical behavior therapy vs. therapy by experts for suicidal behaviors and borderline personality disorder. *Archives of General Psychiatry, 63*, 757–766. doi:10.1001/archpsyc.63.7.757

Linehan, M. M., & Heard, H. L. (1999). Borderline personality disorder: Costs, course, and treatment outcomes. In N. E. Miller & K. M. Magruder (Eds.), *Cost effectiveness of psychotherapy: A guide for practitioners, researchers and policy-makers* (pp. 291–305). New York, NY: Oxford Press.

Linehan, M. M., Heard, H. L., & Armstrong, H. E. (1993). Naturalistic follow-up of a behavioral treatment for chronically parasuicidal borderline patients. *Archives of General Psychiatry, 50*, 971–974.

Lynch, T. R., Morse, J. Q., Mendelson, T., & Robins, C. J. (2003). Dialectical behavior therapy for depressed older adults: A randomized pilot study. *American Journal of Geriatric Psychiatry, 11*, 33–45.

Lynch, T. R., Trost, W. T., Salsman, N., & Linehan, M. M. (2007). Dialectical behavior therapy for borderline personality disorder. *Annual Review of Clinical Psychology, 3*, 181–205. doi:10.1146/annurev.clinpsy.2.022305.095229

Miller, A. L., Wyman, S. E., Huppert, J. D., Glassman, S. L., & Rathus, J. H. (2000). Analysis of behavioral skills utilized by suicidal adolescents receiving dialectical behavior therapy. *Cognitive and Behavioral Practice, 7,* 183–187. doi:10.1016/S1077-7229(00)80029-2

Mischel, W. (1973). Toward a cognitive social learning reconceptualization of personality. *Psychological Review, 80,* 252–283. doi:10.1037/h0035002

Safer, D. L., Telch, C. F., & Agras, W. S. (2001). Dialectical behavior therapy for bulimia nervosa. *American Journal of Psychiatry, 158,* 632–634. doi:10.1176/appi.ajp.158.4.632

Telch, C. F., Agras, W. S., & Linehan, M. M. (2001). Dialectical behavior therapy for binge eating disorder: A promising new treatment. *Journal of Consulting and Clinical Psychology, 69,* 1061–1065. doi:10.1037/0022-006X.69.6.1061

Verheul, R., van den Bosch, L. M. C., Koeter, M. W. J., de Ridder, M. A. J., Stijnen, T., & van den Brink, W. (2003). Dialectical behaviour therapy for women with borderline personality disorder: 12-month, randomised clinical trial in The Netherlands. *British Journal of Psychiatry, 182,* 135–140. doi:10.1192/bjp.182.2.135

IV

PSYCHOTHERAPY PRACTICE

13

PSYCHOTHERAPY PATIENTS

Children

Eugene J. D'Angelo and Gerald P. Koocher

In this chapter, we trace the blooming field of child psychotherapy in historical perspective and speculate about future developments. We begin with a discussion of early treatments and move on to explore the organizing constructs of the therapeutic alliance, use of interpretation, integration of developmental issues, evolution of the child guidance movement, and influences of institutional and social policy.

EARLIEST EFFORTS AT CHILD TREATMENT

Jean-Marc Itard probably began the earliest attempt at child psychotherapy documented in the scholarly literature when he sought to "civilize" the "wild boy of Aveyron" (Itard, 1799/1932). The child, whom Itard called Victor, appeared 10 to 12 years old when discovered living in the wild and presumably on his own since the age of 2 or 3. Itard used an intensive treatment, bringing the child into his home and devoting many hours to working with him daily while trying to establish interpersonal contact and teach communication skills. From today's perspective, the child's behavior would fit a description on the autistic spectrum. Victor made promising progress during his 1st year with Itard, learning to speak some words and to write some with chalk, although he showed little progress beyond the gains of his initial year.

Freud's (1905/1955) classic case of Little Hans provides the earliest account of a psychodynamic treatment with a child. Close inspection reveals that the case represented the beginning of mainstream psychotherapy because Freud used a broader approach than classical psychoanalysis. Modern behavioral therapies rest on experimentation by Watson and Raynor (1920) with Little Albert, who developed fearful behavior by use of conditioning strategies. Subsequently, Mary Cover Jones (1924) demonstrated the ability to eliminate fears using what we might today call *desensitization*. Although couched as laboratory studies of fear, this work probably represents the first records of empirical outcome research in child behavior therapy.

EVOLUTION OF PLAY THERAPY

Play-oriented psychotherapy, which falls largely but not exclusively in the realm of psychodynamic theory, stood as a dominant and enduring approach to child treatment in existing surveys (Kazdin, 1988, 1990; Koocher & Pedulla, 1977) but may well have been overtaken by family and briefer behavioral therapies today.

Influence of Sigmund Freud

Although often underappreciated, Sigmund Freud had a significant influence on the development of child psychotherapy (Novick, 1989). From 1886 to 1893, Freud directed the neurological department at a public institute for children's diseases in Vienna. Letters written to his colleague Wilhelm Fleiss are replete with references to the various statements and activities of his six children (Novick, 1989). Despite assertions to the contrary (e.g., E. Jones, 1955), Freud remained consistently interested in and sensitive to the mental lives of children.

However, Freud did not fully appreciate the differences between the cognitive abilities of young children and adults (Glenn, 1978) but did emphasize allowing children to communicate with adults in age-appropriate ways, including through play. Freud's case study of Little Hans exemplifies the early psychodynamic treatment of children. He did not personally conduct a classical psychoanalysis of Little Hans but instead directed the boy's father, who observed and reported on his son's behavior. The father provided interpretations to Hans in the form of "enlightenments" about the meanings underlying his behaviors, fantasies, feelings, and verbalizations. As with adult analysis, the essence of child analysis focused on interpretation of the child's conflicting drives and defenses. However, Freud recognized several technical problems separating adult from child psychoanalytic techniques, specifically, the inability to use verbal free associations, the need to obtain extra-analytic support and information to sustain the treatment, and the more rapid transference reactions in children (Young-Bruehl, 1988).

Elaborations by Anna Freud and Melanie Klein

In the postwar period, child analytic practice formally emerged, stimulated by the training of lay analysts, primarily women. Two distinct groups dominated this subspecialty, one founded in prewar Berlin led by Melanie Klein and a second presided over in prewar Vienna by Anna Freud. Both women relocated to England as the Nazis came to power.

The work of Anna Freud and Melanie Klein, despite their personal and theoretical differences, formed the basis for much of contemporary psychodynamic child psychotherapy. Klein contributed significantly by moving treatment from the child's home to the consultation room, by introducing toys that did not belong to the child but could serve to stimulate play themes revealing the conflicts needing expression, by expanding the appreciation of the symbolic function of play within the session, by elaborating on the use of interpretation within the therapeutic relationship, and by recognizing the role of transference during the course of treatment.

Anna Freud emphasized the role of a positive treatment alliance as an essential element; the role of a preanalytic phase of treatment to establish this positive alliance; the use of techniques such as drawings and dream interpretations to facilitate the production of clinical material; and the importance of parent guidance and extra-analytic contacts with the caregivers to the psychosocial development of the child. Variants of both traditions informed social efforts, such as the child guidance movement, and still pervade current clinical practice.

Beyond Psychodynamic Approaches

The literature on play therapy has advanced rapidly in response to new approaches and demands for an evidentiary foundation to support such interventions. In July 2009, the PsycINFO database returned more than 10,000 citations in response to the term *play therapy*, and Google Scholar returned more than 1.3 million responses. Case studies of the purely psychoanalytic variety have given way to more rigorous work, and meta-analytic studies have confirmed treatment efficacy (Bratton, Ray, Rhine & Jones, 2005). In practice today, we find a more pragmatic and eclectic version of play therapy, frequently blended with more directive treatments, such as cognitive–behavioral elements (Drewes, 2009).

TREATMENT STRATEGIES

The elaboration and ecumenicalization of play-oriented treatments flowed from four interrelated constructs: changing conceptualizations of the therapeutic alliance, the use of interpretive statements and appreciation of developmental influences on child treatment, and the role of institutional and social policy demands.

Evolution of Therapeutic Alliance

During the 1930s, clinicians became increasingly focused on the therapist as a curative force within treatment and expanded their understanding of play and its influence on the child. Attention also began to focus on factors beyond the therapist, especially about the environment in which the child lived (Hellersberg, 1955). Aichorn (1925/1935) sought to apply child psychoanalysis to major social concerns, particularly delinquency, focusing on elaboration of the role of transference and what came to termed the *corrective emotional experience*. Carl Rogers (1939) began his career focused on children, and his nondirective therapy influenced others (Allen, 1942; Axline, 1947/1969) who advocated giving children relative freedom to determine what type of play to undertake, deemphasizing content of the play, and viewing the positive relationship between child and therapist as the primary change mechanism. Rogers (1946) drew further attention to these principles in his classic paper on significant aspects of client-centered therapy in the *American Psychologist*.

Hellersberg (1955) elaborated on the nondirective approach to child treatment, placing greater emphasis on developmental observations and comments about the current relationship and fostering play as a way to enrich the therapeutic relationship. The therapeutic alliance evolved from serving as the basis for insight-oriented work to exerting a direct beneficial effect on a child's functioning (Greenspan & Wieder, 1984).

Use of Interpretation

When child psychotherapy of the 1930s moved away from the psychoanalytic model and expanded its appreciation of the impact of development on the treatment process, a notable shift occurred in both the understanding of and the methods used to address the child's emotional difficulties. In addition, societal demands that child psychotherapy address social problems (e.g., delinquency) led to treatment for a wide range of problems that did not readily lend themselves to the interpretative processes. New strategies became necessary for patients suffering from high distress and clinical disorganization. In many ways, shifting societal needs triggered a significant shift from open-ended interpretive treatment toward more focal, goal-directed approaches. The process of interpretation evolved from enlightenments described by Sigmund Freud to the father of Little Hans for his carefully timed use, to the metaphorical interpretations of Klein and variations on her technique, and to interpretations within the metaphor of play with more clinically disturbed children. Ultimately, child therapists moved toward client-centered and other treatments that did not rely so heavily on imparting insights via interpretation to bring about behavior change.

Working in an era when free association and focus on the unconscious held sway as conceptual forces, Axline (1947/1969) became a strong proponent of nondirective child treatment. She based her work on assumptions that children have both a positive "growth impulse" and the ability to solve their own problems. She became a strong proponent of nondirective play, focusing on play as the child's natural medium for self-expression. Psychotherapy offering warmth, acceptance, permissiveness, reflection, and only those limitations necessary to anchor the therapy in reality resulted in potentially lengthy courses of treatment. Clark Moustakas (1974, 1997) added a strong humanistic bent to child psychotherapy practice. Charles Schaefer founded the international Association for Play Therapy and qualifies as the most prolific living author in the field of play therapy, with more than 50 books on related topics (see, e.g., Schaefer & Kaduson, 2006).

Impact of Institutional, Economic, and Social Policies

In 1896, when Lightner Witmer opened the first psychological clinic in the United States, he grounded it in the experimentally based psychological tradition. His clinic adopted a reality-based, problem-solving focus. Along with the rise of urban industrial society came a number of social ills, particularly youth delinquency. So-called visiting teachers, a prototype of the social caseworker, collaborated with other professions in the early child guidance clinics to improve the social situations of families, thereby helping to relieve their children's distress (McReynolds, 1996).

In 1909, William Healy established the Juvenile Psychopathic Institute in Chicago (Levine & Levine, 1970). He integrated psychotherapeutic methods with psychoanalytic concepts and engaged children and parents to combat delinquency (Healy & Bronner, 1948). In 1921, the Commonwealth Fund launched a program for prevention of juvenile delinquency that involved establishing child guidance centers as community resources (also see Chapter 13B). Gradually, clinic populations shifted from disruptive children to those with anxiety symptoms, and the child guidance centers became primary treatment and professional training centers. By the latter 1930s, efforts toward social reform slowed, and professional practice focused on children's internal conflicts and only minimally on social contexts. A model emerged whereby the child received psychodynamic play-oriented therapy and the mother engaged in separate individual treatment. This concurrent model became the hallmark of child guidance services and held sway over the field of child psychotherapy (Stevenson & Smith, 1934).

After World War II, a number of theoretical and social changes instigated modifications in child therapy. First came the development of family therapy (see Chapter 6, this volume) and the increased recognition that family members other than the mother and the identified patient–child, most notably fathers, could significantly affect the presenting problems and the success of treatment (Ackerman, 1972). Second, behavior therapy emerged as a treatment emphasizing specificity in therapeutic planning and systematic efforts to measure the efficacy of the interventions (see Chapter 4, this volume). Third, the rapid growth of the community mental health center movement in the 1960s stimulated renewed interest in social and preventive interventions. Fourth, the advent of health insurance coverage for psychotherapy afforded the populace greater opportunity to seek treatment.

Finally, managed care, and specifically HMOs, emerged in the mid-1980s as an increasingly powerful force. Adhering to the philosophy espoused by HMOs, time-limited, intermittent therapy for children became standard for clinical service (Kreilkamp, 1989). Using this model, the child therapist seeks to resolve the presenting problem in a rapid, practical manner, not relying on any one single treatment but using several treatment strategies simultaneously.

By the 1990s, a convergence of forces had exerted considerable influence on child psychotherapy. These included

- increased legal and regulatory mandates necessitating care for youth (e.g., child abuse reporting, custody evaluations in divorce proceedings, wraparound services for seriously emotionally disturbed children);
- expansion of mental health services tied to societal and health-related concerns (e.g., foci on the impact of divorce, violence, trauma, social discrimination);
- concerns about escalating health care costs and seeking ways to curtail them;
- increased demand for accountability in health care, fostering a focus on outcomes assessment; and
- emergence of evidence-based practices (EBPs).

INTO THE FUTURE

The earliest research efforts reported rates of improvement in 67% to 73% of children with treatment (Levitt, 1957, 1963). By 2000, approximately 1,500 treatment outcome studies of youth psychotherapy had appeared in print (Kazdin, 2000a). During the same era, the randomized clinical trial emerged as a new "gold standard" by which to measure treatment effectiveness (Kazdin, 2000b).

The cumulative results on the effectiveness of child therapy are both sobering and promising. On one hand, meta-analysis of usual-care psychotherapy for youth (e.g., psychotherapy provided to clinic patients by professionals who select the treatment) compared with minimal or no treatment revealed a mean effect size of $-.03$ (Weisz, 2004). That is, much of treatment-as-usual treatment does not appear to surpass the effectiveness of no treatment. On the other hand, meta-analyses of many specific child therapies have revealed that the effective treatments were characterized by more structured methods (including treatment manuals), a focus on specific problems, and specific expectations as to what constituted positive clinical outcome (Weisz, 2004). These effective interventions include teaching skills to cope with specific problems, anxiety reduction, and thought monitoring. The mean effect sizes for such studies average between .50 (medium) and .80 (large; Weisz, Donenberg, Han, & Weiss, 1995). There are at least six broad clusters of efficacious interventions: those for fears and anxiety (Ollendick & King, 1998), depression (Kaslow & Thompson, 1998), ADHD (Pelham, Grenier, & Gnagy, 1998), conduct problems (Brestan & Eyberg, 1998), coping with pediatric conditions (Spirito & Kazak, 2006), and multisystemic therapy for youth exhibiting complex and often co-occurring disorders (Henggeler, Schoenwald, Rowland, & Cunningham, 2002).

Although impressive, the emergence of EBPs for children has not occurred without its difficulties (Norcross, Beutler, & Levant, 2006). Colleagues have raised challenges to the research methods used in some outcome studies while expressing concerns about how the dissemination of such treatments and related health policy will occur. Adapting EBPs to meet the unique needs of specific children or families, disseminating them into the practice community, and maintaining their effectiveness will be key challenges during the next 2 decades. Cultural adaptations, in particular, will be required to use treatments with flexibility to meet the complexities of a diverse society (Bernal & Scharrón-del-Río, 2001; LaRoche & Christopher, 2008).

In speculating about the future of child psychotherapy, it seems reasonable to anticipate that we will see a continued focus on treatment outcomes, with an eye toward both effectiveness and efficiency. On the one hand, we expect that efficiency will serve to increase access to youth-based services. On the other hand, we must strive to keep treatments sufficiently flexible to promote individualized treatment planning.

Third-party payers will continue to expect well-controlled, evidence-based outcome studies. These will undoubtedly affect training in child therapy, which will emphasize the development of clinical problem solving and a diverse array of treatments (Elbert, Abidin, Finch, Sigman, & Walker, 1988). Such approaches place less emphasis on training in narrow theoretical traditions but instead use comprehensive treatment planning as the key to both effective and efficient service. Similarly, efforts to improve access to mental health services for culturally diverse families and to explore the theoretical assumptions underlying these practices will prove necessary as the United States ceases to have a single dominant ethnic majority.

CONCLUSIONS

The evolution of child psychotherapy has developed from psycho-analytic beginnings to diverse theoretical views. The evolution resulted chiefly through demands for service to different clinical populations and socioeconomic forces. Despite the methodological difficulties in outcome studies, we have made major advances regarding the efficacy of selected treatments in child and adolescent psychotherapy (Kazdin & Weisz, 2003). These EBPs have emerged as powerful interventions for children and families and have expanded their focus to pediatric conditions and complex behavioral problems. Future practice will likely adapt to reflect cultural sensitivity to increasingly diverse populations.

REFERENCES

Ackerman, N. (1972). The growing edge of family therapy. In C. Sager & H. Kaplan (Eds.), *Progress in group and family therapy* (pp. 440–456). New York, NY: Brunner/Mazel.

Aichorn, A. (1935). *Wayward youth.* New York, NY: Viking. (Original work published 1925)

Allen, F. (1942). *Psychotherapy with children.* New York, NY: Norton.

Axline, V. (1969). *Play therapy.* New York, NY: Ballantine. (Original work published 1947)

Bernal, G., & Scharrón-del-Río, M. R. (2001). Are empirically supported treatments valid for ethnic minorities? Toward an alternative approach for treatment research. *Cultural Diversity and Ethnic Minority Psychology, 7,* 328–342. doi:10.1037/1099-9809.7.4.328

Bratton, S. C., Ray, D., Rhine, T., & Jones, L. (2005). The efficacy of play therapy with children: A meta-analytic review of outcome research. *Professional Psychology: Research and Practice, 36,* 376–390. doi:10.1037/0735-7028.36.4.376

Brestan, E. V., & Eyberg, S. M. (1998). Effective psychosocial treatments of conduct-disordered children and adolescents: 29 years, 82 studies, and 5,272 kids. *Journal of Clinical Child and Adolescent Psychology, 27,* 180–189. doi:10.1207/s15374424jccp2702_5

Drewes, A. A. (Ed.). (2009). *Blending play therapy with cognitive behavioral therapy: Evidence-based and other effective treatments and techniques*. New York, NY: Wiley.

Elbert, J., Abidin, R., Finch, A., Sigman, M., & Walker, C. E. (1988). Guidelines for clinical child psychology internship training. *Journal of Clinical Psychology, 17*, 280–287.

Freud, S. (1955). Analysis of a phobia in a five-year-old boy. In J. Strachey (Ed.), *The standard edition of the complete psychological works of Sigmund Freud* (Vol. 10, pp. I–152). London, England: Hogarth Press. (Original work published 1909)

Glenn, J. (1978). The psychoanalysis of prelatency children. In J. Glenn (Ed.), *Child analysis and therapy* (pp. 164–203). New York, NY: Jason Aronson.

Greenspan, S., & Wieder, S. (1984). Dimensions and levels of the therapeutic process. *Psychotherapy (Chicago, Ill.), 21*, 5–23. doi:10.1037/h0087529

Healy, W., & Bronner, A. (1948). The child guidance clinic: Birth and growth of an idea. In L. Lowrey & V. Sloane (Eds.), *Orthopsychiatry, 1923-48. Retrospect and prospect* (pp. 14–49). New York, NY: American Orthopsychiatric Association.

Hellersberg, E. F. (1955). Child's growth in play therapy. *American Journal of Psychotherapy, 9*, 484–502.

Henggeler, S. W., Schoenwald, S. K., Rowland, M., & Cunningham, P. B. (2002). *Serious emotional disturbance in children and adolescents: Multisystemic therapy*. New York, NY: Guilford Press.

Itard, J. (1932). *The wild boy of Aveyron, Paris* (G. Humphrey & M. Humphrey, Trans.). New York, NY: Century. (Original work published 1799)

Jones, E. (1955). *Sigmund Freud* (Vol. 1). London, England: Hogarth.

Jones, M. C. (1924). A laboratory study of fear: The case of Peter. *Pedagogical Seminary, 31*, 308–316.

Kaslow, N. J., & Thompson, M. P. (1998). Applying the criteria for empirically supported treatments to studies of psychosocial interventions for child and adolescent depression. *Journal of Child Clinical Psychology, 27*, 146–155. doi:10.1207/s15374424jccp2702_2

Kazdin, A. E. (1988). *Child psychotherapy: Developing and identifying effective treatments*. New York, NY: Pergamon Press.

Kazdin, A. E. (1990). Psychotherapy for children and adolescents. *Annual Review of Psychology, 41*, 21–54. doi:10.1146/annurev.ps.41.020190.000321

Kazdin, A. E. (2000a). Developing a research agenda for child and adolescent psychotherapy. *Archives of General Psychiatry, 57*, 829–835. doi:10.1001/archpsyc.57.9.829

Kazdin, A. E. (2000b). *Psychotherapy for children and adolescents: Directions for research and practice*. New York, NY: Oxford University Press.

Kazdin, A. E., & Weisz, J. R. (Eds.). (2003). *Evidence-based psychotherapies for children and adolescents*. New York, NY: Guilford Press.

Koocher, G. P., & Pedulla, B. M. (1977). Current practices in child psychotherapy. *Professional Psychology, 8*, 275–287. doi:10.1037/0735-7028.8.3.275

Kreilkamp, T. (1989). *Time-limited, intermittent therapy with children and families*. New York, NY: Brunner/Mazel.

La Roche, M., & Christopher, M. S. (2008). Culture and empirically supported treatments: On the road to a collision? *Culture and Psychology, 14*, 333–356. doi:10.1177/1354067X08092637

Levine, M., & Levine, A. (1970). *A social history of helping services*. New York, NY: Appleton-Century-Crofts.

Levitt, E. E. (1957). The results of psychotherapy with children: An evaluation. *Journal of Consulting Psychology, 21*, 189–196. doi:10.1037/h0039957

Levitt, E. E. (1963). Psychotherapy with children: A further evaluation. *Behaviour Research and Therapy, 61*, 45–51.

McReynolds, P. (1996). Lightner Witmer: A centennial tribute. *American Psychologist, 51,* 237–240.

Moustakas, C. E. (1974). *Children in play therapy.* Oxford, England: Ballantine.

Moustakas, C. E. (1997). *Relationship play therapy.* Lanham, MD: Jason Aronson.

Norcross, J. C., Beutler, L. E., & Levant, R. F. (Eds.). (2006). *Evidence-based practices in mental health: Debate and dialogue on the fundamental questions.* Washington, DC: American Psychological Association. doi:10.1037/11265-000

Novick, J. (1989). How does infant work affect our clinical work with adolescents? A clinical report. In S. Dowling & A. Rothstein (Eds.), *The significance of infant observational research for clinical work with children, adolescents, and adults* (pp. 27–37). Madison, CT: International Universities Press.

Ollendick, T. H., & King, N. J. (1998). Empirically supported treatments for children with phobic and anxiety disorders. *Journal of Child Clinical Psychology, 27,* 156–167. doi:10.1207/s15374424jccp2702_3

Pelham, W. E., Grenier, A. R., & Gnagy, E. M. (1998). *Children's summer treatment program manual.* Buffalo, NY: State University of New York at Buffalo.

Rogers, C. R. (1939). *The clinical treatment of the problem child.* Boston, MA: Houghton Mifflin.

Rogers, C. R. (1946). Significant aspects of client-centered therapy. *American Psychologist, 1,* 415–422. doi:10.1037/h0060866

Schaefer, C. E., & Kaduson, H. G. (Eds.). (2006). *Contemporary play therapy: Theory, research, and practice.* New York, NY: Guilford Press.

Spirito, A., & Kazak, A. E. (2006). *Effective and emerging treatments in pediatric psychology.* New York, NY: Oxford University Press.

Stevenson, G., & Smith, G. (1934). *Child guidance clinics: A quarter century of development.* New York, NY: Commonwealth Fund.

Watson, J. B., & Raynor, R. (1920). Conditioned emotional reactions. *Journal of Experimental Psychology, 3,* 1–14. doi:10.1037/h0069608

Weisz, J. R. (2004). *Psychotherapy for children and adolescents: Evidence-based treatments and case examples.* Cambridge, England: Cambridge University Press.

Weisz, J. R., Donenberg, G. R., Han, S. S., & Weiss, B. (1995). Bridging the gap between laboratory and clinic in child and adolescent psychotherapy. *Journal of Consulting and Clinical Psychology, 63,* 688–701. doi:10.1037/0022-006X.63.5.688

Young-Bruehl, E. (1988). *Anna Freud: A biography.* New York, NY: Summit Books.

Adolescents

Patrick Tolan and Jennifer Titus

Although adolescents have long received psychological treatments, the idea that their therapeutic needs were distinct from those of child and adult populations did not firmly take hold until the second half of the 20th century. In this brief chapter, we discuss prevailing psychological treatments for adolescent patients in the context of evolving theories and research on adolescent development and mental health. We conclude with a synopsis of current practices and future directions in adolescent psychotherapy.

EARLY CONCEPTS OF ADOLESCENCE

The obvious biological state of puberty has always existed, but adolescence as a distinct developmental stage did not emerge in Western societies until the early 20th century (Keniston, 1971). Until then, children had been considered to be adults, albeit smaller, as soon as they were old enough to work or marry (note Gainsborough's "Blue Boy" portrait as a visual example). The demand for cheap labor and young people's capacity for performing basic duties on farms, in homes, and in factories for little pay meant adulthood often commenced at an early age.

The technological advances of the Industrial Revolution reduced the need for unskilled workers in the United States. Moreover, successive waves of immigration flooded the workforce, further reducing the need for child workers. Around the turn of the century, new education laws granted children the right to public education, which, coupled with new labor laws, gave them a reprieve from the workplace and an early adulthood (Reppucci, 1999). Together, these social and economic forces expanded the number of years that children were dependent on their parents, leading to recognition of a socially defined period of life we now know as adolescence, a period distinct from childhood by biology (puberty) and from adulthood by social and legal status.

At the turn of the 20th century, psychoanalysis was emerging as the predominant psychological theory. Initially, the theory paid little attention to adolescence in explaining the development of personality early in life. For example, although one of Sigmund Freud's first cases involved the treatment of 18-year-old Dora (Freud, 1905/1953), his case description makes no reference to Dora's adolescent developmental status. This may reflect that 18-year-olds were considered adults at the time or that adolescence was not recognized as a distinct developmental stage (Reinecke, 1993). Notably, this lack of reference to development occurs despite the centrality in psychoanalytic theory of focusing on formation of personality into adulthood. When theorists first considered adolescence, they viewed it as an inherently difficult time of development. The first scholarly work on the subject of adolescent development described the period as a time of "storm and stress" (Hall, 1904). Anna Freud (1958) later described dramatic upheaval and conflict as typical and healthy of the period, likening it to "normal psychosis." The view of the period as universally tumultuous predominated for years until debunked by empirical findings about normal development (Offer & Offer, 1975).

As psychoanalytic approaches began to recognize adolescence, neurology began to focus on the link between the brain and behavior, with concordant interest in its development in children and adolescents (Healy, 1915). William Healy, a psychiatrist interested in the causes of juvenile delinquency, was recruited to establish the Juvenile Psychopathic Institute in Chicago in 1909 (now the Institute for Juvenile Research). The institute's goal was to promote research on the origins of delinquency and develop psychotherapeutic practices to treat children with behavior difficulties (Beuttler, 2004). Healy instilled an approach that focused on the interaction of individual characteristics and environmental features such as peer behaviors or community norms about criminal behavior. Accordingly, he advocated multidisciplinary work that examined the child in context and research-driven efforts to better understand behavior.

Like Healy, Aichorn (1963/1935) drew on psychoanalytic theory and neurology to explore aggressive and delinquent youth in his classic book, *Wayward Youth*. This volume became an authoritative text on adolescence but also argued that misbehavior, alienation, and heightened disagreement were typical in adolescence. Later psychoanalytic theorists would elaborate on adolescence as a period of normative crisis, citing the process of separation and identity development as the basis for adolescent angst and family conflict (Blos, 1962; Erikson, 1956). Although retaining this central view of disturbance as typical, and even as a sign of health, these later authors advanced a developmental elaboration and a greater clarification of normative tasks and phasic behavior as different in quality and extent from that of psychopathology. They also advocated for incorporating a developmental understanding in psychotherapy.

Juvenile delinquency has served as a focus for much theory and study of adolescent development and psychotherapy. Thus, many advances in concepts and interventions first emerged in work with this subset of adolescents. In 1922, the Commonwealth Fund invested in child guidance centers as a program for the prevention of juvenile delinquency (Horn, 1989). Building on the work of Healy and other practitioners, child guidance centers of the 1920s and 1930s addressed juvenile delinquency by improving families' social situations. The centers used a team approach to treatment, with the psychologist doing testing, the social worker taking the case history and working with the parents, and the psychiatrist treating the adolescent. Following the accepted psychoanalytic techniques for the treatment of children, child guidance centers usually treated adolescents and parents separately. For the most part, adolescents were treated according to principles of child therapy. One exception was the creation of a separate inpatient ward for adolescent patients in Bellevue Psychiatric Hospital in New York City in 1937 (Curran, 1939). However, it was not until the 1960s that the field would see substantial research on adolescent psychopathology and treatment.

The common assumption among service providers throughout the early years of psychotherapy was that adolescents were resistant to treatment (Mishne, 1986). Mid-century reviews of research indicated that psychotherapy was no more effective than no treatment (Levitt, 1963). Although in retrospect methodological limitations deterred the ability to detect effects, these findings did create pessimism about psychotherapy for adolescents. It was not until 1980 that the first quantitative review on the effectiveness of psychotherapy for adolescents concluded there was some evidence of success (Tramontana, 1980). The evidence base has only grown since then.

NORMATIVE UNDERSTANDING OF ADOLESCENT DEVELOPMENT

Longitudinal studies in the 1960s and 1970s showed that the prevalence of psychopathology among adolescents was comparable with that among adults (Offer & Offer, 1975) and that roughly half of the psychopathology that appeared during adolescence had roots earlier in childhood (Rutter, 1980). At the same time, there was growing recognition of adolescence as the time of first onset of adult psychopathology, in particular for depression among females and in substance use disorders. Concurrently, careful study of emotional lability refuted the stereotype of adolescence as an inherently turbulent period, that hormones were the cause of most adolescent problems (Richards, Abell, & Petersen, 1993), and that relationships between adolescents and their parents were inevitably stormy (Holmbeck, 1996). What has emerged is a more nuanced developmental understanding. For example, evidence has shown that early adolescents experience a fair amount of emotional turmoil, but this characterization does not apply to middle or late adolescents (Larson & Ham, 1993).

The postwar baby boom and increase in attention to and care about mental health as part of child rearing led to a rise in the demand for adolescent services. The growing demand in turn spurred both greater consideration of the special needs of this age group and a wider array of treatments (Mishne, 1986). Learning theory and cognitive–behavioral treatments were increasingly influential, whereas psychoanalytic theories were undercut by empirical studies. In particular, studies of cognition during adolescence began to distinguish adolescence from childhood and adulthood. The work of Piaget (1972) and others posited that it was during adolescence that individuals achieved the capacity to think more complexly, abstractly, and hypothetically. Parent–child relationships and family communication became a focus of scientific study and redirected the emphasis of the child guidance movement to the family, with family therapy beginning in the late 1960s (see Chapter 6, this volume; Tolan, Cromwell, & Brasswell, 1986).

Continued interest in adolescent development and psychotherapy led to more professional attention and substantial growth in the literature. The American Society for Adolescent Psychiatry was established in 1967, and the first volume of the professional journal *Adolescent Psychiatry* was published in 1971. However, it was not until 1986 that the Society for Research on Adolescence first met, and the American Academy of Child Psychiatry did not change its name to the American Academy of Child and Adolescent Psychiatry until 1987.

EMERGENCE OF DISTINCTIVE
PSYCHOTHERAPY FOR ADOLESCENTS

During the past few decades, a general consensus emerged on the importance of using developmentally and contextually sensitive treatments for adolescents (Weisz & Hawley, 2002). As such, treatments for adolescents should account for characteristics and issues unique to adolescents, such as the newly developed capacity for logical, abstract thinking; the development of self-identity and autonomy from parents; and the emergence of sexual interests that accompany puberty. Similarly, applying adult treatments requires modification in light of adolescents' less-developed capacity for risk perception and judgment and the importance of peer influence.

How help seeking for psychotherapy occurs for adolescents differs from how it occurs for adults, with important implications for adolescents' motivation, engagement, and adherence to treatment. For example, parents and guardians generally initiate treatment on adolescents' behalf. This means that many adolescents enter treatment with relatively low levels of motivation. Indeed, adolescents who are more peer oriented than parent oriented may be less motivated to engage in treatment (Weisz & Hawley, 2002). For this reason, a multisystemic approach that incorporates peers or teachers, or both, may be an effective treatment strategy. Studies of adolescent psychotherapy that have examined service use and engagement have underscored the value of engaging both the parent and the adolescent, given that a therapeutic alliance between therapist and adolescent requires a greater level of interaction than for child patients (Kamon, Tolan, & Gorman-Smith, 2006; Meeks, 1971). However, gaining the trust of an adolescent in treatment sometimes requires that the therapist work exclusively with the adolescent and only involve the parents with the adolescent present. The model of parents having their own therapist, with periodic conjoint sessions with the adolescent and his or her therapist, has had success.

Empirical evidence that the transition into adolescence marks a time of heightened risk of mental disorders such as depression and substance use has also affected adolescent interventions. A meta-analysis of epidemiologic studies found that prevalence of major depression among adolescents is as high as 25% by age 18 (Kessler, Avenevoli, & Merikangas, 2001), with adolescent girls being nearly twice as likely as boys to experience clinically significant depressive symptoms (Hankin et al., 1998). The 2007 Monitoring the Future Survey found that nearly three fourths of American students (72%) have consumed alcohol and just under one half (47%) have tried an illicit drug by the end of high school (Johnston, O'Malley, Bachman, & Schulenberg, 2008).

The 1980s and 1990s witnessed a raft of structured and manualized psychotherapies for adolescents. For example, Adolescent Coping With Depression, a group intervention that uses cognitive–behavioral and psychoeducational techniques, emerged during this time period (Clarke, Rohde, Lewinsohn, Hops, & Seeley, 1999). Adolescents with major depression or dysthymia who received 8 weeks of the group treatment reported fewer depression symptoms and were more than twice as likely to recover from their depression than adolescents assigned to the waiting list. For another example, the Coping Cat, a cognitive–behavioral treatment designed for children and young adolescents with anxiety disorders, may be effective for treating anxiety disorders among older adolescents (Kendall, Choudhury, Hudson, & Webb, 2002). For a third and final example, multisystemic therapy (MST) developed as an intensive family-based program to prevent antisocial behavior among adolescents already involved in the juvenile justice system (Henggeler, Schoenwald, Borduin, Rowland, & Cunningham, 1998). MST reflects the belief that multiple systems contribute to serious antisocial behavior among adolescents, including individual characteristics and beliefs, family characteristics, peer relationships, neighborhood characteristics, and school performance. Rigorous evaluations of the program have provided evidence of MST's efficacy in reducing the incidence of arrests, drug use, and periods of incarceration among juvenile offenders, including substantial reductions in arrests and days incarcerated (Curtis, Ronan, & Borduin, 2004).

ADOLESCENT PSYCHOTHERAPIES TODAY

A quantitative review of youth psychotherapy outcome research (from 1962 through 2002) included 236 studies that tested 383 different treatments for disorders (Weisz, Jensen, & Hawley, 2005). The findings provide a rough synopsis of the techniques that are currently used to treat adolescents. Typical treatment spanned 8 to 9 weeks and involved 11 to 12 one-hour sessions. Across common clusters of disorders, youth-focused treatments were much more common than parent-focused and family-focused treatments.

However, the frequency of individual or group treatment varied by disorder. Youth diagnosed with attention-deficit/hyperactivity disorder were more likely to receive individual treatment, whereas youth diagnosed with depression or conduct problems were more likely to receive treatment in a group setting. Behavioral treatments were much more widespread than insight-based approaches, appearing in eight to 10 times as many of the reviewed studies. However, this research did not accurately reflect clinical practice, in which nonbehavioral treatments predominate (Weersing, Weisz, & Donenberg, 2002).

Meta-analyses of controlled studies have supported the efficacy of psychotherapy for adolescents with externalizing and internalizing problems (Weisz, Weiss, Han, Granger, & Morton, 1995). Between 58% and 82% of adolescents who receive psychotherapy have better posttreatment outcomes than untreated adolescents.

Today, the knowledge base about interventions to prevent and treat disorders of adolescence continues to develop by not only focusing on whether interventions are effective (through efficacy and effectiveness trials) but also by determining for whom and under what circumstances they work (moderation) and how they work (mechanisms; Kamon et al., 2006). For example, poverty, high stress, parent psychopathology, and marital discord are known moderators of both treatment use and efficacy for children and adolescents with externalizing problems (Kazdin, 2001).

Most psychological treatments commonly used were not designed with adolescents' developmental needs in mind. Instead, many interventions are adaptations of treatments for adults or children. The lack of a specific developmental orientation does not necessarily mean that these interventions are ineffective with adolescents. Weisz and Hawley (2002) found that 14 of the 25 interventions that the American Psychological Association's Division 12 on Clinical Child Psychology designated as empirically supported for use with children are also efficacious with adolescents. However, only one of those 14 interventions, MST, was designed specifically for adolescents (Henggeler et al., 1998). Psychotherapy is not the only treatment for disorders of adolescence. Psychopharmacology is an increasing component of adolescent treatment and continues to be part of the multimodal approach originally envisioned by Healy (1915). For example, the long-term results of the Treatment for Adolescents With Depression Study (TADS) have indicated that a combination of cognitive–behavioral therapy and antidepressant medication is more effective than either alone (TADS Team, 2007).

There is also growing recognition of interventions that aim to prevent problems during adolescence (Kamon et al., 2006). One such early intervention, the Nurse–Family Partnership, sends nurses to the homes of low-income, first-time mothers during pregnancy and continuing through infancy as a way to improve the children's early health and development (Olds, 2002). Multiple randomized controlled trials of this program have demonstrated that not only does it reduce child problems, but it also reduces adolescent externalizing behaviors in the long term. In addition, repeated trials have shown the beneficial effects of LifeSkills Training in reducing later substance use among adolescents (Botvin et al., 2000).

In the future, we foresee the maturation of adolescent psychotherapy reflected in three directions: the development of developmentally sensitive psychotherapies specifically for adolescents, increased reliance on evidence-based practices, and promotion of prevention in addition to treatment. As the field increasingly recognizes the need for a developmental and ecological understanding of psychopathology, its integration into psychotherapeutic work with adolescents shows promise.

REFERENCES

Aichorn, A. (1963). *Wayward youth*. New York: Viking Press. (Original work published 1935)

Beuttler, F. W. (2004). *For the welfare of every child: A brief history of the Institute for Juvenile Research, 1909-2004*. Chicago: University of Illinois at Chicago.

Blos, P. (1962). *On adolescence*. New York, NY: Free Press.

Botvin, G. J., Griffin, K. W., Diaz, T., Scheier, L. M., Williams, C., & Epstein, J. A. (2000). Preventing illicit drug use in adolescents: Long-term follow-up data from a randomized control trial of a school population. *Addictive Behaviors, 25*, 769–774. doi:10.1016/S0306-4603(99)00050-7

Clarke, G. N., Rohde, P., Lewinsohn, P. M., Hops, H., & Seeley, J. R. (1999). Cognitive-behavioral treatment of adolescent depression: Efficacy of acute group treatment and booster sessions. *Journal of the American Academy of Child & Adolescent Psychiatry, 38*, 272–279.

Curran, F. (1939). Organization of a ward for adolescents in Bellevue Psychiatric Hospital. *American Journal of Psychiatry, 95*, 1365–1388.

Curtis, N. M., Ronan, K. R., & Borduin, C. M. (2004). Multisystemic treatment: A meta-analysis of outcome studies. *Journal of Family Psychology, 18*, 411–419. doi:10.1037/0893-3200.18.3.411

Erikson, E. H. (1956). The problem of ego identity. *Journal of the American Psychoanalytic Association, 4*, 56–121. doi:10.1177/000306515600400104

Freud, A. (1958). Adolescence. *Psychoanalytic Study of the Child, 13*, 255–278.

Freud, S. (1953). A case of hysteria. In J. Strachey (Ed.), *The standard edition of the complete psychological works of Sigmund Freud* (Vol. 7, pp. 1–122). London: Hogarth Press. (Original work published 1905)

Hall, G. S. (1904). *Adolescence*. New York: Appleton.

Hankin, B. L., Abramson, L., Moffitt, T., Silva, P., McGee, R., & Angell, K. (1998). Development of depression from preadolescence to young adulthood: Emerging gender differences in a 10-year longitudinal study. *Journal of Abnormal Psychology, 107,* 128–140. doi:10.1037/0021-843X.107.1.128

Healy, W. (1915). *The individual delinquent. A text-book of diagnosis and prognosis for all concerned in understanding offenders*. Oxford, England: Heinemann.

Henggeler, S. W., Schoenwald, S. K., Borduin, C. M., Rowland, M. D., & Cunningham, P. B. (1998). *Multisystemic treatment for antisocial behavior in children and adolescents*. New York, NY: Guilford Press.

Holmbeck, G. N. (1996). A model of family relational transformations during the transition to adolescence: Parent-adolescent conflict and adaptation. In J. A. Graber, J. Brooks-Gunn, & A. C. Petersen (Eds.), *Transitions through adolescence: Interpersonal domains and context* (pp. 167–199). Mahwah, NJ: Erlbaum.

Horn, M. (1989). *Before it's too late: The Child Guidance Movement in the United States 1922–1945*. Philadelphia, PA: Temple University Press.

Johnston, L. D., O'Malley, P. M., Bachman, J. G., & Schulenberg, J. E. (2008). *Monitoring the Future national results on adolescent drug use: Overview of key findings, 2007* (NIH Pub. No. 08-6418). Bethesda, MD: National Institute on Drug Abuse.

Kamon, J., Tolan, P. H., & Gorman-Smith, D. (2006). Interventions for adolescent psychopathology: Linking treatment and prevention. In D. A. Wolfe & E. J. Mash (Eds.), *Behavioral and emotional disorders in adolescents: Nature, assessment, and treatment* (pp. 56–88). New York, NY: Guilford Press.

Kazdin, A. E. (2001). Treatment of conduct disorders. In J. Hill & B. Maughan (Eds.), *Conduct disorders in childhood and adolescence* (pp. 408–448). Cambridge, England: Cambridge University Press.

Kendall, P. C., Choudhury, M., Hudson, J., & Webb, A. (2002). *The C.A.T. Project manual for the cognitive behavioral treatment of anxious adolescents*. Ardmore, PA: Workbook.

Keniston, K. (1971). Youth as a stage of life. *Adolescent Psychiatry, 1,* 161–175.

Kessler, R. C., Avenevoli, S., & Merikangas, K. R. (2001). Mood disorders in children and adolescents: An epidemiologic perspective. *Biological Psychiatry, 49,* 1002–1014. doi:10.1016/S0006-3223(01)01129-5

Larson, R., & Ham, M. (1993). Stress and "storm and stress" in early adolescence: The relationship of negative events with dysphoric affect. *Developmental Psychology, 29,* 130–140. doi:10.1037/0012-1649.29.1.130

Levitt, E. E. (1963). Psychotherapy with children: A further evaluation. *Behaviour Research and Therapy, 61,* 45–51.

Meeks, J. (1971). *The fragile alliance: An orientation to the outpatient psychotherapy of the adolescent*. Baltimore, MD: Williams & Wilkins.

Mishne, J. M. (1986). *Clinical work with adolescents*. New York, NY: Free Press.

Offer, D., & Offer, J. (1975). Three developmental routes through normal male adolescence. In S. C. Feinstein (Ed.), *Annals of adolescent psychiatry* (Vol. 4, pp. 121–141). New York, NY: Jason Aronson.

Olds, D. L. (2002). Prenatal and infancy home visiting by nurses: From randomized trials to community replication. *Prevention Science, 3,* 153–172. doi:10.1023/A:1019990432161

Piaget, J. (1972). Intellectual evolution from adolescence to adulthood. *Human Development, 15,* 1–12.

Reinecke, M. A. (1993). Outpatient treatment of mild psychopathology. In P. H. Tolan & B. J. Cohler (Eds.), *Handbook of clinical research and practice with adolescents* (pp. 387–410). New York, NY: Wiley.

Reppucci, N. D. (1999). Adolescent development and juvenile justice. *American Journal of Community Psychology, 27*, 307–326. doi:10.1023/A:1022277809281

Richards, M. H., Abell, S., & Petersen, A. C. (1993). Biological development. In P. H. Tolan & B. J. Cohler (Eds.), *Handbook of clinical research and practice with adolescents* (pp. 21–44). New York, NY: Wiley.

Rutter, M. (1980). *Changing youth in a changing society.* Cambridge, MA: Harvard University Press.

TADS Team. (2007). The Treatment for Adolescents With Depression Study (TADS): Long-term effectiveness and safety outcomes. *Archives of General Psychiatry, 64*, 1132–1143. doi:10.1001/archpsyc.64.10.1132

Tolan, P. H., Cromwell, R., & Brasswell, M. (1986). Family therapy with delinquents: A critical review of the literature. *Family Process, 25*, 619–649. doi:10.1111/j.1545-5300.1986.00619.x

Tramontana, M. G. (1980). Critical review of research on psychotherapy outcome with adolescents: 1967–1977. *Psychological Bulletin, 88*, 429–450. doi:10.1037/0033-2909.88.2.429

Weersing, V. R., Weisz, J. R., & Donenberg, G. R. (2002). Development of the Therapy Procedures Checklist: A therapist-report measure of technique use in child and adolescent treatment. *Journal of Clinical Child and Adolescent Psychology, 31*, 168–180.

Weisz, J. R., & Hawley, K. M. (2002). Developmental factors in the treatment of adolescents. *Journal of Consulting and Clinical Psychology, 70*, 21–43. doi:10.1037/0022-006X.70.1.21

Weisz, J. R., Jensen, A. D., & Hawley, K. M. (2005). Youth psychotherapy outcome research: A review and critique of the evidence base. *Annual Review of Psychology, 56*, 337–363. doi:10.1146/annurev.psych.55.090902.141449

Weisz, J. R., Weiss, B., Han, S. S., Granger, D. A., & Morton, T. (1995). Effects of psychotherapy with children and adolescents revisited: A meta-analysis of treatment outcome studies. *Psychological Bulletin, 117*, 450–468. doi:10.1037/0033-2909.117.3.450

Older Adults

Bob G. Knight and T. J. McCallum

Interest in psychotherapy with older adults has been documented for nearly 100 years (Knight, Kelly, & Gatz, 1992), but the treatment of mental health disorders among this group has clearly lagged behind developments with younger adults and with other special populations. Unprecedented increases in life expectancy, improvements in health awareness, the proven effectiveness of psychotherapies among older adults, and changes in Medicare policy have combined to increase the psychological treatment of older adults (Karlin & Humphreys, 2007). The role of clinical geropsychology continues to rise in prominence in accordance with these changes.

LIFE EXPECTANCY

Over the past century, medical advances have led to increased life expectancy in many areas of the world. Infectious diseases are being combated more effectively, and acute illnesses are less common and less likely to cause fatalities than in the past. Our ability to compensate for functional disabilities linked to advanced age continues to improve as well, which has had a positive impact on quality of life.

These increases in life expectancy have led to a greater proportion of older adults in the overall population. Over the past 100 years, average life expectancy rose from 46 to 74 years for men and from 49 to 80 years for women (U.S. Census Bureau, 2003). In fact, men who survive to age 65 can anticipate living another 15 years; women can anticipate living another 19 years (U.S. Census Bureau, 1998). Smaller family size, in conjunction with longer life expectancies, continues to shape U.S. demographics, leading to an increased proportion of older adults to the rest of the population. In the year 2000, about 12% of the U.S. population was age 65 or older (U.S. Census Bureau, 2003). By 2030, it is estimated that older adults will make up closer to 20% of the overall population (U.S. Department of Health and Human Services, 2003).

This major demographic shift is responsible for numerous societal changes, including the emergence of aging as a vital area of psychotherapy practice. When the proportion of older adults to the overall population was smaller, the mental health needs of older adults were easier to dismiss. However, with so much of the population presently older than age 65 and that trend expected to continue, psychotherapy with older adults is receiving greater attention.

HEALTH AWARENESS AND COHORT EFFECTS

Older adults are not just living longer but also enjoying a higher quality of life. Present generations of older adults are more highly educated and healthier than in the past. Most definitions of healthy aging involve maintaining mental acuity and physical fitness, engagement in something that provides meaning, and disease prevention and management (e.g., Rowe & Kahn, 1997). Psychotherapy can play a role in all of these. Furthermore, evidence has suggested that current generations of older adults are more psychologically minded and more likely to believe psychotherapy can be helpful than were earlier cohorts (Zarit & Knight, 1996). Higher rates of chronic disease are another consequence of living longer. As life expectancy increases, so does the percentage of older adults living with one or more functional disability or disease (Zarit, Johansson, & Malmberg, 1995). Depression, anxiety, and a number of other disorders can develop or become exacerbated with the onset of disease or, more commonly, when a functional disability arises. As a result of living with chronic illnesses, this new generation of older adults includes more people with comorbid mental health disorders requiring treatment.

What is the status of psychotherapy with older adults? A brief review of the history of psychotherapy with older clients provides the background for answering that question.

PSYCHOTHERAPY WITH OLDER ADULTS OVER THE PAST CENTURY

The first mention of age as a factor in psychotherapy may have been in a speech by Freud (1905/1953) to the faculty of the Medical College in Vienna in 1904.

> The age of patients has this much importance in determining their fitness for psycho-analytic treatment, that, on the one hand, near or above the age of fifty the elasticity of the mental processes, on which the treatment depends, is as a rule lacking—old people are no longer educable—and, on the other hand, the mass of material to be dealt with would prolong the duration of the treatment indefinitely. (p. 264)

In the past century, we have learned that the first part of Freud's negativity about older clients is factually wrong for healthy older adults and the second part is less relevant given the increasing focus on present-oriented therapies rather than retrospective uncovering of the past.

Psychotherapists have worked with older adults since the early 20th century (Abraham, 1919/1953), and psychologists have been involved in helping older adults since at least the 1920s (e.g., the Martin Method; Knight et al., 1992). However, the frequency and extent of that involvement increased after World War II and accelerated even more from the 1970s onward.

The idea that older adults have specific developmental needs relevant to psychotherapeutic formulations and interventions may well have originated with Erik Erikson (1963, 1968). Erikson's work translated psychosexual stages into ego development and focused attention on later stages in the life cycle: adolescence and early adulthood. He also, of course, suggested stages for middle age and later life, although these were less elaborated. At about the same time, Robert Butler (1963) argued that reminiscence was a normal activity of later life and that life review therapy would be specifically helpful to older adults (Lewis & Butler, 1974).

On a parallel track in the 1960s, behavior therapists began to work with older adults almost as soon as the behavioral revolution began (e.g., Cautela, 1966, 1969; Lindsley, 1964). Behaviorists tended to work with those who are severely impaired, often institutionalized older adults. But behavior therapy was also applied to outpatient problems. On the one hand, the behavioral perspective analyzed the problem behaviors of later life in terms of environmental contingencies. Environmental explanations were an important counterpoint to the then prevalent assumption that the problems of later life were physiological, inevitable, and often irreversible losses that should be accepted but could not be changed. On the other hand, operant behaviorists believed that virtually all behavior was malleable. Behavioral analysis tended to draw attention to the ways in which others reinforce the dependency behaviors of some older adults. Behaviorists began to emphasize the potential for independence in later life and the notion of behaviorally prosthetic environments: When older adults are physically limited, the environment can be changed to accommodate them.

The 1970s brought the development of the life span approach to psychological research on aging and to psychological treatments (e.g., Gentry, 1977). The life span approach emphasized understanding aging through methodological designs that could separate developmental aging, cohort effects, and time effects. The methodological advances brought a new understanding of later life and often challenged pessimistic assumptions about aging. In general, the research of this period found that many of the changes that had been attributed to aging were differences between successive cohorts. Later life emerged as more continuous with early adulthood and middle age than had been thought before.

The 1970s also brought a number of political changes that attended to older adults. The National Institute on Aging was founded in 1974, with Robert Butler as its first director. The National Institute on Aging increased research funding and also encouraged attention to training in aging. The

Older Americans Comprehensive Services Amendments of 1973 expanded the visibility of services for older adults by creating the network of Area Agencies on Aging. Late in the decade, the Carter administration made older adults one of the targeted special populations for mental services nationwide (Santos & VandenBos, 1981).

The 1980s witnessed the emergence of six general themes: the need for careful assessment of the older client; the need for the psychotherapist to act as a caseworker; an appreciation of the common stressors of later life; the need to consider diversity within the population of older adults; the complexities of the interaction of younger therapists with older clients; and the emergence of an empirical literature (Knight et al., 1992). In our opinion, these themes continue to play a critical role in psychotherapy with older adults.

The 1990s added to these themes in several important ways. First, in the United States, there was an explosion of writing about psychological interventions for mental health problems among older adults, with new books appearing every year. This growth included an increasing globalization of psychotherapy and aging, with the inclusion of international authors in U.S. publications and of books edited and written by people from outside the United States (e.g., Nordhus et al., 1998; Woods, 1996). Second, the pre-1990s focus on psychological assessment and treatment of older adults as concerned primarily with distinguishing among dementia, delirium, and depression has broadened to include other disorders such as anxiety, substance abuse, sleep disorders, paranoia, and schizophrenia. Volumes appearing in the 1990s on psychological interventions with older clients reflected this broadening of concern (see Smyer & Qualls, 1999; Zarit & Zarit, 1998). Third, there has been an increased integration of mental health and physical health services (e.g., Haley, 1996). Fourth, the blending of gerontology with mental health and aging led to theoretical developments such as the diathesis–stress model (Gatz et al., 1996) for understanding changes in mental disorders with aging and the contextual, cohort-based, maturity, specific-challenge model (CCMSC; Knight, 1996). Finally, large-scale social and economic changes shaped a reexamination of health and mental health care. In the United States, these changes were primarily driven by the shift from fee-for-service to managed care insurance systems; in Europe, the changes were driven by economic issues, including the economic standards used as tests for membership in the European Union.

The 1st decade of the 21st century has witnessed continued growth in psychotherapy with older adults. The range of diagnoses being treated with psychological intervention has markedly expanded (e.g., Laidlaw & Knight, 2008; Woods & Clare, 2008). There are also signs of increased clinical attention to personality disorders in late life (e.g., Segal et al., 2006). This increasing attention to the complexity of psychological diagnosis in later life takes us beyond the classic focus on depression and dementia to include attention to anxiety disorders, sleep disorders, psychoses, substance abuse, and personality disorders and, it is hoped, foreshadows a life span developmental psychopathology that can guide the understanding of psychological problems and their treatment in later life.

Most of the research on psychotherapy with older adults has focused on cognitive–behavior therapy (CBT), but there is now increasing use of other approaches, including dialectical behavior therapy (Cheavens & Lynch, 2008), schema-based cognitive approaches (James, 2008), and interpersonal therapy (Hinrichsen & Clougherty, 2006). Laidlaw, Gallagher-Thompson, and Thompson (2004) proposed the comprehensive conceptualization framework, which places adaptations to CBT to work with older adults in the context of gerontological theory and science and uses what is known about developmental aging, cohort differences, social contexts of older adults, role transitions, and intergenerational relationships to guide CBT interventions. The comprehensive conceptualization framework model also explores in some depth the role that CBT can play in changing older adults' inappropriate negative thoughts about aging.

Another important development in CBT with older adults is Mohlman's (2005a, 2005b) work on adding to CBT interventions a cognitive skills component emphasizing increasing older clients' executive functioning abilities. The novel element of Mohlman's approach is the focus on modifying the older client's cognitive abilities rather than adapting the therapy to the older client. The use of interventions that draw from applied cognitive aging research to psychotherapeutic interventions is also an encouraging sign of cross-fertilization between these research areas.

We are also witnessing more attention to cultural and individual diversity in understanding psychotherapy with elderly people. The distinctive needs of older adults from different cultural backgrounds has frequently been explored (e.g., Lau & Kinoshita, 2006), and the range of sexual orientations among older clients has begun to receive attention (Kimmel, Rose, & David, 2006). The REACH project for caregivers provides a multisite example of evaluations of ethnic differences (and equivalences) in treatment outcomes with family caregivers of people with dementia (see Knight et al., 2006, for an overview). Knight's CCMSC (2004) model has evolved into the contextual adult life span theory of adaptation of psychotherapy model (e.g., Knight & Poon, 2008), which specifically includes effects of cultural differences and has also clarified the interrelationship of other components of the CCMSC model. This trend often points to the joint neglect of diversity by both aging advocates, who frequently ignore cultural and individual diversity, and advocates for diversity, who frequently focus on younger adults within their community of interest.

There is a nascent attention to positive psychology interventions with older adults. Family caregivers have reported positive aspects of caregiving, and researchers on therapy for caregivers have argued that it is time to focus interventions on increasing the positive aspects rather than reducing the presumed negative effects (Burgio et al., 2008). More generally with regard to psychotherapy with older adults, recent writing has focused on a positive aging approach to CBT with older adults that draws on optimization and reserve capacity (Hill & Mansour, 2008) and a psychotherapy to facilitate the growth of wisdom in later life (Knight & Laidlaw, 2009).

CHANGES IN MEDICARE POLICY

Changes in Medicare policy are a major driving force in the expansion of psychotherapy with older adults in the United States (e.g., Karlin & Humphreys, 2007). The Omnibus Reconciliation Act, Medicare's adoption of Health and Behavior Codes, and mental health parity legislation have combined to improve mental health coverage and increase access to psychotherapy among older adults. At its inception in the 1960s, Medicare covered only the costs associated with inpatient treatment. With the passage of the Omnibus Reconciliation Act of 1987, the program was extended to cover outpatient mental health services commonly provided by psychologists and social workers. Services covered included assessment, consultation, and psychotherapy, but settings from which providers could bill were initially restricted to community mental health centers. In 1989, the rules were broadened to allow psychologists and social workers to submit claims directly for services rendered (Omnibus Reconciliation Act of 1989).

A decade later, the Centers for Medicare and Medicaid Services adopted a series of Health and Behavior Codes that allow for reimbursement to psychologists treating clients who do not meet the criteria for psychiatric diagnoses but who require assistance in maintaining medical regimens associated with acute or chronic medical illnesses. These changes permit psychologists to integrate behavioral health care with medical care (Hartman-Stein & Georgoulakis, 2008). Owing to the higher incidence of chronic disease in older adults, the adoption of these codes has effectively granted psychologists greater access to the subgroup of medically ill older adults.

In 2008, the U.S. Congress enacted mental health parity in Medicare, to be phased in beginning in 2010 (Medicare Improvement for Patients and Providers Act, 2008). The law requires Medicare mental health equity by phasing in, over 6 years, a reduction in the 50% psychotherapy copayment requirement to the 20% required for all other outpatient services. Such parity will enhance access to psychotherapy for older adults in the coming years.

SUMMARY

This brief history of psychotherapy with older adults traces an evolution from early skepticism to contemporary optimism about its efficacy, utilization, and acceptance in public policy, as reflected in the Medicare program. The ongoing advancement of clinical geropsychology and the emergence of positive psychology interventions are a far cry from the pessimistic nihilism of a century ago. Along the way, we have seen a dramatic expansion of its goals, moving from a focus on adjusting to presumed universal losses associated with normal aging to cohort-sensitive psychotherapies targeting a steadily expanding array of specific psychopathologies and behavioral health problems. Psychotherapy with older adults has truly come of age in the past 100 years and is now recognized as a challenging and intellectually rewarding field for psychotherapists.

REFERENCES

Abraham, K. (1953). The applicability of psychoanalytic treatment on patients at an advanced age. In S. Steury & M. L. Blank (Eds.), *Readings in psychotherapy with older people* (pp. 18–20). Washington, DC: U.S. Department of Health, Education, and Welfare. (Original work published 1919)

Burgio, L. D., Schmid, B., & Johnson, M. N. (2008). Issues in assessment and intervention for distress in Alzheimer caregivers. In K. Laidlaw & B. Knight (Eds.), *Handbook of emotional disorders in later life: Assessment and treatment* (pp. 403–419). Oxford, England: Oxford University Press.

Butler, R. N. (1963). The life review: An interpretation of reminiscence in the elderly. *Psychiatry, 119*, 721–728.

Cautela, J. R. (1966). Behavior therapy and geriatrics. *Journal of Genetic Psychology, 108*, 9–17.

Cautela, J. R. (1969). A classical conditioning approach to the development and modification of behavior in the aged. *Gerontologist, 9*, 109–113.

Cheavens, J. S., & Lynch, T. R. (2008). Dialectical behavior therapy for personality disorders in older adults. In D. Gallagher-Thompson, A. M. Steffen, & L. W. Thompson (Eds.), *Handbook of behavioral and cognitive therapies with older adults* (pp. 187–199). New York, NY: Springer. doi:10.1007/978-0-387-72007-4_12

Erikson, E. H. (1963). *Childhood and society* (2nd ed.). New York, NY: Norton. (Original work published 1950)

Erikson, E. H. (1968). *Identity, youth, and crisis*. New York, NY: Norton.

Freud, S. (1953). On psychotherapy. In J. Strachey (Ed. and Trans.), *The standard edition of the complete psychological works of Sigmund Freud* (Vol. 6, pp. 249–264). London, England: Hogarth. (Original work published 1905)

Gatz, M., Kasl-Godley, J. E., & Karel, M. J. (1996). Aging and mental disorders. In J. E. Birren, K. W. Schaie, R. P. Abeles, M. Gatz, & T. A. Salthouse (Eds.), *Handbook of the psychology of aging* (4th ed., pp. 365–382). San Diego, CA: Academic Press.

Gentry, W. D. (Ed.). (1977). *Geropsychology: A model of training and clinical service*. Cambridge, MA: Ballinger.

Haley, W. E. (1996). The medical context of psychotherapy with the elderly. In S. H. Zarit & B. G. Knight (Eds.), *A guide to psychotherapy and aging: Effective clinical interventions in a life-stage context* (pp. 221–239). Washington, DC: American Psychological Association. doi:10.1037/10211-008

Hartman-Stein, P., & Georgoulakis, J. M. (2008). How Medicare shapes behavioral health practice with older adults in the U.S.: Issues and recommendations for practitioners. In D. Gallagher-Thompson, A. M. Steffen, & L. W. Thompson (Eds.), *Handbook of behavioral and cognitive therapies with older adults* (pp. 323–334). New York, NY: Springer. doi:10.1007/978-0-387-72007-4_21

Hill, R. D., & Mansour, E. (2008). The role of positive aging in addressing the mental health needs of older adults. In D. Gallagher-Thompson, A. M. Steffen, & L. W. Thompson (Eds.), *Handbook of behavioral and cognitive therapies with older adults* (pp. 309–322). New York, NY: Springer. doi:10.1007/978-0-387-72007-4_20

Hinrichsen, G. A., & Clougherty, K. F. (2006). *Interpersonal psychotherapy for depressed older adults*. Washington, DC: American Psychological Association. doi:10.1037/11429-000

James, I. A. (2008). Schemas and schema focused approaches with older people. In K. Laidlaw & B. Knight (Eds.), *Handbook of emotional disorders in later life: Assessment and treatment* (pp. 117–140). Oxford, England: Oxford University Press.

Karlin, B. E., & Humphreys, K. (2007). Improving Medicare coverage of psychological services for older adults. *American Psychologist, 62,* 637–649. doi:10.1037/0003-066X.62.7.637

Kimmel, D., Rose, T., & David, S. (2006). *Lesbian, gay, bisexual, and transgender aging: Research and clinical perspectives*. New York, NY: Columbia University Press.

Knight, B. G. (1996). *Psychotherapy with older adults* (2nd ed.). Thousand Oaks, CA: Sage.

Knight, B. G., Kaskie, B., Shurgot, G. R., & Dave, J. (2006). Improving the mental health of older adults. In J. E. Birren & K. W. Schaie (Eds.), *Handbook of the psychology of aging* (6th ed., pp. 407–424). Amsterdam: Elsevier. doi:10.1016/B978-012101264-9/50021-5

Knight, B. G., Kelly, M., & Gatz, M. (1992). Psychotherapy and the older adult. In D. K. Freedheim, H. J. Freudenberger, D. R. Peterson, J. W. Kessler, H. H. Strupp, S. B. Messer, & P. L. Wachtel (Eds.), *History of psychotherapy: A century of change* (pp. 528–551). Washington, DC: American Psychological Association. doi:10.1037/10110-014

Knight, B. G., & Laidlaw, K. (2009). Translational theory: A wisdom-based model to enhance psychological interventions to enhance well-being in later life. In V. Bengtson, M. Silverstein, N. Putney, & D. Gans (Eds.), *Handbook of theories of aging* (pp. 693–705). New York, NY: Springer.

Knight, B. G., & Poon, C. (2008). The socio-cultural context in understanding older adults: Contextual adult life span theory for adapting psychotherapy (pp. 439–456). In B. Woods (Ed.), *The handbook of the clinical psychology of aging*. Chichester, England: Wiley.

Laidlaw, K., Gallagher-Thompson, D., Thompson, L., & Siskin, L. (2003). *Cognitive behavior therapy with older people*. New York, NY: Wiley.

Laidlaw, K., & Knight, B. (2008). *Handbook of emotional disorders in later life: Assessment and treatment*. Oxford, England: Oxford University Press.

Lau, A. W., & Kinoshita, L. M. (2006). Cognitive–behavioral therapy with culturally diverse older adults. In P. A. Hays & G. Y. Iwamasa (Eds.), *Culturally responsive cognitive–behavioral therapy: Assessment, practice, and supervision* (pp. 179–197). Washington, DC: American Psychological Association. doi:10.1037/11433-008

Lewis, M. I., & Butler, R. N. (1974). Life review therapy: Putting memories to work in individual and group psychotherapy. *Geriatrics, 29,* 165–173.

Lindsley, O. R. (1964). Geriatric behavioral prosthetics. In R. Kastenbaum (Ed.), *New thoughts on old age* (pp. 41–60). New York, NY: Springer.

Medicare Improvement for Patients and Providers Act, H.R. 6331, 110th Cong. (2008).

Mohlman, J. (2005a). Does executive dysfunction affect treatment outcome in late-life mood and anxiety disorders? *Journal of Geriatric Psychiatry and Neurology, 18*, 97–108. doi:10.1177/0891988705276061

Mohlman, J. (2005b). The role of executive functioning in CBT: A pilot study with anxious older adults. *Behaviour Research and Therapy, 43*, 447–465. doi:10.1016/j.brat.2004.03.007

Nordhus, I. H., VandenBos, G. R., Berg, S., & Fromholt, P. (1998). *Clinical geropsychology*. Washington, DC: American Psychological Association. doi:10.1037/10295-000

Older Americans Comprehensive Services Amendments of 1973, Pub. L. 93–29, 87 Stat. 30.

Omnibus Budget Reconciliation Act of 1987, Pub. L. 100–203, 101 Stat. 1330.

Omnibus Budget Reconciliation Act of 1989, Pub. L. 103–239, 103 Stat. 2106.

Rowe, J. W., & Kahn, L. (1997). Successful aging. *Gerontologist, 37*, 433–440.

Santos, J. F., & VandenBos, G. R. (1981). *Psychology and the older adult: Challenges for training in the 1980s*. Washington, DC: American Psychological Association.

Segal, D. L., Coolidge, F. L., & Rosowsky, E. (2006). *Personality disorders and older adults: Diagnosis, assessment, and treatment*. Hoboken, NJ: Wiley.

Smyer, M. A., & Qualls, S. H. (1999). *Aging and mental health*. Boston, MA: Blackwell.

U.S. Census Bureau. (1998). *Statistical abstract of the United States*. Washington, DC: Author.

U.S. Census Bureau. (2003). *Statistical abstract of the United States*. Washington, DC: Author.

U.S. Department of Health and Human Services. (2003). The projected future growth of the older population. Retrieved from http://www.aoa.gov/AoARoot/Aging_Statistics/future_growth/future_growth.aspx#state

Woods, R. T. (Ed.). (1996). *Handbook of the clinical psychology of ageing*. Chichester, England: Wiley.

Woods, R., & Clare, L. (2008). *Handbook of the clinical psychology of ageing* (2nd ed.). New York, NY: Wiley. doi:10.1002/9780470773185

Zarit, S. H., Johansson, B., & Malmberg, B. (1995). Changes in functional competency in the oldest old: A longitudinal study. *Journal of Aging and Health, 7*, 3–23. doi:10.1177/089826439500700101

Zarit, S. H., & Knight, B. G. (1996). *A guide to psychotherapy and aging: Effective clinical interventions in a life-stage context*. Washington, DC: American Psychological Association. doi:10.1037/10211-000

Zarit, S. H., & Zarit, J. M. (1998). Mental disorders in older adults: Fundamentals of assessment and treatment. New York, NY: Guilford Press.

Health and Medical Conditions

Carol D. Goodheart and Ronald H. Rozensky

Psychotherapists have long recognized the psychosocial impact of physical disease and disability on individuals and their families. Clinicians have become increasingly involved in helping people to better understand, adapt to, cope with, prevent, and manage medical conditions and to identify their significant risks for illness and their reactions to illness. Health problems often exacerbate psychological distress; conversely, such distress, whether secondary to a medical disorder or premorbid, may worsen medical conditions, obscure the medical picture, or interfere with medical treatment.

Mental health practitioners routinely encounter patients with acute or chronic physical illnesses. The presence of medical conditions often places patients at increased risk of depression, anxiety, substance abuse, interpersonal conflict, and other psychological problems.

Psychotherapists must understand an array of multidimensional interactions to treat people with medical conditions competently. When a disease or injury occurs, its symptom expression, severity, and course may be affected by behavior, cognition, emotion, beliefs, attitudes, interpersonal schemas, family scripts, cultural influences, social support, coping style, and internal and external resources (Belar & Deardorff, 2008). It is well established that when quality psychological care is offered in conjunction with quality medical care, patients' psychological functioning improves and medical services are used more efficiently (Chiles, 1999).

HISTORY OF MEDICAL CONDITIONS IN PSYCHOTHERAPY

Numerous textbooks have traced the modern application of psychological principles within the psychotherapeutic treatment of medically ill patients (e.g., Belar & Deardorff, 2009; Friedman & Silver, 2007; Millon, Green, & Meagher, 1982; Stone, Cohen, & Adler, 1979). That history progresses from Freud and Charcot's clinical studies of hysteria, to the founding of psychosomatic medicine and psychoanalytic approaches to diseases (Wittkower & Warnes, 1977), to behavioral medicine's study of personality and physical illness and the impact of sociocultural factors on disease (Gentry, 1984). It leads to today's evidence-based approaches for enhancing patient adherence to medical regimens, to defined integrative health care practices for the "whole person" (Serlin, 2007), and to delineated competencies needed by clinicians to work with medically ill patients (France et al., 2008).

The early, modern beginning of psychotherapeutic work with medical patients is most often associated with psychosomatic medicine (Wittkower

& Warnes, 1977). This school of thought "originates from a concern with the interaction between biological stressors, symbolic processes, and the body's reaction" (Stone, 1979, p. 68). Early psychoanalytic therapists frequently saw illness as psychogenic. Led by psychoanalysts and theorists such as Franz Alexander, the pioneers in psychosomatic medicine sought to understand how psychological stressors had a direct effect on diseases and looked at problems such as "accidents, hypertension, hay fever, hyperemesis of pregnancy, . . . menstrual problems, cardiospasm, peptic ulcer, ulcerative colitis, migraine, . . . allergy, diabetes, disorders of the colon and of the small intestine, and renal and respiratory disorders" (Stone, 1979, p. 68). With the increasing recognition of biological, neurochemical, and genetic pathways, psychosomatic medicine moved away from its psychodynamic roots and toward updated scientific methods (Friedman & Adler, 2007).

In 1977, Engel proposed a comprehensive biopsychosocial model to understand disease and healing. His perspective reached well beyond the physiological foundation of medicine and incorporated factors outside of the person, including family, community, culture, society, and the environment. This integrative biopsychosocial model has been cited frequently since its introduction but not always practiced. Many health care systems continue to split mental health and physical health services. Nevertheless, there are specialty areas in which the biopsychosocial model has increasingly taken hold, to the benefit of patients and their families. These areas include primary care, internal medicine, pediatrics, family medicine, and psychology (Frank, Baum, & Wallander, 2004; McDaniel, Johnson, & Sears, 2004). The recent focus on integrative health care, with the whole person as a participant in the health care system, is a contemporary iteration of this biopsychosocial model (Serlin, 2007).

By the beginning of this century, models for developing expertise in working with medical patients had been documented (Belar & Jeffrey, 1995; Raczynski & Leviton, 2004; Stone, 1983) and the clinical competencies in health psychology had been framed (American Board of Health Psychology, 1995). Recognizing the importance of health and health care, in 2001 the American Psychological Association (APA) added "health" to its bylaws and mission, stating that APA works "to advance psychology as a science and profession, and as a means of promoting *health* [emphasis added] and human welfare" (APA, 2001; N. G. Johnson, 2004). It is clear that psychology, and its application within psychotherapy, have evolved and "must be viewed, at a minimum, as a physical AND mental health profession" (VandenBos, DeLeon, & Belar, 1991, p. 444).

In 2002, health assessment and intervention billing codes were added to the Current Procedural Terminology Codes in recognition of the centrality of the psychological assessment and treatment for patients with medical diagnoses. These billing codes enable psychologists to receive insurance reimbursement for services provided to patients with physical health diagnoses. The addition of the Health and Behavior Diagnostic Codes corrected a longstanding problem; that is, the use of billing codes based on mental health diagnoses rather than the medical diagnoses for which the patient may have been referred for psychotherapeutic intervention (APA, 2009a). These codes recognize, more specifically, assessment and treatment to address issues with medical patients such as "adherence to medical treatment, symptom management, health-promoting behaviors, health-related risk-taking behaviors, and overall adjustment to physical illness" (APA, 2009b, para. 3).

Illustrating the range of opportunities for psychotherapy to affect health care, Rozensky (2006a, 2008) reviewed 481 consecutive articles published in the *Journal of Clinical Psychology in Medical Settings* during a 13-year period. The medical diagnoses, presenting complaints, or keywords in those articles reflect the range of services provided by psychologists and parallel the most prevalent diseases and their morbidity and mortality as found in the general population (National Center for Health Statistics, 2005). These practice areas include cancer, heart disease, diabetes, asthma, pain, chronic illness, sickle cell disease, cystic fibrosis, brain injury and brain tumor, HIV and AIDS, multiple sclerosis, hepatitis C, infertility, obesity, Parkinson's disease, fibromyalgia, chronic fatigue, arthritis, urinary incontinence, spina bifida, sleep apnea, irritable bowel, prostatectomy, postpartum depression, smoking control, aging, menopause, psychological and behavioral health diagnoses, low birth weight, and eating disorders in women and men, to name just a few.

The clinical assessment of and psychological treatments for the full range of medical diagnosis found in the *International Classification of Diseases, Ninth Revision, Clinical Modification* (World Health Organization, 1996; see also Hart, Schmidt, & Aaron, 1998) have been detailed for both in- and outpatient populations (e.g., S. B. Johnson, Perry, & Rozensky, 2002; Sweet, Rozensky, & Tovian, 1991).

No longer are communicable diseases and acute illnesses the primary cause of death and disability in the United States; they have been replaced by chronic illnesses. By the year 2020, 134 million Americans will be living with chronic illnesses (Institute for Health and Aging, 1996). For example, cancer is increasingly managed as a chronic disease rather than the death threat it once was. In the United States, approximately 12,000 children are newly diagnosed with cancer each year; approximately 75% of them will survive. There are more than 250,000 survivors of childhood cancer in the United States, and the numbers are rising. These children and their families need ongoing medical, psychological, educational, and social support that is culturally sensitive and well coordinated (Woznick & Goodheart, 2002). The same can be said about psychotherapeutic interventions with patients who must manage other chronic diseases.

Today, psychological interventions for medical conditions encompass a very wide range of services for the equally broad range of health problems and populations (S. B. Johnson et al., 2002; Sweet et al., 1991). Goodheart (2005) summarized the kinds of interventions that may be directed toward prevention (e.g., smoking cessation, weight control), surveillance (e.g., screening for medical problems), treatment, and self-management of medical conditions. In general, these interventions include

- Focused psychotherapy: A time-limited approach to problem-solving based on biopsychosocial stressors and resources.
- Decision making: Helping patients and families arrive at the best decisions for their circumstances from among the medical choices they are given.
- Medical symptom reduction: Helping patients decrease pain, lessen side effects of treatment (e.g., anticipatory nausea) and decrease the frequency and intensity of acute episodes (e.g., incidents of asthma exacerbation).
- Coping enhancement: Helping patients (and families) to plan actively, elicit support, seek accurate information, develop new habits, reduce anxiety, and facilitate mourning while preventing depression.
- Treatment adherence: Helping patients to develop understanding and motivation and to overcome obstacles that may interfere with adherence to prescribed medical regimens.
- Stress and pain reduction: Helping patients learn specific, evidence-based techniques, e.g., progressive relaxation, hypnosis, biofeedback, visualization, meditation, and focused breathing.
- Interpersonal techniques: Helping patients learn new or improved skills for communication, assertion, and conflict resolution with medical personnel, family, partners, parents, employers, coworkers, friends.
- Adaptation: Helping patients make quality of life adjustments to an altered reality due to the losses of illness, effects of medications, aftereffects of medical treatment, or disability.
- Crisis management: Helping patients mobilize internal and external supportive resources to regain self control, for use when the patient is overwhelmed by anxiety and when the patient's ability to cope on his or her own is compromised.
- Anger management: Helping patients control anger through the use of shame reduction, guided imagery, anger arousal paired

with exposure techniques, and through improved self-efficacy in communication and problem solving.

- Family involvement: Helping the caregivers, partners, and family members of people with medical conditions by conjoint treatments and the development of coping and support structures within the home care system.
- Support for self disease management: Helping patients contribute to their own well-being through self-selected adjunctive activities (e.g., personal journals or diaries, exercise and nutrition programs [within the limits of medical recommendations], religious or spiritual participation, humorous books and films).
- Referral and consultation: Helping patients decrease their isolation and increase the support network available to them through disease support groups and community services, as well as through better treatment coordination and collaboration between medical and mental health professionals.
- Handling uncertainty and fear of death: Helping patients with the anxiety and depression that often accompany disease progression. The primary technique for death anxiety is to listen fully, which may be difficult under severe and threatening circumstances. To listen fully, means to listen without judgment, without withdrawal, without denial, and without interference to the patient's hopes. To listen fully is to be present, with the patient, in facing death. (Goodheart, 2005, pp. 275–276)

INTO THE FUTURE

We now focus on recent developments in two areas that reflect ongoing trends in psychotherapy with patients suffering from medical conditions: competency-based training in health psychology and primary care.

Competency-Based Training

In 2006, APA's Division of Health Psychology established a competency-based training model for developing the knowledge and skills to become a clinical health psychologist (France et al., 2008). This model expands on the original Arden House Conference discussions of the standards for education and training in health psychology (Stone, 1983) and proposes a series of self-study questions that help focus the clinician on an ethical expansion of psychotherapeutic practice with medical patients (Belar et al., 2001).

The competencies need not be limited to clinical health psychologists; they can be applied to other psychotherapists interested in obtaining the knowledge and skills required to practice with these patients. Developing the range of competencies described would ensure that the psychotherapist has addressed the competency zeitgeist for this practice area, regardless of one's original graduate training.

Primary Care

Increasingly, psychotherapists are working as part of health care teams in primary care settings in which health and mental health concerns are intertwined. The majority of primary care visits are driven by behavioral health needs; primary care has been called the de facto mental health and addictive disorders service system for 70% of the population (Regier et al., 1993).

The psychotherapist's role, the patient's role, and their interconnectedness are particularly important in primary care psychology, especially in the context of integrative, whole-person health care (Rozensky, Vazquez, & Sears, 2007). In primary care settings, psychologists must remain up to date on the relevant evidence-based literature in both medicine and psychology and on the current standards of practice within the local community. They must encourage patients and their families to be active participants in their own health care.

CONCLUSIONS

Psychotherapists are enriched by the history of accelerating advances in the treatment of people with health and medical conditions. Longer life spans, the increasing prevalence of chronic illnesses, and the rising costs of health care make it imperative that people with medical conditions have access to integrated health care. Good integrated care brings together quality psychotherapeutic services and medical care; it takes into account the biopsychosocial dimensions that contribute to health, illness, and recovery. Psychologists in their roles as psychotherapeutic experts play a valuable and ever larger role in the care of people with health and medical conditions. In the future, we expect that the array of effective psychotherapy and related intervention services, and the number of clinicians with the competencies to deliver those services for patients and families living with health-related challenges, will continue to grow.

The world has just as great a need for psychological and behavioral expertise as it does for medical expertise. The integration of both domains is key to a healthy world (Rozensky, Johnson, Goodheart, & Hammond, 2003).

REFERENCES

American Board of Health Psychology. (1995). *Policies and procedures for the creation of diplomates in health psychology.* Columbia, MO: American Board of Professional Psychology.

American Psychological Association. (2001). *APA mission statement.* Retrieved from http://www.apa.org/about/

American Psychological Association. (2009a). *APA Practice Directorate announces new health and behavior CPT codes.* Retrieved from http://www.apa.org/practice/cpt_2002.html

American Psychological Association. (2009b). *FAQs on the health and behavior CPT codes.* Retrieved from http://www.apapractice.org/apo/health_and_behavior/faqs_on_the_health.html#

Belar, C. D., Brown, R. A., Hersch, L. E., Hornyak, L. M., Rozensky, R. H., Sheridan, E. P., . . . Reed, G. W. (2001). Self-assessment in clinical health psychology: A model for ethical expansion of practice. *Professional Psychology: Research and Practice, 32,* 135–141. doi:10.1037/0735-7028.32.2.135

Belar, C. D., & Deardorff, W. W. (2008). *Clinical health psychology in medical settings: A practical guidebook.* Washington, DC: American Psychological Association.

Belar, C. D., & Jeffrey, T. B. (1995). Board certification in health psychology. *Journal of Clinical Psychology in Medical Settings, 2,* 129–132. doi:10.1007/BF01988638

Chiles, J. A. (1999). The impact of psychological interventions on medical cost offset: A meta-analytic review. *Clinical Psychology: Science and Practice, 6,* 204–220. doi:10.1093/clipsy/6.2.204

Engel, G. L. (1977). The need for a new medical model: A challenge for biomedicine. *Science, 196,* 129–136. doi:10.1126/science.847460

France, C. R., Masters, K. S., Belar, C. D., Kerns, R. D., Klonoff, E. A., Larkin, K. T., . . . Thorn, B. E. (2008). Application of the competency model to clinical health psychology. *Professional Psychology: Research and Practice, 39,* 573–580.

Frank, R. G., Baum, A., & Wallander, J. L. (Eds.). (2004). *Handbook of clinical health psychology. Vol. 3: Models and perspectives in health psychology.* Washington, DC: American Psychological Association.

Friedman, H. S., & Adler, N. E. (2007). The history and background of health psychology. In H. S. Friedman & R. C. Silver (Eds.), *Foundations of health psychology* (pp. 3–18). Oxford, England: Oxford University Press.

Friedman, H. S., & Silver, R. C. (Eds.). (2007). *Foundations of health psychology.* Oxford, England: Oxford University Press.

Gentry, W. D. (1984). *Handbook of behavioral medicine.* New York, NY: Guilford Press.

Goodheart, C. D. (2005). Psychological interventions in adult disease management. In G. Koocher, J. Norcross, & S. Hill (Eds.), *The psychologist's desk reference* (pp. 274–277). New York, NY: Oxford University Press.

Hart, A., Schmidt, K., & Aaron, W. (Eds.). (1998). *St. Anthony's ICD-9 CM code book.* Reston, VA: St. Anthony.

Institute for Health and Aging, University of California, San Francisco. (1996). *Chronic care in America: A 21st century challenge.* Princeton, NJ: Robert Wood Johnson Foundation.

Johnson, N. G. (2004). Introduction: Psychology and health—Taking the initiative to bring it together. In R. H. Rozensky, N. G. Johnson, C. D. Goodheart, & W. R. Hammond (Eds.), *Psychology builds a healthy world: Opportunities for research and practice* (pp. 3–31). Washington, DC: American Psychological Association.

Johnson, S. B., Perry, N. W., & Rozensky, R. H. (Eds.). (2002). *Handbook of clinical health psychology. Vol. 1: Medical disorders and behavioral applications.* Washington, DC: American Psychological Association.

McDaniel, S. H., Johnson, S. B, & Sears, S. F. (2004). Psychologists promote biopsychosocial health for families. In R. H. Rozensky, N. G. Johnson, C. D. Goodheart, & W. R. Hammond (Eds.), *Psychology builds a healthy world: Opportunities for research and practice* (pp. 49–76). Washington, DC: American Psychological Association. doi:10.1037/10678-002

Millon, T., Green, C., & Meagher, R. (1982). *Handbook of clinical health psychology*. New York, NY: Plenum.

National Center for Health Statistics. (2005). *Health, United States, 2005 with chartbook on trends in the health of Americans*. Hyattsville, MD: Author.

Regier, D. A., Narrow, W. E., Rae, D. S., Manderscheid, R. W., Locke, B. Z., & Goodwin, F. K. (1993). The de facto US mental and addictive disorders service system: Epidemiologic Catchment Area prospective 1-year prevalence rates of disorders and services. *Archives of General Psychiatry, 50*, 85–94

Rozensky, R. H. (2006a). Clinical psychology in medical settings: Celebrating our past, enjoying the present, building our future. *Journal of Clinical Psychology in Medical Settings, 13*, 343–352. doi:10.1007/s10880-006-9045-4

Rozensky, R. H. (2008). *Healthy People 2020*: Good vision for psychology's future. *Independent Practitioner, Fall*, 188–191.

Rozensky, R. H., Johnson, N. G., Goodheart, C.D., & Hammond, W. R. (Eds.). (2003). *Psychology builds a healthy world: Opportunities for research and practice*. Washington, DC: American Psychological Association.

Rozensky, R. H., Vazquez, L., & Sears, S. F. (2007). Clinical health psychology: From hospital practice into the community. In I. A. Serlin, K. Rockefeller, & S. S. Brown (Eds.), *Whole person healthcare. Vol. 2: Psychology, spirituality, and health* (pp. 1–24). Westport, CT: Praeger.

Serlin, I. A. (2007). Introduction. In I. A. Serlin & M. A. DiCowden (Eds.), *Whole person healthcare. Vol. 1: Humanizing healthcare* (pp. xvii–xxiv). Westport, CT: Praeger.

Stone, G. C. (1979). Psychology and the health system. In G. C. Stone, F. Cohen, & N. E. Adler (Eds.), *Health psychology—A handbook* (pp. 47–76). San Francisco: Jossey-Bass.

Stone, G. C. (1983). National working conference on education and training in health psychology. *Health Psychology, 2*(5, Suppl.), 1–3. doi:10.1037/h0090283

Stone, G. C., Cohen, F., & Adler, N. E. (Eds.). (1979). *Health psychology—A handbook*. San Francisco: Jossey-Bass.

Sweet, J. J., Rozensky, R. H., & Tovian, S. M. (Eds.). (1991). *Handbook of clinical psychology in medical settings*. New York, NY: Plenum.

VandenBos, G. R., DeLeon, P. H., & Belar, C.D. (1991). How many psychologists are needed? It's too early to know! *Professional Psychology: Research and Practice, 22*, 441–448. doi:10.1037/0735-7028.22.6.441

Wittkower, E. D., & Warnes, H. (1977). *Psychosomatic medicine: Its clinical applications*. New York, NY: Harper & Row.

World Health Organization. (1996). *International classification of diseases, ninth revision, clinical modification (ICD–9–CM)*. Geneva, Switzerland: Author.

Woznick, L. A., & Goodheart, C. D. (2002). *Living with childhood cancer: A practical guide to help families cope*. Washington, DC: American Psychological Association. doi:10.1037/10444-000

Client Diversity in Psychotherapy

Laura S. Brown

Understanding the diversity of identities and experiences that each individual brings to psychotherapy is now recognized as a component of effective practice for all psychotherapists (Hays, 2007; Whaley & Davis, 2007). This has not always been the case. It was not until the early 1970s that authors began writing about psychotherapy's failures with women, people of color (also known as *ethnic minorities*), and people who are sexual minorities (lesbian, gay, and bisexual people) and began publishing their critiques of what was being offered in therapists' offices to these and other marginalized groups of people.

Historically, psychotherapies were devised primarily by men of European ancestry and reflected the norms of their gender, ethnicity, and social class. This bias was not perceived as a distorted view of reality by its practitioners. Rather, it reflected both the general culture of the disciplines in which psychotherapists trained and the cultural norms of Western societies in which inequities resulting from factors such as gender, ethnicity, sexual orientation, or social class were generally seen as the purview of politicians or sociologists.

A few exceptions to this norm existed. Alfred Adler's (1956) work attended to the impact of social power and powerlessness, and he was an early critic of the roles assigned to women, both in larger society and in the psychoanalytic theories that were the bedrock of the first half of the 20th century. Similarly, Karen Horney (1922) called into question orthodox psychoanalytic views of women's psyches. Joseph White's "Toward a Black Psychology," published in *Ebony* in 1970, was an early entry into the conversation about racism's impact on well-being and the failures of psychotherapy to address this problem.

For the most part, however, textbooks and training programs reflected a reality in which "even the rat was White," to use Robert Guthrie's (1976) not-quite-humorous words. The prevailing assumption was that a generic European American, heterosexual, middle-class, young male human could cover the experiences of all humans, including those who, unlike men, could menstruate and give birth. Even these uniquely female experiences were viewed through the lenses of men's realities, with, for instance, childbirth described by some authors as inherently masochistic because it is painful.

Although the movement to diversify the scope and practices of psychotherapy began to flourish during the end of the 20th century, the construct of diversity itself was frequently narrowly defined even where it was introduced. Working with diversity was initially generally understood as having to do with practice with North American ethnic minorities of color. Other variables influencing identity, such as gender, culture, social class, sexual orientation, disability, spirituality, and age (to name a few), were construed as less important in early work on psychotherapy with diverse clients. Individuals of European descent were not construed as having a racial identity; they were simply the norm, with identities that were not interrogated for their ethnic meanings. Diversity was about working with the "culturally different," to lift a phrase from the title of an early text on the topic (Sue, Sue, & Ruiz, 1981); "different than whom?" could be answered by "different from White people."

Thus, the history of psychotherapy during most of the 1st century after Pierre Janet's introduction of psychotherapeutic constructs was characterized by an absence of attention to diversity (Hays, 2008). When its absence was initially noted, those authors who raised psychotherapy's narrowness were frequently dismissed as simply political or as practicing sociology rather than psychology—or even, as was true for Joe White in regard to race or Phyllis Chesler in regard to gender—as troublemakers. When diversity was addressed, it was primarily ethnic diversity, with other dimensions, or their intersections, ignored or dismissed as less meaningful than racial difference. More problematic than this narrow construction of diversity, however, was the manner in which competence in working with diverse clients was rarely if ever made mainstream in the training of psychotherapists in any discipline. Rather, diversity became marginalized as a special interest primarily for members of diverse groups who were themselves practicing psychotherapists.

By the 1st decade of the 21st century, some progress toward greater awareness of diversity in psychotherapy has been made, albeit slowly and never straightforwardly. The paradigm of diversity as nonoverlapping identity boxes that informed 20th-century scholarship has become transformed into one that acknowledges the multiplicity and intersectionality of identities for all people. Current models of diversity in psychotherapy understand both therapists and clients through the lenses of that intersectionality of identities and social locations and understand experiences of psychological distress as biopsychosocial phenomena heavily influenced by those variables. Early 21st-century models have redefined *cultural competence* as well, placing it centrally within the skills required of all psychotherapists rather than as a form of special interest for the few. In this chapter, I briefly review how these developments have occurred and discuss current models for understanding diverse clients and identity development.

THE HANDBOOK OF PSYCHOTHERAPY WITH DIVERSE PEOPLE: THE EARLY PARADIGM

The earliest epistemologies of diversity in psychotherapy were referred to as *etic* models. Etic models of diversity assume several truths. First, there is a norm. This is commonly represented by the dominant group in a given culture. Second, other groups that differ from the norm can be understood via an in-depth study of those characteristics that distinguish them from the norm group. Etic models of psychotherapy with diverse groups of people, which represent the first 2 decades of this literature, were almost universally volumes that explicated the special qualities of specific groups and then analyzed how dominant cultural models of psychotherapy would or would not be applicable to working with those groups. I refer to this stage in the history of psychotherapy as the *Handbook of Psychotherapy With Bajorans* paradigm (Bajorans being an imaginary ethnic group from the television series "Star Trek: Deep Space Nine," which I use as a placemarker in discussions of diversity).

Ethnic and Cultural Diversity

Sue et al.'s (1981) *Counseling the Culturally Different* is a classic of the 1980s. Its chapters were surveys of the then-sparse scholarship on psychotherapy with North American ethnic minorities of color, with discussions of why these groups were poorly served by the then-dominant models of humanistic and psychodynamic psychotherapies. By the time of the book's third edition (Sue & Sue, 1999), chapters had been added to include discussions of lesbian, gay, bisexual, and transgender clients, old people, and people with disabilities, although the notion that these were special populations to be understood separately from the general practice of psychotherapy and counseling persisted.

Etic models of diversity were essential and foundational to interjecting the discourse on difference into a field in which the generic human being had been European in ancestry, middle to upper middle in class status, male, heterosexual, young, and able bodied. The "YAVIS" (young, attractive, verbal, intelligent, successful) client, although not explicitly European American, generally embodied those dominant group qualities. "Other" clients were commonly defined as outside the purview of what psychotherapists did because of insufficient motivation or psychological mindedness. The etic literature confronted those stereotypes by focusing on the special qualities of ethnically diverse populations of people and analyzing how different approaches to psychotherapy could and did open up the process to a wider range of individuals. Psychotherapists wishing to work with members of ethnically diverse populations were able to deepen competence and offer practices that had a better chance of being truly helpful to emotionally distressed members not of the cultural mainstream.

Gender Diversity

Introduced simultaneously with etic models of psychotherapy with people of color was the initial literature on psychotherapy with women, beginning with Bardwick's (1971) *The Psychology of Women: A Study of Bio-Cultural Conflicts*. That initial offering shortly led to a flood of literature treating women not as deviant men but as a subject worthy of direct consideration. Chesler's *Women and Madness*, published in 1972, became the first book-length commentary on women's experiences in psychotherapy, and the literature of feminist therapy, initially construed as a psychotherapy for women, blossomed after that. However, as was true for all etic literature, this body of work tended to overemphasize women's similarities. Not until the early 1990s, with the publication of Brown and Root's (1990) *Diversity and Complexity in Feminist Therapy* and Comas-Díaz and Greene's (1994) *Women of Color*, were there in-depth examinations of psychotherapy with women who were not White, heterosexual, young, or middle class.

Sexual Minority Clients

The literature on sexual minority people (lesbian, gay, bisexual, and transgender) had a similar trajectory to that of literature on people of color and women. The psychotherapy literature had long treated homosexuality as a form of mental disorder. Evelyn Hooker's groundbreaking 1957 article demonstrating the normal responses of a nonclinical group of gay men on the Rorschach was followed by a lengthy silence in the field, broken by Weinberg's (1972) *Society and the Healthy Homosexual*, a book that coincided with the burgeoning of the gay and lesbian rights movement. Early texts on psychotherapy with gay men and lesbians followed, with Gonsiorek's 1982 edited volume being among the first to broadly publicize the concept of "affirmative" psychotherapies with this population, differentiating those from prior psychotherapeutic attempts to change sexual orientation. These and similar works were based almost entirely on psychotherapeutic practice with European American clients.

People With Disabilities

Another diverse group of clients who had been marginalized in psychotherapy practice were people with disabilities. This is not to say that there was no psychological literature on working with this population. Rather, what existed was quite similar to the pre-1970s discourse on people of color, women, and sexual minorities. Most of the literature was within the field of rehabilitation psychology; viewed disability through the medical, deficit model; and focused on assisting people with mobility, visual, hearing, or cognitive differences to adjust to their lesser status.

As a disability rights movement began to emerge in the United States, the diverse groups of people with disabilities also began to vociferously criticize the infantilizing and medicalized stance taken by mental health authors. The work of Rhoda Olkin (1999), among others, has been prominent in bringing the particular needs and concerns of people with disabilities to the attention of psychotherapists. Because Olkin's work is more recent than much of the similar early work on psychotherapy with other diverse populations, however, it suffers little if at all from the tendency to view all members of the population as similar in needs and characteristics, reflecting the sophistication about psychotherapy with diverse populations that grew and deepened during the 1990s.

Other Diverse Groups

A variety of other marginalized groups began to see their unique concerns and characteristics in psychotherapy addressed as well. Because this volume contains separate chapters about older adults, children, and adolescents, I do not discuss that literature here. Literatures on psychotherapeutic considerations regarding social class, religion and spirituality, and other aspects of diversity have been slower to emerge, although within some corners of the field, nonpathologizing paradigms for understanding these components of diverse identity can be found (cf. Hill & Rothblum's [1996] edited volume on social class in feminist therapy). Janet Helms's (1990) work on White racial identity development, which began to be published in the 1990s, reflects another important trend in the understanding of human diversity, shifting the conversation from the psychology of the "other" and reframing the experience of members of the dominant group as one of diversity as well.

EXPANDING BEYOND THE ETIC PARADIGM: MULTIPLE AND INTERSECTIONAL IDENTITIES

The inherent problems with etic models became apparent in the decade after psychotherapy with various diverse groups beginning to receive initial attention. Such constructs focused on what is similar among members of an identified group and frequently glossed over within-group differences or the intersections of experiences between one group and another. Within a given group, its dominant members, frequently men, were then defined as the new norm, with women, sexual minorities, people with disabilities, and so on within each group made invisible. This, in turn, gave rise, during the 1980s and early 1990s, to a literature of subgroups, with books and special journal issues devoted to psychotherapy with, for instance, Asian American women, or lesbian, gay, bisexual, and transgender people of color, or women with disabilities.

This refinement of etic diversity in psychotherapy was once again a valuable and necessary step toward a more integrated understanding of human diversity and its effects on psychotherapy practice. As with previous literature, it illuminated experiences previously invisible in the general psychotherapy literature and began to unpack the specific meanings given to experience resulting from intersections between ethnicity and sex, or sexuality, or disability, or age. This deepened literature also began to focus more directly on the experiences of diverse psychotherapists, with Greene's (1986) ground-breaking article examining the multiple layers of meaning in psychotherapy between women who might differ in culture, ethnicity, and sexual orientation and Maria Root's work exploring the multiple and intersecting identities of racially mixed people introducing a discourse that has grown in depth and sophistication over the past 2 decades. Root's (1992) edited volume *Racially Mixed People in America* opened the conversation as to the potentially vast range of identity potentials, and thus responses to psychotherapy, inherent simply in the intersection of two different racial and ethnic heritages in one person. The intervening era has seen an expansion of Root's paradigm, both by Root and others, to explore the range of intersectionalities of identities and to consider what those varieties of trajectories of identity development and experience might mean for people's need in the psychotherapy relationship.

Hays (2001, 2007) introduced the acronym ADRESSING to describe how a wide range of social locations—age, disability, religion and spirituality, ethnicity and race, social class, sexual orientation, indigenous status, national origin, and sex and gender—could intersect in both psychotherapist and client to affect the course of psychotherapy. This paradigm for understanding diversity is reflected in the current status of the Sue and Sue volume, which in 2007 changed its name to *Counseling the Culturally Diverse* and now uses a model of intersecting and multiple identities in which a person of color can also be considered through the lenses of gender, sexual orientation, social class, disability, and so on.

DIVERSITY IN PSYCHOTHERAPY:
A 21ST-CENTURY PERSPECTIVE

The practice of psychotherapy has expanded exponentially since the beginning of the 1970s from the narrow focus on European American, male, middle-class, heterosexual, dominant-culture clients and psychotherapists. Although training for work with the range of diverse clients probably lags behind other aspects in many of the mental health fields, there is a growing acceptance of the need to integrate awareness of diversity with the psychotherapist's own personal and unacknowledged biases into the practice of psychotherapy (Brown, 2008).

Nonetheless, some challenges and threats remain. As noted by a host of authors (including many of those whose work was cited earlier) in a recent volume on evidence-based practices in psychotherapy (Norcross, Beutler, & Levant, 2005), almost none of the empirically supported, primarily cognitive–behavioral treatments for specific disorders in ascendancy respond in any way to client or psychotherapist diversity. A conference held by the National Institutes of Mental Health in 2008 represented an initial attempt to not simply retrofit these therapies to diverse populations but rather to inspire the development of integrations of culture and psychotherapy (Morales, 2008). At the dawn of the 21st century, we can see a resurgence of etic models, in the form of the *Handbook of Cognitive Therapy With Bajorans* paradigm mentioned earlier. It is entirely likely that as research becomes an even more dominant guide in the practice of psychotherapy, the field will repeat its trajectory: creating, first, such etic models for treatment and, second, more finely tuned paradigms that reflect understandings of multiple identities and intersectionalities.

The diverse identities of members of dominant groups, and the impact of White and male identities in psychotherapy, are also increasingly undergoing scrutiny. Good and Brooks's (2005) *The New Handbook of Psychotherapy and Counseling With Men*, which considers male identity development not as a unitary phenomenon but through the lenses of many aspects of diversity, exemplifies this movement toward seeing diversity as not simply about the "other."

Another 21st-century trend is the enhanced attention given to the diversity of the psychotherapist her- or himself and to her or his nonconscious attitudes and biases. Although founded in social psychology rather than in the literature of countertransference in psychotherapy, the research of Gaertner, Dovidio, and their colleagues on what they refer to as "aversive" or modern bias (Dovidio, Gaertner, Kawakami, & Hodson, 2002) has begun to modify our definitions of what constitutes cultural competence. The ability and willingness of the psychotherapist to acknowledge her or his own biases rather than to perceive her- or himself as bias free, will be more fully developed as it is integrated into practice.

CONCLUSION

The field of psychotherapy, seen from the standpoint of many members of marginalized groups, has come but a little ways in its understanding of diversity. Nonetheless, the decades since 1970 have seen an explosion of knowledge, a growth in the complexity and quality of practice with members of diverse groups, and an increasing integration of diversity into the practice of all psychotherapists (Whaley & Davis, 2007). As proportionally greater numbers of members of diverse and marginalized groups enter the field of psychotherapy practice, and as the population of the United States itself becomes more diverse on all dimensions, psychotherapy practice with diverse populations is also likely to become more rich, deepened by the contributions of both these therapists and these clients to the understanding of what makes for a healing relationship in psychotherapy.

REFERENCES

Adler, A. (1956). *The individual psychology of Alfred Adler* (H. L. Ansbacher & R. R. Ansbacher, Eds.). New York, NY: Harper Torchbooks.

Bardwick, J. (1971). *The psychology of women: A study of bio-cultural conflicts*. New York, NY: Harper & Row.

Brown, L. S. (2008). *Cultural competence in trauma therapy: Beyond the flashback*. Washington, DC: American Psychological Association. doi:10.1037/11752-000

Brown, L. S., & Root, M. P. P. (Eds.). (1990). *Diversity and complexity in feminist therapy*. New York, NY: Haworth Press.

Chesler, P. (1972). *Women and madness*. Garden City, NY: Doubleday.

Comas-Díaz, L., & Greene, B. (Eds.). (1994). *Women of color*. New York, NY: Guilford Press.

Dovidio, J. F., Gaertner, S. L., Kawakami, K., & Hodson, G. (2002). Why can't we just get along? Interpersonal biases and interracial distrust. *Cultural Diversity and Ethnic Minority Psychology, 8*, 88–102. doi:10.1037/1099-9809.8.2.88

Gonsiorek, J. (Ed.). (1982). *Homosexuality and psychotherapy: A practitioner's handbook of affirmative models*. Binghamton, NY: Haworth Press.

Good, G. E., & Brooks, G. R. (Eds.). (2005). *The new handbook of psychotherapy and counseling with men: A comprehensive guide to settings, problems, and treatment approaches*. San Francisco, CA: Jossey-Bass.

Greene, B. (1986). When the therapist is White and the patient is Black: Considerations for psychotherapy in the feminist heterosexual and lesbian communities. *Women and Therapy, 5*, 41–65.

Guthrie, R. V. (1976). *Even the rat was White: A historical view of psychology*. New York, NY: Harper & Row.

Hays, P. A. (2001). *Addressing cultural complexities in practice: A framework for clinicians and counselors*. Washington, DC: American Psychological Association. doi:10.1037/10411-000

Hays, P. A. (2007). *Addressing cultural complexities in practice: Assessment, diagnosis, and therapy*. Washington, DC: American Psychological Association.

Hays, P. A. (2008). *Addressing cultural complexities in practice: Assessment, diagnosis, and therapy* (2nd ed.). Washington, DC: American Psychological Association.

Helms, J. E. (Ed.). (1990). *Black and White racial identity: Theory, research and practice*. Westport, CT: Greenwood Press.

Hill, M., & Rothblum, E. D. (Eds.). (1996). *Classism and feminist therapy: Counting costs*. New York, NY: Haworth.

Hooker, E. (1957). The adjustment of the male overt homosexual. *Journal of Projective Techniques, 22*, 18–31.

Horney, K. D. (1922). *Feminine psychology*. New York, NY: Norton.

Morales, E. (2008). *Task force report: Evidence based conference task force translating research and policy for the real world conference.* Retrieved from *http://www.apa.org/divisions/div45/images/Evidenced_Based_Conference_rpt08.doc*

Norcross, J. C., Beutler, L. E., & Levant, R. F. (Eds.). (2005). *Evidence-based practice in mental health: Debate and dialogue on the fundamental questions.* Washington, DC: American Psychological Association.

Olkin, R. (1999). *What psychotherapists should know about disability.* New York, NY: Guilford Press.

Root, M. P. P. (Ed.). (1992). *Racially mixed people in America.* Newbury Park, CA: Sage.

Sue, D. W., & Sue, D. (1999). *Counseling the culturally different: Theory and practice* (3rd ed.). New York: Wiley.

Sue, D. W., & Sue, D. (2007). *Counseling the culturally diverse.* New York, NY: Wiley.

Sue, D. W., Sue, D., & Ruiz, R. (1981). *Counseling the culturally different: Theory and practice* (1st ed.). New York, NY: Wiley.

Weinberg, G. (1972). *Society and the healthy homosexual.* New York, NY: St. Martins Press.

Whaley, A. L., & Davis, K. E. (2007). Cultural competence and evidence-based practice in mental health services: A complementary perspective. *American Psychologist, 62,* 563–574. doi:10.1037/0003-066X.62.6.563

White, J. (1970, September). Toward a Black psychology. *Ebony,* pp. 45, 48–50, 52.

14

TREATMENT MODALITIES

Couple Therapy

Alan S. Gurman and Douglas K. Snyder

Couple therapy refers to a diverse set of interventions provided to partners in an intimate relationship intended to reduce relationship distress and promote relationship well-being. Typically provided to partners in conjoint sessions (i.e., both partners meeting simultaneously with the same therapist), couple-based therapies may be delivered not only to married heterosexual couples but also to cohabiting or same-gender couples, as well as to partners who live separately.

Couple therapy is an essential component of mental health services, emerging partly in response to a divorce rate of approximately 50% for first marriages in the United States. By far the most frequently cited reason for seeking mental health services is relationship difficulties (Swindle et al., 2000). Although couple therapy most often aims to reduce relationship distress, couple-based interventions have also been developed to treat couples in which one or both partners struggle with individual emotional or behavioral disorders.

In this overview, we trace the history of couple therapy through four stages across 80 years of development: (a) initial genesis in the form of marriage education and counseling efforts, (b) emergence as a clinical intervention rooted primarily within the psychoanalytic tradition, (c) reformulation as inspired by theoretical developments within the family therapy movement, and (d) revisions and extensions influenced by evidence-based and integrative treatments.

GENESIS OF MARRIAGE EDUCATION AND COUNSELING

The origins of couple therapy can be traced to the founding of the Marriage Consultation Center in New York City in 1929, followed shortly thereafter by the American Institute of Family Relations in Los Angeles in 1930 and the Marriage Council of Philadelphia in1932 (Broderick & Schrader, 1991). The American Association of Marriage Counselors was established in 1942 and was subsequently renamed the American Association of Marriage and Family Counselors in 1970, and finally the American Association for Marriage and Family Therapy in 1978.

Early marriage counselors were primarily from outside the mental health profession (e.g., obstetricians/gynecologists, clergy, social workers, family-life educators). Their clients were typically couples seeking guidance about the everyday facets of marriage and family life, rather than severely maladjusted individuals suffering from mental disorders. Marriage counselors provided advice and information, largely from an educational perspective, and helped couples solve relatively uncomplicated problems of everyday living. The counseling was typically focused and short term. Moreover, the predominant format for marriage counseling was with individuals, with emergence of the conjoint format rising slowly from only 5% in the 1940s to a meager 15% by 1960.

Adopting a largely pragmatic or educational focus, marriage counseling was generally atheoretical for the first 30 years of its history, maintaining an almost exclusive focus on the present and on patients' conscious experience. In the mid-1960s, this began to change, and in an influential article by Leslie (1964), marriage counseling showed its first major linkage to independently emerging psychoanalytic approaches to couple therapy. From this theoretical perspective, marital conflict was viewed as the consequence of neurotic interactions and psychopathology in one or both partners. Marriage counselors' roles hence shifted from an emphasis on the conscious present to identifying partners' mutual distortions and drawing these out through transference and countertransference reactions manifested within the conjoint counseling process.

INFLUENCE OF PSYCHOANALYTIC THEORY
ON COUPLE THERAPY

As early as 1931, Oberndorf made a seminal presentation at the American Psychiatric Association on the psychoanalysis of married couples, focusing on the role of "interlocking neuroses" in symptom formation and proposing "consecutive" psychotherapy of marital partners treated by the same analyst, in which the second analysis commenced only when the first ended. Not until the end of the next decade did Mittelman (1948) propose *concurrent* marital therapy in which both spouses are treated individually but synchronously by the same therapist. Alternative formats challenging the individual focus of traditional psychoanalysis included *collaborative* therapy, in which partners are treated simultaneously by different therapists who consult with one another for the purpose of maintaining the marriage and coordinating care, and *combined* treatments incorporating family, group, individual, concurrent, or conjoint sessions in various combinations (Greene, 1965). Conjoint sessions did not become the predominant format for couple therapy until about 1970.

Psychoanalytic theory conceptualizes intimate relationships primarily from an object relations framework. Object relations proponents posit that, from interactions first and foremost with the mother or surrogate caretaker, individuals develop internalized images of the self, images of significant others, and sets of transactions connecting these images or objects. Maladaptive relationship patterns of adults reflect enduring pathogenic introjects that give rise to inevitable frustration when these are projected onto an intimate partner and are unwittingly confirmed by the partner's response. Moreover, in distressed marriages, partners' pathogenic introjects interact in an unconscious, complementary manner resulting in repeated disappointments and conflicts. Consequently, a central goal of psychoanalytic couple therapy is to help partners modify each other's projections, distinguish these from objective aspects of their own self, and assume ownership of their own projections.

Although the early proponents of psychoanalytic couple therapy expanded the treatment formats, they did little to extend the fundamental theoretical underpinnings. That is, couple therapy from this perspective continued to emphasize the interpretation of defenses (which now also included joint as well as individual defenses), the use of free association and dream analysis (which now also included each spouse's associations to the other's, as well as their own, productions), and the ventilation and examination of previously unexpressed feelings (which now included feelings toward both one's partner and the therapist).

After reaching its peak in the mid-1960s, psychoanalytic couple therapy experienced a steady decline in response to two challenges. The first involved its limited effectiveness in ameliorating couple difficulties; the emphasis on patient–therapist transference and relative neglect of the partner–partner transference likely constrained its capacity for inducing relationship change. The second challenge came from the outside as alternative theoretical frameworks gained ground within the family therapy movement. Psychoanalytic couple therapy did not disappear but was marginalized by alternative emerging systems of psychotherapy.

IMPACT OF THE FAMILY THERAPY MOVEMENT

Family therapy emerged largely separately from the marriage counseling movement but ultimately had a profound impact on the ways that couple therapy was practiced. Although numerous schools of family therapy emerged during the 1960s and 1970s (see Chapters 6 and 14b, this volume), the work of four individuals—Don Jackson (communications theory), Virginia Satir (experiential therapy), Murray Bowen (transgenerational family systems), and Jay Haley (strategic therapy)—stands apart in advancing new ideas that continue to influence practice.

Don Jackson (1920–1968) was strongly influenced by his collaboration with Gregory Bateson and colleagues studying communication processes in families having a member with schizophrenia. Jackson pioneered efforts to see patients and family members together (in conjoint family therapy) and subsequently founded the Mental Research Institute (MRI) in 1959 and the first family therapy training program funded by the U.S. government. Jackson's conceptualization of family homeostasis—and the mechanisms by which families resist change—became the defining metaphor of family therapy for nearly 3 decades. Family rules, or inferred patterns of redundant interaction, were the homeostatic mechanisms that received the most attention in Jackson's study of marital relationships. Jackson's (1965) defining metaphor of marital relationships was the marital quid pro quo—an unwritten (usually out of awareness) set of ground rules that spouses use to define themselves within their relationship.

In his 1968 text (with William Lederer), *The Mirages of Marriage*, Jackson emphasized that in addressing quid pro quo patterns, "one of the main functions of the marriage counselor is to . . . make them aware of those unconscious rules which are causing friction . . . and help them develop new rules which may be more workable" (p. 442). Jackson described in great detail the specific techniques he used to help couples fashion new, more adaptive, conscious rules for their relationship. These included taking turns expressing one's views on a focused topic, followed by the listener's summarization of what he or she has heard; an emphasis on behavioral specificity in making relational requests; a prohibition against mindreading; the use of "the floor" by the speaker; and the termination of negative interactions to prevent escalation, followed by calmer resumption of the discussion. Not surprisingly, these communication techniques were incorporated in subsequent social-learning based (behavioral) approaches to couple therapy.

Virginia Satir (1916–1988) joined Jackson at the MRI in 1959 and became its first director of training. Satir gave primary emphasis to the functioning and experiencing of the individual, as much as to the individual-in-relational context. She viewed the roles people assume in close relationships (e.g., placater, rescuer) and the dysfunctional communication styles they exhibit as fundamentally expressions of low self-esteem and poor self-concept (Satir, 1964). From Satir's experiential perspective, the main goal of couple therapy was to foster greater self-esteem and self-actualization by increasing the congruence and clarity of self-expression about relational needs, self-perceptions, and perceptions of one's partner; increasing self-awareness; removing protective "masks" that shield authentic self-revelation; and accepting and valuing differences. Toward these ends, a wide variety of techniques were used, ranging from verbal methods such as emphasis on talking to rather than about one's mate and direct expression of feelings, to nonverbal methods, such as family sculpting or dance movement. Among the most influential values Satir represented were the centrality of authentic communication and self-disclosure, salience of relational closeness and security over and above mere problem resolution, and the belief in the restorative potential of committed couple relationships rather than the notion that they almost inevitably resist change. In this respect, her contributions laid the cornerstone for later models of couple therapy grounded in attachment theory and focusing on the exchange of genuine and vulnerable emotions.

Murray Bowen (1913–1990), father of multigenerational or transgenerational family systems therapy, stressed the importance of the history of one's extended family in shaping each successive generation. In both couple and family work, Bowen emphasized differentiation of the self—persons' ability to stand apart from their family to define their own beliefs and values while remaining emotionally connected. Failure to differentiate renders a person more vulnerable to anxious interactions with significant others. Bowen (1978) posited that when experiencing such distress, individuals attempt to "triangulate" a third person to diffuse the tension. For example, a distressed spouse may bring a child or adolescent into the parents' conflict to gain support or deflect criticism.

Bowen began working with couples as an attempt to block pathological multigenerational processes. Marital conflict pointed not only to problems in the dyad but more prominently to problems in the larger family systems of the partners (i.e., to the families of origin). Hence, the therapeutic focus in couple therapy was to disrupt the recursive, repetitive cycles of symptoms between partners and key extended family members. The couple therapist thus needed to resist efforts by either partner toward triangulation, promote understanding of relational patterns from a broader multigenerational perspective, and help individuals separate their own emotions and thoughts from those of the rest of the family.

Jay Haley (1923–2007), probably more than any other individual, influenced an entire generation of marital and family therapists to see relational dynamics as products of a system rather than as features of persons. Haley began his career as a member of Bateson's research group and joined Jackson and Satir in founding the MRI, serving as its first director of research. Haley (1963) argued that the central relational dynamic of marriage involves power and control, and that marital conflicts typically arise when the relationship is marked by rigid symmetry or complementarity—or when the hierarchical structure is ambiguous. Symptoms of individuals in a marriage, as well as straightforward relational complaints, were viewed as serving a functional advantage for the partners-as-a-dyad—that is, as strategies for gaining control or influence. Because symptoms and other problems were seen as functional for the marital unit, resistance to change was seen as almost inevitable. Haley's belief regarding the near-inevitability of patient resistance challenged beliefs in the inherent restorative potential of committed relationships held by some of his closest contemporaries, fueling a philosophical schism that would continue without resolution.

Hence, therapeutic interventions from this perspective emphasized planned, pragmatic, parsimonious, present-focused efforts to disrupt patterns of behavior that maintained the major problem of the couple. The strategic therapist was active in finding creative ways to modify problem-maintaining patterns of interacting so that presenting problems no longer served their earlier maladaptive purposes. Directives were the most important therapist change-inducing tools. Some directives were straightforward, but Haley also helped to create a rich fund of indirect and sometimes paradoxical directives (e.g., reframing, prescribing the symptom, relabeling the phenomenon in ways that challenged assumptions about its causes or meaning).

REFINEMENT AND EXTENSION OF COUPLE THERAPIES

Three trends have dominated couple therapy in the past 3 decades: (a) refinement of treatments for couple distress situated within evidence-based practice, (b) efforts toward integration of existing treatments, and (c) extension of couple-based therapies for purposes other than the amelioration of primary relationship distress.

Development and Evaluation of Treatments for Couple Distress

Since the late 1970s, several couple therapies have emerged with compelling evidence for their efficacy in treating relationship distress. Each builds, in part, on theoretical substrates laid in previous eras. Each emphasizes a different presumed mediator of relationship difficulties: behavior, emotion, and insight.

Behavioral Couple Therapy

Behavioral couple therapy emerged in the late 1960s on the basis of social-learning theory and initially emphasized reinforcement principles of operant conditioning. Richard Stuart (1969) posited that successful marriages could be distinguished from unsuccessful ones by the frequency and range of positive acts exchanged reciprocally by partners. Stuart's treatment consisted of obtaining a list of positive behaviors that each person desired from the partner and instituting an agreement for the two individuals to exchange "tokens" (markers that could be traded for other desired outcomes) as rewards for enacting the desired behaviors. A decade later, in 1979, Neil Jacobson and Gayla Margolin extended behavioral couple therapy by broadening the means of promoting positive behavior exchange and teaching partners communication skills. Behavior-exchange agreements, initially grounded in the quid pro quo concept of Don Jackson (but reformulated to emphasize conscious exchanges of overt behaviors rather than unconscious enactment of implicit relationship rules) were supplemented and eventually replaced by "good faith" contracts in which partners agreed to provide behaviors desired by the other unilaterally in anticipation of reciprocity over time. In addition, partners were taught specific communication skills in highly structured protocols targeting problem solving and, later, emotional expressiveness.

Since its original formulation, behavioral couple therapy has undergone several important extensions. The first involved expanding the social-learning emphasis to target cognitive processes presumed to mediate between overt behaviors and partners' subjective response. A major premise of cognitive–behavioral couple therapy is that partners' dysfunctional emotional and behavioral responses to relationship events are influenced by information-processing errors, whereby cognitive appraisals of the events are either arbitrary or distorted (Epstein & Baucom, 2002). Hence, cognitive–behavioral couple therapy explicitly targets partners' assumptions, standards, and expectancies for intimate relationships and their basis for making attributions (or giving meaning) to their own and each other's behaviors. Another extension of behavior therapy has been to focus on partners' self-regulation (Halford, 1998), encouraging partners to change their own maritally relevant behavior to facilitate increased mutual satisfaction. For example, self-regulation might target altering one's own response to the other partner's undesired behavior or meet-ing one's own unmet needs through alternative means. By far the most impor-tant extension of behavioral couple therapy has involved what its developers, Neil Jacobson and Andrew Christensen (1996), labeled *integrative behavioral couple therapy*. This integrative approach combined traditional behavioral techniques for promoting change (specifically, communication, problem-solving, and behavior-exchange skills training) with strategies aimed at pro-moting acceptance. Acceptance techniques are viewed as essential "when direct efforts to change are blocked by incompatibilities, irreconcilable dif-ferences, and unsolvable problems" (Jacobson & Christensen, 1996, p. 11) and include interventions promoting tolerance and encouraging partners to appreciate differences and to use these to enhance their marriage. The inte-grative behavioral approach also targets empathic joining between partners by promoting "soft" emotional disclosures not unlike those featured in an independently developed approach to be considered next.

Emotionally Focused Couple Therapy

The fundamental premise underlying emotionally focused couple ther-apy, originally codeveloped by Leslie Greenberg and Susan Johnson (1988), is that all human beings have an inherent need for consistent, safe contact with responsive others. Hence, this approach views marital conflict and har-mony as dependent on the degree to which partners' basic needs for bonding or attachment are satisfied. Although ultimately framed from attachment the-ory, emotionally focused couple therapy owes part of its conceptual heritage to object relations theory and is consonant as well with principles posited by Virginia Satir.

The corrective emotional experience sought in emotionally focused couple therapy is achieved through a mixture of gestalt, client-centered, and systemic interventions in which affective immediacy is high. Specific inter-ventions include creating a working alliance, delineating core conflict issues, mapping recurrent problematic interaction patterns, accessing relevant unacknowledged feelings and reframing problems in light of these feelings, encouraging acceptance of one's own needs as well as the partner's emotional experience, and ultimately creating new solutions for developing and main-taining secure attachment (Johnson, 2004). In emotionally focused couple therapy, the therapist does not explore the past, interpret unconscious moti-vations, or directly teach interpersonal skills.

Insight-Oriented Couple Therapy

Psychodynamic couple therapy was reinvigorated and subjected to empirical evaluation in work by Douglas Snyder and colleagues (Snyder, 1999;

Snyder, Wills, & Grady-Fletcher, 1991). This approach emphasizes affective reconstruction of previous relationship injuries resulting in sustained interpersonal vulnerabilities and related defensive strategies interfering with emotional intimacy. In affective reconstruction, developmental origins of interpersonal themes and their manifestation in a couple's relationship are explored using techniques roughly akin to interpretive strategies promoting insight, but emphasizing interpersonal schemas and relationship dispositions rather than instinctual impulses. Previous relationships, their affective components, and strategies for emotional gratification and anxiety containment are reconstructed with a focus on identifying for each partner consistencies in their interpersonal conflicts and coping styles across relationships. In addition, ways in which previous coping strategies vital to prior relationships represent distortions or inappropriate solutions for emotional intimacy and satisfaction in the current relationship are articulated.

Empirical Evaluation of Couple Therapy

The various behavioral, emotionally focused, and insight-oriented couple therapies are distinguished from their historical predecessors by the empirical evaluation of their respective efficacies in controlled clinical trials and by the frequent incorporation of research on basic couple interaction processes (e.g., Gottman, 1998). Although specific findings vary, some important general conclusions have been identified (Snyder, Castellani, & Whisman, 2006). First, meta-analyses of couple therapy affirm that it produces statistically and clinically significant improvement for a substantial proportion of couples, with the average couple receiving therapy being better off at termination than 80% of couples not receiving treatment. However, tempering enthusiasm from this conclusion are findings that in only 50% of treated couples do both partners show significant improvement in relationship satisfaction and that 30% to 60% of treated couples show significant deterioration at 2 years or longer after termination. Second, meta-analyses provide little evidence of differential effectiveness across different theoretical orientations to couple therapy, particularly once other covariates (e.g., reactivity of measures) are controlled.

The Trend Toward Integration

Such findings have fostered two alternative directions in treating couple distress: (a) distillation of common factors contributing to beneficial effects across "singular" or "pure" treatments, and (b) integrative models incorporating multiple components of diverse therapies.

Common factors viewed as specific to couple or family therapies include an emphasis on the interpersonal context in which specific problems occur and fostering an expanded therapeutic alliance across partners or multiple members of the family as a whole (Sprenkle, Davis, & Lebow, 2009). To date, there has been little research documenting specific treatment effects attributable to proposed common factors—nor systematic efforts in designing couple treatments intended to maximize common factors' therapeutic impact.

Various integrative approaches to couple therapy have also been proposed. Integrative approaches specific to couple therapy include the depth-behavioral approach of Alan Gurman (2005, 2008) that strives to modify couple partners' inner representational models and interpersonal schemas by both direct (e.g., behavioral) and indirect (e.g., interpretive) means. The pluralistic approach of Snyder (1999) advocates integration of structural-strategic, cognitive–behavioral, and insight-oriented methods in a sequential manner tailored to couples' presenting difficulties and their unfolding responses to earlier interventions in the therapeutic hierarchy.

Extension of Couple-Based Interventions

A growing body of research has demonstrated high comorbidity between couple distress and individual disorders (Snyder & Whisman, 2003). For example, persons in distressed intimate relationships are 2 to 3 times more likely than nondistressed persons to experience mood, anxiety, or substance abuse disorders. This observation has led to couple-based treatment strategies for addressing these comorbid difficulties: (a) general couple therapy to reduce relationship distress potentially contributing to the development, exacerbation, or maintenance of individual problems; (b) disorder-specific couple interventions that focus on particular partner interactions presumed to directly influence either the co-occurring problems or their treatment; and (c) partner-assisted interventions in which one partner serves as a "surrogate therapist" or coach in assisting the other partner with individual problems.

For example, behavioral couple therapy for both alcoholism and drug abuse produces more abstinence and fewer substance-related problems, happier relationships, fewer couple separations, and lower risk of divorce than does individual-based treatment (O'Farrell & Fals-Stewart, 2006). Behavioral couple therapy has also been shown to be effective in relieving depression when provided to distressed couples with a depressed partner (Beach, 2000). Recent findings have emerged supporting the effectiveness of couple therapy in treating patients suffering from anxiety disorders, chronic pain, cancer, terminal illnesses in general, obesity, coronary artery disease, and posttraumatic stress disorder (Snyder et al., 2006).

Another example of extending couple therapy includes a return to its historical roots in relationship education, but with more explicit emphases on prevention and evidence-based practice. Exemplifying this trend is the Prevention and Relationship Enhancement Program (PREP) of Howard

Markman and colleagues (Markman, Stanley, Blumberg, Jenkins, & Whaley, 2004) that started in 1980 as a premarital program and promotes communication and conflict resolution skills to enhance relationship functioning and prevent divorce. Recent efforts have focused on evaluating the extent to which PREP can be disseminated by clergy and similar providers—another parallel to the early marriage counselors who were primarily from outside the mental health profession. Separate from premarital education have been the development and evaluation of psychoeducational programs targeting couples at known risk of increased distress—for example, couples transitioning to parenthood (Feinberg & Kan, 2008).

CONCLUSIONS

Contemporary couple therapy reflects a growing synthesis of diverse and sometimes conflicting perspectives characterizing its 80-year history: (a) balancing attention to both individual (intrapersonal) as well as broader systemic (interpersonal) dynamics; (b) addressing mutual, recursive influences of individual and relationship dysfunction—particularly in the application of couple-based interventions to mental disorders; and (c) growing recognition of potential enhanced effects through integration of complementary approaches. Evidence regarding the effectiveness of couple therapy is robust in terms of controlled clinical trials, magnitude of effects, and range of applications across diverse spheres of human experience.

REFERENCES

Beach, S. R. H. (Ed.). (2000). *Marital and family processes in depression: A scientific foundation for clinical practice*. Washington, DC: American Psychological Association.

Bowen, M. (1978). *Family therapy in clinical practice*. New York, NY: Jason Aronson.

Broderick, C. B., & Schrader, S. S. (1991). The history of professional marriage and family therapy. In A. S. Gurman & D. P. Kniskern (Eds.), *Handbook of family therapy* (Vol. 2, pp. 3–40). New York, NY: Brunner/Mazel.

Epstein, N. B., & Baucom, D. H. (2002). *Enhanced cognitive-behavioral therapy for couples: A contextual approach*. Washington, DC: American Psychological Association. doi:10.1037/10481-000

Feinberg, M. E., & Kan, M. L. (2008). Establishing family foundations: Intervention effects on coparenting, parent/infant well-being, and parent-child relations. *Journal of Family Psychology, 22*, 253–263. doi:10.1037/0893-3200.22.2.253

Gottman, J. M. (1998). Psychology and the study of marital processes. *Annual Review of Psychology, 49*, 169–197. doi:10.1146/annurev.psych.49.1.169

Greenberg, L. S., & Johnson, S. M. (1988). *Emotionally focused couple therapy*. New York, NY: Guilford Press.

Greene, B. L. (Ed.). (1965). *The psychotherapies of marital disharmony*. New York, NY: Free Press.

Gurman, A. S. (2005). Brief integrative marital therapy: An interpersonal-intrapsychic approach. In J. L. Lebow (Ed.), *Clinical handbook of family therapy* (pp. 353–383). New York, NY: Wiley.

Gurman, A. S. (2008). Integrative marital therapy: A depth-behavioral approach. In A. S. Gurman (Ed.), *Clinical handbook of couple therapy* (4th ed., pp. 383–423). New York, NY: Guilford Press.

Haley, J. (1963). Marriage therapy. *Archives of General Psychiatry, 8*, 213–234.

Halford, W. K. (1998). The ongoing evolution of behavioral couples therapy: Retrospect and prospect. *Clinical Psychology Review, 18*, 613–633. doi:10.1016/S0272-7358(98)00022-1

Jackson, D. D. (1965). Family rules: The marital quid pro quo. *Archives of General Psychiatry, 12*, 589–594.

Jacobson, N. S., & Christensen, A. (1996). *Integrative behavioral couple therapy*. New York, NY: Norton.

Jacobson, N. S., & Margolin, G. (1979). *Marital therapy: Strategies based on social learning and behavior exchange principles*. New York, NY: Brunner/Mazel.

Johnson, S. M. (2004). *The practice of emotionally focused couple therapy* (2nd ed.). New York, NY: Brunner-Routledge.

Lederer, W., & Jackson, D. D. (1968). *The mirages of marriage*. New York, NY: Norton.

Leslie, G. R. (1964). Conjoint therapy in marriage counseling. *Journal of Marriage and the Family, 26*, 65–71. doi:10.2307/349379

Markman, H., Stanley, S., Blumberg, S., Jenkins, N., & Whaley, C. (2004). *Twelve hours to a great marriage*. San Francisco, CA: Jossey-Bass.

Mittelman, B. (1948). The concurrent analysis of married couples. *Psychiatric Quarterly, 17*, 182–197.

Oberndorf, C. P. (1931, June). *Psychoanalysis of married couples*. Paper presented at the meeting of the American Psychiatric Association, Toronto.

O'Farrell, T. J., & Fals-Stewart, W. (2006). *Behavioral couples therapy for alcoholism and drug abuse*. New York, NY: Guilford Press.

Satir, V. (1964). *Conjoint family therapy*. Palo Alto, CA: Science and Behavior Books.

Snyder, D. K. (1999). Affective reconstruction in the context of a pluralistic approach to couple therapy. *Clinical Psychology: Science and Practice, 6*, 348–365. doi:10.1093/clipsy/6.4.348

Snyder, D. K., Castellani, A. M., & Whisman, M. A. (2006). Current status and future directions in couple therapy. *Annual Review of Clinical Psychology, 57*, 317–344. doi:10.1146/annurev.psych.56.091103.070154

Snyder, D. K., & Whisman, M. A. (Eds.). (2003). *Treating difficult couples: Helping clients with coexisting mental and relationship disorders*. New York, NY: Guilford Press.

Snyder, D. K., Wills, R. M., & Grady-Fletcher, A. (1991). Long-term effectiveness of behavioral versus insight-oriented marital therapy: A four-year follow-up study. *Journal of Consulting and Clinical Psychology, 59*, 138–141. doi:10.1037/0022-006X.59.1.138

Sprenkle, D. H., Davis, S., & Lebow, J. (2009). *Common factors in relational therapies*. New York, NY: Guilford Press.

Stuart, R. B. (1969). Operant-interpersonal treatment of marital discord. *Journal of Consulting and Clinical Psychology, 33*, 675–682. doi:10.1037/h0028475

Swindle, R., Heller, K., Pescosolido, B., & Kikuzawa, S. (2000). Responses to nervous breakdowns in America over a 40-year period: Mental health policy implications. *American Psychologist, 55*, 740–749. doi:10.1037/0003-066X.55.7.740

Family Therapy

Florence W. Kaslow

Family therapy can refer to a treatment format or modality, a therapy goal (e.g., improve functioning of and relationships within the family), or a systemic conceptualization of psychopathology and psychotherapy. In this chapter, my task is to focus on the former two meanings and leave it to Chapter 6 (this volume) on systemic theories of psychotherapy to explicate the latter meaning while positing here that systems concepts and conceptualizations are integral to all family therapy.

It is important to note at the outset that the emphasis by any author on the history of a field will reflect his or her particular exposure and experience. Thus, I immediately acknowledge my "bias" in this whirlwind tour of the history of family therapy. *Family* as used herein is broadly encompassing of nuclear and extended/kinship families, stepfamilies, single-parent families, adoptive families, and gay and lesbian families. It includes all those who make a mutual commitment to regard one another as family and to assume certain responsibilities to and for each other on a sustained basis.

A BRIEF HISTORY OF FAMILY THERAPY PRACTICE

As a distinct field, family therapy began to mushroom in the 1950s. The early pioneers who experimented with treating family members conjointly were motivated by a number of factors, which included the following: (a) They were dissatisfied with the slow progress of individual psychotherapy or psychoanalysis; (b) they realized that changes in a patient could have a strong impact on family members, thus significant others might undermine treatment gains if these individuals were not also brought into the process; and (c) there were long waiting lists at agencies post–World War II, so seeing couples or families together seemed a justifiable way to make inroads into the patient backlog and shorten the waiting time for services.

An early taproot of family therapy sprouted in the child guidance movement, first in Chicago in 1909, and then in Boston in 1917, when psychiatrist William Healy established the Judge Baker Guidance Clinic. In child guidance clinics, psychiatrists customarily saw the child alone, and a social worker interviewed the parent, perhaps concurrently, but not conjointly. Most often, *parent* meant *mother*. Few clinics had evening or weekend hours to accommodate working parents, and little outreach was done to encourage fathers to participate.

Another tributary was family casework, an approach utilized in social work with troubled, multiproblem families (Richmond, 1917). Casework often involved home visits to the clients, rather than having whole families come to the agency. However, in family therapy, office-based treatment evolved as the most frequent practice model in the 1950s and continued to be so for the ensuing 60-plus years. Since the early 1990s, there has been a renaissance of the practice of home-based treatment, both in the United States (Lindblad-Goldberg, Dore, & Stern, 1998) and in other countries like Israel (Sharlin & Shamai, 1999), with poor and multiproblem families who are unable or unwilling to get to therapists' offices and by those who are willing to do "in-home therapy." These patients are not categorized as resistant.

The aforementioned discontents crystallized concurrently in the minds and hearts of renegade therapists in different parts of the United States in the 1950s. These dissatisfactions were magnified in the minds of those conducting research into the patterns of interaction between people diagnosed with schizophrenia and their family members. They recognized the crucial role significant others can play in the psychogenesis and maintenance of the disorder.

One pioneering group formed in Palo Alto, California, in 1952 with Gregory Bateson at the helm. In 1953 he was joined by John Weakland and Jay Haley. Their initial interest in metacommunication—the message about the message—propelled them toward developing a communication theory that could possibly lead to deciphering the origin and nature of schizophrenic behavior, particularly as it evolves in the context of the family (Bateson, Jackson, Haley & Weakland, 1956).

Later this group formed the Mental Research Institute (MRI). Other well-known individuals who were part of the early MRI staff included Paul Watzliwick, Virginia Satir, and Don Jackson. Delineation of the concept of the double bind was one of their major contributions (Jackson & Weakland, 1959). Two of their other key constructs were that destructive patterns of relationships are maintained by self-regulating interactions that occur repeatedly within the family group and that there are multiple and often contradictory levels of communications happening simultaneously.

On the East Coast at Yale University, in New Haven, Connecticut, psychiatrists Theodore Lidz and Steven Fleck also investigated the dynamics of families with a member with schizophrenia and focused on the destructive influence of pathological fathering styles, thus challenging the then-prevailing thinking that maternal rejection was a major causative factor. They noted that often the child with a serious mental disorder was inveigled into trying to stabilize the parents' shaky marriage (Lidz, Cornelison, Fleck, & Terry, 1957).

By 1952 at the National Institute of Mental Health in Bethesda, Maryland, Lyman Wynne, psychiatrist and psychologist, was also working with families with a loved one with schizophrenia. He was struck by the unreal, "as if" perfect, quality of these disturbed families and developed the concepts of pseudo mutuality, pseudo hostility and the rubber fence—still utilized today—and connected the concepts of communication deviance, thought disorders, and a continuum of severity of pathology (Wynne, 1984).

Another pioneer was Murray Bowen, a psychiatrist who originally specialized in the treatment of schizophrenia during his years at the Menninger Clinic in the 1940s. He was intrigued by the dynamic of mother—child symbioses. This interest and his working with this pattern of attachment led to his formulation of the concept of differentiation of self (Bowen, 1978, 1988). He spent much of the 1950s in Washington, DC, at the National Institute of Mental Health working on family of origin dynamics before relocating to Georgetown University Medical School, where he remained from 1959–1990.

In New York, at Jewish Family Service, child psychiatrist Nathan Ackerman started experimenting with seeing family members together as the basic patient unit for diagnosis and treatment (Ackerman, Beatman, & Sherman, 1961). For the 1955 meeting of the American Orthopsychiatric Association, he organized one of the first sessions on family diagnosis. In 1960 Ackerman founded a Family Institute in Manhattan, which was renamed the Ackerman Family Institute in 1971, as a tribute to his legacy after his death. Ackerman's work emphasized both intrapsychic and interpersonal issues, the unconscious and the conscious, and confronting and challenging a person and a family's defense mechanisms.

Carl Whitaker was one of the most irreverent, colorful, playful, and daringly innovative of the founders of family therapy. From work with children and with psychotic inpatients, he had learned a great deal about "craziness," and he seemed to be able to enter the inner world of his patients—allowing his unconscious to connect to theirs, doing what he called "psychotherapy of the absurd" (Whitaker, 1975). As early as 1943, he and colleague John Warkentin invited spouses and children to join in patients' treatment sessions in their work in Oak Ridge, Tennessee. Whitaker introduced the use of cotherapy, which was based on the premise that having a colleague involved in the treatment enabled either therapist to interact spontaneously without fear of getting overinvolved, as the cotherapist could pull the other out if need be, and that they could each assume supportive, exploratory, or confrontational roles as needed. *The Family Crucible* (Napier & Whitaker, 1978) provides an excellent depiction of his style of experiential family therapy and of the cotherapy he conducted with Augustus Napier.

In Philadelphia, two active groups of therapists emerged. One group originally came together at the Eastern Pennsylvania Psychiatric Institute (EPPI). This group included Ivan Boszormenyi-Nagy and Geraldine Sparks, who were cotherapists and coauthored the classic *Invisible Loyalties*

(Boszormenyi-Nagy & Spark, 1973), which articulated an ethical existential ledger of balances within the intergenerational family system. Others in this group, most of whom also were initially trained in the psychoanalytic tradition, included James Framo, Ross Speck, and Jack Friedman. Many from EPPI and the family therapy section of the Department of Mental Health Sciences nearby at Hahnemann Medical College formed the Philadelphia Family Institute as a loosely affiliated forum for interchange of ideas and to provide stimulating workshops and, later, to do training for new family therapists. The institute evolved into a strong professional support network, which lasted for many decades.

The Philadelphia Child Guidance Clinic was located a short distance away on the other side of the Schuykill River. When Salvador Minuchin, a brilliant charismatic pioneer, left Wiltwyck School for Boys in New York to assume the directorship in 1965, he brought Braulio Montalvo and Bernice Rosman with him. They were joined by Jay Haley in 1967 and subsequently by many others. Minuchin's early work was reported in *Families of the Slums* (Minuchin et al., 1967), and he has continued to focus his attention on inner-city, poor, underserved populations in New York in the past 2 decades. Out of the heady golden years at Philadelphia Child Guidance came Minuchin's structural family therapy, and the groundwork was probably laid for Haley and Madanes to evolve strategic family therapy (Haley, 1973). Because the theoretical orientations of those in the Philadelphia Family Institute and those at the Child Guidance Center were so different, they rarely met together or collaborated, despite their proximity. Such a schism between those who were psychodynamic and intergenerationally oriented (the former group) and those who were structural, strategic, and systemic family therapists (the latter group) also occurred for decades in other cities in the United States and countries around the world including Canada, Norway, and South Africa.

The history of family therapy practice has evolved during overlapping periods, which have been elucidated as follows (Kaslow, 1990):

- Generation I (pre-1969). The Pioneers and Renegades formulated and refined the premises.
- Generation II (1969–1976). The Innovators and Expanders.
- Generation III (1977–1982). The Challengers, Refiners, and Researchers.
- Generation IV (1983–1995). The Integrators and Seekers of New Horizons.
- Generation V (1995–present). Researchers seeking evidence-based therapies. Postmodernism, social construction of reality, and personal narrative approaches.

FAMILY THERAPY PRACTICE THRIVES

In the United States, several organizations have been formed that are dedicated to the field of family treatment and research: The American Association for Marriage and Family Therapy (AAMFT), begun in 1942 as the American Association of Marriage Counselors, changed its name to AAMFT in the late 1970s, reflecting its changing focus and membership. The American Family Therapy Academy was founded in the mid-1970s by many of the family therapy pioneers as the American Family Therapy Association. The Division of Family Psychology (#43) of the American Psychological Association was formed in the mid-1980s. The American Psychiatric Association has a separate section of the Group for the Advancement of Practice focused on the family.

A significant event connoting recognition of the maturation of family therapy was the birth of the journal, *Family Process*, in 1961. It is still a premier publication almost 50 years later. The *Journal of Marital & Family Therapy* was launched in 1974 as the official journal of AAMFT. Since then at least a half dozen other major family journals have been founded in the United States, including the prestigious empirically based American Psychological Association *Journal of Family Psychology*, which debuted in 1987.

Since the 1960s, the movement has expanded rapidly, with therapists coming from everywhere to observe the masters at work in their own settings via one-way mirrors or to hear them present at workshops and conferences. Trainings sprung up at newly formed family institutes in such places as Boston and Chicago, in addition to those already mentioned, and in graduate, medical, and other professional schools.

By the 1970s, family therapy began to spread to other countries. Initially clinicians from many lands went to the United States and England (now the United Kingdom) to get training. Universities and organizations in far flung countries invited leaders from these two countries to come to present workshops to interested practitioners. Subsequently, many countries and regions established their own family-focused organizations and educational and training programs. Strong theoretician and clinician leaders have emerged in various countries since the 1970s, most notably Italy, Norway, Australia, and New Zealand. Their emphases have been on systemic, social construction, postmodern, and narrative therapies.

Today credentialing is a key concern in many countries. Degree-granting, university-based programs are being more sought after as mobility and internationalization of the professions has increased, partially resulting in the pressure for credentials that are recognized beyond one's own borders. In the United States, some certificate-granting institutes have closed, and others have affiliated with universities as degree-granting programs in order to expand

and solidify their programs and remain viable. Qualitative and quantitative research tailored to studying couples and families by looking at process and outcomes variables now receives more attention in the curriculum.

Currently there are two major international organizations that encompass diverse practitioners of family therapy: the International Family Therapy Association, created in 1987, and the International Academy of Family Psychology, founded in 1990. In addition, there are many active, dynamic regional associations on different continents, such as the European Family Therapy Association. Leading figures in the arena of family therapy emerged during Generation II and in subsequent periods in countries in addition to the United States and the United Kingdom, such as Argentina, Australia, Germany, Israel, Italy, Japan, Norway, and South Africa, among others, and have added other voices and perspectives to the highly valued gender, ethnic, and multicultural dialogues and treatment options being taught and utilized in the field. Family psychologists in the United States have been able to become board certified in couple and family psychology since the early 1990s, another hallmark of the field's acceptance and maturation.

PRACTICE IN THE FUTURE

Family therapy was initially dominated by charismatic leaders, some of whom attained guru status and garnered disciples. They convincingly taught and demonstrated their intervention strategies at family institutes, in graduate school classrooms, at conferences, and in workshops, often before there was any research conducted, which supported the accuracy of their assumptions and the effectiveness of their treatments. However, in the last 2.5 decades, insurance carriers and research-oriented professionals have pushed for evaluation of what works reaching beyond clinical experiences and personal testimonials. In these 25 years, the pressure for evidenced-based treatments, such as functional family therapy has proven to be, has mounted (Alexander & Sexton, 2002).

A recurrent controversy is whether graduate students interested in family therapy should be trained broadly initially, learning many of the theories and then proceeding to gain competence in one or several theories and a set of techniques they believe have greatest value, or whether they should become immersed in one theory and its accompanying techniques and then be exposed to multiple approaches. Some see the latter training model as akin to indoctrination with a rule book of absolute dicta, whereas others deliberately select such a specific unidimensional curriculum and model. This may lead to doctrinaire thinking and practice, akin to ethnocentric politics that hold "our way is the only right way." This is the antithesis of the strong trend toward integrative family therapy that has emerged in the last 15 years (Kaslow & Lebow, 2002; Lebow, 2005; Pinsof, 1995).

Advocates of family therapy continue to be drawn from the disciplines of psychology, psychiatry, social work, counseling, pastoral counseling, and psychiatric nursing. Such diversity enriches the field yet also contributes to interdisciplinary tensions and rivalries around competency, training, what is the appropriate terminal degree, who can use the title, and who can legitimately practice marriage and family therapy. These turf battles are likely to continue.

Since the new millennium began, family therapists have been practicing and teaching in an expanding variety of venues, including medical schools, primary health care settings, with family physicians, and with other kinds of medical specialists. Their expertise is also being utilized outside of health and mental health domains in such settings as school systems and in fields like family business consultation (Kaslow, 2006). Some family practitioners specialize in the forensic arena, focusing on issues such as adoption, intimate partner violence, child custody, divorce, and testamentary capacity (Kaslow, 2000). Others are engaged in such arenas as family trauma, military families, juvenile "delinquency" and rehabilitation, and family public policy (Heldring, 2008). Competence regarding gender issues and treating diverse family populations and immigrant groups has also become central in this expanding field.

Given that we are each born into a family and that most of us grow up in our family of origin, an adoptive family, or stepparent family and then later create our own families, the fascination with the family as a system will undoubtedly continue unabated for many decades to come. Clinicians from various professional disciplines and theoretical orientations share this fascination and many find family therapy to be stimulating and rewarding. More important, so do the families they treat—with a high percentage of them reporting marked improvement and satisfaction in their lives because of the help received in family therapy.

REFERENCES

Ackerman, N. W., Beatman, F. L., & Sherman, S. N. (1961). *Exploring the base for family therapy*. New York, NY: Family Service Association of America.

Alexander, J. F., & Sexton, T. L. (2002). Functional family therapy: A model for treating high-risk, acting-out youth. In F. W. Kaslow & J. Lebow (Eds.), *Comprehensive handbook of psychotherapy: Integrative/eclectic* (Vol. 4, pp. 111–132) New York, NY: Wiley.

Bateson, G., Jackson, D. D., Haley, J., & Weakland, J. (1956). Toward a theory of schizophrenia. *Behavioral Science, 1*, 251–264.

Boszormenyi-Nagy, I., & Spark, G. (1973). *Invisible loyalties: Reciprocity in intergenerational family therapy*. New York, NY: Harper & Row.

Bowen, M. (1978). *Family therapy in clinical practice* (2nd ed.). Northvale, NY: Jason Aronson.

Bowen, M. (1988). *Family therapy in clinical practice* (3rd ed.). Northvale, NY: Jason Aronson.

Haley, J. (1973). *Uncommon therapy: The psychiatric techniques of Milton Erickson.* New York, NY: Norton.

Heldring, M. (2008, Spring/Fall). From the president: A place for family in public policy. *The Family Psychologist, 24,* 27–28.

Jackson, D., & Weakland, J. (1959). Schizophrenic symptoms and family interaction. *Archives of General Psychiatry, 1,* 618–621).

Kaslow, F. W. (1990). *Voices in family psychology* (Vols. 1 & 2). Newberry Park, CA: Sage.

Kaslow, F. W. (2000). *Handbook of couple and family forensics: A guidebook for legal and mental health professionals.* New York, NY: Wiley.

Kaslow, F. W. (Ed.). (2006). *Handbook of family business and family business consultation.* New York, NY: Haworth.

Kaslow, F. W., & Lebow, J. (Eds.). (2002). *Comprehensive handbook of psychotherapy: Integrative/eclectic* (Vol. 4). New York, NY: Wiley.

Lebow, J. L. (2005). *Handbook of clinical family therapy.* New York, NY: Wiley.

Lidz, T., Cornelison, A., Fleck, S., & Terry, D. (1957). The intrafamilial environment of schizophrenic patients: Marital schism and marital skew. *American Journal of Psychiatry, 114,* 241–248.

Lindblad-Goldberg, M., Dore, M., & Stern, L. (1998). *Creating competence from chaos: A comprehensive guide to home-based services.* New York, NY: Norton.

Minuchin, S., Montalvo, B., Guerney, B. G., Rosman, B. L., & Shumer, F. (1967). *Families of the slums.* New York, NY: Basic Books.

Napier, A. Y., & Whitaker, C. A. (1978). *The family crucible.* New York, NY: Harper & Row.

Pinsof, W. M. (1995). *Integrative problem centered therapy.* New York, NY: Basic Books.

Richmond, M. (1917). *Social diagnosis.* New York, NY: Russell Sage Foundation.

Sharlin, S. A., & Shamai, M. (1999). *From distress to hope: Intervening with poor and disorganized families.* New York, NY: Haworth.

Whitaker, C. A. (1975). Psychotherapy of the absurd: With a special emphasis on the psychotherapy of aggression. *Family Process, 14,* 1–16. doi:10.1111/j.1545-5300. 1975.00001.x

Wynne, L. C. (1984). The epigenesis of relational systems: A model for understanding family development. *Family Process, 23,* 297–318. doi:10.1111/j.1545-5300. 1984.00297.x

Group Therapy

Gary M. Burlingame and Scott Baldwin

In this chapter, we identify the notable figures, events, and themes of group therapy using three epochs (1900s–1930s, 1940s–1970s, and 1980s–present) over the past century. As is the case in many historical reviews, recurring and unique themes emerge. We begin with a definition of group therapy that distinguishes it from simply participating in a group and end with future directions for practice.

Group psychotherapy can be defined as the treatment of emotional or psychological disorders or problems of adjustment through the medium of a group setting, the focal point being the interpersonal (social), intrapersonal (psychological), or behavioral change of the participating clients or group members. Although contemporary definitions of group treatments often include personal growth, psycho-educational, and support groups, we believe that the mechanisms of change in such groups differ from the mechanisms of change in group therapy. Thus, we limit our discussion of such groups herein and refer the reader to focused reviews of these specialized group treatments.

1900s–1930s: FOUNDATIONAL YEARS

The first group therapy practitioner cited by most historians is Joseph Pratt, who began treating patients with tuberculosis in a group format in 1905. His "thought control" classes were initially introduced as a labor-saving device to get patients to commit to the medical regimen deemed crucial to curing their disease. Tuberculosis was the second leading cause of death in 1900, and Pratt needed a cost-effective method to treat a large number of patients. He astutely noticed factors that were related to more successful "classes," including patients' ability to identify with one another, establish hope for recovery, and develop faith in the class. After publishing a seminal article (1907), Pratt gradually transformed his classes into formal therapy groups, culminating in an article in 1945 for treating psychosomatic illness with group therapy. Pratt's changing views regarding group were a harbinger of three themes that would recur over the next century: group therapy's cost-efficiency, unique therapeutic properties, and success with focused disorders (psychosomatic illness).

The next 2 decades saw a shift to treating psychiatric patients with groups. Lazell (1921) began to treat hospitalized schizophrenics in 1919 using group educational interventions. Like Pratt, he began to note attributes of successful classes, such as the patients' ability to share their common experiences, thereby gaining support and hope from one another. Lazell also noted that after group, nursing staff reported a decreased patient need for bedtime sedatives.

Trigant Burrow (1928) is credited with the formal development of group analysis and began to treat neurotic patients with group analysis in 1920. Burrow was concerned that individual patient dynamics were being emphasized in contemporary psychoanalytic practice to the exclusion of relational and social forces in a patient's life. He viewed self-disclosure, intermember agreement (consensual validation), and discussion of real-time interactions ("here and now") as important healing properties. At the end of this decade, Hans Syz (1928) proposed that group offered opportunities that mirrored patients outside lives and highlighted here-and-now interventions as a group method to capitalize on this fact. He believed that if one could focus on here-and-now exchanges in the group, thereby shifting dysfunctional interpersonal patterns through insight and acquisition of skills, one ultimately would positively affect the lives of members outside of the group.

The 1930s saw group therapy coming of age with Jacob Moreno, who had been experimenting with psychodrama since 1908, coining the term *group therapy* in 1932 at an American Psychiatric Association conference in Philadelphia. The same year, he published a book explicating the theoretical underpinnings of group therapy, incorporating group dynamics observations made by earlier writers (Moreno & Whitin, 1932). Dreikurs (1959)—Alfred Adler's protégé—described the positive power of group influence for change and as a mirror for patient's family of origin. He is credited with running the first private therapy groups in the 1930s, while Sam Slavson (1943) began treating disturbed children in "activity group therapy" during the same decade. Marsh (1931, 1933) is credited with milieu therapy, using these large groups to stimulate patient emotion and involvement with their treatment. He coined the oft-cited phrase, "By the crowd they have been broken, by the crowd they shall be healed." Marsh believed that healing could be attributed to the interpersonal interactions between group members.

Within a 25-year span, group therapy was championed as a cost-effective format, integrated into the dominant treatment of the day (psychoanalysis), and developed into a new model on the basis of its unique therapeutic properties. These three perspectives on group therapy (cost effective, format to deliver an existing therapy, and a unique therapeutic approach) would continue into the succeeding decades, thereby creating a tension that would spawn active debate and separate professional societies.

1940s–1970s: EXPANSION OF GROUP MODELS AND PRACTICE

Several contextual factors are important in understanding the development of group therapy over the next 4 decades (1940s–1970s). The first is the multiplication of several group psychoanalytic models differentiated by how they focused on individual versus group dynamics. A second contextual factor was the emergence of competing psychotherapies including the gestalt, humanistic, behavioral, interpersonal, and cognitive. Each of these new theories embraced the group format in varying degrees, ranging from using it as a cost-effective treatment to capitalizing on its unique therapeutic potential. A third factor was the social–psychological study of small groups that spawned a host of group models that impacted nonclinical populations. These included training- or T-groups, sensitivity groups, and encounter groups. Finally, group therapy was pushed into the forefront of clinical practice by mental health supply–demand imbalances during this time period. Key imbalances included the demand by veterans of World War II for service during the 1940s (Kline & Dreyfus, 1948) and later pressures emerging in the 1970s from publically funded mental health services that relied heavily on group therapy (e.g., state hospitals, community mental health centers).

Psychoanalytic Group Models

A useful yet admittedly simplified method to differentiate the psychoanalytic groups that came of age during the 1940s–1970s is by their focus on individual versus group dynamics. Slavson (1950, 1964), who founded the American Group Psychotherapy Association in 1943, was a self-taught psychoanalyst who focused on the individual over the group dynamics. Although he is credited with coining the term *group dynamic*, he believed that such phenomena could interfere with individual analysis in a group and viewed the intensity of transference as diminished by the group. Alexander Wolf (1949) also emphasized the importance of the individual psychoanalysis in a group using interpretation of transference, dreams, and the relationship of the past to the present for each individual member. Unlike Slavson, he believed that depth analysis was enhanced by the group environment because of the multiple transferences created by the presence of other group members. He saw the group analysts' task as fostering healthy individual ego and not necessarily the quality of the group effort.

Another set of psychoanalytic writers viewed the interactive properties of the group as a whole as a critical component of the treatment process. Foulkes (1949) worked with veterans from the World War II and embraced gestalt psychology's position that the group was more than the sum of its parts (individual members). He believed that group members could not be understood unless their interactions with each other were taken into consideration. For instance, an individual's dysfunction would appear as the figure or focus, whereas group interaction reflected the ground or context of group exchange. Bion (1961), working with a similar population, expanded on the importance of the group as a whole by suggesting that successful negotiation of group tasks were critical for individual member change. He believed that all groups have three unconscious "basic assumptions" (dependency, flight/fight, and pairing) and that resolution of these as a group paved the way for group and individual therapeutic change. Whitaker and Lieberman (1964) introduced a similar notion with the group focal conflict and postulated that most member activity was intended to solve this conflict. Like Bion, successful resolution of the focal conflict was viewed as a precondition for individual member change.

Emerging Psychotherapy Models

The second epoch also saw the development of a number of new therapeutic approaches that typically originated as individual treatments and were then applied in a group format. This period also spawned two professional associations for group therapists. One emphasized treating individuals in a group, whereas the second advocated the importance of the group as a whole. Indeed, this theme (emphasis on individual vs. group) could be used to distinguish group therapy models for the next 70 years.

The American Society for Group Psychotherapy and Psychodrama (ASGPP; http://www.asgpp.org), founded by Moreno in 1942, was the first professional association for group therapists. Psychodrama—a core emphasis of ASGPP—was intended to alleviate emotional distress by reenacting a member's troublesome relationships with the remaining group members "standing in" as significant others (Moreno, 1946). As a short-term group, it emphasized activity, spontaneity, and creativity. The formality of the therapist role in psychoanalysis was replaced in psychodrama by the therapist becoming a director and the patient role reframed as the protagonist who was working through normal life challenges. Within a year of Moreno starting ASGPP, Slavson organized the American Group Psychotherapy Association (AGPA; http://www.agpa.org). The origins of AGPA were clearly psychoanalytic, with an emphasis on treating individuals in a group. AGPA continues to foster a psychodynamic tradition but has evolved into a multidisciplinary society embracing a broad spectrum of approaches.

During the 1940s–1950s, two therapeutic approaches were developed that contributed to the group therapy literature and to the encounter group movement of the 1960s–1970s. Fritz Perls and colleagues (Perls, Hefferline, & Goodman, 1951) began developing gestalt therapy, which shared similarities with psychodrama. For instance, patient roles were reframed as members who were healthy people experiencing problems in living, and the therapist was viewed as someone assisting members to alleviate blocks or areas of avoidance. Like psychodrama, gestalt therapy was a short-term intervention in which the therapist worked in rounds with one member at a time who wanted to "work"; remaining group members provided an empathic background of support. Members in the "hot seat" took a small portion of the group session, enabling three to six members to participate in group session. However, gestalt group therapy's popularity would await Perls's (1969) move to Esalen Institute in the 1960s.

During the same time frame, Carl Rogers (1951) developed his client-centered therapy. In the early 1950s, Roger's method was integrated as a group therapy and successfully applied to a variety of clinical populations (elderly people, inpatients, handicapped children). The therapeutic relationship was permissive, with a strong emphasis on the clients' internal frame of reference. Rogers espoused a deep sense of trust in the group's organic ability to move in a therapeutic direction. Although client-centered groups had a significant clinical impact, Rogers had an equal impact through his contributions to the encounter group literature.

Arnold Lazarus's (1961) was one of the first to use behavior group therapy (systematic desensitization) to treat members with similar anxieties. Noting an imbalance in mental health service supply and demand, he saw a "double economy" in combining short-term behavior therapy with the time-efficient modality of group. Ozne of his first group studies involved 35 middle class South Africans with phobic disorders who were randomly assigned to desensitization, interpretive, or interpretive-relaxation groups. He found that patients in the behavioral groups produced superior results when assessed by in vivo stress tolerance tests. Five years later, Paul and Shannon (1966) extended Lazarus's research by comparing three individual treatments (systematic desensitization, insight oriented, and placebo attention) with group desensitization. The desensitization group included four sessions of re-educative discussion in which the leader intervened by "generalizing from one client's remarks; emphasizing similarities between problems, experiences, emotions, etc.; referring questions to the group" (p. 128). They found that the combined behavioral group therapy condition produced superior outcomes in treating social anxiety compared with control and alternative treatment groups; gains were maintained for up to 2 years.

The 1970s produced two therapies that would become highly influential in later years: Yalom's interpersonal group therapy and the cognitive–behavioral models of Ellis, Beck, and Meichenbaum. In 1970, Irvin Yalom published what would become a classic textbook on group therapy—*Theory and*

Practice of Group Psychotherapy. Trained in the Sullivan interpersonal tradition, Yalom saw member-to-member interaction as key for change. Yalom refined and advanced earlier writers understanding of how here-and-now interventions could modify maladaptive interpersonal patterns and perceptual distortions. Interpersonal feedback, consensual validation, and self-observation were key processes to assist members in addressing the perceptual distortions that support maladaptive interpersonal patterns. Now in its fifth edition, Yalom's (2005) text remains as one of the most popular texts and frequently cited references (3,598 citations; http://scholar.google.com, retrieved May 12, 2009). By contrast, the work of Aaron Beck (1976), Donald Meichenbaum (Meichenbaum & Genest, 1977), and Albert Ellis (1962, 1992) emphasized a cognitive model: Psychological disturbance is tied to the way that a client thinks about life events and circumstances. Starting in the late 1970s, cognitive–behavioral groups were routinely used for the treatment of anxiety (e.g., Meichenbaum & Genest, 1977; Meichenbaum, Gilmore, & Fedoravicius, 1971).

Social Psychology Groups

An important development for group therapy emerged from Kurt Lewin, one of the parents of social psychology. Lewin with three colleagues (Bradford, Lippitt, and Benne) applied group dynamic principles to promote social change, postulating that an individual had to be understood within his or her social environment. In so doing, they created the National Training Laboratory movement in the 1940s. Lewin's groups were known as *T-groups* and contributed to Lewin's (1951) field theory of group dynamics. In the 1950s–1960s, the focus of T-groups shifted from social change to personal growth and were relabeled as *sensitivity and encounter groups*. The goals of these groups were to help members develop sensitivity and awareness of their own feelings and reactions, increase their understanding of group interactions, and learn to modify their behavior. The focus on thoughts, feelings, and behaviors in a given moment paralleled the here and now emphasis of group therapy.

There was a virtual explosion of practice and research on these experiential groups in the 1960s and 1970s that eclipsed group therapy writings in size and influence. It appeared that group therapy was merging with experiential groups; many notable therapists (e.g., Carl Rogers, 1970) joined in the development of the encounter group movement (Schutz, 1967). Indeed, Perls's gestalt therapy was popularized when he moved to the Esalen Institute, a training center for encounter and sensitivity groups in the 1960s. Theoretical constructs for effective groups were spawned by social psychologists and then studied by psychologists in encounter, sensitivity, and therapy groups. Reviews of the group therapy literature during this time period (Bednar & Kaul, 1978; Bednar & Lawlis, 1971) merged findings from therapy and encounter group research as if they were interchangeable. The late 1960s–1970s was a confusing time for the group therapy literature; the fusion of experiential and therapy group led to a partial identity crisis.

Although there were similarities in themes between the first and second epochs—cost-efficiency, integration of group into existing models, and new group treatments—there were significant differences. The second epoch brought greater (a) theoretical and empirical clarity regarding groups therapeutic mechanism of change from both the clinical (e.g., Corsini & Rosenberg, 1955) and experiential group literature (e.g., Lieberman et al., 1973), (b) specificity for targeting specific disorders with specific treatments, especially behavioral and cognitive therapies, and (c) rigor and control in research designs. These advances set the stage for the last 30 years of research and application.

1980s–2009: ERA OF SPECIFIC GROUPS FOR SPECIFIC POPULATIONS

Up to this point, the identity of most group therapies was organized around a theoretical orientation (humanistic, experiential, interpersonal, process, or psychodynamic groups). This led to conclusions on the general effectiveness of groups without regard for diagnostic or patient population considerations. The change in determining the effectiveness of specific groups for specific mental health needs forced a shift in how group therapy was conceptualized to who was being treated followed by the group approach, which often left the discussion of group processes as a final consideration.

Evidence of the change to specific patient populations is reflected by research published during this period. A review of 400 studies from 1980–1992 identified 30 distinct client populations being treated by group therapies (Fuhriman & Burlingame, 1994). The cognitive–behavioral therapies were applied five times more frequently across these client populations than other types of groups (client centered, psychodrama, gestalt). Conclusions regarding group therapy's effectiveness were summarized from 10 separate reviews covering depression, eating disorders, bereavement, schizophrenia, and elderly people. Superior outcomes were reported over inert control groups, and group proved comparable with or superior to other active treatments. However, seven meta-analyses that compared the differential effectiveness of group and individual revealed four reporting no difference and three favoring individual over group.

The next decade, Burlingame, MacKenzie, and Strauss (2004) summarized 107 studies and 14 meta-analyses across six disorders (mood, anxiety, eating, substance abuse, personality, and psychotic disorders) and four patient populations (older people, domestic violence, sexual abuse, and medical illness) published from 1990 to 2001 and found a similar pattern favoring the frequency with which cognitive, behavioral, and cognitive–behavioral group therapies were being studied The same 5:1 ratio favoring the number of cognitive–behaviorial studies over alternate group approaches was found for mood, anxiety, and eating-disorder treatments. The study of alternative group models (e.g., process, interpersonal) occurred more frequently with other patient populations (e.g., trauma, substance abuse), but cognitive–behaviorial therapies still maintained a presence with these populations. General conclusions on effectiveness found that the amount of improvement varied by patient populations. For instance, cognitive–behavioral therapies received high marks in treating social phobia, whereas in other instances (mood and eating disorders) multiple treatment approaches appeared to produce similar gains. Other diagnostic indications produced promising gains (obsessive–compulsive and substance use disorders), but others were in need of further development (domestic violence and trauma).

The greater specificity of treatments applied to distinct patient populations appeared to have opened up new territory for systematic study of the mechanisms enabling investigators to programmatically test links between pretreatment and in-session process variables with overall improvement. Thus, over the past 20 years, there has been a resurrection of sorts in the study of the unique and defining features of group therapy using programmatic and sophisticated research. Topics such as therapeutic factors (e.g., cohesion), group development, and member interaction have found refined measurement and application as treatments and populations become more distinct. Indeed, in a recent review (Burlingame, Fuhriman & Johnson, 2004), the strength of evidence for 11 group properties was summarized using a four-fold classification scheme (group structure, verbal interaction, therapeutic relationship, and therapeutic factors). Group properties with very good to excellent research support include the systematic use of member-to-member interpersonal feedback and the therapeutic alliance. Factors with promising to good empirical support include pregroup preparation (induction), early group structure, leader verbal style, group climate, and the differential effect of therapeutic factors on the basis of the treatment setting.

FUTURE DIRECTIONS FOR GROUP THERAPY

We are optimistic about the practice of group therapy after a century of development. Specifically, we envision the evidence-based group clinician of the future accessing three types of resources to guide practice. The first is the host of treatments that have been tested for efficacy/effectiveness with distinct populations. The current literature has retraced Pratt's footsteps; he began using group as a cost-efficient approach and ended by developing a group treatment for a distinct clinical population (e.g., Bieling, McCable, & Antony, 2006; White & Freeman, 2000). The second type of resource is practice guidelines published by group therapy associations. For instance, a free download of a practice guideline from AGPA (http://www. agpa.org/guidelines/ index.html) is available for clinicians who practice dynamic, interactional, and relational group psychotherapy. The collective goal of these endeavors is to provide the group therapist with a general evidence-based group structure. A third resource for the evidence-based clinician lies in the emerging field of practice-based evidence, which is the real-time tracking of patient outcomes. At a minimum, it requires the repeated use of an outcome measure that is sensitive to change and reflects the outcomes expected from a group treatment. This type of evidence-based practice is an emerging field but at least one group organization has begun considering it. In 2006, AGPA offered a battery of selection, process, and outcome measures for group clinicians who are interested in empirically tracking the effectiveness of their groups (http://www. agpa.org/pubs/pubsaleold.html).

The past 100 years have seen remarkable accomplishments since Pratt began his experiment with tuberculosis patients. Clinicians have available to them an array of evidence-based treatments for the most common diagnostic presentations and further options for calibrating their practices using evidence-based resources. We envision continued advances in improving the effectiveness of group-based treatments.

REFERENCES

Beck, A. (1976). *Cognitive therapy and the emotional disorders*. New York, NY: International University Press.

Bednar, R., & Kaul, T. (1978). Experiential group research: Current perspectives. In S. Garfield & A. Bergin (Eds.), *Handbook of psychotherapy and behavior change: An empirical analysis* (2nd ed., pp. 769–815). New York, NY: Wiley.

Bednar, R., & Lawlis, G. (1971). Empirical research in group psychotherapy. In A. Bergin & S. Garfield (Eds.), *Handbook of psychotherapy and behavior change* (pp. 812–838). New York, NY: Wiley.

Bieling, P., McCable, R., & Antony, M. (2006). *Cognitive-behavioral therapy in groups*. New York, NY: Guilford Press.

Bion, W. (1961). *Experiences in groups*. New York, NY: Basic Books.

Burlingame, G., Fuhriman, A., & Johnson, J. (2004). Process and outcome in group psychotherapy: A perspective. In J. DeLucia-Waack, C. Kalodner, & M. Riva (Eds.), *Handbook of group work* (pp. 49–61). Thousand Oaks, CA: Sage.

Burlingame, G. M., MacKenzie, K. R., & Strauss, B. (2004). Small group treatment: Evidence for effectiveness and mechanisms of change. In M. J. Lambert (Ed.), *Bergin & Garfield's* handbook of psychotherapy and behavior change (5th ed., pp. 647–696). New York, NY: Wiley.

Burrow, T. (1928). The basis of group-analysis, or the analysis of reactions of normal and neurotic individuals. British Journal of Medical Psychology, 8, 198–206.

Corsini, R., & Rosenberg, B. (1955). Mechanisms of group psychotherapy: Processes and dynamics. Journal of Abnormal and Social Psychology, 15, 406–411.

Dreikurs, R. (1959). Early experiments with group psychotherapy. American Journal of Psychotherapy, 13, 882–891.

Ellis, A. (1962). Reason and emotion in psychotherapy. New York, NY: Lyle Stuart Press.

Ellis, A. (1992). Group rational-emotive and cognitive-behavioral therapy. International Journal of Group Psychotherapy, 42, 63–80.

Foulkes, S. H. (1949). Introduction to group-analytic psychotherapy: Studies in the social integration of individual and groups. New York, NY: Grune & Stratton.

Fuhriman, A., & Burlingame, G. (1994). Group psychotherapy: Research and practice. In A. Fuhriman & G. Burlingame (Eds.), Handbook of group psychotherapy: An empirical and clinical synthesis (pp. 3–40). New York, NY: Wiley.

Kline, N. S., & Dreyfus, A. (1948). Group psychotherapy in veteran's administration hospitals. The American Journal of Psychiatry, 104, 618–622.

Lazarus, A. A. (1961). Group therapy of phobic disorders by systematic desensitization. Journal of Abnormal and Social Psychology, 63, 504–510. doi:10.1037/h0043315

Lazell, E. W. (1921). The group treatment of dementia praecox. Psychoanalytic Review, 8, 168–179.

Lieberman, M., Yalom, I., & Miles, M. (1973). Encounter groups: First facts. New York, NY: Basic Books.

Lewin, K. (1951). Field theory in social science. New York, NY: Harper.

Marsh, L. C. (1931). Group treatment for the psychoses by the psychological equivalent of the revival. Mental Hygiene, 15, 328–349.

Marsh, L. C. (1933). An experiment in group treatment of patients at Worchester State Hospital. Mental Hygiene, 17, 396–416.

Meichenbaum, D., & Genest, M. (1977). Treatment of anxiety. In G. Harris (Ed.), The group treatment of human problems: A social learning approach (pp. 3–15). New York, NY: Grune & Stratton.

Meichenbaum, D. H., Gilmore, B., & Fedoravicius, A. (1971). Group insight versus group desensitization in treating speech anxiety. Journal of Consulting and Clinical Psychology, 36, 410–421. doi:10.1037/h0031112

Moreno, J. L. (1946). Psychodrama (Vol. 1). New York, NY: Beacon House.

Moreno, J. L., & Whitin, E. (1932). Application of the group method to classification. New York, NY: National Commission on Prison and Prison Labor.

Paul, G. L., & Shannon, D. (1966). Treatment of anxiety through systematic desensitization in therapy groups. Journal of Abnormal Psychology, 71, 124–135. doi:10.1037/h0023172

Perls, F. (1969). Ego, hunger and aggression: The beginning of gestalt therapy. New York, NY: Random House.

Perls, F., Hefferline, R., & Goodman, P. (1951). Gestalt therapy: Excitement and growth in the human personality. New York, NY: Dell.

Pratt, J. H. (1907). The organization of tuberculosis classes. Medical communications of the Massachusetts Medical Society, 20, 475–492.

Pratt, J. H. (1945). Group method in the treatment of psychosomatic disorders. Sociometry, 8, 323–331.

Rogers, C. (1951). Client-centered therapy. Boston, MA: Houghton-Mifflin.

Rogers, C. (1970). *Carl Rogers on encounter groups*. New York, NY: Harper & Row.

Schutz, W. (1967). *Joy: Expanding human awareness*. New York, NY: Grove Press.

Slavson, S. R. (1943). *An introduction to group therapy*. New York, NY: Commonwealth Fund. doi:10.1037/10637-000

Slavson, S. R. (1950). *Analytic group psychotherapy*. New York, NY: Commonwealth Fund.

Slavson, S. R. (1964). *A textbook in analytic group psychotherapy*. New York, NY: International Universities Press.

Syz, H. (1928). Remarks on group analysis. *American Journal of Psychiatry, 85*, 141–148.

Whitaker, D. S., & Lieberman, M. A. (1964). *Psychotherapy through the group process*. New York, NY: Atherton Press.

White, J., & Freeman, A. (2000). *Cognitive-behavioral group therapy*. Washington, DC: American Psychological Association. doi:10.1037/10352-000

Wolf, A. (1949). The psychoanalysis of groups. *American Journal of Psychotherapy, 3*, 525–558.

Yalom, I. D. (1970). *The theory and practice of group psychotherapy*. New York, NY: Basic Books.

Yalom, I. (with Leszcz, M.). (2005). *The theory and practice of group psychotherapy* (5th ed.). New York, NY: Basic Books.

Pharmacotherapy

Morgan T. Sammons

Over the past 60 years, advances in understanding of the neurobiological mechanisms associated with mental disorders have led to the development of a large number of pharmacological interventions. Since the beginning of the modern psychopharmacological era in the early 1950s, psychotropics have been among the most commonly prescribed drugs of any class. The increase in the use of drugs to treat mental disorders has been particularly evident in the decades following the introduction of the first selective serotonin reuptake inhibitor (SSRI) fluoxetine (Prozac and others) in the late 1980s. It is no surprise to find, then, that pharmacotherapy is today the most common form of treatment for mental disorders and that the use of pharmacological treatments has come at the expense of psychotherapy. During the 1990s, for example, the proportion of individuals treated for depression who received an antidepressant rose from 37% to 74%. At the same time, the use of psychotherapy declined from 71% to 60%. As a result, treatment for depression was more commonly provided by physicians than by mental health providers (Olfson et al., 2002).

This pattern persists into the present. In 2007, antidepressants were the most commonly prescribed drug in the United States (IMS Health, 2007). Nor is the high use of antidepressants or other psychotropics an American phenomenon. A recent study of Australian women found that antidepressants were the most commonly prescribed drug for women ages 30 to 35 years (they were also common among older women, with prevalence increasing with age; Byles et al., 2008). Antidepressant or antipsychotic drugs are almost always listed among the top 10 selling drugs both within the United States and in the global market.

In this chapter, I briefly trace the history of pharmacotherapy for mental disorders. Given space limitations, the chapter is restricted to an analysis of the three most commonly used classes of agents: anxiolytics, antidepressants, and antipsychotics. Then, I quickly limn the ascendancy of prescriptive authority for psychologists.

THREE PARADOXES

In spite of the increased emphasis placed on drug treatment of mental disorders, several key paradoxes remain. First, psychotropics are not curative agents. They can ameliorate many symptoms of a disorder such as depression or schizophrenia but never correct the neurobiological dysregulation that might have a role in the production of the disorder's symptoms. Thus, an antipsychotic may help a schizophrenic patient to be less troubled by auditory hallucinations or paranoid delusions, but those symptoms, however subdued, remain present. When the patient stops taking the drug, symptoms almost always recur and, without effective psychosocial intervention, long-term outcomes for patients who take psychotropics are frequently no better than for those patients who have never taken them. Paradoxically, however, psychotropic medications remain the mainstay and often the only treatment offered to patients with mental illness.

Second, the mechanism of action of most psychotropics has yet to be fully explained. Although certain of their effects are easily observed, such as an increase or decrease in the amount of a particular neurotransmitter at the synaptic junction, the contribution of this or any other particular effect in improving the symptoms of a disorder is still mostly unknown. It is telling that after 60 years of research, a single unifying explanation for the mechanism of action of most common psychotropics remains elusive (the benzodiazepine anxiolytics are an exception to this observation). Older hypotheses, such as the monoamine hypothesis of depression that held low synaptic levels of the monoaminergic neurotransmitters like serotonin and norepinephrine to be responsible for the behavioral and cognitive features of the disorder, or the dopamine hypothesis of schizophrenia that posited excess activity of dopamine in certain neural tracts to be causal of at least the positive symptoms of psychosis, have been demonstrated to have only limited explanatory power.

A third paradox also persists: In spite of numerous advances in the pharmacology of psychotropic agents, their efficacy has remained overall unchanged. The most recently released antidepressant drug is not likely to be any more effective in treating symptoms than imipramine (sold under the brand of Tofranil and others), the first commonly available antidepressant in the early 1960s. With few exceptions, the same holds true for any other class of psychotropic: Newer mood stabilizers and antipsychotics are no more effective than the first agent of their respective class (lithium and chlorpromazine). This is not to say that the efforts of psychopharmacologists over the past half century have been in vain. Newer drugs are generally far less toxic than their earlier cousins. The first antidepressants, for example, were extraordinarily lethal in overdose and a reliable means of suicide for depressed patients. The introduction of relatively safe antidepressants like fluoxetine revolutionized the treatment of depression and made antidepressants available to a far larger proportion of the population. Newer agents also tend to have less vexacious side-effect profiles, enhancing patient acceptance of and adherence to a drug regimen. New delivery mechanisms, such as extended-release preparations or transdermal routes of administration, have also improved ease of administration and patient acceptance of these drugs. But we are left with the unrelenting observation that in spite of these advances, the latest antidepressant or antipsychotic is no more efficacious than its mid-20th century ancestor.

HISTORY OF MODERN PHARMACOTHERAPY

Although Macht coined the term *psychopharmacology* in 1921 (Healy, 2002), the beginning of modern clinical psychopharmacology dates to the 1930s, when pharmaceutical-company interest in pursuing treatments for depression was piqued by exploration of the psychotropic effects of the amphetamines. Amphetamines today are principally used as a treatment for attention-deficit/hyperactivity disorder, but earlier in the 20th century benzedrine, after initially being marketed as a nasal decongestant, was promoted as a treatment for mild, or psychoneurotic, depression (Rasmussen, 2008). Many current controversies in psychopharmacology, including questions of the utility of a drug for a particular disorder or attempts to expand a clinical condition in order to improve drug sales, are reflected in this early clinical history. In the case of benzedrine, it became clear rather early that stimulants were of limited efficacy in treating severe depressive conditions. The drug was accordingly marketed as a treatment for mild depression or anhedonia—a diagnosis that did not previously exist (Rasmussen, 2008).

It is tempting to ascribe the enduring nature of such controversies to pharmaceutical manufacturers' attempts to maximize profits on patented agents, but the reality is more complex. Numerous factors influence our view of psychopharmacological treatment, among them the limitations posed by a diagnostic nosology that is acknowledged to be imprecise but yet often forces artificial distinctions between common mental disorders (e.g., consideration of anxiety and depression as separate disorders rather than points on a continuum; Shorter & Tyrer, 2003). Additionally, as we have said, treatment with psychotropics is almost always less than definitive. Symptoms improve but rarely resolve with drug treatment, making the calculation of risks and benefits associated with pharmacological treatment an essential clinical consideration. Finally, the view by some professionals (e.g., Keen, 2000) that the choice to use psychotropics is in some manner a moral decision (e.g., the belief that it is morally better to seek relief via psychotherapy than via the use of pharmacology) adds yet another complexity.

The modern psychopharmacological era can be divided into five distinct periods of drug development and clinical practice. In the next few paragraphs, I introduce these periods and then discuss them more fully in the context of each of the three major classes of drugs that make up this chapter. The first phase existed prior to the 1950s, when few effective pharmacological interventions were available. Nonspecific sedating compounds (opiates, bromides, barbiturates) were used to control mania or psychosis (lithium was introduced into clinical practice in the latter part of the 1800s, but for various reasons fell out of favor and was not widely seen again for decades). Institutional treatment and invasive interventions (insulin coma, electroconvulsive therapy, lobotomy) for these conditions or severe depression restricted treatment to the more seriously ill.

The second period started in the 1950s, a period of tremendous pharmacological innovation and one that heralded the introduction of the first effective drug treatment for several disorders. Lithium was reintroduced into clinical practice in 1949, followed in short order by chlorpromazine (brand name of Thorazine in the United States; 1952), reserpine (1954), meprobamate (branded as Miltown, among others; 1956), and in 1957, imipramine and iproniazid (Ban, 2001). Thorazine was the first truly effective agent in managing the delusions and agitation that accompanies many psychotic disorders. The anxiolytic meprobamate (Miltown) was marketed in such a fashion that it became the first "mass-market" psychotropic. Imipramine and iproniazid were the first of the current generation of antidepressant agents, representing the tricyclic antidepressants (TCAs) and monoamine oxidase inhibitors (MAOIs).

A third period of "in-class" drug development then prevailed from the early 1960s to the late 1980s or early 1990s. This period was characterized by the expansion of pharmacological options but almost always within the same class as the index agent introduced in the 1950s. It was also marked by the rapid growth of biological models of mental disorders and their treatment. Imipramine was joined by numerous other tricyclic antidepressants that varied slightly in their chemical composition, giving some a modestly different side-effect profile. In general, however, side effects did not differ significantly between TCAs. Several new MAOIs were introduced. This again produced some minor variability in side-effect profiles but no improvement in effectiveness. With the exception of the introduction of the antidepressant trazodone (Desyrel) in 1982, the antidepressant market continued to be dominated by the TCAs until the introduction of the first SSRI. This period saw the emergence of biological models of mental disorders that competed for dominance and eventually banished earlier psychodynamic explanations of mental disorders. The monoaminergic hypothesis of depression was introduced and elaborated during this period. The most well-known example of this revolution in our conceptualization of mental disorders is the dopamine- or neurotransmitter-based hypothesis of schizophrenia that emerged in the early 1960s and competed with earlier models based on theories of maternal distance or rejection.

A fourth period began with the introduction of a second generation of many psychotropics, accompanied by extraordinary expansion of their use, consolidation of the biological model of mental disorders, and deemphasis on psychotherapy. The index event for this period was, as noted earlier, the introduction of the first SSRI, fluoxetine (Prozac). Fluoxetine achieved the greatest notoriety of these second generation agents, but similar transformations were occurring with other drug classes. In the mid-1990s, a new class of antipsychotic drugs emerged. These drugs, although of no greater efficacy than their earlier counterparts, were and remain so popular that they continue to dominate the antipsychotic marketplace. Earlier antipsychotics were principally thought to work via inhibition of postsynaptic dopaminergic neurotransmission. Even though these drugs were active at multiple receptor sites other than dopamine, the prevailing theory of dopaminergic imbalance led investigators to focus almost exclusively on this aspect of their functioning. But the arrival of fluoxetine and the corresponding prominence of a serotonergic hypothesis of depression led to a reconsideration of the role of other neurotransmitters in psychotic disorders, spurring the development of a second group of antipsychotics that bore closer chemical resemblance to clozapine, a known antipsychotic that had both more serotonergic activity and greater differential efficacy than dopaminergic agents. Clozapine had been synthesized in 1961 and was first used clinically in the 1970s, but continued fears about its toxicity have restricted its use, and most of the newer antipsychotics such as risperidone (Risperdal) and olanzapine (Zyprexa) were developed in an attempt to create a less-toxic, clozapine-like drug.

The fifth and current period in psychopharmacotherapy is characterized by stasis. Few novel psychotropics lie on the horizon. No new class of any agent has been clinically developed. All recently marketed psychotropics are either variants of extant drugs or, in a few instances, drugs relabeled for a mental disorder. The MAOI selegeline, for example, first developed to treat symptoms of Parkinson's disease, is now also sold as the antidepressant Emsam. The current period also reflects a growing skepticism about the explanatory power of biological models, accumulating evidence of the limits of pharmacological intervention, and a renewed interest in combining pharmacological and nonpharmacological interventions.

We see then that the historical development of pharmacotherapy for mental disorders has strikingly common characteristics, regardless of which mental disorder or medication class is under consideration. First, an index drug or class of agents is introduced that has some efficacy but significant toxicity or problematic side effects. Its use is therefore limited to a relatively restricted range of patients, generally with more severe variants of a disorder, with treatment provided almost exclusively by psychiatry. Second, a new class of psychotropics is introduced that is chemically related to earlier drugs but having properties that make them generally less toxic than their predecessors. Often, these drugs have more specific biological mechanisms of action. Although they tend to be no more efficacious than their progenitors, enhanced safety or flexibility in administration leads to an explosion of use in nonspecialty mental health settings, usually for conditions not originally thought to be responsive to pharmacological treatment or for which there is less than compelling evidence of their utility. Third, increasing questions emerge about both the evidence supporting the use of such agents and the opportunity costs associated with displacement of nonpharmacological treatments in preference for newer and more costly medications.

ANXIOLYTICS

The anxiolytics provide a good example of the prototypical trajectory of psycho-pharmaceutical development and clinical use. Because humans in general crave sedation or a reduction in anxiety, a variety of compounds, from alcohol to cannabis to opiates to today's anxiolytics, have been used throughout history for this purpose.

In recent times, anxiolytic pharmacology was typified by either opiates or bromides (bromides are sedating metallic salts, and their chronic use could lead to a toxic condition called *bromism*, marked by tremor, muscular discoordination, cognitive impairment, and hallucinations). In the first half of the 20th century, bromides were replaced by the barbiturates, which are highly effective at promoting sedation or sleep but habit forming and extremely lethal in overdose, particularly when combined with alcohol or other sedatives. The introduction of meprobamate (Miltown) in the mid-1950s was a watershed moment in the history of psychopharmacology. Meprobamate, although closely related to the barbiturate anxiolytics then in use for anxiety and insomnia and like those drugs possessing significant risks of dependence and toxicity in overdose, soon became the most highly prescribed medication of any class. It was marketed in such a fashion that it became an acceptable treatment not just for those defined as having mental illness but also for harried executives and stressed housewives as well, thereby becoming one of the first "popular" or mass market psychotropics. Presaging the public interest surrounding the introduction of fluoxetine (Prozac) 3 decades later, Miltown became a staple item of the culture of the day and was the subject of extensive comment in the popular press as a "miracle cure" for psychoneurotic depression (e.g., *Happiness by Prescription*, 1957).

In 1960, the first benzodiazepine, chlordiazepoxide (Librium), was introduced. Chlordiazepoxide had a specific mechanism of action and had a much lower toxicity index. From the 1960s through the 1990s, numerous other benzodiazepines were introduced, all with some differences in the terms of their pharmacological properties but essentially variations of the benzodiazepine nucleus. Drugs like diazepam (Valium) became the most highly used agent of any class and captured the attention of the media as a drug useful for managing the quotidian stressors of American life. Again, concerns about overprescription, dependence, and abuse led to increased regulatory action and an eventual souring of professional and public opinion regarding these agents. (A nonbenzodiazepine anxiolytic, buspirone [BuSpar], was introduced in the mid-1980s but was less efficacious than benzodiazepines and failed to capture a significant market.)

In the 1990s, a class of agents called GABA receptor agonists (GRAs) was introduced, specifically to combat insomnia. These drugs, including zolpidem (Ambien), do not chemically resemble benzodiazepines. In low doses, they have a specific mechanism of action at the alpha-1 subunit of the GABA receptor complex, causing a relatively specific effect (sleep induction). Benzodiazepines are active at this site but also at others on the receptor complex and therefore have multiple effects (relaxation of skeletal muscles, anxiolysis, cognitive slowing). At higher doses, the action and clinical effects of the GRAs are essentially identical to those of the benzodiazepines, and dose for dose they are not more effective in promoting sleep than benzodiazepines. But their specificity of action simplifies their administration for insomnia (most have very short half lives, preventing unwanted daytime sedation) and help diminish the unwanted side effects of benzodiazepines (muscular incoordination and cognitive slowing), so they represent a clinical advance over earlier agents in the treatment of insomnia.

Like benzodiazepines, these drugs soon became extraordinarily widely prescribed. Although they remain popular, concerns about side effects such as behavioral disinhibition and memory problems, along with the observation that behavioral interventions are more effective long-term treatments for insomnia, have led to a reevaluation of their place in therapy.

Thus, the historical trajectory of the modern anxiolytics—replacement of more toxic alternatives, increased specificity of action, and ease of administration not necessarily accompanied by increase in efficacy, followed by excessive clinical utilization and later questions about their role in treatment—replicates that characteristic of all other classes of psychotropics. The remainder of this chapter provides a history and evaluation of arguably the two most important advances in psychopharmacology over the past half century—the antidepressants and antipsychotics.

ANTIDEPRESSANTS

Modern pharmacological treatment of depression is commonly said to have begun with the clinical introduction of the MAOI iproniazid, a chemical derivative of hydrazine. Hydrazine, used as a rocket propellant by German engineers during World War II, was in abundant supply in the postwar period and had been investigated for a number of potential pharmaceutical applications including the treatment of tuberculosis. The hydrazine isoniazid is still in use for this purpose today (Callahan & Berrios, 2005; Healy, 1997). Iproniazid represented the first specific antidepressant.

Iproniazid did not achieve wide clinical use and has been widely discontinued because of a number of severe side effects, including hepatotoxicity and the occurrence of hypertensive episodes when foods containing tyramine were ingested (the so-called cheese effect). In the late 1950s, the first TCA, imipramine (branded as Tofranil), an antidepressant with a close clinical resemblance to the antipsychotic chlorpromazine, was clinically introduced in the United States, followed in 1961 by amitryptiline (branded as Elavil; Fangmann et al., 2008). These and other tricyclic compounds would dominate the antidepressant market for the next 2 decades until the search for an antidepressant lacking the toxicity and unpleasant anticholinergic side effects of the TCAs (dry mouth, sedation, weight gain, urinary retention, and other symptoms) resulted in the introduction of fluoxetine (marketed as Prozac) in the United States in 1987 (Wong, Perry, & Bymaster, 2005).

Fluoxetine was the first of the SSRIs that have dominated the antidepressant market since the late 1980s. Fluoxetine was followed by a number of other SSRIs, including sertraline (Zoloft), paroxetine (Paxil), citalopram (Celexa), and escitalopram (Lexapro). Although their efficacy was no greater than earlier antidepressants, their ease of administration, enhanced safety profile, and aggressive marketing (Berndt et al., 2002) facilitated their adoption by primary care providers who previously hesitated to use the TCAs. Between 1987 and 1997, the percentage of patients treated for depression who received a medication (predominantly an SSRI) almost doubled. This increase was accompanied by a decline in the use of psychotherapy and a decline in the percentage of depressed patients who received treatment from psychologists as opposed to physicians, from 30% to 20% (Olfson et al., 2002).

The explosive growth in antidepressant use has resulted in numerous controversies concerning not only the perceived overuse of antidepressants but also their safety and efficacy compared with nonbiological treatments or placebos. In particular, the use of antidepressants in children and adolescents has been increasingly questioned. During the 1990s, the increase in prescriptions of antidepressants for U.S. children and adolescents rose at a proportionately far greater rate than for adults (Zito et al., 2002). Prescriptions for antidepressants in adolescents are reported to have risen over 200% from the period 1994–2001, to the point that antidepressants were prescribed in 5.5% of all U.S. outpatient office visits for adolescents in 1999–2001 (Thomas, Conrad, Casler, & Goodman, 2006). This trend is true for classes of medication other than antidepressants, including psychostimulants and antipsychotics, and was mirrored, though to a considerably smaller degree, in prescribing patterns in European countries (Zito et al., 2008).

In 2003, reports of suicidal ideation and suicidal behavior in children or adolescents taking antidepressants began to emerge in the literature. In 2004, the U.S. Food and Drug Administration (FDA) issued a black box warning mandating that information be given to prescribers and consumers of a small but real risk of an increase in suicidal ideation or behavior in children taking such drugs. In 2007, this warning was expanded to include adults from the ages of 18 to 24 years (the warning may be found at http://www.fda.gov/CDER/Drug/antidepressants/antidepressants_label_change_2007.pdf). This warning has engendered a great deal of debate. Antidepressant use in adolescents declined sharply after the warning was published in 2004 (Gibbons, Hur, Bhaumik, & Mann, 2006; Kurian et al., 2007), and suicide rates in this population began to rise after a period of decline observed in the 1990s and early 2000s (National Center for Health Statistics, 2007). This has led to the inference that a rise in suicide rates was related to notable declines in antidepressant use observed after the warning was published (Friedman & Leon, 2007). Whether this is accurate is by no means clear, as the causes of suicidal behavior are complex and multidetermined; a causal association between a reduction in antidepressant prescribing and an increase in suicidal thinking or behavior is not demonstrable.

What is clear is that there was an unprecedented rise in the use of antidepressants in children and adolescents in the last decade of the 20th century. This use has abated somewhat in the past several years, possibly as a result of government regulatory warnings. The effects, either positive or negative, on children's mental health are as yet undecided (Sammons, 2009).

In tandem with the reduction in antidepressant prescriptions to children and adolescents, the rate of increase in the use of antidepressants in adults is slowing somewhat. Nevertheless, antidepressants remain the most prescribed class of any medication in the United States. Total prescriptions of antidepressants in 2007 were 232.7 million, an increase of 25.1 million annually over the 207.6 million prescriptions written for those drugs in 2003 (IMS Health, 2007). The market share of the SSRIs has declined in recent years as a new class of agent, the serotonin and norepinephrine reuptake inhibitors (SNRIs), typified by the drugs venlafaxine (Effexor) and duloxetine (Cymbalta), has entered the therapeutic armamentarium. These so-called dual action agents effect neurotransmission of norepinephrine to a greater degree than do the SSRIs, although their clinical efficacy is no greater than that of any earlier class of antidepressant.

The history of antidepressants illustrates the efficacy problem nicely. In spite of (or perhaps as a result of) the increasing specificity and sophistication of antidepressant agents, response rates have remained unchanged since the introduction of imipramine 50 years ago. Large, ecologically valid studies of antidepressant-treated patients (the STAR-D trials; e.g., Rush et al., 2006) verify that most patients do not show a robust clinical response to a trial of an antidepressant agent, and of those who do not respond to a first agent, fewer still show a positive response to a second agent, even if it is of a different class. The placebo response to antidepressants has also been repeatedly found to be enduring and strong. Significant numbers of depressed patients exposed to placebo rather than an active agent have demonstrated clinical improvement, although as a group more severely depressed patients have responded somewhat better to an active agent than a placebo (Kirsch et al., 2008).

How do we explain the stubborn resistance of depression to pharmacological developments? First, it is important to recognize that in spite of the increased ability of antidepressants to target certain neuronal processes, the mechanism of action of antidepressant drugs remains opaque. Another possible explanation lies in the limits of the monoamingeric hypothesis of depression. Current antidepressants target only monoamine neurotransmitters like serotonin and norepinephrine, and it is increasingly evident that these monoamines are not the final common neuronal mechanism associated with depression. Alternative hypotheses involve brain glucocorticoid imbalances, neurokinins like substance P, or neurohormones like brain-derived neurotrophic factor (Berton & Nestler, 2006). All of these hypotheses are under active investigation. Whether any will lead to more effective treatments for depression is presently unknown, but pharmacological breakthroughs in the short term seem unlikely.

In sum, the current state of pharmacological treatment of depression is static. No immediate pharmacological advances are apparent. Some skeptics might argue that to search for unified biological theories and a conclusive biological treatment is illusory, since the entity we have given the diagnostic appellation of *depression* is multifactorial in origin, presents with a multitude of psychological and physical symptoms unique to each sufferer, and, in the final analysis, will never be wholly responsive to biological interventions alone.

ANTIPSYCHOTICS

The developmental trajectory of effective antipsychotics is remarkably similar to that of antidepressants. Antipsychotic agents first came into common clinical use in the 1950s. Chlorpromazine, the first widely available antipsychotic, marketed in the United States as Thorazine, was introduced into the American market in 1952. Thorazine, a low-potency phenothiazine, was followed several years later by haloperidol (Haldol), a highly potent butyrophenone antipsychotic that became the mainstay of antipsychotic treatment for several decades. Although a variety of different phenothiazine compounds and different dosing preparations (such as depot, or long-acting formulations) were introduced, all were essentially variations on phenothiazines or butyrophenone preparations. The one exception was clozapine (Clozaril), an antipsychotic with a different chemical structure that was generally more effective than other existing medications. Introduced into European clinical practice in 1975 and quickly withdrawn because of toxic side effects, it came on the American market in 1989 but its use remains largely restricted to severe, refractory cases because of a negative side-effect profile including sedation, weight gain, hypotension, and sialorrhea (uncontrollable drooling). Its use is also associated with a severe depletion of certain types of white blood cells (agranulocytosis), leading to an immunosuppressed condition that is not infrequently fatal.

This changed dramatically in 1994, when risperidone (Risperdal), the first of the atypical or second generation antipsychotics (SGAs), was introduced. Structurally resembling clozapine but without the same risk of agranulocytosis, these agents were called *atypical* because their receptor occupancy profile differed substantially from earlier medications. Whereas phenothiazine and butyrophenone antipsychotics had much more affinity for blockade of the postsynaptic dopamine-2 (D2) receptor, SGAs had as much or greater affinity for serotonin and histamine receptors as they did for dopamine receptors. This resulted in a clinical side-effect profile that was dissimilar from earlier antipsychotics, although as was the case for the SSRI antidepressants, their clinical efficacy was no greater than the first generation of phenothiazine antipsychotics. Phenothiazines, particularly those of low to mid-potency, were marked by sedation, weight gain, and cardiac conduction irregularities. High-potency phenothiazines and haloperidol had a side-effect profile that was principally neuromuscular, marked by dystonias (muscular rigidity) and dyskinesias (abnormal muscle movements). Tremor, a shuffling gait, and other so-called drug-induced Parkinsonian-like symptoms were common, resulting in the need for adjunctive treatment with a variety of antiparkinsonian or anticholinergic agents. More serious adverse reactions, such as neuroleptic malignant syndrome (a rare but potentially fatal response to antipsychotics that causes an inability to regulate core body temperature and other basic physiological processes) and tardive dyskinesia (a permanent neuromuscular deficit appearing after long-term use) were less common but were among the principal clinical concerns limiting the use of these classes of antipsychotics.

It was hoped that the SGAs would allow patients to avoid the short- and long-term side effects of the first generation of antipsychotics and in particular to avoid the risk of tardive dyskinesia. Another early hope was that the SGAs would not only be more effective antipsychotics in general but would also be good treatments for the negative symptoms of schizophrenia—the apathy, social withdrawal, and indifference that earlier agents were ineffective in combating. Unfortunately, this was not the case, as SGAs appear to be no more effective in treating negative symptoms than were earlier drugs.

One important difference separates recent advances in antipsychotic drug development from that of other medication classes. Unlike the second generation of antidepressants (the SSRIs and SNRIs), the second generation of antipsychotic agents do not possess an enhanced safety profile over their earlier cousins. The incidence of severe or fatal side effects like neuroleptic malignant syndrome is lower than in the past, but this is probably attributable to less aggressive treatment strategies and the use of lower doses. Neuromuscular side effects and the risk of tardive dyskinesia appear to be lower with SGAs, but these problems still occur and are likely a dose-related phenomenon rather than an improved drug-safety profile. Like earlier antipsychotics, the SGAs are also cardiotoxic. Restrictions have been placed on use of some of the earlier and more cardiotoxic antipsychotics, such as thioridazine (Mellaril and others); nevertheless, the risk of cardiotoxic side effects associated with newer antipsychotics is present, and antipsychotic-related poisoning deaths have increased over the past decade (Flanagan, 2008).

Another set of side effects has also accompanied the SGAs and has been the source of successful litigation against their manufacturers—the so-called metabolic syndrome, marked by dysregulation of serum glucose and serum lipids. Although some have speculated that this was principally a result of the weight gain that is common with the SGAs, a separate and as yet undefined cause for the metabolic syndrome appears to be present. In 2008, the manufacturer of ziprasidone (Zyprexa) reached a $62M settlement with 32 states on the grounds that it had both promoted the drug for unapproved conditions (dementia, bipolar disorder) and that it had minimized the risk of metabolic syndrome as a consequence of taking the drug. Similar actions have been taken or are anticipated against other manufacturers of atypical antipsychotics (Goldstein, 2008).

Unlike antidepressants, then, for which the safety profile of second generation agents is demonstrably improved while efficacy remains constant, the same cannot be said of second generation antipsychotics. With neither improved efficacy nor more benign side effects, many (e.g., Charlton, 2005; Tiihonon et al., 2009) are questioning their role in the pharmacological management of psychotic disorders. Nevertheless, such agents have come to dominate the clinical management of the psychotic spectrum, in spite of their vastly increased cost over earlier agents, with explosive increases in their use for nonpsychotic disorders.

Given concerns about both safety and efficacy, it is rather puzzling that their use has expanded significantly in populations for which first generation antipsychotics had been prescribed only reluctantly—children and adolescents.

As was seen with the SSRIs, the use of antipsychotics in children and adolescents, particularly the SGAs, has markedly expanded in the past decade. In 1993, 200,000 outpatient visits for children and adolescents were associated with the prescription of an antipsychotic. By 2002, this number was over 1.2 million (Olfson et al., 2006), in spite of the fact that none of the SGAs had at the time an FDA indication for use in children under the age of 18 (most atypical antipsychotics are now approved for various conditions in children ages 5 and up). In an analysis by Olfson and colleagues (2006), only 14% of the visits in which an antipsychotic were prescribed was associated with a psychotic spectrum diagnosis; instead, the greatest percentage was associated with diagnoses of disruptive behavior. Other authors have corroborated large increases in antipsychotic prescribing to children and adolescents; one study (Thomas, Conrad, Casler, & Goodman, 2006) found a remarkable 385% rise in the prescription of psychotropics other than antidepressants and anticonvulsants in adolescents between the ages of 14 and 18 years between 1994 and 2001. They attributed the majority of this change to increases in antipsychotic prescriptions among youth.

As with other psychotropics, use in American youth is higher than in other developed countries. The prevalence of antipsychotic use in a representative sample of health claims for U.S. youth was 0.76% in 2000, compared with a prevalence of 0.51% in the Netherlands and 0.34% in Germany (Zito et al., 2008). Striking differences in the use of atypical antipsychotics were also found, ranging from 66% of antipsychotics prescribed in the United States to 5% in Germany. This difference becomes doubly concerning when presented with evidence (Sikich et al., 2008) that first generation antipsychotics are as efficacious as second generation agents in children and have fewer side effects.

Increased regulatory scrutiny of antipsychotics has led the FDA to issue a series of boxed warnings regarding the use of antipsychotics. In 2005, the FDA warned prescribers about increased risk of stroke in elderly patients with dementia who were prescribed atypical antipsychotics. This warning was later extended to all classes of antipsychotic agent. The alert may be found at http://www.fda.gov/cder/drug/InfoSheets/HCP/antipsychotics_conventional.htm. The publication of this and successive warnings may herald a major shift in prescribing patterns as was seen after the publication of similar warnings for antidepressants.

PRESCRIPTIVE AUTHORITY FOR PSYCHOLOGISTS

The developmental trajectory of psychotropics reflects that seen in other areas of health care. Instead of an inexorable scientific march toward enlightenment, progress is uncertain, often halting, and bears the messy inflections of commercial interests, professional fads, and societal trends. This is unavoidable. It is equally unavoidable that trends in psychopharmacology have deeply influenced the development and identity of all health care professions, including psychology. With the expansion of drugs in the management of mental disorders, it was perhaps inescapable that the profession of psychology would consider incorporating them into a redefined scope of practice. Without evidence for the effectiveness of psychotropics, the movement toward prescriptive authority for psychologists would not have begun.

Such a movement did indeed begin in the late 1980s, when a small number of psychologists recognized the inevitable expansion of drug treatment of mental disorders and began to argue that the use of these drugs should not be restricted solely to the psychiatric profession. Psychologists had been involved, of course, in drug development and research for decades. Psychopharmacology before the early 1990s was conducted almost exclusively by physicians, making it unavoidable that their use would be dictated by the core assumptions of medicine, particularly allopathic medicine. These assumptions have been described elsewhere (Sammons, 2001), but briefly they reflect the general conviction that drugs are the primary intervention for mental disorders and therefore implicitly assume that neurobiological dysregulation is the primary etiological factor.

Proponents of prescriptive authority for psychologists, on the other hand, have argued that pharmacological service by psychologists would represent a fundamentally different approach. This approach holds that biological dysregulation is but one factor to consider in the development of mental distress, and that relational and contextual factors figure of equal importance in the genesis and management of most mental disorders. Prescribing psychologists would be expected to integrate pharmacotherapy and psychotherapy to a degree not generally seen in the medical model, and because their assessment is more inclusive of relational and contextual factors, would be likely to use pharmacological interventions less frequently than those trained in a medical model.

In 1991, a program was begun under the auspices of the U.S. Department of Defense (DoD) to train psychologists to prescribe psychotropic drugs (Newman et al., 2000; Sammons & Brown, 1997). The program produced 10 graduates who became fully independent prescribers within DoD. From this program sprang a number of legislative and training initiatives. At the current time, two states (Arizona and New Mexico) authorize psychologists to prescribe, and prescribing psychologists are employed by the Indian Health Service as well as by the DoD. It is estimated that as of 2009, there were approximately 100 clinical psychologists with prescriptive authority, and each year sees a new round of legislative initiatives in other jurisdictions to expand psychological practice to include prescriptive authority. Since 2000, prescribing psychologists have been represented within the American Psychological Association by their own division (55, the American Society for the Advancement of Pharmacotherapy). Within the foreseeable future, prescriptive authority may be within the scope of practice of psychologists in almost every jurisdiction (see Fox et al., 2009)—yet another example of how political, as well as economic and societal forces, interplay with science to shape the complexion and practice of psychology.

CONCLUSIONS

The midpoint of the 20th century marked a watershed in the development of psychotropics. In a short period of time, the pharmacopoeia for mental distress, previously limited to a few sedating agents to control agitation and amphetamines for mild depression, expanded to include all major classes of psychotropics in use today. In particular, the introduction of the first specific antidepressants and antipsychotics radically changed the therapeutic landscape. Indeed, the efficacy of most pharmacotherapy on positive symptoms of severe mental disorders is impressive.

At the same time, the introduction of specific agents and aggressive direct-to-consumer advertising cultivated the hope that definitive treatments for chronic and disabling mental conditions would soon be found. Regrettably, this hope has not been borne out. The second generation of antidepressants, antimanics, and antipsychotics are no more efficacious than their predecessors. Although newer drugs are for the most part less toxic and better accepted by patients, none is entirely benign. Replicated findings have demonstrated high rates of patient nonresponse or placebo response to many drugs. In spite of such findings, the use of psychotropics continues to grow, often at the expense of nonbiological treatments with higher patient acceptability and lower relapse rates. Additionally, many agents continue to be used for populations (e.g., children) or conditions for which little evidence of effectiveness exists.

In the future, professionals will require a detailed understanding of the research supporting pharmacological or nonpharmacological interventions for particular disorders. This viewpoint will be augmented by recognizing that treatment fads exist even in professions largely grounded in empiricism and by avoiding the temptation to frame arguments for or against psychopharmacology in moral or political terms. Most important, clinicians must understand that it is the patient, and not the professional, who is the ultimate decision maker regarding choices of therapy. We best serve our patients by providing impartial and comprehensive information from which they may make treatment decisions optimally suited to their needs.

REFERENCES

Ban, T. A. (2001). Pharmacotherapy of mental illness—a historical analysis. *Progress in Neuro-Psychopharmacology & Biological Psychiatry, 25,* 709–727. doi:10.1016/S0278-5846(01)00160-9

Berndt, E. R., Bhattacharjya, A., Mishol, D. N., Arcelus, A., & Lasky, T. (2002). An analysis of the diffusion of new antidepressants: Variety, quality, and marketing efforts. *Journal of Mental Health Policy and Economics, 5,* 3–19.

Berton, O., & Nestler, E. J. (2006). New approaches to antidepressant drug discovery: Beyond monoamines. *Nature Reviews Neuroscience, 7,* 137–151. doi:10. 1038/nrn1846

Byles, J., Loxton, D., Berecki, J., Dolja-Gore, X., Gibson, R., Hockey, R., . . . Dobson, A. (2008, June). *Use and cost of medications and other health care resources: Findings from the Australian Longitudinal Study on Women's Health* (Report 144 prepared for Australian Government Department of Health and Ageing). Retrieved from http://www.alswh.org.au/other_reports

Callahan, C. M., & Berrios, G. E. (2005). *Reinventing depression: A history of the treatment of depression in primary care, 1940-2004.* New York, NY: Oxford University Press.

Charlton, B. G. (2005). If 'atypical' antipsychotics did not exist, it wouldn't be necessary to invent them: Perverse incentives in drug development, research, marketing and clinical practice. *Medical Hypotheses, 65,* 1005–1009.

Fangmann, P., Assion, H. J., Juckel, G., Gonzalez, C. A., & Lopez-Munoz, F. (2008). Half a century of antidepressant drugs: On the clinical introduction of monoamine oxidase inhibitors, tricyclics, and tetracyclics. Part II: Tricyclics and tetracyclics. *Journal of Clinical Psychopharmacology, 28,* 1–4. doi:10.1097/jcp.0b013e3181627b60

Flanagan, R. J. (2008). Fatal toxicity of drugs used by psychiatry. *Human Psychopharmacology, 23*(Suppl. 1), 43–51. doi:10.1002/hup.916

Fox, R. E., DeLeon, P. H., Newman, R., Sammons, M. T., Dunivin, D., & Baker, D. C. (2009). Prescriptive authority and psychology: A status report. *American Psychologist, 64,* 257–268.

Friedman, R. A., & Leon, A. C. (2007). Expanding the black box—depression, antidepressants, and the risk of suicide. *New England Journal of Medicine, 356,* 2343–2346.

Gibbons, R. D., Hur, K., Bhaumik, D. K., & Mann, J. J. (2006). The relationship between antidepressant prescription rates and rate of early adolescent suicide. *American Journal of Psychiatry, 163,* 1898–1904. doi:10.1176/appi.ajp.163.11.1898

Goldstein, J. (2008, October 7). Lilly paying $62 million to settle state Zyprexa investigations. *Wall Street Journal.* Retrieved from http://blogs.wsj.com/health/2008/ 10/07/ lilly-paying-62-million-to-settle-state-zyprexa-investigations/trackback/

Happiness by prescription (1957, March 11). *Time Magazine.* Retrieved from http://www.time.com/time/magazine/article/0,9171,824739,00.html

Healy, D. (1997). *The antidepressant era.* Boston, MA: Harvard University Press.

Healy, D. (2002). *The creation of psychopharmacology.* Boston, MA: Harvard University Press.

IMS Health. (2007). *2007 U.S. sales and prescription information. Top therapeutic classes by U.S. sales.* Retrieved from http://www.imshealth.com/portal/site/imshealth/menuitem

Keen, E. (2000). *Chemicals for the mind: Psychopharmacology and human consciousness.* Westport, CT: Praeger.

Kirsch, I., Deacon, B. J., Huedo-Medina, T. B., Scoboria, A., Moore, T. J., & Johnson, B. T. (2008). Initial severity and antidepressant benefits: A meta-analysis of data submitted to the Food and Drug Administration. *PLoS Medicine, 5*(2). doi:10.1371/journal.pmed. 0050045

Kurian, B. T., Ray, W. A., Arbogast, P. G., Fuchs, D. C., Dudley, J. A., & Cooper, W. O. (2007). Effects of regulatory warnings on antidepressant prescribing for children and adolescents. *Archives of Pediatrics & Adolescent Medicine, 161*, 690–696. doi:10.1001/archpedi.161.7.690

National Center for Health Statistics. (2007). *Health, United States, with chartbook on trends in the health of Americans*. Hyattsville, MD: Author.

Newman, R., Phelps, R., Sammons, M. T., Dunivin, D., & Cullen, E. (2000). Evaluation of the Psychopharmacology Demonstration Project: A retrospective analysis. *Professional Psychology: Research and Practice, 31*, 598.

Olfson, M., Blanco, C., Liu, L., Moreno, C., & Laje, G. (2006). National trends in the outpatient treatment of children and adolescents with antipsychotic drugs. *Archives of General Psychiatry, 63*, 679–685. doi:10.1001/archpsyc.63.6.679

Olfson, M., Marcus, S. C., Druss, B., Elinson, L., Tanielian, T., & Pincus, H. A. (2002). National trends in the outpatient treatment of depression. *JAMA, 287*, 203–209.

Rasmussen, N. (2008). *On speed: The many lives of amphetamine*. New York, NY: New York University Press.

Rush, A. J., Trivedi, M. H., Wisniewski, S. R., Stewart, J. W., Nierenberg, A. A., Thase, M. E., . . . Fava, M. (2006). Bupropion-SR, sertraline, or venlafaxine-XR after failure of SSRIs for depression. *New England Journal of Medicine, 354*, 1231–1242. doi:10.1056/NEJMoa052963

Sammons, M. T., & Brown, A. B. (1997). The Psychopharmacology Demonstration Project: An evolving experiment in postdoctoral training for psychologists. *Professional Psychology, Research and Practice, 28*, 107–112. doi:10.1037/0735-7028.28.2.107

Sammons, M. T. (2001). Combined treatments for mental disorders: Clinical dilemmas. In M. T. Sammons & N. B. Schmidt (Eds.), *Combined treatments for mental disorders* (pp. 11–32). Washington, DC: American Psychological Association. doi:10.1037/10415-001

Sammons, M. T. (2009). Writing a wrong: Factors influencing the overprescription of antidepressants to youth. *Professional Psychology: Research and Practice, 40*, 327–329.

Shorter, E., & Tyrer, P. (2003). Separation of anxiety and depressive disorders: Blind alley in psychopharmacology and classification of disease. *British Medical Journal, 327*, 158–160. doi:10.1136/bmj.327.7407.158

Sikich, L., Frazier, J. A., McClelland, J., Finding, R. L., Vitiello, B., Ritz, L., . . . Lieberman, J. A. (2008). Double-blind comparison of first and second generation antipsychotics in early onset schizophrenia and schizoaffective disorder. *American Journal of Psychiatry, 165*, 1420–1431.

Thomas, C. P., Conrad, P., Casler, R., & Goodman, E. (2006). Trends in the use of psychotropic medications among adolescents, 1994-2001. *Psychiatric Services, 57*, 63–69. doi:10.1176/appi.ps.57.1.63

Tiihonon, J., Lonngvist, J., Wahlbeck, K., Klaukka, T., Niskanen, L., Tanskanen, A., & Haukka, J. (2009). 11-year follow-up of mortality in patients with schizophrenia: A population-based cohort study (FIN11 study). *The Lancet, 374*, 620–627.

Wong, D. T., Perry, K. W., & Bymaster, F. P. (2005). The discovery of fluoxetine hydrochloride (Prozac). *Nature Reviews. Drug Discovery, 4*, 764–774.

Zito, J. M., Safer, D. J., dosReis, S., Gardner, J. F., Soeken, K., Boles, M., & Lynch, F. (2002). Rising prevalence of antidepressants among US youths. *Pediatrics, 109*, 721–727. doi:10.1542/peds.109.5.721

Zito, J. M., Safer, D. J., de Jong-van den Berg, T. W., Jahnsen, K., Fegert, J. M., Gardner, J. M., . . . Valluri, S. C. (2008). A three-country comparison of psychotropic medication prevalence in youth. *Child and Adolescent Psychiatry and Mental Health, 2*, 26. doi:10.1186/1753-2000-2-26

Integration of Spirituality and Religion Into Psychotherapy

Everett L. Worthington, Jr.

If I were a historian, I would write a different type of minichapter than the present reflection on the history of the integration of spirituality into psychotherapy (for two excellent histories, see Kurtz, 1999; Vande Kemp, 1996). A historian starts with a long perspective that gives a clear idea of what historical influences have survived social evolution to the present. The historian then seeks to trace the reasons that the strong influences survived. Historical documents would be consulted, and then the evidence regarding the interpretations of the events would be argued. A historian would likely consider the changing definitions of religion and spirituality. One could begin in ancient Greece for a psychotherapy (of sorts) being integrated with classical Greek religion, could show that psychological treatment and spirituality were being integrated throughout subsequent history, and could trace the evolution of the integration of the two constructs to the present day.

The present reflection cannot meet the standards of a real history. For one thing, we do not have a long perspective on the integration of modern ideas of religion or spirituality into clinical science. Rather, the integration of modern spirituality into modern psychotherapy spans less than half of the time of the history of psychology. For another thing, readers probably would not have any more patience with careful historical documentation than I have for writing it. As a psychologist, I can write a historical reflection, a recreation of the field as it developed.

Identifying the provenance of any movement always provokes conflict. Take Christianity for example. Depending on one's definitions of Christianity and psychology, cases could be made that a form of Christian therapy was happening with the meditations of the desert fathers (and mothers) in the 3rd century—the confessions of Augustine, the Aristotelian reasoning of Thomas Aquinas, or the disciplines of Ignatian spirituality. Many of those classic soul-care efforts are being incorporated in psychotherapies today (Johnson, 2007). But as valuable as these soul-care integrations are, I do not consider them to be modern spiritual or religious psychotherapy.

What we know with certainty is that most people in the United States report being either spiritual but not religious or both religious and spiritual. For example, about 95% profess to believe in God or a higher power and 69% are members of a church or synagogue, and 85% report that religion plays a significant role in their lives (Gallup & Lindsay, 1999). Even though the percentage of religious psychotherapists is substantially less than for people in the public at large, many do define themselves as spiritual (Delaney, Miller, & Bisonó, 2007). Furthermore, in a recent survey of psychotherapists, 83%

thought that religious and spiritual issues are often relevant to treatment (Delaney et al., 2007).

1940s: INTEGRATION OF TWO PROFESSIONS

In the 1940s, psychoanalytic approaches dominated psychotherapy (Lovinger, 1984). The values of the therapist were not generally considered appropriate to discuss in therapy (cf. one exception was Jung, 1938). Values of the client were grist for the therapeutic mill. So religion was sometimes discussed, but therapy methods were not religiously oriented. Furthermore, when clients and therapists considered religion, they thought primarily in terms of religion, not spirituality. Religion was associated with a set of beliefs, values, and practices and with communities that embraced them. Spirituality— the pursuit of closeness, connection, or unity—became of interest only in the 1990s.

Let me start the examination of the movement to integrate religion and psychotherapy in 1942. In individual therapy, books like Rollo May's (1939) *The Art of Counseling* and Paul Tournier's (1941/1965) *The Healing of Persons* were influential. The incorporation of the American Association of Marital and Family Therapists (AAMFT) brought together family therapists and pastoral counselors. Some pastoral counselors had spearheaded marriage enhancement methods, including marital counseling and marriage enrichment (Broderick & Schrader, 1981). The establishment of the AAMFT achieved some degree of integration at the level of professions, but little integrating of therapeutic methods occurred. Moreover, systems thinking soon muted religious voices in the AAMFT, as the more secular family therapists did more professional writing than did the religiously oriented marriage counselors.

1950s: EVOLUTION OF APPROACHES TO RELIGIOUS VALUES

In the early 1950s, Carl Rogers (1951) moved psychotherapy from the relatively value-free psychodynamic perspective to a value-neutral or phenomenological perspective. Pastoral counselors were comfortable with client-centered therapy, and more and more pastoral counselors began to use this approach. Because pastoral counseling (by title and setting) was explicitly religious, clients could explore spirituality under their own initiative. Pastoral counselors could, using client-centered therapy, facilitate client discussions of spiritual topics. Often, such psychotherapy was religious but not sectarian in denomination (Clinebell, 1966). The therapist tried to see things from the client's perspective. Client-centered therapy freed pastoral counselors to embrace psychology. Psychology rarely returned the embrace.

1960s: EARLY INTEGRATION EFFORTS BY PSYCHOTHERAPISTS

In the 1960s, a few practitioners and theoreticians began explicitly putting religion and psychotherapy together (Mowrer, 1961). Several nonsectarian approaches developed about the same time, as follows:

- Influential psychologists, such as Timothy Leary and Richard Alpert (later Ram Das), advocated for the use of Eastern religious practices and drugs to facilitate the cure of mental disorders. Leary even conducted a government funded study of the use of LSD in prison populations to cure schizophrenia.
- Harvard psychiatrist Herbert Benson (Benson & Klipper, 1975) relied on the relaxation research from behavior therapy, especially work by Joseph Wolpe (1958), to identify what he called a common factor within Eastern meditation, yoga practices, transcendental meditation, and Western-based behavioral relaxation. Benson called this the *relaxation response* and conducted considerable research investigating its efficacy.
- Some psychotherapists began to advocate meditation (Goleman, 1971; Ornstein, 1972). Many of these therapists identified with Eastern religions or were influenced by the Eastern philosophy that entered United States culture in the turbulent 1960s. Because many secular therapists were drawn to these meditative techniques (apart from their religious roots), the empirical research on meditation, relaxation, and yoga has been considerable (for meta-analytic reviews, see Baer, 2003; Grossman, Niemann, Schmidt, & Walach, 2004). Some psychotherapies began using meditation as an integral part of therapy, although their philosophy was not distinctively religious.
- The 12-step addiction treatment enterprise became more widespread (Alcoholics Anonymous, 1939). Originally, 12-step programs to treat addictions were created on the basis of Christian principles. Practitioners quickly moved to eliminate the explicit references to religion. Instead, they emphasized spiritual (not religious) transformations. Peer-led, 12-step treatment became the norm during the anti-establishmentarianism of the 1960s. Many addicted people did not trust mental health professionals.

In the 1960s, religion was seen as part of the establishment. The major forays of spiritual integration into psychotherapy treated spirituality as an anti-establishment subversion or as a technology, thus making it acceptable to the 1960s countercultural values. These limited integrations of spirituality and religion into treatment notwithstanding, mainstream approaches to psychotherapy generally continued to ignore religion.

1970s: CLIENTS PRESSURE PSYCHOTHERAPISTS

In the 1970s, the cognitive revolution ushered into psychotherapy a value-informed position to supplant Rogerian value neutrality. A value-informed position allowed religious therapists to use their religion in psychotherapy—if the clients were informed. The emphasis on client cognition allowed therapists to openly initiate discussions of religion or spirituality.

In the 1970s, eclecticism in psychotherapy was also on the rise (see Chapter 9, this volume). Therapists modified standard approaches, picking techniques hither and yon from different theories. One natural outcome of eclecticism was more implicit permission to integrate religion and spirituality into treatment. However, the freedom to be eclectic had a downside. Practitioners, not academicians, were doing much of the religious and spiritual integration. Thus, few treatment manuals described religiously tailored interventions. Few clinical efficacy trials were conducted. Providing a viable empirical base for religiously accommodated therapy has resembled field trials of effectiveness research more than randomized controlled trials characteristic of efficacy research (e.g., Pecheur & Edwards, 1984; Propst, Ostrom, Watkins, Dean, & Mashburn, 1992).

During the 1970s, professional organizations either formed or increased in popularity (Vande Kemp, 1996). The Christian Association for Psychological Studies was founded in 1953 to promote the explicit integration of psychology and Christianity (mostly from a theological perspective favoring Dutch Reformed theology). The Association for Religious and Value Issues in Counseling arose as an interest group in the American Personnel and Guidance Association during the 1950s. What is now the American Psychological Association's (APA's) Division 36 (Psychology of Religion) formed in 1947 as the American Catholic Psychological Association, and it was later (1970) renamed as Psychologists Interested in Religious Issues, becoming APA Division 36 in 1976.

On the client side, in the 1970s, the vast majority of people in the United States still advocated faith perspectives. Many began to explicitly ask for religiously oriented psychotherapy. This was born of a couple of important social events. The "Jesus movement" of the early 1970s led theologically conservative Christians to demand explicitly Christian adaptations of psychotherapy. Both psychodynamic (Narramore, 1960) and cognitive (Crabb, 1977) therapists wrote about how to integrate Christian faith into psychotherapy practice. The integration movement generated much research (spawning two journals devoted to its integration, the *Journal of Psychology and Christianity* and the *Journal of Psychology and Theology*) and numerous books about practice. Yet, the integration of psychotherapy and religion infrequently touched mainstream psychotherapy.

Increasing acceptance of Eastern religions spawned by the counter-cultural revolution of the 1960s was reinforced in the 1970s because of high immigration of Buddhists from Southeast Asia as a result of the war in that area. Immigration from Latin American countries also intensified, which increased the number of Roman Catholics. Whereas immigrants during the 1970s rarely sought psychotherapy, their American-born children, who grew to adulthood in the 1990s, were more likely to do so. Therefore, pressure from a more eclectic set of psychotherapists, professional organizations of psychologists, and more vocal and demographically changing clients pushed toward more integration of psychology and religion.

1980s: A TURNING POINT

In 1980, Allen Bergin published a major paper on religious therapy in the *Journal of Consulting and Clinical Psychology*. This broke the "religious barrier" and opened the major psychological journals to considering religion in psychotherapy. Secular psychotherapy was building a body of research to support its efficacy (Smith & Glass, 1977). However, research on religiously accommodated psychotherapy was not keeping pace. There were disparate pockets of research on religion or spirituality in psychotherapy, but they tended to remain isolated from each other and from the mainstream psychotherapy movement.

In 1984, the *Journal of Counseling and Development* commissioned a review of the literature (Worthington, 1986). The review organized the meager research addressing the efficacy of religiously oriented therapy, mostly pastoral counseling studies. However, the publication in a mainstream journal may have encouraged psychologists to undertake more research.

The literature grew quickly. Within 5 years, several other reviews were published in leading journals (e.g., Beutler & Bergan, 1991; Worthington, 1989). The literature tended to draw from two groups of clients. On one hand, some studies reported interventions with people in secular settings, which tended to draw a mix of religious and nonreligious people. Beutler found that people's ratings of their religious values became more aligned with the therapist's values over the course of therapy. On the other hand, some research tended to draw from more explicitly religious settings. For example, in Christian settings, the religious values of highly religious clients were not found to change during psychotherapy (Worthington, 1991). This suggested that treatments aimed at explicitly religious clients in religious settings might not be equally effective if used with a mixed religious clientele in explicitly and nonsectarian secular settings.

1990s: MULTICULTURALISM AND MINDFULNESS

In the 1990s, investigators began to study the practice of mindfulness (Hayes, Follette, & Linehan, 2004; Linehan, 1993; Zaretsky, Segal, & Fefergrad, 2007). Mindfulness is a state of mind drawn from the Eastern religions and has to do with being completely aware of one's present. Tuning out internal chatter and focusing attention on beauty and current experiences are consistent with cognitive techniques that attend to attention and self-talk. Inevitably, mindfulness methods have found their way into secular psychotherapy—as a technology or a technique.

The emphasis on multiculturalism in the 1990s empowered people to define themselves in terms of their communities, which included their religious and spiritual—as well as ethnic—contexts. Clients became more comfortable in insisting that their psychotherapy include spiritual interventions, such as meditation or prayer, or be frankly accommodated to a particular religion.

Throughout the 1990s, secular therapy became increasingly spiritual but not religious. Theoreticians were providing general spiritual approaches to conceptualizing life (e.g., Wilber, 1996, 2000). Religiously accommodated therapies were also increasingly used in particular religious communities (e.g., Dwairy, 2008; Worthington & Sandage, 2002). Many committed religious clients attended secular therapy. They did not necessarily want religiously tailored therapy. Neither were they comfortable with spiritual techniques because of the derivation from Eastern religions. Thus, a demand began to be articulated for a generally theistic therapy, and several were proposed (Richards & Bergin, 1997, 2000).

The integration of religion and psychotherapy in mainstream publishing was clear by the mid-1990s, when the American Psychological Association published *Religion and the Clinical Practice of Psychology* by Shafranske (1996). This was closely followed by several other books, notably *A Spiritual Strategy for Counseling and Psychotherapy* (Richards & Bergin, 1997) and *Integrating Spirituality into Treatment* (Miller, 1999). These three titles sold over 21,000 copies collectively in their first 7 years in print. The interest within psychology, and among psychotherapists, had clearly changed from the 1960s. Psychotherapists are reading about religion and spirituality and about techniques for bringing such issues into the clinical setting.

2000s: REBOUND OF RELIGION

By the 21st century, treatments that incorporated either a specific religious emphasis (Worthington & Sandage, 2002) or used generic spirituality (Worthington, Kurusu, McCullough, & Sandage, 1996) were common in clinical practice. At the same time, many treatments continued to ignore religion and spirituality unless it was a focal concern of a client.

The integration of religion and spirituality into therapy has shifted in at least seven noteworthy ways. First, the percentage of solo practices among psychotherapists has certainly declined since the 1980s in favor of affiliated or group practices. With group practices, if a religiously or spiritually oriented client presents for treatment, the chances are higher that someone will be able to deal with the specific religious beliefs of the client. Whereas referral has always been the ethical option for therapists who did not feel competent to treat spiritual and religious clients, the fact is that referral networks are often limited. Group practices yield more options for placing clients with the therapist from whom the clients can benefit. Second, in this multicultural era, some practices form around a particular religious or spiritual approach. Again, this allows clients who are seeking a particular therapy to more likely find what they are looking for. Third, some integrative attempts are moving to a multi-level integration (see McMinn & Campbell, 2008). Previously, most integration tended to blend religiosity or spirituality with a particular approach like cognitive therapy. New trends, however, are to aim at integrating along the lines of symptoms, social interactions, and depth psychological causes. The integrative efforts are breaking out of the bindings that have shackled them for decades. Fourth, some practitioners are moving away from accepting insurance. More clients are opting for pay-as-you-go treatment because they do not want their work or mental health records to reflect psychological treatment. More explicitly religious practitioners have begun to affiliate with large churches and conduct practices under their auspices. This church-subsidized therapy can reduce costs, provide a belief-congruent treatment, and allow therapists to reduce the burden of paperwork in dealing with third-party payers and networks for insurance companies. Fifth, the United States has become increasingly ethnically pluralistic. The rise in numbers of people of Asian origin introduces more Hindu, Buddhist, and Muslim clients into therapy. The rise in numbers of Latino/Latina people suggests that more Roman Catholics will likely seek therapy in future years. Sixth, as we saw in tracing developments throughout the 1990s, more interest seems to be evident among psychotherapists in dealing with highly religious clients. Seventh, multiculturalism has made it easier for clients to specifically request explicitly religious or spiritual therapy. Altogether, these developments lead me to be optimistic about counseling with religious or spiritual clients who have explicitly religious or spiritual problems or who merely want to be treated within a worldview that not only respects their beliefs but also treats their values knowledgeably.

SUMMARY AND CONCLUSIONS

The history of the integration of religion and spirituality into psychotherapy has been driven by several trends. All push toward more religious and spiritual diversity for both clients and therapists. Pressure toward diversity of clients has come from the introduction of Eastern religion and philosophy, which has been largely due to large shifts in immigration and to worldview shifts of the 1960s and 1970s. Among therapists, the cognitive revolution made it more reasonable to deal explicitly with values, hence religion and spirituality have been addressed more openly than in previous decades. Economic pressures—managed care, in particular—have changed practice to accept, if not demand, practitioners willing to integrate religious and spiritual considerations. Openness of secular therapists to spiritual, but less often religious, approaches has been fueled by multicultural evolution. The popularity and availability of peer counseling have moved much helping away from value-free or value-neutral to a value-informed perspective. These social trends have set up two camps: a secular camp emphasizing spirituality and a religious camp focused on particular religions.

The past informs and fuels the future. This historical analysis suggests a number of directions for the future:

1. The incorporation of Eastern-religious informed methods, such as meditation and mindfulness, into Western psychotherapies has begun (e.g., Hathaway & Tan, 2008; Hayes et al., 2004) and likely will increase.
2. Efficacy research on religiously oriented psychotherapies has not kept pace with efficacy research on secular psychotherapies. If religiously oriented and tailored psychotherapies are to continue to receive insurance support, more controlled research is needed.
3. Spirituality has been underemphasized in favor of religious beliefs (Johnson, 2007). We can confidently expect increased incorporation of spirituality into psychotherapy, either at the client's request or the therapist's preference.
4. Secular psychotherapists will develop better ways to deal explicitly with religious issues. In the past, clients withhold religious problems from their psychotherapists; in the future, more clients will be forthcoming about such problems and expect psychotherapists to deal directly with them.

Given the social changes and openness of both clients and therapists to religion and spirituality, it is a reasonable supposition that spiritually tailored therapies will increase to meet clients' needs. There will also need to be continuing sensitivity to clients who do not want to attend religiously or spiritually tailored therapy. These divergent needs provide challenges for both secular and sectarian psychotherapists. But the field of psychotherapy seems committed to providing informed and sensitive care for all clients—whether they embrace religion, spirituality, or neither.

REFERENCES

Alcoholics Anonymous. (1939). *Alcoholics Anonymous*. New York, NY: Alcoholics Anonymous World Services.

Baer, R. A. (2003). Mindfulness training as a clinical intervention: A conceptual and empirical review. *Clinical Psychology: Science and Practice, 10,* 125–143. doi:10.1093/clipsy/bpg015

Benson, H., & Klipper, M. Z. (1975). *The relaxation response*. New York, NY: HarperCollins.

Bergin, A. E. (1980). Psychotherapy and religious values. *Journal of Consulting and Clinical Psychology, 48,* 95–105. doi:10.1037/0022-006X.48.1.95

Beutler, L. E., & Bergan, J. (1991). Value change in counseling and psychotherapy: A search for scientific credibility. *Journal of Counseling Psychology, 38,* 16–24. doi:10.1037/0022-0167.38.1.16

Broderick, C. B., & Schrader, S. S. (1981). The history of professional marriage and family therapy. In A. S. Gurman & D. P. Kniskern (Eds.), *Handbook of family therapy* (pp. 5–35). New York, NY: Brunner/Mazel.

Clinebell, H. (1966). *Basic types of pastoral care and counseling: Resources for the ministry of healing and growth*. Nashville, TN: Abingdon Press.

Crabb, L. J., Jr. (1977). *Effective Biblical counseling: A model for helping caring Christians become capable counselors*. Grand Rapids, MI: Zondervan.

Delaney, H. D., Miller, W. R., & Bisonó, A. M. (2007). Religiosity and spirituality among psychologists: A survey of clinician members of the American Psychological Association. *Professional Psychology, Research and Practice, 38,* 538–546. doi:10.1037/0735-7028.38.5.538

Dwairy, M. (2008). Counseling Arab and Muslim clients. In P. B. Pedersen, J. G. Draguns, W. J. Lonner, & J. E. Trimble (Eds.), *Counseling across cultures* (6th ed., pp. 147–160). Thousand Oaks, CA: Sage.

Gallup, G., Jr., & Lindsay, D. M. (1999). *Surveying the religious landscape: Trends in U.S. beliefs*. Harrisburg, PA: Morehouse.

Goleman, D. (1971). Meditation as meta-therapy. *Journal of Transpersonal Psychology, 3,* 1–25.

Grossman, P., Niemann, L., Schmidt, S., & Walach, H. (2004). Mindfulness-based stress reduction and health benefits: A meta-analysis. *Journal of Psychosomatic Research, 57,* 35–43. doi:10.1016/S0022-3999(03)00573-7

Hathaway, W., & Tan, E. (2008). Religiously oriented mindfulness-based cognitive therapy. *Journal of Clinical Psychology: In Session, 65,* 158–171.

Hayes, S. C., Follette, V. M., & Linehan, M. M. (Eds.). (2004). *Mindfulness and acceptance: Expanding the cognitive-behavioral tradition*. New York, NY: Guilford Press.

Johnson, E. L. (2007). *Foundations for soul care: A Christian psychology proposal*. Downers Grove, IL: InterVarsity Press.

Jung, C. G. (1938). *Psychology and religion*. New Haven, CT: Yale University Press.

Kurtz, E. (1999). The historical context. In W. R. Miller (Ed.), *Integrating spirituality into treatment* (pp. 19–46). Washington, DC: American Psychological Association. doi:10.1037/10327-002

Linehan, M. M. (1993). *Cognitive-behavioral treatment of borderline personality disorder*. New York, NY: Guilford Press.

Lovinger, R. J. (1984). *Working with religious issues in therapy*. New York, NY: Jason Aronson.

May, R. (1939). *The art of counseling: A practical guide with case studies and demonstrations*. Nashville, TN: Abingdon Press.

McMinn, M. R., & Campbell, C. D. (2008). *Integrative psychotherapy: Toward a comprehensive Christian approach*. Downers Grove, IL: InterVarsity Press.

Miller, W. R. (1999). *Integrating spirituality into treatment: Resources for practitioners*. Washington, DC: American Psychological Association. doi:10.1037/10327-000

Mowrer, O. H. (1961). *The crisis in psychiatry and religion*. New York, NY: Van Nostrand.

Narramore, C. M. (1960). *The psychology of counseling*. Grand Rapids, MI: Zondervan.

Ornstein, R. E. (1972). *The psychology of consciousness*. New York, NY: Viking.

Pecheur, D. R., & Edwards, K. J. (1984). A comparison of secular and religious versions of cognitive therapy with depressed Christian college students. *Journal of Psychology and Theology, 12*, 45–54.

Propst, L. R., Ostrom, R., Watkins, P., Dean, T., & Mashburn, D. (1992). Comparative efficacy of religious and nonreligious cognitive-behavioral therapy for the treatment of depression in religious individuals. *Journal of Consulting and Clinical Psychology, 60*, 94–103. doi:10.1037/0022-006X.60.1.94

Richards, P. S., & Bergin, A. E. (1997). *A spiritual strategy for counseling and psychotherapy*. Washington, DC: American Psychological Association. doi:10.1037/10241-000

Richards, P. S., & Bergin, A. E. (Eds.). (2000). *Handbook of psychotherapy and religious diversity*. Washington, DC: American Psychological Association. doi:10.1037/10347-000

Rogers, C. (1951). *Client-centered therapy: Its current practice, implications and theory*. Boston, MA: Houghton Mifflin.

Shafranske, E. P. (1996). *Religion and the clinical practice of psychology*. Washington, DC: American Psychological Association. doi:10.1037/10199-000

Smith, M. L., & Glass, G. V. (1977). Meta-analysis of psychotherapy outcome studies. *American Psychologist, 32*, 752–760. doi:10.1037/0003-066X.32.9.752

Tournier, P. (1965). Healing of persons. (E. Hudson, Trans.). New York, NY: Harper & Row. (Original work published 1941).

Vande Kemp, H. (1996). Historical perspective: Religion and clinical psychology in America. In E. P. Shafranske (Ed.), *Religion and the clinical practice of psychology* (pp. 71–112). Washington, DC: American Psychological Association. doi:10.1037/10199-003

Wilber, K. (1996). *A brief history of everything*. Boston: Shambhala.

Wilber, K. (2000). *Integral psychology: Consciousness, spirit, psychology, therapy*. Boston: Shambhala.

Wolpe, J. (1958). *Psychotherapy by reciprocal inhibition*. Stanford, CA: Stanford University Press.

Worthington, E. L., Jr. (1986). Religious counseling: A review of empirical research. *Journal of Counseling and Development, 64*, 421–431.

Worthington, E. L., Jr. (1989). Religious faith across the life span: Implications for counseling and research. *The Counseling Psychologist, 17*, 555–612.

Worthington, E. L., Jr. (1991). Psychotherapy and religious values: An update. *Journal of Psychology and Christianity, 10*, 211–223.

Worthington, E. L., Jr., Kurusu, T., McCullough, M. E., & Sandage, S. (1996). Empirical research on religion and psychotherapeutic processes and outcomes: A 10-year review and research prospectus. *Psychological Bulletin, 119*, 448–487. doi:10.1037/0033-2909.119.3.448

Worthington, E. L., Jr., & Sandage, S. J. (2002). Religion and spirituality. In J. C. Norcross (Ed.), *Psychotherapy relationships that work: Therapists relational contributions to effective psychotherapy* (pp. 383–399). New York, NY: Oxford University Press.

Zaretsky, A., Segal, Z., & Fefergrad, M. (2007). New developments in cognitive-behavioural therapy for mood disorders [Guest editorial]. *Canadian Journal of Psychiatry, 52*, 3–4.

15

PSYCHOTHERAPY FOR SPECIFIC DISORDERS

Depression

Lynn P. Rehm

Depression has been recognized as a disorder throughout recorded history, but psychological treatments are fairly recent. Early treatments applied generic forms of therapy to different problems. Progress accelerated greatly with the development of depression-specific treatments and with psychotherapy research beginning to evaluate these approaches. Much progress has been made in psychotherapy research, with a number of specific studies of particular importance.

EARLY TREATMENTS

Historically, the earliest conceptualizations of depression by the ancient Greeks viewed it as a somatic phenomenon resulting from to an excess of black bile or an imbalance of bodily fluids. Melancholia, which derives from

I would like to thank Myrna M. Weissman for her contributions to this chapter.

the Greek for black bile, was thus treated by somatic remedies, such as various purging methods. It was not until many centuries later that depression began to be viewed in part as a disorder of emotions as well as of biology. As hospitals and asylums developed across Europe, severe depression was treated generally with kindness and with a few somatic remedies, such as cold bathes and spinning chairs. It was primarily with the coming of psychoanalysis that psychotherapy of depression developed.

In his highly influential paper "Mourning and Melancholia," Freud (1925) described depression as a reaction to a loss, either external or internalized. The depressed person is unable to manage the grieving process successfully. Anger toward the lost object is turned inward as anger toward the self. A number of other psychodynamic theorists wrote about the nature of depression and described case studies. Harry Stack Sullivan (1953) focused on the current interpersonal context of a mental disorder and wrote that interpersonal behaviors of others form the most significant events that trigger emotions in people. Adolf Meyer (Winters, 1950–1952) also put great emphasis on the patient's relationship to the environment. Similarly, Bowlby (1969) stated that individuals form strong affectional bonds, and the separation or threat of separation of these bonds gives rise to depression. However, the nature of psychodynamic therapy was generally held to be the same for individuals with different neurotic diagnoses, with more variation among theorists than for specific disorders.

A more recent psychoanalyst, Silvano Arieti (1982), described ways of adapting psychoanalysis to specific forms of depression. Arieti shared the view with Freud that depression represents unresolved grief that is due to childhood events that prevent successful grief work. He elaborated on the nature of loss by differentiating between individuals whose loss results from submission to a dominant other and individuals whose loss is of a dominant goal. Psychoanalytic therapy for the former type of patient is more active, and Arieti warned that in the process of therapy the patient is likely to become angry at the dominant other or the therapist. Psychotherapy for the latter form of depression progresses through interpretations of the meaning of the dominant other or goal. The therapist helps the patient to recognize denied wishes and desires.

PSYCHOTHERAPY RESEARCH AND THERAPY MANUALS

A sea change occurred when the behavior therapies emerged in the late 1950s and the 1960s. Progress was made in developing new therapies and in assessing their effectiveness in controlled trials. It was not until the next decade that the new behavioral paradigm was applied to depression. In the early 1970s a number of case studies described behavioral techniques applied to depression that were originally developed for treating other disorders. For example, Hannie and Adams (1974) reported on treating a case of agitated depression with the exposure technique of flooding.

Until the early 1970s, there were no group design psychotherapy studies using a homogeneous sample of depressed persons, but in 1973 two small studies appeared. One study (Shipley & Fazio, 1973) used a problem-solving therapy with mildly depressed college students, and the other (McLean, Ogston, & Grauer, 1973) used an eclectic set of behavioral modules from which therapists were allowed to choose. Another sign that new approaches to depression were coalescing was the 1971 workshop on the psychology of depression organized by the National Institute of Mental Health (NIMH), which led to an edited book that gathered a number of the authors of emerging theories of depression (Friedman & Katz, 1974).

The late 1970s marked the appearance of depression-specific models and treatments. Therapies were codified into manuals so that they could be reliably taught and administered in research trials. Research teams were developed and systematic evaluation of the therapies was begun. These therapies were developed in parallel during the later 1970s and 1980s, and therefore the following descriptions of them are not in chronological order.

Peter Lewinsohn and Behavior Therapy

A number of authors around this time wrote speculative papers on the behavioral analysis of depression, but it was Peter Lewinsohn (1974) who developed a theoretical model and translated it into a treatment program. Lewinsohn theorized that depression represented a loss or lack of response contingent reinforcement. In other words, when people suffer a loss, such as a job or a loved one, they lose a source of reinforcement that organizes their behavior. In the absence of that reinforcement, many related behavior chains may deteriorate. For example, a person who has lost a friend might lose interest in the activities that the person had previously done with that friend. Formerly enjoyable experiences may lose their reinforcing value because they are connected with the friend.

Lewinsohn identified three ways in which people might suffer from insufficient reinforcement to maintain behaviors: First, the environment may lack reinforcement because of either the loss of a reinforcer or a deficient and unrewarding environment. Second, people may lack the skills (e.g., social, job, assertion) to obtain sufficient reinforcement. Third, people may suffer from anxiety that keeps them from experiencing the reinforcement that the environment offers.

Each of these ways of not being reinforced leads to a different therapy strategy. For the first, activity scheduling or behavioral activation is used to increase the person's rewarding activities. Often when people are depressed, they do not engage in behavior that was formerly rewarding. This approach returns them to those behaviors. The second problem calls for social skill training, and the third for desensitization of the anxiety. Lewinsohn later developed a psychoeducational therapy that combined these therapy modules and added additional content (Lewinsohn et al., 1984). Outcome research by this group began with case reports and matured to controlled studies (e.g., Brown & Lewinsohn, 1984).

Social Skills Training

Joseph Wolpe, one of the founders of behavior therapy, suggested that depression was caused by a lack of assertiveness (Wolpe, 1958). Being unassertive puts people at a disadvantage in interpersonal relationships, leading to unrewarding experiences. Assertiveness training and various formats for improving social skills have been evaluated in a number of studies and have proven effective for depression. One of the prominent studies done by a group at the University of Pittsburgh (Hersen, Bellack, Himmelhoch, & Thase, 1984) was followed by the publication of a treatment manual for the program (Becker, Heimberg, & Bellack, 1987).

A related idea is that depression results from a lack of problem-solving skills. Nezu, Nezu, and Perri's (1989) problem-solving therapy posits that depressed people tend not to view difficulties in their lives as problems to be solved, but as unfortunate situations to be endured. Thus, they benefit from a program that improves their problem-solving skills (Nezu, 1986).

Martin Seligman and Learned Helplessness

Martin E. P. Seligman (1981) conducted animal research leading to a behavioral model of depression with direct implications for behavior therapy. Seligman was doing research with dogs in an escape-avoidance learning paradigm. In this type of study, the animal is in a shuttle box with two sides separated by a low barrier. A light flashes on one side of the box, signaling that a shock will be presented through a grid in the floor in a few seconds. Typically the dog first learns by trial and error that the shock can be escaped by jumping to the other side of the box. Gradually the dog learns to avoid the shock by jumping to the other side when the light comes on before the shock. Seligman observed that when the animals had previously experienced an unavoidable shock, they were poor at learning the escape and avoidance sequence. Some dogs just lay down and waited for the shock to be over. He termed this phenomenon *learned helplessness* and viewed it as an animal model of depression.

When humans encounter uncontrollable aversive experiences, they feel helpless and fail to make effective efforts to improve their lot. A number of parallels between learned helplessness and depression were cited. Seligman extended his research to humans and noted that following an experience with an unsolvable puzzle, they were less able to succeed at a solvable problem. Their behavior in this regard was similar to the behavior of the helpless animals and was also similar to the behavior of depressed individuals.

This model evolved into a more cognitive form (Abramson, Seligman, & Teasdale, 1978) with the idea that humans are vulnerable to becoming helpless and thus developing depression if they hold a depressive attributional style. A depressive attributional style involves making helpless attributions that are internal, stable, and global for negative events and external, unstable, and specific for positive events. That is, depressed people are prone to blame themselves for negative events and assume that the internal cause is a continuing and pervasive tendency of theirs. At the same time, they are prone not to take credit for positive events that are likely to be seen as transient and specific chance occurrences.

Seligman proposed that the learned helplessness model of depression leads to four possible treatment strategies: (a) environmental enrichment, in which psychotherapy would make the person's environment more controllable; (b) personal control training, in which therapy would teach social skills to make the person more effective and less helpless; (c) resignation training, in which therapy would help the person to give up an unrealistic goal; and (d) attributional retraining, in which therapy modifies depressive biases in making attributions about negative and positive events. Interventions did not immediately arise from Seligman's model, but the last strategy has been used in depression prevention interventions (Seligman, Schulman, DeRubeis, & Hollon, 1999).

Aaron Beck and Cognitive Therapy

Trained in the psychodynamic tradition, psychiatrist Aaron T. Beck became dissatisfied with psychodynamic conceptions of depression when they failed to hold up under research scrutiny. He looked for other treatments and was influenced by reading about the cognitive approach of George Kelly. Beck (1963) adapted the central idea that experience is filtered through our cognitive interpretations of events to produce emotional reactions. Disordered emotional conditions result from distorted interpretations of life situations. Beck viewed depression as a negative view of self, the world, and the future, referred to as the *negative cognitive triad*. The depressed person interprets events in terms of catastrophic loss or potential loss. A person's negative interpretations of specific situations are termed *automatic thoughts* in that they are so well rehearsed that the person is scarcely aware of them. For example, if a depressed person passes a colleague in the hall who is looking down and does not say anything, the depressed person's automatic thought might be, "He is mad at me." This interpretation then leads to sad feelings and a sequence of depressed ruminations such as, "What did I do wrong to make him so angry?" The depressed person does not consider more rational alternatives, such as, "Something must have happened in his meeting with the boss this morning."

Beck identified several forms of cognitive distortions typical of depressed persons. For example, *arbitrary inference* is the illogical assumption that some event is caused by oneself, as in the example cited earlier. *Maximization* and *minimization* involve exaggerating the importance of negative events and brushing off positive events. *Inexact labeling* occurs when a person gives a negative label to an event and then reacts to the label.

Beck's (1963) cognitive therapy (Beck, Rush, Shaw, & Emery, 1979) involves identifying negative automatic thoughts and collaboratively developing more rational alternatives, sometimes through experiments (e.g., "Note each interaction with your boss and see if, indeed, he is *always* critical of you"). As more automatic thoughts are identified, patterns become apparent that reveal underlying assumptions and core beliefs, such as, "I never succeed in making friendships" or "I am basically an unlovable and unlikeable person" (see Chapter 7, this volume, for more details). Cognitive therapy is today the most studied form of psychotherapy for depression.

Lynn Rehm and Self-Control/Self-Management Therapy

Lynn Rehm (1977) proposed an integrative theory of depression incorporating elements from Lewinsohn, Beck, and Seligman using a self-control model as a framework. As described by Kanfer (1970), people engage in behaviors that can be thought of as a three-phase feedback loop involving self-monitoring, self-evaluation, and self-reinforcement. *Self-monitoring* means becoming more conscious of the behavior and observing it over time. Self-monitoring leads into self-evaluation, in which we compare our observation to a formal or informal standard. "I will stay under a pack of cigarettes a day this week," which may result in an evaluation, "I did well and feel good about it" or "I did poorly and feel bad." The third and final phase of the feedback loop is self-reinforcement. People influence their own behavior just as they might influence the behavior of another person, through self-administered rewards and punishments. An informal reward might be just feeling good about an accomplishment or "patting oneself on the back." A formal contingent reward might be, "I met my smoking goals this week, so I will go to a movie on Saturday." Failure to meet a goal might lead to self-punishment, mentally "kicking oneself" or contingently staying home and cleaning out the closet.

Perceived losses that lead to depression require efforts to reestablish rewarding relationships with the environment, a self-control task. Rehm (1977) postulated that depression as conceptualized in part by other theorists could be seen as a series of deficits in self-control skills. Six self-control deficits were proposed. In their self-monitoring, depression-prone persons (a) attend to negative events to the relative exclusion of positive events (as in Beck's selective attention) and (b) attend to the immediate as opposed to the delayed consequences of events (focus on current vs. long-term needs). In their self-evaluation, depression prone people (c) set stringent self-evaluative standards (perfectionism and minimizing one's own performance) and (d) make negative attributions (as described by Seligman). In self-reinforcement, these individuals (e) lack self-reward or positive response contingent reinforcement that supplements external contingent positive reinforcement and (f) excessive self-punishment, which works against self-motivation toward long-term goals. The result is difficulty in working toward long-term goals in any systematic way. This may be expressed as hopelessness about the future.

The resultant self-control or self-management therapy for depression has been evaluated in a group psychoeducational format in which the deficits are addressed in sequence. Sessions involve homework check-in, didactic presentations by the therapist, in-session exercises to get experience with the ideas presented, and homework assignments to implement the ideas. The program has been validated by Rehm and his colleagues as well as in other labs and clinics (Rehm & Adams, 2009).

Klerman and Weissman and Interpersonal Psychotherapy

The story of interpersonal psychotherapy began in 1969 at Yale University, when Gerald Klerman was designing a study to test the relative efficacy of a tricyclic antidepressant as maintenance treatment for unipolar depression (Weissman, 2006). The evidence for the efficacy of tricyclic antidepressants for reducing the acute symptoms of depression was strong, yet it was clear that many patients with depression relapsed after termination of the tricyclic medication. It was unclear how long medication should continue and whether psychotherapy had a role in the prevention of relapse. Klerman was both a psychopharmacologist and a psychotherapist, and his broad view of depression was reflected in the design of the psychotherapy component of the study. Influenced by the interpersonal emphasis of such writers as Sullivan, Myers, and Bowlby, the therapy was based on the idea that social and interpersonal processes were associated with the onset and maintenance of depression.

Klerman's earlier work on life events led naturally to identifying interpersonal problem areas related to depression. The four most prevalent were grief, such as complicated bereavement following a death; role disputes, such as conflicts with a significant other in renegotiation, dissolution, or impasse; role transitions, such as change in life status (e.g., divorce, moving, retirement); and interpersonal deficits, such as lack of social skills, boredom, loneliness, or paucity of attachments.

The maintenance study found that drugs prevented relapse and that psychotherapy (called "high contact") improved social functioning (Klerman, Dimascio, Weissman, Prusoff, & Paykel, 1974). The maintenance study was followed by an acute trial of drugs, and the surprisingly effective psychological treatment was rechristened *interpersonal psychotherapy* or IPT. A psychotherapy manual was subsequently published (Klerman, Weissman, Rounsaville, & Chevron, 1984).

MATURING OF THE FIELD

After these beginnings in the 1970s and 1980s, each of the described psychotherapies went through a variety of expansions, revisions, new applications, and continued evaluation. Several themes and sets of findings emerged.

Comparisons Among Psychological Treatments

After the separate therapies were validated in studies comparing them to no therapy or control conditions, researchers began comparing one form of therapy with another in controlled trials. A milestone study was the NIMH Treatment of Depression Collaborative Research Program. The idea for the study came from Gerald Klerman, who at that time was head of the Alcohol, Drug Abuse and Mental Health Administration. In that position, he was frequently asked for opinions on psychological treatments; for example, should a government health program reimburse for treatment X applied to disorder Y? He found it frustrating that available research and reviews often did not provide clear answers. He argued that NIMH should take the lead in providing solid research answers to what worked for whom, somewhat analogous to the way the Food and Drug Administration approves drugs. This could be done by funding larger and more definitive studies of psychotherapies.

As a result, the NIMH depression collaborative program was initiated. A team of experts designed the study to compare two psychotherapies, Beck's cognitive therapy and Klerman and Weissman's interpersonal psychotherapy, with a reference medication and placebo trial. There were many methodological innovations in this study, which have influenced the field to the present. The design was innovative with the reference comparison with a standard medication, imipramine, and a placebo control providing a yardstick against which to compare the psychotherapies. The study was also multisite, with essentially replications at four different locations. Investigators at the different sites had different areas of expertise and allegiance, balancing one another. Experts who were involved with the development of the treatments oversaw therapist training and therapist adherence to manuals. The placebo control condition was also manualized to standardize clinical management.

In the study, 239 depressed patients were treated for 16 weeks. IPT and cognitive therapy were essentially equally effective in treating depression compared with the reference medication and placebo control. There was limited evidence of the effectiveness of interpersonal but not cognitive therapy when compared with the placebo-clinical management condition. There was also evidence of the superiority of both psychotherapies over placebo in the recovery analysis. The standardized clinical management led to an unusually strong placebo effect in this study (Elkin, Shea, Watkins, & Imber, 1989).

In subsequent years, many of these study features were adopted as standard procedure by psychotherapy researchers, leading to an improved and more comparable collection of studies. Overall, however, as in the NIMH collaborative study, the general finding was that different treatments seemed to lead to similar results. A recent report of a series of meta-analyses of outcome studies for depression found a slight advantage for interpersonal psychotherapy and nondirective supportive treatment somewhat less, but concluded that the effect was so small that the conclusion of treatments being equal should remain (Cuijpers, van Straten, Andersson, & van Oppen, 2008).

Comparisons and Combinations With Medications

The NIMH collaborative study was not just a comparison between two psychotherapies. It was also a comparison between psychotherapy and medication. Studies of this type have become more frequent. As with the psychotherapies, studies comparing one medication to another have generally found them to be equally effective with the only differences among them in side-effect profiles. It is not surprising, then, that in general, studies comparing psychotherapy to medication have found them equivalent in outcome of acute treatment (Agency for Health Care Policy and Research, 1993).

One of the questions asked in studies of psychotherapy and medication is whether their combination is more effective than either one alone. Although smaller studies yielded inconsistent results, meta-analytic reviews suggested a small advantage to combined treatment (Conte, Plutchik, Wild, & Karasu, 1986). One large study with 681 participants (Keller et al., 2000) found a clear advantage for a combination of medication and a cognitive–behavioral treatment designed specifically for treating chronic depression (cognitive–behavioral analysis system of psychotherapy). It may take very large numbers of patients to detect differences among treatment conditions.

Another question about medication versus psychotherapy was raised by the national collaborative study. For participants with an initial Hamilton Depression score of 20 or above, medication yielded the most rapid response and was consistently better than placebo. IPT was similar to medications on most measures and was also superior to placebo. Cognitive therapy produced an intermediate outcome. This finding was interpreted by some to suggest that medication was indicated for more severe depression. However, an analysis aggregating data from four studies (DeRubeis, Gelfand, Tang, & Simons, 1999) concluded that cognitive–behavioral therapy actually was slightly superior in outcome for severe depression, although the effect was not statistically significant. The notion that medications are preferable for severe depression did not hold up. It is also noteworthy that evidence indicates that cognitive–behavioral therapy is superior to medication in preventing relapse, even in comparison with continuation medication (Vittengl, Clark, Dunn, & Jarrett, 2007). Continuation cognitive–behavioral therapy further reduces relapse rates. Another finding comes from a large study of sequenced treatments in which participants who failed to respond to an initial trial of medication were switched to an alternative or augmented treatment (Thase et al., 2007). Cognitive therapy as a second step alternative did as well as augmented medication or an alternative medication.

Dismantling Studies and Mechanisms of Action

Most of the controlled research evaluating psychotherapies for depression has used full treatment packages as described in the treatment manuals. A few studies have tried to dismantle treatment packages to evaluate their components–and an even smaller number have attempted to study the mechanisms of change directly. In what was effectively a dismantling study, Lewinsohn's research group (Zeiss, Lewinsohn, & Munoz, 1979) compared the outcome of activity increase, social skill training, and exposure treatments. They found that there were no differences in effects on the targeted deficits. All of the treatments improved activity, social skill, and anxiety components of depression. As a result, Lewinsohn combined the treatments into a larger package. Rehm's research team evaluated the self-management program components by comparing the self-monitoring topics alone, to self-monitoring plus self-evaluation, and to the full program with the self-reinforcement topics (Rehm et al., 1981). As with the Zeiss study, they found no differences in outcome among the three conditions.

The most frequently cited study of this genre was by Neil Jacobson and colleagues (Jacobson et al., 1996). The study was a component analysis of Beck's cognitive therapy with three therapy conditions: behavioral activation only, behavioral activation plus modification of automatic thoughts, and the full cognitive therapy condition, which added on a focus on changing core schemas. The results were no differences in outcome among the three conditions. The authors concluded that because behavioral activation was sufficient to produce the effects of therapy, it therefore might be more parsimonious and easier to teach therapists only the behavioral-activation component.

The results are consistent with two other dismantling studies in not detecting differences (Rehm et al., 1981; Zeiss, Lewinsohn, & Munoz, 1979). Behavioral activation came first in all three conditions. It is a fairly frequent observation that in therapy studies most of the change occurs in the first few weeks of treatment. It may simply be more difficult to detect differences after the first few weeks, even with a large number of participants (150 in this case). It is also possible that any of the three components if presented first would appear to be sufficient. If the Jacobson study had had a condition in which the automatic thoughts component had been offered first, it would have appeared to be sufficient. In general, it has been difficult to find outcome differences among treatments and equally difficult to find effects that are due to separate treatment components.

Empirically Supported Treatments and Evidence-Based Practice

A milestone for psychotherapy research was the publication by the Society of Clinical Psychology (American Psychological Association [APA] Division 12) of its list of empirically supported treatments (Task Force on Promotion and Dissemination of Psychological Procedures, 1995). A task force was charged with examining the state of empirical support for psychotherapies for different psychological problems. The minimum criteria for considering a psychotherapy as being empirically supported was at least two controlled studies using a manual and finding that it performed better than a control condition.

The 1995 list is now maintained and updated by a permanent Science and Practice Committee of Division 12 and is available on a website (PsychologicalTreatments.org) created for practitioners and the public alike. The list for depression currently consists of six strongly supported treatments and six with modest research support. Psychotherapies with strong research support are behavior therapy/behavioral activation, cognitive therapy, cognitive–behavioral analysis system of psychotherapy, interpersonal psychotherapy, problem-solving therapy, and self-management/self-control therapy. Therapies listed with modest research support are acceptance and commitment therapy, behavioral couple therapy, emotion-focused therapy, reminiscence/life review therapy; self-system therapy, and short-term dynamic therapy.

The Division 12 compilation foreshadowed and paralleled a larger movement in health care, typically referred to as *evidence-based practice*.

Today, with the overwhelming amount of research findings that are published annually, new ways of summarizing available information are coming into use, many relying on websites. For example, the Cochrane Library makes available on its website (http://www.cochrane.org/reviews) short reviews of a large number of treatments for both physical and psychological disorders. Along with summaries of treatment research, various organizations are publishing guidelines for best practices for different disorders; for example, in the United States, the Agency for Health Care Policy and Research is charged with formulating guidelines and has published guidelines for treating depression (Agency for Health Care Policy and Research, 1993).

Applications to Specific Populations

The vast majority of early studies of psychotherapies for depression were conducted with adults and few had sufficient numbers to assess the generalizability of effects for subpopulations defined by age, race/ethnicity, and comorbid disorders. Much has changed in recent years. We now possess evidence for effectiveness of treatments with different populations.

Following the lead of the Division 12 list of empirically supported treatments, APA Division 53, Society of Child and Adolescent Psychology, established a task force to survey treatments for children and adolescents. Their website (http://www.clinicalchildpsychology.org) lists IPT as the sole therapy "well established or best-supported psychotherapy," and cognitive–behavioral therapy and medications as "promising or probably efficacious."

Although not collected in a single source, a number of studies have now established a number of psychotherapies as effective for depression in older people (Areán & Cook, 2002). Many impediments exist in offering psychotherapies for depression to minority groups, but a growing number of studies have demonstrated that culturally adapted psychotherapies are successful in treating depression in various minority groups (Griner & Smith, 2006).

Depression is a complication in the treatment of many chronic medical conditions, and psychotherapy as an adjunct to medical treatment has been shown to be effective with many medical disorders (see Chapters 13c and 13d, this volume).

CURRENT STATUS AND FUTURE DIRECTIONS

After 4 decades of research on psychotherapy for depression, we have learned quite a bit. A number of psychotherapies have been demonstrated to be effective for treating depression. Despite being based on different models, these treatments seem to be equally effective in treating depression. We also know that these psychotherapies are about equal to medications in effectiveness, and combining them yields a small increase in effectiveness. We are beginning to see applications to a variety of populations, and what data there are suggest that the same treatments, sometimes with minor adaptations, are effective in these populations also.

Although many questions have been answered, many new questions now have to be asked. Why are psychotherapies of such different theoretical rationales equal in effectiveness? Why do psychotherapies that target different components of depression seem to be equally effective with other components? Behavior therapy improves negative thinking as well as activity level, and cognitive therapy improves activity level as well as negative thinking. More puzzling still, psychotherapy seems to affect physiology and brain chemistry, and medications improve depressive thoughts. In anxiety treatment research, there is a saying that anxiety is not a lump, that is, each of its components needs to be separately targeted by treatment. Depression, on the other hand, appears to be a lump. Change one part of it, and the other parts come along. To borrow a metaphor from Ricardo Munoz, it is as if depression is a system of gears and to get them moving, all you need to do is connect a crank to one gear and all the rest will turn as well (R. Munoz, personal communication, 1987).

Perhaps it is the fact that all of the programs teach a new way of thinking about depression. "You are not worthless, it is your unrecognized cognitive distortions, or it is your interpersonal conflicts to be resolved, or your self-management skills that need to be improved." Is this rationale enough to set people moving in the right direction?

Many psychotherapy manuals contain very similar components. We need to understand these components better and how they contribute to change. Behavioral activation, cognitive restructuring, problem solving, interpersonal-skill building, and other components are shared among programs. Studying components may lead us to answers to the matching problem. Can we tailor a program to an individual and that individual's problems by putting together appropriate components?

Research on psychotherapy for depression has passed the stage of validating treatment package and extending findings to new groups. In the future, we will increasingly study why they work, who they work for, and how to treat those who are now treatment nonresponders.

REFERENCES

Abramson, L. Y., Seligman, M. E. P., & Teasdale, J. D. (1978). Learned helplessness in humans: Critique and reformulation. *Journal of Abnormal Psychology, 87*, 49–74. doi:10.1037/0021-843X.87.1.49

Agency for Health Care Policy and Research. (1993). *Depression in primary care: Vol. 2. Treatment of major depression*. Rockville, MD: U.S. Department of Health and Human Services, Public Health Service, Agency for Health Care Policy and Research.

Areán, P. A., & Cook, B. L. (2002). Psychotherapy and combined psychotherapy/pharmacotherapy for late life depression. *Biological Psychiatry, 52*, 293–303. doi:10.1016/S0006-3223(02)01371-9

Arieti, S. (1982). Psychotherapy. In E. S. Paykel (Ed.), *Handbook of affective disorders* (pp. 297–306). New York, NY: Guilford Press.

Beck, A. T. (1963). Thinking and depression. *Archives of General Psychiatry, 9*, 324–333.

Beck, A. T., Rush, A. J., Shaw, B. F., & Emery, G. (1979). *Cognitive therapy for depression*. New York, NY: Guilford Press.

Becker, R. G., Heimberg, R. E., & Bellack, A. S. (1987). *Social skills training treatment for depression*. New York, NY: Pergamon Press.

Bowlby, J. (1969). *Attachment*. New York, NY: Basic Books.

Brown, R. A., & Lewinsohn, P. M. (1984). A psychoeducational approach to the treatment of depression: Comparison of group, individual, and minimal contact procedures. *Journal of Consulting and Clinical Psychology, 52*, 774–783. doi:10.1037/0022-006X.52.5.774

Conte, H. R., Plutchik, R., Wild, K. V., & Karasu, T. B. (1986). Combined psychotherapy and pharmacotherapy for depression: A systematic analysis of the evidence. *Archives of General Psychiatry, 43*, 471–479.

Cuijpers, P., van Straten, A., Andersson, G., & van Oppen, P. (2008). Psychotherapy for depression in adults: A meta-analysis of comparative outcome studies. *Journal of Consulting and Clinical Psychology, 76*, 909–922. doi:10.1037/a0013075

DeRubeis, R. J., Gelfand, L. A., Tang, T. Z., & Simons, A. D. (1999). Medications versus cognitive behavior therapy for severely depressed outpatients: Mega-analysis of four randomized comparisons. *The American Journal of Psychiatry, 156*, 1007–1013.

Elkin, I., Shea, M. T., Watkins, J. T., & Imber, S. D. (1989). National Institute of Mental Health Treatment of Depression Collaborative Research Program: General effectiveness of treatments. *Archives of General Psychiatry, 46*, 971–982.

Freud, S. (1925). Mourning and melancholia. In *Collected papers* (Vol. 4). London, England: The Hogarth Press.

Friedman, R. J., & Katz, M. M. (Eds.). (1974). *The psychology of depression*. New York, NY: Winston-Wiley.

Griner, D., & Smith, T. B. (2006). Culturally adapted mental health intervention: A meta-analytic review. *Psychotherapy: Theory, Research, Practice, Training, 43*, 531–548.

Hannie, T. J., Jr., & Adams, H. E. (1974). Modification of agitated depression by flooding: A preliminary study. *Journal of Behavior Therapy and Experimental Psychiatry, 5*, 161–166. doi:10.1016/0005-7916(74)90105-0

Hersen, M., Bellack, A. S., Himmelhoch, J. M., & Thase, M. E. (1984). Effects of social skill training, amitriptyline, and psychotherapy in unipolar depressed women. *Behavior Therapy, 15*, 21–40. doi:10.1016/S0005-7894(84)80039-8

Jacobson, N. S., Dobson, K. S., Truax, P. A., Addis, M. E., Koerner, K., Gollan, J. K., . . . Prince, S. E. (1996). A component analysis of cognitive-behavioral treatment for depression. *Journal of Consulting and Clinical Psychology, 64*, 295–304. doi:10.1037/0022-006X.64.2.295

Kanfer, F. H. (1970). Self-regulation: Research, issues, and speculations. In C. Neuringer & J. L. Michaels (Eds.), *Behavior modification in clinical psychology* (pp. 178–220). New York, NY: Appleton-Century-Crofts.

Keller, M. B., McCullough, J. P., Klein, D. N., Arnow, B., Dunner, D. L., Gelenberg, A. J., . . . Zajecka, J. (2000). A comparison of nefazodone, the cognitive behavioral-analysis system of psychotherapy, and their combination for the treatment of chronic depression. *The New England Journal of Medicine, 342,* 1462–1470.

Klerman, G. L., Dimascio, A., Weissman, M. M., Prusoff, B., & Paykel, E. W. (1974). Treatment of depression by drugs and psychotherapy. *The American Journal of Psychiatry, 131,*186–191.

Klerman, G. L., Weissman, M. M., Rounsaville, B., & Chevron, E. S. (1984). *Interpersonal psychotherapy of depression.* New York, NY: Basic Books.

Lewinsohn, P. M. (1974). A behavioral approach to depression. In R. J. Friedman & M. M. Katz (Eds.), *The psychology of depression: Contemporary theory and research* (pp. 157–178). New York, NY: Winston/Wiley.

Lewinsohn, P. M., Antonuccio, D. O., Steinmetz-Breckenridge, J. L., & Teri, L. (1984). *The Coping with Depression course: A psychoeducational intervention for unipolar depression.* Eugene, OR: Castalia.

McLean, P. D., Ogston, K., & Grauer, L. (1973). A behavioral approach to the treatment of depression. *Journal of Behavior Therapy and Experimental Psychiatry, 4,* 323–330. doi:10.1016/0005-7916(73)90002-5

Nezu, A. M. (1986). Efficacy of a social problem-solving therapy approach for unipolar depression. *Journal of Consulting and Clinical Psychology, 54,* 196–202. doi:10.1037/0022-006X.54.2.196

Nezu, A. M., Nezu, C. M., & Perri, M. G. (1989). *Problem-solving therapy for depression: Theory, research and clinical guidelines.* New York, NY: Wiley.

Rehm, L. P. (1977). A self-control model of depression. *Behavior Therapy, 8,* 787–804. doi:10.1016/S0005-7894(77)80150-0

Rehm, L. P., & Adams, J. H. (2009). Self-Management. In W. O'Donohue & J. Fisher (Eds.), *General principles and empirically supported techniques of cognitive behavioral therapy* (pp. 564–570). New York, NY: Wiley.

Rehm, L. P., Kornblith, S. J., O'Hara, M. W., Lamparski, D. M., Romano, J. M., & Volkin, J. I. (1981). An evaluation of major components in a self-control therapy program for depression. *Behavior Modification, 5,* 459–489. doi:10.1177/014544558154002

Seligman, M. E. P. (1981). A learned helplessness point of view. In Rehm (Ed.), *Behavior therapy for depression* (pp. 123–142). New York, NY: Academic Press.

Seligman, M. E. P., Schulman, P., DeRubeis, R. J., & Hollon, S. D. (1999). The prevention of depression and anxiety. *Prevention and Treatment, 2*(1), Article 8.

Shipley, C. R., & Fazio, A. F. (1973). Pilot study of a treatment for psychological depression. *Journal of Abnormal Psychology, 82,* 372–376. doi:10.1037/h0035168

Sullivan, H. S. (1953). *The interpersonal theory of psychiatry.* New York, NY: Norton.

Task Force on Promotion and Dissemination of Psychological Procedures. (1995). Training in and dissemination of empirically validated treatments: Report and recommendations. *Clinical Psychologist, 48,* 3–23.

Thase, M. E., Friedman, E. S., Biggs, M. M., Wisniewski, S. R., Trivedi, M. H., Luther, J. F., . . . Rush, A. J. (2007). Cognitive therapy versus medication in augmentation and switch strategies as second-step treatments: A STAR*D report. *The American Journal of Psychiatry, 164,* 739–752. doi:10.1176/appi.ajp.164.5.739

Vittengl, J. R., Clark, L. A., Dunn, T. W., & Jarrett, R. B. (2007). Reducing relapse and recurrence in unipolar depression: A comparative meta-analysis of cognitive-behavioral therapy's effects. *Journal of Consulting and Clinical Psychology, 75,* 475–488. doi:10.1037/0022-006X.75.3.475

Weissman, M. M. (2006). A brief history of interpersonal psychotherapy. *Psychiatric Annals*, *36*, 553–557.

Winters, E. E. (Ed.). (1950–1952). *The collected papers of Adolf Meyer*. Baltimore, MD: The Johns Hopkins University Press.

Wolpe, J. (1958). *Psychotherapy by reciprocal inhibition*. Stanford, CA: Stanford University Press.

Zeiss, A. M., Lewinsohn, P. M., & Munoz, R. F. (1979). Nonspecific improvement effects in depression using interpersonal skills training, pleasant activity schedules, or cognitive training. *Journal of Consulting and Clinical Psychology*, *47*, 427–439. doi:10.1037/0022-006X.47.3.427

Anxiety Disorders

Barry E. Wolfe

The history of psychotherapy with anxiety disorders can be organized into three overlapping stages. The first stage involved a psychoanalytic focus on anxiety as an integral part of most neurotic and psychotic disorders with only an occasional focus on specific anxiety neuroses. The second stage was a period in which behavioral and cognitive–behavioral therapies were developed to treat more narrowly defined anxiety disorders. This influenced modern psychoanalytic therapies that only recently have been applied to specific anxiety disorders. Most recently, a third stage has begun in which a variety of cognitive–behavioral and integrative psychotherapies have been applied to specific anxiety disorders and to a unified conception of anxiety disorder. This focus on a unifying diagnostic classification has even produced a new classification of a general neurotic syndrome. This new classification encompasses both anxiety and mood disorders and has been called *negative affect syndrome*.

STAGE 1: PSYCHOANALYTIC THERAPIES FOR ANXIETY

Psychoanalytic therapies for the most part did not focus on specific disorders per se, even though Freud (1926/1959) and his followers described a few anxiety-based neuroses that we would now refer to as anxiety disorders. Instead, psychoanalytic therapies analyze the developmental roots of the anxiety and uncover the related unconscious conflicts. The means of change is the therapeutic relationship itself. The analytic or psychodynamic conversation will eventually result in the appearance of the transferential roots of the patient's anxiety, and it is the analysis of these transferential feelings that will lead to uncovering of the unconscious conflicts that maintain the patient's anxiety. Preceding the analysis of transference, however, the psychoanalytic therapist analyzes the psychological defenses that patients use both to reduce the anxiety and to protect them from revealing (to themselves and others) the conflicts that exist outside of their awareness.

The basic therapeutic stance of the psychoanalytic therapist is one of passive listener who occasionally interprets the symbolic meaning of the patient's communications. Interpretive links are made between the patient's present modes of interpersonal functioning and previously adopted interpersonal scenarios. As insights emerge in the therapy session and are thoroughly "worked through," the patient gradually experiences a stronger sense of self, a greater sense of control over life, and increased energy with which to live it. Thus, the change process is construed to be a slow but steady accretion of new thoughts, feelings, and experiences and their integration. Even when specific anxiety-based neuroses such as phobias, obsessional neurosis, or agoraphobia were the subject of psychoanalytic therapy, the same basic treatment was applied. As a result of successful therapy, the client now has the choice of whether to use this new information to change his or her behavior outside of therapy. For this reason, behavior change per se has been of less relevance to psychodynamic therapies than it has for the behavior and cognitive–behavioral therapies.

By the 1940s and 1950s, a conceptual paradigm shift had taken place with the appearance of the object relations school. Its most distinctive point of departure is expressed in Fairbairn's (1952) contention that libido is object seeking, not pleasure seeking. The clear implication was that human beings are social creatures hard-wired by evolution to attach to other people and endeavor to maintain relationships that are felt to be critical to one's sense of security. Anxiety in the object relations model represents the anticipated danger of experiencing or expressing any thought, feeling, or action that might threaten an individual's attachment to the significant people in his or her life.

An even greater shift from Freud's (1926/1959) drive theory and the later ego psychology came with the appearance of self psychology (Kohut, 1979). Kohut posited a developmental deficit model, particularly for individuals suffering from narcissistic defects that prevent them from developing a cohesive self. Anxiety in this perspective is viewed as the fear of losing contact with one's authentic self. The major implication and difference in Kohut's treatment of anxiety is that through empathic attunement, the therapist exhibits qualities and characteristics that patients internalize. These conceptual battles appear to have resulted in relatively minimal changes either in the process of psychoanalytic therapy or in its approach to the treatment of anxiety. Interpretation, for example, appears to be the major intervention used by most psychodynamic therapists. The focus of these interpretations, however, would tend more toward relationships with internal objects, for example, than toward sexual and aggressive wishes.

A second change is that relational therapists place less emphasis on insight and a greater focus on therapist support and empathy. By offering something different and more benign by way of a relationship, the therapist provides a positive model to be internalized by the client, which in turn will bring about positive changes in his or her view of self and others (Greenberg & Mitchell, 1983; Kohut, 1979).

The phrase *anxiety disorder* appeared for the first time in the third edition of the *Diagnostic and Statistical Manual of Mental Disorders* (3rd ed.; DSM–III; American Psychiatric Association, 1980). A sizable number of specific anxiety disorders (e.g., specific phobias, panic disorder, obsessive–compulsive disorder (OCD), generalized anxiety disorder [GAD]) were defined in this and all subsequent editions of the *DSM*. The major implication of this splintered diagnostic classification in terms of psychotherapy is that specific therapies might be developed for specific anxiety disorders.

As practitioners, policymakers, and managed care-based insurance companies began to rely on the *DSM–III* and subsequent editions of the *DSM*, the pressure for psychoanalytic practitioners and researchers to do the same became enormous. Some psychodynamic clinicians have begun to develop manualized psychodynamic psychotherapies for specific *DSM–IV* (American Psychiatric Association, 1994) diagnosed disorders, including, for example, GAD and panic disorder.

For example, a short form of Luborsky's (1984) supportive–expressive treatment has been developed for GAD (Crits-Christoph et al., 1995). Individuals who meet criteria for GAD possess serious doubts about their ability to obtain love, security, stability, and protection from others. These individuals defend against the rising fear produced by these assumptions by "worrying" rather than facing painful emotional conflicts. But these conflicts continue to influence individuals with GAD and lead them to develop repetitive maladaptive relationship patterns. The patterns are actually vicious cycles in which the individual behaves toward others on the basis of his or her maladaptive basic assumptions, which then encourage responses from others that confirm the individual's original beliefs.

Other psychodynamic clinicians have attempted to develop a manualized psychodynamic therapy for panic disorder. They call their treatment *panic-focused psychodynamic psychotherapy* (Milrod et al, 1997). Whereas traditional psychoanalytic therapies tended to ignore the manifest symptoms of a disorder in favor of an exploration of their underlying, unconscious determinants, this therapy maintains a focus on the symptoms of panic disorder with or without agoraphobia. This therapy can be used as a short-term treatment for the elimination of panic and agoraphobic symptoms or as a longer term treatment to resolve the panic patient's vulnerability to relapse. To do the latter, however, the therapy must address the unconscious dynamisms that predispose the panic patient to panic symptoms.

STAGE 2: BEHAVIORAL AND COGNITIVE–BEHAVIORAL THERAPIES FOR ANXIETY DISORDER

The behavioral perspective began as a revolt against the study of consciousness as the basic data of psychology. Its philosophical and methodological commitments spawned a number of learning theories that served as the intellectual scaffolding for the various behavior therapies in the 1950s and

1960s. These theories attempted to focus on publicly observable behaviors and consequently redefined emotional experiences as behavioral responses. Thus, anxiety was reconceptualized as a conditioned fear response, an observable behavioral response. All of the behavior therapies that subsequently emerged were considered to be applications of modern learning theory to clinical disorders (Eysenck, 1959).

Behavioral Therapies for Phobias and Anxiety Problems

Although behavioral therapies for phobias did not come into existence until the late 1950s, research was conducted much earlier on the conditioning of fear responses. From the behavioral point of view, anxiety or fear (because the terms are often used interchangeably) is both a basic biological given and a learned response. Behavioral researchers defined two basic learning processes: classical and instrumental conditioning. A classically conditioned fear response is produced by contiguously pairing a neutral stimulus with a stimulus that inherently causes fear or pain. An instrumental conditioned fear response is learned through the provision of environmental reinforcements for selected, self-initiated behaviors. Combining these two learning processes, Mowrer offered a two-factor theory that explained both the acquisition and maintenance of a conditioned fear. Anxiety in this account is acquired through classical conditioning but then serves as a secondary motivation or drive that produces tension in the organism. Avoiding the fear stimulus then reduces the autonomically mediated tension, and this "drive reduction" reinforces the avoidance behavior (Mowrer, 1939).

If fear responses could be learned through either learning process, behavioral therapists argued that fear could be unlearned through the lack of reinforcement of the fear response. Thus, if the conditioned stimulus results in no pain, the learned pattern eventually will be extinguished. Wolpe (1958) provided experimental evidence for another method of reducing fear: Have individuals emit responses that are antagonistic to fear. Through his research with cats, he found that a phobic response could be learned and unlearned, the latter through the previously mentioned principle of reciprocal inhibition (now more widely known as counterconditioning). Although Wolpe suggested that many different kinds of responses are antagonistic to anxiety, he eventually settled on relaxation as the primary anxiety antagonist in his therapy, systematic desensitization.

Behavioral treatments of specific phobias typically involve exposure to the phobic object or situation and the simultaneous use of a specific relaxation strategy. Wolpe instructed the patient to imagine a series of scenes involving a feared object, arranged hierarchically from the least to the most frightening. Patients would begin by imagining the least frightening scene that still induced anxiety and would then use a previously learned relaxation strategy to reduce the anxiety. The imagery trials with a given scene would continue until the patient could imagine the scene without anxiety. At that point, the procedure would move to the next scene in the hierarchy. This would continue until the patient could imagine the most frightening scene in the hierarchy in an anxiety-free state (Wolpe, 1958).

Eventually, a number of effective behavior therapy techniques were developed for phobias, yet they all seemed to possess the common factor of exposing the individual either in imagination or in vivo to the feared object or situation. As the various behavioral treatments were applied to specific anxiety disorders, it was clear to most behavior therapy practitioners and researchers that exposure to the anxiety-producing stimuli was a necessary component of effective treatment.

Social Phobias (Social Anxiety Disorder)

Early on, systematic desensitization was used to treat social anxiety as well as other phobias (Wolpe, 1958). In 1971, Goldfried introduced a self-control variation of the desensitization. It used the same desensitization paradigm, but there were some significant differences in procedure added. Goldfried reconceptualized desensitization as training in coping skills. Desensitization sessions therefore can be seen as providing practice in coping with anxiety.

Agoraphobia

When behavior therapists first began to treat agoraphobia, they focused on the avoidance behavior. A number of exposure in vivo programs were developed that entailed a gradual movement away from a point of safety toward a feared location. Although exposure in vivo was initially found to be effective in increasing the distance that a patient could travel away from his or her point of safety, a number of limitations were also uncovered for this treatment. For example, panic attacks were unaffected by exposure in vivo.

Behavior therapists began to notice that agoraphobic patients seemed to be very frightened of specific bodily sensations. Interoceptive exposure (exposure to the feared body sensation) was added to desensitize individuals to these specific bodily sensations. Still, not everyone benefited from exposure therapy and there typically was a fairly high dropout rate for agoraphobic patients in studies of this treatment (Barlow, 1988).

Obsessive–Compulsive Disorder

A treatment package of exposure and response prevention was developed for OCD in the 1960s (Meyer, 1966). This treatment combined in vivo exposure to a feared stimulus with subsequent prevention of the compulsive behavior. This combination compels the patient to experience the anxiety that he or she has been avoiding through ritualization. Prolonged exposure is presumed to reduce anxiety through habituation, whereas response prevention reduces ritualistic behavior through extinction. In a review of 16 studies reporting long-term outcome, 76% were responders (Foa & Kozak, 1996). There are, however, still a significant number of patients who relapse, perhaps as many as a third of those treated.

Social Learning Theory

Bandura's (1977) social learning theory represented a bridge between the earlier behavior therapies and the later cognitive–behavioral therapies. His core assumption was that learning through observation was not only feasible but necessary. Vicarious learning can produce three kinds of cognitive representations: (a) behavior possibilities, (b) outcome expectancies, and (c) self-efficacy expectancies. Self-efficacy expectancies were critical in the development of anxiety. Bandura contended that anxiety results from a person's perception that he or she cannot cope with a potentially aversive situation. Low self-efficacy expectancies create problems, and improvement in self-efficacy is the critical mechanism in positive therapy changes.

On the basis of his self-efficacy theory, Bandura used a variety of performance-based treatments to show the importance of self-efficacy expectations in therapeutic change, particularly in patients with agoraphobia and snake phobia. This treatment does not focus on exposure per se, but rather on the amount of information that a person obtains about his or her ability to cope with challenges in the environment. Instead of being passively exposed to fear stimuli, the individual attempts challenging tasks. Success presumably brings an increase in self-efficacy beliefs.

The behavioral therapies produced useful results in the treatment of anxiety. However, they were found wanting when it became clear how much an individual's thought processes were involved in the maintenance of anxiety disorders. This insight led to the rise of cognitive and cognitive–behavioral models.

Cognitive–Behavioral Treatments

All cognitive–behavioral therapies assume that "1. Cognitive activity affects behavior. 2. Cognitive activity can be monitored and altered. 3. Desired behavior change may be affected through cognitive change" (Dobson, 2001, p. 4). The early approaches to cognitive therapy focused on the patient's conscious cognitions and self-statements (Meichenbaum, 1977). More recently, cognitive therapists have added a focus on unconscious cognitive schemas that presumably generate the dysfunctional automatic thoughts associated with a given psychological disorder. In the case of anxiety disorders, the relevant schemas relate to perceived, experienced, or imagined dangers in the world (Beck & Emery, 1985). There are now in existence a number of versions of cognitive–behavioral therapy that attempt to directly change cognitive schemas by cognitive means or conduct behavioral procedures to achieve the same ends.

In the cognitive–behavioral treatment of any given anxiety disorder, one is likely to find a relaxation strategy to inhibit the somatic anxiety, some form of exposure therapy for the relevant fear stimuli, and cognitive restructuring methods for modifying inaccurate, danger-related cognitive schemata and negative thoughts. More recently, cognitive–behavioral therapists have included affect as a dimension and target of therapeutic change (Barlow, 2000).

The therapy is relatively directive; therefore, the therapist's role is one of an expert who guides the unfolding of the therapy. The relationship, however, has been described as *collaborative empiricism* in which the therapist and client collaborate on the setting of therapeutic goals, and on the means and timing of specific therapeutic tasks. The therapist, for example, often suggests behavioral experiments for the client to test the accuracy of his or her cognitive schemas. Therapeutic empathy is an important skill, not only for building rapport but also for helping the therapist understand the nuances of the patient's problems.

Exposure to the primary fear stimuli is a common feature of cognitive–behavioral therapy, although the focus and content of exposure may vary with the disorder. Recently, for example, the technique of worry exposure has been added to the protocol for GAD (Brown, O'Leary, & Barlow, 2001). For phobic patients, exposure is applied imaginally or in vivo to the phobic object or situation. In panic disorder patients, interoceptive exposure is used for the feared body sensations, whereas for OCD patients, exposure to the obsessional thought is uniformly used. Cognitive techniques, such as the downward arrow technique or Socratic questioning are often used to explore the patient's danger cognitions. Cognitive restructuring techniques are used to modify dysfunctional cognitive schemata, and behavior-rehearsal techniques are used to teach new and more effective behaviors.

Specific Phobias

The cognitive–behavioral therapies of specific phobias focus on maladaptive cognitions in addition to the earlier behavioral focus on exposure to fear stimuli. Maladaptive cognitions are seen as elicitors of anticipatory anxiety and anxiety experienced when faced with the phobic object or situation. The reduction of fear may occur through the reduction of negative self-statements. Fewer negative self-statements would produce less physiologically based fear, which in turn would result in less avoidance behavior. This hypothesis has been difficult to empirically test because most cognitive treatments of specific phobias include exposure.

Social Phobias (Social Anxiety Disorder)

Heimberg and colleagues have developed a 12-session group cognitive–behavioral therapy for social anxiety disorder. The group format allows for (a) learning vicariously, (b) seeing that one is not alone with this type of problem, (c) making a public commitment to change, (d) having others to help correct one's distorted thinking, and (e) having several built-in role play partners (Turk, Heimberg, & Hope, 2001). The major techniques, however, include exposure to fear stimuli and cognitive restructuring. After each session, homework is given, which involves recording automatic thoughts in anxiety-provoking situations, identifying the thinking errors, questioning the automatic thoughts, and creating rational responses. The authors report that 80% of treatment completers experience meaningful reductions in their social anxiety.

Panic Disorder with Agoraphobia

Cognitive–behavioral therapies focus on the multifaceted features of this disorder, including the elimination of the panic attacks, the reduction of the anticipatory anxiety, the cognitive restructuring of the catastrophic cognitions related to frightening body sensations, and the elimination of avoidance behavior. Barlow's panic control treatment provides a highly structured therapy for panic disorder and agoraphobia (Craske & Barlow, 2001). The 15-session treatment protocol includes psychoeducation about the nature of panic disorder, breathing retraining, cognitive restructuring of the patient's overestimation of danger and catastrophic thinking, interoceptive exposure to the frightening body sensations, and in vivo exposure to agoraphobic situations. Most patients are panic free at the end of treatment, and these gains are maintained for at least 2 years. However, about 50% of patients continue to suffer from substantial symptomatology despite improving initially. This is particularly true for patients with severe agoraphobia. Similar cognitive–behavioral therapy models of panic disorder developed by Clark (1986) and Beck (Beck & Emery, 1985) have achieved similar results.

Obsessive–Compulsive Disorder

Exposure plus response prevention (ERP) is generally viewed as the treatment of choice for OCD. However, several cognitive–behavioral therapists (e.g., Foa & Kozak, 1996) maintain that cognitive change is an integral part of ERP, particularly the disconfirmation of erroneous beliefs. Several cognitive therapies that do not include exposure as a component have also been developed. At least one study has shown that rational emotive therapy was as effective as ERP (Emmelkamp, Visser, & Hoekstra, 1988). Beyond this, there is little research on the efficacy of any purely cognitive therapy with OCD.

Generalized Anxiety Disorder

Two major cognitive–behavioral treatments have been developed for GAD. The cognitive–behavioral therapy package developed by Borkovec attempts to teach clients to identify internal and external anxiety cues and to implement new coping skills. The treatment involves self-monitoring of worrying and other anxiety symptoms, applied relaxation training, cognitive restructuring for the client's negative thinking, and imagery rehearsal of coping skills. On average, about 50% of GAD patients who participate in clinical trials achieve high end-state functioning by the end of treatment (Borkovec & Ruscio, 2001).

The cognitive–behavioral therapy program developed by Barlow and his colleagues (Brown et al., 2001) includes self-monitoring, progressive muscle relaxation, cognitive countering of the individual's misinterpretations of situations, and worry exposure. The latter technique is a relatively new addition to the cognitive–behavioral therapy armamentarium for GAD. Worry exposure entails (a) the identification of two or three major areas of worry for the individual, which are then hierarchically ordered in ascending levels of stress; (b) imagery training of pleasant scenes; and (c) self-exposure to one's anxious thoughts while imagining the worst possible outcome for that particular area of worry. The individual moves up each step of the hierarchy only after he or she can vividly imagine the worry with no or low levels of anxiety. The key mechanisms of change for this therapy include the habituation of anxiety, cognitive restructuring of inaccurate thoughts, and worry behavior prevention. To date, there are only promising pilot data in support of this new added technique (Brown et al., 2001).

A third model is worth mentioning for its promising conceptual extensions of the cognitive treatment of GAD. Wells (2004) proposed that pathological worry is based in dysfunctional metacognitive beliefs about the meaning and significance of worry. Negative "meta-worrying" escalates the individual's distress, which in turn prevents the disconfirming of negative beliefs about the imagined dangers of worrying. Wells's specialized form of cognitive therapy helps patients become aware of how metacognitions about worrying and the resulting maladaptive behavioral responses maintain their GAD. A recent open trial of community outpatients with GAD treated with metacognitive therapy has shown promising results.

Behavioral and cognitive–behavioral therapies have been quite effective in ameliorating the symptoms associated with each specific anxiety disorder. They have been less successful, however, in changing the core dysfunctions generating these disorders, whether they are conceptualized as negative core self-schema, the propensity to meta-worry, or a fundamental intolerance of uncertainty.

STAGE 3: INTEGRATIVE PSYCHOTHERAPY FOR SPECIFIC ANXIETY DISORDERS AND FOR A UNIFIED CONCEPTION

The rise of psychotherapy integration was based, among other reasons, on the limitations of so-called single-school approaches to psychotherapy (Norcross, 2005). Since its inception, a number of integrative psychotherapies have been developed. Early on, only generic psychotherapies were developed, but more recently, integrative therapies have been developed for specific behavioral disorders.

One of these is a therapy that attempts to expand the benefits of cognitive–behavioral therapy for GAD. Castonguay and colleagues (Castonguay, Newman, Borkovec, Holtforth, & Maraba, 2005) hypothesized that cognitive–behavioral therapy's efficacy with GAD would improve by facilitating an emotionally immediate exploration of the patient's problematic relationships with significant others. Cognitive–behavioral therapy was therefore supplemented by a focus on interpersonal functioning and emotional deepening. GAD patients can benefit from deepening of their emotional experience of their relationships because they routinely ignore or fear their emotions. The 1st hour of the 2-hour therapy session involves a cognitive–behavioral therapy session that includes self-monitoring and early cue detection, stimulus control methods, relaxation methods, self-control desensitization, and cognitive therapy. The 2nd hour focuses on exploring and changing interpersonal functioning and facilitating emotional deepening. Only preliminary outcome results are available at this point in time.

The current decade has witnessed the emergence of transdiagnostic models of anxiety disorder based on the premise that the similarities among the various anxiety disorders far outweigh the differences. A generic cognitive therapy that focuses on these similarities is in the process of development. This reduces the need for separate treatment manuals for different anxiety disorders. This is a new development, and efficacy data are relatively sparse (Norton, 2006).

For the past 2 decades, I have been developing an integrative theory and psychotherapy for anxiety disorders in general as opposed to specific anxiety disorders. My integrative model postulates that the root of anxiety disorders lies in unbearably painful self-perceptions and conceptions (self-wounds) that are initially experienced as feared catastrophes. These unbearably painful self-views contain an associative network of ideas, images, and feelings linked to specific unavoidable human experiences (existential crises) with which the individual cannot cope, such as mortality, loss, and responsibility for harming others (Wolfe, 2008). The immediate experience of anxiety produces self- preoccupied cogitation about one or more feared catastrophes, which increases the intensity and/or duration of the individual's anxiety. More important, their cogitation prevents them from understanding and experiencing the implicit meaning of their anxiety or panic (Wolfe, 2005).

A four-stage treatment has been developed that entails (a) establishing the therapeutic alliance; (b) using cognitive–behavioral therapy for the symptoms of an anxiety disorder; (c) eliciting the preconscious self-wounds through focusing and other experiential techniques; and (d) healing the self-wounds, which involves therapeutic strategies from the three major schools of psychotherapy (i.e., psychodynamic, experiential, and cognitive behavioral). Although this therapy has been successfully applied by the author and several of his students, it has not been empirically evaluated.

ANXIETY DISORDERS AND BEYOND

Several therapies for anxiety disorders appear to apply to depressive disorders as well. Similar self-wounds often appear to be the underlying roots of depressive disorders (Wolfe, 2005). Castonguay et al.'s (2005) therapy has also been applied to depression, suggesting that the two classes of disorders share more similarities than differences. David Barlow, who ironically was a leading voice in the differentiation of the older term *neurosis* into several more narrowly defined disorders (Barlow, 1988), has recently suggested that a broad category of emotional disorders that he calls *negative affect syndrome* can be treated by a manualized unified treatment. Barlow and his colleagues contend that the etiology of the negative affect syndrome is based in interacting vulnerabilities that include a generalized biological vulnerability, a generalized psychological vulnerability, and a specific psychological vulnerability resulting from early learning. To ameliorate this syndrome, Barlow has developed a four-component therapy (a) using a standard psycho-educational phase; (b) altering antecedent cognitive reappraisals—an intensive emotion-regulation procedure; (c) preventing emotional avoidance that targets cognitive, behavioral, and somatic experiential avoidance; and (d) facilitating action tendencies not associated with the emotion that is disordered. Thus far, they have collected data from small groups of patients with a variety of different emotional disorders (Barlow, Allen, & Choate, 2004).

Although the evolution of psychotherapy with the anxiety disorders has certainly improved the lives of millions of patients so afflicted, the next hundred years may see the elimination of this diagnostic category. If such unifying constructs as negative affect syndrome becomes an accepted diagnostic category, then the term *anxiety disorders* may be consigned to the status of an historical footnote.

REFERENCES

American Psychiatric Association. (1980). *Diagnostic and statistical manual of mental disorders* (3rd ed.). Washington, DC: Author.

American Psychiatric Association. (1994). *Diagnostic and statistical manual of mental disorders* (4th ed.). Washington, DC: Author.

Bandura, A. (1977). Self-efficacy: Toward a unifying theory of behavioral change. *Psychological Review, 84,* 191–215. doi:10.1037/0033-295X.84.2.191

Barlow, D. H. (1988). *Anxiety and its disorders.* New York, NY: Guilford Press.

Barlow, D. H. (2000). Unraveling the mysteries of anxiety and its disorders from the perspective of emotion theory. *American Psychologist, 55,* 1247–1263. doi:10.1037/0003-066X. 55.11.1247

Barlow, D. H., Allen, L. B., & Choate, M. L. (2004). Toward a unified treatment for emotional disorders. *Behavior Therapy, 35,* 205–230. doi:10.1016/S0005-7894(04)80036-4

Beck, A. T., & Emery, G. (with Greenberg, R.). (1985). *Anxiety disorders and phobias: A cognitive perspective.* New York, NY: Basic Books.

Borkovec, T. D., & Ruscio, A. M. (2001). Psychotherapy for generalized anxiety disorder. *The Journal of Clinical Psychiatry, 62*(Suppl. 11), 37–42.

Brown, T. A., O'Leary, T. A., & Barlow, D. H. (2001). Generalized anxiety disorder. In D. H. Barlow (Ed.), *Clinical handbook of psychological disorders* (3rd ed., pp. 154–208). New York: Guilford Press.

Castonguay, L. G., Newman, M. G., Borkovec, T. D., Holtforth, M. G., & Maraba, C. G. (2005). Cognitive-behavioral assimilative integration. In J. C. Norcross & M. R. Goldfried (Eds.), *Handbook of psychotherapy integration* (2nd ed., pp. 241–260). New York, NY: Oxford University Press.

Clark, D. M. (1986). A cognitive approach to panic. *Behaviour Research and Therapy, 24,* 461–470. doi:10.1016/0005-7967(86)90011-2

Craske, M. G., & Barlow, D. H. (2001). Panic disorder and agoraphobia. In D. H. Barlow (Ed.), *Clinical handbook of psychological disorders* (3rd ed., pp. 1–59). New York, NY: Guilford Press.

Crits-Christoph, P., Crits-Christoph, K., Wolf-Palacio, D., Fichter, M., & Rudick, D. (1995). Brief supportive-expressive psychodynamic therapy for generalized anxiety disorder. In J. P. Barber & P. Crits-Christoph (Eds.), *Dynamic therapies for psychiatric disorders: Axis I* (pp. 43–83). New York, NY: Basic Books.

Dobson, K. S. (2001). *Handbook of cognitive-behavioral therapies* (2nd ed.). New York, NY: Guilford Press.

Emmelkamp, P. M. G., Visser, S., & Hoekstra, R. J. (1988). Cognitive therapy vs. exposure in vivo in the treatment of obsessive-compulsives. *Cognitive Therapy and Research, 12,* 103–114. doi:10.1007/BF01172784

Eysenck, H. J. (1959). Learning theory and behavior therapy. *British Journal of Medical Science, 105*, 61–75.

Fairbairn, W. R. D. (1952). *An object-relations theory of the personality.* New York, NY: Basic Books.

Foa, E. B., & Kozak, M. J. (1996). Psychological treatment of obsessive-compulsive disorder. In M. R. Mavissakalian & R. P. Prien (Eds.), *Long-term treatments of anxiety disorders* (pp. 285–309). Washington, DC: American Psychiatric Press.

Freud, S. (1959). Inhibitions, symptoms, and anxiety. In J. Strachey (Ed. & Trans.), *The standard edition of the complete psychological works of Sigmund Freud* (Vol. 20, pp. 87–172). London: Hogarth Press. (Original work published 1926)

Goldfried, M. R. (1971). Systematic desensitization as training in self-control. *Journal of Consulting and Clinical Psychology, 37*, 228–234. doi:10.1037/h0031974

Greenberg, J., & Mitchell, S. (1983). *Object relations in psychoanalytic theory.* Cambridge, MA: Harvard University Press.

Kohut, H. (1979). The two analyses of Mr. Z. *The International Journal of Psychoanalysis, 60*, 3–27.

Luborsky, L. (1984). *Principles of psychoanalytic psychotherapy: A manual for supportive-expressive treatment.* New York, NY: Basic Books.

Meichenbaum, D. H. (1977). *Cognitive-behavior modification: An integrative approach.* New York, NY: Plenum Press.

Meyer, V. (1966). Modification of expectations in cases with obsessional rituals. *Behaviour Research and Therapy, 4*, 273–280.

Milrod, B., Busch, F., Cooper, A., & Shapiro, T. (1997). *Manual of panic-focused psychodynamic psychotherapy.* Washington, DC: American Psychiatric Press.

Mowrer, O. H. (1939). Stimulus response theory of anxiety. *Psychological Review, 46*, 553–565. doi:10.1037/h0054288

Norcross, J. C. (2005). A primer on psychotherapy integration. In J. C. Norcross & M. R. Goldfried (Eds.), *Handbook of psychotherapy integration* (2nd ed., pp. 3–23). New York, NY: Oxford University Press.

Norton, P. J. (2006). Toward a clinically-oriented model of anxiety disorders. *Cognitive Behaviour Therapy, 35*, 88–105. doi:10.1080/16506070500441561

Turk, C. L., Heimberg, R. G., & Hope, D. A. (2001). Social anxiety disorder. In D. H. Barlow (Ed.), *Clinical handbook of psychological disorders* (pp. 114–153). New York, NY: Guilford Press.

Wells, A. (2004). A cognitive model of GAD: Metacognitions and pathological worry. In R. G. Heimberg, C. L. Turk, & D. S. Mennin (Eds.), *Generalized anxiety disorders: Advances in research and practice* (pp. 164–186). New York, NY: Guilford Press.

Wolfe, B. E. (2008). Existential issues in anxiety disorders and their treatment. In K. J. Schneider (Ed.), *Existential-integrative psychotherapy: Guideposts to the core of practice* (pp. 204–216). New York, NY: Routledge.

Wolfe, B. E. (2005). *Understanding and treating anxiety disorders: An integrative approach to healing the wounded self.* Washington, DC: American Psychological Association. doi:10.1037/11198-000

Wolpe, J. (1958). *Psychotherapy by reciprocal inhibition.* Stanford, CA: Stanford University Press.

Substance Abuse

Peter E. Nathan and Anne Helene Skinstad

This chapter traces the development of psychosocial treatments for substance abuse from the 1960s to the present. From an array of techniques and procedures without empirical backing or proven effectiveness in the 1960s, a significant number of empirically supported interventions today have shown substantial effectiveness.

THE 1960s: DIVERSE TREATMENTS, UNPROVEN EFFECTIVENESS

Most of the individual and group psychotherapy done in the early 1960s with patients with a wide range of diagnoses, including substance abuse and dependence, was broadly based on psychoanalytic principles. To this end, most psychoanalytic psychotherapists believed that alcoholism was an expression of underlying unconscious conflict and that the primary treatment goal was resolution of this unconscious conflict so that the patient no longer needed to drink to deal with the depression, anxiety, and/or psychotic behaviors for which it was responsible.

At the same time, many psychotherapists with extensive experience with alcohol-dependent patients believed that they tended not to be good candidates for insight-oriented treatment. Many suffered from long-term cognitive dysfunction, came to treatment intoxicated, and were unmotivated to do anything about their drinking. In truth, for many chronic alcoholics, especially those who were poor and without much in the way of resources, alcohol was one of the few things in their lives that they valued. The minority of alcoholics who actually sought treatment often joined Alcoholics Anonymous (AA), a self-help group founded 30 years earlier that claimed considerable success with alcohol dependence. Although most mental health professionals paid lip service to AA as a way to reach patients unreachable by other means, to each other they expressed the belief that its efficacy was limited to "character disorders" and "psychopaths."

The psychosocial treatment accorded individuals with alcohol abuse and dependence in the early 1960s was not all that different from that used in earlier decades. There was rather expensive individual psychoanalytic psychotherapy, generally considered of limited value for more deteriorated alcoholics, albeit of somewhat greater efficacy for individuals whose alcoholism was not yet chronic or associated with cognitive dysfunction. There was group therapy, with 12-step or psychoanalytic foci, of limited value for chronic alcoholics. There was AA, which seemed to be helpful to quite a number of alcoholics, but of unproven efficacy—and the object of disdain by many professionals. And there were inpatient facilities, either 12 step or psychoanalytically oriented. They were considered the treatment of choice for most alcoholics because they took patients out of their typically alcohol-centered environments for a time. These inpatient facilities were often located far away from urban areas, in the belief that a return to sobriety was best achieved in a serene, uncomplicated setting. In general, for most persons with an alcohol problem that had lasted for several years, regardless of the treatment, prognosis was guarded. Most experienced psychologists and psychiatrists worked hard to avoid having to treat such persons.

The efficacy of treatments for other kinds of substance abuse was not much different. Their theoretical underpinnings generally reflected psychoanalytic theory, so these treatments also endeavored to help the heroin or cocaine addict bring the unconscious conflict to consciousness. Substance abuse other than alcoholism was less common and attracted much less attention than it does today. Consequently, there were relatively few treatment facilities for patients addicted to drugs other than alcohol. But the results of treatment, mediocre at best, were generally the same as those for alcoholism.

Then as now, a small percentage of substance abuse patients were in treatment at any given time. A few empirical studies of psychosocial alcoholism treatment had been reported; their findings were quite disappointing. Typically, less than a third of the patients receiving treatment remained drug or alcohol free for any length of time (Sterne & Pittman, 1965). The explanation by those who supported the treatment status quo was that substance abusers were poor psychotherapy patients because of their character disorders.

By the middle 1960s, however, things had begun to change. The phenothiazines had started emptying the state hospitals of patients suffering from schizophrenia, many of whom could function independently in the community with outpatient services; the monoamine oxidase inhibitors and tricyclic antidepressants appeared to be more effective than previous treatments for depression; and the benzodiazepines and carbamates, whose profound abuse potential had not yet been fully recognized, were viewed by many as wonder drugs that could alleviate disabling anxiety in patients. All of these and other new psychopharmacologic agents were given to substance abusers in the belief that treating their comorbid depression, anxiety, or schizophrenia more effectively would reduce their propensity to use drugs to deal with their symptoms. Typically, the initial use of these medications with substance abusers yielded promising early results. However, after a few years, reality would set in, accompanied by the more nuanced judgment that, although these drugs might be useful for some addicts with comorbid anxiety, depression, or schizophrenia, they did not and would not constitute definitive treatments for substance abuse (Gallant, 1995).

Meanwhile, on the psychosocial front, the efficacy of psychoanalytic psychotherapy had begun seriously to be questioned, following Hans Eysenck's influential attacks on it in the 1950s and early 1960s (e.g., Eysenck, 1952, 1960). Although no other equally well-regarded treatments had yet been developed, Joseph Wolpe (1969) published intriguing findings from his experiments with systematic desensitization. Fellow behavioral clinicians had reported promising data attesting to the power of behavior therapy and behavior modification with a variety of disorders, including substance abuse (Nathan, 1969). Hence, it was not surprising that a new generation of clinicians, many of them psychologists, joined the behavior therapy bandwagon and began developing behavioral treatments for substance abuse.

THE 1970s

Hallmarks of 1970s treatments for substance abuse include aversion conditioning—promising but difficult to implement; community reinforcement therapy—effective, empirically supported, and a model for more recent community-wide interventions; nonabstinence treatment goals—controversial and ultimately discredited; and harm reduction—promising and still in development.

Aversion Conditioning

Behavioral treatments for alcoholism, especially those termed *broad spectrum*, proliferated in the 1970s. These treatments were not the first behavioral treatments for alcoholism, however. In the early 1930s, a Russian physician named Kantorovich, using classical conditioning, paired painful electric shock with the sight, taste, and smell of alcoholic beverages over repeated conditioning trials, reporting very positive results with alcoholic patients. Electrical aversion conditioning of alcoholics then went into decline until the 1950s and 1960s, when it experienced a bit of a renaissance; however, it never grew enough to constitute a movement. By contrast, chemical aversion, which pairs the sight, taste, and smell of alcoholics' favorite beverages with a nausea-inducing chemical (usually apomorphine) over several conditioning sessions, has been used more widely from the 1940s to the present (Davidson, 1974). Aversive treatments are exceedingly unpleasant and very expensive; as a result, they tend to attract only highly motivated patients. Hence, they have not become very popular, although several treatment centers continue to offer chemical aversion, largely because its results are quite positive, despite its costs and patient recruitment problems.

When behavioral treatments for substance abuse were first introduced, it was believed that abusive drinking and drug use were learned maladaptive behaviors that could be modified or extinguished by treatment methods derived from learning theory. Nowadays, in recognition of research implicating genetic, personality, and concurrent psychopathology as well in the etiology of these conditions, these earlier beliefs are no longer widely held. Nonetheless, behavioral methods have become treatments of choice for these conditions because they have yielded superior outcomes (McCrady & Nathan, 2006). The term *broad spectrum* was coined by Arnold Lazarus (1971) to describe his decision to combine systematic desensitization with other behavioral methods to confront his patients' typically wide array of problems, including substance abuse. Lazarus' multimodal therapy was modified and extended in the early 1970s by investigators developing new alcoholism treatments (e.g., Sobell & Sobell, 1973).

Community-Reinforcement Therapy

One of the few broad-spectrum treatment programs developed during this period to have stood the test of time is community-reinforcement therapy, developed by Hunt and Azrin (1973). Comparing a small group of hospitalized chronic alcoholics who were offered community-reinforcement treatment with a matched group of patients who received standard hospital ward–milieu therapy, these investigators reported that the community-reinforcement group did substantially better than the standard-treatment group in eliminating their abusive drinking. Community reinforcement involved systematic modification of patients' natural reinforcers—vocational, familial, and social—so that access to them could be withdrawn whenever they began to drink again. To heighten the effects of this intervention, patients received training in job acquisition and maintenance skills, marital and family therapy, and social skills training. The concept of community reinforcement—providing alcoholics and drug abusers with access to reinforcers such as money or vouchers for positive changes in their substance use patterns—has led to the creation of several present-day variants, the most important of which is termed *motivational incentives*, that reward cocaine addicts with cash or vouchers for abstinence (Higgins, Budney, Bickel, & Hughes, 1993).

Nonabstinence Treatment Goals

The most controversial development in substance abuse treatment during this period involved teaching alcoholics controlled or nonproblem drinking instead of abstinence. A basic tenet of AA, abstinence had long been the sole alcoholism treatment goal. Notwithstanding, discouraged by the modest outcomes of existing treatments for alcoholism, several behavioral clinicians developed broad-spectrum behavioral treatments in the 1970s that were designed to replace alcoholics' abusive drinking with controlled, nonproblem drinking.

In the early years of the decade, a broad-spectrum behavioral treatment program with a goal of nonproblem drinking was initiated by Mark and Linda Sobell at the Patton (California) State Hospital. Treatment methods and initial results were reported by Sobell and Sobell (1973). The treatment included several behavioral components embedded in a 17-session package, which emphasized the development of more appropriate responses to drinking-related stimuli than alcoholic, uncontrolled drinking. Some patients in the behavior-modification treatment group decided to work toward controlled, nonproblem drinking, whereas others in the same treatment group chose abstinence; a control group offered standard hospital-based treatment could also choose between the same two treatment goals. Components of the broad-spectrum behavior-modification program included the following elements, in order: videotaping of drunken behavior by each alcoholic subject and subsequent discussion with the subject of factors responsible for his uncontrolled alcoholic drinking; a thorough explanation of the treatment plan, with patients aspiring to controlled drinking trained to recognize and identify the separate ingredients of mixed drinks; replaying the videotape of drunken deportment to demonstrate the inappropriateness of the behavior and thereby to increase motivation to change; and programmed exposure to failure experiences designed to emphasize one of the most common consequences of alcoholism.

The bulk of the treatment program for controlled drinker subjects, lasting 10 sessions, involved the imposition of painful electric shocks for behaviors characteristic of uncontrolled drinkers and reinforcement with alcohol (up to 65 mg/%) for drinking like social drinkers. Patients were also taught to recognize the crucial environmental, social, and personal stimulus variables associated with their decision to drink and were trained in alternative responses to drinking in the presence of stimuli previously associated with drinking. A final session reviewed these components of treatment and reemphasized the lessons learned during treatment.

Follow-up of these 70 chronic alcoholic patients at 6 weeks and 6 months, reported in the 1973 report by Sobell and Sobell, revealed, unsurprisingly, that subjects were more likely to be abstinent or drinking in a controlled fashion at 6 weeks than 6 months. Members of the two treatment groups ($n = 40$) reported adhering more closely to their respective treatment goals than did control subjects ($n = 30$). Additionally, the treatment group members reported significantly better "drinking dispositions" at both 6 weeks and 6 months: They were either abstinent or drinking in controlled fashion at higher rates than were control subjects. In a subsequent report by the same researchers, reporting on 18-month and 2-year follow-up data, the 1993 data for experimental and control groups were reaffirmed. In addition, patients in the controlled drinking group were reported to have spent fewer drunk days, days in the hospital, or days in jail, and to have more abstinent or controlled drinking days than the experimental (abstinence) group.

The Sobell articles and broad-spectrum behavioral treatment programs by others that shared controlled drinking goals generated a great deal of controversy within the alcoholism treatment community in the 1970s. Nonabstinence treatment goals directly challenged a central AA tenet, the goal of abstinence that had prevailed since the founding of AA in the mid-1930s. Although opposition to nonabstinence goals was generally couched in terms of concern about patient welfare, the real conflict was between alcoholism treatment providers, most of them alcoholics who had recovered through AA, and behavioral scientists, few of whom were recovering alcoholics, who had dared to challenge an established verity. The attack on the Sobells ultimately led to a lawsuit, a distinguished review panel, and many articles on both sides of the issue. Although the Sobells were ultimately cleared of the accusation of research fraud, bruised feelings on all sides persisted for many years.

The controversy over controlled drinking treatment has largely died down. Few treatment facilities in the United States offer treatment with nonabstinent goals nowadays, largely because the weight of the research evidence from nonabstinent treatments in the late 1970s and early 1980s led most scientists and clinicians to conclude that nonabstinence treatment for chronic alcoholics had been largely unsuccessful, despite its early promise. Nonetheless, a self-help group with controlled drinking as a goal—Moderation Management—was founded during this time and continues to the present, although it is unclear how many adherents it has attracted.

Harm Reduction

As controlled drinking treatments gradually diminished, exploration of *harm reduction* or *risk reduction* methods began to increase (Marlatt, 2002). These interventions were intended to help patients moderate but not stop their drinking and, concomitantly, limit the extent of the physical, psychological, and interpersonal harm their drinking caused them. Harm reduction methods have been used extensively to the present day, for example, with binge drinking college students in an effort to limit the negative consequences of their abusive drinking.

THE 1980s

The 1980s witnessed considerable controversy over whether outpatient treatment was as effective an intervention for substance abuse as inpatient treatment, long the treatment of choice for alcohol dependence; non-abstinence treatment goals for early-stage problem drinkers, now a credible treatment option; motivational interviewing and the stages of change model, now accepted as empirically supported and widely used; and relapse prevention, an important contributor to the effectiveness of cognitive–behaviorial therapy for substance abuse, an empirically supported treatment.

Inpatient Versus Outpatient Treatment

Serious questions were raised early in the decade about whether inpatient treatment for alcoholism was more effective than outpatient treatment. Buttressing this new understanding was an influential article by Moos and Billings (1982), which reported their inability to find consistent differences in outcomes of treatment for alcoholism as a function of differences in treatment method, treatment setting, or treatment intensity.

Nonabstinence Treatment Goals for Early-Stage Problem Drinkers

Reports appeared early in the decade of the 1980s indicating that relatively brief behavioral interventions designed to teach early-stage problem drinkers how to moderate their drinking might be effective (e.g., Sanchez-Craig, Annis, Bornet, & MacDonald, 1984). These reports were significant because most clinicians had decided that nonabstinence treatment goals for chronic alcoholics were ineffective and possibly harmful in the long run. By contrast, teaching individuals at the very beginning of a potential lifetime of abusive drinking how to drink in a controlled, nonproblem fashion made a good deal of sense. Such individuals tended to minimize their drinking problems so they were less willing to adopt abstinence as a goal for treatment. Their drinking patterns had not yet crystallized around a serious abuse pattern, so they were more amenable to modification. And society did not find it as difficult to accept nonabstinent goals for individuals who had recently become abusive drinkers as for individuals who had abused alcohol and suffered the consequences of doing so for many years.

Motivational Interviewing and the Stages of Change Model

It has long been recognized that motivation to modify abusive drinking is the sine qua non of successful alcoholism treatment. Unless the alcohol-dependent individual recognizes the problem and is motivated to do something about it, treatment is likely to be unsuccessful. Focusing on the important role of motivation in the treatment of alcoholism, William Miller (1983) developed motivational interviewing in the late 1970s and early 1980s. A 3-hour interview and assessment were designed to gather a great deal of information from patients that could be used both to determine the severity and prognosis of their alcohol problem and to motivate them to change their abusive drinking behavior. Publication of the first edition of *The Motivational Interview* (Miller & Rollnick, 1991) provided substantial detail on the methods and contributions of the motivational interview. Research on the clinical utility of the motivational interview suggested that many patients confronted with detailed findings on current and projected effects of their drinking would consider changing their drinking pattern to head off the likely negative consequences of continuing to drink abusively.

Concurrently, Prochaska and DiClemente (1986) began developing what came to be called the stages of change model. It was designed initially to characterize the change processes used to quit addictive behaviors. Prochaska and DiClemente identified five stages of change: precontemplation, contemplation, preparation, action, and maintenance. They suggested that the goal of treatment for substance-dependence should be to move patients from the precontemplation or contemplation stages to a later one more responsive to treatment. Further, different change processes were differentially effective at each stage of change; what helped a precontemplator, for example, would be quite different from what assisted someone in the action stage. Miller incorporated the stages of change into his motivational interview, believing that it provided important information to clinicians as they considered how to change patients' motivation to change their drinking behavior. Subsequently, an assessment instrument, the URICA, was developed to enable more reliable assessment of a patient's stage of change prior to and following treatment.

Relapse Prevention

Late in the 1970s, G. Alan Marlatt and his colleagues concluded that relapse from sobriety after substance abuse treatment was an understudied but important factor in determining whether treated alcoholics would maintain therapeutic gains after treatment. Recognizing the high frequency of relapse back to abusive drinking by newly sober alcoholics, Marlatt and Gordon (1985) outlined a series of steps to prevent a lapse or, if one occurred, to confront it before it became a full-flown relapse. They also recommended making clear to recovering alcoholics that, instead of viewing persons who experienced a brief return to drinking or drug use as treatment failures, they should consider such events to be temporary setbacks in someone learning new mechanisms for coping with a new, drug-free lifestyle.

Marlatt and Gordon (1985) developed a decision-matrix exercise to help patients consider the costs and benefits of changing or not changing their abusive substance use; the matrix helps build motivation for behavior change as well as identifies potential sources of challenge along the route to abstinence. Once this exercise has been completed, relapse prevention patients are encouraged to take personal responsibility for what comes next, including the choices of when and how to stop using their substance of choice and decisions about which stimulus control procedures to use to eliminate cues previously associated with alcohol or drug use. Once abstinence has been initiated, a variety of cognitive–behavioral techniques are taught patients to help them cope with the cravings that so often lead to lapses.

The relapse-prevention model also envisions the steps patient and therapist are to take when a lapse occurs. In anticipation, the patient is asked to develop specific behavioral responses to a lapse. The plan might include such coping strategies as leaving the area in which the lapse occurred, engaging in a nonalcohol-related alternative activity, or asking for help from others. If a lapse occurs, the patient is urged not to give in to guilt and self-recrimination but instead to view it as an opportunity to demonstrate effective coping. Avoiding situations that represent high risk for a lapse and recognizing seemingly irrelevant decisions that increase the likelihood of a lapse are additional components of a lapse-prevention strategy. The data on the effectiveness of relapse prevention have been sufficiently encouraging that relapse prevention has been incorporated into a number of cognitive–behavioral treatment programs tested during the 1980s and 1990s, including Project MATCH.

THE 1990s TO THE PRESENT

The first two substantial, methodologically superior randomized clinical trials of treatments for alcoholism were reported in the decade of the 1990s. Until then, no existing treatment could claim to meet standards establishing it as empirically supported. In the early 1990s, however, investigators supported by the National Institute on Alcohol Abuse and Alcoholism planned a large-scale, multisite study designed primarily to confirm the validity of 16 well-accepted patient-treatment matches in a diverse group of more than 1,700 alcoholics at treatment sites across the country (Project MATCH Research Group, 1997). Among subsidiary goals of Project MATCH was a randomized clinical trial of three widely used treatments for alcoholism. Concurrently, the Veterans Administration (Ouimette, Finney, & Moos, 1997) undertook a large scale, multisite, naturalistic comparison of treatments that, although not randomized, was nonetheless of sufficient size, power, and methodological quality to effectively supplement Project MATCH's clinical trial.

Project MATCH

Project MATCH compared outcomes of three different, manual-guided, individually delivered treatments: cognitive–behavioral coping skills treatment (CBCST; Kadden et al., 1994), motivational enhancement therapy (MET; Miller, Zweben, DiClemente, & Rychtarik, 1994), and 12-step facilitation therapy (TSF: Nowinski, Baker, & Carroll, 1994). CBCST and TSF were conducted over 12 sessions; MET, a brief intervention, was designed to last four sessions. Two independent, parallel matching studies were run, one with 952 patients (72% male) recruited from outpatient settings, the other with 774 patients (80% male) in aftercare treatment after a period of inpatient treatment. After treatment ended, patients were contacted for follow-up every 3 months for a year, then each year to the 39-month mark. The primary outcome measures were percentage of days abstinent and drinks per drinking day (Project MATCH Research Group, 1997; see Chapter 12g for details).

The initial sessions of CBCST helped patients identify situations that put them at high risk of continued abusive drinking; later sessions were devoted to facilitating development of both the skills to cope with those risky situations and the self-efficacy to believe that they could do so successfully. Among the topics covered in the first few treatment sessions were (a) coping with cravings and urges to drink, (b) managing thoughts about alcohol and drinking, (c) problem solving, (d) drink-refusal skills, (e) planning for emergencies and lapses, and (f) considering seemingly irrelevant decisions. The first four topics are components of most cognitive–behavioral treatments for substance abuse; the fifth and sixth are elements of Marlatt's relapse-prevention protocol. CBCST also offered several elective sessions, chosen to provide patients with essential coping skills, including assertiveness training, anger management, managing negative moods, enhancing social support networks, job-seeking skills, and couples/family involvement.

MET was a four-session brief intervention based on principles of motivational psychology; it aimed to produce internally motivated change. Motivational interviewing (Miller, 1983) served as the template for Project MATCH's MET. MET therapists were thoroughly trained to respond to patients in a consistent, nonjudgmental, supportive, and maximally facilitative manner by (a) expressing empathy, (b) developing the discrepancy between the patient's goals and aspirations and his or her current self-destructive behavior, (c) avoiding argumentation, (d) rolling with the patient's resistance to behavior change, and (e) supporting the patient's self-efficacy in bringing about constructive behavior changes. MET therapists were also familiar with the six elements of successful brief intervention (FRAMES; Miller & Sanchez, 1994): (a) Feedback of personal risk, (b) Responsibility of the patient, (c) Advice to change, (d) Menu of ways to reduce drinking, (e) Empathetic counseling style, and (f) Self-efficacy of the patient. MET therapists were trained intensively in skills to facilitate the establishment of a strong therapist–patient bond capable of supporting the patient in the decision to choose to change his or her drinking behavior.

TSF was a 12-session treatment designed to prepare alcoholics to benefit from the interpersonal and emotional rigors of active involvement in AA. TSF was developed in recognition of the difficulty some alcohol-dependent individuals experience committing to a continuing relationship with an AA group strong enough to enable them to benefit from AA's sponsor system and alcohol-free environment, the social support that the members of the AA group provide, and the personal insights that detailed examination of the 12 steps of AA can bring about. TSF provided information on AA's history, a clear description of its methods and aspirations, group practice in analogue 12-step meetings, and mandatory attendance at actual AA meetings, followed by discussion of patients' reactions to the experience.

Project MATCH treatment follow-ups to the 39-month mark confirmed reductions of more than 70% in number of drinking days from pretreatment baseline and the same or greater percentage of reductions in amount of alcohol consumed each drinking day for all three treatments (Project MATCH Research Group, 1997). Participants in the study had been abstinent on average only 20% to 25% of the days before treatment began; following treatment, participants maintained abstinence between 80% and 95% of the time. Drinks per drinking day dropped from 11–20 on average during the pretreatment period to an average of 2–4 posttreatment. No significant differences in outcomes among the three treatments were observed. These positive findings for all three Project MATCH therapies, over a lengthy follow-up period, have confirmed CBCST and MET as empirically supported professional treatments and AA as an empirically supported self-help therapy. All three treatments have continued to influence treatment to the present day.

Veterans Administration Medical Centers Cooperative Study

This study constituted a multisite, naturalistic evaluation of more than 3,000 Veterans Administration inpatients diagnosed with alcohol abuse or dependence. Patients received site-specific treatments—traditional 12-step treatment, cognitive–behavioral treatment, or combined cognitive–behavioral/ AA treatment—at Veterans Administration Medical Centers (VAMC) facilities around the United States. Only one of the three treatments was offered at each site. A 1-year follow-up revealed no differences in outcomes as a function of treatment type in nine of 11 outcome criteria (Ouimette, Finney, & Moos, 1997). Patients in all three treatment groups showed marked beneficial changes in drinking and lifestyle at the 1-year mark. Hence, the VAMC Cooperative Study, whose outcome data were reported the same year that Project MATCH outcome data were reported, are usually seen as confirming both AA and cognitive–behavioral therapy as empirically supported treatments for alcohol dependence.

Behavioral Couples and Family Therapy

Although diverse treatments for couples and families with a substance-abusing member had been developed through the years, behavioral couples therapy and behavioral family therapy came into their own during the decade of the 1990s (e.g., O'Farrell & Fals-Stewart, 1999). Behavioral marital and family therapy derives from learning-based behavioral models of etiology and uses cognitive–behavioral techniques to bring about change in maladaptive interpersonal responses. The assumption is that these response patterns lead to marital and family discord, thereby reinforcing a destructive behavioral cycle within the family or between partners. The patterns must be identified, evaluated, and then if possible eliminated. The drinking or drug use of the addicted family member and the destructive relationship patterns of the couple or the family are both addressed in therapy. Behavioral contracts are often used in the effort to maximize the clarity of the treatment's focus on changes in substance use and inappropriate relationship patterns. Data on the effectiveness of behavioral couples or family therapy have been quite encouraging.

2007 Review of Psychosocial Treatments for Substance Use Disorders

In a comprehensive review of research on psychosocial treatments for substance use disorders, Finney, Wilbourne, and Moos (2007) concluded that "among the most effective treatments for alcohol and illicit drug use disorders are cognitive–behavioral treatments, community reinforcement and contingency management approaches, 12-step facilitation and 12-step treatment, behavioral couples and family treatment, and motivational enhancement interventions" (p. 179). They attributed the success of these diverse treatments to the fact that they "address not only drinking and/or drug use behavior but also patients' life contexts, sense of self-efficacy, and coping skills; motivational interventions focus primarily on attempts to enhance individuals' commitment to behavior change" (p. 179). Finney and his colleagues also make the point that "an effective strategy for many patients may be to provide lower intensity treatment for a longer duration . . . to match better the chronic, relapsing nature of many individuals' substance use disorders" (p. 179).

Although there are no surprises in these conclusions, given the findings from research on treatment outcomes reviewed in this chapter, Finney and his colleagues, long-time observers of the substance use treatment scene, did the field a service by highlighting the several effective treatments for substance abuse that have become available and the most efficacious means by which they may be delivered.

CONCLUSIONS

Few clinicians who worked in the substance treatment field in the 1960s could have anticipated that effective, empirically supported psychosocial treatments for substance abuse would be developed and that patients and therapists would thereby have access to treatments that provide good outcomes. Few who worked in the field more than 40 years ago could have anticipated the efficacy, availability, or research support enjoyed by substance-abuse treatments. That is not to say, though, that we have reason to be sanguine about where we are and how far we have come. True, we now have therapy models that enjoy research support, but too few of those on the front lines of substance abuse treatment have been adequately trained to translate them into consistently efficacious interventions. In our judgment, that is the next challenge facing the field, and it is one that is every bit as compelling as was the need to develop effective treatments in the first place.

REFERENCES

Davidson, W. S. (1974). Studies of aversive conditioning for alcoholics: A critical review of theory and research methodology. *Psychological Bulletin, 81*, 571–581. doi:10.1037/h0037092

Eysenck, H. J. (1952). The effects of psychotherapy: An evaluation. *Journal of Consulting Psychology, 16*, 319–324. doi:10.1037/h0063633

Eysenck, H. J. (1960). *Behavior therapy and the neuroses.* Oxford, England: Pergamon Press.

Finney, J. W., Wilbourne, P. L., & Moos, R. H. (2007). Psychosocial treatments for substance use disorders. In P. E. Nathan & J. M. Gorman (Eds.), *A guide to treatments that work* (3rd ed., pp. 179–202). New York, NY: Oxford University Press.

Gallant, D. (1995). Alcoholism. In G. E. Gabbard (Ed.), *Treatments of psychiatric disorders* (pp. 662–683). Washington, DC: American Psychiatric Press.

Higgins, S. T., Budney, A. J., Bickel, W. K., & Hughes, J. R. (1993). Achieving cocaine abstinence with a behavioral approach. *The American Journal of Psychiatry, 150*, 763–769.

Hunt, G. M., & Azrin, N. H. (1973). The community-reinforcement approach to alcoholism. *Behaviour Research and Therapy, 11*, 91–104. doi:10.1016/0005-7967(73)90072-7

Kadden, R., Carroll, K. M., Donovan, D., Cooney, N., Monti, P., Abrams, D., . . . Hester, R. (1994). Cognitive-behavioral coping skills therapy manual: A clinical research guide for therapists treating individuals with alcohol abuse and dependence. *Project MATCH Monograph Series: Vol. 3* (DHHS Publication No. 94-3724). Rockville, MD: NIAAA.

Lazarus, A. A. (1971). *Behavior therapy and beyond*. New York, NY: Brunner/Mazel.

Marlatt, G. A. (Ed.). (2002). *Harm reduction: Pragmatic strategies for managing high risk behaviors*. New York, NY: Guilford Press.

Marlatt, G. A., & Gordon, J. R. (Eds.). (1985). *Relapse prevention: Maintenance strategies in the treatment of addictive behaviors*. New York, NY: Guilford Press.

McCrady, B. M., & Nathan, P. E. (2006). Impact of treatment factors on outcomes of treatment for substance abuse disorders. In L. G. Castonguay & L. E. Beutler (Eds.), *Principles of therapeutic change that work* (pp. 319–340). New York, NY: Oxford University Press.

Miller, W. R. (1983). Motivational interviewing with problem drinkers. *Behavioural Psychotherapy, 11*, 147–172. doi:10.1017/S0141347300006583

Miller, W. R., & Rollnick, S. (1991). *Motivational interviewing: Preparing people to change addictive behaviors*. New York, NY: Guilford Press.

Miller, W. R., & Sanchez, V. V. (1994). Motivating young adults for treatment and lifestyle change. In G. Howard & P. E. Nathan (Eds.), *Alcohol use and misuse by young adults* (pp. 55–81). Notre Dame, IN: University of Notre Dame Press.

Miller, W. R., Zweben, A., DiClemente, C. C., & Rychtarik, R. G. (1994). Motivational enhancement therapy manual: A clinical research guide for therapists treating individuals with alcohol abuse and dependence. *Project MATCH Monograph Series: Vol. 2* (DHHS Publication No. 94-3723). Rockville, MD: NIAAA.

Moos, R. H., & Billings, A. G. (1982). Conceptualizing and measuring coping resources and processes. In L. Goldberger & S. Breznitz (Eds.), *Handbook of stress* (pp. 234–257). New York, NY: Free Press.

Nathan, P. E. (1969). The behavior therapies. In P. Solomon & V. D. Patch (Eds.), *Handbook of psychiatry* (pp. 560–565). Los Altos, CA: Lange.

Nowinski, J., Baker, S., & Carroll, K. M. (1994). Twelve-step facilitation therapy manual: A clinical research guide for therapists treating individuals with alcohol abuse and dependence. *Project MATCH Monograph Series: Vol. 1* (DHHS Publication No. 94-3722). Rockville, MD: NIAAA.

O'Farrell, T. J., & Fals-Stewart, W. (1999). Treatment models and methods: Family models. In B. S. McCrady & E. E. Epstein (Eds.), *Addictions: A comprehensive guidebook* (pp. 287–305). New York, NY: Oxford University Press.

Ouimette, P. C., Finney, J. W., & Moos, R. H. (1997). Twelve-step and cognitive-behavioral treatment for substance abuse: A comparison of treatment effectiveness. *Journal of Consulting and Clinical Psychology, 65*, 230–240. doi:10.1037/0022-006X.65.2.230

Prochaska, J. O., & DiClemente, C. C. (1986). Toward a comprehensive model of change. In W. R. Miller & N. Heather (Eds.), *Treating addictive behaviors: Processes of change* (pp. 3–27). New York, NY: Plenum Press.

Project MATCH Research Group. (1997). Matching alcoholism treatments to client heterogeneity: Project MATCH posttreatment drinking outcomes. *Journal of Studies on Alcohol, 58*, 7–29.

Sanchez-Craig, M., Annis, H. A., Bornet, A. R., & MacDonald, K. R. (1984). Random assignment to abstinence and controlled drinking: Evaluation of a cognitive-behavioral program for problem drinkers. *Journal of Consulting and Clinical Psychology, 52*, 390–403. doi:10.1037/0022-006X.52.3.390

Sobell, M. B., & Sobell, L. C. (1973). Individualized behavior therapy for alcoholism. *Behavior Therapy, 4*, 49–72. doi:10.1016/S0005-7894(73)80074-7

Sterne, M. W., & Pittman, D. J. (1965). The concept of motivation. *Quarterly Journal of Studies on Alcohol, 26*, 41–57.

Wolpe, J. (1969). *The practice of behavior therapy*. Elmsford, NY: Pergamon Press.

Borderline Personality Disorder

Anthony W. Bateman

In 1938, an American psychoanalyst, Adolph Stern, identified a group of patients who did not respond to classical psychoanalytic treatment. He described a constellation of symptoms found in this group closely related to the current diagnostic criteria of borderline personality disorder (BPD) and referred to the patients as the "border line group." He later described modifications of psychotherapy for his borderline group that remain relevant today (Stern, 1945). In doing so, he started a search for more effective treatments that continues to this day. Although there has been persistent pessimism over the years about the treatment of personality disorders, there is increasing optimism about psychotherapeutic treatments for BPD, which continues to be the only serious mental disorder for which the primary treatment recommendation is psychotherapy (Oldham, Phillips, Gabbard, & Soloff, 2001).

I discuss contemporary treatments later in the chapter, but first they are placed in the context of earlier pioneering treatments that developed within a different health care context but which continue to inform current psychotherapies.

EARLY PIONEERS

The majority of early attempts to treat patients suffering from BPD followed a psychoanalytic model primarily because this was the most influential treatment paradigm for understanding personality disorder until the 1980s, but second because the disorder was first described within a psychoanalytic context. Given the common practice for psychoanalysts to publish case material, it is not surprising that the early literature is full of individual case reports commenting on the demanding nature of patients, their tendency to break boundaries, and their propensity to regress. To address these problems, more ambitious long-term treatments became the norm, aiming to effect permanent changes in personality structure.

Knight (1953) first described reasonable results for patients, many of whom probably would today have a diagnosis of BPD, treated with psychoanalysis in an inpatient context. Patients spent months or years in the hospital undertaking intensive psychotherapy, despite some senior clinicians noting that long-term institutional care could be counterproductive, inducing regression and stimulating dependence rather than engendering independence. In short, the predominance of long-term inpatient treatments led to the recognition that intense emotional relationships could induce harm in patients with BPD. However, regressive phenomena were not confined to inpatient settings and similar observations were being made in outpatient settings with therapies ending abruptly and without warning. Despite all these concerns it is clear that some, but not all, patients benefited from long-term inpatient treatment, although the evidence for this remains primarily descriptive and naturalistic in nature (e.g., Tucker, Bauer, Wagner, Harlam, & Sher, 1987).

Gradually practitioners developed compelling theories, often based on observed developmental origins of BPD, which were translated into treatments. Different theories led to contrasting emphases in approach, with marked differences emerging between treatments for BPD. Kernberg (1967) emphasized the low level of ego function in patients and the predominance of primitive defense mechanisms deployed to manage excessive development of early aggression and intolerable conflict. His treatment for BPD became increasingly focused on these areas of psychological function, leading eventually to the development of transference-focused psychotherapy (TFP). Kernberg suggested that the integration of split internal states, themselves characteristic of BPD, was essential for improvement, and that interpretation and insight were the primary techniques to effect this change. In contrast, Kohut (1977) emphasized deficit, rather than conflict, as the core of narcissistic and borderline patients and highlighted empathy and attunement in treatment, rather than interpretation and insight, as the curative factors in successful treatment.

Contemporaneously, other pioneers, such as Masterson (1981), Rinsley (1980), and Gerald Adler (1985), developed psychotherapeutic treatments. Whereas Masterson and Rinsley focused treatment on exploration of relational units, one being rewarding and the other being withdrawing and withholding, Adler was more concerned with the borderline patient's inability to develop and maintain a "holding-soothing" internal object. Exactly how these differences in emphasis translated into variation in treatment itself is somewhat unclear. None of the treatments were carefully defined in terms of techniques and principles until much later. But the major distinctions were related first to the controversy between whether expressive or supportive techniques should take primacy in treatment of BPD, and second to the concern about the context in which treatment should take place.

The Menninger Project

This distinction between support and expression of underlying conflicts was highlighted in the Menninger Project, and the debate is still alive today. But it was the Menninger Project (Wallerstein, 1986), which began in 1954 as a prospective study and spanned a 25-year period looking at assessment, treatment, and outcome, that fuelled the debate and continues to be an outstanding example of detailed naturalistic observation. Forty-two patients were selected for detailed study, some of whom were in psychoanalysis and some in less intensive psychodynamic psychotherapy. The patients, their families, and their therapists were subjected to a battery of tests; process notes and supervisory records were kept that charted the progress of therapy. (Wallerstein's [1992] chapter in the first edition of this volume provides details of the study.)

The conclusions about this group of patients were that the best form of therapy is supportive-expressive for however long it is necessary, a lifetime if need be; that periods of hospitalization will be required alongside long-term therapy; and that a network of informal supports, often centered around the subculture associated with mental health centers, is also an important ingredient if these patients are to survive at all, let alone thrive. These conclusions have, to some extent, stood the test of time. Current psychotherapeutic treatments emphasize the need for intervention to be well-structured, to devote considerable effort to enhancing compliance, and to have a clear focus. That focus may be problem behavior such as self-harm or a disruption of interpersonal relationship patterns. Treatments tend to be relatively long term and to be well integrated with other services available to the patient.

Expressive and Supportive Techniques

Support, directiveness, and expressiveness are found in all psychotherapies in different proportions. Following on from the Menninger Project, debate in the 1970s focused on the level of direct support that a patient required in treatment, the techniques that were believed to effect change, and the level of emphasis recommended on actively fostering a therapeutic alliance.

Establishing and maintaining a therapeutic alliance with a patient with BPD is problematic although universally acknowledged as an essential part of the framework for treatment. Masterson (1981), Modell (1968), and others advocated supportive techniques rather than focusing on expressive work in order to establish an alliance. In supportive work, a passive, opaque stance is avoided and the therapist tries to provide an honest, open relationship, combining warmth, empathy, and firmness. The therapist serves as a secure container for the patients' anxieties, experiences, and feelings. Positive transference is actively nurtured and not interpreted by the therapist. When negative reactions occur, the therapist has to accept the patient's frustration, anger, distress, and disappointment. Mistakes and misunderstandings are handled with honesty and tact, with therapists owning up to their own contribution and some of their own imperfections.

This stance contrasts with the approach of Kernberg, who promoted a more confrontational approach, addressing anxieties and negative responses. He advocated more interpreting the distortions within the relationship between the patient and therapist, so that the patient could view the therapist more accurately and recognize that his or her reactions were governed by past experiences rather than the current reality. Although the debate about the most appropriate balance between expressive and supportive techniques continues within the dynamically orientated therapies, more emphasis is now being placed on the importance of repairing alliance ruptures to prevent dropout from therapy, which hitherto had been unacceptably high.

Therapeutic Communities

A related development to inpatient psychoanalytic treatment for personality disorder, emerging as a treatment initially in response to the psychological trauma of war, was the therapeutic community (TC). This is commonly defined as a consciously designed social environment (Main, 1957) in which the community itself becomes the primary therapeutic instrument through processes of democratization, permissiveness, reality confrontation, and communalism. Programs within the community often included a range of therapies including small analytic groups, psychodrama, art therapy, music therapy, and gestalt. The TC movement quickly adapted to treating people with personality disorders, initially within full-time residential settings but currently more often operating as partial hospital programs. Most TCs succumbed to the developing changes in health care in the 1980s. Proponents of the TC movement were unable to gather robust evidence for their effectiveness over many years, and the challenge of evidence-based treatment led to the closure of facilities around the world. Recent valiant attempts to summarize the research that has been done over the years (Lees, Manning, & Rawlings, 1999) and to reinvent TCs have met with limited success (Kennard, 1998). Yet spirited defenses of the TC movement (Haigh, 2002) continue, suggesting that the focus on helping people humanely and with compassion through a permissive milieu, hallmarks of the movement, may be revived.

THE RISE OF OTHER PSYCHOTHERAPIES

The dominance of the psychoanalytic treatments for people with BPD continued unchallenged for nearly 2 decades with few other practitioners taking an interest in the condition, perhaps because the patients continued to be considered "heart sink" patients who were impossible to treat.

Cognitive Therapy

With the emergence of cognitive–behavioral therapy (CBT) for depression in the late 1970s, more as a result of dissatisfaction with the results of psychoanalysis for neurotic patients than as a development of behavior therapy, it was inevitable that attention would turn to cognitive understanding of personality and personality disorders. Beck and Freeman (1990) published *Cognitive Therapy of Personality Disorders*, and shortly after, Layden, Newman, Freeman, and Morse (1993) laid out a more specific cognitive understanding of BPD. While maintaining the basic core of cognitive therapy as presented by Beck (e.g., identifying automatic thoughts and beliefs typical of patients with BPD), they identified an additional level of cognition and termed it the *schema*. There was no consensus on definition: Some practitioners suggested schemas were a mental filter or template that guided processing of information, whereas others considered them as latent core beliefs. All agreed that they were difficult to assess and to access in treatment to effect change.

These developments were predicated on the basis that unmodified CBT was relatively ineffective with patients with personality disorder; just as unmodified psychoanalysis had been found to be ineffective in BPD decades earlier, so it was that unchanged CBT was also found to be wanting. However, traditional CBT continues to be developed and, to a certain extent, there is an unhelpful schism between the modified CBT approaches and the more traditional CBT practitioners, just as there is between some of the dynamically orientated treatment developers (see later in this chapter).

Jeffrey Young (1990) challenged some of the traditional assumptions associated with CBT—for example, that patients can change their problematic cognitions and behaviors through empirical analysis, logical discourse, and experimentation. In BPD he thought these techniques are undermined by persistent self-defeating behaviors, and thus different techniques are required. This led to the development of schema-focused psychotherapy (SFT) as a more systematic approach to the maladaptive schemas associated with BPD.

There has thus been a profound change over time within the cognitive tradition. Initially, personality disorders were at worst ignored or at best seen as a collection of isolated symptoms such as cognitive distortions. This changed to the view of personality as a disorder of interpersonal behaviors, arising out of dysfunctional cognitive schemas and self-perpetuating cognitive-interpersonal cycles.

Behavior Therapy

Behaviorists traditionally rejected the idea that personality traits could determine behavior, preferring to think of actions as being determined by situations. As a result, they paid little attention to personality disorders, considering personality variables as accounting for only a small component of the variance in human behavior. But with the advent of the *Diagnostic and Statistical Manual of Mental Disorders* (3rd. ed.; American Psychiatric Association, 1980) in which personality disorders were defined as "enduring patterns of perceiving, relating to, and thinking about the environment and oneself" which are "exhibited in a wide range of important social and personal contexts" and "which are inflexible and maladaptive and cause significant functional impairment or subjective distress," behaviorists began to recognize that dysfunctional patterns and groups of symptoms might respond to behavioral methods.

As this recognition was gaining ground, principally in the treatment of patients who attempted suicide or self-harmed, a further development was taking place within the radical behavioral tradition. Behavioral practitioners were dissatisfied with results of traditional behavioral methods for patients with BPD who self-harmed. Marsha Linehan (1993) developed a complex treatment program for patients who self-harmed known as dialectical behavior therapy (DBT). DBT includes techniques at the level of behavior (functional analysis), cognitions (e.g., skills training), and support (empathy, teaching management of trauma) with the creative use of aspects of Buddhism (e.g., mindfulness), which has become a treatment for depression in its own right. DBT provided the biggest challenge to the dominance of psychodynamic treatments for BPD simply because it was the first treatment for BPD to be subjected to a randomized controlled trial at a time when empirically supported treatments were in the ascendancy. This brings our historical narrative to the current psychotherapeutic treatments for BPD.

Current Psychotherapies for BPD

Stimulated by the controlled studies conducted on DBT, most contemporary treatments for BPD have embraced an evidence-based approach. The rigors of managed care in the United States and the increasing controls on spending in health care elsewhere in the world have meant that only treatments with research evidence of effectiveness will be increasingly paid by insurance companies or form part of a national service provision. The complexity of treatments for BPD makes this problematic. So, in keeping with their long history of neglect, patients suffering from BPD continue to have limited access to intensive psychotherapy due to patchy provision, inadequate funding, and nonreimbursement from insurance companies. Self-help and pressure groups have developed to counter these trends, and family support groups for relatives of people with BPD thrive. But overall, not only are natural outcomes better overtime than previously believed (e.g., Zanarini, Frankenburg, Hennen, & Silk, 2003), but a number of psychotherapies are helpful at least for the more acute symptoms of the disorder, such as self-harm and suicide attempts.

Dialectical Behavior Therapy

The aim of DBT is initially to control self-harm, but its main aim is to promote change in the emotional dysregulation judged to be at the core of the disorder. In the first trial undertaken by its founder, DBT reduced episodes of self-harm initially, but was less effective in the long term. Control patients were significantly more likely to make suicide attempts, spent significantly longer periods of time as inpatients over the year of treatment, and were significantly more likely to drop out of the therapies to which they were assigned. At 6-month follow-up, DBT patients continued to show less parasuicidal behavior than controls, though at 1 year there were no between-group differences.

The widespread adoption of DBT is both a tribute to the energy and charisma of its founder, Marsha Linehan, and to the attractiveness of the treatment, with its combination of acceptance and change, skills training, excellent manualization, and a climate of opinion that is willing and able to embrace this multifaceted approach (Swenson, 2000). Whereas some have felt that the popularity of DBT is not justified by the strength of the evidence (Tyrer, 2002) and some have felt that the conclusions are premature (Scheel, 2000), currently it is the best validated treatment for BPD. A recent replication of the original study that found, in most respects, results very similar to the original study gives further support to its effectiveness (Linehan et al., 2006). An additional randomized study by an independent group supports the findings as well (Verheul et al., 2003).

Cognitive–Behavioral Therapy

The evidence for modified CBT as a potential treatment for BPD began with a small ($N = 34$) randomized controlled trial using manual assisted cognitive–behavioral therapy (MACT) in the treatment of recurrent self-harm in those with Cluster B personality disorders (the rate of suicide acts was lower with MACT and self-rated depressive symptoms also improved; Evans et al., 1999). In a more recent large study ($N = 480$), following from the first, brief MACT slightly increased the likelihood of self-harm relative to treatment as usual with personality-disorder patients and in BPD increased the costs associated with ongoing treatment (Tyrer et al., 2003; Tyrer et al., 2004). In a more recent randomized controlled trial of BPD with longer treatment (up to 30 sessions), from therapists trained in advance, there was significant benefit on suicidal behavior ($N = 104$) but a nonsignificant increase in emergency presentations in those allocated to cognitive–behaviorial therapy (Davidson et al., 2006). There is an interesting contrast in terms of the duration of treatments focusing on a cognitive approach, which might limit availability and certainly reduces utility. SFT appears to be an efficacious long-term treatment when offered for a period of 3 years, but the 30-session version of MACT, still a relatively long-term therapy, is limited in its effectiveness. Both cognitive therapies are, however, promising and may occupy different niches in the treatment of BPD.

Dynamic Psychotherapy

Just as behavioral and cognitive treatments have been adapted to the special needs of patients with BPD, so too have the classical techniques of psychoanalytic psychotherapy. This has led to more detailed elaboration of treatments with manualization of TFP (Clarkin, Kernberg, & Yeomans, 1999) and dynamic deconstructive psychotherapy (Gregory & Remen, 2008) in the United States and mentalization-based treatment (MBT; Bateman & Fonagy, 2004a, 2006) in the United Kingdom and psychodynamic interpersonal psychotherapy in the United Kingdom and Australia.

Differences between the dynamic treatments are reminiscent of the earlier debates about the relative treatment emphasis placed on either supportive or expressive techniques. Some favor a supportive approach, whereas others promote emotional understanding. It still remains unclear whether this is a debate over small differences or over an important technical aspect.

The initial variant of dynamic therapy was TFP, which emphasizes expressive and interpretive techniques; it has now been manualized and subjected to clinical trials (Clarkin, Levy, Lenzenweger, & Kernberg, 2004, 2007). Ninety patients, 92% of whom were female, were randomized to TFP, DBT, or supportive psychotherapy. At completion of treatment at 1 year, there were no differences among groups on global assessment of functioning, depression scores, social adjustment, anxiety, and measures of self-harm. However, whereas TFP showed significant improvement in irritability and verbal and direct assault, this was not observed in either DBT or supportive psychotherapy. The lack of significant difference may be due to lack of power in the study, but equally might be because all three treatments in this comparative trial met the general criteria for effective treatment.

A further randomized controlled trial (Gieson-Bloo et al., 2006) compared TFP with SFT. Patients who received TFP showed significantly less improvement than did those who received schema-focused CBT over 3 years, and TFP was more expensive. Both groups showed improvement, but changes in the combined measure of outcome in the group treated with SFT were greater and more prolonged than in the TFP group. However, the results should be interpreted with caution (Fonagy & Bateman, 2006), especially as longer term follow-up is needed and follow-on research has suggested that over the same period approximately 40% of patients would have been expected to have improved (Zanarini et al., 2003). MBT uses more supportive techniques and delays detailed exploration of transference until later in treatment than does TFP. The focus of therapy is on the patient's moment-to-moment state of mind. Patient and therapist collaboratively generate alternative perspectives to the patient's subjective experience of themselves and others by moving from validating and supportive interventions to exploring the therapy relationship itself as it suggests alternative understanding. The evidence for this approach comes primarily from the developers of the treatment (Bateman & Fonagy, 1999, 2001), and replication is necessary, although promising data has recently become available on the effectiveness of a similar program established in the Netherlands. The treatment has now been manualized (Bateman & Fonagy, 2004b, 2006). Long-term follow-up suggested that gains made during treatment are maintained over a further period of 5 years after all treatment has ceased (Bateman & Fonagy, 2008).

Other dynamically orientated treatments have been developed, the best known of which is psychodynamic interpersonal therapy (PI; Hobson, 1985). This treatment has more supportive elements than does TFP and overlaps considerably with MBT. There are a number of nonrandomized trials of PI in the literature, which have suggested that treated patients show significant reduction in symptom severity and increase in global assessment of function scores relative to a waiting-list group (Meares, Stevenson, & Comerford, 1999; Stevenson & Meares, 1992).

Group Psychotherapy

Group psychotherapy in a partial hospital context is perhaps the remaining representative of long-term inpatient treatment for BPD. Marziali and Monroe-Blum concentrated on group therapy alone without the additional milieu and social components of therapy, although their therapy was not formally psychoanalytic but focused instead on relationship management. In a randomized controlled trial, they found equivalent results between group and individual therapy and concluded that on cost-effectiveness grounds, group therapy is the treatment of choice (Monroe-Blum & Marziali, 1995). Further studies are needed to confirm their findings, especially because the treatment offered was less structured than most other treatments and dropout rates were high.

Other Psychotherapies

A number of other therapies have been modified for patients with BPD. For one example, cognitive analytic therapy (CAT) has been manualized for treatment of BPD, and many are enthusiastic about its effectiveness. A case series of 27 patients with BPD treated with 24 sessions of CAT (Ryle & Golynkina, 2000) found that at 6-month follow-up, 52% of the sample no longer met diagnostic criteria for personality disorder and were classified as improved. Benefits of CAT have also been found in the treatment of adolescents with borderline traits (Chanen et al., 2008). For another example, interpersonal psychotherapy has been applied to patients suffering from BPD (Markowitz, Skodol, & Bleiberg, 2006).

IN THE FUTURE

A wide variety of psychotherapies have shown some effectiveness for BPD, with minimal differences in overall outcomes when they have been directly compared by unbiased investigators. This pattern, along with the general finding that structured clinical care is superior to rather chaotic treatment as usual, suggests that effective treatments have certain features in common. The effective therapies tend to (a) be well structured; (b) devote considerable effort to enhancing compliance; (c) have a clear focus whether that focus is a problem behavior, such as self-harm or an aspect of relationship patterns; (d) be theoretically highly coherent to both therapist and patient, sometimes deliberately omitting information incompatible with the theory; (e) be relatively long term; (f) encourage a powerful attachment between therapist and patient, enabling the therapist to adopt a relatively active rather than a passive stance; and (g) be well integrated with other services available to the patient.

Clearly, there is much research to be done in better understanding the effect of various therapeutic approaches to this complex psychological problem. But more important, future research needs to address the question of how treatments can be disseminated more widely. Evidence-based therapies for BPD require extensive training and stringent monitoring of adherence and standards, all of which are obstacles to comprehensive implementation across mental health services. To have the potential for broad dissemination, treatments have to have minimal training and supervision demands. Research needs to address these issues if patients with BPD are going to have access to the treatment they deserve and so sorely need.

REFERENCES

Adler, G. (1985). *Borderline psychopathology and its treatment*. New York, NY: Jason Aronson.
American Psychiatric Association. (1980). *Diagnostic and statistical manual of mental disorders* (3rd ed.). Washington, DC: Author.

Bateman, A., & Fonagy, P. (1999). The effectiveness of partial hospitalization in the treatment of borderline personality disorder: A randomised controlled trial. *The American Journal of Psychiatry, 156,* 1563–1569.

Bateman, A., & Fonagy, P. (2001). Treatment of borderline personality disorder with psychoanalytically oriented partial hospitalisation: An 18-month follow-up. *The American Journal of Psychiatry, 158,* 36–42. doi:10.1176/appi.ajp.158.1.36

Bateman, A., & Fonagy, P. (2004a). Mentalisation-based treatment of borderline personality disorder. *Journal of Personality Disorders, 18,* 35–50.

Bateman, A., & Fonagy, P. (2004b). *Psychotherapy for borderline personality disorder: Mentalisation based treatment.* Oxford, England: Oxford University Press.

Bateman, A., & Fonagy, P. (2006). *Mentalization-based treatment: A practical guide.* Oxford, England: Oxford University Press.

Bateman, A., & Fonagy, P. (2008). 8-year follow-up of patients treated for borderline personality disorder: Mentalization-based treatment versus treatment as usual. *The American Journal of Psychiatry, 165,* 631–638. doi:10.1176/appi.ajp.2007.07040636

Beck, A. T., & Freeman, A. (1990). *Cognitive therapy of personality disorders.* New York, NY: Guilford Press.

Chanen, A. M., Jackson, H. J., McCutcheon, L. K., Jovev, M., Dudgeon, P., Yuen, H. P., . . . McGorry, P. D. (2008). Early intervention for adolescents with borderline personality disorder using cognitive analytic therapy: Randomised controlled trial. *The British Journal of Psychiatry, 193,* 477–484. doi:10.1192/bjp.bp.107.048934

Clarkin, J. F., Kernberg, O. F., & Yeomans, F. (1999). *Transference-focused psychotherapy for borderline personality disorder patients.* New York, NY: Guilford Press.

Clarkin, J. F., Levy, K. N., Lenzenweger, M. F., & Kernberg, O. (2004). The Personality Disorders Institute/Borderline Personality Disorder Research Foundation randomised controlled trial for borderline personality disorder: Rationale, methods, and patient characteristics. *Journal of Personality Disorders, 18,* 52–72. doi:10.1521/pedi.18.1.52.32769

Clarkin, J. F., Levy, K. N., Lenzenweger, M. F., & Kernberg, O. (2007). Evaluating three treatments for borderline personality disorder. *The American Journal of Psychiatry, 164,* 922–928. doi:10.1176/appi.ajp.164.6.922

Davidson, K., Norrie, J., Tyrer, P., Gumley, A., Tata, P., Murray, H., & Palmer, S. (2006). The effectiveness of cognitive behavior therapy for borderline personality disorder: Results from the borderline personality disorder study of cognitive therapy (BOSCOT) trial. *Journal of Personality Disorders, 20,* 450–465. doi:10.1521/pedi.2006.20.5.450

Evans, K., Tyrer, P., Catalan, J., Schmidt, U., Davidson, K., Dent, J., . . . Thompson, S. (1999). Manual-assisted cognitive-behaviour therapy (MACT): A randomised controlled trial of a brief intervention with bibliotherapy in the treatment of recurrent deliberate self-harm. *Psychological Medicine, 29,* 19–25. doi:10.1017/S003329179800765X

Fonagy, P., & Bateman, A. (2006). Progress in the treatment of borderline personality disorder. *The British Journal of Psychiatry, 188,* 1–3. doi:10.1192/bjp.bp.105.012088

Gieson-Bloo, J., van Dyck, R., Spinhoven, P., van Tilburg, W., Dirksen, C., van Asselt, T., . . . Arntz, A. (2006). Outpatient psychotherapy for borderline personality disorder: Randomized trial of schema-focused therapy vs. transference focused therapy. *Archives of General Psychiatry, 63,* 649–658. doi:10.1001/archpsyc.63.6.649

Gregory, R. J., & Remen, A. L. (2008). A manual-based psychodynamic therapy for treatment-resistant borderline personality disorder. *Psychotherapy: Theory, Research, Practice. Training, 45,* 15–27.

Haigh, R. (2002). Therapeutic community research: Past, present and future. *Psychiatric Bulletin, 26,* 65–68. doi:10.1192/pb.26.2.65

Hobson, R. F. (1985). *Forms of feeling: The heart of psychotherapy*. New York, NY: Basic Books.

Kennard, D. (1998). Therapeutic communities are back—and there's something a little different about them. *Therapeutic Communities, 19*, 323–329.

Kernberg, O. F. (1967). Borderline personality organization. *Journal of the American Psychoanalytic Association, 15*, 641–685. doi:10.1177/000306516701500309

Knight, R. P. (1953). Borderline states. In R. P. Knight & C. R. Friedman (Eds.), *Psychoanalytic psychiatric and psychology* (pp. 203–215). New York, NY: International Universities Press.

Kohut, H. (1977). *The restoration of the self*. New York, NY: International Universities Press.

Layden, M. A., Newman, C. F., Freeman, A., & Morse, S. B. (1993). *Cognitive therapy of borderline personality disorder*. Needham Heights, MA: Allyn and Bacon.

Lees, J., Manning, N., & Rawlings, B. (1999). *Therapeutic community effectiveness. A systematic international review of therapeutic community treatment for people with personality disorders and mentally disordered offenders* (CRD Report 17). York, England: NHS Centre for Reviews and Dissemination, University of York.

Linehan, M. M. (1993). *Cognitive-behavioural treatment of borderline personality disorder*. New York, NY: Guilford Press.

Linehan, M. M., Comtois, K. A., Murray, A. M., Brown, M. Z., Gallop, R. J., Heard, H. L., . . . Lindenboim. M. S. (2006). Two-year randomized controlled trial and follow-up of dialectical behavior therapy vs. therapy by experts for suicidal behaviors and borderline personality disorder. *Archives of General Psychiatry, 63*, 757–766. doi:10.1001/archpsyc.63.7.757

Main, T. F. (1957). The ailment. *The British Journal of Medical Psychology, 30*, 129–145.

Markowitz, J. C., Skodol, A. E., & Bleiberg, K. (2006). Interpersonal psychotherapy for borderline personality disorder: Possible mechanisms of change. *Journal of Clinical Psychology, 62*, 431–444. doi:10.1002/jclp.20242

Masterson, J. (1981). *The narcissistic and borderline disorders*. New York, NY: Brunner/ Mazel.

Meares, R., Stevenson, J., & Comerford, A. (1999). Psychotherapy with borderline patients: A comparison between treated and untreated cohorts. *The Australian and New Zealand Journal of Psychiatry, 33*, 467–472. doi:10.1046/j.1440-1614.1999.00594.x

Modell, A. (1968). *Object love and reality*. New York, NY: International Universities Press.

Monroe-Blum, H., & Marziali, E. (1995). A controlled trial of short-term group treatment for borderline personality disorder. *Journal of Personality Disorders, 9*, 190–198.

Oldham, J., Phillips, K., Gabbard, G., & Soloff, P. (2001). *Practice guideline for the treatment of patients with borderline personality disorder*. Washington, DC: American Psychiatric Association.

Rinsley, D. B. (1980). The developmental etiology of borderline and narcissistic disorders. *Bulletin of the Menninger Clinic, 44*, 127–134.

Ryle, A., & Golynkina, K. (2000). Effectiveness of time-limited cognitive analytic therapy of borderline personality disorder: Factors associated with outcome. *The British Journal of Medical Psychology, 73*, 197–210. doi:10.1348/000711200160426

Scheel, K. (2000). The empirical basis of dialectical behavior therapy: Summary, critique, and implications. *Clinical Psychology: Science and Practice, 7*, 68–86. doi:10.1093/clipsy/7.1.68

Stern, A. (1938). Psychoanalytic investigation and therapy in borderline group of neuroses. *The Psychoanalytic Quarterly, 7*, 467–489.

Stern, A. (1945). Psychoanalytic therapy in the borderline neuroses. *The Psychoanalytic Quarterly, 14*, 190–198.

Stevenson, J., & Meares, R. (1992). An outcome study of psychotherapy for patients with borderline personality disorder. *The American Journal of Psychiatry, 149*, 358–362.

Swenson, C. (2000). How can we account for DBT's widespread popularity. *Clinical Psychology: Science and Practice, 7*, 87–91. doi:10.1093/clipsy/7.1.87

Tucker, L., Bauer, S. F., Wagner, S., Harlam, D., & Sher, I. (1987). Long-term hospital treatment of borderline patients: A descriptive outcome study. *The American Journal of Psychiatry, 144,* 1443–1448.

Tyrer, P. (2002). Practice guideline for the treatment of borderline personality disorder: A bridge too far. *Journal of Personality Disorders, 16,* 113–118. doi:10.1521/pedi.16.2.113.22547

Tyrer, P., Thompson, S., Schmidt, U., Jones, V., Knapp, M., Davidson, K., . . . Wessely, S. (2003). Randomized controlled trial of brief cognitive behaviour therapy versus treatment as usual in recurrent deliberate self-harm: the POPMACT study. *Psychological Medicine, 33,* 969–976. doi:10.1017/S0033291703008171

Tyrer, P., Tom, B., Byford, S., Schmidt, U., Jones, V., Davidson, K., . . . Catalan, J. (2004). Differential effects of manual assisted cognitive behaviour therapy in the treatment of recurrent deliberate self-harm and personality disturbance: The POPMACT study. *Journal of Personality Disorders, 18,* 102–116. doi:10.1521/pedi.18.1.102.32770

Verheul, R., Van Den Bosch, L. M., Koeter, M. W., De Ridder, M. A., Stijnen, T., & Van Den Brink, W. (2003). Dialectical behaviour therapy for women with borderline personality disorder: 12-month, randomised clinical trial in The Netherlands. *The British Journal of Psychiatry, 182,* 135–140. doi:10.1192/bjp.182.2.135

Wallerstein, R. S. (1986). *Forty-two lives in treatment: A study of psychoanalysis and psychotherapy.* New York, NY: Guilford Press.

Wallerstein, R. S. (1992). The Menninger Project. In D. K. Freedheim (Ed.), *History of psychotherapy,* pp. 401–407.

Young, J. E. (1990). *Cognitive therapy for personality disorders: A schema-focused approach.* Sarasota, FL: Professional Resource Exchange.

Zanarini, M. C., Frankenburg, F. R., Hennen, J., & Silk, K. (2003). The longitudinal course of borderline psychopathology: 6-year prospective follow-up of the phenomenology of borderline personality disorder. *The American Journal of Psychiatry, 160,* 274–283. doi:10.1176/appi.ajp.160.2.274

Schizophrenia

Kim T. Mueser and Gary R. VandenBos

Strange, bizarre, and insane behavior scares everyone. Historically, the claimed causes of these behaviors have ranged from curses inflicted by the gods, disordered metabolism (humors), possession by demons, and diseased brains. The treatment of "crazy" individuals has ranged from kindness to restraints, isolation to torture (and even murder).

In this chapter, we trace the modern history of psychotherapy for schizophrenia and psychotic disorders. The focus is largely on psychological and integrated therapies, as opposed to pharmacological treatments alone. In closing, we offer a brief glimpse into three future directions.

EARLY MODERN TREATMENTS

Philippe Penal (1745–1826) is generally credited with beginning the modern care and treatment of individuals with severe mental illness. He greatly improved the status and living conditions of the majority of patients under his care and introduced *moral treatment* as a new way of handling insane patients (Magaro, 1976).

Moral treatment meant psychological treatment, and its principles were deceptively simple. The first principle was to eliminate cruelty. If physical force was needed, it was only used to prevent patients from hurting themselves or others. The goal was to use physical force rarely, and if it had to be used, to do so in as gentle a manner as possible—and certainly not used as punishment or in a sadistic manner. The second principle was to not do anything that would injure patients or subject them to humiliation, contempt, or cruelty. The third principle was to keep accurate case histories. Patients were viewed as sick people; keeping accurate records on them would allow one to learn more about the individual as well as the disorder. The fourth principle was that caregivers were to try to understand the patient as an individual human being, and patients were encouraged to live as normal a life as their condition permitted, with the aim of restoring them to a normal role in society. Productive work was seen as a value, and discharge from the institution was the goal of treatment.

Records were kept at institutions using moral treatment in France, England, Scotland, and the United States that documented the recovery and discharge rates in these hospitals during the 1800s. Discharge rates between 60% and 80% were often reported (Bockoven, 1972). In the 1830s, Worcester State Hospital in Massachusetts reported that 70% of the patients who were ill less than 1 year "recovered" and were discharged.

However, by the end of the 1800s, moral treatment was replaced by a more "scientific" psychiatric treatment, which only achieved discharge rates between 15% and 20%. Economics also played a role in the abandonment of moral treatment. Following the social reforms of Dorothea Dix (1802–1887) in the United States, increasing numbers of patients were removed from jails and reformatories and put in mental hospitals. As the ratio of patients to staff increased, treatment became less personal and individualized.

Eugen Bleuler (1911/1950) provided one of the best descriptive presentations of schizophrenia spectrum disorders, and his hospital in Switzerland became a model in Europe for the long-term care and psychological treatment of such seriously disturbed patients. In the United States, starting in the 1930s, Harry Stack Sullivan (1953) and Frieda Fromm-Reichmann (1948) developed psychoanalytic psychotherapy for people with schizophrenia, which involved first building a meaningful interpersonal relationship with patients, and then using that relationship to help patients reconnect with the external world and social relationships. Hospitals and residential settings such as the Chestnut Lodge Sanatorium in Washington, DC, the Austen Riggs Center in Stockbridge, Massachusetts, and the Menninger Clinic in Topeka, Kansas, emerged in the United States during this era as models for psychological treatment for patients with schizophrenia and as major centers of education, training, and research in the treatment of schizophrenia (Kubie, 1960).

The psychological casualties of World War II forced the military to address the mental health needs of soldiers. The army reported that almost half of the first 1.5 million medical discharges during the war were due to psychiatric disabilities, and they estimated that by the end of the war, at least 2 million veterans would require psychiatric and psychological treatment (Grinker & Spiegel, 1945). The Veterans Administration was greatly expanded during and after World War II (see Chapter 16f), and training programs in the psychotherapy of schizophrenia were developed for psychologists and psychiatrists. The National Institute of Mental Health was also established immediately after World War II, and it played an important role in funding of a national research program on psychotherapy, including psychotherapy for schizophrenia.

In a case study truly ahead of its time, Beck (1952) described the successful application of cognitive–behavioral therapy (CBT) to a patient suffering from severe paranoid delusions. A collaborative relationship between the client and therapist was established that initially aimed at developing a shared understanding of the circumstances in which the psychotic symptoms emerged. Thereafter, the client examined the evidence supporting and not supporting the accuracy of delusional beliefs, with a gradual accumulation of evidence against the beliefs. As the client's conviction in the delusional beliefs weakened, avoidance of social interactions decreased, without any concomitant increase in anxiety or depression. The effects were durable after the end of treatment. It would be 30 years before CBT would systematically address schizophrenic psychopathology.

The International Symposium for the Psychotherapy of Schizophrenia (ISPS) was established in 1956 by Gaetano Benedetti and Christian Muller, two leading European figures in the psychological understanding and treatment of schizophrenia. For over 50 years, the ISPS has been the international professional forum for presenting the latest research and clinical findings about schizophrenia and its psychological treatment, through its annual meeting as well as through local chapters, newsletters, a journal, and a book series. The organization is known today as the International Society for the Psychological Treatments of the Schizophrenias and Other Psychoses.

The 1950s also witnessed the rise of psychopharmacological treatments for individuals with schizophrenia (see also Chapter 14d). Chlorpromazine appeared in the United States under the trade name Thorazine, and other psychoactive drugs with similar actions and effects were soon to appear. Psychoactive drugs showed dramatic effects on the florid psychotic symptoms of schizophrenia, including thought disorders, hallucinations, and social withdrawal.

In 1955, public mental hospitals in the United States housed over 550,000 patients; just 20 years later this number had dropped to slightly over 200,000 individuals (Gelman, 1999). The decrease was attributed primarily to the use of psychopharmacological agents, coupled with the deinstitutionalization movement fueled by the high cost in institutional care (Johnson, 1990). The introduction of such psychoactive drugs raised new questions about the role of psychotherapy in the treatment of schizophrenia.

1960–2010: THE LAST 50 YEARS

Three major federally funded research projects on the effectiveness of psychotherapy for patients with schizophrenia occurred in the 1960s, including the combination of pharmacotherapy and psychotherapy. May (1968) found that patients with schizophrenia treated solely with medication and patients treated with supportive psychodynamic psychotherapy plus antipsychotic drugs had significantly greater improvement rates than patients who only received supportive psychodynamic psychotherapy. Karon and VandenBos (1972, 1981) obtained an opposite finding. Patients treated with psychotherapy alone and patients treated with a combination of psychotherapy and psychoactive drugs improved in comparison with those who received standard hospital care, which consisted primarily of antipsychotic drugs alone. The patients who received psychotherapy without medication showed greater long-term improvement. During this same period, Carl Rogers and his associates

(Rogers, Gendlin, Kiesler, & Truax, 1967) also studied the effectiveness of client-centered psychotherapy with schizophrenic patients.

Another thrust during the 1960s involved rehabilitation of patients with schizophrenia, focusing on independent living skills and social interaction skills. Problem-solving therapies involved skills training and practice rehearsals (e.g., D'Zurilla & Goldfried, 1971). Five stages or types of skills were taught to patients in this social learning program. In a similar research effort, individuals with schizophrenia often received training in the basic components of individual skills of daily living. Programs typically involved classroom presentations and individual coaching around a broad array of skills, such as medication management, social skills, leisure for recreation, and friendship and dating (e.g., Wallace & Liberman, 1985). More comprehensive rehabilitation approaches combined directive and nondirective psychotherapy techniques, patient input and active participation in treatment planning, skill-building approaches, and psychopharmacological interventions (Anthony, Cohen, Farkas, & Gagne, 2002).

Contingency management techniques, primarily token economies, also started to be developed in the 1960s (Ayllon, 1968). Several studies empirically demonstrated the effectiveness of such procedures in altering maladaptive inpatient behavior and promoting adaptive behavior, leading to successful discharge and sustained living in the community (e.g., Paul & Lentz, 1977). Likewise, psychosocial "clubhouse" programs emphasizing peer support, residential living, and occupational training were developed and demonstrated to be effective (Fairweather, Sanders, Maynard, & Cressler, 1969). These early programs were the forerunners of assertive community treatment (ACT; Stein & Test, 1980) and social learning therapies (Paul & Menditto, 1992), now among the most widely researched and empirically supported psychosocial therapies for schizophrenia. Pfammatter, Junghan, and Brenner (2006) presented a meta-analysis of the research done on these approaches since 1990, which demonstrates their positive effects.

The nature of the interpersonal relationship between schizophrenic individuals and their families and friends has long been an active area of research, with important clinical implications. Some researchers have viewed strained family relationships as being causal in the development of schizophrenia, whereas others have viewed such difficult relationships as a major source of stress for the severely disturbed patients, which overwhelms their coping abilities and triggers the onset of serious symptoms.

Leff and colleagues (Leff et al., 1990; Leff, Kuipers, Berkowitz, & Sturgeon, 1985) in England, working with Brown, Monck, Carstairs, and Wing's (1962) concept of *expressed emotion*, developed a 4.5-month psychoeducational program for patients and family members. The program involved lectures on the causes, symptoms, and course of schizophrenia; training in recognizing high versus low patterns of expressed emotions; and family sessions geared toward practical mutual problem solving (and that used the communication concept of expressed emotion). Expressed emotion is measured in terms of the number of critical or negative comments from family members toward the patient and the intensity of the emotional involvement of others in the family in the patient's life. Leff and colleagues found that patients who participated in the program with their families had only an 8% relapse rates in the 6 months immediately after discharge from the hospital, compared with a 50% relapse rate for other comparable patients receiving routine care at the same hospital.

Similar psychoeducational programs were developed in the United States. Rehospitalizations were dramatically reduced by such programs in comparison with control patients who received routine care at the same hospital (Hogarty et al., 1986, 1991). In meta-analyses of dozens of clinical trials (e.g., Barbato & D'Avanzo, 2000), the addition of a family therapy component cut the relapse rates by more than half.

During the 1970s and 1980s, research on the natural course of schizophrenia began to emerge from research centers around the world. Manfred Bleuler (1970), who continued the work of his father (Eugen Bleuler), reported on a follow-up of 208 patients over an average of 22 years in Zurich. He found that 20% of the patients had complete remission of schizophrenic symptoms and another 33% had mild end-states—or, in short, over one half of the patients were much improved. He also reported that another 24% had intermediate end-states and 24% were chronic and severe cases with little or no improvement. A similar study reported on 289 highly representative first-admission schizophrenic patients in Lausanne, Switzerland, who were followed up an average of 37 years (Ciompi & Muller, 1976). Outcome was assessed across five dimensions: severity of psychotic symptoms, development of additional disorders, further deterioration, social adjustment over time, and global evaluation. All told, 27% of patients fully recovered, 22% had only mild remaining symptoms, 24% had intermediate end-states, and 18% had chronic and severe unimproved end-states.

U.S. researchers (Harding, Brooks, Ashikaga, Strauss, & Breier, 1987a, 1987b) reported on the long-term outcome of a project in the state of Vermont that began in 1955. They examined people with chronic schizophrenia who had been hospitalized an average of 6 years, and they systematically followed the 269 most chronic patients through their rehabilitation program, discharge into the community, and later in life. Patients were rediagnosed using the *Diagnostic and Statistical Manual of Mental Disorders* criteria (*DSM–III*; American Psychiatric Association, 1980), 20 years after discharge. The researchers found that 17% were fully recovered and functioning in a "superior" manner, whereas only 3% were still residing in a psychiatric hospital. They also found that 56% met with friends at least once a week, and only 5% reported never meeting with friends. Further, they found that 76% reported having close or moderately close friends, and only 21% reported having only superficial social relations with others. These research studies provided important information on the more positive long-term outcome of schizophrenia, as well as evidence of the value of planned rehabilitation, psychosocial support, and psychotherapeutic efforts.

An individual psychodynamic-informed supportive psychotherapy combined with family therapy—generally referred to as *need-adapted treatment*—was developed and researched in Finland in the 1980s by Alanen (1997; Alanen, Lehtinen, Räkköläinen, & Aaltonen, 1991). A 5-year follow-up outcome study (Salokangas, Palo-Oja, & Ojanen, 1991) found that 46% of the patients had no remaining psychotic symptoms and 29% had worked in fully employed jobs during the previous full year.

In the 1980s, researchers, mainly in England, began to develop more systematic attempts to apply CBT to psychotic symptoms and the commonly associated problems of anxiety and depression. A series of rigorous single-case studies demonstrated the feasibility and suggested clinical effects of providing CBT for psychosis (Chadwick & Lowe, 1990; Slade & Bentall, 1988). Applications of CBT in schizophrenia have mainly focused on the treatment of persistent psychotic symptoms, which are present in 15% to 60% of patients with schizophrenia who are adherent to antipsychotic medication (Curson, Patel, Liddle, & Barnes, 1988; Johnstone, Macmillan, Frith, Benn, & Crow, 1990). The application of CBT to psychosis was influenced by the growth in cognitive models of schizophrenia, which posited that the emergence of psychotic symptoms was a result of efforts to understand anomalous experiences and cognitive biases in which internal images and thoughts (e.g., thinking "I'm worthless") were misattributed to external sources (e.g., a hallucination). An additional influence was the emergence of evidence demonstrating that patients with schizophrenia who were actively involved in the management of their psychotic symptoms, including the spontaneous development of coping strategies (Breier & Strauss, 1983), reduced their distress and dysfunction.

According to Hagen and Nordahl (2008), typical features of CBT for psychosis involve the following:

- developing a collaborative relationship between the patient and therapist,
- normalizing psychotic symptoms as common reactions to stress to reduce patients' shame or embarrassment when discussing these experiences,
- cognitive restructuring for teaching patients how to identify and critically examine thoughts that contribute to negative feelings,

- eschewing direct confrontation about delusional beliefs in favor of guided discovery of evidence against them,
- teaching coping strategies for the management of persistent symptoms, and
- conducting behavioral experiments when more information is needed concerning the accuracy of a belief.

The success of pilot studies on CBT for psychosis led to the development of several treatment manuals (e.g., Beck et al., 2009; Chadwick, 2006; Kingdon & Turkington, 2005) as well as more than 30 randomized controlled trials, which demonstrated positive effects on reducing the severity of persistent psychotic symptoms and associated distress. Meta-analyses of the research on CBT for psychosis have consistently supported its efficacy; the most recent meta-analysis indicated that it was effective at reducing the severity of psychotic symptoms, as well as reducing negative symptoms and improving psychosocial functioning (Wykes, Steel, Everitt, & Tarrier, 2008). CBT for psychosis is a recommended treatment in both the Patient Outcomes Research Team (PORT) guidelines for schizophrenia in the United States (Dixon et al., 2009) and the National Institute for Health and Clinical Excellence (NICE) guidelines for the treatment of schizophrenia in Great Britain (National Collaborating Centre for Mental Health, 2009).

Calls have been made to increase access to research-supported treatments for psychosis in part by recommending a greater commitment by the mental health professions to mandate training in evidence-based practices (Mueser & Noordsy, 2005). The Society of Clinical Psychology (http://www.div12.org/) of the American Psychological Association designated the following therapies as empirically supported therapies for schizophrenia with strong research support:

- social skills training,
- cognitive–behavioral therapy (CBT),
- assertive community treatment (ACT),
- family psychoeducation,
- supported employment,
- social learning/token economy programs, and
- cognitive remediation.

LOOKING INTO THE FUTURE

Tremendous strides have been made in the development and validation of effective psychotherapies for schizophrenia, but there is still much work to be done. One area clearly in need of further development is the application of psychotherapies to a broader range of problem areas, such as depression and anxiety among those suffering from schizophrenia. CBT, for example, has been shown to be effective in reducing the severity of psychotic symptoms and in modestly improving psychosocial functioning and negative emotions. This leaves open a wide range of applications for CBT to address other problems in schizophrenia, such as enhancing social skills training and facilitating client efforts to find and keep work. In doing so, psychologists will return to the emphasis of earlier eras in treating the entire person, not simply the florid symptoms.

Another future direction is early identification and preventive intervention for individuals who have recently experienced a psychotic episode and who either already have a schizophrenia spectrum diagnosis or may qualify for such a diagnosis in the near future. Rapid detection and comprehensive treatment at the first episode of psychosis represent a unique opportunity to improve the long-term trajectory of schizophrenia. Multiple efforts are under way throughout the world to develop and evaluate such programs (e.g., Petersen et al., 2005).

A final frontier for future work on psychotherapy for schizophrenia is to shift the balance away from its traditional focus on psychopathology and deficits to a greater emphasis on helping individuals increase their positive emotions and sense of purpose. In recent years, consumers of mental health services have argued for a redefinition of the traditional medical term *recovery* to incorporate personal growth and life meaning (Ralph & Corrigan, 2005). The broadened definition of recovery centers on the capacity of people with a serious mental disorder to grow as individuals and to embrace life. Much that has been learned from positive psychology—the savoring of pleasant experiences, the cultivation of interpersonal connections, the development of mindfulness, the acquisition of learned optimism (Seligman, 2002)—has the potential not only to improve the quality of people's lives but also to increase their resiliency in dealing with the multiple challenges posed by schizophrenia.

REFERENCES

Alanen, Y. O. (1997). *Schizophrenia: Its origins and need-adapted treatment*. London, England: Karnac Books.

Alanen, Y. O., Lehtinen, K., Räkköläinen, V., & Aaltonen, J. (1991). Need-adapted treatment of schizophrenic patients: Experiences and results of the Turku project. *Acta Psychiatrica Scandinavica, 83*, 363–372. doi:10.1111/j.1600-0447.1991.tb05557.x

American Psychiatric Association. (1980). *Diagnostic and statistical manual of mental disorders* (3rd ed.). Washington, DC: Author.

Anthony, W., Cohen, M., Farkas, M., & Gagne, C. (2002). *Psychiatric rehabilitation* (2nd ed.). Boston, MA: Boston University Center for Psychiatric Rehabilitation.

Ayllon, T. (1968). *The token economy: A motivational system for therapy and rehabilitation*. New York, NY: Appleton-Century-Crofts.

Barbato, A., & D'Avanzo, B. (2000). Family interventions in schizophrenia and related disorders: A critical review of clinical trials. *Acta Psychiatrica Scandinavica, 102*, 81–97. doi:10.1034/j.1600-0447.2000.102002081.x

Beck, A. T. (1952). Successful outpatient psychotherapy with a schizophrenic with a delusion based on borrowed guilt. *Psychiatry, 15*, 305–312.

Beck, A. T., Rector, N. A., Stolar, N., & Grant, P. (2009). *Schizophrenia: Cognitive theory, research, and therapy*. New York, NY: Guilford Press.

Bleuler, E. (1950). *Dementia praecox or the group of schizophrenias*. Oxford, England: International Universities Press. (Original work published 1911)

Bleuler, M. (1970). Some results of research in schizophrenia. *Behavioral Science, 15*, 211–219. doi:10.1002/bs.3830150302

Bockoven, J. S. (1972). *Moral treatment in community mental health*. Oxford, England: Springer.

Breier, A., & Strauss, J. S. (1983). Self-control of psychotic behavior. *Archives of General Psychiatry, 40*, 1141–1145.

Brown, G. W., Monck, E. M., Carstairs, G. M., & Wing, J. K. (1962). Influence of family life on the course of schizophrenic illness. *British Journal of Preventive and Social Medicine, 16*, 55–68.

Chadwick, P. D. (2006). *Person-based cognitive therapy for distressing psychosis*. Chichester, England: Wiley. doi:10.1002/9780470713075

Chadwick, P. D., & Lowe, C. F. (1990). Measurement and modification of delusional beliefs. *Journal of Consulting and Clinical Psychology, 58*, 225–232. doi:10.1037/0022-006X.58.2.225

Ciompi, L., & Muller, C. (1976). [Lifestyle and age of schizophrenics: A catamnestic long-term study into old age] [In German]. *Monographien aus dem Gesamtgebiete der Psychiatrie. Psychiatry Series, 12*, 1–242.

Curson, D. A., Patel, M., Liddle, P. F., & Barnes, T. R. E. (1988). Psychiatric morbidity of a long stay hospital population with chronic schizophrenia and implications for future community care. *British Medical Journal, 297*, 819–822. doi:10.1136/bmj.297.6652.819

Dixon, L. B., Dickerson, F., Bellack, A. S., Bennett, M. E., Dickinson, D., Goldberg, R., . . . Kreyenbuhl, J. (2009). The 2009 PORT psychosocial treatment recommendations and summary statements. *Schizophrenia Bulletin, 36*, 48–70. doi:10.1093/schbul/sbp115

D'Zurilla, T. J., & Goldfried, M. R. (1971). Problem solving and behavior modification. *Journal of Abnormal Psychology, 78*, 107–126. doi:10.1037/h0031360

Fairweather, G. W., Sanders, D. H., Maynard, H., & Cressler, D. L. (1969). *Community life for the mentally ill: An alternative to institutional care*. Chicago, IL: Aldine.

Fromm-Reichmann, F. (1948). Notes on the development of treatment of schizophrenics by psychoanalytic psychotherapy. *Psychiatry, 11*, 263–273.

Gelman, S. (1999). *Medicating schizophrenia: A history*. New Brunswick, NJ: Rutgers University Press.

Grinker, R., & Spiegel, J. (1945). *Men under stress*. Philadelphia, PA: Blakiston. doi:10.1037/10784-000

Hagen, R., & Nordahl, H. M. (2008). Behavioral experiments in the treatment of paranoid schizophrenia: A single case study. *Cognitive and Behavioral Practice, 15*, 296–305. doi:10.1016/j.cbpra.2007.09.004

Harding, C. M., Brooks, G. W., Ashikaga, T., Strauss, J. S., & Breier, A. (1987a). The Vermont longitudinal study of persons with severe mental illness: I. Methodology, study sample and overall status 32 years later. *American Journal of Psychiatry, 144*, 718–726.

Harding, C. M., Brooks, G. W., Ashikaga, T., Strauss, J. S., & Breier, A. (1987b). The Vermont longitudinal study of persons with severe mental illness: II. Long-term outcome of subjects who retrospectively met *DSM–III* criteria for schizophrenia. *American Journal of Psychiatry, 144,* 727–735.

Hogarty, G. E., Anderson, C. M., Reiss, D. J., Kornblith, S. J., Greenwald, D. P., Javna, C. D., & Madonia, M. J. (1986). Family psychoeducation, social skills training, and maintenance chemotherapy in the aftercare treatment of schizophrenia: One-year effects of a controlled study on relapse and expressed emotion. *Archives of General Psychiatry, 43,* 633–642.

Hogarty, G. E., Anderson, C. M., Reiss, D. J., Kornblith, S. J., Greenwald, D. P., Ulrich, R. F., & Carter, M. (1991). Family psychoeducation, social skills training, and maintenance chemotherapy in the aftercare treatment of schizophrenia: II. Two-year effects of a controlled study on relapse and adjustment. *Archives of General Psychiatry, 48,* 340–347.

Johnson, A. B. (1990). *Out of bedlam: The truth about deinstitutionalization.* New York, NY: Basic Books.

Johnstone, E. C., Macmillan, J. F., Frith, C. D., Benn, D. K., & Crow, T. J. (1990). Further investigation of the predictors of outcome following first schizophrenic episodes. *British Journal of Psychiatry, 157,* 182–189. doi:10.1192/bjp.157.2.182

Karon, B. P., & VandenBos, G. R. (1972). The consequences of psychotherapy for schizophrenic patients. *Psychotherapy: Theory, Research, and Practice, 9,* 111–119. doi:10.1037/h0086728

Karon, B. P., & VandenBos, G. R. (1981). *Psychotherapy of schizophrenia: The treatment of choice.* New York, NY: Aronson.

Kingdon, D. G., & Turkington, D. (2005). *Cognitive therapy of schizophrenia.* New York, NY: Guilford Press.

Kubie, L. S. (1960, December). Psychoanalysis and scientific method. *Journal of Nervous and Mental Disease, 131,* 495–512. doi:10.1097/00005053-196012000-00004

Leff, J. P., Berkowitz, R., Shavit, N., Strachan, A., Glass, I., & Vaughn, C. (1990). A trial of family therapy versus a relatives' group for schizophrenia: Two-year follow-up. *British Journal of Psychiatry, 157,* 571–577. doi:10.1192/bjp.157.4.571

Leff, J. P., Kuipers, L., Berkowitz, R., & Sturgeon, D. (1985). A controlled trial of social intervention in the families of schizophrenic patients: Two-year follow-up. *British Journal of Psychiatry, 146,* 594–600. doi:10.1192/bjp.146.6.594

Magaro, P. A. (1976). The cultural context of madness and its treatment. In P. A. Magaro (Ed.), *The construction of madness.* Elmsford, NY: Pergamon.

May, P. R. A. (1968). *Treatment of schizophrenia: A comparative study of five treatment methods.* New York, NY: Science House.

Mueser, K. T., & Noordsy, D. L. (2005). Cognitive behavior therapy for psychosis: A call to action. *Clinical Psychology: Science and Practice, 12,* 68–71. doi:10.1093/clipsy/bpi008

National Collaborating Centre for Mental Health. (2009). *Schizophrenia: Core interventions in the treatment and management of schizophrenia in adults in primary and secondary care* (Updated ed. Vol. 82). London, England: National Institute for Health and Clinical Excellence.

Paul, G. L., & Lentz, R. J. (1977). *Psychosocial treatment of chronic mental patients: Milieu versus social-learning programs.* Cambridge, MA: Harvard University Press.

Paul, G. L., & Menditto, A. A. (1992). Effectiveness of inpatient treatment programs for mentally ill adults in public psychiatric facilities. *Applied and Preventive Psychology: Current Scientific Perspectives, 1,* 41–63.

Petersen, L., Jeppesen, P., Thorup, A., Abel, M. B., Ohlenschlager, J., Christensen, T. O., . . . Nordentoft, M. (2005). A randomized, multi-center trial of integrated versus standard treatment for patients with a first episode of psychotic illness. *British Medical Journal, 331,* 602–609. doi:10.1136/bmj.38565.415000.E01

Pfammatter, M., Junghan, U. M., & Brenner, H. D. (2006). Efficacy of psychological therapy in schizophrenia: Conclusions from meta-analyses. *Schizophrenia Bulletin, 32*(Suppl. 1), S64–S80. doi:10.1093/schbul/sbl030

Ralph, R. O., & Corrigan, P. W. (Eds.). (2005). *Recovery in mental illness: Broadening our understanding of wellness.* Washington, DC: American Psychological Association. doi:10.1037/10848-000

Rogers, C. R., Gendlin, E. T., Kiesler, D. J., & Truax, C. B. (1967). *The therapeutic relationship and its impact: A study of psychotherapy with schizophrenics.* Madison, WI: University of Wisconsin Press.

Salokangas, R. K., Palo-Oja, T., & Ojanen, M. (1991). The need for social support among out-patients suffering from functional psychosis. *Psychological Medicine, 21,* 209–217. doi:10.1017/S0033291700014793

Seligman, M. E. P. (2002). Positive psychology, positive prevention, and positive therapy. In C. R. Snyder, & S. J. Lopez (Eds.), *Handbook of positive psychology.* (pp. 3–9). New York, NY: Oxford University Press.

Slade, P. D., & Bentall, R. P. (1988). *Sensory deception: A scientific analysis of hallucinations.* London, England: Croom Helm.

Stein, L. I., & Test, M. A. (1980). Alternatives to mental hospital treatment: Conceptual, model, treatment program and clinical evaluation. *Archives of General Psychiatry, 37,* 392–397.

Sullivan, H. S. (1953). *The interpersonal theory of psychiatry.* Washington, DC: William Alanson White Psychiatric Foundation.

Wallace, C. J., & Liberman, R. P. (1985). Social skills training for patients with schizophrenia: A controlled clinical trial. *Psychiatry Research, 15,* 239–247. doi:10.1016/0165-1781(85)90081-2

Wykes, T., Steel, C., Everitt, B., & Tarrier, N. (2008). Cognitive behavior therapy for schizophrenia: Effect sizes, clinical models and methodological rigor. *Schizophrenia Bulletin, 34,* 523–537. doi:10.1093/schbul/sbm114

V

PSYCHOTHERAPY
EDUCATION
AND TRAINING

16

TRAINING SYSTEMS AND SITES

PhD Programs

Elizabeth A. Klonoff

For the first 50 or 60 years in professional psychology, the training of a doctoral-level psychologist meant receiving a PhD from a traditional university. Thus, the early history of the field was the early history of PhD training. The primary focus of this chapter is on the history of PhD programs and secondarily the attendant conflict that has plagued professional psychology from its early days: What is the relationship between science and practice in the education of doctoral psychologists performing psychotherapy?

THE EARLY YEARS

Various committees and groups worked to define the content, rationale, and nature of the field. As early as 1945, the subcommittee charged with helping to define the internship experience called for a detailed survey of job actualities and possibilities for the then-developing field of clinical psychology

(Shakow et al., 1945). That report called for 2 years of graduate study, a 3rd year spent in a full-time clinical internship, and finally a 4th year back at the university where the student would complete his or her dissertation. The goal of the internship was to augment the years spent learning about people with learning derived from experience with people. The Shakow et al. (1945) report also raised the notion that the doctoral degree might not be the optimal degree for a clinical psychologist; specifically, the report noted that "the arguments for a truly professional degree, for example, a PsD, are many, and should be given careful consideration" (pp. 264–265). The establishment of an American Board of Clinical Psychology to provide diplomas or certificates for a certain level of experience was also proposed.

The 1947 report of the American Psychological Association's (APA's) Committee on Training in Clinical Psychology formed the foundation for future recommendations for the academic training of clinical psychologists. That report described the prominent place of science: "If we recognize that clinical psychology is both a science and an art calling for scientific rigor tempered by personal and social sensitivity, we can specify these [training] goals fairly clearly" (APA, 1947, p. 540). Rather than providing a detailed, prescriptive program, the report articulated 14 general training goals. It argued vehemently that at that stage of development, the curriculum for clinical psychology training programs should be open to experimentation with respect to who is accepted into a program and what should be taught. The field was cautioned against "settling clinical psychology at a time when it should have great lability" (APA, 1947, p. 543).

The final phase in the development of professional psychology as its own academic discipline was prompted to a large extent by World War II. In 1942, the federal government realized that the war would necessitate greatly increased mental health needs. As a result, the Veterans' Administration (VA) and the U.S. Public Health Service were asked to increase the number of mental health workers. Because it was believed that increasing the number of individuals attending medical schools and becoming psychiatrists would not be sufficient to meet the need, this was interpreted as a mandate to increase the number of clinical psychologists. Collaborating with a newly revamped APA (see the Professional Organizations and PhD Programs section), the VA and the Public Health Service began working with psychology doctoral programs already training clinicians to improve the quality of their training and encouraging universities that did not have clinical training programs to begin them. A two-pronged effort was undertaken: The Public Health Service provided funding to psychology departments to develop and expand their training programs, and the VA provided funding for practica and internship training experiences.

In 1945, the VA asked APA to provide a listing of universities that provided adequate training in clinical psychology. The APA Committee on

Graduate and Professional Training was tasked with determining these institutions. Universities were required to complete a questionnaire that described the clinical and nonclinical faculty, the curriculum specific to clinical psychology, and the nature of the practicum experiences (Cohen, 1992). By 1946, 22 universities had been so identified. The Committee on Graduate and Professional Training increased the number of approved universities to 29 (out of a total of 40 that had applied) by 1947; as the remaining 11 universities met the committee's criteria, they were approved as well. Table 16.1 lists the clinical programs applying for recognition and those recommended to the VA.

The VA began allowing students from these universities to work in its hospitals and clinics, with approximately 200 students doing so that first year. Programs were required to place students into practica that (a) involved treating patients within a team environment, (b) provided experience with children, and (c) included at least one other setting chosen by the university. Some of the practica sites were at state mental hospitals and some at institutions for people with mental retardation. Many universities had college counseling clinics to serve their own students, and clinical psychology students were placed in these as well. Some psychology departments, particularly those located far from state hospital facilities, developed their own clinics to provide services to the community and to the campus.

The strong consensus throughout the early period was to locate the training of clinical psychologists in university departments of psychology, as opposed to separate schools within universities, in a manner similar to medical and law schools, or outside of universities entirely. This decision, although expedient, had long-standing ramifications. The Flexner Report (Flexner, 1910/1972) had been critical of the development of medical schools independent of universities. It decried what was termed the *overproduction* of poorly trained practitioners and the existence of for-profit, commercial medical schools. It argued that universities had to invest resources into these emerging medical schools and incorporate them into the university and that all schools should have a similar, agreed-on curriculum, which led to relative conformity among the medical schools within the United States. Although various schools of medicine have experimented with different curricula, the core has remained pretty much the same, and in general students graduating from an accredited medical program in the United States can be expected to have a common core of knowledge and experiences. By contrast, university departments have long supported the philosophy of academic freedom. This has often resulted in resistance to a uniform curriculum and a lack of consensus on exactly what someone who completes PhD training in professional psychology knows and can do.

By 1949, universities, the VA, and the National Institute of Mental Health had sufficient experience training clinical psychologists to bring together representatives from the major training sites to consolidate the

TABLE 16.1

PhD Programs Applying for Recognition, Recommended to the Veterans Administration, and Members of the Academy of Psychological Clinical Science

Program	Applied to Committee on Graduate and Professional Training for Recognition, 1947	Recommended to Veterans Administration, 1947	Member, Academy of Psychological Clinical Science
University of Arizona			X
Arizona State University			X
Boston University			X
University of California, Berkeley	X	X	X
University of California, Los Angeles	X	X	X
Catholic University of America	X	X	
Case Western Reserve University	X	X	
University of Cincinnati	X	X	
Clark University	X	X	
University of Colorado	X		
Columbia University	X	X	
Columbia University, Teachers College	X	X	
University of Delaware			X
University of Denver (Department of Psychology)	X		X
Duke University	X	X	X
Emory University			X
University of Florida	X		
Florida State University			X
George Washington University	X		
University of Georgia	X		X
Harvard University	X	X	X
University of Hawaii			X
University of Illinois at Chicago			X
University of Illinois at Urbana–Champaign	X	X	X
Indiana University	X	X	X
University of Iowa	X	X	X
Kent State University			X
University of Kentucky	X	X	X
University of Maryland			X
McGill University			X
University of Memphis			X
University of Miami (Health Psychology)			X
Michigan State University	X		
University of Michigan	X	X	
University of Minnesota	X	X	X
University of Missouri			X

TABLE 16.1
PhD Programs Applying for Recognition, Recommended to
the Veterans Administration, and Members of the Academy
of Psychological Clinical Science   *(Continued)*

Program	Applied to Committee on Graduate and Professional Training for Recognition, 1947	Recommended to Veterans Administration, 1947	Member, Academy of Psychological Clinical Science
University of Nebraska	X		
University of Nevada, Reno			X
Northwestern University	X	X	X
Ohio State University	X	X	X
University of Oregon			X
University of Pennsylvania	X	X	X
Pennsylvania State University	X	X	X
University of Pittsburgh	X	X	X
Purdue University	X	X	X
University of Rochester	X	X	
Rutgers University			X
San Diego State University and University of California, San Diego (joint program)			X
University of Southern California	X	X	X
University of South Florida			X
Stanford University	X	X	
Syracuse University	X	X	
University of Texas	X		X
Tulane University	X		
Binghamton University, State University of New York			X
University at Buffalo, State University of New York			X
Stony Brook University, State University of New York			X
University of Toronto			X
Vanderbilt University			X
Virginia Commonwealth University			X
Virginia Polytechnic Institute and State University			X
University of Virginia (Department of Psychology)			X
University of Washington	X		X
Washington University in St. Louis	X	X	X
Wayne State University	X		
West Virginia University			X
University of Wisconsin	X	X	X
Yale University	X	X	X

Note. Information taken from Cohen (1992) and Academy of Psychological Clinical Science (n.d.).

recommendations for improvement in training. A 2-week conference was held in Boulder, Colorado, that has since become the watershed in the development of academic clinical psychology. The results of the conference (Raimy, 1950) codified much of the writings that defined what clinical psychology was to be. The resulting *Boulder model* described the preparation of scientist–practitioners, individuals trained to conduct research, perform clinical work, and integrate the two. The scientist–practitioner was to be trained in a 4-year course of study similar to the nonclinical areas of psychology. The 3rd year was designed to be a full-time clinical internship, with the goal of providing real-world experience that could inform the student's dissertation research, which was to be done in the 4th year when the student returned to campus.

Although the scientist–practitioner model still predominates PhD programs, the nature of the training has changed. For example, somewhere between this original outline and today, the internship has migrated from a clinical experience meant to inform future research to a "capstone" experience meant to be done immediately before the degree is awarded. The majority of PhD programs in professional psychology are now accredited by APA, which means that they do present a modicum of uniform content. Also, the 4 years originally anticipated for the PhD has grown to an average of 6 years, including internship (Norcross, Ellis, & Sayette, 2009).

One thing that has not changed, however, is the requirement that the dissertation be an empirical research project that makes a new and creative contribution to the field. Few universities would accept the kind of projects typically done in PsyD programs as a dissertation. The dissertation requirement ensures that individuals receiving PhDs have some experience conducting their own original research.

ROLE OF TRAINING CONFERENCES

The Boulder conference was not the only meeting that has had a significant impact on the growth and development of PhD programs. Table 16.2 lists the majority of these conferences, along with references for the proceedings of the various meetings. Some of these conferences helped to define the training and experience of what have come to be called *developed practice areas*. Conferences have been held to define the content and sequence of training for the areas of counseling psychology, school psychology, neuropsychology, and health psychology. Both the Vail conference, which provided the initial framework for the professional degree in psychology, the PsyD, and the Clinical Science conference, which helped to solidify that model, are represented among the conferences listed. Each of these conferences has contributed to the field as it is currently understood. Unfortunately, many of the unresolved issues that were raised in some of the early conferences remain to this day.

TABLE 16.2

Training Conferences Related to the Development
of PhD Programs in Professional Psychology

Year	Conference
1918	APA: The Future of Pure and Applied Psychology
1949	Boulder conference: Graduate Education in Clinical Psychology (Raimy, 1950)
1951	Northwestern conference: Doctoral Education and Training in Counseling Psychology (American Psychological Association, Committee on Counselor Training, Division of Counseling and Guidance, 1952a; 1952b)
1954	Thayer conference: Functions, Qualifications, and Training of School Psychologists (Cutts, 1955)
1955	Stanford conference: Institute on Education and Training for Psychological Contributions to Mental Health (Strother, 1956)
1958	Miami conference: Graduate Education and Training in Psychology (Roe, Gustad, Moore, Ross, & Skodak, 1959)
1964	Greyston conference: Professional Preparation of Counseling Psychologists (Thompson & Super, 1964)
1965	Chicago conference: Professional Preparation of Clinical Psychologists (Hoch, Ross, & Winder, 1966)
1972	Topeka, KS: Menninger Conference on Postdoctoral Education in Clinical Psychology
1973	Vail conference: Levels and Patterns of Professional Education and Training (Korman, 1976)
1976	APA convened a series of meetings to address education and credentialing in professional psychology from which evolved agreement on a core curriculum
1977	Vancouver conference: Organization and Representation of Professional Psychology
1978	Virginia Beach conference: Education of Professional Psychologists (Watson, Caddy, Johnson, & Rimm, 1981)
1980	Spring Hill Symposium: The Future of Psychology in the Schools
1981	Olympia conference: School Psychology
1981	La Jolla conference: Quality of Professional Psychology Training (Callan, Peterson, & Stichy, 1986)
1983	Arden House conference: Education and Training in Health Psychology (Stone, 1983)
1985	Hilton Head conference: Training Clinical Child Psychologists
1986	Mission Bay: Standards and Evaluation in Professional Education and Training (Bourg, Bent, McHolland, & Strichy, 1989)
1987	Gainesville conference: Internship Training in Professional Psychology (Belar et al., 1987)
1987	Atlanta conference: Planning for the Future of Counseling Psychology (Gazda, Rude, & Weissberg, 1988)
1987	Salt Lake City conference: Graduate Education and Training in Psychology (Bickman, 1987)
1990	Gainesville conference: Scientist-Practitioner Education and Training for the Professional Practice of Psychology (Belar & Perry, 1992)
1992	Ann Arbor conference: Postdoctoral Training in Professional Psychology (Larsen et al., 1993)
1994	New Orleans: First International Congress on the Licensing, Certification, and Credentialing of Psychologists (Association of State and Provincial Psychology Boards)

(continues)

TABLE 16.2
Training Conferences Related to the Development of
PhD Programs in Professional Psychology   *(Continued)*

Year	Conference
1994	Bloomington, IN: Clinical Science in the 21st Century
1994	Norman, OK: American Psychological Association National Conference on Postdoctoral Training
1997	Supply and Demand: Education, Training and Employment Issues in Professional Psychology
1997	Houston, TX: Specialty Education and Training in Clinical Neuropsychology (Hannay et al., 1998)
2001	Houston Conference on Counseling Psychology (Fouad et al., 2004)
2000	Miami, FL: Doctoral-Level Education of Clinical, Counseling, and School Psychologists
2002	Scottsdale, AZ: Competencies Conference (Kaslow, 2004)
2005	Snowbird Summit on Accreditation
2006	Colorado Springs, CO: Pike's Peak Conference on Geropsychology (Knight, Karel, Hinrichsen, Qualls, & Duffy, 2009)

Note. Information taken from Cohen (1992), Altmaier (2003), Commission for the Recognition of Specialties and Proficiencies in Professional Psychology (n.d.), and Catherine Grus (personal communication, February 11, 2009).

It was the Chicago conference (Hoch, Ross, & Winder, 1966) that reaffirmed the position against master's-level training as the entry level for professional psychologists. The conference went so far as to condemn the practice of granting consolation master's degrees to individuals judged unsuitable to complete the doctorate, stating that "if such students are judged suitable for master's-level training, they should complete the requirements of the specialty program awarding the degree" (p. 44). This conference described the distinction between postgraduate education, designed to prepare nonclinically trained psychologists for clinical practice, and postgraduate training, designed to allow clinicians to perfect their skills, to specialize in working with specific populations, or both.

The Chicago conference also developed a listing of the conditions believed to be necessary for implementing good clinical training. Faculty should represent the full range of the scientist–practitioner continuum, and clinical practice should be afforded the same rewards as other academic enterprises. The setting in which students learned to practice was also considered important. To that end, the conference called for the development of "psychological service centers," which were to be associated with universities and staffed by psychologists. The ideal would be for these centers to treat a broad range of problems as well as serving as a primary location in which to conduct research. The conference also reaffirmed the importance of a 1-year clinical internship, with practica experiences designed to lead to the internship, which was thought to be best done away from campus.

Two points recurred during the conference: (a) the "core" did not need to be enumerated, but departments were responsible for ensuring that students received instruction in the broad areas of psychology; and (b) clinical psychology had to have its base in general psychology and clinical skills could not be taught independent of their scientific base. The importance of integrating science and practice was reaffirmed, as was the requirement that each student receive training in "one-to-one psychotherapy" (Hoch et al., 1966, p. 49). Finally, the conference began the dialogue on the relative need for the development of the professional psychologist model of training, one that might lead to a non-PhD professional degree. Although the conference continued to endorse the PhD as the desired degree, it did note that some universities might want to begin to experiment with other types of training and degrees.

PROFESSIONAL ORGANIZATIONS AND PhD PROGRAMS

The tension between the scientific and the clinical requirements of training, and the integration of the two at the program and department level, has been played out many times at the organizational level as well. Fernberger (1932) summarized the history of the APA from its founding by a group of "rugged pioneers" meeting at Clark University in July 1892 to its growth to 530 members and 571 associates in 1930. As the organization increased in size and influence, its relationship with those who labeled themselves *clinicians* became more tumultuous.

During the 1920s and 1930s, various local groups, consisting mainly of practitioners, continued to develop, and these often formed coalitions with the group out of New York state because it was so large. In 1930, this coalition became the Association of Consulting Psychologists. The newsletter for the organization became the *Journal of Consulting Psychology*, which eventually became the *Journal of Clinical and Consulting Psychology*. In 1937, the Association of Consulting Psychologists joined with various state organizations to become the American Association for Applied Psychology (AAAP). In 1939, the looming threat of war brought both APA and AAAP to the table to plan for the role of psychologists in the possible war effort (Olson, 1940; Routh, 1994). In 1945, AAAP merged with a newly reorganized APA. The reorganization reframed the mission of the organization as "the object of the American Psychological Association shall be to advance psychology as a science, as a profession, and as a means of promoting human welfare" (Olson, 1944, p. 746). This is when APA became both a professional and a scientific organization.

APA Division 11 was originally conceptualized to be for the scientists, and Division 12 (the continuation of AAAP, first called Clinical Psychology) was thought to be directed primarily at the practitioners (Routh, 1994). Because of the large overlap in membership, it was decided to make Division 12 the Division of Clinical and Abnormal Psychology (this was shortened in 1955 to the Division of Clinical Psychology) and to keep both scientists and practitioners in the same division. Today, the Society of Clinical Psychology (APA Division 12) thrives as the second largest division within APA. Its stated mission is "to encourage and support the integration of psychological science and practice in education, research, application, advocacy and public policy, attending to the importance of diversity" (Norcross, 2009, para. 3).

The directors of PhD clinical psychology programs started meeting at the annual APA convention (Routh, 1994); the group became the organization now known as the Council of University Directors of Clinical Psychology and officially incorporated in 1986 (R. Bauer, personal communication, January 5, 2009). The Council of University Directors of Clinical Psychology now represents more than 165 scientist–practitioner programs housed in traditional universities.

Subsequently, directors of other psychology doctoral programs began their own training groups, such as the Council of Counseling Psychology Training Programs established in 1978. The Council of Directors of School Psychology Programs, with the express purpose of advancing doctoral education in school psychology, was formed around the same time (August 1977). The Consortium of Combined-Integrated Doctoral Programs in Psychology was officially formed in August 2002; this organization represents those programs that intentionally combine or integrate education across at least two of the recognized practice areas of clinical, counseling, and school psychology.

In the mid-1980s, the four groups that emphasized the PhD, scientist–practitioner model were joined by 11 others, and the 15 training organizations along with the seven liaison groups are now known as the Council of Chairs of Training Councils. This organization facilitates communication among the various training communities.

The definition of and need for a return to the traditional scientific base that first gave rise to academic clinical psychology were articulated by McFall (1991) in his "manifesto" for clinical psychology. In that article, McFall presented one "cardinal principle" and two corollaries. The cardinal principle is that scientific clinical psychology is the only legitimate and acceptable form that the field can take. He decried the dichotomy implied by the scientist–practitioner model, arguing that if science is only one aspect of being a psychologist, does that mean it is possible to have an "unscientific" clinical psychology? He described a number of instances in which APA appeared to have drawn a distinction between psychology and science and asked whether that would happen in any other scientific field. One of the corollaries of his position was the belief that the goal of doctoral training in clinical psychology should be to produce the most competent clinical scientists possible.

A 1994 conference involving 25 representatives from clinical and health psychology programs was held in Bloomington, Indiana, to define the future of clinical science in psychology. The Academy of Psychological Clinical Science grew out of this meeting. A total of 51 universities (see Table 16.1) and a number of internship and postdoctoral training sites are now members of the academy (http://psych.arizona.edu/apcs/origins.php). Not surprisingly, more than half (22) of the original 40 departments of psychology that applied for approval by the Committee on Education and Training in Clinical Psychology in the mid-1940s have become academy programs today. This pattern underscores the centrality of the scientific training in the original establishment of the discipline, an importance that has continued for many academic programs.

FUTURE OF PhD PROGRAMS

Altman (1987) described two phases of psychology history: (a) the centripetal period, where unifying trends were developed and the field was consolidated, and (b) the centrifugal period, characterized by increasing disorganization, an increased emphasis on individualism, and a weaker attachment to the profession. This trend of moving away from a monolithic discipline of psychology has continued in the past 20 years (Belar, 1998). As a result, a number of continuing and new issues affect PhD training in professional psychology.

Changes in Instruction That Reflect Emerging Technologies

The advent of online instruction has the potential to revolutionize university education, making it available to many students in different formats. The potential problems are underscored by the increasing need for such things as websites to check for plagiarism; methods to prevent students from using cell phones to e-mail photographs of exams to other students; and the ability to check social networking sites to find out about students, instructors, psychotherapists, or patients. How this will affect training in professional psychology has yet to be determined. Although some courses and topics may be more easily amenable to online instruction, the field has yet to make decisions about assessment, treatment, and clinical supervision online. In addition, the field has yet to grapple with problems that could arise when a professor or supervisor is in one state and the supervisee and patient are in another, each with differing laws and requirements. The new technology has raised practical and ethical questions.

Increased Emphases on Interdisciplinary Research and Practice

Many National Institutes of Health initiatives expect translational work and demand that doctoral students interested in pursuing research careers obtain training outside of the traditional, separate academic disciplines. Access to an array of other disciplines and research training opportunities may soon produce a change in the training of PhD scientist–practitioners. Already one can see that students are now no longer presenting their data solely at psychological meetings; rather, they are presenting at meetings ranging from the Society of Neuroscience to the Association of Behavior and Cognitive Therapies, International Neuropsychological Society, Society of Behavioral Medicine, and the American Public Health Association.

Continuing Questions About the Integration of Science and Practice

Related to interdisciplinary research are increasing concerns about the optimal way to integrate science and practice in PhD training and beyond. As the science increases rapidly, students need to know how to assess and integrate the research into clinical practice. Merely being consumers of research will not be sufficient in the future. Doctoral-level professionals should have the ability to evaluate treatments, to develop and test new ones, and to ensure that science is included in practitioner training.

Concerns About Health Care in the United States

Many years ago when fee-for-service was the primary way in which practitioners were reimbursed, private practice was a reasonable option for most practicing psychologists, even new graduates. Recent changes in health care reimbursement make private practice a less than viable option for many practitioners. Exactly how health care will eventually be delivered and reimbursed, particularly for doctoral-level practitioners, has yet to be determined. However, it will be necessary for doctoral-level practitioners to demonstrate that they offer services and outcomes beyond those offered by practitioners with less education.

Increased Diversity and International Contact

As has often been described, much of scientific psychology represents research done primarily with middle- and upper-middle-class White college students. The ability to involve a broader segment of the population in studies is vitally important to keeping psychology relevant. Similarly, the ability to attract a diverse group of students to research-oriented training programs is equally important. PhD programs will need to include diverse faculty who conduct research on equally diverse populations if the field is to maintain its edge.

SUMMARY

Today, PhD programs in clinical, counseling, school, and combined psychology represent more than 70% of APA-accredited training programs (Norcross et al., 2009). The 80 or so PsyD programs in the United States pale in comparison to the 250 PhD programs. However, professional PsyD programs typically accept and graduate far more students than PhD programs, meaning that currently equal numbers of PhD and PsyD graduates are being produced (see Chapter 16b).

PhD training in professional psychology continues to prosper despite the increase in the number of students obtaining PsyDs. Although PhD programs accept a lower percentage of applicants, these programs have significantly smaller class sizes and are much more likely to provide students with both tuition waivers and assistantships. Students in PhD programs tend to have higher GRE scores and higher GPAs (Norcross, Ellis, & Sayette, in press). Despite the emphasis on practice in PsyD programs, students who graduate from PhD programs tend to score higher on the Examination for Professional Practice in Psychology, which is necessary for licensure in all states. The differences between these types of programs have actually increased over time (e.g., Templer, Stroup, Mancuso, & Tangen, 2008). PhD programs also train the overwhelming majority of those who conduct research.

These data, taken together, suggest that PhD programs continue to adhere to the scientist–practitioner ideal as envisioned at the Boulder conference. The large number of applicants means that professional psychology PhD programs are highly selective in who they admit; it also means that PhD training is alive and well and likely to remain that way for many years to come.

REFERENCES

Academy of Psychological Clinical Science. (n.d.). *Origins and background*. Retrieved from http://psych.arizona.edu/apcs/origins.php

Altmaier, E. M. (Ed.). (2003). *Setting standards in graduate education: Psychology's commitment to excellence in accreditation*. Washington, DC: American Psychological Association. doi:10.1037/10568-000

Altman, I. (1987). Centripetal and centrifugal trends in psychology. *American Psychologist, 42*, 1058–1069. doi:10.1037/0003-066X.42.12.1058

American Psychological Association, Committee on Training in Clinical Psychology. (1947). Recommended graduate training program in clinical psychology. *American Psychologist, 2*, 539–558. doi:10.1037/h0058236

American Psychological Association, Committee on Counselor Training, Division of Counseling and Guidance. (1952a). The practicum training of counseling psychologists. *American Psychologist, 7*, 182–188. doi:10.1037/h0060510

American Psychological Association, Committee on Counselor Training, Division of Counseling and Guidance. (1952b). Recommended standards for training counseling psychologists at the doctoral level. *American Psychologist, 7*, 175–181. doi:10.1037/h0056299

Association for Psychological Science. (n.d.) *History of APS.* Retrieved from http://www.psychologicalscience.org/about/history.cfm

Belar, C. D. (1998). Graduate education in clinical psychology: "We're not in Kansas anymore." *American Psychologist, 53*, 456–464. doi:10.1037/0003-066X.53.4.456

Belar, C. D., Bieliauskas, L. A., Larsen, K. G., Mensh, I. N., Poey, K., & Roehlke, H. J. (Eds.). (1987). *Proceedings: National Conference on Internship Training in Psychology.* Washington, DC: Association of Psychology Postdoctoral and Internship Centers.

Belar, C. D., & Perry, N. W. (1992). National conference on scientist–practitioner education and training for the professional practice of psychology. *American Psychologist, 47*, 71–75. doi:10.1037/0003-066X.47.1.71

Bickman, L. (1987). Proceedings of the National Conference on Graduate Education in Psychology. *American Psychologist, 42*, 1041–1047. doi:10.1037/0003-066X.42.12.1041

Bourg, E. F., Bent, R. J., McHolland, J. D., & Strichy, G. (1989). Standards and evaluation in the education and training of professional psychologists: The National Council of Schools of Professional Psychology Mission Bay Conference. *American Psychologist, 44*, 66–72. doi:10.1037/0003-066X.44.1.66

Callan, J. E., Peterson, D. R., & Stichy, G. (1986). *Quality of professional psychology training: A national conference and self-study.* Norman, OK: Transcript Press. doi:10.1037/10558-000

Cohen, L. D. (1992). The academic department. In D. K. Freedheim (Ed.), *History of psychotherapy* (pp. 731–764). Washington, DC: American Psychological Association. doi:10.1037/10110-021

Commission for the Recognition of Specialties and Proficiencies in Professional Psychology. (n.d.). *Highlights of psychology's evolutional as a profession.* Retrieved from http://www.apa.org/crsppp/evolution.html

Cutts, N. (1955). *School psychologists at midcentury: A report on the Thayer Conference on the functions, qualification, and training of school psychologists.* Washington, DC: American Psychological Association.

Fernberger, S. W. (1932). The American Psychological Association: A historical summary, 1892-1930. *Psychological Bulletin, 29*, 1–89. doi:10.1037/h0075733

Flexner, A. (1972). *Medical education in the United States and Canada: A Report to the Carnegie Foundation for the Advancement of Teaching* (Bulletin Number 4). New York, NY: Carnegie Foundation for the Advancement of Teaching. (Original work published 1910)

Fouad, N. A., McPherson, R. H., Gerstein, L., Blustein, D. L., Elman, N., Helledy, K. I., & Metz, A. J. (2004). Houston, 2001: Context and legacy. *Counseling Psychologist, 32*, 15–77. doi:10.1177/0011000003259943

Gazda, G. M., Rude, S. S., & Weissberg, M. (Eds.). (1988). Third National Conference for Counseling Psychology: Planning for the future. *Counseling Psychologist, 16*, 423–430.

Hannay, H. J., Bieliauskas, L. A., Crosson, B. A., Hammeke, T. A., & Hamsher, K. D., & Koffler, S.P. (1998). Proceedings of the Houston Conference on Specialty Education and Training in Clinical Neuropsychology. *Archives of Clinical Neuropsychology, 13*, 157–250.

Hoch, E. L., Ross, A. O., & Winder, C. L. (1966). Conference on the professional preparation of clinical psychologists: A summary. *American Psychologist, 21,* 42–51. doi:10.1037/h0021107

Kaslow, N. J. (Ed.). (2004). Competencies Conference: Future Directions in education and credentialing in professional psychology [Special issue]. *Journal of Clinical Psychology, 60.*

Knight, B. G., Karel, M. J., Hinrichsen, G. A., Qualls, S. H., & Duffy, M. (2009). Pikes Peak model for training in professional geropsychology. *American Psychologist, 64,* 205–214. doi:10.1037/a0015059

Korman, M. (1976). *Levels and patterns of professional training in psychology.* Washington, DC: American Psychological Association. doi:10.1037/10047-000

Larsen, K. G., Belar, C. D., Bieliauskas, L. A., Klepac, R. K., Stigall, T. T., & Zimet, C. N. (Eds.). (1993). *Proceedings of the National Conference on Postdoctoral Training in Professional Psychology.* Washington, DC: Association of Psychology Postdoctoral and Internship Centers.

McFall, R. (1991). Manifesto for a science of clinical psychology. *Clinical Psychologist, 44,* 75–88.

Norcross, J. C. (2009). *Welcome from the president of APA's Division 12.* Retrieved from http://www.div12.org/

Norcross, J. C., Ellis, J. L., & Sayette, M. A. (in press). Getting in and getting money: A comparative analysis of admission standards, acceptance rates, and financial assistance across the research-practice continuum in clinical psychology programs. *Training and Education in Professional Psychology.*

Olson, W. C. (1940). Proceedings of the forty-eighth annual meeting of the American Psychological Association. *Psychological Bulletin, 37,* 699–741. doi:10.1037/h0063182

Olson, W. C. (1944). Proceedings of the fifty-second annual meeting of the American Psychological Association. *Psychological Bulletin, 41,* 725–793. doi:10.1037/h0061320

Raimy, V. (Ed.). (1950). *Training in clinical psychology.* New York, NY: Prentice Hall.

Roe, A., Gustad, J. W., Moore, B. V., Ross, S., & Skodak, M. (Eds.). (1959). *Graduate education in psychology.* Washington, DC: American Psychological Association. doi:10.1037/11398-000

Routh, D. K. (1994). *Clinical psychology since 1917: Science, practice, and organization.* New York, NY: Springer.

Shakow, D., Brotemarkle, R. A., Doll, E. A., Kinder, E. F., Moore, B. V., & Smith, S. (1945). Graduate internship training in psychology: Report by the Subcommittee on Graduate Internship Training to the Committees on Graduate and Professional Training of the American Psychological Association and the American Association for Applied Psychology. *Journal of Consulting Psychology, 9,* 243–266. doi:10.1037/h0058618

Stone, G. C. (Ed.). (1983). *National working conference on education and training in health psychology.* Baton Rouge, LA: Land & Land.

Strother, C. R. (1956). *Psychology and mental health.* Washington, DC: American Psychological Association. doi:10.1037/10791-000

Templer, D. I., Stroup, K., Mancuso, L. J., & Tangen, K. (2008). Comparative decline of professional school graduates' performance on the examination for professional practice in psychology. *Psychological Reports, 102,* 551–560. doi:10.2466/PR0.102.2.551-560

Thompson, A. S., & Super, D. E. (Eds.). (1964). *The professional preparation of counseling psychologists: The report of the 1964 Greyston Conference.* New York, NY: Columbia University Press.

Watson, N., Caddy, G. R., Johnson, J. H., & Rimm, D. C. (1981). Standards in the education of professional psychologists: The resolutions of the Conference at Virginia Beach. *American Psychologist, 36,* 514–519. doi:10.1037/0003-066X.36.5.514

PsyD Programs

George Stricker

The first edition of this volume (Freedheim, 1992) contained chapters on the doctor of psychology degree (Peterson, 1992) and the professional school movement (Stricker & Cummings, 1992). That configuration was necessary and appropriate to the time, as many professional schools offered the doctor of philosophy (PhD) degree rather than the doctor of psychology (PsyD) degree. However, at the present time the two approaches have converged. The National Council of Schools and Programs in Professional Psychology, the organization that represents professional schools, has 62 member schools (accreditation by the American Psychological Association [APA] is required for membership) and 20 additional associate member or observer schools. The great majority of these offer the PsyD degree, although several offer both degrees. If one looks at the list of APA-accredited programs in clinical psychology, approximately one quarter are PsyD programs, and because of the large size of PsyD classes, these programs graduate about one half of all doctorates in clinical psychology each year (Norcross, Kohout, & Wicherski, 2005).

Clearly, the PsyD degree, once a subject of great controversy, is here to stay. This conclusion represents something of a palinode for both authors of the original chapters. The late Donald Peterson, whose contributions led to the establishment of the PsyD degree, became a critic of the movement toward the award of the PsyD degree (Peterson, 2003) and suggested several actions to be taken to correct what he saw as an erosion of standards. In contrast, I was an initial critic of the PsyD degree (Stricker, 1975) but am now a happy faculty member in a program that awards the PsyD and have changed my initial position. The reasons for Peterson's discontent and my shifting allegiance are elaborated in a later section of this chapter. However, it is clear that times have changed.

HISTORY OF THE PsyD

Before going into detail, it probably would be helpful to briefly indicate what the PsyD represents. Programs in practice areas of clinical psychology typically culminated in the PhD degree (a few offered the EdD), emphasizing research and not giving as much attention to practice. Nonetheless, the majority of graduates of these PhD programs then went into practice careers. The PsyD was developed in an attempt to redress the balance, emphasizing practice without neglecting research.

Peterson (1992) provided an extensive history of the PsyD degree, from which I will quote at length, dating the first suggestion back to 1925 (Crane, 1925). According to Peterson, Crane

> proposed a 4-year graduate curriculum with heavy emphasis on psychology and those aspects of medicine most clearly pertinent to the study and treatment of psychological problems. He suggested that the Doctor of Psychology degree be awarded upon completion of the program. (p. 830)

Luminaries such as Freud and Menninger are also seen as having recognized the potential contribution of psychologists to clinical practice, but their suggestions were unheeded because "professional psychology was small in size, indefinite in function, uncertain as to usefulness, and unclear about its own identity. Then, and for the two decades to follow, the discipline was too weak to be taken seriously as a profession" (Peterson, 1992, p. 832).

A marked change in the role of psychology was brought about by World War II. The need to provide services to returning veterans led to a need for additional personnel for Veterans Administration (VA) hospitals (see Chapter 16f). To help the VA to select appropriately trained psychologists, APA was asked to accredit training programs. This, in turn, led to a need for a training model for clinical psychology, and a conference was convened for this purpose. The resulting conference led to the development of the Boulder model (Raimy, 1950), which remains the single most important development in psychological training (see Chapter 17, this volume). Since that time, every training program in each practice area of psychology either claims to follow that model or a model that was developed in response to it.

The Boulder model, also known as the scientist–practitioner model, emphasized the need to train students in both science and practice, recognizing that there would be variations in the interests of students and the emphases of different programs. The valued balance between science and practice remains an excellent one in theory, but in implementation it has fallen far short of the intention of the conferees (Stricker, 2000b). In the decade that followed the Boulder conference, almost every program that developed followed a science-first approach, even though students usually intended to follow a practice-oriented career path. As Peterson (1992) noted, the students, "once admitted, either had to maintain the pretense, reveal their aims and incur the disfavor of their professors, or withdraw from training altogether" (p. 833). Surveys conducted at that time showed that most graduates were not becoming productive scientists and felt ill prepared for the careers they chose in practice. Peterson concluded that "the scientist–practitioner model was designed to meet the dual purposes of scientific inquiry and professional service. In trying to reach both aims, it evidently accomplished neither. As scientists, the Boulder style PhDs were unproductive. As professionals, they were incompetent" (p. 834). An exception to this trend was at Adelphi University, the only accredited clinical program explicitly intended to train practitioners, culminating in the award of the PhD degree.

Another training model seemed called for, and another committee, the Clark committee, was convened. Their report (APA, 1967) concluded that the PhD programs then in effect for educating scientist–practitioners were neither preparing scientists for contributory research nor professionals for effective practice. They recommended creation of a two-track educational system.

> Students interested predominantly in research would be prepared to do research and receive the PhD degree. Students interested predominantly in practice would be prepared for professional service and receive the PsyD degree. Students interested in combining careers of research and practice would complete both courses of study and receive both degrees. (Peterson, 1992, p. 834)

The report led to a great deal of discussion but little action because most programs continued with business as usual. One exception was at the University of Illinois, where active consideration was given to developing a PsyD program.

A conference was then convened in Chicago (Hoch, Ross, & Winder, 1966) to discuss the Clark report (APA, 1967), and it produced rather ambivalent results. Peterson (1992) noted that there was some support for the report, but

> the majority, however, 57%, were merely willing to extend "recognition" to the idea that explicit professional training programs might be attempted in some university departments, and that the results of those efforts should provide a basis for evaluating the programs at a later time. (p. 835)

The University of Illinois then voted to go ahead with a PsyD program and, in 1968, under the direction of Peterson, admitted students. The program received provisional APA accreditation in 1972 and became a template for many professional schools that then developed. At the same time, other professional schools were being developed, most noteworthy of which is the California School of Professional Psychology, but these led to the PhD degree. As a side note, the program at Illinois has been discontinued, and the California School of Professional Psychology programs are now known as Alliant University and award PsyD and PhD degrees.

The APA response to the growing interest in and need for professional programs was to convene one more conference, this time in Vail, Colorado (Korman, 1976). Peterson (1992) cited the most important of the Vail resolutions:

First, "the development of psychological science has sufficiently matured to justify creation of explicit professional programs, in addition to programs for training scientists and scientist-professionals." Second, "we recommend that completion of doctoral level training in explicitly professional programs be designated by award of the Doctor of Psychology degree and that completion of doctoral level training in programs designed to train scientists or scientist-professionals be designated by award of the Doctor of Philosophy degree . . . .Where primary emphasis in training and function is upon direct delivery of professional services and the evaluation and improvement of those services, the Doctor of Psychology degree is appropriate. Where primary emphasis is upon the development of new knowledge in psychology, the PhD degree is appropriate" (Korman, 1974, p. 443). (Peterson, 1992, p. 838)

The Vail conference gave an official imprimatur to professional schools, the PsyD degree, and the practitioner model of training as an alternative to the scientist–practitioner model. This was followed by an explosion of new programs in many settings, including research universities (e.g., Rutgers), small colleges (e.g., Florida Institute of Technology), and free-standing programs (e.g., Argosy University). Most of the newly developed programs preferred the PsyD degree, perhaps because it is less expensive to develop (there is no need for extensive laboratories), attracts more students, and can manage larger classes.

Peterson (1992) detailed several of the local fights that took place, at the level of both the university and state boards of education, but that now seems to be an event of the past. Several studies have demonstrated that initial worries about public stigmatization, licensure uncertainty, and employment difficulty have not materialized—at least not any more than encountered by PhD recipients (Norcross, Castle, Sayette, & Mayne, 2004).

Today, the APA accredits 63 PsyD programs in clinical psychology, three in counseling psychology, six in school psychology, and three in combined professional–scientific psychology ("Accredited Internship and Postdoctoral Programs," 2007). Another 20 or so are not (yet) accredited by APA, mostly because they are relatively new programs.

The PsyD has attained acceptance and is increasingly familiar to the public and within the discipline. Nonetheless, active criticism persists, and it is to this that I turn next.

CRITIQUES OF PsyD PROGRAMS

There have been two approaches to criticizing PsyD programs. The first of these consists of articles in peer-reviewed journals, and these usually are thoughtful and measured, even if critical. I review several exemplars of this approach in this section. The second source of criticism hails from the ongoing tension between scientists and practitioners within APA. From the founding of the organization, the APA presidency was occupied by a series of distinguished researchers and academicians. However, in 1977, Theodore Blau, a well-known practitioner, was elected to that office, followed over the next decade by Nicholas Cummings, who was instrumental in beginning the California School of Professional Psychology, and Max Siegel, also a noted practitioner. Not coincidentally, the American Psychological Society (APS), now known as the Association for Psychological Science, was founded in 1988. The mission of APS is "to dedicated to the advancement of scientific psychology and its representation at the national and international level" (Association for Psychological Science, n.d., para. 1). Although this is a worthy goal, the subtext is that APA, now dominated by practitioners, was not doing a very good job with science. The criticism of professional education from this source is not covered because it belongs primarily in the realm of politics.

One early criticism of the then–newly developing PsyD degree, as mentioned earlier, was my own (Stricker, 1975). At the time, as now, I was a strong supporter of professional education, but I believed that there was a need to disentangle the value of professional education from the need for a new degree. I took exception to many of the points that Peterson (1968) raised in his presentation of the PsyD program at Illinois. The most critical point concerned the doctoral dissertation. Peterson thought that the research demands of a PhD program could not be altered in a practitioner program. I contended that the final paper required of PsyD students was comparable in scholarship to that of a doctoral dissertation, although the requirement for empirical research had to be altered to allow papers more in line with clinical concerns. The PhD is not a research degree but one that rewards scholarship, and the final papers in the better professional programs met any reasonable standard of scholarship. However, I recognized that many universities would not allow this to happen, and clinical training resulting in a PsyD would then occur in a second-class program within the university. I still believe that students who produce excellent final papers deserve the PhD, but I also recognize that it is unlikely that many universities will grant such a degree for that effort. With several notable exceptions, most PsyD programs exist in settings other than major universities, and so the programs become the centerpiece of the academic institution rather than a minor offering as they would be in a research setting.

Many of the other problems cited by Peterson (1968), such as the differentiation of goals of training and the valuing of clinical practice, follow from this difficulty and could have been overcome if the large universities had been willing to do so. They were not, and thus the need for an alternative degree increased.

I summarized my concerns by stating,

> There is no denying that the PhD is the highest and most prestigious academic degree that is awarded, that it is well accepted by the general public, and that a strange-sounding degree will raise inevitable and undeserved suspicion in our era of rampant quackery in the mental health field. Before we accept the creation of a new degree, we must demand evidence that it will lead to benefits unattainable within the well-accepted and well-understood contemporary framework. (Stricker, 1975, p. 1065)

Time has proven me wrong. Major universities, with few exceptions, have not turned to professional training, and the PsyD is often the only doctoral degree available in the settings in which it is offered. The "undeserved suspicion" may have occurred earlier, but at this time, most internship directors, employers, and the general public either recognize the value of the PsyD or at least do not make distinctions according to degree. I still believe that a well-done dissertation is deserving of a PhD, and a poorly done project is not deserving of any doctoral degree, but I also am convinced that practicality will not allow for this solution. Accordingly, I am glad that the PsyD has become an appropriate vehicle to allow for professional training to occur.

Recently, an empirically based criticism of professional school graduates (almost always now PsyD recipients) was published and widely circulated (Templer, Stroup, Mancuso, & Tangen, 2008). It is the most recent of a series of studies by the same senior author, who compared the scores of professional school graduates with those of graduates of more traditional PhD programs on the Examination for Professional Practice in Psychology (EPPP), which is a part of the licensing examination for psychologists in every jurisdiction in North America. The results indicate that professional school graduates score lower on average on the EPPP than graduates of traditional PhD programs.

The major problem with this conclusion, as I see it, is the overvaluing of EPPP scores as a measure of quality of the student, particularly when it comes to students pursuing a clinical career. I would prefer to see scores on clinical functioning assessed, either rather than or as well as scores on an examination that correlates highly with GREs, which are typically used as a principal selection tool for traditional programs. It is no surprise that students selected for excellence on GREs also score well on the EPPP, but it is not clear what either has to do with clinical functioning. Clinical training is multifaceted, and it is unlikely that any single test could ever capture the variability in clinical programs of equal but differing sources of excellence (Stricker, 2000a).

Peterson (2003) recommended that action be taken to reduce the number of inadequate PsyD programs, a recommendation that no serious person can oppose, but one that requires the identification of such programs. He then suggested an evaluation of clinical training programs, again a recommendation that is appropriate but difficult to implement. The closest we have to such evaluation is accreditation by APA, and most of the extant PsyD programs have survived this challenge (many of the others are in an early developmental phase and may eventually become accredited). I am sympathetic to Peterson's wish for increased quality but not to his conclusion that PsyD programs fall short of the goal, because there is little evidence that they do not produce graduates who achieve excellence in the mission of their training program. All of us endorse determining quality through graduates' performance as professionals (Kenkel, DeLeon, Albino, & Porter, 2003, p. 805), but nobody has suggested a viable method of doing such an assessment.

Additional data-based criticisms of PsyD programs concern (a) the larger size of these programs; (b) their comparatively high acceptance rates; and (c) the paucity of financial support for students, leading to increased student debt compared with PhD clinical programs. PsyD programs are, as a rule, considerably larger than PhD programs, typically by a factor of two or three (with the size made possible by the lack of need for extensive research training or an empirical doctoral dissertation, both of which are very labor-intensive activities for faculty members). There is widespread concern about the shortage of APA-accredited internship positions, and PsyD students, as a rule, are those experiencing the shortage most acutely. PsyD programs have been particularly active in creating internship consortia for their students to reduce the gap between the number of applicants and the number of internship positions.

STRENGTHS OF PsyD PROGRAMS

The contributions of PsyD programs are difficult to separate from their strengths. These contributions have been listed as

> (a) a comprehensive competence-based training model for professional psychologists (a concept that the rest of psychology has only more recently begun to consider), (b) pedagogies appropriate to training goals, (c) ways of attracting more diverse students into psychology and more diverse faculty to professional programs, (d) measures of quality control for both academic and clinical skills, (e) methods for integrating diversity training throughout the curriculum, (f) interdisciplinary training and collaboration, and (g) methods for keeping the curriculum current with societal demands. (Kenkel et al., 2003, p. 802)

The emphasis on diversity is particularly noteworthy. PsyD programs have as high a proportion of minority students in the student body as traditional PhD programs, and perhaps a higher proportion of minority faculty members (Norcross et al., 2004). PsyD programs have taken the lead in changing the face of psychology and, in doing so, have adopted a socially responsible role consistent with the goal of making excellent services available to the public.

Finally, I should note that training in PsyD programs does not ignore either research or the corpus of psychological knowledge. To do so would result in a loss of accreditation, and that has not happened. However, the approach to research has been to produce consumers of research rather than producers of research (traditional programs, despite stated intentions, have not been very successful at developing many producers of research either). Along this line, the graduate of a PsyD program will probably not be an active research scientist but should be a local clinical scientist (Stricker & Trierweiler, 1995; Trierweiler & Stricker, 1998).

CONCLUSIONS

Accredited PsyD programs have successfully met their stated goal: to produce competent practitioners prepared to meet public needs for psychological services. Graduates of these programs are gaining in getting internships, passing the licensure exam, and finding employment in the area for which they have been prepared. They have grown the clinical practice of psychology, filling unmet societal needs. Despite this success, they have drawn criticism on the basis of the alleged lack of quality of some graduates, a charge that has only indirect and flawed data to support it, and the larger size of the student bodies, lower acceptance standards, and higher debt load. The question of size is only of importance if it relates to performance in the clinical setting for which the students have been prepared, and these have not been systematically attempted.

The organization charged with quality control in psychological education and training is APA's Committee on Accreditation. There are two suggestions that I can make to this group about weeding out programs that are not successful, and these suggestions should be applied to PsyD and PhD programs alike: (a) Programs that are consistently unsuccessful in placing students within accredited internships should be phased out, and (b) programs that are consistently unsuccessful in placing students in employment settings for which they have been trained should be phased out. These represent operational definitions of the problem of size. If these criteria are used, I suspect that neither PsyD programs nor PhD programs will have difficulty meeting the first criterion. However, the second criterion will be far more difficult for PhD programs, as many of their graduates, who are being prepared for research or academic careers, end up in service delivery positions.

The PhD scientist–practitioner model and the PsyD practitioner model entail trade-offs in their mission and subsequent training. An unfortunate penchant of humans, including psychotherapists, is to demonize differences rather than embrace them. Let the evidence speak, and that evidence largely favors the simultaneous existence of two training models toward different but overlapping ends.

REFERENCES

Accredited internship and postdoctoral programs for training in psychology: 2007. (2007). *American Psychologist, 63*, 1016–1040.

Anonymous. (1967). The scientific and professional aims of psychology. *American Psychologist, 22*, 49–76. doi:10.1037/h0024248

Association for Psychological Science. (n.d.). *About APS*. Retrieved from http://www.psychologicalscience.org/about/

Crane, L. (1925). A plea for the training of professional psychologists. *Journal of Abnormal and Social Psychology, 20*, 228–233. doi:10.1037/h0068539

Freedheim, D. K. (1992). *History of psychotherapy: A century of change.* Washington, DC: American Psychological Association. doi:10.1037/10110-000

Hoch, E. L., Ross, A. O., & Winder, C. L. (1966). *Professional preparation of clinical psychologists.* Washington, DC: American Psychological Association. doi:10.1037/10537-000

Kenkel, M. B., DeLeon, P. H., Albino, J. E. N., & Porter, N. (2003). Challenges to professional psychology education in the 21st century: Response to Peterson. *American Psychologist, 58*, 801–805. doi:10.1037/0003-066X.58.10.801

Korman, M. (1974). National Conference on Levels and Patterns of Professional Training in Psychology: The major themes. *American Psychologist, 29*, 441–449. doi:10.1037/h0036469

Korman, M. (1976). *Levels and patterns of professional training in psychology.* Washington, DC: American Psychological Association. doi:10.1037/10047-000

Norcross, J. C., Castle, P. H., Sayette, M. A., & Mayne, T. J. (2004). The PsyD: Heterogeneity in practitioner training. *Professional Psychology: Research and Practice, 35*, 412–419. doi:10.1037/0735-7028.35.4.412

Norcross, J. C., Kohout, J. L., & Wicherski, M. (2005). Graduate study in psychology: 1971 to 2004. *American Psychologist, 60*, 959–975.

Peterson, D. R. (1968). The Doctor of Psychology program at the University of Illinois. *American Psychologist, 23*, 511–516.

Peterson, D. R. (1992). The Doctor of Psychology degree. In D. K. Freedheim (Ed.), *History of psychotherapy: A century of change* (pp. 829–849). Washington, DC: American Psychological Association.

Peterson, D. R. (2003). Unintended consequences: Ventures and misadventures in the education of professional psychologists. *American Psychologist, 58*, 791–800.

Raimy, V. (1950). *Training in clinical psychology.* New York, NY: Prentice-Hall.

Stricker, G. (1975). On professional schools and professional degrees. *American Psychologist, 30*, 1062–1066.

Stricker, G. (2000a). The measurement of clinical psychology training programs. *Clinical Psychology: Science and Practice, 7*, 361–363.

Stricker, G. (2000b). The scientist–practitioner model: Gandhi was right again. *American Psychologist, 55*, 253–254.

Stricker, G., & Cummings, N. A. (1992). The professional school movement. In D. K. Freedheim (Ed.), *History of psychotherapy: A century of change* (pp. 801–828). Washington, DC: American Psychological Association.

Stricker, G., & Trierweiler, S. J. (1995). The local clinical scientist: A bridge between science and practice. *American Psychologist, 50,* 995–1002.

Templer, D. I., Stroup, K., Mancuso, L. J., & Tangen, K. (2008). Comparative decline of professional school graduates' performance on the Examination for Professional Practice in Psychology. *Psychological Reports, 102,* 551–560.

Trierweiler, S. J., & Stricker, G. (1998). *The scientific practice of professional psychology.* New York, NY: Plenum.

Internship and Postdoctoral Residency

Nadine J. Kaslow and Carol Webb

We begin this chapter by summarizing the history of internship and postdoctoral training in professional psychology. Attention is paid to historical background, key conferences, national standards, and current challenges. Then we discuss the history of psychotherapy training in internship and residency programs. We close with concluding comments.

HISTORY OF INTERNSHIP TRAINING IN PROFESSIONAL PSYCHOLOGY

Shortly after World War II, the need for professional services to returning veterans prompted the American Psychological Association (APA) to address internship training, and in 1946 APA sponsored a roundtable on the internship training of clinical psychologists. One year later, APA appointed a Special Committee on Training in Clinical Psychology, tasked in part to formulate standards for internship training. Using a developmental and competency-oriented approach, this group focused on direct service with supervision and training in advanced diagnostic and psychotherapy techniques (Committee on Training in Clinical Psychology, 1947). The Shakow (1965) report, generated from this workgroup, served as the basis for subsequent education and training conferences. In 1949, APA held the Boulder conference (see Chapter 17, this volume), which led to the systematic inclusion of internship training as a required condition of the doctoral degree in applied psychology (Raimy, 1950). In keeping with developments in clinical psychology, in 1951 the Division of Counseling and Guidance recommended a doctoral internship experience for its students, and in 1952 standards for practicum training in counseling psychology were devised that indicated that the internship was the terminal phase of the practicum experience.

APA, through its Office of Accreditation, began accrediting internship programs in 1956. Central to the guidelines of the APA Commission on Accreditation (formerly the Committee on Accreditation) was the teaching, training, and supervision of psychotherapy. The accreditation criteria have evolved from a focus on numbers and types of psychotherapy experiences to specific competencies and their assessment via outcome measures. The competency-based accreditation system includes intervention as a core competency for internship programs. At the beginning of internship accreditation in 1956, there were 28 accredited programs (Belar & Kaslow, 2003); by the end of 2008, there were 469 APA-accredited internship programs.

Internship training in the 1950s focused on psychological assessment. However, trainee interest and the need for more psychotherapeutic services led to a greater emphasis on psychotherapy training. With the advent of internship accreditation, more consistent standards were applied to the training such that interns were expected to see clients with a variety of presenting problems and use a variety of assessment and psychotherapy methods. Although much of the internship training occurred initially in the Veterans Administration system, more hospital- and community-based programs were developed. In the 1960s, the emphasis on psychotherapy training in internships grew significantly.

The Chicago Conference on the Professional Preparation of Clinical Psychologists held in 1965 reaffirmed the importance of the 1-year (as opposed to a 9-month) internship and acknowledged that off-campus placements were valuable to the internship experience (Hoch, Ross, & Winder, 1966). Participants at this conference also advocated that interns be exposed to both "normal" and "psychologically disturbed" individuals who were demographically diverse. In terms of psychotherapy training, it was noted that trainees should be trained in individual therapy and at least one other psychotherapy format.

The centrality of internship training to professional psychologists spurred the establishment of the Association of Psychology Internship Centers, which was formed in 1968 as an informal group of psychologists for the purposes of information sharing of mutual concerns related to internship training. In the late 1970s, the Association of Psychology Internship Centers began to develop goals for assessing intern competency and developed a clearinghouse program to assist in matching students to sites with unfilled slots following the internship offer and acceptance period. The Association of Psychology Internship Centers expanded its mission in 1992 to encompass both internship and postdoctoral training and changed its name to the Association of Psychology Postdoctoral and Internship Centers (APPIC; http://www.appic.org). At the internship level, APPIC ensures quality training by establishing standards for quality programs, fostering the development of new programs, facilitating the matching of intern candidates to sites, collaborating with other organizations to enhance training in diverse competencies including psychotherapy, and representing the views of internship and postdoctoral agencies at key meetings.

APPIC coordinated a number of internship training conferences. Cosponsored by the Department of Clinical and Health Psychology at the University of Florida, the 1987 National Conference on Internship Training in Psychology was the first to address specifically the policies of internship training (Belar et al., 1989). Delegates developed a policy statement related to the purpose of internship, which psychologists needed an internship, when internships should occur, entrance criteria, core requirements, outcome criteria, and characteristics of the internship. Delegates also asserted that a 2-year supervised training experience was essential to ensure that individuals were capable of functioning autonomously as psychologists. The second conference, organized in collaboration with APA, was held in 1997 and was titled "Supply and Demand: Training and Employment Opportunities in Professional Psychology" (Pederson et al., 1997). This conference addressed what continues to be a major challenge: the internship supply and demand imbalance.

CURRENT CHALLENGES IN INTERNSHIP TRAINING

Internship training programs and their accreditation are now well established in professional psychology. At the same time, a number of challenges confront internship training and, to some extent, postdoctoral training. First, for more than a decade, there has been a supply–demand imbalance: a significant discrepancy between the number of applicants (supply) and the number of available training slots (demand; e.g., Boggs & Douce, 2000; Kaslow & Keilin, 2006; Keilin, Baker, McCutcheon, & Peranson, 2007; Keilin & Kaslow, 2008). Although potential solutions have been proposed for this problem, the imbalance continues to plague training programs (Rodolfa, Bell, Bieschke, Davis, & Peterson, 2007).

Second, there is an ongoing debate regarding the need for a required internship given the purported escalation in practicum hours (Thorp, O'Donohue, & Gregg, 2005). Nevertheless, many internship trainers maintain that a full-time (or 2-year half-time) experience of focused, well-supervised, sequential training is critical to readiness for independent practice (Boggs & Douce, 2000; Stedman, 2007).

Third, there has been a marked shift within the profession toward competency-based training, with implications for the internship and postdoctoral levels (Kaslow et al., 2004; Rodolfa et al., 2005). These efforts were bolstered by the APPIC-sponsored 2002 Competencies Conference. Competency benchmarks address the foundational and functional competencies in professional psychology across three levels of professional development: readiness for practicum, readiness for internship, and readiness for entry to practice. Within each level, the benchmarks provide operational descriptions and delineate the essential components (Fouad et al., 2009). A Competency Assessment Toolkit for Professional Psychology (Kaslow et al., 2009) offers a wide range of assessments for evaluating these competencies. Despite this progress, training sites are only beginning to implement competency-based assessments.

Fourth, the Committee on Accreditation remains firm that internship training should be broad and general. However, proponents of specialty training remain vocal in their advocacy for more specialized training during internship. For example, some have argued that more specialty-oriented internships (e.g., child clinical, clinical neuropsychology) should be available and are needed to ensure competent psychologists whose practice is generally limited to their specialty area.

Finally, many jurisdictions are changing their licensure laws to make postdoctoral supervised experience optional rather than required. We thus expect more specific attention will be paid to the nature and extent of psychotherapy training during internship.

HISTORY OF POSTDOCTORAL TRAINING IN PROFESSIONAL PSYCHOLOGY

The postdoctoral movement in psychology occurred in response to myriad factors (Graham & Fox, 1991). The emergence of new practice areas, the prominence of specialization, and the ascendancy of interdisciplinary collaboration all called for specialized postdoctoral training. Furthermore, the postdoctoral year frequently solidifies professional identity (Kaslow, McCarthy, Rogers, & Summerville, 1992).

Postdoctoral training was considered in a minor way in several conferences held since the middle of the 20th century. At the 1949 Boulder conference, a case was built for the necessity of postdoctoral training. Participants argued that supervised postdoctoral experience was required for individual proficiency in psychotherapy. At both the 1955 Stanford conference and the 1958 Miami conference, attendees further underscored the value of postdoctoral training. However, there was no consensus reached regarding the criteria for attaining competence and ultimate licensure at the independent practice level. In 1965, at the Chicago conference, participants noted that postdoctoral training was needed for individuals to attain advanced and specialized competence. At the 1987 Gainesville conference, participants argued that supervised experience needed to be 2 years, 1 of which was postdoctoral (Belar et al., 1989). They called for standards for accrediting postdoctoral programs and for a conference to develop such standards.

Starting in the early 1970s, key meetings were organized specifically on postdoctoral education and training. The first conference was the 1972 conference held at the Menninger Clinic, titled "Postdoctoral Education in Clinical Psychology" (Weiner, 1973). Attendees shared their thoughts and experiences, but there were no specific outcomes or products. In 1991 in Minneapolis, the American Board of Professional Psychology sponsored a conference addressing the accreditation of postdoctoral programs in professional psychology. Participants recommended that an interorganizational council be formed for the accreditation of these programs. A third conference was held in 1992 at Ann Arbor, the first National Conference on Postdoctoral Training in Professional Psychology (Belar et al., 1993). The outcome was the creation of a policy statement that addressed the rationale for postdoctoral training; entrance requirements; program content, structure, and organization; faculty and staff; and evaluation mechanisms. Attendees crafted recommendations for initiatives to foster excellence and innovation in postdoctoral education and called for guidelines for accrediting postdoctoral programs.

A fourth conference that addressed postdoctoral education in psychology more broadly was held in Norman, Oklahoma, in 1994: the APA National Conference on Postdoctoral Education and Training in Psychology (Reich, Sands, & Wiens, 1995). The diverse participants examined the need, role, and potential of postdoctoral education; established a taxonomy and terminology; offered mechanisms for trainee and program outcomes assessment; considered models for postdoctoral education; and examined ways to enhance the competence needed for psychologists to contribute maximally to teaching, research, and practice.

APPIC was the first body to develop standards for the approval, but not accreditation, of postdoctoral training programs. They began approving programs in 1974–1975, and as of 2009, there were 124 APPIC postdoctoral programs (32 of which are APA accredited).

Beginning in the mid-1980s, various constituency groups expressed a desire for accreditation standards for postdoctoral programs. In response to these calls and the previous conference recommendations, the Inter-Organizational Council for the Accreditation of Postdoctoral Training Programs was formed in 1992. Working collaboratively with APA's Committee on Accreditation, this group developed guidelines and procedures for accrediting postdoctoral programs that set the stage for APA's accreditation of such programs.

In 1996, the APA Committee on Accreditation adopted and implemented new accreditation guidelines for postdoctoral education and training programs (Belar & Kaslow, 2003). To be accredited, the program must be embedded in a context that values training and must publically state its commitment to training individuals in a substantive traditional or specialty practice area. Accredited programs must demonstrate that their residents attain an advanced level of competence in theories and effective methods of psychological assessment, diagnosis, and intervention; consultation; program evaluation; supervision, teaching, or both; strategies of scholarly inquiry; organizational management and administration; professional conduct, ethics, and law; and cultural and individual diversity. By the end of 2008, there were 51 accredited postdoctoral residencies, 28 in traditional substantive areas and the rest in specialty areas.

Typically, specialization occurs at the postdoctoral level of training and beyond. Not surprisingly, since the 1980s multiple specialties have developed specialty-specific guidelines for postdoctoral training, such as clinical neuropsychology and pediatric psychology (Hannay et al., 1998; Spirito et al., 2003). No group has developed specialty-specific guidelines for psychotherapy, which reflects that it is not considered a specialty but rather an expected competency associated with multiple specialties.

Both APA's early Model Act for State Licensure of Psychologists and the 1992 Association of State and Provincial Psychology Boards Model Licensure Act emphasized the need for supervised postdoctoral work experience (see Chapter 16d). As a result, in the early 2000s all but one state required at least 1 year of supervised work experience for licensure, although the specifics of this requirement differed by jurisdiction. In 2000, APA began reconsidering the necessity for the postdoctoral experience before licensure, and in 2007, APA changed its policy to recommend the equivalent of 2 full-time years of sequential, organized, supervised professional experience before obtaining the license. This training may be completed before or after the granting of the doctoral degree. As such, postdoctoral work experience is now considered optional by APA. As of 2009, four jurisdictions have already changed their legislation to adopt this new policy, with several others in the process.

CURRENT CHALLENGES IN POSTDOCTORAL TRAINING

Postdoctoral residencies in professional psychology are now established and accredited. But we foresee three critical challenges facing them in the near future.

First, there is continued debate about the elimination of the postdoctoral year of supervised work experience for licensure. Although APA changed its policy, many jurisdictions are committed to retaining this requirement. This policy change was made because many psychologists believed the 1987 Model Act did not reflect the developments in professional practice that had occurred during the prior 2 decades. Advocates for eliminating the postdoctoral requirement cite greater number of practicum hours, limited supervised postdoctoral experiences, lack of sufficient reimbursement opportunities, protracted training time, and heavy student debt load on graduation. However, advocates for maintaining the postdoctoral year of supervised experience cite student need to be competent to practice independently (Rodolfa, Ko, & Petersen, 2004), the lack of uniform practicum guidelines, and the difficulties differential requirements across jurisdictions place on mobility.

Second, there is variability in the content, structure, and quality of postdoctoral experiences, particularly those that are informal (Drotar, Palermo, & Ievers-Landis, 2003; Kaslow & Keilin, 2008). Formal programs provide organized, sequential training that includes didactic, supervisory, and experiential components. By contrast, informal opportunities often involve service delivery demands with insufficient education and supervision.

Third, there is a lack of clarity in the field regarding the tasks to be accomplished during the postdoctoral year (Drotar et al., 2003). Concomitantly, there is a paucity of direction regarding benchmark performance in each competency domain expected of postdoctoral fellows.

PSYCHOTHERAPY TRAINING IN INTERNSHIPS AND POSTDOCTORAL RESIDENCIES

Before World War II, few psychologists conducted psychotherapy. As a result, internship training was primarily limited to enhancing competence in diagnosis and assessment (Humphreys, 1996). Psychotherapy training for interns, when permitted, was done under the supervision of psychiatrists. After the war, with the increased demand for psychotherapy, the Veterans Administration began to support the conduct of psychotherapy by psychologists and psychology interns, although the focus of their clinical endeavors remained on psychodiagnostic assessment (Humphreys, 1996). However, psychotherapy training at the internship and ultimately postdoctoral levels expanded, markedly driven by the clear need for psychotherapeutic services, along with the inviting financial opportunity these services provided, such that by the mid- to late 1970s, psychotherapy dominated the training. Meanwhile, scant empirical attention has addressed the nature of this training (Stedman, 1997, 2007).

Historically, psychotherapy training in internship sites was predominantly psychodynamic with relatively high-functioning patients (Levenson & Burg, 2000). Over time, the changes in patients, theories, reimbursement, and competency-based training have propelled shifts in training. Today, most psychotherapy training in internship programs is eclectic or integrative in orientation and thus more broad based (Stedman, Hatch, & Schoenfeld, 2007).

Most programs teach individual psychotherapy, but fewer programs teach couples and family therapy (Stedman, Hatch, Schoenfeld, & Keilin, 2005). Although a number of programs teach group therapy, this training tends to be inadequate (Markus & King, 2003). With deinstitutionalization and the advent of the community mental health system in the 1970s, the psychotherapy conducted by interns and postdoctoral fellows shifted from long-term and supportive treatments in hospitals to outpatient work. This has resulted in fewer trainees being well trained in the treatment of severe mental illness (Hoge, Stayner, & Davidson, 2000).

In general, little attention is paid at the internship and postdoctoral levels toward preparing students for working in managed care settings. For interns and postdoctoral fellows to be trained for managed care systems, they need better training in developing treatment plans; conducting time-limited interventions, including those that are evidence based; providing psychotherapy on an intermittent basis; and negotiating psychotherapy services for their patients with administrative personnel (Sanderson, 2003; Spruill & Pruitt, 2000).

The empirically supported treatment initiative (Chambless et al., 1996) and the newer evidence-based practice movement (APA Presidential Task Force on Evidence-Based Practice, 2006) have both made a major impact on training programs (Calhoun, Moras, Pilkonis, & Rehm, 1998). An increasing number of interns are being taught the fundamentals of empirically supported treatments; at the postdoctoral level, training in empirically supported treatments is typically more in depth, focused on adapting these interventions to nonprototypical patients (Calhoun et al., 1998). There has also been a shift to examining how psychotherapies developed in controlled settings can be disseminated into the community, where many internships and postdoctoral residencies are located. Clinical competencies associated with evidence-based practice (DiLillo & McChargue, 2007) are likely to be the wave of the future in psychotherapy training at the internship and postdoctoral levels.

CONCLUSIONS

In general, internship training directors believe that students come to internship with adequate amounts of psychotherapy preparation (Stedman, Hatch, & Schoenfeld, 2000, 2002). However, there is often a marked difference between the psychotherapy training students receive on internship and in their graduate programs, with the former placing less emphasis on empirically supported treatments and more focus on interventions reflective of a broader range of theoretical orientations and patient populations. This disconnect can be both challenging and stimulating for students as they move from their graduate to their internship program.

One frequent reason that psychologists seek formal postdoctoral training is to secure more advanced psychotherapy training (Logsdon-Conradsen et al., 2001). Unfortunately, we know relatively little about psychotherapy training at the postdoctoral level. Thus, in the future, there needs to be more focus on developmental differences in the psychotherapy training appropriate for individuals at the postdoctoral level compared with other phases of the training sequence. Such examination will shed light on optimal psychotherapy training and supervision for this phase of development.

For psychotherapy training to move forward as a competency-based and evidence-based activity, it behooves us as a profession to foster dialogue among educators at all training levels regarding the essential components of psychotherapy competence. The field must collectively delineate the benchmarks for readiness for internship training, readiness for postdoctoral training, and readiness for licensure and independent practice.

REFERENCES

American Psychological Association Presidential Task Force on Evidence-Based Practice. (2006). Evidence-based practice in psychology. *American Psychologist, 61,* 271–285. doi:10.1037/0003-066X.61.4.271

Belar, C. D., Bieliauskas, L. A., Klepac, R. K., Larsen, K. G., Stigall, T. T., & Zimet, C. N. (1993). National Conference on Postdoctoral Training in Professional Psychology. *American Psychologist, 48,* 1284–1289. doi:10.1037/0003-066X.48.12.1284

Belar, C. D., Bieliauskas, L. A., Larsen, K. G., Mensh, I. N., Poey, K., & Roehlke, H. J. (1989). The National Conference on Internship Training in Professional Psychology. *American Psychologist, 44,* 60–65. doi:10.1037/0003-066X.44.1.60

Belar, C. D., & Kaslow, N. J. (2003). The history of accreditation of internship programs and postdoctoral residencies. In E. M. Altmaier (Ed.), *Setting standards in graduate education* (pp. 61–89). Washington, DC: American Psychological Association. doi:10.1037/10568-003

Boggs, K. R., & Douce, L. A. (2000). Current status and anticipated changes in psychology internships: Effects on counseling psychology training. *Counseling Psychologist, 28,* 672–686. doi:10.1177/0011000000285005

Calhoun, K. S., Moras, K., Pilkonis, P. A., & Rehm, L. P. (1998). Empirically supported treatments: Implications for training. *Journal of Consulting and Clinical Psychology, 66,* 151–162. doi:10.1037/0022-006X.66.1.151

Chambless, D., Sanderson, W., Shoham, V., Johnson, S., Pope, K., Crits-Cristoph, P., . . . McCurry, S. (1996). An update on empirically validated therapies. *Clinical Psychologist, 49,* 5–18.

Committee on Training in Clinical Psychology. (1947). Recommended graduate training program in clinical psychology. *American Psychologist, 2,* 539–558. doi:10.1037/h0058236

DiLillo, D., & McChargue, D. (2007). Implementing elements of evidence-based practice into scientist-practitioner training at the University of Nebraska-Lincoln. *Journal of Clinical Psychology, 63,* 671–684. doi:10.1002/jclp.20375

Drotar, D., Palermo, T., & Ievers-Landis, C. E. (2003). Commentary: Recommendations for the training of pediatric psychologists: Implications for postdoctoral training. *Journal of Pediatric Psychology, 28,* 109–113. doi:10.1093/jpepsy/28.2.109

Fouad, N. A., Grus, C. L., Hatcher, R. L., Kaslow, N. J., Hutchings, P. S., Madson, M., . . . Crossman, R. E. (2009). Competency benchmarks: A model for the understanding and measuring of competence in professional psychology across training levels. *Training and Education in Professional Psychology, 3,* S5–S26.

Graham, S. R., & Fox, R. E. (1991). Postdoctoral education for professional practice. *American Psychologist, 46,* 1033–1035. doi:10.1037/0003-066X.46.10.1033

Hannay, H. J., Bieliauskas, L. A., Crosson, B. A., Hammeke, T. A., Hamsher, K., & Koffler, S. P. (1998). Proceedings from the Houston Conference on Specialty Education and Training in Clinical Neuropsychology. *Archives of Clinical Neuropsychology, 13,* 157–250.

Hoch, E. L., Ross, A. O., & Winder, C. L. (1966). Conference on the professional preparation of clinical psychologists: A summary. *American Psychologist, 21,* 42–51. doi:10.1037/h0021107

Hoge, M. A., Stayner, D., & Davidson, L. E. (2000). Psychology internships in the treatment of severe mental illness: Implications for training in academic medical centers. *Journal of Clinical Psychology in Medical Settings, 7,* 213–222. doi:10.1023/ A:1009580413935

Humphreys, K. (1996). Clinical psychologists as psychotherapists. *American Psychologist, 51*, 190–197. doi:10.1037/0003-066X.51.3.190

Kaslow, N. J., Borden, K. A., Collins, F. L., Forrest, L., Illfelder-Kaye, J., Nelson, P. D., . . . Willmuth, M. E. (2004). Competencies Conference: Future directions in education and credentialing in professional psychology. *Journal of Clinical Psychology, 60*, 699–712. doi:10.1002/jclp.20016

Kaslow, N. J., Grus, C. L., Campbell, L. F., Fouad, N. A., Hatcher, R. L., & Rodolfa, E. R. (2009). Competency assessment toolkit for professional psychology. *Training and Education in Professional Psychology, 3*, S27–S45.

Kaslow, N. J., & Keilin, W. G. (2006). Internship training in clinical psychology: Looking into our crystal ball. *Clinical Psychology: Science and Practice, 13*, 242–248. doi:10.1111/j.1468-2850.2006.00031.x

Kaslow, N. J., & Keilin, W. G. (2008). Postdoctoral training. In F. T. L. Leong, E. M. Altmaier, & B. D. Johnson (Eds.), *Encyclopedia of counseling: Changes and challenges for counseling in the 21st century* (pp. 337–341). Los Angeles, CA: Sage.

Kaslow, N. J., McCarthy, S. M., Rogers, J. H., & Summerville, M. B. (1992). Psychology postdoctoral training: A developmental perspective. *Professional Psychology: Research and Practice, 23*, 369–375. doi:10.1037/0735-7028.23.5.369

Keilin, W. G., Baker, J., McCutcheon, S., & Peranson, E. (2007). A growing bottleneck: The internship supply–demand imbalance in 2007 and its impact on psychology training. *Training and Education in Professional Psychology, 1*, 229–237. doi:10.1037/1931-3918.1.4.229

Keilin, W. G., & Kaslow, N. J. (2008). Predoctoral internship. In F. T. L. Leong, E. M. Altmaier, & B. D. Johnson (Eds.), *Encyclopedia of counseling: Changes and challenges for counseling in the 21st century* (pp. 342–346). Los Angeles, CA: Sage.

Levenson, H., & Burg, J. (2000). Training psychologists in the era of managed care. In A. J. Kent & M. Hersen (Eds.), *A psychologist's proactive guide to managed mental health care* (pp. 113–140). Mahwah, NJ: Erlbaum.

Logsdon-Conradsen, S., Sirl, K. S., Battle, J., Stapel, J., Anderson, P. L., Ventura-Cook, E., . . . Kaslow, N. J. (2001). Formalized postdoctoral fellowships: A national survey of postdoctoral fellows. *Professional Psychology: Research and Practice, 32*, 312–318. doi:10.1037/0735-7028.32.3.312

Markus, H. E., & King, D. A. (2003). A survey of group psychotherapy training during predoctoral psychology internship. *Professional Psychology: Research and Practice, 34*, 203–209. doi:10.1037/0735-7028.34.2.203

Pederson, S. L., DePiano, F., Kaslow, N. J., Klepac, R. K., Hargrove, D. S., & Vasquez, M. (1997, October). *Proceedings from the National Working Conference on Supply and Demand.* Paper presented at the National Working Conference on Supply and Demand: Training and Employment Opportunities in Professional Psychology, Orlando, Florida.

Raimy, V. C. (Ed.). (1950). *Training in clinical psychology.* New York, NY: Prentice Hall.

Reich, J. N., Sands, H., & Wiens, A. N. (Eds.). (1995). *Education and training beyond the doctoral degree: Proceedings of the APA National Conference on Postdoctoral Education and Training in Psychology.* Washington, DC: American Psychological Association.

Rodolfa, E. R., Bell, D. J., Bieschke, K. J., Davis, C., III, & Peterson, R. L. (2007). The internship match: Understanding the problem-seeking solutions. *Training and Education in Professional Psychology, 1*, 225–228. doi:10.1037/1931-3918.1.4.225

Rodolfa, E. R., Bent, R. J., Eisman, E., Nelson, P. D., Rehm, L., & Ritchie, P. (2005). A cube model for competency development: Implications for psychology educators and regulators. *Professional Psychology: Research and Practice, 36*, 347–354. doi:10.1037/0735-7028.36.4.347

Rodolfa, E. R., Ko, S. F., & Petersen, L. (2004). Psychology training directors' views of trainees' readiness to practice independently. *Professional Psychology: Research and Practice, 35*, 397–404. doi:10.1037/0735-7028.35.4.397

Sanderson, W. C. (2003). Why empirically supported psychological treatments are important. *Behavior Modification, 27*, 290–299. doi:10.1177/014544550 3027003002

Shakow, D. (1965). Seventeen years later: Clinical psychology in light of the 1947 Committee on Training in Clinical Psychology Report. *American Psychologist, 20*, 353–362.

Spirito, A., Brown, R. T., D'Angelo, E., Delamater, A., Rodrigue, J., & Siegel, L. J. (2003). Society of Pediatric Psychology Task Force Report: Recommendations for the training of pediatric psychologists. *Journal of Pediatric Psychology, 28*, 85–98. doi:10.1093/jpepsy/28.2.85

Spruill, J., & Pruitt, S. D. (2000). Preparing psychologists for managed care settings: Enhancing internship training programs. *Professional Psychology: Research and Practice, 31*, 305–309. doi:10.1037/0735-7028.31.3.305

Stedman, J. M. (1997). What we know about predoctoral internship training: A review. *Professional Psychology: Research and Practice, 28*, 475–485. doi:10.1037/0735-7028.28.5.475

Stedman, J. M. (2007). What we know about predoctoral internship training: A 10-year update. *Training and Education in Professional Psychology, 1*, 74–88. doi:10.1037/1931-3918.1.1.74

Stedman, J. M., Hatch, J. P., & Schoenfeld, L. S. (2000). Preinternship preparation in psychological testing and psychotherapy: What internship directors say they expect. *Professional Psychology: Research and Practice, 31*, 321–326. doi:10.1037/ 0735-7028.31.3.321

Stedman, J. M., Hatch, J. P., & Schoenfeld, L. S. (2002). Preinternship preparation of clinical and counseling students in psychological testing, psychotherapy, and supervision: Their readiness for medical school and nonmedical school internships. *Journal of Clinical Psychology in Medical Settings, 9*, 267–271. doi:10.1023/ A:1020730800241

Stedman, J. M., Hatch, J. P., & Schoenfeld, L. S. (2007). Toward practice-oriented theoretical models for internship training. *Training and Education in Professional Psychology, 1*, 89–94. doi:10.1037/1931-3918.1.2.89

Stedman, J. M., Hatch, J. P., Schoenfeld, L. S., & Keilin, W. G. (2005). The structure of internship training: Current patterns and implications for the future of clinical and counseling psychologists. *Professional Psychology: Research and Practice, 36*, 3–8. doi:10.1037/0735-7028.36.1.3

Thorp, S. R., O'Donohue, W. T., & Gregg, J. (2005). The predoctoral internship: Is current training anachronistic? *Professional Psychology: Research and Practice, 36*, 16–24. doi:10.1037/ 0735-7028.36.1.16

Weiner, I. B. (Ed.). (1973). *Postdoctoral education in clinical psychology*. Topeka, KS: Menninger Foundation.

Licensing and Credentialing

Jack B. Schaffer, Stephen T. DeMers, and Emil Rodolfa

Humans have struggled with problems in living since the beginning of time and have sought guidance from others to assist in overcoming or managing their problems. For most of history, that guidance came in the form of philosophy, medicine, or theology. For the past 120 years, the rapidly developing profession of psychology has also served that purpose.

Early in the evolution of professional psychology, there was concern about standards of care and quality of services offered. Licensure of physicians began in the United States around 1888 after a landmark decision by the U.S. Supreme Court (*Dent v. West Virginia*, 1889) in which the court upheld the legitimate policing powers of the states to protect the public from medical malpractice. Other professions, such as dentistry, pharmacy, and architecture, soon followed medicine's lead, with psychology close behind (Sinclair, Simon & Pettifor, 1996). In 1938, the American Psychological Association (APA) established a Committee on Scientific and Professional Ethics, making psychology the first mental health profession to address the ethical practice of its members (Ford, 2001). During and just after World War II, the Conference of State Psychology Associations was actively involved in discussions regarding standards and controls in the practice of psychology (Carlson, 1978). Then, as now, it was recognized that not every psychologist provides services in a competent or ethical manner because of lack of knowledge, skills, or adequate ethical standards. This concern led to a growing interest in creating structures to regulate the practice of psychologists, and hence the beginning of efforts to pass psychology licensing acts.

In this chapter, we describe the history, current status, and future of psychology licensure and postlicensure credentialing. We conclude by briefly reviewing the history of credentialing advanced practice in psychology.

PURPOSE AND EARLY HISTORY OF PSYCHOLOGY LICENSURE

Licensure laws exist to protect the public from psychologists who practice incompetently or unethically. As stated on the website of the Association of State and Provincial Psychology Boards (ASPPB) regarding the organization of licensing boards in the United States and Canada,

> The laws are intended to protect the public by limiting licensure to persons who are qualified to practice psychology as defined by state or provincial law. The legal basis for licensure lies in the right of a jurisdiction to enact legislation to protect its citizens. The concept of caveat emptor, or buyer beware, is considered an unsound maxim when the

consumer of services cannot be sufficiently informed to beware. Hence, jurisdictions have established regulatory boards to license qualified practitioners. (Association of State and Provincial Psychology Boards, n.d., para. 1)

Thus, the primary legislative mandate for licensure involves protection of the public. In that regard, licensing boards have a different focus than do state and national psychological associations, which exist to promote the profession and the members of the profession. At the same time, as the ASPPB website goes on to say,

by ensuring high standards for those who practice, the board serves the best interests of both the public and the profession. The major functions of a professional regulatory agency are: 1) to determine standards for admission into the profession and to administer appropriate procedures for selection and examination, and 2) to regulate practice and to conduct disciplinary proceedings involving violations of standards of professional conduct embodied in the law and regulations of the board. (Association of State and Provincial Psychology Boards, n.d., para. 1)

Formal regulation of psychology practice began in the 1940s. Connecticut was the first state to pass legislation to institute a psychology licensing board in 1945 (Carlson, 1978). Over the next 5 years, only two additional states—Virginia and Kentucky—approved legislation to develop psychology licensing boards. By 1960, 32 more jurisdictions had passed similar laws. Not until 1977 had all 50 states enacted psychology licensing acts (Sinclair et al., 1996). Table 16.3 presents the dates of initial licensure laws and number of licensed psychologists by jurisdiction.

Initially, most psychology licensing laws were title acts that focused primarily on who could use the title *psychologist*. Subsequently, most psychology licensing acts were modified to become "practice acts" that sought to regulate both the title *psychologist* and the types of services defined as the practice of psychology. Because other mental health professions are also recognized by state licensing laws to provide services such as psychotherapy (e.g., professional counselor, clinical social worker, marriage and family therapist), most psychology licensing laws include an exemption for such people to provide services defined within the practice of psychology as long as they do not refer to themselves as psychologists.

CURRENT STATUS OF PSYCHOLOGY REGULATION

The process by which a person becomes licensed is well defined in each of the states and territories of the United States. Although there is considerable similarity in licensure requirements across the jurisdictions, there are also

TABLE 16.3
Initial Licensure Laws by State

Jurisdisction	Year of original licensure law	No. licensed psychologists as of January 2001[a]	No. licensed psychologists in 2008[a]
Alabama	1963	732	849
Alaska	1967	191	219
Arizona	1965	1,306	1,800
Arkansas	1955	833	972
California	1957	15,030	16,896
Colorado	1961	1,947	Approximately 2,500
Connecticut	1945	1,481	1,769
Delaware	1962	383	419
District of Columbia	1975	1,067	1,177
Florida	1961 Sunset 2 years (1980–1982)	3,446	4,051
Georgia	1951	1,824	2,070
Hawaii	1967	528	799
Idaho	1963	282	312
Illinois	1963	6,146	4,197
Indiana	1969	1,723	1,534
Iowa	1975	482	494
Kansas	1967	1,405	737
Kentucky	1948	1,290	1,400
Louisiana	1964	540	630
Maine	1953	611	636
Maryland	1957	2,749	2,525
Massachusetts	1974	5,224	5,088
Michigan	1959	6,608	6,831
Minnesota	1951	3,740	3,769
Mississippi	1966	384	398
Missouri	1977	1,921	1,748
Montana	1971	213	238
Nebraska	1967	417	560
Nevada	1963	292	347
New Hampshire	1957	611	577
New Jersey	1966	2,791	3,122
New Mexico	1963	560	634
New York	1956	9,786 active	9,784
North Carolina	1967	3,396	3,512
North Dakota	1967	185	205
Ohio	1972	3,887	3,689
Oklahoma	1965	559	565
Oregon	1963	1,137	1,225
Pennsylvania	1976	5,516	5,484
Rhode Island	1969	532	600
South Carolina	1968	557	648
South Dakota	1967 Sunset 2 years (1979–1981)	180	187

(*continues*)

TABLE 16.3
Initial Licensure Laws by State *(Continued)*

Jurisdisction	Year of original licensure law	No. licensed psychologists as of January 2001[a]	No. licensed psychologists in 2008[a]
Tennessee	1953	Approximately 1,900	1,313
Texas	1969	6,826	7,891
Utah	1959	774	827
Vermont	1975	565	588
Virgin Islands	1997	12	22
Virginia	1946	2,209	2,595
Washington	1955	1,613	1,836
West Virginia	1970	689	630
Wisconsin	1969	1,616	1,325
Wyoming	1965	176	208

Note. Data gathered from Board of Psychology Administrators in April 2009.
[a]Includes all levels of licensure unless otherwise noted.

substantial differences (ASPPB, 2008b). Standardizing licensure requirements across jurisdictions will enhance mobility of psychologists (DeMers, Van Horne, & Rodolfa, 2008), but such standardization is an ongoing challenge because of the authority of individual jurisdictions to regulate the professions and the differences across states in demographics, geography, and the availability of health services.

Academic Degree

In 47 of the 50 states, a doctoral degree in psychology is required for the independent practice of psychology, and in all but one jurisdiction, only a licensee with a doctoral degree can be called a *licensed psychologist*. There are 12 jurisdictions that allow supervised practice at the master's level, most commonly with the title *psychologist associate*. In a few jurisdictions, graduation from a doctoral program accredited by the American Psychological Association or the Canadian Psychological Association is a requirement for licensure. Laws in many more jurisdictions require that the academic training program be designated as a doctoral program in psychology through the ASPPB/National Register Designation Program. Most often, an applicant from an APA- or Canadian Psychological Association–accredited program or an ASPPB/National Register–designated program is considered to have met the educational requirements for licensure without having to provide further evidence of the adequacy of their academic training. Consistent with the requirements for accreditation and designation, graduate education must cover both the core knowledge domains of psychology and the specialty domains related to the intended area of practice.

Supervised Experience

All states have supervised experience requirements for licensure, but these vary across the jurisdictions. The most common standard is a year of predoctoral experience after coursework is completed, typically an internship, plus 1 year of supervised experience postdoctorally. But even the numerous jurisdictions with this standard vary in the structure of the regulations because requirements vary from 1,500 hr to 2,000 hr for each year of experience. As a result, an individual may be eligible for licensure in one state with 3,000 hr of supervised experience but not be eligible in a neighboring state that requires 4,000 hr.

Practicum Experience

In 2006, the APA adopted a policy that resulted in a change in its Model Licensing Act to exclude the requirement of a supervised year of postdoctoral experience. Under this policy, an individual can be eligible for licensure on graduation from a doctoral program, assuming they have attained the required amount and type of supervised experience before graduation. By the time this chapter was written, seven states (Washington, Utah, Ohio, Maryland, North Dakota, Indiana, and Arizona) had changed their licensure laws to allow individuals to apply for licensure with this sequence of training, although no psychologist in any of these states had been licensed using practicum experiences. The majority of the remaining jurisdictions are adamantly opposed to such a change. As a result, there is the possibility of even more variability in licensure laws in the coming years, leading to even more difficulties in becoming licensed for some individuals and mobility for others. The ASPPB developed guidelines for practicum training to provide licensing boards a common understanding of what constitutes adequate practicum experience (ASPPB, 2009).

Supervisor Competence

Another concern in licensure regards the demonstrated competence of the supervisor. Some jurisdictions require that the supervisor possess specific training and experience providing supervision before the supervised experience can count toward licensure. In many jurisdictions, there are no such requirements. In some jurisdictions, the requirement is that a licensed psychologist must provide all supervised experience; in many jurisdictions, however, part of the supervision can be provided by a nonlicensed psychologist (faculty member, intern, or postdoctoral fellow) or by a licensed allied health professional (e.g., psychiatrist). There is clearly a lack of standardization of supervisor requirements across the jurisdictions nationally.

Examinations

In every state in the United States, passing the Examination for Professional Practice in Psychology (EPPP) is a requirement for licensure, one of the few areas in which there is universal consistency across jurisdictions. As with all requirements for licensure, the EPPP passing score is set by the individual jurisdictional board, but almost all have adopted the ASPPB recommended pass point, which is a standard score of 500 or approximately 70% of the scored items (ASPPB, 2008a).

The EPPP examines a licensing candidate's knowledge of the breadth of the field of psychology: biological bases of behavior, cognitive–affective bases of behavior, social and multicultural bases of behavior, growth and life span development, assessment and diagnosis, treatment, intervention and prevention, research and statistics, and ethical–legal–professional issues (ASPPB, 2008a). An analysis of the practice of psychology validates the composition of the EPPP. To sit for the EPPP, an individual must be a candidate for licensure in one of the jurisdictions in the United States or Canada.

Many jurisdictions require additional examinations to test candidates' understanding of the laws and ethics of practice or the limits of their competence. A number of jurisdictions require a jurisprudence examination covering the laws and rules that govern the practice of psychology in that state. Several psychology licensing boards administer an oral examination to test competency, and some boards administer an ethics examination in addition to the jurisprudence examination. Because of concerns about the validity and reliability of the oral examination, a number of boards have eliminated the oral examination requirement during the past several years.

Other Requirements

In addition to these general requirements, select licensing boards have additional requirements for such variables as citizenship or age. Many require that the applicant demonstrate "good moral character," a requirement that is usually met through letters of recommendation from training directors or supervisors. Most jurisdictions have an exemption from licensure for faculty who teach or do research but who otherwise do not provide or supervise psychological services to the public.

POSTLICENSURE CREDENTIALING

Most psychology licensing laws are generic, meaning psychologists who are trained to provide services in a variety of specialty areas of practice all receive the title of licensed psychologist. Thus, anyone with a doctoral degree in psychology and the requisite supervised experience can be licensed, whether the terminal degree is in clinical or counseling psychology or in social, developmental, or industrial–organizational psychology. With the inclusion of psychologists in both government-sponsored (e.g., Medicare) and private health insurance systems, there grew a need to identify those psychologists trained to provide health services from those who were not.

In the early 1970s, the National Register of Health Service Providers in Psychology (NRHSP) was established in the United States as a voluntary registry of licensed psychologists who met prescribed standards of training and credentialing as health service providers. Currently, about a dozen U.S. licensing laws have established mechanisms to distinguish health service providers from non–health service providers in a statutory way rather than relying on a voluntary certification or registration process. However, most jurisdictions continue to issue generic licenses and require their licensees to provide psychological services only in those areas for which they have the requisite education and supervised experience to function competently.

Board certification provides peer and public recognition of demonstrated advanced competence in an approved specialty area in professional psychology. The most notable specialty certification program is the American Board of Professional Psychology (ABPP), which was incorporated in 1947 with the support of the APA. The 13 member boards of the ABPP each establish and maintain specialty standards and provide examinations of psychologists.

Besides the ABPP and the NRHSP, numerous other specialty boards offer voluntary certification for psychologists. Such voluntary certifications do provide a means for the practitioner to demonstrate external endorsement of his or her expertise in a specialty area of practice. However, these groups vary widely in the rigor of their standards and assessment strategies and should be evaluated on their individual merits as a true measure of specialty competence rather than a so-called vanity board.

FUTURE OF LICENSING

The licensure of psychologists in the United States is now firmly established even if not always identical across jurisdictions. Five significant issues confront licensure and credentialing now and into the foreseeable future: mobility, telehealth, distance education, competence, and specialization.

Mobility

The interjurisdictional variability in licensure requirements has presented a major challenge to mobility of licensed psychologists. Unfortunately, a common scenario is a psychologist who has practiced in one jurisdiction for many years, competently and without disciplinary action, deciding to relocate to another state and not being able to become licensed, or at least not able to become licensed without extraordinary effort. Such efforts often include documenting supervised experience from decades earlier or even completing another year, or substantial part of a year, of supervised experience because of differences across jurisdictions in the number of hours of supervised experience required for licensure.

In the early 1990s, ASPPB sponsored a reciprocity agreement among some jurisdictions that allows a psychologist licensed in one state to be licensed easily in another participating jurisdiction. By 2008, only 12 states had joined this agreement (DeMers et al., 2008) because most jurisdictions were reluctant to allow another jurisdiction to determine eligibility for licensure and independent practice in their jurisdictions.

To respond to these mobility barriers, NRHSP, ASPPB, and ABPP launched efforts to facilitate the relicensure of competent and ethical psychologists (Jonason, DeMers, Vaughn, & Reaves, 2003). Individuals holding certification from ABPP, ASPPB, or NRHSP can obtain a waiver of some requirements for licensure, such as documenting EPPP scores, in approximately 35 states for the NRHSP or ABPP and 45 states for the ASPPB certificate. After documenting a valid NRHSP, ABPP, or ASPPB credential, a psychologist typically has to pass only the local jurisprudence examination to meet the requirements for licensure.

Another mobility-related challenge has been to provide a second licensing board the necessary documentation required for licensure after years of practice in one jurisdiction. Typical problems include difficulty locating a former supervisor, the inaccessibility of training records because of a closed training site, or a natural disaster. To preserve psychologists' licensure-related records, ASPPB and the NRHSP have developed credentials verification programs in which records for licensure are primary source verified (DeMers & Jonason, 2006). NRHSP and ABPP also offer credentials banking services for early career psychologists.

Telehealth

Telehealth is an important mechanism of practice requiring increasing oversight of psychology boards. Boards have not yet settled on the answer to the following question: Should telehealth practice be regulated by the jurisdictional board where the psychologist is practicing, where the client is located, or both? Most psychologists agree that additional licensure is not needed for the practice of telehealth (e.g., Reed, McLaughlin, & Milholland, 2000), but standards of care have not yet been consensually identified or legally regulated (Glueckauf, Pickett, Ketterman, Loomis, & Rozensky, 2003). Jurisdictions will need to embrace consistent regulations for telepractice services if practitioners can be reasonably expected to comply (DeMers et al., 2008).

Distance Education

Some licensing boards are discussing whether professional psychology can be taught effectively in academic programs that deliver instruction predominantly via web-based courses without a traditional residency requirement. Psychology boards are also discussing the utility of distance education for continuing education. Most jurisdictions allow psychologists to accrue a certain percentage of their continuing education hours through distance education experiences (Murphy, Levant, Hall, & Glueckauf, 2007).

Competence

The profession of psychology has moved toward a culture of competence (Roberts, Borden, Christiansen, & Lopez, 2005). The implications of this culture shift for psychology boards will be a change from focusing on meeting specific course and hour requirements to determine eligibility for licensure to assessing professional competence (Rodolfa et al., 2005).

The EPPP has long served as the single, internationally accepted measure of licensure eligibility, but it has never claimed to be a measure of competence to practice. Rather, it is a test of knowledge in psychology, with the assumption that this knowledge "should have been acquired by any candidate who is seeking to practice psychology" (ASPPB, 2008a, p. 3) and is related to the ability to practice with competence (Rehm & Lipkins, 2006). Currently, practice competency is assessed through the supervisors' evaluation and other mechanisms (e.g., jurisprudence examination, degree review). The time is coming when a test of knowledge may be augmented by a direct assessment of professional competencies as well.

Psychology boards have historically taken the position that once licensed, the practitioner is assumed to be competent and ethical unless complaints are received regarding his or her services. In other words, a psychologist is not required to demonstrate continuing competence unless some question of competence is raised. Typically, most jurisdictions require attendance at continuing education programs (see Chapter 16e), but there is no formal assessment of sustained professional competence. Yet, disciplinary data have suggested that one variable that predicts incompetent or unethical practice is the length of time since initial license (Pope, 1993) because many psychologists who violate boundaries are middle aged and mid-career. Some psychologists may not keep up with changes in the profession and their ethical obligations. This suggests that there may be a need for assessing continuing competence, as recommended by the Pew Health Professions Commission (1998).

Specialization

The focus on competence raises two additional matters relevant to licensure and credentialing. As psychology practice has become more complex, specialization plays an increasingly important role (ABPP, 2008), and licensing boards will be charged with regulating a more varied practice of psychology (DeMers et al., 2008). Almost all psychology boards grant generic licenses, but as the profession moves toward specialization, licensing boards may decide that it is time to regulate not only the generic practice of psychology but also the specialty practices of psychology. For instance, the state of Florida has required a specialty credential for a psychologist to be called a specialist.

CONCLUSIONS

The profession of psychology has successfully instituted licensing in all U.S. jurisdictions and has effectively established a system of credentialing more advanced practice, with the NRHSP, ABPP, and ASPPB representing the three most prevalent postlicensure credentials. The history of licensure and credentialing has been characterized by increasing standards and escalating rigor.

At the same time, many challenges face the profession of psychology and licensing boards. To respond to these challenges, the future of psychology regulation will need to involve increased cooperation among licensure and credentialing bodies, as well as communication and collaboration with professional psychology associations (Smith, 2006). As psychology licensing boards and professional associations work together, boards will more effectively achieve their primary mandate of licensing competent psychologists and, in turn, protect those seeking help from psychologists for their problems of living.

REFERENCES

American Board of Professional Psychology. (2008). *Standards for the purpose and structure of a body certifying psychologists as specialists in professional psychology.* Retrieved from http://www.abpp.org/brochures/general_brochure.htm

Association of State and Provincial Psychology Boards. (n.d.). *Obtaining a license: The purpose of licensure or certification.* Retrieved from http://www.asppb.net/i4a/pages/ index.cfm? pageid=3390

Association of State and Provincial Psychology Boards. (2008a). *ASPPB information for candidates.* Retrieved from http://www.asppb.net/files/public/IFC.pdf

Association of State and Provincial Psychology Boards. (2008b). *Handbook on licensure and certification.* Retrieved from http://www.asppb.org/Handbook Public/before.aspx

Association of State and Provincial Psychology Boards. (2009). *Guidelines on practicum experience for licensure.* Retrieved from http://www.asppb.net/files/public/Final_ Prac_ Guidelines_1_31_09.pdf

Carlson, H. (1978). The ASPPB story: The beginnings and first 16 Years of the American Association of State Psychology Boards, 1961-1977. *American Psychologist, 33*, 486–495. doi:10.1037/0003-066X.33.5.486

DeMers, S. T., & Jonason, K. R. (2006). The ASPPB Credentials Bank and Certificate of Professional Qualification in Psychology (CPQ). In T. Vaughn (Ed.), *Psychology licensure and certification: What students need to know* (pp. 107–115). Washington, DC: American Psychological Association. doi:10.1037/11477-009

DeMers, S., Van Horne, B., & Rodolfa, E. (2008). Changes in the training and practice of psychologists: Current challenges for licensing boards. *Professional Psychology: Research and Practice, 39*, 473–479.

Dent v. West Virginia, 129 U.S.114, 9 S. Ct. 231 (1889).

Ford, G. C. (2001). *Ethical reasoning in the mental health professions* (p. 6). Boca Raton, FL: CRC Press.

Glueckauf, R. L., Pickett, T. C., Ketterman, T. U., Loomis, J. S., & Rozensky, R. H. (2003). Preparation for the delivery of telehealth services: A self-study framework for expansion of practice. *Professional Psychology: Research and Practice, 34*, 159–163.

Jonason, K. R., DeMers, S. T., Vaughn, T. J., & Reaves, R. P. (2003). Professional mobility for psychologists is rapidly becoming a reality. *Professional Psychology: Research and Practice, 34*, 468–473. doi:10.1037/0735-7028.34.5.468

Murphy, M., Levant, R., Hall, J., & Glueckauf, R. (2007). Distance education in professional psychology training in psychology. *Professional Psychology: Research and Practice, 38*, 97–103. doi:10.1037/0735-7028.38.1.97

Pew Health Professions Commission. (1998). *Recreating health professional practice for a new century: Fourth report of the Pew Health Professions Commission* (Executive Summary). Retrieved from http://futurehealth.ucsf.edu/compubs.html

Pope, K. (1993). Licensing disciplinary actions for psychologists who have been sexually involved with a client: Some information about offenders. *Professional Psychology: Research and Practice, 24*, 374–377. doi:10.1037/0735-7028.24.3.374

Reed, G. M., McLaughlin, C. J., & Milholland, K. (2000). Ten interdisciplinary principles for professional practice in telehealth: Implications for psychology. *Professional Psychology: Research and Practice, 31*, 170–178. doi:10.1037/0735-7028.31.2.170

Rehm, L., & Lipkins, R. (2006). The Examination for Professional Practice in Psychology. In T. Vaughn (Ed.), *Psychology licensure and certification: What students need to know* (pp. 39–53). Washington, DC: American Psychological Association. doi:10.1037/ 11477-004

Roberts, M. C., Borden, K. A., Christiansen, M. D., & Lopez, S. J. (2005). Fostering a culture shift: Assessment of competence in the education and career of professional psychologists. *Professional Psychology: Research and Practice, 36*, 355–361. doi:10.1037/0735-7028.36.4.355

Rodolfa, E., Bent, R., Eisman, E., Nelson, P., Rehm, L., & Ritchie, P. (2005). A cube model for competency development: Implications for educators and regulators. *Professional Psychology: Research and Practice, 36,* 347–354. doi:10.1037/ 0735-7028.36.4.347

Sinclair, C., Simon, N. P., & Pettifor, J. (1996). The history of ethical codes and licensure. In L. Bass, S. DeMers, J. Ogloff, C. Peterson, J. Pettifor, R. Reaves, T. Retfalvi, N., . . . R. Tipton (Eds.), *Professional conduct and discipline in psychology* (pp. 1–15). Washington, DC: American Psychological Association.

Smith, L. (2006, October). *Tour of assessments used in regulation by selected healthcare professions.* Paper presented at the annual meeting of Association of State and Provincial Psychology Boards, San Diego, CA.

Continuing Education in Psychology

Greg J. Neimeyer and Jennifer M. Taylor

If continuing education (CE) is a natural expression of a profession's ongoing evolution (Houle, 1980), then professional psychology can be viewed as suffering a significant developmental delay. Sporadic discussions of lifelong professional development predate the Boulder conference, but emergence of a systematic discussion of CE in psychology is a relatively recent phenomenon. Largely a product of the 1960s and 1970s, the field's long-standing inattention to CE served as one of the earliest recurring themes in its nascent literature. Since that time, the field has experienced maturation, bringing greater clarity to its mission and achieving major milestones over the course of its developmental trajectory. In this chapter, we provide a précis of the history of CE in psychology, from the originating events that first animated it, through the foreseeable future that now confronts it.

EVOLUTION OF CE IN PSYCHOLOGY

The history of CE in psychology has been written by many hands across its 50-year span. Individuals, agencies, and associations have all played central roles in supporting the fledgling efforts of the field to dedicate concerted attention to ongoing postdoctoral training and professional development. In this chapter, we outline the overall themes and contributions that have signaled the field's development. These themes can represent three overlapping phases of growth. The first phase speaks to the early years (1960s and 1970s), beginning with the key factors that triggered a consideration of CE. The middle years (1980s and 1990s) witnessed the emergence of an empirical literature on CE in psychology, partly in response to demands of accountability, as states considered the enactment of legislated CE mandates for license renewal. These middle years gradually elided into the current era (2000 to the present), which has introduced a distinctive set of concerns that align CE with broader movements regarding professional competencies.

The Early Years (1960s–1970s): Laying the Foundation

Although the first CE mandate in psychology was enacted in 1957 by the state of Maryland, the seeds of CE in psychology were largely sown in the era of consumer activism in the 1960s. During that time, the public initiated efforts to develop greater accountability in relation to the services provided by a broad range of health care professions (Jones, 1975). The 1960s can best be regarded as the foundational era for CE in professional psychology, marked largely by the development of early blueprints for postgraduate training in the field and by a range of projects guided by those blueprints. As one example, in 1966 the National Institute of Mental Health established a Continuing Education Branch (Lewinsohn & Pearlman, 1972). These efforts were followed in 1972 by the American Board of Professional Psychology's development of the National Academy of Professional Psychologists, which was formed "with the express purpose of providing postdoctoral opportunities of continuing professional development to practitioners" (Ross, 1974, p. 124). Four years later, the Board of Directors of the American Psychological Association (APA) voted to establish a program for CE within its Central Office, followed in 1978 by its approval of the Continuing Education Committee that remains in operation today. These early organizational efforts reflected the field's developing commitment to the core values and purposes of CE.

From its inception, a central warrant for CE concerned its role in protecting the public against the dangers of "professional obsolescence" (Ross, 1974, p. 123), which, in the absence of ongoing updating, might otherwise affect professional knowledge and skills. The widespread recognition that professional knowledge is time limited brought with it the realization that professional psychology needed to demonstrate a visible commitment to instantiating the values of CE and to developing mechanisms for supporting it. An early watershed event in this regard was the National Agenda for Developing Continuing Education in Psychology (Webster, 1971). To advance CE in psychology, Webster (1971) outlined four priorities: (a) the clear need for program planning, (b) concerted efforts to support the development of leadership to provide CE training, (c) the identification of high-priority content areas for CE, and (d) the establishment of an ongoing research agenda concerning CE in psychology. Webster envisioned program planning occurring at multiple levels, with national, regional, state, and local agencies all playing critical roles. As a prophetic preface, Webster advocated that organizations such as the APA, National Institute of Mental Health, American Association of State Psychology Boards, and National Science Foundation specifically identify their organizations' roles and functions in relation to addressing the CE needs of psychologists.

Leadership development was a second priority from Webster's (1971) standpoint. This involved developing mechanisms for recruiting and cultivating instructional excellence to sustain high-quality postdoctoral education. Early discussions focused on the roles that universities might play in this regard. Maintaining university participation in CE was regarded as vital to ensuring a direct pipeline to the most recent scientific advances in the field and to enhancing the ongoing interface between scholarly and practitioner communities (Jones, 1975).

The identification of high-priority content areas represented the third prong of Webster's (1971) call to arms. Recognizing that the field could not provide broad access to all of its available knowledge simultaneously, Webster advocated focusing instead on designated areas of greatest importance, an approach that remains evident in the literatures to this day.

Last, Webster (1971) suggested developing systematic programs of research concerning CE in psychology, viewing this as a natural extension of one of the discipline's most distinctive strengths: its emphasis on research and scientific inquiry. Webster highlighted the need for basic research on processes of adult learning, communication, and organizational behavior, as well as the ongoing evaluation of CE programs and their outcomes.

Now, 40 years after Webster's (1971) call to arms, organized psychology has made identifiable advances along several of these lines and remained conspicuously delinquent along others. Even the definition of CE remains a point of contention, although the definition developed by APA is perhaps the most broadly accepted:

> an ongoing process consisting of formal learning activities that (1) are relevant to psychological practice, education, and science, (2) enable psychologists to keep pace with emerging issues and technologies, and (3) allow psychologists to maintain, develop, and increase competencies in order to improve services to the public and enhance contributions to the profession. (APA, 2000)

Given the importance of maintaining professional competencies and demonstrating a visible commitment to the welfare of the consumer, CE quickly became a widespread ethical, although not yet legal, mandate during this foundational era. APA introduced CE language into its Ethics Code early, with efforts that carry through to its most recent guidelines (see APA, 2002, Principle 2.03).

Early calls to extend this ethical imperative to a legal one can be traced to this era as well. By the early 1970s, for example, the Association of State Psychology Boards began urging member boards to implement CE requirements for license renewal (Jones, 1975). Resistance to those calls was evident from the outset, however, serving as a harbinger of the field's subsequent experience. In December 1968, for example, the Oregon Board of Psychologist Examiners surveyed certified psychologists in their state and learned that only about one quarter of their respondents supported a proposal for mandated CE, whereas nearly one half of them took a negative stance, regarding mandated CE as a potentially coercive and punitive requirement (Lewinsohn & Pearlman, 1972).

Nonetheless, efforts continued to explore the potential for legally mandated CE and to fashion national leadership for CE within the existing organizations central to postdoctoral psychology. Examples include a resolution passed by the American Association of State Psychology Boards in 1971 to form an active collaboration with APA in CE and the development of the Center for Advanced Study and Continuing Education in Mental Health in Nashville, Tennessee (Lewinsohn & Pearlman, 1972). These and a range of other regional efforts represented the field's early efforts to construct fledgling organizations that would support the ongoing training and educational needs of postdoctoral psychologists.

The Middle Years (1980s–1990s): Building the Structure

If the earlier era laid the groundwork for CE in psychology, the bulk of the building project was left to the middle years to accomplish. The scaffolding erected in the early years gradually supported the development of various CE structures that experienced significant delays over time. As a case in point, the state of New York first presented legislation in 1971 in support of mandating CE for all health professionals. Forty years later, psychologists in New York are still operating without CE mandates, and they are joined by a range of other states that have similarly struggled to enact legislated mandates (Lewinsohn & Pearlman, 1972).

The development of these mandates nonetheless represents the signal achievement of this middle era. Although only three states had adopted mandated CE in 1975 (Jones, 1975), 19 states had enacted CE mandates by 1990 (VandeCreek, Knapp, & Brace, 1990). By 2003, CE was mandated in 41 states and the District of Columbia (Sharkin & Plageman, 2003). Today, 43 states have legislated CE mandates, and others are currently considering some form of mandatory quality assurance or CE stipulation as a requirement for license renewal for professional psychologists.

The defining features of these middle years regarding CE in psychology reflected the development of CE mandates and the resistance associated with those developments (VandeCreek, Knapp, & Brace, 1990). One of the recurring themes in these debates concerned whether psychologists would voluntarily participate in CE in the absence of legal mandates to do so, thereby rendering the mandates superfluous and unnecessarily intrusive. Early researchers, however, estimated that approximately 25% to 30% of licensed psychologists might not participate in CE the absence of a mandate to do so (Phillips, 1987; VandeCreek et al., 1990), a finding consistent with subsequent surveys in the field. A recent study of more than 6,000 psychologists across North America, for example, found that in the absence of a legislated mandate, fully one quarter of licensed psychologists completed fewer than five CE credits per year (Neimeyer, Taylor, & Wear, 2008a).

The increased attention given to CE mandates during these middle years brought with it an interest in understanding their impact on psychologists and their professional training. The only direct study of this sort was conducted by Brown, Leichtman, Blass, and Fleisher (1982), who surveyed Maryland psychologists before, and following, the enactment of a CE mandate in that state. Among their findings was an indication that the enactment of the CE mandate was associated with increased participation in formal CE programs, without any corresponding decreases in other forms of professional development (e.g., professional consultation, reading, supervision). More important, this increased CE activity appeared to relate to the greater availability of CE programs as a consequence of the mandate, rather than the mandate per se, raising questions regarding the broader impact of CE mandates that remain unanswered to this day.

The efforts to formalize and nationalize CE in psychology during these middle years took many forms. Legislated CE mandates were among them, as were other mechanisms, such as the call for greater attention to CE, the formation of organizations to provide CE, and the development of committees within existing associations to address the growing interest in offering and monitoring CE programs. Signature accomplishments in this regard included reports dedicated to psychology. Phillips (1994) drafted *A Study of Mandatory Continuing Education*, and APA (1995) sponsored the *Final Report of the Board of Educational Affairs Task Force on Developing State and Provincial Continuing Education (CE) Regulations*, as well as *A Review of the APA Sponsor Approval System* (as cited in Levant, 1999).

In 1986, the APA Board of Directors voted to approve the establishment of the Committee for the Approval of Continuing Education Sponsors, an organization that today supports the regulation of nearly 900 APA-approved sponsors of CE (A. Tongue, personal communication, December 22, 2008). Although the APA Board of Directors voted not to recommend mandatory CE in psychology, they did support states deciding to implement it. It was not until 1998 that the Association of State and Provincial Psychology Boards included mandatory CE in the revision of its Model Act for Licensure of Psychologists, providing substantial impetus to nonmandating states to consider joining the substantial majority of states that mandated CE.

As the middle years drew to a completion, dozens of states had adopted CE mandates, and many of the contemporary mechanisms and processes of CE delivery had been established. However, this era did not quell the controversy regarding CE, its mandates, or its putative outcomes. These issues continue to dominate much of the landscape today.

The Current Era (2000–Present): Inspecting the Structure

If the early and middle years laid the groundwork and then framed the structure of CE in professional psychology, the current era can be viewed as an ongoing building inspection. Examining the processes and outcomes associated with CE has dominated the most recent literature and set the stage for the field's foreseeable future.

Although CE mandates are favored by 75% to 88% of psychologists (e.g., Fagan, Ax, Liss, Resnick, & Moody, 2007; Neimeyer et al., 2008a; Sharkin & Plageman, 2003), detractors of mandated CE still question its value. A central concern follows from the field's failure to produce reliable evidence that CE translates into discernibly superior psychotherapy or outcomes, which serves as the cornerstone of the warrant underlying CE and its related commitment to the welfare of the consumer. As psychology turns renewed attention to accountability and competency, it has discovered a conspicuous absence of research data regarding the effectiveness of CE. This owes, in part, to the limited number of studies in this area and to the significant limitations associated with these studies (Daniels & Walter, 2002; Neimeyer et al., 2008a).

Research on CE outcomes can be classified into four categories, each marked by its distinctive outcome measures. These studies assess (a) participants' satisfaction with their CE experiences, (b) the extent of learning and new knowledge acquisition, (c) the development and translation of new skills into practice, and (d) the impact of new knowledge and skills on practice outcomes, such as the effectiveness of psychotherapy.

The most common category of research concerning CE outcomes is also the weakest: participant satisfaction ratings. In a study of Pennsylvanian psychologists, for example, 69% of Sharkin and Plageman's (2003) respondents were satisfied with the quality of CE programs they had attended, results that are consistent other studies (e.g., Fagan et al., 2007), which found 79% of their participants characterizing their CE experiences as being good to excellent (see also Neimeyer et al., 2008a). However, people can be satisfied with their CE experiences for a wide variety of factors (e.g., entertainment value, proximity to home) that do not necessarily reflect new learning or translate into more informed or effective practice (Vande-Creek et al., 1990).

Direct measures of learning more closely target the intended objectives of CE, although they are uncommon in research on CE in psychology. The enduring absence of direct measures of learning runs counter to movements toward demonstrated competencies (Rubin et al., 2007).

In the absence of measures of direct learning, the translation of that learning into new skills or practices is even more difficult to demonstrate. Although recent work has clearly demonstrated that psychologists report the frequent translation of their CE experiences into their practice (Neimeyer et al., 2008a; Sharkin & Plageman, 2003), no work has yet documented this translation in objective or behavioral terms.

Furthermore, without direct evidence to this effect, researchers have advocated looking to allied fields for relevant evidence. Within continuing medical education, for example, randomized clinical trials assessing the impact of interactive, skill-based continuing medical education on physicians have yielded favorable results. Compared with family physicians who did not receive a training program on cardiovascular and cancer medicine, family doctors who received the training performed the recommended procedures more often than their counterparts, for example, and maintained these differences across a 12-month follow-up period (Jennett, Laxdal, Hayton, & Klaassen, 1988).

Not all forms of CE training are equally effective, however. From his systematic review of a 20-year period of controlled research on the effects of continuing medical education, Bloom (2005) concluded that interactive techniques were the most effective at changing physician care and patient outcomes but that didactic presentations had "little or no beneficial effect in changing physician practice" (p. 380). In other words, passive dissemination of new or even evidence-based practices by itself exerts no significant effect on practitioner behavior, but teaching skills via feedback and practice frequently do (see Norcross, Hogan, & Koocher, 2008).

More recent assessments have provided more pointed appraisals. In their review of the research on CE in psychology, Neimeyer et al. (2008a) concluded that the field

> remains in its infancy and can best be described as a pre-experimental patchwork of isolated surveys conducted largely on localized samples of convenience. These efforts have not yet risen to the level of programmatic research and for that reason have not yet demonstrated the methodological progression or systematic knowledge gains that would ordinarily accompany a sustained program of research. (p. 18)

THE FUTURE OF CE IN PSYCHOLOGY

Coupled with the fact that the weakest assessments of CE outcomes (participant satisfaction ratings) are also the most frequent, the foreseeable future will probably be marked by efforts to document the translation of CE efforts into demonstrable outcomes in a way that satisfies its original warrant. That is, psychologists completing CE programs should behave in different and presumably more effective manners.

In addition to documenting CE outcomes, future work is likely to examine the mechanisms associated with CE selection and delivery. Concerning CE selection, CE is largely self-regulated. Unlike the highly regulated nature of their doctoral training, psychologists choose which CE programs to complete (Daniels & Walter, 2002). Early work in the field focused largely on examining the availability of CE programs to psychologists. Only recently, with the rapid proliferation and increased accessibility of CE programs, has attention turned to understanding the factors involved in the selection of particular CE programs over others. Psychologists presumably choose those programs on the basis of their self-assessed needs and interests and on an awareness of developments that require additional training. However, research assessing these assumptions is only now beginning to take shape. The most commonly cited reason for selecting a particular CE program was its topical interest (Sharkin & Plageman, 2003), followed by its cost and location. Subsequent efforts have similarly reported that topical interest was a primary driving force, followed by perceived need and recognized advances in selected fields that required updating (Neimeyer et al., 2008a). Future work is likely to continue to explore the factors responsible for the selection of particular CE programs as a way of demonstrating that it is a rational process responsive to developing needs within society (see Daniels & Walter, 2002) and distinctive workplace demands (Neimeyer, Taylor, & Wear, 2008b).

Concerning CE delivery, innovative technologies represent one rapidly developing, but largely unexplored, area of future development. There is a growing consensus that in "continuing education, technology will play an increasingly pivotal role. It will rely on the Internet and other developing mediums to support distance learning, interactive videoconferences, Web-based distribution of information and curriculum resources, interactive learning, and simulation techniques" (Daniels & Walter, 2002, pp. 371–372). In short, the traditional reliance on onsite, face-to-face training sessions may yield to a variety of technology-mediated forms of CE delivery.

In addition to its mechanisms of delivery, the content of CE programs will likely continue to be the source of considerable debate. Central to this concern is the function that CE is designed to fulfill. Some have argued that CE should be limited to new knowledge generated within the discipline through recognized scientific methods. Others, however, have argued for the inclusion of programs that support the growth and eventual success of the profession itself (e.g., how to market psychological services). Because CE in psychology does not have a single, unified definition, various organizations and licensing jurisdictions differ in regards to CE fulfillment. The ongoing tension between CE that is based on science and on the needs of the practitioner is nonetheless bridged by a range of common interests, including both protecting consumer welfare and promoting effective psychological services.

Last, both the processes and outcomes associated with CE in psychology are likely to align themselves increasingly with the movement toward documenting professional competencies across the life span. Given that the "mandatory requirement of continuing education is the sole licensing action addressing continued competencies by licensees" (Rubin et al., 2007, p. 456), it is likely that CE will become an increasingly load-bearing mechanism for documenting continuing professional competencies.

Indeed, the field may gradually give rise to the development of evidence-based CE, which can be regarded as professional education that has an ongoing commitment to evaluating educational practices and assessing educational outcomes in support of understanding, prompting, and demonstrating the effectiveness of CE in psychology (Neimeyer et al., 2008a). By embracing an evidence-based approach to lifelong professional learning, the future of CE in psychology would be joined to larger competency movements that share similar commitments to ensuring and documenting enhanced professional skills, practices, and outcomes across the lifelong course of professional development.

REFERENCES

American Psychological Association. (1995). *Final report of the Board of Educational Affairs Task Force on Developing State and Provincial Continuing Education (CE) Regulations.* Washington, DC: Author.

American Psychological Association. (2000). *Minutes of APA Council of Representatives.* Washington, DC: Author.

American Psychological Association. (2002). Ethical principles of psychologists and code of conduct. *American Psychologist, 57,* 1060–1073. doi:10.1037/0003-066X. 57.12.1060

Bloom, B. S. (2005). Effects of continuing medical education on improving physician clinical care and patient health: A review of systematic reviews. *International Journal of Technology Assessment in Health Care, 231,* 380–385.

Brown, R. A., Leichtman, S. R., Blass, T., & Fleisher, E. (1982). Mandated continuing education: Impact on Maryland psychologists. *Professional Psychology: Research and Practice, 13,* 404–411. doi:10.1037/0735-7028.13.3.404

Daniels, A. S., & Walter, D. A. (2002). Current issues in continuing education for contemporary behavioral health practice. *Administration and Policy in Mental Health, 29,* 359–376. doi:10.1023/A:1019653123285

Fagan, T. J., Ax, R. K., Liss, M., Resnick, R. J., & Moody, S. (2007). Professional education and training: How satisfied are we? An exploratory study. *Training and Education in Professional Psychology, 1,* 13–25. doi:10.1037/1931-3918.1.1.13

Houle, C. O. (1980). *Continuing learning in the professions.* San Francisco, CA: Jossey-Bass.

Jennett, P. A., Laxdal, O. E., Hayton, R. C., & Klaassen, D. J. (1988). The effects of continuing medical education on family doctor performance in office practice: A randomized control study. *Medical Education, 22,* 139–145. doi:10.1111/j.1365-2923.1988.tb00424.x

Jones, N. F. (1975). Continuing education: A new challenge for psychology. *American Psychologist, 30,* 842–847. doi:10.1037/h0077108

Levant, R. F. (1999). Proceedings of the American Psychological Association, Incorporated, for the legislative year 1998: Minutes of the Annual Meeting of the Council of Representatives February 20–22, 1998, Washington DC, and August 13 and 16, 1998, San Francisco,

CA, and Minutes of the February, June, August, and December 1998 Meetings of the Board of Directors. *American Psychologist, 54*, 605–671. doi:10.1037/0003-066X.54.8.605

Lewinsohn, P. M., & Pearlman, S. (1972). Continuing education for psychologists. *Professional Psychology, 3*, 48–52.

Neimeyer, G. J., Taylor, J. M., & Wear, D. W. (2008a). *Continuing education in psychology: Outcomes, evaluations and mandates.* Unpublished manuscript, University of Florida, Gainesville.

Neimeyer, G. J., Taylor, J. M., & Wear, D. W. (2008b). *Patterns of participation and preferences in the selection of continuing education programs in psychology.* Unpublished manuscript, University of Florida, Gainesville.

Norcross, J. C., Hogan, T. P., & Koocher, G. P. (2008). *Clinician's guide to evidence based practices: Mental health and the addictions.* New York, NY: Oxford University Press.

Phillips, L. E. (1987). Is mandatory continuing education working? *Mobius, 7*, 57–64.

Phillips, L. (1994). *A study of mandatory continuing education.* Washington DC: American Psychological Association.

Ross, A. O. (1974). Continuing professional development in psychology. *Professional Psychology, 5*, 122–128. doi:10.1037/h0037559

Rubin, N. J., Bebeau, M., Leigh, I. W., Lichtenberg, J. W., Nelson, P. D., Portnoy, S., . . . Kaslow, N. J. (2007). The competency movement within psychology: An historical perspective. *Professional Psychology: Research and Practice, 38*, 452–462. doi:10.1037/h0037559

Sharkin, B. S., & Plageman, P. M. (2003). What do psychologists think about mandatory continuing education? A survey of Pennsylvania psychologists. *Professional Psychology: Research and Practice, 34*, 318–323. doi:10.1037/0735-7028.34.3.318

VandeCreek, L., Knapp, S., & Brace, K. (1990). Mandatory continuing education for licensed psychologists: Its rationale and current implementation. *Professional Psychology: Research and Practice, 21*, 135–140. doi:10.1037/0735-7028.21.2.135

Webster, T. G. (1971). National priorities for the continuing education of psychologists. *American Psychologist, 26*, 1016–1019. doi:10.1037/h0032256

Department of Veterans Affairs

Rodney R. Baker and Wade E. Pickren

The Department of Veterans Affairs (VA), VA psychology, and the VA psychology training program have served important roles in the evolution of the profession of psychology since World War II. VA psychologists advanced the use of individual and group psychotherapy to meet the mental health treatment needs of veterans. The VA's early psychologist employment requirement of the doctoral degree with practical training was followed by requirements for accreditation of doctoral programs and internships and set the credentialing standard for the profession. In its psychology training program, however, the VA made one of its most significant contributions to psychology and psychotherapy. From the beginning of its training program in 1946, the VA promoted training and accreditation standards that served as a model for others, while providing the largest single source of funding for psychology training in the country.

BEGINNING OF VA PSYCHOLOGY AND ITS TRAINING PROGRAM

The VA psychology training program grew out of the lack of trained psychologists to meet the need for mental health treatment of millions of soldiers returning from World War II. In spring 1946, James Grier Miller, on leave from his position at Harvard University, was released from the Army Medical Corps and Office of Strategic Services and appointed the first chief of the VA clinical psychology program. He was given the task of hiring 500 doctoral-level psychologists for the VA—a number almost equaling that of psychologists with doctoral-level clinical training in the entire country at that time (Baker & Pickren, 2007). In addition to the short supply of doctoral-level clinical psychologists, Miller observed that the clinical training being provided by universities lacked an organized curriculum, a conclusion that had also been reached by others (Sears, 1946). Miller decided that the VA would have to play a role in helping to train the psychologists needed to provide quality treatment for veterans.

The 1946 legislation that created the Neuropsychiatry Division and other clinical departments within the VA gave these departments responsibility for oversight of medical care (Baker & Pickren, 2007). The legislation also allowed the clinical departments to establish affiliations with medical schools to help train physicians and nurses to work in VA hospitals. With the publication of Policy Memorandum Number 2 on January 30, 1946, the VA began to establish affiliations between its hospitals and medical schools using procedures that are still in place today (Veterans Administration, 1967). In the 1st year, affiliations were established with 63 of the 77 medical schools in the country. In these affiliations, the VA retained responsibility for the care of patients, and the medical schools were assigned responsibility for graduate education and training.

Although the legislation enabling affiliations for training specifically applied to physicians and nursing personnel, Miller convinced General Omar A. Bradley, newly appointed administrator of the VA, that language in the legislation would also permit psychology students to be employed as part-time training staff to provide psychological services under supervision (Moore, 1992). Together with consultants George A. Kelly, Chauncey M. Louttit, and E. Lowell Kelly, Miller successfully argued that doctoral-level psychologists could provide psychotherapy services to patients. At the same time, psychologists were beginning to seek licensure in states to practice their profession without medical supervision. Miller also noted that with their research skills, psychologists could conduct research and program evaluation in the VA that would benefit patients. These arguments anticipated the scientist–practitioner model promoted in the 1949 Boulder Conference (Raimy, 1950).

Because of insufficient numbers of doctorally trained clinical psychologists, Miller and his colleagues proposed that the VA hire those possessing some psychology coursework, with the proviso that their appointments would be on a temporary basis without promotion possibilities until they had obtained their doctorate (Ash, 1968b). The proposal stipulated that they would be given until 1951 to obtain that degree, after which only doctorally trained psychologists would be employed in the VA.

In outlining his vision for VA psychology and its training program, Miller (1946) introduced a new requirement that some practical training augment the coursework of student psychologists to be hired in the VA. Those recruited for the VA psychology training program would need to come from universities that were preparing students in both scientific and clinical areas. Miller also began working with Dael Wolfle of the American Psychological Association (APA) to identify graduate schools providing this scientist–practitioner training. Under the direction of Robert Sears, APA identified 22 universities meeting this criterion, and the first VA psychology training class in 1946 was selected from these universities (Farreras, 2005).

Following the first selection of students, the VA, with the support of the U.S. Public Health Service, asked APA to develop a formal evaluation of universities that were providing clinical psychology training (Farreras, 2005). The APA Committee on Graduate Professional Training reviewed 40 universities against 13 criteria developed for this purpose and recommended 31 universities for student recruitment (Sears, 1947). The VA's request of APA to identify universities training their students in both scientific and clinical areas is generally acknowledged to have led to APA's doctoral accreditation program (Baker & Pickren, 2007).

Miller's (1946) outline for the VA's clinical psychology training program included the expectation that faculty from the affiliated universities would be appointed as part-time consultants to supervise the clinical work of their students at the VA. These faculty were expected to supervise their students' research and to conduct research at the VA themselves. The consultant's role, and the fees paid to the faculty in that role, proved quite attractive to many faculty, who were often poorly paid at their universities.

FIRST YEARS OF VA TRAINING

Miller obtained funding for 225 psychology training positions for the first VA training class in fall 1946. Universities recommended by APA for recruitment were given an allotment of training positions on the basis of their training capacity, and students interested in the VA training program submitted their applications to the chair of the Department of Psychology at those universities. The chief of the Psychology Section in the VA Central Office in Washington then reviewed and approved the candidates for part-time hiring by the VA. Students were given an hourly pay matching their level of academic preparation and could be appointed for 1 or more years of training. The first 2 years of training approximated what would later be called *practicum training*. An additional 2 years of advanced training were considered internship years, with students paid an hourly salary equal to one half the salary of predoctoral staff (Baker & Pickren, 2007).

The number of funded psychology training positions in the VA more than doubled in the 2nd training year. As Miller was preparing to return to academia in December 1947, his final letter to chairs of psychology in the cooperating universities with clinical psychology training programs reported that high numbers of their students were hired in the VA after their training (Miller, 1947). Miller had still not been able to hire the original number of 500 psychologists for the VA, however, and he noted in his letter that psychology staffing for the VA was not limited by VA appropriations but by the number of trainees that the universities could handle.

The number of VA-funded psychology trainees rose from 225 in 1946 to 650 in 1950. In their training assignments in the VA, students essentially functioned as technicians and psychometrists, replacing those hired in these positions in the VA before 1946. Many of the master's-level psychologists who were working in the VA at the time this program was introduced returned to graduate school to earn their doctorate; some, however, continued in their careers at the VA, offering important bridging functions to the new training program. The assignments were diverse and included testing, diagnosis, and psychotherapy with patients in both traditional mental health programs and medical and surgical programs (Baker & Pickren, 2007).

In support of its mental health training programs, the VA funded research to assess the effectiveness of training for both psychiatry and psychology students. E. Lowell Kelly at the University of Michigan was funded to evaluate psychology trainees before their entry into the program and then followed them for a number of years to determine their performance as clinicians (Kelly & Fiske, 1951).

Psychology trainee research activities ranged from investigations of the psychological impact of medical procedures to mental health treatment. Although the focus of this chapter is on training, the viability of psychology within the VA has frequently been validated and enhanced by the clinical and basic research conducted by psychologists over the years. For example, in the 1950s and 1960s, it was the research of VA psychologists in the then new area of psychopharmacology that helped to establish the validity of the new drug treatments for a variety of serious mental illnesses. It was also the research and clinical applications of VA psychologists that helped push the third edition of the *Diagnostic and Statistical Manual of Mental Disorders* (American Psychiatric Association, 1980) to focus on behavior. The point is that although training was a critical part of the VA mission, the payoff to the VA and to society also came in the improved treatment and understanding of mental disorders that flowed from VA psychology research. The two—training and research—have historically been inextricably linked within the VA, and this continues today.

Before 1952, the VA employed master's-trained vocational rehabilitation counselors only in VA regional offices responsible for administering benefits for veterans. Robert S. Waldrop, dean of students at Vanderbilt University, was hired as a consultant to evaluate whether counseling psychologists should be hired and located in VA hospitals to assist veterans in their rehabilitation. Waldrop, a former director of the Veterans Service Bureau at the University of Michigan, not only strongly supported this concept but also insisted that counseling psychologists have doctoral training with the same practical training and earn the same salary as their clinical psychology colleagues in the hospital (Waldrop, 2007).

In 1952, Waldrop accepted the position offered him as director of vocational counseling in the VA Central Office and was given the mandate to carry out his recommendations. His difficulty hiring counseling psychologists with the needed doctoral and practical training paralleled that faced earlier by Miller, and a counseling psychology training program was begun in the VA in fall 1953 with 55 counseling psychology training positions (Baker & Pickren, 2007).

For the 1955–1956 training year, 771 clinical and counseling psychology students were appointed to training positions in the VA. In 1957, the staff and training positions for the clinical and counseling psychology programs were combined into one service.

To reduce the need for hospitalization, the VA had developed the largest outpatient mental health clinic network in the country by 1955. It was in these clinics that psychologists made a major contribution to meeting the mental health treatment needs of veterans. The clinics also became a major resource for training mental health professionals. By design, each clinic was to have a psychologist, psychiatrist, and social worker on staff. Psychology trainees, however, were added to these clinics in larger numbers than other training staff, in part because of their contributions and significant involvement in individual and group psychotherapy. A 1954 report (Veterans Administration, 1955) indicated that the VA was operating 62 mental health outpatient clinics that included staffing of 151 clinical psychologists, 165 psychiatrists, and 162 social workers. The staffing was augmented by 160 psychology trainees, with only 45 psychiatry residents and 42 social work students.

The 1954 report (Veterans Administration, 1955) further noted that individual therapy was the backbone of the mental health clinic program but that increasing use was being made of group psychotherapy. This was consistent with clinical practice at that time because group therapies with a diverse range of theoretical orientations were developed and implemented across the spectrum of mental health service sites. At the time, there was a large body of research on group psychotherapy, but there was little available for training in the practical details of conducting group psychotherapy. To meet this need, the VA published the *Manual of Group Therapy*, written by two VA psychologists and a psychology consultant (Luchins, Aumack, & Dickman, 1960). The manual provided guidance in such areas as where to conduct groups, the frequency and duration of group meetings, the optimal number of patients in a group, and how to handle hostile, dependent, silent, and talkative patients. In addition, the manual's chapters reviewed the theoretical basis for group therapy and described some of the types of group therapy being used in the VA, such as psychodrama. The usefulness of the manual in training and in VA treatment programs necessitated a second printing a year later and helped establish the theoretical and therapeutic basis for group therapy in the VA.

One early criticism of the VA training program surfaced in a status report on general doctoral training by the APA Committee on Training in Clinical Psychology. Some believed that a too-narrow definition of clinical psychology was emerging with VA trainee involvement in treating large numbers of psychotic and seriously disturbed patients (American Psychological Association, 1949). Psychology and its training program were clearly meeting an important need in the VA, however, and the report had no impact on the direction of training in the VA. That report also stressed the importance of training and supervision in psychotherapy, a training goal already clearly established by that time in the VA.

The decision to incorporate university consultants into its training program served both the VA and the university. University faculty provided clinical supervision for their students and helped ensure the quality of treatment in the VA. Equally as important was the participation of faculty consultants in research programs. Faculty, however, were often limited in their clinical experience with the major mental illnesses found in the VA patient population, and supervising their students gave them more knowledge that they could bring back to the classroom (Baker & Gurel, 2003).

The VA's psychology training program was evaluated in 1956 to determine whether the program had met its goals and whether it should be continued. The physician panel conducting the evaluation not only reported that the program was highly successful (80% of the psychology trainees went to work for the VA after their training), but it also further recommended that the program be continued to keep pace with veterans' growing need for psychological services (Baker & Pickren, 2007).

The finding of the panel that large numbers of trainees were being employed by the VA after their training was especially noteworthy in view of the absence of a payback service requirement. This finding was sustained in a 20-year review of the training program that showed that 72% of the clinical and counseling psychologists on staff had been VA trained (Ash, 1968a).

ACCREDITATION OF INTERNSHIP TRAINING

Beginning in the 1960s, several changes occurred in the VA psychology training program that would alter its eventual mission (Moore, 1992). In 1963, psychology trainees were converted to a stipend appointment to replace their part-time employment status. Legislation in 1966 gave the VA a mandate to train health care manpower for the entire nation in addition to meeting its own staffing needs, and the retention of trainees for VA employment assumed a lesser importance in defining the success of training programs. In 1970, a full-time psychology internship appointment was officially defined as a minimum of 1,900 hr. Finally, a 1973 reorganization in the VA moved the funding and oversight of all training programs from the professional disciplines to a centralized Office of Academic Affairs. In that reorganization, the selection of students for training programs was removed from the universities and given to each medical center on the basis of centrally funded positions assigned or funded for each profession's training program in the VA medical center.

The new centralized office for VA training also began making shifts in priorities for funding. In psychology, support for internship-level training was given the highest priority. With the national budget problems in the late

1970s, proposals to eliminate funding for psychology practicum training emerged. Although these proposals were reversed as the result of advocacy by APA and VA psychology leaders, the VA's psychology training program soon became primarily focused on internship training. Of special significance was a new funding that favored training programs that had national accreditation status, which for psychology meant APA approval of the psychology training program at the medical center. The incentive to achieve accreditation had now been given a new level of urgency (Moore, 1992).

In 1974, the psychology internship training program at the VA medical center at Topeka received APA accreditation, the first in the VA. By fall 1977, 13 VA medical centers had received accreditation (Moore, 1992). Two years later, that number had doubled.

In 1982, the VA added an APA-approved internship to the requirement of an APA-approved doctoral degree as a condition for employment, along with receiving licensure within 2 years of appointment. The new employment condition for accredited internships further stimulated applications for accreditation, and by 1985, 84 VA internship training programs had received APA accreditation (Moore, 1992).

Training psychologists for the special treatment needs of veterans began in 1984 with 25 internship positions funded for geriatric-focused predoctoral training for which VA medical centers could compete. These were followed by competition for new internship positions to promote psychology training in primary care. By 1991, the VA was funding 348 predoctoral, accredited psychology training positions. More than one third of all APA-approved training programs were now located in the VA (Baker & Pickren, 2007).

POSTDOCTORAL TRAINING IN THE VA

The VA recognized the importance of postdoctoral training for psychologists to meet the specialized treatment needs of veterans as early as the 1980s. The psychology training program at the VA medical center in Palo Alto received a National Institute of Mental Health (NIMH) postdoctoral training grant in geriatric mental health in 1983 (Moore, 1983). The following year, the VA psychology training program at Knoxville, Iowa, received similar NIMH postdoctoral funding.

Although the VA's Office of Academic Affairs was initially opposed to funding postdoctoral training for psychologists, arguments by VA psychology leaders led to a reversal of that position. For the 1991–1992 training year, the VA medical centers in Dallas and Seattle were each funded for one psychology postdoctoral training position in substance abuse. Competition for six postdoctoral positions in geriatrics was held for the following training year. Other postdoctoral training positions were subsequently funded in posttraumatic stress disorder, palliative care, and psychosocial rehabilitation (Baker & Pickren, 2007).

A problem with the funding of postdoctoral positions in the VA was the policy of the Office of Academic Affairs that such positions would be awarded only where the training program had received national accreditation status. The first VA-funded postdoctoral training positions were allowed with the understanding that APA would soon establish that accreditation. VA psychology leaders began pushing APA to move more quickly on developing its postdoctoral accreditation program (Baker & Pickren, 2007).

With the establishment of APA postdoctoral accreditation, the postdoctoral psychology training program at the VA medical center in San Antonio was the first to receive accreditation in 1999 (Baker & Pickren, 2007). It was only the third training program in the country to receive the new accreditation status.

Through 2004, the VA had funded more than 300 postdoctoral training positions. For the 2004–2005 training year, the VA funded 359 predoctoral internship training positions and 73 postdoctoral positions (Baker & Pickren, 2007). On the APA accreditation website (American Psychological Association, Office of Program Consultation and Accreditation, 2005), the following year, almost half of the listed accredited psychology postdoctoral training programs were in the VA.

IMPACT OF VA PSYCHOLOGY AND TRAINING

The impact of VA psychology on developing training standards for the profession has been augmented by the large numbers of clinical and counseling psychologists who received at least part of their professional training in the VA. From 1946 through 2005, the VA funded almost 36,000 psychology training positions (Baker & Pickren, 2007). By comparison, NIMH had funded 32,727 clinical psychology training appointments from 1948 through 1986, when it discontinued funding of psychology and other mental health disciplines (Schneider, 2005).

Recent data provided by the VA Office of Academic Affiliations indicated that the role of the VA in training and hiring psychologists has significantly increased since 2005, adding another 2,000 funded training positions through the 2008–2009 training year. The 16% increase in funded pre- and postdoctoral training positions from 1980 through 2005 (374 to 432) rose to 48% from 2005 through 2009 (432 to 641). The number of psychologists hired in the VA who received VA training support has also remained high. In the 2-year period beginning June 1, 2005, 680 psychologists had been hired by the VA, with 74% receiving either or both VA pre- or postdoctoral training (R. A. Zeiss, personal communication, July 30, 2008).

The early use of psychotherapy and other treatment services by VA psychology and its trainees grew substantially over the first 40 years and established psychotherapy as a primary activity for the profession. The very first reports detailing the time that psychologists spent in their work indicated that the majority of their time was spent in diagnostic activities. At the end of the 1st decade, however, psychotherapy and treatment services equaled the time spent in assessment. By 1986, doctoral-level psychologists in the VA were spending more than three times the hours in direct patient care in individual, family, and group therapy as they were in all types of instrument-based assessment, including neuropsychology assessments. That figure was two and a half for psychology interns (Baker, Barrett, & Klauck, 1986).

CONCLUSIONS

The clinical psychology training begun by the VA in 1946 has had an enduring impact on the field of mental health, both in training and in research. The modernization of clinical psychology by the VA was, as we pointed out in this chapter, critical for serving VA needs while also meeting the needs of the larger society. The program, along with the massive funding of psychology research and training by the NIMH, was inspired by an ethos of government responsibility to its citizens (Pickren & Schneider, 2005). The era initiated by the administration of Franklin Delano Roosevelt of government intervention and support for mental and physical health was informed by a belief that government should play a pivotal role in the health of its citizenry. The history of the training of clinical psychologists after World War II is part of this larger history of changes in health care that dramatically changed several professions, including psychology (Capshew, 1999; Herman, 1995; Pickren & Schneider, 2005).

REFERENCES

American Psychiatric Association. (1980). *Diagnostic and statistical manual of mental disorders* (3rd ed.). Washington, DC: Author.
American Psychological Association. (1949). Doctoral training programs in clinical psychology. *American Psychologist, 4,* 331–341. doi:10.1037/h0057831

American Psychological Association, Office of Program Consultation and Accreditation. (2005). *Accredited postdoctoral residency training programs.* Retrieved from http://www.apa.org/ed/accreditation/intern.html

Ash, E. (1968a). Issues faced by the VA psychology training program in its early development. *Clinical Psychologist, 21,* 121–123.

Ash, E. (1968b). The Veterans Administration psychology training program. *Clinical Psychologist, 21,* 67–69.

Baker, R. R., Barrett, J., & Klauck, K. (1986, August). *Productivity standards for psychology staffing in treatment institutions.* Paper presented at the 94th Annual Convention of the American Psychological Association, Washington, DC.

Baker, R. R., & Gurel, L. (2003, August). The VA affiliation contribution to the development of clinical psychology. In W. E. Pickren (Chair), *Growth stimulus: Federal funding of American psychology after World War II.* Symposium conducted at the meeting of the American Psychological Association, Toronto, Ontario, Canada.

Baker, R. R., & Pickren, W. E. (2007). *Psychology and the Department of Veterans Affairs: A historical analysis of training, research, practice, and advocacy.* Washington, DC: American Psychological Association. doi:10.1037/11544-000

Capshew, J. H. (1999). *Psychologists on the march: Science, practice, and professional identity in America, 1929-1969.* New York, NY: Cambridge University Press.

Farreras, I. G. (2005). The historical context for National Institute of Mental Health support of American Psychological Association training and accreditation efforts. In W. E. Pickren & S. F. Schneider (Eds.), *Psychology and the National Institute of Mental Health: A historical analysis of science, practice, and policy* (pp. 153–179). Washington, DC: American Psychological Association. doi:10.1037/10931-005

Herman, E. (1995). *The romance of American psychology: Political culture in the age of experts.* Berkeley: University of California Press.

Kelly, E. L., & Fiske, D. W. (1951). *The prediction of performance in clinical psychology.* Ann Arbor: University of Michigan Press.

Luchins, A. S., Aumack, L., & Dickman, H. R. (1960). *Manual of group therapy.* Roseburg, OR: Veterans Administration Hospital.

Miller, J. G. (1946). Clinical psychology in the Veterans Administration. *American Psychologist, 1,* 181–189. doi:10.1037/h0055143

Miller, J. G. (1947, December). [Letter to Chairman of Departments of Psychology in cooperating universities with clinical psychology training programs in the Veterans Administration]. Archives of the History of American Psychology (David Shakow collection, Box M1325, folder labeled Miller, James G.). University of Akron.

Moore, D. L. (1983, July). Psychology training program. *Newsletter for the Association of VA Chief Psychologists, 6,* 23.

Moore, D. L. (1992). The Veterans Administration and the training program in psychology. In D. K. Freedheim (Ed.), *History of psychotherapy* (pp. 776–800). Washington, DC: American Psychological Association. doi:10.1037/10110-023

Pickren, W. E., & Schneider, S. F. (Eds.). (2005). *Psychology and the National Institute of Mental Health: A historical analysis of science, practice, and policy.* Washington, DC: American Psychological Association. doi:10.1037/10931-000

Raimy, V. C. (Ed.). (1950). *Training in clinical psychology.* New York: Prentice-Hall.

Schneider, S. F. (2005). Reflections on psychology and the National Institute of Mental Health. In W. E. Pickren & S. F. Schneider (Eds.), *Psychology and the National Institute of Mental Health: A historical analysis of science, practice, and policy* (pp. 17–28). Washington, DC: American Psychological Association. doi:10.1037/10931-001

Sears, R. R. (1946). Graduate training facilities: I. General information; II. Clinical psychology. *American Psychologist, 1*, 135–150. doi:10.1037/h0058566

Sears, R. R. (1947). Clinical training facilities: 1947. *American Psychologist, 2*, 199–205. doi:10.1037/h0061605

Veterans Administration. (1955). *Department of Medicine and Surgery Program Guide for Psychiatric and Neurology Service, G-2, M-2, Part X, May 1955*. Washington, DC: Author.

Veterans Administration. (1967). *Medical care of veterans*. Washington, DC: U.S. Government Printing Office.

Waldrop, R. S. (2007). The beginning of counseling psychology in VA hospitals. In R. R. Baker (Ed.), *Stories from VA psychology* (pp. 127–133). Bloomington, IN: AuthorHouse.

Medical Schools and Academic Health Centers

Danny Wedding

Thousands of clinical and counseling psychologists have been trained in medical schools and other academic health centers, such as dental schools, schools of public health, and other health professional schools. Many thousands more psychologists currently teach or have taught in these schools. Training typically occurs at the internship or postdoctoral level, although some clinical psychology graduate programs (e.g., University of Florida, University of Missouri) are embedded within academic health centers rather than the more traditional schools of arts and sciences.

Psychotherapy is a formal part of the training of psychologists in all of these programs. However, psychotherapy training is also provided for social workers, psychiatric residents, pastoral counselors, and other health professionals; the training may sometimes be concurrent but is most often discipline specific and offered separately. Training in an academic health center offers students the opportunity to see a wider range of psychopathology than can be observed in, say, a university counseling center, and a large teaching hospital provides an unparalleled opportunity to interact with—and learn from—other health professionals. It is also a setting that maximizes student learning about the interaction of physical and mental disorders, the extent to which psychological factors affect the development and maintenance of medical conditions, and the ways in which a variety of diseases produce psychological symptoms. These factors may account for the fact that medical schools represent the settings in which the largest number of predoctoral interns and postdoctoral fellows apply for internship training.

There are 130 U.S. medical schools and 17 Canadian medical schools accredited by the Association of American Medical Colleges; all of these schools offer the doctor of medicine degree. In addition, there are 25 accredited colleges of osteopathic medicine in the United States that offer the doctor of osteopathic medicine degree. Psychologists tend to be better represented in allopathic (doctor of medicine) than in osteopathic (doctor of osteopathic medicine) medical schools. There are also a large number of medical schools in the Caribbean and in the Philippines; English is the language of instruction in most of these schools. Almost all of these schools have psychologists serving on the faculty, and teaching psychotherapy is typically one of their core duties. Convincing medical students that psychology and the behavioral sciences are germane to the practice of medicine is one of the challenges facing every psychologist working in such a setting (Carr, Emory, Errichetti, Johnson, & Reyes, 2007; Wedding, 2008).

In this chapter, I trace the history of psychotherapy education and training in medical schools and other academic health centers. Specifically, I review the organizational history of psychology and psychiatry in U.S. and Canadian medical schools and then point to several probable trends that will affect the future of all psychologists teaching, conducting research, or providing clinical services in academic health centers.

A BRIEF HISTORY

It was necessary for psychiatry to become recognized as a medical specialty before psychology could establish its presence in U.S. medical schools; however, this recognition was not immediately forthcoming, and psychiatry was not fully recognized as a legitimate branch of medicine until the second half of the 20th century. A respected medical historian (William Rothstein, 1987) noted,

> In 1932, a survey of 66 medical schools in the U.S. and 2 in Canada found that only 21 of them had departments of psychiatry and 15 had departments in which psychiatry was joined with neurology. In the remaining 32 schools, psychiatry was taught in the department of medicine. Teachers of psychiatry generally were part-time, poorly trained, and . . . "uninterested in improving their teaching." (p. 154)

A few teaching hospitals had set up teaching clinics for training in psychiatry, but medical schools in the first half of the 20th century were seldom connected with the large asylums in which most psychiatric care for people with serious mental illness was delivered. Many of the patients in these institutions suffered from undiagnosed neurological disorders.

Psychiatry and neurology have always been closely linked; even today, one third of the questions on the examination psychiatrists take to become board certified are drawn from neurology, and one third of the questions on the examination neurologists take to become board certified are taken from psychiatry. In general, psychiatry addresses diseases in which the etiology and pathogenesis are not well understood, whereas neurology addresses problems for which the underlying mechanisms—if not the causes—are well established (e.g., the amyloid plaques and neurofibrillary tangles associated with Alzheimer's disease). The obvious overlap between a specialty that focuses on the central nervous system and one that focuses on the mind has led some medical school deans to once again combine the two departments.

During the second half of the 20th century, psychiatry came to be recognized as a legitimate medical specialty, and the Association of American Medical Colleges Licensing Committee on Medical Education now requires training in psychiatry as a formal part of the education of medical students for every accredited medical school. The growing recognition of psychiatry as a medical specialty and enhanced appreciation for the importance of behavior to the practice of medicine paved the way for psychology to establish a toe-hold in medical schools.

The history of psychotherapy in medical schools is intimately related to the history of psychology in medical schools, and this history is chronicled in the evolution of the Association of Psychologists in Academic Health Centers. This organization began in 1982 as the Association of Medical School Professors of Psychology; the name was later changed to the Association of Medical School Psychologists (AMSP). The most recent name change to the Association of Psychologists in Academic Health Centers was a deliberate attempt to acknowledge the important contributions made by psychologists working in medical settings other than medical schools per se. In a recent history of the organization, Silver, Carr, and Leventhal (2005) noted,

> Prior to 1982, there had been several unsuccessful efforts to form an association that would represent psychologists in academic medical centers. Attempts by psychiatry to limit the growing number and influence of psychologists in medical schools created a sense of threat among psychologists that catalyzed the formation of the Association. Membership was initially restricted to one senior psychologist from each medical school, a restriction that limited AMSP's development, but AMSP later opened its doors to all academic medical center psychologists. The Association was rebuffed in initial efforts to join the Association of American Medical Colleges, and at a later date, to become a Division of the American Psychological Association (APA). In time, however, AMSP did establish formal ties to both of those organizations, and it has collaborated with APA in important surveys of academic medical center psychologists. (p. 235)

A dramatic 10-fold growth occurred in the number of psychologists in medical schools between 1953 and 1976 (Lubin et al., 1979); this period roughly coincides with the change in the role of psychologists after World War II from psychometricians to psychotherapists (Benjamin, 2005). Fifteen years later, Matarazzo (1994) estimated that there were approximately 3,500 psychologists on medical school faculties. Since 1994, the number of psychologists teaching, conducting research, and providing psychotherapy and assessment services in U.S. and Canadian medical schools has continued to grow. In 1998, approximately 5,000 psychologists were working in 125 U.S. medical schools, and it is likely that this number is now even larger (Williams, Wicherski, & Kohout, 1998). Although it is difficult to quantify precisely because of the variegated roles of psychologists in academic health centers and the increasing tendency of psychologists to adopt other professional labels (e.g., *neuroscientist*), it appears that psychologists represent approximately 3% of all medical school faculty (Hong & Leventhal, 2004).

After teaching at Washington University and Harvard, Joseph D. Matarazzo established an autonomous department of psychology in 1957 at the Oregon Health and Science University that thrived for 40 years. This program served as a model for all of the other independent psychology programs in U.S. and Canadian medical schools (Matarazzo, 1994); regrettably, in 1997, it was absorbed into a behavioral neuroscience department, and its unique identity was lost.

As in other academic settings, the number of female psychologists in academic health centers has burgeoned. In the mid-1970s, women made up 23% of medical school psychologists, which was comparable to their representation within the APA at that time (Zimet, 1979). Today, approximately 43% of medical school psychologists are women (Pate & Kohout, 2005); these findings are comparable to an earlier survey that documented that in the mid-1990s 41% of medical psychologists were women (Williams & Wedding, 1999). Pediatrics is the only medical school department in which female psychologists outnumber male psychologists, and, perhaps predictably, salaries in pediatrics are lower than in other medical specialties; however, even in pediatrics, male psychologists earned more than female psychologists (Williams, Wedding, & Kohout, 2000).

Many but not all psychologists in medical schools will teach and supervise psychotherapy conducted by medical students, residents, and students from other disciplines as well as the work of psychology interns and postdoctoral trainees. In fact, one of the most salient rewards associated with teaching in a medical school is the opportunity to interact with students and faculty from a number of health care disciplines.

A national survey of approximately 3,000 medical school psychologists (Pate & Kohout, 2005) documented that they spent about 40% of their time on research, with about 20% of their time spent on providing clinical services, and 20% of their time devoted to teaching and administration. Teaching psychotherapy would undoubtedly make up part of the training time for most psychologists in these settings. The majority of respondents taught both psychology students and medical students; 44% taught psychiatric residents, and 33% worked with medical or surgical residents. Although most psychologists (54%) worked in psychiatry departments, psychologists also frequently worked in pediatrics, neurology, family and community medicine, and rehabilitation departments. A major change that has occurred over the past 30 years has been the proliferation of psychologists across medical school departments other than psychiatry (Carr & Benjamin, 1997).

Although many psychologists have found departments of psychiatry to be congenial academic homes (e.g., Hong & Leventhal, 2004), many others have felt that the profession is best served when psychology maintains autonomy and independence. Rozensky (2004), for one, argued that it is in the best interest of psychology to ensure that its programs, faculty and staff, clinical services, research enterprises, and training programs are freestanding and not organized within any other department. Without such autonomy, psychology might never reach its full potential as a health care science and profession in academic health care center settings. Rozensky's argument is based on finances, credentialing and privileging, role modeling for psychologist trainees, the importance of psychology's persona within the health science center and in the eyes of the public, and finally, academic freedom (Rozensky, 2004).

The longstanding tension between psychology and psychiatry has recently been exacerbated by the success of psychology in gaining prescriptive authority in the military and in several states. The growing prescriptive movement has threatened psychiatry and has strained the normally congenial relationships between the two disciplines.

Despite the professional tensions between psychiatry and psychology, academic health centers remain an excellent training venue for psychologists, with multiple opportunities for psychotherapy training and with a wide variety of patients who often present with symptoms that reflect the complex interactions between psyche and soma. The number of opportunities to work outside psychiatry departments is increasing, and many medical school psychologists believe primary care departments, and especially departments of family and community medicine, offer especially rewarding training opportunities for those psychologists interested in collaborative care (e.g., Bray, 2004; Wedding & Mengel, 2004). These settings do not typically offer training in long-term psychotherapy; instead, they focus on short-term, problem-focused therapies.

RECENT DEVELOPMENTS

Of the multiple sea changes confronting psychotherapy in academic health centers, three strike me as particularly important in the next decade: the medicalization of psychiatry, the ascendancy of evidence-based treatments, and the future training needs of psychologists in medical school settings.

Medicalization of Psychiatry

One of the changes occurring in psychotherapy is the widely acknowledged abdication of the practice of psychotherapy by psychiatrists. The reduction in the amount of time psychiatrists devote to psychotherapy has resulted from converging forces, including the increasing medicalization of psychiatry and the need to differentiate psychiatry from other mental health disciplines. However, the major reason psychiatry has deemphasized psychotherapy is economic because managed care companies will typically not pay physicians higher rates for psychotherapy services than those rates paid to psychologists and social workers, forcing psychiatrists to focus on medication management to maintain high incomes. Increasingly, patients in academic health settings receive medication management from primary care physicians, and psychologists and social workers provide psychotherapy and counseling services. However, this is not without its costs. For example, Meyer and Sotsky (1995) noted,

> HMOs emphasized the role of the primary care physician and restricted access to specialists, including psychiatrists, through gatekeeping. In the best of these organizations, mental health services were delivered by a team comprising a primary care physician, who could provide medication, and a psychologist or social worker, who could provide psychotherapy. More recently, a growing literature has highlighted the difficulties that primary care physicians face in addressing the needs of mentally ill and addicted patients. Recent health services research has shown that primary care physicians in a general medical setting have a lower rate of recognition of mental and addiction disorders and less clinical effectiveness than do psychiatrists in a mental health setting. Primary care physicians . . . receive virtually no training in office counseling or psychotherapy. Finally, the financial and time disincentives of primary care practice do not readily permit the time-intensive clinical interview process that is essential to the detection and evaluative understanding of mental illness, its course, and its determinants. (p. 66)

Despite the realities of managed care, psychiatric residents do want to learn about psychotherapy, and training in cognitive–behavior therapy is required for psychiatry residency program accreditation; the fact that cognitive–behavior therapy was privileged vis-à-vis other empirically supported treatments may be linked to the fact that its founder, Aaron Beck, is an esteemed psychiatrist.

Bernard Beitman has been a strong proponent of continued high-quality training in psychotherapy for psychiatrists, and he developed a series of modules designed to teach psychotherapy to psychiatry residents in a series of weekly seminars held over the course of a year (Beitman & Yue, 1999a, 1999b). These modules focus on the core principles of integrative psychotherapy and various techniques that are shared by almost all schools of psychotherapy.

Evidence-Based Practices

Although there has been a diminution of emphasis on overall psychotherapy training in psychiatry, medical school departments of psychiatry do appear to be doing a somewhat better job than psychology departments and schools of social work in training in evidence-based practices. A national survey of psychotherapy training was conducted using a "cross-sectional survey of a probability sample of all accredited training programs in psychiatry, psychology, and social work in the United States" (Weissman et al., 2006). The evidence-based therapies were identified as behavior therapy, cognitive–behavior therapy (CBT), dialectical behavior therapy, manual-based family therapy, interpersonal psychotherapy, multisystem systemic therapy, and parent training. All other therapies were identified as lacking sufficient evidence to qualify as evidence-based therapies; these included existential psychotherapy, gestalt therapy, psychoanalytic–psychodynamic psychotherapy, humanistic psychotherapy, and supportive psychotherapy. In general, PhD clinical psychology training directors were more positive about evidence-based practices than were their counterparts in psychiatry programs, PsyD psychology programs, and social work programs. This survey also documented the popularity of CBT, which was offered by more than 90% of programs in the three disciplines studied: psychology, psychiatry, and social work. However, "required clinical supervision in CBT was significantly more likely in psychiatric residency as compared with the other disciplines. More than 80% of the disciplines offered couples therapy, family therapy, and group therapy, but far fewer required them" (p. 926). The high number of psychiatry residencies offering CBT training undoubtedly results from the fact that this training is now required for psychiatry residency accreditation in the United States by the Accreditation Council for Graduate Medical Education (Weissman et al., 2006).

Training for the Future

Belar (2004) speculated on the additional skills needed by psychologists being trained in academic health centers in the future. She wrote,

> There will be more focus on training for competence in patient-centered care, evidence-based care, interdisciplinary teamwork, informatics, and continuous quality improvement. Other trends that will affect training of psychologists and other health disciplines in AHC [academic health center] settings include emphasis on better ways to assess the quality of clinical skills, support for improvement of teaching and training, and an increase in educators' status. (p. 77)

The Collaborative Psychotherapist: Creating Reciprocal Relationships with Medical Professionals (Ruddy, Borresen, & Gunn, 2008) describes in detail how psychologists can develop and profit from collaborative relationships with physician colleagues; these relationships and the skills of psychologists are highly valued in almost all medical schools and academic health centers. The ability to see patients in these settings and provide psychotherapy services is an important part of the psychologist's role in almost all such settings.

Training junior colleagues in skillfully providing psychotherapy remains a crucial component of the professional identity of almost all psychologists working in academic health centers.

REFERENCES

Beitman, B. D., & Yue, D. (1999a). *Learning psychotherapy: A time-efficient, research-based and outcome-measured psychotherapy training program.* New York, NY: Norton.

Beitman, B. D., & Yue, D. (1999b). A new psychotherapy training program: Description and preliminary results. *Academic Psychiatry, 23,* 95–102.

Belar, C. D. (2004). The future of education and training in academic health centers. *Journal of Clinical Psychology in Medical Settings, 11,* 77–82. doi:10.1023/B:JOCS.0000025718. 34590.2b

Benjamin, L. T., Jr. (2005). A history of clinical psychology as a profession in America (and a glimpse at its future). *Annual Review of Clinical Psychology, 1,* 1–30. doi:10.1146/ annurev.clinpsy.1.102803.143758

Bray, J. H. (2004). Training primary care psychologists. *Journal of Clinical Psychology in Medical Settings, 11,* 101–107. doi:10.1023/B:JOCS.0000025721.17763.d7

Carr, J. E., & Benjamin, G. A. H. (1997). Future of psychology in departments of psychiatry. *Journal of Clinical Psychology in Medical Settings, 4,* 143–153. doi:10.1023/ A:1026248524057

Carr, J. E., Emory, E. K., Errichetti, A., Johnson, S. B., & Reyes, E. (2007). Integrating behavioral and social sciences in the medical school curriculum: Opportunities and challenges for psychology. *Journal of Clinical Psychology in Medical Settings, 14,* 33–39. doi:10.1007/ s10880-006-9049-0

Hong, B. A., & Leventhal, G. (2004). Partnerships with psychiatry and other clinical disciplines: A key to psychology's success in U.S. medical schools. *Journal of Clinical Psychology in Medical Settings, 11,* 135–140. doi:10.1023/B:JOCS. 0000025725.81087.21

Lubin, B., Nathan, R. G., Millhan, J., Malmed, M., Nathan, S., Rouce, L., . . . Zimet, C. N. (1979). A symposium on psychologists in schools of medicine in 1977. *Professional Psychology: Research and Practice, 10,* 94–96.

Matarazzo, J. D. (1994). Psychology in a medical school: A personal account of a department's 35-year history. *Journal of Clinical Psychology, 50,* 7–36. doi:10.1002/1097-4679(199401) 50:1<7::AID-JCLP2270500104>3.0.CO;2-6

Meyer, R. E., & Sotsky, S. M. (1995). Managed care and the role and training of psychiatrists. *Health Affairs, 14,* 65–77. doi:10.1377/hlthaff.14.3.65

Pate, W. E., II, & Kohout, J. L. (2005). Results from a national survey of psychologists in medical school settings—2003. *Journal of Clinical Psychology in Medical Settings, 12,* 203–208. doi:10.1007/s10880-005-5739-2

Rothstein, W. G. (1987). *American medical schools and the practice of medicine.* New York, NY: Oxford University Press.

Rozensky, R. H. (2004). Freestanding psychology: The only way in academic health centers. *Journal of Clinical Psychology in Medical Settings, 11,* 127–133. doi:10.1023/B:JOCS. 0000025724.09384.3d

Ruddy, N. B., Borresen, D. A., & Gunn, W. B., Jr. (2008). *The collaborative psychotherapist: Creating reciprocal relationships with medical professionals.* Washington, DC: American Psychological Association. doi:10.1037/11754-000

Silver, R. J., Carr, J. E., & Leventhal, G. (2005). History of the Association of Medical School Psychologists (AMSP), 1982-2005. *Journal of Clinical Psychology in Medical Settings, 12,* 235–245. doi:10.1007/s10880-005-5742-7

Wedding, D. (2008). Innovative methods for making behavioral science relevant to medical education. *Journal of Clinical Psychology in Medical Settings, 15,* 89–91. doi:10.1007/s10880-008-9107-x

Wedding, D., & Mengel, M. (2004). Models of integrated care in primary care settings. In L. J. Haas (Ed.), *Handbook of primary care psychology* (pp. 47–60). New York, NY: Oxford University Press.

Weissman, M. M., Verdeli, H., Gameroff, M. J., Bledsoe, S. E., Betts, K., Mufson, L., . . . Wickramaratne, P. (2006). National survey of psychotherapy training in psychiatry, psychology, and social work. *Archives of General Psychiatry, 63,* 925–934. doi:10.1001/archpsyc.63.8.925

Williams, S., & Wedding, D. (1999). Employment characteristics and salaries of psychologists in United States medical schools: Past and current trends. *Journal of Clinical Psychology in Medical Settings, 6,* 221–238. doi:10.1023/A:1026252429003

Williams, S., Wedding, D., & Kohout, J. L. (2000). Gender differences in employment and salaries of psychologists within medical school settings. *Journal of Clinical Psychology in Medical Settings, 7,* 149–157. doi:10.1023/A:1009551828123

Williams, S., Wicherski, M., & Kohout, J. (1998). *1997 employment characteristics and salaries of medical school psychologists* (APA Research Office Technical Reports). Washington, DC: American Psychological Association.

Zimet, C. N. (1979). Psychologists in schools of medicine in 1977: An overview. *Professional Psychology, 10,* 115–117. doi:10.1037/0735-7028.10.1.115

Training Audiotapes and Videotapes

John C. Norcross and Gary R. VandenBos

Just as there is no better teacher of surgery than watching an operation in progress, there is no better teacher of psychotherapy than observing a session in progress. Unfortunately, because of technological limitations and confidentiality concerns, psychotherapy training historically avoided demonstrations of how psychotherapy is practiced. Instead, psychotherapy teachers traditionally relied on lectures and readings to convey the complex interpersonal process known as psychotherapy. Academic training in psychotherapy was often just that: academic—long on exposition and theory, short on demonstration and practice.

For the first 60 or so years in modern psychotherapy, clinicians and trainees relied on their recollections or re-creations of the therapy hour in clinical supervision, case presentations, and training workshops. Some would record intensive process notes during the hour or so immediately after the end of the session (Goldberg, 1985). Audiotaping, filming, and videotaping were either not available or not desirable. For generations, this created a rather remarkable situation in training psychotherapists. Can you imagine surgeons, musicians, or teachers not observing the very skills they are expected to acquire?

Beginning in the 1940s with the advent of mobile recording technology, select psychotherapists began to audiotape their sessions for the purpose of training, supervision, and research. Then, in the 1960s, psychotherapy sessions began to be filmed or videotaped, often at considerable expense. The "Gloria" films produced by Shostrom and the multiple family therapy videotapes of conjoint sessions stand out as exemplars. Beginning in the 1970s and 1980s, the advent of small and inexpensive videotaping equipment engendered widespread taping of sessions for supervision and training purposes. The 1990s brought several extensive videotape series for clinical education, such as the APA Psychotherapy Videotape Series, now featuring more than 100 demonstration tapes.

In this chapter, we trace the development of audiotapes and videotapes for psychotherapy training over 5 decades and several technological iterations. Individual sessions conducted by psychotherapists in training are now routinely videotaped for the purpose of clinical supervision, but these do not occupy us here. Nor do tape series featuring lectures or discussions by famous clinicians. Rather, our focus is on those publicly available and commercially produced videotapes used for teaching and training purposes.

EARLY AUDIOTAPE STIRRINGS: 1940s–1960s

The inner sanctum of psychoanalysis and psychotherapy was considered inviolate, but Carl Rogers's tape recorder breached it in the early 1940s. He and his research team began using large reel-to-reel machines to record client-centered therapy sessions. Rogers's 1942 article, "The Use of Electrically Recorded Interviews in Improving Psychotherapeutic Techniques," summarized one of the earliest systematic uses of audiotaping for research and education.

Another research pioneer, Hans Strupp, recorded therapists' responses to an experimental film of an initial patient interview. Strupp collected data from psychologists, psychiatrists, and social workers in four cities. About a dozen psychoanalysts at the Chicago Institute of Psychoanalysis complied with the experimental task of providing responses to the film segments. "However, several showed overt anger, and one or two wrote letters documenting their displeasure at what they regarded as a highly artificial and meaningless assignment" (Strupp, 1991, p. 304).

Strupp's audacity to study what psychoanalysts and psychotherapists actually "do" foreshadowed three trends that characterize the history of audio- and videotaping psychotherapy. First, many practitioners equate recording as invading the privacy of their consulting rooms. Second, critics frequently complain that any recording contaminates or taints the therapy experience, rendering the tapes artificial and experience-distant. Third, most of the early recording began as research studies and only then indirectly translated into training.

The resistance to recording psychotherapy did not dissuade everyone from collecting and sharing audiotapes of sessions. The American Academy of Psychotherapists (http://www.aapweb.com) began compiling in the early 1960s an extensive audiotape collection of a variety of therapy styles and theoretical orientations. About 100 audiocassettes of actual sessions were available for purchase for teaching and supervision (A. Mahrer, personal communication, July 9, 2009).

EARLY PSYCHOTHERAPY FILMS: 1960s–1980s

Starting in the mid-1960s, Everett Shostrom produced a series of groundbreaking films featuring prominent psychotherapists conducting a session with the same patient. The first and inarguably most famous films in the annals of psychotherapy were the "Gloria" films, named after a patient seen by Carl Rogers, Frederick Perls, and Albert Ellis on the same day. Formally titled *Three Approaches to Psychotherapy*, each 16-mm film portrayed introductory comments by the therapist, a session with Gloria, and then the therapist's impressions of that session immediately afterward. That format continues in most psychotherapy videorecordings to this day.

Several researchers conducted statistical analyses of the psychotherapy sessions conducted by Rogers, Perls, and Ellis with Gloria (e.g., Hill, Thames, & Rardin, 1979; LaCrosse & Barak, 1976; Zimmer & Cowles, 1972). The findings were consistent with theoretical prescriptions and, more important, helped viewers to track the therapist behaviors and learn specific skills. Carl Rogers used mainly encouragers, reflections, and questions; he offered no direct guidance and little in the way of confrontation. Fritz Perls relied mainly on direct guidance and interpretation; he was by far the highest of the three on nonverbal referents and confrontations. Albert Ellis provided mainly information and direct guidance; he was extremely talkative in comparison with Perls and Rogers.

Shostrom produced several subsequent film series: *Three Approaches to Psychotherapy II* in 1978 featured Carl Rogers, Everett Shostrom, and Arnold Lazarus interviewing Kathy, and *Three Approaches to Psychotherapy III* in 1986 showed Hans Strupp, Donald Meichenbaum, and Aaron Beck describing their therapy method and interviewing Richard. Shostrom also launched *Three Approaches to Group Therapy*, showing, within a 1-day period, three therapists work with a newly formed psychotherapy group.

In 1969, leading family therapists Nathan Ackerman, Carl Whitaker, Don Jackson, and Murray Bowen interviewed the same family, the Hillcrest family (a pseudonym), who sought help because of problems with their children. Content analysis of those interviews with the Hillcrest family revealed both convergence and divergence (Friedlander, Highlen, & Lassiter, 1985). In all four demonstrations, the parents were the most active participants, the therapists focused on the parental subsystem, and they used relatively few silences and empathetic restatements. Instead, these family therapists were quite active and directive. Two major differences involved Bowen's emphasis on the past in contrast to the others' focus on present interactions and Whitaker's use of more indirect messages and self-revealing responses. Both the films and the subsequent process research performed on them served educational purposes for decades.

Family therapists led the charge in making and disseminating video recordings of their psychotherapy sessions. In a classic consultation titled *Taming Monsters*, Salvador Minuchin joined the family of an "uncontrollable" 5-year-old girl. He reframed the problem, staged enactments, used play, and challenged the family's rules for interaction and perception of reality. In this context, "taming monsters" had a double meaning: controlling the monster of a child and the monster of the mother (she "feels like a monster" when disciplining children).

PSYCHOTHERAPY VIDEOTAPES COME OF AGE: 1990s–2000s

By the 1990s, the technological feasibility, economic possibility, and professional acceptability of videotaping sessions had all improved to the point to which literally hundreds of recorded sessions became commercially available. Chief among the offerings were, in alphabetical order:

- *Brief Therapy for Addictions* video series (seven videotapes; Allyn & Bacon/Pearson);
- *Brief Therapy Inside Out* video series (14 videotapes; Zeig, Tucker & Co.);
- *Child Therapy With the Experts* video series (12 videotapes; Allyn & Bacon/Pearson);
- *Family Therapy With the Experts* video series (13 videotapes; Allyn & Bacon/Pearson);
- *Living Love Video Series* (seven videos of couples therapy; Zeig, Tucker, & Thiesen)
- *Master Therapists Workshop Series* (approximately 75 videotapes, The Master Therapists); and
- *Psychotherapy With the Experts* (12 videotapes, Allyn & Bacon/Pearson).

Professional associations began slowly entering the videotape market as well. For example, starting in 1994, the Association for Advancement of Behavior Therapy, now the Association of Behavioral and Cognitive Therapies (http://www.abct.org/dHome/), has produced approximately 26 videotaped "archive" interviews with founders of behavior therapy and 20-plus videotaped clinical demonstrations of cognitive and behavior therapies. For another example, the American Association for Marriage and Family Therapy (http://www.aamft.org/) offers approximately 40 live, unedited conjoint therapy sessions recorded at its conferences over the years.

Teaching programs began routinely using psychotherapy videotapes and films in conjunction with written materials and role plays. Research has generally demonstrated that watching videotapes produced improvements in learning specific therapy skills (e.g., Maguire et al., 1984) and even entire psychotherapy systems (e.g., Hilsenroth, Defife, Blagys, & Ackerman, 2006). Scholarly journals, such as the *International Journal of Group Psychotherapy* in 1996 and *Contemporary Psychology* in 2005, began to review videotape resources. And treatment researchers across the theoretical spectrum consistently encouraged videotape use for teaching and supervision (e.g., Anderson, Rigazio-DiGilio, & Kunkler, 1995; Levenson & Strupp, 1999).

In recommending that videotapes be used in training programs to illustrate the conduct of empirically supported therapies, one set of researchers concluded that videotapes are probably the most efficiently effective elements of the initial phase of any training program, in terms of the amount of information conveyed per unit of training time and number of trainee questions answered about conducting the empirically supported therapies. Viewing videotapes answers many questions that trainees do not know they have until they see in vivo implementation of the empirically supported therapies, as well as questions they spontaneously formulate during training sessions. Tapes also answer questions that even the most detail-oriented, conscientious trainer cannot anticipate (Calhoun, Moras, Pilkonis, & Rehm, 1998, p. 156).

APA PSYCHOTHERAPY VIDEOTAPE SERIES

Reflecting and reinforcing the movement toward educating students with actual demonstrations of psychotherapy, the American Psychological Association (APA) initiated a Psychotherapy Videotape Series in 1992–1993. The series codevelopers (Gary VandenBos, Donald Freedheim, and John Norcross) began small with seed money and sponsorship of the APA Division of Psychotherapy. Each demonstration video showed an unrehearsed second or third session of therapy. Ten years later, Jon Carlson began coordinating and hosting the videotapes. The APA series has now blossomed into the largest—more than 100 individual demonstration sessions and more than 25 six-session demonstration sets—and probably most influential psychotherapy videotape series in the world.

The series consists of, in fact, a number of series. In general order of their development, these are *Systems of Psychotherapy* (e.g., psychodynamic, experiential, cognitive, systems, integrative); *Specific Treatments for Specific Populations* (e.g., cognitive therapy for depression, behavior therapy for obsessive–compulsive disorder); *Behavioral Health* (e.g., breast cancer, pain management); *Multicultural Counseling* (e.g., working with African American clients, counseling Latina–Latino clients); *Children and Adolescents* (e.g., parent–child interaction therapy, adolescent girls who are suicidal); *Relationships* (e.g., emotionally focused therapy for couples, working with stepfamilies); *Psychology in the Schools* (e.g., bullying prevention, harm reduction with high school students); and *Spirituality* (e.g., Christian counseling, mindfulness therapy). The most recent series is *Psychotherapy in Six Sessions*—a set of sessions looking at how psychological treatment affects the client over the course of therapy.

Despite its growth and diversification, the APA series remains tied to its original mission of "presenting distinguished psychologists of various orientations demonstrating their particular approach in entire sessions" explicitly "for clinical training and continued education" (VandenBos, Frank-McNeil, Norcross, & Freedheim, 1995, p. vii). Like the human anatomy laid bare, the videotapes expose psychotherapy and its methods for the purpose of education.

A number of features enhance the educational value of the videotapes. First, each videotape is accompanied by a booklet containing the purpose of the series; an autobiographical sketch of the therapist; a synopsis of the therapeutic approach demonstrated; suggested readings; client history, precipitating events; preceding sessions; and discussion questions on choice points during the therapy session. The booklet contains all the information available to the psychotherapist before the taped session so that the viewer and the therapist occupy a level playing field. Second, at the conclusion of the demonstration session and on the videotape itself, the therapist responds to questions from the series editors about the session and the psychotherapy. Third, the original 12 videotapes in *Systems of Psychotherapy* were accompanied by a separate Viewer's Guide (VandenBos et al., 1995); it presents the foregoing information on each of the videotapes plus additional material in an inexpensive spiral-bound format.

Beyond the general goal of enhancing clinical training and continuing education, the APA series was envisioned as addressing more specific objectives as well. These include learning how prominent practitioners carry out their session; concretely illustrating theoretical concepts in psychotherapy; gaining a first-hand look at what ensues in psychotherapy; comparing the technical interventions and relationship stances associated with different systems of psychotherapy; training in specific psychological procedures (e.g., empty-chair technique); providing material for psychotherapy process research; and observing how therapists handle particular critical incidents in treatment, for example, dealing with anger toward the therapist.

The latter objective led to the production of several stimulus training tapes: *Responding Therapeutically to Patient Anger*, *Responding Therapeutically to Patient Expression of Sexual Attraction*, and *Therapist–Client Boundary Challenges*. These tapes present brief vignettes demonstrating several ways of dealing with common critical incidents during psychosocial treatment.

When we began developing the APA Psychotherapy Videotape Series, we initiated numerous discussions and conducted a small survey of fellow clinicians ($N = 28$) on which in-therapy incidents they would most like to observe on videotape for the purposes of training. Clinicians of various disciplines and orientations rated "expresses sexual attraction toward the therapist" as among the most instructive incidents. And no wonder: Explicit training in this area is rare despite the high prevalence of client expression of sexual feelings toward clinicians. In one national study of 600 psychologists, 73% of practitioners were told by a client that he or she was sexually attracted to them (Pope & Tabachnick, 1993). Even higher percentages of practitioners— between 87% and 90%—reported having felt sexually attracted to a client. However, more than one half of psychologists reported no training in this area, and only 9% believed they had received adequate training (Pope et al., 1986).

As a result, students are inadequately prepared for intense and intimate feelings clients may express toward them.

Each of the vignettes in the stimulus training or critical incident tape (APA, 2000), between 3 and 7 minutes in length, shows the content and process of the client's expression of sexual attraction, the therapist's initial responses to that expression, and some ensuing transaction. In demonstrating an assortment of skilled therapist responses to patient expression of sexual attraction, we hoped to

- provide a sample of appropriate therapist behaviors when confronted with sexually provocative material;
- model ethical responses that strengthen the therapeutic alliance and enhance the treatment process;
- stimulate consideration of pertinent ethical and legal guidelines;
- generate discussion of alternative ethical responses to those portrayed in the videotape;
- identify countertransferential feelings and potentially nontherapeutic responses; and
- raise awareness of the importance of therapists monitoring their internal states and promoting self-care.

Instructors and viewers experiment with at least three pedagogical methods. The first is pausing the tape after a particular provocative statement by the client—the "freeze frame" method; for example, in Vignette 2 when Linda declares, "I'm becoming sexually attracted to you" or in Vignette 5 when Scott suggests "to take the relationship outside of this" (American Psychological Association, 2000). Viewers are then prompted for their own spontaneous response to complete the response couplet, which can then be evaluated on its own merits and in comparison with the videotaped response. Second, the tape can be paused following each vignette long enough to consider the interaction and the implication of the therapist's response. Viewers can ask several of the Questions Following Each Vignette presented in the booklet accompanying the videotape or DVD, for example, What feelings and thoughts did the patient's sexual attraction provoke in you? What would have been your immediate, uncensored reply to the client's declaration of sexual feelings toward you? How did the patient in this vignette appear to respond to the therapist's interventions? What were your reactions to the therapist's handling of the situation? What might you have done differently? What are some strengths of the therapist's response in this case? What are some weaknesses? Third, viewers can generate alternative responses to the videotaped interaction with subsequent role-playing to parallel the demonstrated response. The aim is to help therapists to acquire comfortable and confident responses that advance the treatment process.

FUTURE DIRECTIONS: 2010 AND BEYOND

Nowhere is the adage "a picture is worth a thousand words" more applicable than in teaching and learning psychotherapy. However, until quite recently in historical terms, psychotherapists rarely observed seasoned clinicians conducting psychotherapy.

As is often said in psychotherapy research, the time has arrived when we should study not what psychotherapists say they do but what they actually do. In the steady progression of learning psychotherapy through process notes in the 1950s, to audiotapes in the 1970s, to live observation and supervision in the 1980s, the present brings us literally hundreds of widely available recordings of authentic psychotherapy sessions. The historical progression of recording psychotherapy for training purposes is now clearly evident, as summarized here:

- audiotapes to films to videotapes to DVDs;
- use of composite patients or actors to real, undisguised clients;
- stand-alone therapy tapes to coordinated multimedia products;
- global psychotherapy systems to specific psychotherapies for particular problems and populations;
- primarily White male therapists to multiculturally diverse therapists;
- classic mental health disorders to a broad array of relational, addictive, health, and spiritual problems; and
- single sessions to multiple sessions over time.

We predict that, in the future, recordings of the sustained, detailed work of psychotherapy will increasingly be required for clinical training. Indeed, we cannot imagine teaching a systems of psychotherapy course or a particular treatment method without showing an exemplary video or DVD of it. Those recordings will become more interactive, requiring trainee responses and role-plays.

We also anticipate that critical incident or stimulus training tapes will become increasingly popular in education. Students will attempt not to observe and master an entire therapy system but to learn specific, evidence-based skills, such as handling silences, providing feedback, and negotiating termination. In the *Responding Therapeutically to Patient Expression of Sexual Attraction* videotape (APA, 2000), for example, we observed that the six featured psychologists—and others we have watched—handled the critical incident in common, if not consensual, ways. The therapists encouraged the expression, normalized the sexual feelings as common, stated that acting on those feelings was impossible and contrary to the patient's and the treatment's best interest, and reiterated the specialness and safety of the therapeutic relationship. Significantly, the psychotherapists also behaved similarly in how they did not respond. None of the therapists belittled or criticized the patient for vocalizing sexual feelings; none ignored or avoided the attraction— although they may have been tempted to avoid their discomfort; none shamed, blamed, or rejected the client. These are the skills that videos can convincingly demonstrate and teach.

In the not-too-distant future, too, we predict that virtual reality technology will seamlessly integrate itself into the training enterprise. Simulated patients will appear before trainees' very eyes (e.g., Beutler & Harwood, 2004). In this way, like the human anatomy laid bare, videotapes will continually and masterfully expose psychotherapy and its methods for the purpose of education.

REFERENCES

American Psychological Association. (Producer). (2000). *Responding therapeutically to patient expression of sexual attraction* [DVD]. Available from http://www.apa.org/videos/

Anderson, S. A., Rigazio-DiGilio, S. A., & Kunkler, K. P. (1995). Training and supervision in family therapy: Current issues and future directions. *Family Relations, 44*, 489–500. doi:10.2307/585003

Beutler, L. E., & Harwood, T. M. (2004). Virtual reality in psychotherapy training. *Journal of Clinical Psychology, 60*, 317–330. doi:10.1002/jclp.10266

Calhoun, K. S., Moras, K., Pilkonis, P. A., & Rehm, L. P. (1998). Empirically supported treatments: Implications for training. *Journal of Consulting and Clinical Psychology, 66*, 151–162. doi:10.1037/0022-006X.66.1.151

Friedlander, M. L., Highlen, P. S., & Lassiter, W. L. (1985). Content analytic comparison of four expert counselors' approaches to family treatment: Ackerman, Bowen, Jackson, and Whitaker. *Journal of Counseling Psychology, 32*, 171–180. doi:10.1037/0022-0167.32.2.171

Goldberg, D. A. (1985). Process notes, audio, and videotape: Modes of presentation in psychotherapy training. *Clinical Supervisor, 3*, 3–13. doi:10.1300/J001v03n03_02

Hill, C. E., Thames, T. B., & Rardin, D. K. (1979). Comparison of Rogers, Perls, and Ellis on the Hill Counselor Verbal Response Category System. *Journal of Counseling Psychology, 26*, 198–203. doi:10.1037/0022-0167.26.3.198

Hilsenroth, M. J., Defife, J. A., Blagys, M. D., & Ackerman, S. J. (2006). Effects of training in short-term psychodynamic psychotherapy: Change in graduate clinician technique. *Psychotherapy Research, 16*, 293–305. doi:10.1080/10503300500264887

LaCrosse, M., & Barak, A. (1976). Differential perception of counselor behavior. *Journal of Counseling Psychology, 23*, 170–172. doi:10.1037/0022-0167.23.2.170

Levenson, H., & Strupp, H. H. (1999). Recommendations for the future of training brief dynamic psychotherapy. *Journal of Clinical Psychology, 55*, 385–391. doi:10.1002/(SICI)1097-4679(199904)55:4<385::AID-JCLP2>3.0.CO;2-B

Maguire, G. P., Goldberg, D. P., Hobson, R. F., Margison, F., Moss, S., & O'Dowd, T. (1984). Evaluating the teaching of a method of psychotherapy. *British Journal of Psychiatry, 144*, 575–580. doi:10.1192/bjp.144.6.575

Pope, K. S., Keith-Spiegel, P., & Tabachnick, B. G. (1986). Sexual attraction to clients: The human therapist and the (sometimes) inhuman training system. *American Psychologist, 41*, 147–158. doi:10.1037/0003-066X.41.2.147

Pope, K. S., & Tabachnick, B. G. (1993). Therapists' anger, hate, fear, and sexual feelings: National survey of therapist responses, client characteristics, critical events, formal complaints, and training. *Professional Psychology: Research and Practice, 24,* 142–152. doi:10.1037/0735-7028.24.2.142

Rogers, C. R. (1942). The use of electrically recorded interviews in improving psychotherapeutic techniques. *American Journal of Orthopsychiatry, 12,* 429–435.

Strupp, H. H. (1991). Reflections on my career in clinical psychology. In C. E. Walker (Ed.), *The history of clinical psychology in autobiography* (pp. 293–329). Pacific Grove, CA: Brooks/Cole.

VandenBos, G. R., Frank-McNeil, J., Norcross, J. C., & Freedheim, D. K. (1995). *The anatomy of psychotherapy: Viewer's guide to the APA Psychotherapy Videotape Series.* Washington, DC: American Psychological Association.

Zimmer, J. M., & Cowles, K. H. (1972). Content analyses using FORTRAN: Applied to interviews. *Journal of Counseling Psychology, 19,* 161–166. doi:10.1037/h0032429

17

PSYCHOTHERAPY SUPERVISION

ALLEN K. HESS

The story of psychotherapy supervision wends its way back into the mists of time. Supervision books typically begin with a chapter on contemporary theories of supervision, not the history of supervision. Perhaps Ebbinghaus's dictum about psychology having a long past but short history captures the nature of supervision. As the major systems are reviewed in this chapter, the reader will easily see that Lightner Witmer, Sigmund Freud, John Watson, and Carl Rogers were supervising students in their systems. Yet, it was not until the 1980s that supervision as a field was recognized—indeed a long past but a short history. Thus, the prescient editors mark the maturing of clinical supervision and the need to represent it in this volume, a field in its infancy when the first edition of this volume was composed.

The first half of this chapter recounts the teaching and learning of psychotherapy at the beginning of psychology and within the three major systems of psychotherapy. The second part is devoted to the history of supervision as a specialty itself, the theories of supervision, and the status of its research, concluding with a consideration of key issues confronting psychotherapy supervision.

SUPERVISION'S PAST: WITMER AND THREE PSYCHOTHERAPY SYSTEMS

Lightner Witmer

With his master's degree completed under J. McKeen Cattell, Lightner Witmer completed his doctoral studies with Wilhelm Wundt, accumulating impeccable credentials from two of the founders of psychology. Lightner Witmer saw his first case in 1896, established the world's first psychology clinic, coined the term *clinical psychology*, founded a journal, and "establish[ed] the first training program in clinical psychology, with the understanding from the beginning that its practitioners should have doctoral level education with supervised clinical experience" (McReynolds, 1996, p. 237).

Many lessons can be drawn from Witmer, but as our focus is supervision, we learn

> before offering to treat these children on a large scale, and I needed some years of experience and extensive study, which could only be obtained through the prolonged observation of a few cases. Above all, I appreciated the great necessity of training a group of students upon whose assistance I could rely. (Witmer, 1907/1996, p. 250)

Using assessment methods of his time (reaction time, cognitive processing, word breadth and meaning), Witmer mainly relied on behavioral observations. His students were all enrolled in didactic programs at the University of Pennsylvania prior to or while engaged in clinical training. Witmer led case discussions and published case studies in his journal, *The Psychological Clinic*. A number of features of contemporary clinical psychology are woven into the fabric of our field from its birth under Witmer, and none more central than supervision in the service of building professionals.

Psychoanalytic Therapy

> In the beginning, Freud wrote about losing his "splendid isolation" as
>
> Regular meetings took place on certain evenings in my house, discussions were held according to certain rules. . . . On the whole I could tell myself that (the group) was hardly inferior in wealth and variety of talents to the staff of any clinical teacher one can think of. (reported by Fleming & Benedek, 1966, p. 7)

Freud's excitement and dedication in founding a science of mental structure and functioning led them to the technique of psychoanalysis and its instrument, the psychoanalyst. Freud assiduously pursued his own analysis and felt it indispensable that analysts be analyzed as part of their training. As a type of supervision, by the 1920s, each analyst was to experience a training analysis, done by an experienced analyst.

Up to the 1920s, analytic candidates were largely self-selected; those attending the Wednesday evening discussion group at Freud's home were effectively selected by him. However, groups began to materialize as Freud's views spread to other cities and countries. Often the student of analysis and the analysand (patient) were one and the same. The analyst could observe in both settings the capacity for free association, for self-observation, and for access to the unconscious. Learning was highly personalized, and referrals of patients and to the analytic group were by personal invitation. Then as now, one's style of supervisory conduct was and is a product of the supervisor's personality.

In 1925, Max Eitingon distinguished personal analysis from *Kontrollanalyse* or supervised analysis. The aim of control analysis was more to be educational, teach technique, and help the student–analyst understand any unresolved complexes in the analyst that influenced his or her work. The 1927 Congress of the International Psychoanalytic Association heard papers by Sandor Rado, Hans Sachs, and Helene Deutsch, all leading teachers and supervisors of psychoanalysis, but these were never published. Their concerns centered on establishing high minimal standards versus the need to freely explore the dimensions of psychoanalysis that were not yet clear. As a rule, rendering five years of psychoanalytic service was deemed adequate by the education committee of an institute to qualify a person as a training analyst. Now the enthusiastic supervisor eagerly showed the neophyte how he or she would handle the case. This "psychoanalysis à trois" could lose sight of the student's learning needs and was dependent on the student's positive transference toward the supervisor.

By 1935, Alice Balint's position was that the didactic analysis was losing sight of the fact that "the character of the analyst is an integral factor in the analytic situation and with the best will in the world it cannot be eliminated" (Fleming & Benedek, 1966/1983, pp. 13–14). Helene Deutsch was likely the first to point out the evaluative component of supervision. Other psychoanalysts held that the work of supervision is didactic and evaluative. Edward Bibring warned of the hypertrophy of the teaching function and the disadvantages of analyzing the candidate in the control situation. These sincere concerns were interrupted by the horror of Hitler's Germany as many of the analysts who survived emigrated to America in the 1930s.

As psychoanalysts reached the secure shores of America, there was a burgeoning of applications to the newly established institutes, and the military had a great need for help with combat neurosis, as posttraumatic stress disorder was then known. These forces launched psychoanalysis to preeminence on the North American continent. Bibring, now in America with its pragmatic bent, emphasized quantitative and institute-centered requirements, and soon minimum standards, such as 200 supervisory hr, were codified.

Meanwhile, the institutes became increasingly rigid. They admitted social workers and psychologists, but only to study and conduct research, not to earn clinical certificates. As late as 1984, a restraint-of-trade suit was filed against the American Psychoanalytic Association. After 4 years, an out-of-court settlement was reached, and psychologists and social workers desiring psychoanalytic training and clinical certification prevailed. Thus were psychologists and social workers admitted to the clinical training tracks in the institutes.

Ironically, this lawsuit was an odd reverberation from over a half-century before. Medical authorities in Germany sued the PhD-holding Theodor Reik for the unauthorized practice of medicine when he saw patients in psychoanalysis. Freud championed such non-MDs as daughter Anna, pastor Oskar Pfister, child educator and painter Erik Erikson, engineer Hellmuth Kaiser, and lawyer Max Eitingon as easily as he embraced physicians. Further, Freud favored a curriculum

> from psychology, the history of civilization and sociology, as well as from anatomy, biology and the study of evolution. . . . Psychoanalysis is part of psychology; not medical psychology in the old sense, not of the psychology of morbid processes, but simply of psychology. (Gay, 1989, p. 680)

The distinctions between personal, training, and control analyses may be helpful in understanding its relationship to supervision. Through training analysis, clinicians were to unearth their own blind spots and empathically understand what the psychoanalytic task demanded from the analysand, such as free associating, examining resistances, and readying one's self to receive interpretations. What unearthed issues might weigh upon the student's subsequent work? How did the student's personality limit his or her ability to see the analysand's world? The training analyst reported to the education committee, creating tremendous anxieties in the student and compromises in the free flow of associations and perhaps an uneasy feeling in the supervisor of being a double agent.

Control analysis was mandated by the institute for at least two cases. The cases were to be supervised by at least two different supervisors, neither of whom was the student's personal or training analyst, and with at least one of the cases being a child case. The supervising analysts' job was to catalyze the case. This meant to help the student free up his or her listening processes, to better enable the student–trainee in understanding the patient's world and to identify transferences, as well as explore with the student any of the student's countertransferences. Group control analysis, at least in some programs, allowed the student to relieve some of the pressure of control analysis and see how peers handled issues. Control analysis continued throughout one's career, providing continuing education, continual clarification of one's emotions, and personal growth and self-discovery. Personal analysis was expected and mandated. In contemporary programs, particularly those with psychoanalytic leanings, students are expected to uncover blind spots and stimulate personal growth. The only reporting function by the analyst is to certify the student is in attendance.

The term *didactic analysis* was used to indicate personal analysis plus a teaching or learning function, but this was controversial as it might dilute the uncovering and growth functions of personal analysis. They are similar in that they are each "in-the-job training" rather than "on-the-job training" (Fleming & Benedek, 1966/1983, p. 27).

Henry Stack Sullivan (1934–1935/1967) was keenly aware of the dire necessity of training his professional and paraprofessional staff, and the problems attendant to clear communication. With his trenchant sense of irony he noted how the most disturbed are in the greatest need, but they most often get the trainees as psychotherapists. Sullivan coined the term *transference jam* to indicate that

> interpersonal relationships involving the patient are so complicated and so stressful that even though they may embarrass the patient gravely, they also—if there is any sort of competent supervision—embarrass the young physician and lead him to inquire into his deficiencies. (p. 316)

These deficiencies are intrapsychic, as well as from the person's own upbringing, and cultural/racial/socioeconomic class derived. They are barriers that jar both participants and jam the communications. Sullivan saw clinical skills as "vast augmentation of alertness. . . . I am convinced that methodic steps amounting to intensive supervision of the potential psychotherapist from the very day of his entrance to the mental hospital is urgently necessary" (p. 317).

Searles (1955) famously noted a parallel process that resonated between the analysand, the analyst, and the supervisor. For example, a client who was late to sessions might challenge the student–psychotherapist's capacity to confront the client. The student might then be late to the supervisory session, replicating the client's behavior. The same issue arising in psychotherapy would recur in supervision, providing a parallel in the processes between the dyadic situations (Ekstein & Wallerstein, 1963). Obvious institutional influences might include limits on supervisory hours accorded the student per number of hours of clinical services rendered by the student, or how fees (and pay to the supervisee) are handled. More subtle effects of the institution might include how evaluations are handled and how much freedom to innovate or deviate from clinic treatment protocols is allowed the student. Feelings toward a training institute can be profound and influence one's experience. Such *institutional transference* (Gendel & Reiser, 1981) ought to be familiar to every university fund-raiser whose success depends on the alumni's positive feelings toward their alma mater. Any student who failed out of a program can well describe the malevolent institutional transferences he or she feels.

Behavior Therapy

Behaviorism heralded several noteworthy developments. On a general level, it anticipated a century-long skirmish between psychoanalytic and behavioral views. On a practical level, Watson engaged in the first behavioral intervention with Rosalie Raynor at his side (Watson & Raynor, 1920), perhaps the first modern behavioral supervision or cosupervision. We can certainly date behavioral supervision to the time Mary Cover Jones conducted her dissertation under Watson's tutelage (Jones, 1924a, 1924b), desensitizing little Peter from a phobia.

Knight Dunlap carried on the behaviorist's program at Johns Hopkins when his book *Habits: Their Making and Unmaking* focused on negative practice as a scientific way of curing neurosis (Dunlap, 1932). His work with stuttering and other "nervous conditions" showed students the way to employ in clinical cases the exciting conditioning techniques delineated in the scientific laboratory. Shortly after, Jacobson (1938) wrote about progressive relaxation techniques, which were to undergird Wolpe's systematic desensitization in 1948.

Krasner and Ullmann's (1965) collection linked learning theory and behavior change, while their casebook (Ullmann & Krasner, 1965) provided several generations of students as clearheaded a guide to treatment as has been written (both books became Citation Classics). A more social-learning variety of behavioral psychology then emerged. It was initially termed *methodological behaviorism*, then *social learning* (Peterson, 1968; Rotter, 1954), and finally *cognitive–behavioral therapy*. These approaches explored the use of imagery as in covert sensitization (and desensitization) by having the patient imagine phobic objects, such as dirt or heights or snakes, rather than having the patient physically confront the objects.

The central supervisory techniques focused on skill implementation through modeling, shaping, or successively approaching a desired repertoire of behavior by the student. Behaviorism (and family and marital therapy) contributed the bug-in-the-ear method by which the supervisor could watch the student behind a one-way mirror and speak telephonically through a small hearing aid speaker in the student's ear. These comments were intended to guide the student toward making more adaptive responses in vivo.

Two contemporary behavioral approaches developed training programs with noteworthy supervision models. Linehan's (1980; Chapter 121, this volume) dialectical behavior therapy is designed to treat borderline personality patients. Her program involves a functional analysis of the problem, a planful treatment, and a flexible psychotherapist who can tolerate the borderline patient's risky behaviors and resistances to the treatment, yet maintains validation for the patient. Because this population tends to be obdurate and dramatic, the patients are draining on the psychotherapist. Consequently, Linehan built into her program an ongoing supervision that involves redefining the presenting problem and cheerleading for the psychotherapist who, after multiple failures with a client, might be demoralized yet must prevail.

Beck's (Beck, Sarnat, & Barenstein, 2008; Chapter 7, this volume) cognitive therapy provides a programmatic analysis and treatment plan and multiple assessments and feedback to both the client and the psychotherapist. Both Aaron Beck and his daughter, Judy, reconceptualized behaviorism toward recognizing the interpersonal processes through which the treatment works. The Becks disabused archaic conceptions: Behavioral treatment is superficial, focuses only on symptoms, neglects interpersonal factors, and dismisses emotions in favor of correcting distorted thinking. They developed therapist competence, covering the structure of treatment, the tenor of the relationship, how well the case is conceptualized, and how well the techniques fit, have been applied, and have been modified to meet the goals of treatment.

Cognitive psychology provided us with the concept that there might be three types of learning: episodic, semantic, and procedural. That is, a case that provides episodic learning might be the student's first case or first supervision. These defining moments provide prototypes for how the student ought to behave as a psychotherapist. Semantic learning best captures the student's attempts to learn theory and techniques through reading or lectures, as cognitive bits. Procedural learning allows the supervisor to examine the student's technique and way of construing the case and then correcting, much as a golf or knitting coach polishing the client's swing or stitching.

Existential–Humanistic Therapy

If possible, Rogers (1942a) was even more resolute than were psychoanalysts in holding that the instrument of change was the psychotherapist and the conditions he or she established in the consulting room. Training and supervised practice in developing and refining the psychotherapist were quintessential to Rogers and existential humanists. Whereas psychoanalytic conceptualizations grew increasingly complex, Rogers's system seems deceptively simple. All one had to do was establish three conditions: unconditional positive regard, empathic understanding, and congruence. In this nutritious firmament, the client, much like a seed ready to sprout, would flourish.

Rogers was wholly committed, as was behaviorism, to basing his system of psychotherapy and its supervision on scientific foundations. Rogers brought the scientific bent of his youth, during which he experimented with the best conditions of nutrients for his plants in a farm plot, with the zeal of helping people in pain. Heretofore, the inner sanctum of psychotherapy had been inviolate, but now Rogers's tape recorder breached it (Rogers, 1942b). In his words,

> I cannot exaggerate the excitement of our learning as we clustered about the machine which enabled us to listen to ourselves, playing over and over some puzzling point at which the interview clearly went wrong, or those moments in which the client moved significantly forward. (Rogers, 1975, p. 3)

This excitement resulted in research about teasing out the ways by which the three conditions work. In teaching listening skills, take the example of a patient beginning a session with the observation that she saw a lonely looking puppy on the way to the office. The less skilled psychotherapist might say, "Let us get on with the session," blithely ignoring a feeling complex, cuing the patient that it might not be safe to explore loneliness (if that were the underlying motif). A psychotherapist who has just begun learning how to interpret might say, "Were you the little puppy?," ignoring that the client might not be adequately prepared for the depth of that interpretation. A more empathically connected and advanced psychotherapist might respond, "Might that have any meaning for you?"

Rogerians embarked on exciting training programs (see Carkhuff, 1969; Mueller & Kell, 1972). Research based on Rogers's program showed that laypersons who were taught basic therapeutic conditions can effect client change and can be as effective as professional trainees for many clients.

N. Kagan (1980) developed his interpersonal process recall method—a training program that exquisitely tunes people into their emotions and cognitions. Kagan noticed that people can vividly recall their experiences as they watch themselves on a videotape. They can then process information that sensitizes them to the nuances of the relationship. H. Kagan (Klein) and Kagan (1997) described the sound research program supporting interpersonal process recall and the manuals that allow for deeper processing and assessment.

Following the person-centered tradition, Ivey and associates (Forsyth & Ivey, 1980) developed microcounseling. True to its name, microcounseling selects a skill such as offering minimal, nonintrusive encouragement to have a client continue self-disclosure. A tape is made and played so the student can self-appraise. He or she then practices, for example, offering five encouraging prompts within three minutes, until the student and instructor assess mastery of the microskill. Microcounseling has been thoroughly researched. The client-centered approach provides the dominant model in training lay and clerical staff, for example at crisis centers, and remains an optimal way to begin to train any psychotherapist.

From recounting the past, we can see common themes pertinent to clinical supervision: (a) There is a leader with a vision, (b) who writes well and inspires others to study, (c) often by writing in public arenas by describing compelling cases (e.g., Freud's *The Interpretation of Dreams*, Watson's advice columns in *Redbook* magazine, Rogers's *Client-Centered Therapy*), (d) involvement in case discussions that give a "face" or palpable feel to a theory or technique, (e) with a strong academic tradition, (f) with assessment built in, (g) toward producing a competent practitioner. Supervision is embedded within the warp and woof of each approach. Across perspectives, supervision uses (h) modeling on key cases, (i) didactic work on the theoretical underpinning of the approach, (j) shaping of responses, and (k) assessment of the patient and the psychotherapist.

THE PROFESSIONAL RECOGNITION OF SUPERVISION

In the 1970s, I was finishing my internship, and a fellow intern and I would soon take academic positions requiring us to supervise. Having scant mastery of the psychotherapeutic process and wanting some training in supervision, we asked the internship faculty for a course or module on how to supervise, so we would be a bit less incompetent in our work. The faculty member responded, "That is a really hostile way to respond to our supervisions of you." Stunned, chastised, we embarked on our careers. After a few years of supervising assessments, another assistant professor and I began to supervise psychotherapy. Doubts resurfaced. I did a poor search of the literature, in part because the psychology literature (in the old *Psychological Abstracts*, not the computer-based searches we have now) did not turn up the rich sources cited above (e.g., Ekstein & Wallerstein, 1963; Fleming & Benedek, 1966).

Feeling a vacuum in the literature, I approached various masters of their area and asked them to prepare chapters in what became *Psychotherapy Supervision: Theory, Research and Practice* (Hess, 1980). The experts in this volume examined psychotherapy supervision across theories and presented stage theories of supervision. I prepared a chart depicting the various roles encompassed in the term *supervisor* and the roles and role conflicts attendant to them. The chart summarized the conflicts of the past century, for example, the supervisor as helpful teacher versus the supervisor as monitor, which places the student in an impossible dilemma of telling on him- or herself. This chart (Hess, 2008) is reproduced in Table 17.1 for the reader to consider in terms of the various "pulls" on the supervisory pair in structuring the supervision and the model's attendant duties.

About this time, the only journal with "supervision" in its title, *Counselor Education and Supervision*, was joined by *The Clinical Supervisor*. The "quiet profession" (Alonso, 1985) was now established.

TABLE 17.1
Eight Models of Psychotherapy Supervision

Model	Goal	Nature of relationship
I. Lecturer	Conveys global conceptual schemes and demonstrates technique Generates enthusiasm and provides an ideal or model	The listener can decide to tune out, to become an acolyte, or to choose some middle range of engagement with the lecturer.
II. Teacher	Presents specific goals and content within a curriculum for competency or mastery	Superordinate to subordinate
III. Case reviewer	Reviews cases focusing on recognizing the session's events and guiding future interactions	Elder, experienced to younger, less experienced
IV. Collegial peer	Consults with peers to gain support or for a critical review that does not jeopardize one's career	Shared intimacy and trust
V. Monitor	Maintains standards and ensures mandated guidelines (e.g., for accreditation) are met	Censor; censures and corrects
VI. Psychotherapist	Helps student psychotherapist apprehend the client's perspective and tasks	Secure and trusted model in which doubts and hopes can be expressed without external consequence
VII. Coach	Focuses on linking explicit or semantic learning (content) with procedural knowledge while building confidence and hope and benignly correcting	Trusted elder who has walked in the student's shoes; may be a cotherapist
VIII. Educator	Enables student to attain skills, builds higher order judgment skills, and establishes a psychotherapeutic identity	A role superordinate (and inclusive of the other roles) that is careful to see that cognitive and emotional growth proceed apace with skill development

Note. From *Psychotherapy Supervision: Theory, Research, and Practice* (2nd ed.), by A. K. Hess, K. D. Hess, and T. H. Hess, 2008, New York, NY: Wiley. Copyright 2008 by Wiley. Adapted with permission.

The 1992 American Psychological Association (APA) Ethics Code was the first to explicitly mention supervisees as meriting attention. The 2002 revision of the code's Section 7 describes standards of education and training, with particular note to students being required to reveal personal information (Section 7.04), mandated psychotherapy (Section 7.05), timely and criterion-based evaluations of supervision evaluations (Section 7.06), and forbidden sexual relations (Section 7.07 on supervision, in tandem with Section 3.05 on multiple relationships).

A well-organized and thorough bibliography (Robiner & Schofield, 1990) signaled that the literature had reached a critical mass (see an updated bibliography by Peake, Nussbaum, & Tindell, 2002). In 2006, APA launched *Training and Education in Professional Psychology*, which features psychotherapy supervision in a plurality of its articles. The standing of psychotherapy supervision in the profession's code of ethics and its literature is now secure.

PSYCHOTHERAPY SUPERVISION: THEORY AND RESEARCH

Developmental Models

Supervisee Stages

A field of inquiry often begins with attempts at taxonomy or classifications, particularly of the developmental variety. Many authors from the 1960s to the 1980s have sketched the stages of supervisee development (e.g., Delaney 1972; Hogan, 1964; Gaoni & Neumann, 1974; Loganbill, Hardy, & Delworth, 1983; Yogev, 1982). The first stage is termed *inception* and is described variously as insecurity–dependence, pupil, adequacy–inadequacy, role defining, and stagnation. Structure, support, and guidance seem to be the order of the day for students in this stage. The second stage, termed *skill development,* is characterized by movement toward autonomy in using guidance, goal identification, and implementation of skills as confusion lessens and an apprentice functioning emerges. The third stage involves conditional dependence versus individuation (or being creative in using the supervisor and in venturing from the supervisor), a solidifying and evaluating of one's style into the development of a therapeutic personality. A fourth stage is identified by some theorists when a mutuality develops such that the supervisee and supervisor are more collegial.

Supervisor Stages

Parallel models have been developed for stages of supervisor development (e.g., Bernard & Goodyear, 2009; Falender & Shafranske, 2004). The first stage, across the 11 theorists' schemas, appears to characterize the supervisor as feeling unsure and mimicking one's own supervisors, preferring a teacher role, feeling self-conscious, and being quite sensitive to feedback. The second stage involves using more therapy skills in listening and intervening, as developing structure and expectancies in supervision with increased abilities for self-appraisal, working toward a supervisory identity though still prone to moments of doubt. The third stage focuses more on the relationship and less on feeling that the supervision is work, excitement about the supervision, and an ability to use the supervisory process at the readiness level of the supervisee so there is an increased ability to use material to accomplish learning goals, with an increased reliance on the supervisee to use the sessions efficaciously. A few theorists posit a fourth stage using terms such as *mastery, integrated,* and *comfortable with mistakes.* The third and fourth stages certainly include the supervisor's feeling of generativity about the next generation.

Experience Level

Reviews concerning experience in supervision conclude that there is a perception of change over the course of supervision (e.g., Worthington, 1987). As students advance, the supervisors increasingly "confront, deal with personal issues, tackle client resistances and transference/countertransference issues, give negative feedback and treat them [students] like peers more often . . . [as well as] give . . . less instruction, provide less structure" (Worthington, 1987, p. 202). Supervisors differ in skills, but this difference is not a function of degrees, licensure, or experience. There may well be two types of wine—supervisees who improve with age and experience and supervisors who do not.

Mapping Supervision's Dimensions

Fortunately, there are guides for the supervisor and the student to see how each views the dimensions of supervision and how beneficent supervisors work. The nature of supervision does not lend itself to large-N parametric research but more toward particular events that are characterized as good or bad. Several researchers have used the critical methodology to see how supervisors and supervisees view facilitative and disjunctive events.

Moore (1988) asked 25 supervisors to list critical incidents that occurred in actual supervisions that they found positive or negative. She collected a catalog of events and then eliminated redundant ones. Using an iterative procedure, judges then sorted the incidents into five dimensions by which students are viewed:

- *clinical sense* (good = provides client with hope, bad = tells client to "grow up");
- *preparation for supervision* (good = reviews case for problem points before supervision, bad = sees supervision as taking time from more important chores);
- *self-exploration and awareness* (good = can process feelings in supervision, bad = continually makes negative statements about self);
- *theoretical and cognitive knowledge* (good = hypothesizes about how client behavior and literature articulate, bad = mistakes healthy for unhealthy client behaviors); and

- *boundary management* (good = is able to tactfully establish time limits with clients; bad = misses appointments).

One researcher (Aldrich, 1982) plumbed 30 graduate student supervisees for over 700 critical incidents and had experienced clinicians cull them down to basic dimensions. Supervisees see supervisors on eight dimensions:

- *defensiveness* (good = uses a student challenge as a teaching moment, bad = quickly contradicts any student interpretation at variance with his or hers);
- *professionalism* (good = discusses parameters of supervision such as case responsibilities before beginning, bad = uses harsh, blaming language);
- *clinically experienced* (good = has grasp of client disorders of the student's cases, bad = unable to offer suggestions for clinical management when case goes beyond student's abilities);
- *theoretically facile* (good = is facile with theories and can articulate them with case phenomena, bad = never refers to theories or research);
- *experienced as a teacher* (good = gives tactful feedback at a level the student can metabolize, bad = cannot pinpoint student problem areas);
- *interested in the supervisee's life* (good = aware of student concerns via observation or through a third party and gently inquires, bad = cuts off the student whenever any mention about student experience or emotion is made);
- *likable* (good = friendly in and out of supervision and seems to value the student, bad = noxious personal mannerisms that make modeling difficult); and
- *motivating* (good = encourages student to meet goals and models appropriate enthusiasm, bad = forgets the facts that were reviewed in prior sessions repeatedly).

Simply put, the good supervisor (Carifio & Hess, 1987) is competent in the substantive (clinical problem) area, is open to experiencing and exploring what the supervisee is experiencing, sets appropriate goals and provides appropriate feedback consonant with the readiness level of the supervisee, and is supportive and noncritical while being concrete in making suggestions. This fits well with research on 142 doctoral students, who found that good supervisors were supportive, were clear in their expectations, and gave feedback (Allen, Szollos, & Williams, 1986). They were seen as trustworthy, expert, possessing clinical experience, confronting with a sense of safety for the student, and concerned about supervisee growth (Allen et al., 1986). Poor supervisors seemed inept, unfocused, devaluing of supervision, and exercising an authoritarian style; most devastating were those who were sexually exploitive (Allen et al., 1986). Trainees asked about role conflicts in supervision described supervisors as uninvested in supervision and unwilling to take responsibility for supervisory conflicts or for their anger directed at students, leaving the students in stress and self-doubt (M. L. Nelson & Friedlander, 2001). Often these students coped by finding support with peers, spouses, or mentors.

Supervision Process

As a field matures, taxonomies call for mechanisms to explain how the types function. That is, the processes by which the types work are postulated and studied. Nowhere is process more central than in psychotherapy supervision. For example, Kadushin's (1968) classic article "Games People Play in Supervision" shows the interpersonal ploys supervisees use when facing stress. Students might unduly compliment the supervisor, as if to say, "I am nice to you, so be nice to me." Reducing supervisory power might be shown by the student parrying a suggestion by saying, "In class, Professor X said that was not an evidence-based technique," rather than making an open and less challenging response, inviting dialogue. To be sure, there are supervisor games, too, such as, "No matter what you do, it will be wrong or insufficient" or "If you admire me, I will reward your hero-worship."

The skilled supervisor is mindful of the distinction between problems in learning (educational; Ekstein & Wallerstein, 1963) and learning problems (character based; Fleming & Benedek, 1966). Among these discordant elements rupturing the interpersonal process are supervisee shame, doubt, dependence, and sloth, oft-times accompanying insecurities and sometimes induced by graduate training and toxic supervision.

There have always been students who are not suited to be psychotherapists. Many experienced supervisors may be unprepared to recognize and cope with trainee impairment vis-à-vis their agencies' policies (Gizara & Forrest, 2004). In dealing with impaired supervisees, supervisors may feel less prepared than they ought to be, and they may find that collegial and supervision groups can be as frustrating as supportive, because the members feel they must have input, resulting in "too many cooks in the kitchen" (Gizara & Forrest, 2004, p. 135) when making a clinically informed administrative decision. Some group members speculate about the supervisor's personality with no clear understanding of student impairment. These events can be painful, sad, and wrenching for empathic and ethical supervisors. The APA Task Force on the Assessment of Competence in Professional Psychology produced a set of articles in *Professional Psychology*'s October 2007 issue. They provide a context for assessing and intervening in areas of problematic trainee competence.

Clear goals of supervision with multiple sources of measurement articulated to those goals lead to a clear but modest effect size associated with training (Lambert & Ogles, 1997). In trying to improve this effect, Worthen and Lambert (2007) developed a tracking system by which the psychotherapist and supervisor gather session-by-session client progress information so psychotherapy can be monitored and client distress that is not being addressed can be flagged. Such information seems critical in improving both psychotherapy and supervision, and makes decision making about student competence more informed by metric information.

Another set of reviewers (Neufeldt, Beutler, & Banchero, 1997) concluded that we have a good idea what goes on in supervision. However, as different clients with different problems are assigned to students who vary in both their skill and experience levels, we are confronted with a tangle of variables with no clear baselines. Thus, assessing how effectively a supervisor has performed and comparing him or her with other supervisors becomes a conundrum. Compound this conundrum with assessing the student on higher order functioning, such as judgment and depth and timing of interventions, which further complicates the clinical research task. Ellis, D'Iuso, and Ladany (2008) provided a review of psychometrically sound and useful measures to better assess the contours of supervision and begin unraveling the knot.

This sampler of the literature in guiding supervisors tells us that competence and caring carry the day. Words from the poet laureate John Masefield are apt: "Once in a century a person may be ruined or made insufferable by praise. But surely once in a minute something precious dies for want of it."

Supervision Resources

As psychotherapy supervision gathers momentum, this recounting will conclude by providing a few of the latest resources for guiding supervisees and supervisors, reviewing surveys that point out longitudinal trends, and offering observations about supervision.

Two recent casebooks provide a textured analysis of supervision (Falender & Shafranske, 2008; Ladany, Friedlander, & Nelson, 2005). These will benefit students wanting some structure about how supervision works. Hess, Hess, and Hess's (2008) comprehensive volume has a variety of theorists who provide detailed case vignettes on managing clinical cases and update the assessment of supervision and the theories and research base. Bernard and Goodyear's (2009) text summarizes the supervision literature from a counseling viewpoint and furnishes a toolkit with supervision contracts. Falender and Shafranske's (2004) text takes a competence-based approach, articulating their model with the APA Competence Taskforce's philosophy. These three texts are in multiple editions, signifying the establishment of supervision.

Surveys

Surveys of clinical supervision over the past 3 decades summarize and extend many of these changes. A study conducted in the early 1980s (Hess & Hess, 1983) surveyed internship supervision practices. Students received 1 hour of supervision for some 3 hours of psychotherapy, comprising 3.76 hours of supervision per week. The dominant mode of supervision was face-to-face, one-to-one. No specific evaluation procedures were then used; faculty were not remunerated, as supervision was seen as part of the job; and one third of the surveyed internships provided training in supervision. Another survey conducted about the same time (G. L. Nelson, 1978) found that students would like to see their supervisors in action with a case; that they preferred direct observation and videotaping of their performance; and that they preferred supervisors who were interested in supervision, who were open, flexible, permissive, and outgoing, and who explored trainee feelings toward the client while letting the trainee develop a therapeutic style fitting the student.

Hess and Hess (1996, 2009) followed up their surveys of internships with another survey in 1990, then in 2002, plus they surveyed doctoral programs as well in 1980, 1990, and 2002, providing a longitudinal view as well as a comparative one between doctoral and intern programs. A précis of their findings include the following: Faculty are still being "paid in collegial esteem" as opposed to cash, but some get release time. The number of female supervisors has increased. While doctoral departments provide a bit more supervision over the years, internship faculty provide about double the supervision hours per week per faculty, although the variances and overlaps are large. Despite increasing availability of technology, the methods of supervision remain stable, with the dominant modes being one-to-one, then seminar type, use of audiotape, and group supervision with an increase in doctoral programs in recent years.

THE FUTURE OF PSYCHOTHERAPY SUPERVISION

The reader can sense the rapid evolution of clinical supervision in the scant 3 decades of its recognition as a specialty practice and a research domain. In closing, I present six observations about future developments in clinical supervision.

1. The practice of psychotherapy has been profoundly altered as governmental regulations and third-party payers have limited the ability of practitioners to govern their own practice. As our activities are seen increasingly through economic prisms, the cost of providing supervision and the ability to bill for unli-

censed and non-autonomously-functioning psychotherapists needs to be factored into administrators' budgets and into private providers' allocation of their time in undertaking clinical supervision.

2. Though psychotherapists have always maintained confidentiality and privilege, electronic communications and record-keeping guidelines affect practice. With respect to supervision, are one's process notes subject to the same level of revelation as are progress notes? What communications to a supervisor or a consultant are potentially knowable and to whom?

3. An increasingly paradoxical world in which we are electronically connected but personally alone may yet put an even greater premium on the authenticity and caring that psychotherapy provides. The communicative processes of both electronic and personal, "in-the-flesh" theaters are rich fields for clinical and research explorations—their impact on supervision is direct. How will a supervisor cope with a remote supervisee who might be seeing a remote client? Further, what standards govern the supervision and in what venues are each of the people (client, psychotherapist, supervisor) located which might determine the legal and ethical strictures? If a client is "seen" electronically while living in one state, the psychotherapist lives in another, and the supervisor lives in a third state or another country, what legal and professional codes prevail—the client's, the psychotherapist/supervisee's, or the supervisor's locality?

4. Our evidence-based services will extend to supervision. We must explore what "value added" a professional brings. The value added might be the professional's knowledge that allows the practitioner to efficaciously recognize and intervene in such subtle yet damaging interpersonal problems, where the sensitive laity might realize something is amiss but not quite identify what is happening. Moreover, the professional might be able to teach these skills to others—in a word, supervise. Are such skills as timing and client readiness for change the areas on which professionals are more effective than the rendering of direct services?

5. Supervision is finding its way into many state licensing laws. Some consensus about entry levels into psychotherapeutic practice would clear the fog now existing. What do *competence, proficiency,* and *mastery* mean, and might they be different levels on which practitioners are skilled? That is, does every clinician need to be an expert, and at which skills need one be an expert?

6. Who can supervise? Are there standards, and are these realistic? Do they make for a better clinician? Can we ensure that the standards we develop will still allow the creative student to flourish (Ryff & Singer, 2000)?

We have surveyed both the past and the future of psychotherapy supervision. Ebbinghaus might have said about supervision that it has a short history, a long past, and a vibrant future.

REFERENCES

Aldrich, L. (1982). *Construction of mixed standard scales for the psychotherapy supervisors* (Unpublished master's thesis). Auburn University, Auburn, AL.

Allen, G. J., Szollos, S. J., & Williams, B. E. (1986). Doctoral students' comparative evaluations of best and worst supervision experiences. *Professional Psychology, 17,* 91–99. doi:10.1037/0735-7028.17.2.91

Alonso, A. (1985). *The quiet profession: Supervisors of psychotherapy.* New York, NY: Macmillan.

American Psychological Association (APA). (1992). Ethical principles of psychologists and code of conduct. *American Psychologist, 47,* 1597–1611. doi:10.1037/0003-066X. 47.12.1597

American Psychological Association (APA). (2002). Ethical principles of psychologists and code of conduct. *American Psychologist, 57,* 1060–1073. doi:10.1037/0003-066X.57.12.1060

Beck, J. S., Sarnat, J. E., & Barenstein, V. (2008). Psychotherapy based approaches to supervision. In C. Falender & E. M. Shafranske (Eds.), *Casebook for clinical supervision: A competency-based approach* (pp. 57–96). Washington, DC: American Psychological Association. doi:10.1037/11792-000

Bernard, J. M., & Goodyear, R. K. (2009). *Fundamentals of clinical supervision* (4th ed.). Boston, MA: Allyn & Bacon.

Carifio, M. S., & Hess, A. K. (1987). Who is the ideal supervisor? *Professional Psychology, 18,* 244–250. doi:10.1037/0735-7028.18.3.244

Carkhuff, R. R. (1969). *Helping and human relations: A primer for lay and professional helpers.* New York, NY: Holt, Rinehart & Winston.

Delaney, D. J. (1972). A behavioral model for the practicum supervision of counselor candidates. *Counselor Education and Supervision, 12,* 46–50.

Dunlap, K. (1932). *Habits: Their making and unmaking.* New York, NY: Liveright.

Ekstein, R., & Wallerstein, R. S. (1963). *The teaching and learning of psychotherapy.* New York, NY: Basic Books.

Ellis, M. V., D'Iuso, N., & Ladany, N. (2008). State of the art in the assessment, measurement, and evaluation of psychotherapy supervision. In A. K. Hess, K. D. Hess, & T. H. Hess (Eds.), *Psychotherapy supervision* (2nd ed., pp. 473–499). New York, NY: Wiley.

Falender, C. A., & Shafranske, E. P. (2004). *Clinical supervision: A competency-based approach.* Washington, DC: American Psychological Association. doi:10.1037/10806-000

Falender, C. A., & Shafranske, E. P. (2008). *Casebook for clinical supervision: A competency-based approach.* Washington, DC: American Psychological Association. doi:10.1037/11792-000

Fleming, J., & Benedek, T. (1966). *Psychoanalytic supervision.* New York, NY: Grune & Stratton.

Forsyth, D. R., & Ivey, A. E. (1980). Microtraining: An approach to differential supervision. In A. K. Hess (Ed.), *Psychotherapy supervision* (pp. 242–261). New York, NY: Wiley.

Gaoni, B., & Neumann, M. (1974). Supervision from the point of view of the supervisee. *American Journal of Psychotherapy, 28*, 108–114.

Gay, P. (1989). *The Freud reader*. New York, NY: Norton.

Gendel, M. H., & Reiser, D. G. (1981). Institutional countertransferences. *American Journal of Psychiatry, 138*, 508–511.

Gizara, S. S., & Forrest, L. (2004). Supervisors' experience of trainee impairment and incompetence at APA-accredited internship sites. *Professional Psychology, 35*, 131–140. doi:10.1037/0735-7028.35.2.131

Hess, A. K. (1980). *Psychotherapy supervision: Theory, research and practice*. New York, NY: Wiley.

Hess, A. K. (2008). Psychotherapy supervision: A conceptual review. In A. K. Hess, K. D. Hess, & T. H. Hess (Eds.), *Psychotherapy supervision* (2nd ed., pp. 3–22). New York, NY: Wiley.

Hess, A. K., & Hess, K. D. (1983). Psychotherapy supervision: A survey of internship training practices. *Professional Psychology, 14*, 504–513. doi:10.1037/0735-7028.14.4.504

Hess, A. K., & Hess, K. D. (1996, August). *Training of psychotherapists*. Presented at the 104th Annual Convention of the American Psychological Association, Toronto, Ontario, Canada.

Hess, A. K., & Hess, K. D. (2009, August). *The training of psychotherapists: Doctoral and internship practices from 1980 to 2000*. Poster presented at the 117th Annual Convention of the American Psychological Association, Toronto, Ontario, Canada.

Hess, A. K., Hess, K. D., & Hess, T. H. (2008). *Psychotherapy supervision: Theory, research and practice* (2nd ed.). New York, NY: Wiley.

Hogan, R. A. (1964). Issues and approaches in supervision. *Psychotherapy: Theory, Research and Practice, 1*, 139–141.

Jacobson, E. (1938). *Progressive relaxation*. Chicago, IL: University of Chicago Press.

Jones, M. C. (1924a). The elimination of children's fears. *Journal of Experimental Psychology, 7*, 382–390. doi:10.1037/h0072283

Jones, M. C. (1924b). A laboratory study of fear: The case of Peter. *Pedagogical Seminary, 31*, 308–315.

Kadushin, A. (1968). Games people play in supervision. *Social Work, 13*, 23–32.

Kagan, H. (Klein) & Kagan, N. I. (1997). Interpersonal process recall: Influencing human interaction. In C. E. Watkins (Ed.), *Handbook of psychotherapy supervision* (pp. 296–309) New York, NY: Wiley.

Kagan, N. (1980). Influencing human interaction: Eighteen years with IPR. In A. K. Hess (Ed.), *Psychotherapy supervision* (pp. 262–283). New York, NY: Wiley.

Krasner, L., & Ullmann, L. C. (1965). *Research in behavior modification*. New York, NY: Holt, Rinehart & Winston.

Ladany, N., Friedlander, M. L., & Nelson, M. L. (2005). *Critical events in psychotherapy supervision*. Washington, DC: American Psychological Association. doi:10.1037/10958-000

Lambert, M. J., & Ogles, B. M. (1997). The effectiveness of psychotherapy supervision. In C. E. Watkins Jr. (Ed.), *Handbook of psychotherapy supervision* (pp. 421–446). New York, NY: Wiley.

Linehan, M. (1980). Supervision of behavior therapy. In A. K. Hess (Ed.), *Psychotherapy supervision: Theory, research and practice* (pp. 148–180). New York, NY: Wiley.

Loganbill, C., Hardy, E., & Delworth, V. (1983). Supervision in counseling I. *Counseling Psychologist, 10*, 1–67.

McReynolds, P. (1996). Lightner Witmer: A centennial tribute. *American Psychologist, 51*, 237–240. doi:10.1037/0003-066X.51.3.237

Moore, D. S. (1988). *Validation of the behaviorally anchored rating scales for psychotherapy supervisees* (Unpublished doctoral dissertation). Auburn University, Auburn, AL.

Mueller, W., & Kell, B. (1972). *Coping with conflict: Supervising counselors and psychotherapists*. New York, NY: Appleton-Century-Crofts.

Nelson, G. L. (1978). Psychotherapy supervision from the trainee's point of view. *Professional Psychology, 9*, 539–550. doi:10.1037/0735-7028.9.4.539

Nelson, M. L., & Friedlander, M. L. (2001). A close look at conflictual supervisory relationships: The trainee's perspective. *Journal of Counseling Psychology, 48*, 384–395. doi:10.1037/0022-0167.48.4.384

Neufeldt, S. A., Beutler, L. E., & Banchero, R. (1997). Research on supervisor variables in psychotherapy supervision. In C. E. Watkins Jr. (Ed.), *Handbook of psychotherapy supervision* (pp. 508–524). New York, NY: Wiley.

Peake, T. H., Nussbaum, B. D., & Tindell, S. D. (2002). Clinical and counseling supervision references: Trends and needs. *Psychotherapy: Theory, Research, Practice, Training, 39*, 114–125. doi:10.1037/0033-3204.39.1.114

Peterson, D. R. (1968). *The clinical study of social behavior*. New York, NY: Appleton-Century-Crofts.

Robiner, W. N., & Schofield, W. (1990). References on supervision in clinical and counseling psychology. *Professional Psychology: Research and Practice, 21*, 297–312. doi:10.1037/0735-7028.21.4.297

Rogers, C. R. (1942a). *Counseling and psychotherapy: Newer concepts in practice*. Boston, MA: Houghton Mifflin.

Rogers, C. R. (1942b). The use of electrically recorded interviews in improving psychotherapeutic techniques. *American Journal of Orthopsychiatry, 12*, 429–434.

Rogers, C. R. (1975). Empathic: An unappreciated way of being. *Counseling Psychologist, 5*, 2–9.

Rotter, J. B. (1954). *Social learning and clinical psychology*. New York, NY: Prentice-Hall.

Ryff, C. D., & Singer, B. (2000). Interpersonal flourishing: A positive health agenda for the new millennium. *Personality and Social Psychology Review, 4*, 30–44. doi:10.1207/S15327957PSPR0401_4

Searles, H. F. (1955). The informational value of the supervisor's emotional experiences. *Psychiatry, 18*, 135–146.

Sullivan, H. S. (1962). Psychiatric training as a prerequisite to psychoanalytic practice. In *Schizophrenia as a human process*. New York, NY: Norton. (Original work published 1934–1935)

Ullmann, L. C., & Krasner, L. (1965). *Case studies in behavior modification*. New York, NY: Holt, Rinehart & Winston.

Watson, J. B., & Raynor, R. (1920). Conditioned emotional reactions. *Journal of Experimental Psychology, 3*, 1–14. doi:10.1037/h0069608

Witmer, L. (1996). Clinical psychology. *American Psychologist, 51*, 248–251. (Original work published 1907)

Worthen, V. F., & Lambert, M. J. (2007). Outcome oriented supervision: Advantages of adding systematic client tracking to supportive consultations. *Counselling & Psychotherapy Research, 7*, 48–53. doi:10.1080/14733140601140873

Worthington, E. L. (1987). Changes in supervision as counselors and supervisors gain experience: A review. *Professional Psychology: Research and Practice, 18*, 189–208. doi:10.1037/0735-7028.18.3.189

Yogev, S. (1982). An eclectic model of supervision: A developmental sequence for beginning psychotherapy students. *Professional Psychology, 13*, 236–243. doi:10.1037/0735-7028.13.2.236

18

ETHICS IN PSYCHOTHERAPY

NORMAN ABELES AND GERALD P. KOOCHER

In the first 60 years after the founding of the American Psychological Association (APA) in 1892, no formal code of ethics existed (Pope & Vetter, 1992). Not until 1938 did APA establish a Committee on Scientific and Professional Ethics and begin dealing with ethical complaints on an informal basis (Golann, 1969). In 1948, development of a formal ethical code began under the leadership of Nicholas Hobbs (1948). The first provisional *Ethical Standards of Psychologists* ultimately won adoption by the APA Council of Representatives in 1952 for a 3-year trial period (APA, 1953).

The standards originated using a critical incident methodology (Flanagan, 1954). APA encouraged its members to critique the 1953 publication and provide additional incidents leading to a vote of the membership principle by principle, with formal adoption by the Council to follow in 1955. The APA has revised its code a number of times in ensuing years, but not until the 2002 revision did it again use a critical incident survey. In the 5 years leading to adoption of that revision, APA invited both critiques and case examples that did not seem well addressed in prior versions. During that revision APA members and the public could submit comments and cases via the APA website for electronic review by the Ethics Code Revision Task Force. The APA approach proved more relevant to actual practice than codes developed by other professional associations by virtue of the early reliance on actual incidents, and the resulting document became a model for the ethical codes of other health professions.

As the practice of psychotherapy bloomed, and as more psychologists and other professions entered the field, attention to the unique ethics of psychotherapy broadened. Other professional groups added their own perspectives, and the major professions of psychotherapists have all evolved distinct ethical codes. These include the American Association for Marriage and Family Counseling (2001), American Counseling Association (2005), American Psychiatric Association (2006), and National Association of Social Workers (1999). Many more specialized psychotherapy ethical codes exist, and one can easily locate these via Web searches (Pope, 2008).

An important survey of ethical dilemmas encountered by APA members (Pope & Vetter, 1992) yielded categories of ethically troubling incidents closely tied to psychotherapy. The prominent categories involved confidentiality; blurred, multiple, and/or conflicted relationships; and payment for services. Reports of the APA Ethics Committee describing the nature and incidence of ethical complaints, published annually in *American Psychologist*, suggest that these three categories remain the most salient bases for complaints in psychotherapy practice. In the pages that follow, we trace the evolution of these three concerns over the past 6 decades and then consider controversial professional and public issues related to psychotherapy.

CONFIDENTIALITY

American history provides many examples of how breaches in confidentiality of mental health information have hurt both clients and society. Thomas Eagleton, a senator from Missouri, was dropped as George McGovern's vice presidential running mate in 1968 following public disclosure that he had previously undergone hospitalization for the treatment of depression. Dr. Lewis J. Fielding, better known as "Daniel Ellsberg's psychiatrist," certainly did not suspect that the break-in at his office by federal agents on September 3, 1971, might ultimately contribute to the only resignation of an American president (Morganthau, Lindsay, Michael, & Givens, 1982; G. R. Stone, 2004). Disclosures of confidential information received by therapists also played prominently in the press during the well-publicized murder trials of the Menendez brothers (Scott, 2005) and O. J. Simpson (Hunt, 1999).

No discussion of confidentiality in the mental health arena can occur without reference to the Tarasoff case (*Tarasoff v. Board of Regents of the*

University of California, 1976) and the family of so-called progeny cases that followed in its wake (see Quattrocchi & Schopp, 2005; A. A. Stone, 1976; VandeCreek & Knapp, 2001), as these contributed to significant changes in how psychotherapists deal with confidentiality. The case began in fall 1969, when a student at the University of California's Berkeley campus killed Ms. Tarasoff, a young woman who had spurned his affections. The perpetrator had sought psychotherapy at the university's student health facility and gave his psychologist cause to seek civil commitment by notifying police about fears that his client posed a danger to Ms. Tarasoff. The police concluded that the patient did not pose a danger and secured a promise that he would stay away from Ms. Tarasoff. After his release by the police, the man understandably never returned for further psychotherapy, and 2 months later killed Tarasoff. California courts determined that the psychologist had a duty to protect Ms. Tarasoff and awarded damages. With respect to risk to public safety, little hard data exist to demonstrate that warnings effectively prevent harm, although reasonable indirect evidence does suggest that treatment can prevent violence (Douglas & Kropp, 2002; Otto, 2000). Obviously, ethical principles preclude direct empirical validation of management strategies that may or may not prevent people at a high risk from doing harm to others (Koocher & Keith-Spiegel, 2008).

In addition, many states had already begun passing legislation mandating that certain professionals, including psychologists, report knowledge of physical or emotional abuse of vulnerable persons (e.g., children, older people, people with disabilities). APA subsequently amended its Ethics Code to reflect authorized breaches to prevent imminent harm to self or others, or as mandated by law.

In 1996, Congress enacted Public Law 104-191, better known as the Health Insurance Portability and Accountability Act or HIPAA. Regulations and implementation took several years, but many focus on protecting the privacy of personal health information (PHI). HIPAA specifies that health care providers, including psychotherapists, must give clients specific notices about the confidentiality of records and standards for authorizing the release of PHI. It is interesting to note that the APA Ethics Code already addressed most of the key principles mandated under HIPAA, albeit with less specificity (e.g., the need to alert clients about limits of confidentiality at the outset of the professional relationship, releasing information to third parties only with a client's consent). As a result of these cases and statutes, psychotherapists in the United States must ethically give all clients information on the limits of confidentiality at the outset of a professional relationship and must breach confidentiality in certain circumstances to protect the client or other vulnerable parties.

MULTIPLE RELATIONSHIPS

The APA (2002) "Ethical Principles of Psychologists and Code of Conduct" defines multiple role relationships as occurring when a psychologist stands in a professional role with a person and also (a) holds another role with the same person, (b) has a relationship with someone closely associated with or related to the person with whom the psychologist has the professional relationship, or (c) makes promises to enter into another relationship in the future with the person or a person closely associated with or related to the person. One often cannot avoid such role overlap, and the APA Ethics Code recognizes this by noting that not all multiple role relationships with clients are necessarily unethical so long as no risk of harm can be reasonably expected. The code admonishes psychologists to refrain from entering a multiple role relationship when their objectivity, competence, or effectiveness in performing their professional functions could be impaired or if a risk of exploitation exists.

Some mental health professionals decry the concept of professional boundaries, asserting that they promote the conduct of psychotherapy as a mechanical technique rather than relating to clients as unique human beings. Such critics call attention to boundaries' rigid, cold, and aloof "cookbook therapy," harmful to the natural process of psychotherapy (Koocher & Keith-Spiegel, 2008). Lazarus (1994) put it bluntly: "Practitioners who hide behind rigid boundaries, whose sense of ethics is uncompromising, will, in my opinion, fail to really help many of the clients who are unfortunate enough to consult them" (p. 260).

The evolution of strong concern about boundaries appeared most intensely in the mid-20th century. As described in Chapter 13a, Jean-Marc Itard thought nothing of taking "the wild boy of Aveyron" into his home for treatment in 1799. In 1914, Sigmund Freud sent his daughter, Anna, on a trip to England in the care of one of his patients, Leo Kann. Freud later conducted the psychoanalysis of Anna from 1918 to 1922. Anna in turn analyzed Erik Erikson and allowed him to travel with the family on vacations so that he could continue his treatment. One of the most sensational accounts of multiple role conflicts concerns Henry A. Murray (related by his authorized biographer Forrest Robinson [1992]). In spring 1925 Murray visited Carl Jung in Zurich and told Jung of his infatuation with Christiana Morgan, the wife of a friend, with whom Murray would later create the Thematic Apperception Test. Murray's story triggered a self-disclosure by Jung of his intimate relationship with his patient Antonia "Toni" Wolff, conducted with the full approval of his wife, Emma Jung. At Murray's urging, Jung agreed to see Christina in October 1925 and encouraged her to become Murray's professional and sexual muse, while both were married to other people.

In the latter part of the 20th century, complaints by patients alleging harmful sexual intimacies with psychotherapists became significant ethical and professional problems. Increasingly, the field became aware of how social and business relationships can compromise the quality of professional services and integrity (Koocher & Keith-Spiegel, 2008). These factors led to the founding of the interdisciplinary Neuroethics Society, which held its first meeting in November 2008. The society's president, Steven Hyman, a psychiatrist turned neurobiologist and provost of Harvard University, spoke on "Neuroethics of Pediatric Bipolar Disorder." He discussed the controversy of assigning the diagnosis of bipolar disorder to hundreds of thousands of American children who never before had signs of major mood disorder, and simultaneously treating these children with powerful drugs in off-label usage (i.e., treatment with drugs neither tested nor approved by the Food and Drug Administration for use in children). Other speakers noted the extremely rare incidence of the same diagnosis outside of the United States.

As new medications abound, adult diagnoses such as bipolar disorder and attendant off-label drug treatments have found their way to children as young as 2 or 3 years old. Such medications pose significant unevaluated risks for children at young ages. How has this ethically risky practice evolved? Recent congressional investigations by Senator Chuck Grassley (R-Iowa) have revealed enormous conflicts of interests involving several of the strongest proponents of such medical applications. Two *Boston Globe* reporters broke the story of a world-renowned Harvard Medical School professor and child psychiatrist at the Massachusetts General Hospital whose work fueled "an explosion in the use of powerful antipsychotic medicines in children," earning him at least $1.6 million in consulting fees from pharmaceutical companies between 2000 and 2007. The psychiatrist and two of his colleagues allegedly never reported much of their income from the drug companies, estimated at a combined $4.2 million over 7 years, to university officials (Harris & Carey, 2008). The psychiatrists earned much of the money giving continuing medical education lectures teaching other physicians about prescribing such drugs to children.

Couple these circumstances with long-sought mental health parity legislation (i.e., granting fiscal parity to coverage of mental conditions with that afforded physical conditions), and one sees interesting contradictions. The same professionals who support a biopsychosocial model of emotional problems willingly adopted enough focus on "illness" to seek insurance reimbursement parity (i.e., more money to pay providers). Many psychiatrists, who have increasingly eschewed psychotherapy training over psychopharmacology practice (Gabbard, 2005), have flocked to incorporate the new off-label uses into their practices. Just as others have argued against viewing psychological problems as mental illnesses (Szasz, 1960), we now see economic forces aligning to promote remedicalization of such difficulties and even create new ones to fit existing or newly created drug protocols (Harris & Carey, 2008). Many years will pass before one can assess whether these shifting roles, trends, and motivations benefit patients or practitioners more.

PAYMENT PROBLEMS

Payment for psychotherapy services has played a significant role in the evolution of service delivery. In particular, the advent of health insurance and coverage for mental conditions influences who practices psychotherapy and how. During the early years of the psychoanalytic movement, few people sought or could afford individual therapy, and professional regulation as we know it today did not exist. So-called lay analysts abounded. From the perspective of psychology, the post–World War II era saw a boom in the training of psychologists and struggles with psychiatry over which profession owned psychotherapy. The key became insurance reimbursement, as psychologists sought licensing recognition, demanded "freedom of choice" laws, and created organizations such as the National Register of Health Service Providers in Psychology to help secure insurance coverage for their services. The 1990s brought managed care and growing ranks of licensed mental health providers who needed to account to third parties (i.e., the client and therapist being the first and second parties) for their therapeutic decisions and treatment plans.

Today, newly licensed mental health professionals worry about their ability to secure a listing on overcrowded rolls of approved health insurance providers. And practice patterns have changed dramatically. Most younger psychiatrists have reduced or completely ceased practicing psychotherapy in favor of pharmacotherapy (Gabbard, 2005), and licensed psychotherapists at the master's degree level abound. This has led to many efforts by psychotherapists to differentiate themselves with brand-name psychotherapies, discussed below, and has led to a host of ethical problems related to third-party payments. Some of these concern co-insurance (i.e., copayments and deductibles), billing for missed appointments, and other potential contract violations (Koocher & Keith-Spiegel, 2008). The key to ethical conduct in financial matters involves carefully informing clients of fees and other costs in advance and securing their agreement to these prior to billing. In addition, when psychologists sign a contract with a third-party payer, they must honor provisions of that contract by such acts as collecting specified copayments and not billing clients for amounts in excess of contractual agreements.

The modern reality involves ethical dealings with clients, government, and insurers who have a powerful say in what services they will pay for and what data they will demand to process such payments. In every case, obeying contractual agreements, clear communication with clients, and accurate billing form the essentials of ethical conduct.

OTHER ETHICAL CHALLENGES IN PSYCHOTHERAPY

Changes in social values also led to changes in the way psychotherapists conceptualize their ethical values and practices. Such issues have included perceptions of mental illness, same-sex attraction, and the rights of individuals to express a preference for rational suicide in cases of painful terminal illness. As society has changed, psychotherapists have found themselves facing situations and client preferences they could not have envisioned during their professional years earlier.

Myth of Mental Illness Debate

In 1960, Thomas Szasz, a psychiatrist, published an article titled "The Myth of Mental Illness." He argued against the medical or disease model of mental illness, which presumes that underlying biological defects can explain all disorders in thinking and behavior. Szasz differentiated between physical symptoms, such as pain or fever, and mental symptoms, asserting that believing one's delusion requires a cognitive judgment. He saw mental symptoms as tied to the social and ethical contexts in which they occur.

Szasz objected to claims that any health treatment (including psychotherapy) could ever become value neutral, noting that it is actually tied closely to cultural and moral values that one often fails to recognize explicitly. He regarded disorders of the brain as falling chiefly under the rubric of neurology and insisted that the psychotherapists of the 1960s dealt primarily with problems in living, not mental illnesses.

The same year Szasz published his article, O. H. Mowrer (1960), a former APA president, published, "'Sin,' the Lesser of Two Evils." He argued that troubled people, described as "neurotics," experience self-torture and suffer from excessive rigidity. He suggested that confessing one's sins causes the conscience to loosen its stranglehold, letting society and the superego relax, and allowing the person to become free and well. Mowrer's assumption: Psychologists could seek to remedy unacknowledged sin with psychotherapy.

Suicide Prevention and the Duty to Protect

Ethical principles across mental health professions clearly emphasize the importance of protecting clients from harm, including self-harm. Most mental health ethics texts (e.g., Koocher & Keith-Spiegel, 2008; Pope & Vasquez, 2007) devote significant discussion to suicidal risk assessment and intervention, and rightly so, because failure to prevent suicide often leads to complaints against a deceased patient's psychotherapist. Thoughtful clinicians will screen all clients for suicidal risk during initial contact and remain alert to possible risks throughout treatment.

A recent *New York Times* article (Anderson, 2008) described a premeditation–passion dichotomy to explain how some individuals carefully plan their suicide while others act impulsively using any means available to kill themselves. One must consider how people commit suicide rather than primarily focusing on why they attempt it. The article cites the National Institute of Mental Health (NIMH) as reporting that about 90% of all completed U.S. suicides involve people with a diagnosable mental disorder. It seems clear that psychotherapists will continue to encounter suicidal patients and bear a duty to prevent suicide by comprehensive interventions involving psychotherapy and medication, and separating them from the means of harming themselves through hospitalization if necessary.

Szasz (1986) pointed out that a director of NIMH had in 1967 described suicide as a "disease and public health problem" (p. 806) and reviewed the resulting difficulties in addressing suicide risk by ethicists, if it qualifies as a disease. For example, competent adults have the right to decline treatment, even for fatal illnesses. Szasz argued against suicide prevention (at least coercive prevention), asserting that the mental state of any potentially suicidal individual has no bearing on instituting coercive action. Szasz did not object to helping suicidal patients in psychotherapy but believed that all people should assume responsibility for their own behavior unless delirium or acute psychosis requires physical restraint as an integral part of caring for that patient (p. 810). He insisted, however, that the state should not have the right to prohibit or prevent suicide.

Can rational suicide qualify as a valid quality-of-life decision requiring psychotherapists to eschew aggressive intervention? Let's fast forward to the topic of assisted suicide. In 1997, Oregon enacted the Death With Dignity Act, allowing patients to obtain prescriptions from physicians to achieve a humane and dignified death under specified circumstances (Abeles & Barlev, 1999). Under the Oregon law, such patients must not suffer from impaired judgment and must have a terminal disease. Consider that law in the context of a 21-year-old man in Michigan, who had become ventilator dependent as the result of quadriplegia (Abeles & Barlev, 1999). Reportedly, he became depressed and sought to discontinue using the ventilator knowing that doing so would cause his death. He insisted he wanted to die and sought discharge to home. His mother agreed with his decision, but the hospital objected. The courts allowed his discharge, he returned home, and died following a visit from Dr. Kervorkian (Reye, 1998). The courts ruled his death a homicide.

The ethics codes of both the American Psychiatric Association (2006) and APA (2002) authorize intervention to prevent suicide. The National Association of Social Workers (1994), however, provided a position statement authorizing nonintervention in jurisdictions where laws permit assisted suicide. The debate concerning physician-assisted suicide has increased since the U.S. Supreme Court's holding that physician-assisted suicide remains a state, rather than a federal, matter (*Gonzales v. Oregon*, 2006).

Many professionals (e.g., Werth, 1996) argue that suicide can constitute a rational act in some circumstances and present several criteria to support the argument. These include the existence of a hopeless condition, circumstances in which the decision constitutes a free choice, and clear indications that the person has engaged in a sound decision-making process. A decision of suicide should include consultation, nonimpulsive consideration of all alternatives, and consideration of the impact the act would have on significant others. The only existing state law on assisted suicide (Oregon) requires evaluation by competent professionals to determine that the patient's judgment remains unimpaired. The APA (2005) report on the role of psychology in end-of-life decisions and quality of care identified four roles that psychologists play in this area: clinical care, education and training, research, and policy.

Sexual Orientation Conversion or Reparative Therapy

Sexual orientation conversion therapies, once considered a treatment of choice when society deemed homosexuality an illness or form of psychopathology, raise a number of ethical challenges. For over a century, medical, psychotherapeutic, and religious practitioners sought to reverse unwanted same-sex attraction or homosexual orientation through a variety of methods, including psychoanalysis, prayer, electric shock, nausea-inducing drugs, hormone therapy, surgery, and a variety of behavioral treatments, including masturbatory reconditioning, visits to prostitutes, and even excessive bicycle riding. The American Psychiatric Association's 1973 decision to remove homosexuality from its seventh printing of the second edition of the *Diagnostic and Statistical Manual of Mental Disorders* (DSM–II) in 1974 marked the official demise of the illness model of homosexuality. Despite this official "depathologizing" of homosexuality, efforts by both mental health professionals and pastoral care providers to convert lesbians and gay men to heterosexuality have persisted (Greene, 2007).

Such efforts, variously described as *conversion therapy, reparative therapy,* or *therapy to eliminate same-sex attraction,* span a variety of treatments. So-called reparative therapy emerged in the early 1980s as a "new method of curing" homosexuals. Elizabeth Moberly, a conservative British Christian theologian with a PhD in experimental psychology, became a key proponent of the approach after publishing her theory "that the homosexual . . . whether man or woman . . . has suffered from some deficit in the relationship with the parent of the same sex; and that there is a corresponding drive to make good this deficit . . . through the medium of same-sex, or 'homosexual,' relationships" (Moberly, 1983, p. 2). Organizations currently promoting psychotherapy for individuals with same-sex attraction often have moralistic or religious underpinnings and include the National Association for Research and Therapy of Homosexuality and Jews Offering New Alternatives to Homosexuality.

The ethical imperative of respect for clients requires psychotherapists to take guidance from and engage clients in goal setting. Some clients present themselves for treatment, describing emotional problems associated with same-sex attraction. In such circumstances the therapist has an obligation to carefully explore how patients arrive at their choices. Some motives may result from social pressures or experiences with homophobic environments. No type or amount of individual psychotherapy will modify societal prejudices. In addition, as part of informed consent to treatment, therapists must help clients understand the potential consequences of any treatment, including those intended to modify sexual orientation. Clients have a right to know that reparative treatments lack any validated scientific foundation and may prove harmful. Finally, clients have the right to know that organizations representing the mental health professions do not consider homosexuality a mental disorder.

Two additional ethical concerns accompany so-called reparative treatments. First, to what extent does offering such treatments comport with therapist responsibility and consumer welfare? Second, given that rigorous empirical studies fail to show that conversion therapies work, do therapists offering such interventions without clear disclaimers and cautions mislead clients (Greene, 2007; Koocher & Keith-Spiegel, 2008)? APA (1998) addressed these concerns with a Resolution on Appropriate Therapeutic Responses to Sexual Orientation, and similar positions have emanated from other professional groups (e.g., American Psychiatric Association, 1998, 2000; National Association of Social Workers, 2000). These standards essentially allow therapists to address the stated needs of clients, so long as they fully inform clients regarding known limitations.

Teletherapy

Rapid advances in microelectronics have made portable communication, data, image, sound storage, and transmission devices affordable and readily available in much of the world. A broad array of personal communications and business transactions now occur in cyberspace. Mental health practitioners increasingly face expectations by clients to provide services in the context of their preferred modes of communication. As psychotherapists move away from the traditional context of sitting face-to-face with a client across a room, the Greek prefix *tele*, meaning from a distance, leads naturally to considering the ethics of teletherapy. Telehealth is used in medicine and mental health for a variety of professional services via telephone and other electronic means (e.g., Barnett & Scheetz, 2003; C. B. Fisher & Fried, 2003). Many medical specialties have regularly used these techniques for consultation among professionals, and a number of services now offer such consultation directly to patients for a fee (e.g., http://www.eclevelandclinic.org/eCCHome.jsp). The traditional way of forming alliances and contracts with individual clients and professional standards will certainly require rethinking.

From the perspective of professional ethics, consider the four Cs: contracting, competence, confidentiality, and control (Koocher, 2007). In the context of teletherapy, these questions arise: What contracts or agreements for providing distance services will we as psychotherapists make with our clients? What competencies will we need to offer services remotely? What new factors will constrain confidentiality protections? Who will control the practice of teletherapy (i.e., the regulation of practice and data access)?

When psychotherapists agree to work with clients via teletherapy, the nature and terms of how they relate to clients will change. Psychotherapists will need to reach accords on new contracts regarding the nature of psychological services and the manner of providing them. For example, psychotherapists will have to obtain and document clients' informed consent to communicate with them electronically. Such consent will doubtless require many changes, such as establishing reasonable security and encryption precautions, keeping information posted on professional websites up to date, and providing instructions regarding access and emergency coverage.

Still other questions must be answered: Will we as psychotherapists contract to correspond electronically only with existing therapy clients, or will we readily accept new referrals of people whom we have never met for professional services? Will we agree to conduct assessment, consultation, or therapy entirely via telemetry or only a limited range of services? Will we promise real-time electronic access 24/7/365? How will record keeping change, given the ease with which we can record, store, and alter such communications? Will our fees and reimbursement policies differ from office-based services? Will we offer emergency coverage? If so, what backup must we organize for clients who live hundreds or thousands of miles away?

New standards of care and professional competencies will certainly apply when we offer therapy services remotely. APA has not chosen to address teletherapy directly in its Ethics Code (APA Ethics Committee, 1997), and by this intentional omission has created no rules prohibiting such services.

Telehealth brings the obvious potential for mischief. Those offering to provide services and those seeking to obtain them may more easily engage in misrepresentation. How can one be certain that the person on the other end of the phone line or computer terminal is the person he or she claims to be? How accurate are the claims of teletherapy practitioners regarding their credentials, skills, and success rates with remote interventions? How will therapists feel when an angry former client posts edited excerpts of their "sessions" on youtube.com or stupidvideos.com? Will teletherapy lead to greater caution and reduced liability (e.g., by reducing the risk of client–therapist sexual intimacy) or greater risk (e.g., reduced ability to respond across distances with suicidal clients)? We will probably have answers to such intriguing questions in the not-so-distant future.

Answers about the control or regulation of teletherapy remain highly fluid. Considerable variability exists across licensing jurisdictions in the United States with respect to electronic practice across state lines. With state, provincial, and territorial governments regulating professional practice within United States and Canadian jurisdictions, the Association of State and Provincial Psychology Boards has taken the lead in attempting to foster interstate practice and mobility credentials for psychologists in North America. However, little agreement exists regarding standards for interstate or international telepractice. When a client in Massachusetts enters teletherapy with a psychotherapist in Michigan, or Mumbai, who regulates the practice? Does the treatment take place where the client sits, where the therapist sits, or in cyberspace? If something goes wrong, to whom can one complain? Will telepractice qualify as interstate (or international commerce) exempt from state licensing authorities? We simply do not know the answers at this time.

Brand-Name or Proprietary Psychotherapies

Many psychotherapies have acquired brand-name status over the years. Psychoanalysis probably qualifies as the first established brand of therapy, even though (as described earlier) the practice of psychoanalysis today differs significantly from treatment at Freud's Vienna Polyclinic (see Chapter 3, this volume). We have chosen two different proprietary therapies to illustrate the ethical challenges they pose.

Eye Movement Desensitization and Reprocessing.

Eye movement desensitization and reprocessing (EMDR), developed by Francine Shapiro (Shapiro, 1995; Shapiro & Forrest, 2004), is described as a comprehensive method for treating disturbing experiences such as trauma associated with sexual abuse, violence, combat, and grief. The treatment incorporates eight stages (using Shapiro's terminology): taking the client's history and treatment planning, preparation, assessment, desensitization and reprocessing, installation of positive cognition, body scan, closure, and reevaluation. The treatment asks the client to describe aspects of traumatic memories, including recounting mental images associated with the event, the client's emotional and physiological responses, and the negative feelings of self contained in the memories The technique repeats the sequence of steps until the client's subjective units of distress scale (so-called SUDS rating) approaches zero.

EMDR has become one of the fastest growing treatments in the annals of psychotherapy, and its progression has many similarities with the history of mesmerism (McNally, 1999). EMDR as a treatment for posttraumatic stress disorder has received widely divergent reactions from the scientific and professional community. Perkins and Rouanzoin (2002) noted that many points of confusion exist in the published literature on EMDR, including its theoretical and historical foundation, placebo effects, exposure procedures, the eye movement component, treatment fidelity, and outcome studies. They described the charges of "pseudoscience" surrounding EMDR and attributed the controversy to confusion in the published literature focused on five factors: the lack of an empirically validated model capable of convincingly explaining the effects of EMDR; inaccurate or selective reporting of research; some poorly designed studies; inadequate treatment fidelity in some of the outcome studies; and multiple biased or inaccurate reviews by a relatively small group of authors.

EMDR involves many elements of exposure and cognitive–behavioral therapies, along with the lateral eye movements, causing some to wonder whether the effective component of EMDR actually qualifies as new, and whether the genuinely new aspects of EMDR qualify as effective (McNally, 1999). Shapiro (personal communication, January 17, 2007) argued that EMDR actually integrates many components in addition to cognitive–behavioral elements, including those used in psychodynamic and experiential therapies. In one book, Shapiro (2002) asked experts of the various orientations in experiential, cognitive, and psychodynamic treatment to identify the elements in EMDR that made it effective. Each one identified elements of his or her own orientation as the pivotal factors.

Reviews of the related eye movement research have provided a range of conclusions. Some reviewers (Lohr, Lilienfeld, Tolin, & Herbert, 1999) found no compelling evidence that eye movements contribute to outcome in EMDR, and the lack of unequivocal findings has led some reviewers to dismiss eye movements altogether (e.g., McNally, 1999). Other reviewers (e.g., Chemtob et al., 2000; Perkins & Rouanzoin, 2002) identified methodological failings (e.g., lack of statistical power, floor effects) and called for more rigorous study. Nonetheless, many studies have demonstrated beneficial outcomes for some people using EMDR (e.g., Brown & Shapiro, 2006; Konuk et al., 2006; Raboni, Tufik, & Suchecki, 2006). The Department of Veterans Affairs and Department of Defense (2004) listed EMDR as a potentially effective treatment in their clinical practice guideline for the management of posttraumatic stress.

Although EMDR has clearly proved beneficial for many clients, its aggressive marketing, early restrictions on teaching, and resulting aura of secretiveness have contributed to a sense of mystique and controversy. Shapiro had attempted to assure a standard quality in the training of EMDR (Shapiro, 1995; Shapiro & Forrest, 2004). Proponents founded a nonprofit professional organization named EMDR International Association (EMDRIA) as a forum "where practitioners and researchers seek the highest standards . . . by promoting training, research and the sharing of the latest clinical information . . . assuring that therapists are knowledgeable and skilled in the methodology" (according to its website: http://www.emdria.org/). Sadly, Shapiro's work has spawned some creative imitators with questionable rigor who probably cause consternation to well-trained clinicians (Koocher & Keith-Spiegel, 2008).

est

Werner Erhard, the developer of *est* (Erhard seminar training), was a skilled salesman with no professional training as a psychotherapist. His program evolved to become the "Forum" seminars (Efran, Lukens, & Lukens, 1986; Wistow, 1986) and exists currently as the Landmark Forum, a genre of so-called large group awareness programs (Finkelstein, Wenegrat, & Yalom, 1982). The basic approach challenged participants' sense of psychological identity or, as one commentator noted, systematic escalation and discounting of each participant's "adapted child," eventually forcing the participant into their "free child" state, thereby releasing a large amount of "bound energy" (Klein, 1983, p. 178). Other articles have described est as brainwashing (Moss & Hosford, 1983). One of the few careful attempts to study Erhard's techniques in a rigorous fashion showed no long-term treatment effects and declared claims of far-reaching effects for programs of the Forum as exaggerated (J. D. Fisher et al., 1989).

The ability of skilled salesmen, such as Erhard, to promote and morph their programs in the absence of controlled outcome research and in the face of criticism by behavioral scientists is quite impressive. The central message from an ethical perspective remains the obligation of therapists to have a sound scientific foundation for their work. Rigorous proof of efficacy should precede mass marketing of new techniques to the public or to colleagues.

CONCLUSION

In covering the history of ethics in psychotherapy, we have traversed the emergence of ethical consensus and code of conduct on confidentiality, multiple conflicts, and payment problems. We have selected contentious debates and controversies that had raised significant ethical issues related to psychotherapy. We have no doubt that changes in the health care system, society, and technology will continue to force ethical reexamination about the manner in which psychotherapy is practiced.

REFERENCES

Abeles, N., & Barlev, A. (1999). End of life decisions and assisted suicide. *Professional Psychology: Research and Practice, 30*, 229–234. doi:10.1037/0735-7028.30.3.229

American Association for Marriage and Family Therapy. (2001). *Code of ethics.* Alexandria, VA: Author.

American Counseling Association. (2005). *Code of ethics.* Alexandria, VA: Author.

American Psychiatric Association. (1998). *Position statement on psychiatric treatment and sexual orientation: December 11, 1998.* Arlington, VA: Author.

American Psychiatric Association. (2000). Commission on Psychotherapy by Psychiatrists (COPP): Position statement on therapies focused on attempts to change sexual orientation (Reparative or conversion therapies). *American Journal of Psychiatry, 157*, 1719–1721.

American Psychiatric Association. (2006). *Principles of medical ethics: With annotations especially applicable to psychiatry.* Arlington, VA: Author.

American Psychological Association. (1953). *Ethical standards of psychologists.* Washington, DC: Author.

American Psychological Association. (1998). Proceedings of the American Psychological Association, Incorporated, for the legislative year 1997. *American Psychologist, 53*, 882–939.

American Psychological Association. (2002). *Ethical principles of psychologists and code of conduct.* Washington, DC: Author.

American Psychological Association. (2005). *The role of psychology in end-of-life decisions and quality of care.* Retrieved from http://www.apa.org/pi/eol/role.html

American Psychological Association Ethics Committee. (1997). *Statement on services by telephone, teleconferencing, and Internet.* Retrieved from http://apa.org/ethics/stmnt01.html

Anderson, S. (2008, July 6). The urge to end it all. *New York Times Magazine.* Retrieved from http://www.nytimes.com/2008/07/06/magazine/06suicide-t.html

Barnett, J. E., & Scheetz, K. (2003). Technological advances and telehealth: Ethics, law, and the practice of psychotherapy. *Psychotherapy: Theory, Research, Practice, Training, 40*, 86–93.

Brown, S., & Shapiro, F. (2006). EMDR in the treatment of borderline personality disorder. *Clinical Case Studies, 5*, 403–420. doi:10.1177/1534650104271773

Chemtob, C. M., Tolin, D. F., van der Kolk, B. A., & Pitman, R. K. (2000). Eye movement desensitization and reprocessing. In E. B. Foa, T. M. Keane, & M. J. Friedman (Eds.), *Effective treatments for PTSD: Practice guidelines from the International Society for Traumatic Stress Studies* (pp. 139–154). New York, NY: Guilford Press.

Department of Veterans Affairs & Department of Defense. (2004). *Clinical practice guideline for the management of post-traumatic stress* (Office of Quality and Performance Report

No. 10Q-CPG/PTSD-04). Washington, DC: Veterans Health Administration, Department of Veterans Affairs and Health Affairs, Department of Defense.

Douglas, K. S., & Kropp, P. R. (2002). A prevention-based paradigm for violence risk assessment: Clinical and research applications. *Criminal Justice and Behavior 29*, 617–658.

Efran, J. S., Lukens, M. D., & Lukens, R. J. (1986). It's all done with mirrors. *Family Therapy Networker, 10*, 41–49.

Finkelstein, P., Wenegrat, B., & Yalom, I. (1982). Large group awareness training. *Annual Review of Psychology, 33*, 515–539. doi:10.1146/annurev.ps.33.020182.002503

Fisher, C. B., & Fried, A. L. (2003). Internet-mediated psychological services and the American Psychological Association ethics code. *Psychotherapy: Theory, Research, Practice, Training, 40*, 103–111.

Fisher, J. D., Silver, R. C., Chinsky, J. M., Goff, B., Klar, Y., & Zagieboylo, C. (1989). Psychological effects of participation in a large group awareness training. *Journal of Consulting and Clinical Psychology, 57*, 747–755. doi:10.1037/0022-006X.57.6.747

Flanagan, J. C. (1954). The critical incident technique. *Psychological Bulletin, 51*, 327–358. doi:10.1037/h0061470

Gabbard, G. O. (2005). How not to teach psychotherapy. *Academic Psychiatry, 29*, 332–338. doi:10.1176/appi.ap.29.4.332

Golann, S. E. (1969). Emerging areas of ethical concern. *American Psychologist, 24*, 454–459. doi:10.1037/h0027869

Gonzales v. Oregon, 546 U.S. 243, 126 S. Ct. 904 (2006).

Greene, B. (2007). Delivering ethical psychological services to lesbian, gay, and bisexual clients. In K. J. Bieschke, R. M. Perez, & K. A. DeBord (Eds.), *Handbook of counseling and psychotherapy with lesbian, gay, bisexual, and transgender clients* (2nd ed., pp. 181–199). Washington, DC: American Psychological Association. doi:10.1037/11482-007

Harris, G., & Carey, B. (2008, June 8). Researchers fail to reveal full drug pay. *The New York Times*. Retrieved from http://www.nytimes.com/2008/06/08/us/08conflict.html

Hobbs, N. (1948). The development of a code of ethical standards for psychology. *American Psychologist, 3*, 80–84. doi:10.1037/h0060281

Hunt, D. M. (1999). *O. J. Simpson: Facts and fictions*. Cambridge, UK: Cambridge University Press.

Klein, M. (1983). How EST works. *Transactional Analysis Journal, 13*, 178–180.

Konuk, E., Knipe, J., Eke, I., Yuksek, H., Yurtsever, A., & Ostep, S. (2006). The effects of eye movement desensitization and reprocessing (EMDR) therapy on posttraumatic stress disorder in survivors of the 1999 Marmara, Turkey, earthquake. *International Journal of Stress Management, 13*, 291–308. doi:10.1037/1072-5245.13.3.291

Koocher, G. P. (2007). 21st century ethical challenges for psychology. *American Psychologist, 62*, 375–384. doi:10.1037/0003-066X.62.5.375

Koocher, G. P., & Keith-Spiegel, P. (2008). *Ethics in psychology and the mental health profession: Standards and cases* (3rd ed.). New York, NY: Oxford University Press.

Lazarus, A. A. (1994). How certain boundaries and ethics diminish therapeutic effectiveness. *Ethics and Behavior, 4*, 255–261. doi:10.1207/s15327019eb0403_10

Lohr, J. M., Lilienfeld, S. O., Tolin, D. F., & Herbert, J. D. (1999). Eye movement desensitization and reprocessing: An analysis of specific versus nonspecific treatment factors. *Journal of Anxiety Disorders, 13*, 185–207. doi:10.1016/S0887-6185(98)00047-4

McNally, R. J. (1999). EMDR and mesmerism: A comparative historical analysis. *Journal of Anxiety Disorders, 13*, 225–236. doi:10.1016/S0887-6185(98)00049-8

Moberly, E. (1983). *Homosexuality: A new Christian ethic*. Greenwood, SC: Attic Press.

Morganthau, T., Lindsay, J. J., Michael, R., & Givens, R. (1982, June 14). The unanswered questions. *Newsweek*, p. 40.Moss, C. S., & Hosford, R. E. (1983). Reflections on est training from the viewpoint of two correctional psychologists. *Journal of Integrative and Eclectic Psychotherapy*, 2, 18–39.

Mowrer, O. H. (1960). "Sin," the lesser of two evils. *American Psychologist*, 15, 301–304. doi:10.1037/h0045069

National Association of Social Workers. (1994). *Client self-determination in end-of-life decisions: Social work speaks* (3rd ed.). Washington, DC: Author.

National Association of Social Workers. (1999). *Code of ethics*. Washington, DC: Author.

National Association of Social Workers. (2000). *"Reparative" or "conversion" therapies for lesbian and gay men*. Washington, DC: Author.

Otto, R. K. (2000). Assessing and managing violence risk in outpatient settings. *Journal of Clinical Psychology*, 56, 1239–1262.

Perkins, B. R., & Rouanzoin, C. C. (2002). A critical evaluation of current views regarding eye movement desensitization and reprocessing (EMDR): Clarifying points of confusion. *Journal of Clinical Psychology*, 58, 77–97. doi:10.1002/jclp.1130

Pope, K. S. (2008). *Ethics codes and practice guidelines for assessment, therapy, counseling, and forensic practice*. Retrieved from http://kspope.com/ethcodes/index.php

Pope, K. S., & Vasquez, M. (2007). *Ethics in psychotherapy and counseling* (3rd ed.). San Francisco, CA: Wiley.

Pope, K. S., & Vetter, V. (1992). Ethical dilemmas encountered by members of the American Psychological Association. *American Psychologist*, 47, 397–411. doi:10.1037/0003-066X.47.3.397

Quattrocchi, M. R., & Schopp, R. F. (2005). Tarasaurus Rex: A standard of care that could not adapt. *Psychology, Public Policy, and Law*, 11, 109–137.

Raboni, M. R., Tufik, S., & Suchecki, D. (2006). Treatment of PTSD by eye movement desensitization reprocessing (EMDR) improves sleep quality, quality of life, and perception of stress. In *Annals of New York Academy of Sciences: Vol. 1071. Psychobiology of posttraumatic stress disorders: A decade of progress* (pp. 508–513). Malden, MA: Blackwell.

Reye, B. (1998, February 28). 21-year-old quadriplegic's death ruled a homicide. *The Detroit News*, p. 1.

Robinson, F. G. (1992). *Love's story told: A life of Henry A. Murray*. Cambridge, MA: Harvard University Press.

Scott, G. G. (2005). *Homicide by the rich and famous: A century of prominent killers*. Westport, CT: Praeger.

Shapiro, F. (1995). *Eye movement desensitization and reprocessing: Basic principles, protocols, and procedures*. New York, NY: Guilford Press.

Shapiro, F. (2002). (Ed.). *EMDR as an integrative psychotherapy approach: Experts of diverse orientations explore the paradigm prism*. Washington, DC: American Psychological Association.

Shapiro, F., & Forrest, M. S. (2004). *EMDR: The breakthrough therapy for overcoming anxiety, stress, and trauma*. New York, NY: Basic Books.

Stone, A. A. (1976). The Tarasoff decisions: Suing psychotherapists to safeguard society. *Harvard Law Review*, 90, 358–378.

Stone, G. R. (2004). *Perilous times: Free speech in wartime from the Sedition Act of 1798 to the war on terrorism*. New York, NY: Norton.

Szasz, T. (1960). The myth of mental illness. *American Psychologist*, 15, 113–118. doi:10.1037/h0046535

Szasz, T. (1986). The case against suicide prevention. *American Psychologist, 41*, 806–812. doi:10.1037/0003-066X.41.7.806

Tarasoff v. Regents of University of California, 17 Cal.3d 425.

VandeCreek, L., & Knapp, S. (2001). *Tarasoff and beyond: Legal and clinical considerations in the treatment of life-endangering patients*. Sarasota, FL: Professional Resource Press.

Werth, J. (1996). *Rational suicide?* New York, NY: Taylor & Francis.

Wistow, F. (1986). Being there. *Family Therapy Networker, 10*, 20–29, 77–80.

VI

EPILOGUE: CONCLUSIONS
AND THE FUTURE

19

INTO THE FUTURE: RETROSPECT AND PROSPECT IN PSYCHOTHERAPY

JOHN C. NORCROSS, DONALD K. FREEDHEIM,
AND GARY R. VANDENBOS

History, according to G. K. Chesterton, is a hill or high point of vantage from which people can see the place in which they live or the age in which they are living. We would advance Chesterton's line of reasoning to suggest that the history of psychotherapy is also an indispensable vantage point from which to view—and to guide—the future of psychotherapy. "One faces the future with one's past," as Pearl Buck observed.

In this concluding chapter, we reverse the temporal focus from the past to the future. Our objective is not to predict events in a soothsayer's manner; history is replete with confident but erroneous predictions about the future and people who then act on them as truth without question or cavil. Rather, our goal is to extract and amplify salient trends that may occupy us in the next decade. We draw on three principal sources in tentatively addressing the future of psychotherapy: (a) the preceding chapters in this volume, (b) the extant literature on the future of psychotherapy, and (c) a review of our own predictions from the first edition of this book, published 20 years ago.

IN RETROSPECT

In the first edition of this book, published in 1992, we sought emerging themes for psychotherapy practitioners, researchers, and trainers. After reading, and rereading, the preceding chapters—our hill or high point of vantage—we detected several nascent directions for the future of psychotherapy. These themes ran deeply and ofttimes subtly throughout the contributions, but their ramifications were invariably audible. We gave voice and presence to six recurring future themes that emerged throughout the book: pluralism, contextualism, prescriptionism, therapeutic alliance, socioeconomic pressures, and process–outcome linkages (Norcross & Freedheim, 1992).

Before attempting to look forward into the future, it might be well to review those six themes and see just how accurate, or inaccurate, we were in 1992. We discuss each briefly in the context of the ensuing 20-plus years and the relevant chapters in this edition. It is interesting to note the continuity and change in each theme.

Pluralism

We predicted, first, a continuing expansion of treatment settings, theoretical orientations, and therapy providers. We were certainly on target here.

One of the remarkable events of modern society is how quickly professions change and diversify. Only 120 years ago, a veritable wink of the eye in a historical sense, psychotherapy was practiced almost exclusively in an individual format by medically trained men in independent practice from a psychoanalytic perspective with middle-class women (and a few men) in Vienna. The chapters in the first edition—and now in the second edition—underscore the escalating pluralism of the psychotherapeutic scene.

Chapters 1 and 2 highlight the expanding locales in which psychotherapy is now practiced: private practice, universities, psychiatric units, primary care offices, child and family guidance centers, schools, hospitals, HMOs, counseling centers, community mental health centers, prisons, the military, and so forth. Some psychotherapists practice in situ or on location, aiding both victims and rescue workers at natural and accidental disaster sites, such as floods, hurricanes, fires, and air crashes. Other psychotherapists practice nowhere and everywhere—online with individual clients or 24/7 though their computerized treatment packages and Web sites (Jerome et al., 2000).

Theoretical orientations continue to evolve. Over the past 20 years, psychoanalytic (Johns, 2000; Chapter 3) and humanistic therapies (Chapter 5) have diminished in professional popularity as integrative–eclectic (Chapter 9) and cognitive–behavioral treatments have replaced them in preeminence. A nationwide survey of American psychologists, counselors, and social workers, for example, showed integrative and cognitive at the top of primary orientations with 24% each. Psychoanalytic–psychodynamic followed with 16% endorsement and humanistic with 9% endorsement (Bike, Norcross, & Schatz, 2009).

The present is increasingly characterized by theoretical pluralism. In fact, we needed to expand the theory section in this edition to seven theoretical orientations to capture this diversity. Still other chapters (e.g., interpersonal, developmental) could have been added. Within theories, as several authors have pointed out, it is patently inaccurate to speak of a single theory or uniform practice of any particular theoretical orientation. To do so is to fall prey to the uniformity myth (Kiesler, 1966).

The number of professions conducting psychotherapy increases steadily. Recent entries hail from life coaches and executive coaches. The only profession diminishing in delivering psychotherapy is psychiatry. Between 1997 and 2005, the percentage of psychiatrists who provided psychotherapy to all their patients declined from 19.1% to 10.8% (Moran, 2009). Although initially dominated by psychiatrists and psychoanalysts, psychotherapy is now primarily conducted by nonmedical and nonpsychoanalytic clinicians. Psychologists outnumber psychiatrists as health service providers, and the number of clinical social workers outnumber both combined (see Chapter 3).

Pluralism must be reconciled, of course, with client benefit and research evidence. Uncritical acceptance of every new development is not prized. This view is embodied in the distinction between informed pluralism and uninformed faith. As the Maharishi of Jaipur was once reported to have said, "Keep an open mind. An open mind is a very good thing, but don't keep your mind so open that your brains fall out."

Contextualism

The second theme we discerned 20 years ago concerned the centrality of context, particularly the sociocultural context, of psychotherapy. The recent past has largely confirmed our prediction because the lesson of contextualism is being learned, and relearned, in psychotherapy. Cultural norms and political institutions shape both individual lives and professions' trajectories. Harshly put, "contextless is meaningless," or at least less meaningful than a full appreciation of the surrounding sociocultural environment.

Psychotherapists now acknowledge that treatment is never conducted in a vacuum; it is a cultural invention situated within a particular contextual frame. The therapist and patient are never alone. "Third parties" frequently interlope with their own needs and agendas.

Twenty years ago, we expected contextualism to be manifested in equal parts political and cultural. We were wrong. Only the latter—culture—reigned in the past 2 decades. The political context stalled, along with legislation for a national health insurance and a single-payor system. Although some will argue that the historic election of an African American to the U.S. presidency reflects the power of the political context, its influence on psychotherapy has been muted and indirect so far.

The 1990s and 2000s witnessed the multicultural revolution in psychotherapy. As amply documented in this edition, culturally sensitive treatments (Chapter 8) and culture-specific research programs (Chapter 12k) blossomed. During this era, psychotherapists paid more than the historic lip service to diversity within themselves (Chapter 2) and in their clients (Chapter 13e). And we have every reason to believe that multiculturalism will continue to thrive and be infused throughout theory, research, practice, and training.

Prescriptionism

Abraham Maslow was fond of repeating the adage "If you only have a hammer, you treat everything like a nail." The early history of psychotherapy repeatedly confirmed Maslow's observation, as clinicians recommended the identical treatment—their treasured proficiency—to virtually every patient who crossed their paths. But recent decades saw a greater emphasis on prescriptionism—that elusive, empirically driven match among patient, disorder, and treatment. We predicted 20 years ago that psychotherapists would use an expanded toolbox instead of senselessly hammering away at anything remotely similar to a nail.

On balance, we think we got that prediction correct. The era of grand psychotherapy theories is waning; evidence-based practice and pragmatic integration are upon us. Effective therapy is "defined not by its brand name, but by how well it meets the need of the patient" (Weiner, 1975, p. 44). In other words, the question is no longer "Does it work in general?" but rather "Does it work best for this client with that problem?"

The need to match patient and treatment was recognized by Freud from the beginning of psychotherapy (Chapter 3) but has become more systematic and evidence based in recent years. As early as 1919, Freud introduced psychoanalytic psychotherapy as an alternative to classical analysis on the recognition that the more rarified approach lacked universal applicability and that many patients did not possess the requisite psychological mindedness. In the 1980s and 1990s, the identification of empirically supported treatments by the American Psychological Association (APA) Division 12 (Clinical Psychology; http://www.div12.org/) began a host of efforts to compile lists of research-supported therapies for particular disorders. The newer evidence-based practice (EBP) does that as well, placing research evidence at the center of treatment selection.

Psychotherapy research has gravitated to more specific populations and disorders. In this edition, we feature research groups working specifically to match psychotherapy to child conduct disorders (Chapter 12b), alcohol abuse (Chapter 12g), clinical depression (Chapter 12h), intransigent anxiety disorders (Chapter 12i), and borderline personality disorder (Chapter 12l). Programmatic research has demonstrated that different therapies can be prescribed not only to disorders but also to patient personalities. For example, directive treatments are more effective than nondirective ones with low-reactant patients, and treatments focusing most explicitly on overt behavior are differentially effective over internally focused approaches for clients with externalizing coping styles (Chapter 12h).

Gone are the days of generic psychotherapy research; specificity and sensitivity now rule. The desideratum of specificity has enormous potential implications for the future. These include generating more focused therapeutic strategies, providing sharper answers to the question of what psychotherapy can do for particular patients, selecting the most cost-effective therapies for each client, and generating optimal matches among therapists, patients, and treatments (Chapters 10 and 11). Psychotherapists have come to embrace the ancient wisdom in "different folks require different strokes."

Therapeutic Alliance

We concurred with many contributors to the first edition of this book that the centrality of the therapeutic alliance would emerge as a recurrent future theme. In all probability, we correctly predicted this trend, but in the interest of full disclosure, we also worked to actualize the prediction. John C. Norcross edited a comprehensive text on the topic—*Psychotherapy Relationships That Work* (Norcross, 2002)—that both reflected and reinforced our prediction.

Two previous themes we predicted in 1992 would converge to produce a renewed but modified emphasis on the therapeutic alliance in the future. Contextualism would contribute a heightened sensitivity to the interpersonal relationship and remind us that the value of a clinical intervention is inextricably bound to the relational context in which it is applied. Prescriptionism would remind us that a unitary therapeutic relationship will not suffice for diverse clients and will mandate that therapists tailor interpersonal styles to fit the unique needs of individual clients.

Specific delineations among therapeutic method, strategy, and relationship are nearly impossible in practice because they are interwoven in the contextual fabric of psychotherapy. Hans Strupp (1986) offered an analogy to illustrate the inseparability of the constituent elements of psychotherapy: Suppose you want your teenager to clean his or her room. One method for achieving this is to establish clear standards and impose consequences. Fine, but the effectiveness of these two empirically supported methods will vary depending on whether the relationship between you and the teenager is characterized by warmth and mutual respect or by anger and distrust. This is not to say that the methods are useless, merely that how well they work depends on the context in which they are is used.

There is virtual unanimity among reviewers of the outcome research (Chapter 10) that the therapist–patient relationship is central to positive change. Moreover, the relationship is the single most frequent common factor in the literature (Grencavage & Norcross, 1990). The research conclusions converge with what every practitioner knows in his or her bones: Effective psychotherapy is rooted in the nurture and comfort of another human. The importance of the therapeutic alliance is now an unquestioned component of successful therapy, independent of theoretical orientation and treatment length.

In the 1990s, an APA Division of Psychotherapy Task Force was established to identify, operationalize, and disseminate information on empirically supported therapy relationships. The aim was to identify empirically supported (therapy) relationships rather than empirically supported treatments. Specifically, the twin aims of the Division 29 Task Force were to identify elements of effective therapy relationships and to identify effective methods of tailoring therapy to the individual patient on the basis of his or her (nondiagnostic) characteristics. In other words, we sought to answer the dual pressing questions of "What works in general in the therapy relationship?" and "What works best for particular patients?" The 2002 book edited by Norcross brought science and practice together in presenting what works in the therapy relationship.

The challenge ahead is to articulate the grounds on which the relationship is fitted to various client presentations. In this sense, the meaning of prescriptive matching has been broadened to denote not only specific clinical procedures but also therapist relationship stances (Lazarus, Beutler, & Norcross, 1992). Systematic studies on relational matching will examine the commonly shared perception among therapists of feeling oneself to be better suited to deal interpersonally with some patients rather than others. The research literature will then confidently generate prescriptive matches for technical and interpersonal interventions in specific circumstances.

Socioeconomic Pressures

In the first edition of this book, we predicted an increasing influence of economics for both clients and therapists. Little did we know how major a role economics would play in the practice of psychotherapy! In retrospect, we should have prioritized this prediction because it has emerged as the proverbial elephant in the room.

The health care dollar now determines, in large measure, the type, focus, and availability of psychotherapy. Sadly, one of the first questions asked of patients is "What is your health insurance?" Economics shape the parameters of psychotherapy—what can be bought, taught, funded, and reimbursed. Theoretical developments and clinical innovations are increasingly fueled by—and a consequence of—economic considerations.

Until the 1990s, there was little demand on the part of insurance carriers and federal agencies for evidence demonstrating the efficacy of psychotherapy. However, the situation has changed rapidly, and the demands have grown dramatically. No longer is it sufficient to demonstrate the general efficacy of psychotherapy; cost efficiency and pragmatic resolution of specific disorders have become necessary.

Economic pressures have led, *inter alia,* to a reduction in long-term psychotherapy, restricted choice of psychotherapists, imposition of external controls and limited reimbursement, and acceleration of minimal treatment. Long-term, open-ended psychotherapy is an option largely limited to the wealthy. Inpatient hospitalization for mental disorders averages less than a week of medication stabilization without individual psychotherapy. In the service of cost containment, many patients are denied individual psychotherapy, instead referred to self-help organizations, self-change materials, and psychoeducational groups for specific disorders.

What takes place in the consulting room is not only a matter of financial interest to practitioners but also of empirical interest to researchers. Researchers must develop a fuller understanding of how psychotherapy is financed and distributed, how patients find their way into the system, and how this service affects the productive functioning of patients. We must provide policymakers with the best information on which to base their decisions, in a manner that can be communicated to the public, so that they can become effective advocates for our profession.

As our nation moves gradually toward universal health care, as most other developed nations have, only the future will tell how we balance the realities of economic pressures with client needs. That clinical and ethical balancing act will challenge the integrity of professionals to offer the best treatment predicated on available research, clinical expertise, and patient preferences within economic realities insisting they "do less and quicker." Some psychotherapists will find opportunities in the transformation, and others will curse the change, but all will be profoundly influenced by these accelerating economic forces.

Process–Outcome Linkages

Historically, psychotherapy process researchers and outcome researchers were segregated into parallel and discrete camps. Members of the outcome camp were taught to distrust process enthusiasts as being entrapped by fuzzy concepts, adherence to unsupportable theories, and use of largely nonempirical methods. Members of the process camp, in turn, criticized outcome enthusiasts for favoring sterile number crunching over clinical utility, operating under academic ideals rather than theory-driven treatment, and being unresponsive to the issues that could benefit practicing clinicians (Beutler, 1990; Chapter 11).

Our final prediction in 1992 was that the distinctions between process and outcome research would fade and that explicit linkages between the two would be forged. We were only half right.

On the one hand, the distinctions readily persist, and outcome researchers tend to avoid process research. Many researchers have been forced by federal grant guidelines to pursue outcome research—testing the efficacy of a particular treatment method for a specific diagnosis. Process research is rarely funded these days by the National Institutes of Health or other large funding sources. Instead, process researchers fund themselves (Chapter 12a), participate in collaborative programs (Chapter 12d), or conduct the research as a secondary analysis to randomized controlled trials (Chapter 12c).

On the other hand, in the intervening 20 years process–outcome studies have taken center stage (Chapter 11). The dual thrust of process and outcome research has become the hallmark of psychotherapy research, together with the realization that the two must necessarily complement each other. Whether psychotherapy works (outcome) is informed by how that psychotherapy works (process). Systematic examination of the causal linkages between process and outcome will increasingly characterize sophisticated psychotherapy research.

As the sophistication of our computerized data collection and analysis increases, so too do opportunities for integrative studies.

In clinical training, too, the growing commitment to evidence-based education will yield systematic examination of the connections between training components (process) and clinical competence (outcome; Chapters 12a, 12c, 12e, and 12h). More attention, we and the contributors to Section V presage, will be accorded to evaluations of training programs and to certification of competence. Advancing the process–outcome linkages may well help bridge the gap between research and practice in psychotherapy.

IN PROSPECT

And what of psychotherapy from 2011 onward? What might the future of psychotherapy look like? What is hot and what is not in the 2000s? Where are the growth opportunities? As nations painfully transition from the industrial era to an information era, it is imperative that we remain knowledgeable of how changes will affect psychotherapy, professionals, and our patients. Those who cannot learn from history are doomed to repeat it, as George Santayana famously forewarned.

Having reviewed the accuracy of our predictions rendered in 1992, we boldly venture to offer several predictions on the foreseeable future. Our forecasts are firmly grounded in the foregoing chapters of this book and in a series of Delphi polls on the future of psychotherapy (e.g., Norcross, Hedges, & Prochaska, 2002). Research has indicated that the results of Delphi polls usually provide the most accurate answers to forecasting questions compared with other prognostication techniques, such as opinions of individual experts (Ascher, 1978; Linstone & Turoff, 1975). Another advantage is that "the Delphi method attempts to negotiate a reality that can then be useful in moving a particular field forward, planning for the future or even changing the future by forecasting its events" (Fish & Busby, 1996, p. 470).

Here, then, are eight specific predictions about the future of psychotherapy.

Applicability and Adaptability of Psychotherapy

Psychotherapy has evolved from an open-ended treatment for mental disorders to time-limited treatment for an infinite array of human maladies—mental, emotional, relational, addictive, physical, existential, financial, educational, spiritual, vocational, and onward. The expanding role and range of psychotherapy stagger us. Scan a psychotherapy journal's contents online, and you are likely to encounter articles on promoting health, preventing bullying, treating diabetic behaviors, reversing chronic medical conditions, enhancing character strengths, and reducing unwanted pregnancies. This trend, we presage, will continue into the future.

One emerging area for psychological intervention entails preventing physical diseases and maintaining good health throughout life (see Chapter 13d). A 2009 Future of Psychology Summit (Bray et al., 2009) focused on the opportunities for collaboration with other health care professionals. Psychotherapy has matured to a health care profession, not only a mental health specialty. The term *behavioral health care* is gradually replacing *mental health care* in an effort to communicate its broader focus and wider range of disorders treated. Perhaps there will even come a time when visits to the psychotherapist (like the dentist) for routine check-ups will be part of a healthy lifestyle. Meanwhile, professional organizations and parity legislation can raise public awareness and reduce stigma so that psychological health is placed on a par with physical health.

Primary Care

Psychotherapists, it seems, are working everywhere, particularly in primary care. A health care system that bifurcates mind and body cannot endure. In the next 20 years, psychotherapists will be largely integrated into primary care settings, working seamlessly side by side with primary care physicians at the same location.

In part, the interest in the psychological consequences and treatment of health problems is financial. More than 50% of health care costs are the result of behaviors (Prochaska, 1996). Smoking, alcohol abuse, obesity, chronic pain, and stress are the most costly conditions in our society. In part, the interest is the result of recognizing that traditional medical care of chronic health conditions is unsatisfactory. As currently practiced, only 15% of the aforementioned conditions are treated effectively in the population at large. And, in part, the interest is spurred by the effectiveness of psychological treatments for chronic medical conditions (Prochaska & Norcross, 2010).

Both objective evidence and Delphi poll experts predict psychotherapists will routinely treat the behavioral components of health problems in the future, mainly as part of a primary care team. Psychological services are emerging as part of the overall health care system, not apart from it. No health care system will work unless behavior is integrated throughout it. Only a biopsychosocial model will address the central roles of lifestyle choices, compliance with medical regimens, and management of chronic diseases—and only psychotherapists are trained to change such behaviors. The future will bring health care for the whole person (Kaslow, Blount, & Sue, 2005).

Evidence-Based Practice

The EBP movement is an international juggernaut racing to achieve accountability in all forms of health care. The aim of EBP is to require professionals to base their practice on solid, typically research, evidence to improve treatment effectiveness and enhance public health (Kazdin, 2008). The APA Task Force on Evidence-Based Practice (2006) defined *EBP* as the integration of the best available research with clinical expertise in the context of patient characteristics, culture, and preferences. As shown in Figure 19.1, EBP occurs at the intersection of three evidentiary sources: best available research, clinical expertise, and patient characteristics, culture, and preferences (Norcross, Hogan, & Koocher, 2008).

In our Delphi poll (Norcross et al., 2002), the single most likely scenario in all of psychotherapy was that evidence-based psychotherapies would be required by health care systems. For the most part, the ascending theoretical orientations are those with the most intense involvement in controlled

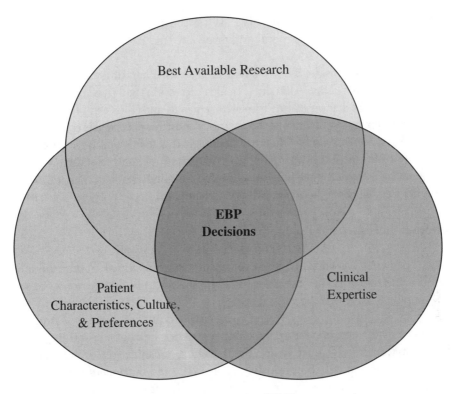

Figure 19.1. The three evidence-based practice (EBP) components.

research. This does not necessarily mean that these therapies have greater efficacy, but they do have greater evidence. So the Dodo bird prediction (Luborsky, Singer, & Luborsky, 1975) from the past is probably untrue in the health care market, and it is unlikely to be the case that "all have won and all must receive prizes." Theories that will win the most prizes are those that have won the support of the most researchers (Prochaska & Norcross, 2010).

At first blush, there is universal agreement that psychotherapists should use evidence as a guide in determining what works. It's like publicly prizing Mother and apple pie. Can anyone seriously advocate the reverse: non-EBP? But it is neither as simple nor as consensual as that. Defining *evidence*, deciding what qualifies as evidence, and applying that which is privileged as evidence are complicated matters with deep philosophical and huge practical consequences (Norcross, Beutler, & Levant, 2006). For example, many psychological treatments deigned as evidence-based have never been tested on diverse populations, including ethnic minority; gay, lesbian, bisexual, and transgender; and physically disabled clients. For another example, 60% to 80% of EBPs in psychotherapy identified by one organization are cognitive–behavioral treatments. These typically involve skill building, have a specific focus, involve relatively brief treatment, and rarely use traditional assessment measures (O'Donohue et al., 2000).

Controversies aside, what we can predict with certainty is that EBP in health care is here to stay. All mental health professions will need to respond to this clarion call by demonstrating the safety, efficacy, and efficiency of their work. In fact, the demands for evidence from various constituencies will escalate in the future. What we can also confidently predict is that EBPs will have profound implications for mental health practice, policy, training, and research. What is designated as evidence based will increasingly determine what is conducted, what is reimbursed, what is taught, and what is researched.

Internationalization of Psychotherapy

The world has flattened and everything has gone global. Psychotherapy is following suit in going international. The historical U.S. centricity of psychotherapy is slowly giving way.

Consider psychotherapy research as a case in point. Two of the 12 psychotherapy research centers featured in this book are located outside of the United States (in the United Kingdom and Switzerland), one of the research programs is an international collaboration (Chapter 12d), and authors of three of the other reports on research centers explicitly mention international work.

Or consider the number of psychologists around the globe. We do not yet have definitive information on either the numbers of psychologists or licensure by country, but estimates range from 300,000 to 800,000 (APA Policy and Planning Board, 2008). The wide range of estimates is largely because of the disparate definition of *psychologist*—ranging from a postbaccalaureate to doctoral level. It is becoming abundantly clear that the 95,000 or so licensed psychologists in the United States constitute a minority of those around the world and should not, cannot, speak for the world of psychology.

We are not yet at the point at which psychotherapies are interchangeable around the world. That is, unlike medical care, therapy is nation bound, mainly because of language and cultural differences. However, with research, training, and communications spanning the borders, it may not be long before some psychotherapy principles become universal.

Neuroscience

Advances in neuroscience will further permeate the theory and practice of psychotherapy. In fact, psychotherapy might be called "brain therapy" in the future, and many mental disorders might be redefined as "brain illnesses" (Prochaska & Norcross, 2010).

Psychotherapy typically results in detectable changes in the brain (Etkin et al., 2005). In a seminal and replicated study by Lewis Baxter et al. (1992), patients with obsessive–compulsive disorder who were treated with medication or psychotherapy (exposure and response prevention) showed normalized changes in the functioning of multiple brain regions. In most studies, psychotherapy is similar to medication in normalizing functional abnormalities in brain circuits that give rise to symptoms.

Positive human interactions, such as psychotherapy, can create new synaptic connections and release neurotransmitters, helping people respond with increasing resilience and self-soothing abilities. Several neuroimaging studies on mood and anxiety disorders have found that activity in certain brain regions can predict who is most likely to respond positively to treatment (Grawe, 2007). These lines of research remind us that we are not only treating mental disorders but literally brain illnesses (regardless of what originally caused the disorder).

As we enter the age of neuroscience, we will treat brain illnesses more specifically on the basis of their molecular biology, and we will enhance prevention by identifying biological indicators of vulnerability. The burgeoning field of neuroscience will likely dissolve the gap between mind and brain. It will also require a whole new way of thinking about, and talking about, how psychotherapy works (Prochaska & Norcross, 2010).

Combined Treatment

Probably the most dramatic change in psychotherapy over the past 20 years entails combined treatment: psychotherapy plus pharmacotherapy. The ascendency of pharmacotherapy has been staggering. As Sammons documents in Chapter 14d, pharmacotherapy tends to be the rule rather than the exception in patients receiving psychotherapy. From 1996 to 2006, prescriptions for psychotropic medications increased by 73% among adults and 50% among children. The most striking result is the dramatic expansion of spending on prescription drugs for all payer groups. During this 10-year period, per capita spending on psychotropic drugs tripled (Frank, Goldman, & McGuire, 2009). We foresee continued use of pharmacotherapy, frequently at the expense of psychotherapy, and the practice pattern of combined treatment.

The debate on mind versus brain is outdated. It is no longer a question as to which is dominant in determining personality and pathology. The only questions remaining are where and how. Medications that alter brain function and, in turn, alter thinking and emotion have revolutionized the treatment of those with severe mental illness. The widespread use of psychotropic drugs has increased over the past 2 decades to the point that we are an overmedicated society. The situation is most acute with children, who are given medication for behavior disorders and learning difficulties before any attempt is made to determine the causes or to attempt psychological interventions.

As our society sees that behavior and emotion can easily be changed with medication, why spend time and money on talking cures? While in graduate school, an admired clergyman told Donald K. Freedheim, "The couch has replaced the pulpit." In the future, will it be said that the pill has replaced the couch? At this point, the prospect seems more far fetched than frightening. However, so did trips to the moon not long ago. One would hope that the inevitable march of science will be tempered with judgment.

This matter is complicated for organizing psychology, which has successfully sought prescription privileges for appropriately trained psychologists in three jurisdictions and which is intensifying efforts for similar privileges in many other states (Chapter 14d). When the first edition of this volume was prepared in the early 1990s, the U.S. Department of Defense was poised to inaugurate an experimental program for psychologists to learn to prescribe medication. Since then, APA has approved training guidelines for prescribing, and many graduate programs have started throughout the country. If these trends continue, all professional psychologists will have to consider whether to include psychopharmacology in their education and treatment skills.

Broadening of Multiculturalism

Our nation is becoming a true pluralistic society, with the certainty that there will be no dominant ethnic or racial group in the next 40 years. Pluralism exists when numerous ethnic and racial groups are present and accepted within society, accompanied by the belief that such a condition is desirable. Changing demographics signal an ever-increasing need for cultural awareness in all pursuits, but especially those as rooted in interpersonal relations as psychotherapy. If present trends in immigration and birth rates persist in the United States, people of color will no longer be the minority, but the majority, by the year 2050 (U.S. Census Bureau, 2001).

The understandable focus in psychotherapy of late has been multiculturalism in terms of race or ethnicity (Chapter 8). Existing paradigms have been questioned and modified by pluralistic theories that are less ethnocentric and more inclusive. Many extant "universal" principles of human behavior have been reinterpreted as examples of clinical myopia or cultural imperialism (Chapter 13e).

In the future, we predict, the meaning of *multiculturalism* will expand to embrace all salient dimensions of personal identity, such as sexual orientation, chronological age, disability status, and so forth. Lesbian, gay, bisexual, and transgender clients; elderly clients; and clients with disability are subject to the same prejudice and oppression as those who are racial or ethnic minorities. An acronym organizing the factors to be considered in culturally responsive practice (Hays, 1996) forms the slightly misspelled word *ADRESSING: a*ge and generational influences, *d*isability, *r*eligion, *e*thnicity, *s*ocial status, *s*exual orientation, *i*ndigenous heritage, *n*ational origin, and *g*ender.

In the future, practitioners will indeed be "adressing" the complex intersections of these multiple factors in their assessment and treatment of heterogeneous clients. Although the content of each category varies, there are many commonalities relating to acculturation–separateness, inclusion–exclusion, and power–oppression. A concurrent challenge will be to create training programs that attend to all facets of diversity and research programs that investigate the effectiveness of psychotherapies with diverse populations. Expanded, evidence-based multicultural therapies will take us deeper into compassion and connection.

Web Technology

Until recently, psychotherapy was relatively immune from the information revolution. Two people speaking to each other in the privacy and immediacy of the consulting room remains the quintessential format. However, the information age is dramatically changing psychotherapy in the forms of computer-assisted treatment, telepsychotherapy, virtual reality treatment, and online consultation. In place of, as the old saying goes, psychotherapy only needing two people, an office, and a box of tissues, in the 21st century we might only require one person and a computer (Prochaska & Norcross, 2010).

The World Wide Web helps to assess and treat behavioral or mental disorders in multiple ways. Web resources offer psychoeducation, improve access to psychotherapy, promote self-monitoring, rehearse coping skills, provide outcome measures, furnish self-help guides, provide psychological assessment and screening, and generate support groups and social networks. *Behavioral e-health* is the popular term that captures the variety of therapeutic services being delivered over the Internet, ranging from psychoeducational information to actual psychotherapy (Maheu & Gordon, 2000). Some patients are now on the virtual couch. Although fraught with ethical and logistical concerns, various forms of Web-based therapy are destined to proliferate.

As evidenced throughout the chapters of this book, psychotherapy research has become more sophisticated and complex over the recent past (Chapters 10, 11, and 12). The Web has facilitated quick and massive recording of therapy data, such that nuances of therapeutic interactions and communications can be analyzed in relation to clients' attitude and behavior change, even at the level of therapy sessions (Barkham et al., 2008).

And these data can be sorted by multiple criteria on large samples of therapists, methodologies, and clients. An ongoing example of using the latest technologies for large data is a national collaboration among more than 100 universities gathering clinical information on more than 20,000 cases (Locke, 2009).

CONCLUDING COMMENTS

From the high vantage point of history, we have tried to extract and amplify megatrends in the future of psychotherapy. In the Janusian tradition (Rothenberg, 1988), we have examined the dialectical interplay of retrospect and prospect, simultaneously looking backward and forward. We have attempted to conceptualize these changes in ways that counter a defensive propensity and that assist the reader in actively considering the evolution of the field.

Psychotherapy has a short history but, we are confident, a long and prosperous future. How that future will look in 50 years, or even in 20, is not easy to predict. In many ways, we hope that human behavior will remain as mysterious as it often is. The mind–brain may be as vast as the universe and, we hope, the complete understanding of human behavior will never be an undisputed certainty. There is only one guaranteed prediction for the future of psychotherapy: continuity and change.

REFERENCES

American Psychological Association Policy and Planning Board. (2008). From the American Psychological Association to the American Psychology Association: An organization for psychologists or for the discipline? *American Psychologist, 63*, 443–451. doi:10.1037/0003-066X.63.5.443

American Psychological Association Task Force on Evidence-Based Practice. (2006). Evidence-based practice in psychology. *American Psychologist, 61*, 271–285. doi:10.1037/0003-066X.61.4.271

Ascher, W. (1978). *Forecasting*. Baltimore, MD: Johns Hopkins University Press.

Barkham, M., Stiles, W., Connell, J., Twigg, E., Leach, C., Lucock, M., . . . Angus, L. (2008). Effects of psychological therapies in randomized trials and practice-based studies. *British Journal of Clinical Psychology, 47*, 397–415. doi:10.1348/014466508X311713

Baxter, L. R., Schwartz, J. M., Bergman, K. S., . . . Phelps, M. E. (1992). Caudate glucose metabolic rate changes with both drug and behavior therapy for obsessive-compulsive disorder. *Archives of General Psychiatry, 49*, 681–689.

Beutler, L. E. (1990). Introduction to the special series on advances in psychotherapy process research. *Journal of Consulting and Clinical Psychology, 58*, 263–264.

Bike, D. H., Norcross, J. C., & Schatz, D. M. (2009). Processes and outcomes of psychotherapists' personal therapy: Replication and extension 20 years later. *Psychotherapy, 46,* 19–31. doi:10.1037/a0015139

Bray, J., Goodheart, C., & Heldring, M. (2009, July). Presidential Summit on the Future of Psychology Practice: Collaborating for change. *OPA Notes.*

Etkin, A., Pittenger, C., Polan, H. J., & Kandel, E. R. (2005). Toward a neurobiology of psychotherapy: Basic science and clinical applications. *Journal of Neuropsychiatry and Clinical Neurosciences, 17,* 145–158. doi:10.1176/appi.neuropsych.17.2.145

Fish, L. S., & Busby, D. M. (1996). The Delphi method. In D. H. Sprenkle & S. M. Moon (Eds.), *Research methods in family therapy* (pp. 469–484). New York, NY: Guilford Press.

Frank, R. G., Goldman, H. H., & McGuire, T. G. (2009). Trends in mental health cost growth: An expanded role for management? *Health Affairs, 28,* 649–659. doi:10.1377/hlthaff.28.3.649.

Grawe, K. (2007). *Neurotherapy: How the neurosciences inform effective psychotherapy.* Mahwah, NJ: Erlbaum.

Grencavage, L. M., & Norcross, J. C. (1990). Where are the commonalities among the therapeutic common factors? *Professional Psychology, Research and Practice, 21,* 372–378. doi:10.1037/0735-7028.21.5.372

Hays, P. A. (1996). Culturally responsive assessment with diverse older clients. *Professional Psychology: Research and Practice, 27,* 188–193. doi:10.1037/0735-7028.27.2.188

Jerome, L. W., DeLeon, P. H., James, L. C., Folen, R., Earles, J., & Gedney, J. J. (2000). The coming of age of telecommunications in psychological research and practice. *American Psychologist, 55,* 407–421. doi:10.1037/0003-066X.55.4.407

Johns, J. (2000). Future choices for psychoanalytic psychotherapy. *British Journal of Psychotherapy, 17,* 62–70. doi:10.1111/j.1752-0118.2000.tb00560.x

Kaslow, N. J., Blount, A., & Sue, S. (2005). *Health care for the whole person: Moving toward improved health outcomes.* Washington, DC: American Psychological Association.

Kazdin, A. E. (2008). Evidenced-based treatment and practice: New opportunities to bridge clinical research and practice, enhance the knowledge base, and improve patient care. *American Psychologist, 63,* 146–159. doi:10.1037/0003-066X.63.3.146

Kiesler, D. J. (1966). Some myths of psychotherapy research and the search for a paradigm. *Psychological Bulletin, 65,* 110–136. doi:10.1037/h0022911

Lazarus, A. A., Beutler, L. E., & Norcross, J. C. (1992). The future of technical eclecticism. *Psychotherapy: Theory, Research, Practice, Training, 29,* 11–20.

Linstone, H. A., & Turoff, M. (Eds.). (1975). *The Delphi method: Techniques and applications.* Reading, MA: Addison-Wesley.

Locke, B. (2009). *Centre for the Study of Collegiate Mental Health.* Retrieved from http://www.sa.psu.edu/caps/research_center.shtml

Luborsky, L., Singer, B., & Luborsky, L. (1975). Comparative studies of psychotherapies. *Archives of General Psychiatry, 32,* 995–1008.

Maheu, M., & Gordon, B. L. (2000). Counseling and therapy on the Internet. *Professional Psychology: Research and Practice, 31,* 484–489. doi:10.1037/0735-7028.31.5.484

Moran, M. (2009). *Psychiatrists lament decline of key treatment modality. Psychiatric News, 44,* 8.

Norcross, J. C. (Ed.). (2002). *Psychotherapy relationships that work.* New York, NY: Oxford University Press.

Norcross, J. C., Beutler, L. E., & Levant, R. F. (Eds.). (2006). *Evidence-based practices in mental health: Debate and dialogue on the fundamental questions.* Washington, DC: American Psychological Association.

Norcross, J. C., & Freedheim, D. K. (1992). Into the future: Retrospect and prospect in psychotherapy. In D. K. Freedheim (Ed.), *History of psychotherapy: A century of change* (pp. 881–900). Washington, DC: American Psychological Association.

Norcross, J. C., Hedges, M., & Prochaska, J. O. (2002). The face of 2010: A Delphi poll on the future of psychotherapy. *Professional Psychology: Research and Practice, 33,* 316–322. doi:10.1037/0735-7028.33.3.316

Norcross, J. C., Hogan, T. P., & Koocher, G. P. (2008). *Clinician's guide to evidence-based practices: Mental health and the addictions.* New York, NY: Oxford University Press.

O'Donohue, W., Buchanan, J. A., & Fisher, J. E. (2000). Characteristics of empirically supported treatments. *Journal of Psychotherapy Practice and Research, 9,* 69–74.

Prochaska, J. O. (1996). A revolution in health promotion: Smoking cessation as a case study. In R. J. Resnick & R. H. Rozensky (Eds.), *Health psychology through the lifespan: Practice and research opportunities* (pp. 361–375). Washington, DC: American Psychological Association.

Prochaska, J. O., & Norcross, J. C. (2010). *Systems of psychotherapy: A transtheoretical analysis* (7th ed.). Pacific Grove, CA: Brooks/Cole.

Rothenberg, A. (1988). *The creative process of psychotherapy.* New York, NY: Norton.

Strupp, H. H. (1986). The nonspecific hypothesis of therapeutic effectiveness: A current assessment. *American Journal of Orthopsychiatry, 56,* 513–520.

U.S. Census Bureau. (2001). *Your gateway to Census 2000.* Retrieved from http://www.census.gov/main/www/cen2000.html

Weiner, I. B. (1975). *Principles of psychotherapy.* New York, NY: Wiley.

INDEX

Clinical psychology, *continued*
    turf battles between psychiatry
        and, 21
    VA training program for, 675–678
Clinical Psychology (APA Division
    12), 30, 49, 272, 307–308,
    554–555, 624
Clinical Science conference (1994),
    620
Clinical social workers, 48, 57
The Clinical Supervisor journal, 711
The Clinical Treatment of the Problem
    Child (Rogers), 16
Clinics
    child guidance, 19–20
    community-based, 21
    psychoanalytic, 15
    psychological, 6, 11
    VA, 677
    work with children in, 443–444
Clozapine, 520, 526
CMHCs. *See* Community mental health
    centers
Cochrane Library, 556
Cognitive analytic therapy (CAT), 596
Cognitive–behavior modification, 205
Cognitive behavioral analysis, 125
Cognitive–behavioral coping skills
    treatment, 583
Cognitive–behavioral couple therapy,
    491–492
Cognitive–behavioral group therapy,
    509–510
Cognitive–behavioral therapies (CBTs),
    102, 114, 203–210
    acceptance and commitment therapy
        vs., 128–131
    for alcoholism, 397–400
    alone vs. with experiential therapy,
        391
    for anxiety, 606
    for anxiety disorders, 566–570
    and attribution theories, 207–208
    for borderline personality disorder,
        592, 594–595
    for childhood disorders, 229
    and cognitive deficit model, 205–206
    cognitive theory in, 109
    conferences on, 204
    with couples and families, 121
    for depression, 307, 350, 606

    and dysfunctional thoughts, 206–207
    early ridicule of, 214
    for eating disorders, 228
    as evidence-based therapy, 690
    evolution of, 708
    for families, 195
    future of, 230–232
    for generalized anxiety disorder, 226
    manualized, 320–321
    multicultural awareness and culture-
        specific strategies with, 254
    for obsessive–compulsive disorder,
        227–228, 409–410
    with older adults, 462
    origin of, 108, 204
    other therapies vs., 386–387
    for paranoid delusions, 602–603
    and personal construct therapy, 207
    for posttraumatic stress disorder, 228
    psychodynamic–interpersonal ther-
        apy vs., 382–386
    psychodynamic therapies vs.,
        284–285
    for psychosis, 606–607
    for schizophrenia, 606
    social learning theory in, 109
    for social phobia, 226
    and social problem-solving
        model, 206
    for specific client populations,
        511–512
    use of term, 103
    as worldwide movement, 111–112
Cognitive–behavioral therapists, task
    of, 110
Cognitive deficit model, 205–206
Cognitive dysfunction model, 206–207
Cognitive theories, 108, 110
    of Beck, 220
    in cognitive behavior therapy, 109
    mediators of behavior change in, 110
Cognitive therapies, 114, 203–233
    of Beck, 220–230
    and behavior therapy, 102, 203
    for borderline personality disorder,
        592
    cognitive behavior therapies,
        203–210. *See also*
        Cognitive–behavioral
        therapies

Depressive attributional style, 549
Desensitization
    for depression, 548
    eye movement desensitization and
        reprocessing, 734–736
    group, 509
    systematic, 107, 274, 509
Deutsch, H., 705
Developed practice areas, 620
Development
    and cultural school of psycho-
        analysis, 245
    cumulative–hierarchical, 109
    of minority groups, 246
    of older adults, 460
Developmental models of supervision,
    713–714
Developmental theory, 197–198
Development of Psychotherapists
    Common Core Questionnaire
    (DPCCQ), 375–376
Devereux, G., 245
Diagnostic and Statistical Manual of Men-
    tal Disorders (3rd ed., *DSM-III*),
    562–563, 593, 676
Diagnostic and Statistical Manual of
    Mental Disorders (3rd ed., rev.,
    DSM-III-R), 323
Diagnostic evaluations, 323
Dialectical behavior therapy (DBT),
    110, 125, 127, 428–433, 708–709
    for borderline personality disorder,
        228, 593, 594
    as evidence-based therapy, 690
Dialogical gestalt therapy, 160
Dialogue
    in experiential psychotherapy, 147
    in gestalt therapy, 149, 160
    in process experiential psycho-
        therapy, 157
Diazepam, 521–522
Dichos psychotherapy, 258
DiClemente, C. C., 581
Didactic analysis, 705, 707
Differentiation
    in Bowenian family systems
        therapy, 185
    of self, 499
Digital technologies, 53, 58
Direct conditioning, 16

Direct observation, in behavior
    therapy, 125
Disability rights movement, 479
Disabled people. *See* People with
    disabilities
Disclosure, in relational psychoanalysis,
    86–87
Disconnection, 358
Disease. *See* Physical illnesses
Disengaged families, 179
Dissociation
    Boston school investigation of, 10
    in relational psychoanalysis, 86
Distance education, 659
Diversity
    among older adults, 462
    of clients, 475–481
    and cultural competence, 50–51
    ethnic and cultural, 477–478. *See also*
        Multicultural psychotherapy
    gender, 478
    multiple and intersectional
        identities, 480
    people with disabilities, 478–479
    in PhD programs, 626–627
    in PsyD programs, 636
    sexual minority clients, 478
Division 11. *See* Society for the Psychol-
    ogy of Aesthetics, Creativity and
    the Arts (APA Division 11)
Division 12. *See* Clinical Psychology
    (APA Division 12)
Division 29. *See* Psychotherapy (APA
    Division 29)
Division 36. *See* Psychology of Religion
    (APA Division 36)
Division 38. *See* Health Psychology
    (APA Division 38)
Division 43. *See* Family Psychology
    (APA Division 43)
Division 45. *See* Society for the Psycho-
    logical Study of Ethnic Minority
    Issues (APA Division 45)
Division 53. *See* Society of Child and
    Adolescent Psychology (APA
    Division 53)
Division of Mental Hygiene (USPHS),
    26–27
Division of Psychotherapy Task Force
    (APA), 748

Doctoral degrees, 26. *See also* PhD programs; PsyD programs
  CTCP evaluation of, 28
  EdD, 630
  as state licensure requirement, 654
Doctoral psychologists
  in 1970s, 42
  in 1980s, 46
  in 1990s, 48
  in 2000s, 51
  for VA programs, 673–675
Dollard, J., 271–272
Dose–effect question, 316–318, 385
Double bind, 175, 498
DPCCQ (Development of Psychotherapists Common Core Questionnaire), 375–376
Dreikurs, R., 506
Drug use and abuse, 575
  among adolescents, 453
  community-reinforcement therapy for, 577
DSM-III. *See Diagnostic and Statistical Manual of Mental Disorders* (3rd ed., *DSM-III*)
DSM-III-R. *See Diagnostic and Statistical Manual of Mental Disorders* (3rd ed., rev., *DSM-III-R*)
Duloxetine, 524
Dunlap, K., 708
Duration of therapy, 317, 383–384
Duty to protect, 725, 729–731
Duvall, E. M., 197
Dyadic Parent–Child Interaction Coding System, 417
Dynamic psychiatry, 11
Dynamic psychotherapy, for borderline personality disorder, 595–596
Dynamic theory, 210
Dynamic unconscious, 71

EABCT (European Association for Behavioural and Cognitive Therapy), 111
Eastern Pennsylvania Psychiatric Institute (EPPI), 499–500
Eastern religions and philosophies, 535, 537, 538
Eating disorders, 228
EBP. *See* Evidence-based practice

Eclecticism, 402. *See also* Psychotherapy integration
  and religion and spirituality in psychotherapy, 536
  technical, 273–274, 287
EdD degree, 630
Eddy, M. B., 8–9
Education. *See also* Continuing education (CE); Training
  in cultural competence, 51
  distance, 659
  for the oppressed, 248
Effect, Thorndike's law of, 104
Effectiveness of treatment
  behavior therapy, 130–131
  with children, 445
  comparative research on, 56–57, 305–307
  contributors to, 340
  couple therapy, 493
  with electronic technologies, 54, 55
  and managed care, 49
  negative effects research question, 314–316
  psychodynamic psychotherapies, 68–69
  with psychotropics, 529
  as research question, 300–303
  for schizophrenia, 603–604
Effectiveness trials, 337
Efficacy of psychotherapy, 749
  for adolescents, 454–455
  antidepressant therapy, 524–525
  behavior therapy, 130–131
  cognitive therapy, 222–223
  couple therapy, 493
  differential, 338
  interest in demonstrating, 30
  Surgeon General's report on, 50
  tests of, 45
Efficacy studies, 337
Efficiency of health care, electronic technologies for, 55
Ego, 71, 76
The Ego and the Mechanisms of Defense (A. Freud), 76
Ego psychology, 71
Ehlers, A., 224
Eitingon, M., 705
Electronic communications, 53

Federal policy
 in 1960s, 41
 in 1970s, 42, 43
 in 1980s, 46–47
 in 1990s, 48
 in 2000s, 53
 post-World War II, 40
Feminism, family therapy and, 193
Feminist therapy, 247, 249–250
Ferenczi, S., 75
Field theory, in gestalt therapy, 148
File drawer problem, 339
Filipino American Community
  Epidemiological Study
  (FACES), 424
Finney, J. W., 585
First generation approaches, 390
First-order change, 176
Fisch, R., 176
Fishman, D. B., 119
Fleck, S., 498
Fleming, J., 704
Flexner Report, 617
Flooding, 305, 547
Fluoxetine, 516, 520, 523
Foa, E. B., 408–412
Focusing, 155–156
Focusing Institute, 146
Fogarty, Tom, 186, 187
Folk healing, 256
Fonagy, P., 68
Forsyth, J., 209
Foulkes, S. H., 508
Fox sisters, 8
Framo, J., 183–184
Frank, J. B., 284
Frank, J. D., 272, 284
Frankl, V., 151
Franklin, Benjamin, 7
Franks, C., 106
Free association, 70, 78
Freedom-of-choice legislation, 42, 46
French, T., 270
Freud, A., 76, 441, 450, 726
Freud, S., 12, 13, 69–71, 211, 270, 546,
  704–706, 726, 746
 and Clark Conference, 12–13
 and development of child
   psychotherapy, 440–441
 Dora case, 449

on interpretation, 73
 Little Hans case, 440–441
 on narcissism, 89–90
 on neutral analytic stance, 73
 on older patients, 459
 on the practice of psychoanalysis, 21
 Reik's defense by, 22
 on resistance, 74
 on suggestion, 67–68
 on therapeutic alliance, 74
Freudian drive theory, 66, 71
Freudian psychoanalysis, 3
 contemporary, 76–81
 traditional, 12–15, 66, 69–71
Fromm, E., 245
Fromm-Reichmann, F., 602
Functional analytic psychotherapy, 125
Functional nervous disorders
 Boston school investigation of,
   10–11
 Mesmer's work with, 7
 somatic explanations of, 5
 Worcester's treatment of, 9
Funding
 for behavior therapies, 44
 for mental health research, 29–30
 of NIMH training, 680
 post-World War II, 24
 for substance abuse services, 47
Future of psychotherapy, 57–58,
   743–758
 applicability and adaptability, 751
 broadening of multiculturalism,
   756–757
 combined treatment, 755–756
 evidence-based practice, 752–754
 first edition predictions of, 744–750
 internationalization, 754
 and neuroscience, 754–755
 in primary care, 752
 Web technology, 757–758

GABA receptor agonists (GRAs), 522
GAD. See Generalized anxiety disorder
Gainesville Conference on Internship
  Training in Professional Psychol-
  ogy (1987), 643
Garfield, S. L., 272, 279
Gay, P., 706
Gay and lesbian affirmative therapy, 247

Health care system, 39–40
  costs in, 44–45
  integration of physical and psycho-
    logical health in, 56
  quality problems in, 55
Health Insurance Portability and
    Accountability Act (HIPAA),
    55, 725
Health psychology, 47–48
Health Psychology (APA Division 38),
    47–48
Health Psychology journal, 47
Healy, W., 19, 450, 497
Hefferline, R. F., 148
Heidegger, M., 150
Heimberg, R. G., 568
Hellinger, B., 262
Helms, J. E., 247
Henggeler, S., 199
Hermeneutic paradigm, 117
Hess, A. K., 711, 718
Hess, K. D., 718
Hilgard, E., 18
Hill, C. E., 343
Hill, R. L., 197
HIPAA. *See* Health Insurance Portabil-
    ity and Accountability Act
History of psychotherapy. *See also spe-
    cific topics, e.g.:* Training
  in the 1960s, 40–42
  in the 1970s, 42–46
  in the 1980s, 46–48
  in the 1990s, 48–51
  in the 2000s, 51–57
  with adolescents, 449–453
  American behaviorism, 15–16
  American psychoanalysis, 12–15
  American psychotherapy movement,
    5–12
  for anxiety disorders, 561–572
  for borderline personality disorder,
    588–597
  child guidance movement, 18–21
  for children, 439–444
  client-centered therapy, 16–17
  clinical psychology, 17–18
  couple therapy, 485–495
  for depression, 545–557
  family therapy, 497–503
  group therapy, 505–512

  and health care system, 39–40
  integration of spirituality and reli-
    gion in psychotherapy,
    534–540
  medical conditions in, 467–471
  mental testing, 17–18
  moral treatment, 4–5
  and National Institute of Mental
    Health, 26–30
  with older adults, 459–463
  overview, 3–4
  pharmacotherapy, 516, 518–521
  post-World War II, 23–24
  professional standing of clinical psy-
    chology, 22–23, 30–32
  for schizophrenia, 601–607
  for substance abuse, 574–586
  and Veterans Administration, 24–26
HMOs
  child therapies in, 444
  federal recognition of, 43
  gatekeeping in, 688
Hoffman, S. G., 130
Holtforth, M. G., 570
Home-based family therapy, 498
Homework assignments (for clients),
    213
Homosexuality, 731–732
Hope, D. A., 568
Horney, K., 245, 475
Human Change Processes (Mahoney),
    284
Humanistic–experiential psychothera-
    pies, 141–166, 335
  client-centered therapy, 143–145,
    152–155
  existential psychotherapy, 149–152,
    161–163
  experiential psychotherapies,
    146–148, 155–157
  gestalt therapy, 148–149, 157–160
  major tenets/assumptions of,
    142–143
  recent and future developments in,
    163–165
  therapeutic process in, 152–163
Humanistic movement, 141
"Hydesville Rappings," 8
Hydrazine, 522–523
Hyman, Steven, 727

Newman, R., 56
New York Institute for Gestalt
    Therapy, 149
New York Psychoanalytic Society, 14
New York state, 22
NIAAA (National Institute on Alcohol
    Abuse and Alcoholism), 395
Nichols, M., 175–176
NIMH. *See* National Institute of Mental
    Health
NLAAS (National Latino and Asian
    American Study), 424
Nonabstinence treatment goals, for
    substance abuse, 577–580
Nondirective therapy, with children,
    442, 443
Nondirectivity, in client-centered
    therapy, 153–155
Noninterpretive elements, in traditional
    psychoanalysis, 75–76
Norcross, J. C., 288
Nordal, K., 56
NRHSP. *See* National Register of
    Health Service Providers in
    Psychology
Nurse–Family Partnership, 455
Nurses. *See also* Psychiatric nurses
    in 2000s, 51
    VA training for, 674

Object relations
    in contemporary psychoanalysis,
        76–77, 80
    and couple therapy, 487
    and family systems therapy, 181–184
    in relational psychoanalysis, 82–83
    in treatment of anxiety, 562–563
Object relations theories, 81–82
Observational learning, 109
    with audiotapes, 693–694
    with videotapes, 693–701
Obsessive–compulsive disorder (OCD),
    227–228
    behavioral therapy for, 565–566
    cognitive–behavioral therapies for,
        567–569
    CTSA research on, 409–412
    neural mechanisms of, 350
OCD. *See* Obsessive–compulsive
    disorder

Ogden, T. H., 85–86
Older adults
    and changes in Medicare policy,
        463
    cohort effects with, 459
    depression treatments for, 556
    failures of psychotherapy with, 477
    health awareness of, 459
    history of psychotherapy with,
        459–463
    life expectancy of, 458
    Medicare reimbursements for care of,
        48
    as patients, 458–463
O'Leary, K. D., 114–115
Omnibus Budget Reconciliation Act
    (1981), 47
Omnibus Reconciliation Act (1987),
    463
"One-person" psychology, 73, 84
Online counseling, 54
"On Narcissism" (S. Freud), 89–90
Operant conditioning, 104, 108
    behavior influenced by, 109
    in first-wave behavior therapy, 122,
        124–125
Operationalization
    of outcomes, 322–323
    of treatment, 319
Opiates, 521
Oppressions, mental health and,
    247–248
Oral examinations, 656
Ordeal therapy, 177–178
Oregon Board of Psychologist
    Examiners, 665
Organismic theory, 116, 119–122
Oscillation theory, 197–198
Outcome management, 316
Outcome operationalization, 322–323
Outcome research, 750
    and equal outcomes phenomenon,
        309–310
    negative effects in, 315
    on psychotherapy integration,
        286–287
    on rating scales, 322–323
    and Sheffield–Leeds work, 382–385
    and "spontaneous remission rate," 301
    on youth psychotherapy, 454–455

Outcomes
  for adolescents, 454–455
  integrating process and, 345–349
  of schizophrenia treatment, 605–606
  and therapeutic relationship,
    343–344
Outpatient facilities for care
  in 1960s, 41
  VA mental health clinics, 676
Outpatient substance abuse treatment,
  580

Panic control treatment, 568
Panic disorder
  cognitive–behavioral therapies for,
    568
  cognitive therapy for, 225–226
  manualized CBT for, 320–321
  manualized psychodynamic therapy
    for, 563
Panic-focused psychodynamic psycho-
  therapy, 563
Paradigmatic behaviorism, 109
Parasuicidal borderline clients,
    dialectical behavior therapy
    with, 127
Parental empathy, in self psychology, 91
Parent–child interactions, in contempo-
    rary psychoanalysis, 80
Parent–Child Interaction Therapy
    (PCIT), 125, 415–419
Parent-Directed Interaction (PDI), 415
Parent management training (PMT),
    363–366, 690
Paroxetine, 523
Pastoral counselors, 534
Patient-focused research, 316
Patients, 439–477
  adolescents, 449–455
  characteristics of, 341–342, 344
  children, 439–446
  constitutional and civil rights of
    patients, 40
  diversity of, 475–481
  health and medical conditions of,
    468–472
  older adults, 458–463
  and quality of therapeutic relation-
    ships, 312–313
Paul, G. L., 123–125, 509

Pavlov, I., 104, 106, 270
Payment problems, 728–729
PCIT. *See* Parent–Child Interaction
    Therapy
PCT (personal construct therapy), 207
PDI (Parent-Directed Interaction), 415
Penal, P., 601
People of color
  as CBT drop-outs, 254
  colonization of, 248
  failures of psychotherapy with,
    475–477
  family structure among, 255
  and feminist therapy, 249–250
  racial microaggressions of, 260
People with disabilities, 478–479
  failures of psychotherapy with, 477
  Medicare reimbursements for
    care of, 48
  therapy for clients with, 468–472
Perls, F. S., 148, 149, 157–158, 160,
    509, 694–695
Perls, L., 149
Permanence question, 318–319
Personal construct therapy (PCT), 207
Personality
  Freud's conception of, 69–71
  Rogers' conception of, 17
  Sullivan's view of, 81
  Winnicott's view of, 82
Personality and Psychotherapy (Dollard
    and Miller), 271–272
Personality assessment, 18
Person-centered therapy, 145, 386–387.
    See also Client-centered
    (person-centered) therapy
Persons, Jacqueline, 134
Persuasion and Healing (Frank), 272
Persuasion and Healing (Frank and
    Frank), 284
Peterson, D. R., 121, 630–636
Pharmacotherapy, 516–530
  for adolescents, 454–455
  antidepressants, 350, 522–525
  antipsychotics, 525–528
  anxiolytics, 521–522
  for bipolar disorder and schizophre-
    nias, 229
  for children, 727
  cognitive therapy vs., 222, 225

Pratt, J., 505
Precontemplation stage (patient readiness for change), 341
PREP (Prevention and Relationship Enhancement Program), 494–495
Preparation stage (patient readiness for change), 341
Prescriptionism, 746–747
Prescriptive authority, 49–50, 58, 528–530, 688, 756
Prescriptive matching, 402–406
President's Commission on Mental Health, 44
President's New Freedom Commission on Mental Health, 52
Prevention and Relationship Enhancement Program (PREP), 494–495
PRIDE skills, 415
Primary health care setting
  mental health problems treated in, 44
  psychotherapists in, 472, 752
  screening for mental disorders in, 52
Prince, M., 11, 13
Principles of Behavior Modification (Bandura), 204
Principles of Personality Counseling (Thorne), 272
Privacy
  of health data, 55, 725
  and recording of therapy, 694
Private practice
  in 1980s, 47
  psychiatrists in, 21
  psychologists in, 21, 42
Problem-centered therapy, 198
Problem-solving skills training (PSST), 364–366
Problem-solving therapy
  for depression, 547, 548
  for schizophrenia, 604
Procedural learning, 709
Process experiential psychotherapy, 146, 147, 156–157
Process model of therapeutic change, 122
Process notes, 55
Process–outcome research, 391–392, 750
Process rating scales, 321–322

Process research, 340–345, 750
  of Bern Psychotherapy Research Group, 391–392
  integrating RCTs and, 345–349
Process variables
  multilevel models of, 348
  transactional nature of, 346–347
Prochaska, J. O., 278, 581
Professional boundaries, 21, 726–727
Professional counselors
  in 1970s, 46
  in 1990s, 48
  in 2000s, 51
Professional development
  model of, 378–380
  SPR/CRN study of, 378
Professionalization of clinical psychology, 27, 30–32
Professional organizations. *See also* *specific organizations*
  and PhD programs, 623–625
  and psychoanalytic movement, 14
Professional Psychology journal, 42
Professional school movement, 630
Progeny cases (confidentiality), 725
Program for the Prevention of Delinquency, 19
Projective identification, 182
Project MATCH, 395–400, 582–585
Proprietary psychotherapies, 734–736
Protected health information, 55
Pseudohostility, 181
Pseudomutuality, 181
Psychiatric anthropologists, 245
Psychiatric nurses
  in 1960, 40
  in 1970s, 42–43
  in 1980s, 46
  in 1990s, 48
  in 2000s, 51
Psychiatric nursing, 27
Psychiatric social work, 27
Psychiatric social workers, 20. *See also* Social workers, psychotherapy-trained
Psychiatrists
  in 2000s, 51
  and American psychotherapy movement, 6
  and behavior therapy, 16

Relational frame theory (RFT), 129–130
Relational Health Indices (RHI), 360
Relational psychoanalysis, 72, 81–89
Relationship factors
in contemporary psychoanalysis, 76–79
in humanistic–experiential psychotherapies, 143
Relationships. *See also* Family systems therapy; Therapeutic relationship
obtaining control in, 177
in relational psychoanalysis, 87
Relationships (videotapes), 697
Relaxation response, 535
Religion. *See also* Spirituality and religion in psychotherapy
Ellis' attacks on, 218
and folk healing, 256
religiosity vs., 218
spirituality vs., 533
Religion and Medicine (Worcester, McComb, and Coriat), 9
Religiosity, religion vs., 218
Religious therapy, 537, 539. *See also* Spirituality and religion in psychotherapy
Reparative therapy, 731–732
Repression, Freud's view of, 69–70
Research
on CE in psychology, 665, 668–669
on effectiveness of VA training, 676
in mental health, 29–30
psychoanalytic, 68–69, 93, 94
in psychotherapy. *See* Psychotherapy research; Psychotherapy research achievements
in PsyD programs, 637
by VA trainees, 676
Research centers and groups, 357–433
Asian American Center on Disparities Research, 421–427
The Bern Psychotherapy Research Group, 389–393
Center for the Treatment and Study of Anxiety, 408–413
Parent–Child Interaction Therapy, 415–419
prescriptive matching and systematic treatment selection, 402–406

Project MATCH, 395–400
The Sheffield–Leeds Psychotherapy Research Program, 382–387
Society for Psychotherapy Research Collaborative Research Program on the Development of Psychotherapists, 375–380
The Stone Center for Developmental Studies, 357–361
University of Pennsylvania Center for Psychotherapy Research, 370–373
University of Washington Behavioral Research and Therapy Clinics, 428–433
Yale Parenting Center and Child Conduct Clinic, 363–368
Research process
achievements reflected in, 319–323
integrating outcome and, 345–349
Research questions, 300–319
common factors, 310–314
comparative effects, 305–307
dose–effect, 316–318
general effects, 300–303
negative effects, 314–316
permanence, 318–319
placebo, 303–304
Reserpine, 519
Resistance
in contemporary psychoanalysis, 79
and solution-focused therapy, 192
in traditional psychoanalysis, 73–74
Resolution on Appropriate Therapeutic Responses to Sexual Orientation (APA), 732
Respondent conditioning, in first-wave behavior therapy, 122
Responding Therapeutically to Patient Anger (videotapes), 698
Responding Therapeutically to Patient Expression of Sexual Attraction (videotapes), 698, 700–701
RFT (relational frame theory), 129–130
RHI (Relational Health Indices), 360
Rice, Laura, 146–147, 156
Rights of patients, 40, 55
Rinsley, D. B., 589
Risk reduction methods, 579

Self-instructional training, 205
Self-monitoring, 551
Self-object experiences, in self
    psychology, 90–91
Self psychology, 89–92
    in contemporary psychoanalysis, 80
    in treatment of anxiety, 562
Self-reflection
    in client-centered therapy, 153
    in humanistic–experiential psycho-
        therapies, 142
Self-regulation, in gestalt therapy, 160
Self-states, in relational psychoanalysis,
    86, 89
Self-support, in gestalt therapy, 159
Self-talk, second- vs. third-wave behav-
    ioral approaches to, 128–129
Self-wounds, 570–571
Seligman, M. E. P., 207–208, 548–549
Semantic learning, 709
Senate Finance Committee, 45
Sensitivity groups, 510
SEPI. *See* Society for the Exploration of
    Psychotherapy Integration
Sequential and parallel-concurrent
    integration, 286–287
Serotonin and norepinephrine reuptake
    inhibitors (SNRIs), 524
Sertraline, 523
SEU. *See* Systematic evocative
    unfolding
Sexual dysfunctions, comparative
    research on therapies for, 306
Sexual minority clients, 475–478
Sexual misconduct, 726–727
Sexual orientation conversion
    (reparative) therapy, 731–732
Sexual repression, 69–70
SFT. *See* Schema-focused
    psychotherapy
SGAs (second generation anti-
    psychotics), 526–528
Shakow, D., 27–29, 640
Shamanism, 256
Shannon, D., 509
Shapiro, F., 734–736
The Sheffield–Leeds Psychotherapy
    Research Program, 382–387
Shell shock, 14
Short-term therapy, 317

Shostrom, E., 695
Sidis, B., 11
Siegel, M., 634
Silver, R. J., 686
Skills development, as common factor
    in therapy, 314
Skinner, B. F., 104, 214
Slavson, S. R., 506–508
SNRIs (serotonin and norepinephrine
    reuptake inhibitors), 524
Snyder, D. K., 492–493
Sobell, L. C., 578–579
Sobell, M. B., 578–579
Social anxiety disorder
    behavioral therapy for, 565
    cognitive–behavioral therapies
        for, 568
Social behaviorism, 109
Social constructionism, 117, 121–122
Social context
    and family dynamics, 183, 189
    and family life course, 197
Social exchange theory, 194
Social learning program, 124–125, 708
Social learning theory, 108–110,
    124, 566
Social learning therapies, for schizo-
    phrenia, 604
Social pain, 360–361
Social phobias, 565
    cognitive–behavioral therapies for,
        568
    cognitive therapy for, 226
Social problem-solving (SPS), 205, 206,
    510–511
Social skills training
    for depression, 548
    for patients with schizophrenia, 604
Social workers
    clinical, 48, 57
    mental health, 51
    psychiatric, 20
    psychotherapy-trained, 40,
        42–43, 46
Society for Psychotherapy Research
    Collaborative Research Program
    on the Development of Psycho-
    therapists, 375–380
Society for Research on Adolescence,
    452

EDITORS

John C. Norcross, PhD, ABPP, is a professor of psychology and distinguished university fellow at the University of Scranton, editor of the *Journal of Clinical Psychology: In Session*, and a clinical psychologist in part-time practice. His recent coauthored books include *Leaving It at the Office: Psychotherapist Self-Care*; *Clinician's Guide to Evidence-Based Practice in Mental Health and Addictions*; *Insider's Guide to Graduate Programs in Clinical and Counseling Psychology*; and *Systems of Psychotherapy: A Transtheoretical Analysis*, now in its seventh edition. Among Dr. Norcross's awards are American Psychological Association's Distinguished Career Contributions to Education and Training, Pennsylvania Professor of the Year from the Carnegie Foundation, and election to the National Academies of Practice.

Gary R. VandenBos, PhD, is the executive director of the Office of Publications and Databases of the American Psychological Association. Among his books are *Psychotherapy of Schizophrenia: The Treatment of Choice* (with Bertram Karon), *Psychology and National Health Insurance*, *Clinical Geropsychology*, *Professional Liability and Risk Management*, and *Violence on the Job*. He maintains a part-time practice and consults on treatment and research with violent patients. He received the Early Career Contribution to Psychotherapy and the Lifetime Contributions to Psychotherapy from Division 29 (Psychotherapy) of the American Psychological Association.

Donald K. Freedheim, PhD, is professor emeritus of psychology at Case Western Reserve University and a past president of the American Psychological Association (APA) Division of Psychotherapy. He edited the first edition of *History of Psychotherapy: A Century of Change*, published in 1992 in honor of APA's centennial. In 2003, he edited *History of Psychology*, the first volume of the *Handbook of Psychology*. He also coedited *The Clinical Child Documentation Sourcebook*. For 10 years he edited the journal *Psychotherapy*. He also founded *The Clinical Psychologist* and *Professional Psychology*. He is a Distinguished Practitioner of the National Academies of Practice and serves on the Trauma Response Team of the Cleveland Chapter of the American Red Cross.